SOCIOLOGY

NINTH CANADIAN EDITION   **JOHN J. MACIONIS**

Kenyon College

LINDA M. GERBER

Professor Emerita,
University of Guelph

EDITORIAL DIRECTOR: Claudine O'Donnell
ACQUISITIONS EDITOR: Keriann McGoogan
MARKETING MANAGER: Euan White
PROGRAM MANAGER: Madhu Ranadive
PROJECT MANAGER: Andrea Falkenberg
MANAGER OF CONTENT DEVELOPMENT: Suzanne Schaan
MEDIA DEVELOPER: Tiffany Palmer
PRODUCTION SERVICES: Cenveo® Publisher Services
PERMISSIONS PROJECT MANAGER: Kathryn O'Handley

PHOTO PERMISSIONS RESEARCH: Integra Publishing Services, Inc.
TEXT PERMISSIONS RESEARCH: Integra Publishing Services, Inc.
COVER AND INTERIOR DESIGN: Anthony Leung
COVER IMAGE: Javindy/Fotolia; Neyro/Fotolia
VICE-PRESIDENT, CROSS MEDIA AND PUBLISHING SERVICES: Gary Bennett

Pearson Canada Inc., 26 Prince Andrew Place, Don Mills, Ontario M3C 2T8.

ISBN 978-0-13-430804-3

3 17

Library and Archives Canada Cataloguing in Publication

Macionis, John J., author
    Sociology / John J. Macionis, Linda M. Gerber. —Ninth Canadian edition.

Includes bibliographical references and index.
ISBN 978-0-13-430804-3 (loose-leaf)

    1. Sociology. I. Gerber, Linda M. (Linda Marie), 1944-, author II. Title.

HM586.M325 2017   301   C2016-906937-0

Dedication

This book is offered to teachers of sociology in the hope that it will help our students understand their place in today's society and in tomorrow's world.

—John J. Macionis & Linda M. Gerber

Brief Contents

Contents

Boxes

THINKING GLOBALLY

THINKING ABOUT DIVERSITY: RACE, CLASS, AND GENDER

CONTROVERSY & DEBATE

SOCIOLOGY AND THE MEDIA

SOCIOLOGY IN FOCUS

THINKING CRITICALLY

Maps

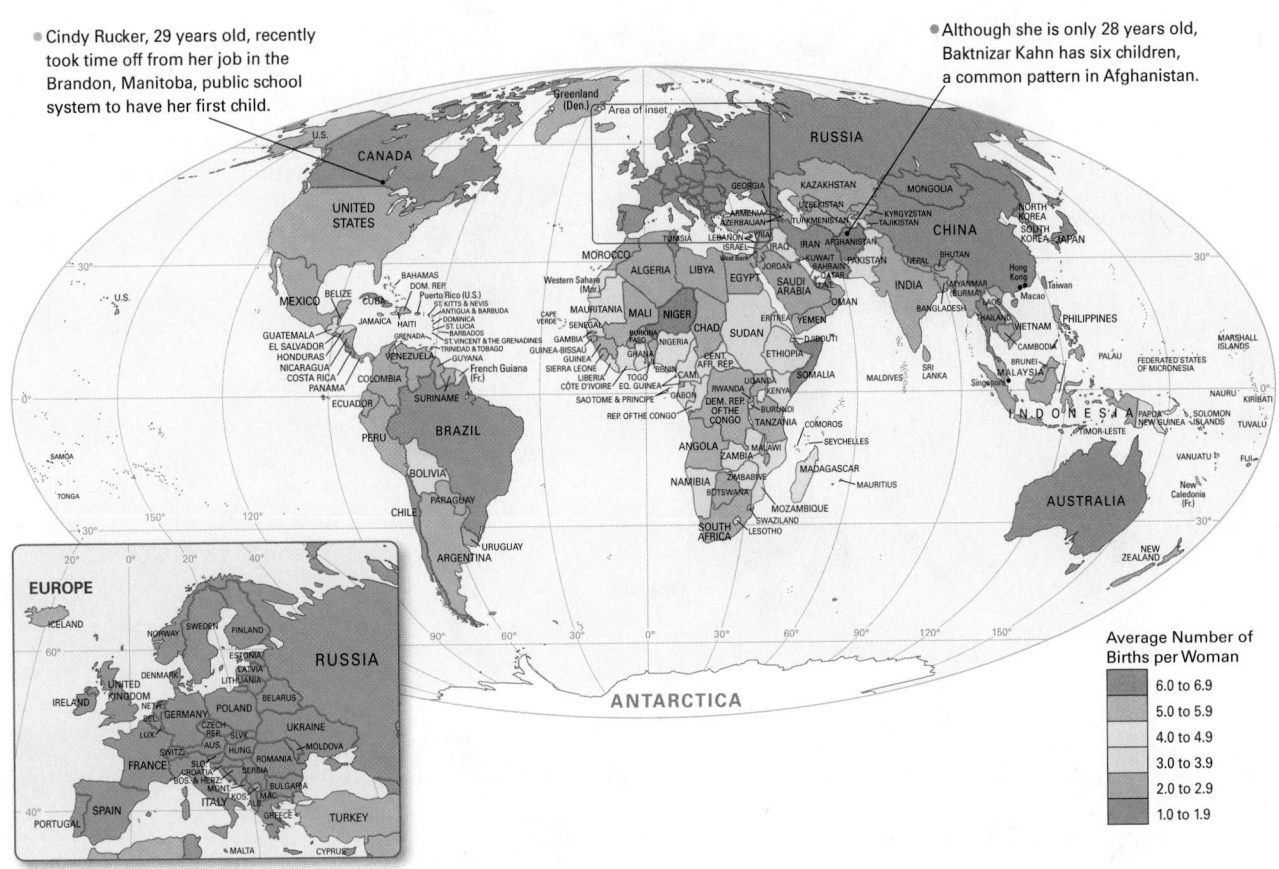

Cindy Rucker, 29 years old, recently took time off from her job in the Brandon, Manitoba, public school system to have her first child.

Although she is only 28 years old, Baktnizar Kahn has six children, a common pattern in Afghanistan.

Average Number of Births per Woman

6.0 to 6.9
5.0 to 5.9
4.0 to 4.9
3.0 to 3.9
2.0 to 2.9
1.0 to 1.9

GLOBAL MAPS: Window on the World

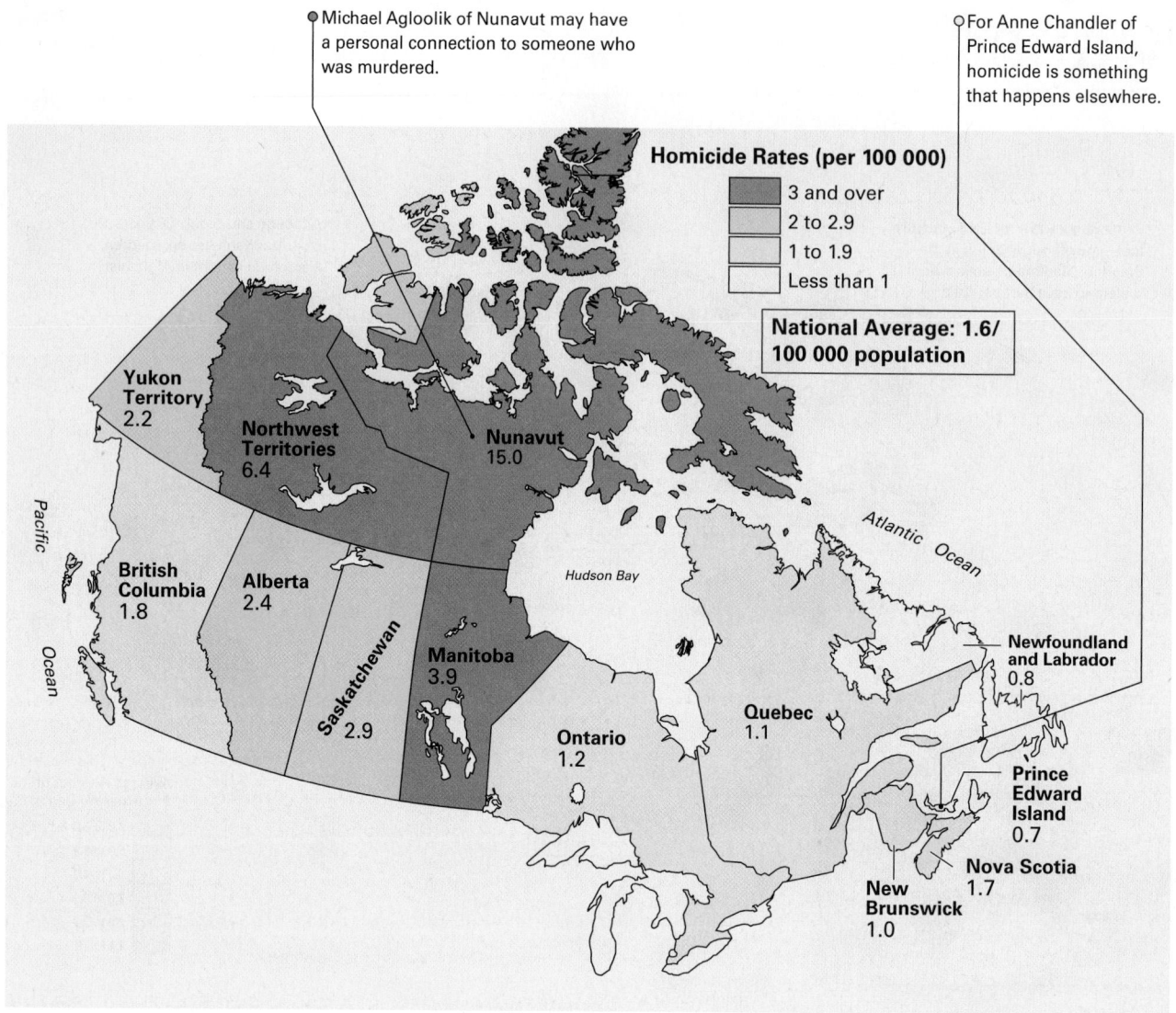

Michael Agloolik of Nunavut may have a personal connection to someone who was murdered.

For Anne Chandler of Prince Edward Island, homicide is something that happens elsewhere.

Homicide Rates (per 100 000)
- 3 and over
- 2 to 2.9
- 1 to 1.9
- Less than 1

National Average: 1.6/ 100 000 population

Yukon Territory 2.2

Northwest Territories 6.4

Nunavut 15.0

Pacific

Ocean

British Columbia 1.8

Alberta 2.4

Saskatchewan 2.9

Manitoba 3.9

Ontario 1.2

Hudson Bay

Quebec 1.1

Atlantic Ocean

Newfoundland and Labrador 0.8

Prince Edward Island 0.7

Nova Scotia 1.7

New Brunswick 1.0

CANADA MAPS: Seeing Ourselves

Preface

The world today challenges us as never before. The economy is uncertain, not only here at home but around the world. Technological disasters of our own making threaten the natural environment. There is much anger about how—and whether—our leaders are doing their jobs. Perhaps no one should be surprised to read polls that tell us most people are anxious about their economic future, unhappy with government, and worried about the state of the planet. Many of us simply feel overwhelmed, as if we are up against forces we can barely grasp.

That's where sociology comes in. For more than 150 years, sociologists have been working to better understand how society operates. Sociologists may not have all the answers, but we have learned quite a lot. A beginning course in sociology is your introduction to the fascinating and very useful study of the world around you. After all, we all have a stake in understanding our world and, as best we can, improving it.

Sociology, Ninth Canadian Edition, provides a comprehensive view of how the world works. You will find this book informative and even entertaining. Before you have even finished the first chapter, you will discover that sociology is not only useful—it's also fun. *Sociology is a field of study that can change the way you see the world and open the door to many new opportunities.* What could be more exciting than that?

Sociology in REVEL: A Powerful and Interactive Learning Program

Sociology, Ninth Canadian Edition, places a thorough revision of the discipline's leading textbook at the centre of an interactive learning program. Our outstanding learning program has been constructed with care and directed toward both high-quality content and easy and effective operation. Each major section of every chapter has a purpose, which is stated simply in the form of a Learning Objective. All the learning objectives are listed on the first page of each chapter; they guide students through their reading of the chapter, and they appear again as the organizing structure of the Making the Grade summary at the chapter's end. These learning objectives also involve a range of cognitive abilities.

Some sections of the text focus on more basic cognitive skills—such as remembering the definitions of key concepts and understanding ideas to the point of being able to explain them in one's own words—while others

ask students to compare and contrast theories and apply them to specific topics. In addition, questions throughout the text provide students with opportunities to engage in discovery, analysis, and evaluation. The Sociology in Focus blog, to which readers can link to at the end of each chapter, gives readers the chance to evaluate many of the most current debates and controversies as they read frequent postings by a team of young and engaging sociologists.

We also strive to get students writing. First, students will consistently encounter Journal Prompts throughout each chapter, where they're encouraged to write a response to a short-answer question applying what they've just learned. A Shared Writing question at the end of each chapter asks students to respond to a question and see responses from their peers on the same question. These discussions—which include moderation tools and must first be enabled by the instructor—offer students an opportunity to interact with each other in the context of their reading. Finally, at the end of each chapter there is a more comprehensive Seeing Sociology in Your Everyday Life interactive essay.

Finally, another key part of the REVEL content is our video program—the Core Concept Video Series. This is a series of short videos that fall into six categories.

- In The Big Picture videos, sociologist Jodie Lawston provides an introductory overview of the text chapter.

- The Basics videos present a review of the most important concepts for each core topic in the course, using an animated whiteboard format.

- Sociology on the Job videos, created by Professor Tracy Xavia Karner, connect the content of each chapter to the world of work and careers.

- Sociology in Focus videos feature a sociological perspective on today's popular culture.

- Social Inequalities videos, featuring Lester Andrist, introduce notable sociologists who highlight their own research, emphasizing the importance of inequality based on race, class, and gender.

- Thinking Like a Sociologist videos introduce students to examples and issues using data. These friendly videos help build students' quantitative analysis skills.

Videos from this series are placed within the narrative where they are most relevant, ensuring that students encounter the videos at the most appropriate moment in their reading.

What's New in This Edition?

Here's a quick summary of the new features found throughout *Sociology*, Ninth Canadian Edition.

- Learning Objectives. Each major section of every chapter begins with a specific Learning Objective. These Learning Objectives have been reorganized and streamlined for this new edition. All Learning Objectives are listed at the beginning of each chapter and they organize the summary at the end of each chapter.

- New Power of Society figures. If you could teach your students only one thing in the introductory course, what would it be? Probably, most instructors would answer, "to understand the power of society to shape people's lives." Each chapter begins with a Power of Society figure that does exactly that—forcing students to give up some of their cultural common sense that points to the importance of "personal choice" by showing them evidence of how society shapes our major life decisions.

- A new design makes this edition of the text the cleanest and easiest ever to read. Also, the photo and art programs have been thoroughly reviewed and updated.

- Canadian references and examples appear throughout the Ninth Canadian Edition of *Sociology,* and for some chapters—especially Chapter 11: Social Class in Canada, Chapter 14: Race and Ethnicity, and Chapter 17: Politics and Government—substantial parts are entirely Canadian. In addition to Canadian content throughout the body of the text, most of the chapter openers, boxes, figures, and tables are unique to the Canadian edition. This edition includes numerous updated boxes dealing with Canadian issues or research by Canadian scholars—as well as 100 tables, figures, and Canada maps that have been updated on the basis of Census 2011, the National Household Survey (NHS 2011), and other Statistics Canada data.

Finally, the REVEL electronic version of *Sociology* is now available with a full package of interactive learning material that expands key themes of the text. These interactive elements include the following types:

- A Global Perspective. These items provide international contrasts. In some cases, they highlight differences between high-income and low-income nations. In other cases, they highlight differences between Canada and other high-income countries.

- Diversity. These items expand the focus on race, class, gender, and other dimensions of difference within the Canadian population.

- Surveys. These items ask students timely questions about policy and politics. Students are asked what

they think, and they are able to assess their own attitudes against those of various populations.

- Sociology in the Media. The author suggests short, high-quality videos that are readily available on the Internet and current articles on sociological topics from respected publications.

- Readings. Short, primary-source readings by notable sociologists are provided to allow students to engage directly with analysts and researchers.

- In Review. Engaging "drag and drop" interactives offer a quick review of the insights gained by applying sociological theories to the issue at hand.

Chapter-by-Chapter Highlights

Chapter 1 The Sociological Perspective

- Power of Society figure: Couples Living Common-Law by Province, 1981 to 2006 (new figure based on Canadian data)

- Chapter opener: male-female hand-holding as patterned behaviour

- Figure 1–1: Suicide Rates for Canada by Sex: 1951–2011 (updated figure)

- Figure 1–2: Suicide Rates for Canada by Age and Sex, 2011

- Sociology and Canadian public policy

- Canadian Sociology: Distinctive Touches—Harold Innis, John Porter, Marshall McLuhan, Erving Goffman, Dorothy Smith, and Raymond Breton

- Sociology and the Media: Marshall McLuhan: Media Theorist (box)

- Thinking About Diversity: Early Contributions of Women to the Social Sciences (box based on Canadian research)

- Table 1–1: Women and Men as Early Founders of the Social Sciences (table combining data from multiple sources)

- Feminist and postmodernist theories included in the Applying Theory table

- Sociological perspectives on Canadian sports

Chapter 2 Sociological Investigation

- Power of Society figure: Education and poverty among Aboriginal peoples (new figure based on Canadian data)

- Chapter opener: student research into election results

- Table 2–1: Correlates of Piercings and Tattoos

- Women as methodologists (based on Canadian sources)

- Sociology in Focus: Feminist Research: Critical and Interpretive Examples (box based on the work of Canadian sociologists)
- Thinking About Diversity: Conducting Research with Aboriginal Peoples (box)
- Illustration of Survey Research: The Case of Anti-Semitism in Quebec
- Thinking Critically: Reading Tables: Aboriginal Employment and Income in Canada (box)
- Table 2–2: Labour Force Participation and Income of Aboriginal Men and Women (revised table)
- Sociology and the Media: From Card Punching to Cyberspace: Evolution in the Media of Research (box based on personal experience)

Chapter 3 Culture

- Chapter opener: excerpt from *Kiss of the Fur Queen* (Tomson Highway)
- Thinking About Diversity: Aboriginal Languages in Danger of Extinction (box)
- Thinking Globally: Canadians and Americans—What Makes Us Different? (box)
- Cultural Diversity in Canada (updated section)
- Figure 3–2: Immigrant Population by Place of Birth and Period of Immigration (updated figure)
- Table 3–1: Mother Tongues in Canada, 1996, 2001, 2006, and 2011 (updated table)

Chapter 4 Society

- Power of Society figure: Education and internet access, United States and Canada (new figure)
- Chapter opener: What is it about Canadian society that is so intriguing?
- Sociology in Focus: What Makes Quebec a "Distinct Society" within Canada? (box)

Chapter 5 Socialization

- Power of Society figure: television viewing by age among Canadians (new figure)
- Thinking About Diversity: Ethnic and Racial Identities: Evidence of Renewal and Dilution (box)
- Table 5–1: Ethnic and Racial Identities: Immigration and Intermarriage (table based on Canadian data)
- Sociology and the Media: How Do the Media Portray Minorities? (box)
- Controversy and Debate: Ontario's First Boot Camp as a Total Institution (box)

Chapter 6 Social Interaction in Everyday Life

- Figure 6–2: The Prevalence of Common-Law Unions in Canada, Quebec, and the Rest of Canada (updated figure)
- Sociology and the Media: Disease and Disability in Hollywood Film—20 Years of Change (box)
- Thinking Critically: Social Interaction: Life, Work, and Leisure in Cyberspace (box based on the Canadian scene)
- Sociology in Focus: The Social Construction of Reality: Reflections on Canadian Humour (box)

Chapter 7 Groups and Organizations

- Chapter opener: McDonald's and McDonald's Canada
- Sociology in Focus: The Club DJ—Local Musician, Global Ties (box based on Canadian research)
- Canadian illustrations of "groupthink"
- Sociology in Focus: The Tattoo and Social Organization (based on Canadian research)
- Sociology and the Media: Virtual Community—Building Networks through Cyberspace (box based on Canadian network research)
- Canada map 7–1: Employment in Government Service for Canada, the Provinces, and Territories, 2011 (updated map)
- Japanese organizational principles applied in Canada
- Thinking Critically: Computer Technology, Large Organizations and the Assault on Privacy (box based on Canadian policy)

Chapter 8 Sexuality and Society

- Power of Society figure: attitudes towards same-sex relations (new figure)
- Chapter opener: sex reassignment—the experience of Canadians Sylvia Durand and Cynthia Cousens
- Sociology and the Media: The Boy Who Was Raised as a Girl (box based on a Canadian story)
- Sexual Attitudes in Canada (updated sections)
- Table 8–1: Canadian Attitudes toward Non-marital Sex, Extramarital Sex, and Homosexuality
- Table 8–2: How Canadians and Americans View Premarital Sex (updated table)
- Thinking About Diversity: Same-Sex Marriage in Canada (updated box)
- Teen pregnancy (updated), pornography, prostitution, and sexual assault as Canadian issues
- Controversy and Debate: The Abortion Controversy (updated box based on Canadian policy)

- Sociology in Focus: Rape and Date Rape—Exposing Dangerous Myths (box based on Canadian research)

Chapter 9 Deviance

- Power of Society figure: imprisonment of Aboriginals (new figure)
- Thinking About Diversity: Suicide among Aboriginal People (box)
- Rocco Perri: Canada's link to Al Capone (under Merton's Strain Theory)
- Figure 9–2: Graphic representation of labelling theory, linking primary and secondary deviance (created by L.M. Gerber)
- Sociology and the Media: Crime in High Places (box – Adscam, Conrad Black)
- Figure 9–3: Incidence of Hate Crimes Motivated by Race, Ethnicity, Religion, and Sexual Orientation, Canada, 2013 (new figure)
- Sociology in Focus: Dangerous Masculinity—Violence and Crime in Hockey (box based on Canadian research)
- Canadian criminal statistics (including homicide by women)
- Figure 9–4: Violent and Property Crime Rates in Canada, 1962–2012 (updated figure)
- Canada Map 9–1: Homicide Rates for Canada, Provinces, and Territories, 2010 to 2014 (updated map)
- Crime and punishment in Canada, by social class, race, ethnicity, Aboriginal identity, and gender (updated sections)
- Table 9–1: Homicide by Method for Canada, 2000–2014 (updated)
- Controversy and Debate: Homicide in Toronto by Method and Region: Surprising Findings (analysis by LM Gerber)
- Table 9–2: Homicide by Method and Non-Fatal Shootings in Toronto, January to June 2012 (created by LM Gerber)
- Sociology in Focus: Cops are People Too! Reconciling Role Constructs with the Reality of Police Work and Explaining Police Deviance (box based on Canadian research)
- Punishment from a Canadian perspective
- The criminal justice system, including Aboriginal sentencing circles

Chapter 10 Social Stratification

- Power of Society figure: life expectancy in selected countries (new figure)
- Thinking About Diversity: *Titanic*—Personal and Canadian Connections (box)

- Sociology in Focus: Salaries—Are the Rich Worth What They Earn? (updated box based on Canadian data)

Chapter 11 Social Class in Canada

- Power of Society figure: ethnic origins and poverty (new figure based on Canadian data)
- Chapter opener: Winnipeg's homeless hero, Faron Hall
- Figure 11–1: Pre- and After-Tax Income by Family Structure in Canada, 1985 to 2010 (new figure)
- Table 11–1: Distribution of Income by Quintile in Canada: 1961 to 2011 (updated table)
- Table 11–2: Average Family Income (in after-tax dollars) by Quintile for Canada (2011) (new table)
- Canada Map 11–1: Average Family Income for Canada, the Provinces and Territories (2010) (updated map)
- Occupational prestige in Canada (Creese/Goyder)
- Figure 11–2: Distribution of Occupational Prestige, 1975 and 2000 (based on Canadian research)
- Table 11–3: Income by Highest Level of Educational Attainment (in 2010 dollars) (new table based on Canadian data)
- Figure 11–3: Average Employment Income in Canada for Selected Categories, 2010 (updated figure based on Canadian data)
- Figure 11–4: Percentage with Income of $80 000 or More for Selected Categories: Canada, 2010 (new figure based on Canadian data)
- Thinking About Diversity: Social Class and Aboriginal Peoples (updated box)
- Social classes in Canada (updated sections)
- Sociology and the Media: Computers and Social Class (updated box based on Canadian research)
- Table 11–4: You Are Richer Than You Think (Canada/US comparison)
- Social mobility in Canada
- Poverty in Canada (updated)
- Figure 11–5: Average Income of Immigrants by Period of Immigration and Educational Achievement
- Figure 11–6: Average Family Income by Family Structure (2000, 2005, and 2010 in Constant 2010 dollars) (new figure based on Canadian data)
- Figure 11–7: Prevalence of Low Income by Family Structure, 2010 (new figure based on Canadian data)
- Thinking Critically: The Welfare Dilemma: Canadian Perspectives (box)
- Sociology and the Media: Counting the Homeless in Toronto (box)

Chapter 12 Global Stratification

- Canada and Low-Income Countries (updated sections)
- Thinking Globally: Canadian Contributions to Livelihood and Food Security in Isolated Communities of Latin America and India (box based on Canadian research)

Chapter 13 Gender Stratification

- Chapter opener: the fight for personhood (1927) and sexual equality in the Charter of Rights and Freedoms (1982)
- Working Women and Men in Canada (updated section)
- Gender, occupation, and income in Canada (updated section)
- Figure 13–2: Employment Rates of Men and Women (15 Years of Age and Over) in Canada, 1971 to 2011 (updated figure)
- Figure 13–3: Employment Rates of Men and Women (35 to 44 Years of Age) in Canada, 1971 to 2011 (updated figure) Women's "Second Shift" (updated section)
- Table 13–1: Average Income for Full-time Work, the Gender Gap, and Percentage Female in Selected Occupations (table compiled by LM Gerber)
- Table 13–2: Educational Certification by Sex and Age (Populations 15 and Over, and 35 to 44 Years of Age) in Canada, 2006 and 2011 (updated table)
- Table 13–3: Benchmarks for Women in Canadian Politics and Public Life (table)
- Gender and politics in Canada
- Minority women/intersection theory/Aboriginal women
- Violence against and by women in Canada (updated section)
- Sociology in Focus: Understanding the Gender Gap in Occupation and Income and All the Fuss about Women as Breadwinners (box based on Canadian research)
- Thinking About Diversity: Powerful Canadian Women (updated box)
- Sexual Harassment (updated section)
- Intersection Theory (new section)
- Thinking About Diversity: Canadian Women in Hockey—Going for Gold (box)

Chapter 14 Race and Ethnicity

- Power of Society figure: ethnic origins and the choice between marriage and common-law union (new figure based on Canadian data)
- Chapter opener: Stuart McLean on racism and discrimination against Blacks

- Ethnic and racial mixing or intermarriage in Canada (updated section)
- Table 14–1: The Top 30 Ethnic Origins in Canada: Single- and Multiple-Origin Responses, 2011 (new table compiled by LM Gerber))
- Prejudice and racism in Canada
- Profiles of Lincoln Alexander and Michaëlle Jean
- Prejudice and stereotypes in Canadian perspective
- Pluralism, multiculturalism, institutional completeness in Canada
- Assimilation and segregation in Canada and the United States
- Race and Ethnicity in Canada (updated section)
- Thinking About Diversity: Black Citizens of Canada— A History Ignored (box)
- Figure 14–2: Visible Minority Population of Canada, Provinces, and Territories, 2011 (new figure)
- Social Standing (revised and updated section)
- Thinking About Diversity: Visible Minorities—Toronto, Vancouver, and Montreal (revised box)
- Table 14–2: Visible Minority Population of Montreal, Toronto, and Vancouver, 2011 (new table)
- Table 14–3: Education, Employment, and Income among Selected Ethnic Categories, 2011 (new table)
- Special Status Societies: Aboriginal peoples (updated section)
- Special Status Societies: the Québécois
- Sociology and the Media: The Aboriginal Peoples Television Network (box based on Canadian research)
- Immigration to Canada: a hundred-year perspective
- Figure 14–3: Immigration to Canada, 1885–2009 (updated figure)
- Sociology in Focus: Distinct Societies and National Unity (box)
- Table 14–4: The Top 25 Places of Birth for Immigrants Arriving from 2006 to 2011 (new table based on Canadian data)
- Canada Map 14–1: Percentage of Foreign-Born Population for Canada, the Provinces, and Territories, 2011 (updated map)

Chapter 15 Aging and the Elderly

- Power of Society figure: emotional support for the elderly (new figure based on Canadian data)
- Chapter opener: Gladys Powers—WWI veteran—who died at age 109 in BC
- Population aging in Canada
- Consequences for Canada

- Chapter opener: lesbian mothers and child custody
- Controversy and Debate: International Adoption (box based on Canadian research)
- Marriage (Canadian perspectives on sex and infidelity)
- Figure 18–1: Sexual Activity by Marital Status (figure)
- Child rearing (women, men, employment, parental leave in Canada)
- Canadian Families: Class, Race, and Gender
- Controversy and Debate: The Child-Care Debate (box)
- Table 18–1: Employment Among Women (25 to 35 Years of Age) with Spouse or Partner Present, for Canada, Quebec, Ontario and Alberta: 1981, 1991, 2001, and 2006 (table)
- Table 18–2: Employment Among Women (25 to 34 Years of Age) with Spouse or Partner Present, by Presence of Children, for Canada, Quebec, Ontario, and Alberta, 2006 (table)
- Aboriginal families in Canada (ethnicity and race)
- Table 18–3: Approval of Intergroup Marriage, 1975 through 1995 (table based on Canadian data)
- Figure 18–2: The Divorce Rate in Canada, 1968–2006 (figure)
- Canada Map 18–1: Percentage of the Population that is Married by Province and Territory, 2011 (new map)
- Sociology in Focus: Spousal Violence in Canada (box)
- Alternative Family Forms
- Figure 18–3: Lone-Parent Families (Female- and Male-Headed) as Proportions of the Total in Canada, 1961, 1976, 1996, 2001, 2006, and 2011 (updated figure)
- Table 18–4: Alternative Family Forms, 2011 (new table based on Canadian data)
- Table 18–5: Couples Living Common-Law by Province and Territory: 1981, 2001, and 2011 (Percentage of all Couples) (new table)
- Sociology in Focus: Cohabitation among Canadians (box)
- Table 18–6: Singlehood over Generations (Percentage Never Married) by Selected Age Cohorts and Sex: 2001, 2006, 2011 (new table based on Canadian data)
- Table 18–7: Singlehood over Generations (Never Married, and "in"or "not in" Common-Law Unions) by Selected Age Cohorts and Sex, 2011 (new table based on Canadian data)

Chapter 19 Religion

- Power of Society figure: proportion married by religion (new figure based on Canadian data)
- Chapter opener: "Make Jesus your CEO"—evangelical megachurches in Ontario

- Table 19–1: Religious Affiliation and Immigrant Status for Selected Religions in Canada, 2001 and 2011 (new table)
- Sociology in Focus: Religion in Canada—Decline or Renaissance? (box)
- Canada Map 19–1: Canadians Claiming "No Religion" by Province and Territory, 2011 (updated map)
- Religion in Canada: religious affiliation, religiosity, class and ethnicity, education, and labour force participation
- Table 19–2: Educational Attainment and Labour Force Participation among 25- to 54-Year-Olds for Selected Religions in Canada, 2011 (new table)
- Sociology and the Media: Check the Media—Religion is Hot! (box)

Chapter 20 Education

- Power of Society figure: higher education among visible minorities (new figure based on Canadian data)
- Chapter opener: education on reserves
- Schooling in Canada (section)
- Thinking Critically: Functional Illiteracy—Must We Rethink Education? (box based on Canadian materials)
- Schooling and Social Inequality (updated section)
- Canada Map 20–1: Population Aged 25 to 64 with Bachelor's Degree or Higher by Province and Territory, 2011 (new map)
- Access to Education (updated section)
- Thinking About Diversity: School Attendance among Youth across Canada—Where You Live Makes a Difference (box)
- Table 20–1: Full-Time School Attendance among Youth Aged 15 to 24 for Canada, Provinces, and Territories, 1991 to 2001 (table)
- Figure 20–1: Educational Attainment for Selected Ethnic Categories Aged 25 to 64, 2011 (new figure based on Canadian data)
- Thinking About Diversity: Aboriginal Education—From Residential School to College and University (updated box)
- Table 20–2: Educational Attainment of On-Reserve and Urban First Nations, all Aboriginals and non-Aboriginals, 25 to 44 Years of Age, 2001 and 2006 (new table based on Canadian data)
- Sociology in Focus: Explaining Educational Attainment (box based on Canadian materials)
- Table 20–3: Employment of 25- to 64-Year-Olds by Level of Educational Attainment and Sex, 2011 (new table)
- Dropping out

- Academic standards
- Table 20–4: Highest Level of Educational Attainment by Age Cohort and Sex, 2011 (new table)
- Sociology and the Media: Welcome to Cyber-School (updated box)

Chapter 21 Health and Medicine

- Power of Society figure: obesity by age and sex (new figure based on Canadian data)
- Health in Canada—age, gender, social class, and race (section)
- Sociology in Focus: SARS, West Nile, One Mad Cow, and Bird and Swine Flu (box)
- Table 21–1: Self-Reported Health: Canadian Women and Men by Age, 1975 to 1995 (table)
- Mental health in Canada
- Table 21–2: Mortality and Life Expectancy, First Nations and All Canadians, 1960 and 1991 (table)
- Cigarette smoking
- Canada Map 21–1: Percentage of Population 12 years and Over Who are Current Smokers, 2014 (new map)
- Sexually Transmitted Diseases in Canada (updated and revised section)
- Table 21–3: HIV Cases Reported to PHAC, 1985–2014 (1985–1995, 1996–2004, 2005–2011, and 2012–2014) (new table)
- Table 21–4: Reported AIDS Cases by Sex: 1979 to 2004; 2005 to 2011; and 2012 to 2014 (new table)
- Table 21–5: Deaths from AIDS, 1987 to 2011, including peak years, 1991 to 1996 (new table)
- Table 21–6: Reported Cases of HIV by Race or Ethnicity (1998 to 2014) (new table)
- The Right to Die in Canada
- Mercy killing in Canada
- The rise of scientific medicine in Canada
- Medicine in Canada
- Sociology and the Media: Two-Tiered Health Care: Threat, Fact, or Fiction? (box based on Canadian materials)
- The shortage of nurses
- Canadian women in medicine
- Table 21–7: The Representation of Canadian Women in Medicine by Age, 2003 , 2009, 2012, and 2015 (updated table)
- Health and inequality in Canada
- Controversy and Debate: Waiting for a Kidney Transplant: Canadian Patients and the International Organ Trade (box based on Canadian research)

Chapter 22 Population, Urbanization, and Environment

- Chapter opener: Walkerton water contamination
- Population, fertility, mortality, and the baby boom
- Canada Map 22–1: Crude Birth Rates (births per 1000 population) by Province and Territory, 2011 (updated map)
- Figure 22–2: Age-Sex Population Pyramids for Canada, 1971–2011 (updated figure)
- Figure 22–4: Map of York (Toronto), 1834 (map)
- Canadian content in all sections under The Growth of North American Cities
- Table 22–1: Population of Census Metropolitan Areas in Canada, 1956 and 2011—Top 20 Ranked by 2011 Population (updated table)
- Thinking About Diversity: NHS 2011—Minorities a Major Presence in Canada's Largest Metropolitan Areas (updated box)
- Table 22–2: Ethnic and Racial Diversity in Canada's Ten Largest Metropolitan Areas, 2011 (new table)
- Profile of Jane Jacobs
- Sociology and the Media: Environmentally Friendly Canada, Eh! (updated box)
- Environmental racism (and Aboriginal communities)

Chapter 23 Collective Behaviour and Social Movements

- Chapter opener: Elijah Harper and Oka: the birth of the Aboriginal social movement in Canada
- Crowds, mobs, and riots in Canada
- Public opinion and propaganda (Canadian examples)
- Social movements in Canada
- Claims making—the Quebec student strike
- Controversy and Debate: Are You Willing to Take a Stand? (box based on Canadian materials)

Chapter 24 Social Change: Traditional, Modern, and Postmodern Societies

- Thinking Globally: Indonesian Democracy and Development—Welcome but Unexpected! (box based on Canadian research)
- Sociology in Focus: The True North LGBT—We're "Post-Gay" (box based on Canadian attitudes)
- Sociology and the Media: The Canadian Revolution through the Information Revolution—The Point of No Return (box)
- Controversy and Debate: We're Different, Eh? (box based on Canada/US attitudes and values)

Instructor Supplements

These instructor supplements are available for download from a password-protected section of Pearson Canada's online catalogue (catalogue.pearsoned.ca). Navigate to your book's catalogue page to view a list of those supplements that are available. Speak to your local Pearson sales representative for details and access.

Instructor's Manual.   The Instructor's Manual provides detailed chapter outlines, essay topics, student exercises, and supplemental lecture material with discussion questions.

PowerPoint® Presentations.   Chapter-by-chapter PowerPoint presentations cover the key topics and incorporate figures, tables, and maps from the main text.

Computerized Test Bank.   Pearson's computerized test banks allow instructors to filter and select questions to create quizzes, tests or homework. Instructors can revise questions or add their own, and may be able to choose print or online options. The test bank for Sociology contains more than 2400 items in multiple-choice, true/false, and essay format. These questions are also available in Microsoft Word format.

Image Library.   The image library provides chapter figures and tables.

Learning Solutions Managers.   Pearson's Learning Solutions Managers work with faculty and campus course designers to ensure that Pearson technology products, assessment tools, and online course materials are tailored to meet your specific needs. This highly qualified team is dedicated to helping schools take full advantage of a wide range of educational resources, by assisting in the integration of a variety of instructional materials and media formats. Your local Pearson Canada sales representative can provide you with more details on this service program.

In Appreciation

The conventional practice of designating just two authors obscures the efforts of dozens of women and men that have resulted in *Sociology,* Ninth Canadian Edition. We would like to express our thanks to the Pearson Canada team, including Claudine O'Donnell, Matthew Christian, Darcey Pepper, Madhu Ranadive, Andrea Falkenberg, and Kathy O'Handley. A special "thank you" goes to Keriann McGoogan – Senior Developmental Editor – for her unwavering patience, encouragement, and gentle nudging where required. Her supportive approach made dealing with the inevitable hurdles and looming deadlines much easier.

We are grateful to the authors of the supplements for this edition, and particularly to Peter Ove from Camosun College for his hard work on and contributions to the REVEL.

We are also indebted to Euan for managing our marketing campaign, and to the members of the sales staff, the men and women who have given this text such remarkable support over the years.

It goes without saying that every colleague knows more about some topics covered in this book than the authors do. For that reason, we are grateful to the hundreds of faculty and students who have written to offer comments and suggestions.

Without the support, encouragement, and patience of Linda Gerber's family—her husband, Gerhard; her daughter, Laura; grandchildren, Grace, James, and Charlie; her son, Martin, and his wife, Alyshia—the road to the 9th Canadian edition of *Sociology* would have been much bumpier. As always, the greatest debt is owed to Gerhard, who, by holding home and family together, allows Linda to devote herself to research and writing.

John Macionis

Linda Gerber

About the Authors

John J. Macionis John J. Macionis (pronounced "ma-SHOW-nis") has been in the classroom teaching sociology for more than forty years. Born and raised in Philadelphia, Pennsylvania, John earned a bachelor's degree from Cornell University, majoring in sociology, and then completed a doctorate in sociology from the University of Pennsylvania. His publications are wide-ranging, focusing on community life in the United States, interpersonal intimacy in families, effective teaching, humour, new information technology, and the importance of global education. In addition to authoring this best-seller, Macionis has also written *Society: The Basics*, the most popular paperback text in the field, now in its fourteenth edition. He collaborates on international editions of the texts: *Sociology*: Canadian Edition; *Society: The Basics*, Canadian Edition; and *Sociology: A Global Introduction*. *Sociology* is also available for high school students and in various foreign-language editions. All the Macionis texts are now available in low-cost electronic editions in the REVEL program. These exciting programs offer an interactive learning experience. Unlike other authors, John takes personal responsibility for writing all electronic content, just as he authors all the supplemental material. John proudly resists the trend toward "outsourcing" such material to non-sociologists.

In addition, Macionis edited the best-selling anthology *Seeing Ourselves: Classic, Contemporary, and Cross-Cultural Readings in Sociology*, also available in a Canadian edition. Macionis and Vincent Parrillo have written the leading urban studies text, *Cities and Urban Life*, soon available in a sixth edition. Macionis is also the author of *Social Problems*, now in its sixth edition and the leading book in this field. The latest on all the Macionis textbooks, as well as information and dozens of internet links of interest to students and faculty in sociology, is found at the author's personal website: **www.macionis.com** or **www.TheSociologyPage.com**. Follow John on this Facebook author page: John J. Macionis. Additional information and instructor resources are found at the Pearson site: **www.pearsonhighered.com**.

John Macionis recently retired from full-time teaching at Kenyon College in Gambier, Ohio, where he was Professor and Distinguished Scholar of Sociology. During that time, he chaired the Sociology Department, directed the college's multidisciplinary program in humane studies, presided over the campus senate and the college's faculty, and taught sociology to thousands of students.

Courtesy of John Macionis

In 2002, the American Sociological Association presented Macionis with the Award for Distinguished Contributions to Teaching, citing his innovative use of global material as well as the introduction of new teaching technology in his textbooks.

Professor Macionis has been active in academic programs in other countries, having travelled to some fifty nations. He writes, "I am an ambitious traveller, eager to learn and, through the texts, to share much of what I discover with students, many of whom know little about the rest of the world. For me, travelling and writing are all dimensions of teaching. First, and foremost, I am a teacher—a passion for teaching animates everything I do."

At Kenyon, Macionis taught a number of courses, but his favourite classes have been Introduction to Sociology and Social Problems. He continues to enjoy extensive contact with students across the United States and around the world.

John now lives near New York City, and in his free time, he enjoys tennis, swimming, hiking, and playing oldies rock-and-roll. He is an environmental activist in the Lake George region of New York's Adirondack Mountains, where he works with a number of organizations, including the Lake George Land Conservancy, where he serves as president of the board of trustees.

Professor Macionis welcomes (and responds to) comments and suggestions about this book from faculty and students. Contact him at his Facebook pages or email: macionis@kenyon.edu.

Linda M. Gerber was born in Toronto (to Finnish parents) and raised in Thornhill (just north of Toronto). Finnish was her first language, and she remains sufficiently fluent to speak the language with relatives on regular trips to Finland.

After graduating from the Nightingale School of Nursing (in Toronto), she toured Europe on a Eurail-pass over the summer—and spent the next year nursing in Helsinki, Finland. Upon her return, she completed a nursing degree at the University of Toronto—before switching to sociology at the MA and PhD levels. While still an undergraduate in nursing, she married Gerhard Gerber, whose family (pictured here) had escaped from East Germany when he was 10 years old.

As a graduate student, she was a consultant in highway planning, doing socio-impact assessment for a range of highway planning projects in southern and central Ontario. She also taught a course on Canadian Native peoples at York University's Glendon campus.

On completion of their PhDs in sociology and in biochemistry (and three weeks after the birth of their daughter, Laura), the Gerbers moved to Boston, Massachusetts, for continued study. After three years at Harvard's Centre for Population Studies, Linda Gerber accepted a position in the Department of Sociology and Anthropology at the University of Guelph. Over her 35 years at Guelph, she taught a wide range of courses at the undergraduate and graduate levels—most recently introductory sociology, political sociology, contemporary Aboriginal peoples, and Canadian society. She retired as Professor Emerita in August 2014.

Professor Gerber's research has focused on Canada's Aboriginal peoples, politics, and ethnic relations, but she has a broader interest in Canadian society (its demographics, its identity, and its regional tensions). Her publications are in the areas of Aboriginal studies, voting behaviour, ethnic relations, and Quebec separatism. All of these interests inform the nine Canadian editions of *Sociology*.

On October 12, 2006, when other Canadians were celebrating Thanksgiving, the Gerber family met for its own special reunion marking 50 years since Maria and Herbert Gerber arrived in Canada—with four of their children—after escaping from East Germany. Two sons had gone ahead separately (at 19 and 20 years of age) with no assurances that they would see the rest of the family again. The escape, which was meticulously

Linda Gerber's family—clockwise from the upper left—includes son Martin, daughter-in-law Alyshia, Linda, daughter Laura, husband Gerhard, and grandchildren Charlie, James, and Grace.

Courtesy of Linda Gerber

planned and executed, took place just before the Berlin Wall was erected.

The family has grown and prospered over the past 60 years. Maria and Herbert Gerber are responsible for adding six children, 21 grandchildren, and 41 great-grandchildren to the North American population. The 47 "Gerbers" who met for the October reunion are part of a much larger clan living mainly in southern Ontario, as well as in Vancouver, Chicago, Texas, and the southeastern United States. Interestingly, 4 of the 6 children (Gerhard's generation) married Germans, but only 2 of the 21grandchildren married people of German origins.

Chapter 1
The Sociological Perspective

∨ Learning Objectives

1.1 Explain how the sociological perspective differs from common sense.

1.2 State several reasons for the importance of a global perspective in today's world.

1.3 Identify the advantages of sociological thinking for developing public policy, for encouraging personal growth, and for advancing in a career.

1.4 Link the origins of sociology to historical social changes.

1.5 Summarize sociology's major theoretical approaches.

1.6 Apply sociology's major theoretical approaches to the topic of sports.

The Power of Society

to guide our choices of marriage or cohabitation

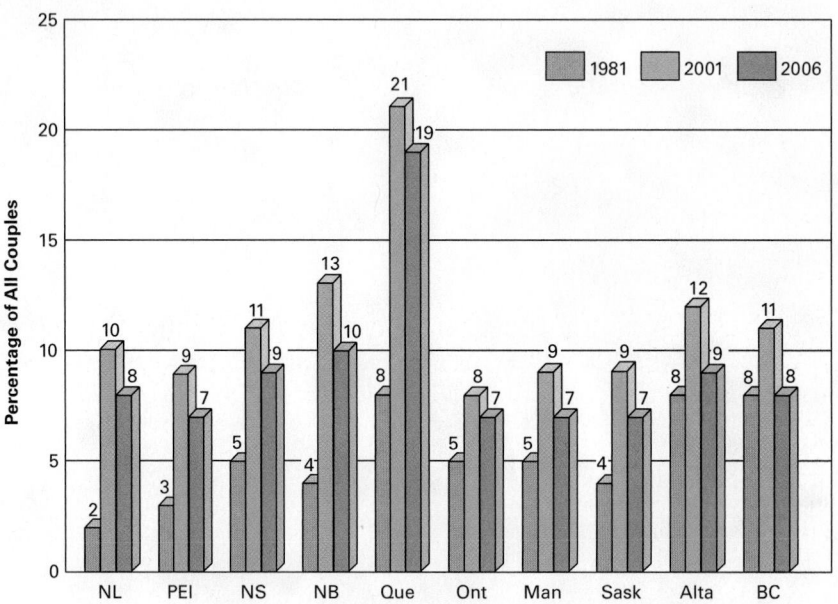

SOURCE: Adapted from Statistics Canada, catalogue nos. 93-312 and 93-320, cited in Stout (1994:9); calculations by L.M. Gerber based on Statistics Canada, Census 2006, catalogue no. 97-552-XCB2006007.

How is it that some young couples choose marriage while others opt for cohabitation or living common-law? Why are Québécois, First Nations, and Inuit more likely to opt for common-law unions than other Canadians? In the figure above, you see that, in every one of our provinces, cohabitation rates increased dramatically from 1981 to 2001 before falling off in 2006. That said, all provinces are not "equal." Quebecers choose common-law unions at roughly twice the rate of those living in other provinces. New Brunswick and Alberta rank second and third in terms of cohabitation rates, while Ontario posts a low of 8 percent of all couples in such unions. Are the vastly different levels of cohabitation among Canada's provinces or the similarities in patterns—up from 1981 to 2001 and down a little by 2006—the result of random choices made by millions of couples? Not a chance. What you are seeing here is the power of society (or segments of society) to guide individual behaviour.

Chapter Overview

You are about to begin a course that could change your life. Sociology is a new and exciting way of understanding the world around you. It will change what you see, how you think about the world, and perhaps even how you think about yourself. This chapter introduces the discipline of sociology. The most important skill to gain from this chapter is the ability to use what we call the *sociological perspective*. This chapter also introduces *sociological theory*, which will help you see the world from a sociological perspective.

Imagine you are walking along and have taken the hand of a member of the opposite sex. Now stop and take a close look at what has just happened. If you are a man, it is almost certain that you will be holding your partner's hand from the front; if you are a woman, you will be holding hands from behind. Was this hypothesis supported in your case?

If you want to do a little experiment, try this. As you are about to clasp hands, stop, reconsider, and take your partner's hand opposite to the way you normally would. Now check for reactions in each of you. Are there any signs that this feels unnatural? Both of you are likely to feel uncomfortable with the new arrangement, and signs of this discomfort will be obvious.

So what does this reaction mean? Why does holding hands this way feel awkward? Since holding hands is a highly personal or individual act, people should be able to hold hands in one way or the other, as a matter of choice. Surely there are no unwritten rules about how males and females are meant to hold hands. Assuming an absence of hand-holding rules, it is worth noting that the vast majority of us *conform* to predictable patterns of behaviour. If, on the other hand, there *are* rules underlying this conformity, how do we learn about them? And why is the man's hand in front? Is it a matter of height differences, leadership, or power and dominance?

Understanding *society* is a much more difficult task than understanding hand-holding behaviour, but this example suggests that people act in highly predictable ways; life does not unfold on the basis of sheer chance or complete freedom of choice. The essential wisdom of sociology is that society guides our actions and shapes our values; knowledge of the social forces at work allows sociologists to understand and predict the behaviour of individuals, groups, or categories of people. ■

Linda Gerber

When it comes to holding hands, or even falling in love, the decisions people make do not simply result from the process that philosophers call *free will*. Sociology teaches us that the social world guides all our life choices in much the same way that the seasons influence our clothing and activities.

The Sociological Perspective

1.1 **Explain how the sociological perspective differs from common sense.**

Sociology is *the systematic study of human society*. At the heart of sociology is a special point of view called the *sociological perspective*.

Seeing the General in the Particular

Years ago, Peter Berger (1963) described the **sociological perspective** as *seeing the general in the particular*. By this he meant that sociologists identify general patterns in the behaviour of particular individuals. While acknowledging that each individual is unique, sociologists recognize that society acts differently on various *categories* of people (say, children compared to adults, women versus men, the rich as opposed to the poor). We think sociologically when we realize how the general categories into which we happen to fall shape our particular life experiences.

sociology the systematic study of human society

sociological perspective sociology's special point of view that sees general patterns of society in the lives of particular people

WE CAN EASILY SEE THE POWER OF SOCIETY OVER THE INDIVIDUAL BY IMAGINING HOW DIFFERENT OUR LIVES WOULD BE HAD WE BEEN BORN IN PLACE OF ANY OF THESE CHILDREN FROM, RESPECTIVELY, KENYA, ETHIOPIA, MYANMAR, PERU, SOUTH KOREA, AND INDIA.

At a 1997 conference in Toronto, sociology professor Donna Winslow illustrated this perspective in her report on a study commissioned by the federal government. Her 400-page tome, *The Canadian Airborne Regiment: A Socio-Cultural Inquiry,* attempts to explain the atrocities committed by two Canadian peacekeepers in Somalia—not in terms of the characteristics of the individual soldiers who brutally tortured and murdered a Somali teenager but in terms of the combat or warrior culture within which they functioned. At that time (i.e., 1993), the culture of the Airborne Regiment, which focused on war making, was enhanced by recruitment, the chain of command, training, and even the nature of weapons at hand. Training for the peacekeeping role, in the areas of ethics and technique, was minimal: Soldiers were unprepared in terms of recruitment, attitude, skill, training, or equipment to engage in problem solving and negotiation or to deal with high-stress civilian situations using milder force (Winslow, 1997). Despite Canada's commitment to peacekeeping, its military—until the 1970s—had continued to prepare soldiers for war instead of peace, thereby setting the scene for violence toward civilians (Skelton, 1997). The explanation lies in the position of Canadian soldiers within a structural and cultural environment—not in individual personalities.

In March 2012, a U.S. soldier in Afghanistan left his base and entered the homes of two Afghan families in nearby villages: He opened fire and killed 16 civilians (seven adults and nine children) in a district of Kandahar where Canadian troops had patrolled from 2006 to 2011 (Clark, 2012). The goodwill among the Afghan people that had been built up by Canadian soldiers was shattered. If Winslow were to explain the actions of this soldier, she would not look to the characteristics of the soldier himself. He had been trained to be a warrior and had experienced the horrors of battle. Any one of the soldiers could have snapped under the stress of the Afghan mission. Here again, we can see the general in the particular—the behaviour of a particular individual must be understood in terms of the social, cultural, and structural context of military life.

We begin to think sociologically when we realize that our individual life experiences are shaped by the society in which we live—as well as by the general categories into which we fall.

Seeing the Strange in the Familiar

At first, using the sociological perspective is seeing the strange in the familiar. Imagine a young woman walking up to a young male friend and saying, "You fit all the right social categories, which means you would make a wonderful husband for me!" We are used to thinking that people fall in love and decide to marry based on personal feelings. But the sociological perspective reveals the initially strange idea that society shapes what we think and do. Before reading the opener to this chapter, you may not have noticed that men and women hold hands in specific ways (men from the front and women from behind). Hand-holding is very "familiar": The argument that society determines the way we hold hands is strange.

Because we live in an individualistic society, learning to see how society affects us may take a bit of practice. Asked why you chose to enrol at your particular university or college, you might offer any of the following reasons: To stay near home, to ensure a good job, or to attend with friends from high school. Such responses are certainly grounded in reality for the people expressing them. But do they tell the whole story? The sociological perspective provides additional insights that may not be readily apparent.

Thinking sociologically about university and college attendance, we should understand that, for young people throughout most of the world, post-secondary education is out of reach. Moreover, had we lived a century ago, university or college would not have been an option. Even now, a look around your classroom suggests that social forces determine whether or not one pursues higher education. Typically, university and college students are young— between 18 and 24 years of age. Why? Because, in our society, university or college attendance is associated with this period of life. But more than age is involved, because the majority of Canadians in their late teens or early twenties are not enrolled at post-secondary institutions.

Other factors affecting the pursuit of post-secondary education include socio-economic background—higher education is expensive—race or ethnicity, and region. Is it reasonable, in light of these facts, to say that attending college or university is simply a matter of personal choice?

Seeing Society in Our Everyday Lives

To see how society shapes personal choices, consider the number of children women have. In Canada and the United States, as shown in Global Map 1–1, the average woman has about two children during her lifetime. In Honduras, however, the average is about three; in Kenya, about four; in Yeman, five; and, in Niger, the average woman has more than seven children.

Why these striking differences? Women in poor countries have less schooling and fewer economic opportunities, are more likely to remain in the home, and are less likely to use contraception. Clearly, society has much to do with the decisions women and men make about child-bearing.

Another illustration of the power of society to shape even our most private choices comes from the study of suicide. What choice could be more personal than the decision to end your own life? But Émile Durkheim (1858–1917), one of sociology's pioneers, showed that, even here, social forces are at work.

Examining official records in France, his own country, Durkheim (1966; orig. 1897) found that some categories of people were more likely than others to take their own lives. Men, Protestants, wealthy people, and the unmarried had much higher suicide rates than did women, Catholics and Jews, the poor, and married people. Durkheim explained the differences in terms of social integration: Categories of people with strong social ties had low suicide rates, and more individualistic categories of people had high suicide rates.

In any given year, Canadian men are more likely than Canadian women to commit suicide.

In Durkheim's time, men had much more freedom than women. But despite its advantages, freedom weakens social ties and thereby increases the risk of suicide. Likewise, more individualistic Protestants were more likely to commit suicide than more tradition-bound Catholics and Jews, whose rituals encourage stronger social ties. The wealthy have much more freedom than the poor but, once again, at the cost of a higher suicide rate.

A century later, statistical evidence continues to support Durkheim's analysis. Figure 1–1 reveals changes in suicide rates for males and females from 1951 to 2011 in

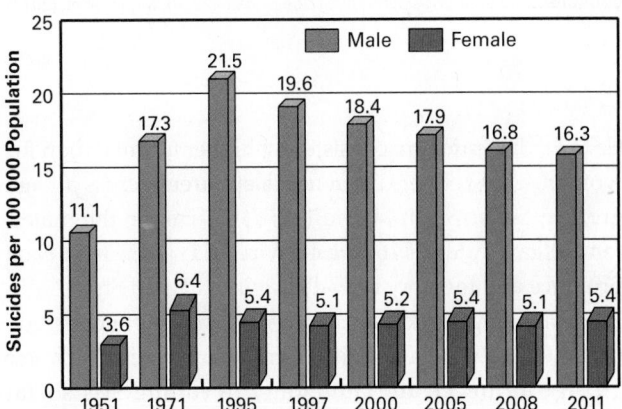

Figure 1–1 Suicide Rates for Canada by Sex: 1951–2011

Suicide rates are consistently higher for men than for women. The number of suicides per 100 000 men and women increased substantially between 1951 and 1995 and remained relatively high thereafter.

SOURCE: Compiled by L.M. Gerber from Colombo (1992:61), Statistics Canada, Catalogue no. 84F0209X and CANSIM table 102-0552.

Window on the World

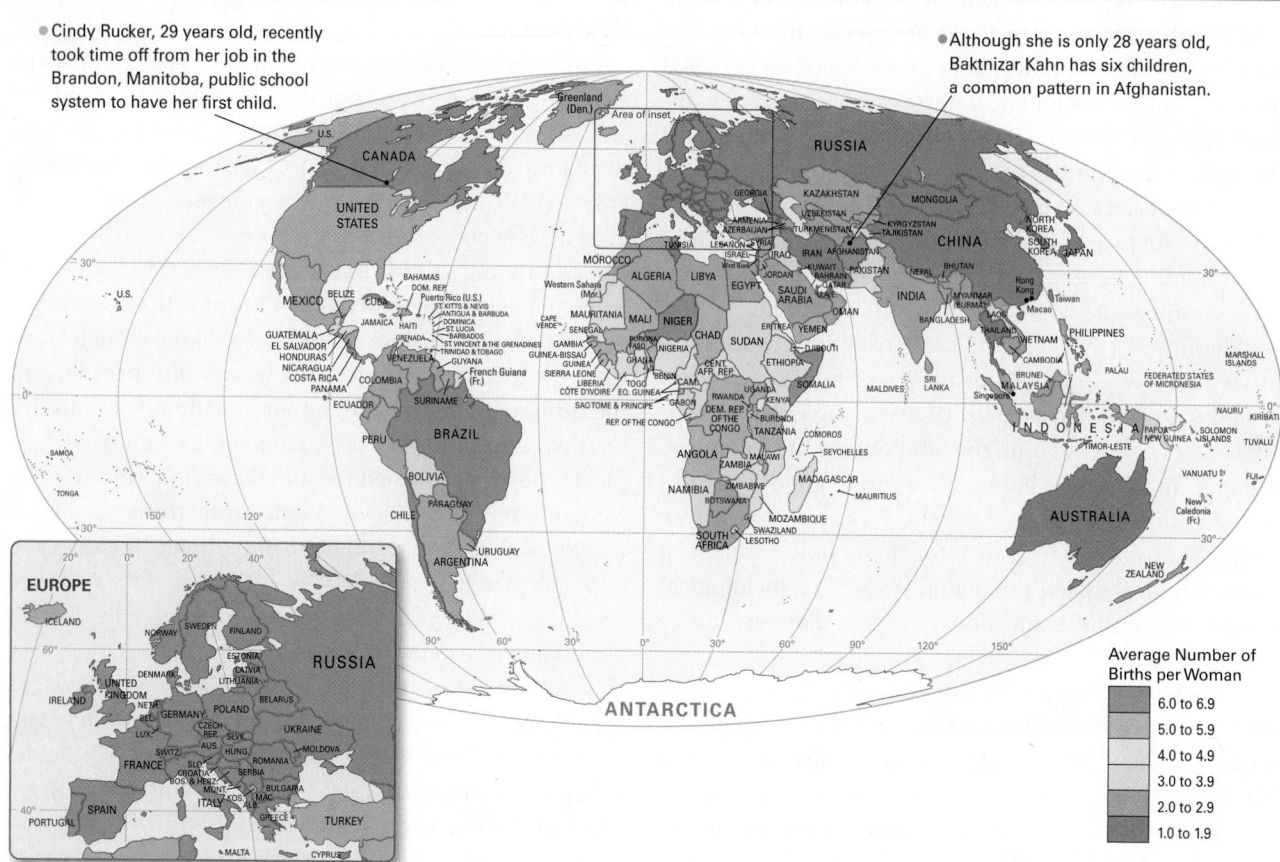

- Cindy Rucker, 29 years old, recently took time off from her job in the Brandon, Manitoba, public school system to have her first child.

- Although she is only 28 years old, Baktnizar Kahn has six children, a common pattern in Afghanistan.

Average Number of Births per Woman

- 6.0 to 6.9
- 5.0 to 5.9
- 4.0 to 4.9
- 3.0 to 3.9
- 2.0 to 2.9
- 1.0 to 1.9

Global Map 1–1 Women's Child-Bearing in Global Perspective

Is child-bearing simply a matter of personal choice? A look around the world shows that it is not. In general, women living in poor countries have many more children than women in rich nations. Can you point to some of the reasons for this global disparity? In simple terms, such differences mean that if you had been born into another society (whether you are female or male), your life might be quite different from what it is now.

SOURCES: Data from Population Reference Bureau (2014), Martin et al. (2015).

Canada: The rates are consistently higher for men than for women. This gender difference is apparent across all age groups, as shown in Figure 1–2; furthermore, the male/female gap (rates of 16.3 and 5.4 in 2011) persists in each province and territory as well as in the United States.

Following Durkheim's argument, we might conclude that the higher suicide rate among men is a result of their greater affluence and autonomy (meaning less social integration). Likewise, the high suicide rates among men from 80 to 90 years of age (20 and 23 per 100 000) can be attributed to lower levels of social integration due to widowhood, the death of friends, declining health, and declining mobility. This theory is consistent with the fact that male suicide rates are highest in Quebec and the Northwest Territories, where marriage rates are the lowest, as well as in the Yukon, where the divorce rate

is the highest. In addition, the territories are undergoing substantial social change. For several decades, young people in Canada's First Nations communities have had suicide rates five or more times higher than those of other Canadians. Aboriginal communities are still experiencing massive social change and upheaval, which, Durkheim would have argued, affect levels of social integration by putting norms and values into a state of flux. In contrast to the situation of Aboriginal peoples in Canada, suicide rates among Black men and women in the United States are less than half of those for White men and women (Centres for Disease Control and Prevention, 2012). This suggests that Black Americans experience more poverty, less freedom, and less mobility—which results in stronger social ties and greater social cohesion or solidarity.

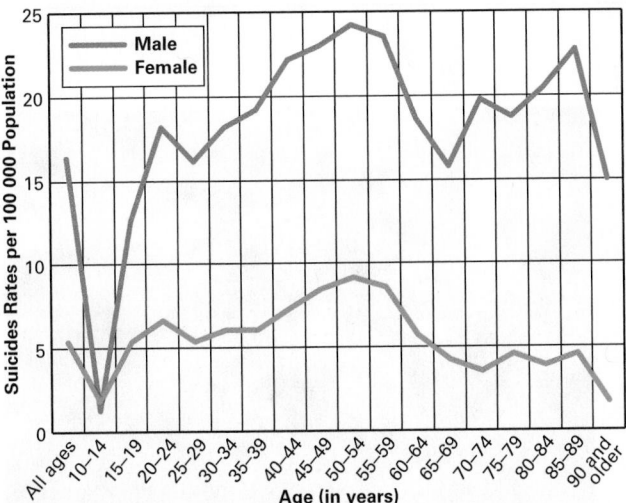

Figure 1–2 Suicide Rates for Canada by Age and Sex, 2011

In each of the age categories shown—with two or three exceptions—suicide rates for males are at least three times higher than for females. The suicide rates of both men and women are relatively high from 40 to 60 years of age. Suicide rates for men—but not for women—peak once more from 80 to 90 years of age.

SOURCE: Compiled by L.M. Gerber from Statistics Canada, CANSIM table 102-0551.

Thus, we observe general social patterns in even the most personal actions of individuals. Social forces are complex, of course, but we can see that they produce patterns in suicide. Gender operates consistently: Men throughout North America are more prone to suicide than are women. The rates may change over time, by location, or by age, but even suicide rates reveal the impact of social conditions and social forces.

Seeing Sociologically: Marginality and Crisis

Anyone can learn to see the world using the sociological perspective. But two situations help people see clearly how society shapes individual lives: living on the margins of society and living through a social crisis.

From time to time, everyone feels like an "outsider." For some categories of people, however, being an "outsider"—not part of the dominant group—is an everyday experience. The greater people's social marginality, the better able they are to use the sociological perspective. For example, Black youth growing up in the Finch and Dufferin area of Toronto understand the importance of race in shaping people's lives. Rap lyrics by artists such as k-os reinforce the notion that their hopes and dreams have been crushed by society. Contrast this with members of the dominant White majority, who think less often about their race and the privileges

it provides, believing that race affects only people from visible minorities and not themselves. People at the margins of social life, including women, gay and lesbian people, people with disabilities, and the very old, are aware of social patterns that others rarely think about. To become better at using the sociological perspective, we must step back from our familiar routines and look at our lives with new curiosity.

Periods of change or crisis make everyone feel a little off balance, encouraging us to use the sociological perspective. Sociologist C. Wright Mills (1916–1962) illustrated this idea using the Great Depression of the 1930s. As the unemployment rate soared to 25 percent, people without jobs could not help but see general social forces at work in their lives. Rather than saying, "Something is wrong with me; I can't find a job," they took a sociological approach and realized, "The economy has collapsed; there are no jobs to be found!" Mills (1959) believed that using what he called the "sociological imagination" in this way helps people understand not

PEOPLE WITH THE GREATEST PRIVILEGES TEND TO SEE INDIVIDUALS AS RESPONSIBLE FOR THEIR OWN LIVES Those at the margins of society, in contrast, see clearly that race, class, and gender imply disadvantages. Rap artist k-os gives voice to the frustration felt by many Black Canadians.

David Cooper/Toronto Star/Getty Images

Thinking Critically

The Sociological Imagination: Turning Personal Problems into Public Issues

As Mike opened the envelope, he felt his chest tighten. The letter he had dreaded was in his hands: His job was finished after 11 years of hard work he had believed would move him up in the company. All of those hopes and dreams were suddenly gone: Mike felt like a failure. He became increasingly angry with *himself* for failing and for wasting 11 years in a dead-end job.

As he returned to his workstation to pack his things, he realized he was not alone. Almost all of his colleagues in the tech support group had received the same letter. Their jobs were moving to India, where the company was able to provide telephone tech support at less than half the cost of the same service provided by Ontario workers.

A few days later, Mike was sitting in his living room with a dozen ex-employees. While comparing notes and sharing ideas, they realized they were simply victims of a massive outsourcing of jobs that is part of what analysts call the "globalization of the economy."

In good times and bad, the power of the sociological perspective lies in making sense of our individual lives. We see that many of our personal problems—and successes— are not unique to us but rather the result of larger social trends. Half a century ago, C. Wright Mills pointed to the power of the "sociological imagination" to explain everyday events. As he saw it, *society*—rather than personal failure— is the main cause of poverty and other social problems. By turning *personal problems* into *public issues,* the sociological imagination brings people together to press for needed change.

In this excerpt,[1] Mills explains the need for a sociological imagination:

> When a society becomes industrialized, a peasant becomes a worker; a feudal lord is liquidated or becomes a businessman. When classes rise or fall, a man is employed or unemployed; when the rate of investment goes up or down, a man takes new heart or goes broke. When wars happen, an insurance salesman becomes a rocket launcher; a store clerk, a radar man; a wife lives alone; a child grows up without a father. Neither the life of an individual nor the history of a society can be understood without understanding both.
>
> Yet men do not usually define the troubles they endure in terms of historical change. . . . The well-being

they enjoy, they do not usually impute to the big ups and downs of the society in which they live. Seldom aware of the intricate connection between the patterns of their own lives and the course of world history, ordinary men do not usually know what this connection means for the kind of men they are becoming and for the kinds of history-making in which they might take part. They do not possess the quality of mind essential to grasp the interplay of men and society, of biography and history, of self and world. . . .

What they need . . . is a quality of mind that will help them to [see] what is going on in the world and . . . what may be happening within themselves. It is this quality . . . that . . . may be called the sociological imagination. (1959:3–5)

What Do You Think?

1. As Mills sees it, how are personal troubles different from public issues?

2. Why do we blame ourselves for the personal problems we face?

3. How are we empowered by using the sociological imagination?

---

[1]In this excerpt, Mills uses "man" and male pronouns to apply to all people. Note that even an outspoken critic of society such as Mills reflected the conventional writing practices of his time as far as gender was concerned.

---

only their society but also their individual lives, because the two are closely related. The Thinking Critically box takes a closer look.

Just as social change encourages sociological thinking, sociological thinking can bring about social change.

The more we learn about how "the system" operates, the more we may want to change it in some way. Becoming aware of the power of gender, for example, has encouraged many women and men to try to reduce gender inequality.

The Importance of a Global Perspective

1.2 State several reasons for the importance of a global perspective in today's world.

As new information technology draws the farthest reaches of Earth closer together, many academic disciplines are taking a **global perspective:** *The study of the larger world and our society's place in it.* What is the importance of a global perspective for sociology?

First, global awareness is a logical extension of the sociological perspective. Since sociology shows us that our place in society shapes our life experiences, it stands to reason that the position of our society in the larger world system affects everyone in Canada. Consider Canada's often ambivalent relationship with the United States—the destination for over 80 percent of our exports—and our nation's attempts to come to terms with the emerging economic powers of China and India.

The world's 195 nations can be divided into three broad categories according to their level of economic development (see Global Map 12–1). **High-income countries** are the *nations with the highest overall standards of living.* The 72 countries in this category include the United States and Canada, Argentina, the nations of Western Europe, Israel, Saudi Arabia, Japan, and Australia. Taken together, these nations produce most of the world's goods and services, and the people who live there own most of the planet's wealth. Economically speaking, people in these countries are very well off, not because they are smarter or work harder than anyone else but because they were lucky enough to be born in a rich region of the world.

A second category is **middle-income countries**, *nations with a standard of living about average for the world as a whole.* People in any of these 72 nations—many of the countries of Eastern Europe, some of Africa, and almost all of Latin America and Asia—are as likely to live in rural villages as in cities, and to walk or ride tractors, scooters, bicycles, or animals as to drive automobiles. On average, they receive eight years of schooling. Most middle-income countries also have considerable social inequality within their own borders, so that some people are extremely rich (members of the business elite in nations across North Africa, for example), but many more

lack safe housing and adequate nutrition (people living in the shanty settlements that surround Lima, Peru, or Mumbai, India).

The remaining 53 nations of the world are **low-income countries**, *nations with a low standard of living in which most people are poor.* Most of the poorest countries in the world are in Africa, and a few are in Asia. Here again, a few people are very rich, but the majority struggle to get by with poor housing, unsafe water, too little food, and, perhaps most serious of all, little chance to improve their lives.

The position of Canada among the "haves" of the world is apparent in an annual list of the best countries in which to live—ranked according to the United Nations' Human Development Index (United Nations, 2014). This index determines quality of life by combining measures of income, life expectancy, literacy, and school enrolment. Canada ranked at the top of the list for many years (to the delight of Prime Minister Jean Chrétien) before dropping to third place in 2001 and fifth place in 2003. By 2008, Canada had recaptured its third-place standing—before declining to sixth place again in 2011 and eighth place in 2014, behind Norway (first place since 2003), Australia, Switzerland, Netherlands, the United States, Germany, and New Zealand. Since the top 50 are considered to be the "very high human development" countries, Canada—in eighth place in 2014—is in very good company.

The chapter on Global Stratification explains the causes and consequences of global wealth and poverty. But every chapter of this text makes comparisons between North America and other world regions for four reasons:

1. **Where we live shapes the lives we lead.** As we saw in Global Map 1–1, women living in rich and poor countries have different-sized families, in part determined by the very different lives they lead. To understand ourselves and appreciate how others live, we must understand something about how countries differ, which is one good reason to pay attention to the global maps found throughout this text.

2. **Societies throughout the world are increasingly interconnected.** Although, in the past, we may have paid little attention to the countries beyond our borders, in recent decades Canadians have become linked as never before to people in the rest of the world. Electronic technology now transmits sounds, pictures, and written documents around the globe in seconds. Email and internet chat groups have freed social interaction from the constraints of geography.

One effect of new technology is that people the world over now share many tastes in food, clothing, and music. Rich countries such

global perspective the study of the larger world and our society's place in it

high-income countries	middle-income countries	low-income countries
nations with the highest overall standards of living	nations with a standard of living about average for the world as a whole	nations with a low standard of living in which most people are poor

Thinking Globally

The Global Village: A Social Snapshot of Our World

Earth is currently home to 7 billion people, who live in the cities and villages of 195 nations. To grasp the social shape of the world on a smaller scale, imagine shrinking the planet's population to a "global village" of just 1000 people. In this village, more than half (604) of the inhabitants would be Asian, including 191 citizens of the People's Republic of China. Next, in terms of numbers, we would find 152 Africans, 105 Europeans, 85 people from Latin America and the Caribbean, 5 people from Australia and the South Pacific, and just 49 North Americans, including 44 people from the United States.

A close look at this settlement would reveal some startling facts: The village is a rich place, with a spectacular range of goods and services for sale. Yet most of the villagers can only dream about such treasures, because they are so poor: 50 percent of the village's total income is earned by just 90 people.

For most, the greatest problem is getting enough food. Every year, village workers produce more than enough to feed everyone; even so, about 125 people in the village do not get enough to eat, and many go to sleep hungry every night. These 125 residents (who together have less money than the single richest person in the village) lack both clean drinking water and safe shelter. Weak and often unable to work, they are at risk of contracting deadly diseases and dying.

The village has many schools, including a fine university. About 67 inhabitants have completed a college degree, but one-sixth of the village's adults are not even able to read or write.

Canadians and Americans would be among the village's richest people. Although we may like to think that our comfortable lives are the result of our individual talent and hard work, the sociological perspective reminds us that our achievements also result from our nation's privileged position in the worldwide social system.

What Do You Think?

1. Do any of the statistics presented in this box surprise you? Which ones? Why?
2. How do you think the lives of poor people in a lower-income country differ from those typical of people in the North America?
3. Is your "choice" to attend college or university affected by the country in which you live? How?

SOURCES: Calculations by the author based on international data from the Population Reference Bureau (2012), UNESCO (2012), United Nations Development Programme (2012), U.S. Census Bureau (2012), World Bank (2012).

---

as the United States influence other nations, whose people are ever more likely to gobble up its Big Macs and Whoppers, dance to the latest popular American music, and speak the English language. Living next door makes Canadians especially sensitive to American cultural influence. As the North American way of life is projected onto much of the world, the larger world, too, has an impact here. In the past two decades, more than 4 million immigrants added to the historical flow that built our country. In response, Canada has adopted many of the favourite sights, sounds, and tastes of its new members. The enhanced ethnic and cultural diversity of this country is apparent in our streets, our festivals, our grocery stores, and the media.

Trade across national borders has created a global economy. Large corporations manufacture and market goods worldwide, just as global financial markets linked by satellite now operate around the clock. Today, no stock trader in Toronto dares to ignore what happens in the financial markets in New York, Tokyo, and Hong Kong, just as no wheat farmer in Manitoba can afford to overlook the price of grain in the former Soviet republic of Georgia.

When you receive routine calls from "Canadian" corporations, they may well come from call centres in India—and many familiar North American products (clothing, shoes, and electronics) may be made, entirely or in part, in low-wage countries halfway around the world. Because many new Canadian jobs involve international trade, gaining greater global understanding has never been more important.

3. **Many of the social problems we face in Canada are far more serious elsewhere.** Poverty is a serious problem in Canada but, as the chapter on Global Stratification explains, poverty in Latin America, Africa, and Asia is both more common and more severe. Moreover, although Canadian women have lower social standing than men, gender inequality is even greater in the world's poor countries.

4. **Thinking globally helps us learn more about ourselves.** We cannot walk the streets of a distant city without thinking about what it means to live in Canada. Comparing life in various settings also leads to unexpected lessons. For instance, a squatter settlement in Madras, India, reveals people who thrive in the love and support of family members—despite desperate poverty. Why, in contrast, are so many of

our own poor angry and alone? Are material things—so central to our definition of the "good life"—the best way to measure human well-being?

In sum, in an increasingly interconnected world, we can understand ourselves only to the extent that we understand others. Sociology is an invitation to learn new ways of looking at the world around us. But is this invitation worth accepting? What are the benefits of applying the sociological perspective?

Applying the Sociological Perspective

1.3 Identify the advantages of sociological thinking for developing public policy, for encouraging personal growth, and for advancing in a career.

Applying the sociological perspective is useful in many ways. First, sociology is at work guiding many of the laws and policies that shape our lives. Second, on an individual level, making use of the sociological perspective leads to important personal growth and expanded awareness. Third, for anyone, studying sociology is excellent preparation for the world of work. We will look briefly at these different ways of putting sociology to work.

Sociology and Public Policy

Sociology has played an important role in the development of Canadian social policy. For example, sociological research strongly influenced the Royal Commission on Health Services (1964–1965), from which Canada's medicare system arose. The findings of sociologists also underpinned the Royal Commission on Bilingualism and Biculturalism (1963–1969) and the Royal Commission on the Status of Women in Canada (1967–1970), which brought far-reaching policy changes. In Quebec, La Commission d'évaluation de l'enseignement collégial du Québec (1963–1966) drastically altered the educational system in that province. Aboriginal peoples are still waiting for research results for the Royal Commission on Aboriginal Peoples (1993–1996) to have positive effects on public policy. Many sociologists have done policy-relevant work outside the context of royal commissions. Raymond Breton, who for a number of years was the director of Montreal's Institute for Research on Public Policy, has done influential work in the areas of ethnicity, cultural boundaries, Quebec nationalism, regionalism, and constitutional change. Hundreds of people with sociological training, who are employed by government, polling agencies, the media, and universities, have impacts on public policy and Canada's response to a wide range of social issues.

Toronto Star/Getty Images

MORE THAN 2000 EMPLOYEES AT A GM TRUCK PLANT IN OSHAWA, ONTARIO, LOST THEIR JOBS WHEN THE PLANT CLOSED IN 2009 DUE TO THE ECONOMIC DOWNTURN.

Living in a society that stresses individual freedom and responsibility, we grow up thinking that people are entirely responsible for their lives. The sociological perspective helps us see that the operation of society, including the way the economy works (or fails to work), can shape the fate of many people.

Sociology and Personal Growth

By applying the sociological perspective, we become more active, aware, and critical in our thinking. Using sociology benefits us in four ways:

1. **The sociological perspective helps us assess the truth of "common sense."** We all take many things for granted, but that does not make them true. Take the idea that we are free individuals, personally responsible for our own lives. Assuming that you decide your own fate, you might praise very successful people as superior and less successful ones as personally deficient. A sociological approach, in contrast, encourages us to ask whether such common beliefs are true and, to the extent that they are not, why they are so widely held.

2. **The sociological perspective helps us see the opportunities and constraints in our lives.** Sociological thinking leads us to see that, in the game of life, we have a say in how to play our cards, but it is society that deals us the hand. The more we understand the game, the better players we will be. Sociology helps us "size up" our world so that we can pursue our goals more effectively.

3. **The sociological perspective empowers us to be active participants in our society.** The more we understand about how society works, the more active citizens we become. As C. Wright Mills (1959) explained, it is the sociological perspective that turns a "personal problem" (such as being out of work) into a "public issue" (a lack of good jobs or a high unemployment rate). As we come to see how society affects us, we may support society as it is, or we may set out with others to change it.

4. **The sociological perspective helps us live in a diverse world.** North Americans represent just 5 percent of the world's people; Canadians alone represent only 0.5 percent. As the remaining chapters of this text explain, many of the other 95 percent of the world's people live lives very different from ours. Still, like people everywhere, we tend to define our own way of life as "right," "natural," and "better." The sociological perspective encourages us to think critically about the relative strengths and weaknesses of all ways of life, including our own.

Careers: The "Sociology Advantage"

Most post-secondary students are interested in getting a good job. A background in sociology is excellent preparation for the working world. Of course, completing a bachelor's degree in sociology is the right choice for people who would like to go on to graduate work to eventually become professors or researchers in the field. Throughout Canada, thousands of men and women teach sociology in universities, colleges, and high schools. But just as many professional sociologists work as researchers for government agencies or private foundations and businesses, gathering important information on social behaviour and carrying out evaluation research. In today's cost-conscious world, agencies and companies want to be sure that the programs and policies they set in place can get the job done at the lowest cost. Sociologists, especially those with advanced research skills, are in high demand for this kind of work.

But sociology is not just for people who want to be sociologists. People who work in criminal justice—including jobs in police departments, probation offices, and corrections facilities—gain the "sociology advantage" by learning which categories of people are most at risk of becoming criminals or victims, how effective various policies and programs are at preventing crime, and why people turn to crime in the first place. Similarly, people who work in health care—including doctors, nurses, and technicians—also gain a "sociology advantage" by learning about patterns of health and illness, as well as the effects of race, gender, and social class on human health and attitudes toward health care providers. Social work is a field chosen by many young people with a solid foundation in sociology.

Sociology is also excellent preparation for jobs in dozens of additional fields, including advertising, banking, business, education, government, journalism, law, public relations, and personnel management. In almost any type of work, success depends on understanding how various categories of people differ in beliefs, family patterns, and other ways of life. Unless you plan to have a job that never involves dealing with people, you should consider the workplace benefits of learning more about sociology.

The Origins of Sociology

1.4 Link the origins of sociology to historical social changes.

Like the "choices" made by individuals, major historical events rarely just "happen." The birth of sociology was itself the result of powerful social forces.

Social Change and Sociology

Striking changes took place in Europe during the eighteenth and nineteenth centuries. Three kinds of change were especially important in the development of sociology: the rise of a factory-based industrial economy, the explosive growth of cities, and the spread of new ideas about democracy and political rights.

A NEW INDUSTRIAL ECONOMY During the Middle Ages in Europe, most people worked the fields near their homes or toiled in small-scale manufacturing (a word derived from Latin words meaning "to make by hand"). By the end of the eighteenth century, inventors used new sources of energy—the power of moving water and then steam—to operate large machines in mills and factories. Instead of labouring at home, workers became part of a large and anonymous labour force, under the control of strangers who owned the factories. This change in the system of production took people out of their homes, weakening the traditions that had guided community life for centuries.

THE GROWTH OF CITIES Across Europe, landowners took part in what historians call the *enclosure movement:* They fenced off more and more farmland to create grazing areas for sheep, the source of wool for the thriving textile mills. Without land, countless tenant farmers had little choice but to head to the cities in search of work in the new factories. As cities grew larger, these urban migrants faced many social problems, including pollution, crime, and homelessness. Moving through streets crowded with strangers, they saw a new, impersonal social world.

POLITICAL CHANGE Europeans in the Middle Ages viewed society as an expression of God's will: From royalty to serf, each person on the social ladder played a part in the holy plan. This view of society is captured in lines from the old Anglican hymn "All Things Bright and Beautiful":

> The rich man in his castle,
> The poor man at his gate,
> God made them high and lowly
> And ordered their estate.

But as cities grew, this sort of traditional thinking came under spirited attack. In the writings of Thomas Hobbes (1588–1679), John Locke (1632–1704), and Adam Smith (1723–1790) we see a shift in focus from a moral obligation to God and monarch to the pursuit of self-interest. In the new political climate, philosophers spoke of *individual liberty* and *individual rights*. The French Revolution, which began in 1789, was an even greater break with political and social tradition. French social analyst Alexis de Tocqueville (1805–1859) thought that the changes in society brought about by the French Revolution were so great

that they amounted to "nothing short of the regeneration of the whole human race" (1955:13; orig. 1856).

We hear an echo of these sentiments today in the Canadian constitution, which asserts that each individual has certain rights, freedoms, and protections. Section 2, "Fundamental Freedoms," of the Canadian *Charter of Rights and Freedoms* states

> Everyone has the following fundamental freedoms:
>
> **(a)** freedom of conscience and religion;
> **(b)** freedom of thought, belief, opinion and expression, including freedom of the press and other media of communication;
> **(c)** freedom of peaceful assembly; and
> **(d)** freedom of association. (Canada, 1982)

A NEW AWARENESS OF SOCIETY Huge factories, exploding cities, a new spirit of individualism—these changes combined to make people aware of their surroundings. The new discipline of sociology was born in England, France, and Germany—precisely where the changes were greatest.

Science and Sociology

It was the French social thinker Auguste Comte (1798–1857) who coined the term *sociology* in 1838 to describe a new way of looking at society. This makes sociology one of the youngest academic disciplines—far newer than history, physics, or economics, for example. Of course, Comte was not the first person to think about the nature of society. Such questions fascinated the brilliant thinkers of ancient civilizations, including the Chinese philosopher K'ung Fu-tzu (Confucius, 551–479 BCE) and the Greek philosophers Plato (c. 427–347 BCE) and Aristotle (384–322 BCE).[2] Centuries later, Roman emperor Marcus Aurelius (121–180), medieval thinkers Saint Thomas Aquinas (c. 1225–1274) and Christine de Pisan (c. 1363–1431), and English playwright William Shakespeare (1564–1616) wrote about the workings of society. Yet these thinkers were more interested in imagining the ideal society than in looking at reality.

Comte and other pioneers of sociology all cared about how society could be improved, but their major goal was to understand how society actually operates. Comte (1975; orig. 1851–1854) saw sociology as the product of a three-stage historical development:

- During the earliest, the *theological stage,* from the beginning of human history to the end of the

---

[2]The abbreviation BCE means "before the common era." To reflect the religious diversity of our society, we use this throughout the text instead of the traditional BC ("before Christ"). Similarly, in place of the traditional AD (*anno Domini,* or "in the year of our Lord"), we use the abbreviation CE ("common era").

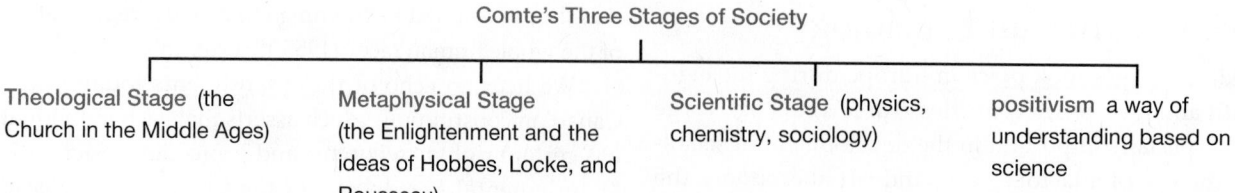

Comte's Three Stages of Society

Theological Stage (the Church in the Middle Ages)

Metaphysical Stage (the Enlightenment and the ideas of Hobbes, Locke, and Rousseau)

Scientific Stage (physics, chemistry, sociology)

positivism a way of understanding based on science

European Middle Ages (about 1350 CE), people took a religious view that society expressed God's will.

- With the dawn of the Renaissance in the fifteenth century, the theological approach gave way to a *metaphysical stage* of history in which people saw society as a natural rather than a supernatural system. Thomas Hobbes (1588–1679), for example, suggested that society reflected not the perfection of God so much as the failings of a selfish human nature.

- What Comte called the *scientific stage* of history began with the work of early scientists such as Polish astronomer Copernicus (1473–1543), Italian astronomer and physicist Galileo (1564–1642), and English physicist and mathematician Isaac Newton (1642–1727). Comte's contribution came in applying the scientific approach—first used to study the physical world—to the study of society.[3]

Comte's approach, called **positivism**, is *a way of understanding based on science*. As a positivist, Comte believed that society operates according to its own laws, much as the physical world operates according to gravity and other laws of nature.

By the beginning of the twentieth century, sociology had spread to North America and showed the influence of Comte's ideas. Today, most sociologists still consider science a crucial part of sociology. But as the chapter on Sociological Investigation explains, we now realize that human behaviour is far more complex than the movement of planets or even the actions of other living things. We are creatures of imagination and spontaneity, so human behaviour can never fully be explained by rigid "laws of society." In addition, early sociologists such as Karl Marx (1818–1883), whose ideas are discussed in the chapter on Society, were troubled by the striking inequality of industrial society. They wanted the new discipline of sociology not just to understand society but to bring about change toward social justice.

Canadian Sociology: Distinctive Touches

Canadian sociology arose from different traditions and continues to be distinct from American sociology in many ways. As a discipline that reflects a country with two major cultures and linguistic communities, Canadian sociology includes a unique francophone component. Sociology began in Canada, as in the United States, in the early part of the twentieth century. By 1920, sociology courses were being offered in a number of disciplines, including theology. During this period the Canadian Political Science Association, formed in 1913, accepted sociologists as members. Teaching and research in sociology were undertaken earlier in Quebec—at Laval, at l'Université de Montréal, and then later at l'Université du Québec—than in the rest of the country. French-Canadian sociology was influenced, initially, by the Roman Catholic Church and, in the longer term, by developments in Europe and France, where sociologists tended to investigate and compare economic and political trends. English-Canadian sociology began both at McGill, following the U.S. tradition, and at the University of Toronto, following the British tradition.

Sociology did not have its own department at the University of Toronto until the 1960s. Before that time, social thinkers of sociological cast worked out of the department of political economy. Sociology at the University of Toronto differed from the American-influenced social issues and the community study approach that characterized studies at McGill.

Harold Innis, a political economist at the University of Toronto, tackled questions of political and economic history. In *The Fur Trade in Canada* (1930), Innis argued that Canadian economic development depended on resource extraction and exportation (the staples thesis)—thereby forming the backdrop for the development of the sociological perspective in Canada. This perspective focused on economic developments such as the branch-plant nature of the Canadian economy. Innis also explored the role of communications, communications technology, and the media in the development of Canadian society. He established the Toronto "school" of communication, defended the independence of universities from political and economic pressures, and worked to establish funding for Canadian social research.

---

[3]Illustrating Comte's stages, the ancient Greeks and Romans viewed the planets as gods; Renaissance metaphysical thinkers saw them as astral influences (giving rise to astrology); by the time of Galileo, scientists understood planets as natural objects moving according to natural laws.

Sociology and the Media

Marshall McLuhan: Media Theorist

When, in the 1960s, Marshall McLuhan (1911–1980) claimed that the electronic media would transform the world as we knew it, he captured the attention of the world, achieving a fame that would fade by the late 1970s. Then, personal computers, laptops, and the Canadian BlackBerry were decades away. McLuhan was a renegade, too far ahead of everyone else. He spoke of running a factory, or indeed the world, from a cottage computer—at a time when computers, mostly operated by universities or large institutions, were the size of a small room. McLuhan's students at the University of Toronto struggled to understand his science fiction. Today, you might have difficulty comprehending the revolutionary impact of his thought, because—like fish oblivious to water—you are totally immersed in the very world he foresaw. Now that we live in the information age, scholars are revisiting McLuhan's thoughts and reviving his fame three decades after his death.

McLuhan taught us that "the instantaneous world of electronic information media involves all of us, all at once" in a "global village" or "instantaneous happening" (cited in Benedetti and DeHart, 1996). The instant movement of electronic information involves anyone connected to it in the business of others. Electronic communication extends our nervous systems so that we can be aware, immediately, of things that are happening in the world. This instant awareness explodes local or even national boundaries—which cease to exist—making each of us part of the global village: Recall our experience of the December 2004 tsunami and the phenomenal generosity of Canadian donors. At the same time, the world implodes or collapses in on us as instantaneous communication can come from everywhere. Explosion and implosion occur simultaneously.

"The medium is the message": This enigmatic or contradictory statement is typical of those with which McLuhan would tease his students. Because he wanted to teach rather than to inform or entertain, he sought to engage his students in the process of discovery, or puzzle solving. In observing that the medium is the message, he is saying that content is not everything. The book, the television, the cellphone, the camera, or the computer—in and of itself—changes the way we interact with the world around us. The bits of information we acquire may be of less importance than the media through which we obtain them. Think about the death of Princess Diana or New Orleans after Hurricane Katrina. How differently did you absorb the news from the television and from the newspaper? Each medium covered the same "news," but the impacts on their recipients had little in common. Instantaneous coverage via satellite television and social networking can make us feel part of the global village in a way that newspapers cannot.

Take a look at the following aphorisms, or brief statements of principle (cited in Benedetti & DeHart, 1996:102), to get a sense of McLuhan's approach to teaching—making you a puzzle solver rather than a passive recipient of information as you come to grips with his intent.

The telephone: speech without walls.

The phonograph: music hall without walls.

The photograph: museum without walls.

The electric light: space without walls.

The movie, radio, and TV: classroom without walls.

What Do You Think?

1. Does instantaneous electronic communication make *you* feel like a part of the global village?
2. *Is* the medium the message? For example, is the cell phone itself the message—apart from content?
3. Do McLuhan's aphorisms make sense to you?

Marshall McLuhan was a controversial figure who achieved international recognition as a media theorist in the 1960s and 1970s. He foresaw the impact of electronic communication on culture, politics, countries, and personal identities. In reality a social theorist, he provoked Canadians with his musings on the interplay of the media—the electronic media in particular—with human thought, human behaviour, and the shape of society. He had his students chew on tidbits such as "the medium is the message" and "global village," while his thinking laid the groundwork for our understanding of the current concepts of cyberspace and virtual reality and their impacts on social cohesion and identity (Benedetti & DeHart, 1996; Goyder, 1997). See the Sociology and the Media box for further insight into his work.

In the Sociology and the Media box in the chapter on Groups and Organizations, Barry Wellman carries on the Innis–McLuhan study of community and communication in his analysis of non-local community based on networks built through cyberspace. He is an expert in the areas of community, network analysis, and the impact of computers and the internet on the conduct of organizations or professional associations—as well as on the personal lives of individuals.

John Porter, in many minds, is Canada's leading sociologist. His book *The Vertical Mosaic: An Analysis of Social Class and Power in Canada* (1965) laid the groundwork for the focus on Canadian society in the context of development and underdevelopment (particularly as compared to the United States), social stratification, ethnic inequality, elites, French–English relations, and bureaucracy. He noted that the elites of the 1950s were made up largely of wealthy Anglo-Saxon men (hence the vertical mosaic) and that there were multiple elites (e.g., those who controlled our financial, industrial, and political institutions) instead of one unified elite. Porter initiated the study of social class in Canada, thereby challenging the notion that Canada is a classless society.

One of John Porter's many influential students, Wallace Clement, replicated the vertical mosaic and contributed further to the study of power elites and stratification in Canadian society (Clement, 1975, 1990).

Erving Goffman, one of North America's most influential sociologists, pioneered micro-analysis, or the study of face-to-face interaction. He is a symbolic interactionist who argued that the maintenance of the social world requires each individual to play his or her own part. Taking this one step further, he conceived of individuals as actors on stage and developed the dramaturgical perspective and dramaturgical analysis. As a participant-observer, Goffman would conduct experiments to understand social order in specific settings. By breaking the "rules" and observing the responses of others, Goffman developed a method for revealing the existence of the rules that shape the social order. His major books include: *The Presentation of Self in Everyday Life* (1959), *Asylums: Essays on the Social Situation of Mental Patients and Other Inmates* (1961), and *Stigma: Notes on the Management of Spoiled Identity* (1963). Goffman was born in Alberta, did his undergraduate work at the University of Toronto, and went on to graduate studies and teaching in the United States.

Dorothy Smith, teaching at University of California at Berkeley when the women's movement was in its early stages, looked at the experience of female academics (who were few in number there) and began to ask about the life stories of these women. Later, at the University of British Columbia, she taught one of the first women's studies courses in Canada and inspired the establishment of women's studies courses across the country. As a feminist inspired by Karl Marx, Smith turned her attention to the development of "a sociology for women."

HAROLD A. INNIS

MARSHALL MCLUHAN

JOHN PORTER

ERVING GOFFMAN

DOROTHY SMITH

RAYMOND BRETON

She founded feminist standpoint theory, which looks at the social world from the perspectives of women in their everyday lives and the ways in which women socially construct their worlds. In 2005, she published a book, *Institutional Ethnography: A Sociology for People,* that outlines a method of studying social organization through everyday life. Her approach has been adopted worldwide by a variety of disciplines to study a range of institutions as well as for public policy research. Within sociology, she contributed to family studies, methodology, and feminist theory—founding the field of institutional ethnography in addition to feminist standpoint theory.

Raymond Breton, of the University of Toronto, is world-renowned as an expert on ethnocultural and immigrant communities, ethnic and linguistic diversity, multiculturalism, French–English relations, Quebec nationalism, regionalism, national unity, and constitutional issues. His analysis of factors contributing to the viability of immigrant communities led to his coining the immensely useful term *institutional completeness* (Breton, 1964). This concept has been expanded to become a general framework for institutional analysis in the study of inter-ethnic relations (Breton & Reitz, 2007). Not content simply to teach and carry out his research, Breton served sociology and Canadian society as the director of Montreal's Institute for Research on Public Policy. In 2008, he was named an Officer of the Order of Canada for his "contributions to the advancement of sociology and to the understanding of the impact of multiculturalism and linguistic diversity on Canadian society."

Canada's massive size, its sparse but diverse population, its proximity to the United States, and its global situation (economic, cultural, and political) ensure that Canadian sociology will continue to be concerned with questions of unity, political movements, economic development, and inequality.

Sociological Theory

1.5 Summarize sociology's major theoretical approaches.

Weaving observations into understanding brings us to another aspect of sociology: theory. A **theory** is *a statement of how and why specific facts are related.* The job of sociological theory is to explain social behaviour in the real world. For example, recall Émile Durkheim's theory that categories of people with low social integration (men,

Protestants, the wealthy, and the unmarried) are at higher risk of suicide. As the next chapter on Sociological Investigation explains, sociologists test their theories by gathering evidence using various research methods. Durkheim did exactly this, finding out which categories of people were more likely to commit suicide and which were less likely, and then devising a theory that best squared with all available evidence.

In building theory, sociologists face two fundamental questions: What issues should we study? How should we connect the facts? In the process of answering these questions, sociologists look to one or more theoretical paradigms, or approaches, as "road maps." Think of a **theoretical approach** as *a basic image of society that guides thinking and research.* Sociologists use three major theoretical approaches: The structural-functional approach, the social-conflict approach, and the symbolic-interaction approach, each of which will be explored in the remainder of this chapter. We also discuss two more recent paradigms: Feminism and postmodernism.

The Structural-Functional Approach

The **structural-functional approach** is *a framework for building theory that sees society as a complex system whose parts work together to promote solidarity and stability.* As its name suggests, this approach points to **social structure**—*any relatively stable pattern of social behaviour.* Social structure gives our lives shape—in families, the workplace, the classroom, and the community. This approach also looks for a structure's **social functions**, *the consequences of any social pattern for the operation of society as a whole.* All social structure, from a simple handshake to complex religious rituals, functions to keep society going, at least in its present form.

The structural-functional approach owes much to Auguste Comte, who pointed out the need to keep society unified when many traditions were breaking down. Émile Durkheim, who helped establish the study of sociology in French universities, also based his work on this approach. A third structural-functional pioneer was the English sociologist Herbert Spencer (1820–1903). Spencer compared society to the human body. Just as the structural parts of the human body—the skeleton, muscles, and various internal organs—function interdependently

---

theory a statement of how and why specific facts are related

theoretical approach a basic image of society that guides thinking and research

structural-functional approach a framework for building theory that sees society as a complex system whose parts work together to promote solidarity and stability

social structure any relatively stable pattern of social behaviour

social functions the consequences of a social pattern for the operation of society as a whole

manifest functions the recognized and intended consequences of any social pattern

latent functions the unrecognized and unintended consequences of any social pattern

to help the entire organism survive, social structures work together to preserve society. The structural-functional approach, then, leads sociologists to identify various structures of society and investigate their functions.

Robert K. Merton (1910–2003) expanded our understanding of the concept of social function by pointing out that any social structure probably has many functions, some more obvious than others. He distinguished between **manifest functions**, *the recognized and intended consequences of any social pattern*, and **latent functions**, *the unrecognized and unintended consequences of any social pattern*. For example, the manifest function of our system of higher education is to provide young people with the information and skills they need to perform jobs after graduation. Less often acknowledged is its latent function as a "marriage broker," bringing together people of similar social backgrounds. Higher education also limits unemployment by keeping young people out of the labour market, where many of them would have difficulty finding jobs.

But Merton also recognized that the effects of social structure are not all good, and certainly not good for everybody. Consequently, a **social dysfunction** is *any social pattern that may disrupt the operation of society*. People often disagree about what is helpful and what is harmful to society as a whole. In addition, what is functional for one category of people (say, high profits for factory owners) may well be dysfunctional for another category of people (say, low wages for factory workers).

EVALUATE

The main idea of the structural-functional approach is its vision of society as stable and orderly. The main goal of the sociologists who use this approach, then, is to figure out what makes society tick.

In the mid-1900s, most sociologists favoured the structural-functional approach. In recent decades, however, its influence has declined. By focusing on social stability and unity, critics say, structural functionalism ignores inequalities of social class, race, and gender, which cause tension and conflict. In general, its focus on stability at the expense of conflict makes this approach somewhat conservative. As a critical response, sociologists developed the social-conflict approach.

CHECK YOUR LEARNING How do manifest functions differ from latent functions? Give an example of a manifest function and of a latent function of automobiles. Can you do the same for a laptop or cellphone?

Courtesy of the Adirondack Museum

THE APPROACH OF THE STRUCTURAL-FUNCTIONAL PARADIGM IS CONVEYED BY THE PAINTING *ST. REGIS INDIAN RESERVATION* BY AMY JONES (1937) Here we see society composed of major rounds of life, each serving a particular purpose that contributes to the operation of the entire system.

SOURCE: Amy Jones, *St. Regis Indian Reservation*, 1937.

The Social-Conflict Approach

The **social-conflict approach** is *a framework for building theory that sees society as an arena of inequality that generates conflict and change*. Unlike the structural-functional emphasis on solidarity and stability, this approach highlights inequality and change. Guided by this approach, sociologists investigate how factors such as social class, race, ethnicity, gender, sexual orientation, and age are linked to a society's unequal distribution of money, power, education, and social prestige. Conflict analysis rejects the idea that social structure promotes the operation of society as a whole, focusing instead on the fact that social patterns may benefit some people while hurting others.

Sociologists using the social-conflict approach look at ongoing conflict between dominant and disadvantaged categories of people—the rich in relation to the poor, White people in relation to people of colour, and men in relation to women. Typically, people in dominant positions try to protect their privileges while the disadvantaged try to gain more for themselves.

To illustrate, conflict analysis of our educational system might highlight the ways in which schooling perpetuates inequality by helping to reproduce the class structure in every new generation. The process begins as secondary schools assign some students to university preparatory programs and others to vocational training. From a functional point of view, such "streaming" may benefit all of society because, ideally, students receive the training appropriate

social dysfunction any social pattern that may disrupt the operation of society

social-conflict approach a framework for building theory that sees society as an arena of inequality that generates conflict and change

THE SOCIAL-CONFLICT APPROACH POINTS OUT PATTERNS OF INEQUALITY In general, students are relatively privileged women and men who routinely come into contact with other people who have far fewer opportunities for success. What patterns of social inequality do you see in your everyday life?

to their academic abilities. Conflict analysis counters that streaming has less to do with talent than with social background—well-to-do students are placed in higher streams and poor students end up in the lower ones. Through streaming, privileged families gain favoured treatment for their children from schools and, subsequently, universities. With the best schooling behind them, these young people leave university to pursue occupations that confer both prestige and high income. In comparison, children from poor families and communities are unprepared for university or college; like their parents before them, these young people typically move from high school into low-paying jobs. In each case, the social standing of one generation is passed on to another, with schools justifying the practice in terms of individual merit, not privilege.

Many sociologists use the social-conflict approach not just to understand society but to bring about societal change that would reduce inequality. Karl Marx, whose ideas are discussed at length in the chapter on Society, championed the cause of the workers in what he saw as their battle against factory owners. In a well-known statement (inscribed on his monument in London's Highgate Cemetery), Marx asserted: "The philosophers have only interpreted the world, in various ways; the point, however, is to change it."

Feminism and the Gender-Conflict Approach

One important type of conflict analysis is the **gender-conflict approach**, *a point of view that focuses on inequality and conflict between women and men*. The gender-conflict approach is closely linked to **feminism**, *the advocacy of social equality for women and*

men. The importance of the gender-conflict approach lies in making us aware of the many ways in which our way of life places men in positions of power over women: in the home (where men are usually considered the "head of household"), in the workplace (where men earn more and hold most positions of power), and in the mass media (where few executives are women).

Another contribution of the gender-conflict approach is making us aware of the importance of women to the development of sociology. Harriet Martineau (1802–1876) is regarded as the first woman sociologist. Martineau, who was born to a wealthy English family, made her mark in 1853 by translating the writings of Auguste Comte from French into English. She established her reputation as a sociologist with studies that documented the evils of slavery and argued for laws to protect factory workers, defending workers' right to unionize. She was particularly concerned about the position of women in society and fought for changes in education policy so that women could look forward to more in life than marriage and raising children. She also found time to write novels, travel widely, and pursue a full-time career as a journalist, in spite of deafness and recurrent ill health.

In the United States, Jane Addams (1860–1935) was a sociological pioneer whose contributions began in 1889 when she helped found Hull House, a Chicago settlement house that provided assistance to immigrant families. Although widely published (she wrote 11 books and hundreds of articles), Addams chose the life of a public activist over that of a university sociologist, speaking out on issues involving immigration and the pursuit of peace. Despite the controversy caused by her pacifism during World War I, she was awarded the Nobel Peace Prize in 1931.

In the past several decades, feminist sociology has been challenging the male-dominated discipline with critiques of methodology, theory, and all substantive areas of

the field. Thanks to the efforts of Dorothy Smith, among others, feminist sociology (along with feminist analysis in other academic disciplines) established the field of women's studies. There are now women's studies programs in universities and colleges across Canada. While almost all chapters of this text reflect upon gender and gender inequality, you will find a detailed look at feminism and the social standing of women and men in the chapter on Gender Stratification.

The Race-Conflict Approach

Another important type of social-conflict analysis is the **race-conflict approach**, *a point of view that focuses on inequality and conflict between people of different racial and ethnic categories.* Just as men have power over women, White people have numerous social advantages over people from visible minorities including, on average, higher incomes, more schooling, better health, and longer life. An important contribution to understanding race in the United States was made by William Edward Burghardt Du Bois (1868–1963). Born to a poor Massachusetts family, Du Bois eventually enrolled at Harvard University, where he earned the first doctorate awarded by that university to a person from a visible minority. Like most people who follow the social-conflict approach—whether focusing on class, gender, or race—Du Bois believed that sociologists should try to solve society's problems. He therefore studied the Black community (1967; orig. 1899), spoke out against racial inequality, and served as a founding member of the National Association for the Advancement of Colored People.

Ethnic and racial diversity have long been important themes in Canadian sociology. John Porter, in *The Vertical Mosaic* (1965), argued that class and power are functions of ethnicity and race, with people of British descent at the top of the hierarchy. Aboriginal peoples, still at the bottom of that hierarchy, are the subject of extensive research. Trent University (in Peterborough, Ontario) has special programs in Native Studies, while other universities have programs designed for Aboriginal students: The First Nations University of Canada (in Saskatchewan) specifically serves the needs of Aboriginal communities. Meanwhile, the existence of a journal titled *Canadian Ethnic Studies* reflects the continuing importance of broader issues related to diversity.

EVALUATE

The various social-conflict approaches have gained a large following in recent decades but, like other approaches, they have met with criticism. Because any conflict analysis focuses on inequality, it largely ignores how shared values and interdependence unify members of a society. In addition, to the extent that the conflict approaches pursue political goals, they cannot claim scientific objectivity. Supporters of social-conflict approaches respond that *all* theoretical approaches have political consequences.

A final criticism of both the structural-functional and the social-conflict approaches is that they paint society in broad strokes—in terms of "family," "social class," "race," and so on. A third theoretical approach views society in terms of the everyday experience of individual people.

CHECK YOUR LEARNING Why do you think sociologists characterize the social-conflict approach as "activist"? What is it actively trying to achieve?

The Symbolic-Interaction Approach

The structural-functional and social-conflict approaches share a **macro-level orientation**, *a broad focus on social structures that shape society as a whole.* Macro-level sociology takes in the big picture, rather like observing a city from high above in a helicopter and seeing how highways help people move from place to place or how housing differs from rich to poor neighbourhoods. Sociology also uses a **micro-level orientation**, *a close-up focus on social interaction in specific situations.* Exploring urban life in this way occurs at street level, where you might watch how children invent games on a school playground or observe how pedestrians respond to homeless people they pass on the street. The **symbolic-interaction approach**, then, is *a framework for building theory that sees society as the product of the everyday interactions of individuals.*

How does "society" result from the ongoing experiences of tens of millions of people? One answer, explained in the chapter Social Interaction in Everyday

gender-conflict approach a point of view that focuses on inequality and conflict between women and men

race-conflict approach a point of view that focuses on inequality and conflict between people of different racial and ethnic categories

feminism the advocacy of social equality for women and men

macro-level orientation a broad focus on social structures that shape society as a whole

micro-level orientation a close-up focus on social interaction in specific situations

symbolic-interaction approach a framework for building theory that sees society as the product of the everyday interactions of individuals

postmodernism an approach that is critical of modernism, with a mistrust of grand theories and ideologies, that can have either a micro or a macro orientation

THE BASIC INSIGHT OF THE SYMBOLIC-INTERACTION APPROACH IS THAT PEOPLE CREATE THE REALITY THEY EXPERIENCE AS THEY INTERACT In other words, as these three students engage one another in conversation, they are literally determining "what's going on."

Life, is that society is nothing more than the shared reality that people construct as they interact with one another. That is, human beings live in a world of symbols, attaching meaning to virtually everything, from the words on this screen to the wink of an eye. "Reality," therefore, is simply how we define our surroundings, our obligations toward others, and even our own identities.

The symbolic-interaction approach has roots in the thinking of Max Weber (1864–1920), a German sociologist who emphasized the need to understand a setting from the point of view of the people in it. Weber's approach is discussed in detail in the chapter on Society. Since Weber's time, sociologists have taken micro-level sociology in a number of directions. The chapter on Socialization discusses the ideas of George Herbert Mead (1863–1931), who explored how our personalities develop as a result of social experience. The chapter on Social Interaction in Everyday Life presents the work of Erving Goffman (1922–1982), whose dramaturgical analysis describes how we resemble actors on a stage as we play out our various roles. Other contemporary sociologists, including George Homans and Peter Blau, have developed social-exchange analysis. In their view, social interaction is guided by what each person stands to gain and lose through relationships with others. In the ritual of courtship, for example, people seek mates who offer at least as much—in terms of physical attractiveness, intelligence, and social standing—as they offer in return.

EVALUATE

Without denying the existence of macro-level social structures such as "the family" and "social class," the symbolic-interaction approach reminds us that society essentially amounts to *people interacting*. That is, micro-level sociology tries to show how

individuals actually experience society. On the other side of the coin, by focusing on what is unique in each social scene, this approach risks overlooking the widespread influence of culture, as well as factors such as class, gender, and race.

CHECK YOUR LEARNING How does micro-level analysis differ from macro-level analysis? Provide an explanation of a social pattern at each level.

The Postmodern Approach

Postmodernism is *an approach that is critical of modernism, with a mistrust of grand theories and ideologies, that can have either a micro or a macro orientation.* As applied by social scientists, postmodernism is at its core both anti-theory and anti-methods: Human sciences, it proposes, cannot be scientific because of human subjectivity, which makes discovering objective truth impossible. Proponents argue that they are not trying to create systematic new knowledge but are writing to permit multiple interpretations by their readers. Postmodernists seek to observe other societies without applying the conceptual baggage of their own. They observe with the goal of achieving understanding and a vision rather than data collection. Through deconstruction of existing text, postmodernists can demystify the assumptions, hierarchies of knowledge, and ideological motivation of the social sciences.

Michel Foucault (1926–1984), a French philosopher and one of the most influential postmodernists, would agree with Weber that scientific rationality is a means to an end that tells us nothing about the values that should guide our lives. Furthermore, his treatment of power, which for him permeates all of society, takes it out of the exclusive hands of capitalists, males, or any other category of people (Foucault, 1980).

The Applying Theory table summarizes the main characteristics of the classical approaches—structural functionalism, social conflict, and symbolic interactionism—as well as the feminist and postmodernist approaches. Each deals with specific kinds of questions about society. However, the fullest understanding of our social world comes from combining approaches, as we show with the following analysis of sports in North America.

Applying the Approaches: The Sociology of Sports

1.6   Apply sociology's major theoretical approaches to the topic of sports.

Who among us doesn't enjoy sports? Children as young as six or seven may be involved in as many as two or

Thinking about Diversity: Race, Class, and Gender

Early Contributions of Women to the Social Sciences

Those of you who continue to study sociology will find that your textbooks and courses rarely mention the significant contributions of women founders of the social sciences. The one exception to this rule, for *some* of the founding women, occurs in books and courses contributing to women's studies. Even though the women listed in Table 1–1 were public figures who debated the issues of their times, carried out research, published papers, pushed for social change, and influenced recognized male founders (through publication, conversation, or correspondence), they were effectively "written out" or erased from the record. Worse, their theoretical and methodological contributions were attributed to the male contemporaries who adopted their approaches.

Table 1–1 contains the names of male and female founders in two colours and several print variations. Plain black print indicates women founders or pioneers identified by Patricia Madoo Lengermann and Jill Niebrugge-Brantley (1998) in *The Women Founders: Sociology and Theory, 1830–1930*. Italic print marks the women identified by Lynn McDonald (1994) in *The Women Founders of the Social Sciences*. Red print identifies the women who are covered in both books. (Note that the women named in italics lived between the mid-1500s and 1900, while almost all of those in plain black or red print lived and worked between 1830 and 1930. In effect, McDonald reached back further in time in her search for women founders.) Bold black print identifies male founders, who are included in the table to show that the women on the list made their contributions before and during the lifetimes of the men so widely acknowledged as the "fathers" of sociology.

Throughout this text, you will find references to all of the men and many of the women listed here. In particular, you will find numerous references to Karl Marx, Émile Durkheim, and Max Weber because the main theoretical approaches of sociology—social conflict, structural functionalism, and symbolic interactionism—are attributed to them. The message here is that the men who have been credited with these insights were profoundly influenced by

the women who laid the groundwork in some earlier period or as their contemporaries. In the case of Max Weber, his wife, Marianne, was a prominent German feminist, a politician, and a prolific writer of nine books on social and women's issues. After his death, Marianne Weber edited and published 10 of his books and wrote his biography. How, one might ask, can her influence on Max Weber's thinking and writing be ignored?

Margrit Eichler (2001) turned her attention to pioneering women on the Canadian scene, interviewing 10 anglophone women sociologists who were born before 1930: Helen Abell, Grace Anderson, Jean Burnet, Eleanor Cebotarev, Kathleen Herman, Helen McGill Hughes, Thelma McCormack, Helen Ralston, Aileen Ross, and Dorothy Smith. Although these women faced sexism, they had no difficulty landing academic appointments—at a time when sociology departments were expanding along with the Canadian university system as a whole. Despite their important contributions to the development of sociology and the feminist perspective in particular, Eichler found it necessary to conduct her interviews because no published information was available on most of these women at that time. Like the earlier women founders, these Canadian sociologists have been "written out" or erased from the literary record.

Sadly, women themselves contribute to our ignorance regarding the contributions of the early women founders introduced here. Many radical feminists have been reluctant to recognize their work because their methods—"the very enterprise of empirical social science"—are under attack: "I am convinced that much of the 'feminist critique' of methodology is based on a false premise: That the social sciences have been developed by and for men" (McDonald, 1994:ix). In reality, many of the pioneers of scientific sociology were women.

What Do You Think?

1. Are you surprised by the early contributions of women to the development of social science?
2. Why might women fail to recognize the contributions of other women in their field?
3. Do women offer a unique and valuable perspective to scholarly discourse?

Table 1–1 Women and Men as Early Founders of the Social Sciences

Gournay, Marie le Jars de (1565–1645)	*Wollstonecraft, Mary (1759–1797)*	*Blackwell, Antoinette Brown (1825–1921)*	Wells Barnett, Ida B. (1862–1931)
Conway, Anne (1631–1679)	*Hays, Mary (1760–1843)*	*Gage, Matilda Joslyn (1826–1898)*	**Mead, George Herbert (1863–1931)**
Marsham, Damaris Cudworth (1658–1708)	*de Staël Holstein, Germaine Necker (1766–1817)*	Cooper, Anne Julia (1858–1964)	**Thomas, W.I. (1863–1947)**
Astell, Mary (1668–1731)	*Wright, Frances (1795–1852)*	**Durkheim, Emile (1858–1917)**	**Park, Robert E. (1864–1944)**
Cockburn, Catherine Trotter (1679–1749)	**Comte, August (1798–1857)**	Lathrop, Julia (1858–1932)	**Weber, Max (1864–1920)**
Wortley Montagu, Mary (1689–1762)	Martineau, Harriet (1802–1876)	**Simmel, Georg (1858–1918)**	Breckinridge, Sophonisba (1866–1948)
Châtelet, Emilie du (1706–1749)	*Tristan, Flora (1803–1844)*	Talbot, Marion (1858–1947)	MacLean, Annie Marion (c. 1870–1934)
Macaulay, Catharine (1731–1791)	*Taylor Mill, Harriet (1807–1858)*	Webb, Beatrice Potter (1858–1943)	Weber, Marianne (1870–1954)
Roland de la Platière, Marie Jeanne (1754–1793)	**Marx, Karl (1818–1883)**	Kelly, Florence (1859–1932)	Kellor, Francis (1873–1952)
	Nightingale, Florence (1820–1910)	Adams, Jane (1860–1935)	Abbott, Edith (1876–1957)
	Spencer, Herbert (1820–1903)	Gilman, Charlotte Perkins (1860–1935)	Abbott, Grace (1878–1939)

APPLYING THEORY
Major Theoretical Approaches

	Classical Approaches			Recent Approaches	
	Structural-Functional Approach	**Social-Conflict Approach**	**Symbolic-Interaction Approach**	**Feminist Approach**	**Postmodernist Approach**
What is the level of analysis?	Macro level	Macro level	Micro level	Micro and macro levels	Micro and macro levels
What image of society does the approach have?	Society is a system of interrelated parts that is relatively stable. Each part works to keep society operating in an orderly way. Members have general agreement about what is morally right.	Society is a system of social inequality. Society operates to benefit some categories of people and to harm others. Social inequality causes conflict that leads to social change.	Society is an ongoing process. People interact in countless settings using symbolic communications. The reality that people experience is variable and changing.	A gender-based hierarchy where men dominate women in all realms of social life (including the family, religion, the polity, the economy, and education).	Shifting patterns of social order, institutions, and personal relations, about which truths and assumptions are subject to change.
What core questions does the approach ask?	How is society held together? What are the major parts of society? How are these parts linked? What does each part do to help society work?	What factors give rise to social inequality? How do advantaged people protect their privileges? How do disadvantaged people challenge the system to seek change?	How do people experience society? How do people shape the reality they experience? How do behaviour and meaning change from person to person and from one situation to another?	What factors give rise to gender-based inequality? What are the effects of male domination on men and on women? How can such a structure be overturned?	How does power permeate social relations or society, and change with circumstances? How do we understand societies or interpersonal relations, while rejecting the theories and methods of the social sciences and our assumptions about human nature?

three organized sports at a time. Almost everyone has engaged in some type of sport: In Canada, about 45 percent of those aged 15 and over indicate regular participation in sport; the number reaches a high of 53 percent in British Columbia and dips to 36 percent in Newfoundland (Corbeil, 2000). Recognizing the importance of sports for Canada's children, Former Prime Minister Harper—an ardent hockey fan and hockey dad who wrote a book on the history of professional hockey—introduced a fitness tax credit ($500 per child) to help parents cover the expenses of organized sport.

Weekend television is filled with sporting events, and whole sections of our newspapers report the scores. Wayne Gretzky, Cassie Campbell, and Hayley Wickenheiser (hockey); Eric Gagné and David Ortiz (baseball); David Pelletier and Jamie Salé (pairs figure skating); Mike Weir and Tiger Woods (golf); and Serena Williams and Roger Federer (tennis) are all top athletes who are famous celebrities—even after they retire from active participation. Sports, both amateur and professional, have become a multibillion-dollar industry. What sociological insights can our three major theoretical approaches give us into this familiar part of everyday life?

The Structure and Function of Sports

A structural-functional approach directs our attention to the ways in which sports help society operate. The manifest functions of sports include providing recreation, a means of getting in physical shape, and a relatively harmless way to let off steam. Sports have important latent functions as well, from building social relationships to creating tens of thousands of jobs. Sports encourage both competition and teamwork, which are central to our society's way of life.

Another very important function of sports is apparent whenever our athletes compete at the international level—especially in the Olympics. Canadians find themselves waving the flag and talking to strangers while experiencing a burst of pride and solidarity. One needs only think back to the 2010 Winter Olympics to relive the emotions of the time. We took pride in a record number of medals, the opening ceremonies, and the fact that we welcomed the world to Canada with open arms. In that context, we experienced a very strong sense of Canadian identity and belonging: Sports brought us together in solidarity.

Function is one-half of the structural-functional model; the other is structure. This perspective draws our attention to social organization or social structure. Even though we can't touch, feel, or see it, we assume that our government is structured and that it is relatively stable. Concepts such as the National Hockey League (NHL) or even the Olympic movement imply some sort of structure. Moreover, the NHL will continue to exist for generations, as players, coaches, owners, and managers pass though the system—there is something "real" there that is more than the sum of its parts. From this perspective the sports complex has functions and is structured.

Sports and Social Conflict

A social-conflict analysis of sports begins by pointing out that the games people play reflect their social standing. Some sports—including hockey, tennis, golf, sailing, and skiing—are expensive, so participation is largely limited to the affluent. On the other hand, soccer, football, baseball, and basketball are accessible to people at almost all income levels. Thus, social class matters: Children from rich and poor neighbourhoods are introduced to very different sports. Race matters as well: To the extent that visible minorities are overrepresented in relatively poor neighbourhoods, they should excel in baseball or basketball rather than hockey or downhill skiing. The impact of neighbourhood is compounded by racism in professional sports.

Gender inequality persists in Canada and the United States, where sports are oriented primarily toward males. The first modern Olympic Games held in 1896 excluded women from competition and, even today, girls' teams have limited access to ice rinks and playing fields. Such gender-biased practices have been defended by unfounded notions that girls and women lack the ability to engage in sports or risk losing their femininity if they do so. Thus, our society encourages men to be athletes and expects women to be attentive observers and cheerleaders.

More women now play competitive sports than ever before—in women's hockey, Canada won gold at the Winter Olympics of 2002, 2006, and 2010—yet they continue to take a back seat to men, particularly in sports that yield the greatest earnings, media coverage, and prestige.

At the 2006 Winter Olympics in Turin, Italy, women won five of Canada's seven gold medals and 16 (two-thirds) of our country's 24 medals overall. The results in the 2010 Winter Olympics were similar: Women won six and a half of Canada's 14 gold medals (one gold was for pairs figure skating) and 15.5 of our 26 medals. In the 2008 Summer Olympics in Beijing, women won seven of our 18 medals.

In sum, sports in Canada are characterized by inequalities based on gender, race, and class.

Physical disabilities also contribute to inequalities—in life as in sports. One might argue that the Paralympics, which segregate disabled athletes in their own Olympic games, represent unequal opportunity. Nevertheless, despite relatively little media coverage, some Paralympians capture the attention of the nation. Downhill skier Lauren Woolstencroft won five gold medals for Canada at the 2010 Paralympics in Vancouver. She did this despite the fact that she was born with one hand and no legs below the knees. In November 2011, Woolstencroft was inducted into Canada's Sports Hall of Fame (Maki, 2011).

Sports as Symbolic Interaction

Most people—whether or not they are fans—will recognize hockey as a powerful symbol of Canada. The "meaning" of that symbol is shared by millions of Canadians; in turn, the symbol (hockey) provides the context for a wide range of interactions—among team members, players and fans, fans themselves, and parents at an early-morning practice. Interaction based on a shared understanding of

Isabella Vosmikova/ABC Family/Getty Images

AS THE TELEVISION SHOW *MAKE IT OR BREAK IT* **MAKES CLEAR, SPORTS ARE AN IMPORTANT ELEMENT OF SOCIAL LIFE IN COUNTLESS COMMUNITIES ACROSS NORTH AMERICA AND AROUND THE WORLD (E.G., RUSSIA AND FINLAND)** Each of sociology's three theoretical approaches contributes to our understanding of the role of sports in society.

CANADIANS, WHO ARE NORMALLY SUBDUED IN THEIR EXPRESSIONS OF PATRIOTISM, GO WILD WITH ENTHUSIASM AS THEY CHEER ON THE HOME TEAM AT THE VANCOUVER OLYMPICS (IN 2010).

hockey takes place between players and Don Cherry or players and the mass media. Without shared symbols, none of these patterned interactions would take place; nor would we experience a burst of pride when our hockey team wins Olympic gold or devastation when it loses.

Keeping in mind that words and language are symbols we use to communicate—as are shrugs, nods, and hand signals—try to imagine a hockey game without shared symbols. Without them the coach, team members, referee, and fans would be unable to communicate, and paralysis would result. Without shared understandings about symbols, such as the rules, the net, the score, offence, defence, or the goalie, the game could not proceed. Because meaningful social interaction requires shared symbols, we call it *symbolic interaction*.

The three major theoretical approaches—the structural-functional approach, the social-conflict approach, and the symbolic-interaction approach—provide different insights into sports, and none is more correct than the others. Applied to any issue, each approach generates its own interpretation. To appreciate fully the power of the sociological perspective, you should become familiar with all three.

Seeing Sociology in Everyday Life

CHAPTER 1 The Sociological Perspective

Why do couples marry?

The commonsense answer is that people marry because they are in love. But as this chapter has explained, society guides our everyday lives, affecting what we do, think, and feel. Look at the three photographs, each showing a couple that, we can assume, is "in love." In each case, can you provide some of the rest of the story? By looking at the categories that the people involved represent, explain how society is at work in bringing the two people together.

> **Hint** Society is at work on many levels. Consider (1) rules about same-sex and other-sex marriage, (2) laws defining the number of people who may marry, (3) the importance of race and ethnicity, (4) the importance of social class, (5) the importance of age, and (6) the importance of social exchange (what each partner offers the other). All societies enforce various rules that state who should or should not marry whom.

BEYONCÉ GISELLE KNOWLES, WIDELY KNOWN AS BEYONCÉ, PERFORMS IN NEW YORK'S MADISON SQUARE GARDEN WITH HER HUSBAND JAY-Z (SHAWN COREY CARTER) Looking at this couple, who married in 2008, what social patterns do you see?

Face to face/Zuma Press/Newscom

IN 2014, DAVID BURTKA AND NEIL PATRICK HARRIS WERE MARRIED They are raising two young children. Ten years ago, when this couple began dating, it is likely that few people imagined that same-sex marriage would become legal in many parts of the United States within a decade.

Bettmann/Getty Images

WHILE HE WAS CANADA'S PRIME MINISTER, PIERRE TRUDEAU (AT AGE 52) SECRETLY MARRIED A 22-YEAR-OLD "FLOWER CHILD," MARGARET SINCLAIR, WHOM HE HAD COURTED SINCE SHE WAS 18 If you are surprised by the age difference, ask yourself how likely it is that a 52-year-old *woman* would marry a man who is 30 years younger than she is.

Seeing Sociology in *Your* Everyday Life

1. Think about the marriages of your parents, other family members, and friends in terms of class, race, age, and other factors. What evidence can you find that society guides the feelings we call "love"?

2. Create a more complex and realistic appreciation of your own personal life by using sociological thinking to answer this question: Can you point to several "decisions" in your life that were largely guided by society due to your class, race, age, or other factors?

3. As this chapter explained, the time in human history when we are born, the society in which we are born, as well as our class position, race, and gender all shape the personal experiences we have throughout our lives. Does this mean we have no power over our own destiny? No. In fact, the more we understand how society works, the more power we have to shape our lives. The material in this chapter can help deepen your understanding of yourself and others around you so that you can more effectively pursue your life goals.

Making the Grade

CHAPTER 1 The Sociological Perspective

The Sociological Perspective

1.1 Explain how the sociological perspective differs from common sense.

The **sociological perspective** reveals the power of society to shape individual lives.

- What we commonly think of as personal choice—whether or not to go to college, how many children we will have, even the decision to end our own lives—is affected by social forces.
- Peter Berger described the sociological perspective as "seeing the general in the particular."
- C. Wright Mills called this point of view the "sociological imagination," claiming it transforms personal troubles into public issues.
- The experience of being an outsider or of living through a social crisis can encourage people to use the sociological perspective.

sociology the systematic study of human society
sociological perspective the special point of view of sociology that sees general patterns of society in the lives of particular people

The Importance of a Global Perspective

1.2 State several reasons for the importance of a global perspective in today's world.

Where we live—in a **high-income country** like Canada, a **middle-income country** such as Brazil, or a **low-income country** such as Mali—shapes the lives we lead.

Societies throughout the world are increasingly interconnected.

- New technology allows people around the world to share popular trends.
- Immigration around the world increases the racial and ethnic diversity of Canada.
- Trade across national boundaries has created a global economy.

Many social problems that we face in the Canada are far more serious in other countries. Learning about life in other societies helps us learn more about ourselves.

global perspective the study of the larger world and our society's place in it
high-income countries nations with the highest overall standards of living

middle-income countries nations with a standard of living about average for the world as a whole
low-income countries nations with a low standard of living in which most people are poor

Applying the Sociological Perspective

1.3 Identify the advantages of sociological thinking for developing public policy, for encouraging personal growth, and for advancing in a career.

Research by sociologists plays an important role in shaping **public policy**.

On a **personal level,** using the sociological perspective helps us see the opportunities and limitations in our lives and empowers us to be active citizens.

A background in sociology is excellent preparation for success in many different **careers**.

The Origins of Sociology

1.4 Link the origins of sociology to historical social changes.

Rapid social change in the eighteenth and nineteenth centuries made people more aware of their surroundings and helped trigger the development of sociology:

- The **rise of an industrial economy** moved work from homes to factories, weakening the traditions that had guided community life for centuries.
- The **explosive growth of cities** created many social problems, such as crime and homelessness.
- **Political change** based on ideas of individual liberty and individual rights encouraged people to question the structure of society.

Auguste Comte named sociology in 1838 to describe a new way of looking at society.

- Early philosophers had tried to describe the ideal society.
- Comte wanted to understand society as it really is by using **positivism**, a way of understanding based on science.
- Karl Marx and many later sociologists used sociology to try to make society better.

Canadian sociology arose from different traditions than did American sociology. It reflects a country with two major cultures and linguistic communities and includes a unique francophone component.

Women made important contributions to the social sciences as early as the 1500s—predating the men who are considered the founders of sociology.

positivism a way of understanding based on science

Sociological Theory

1.5 Summarize sociology's major theoretical approaches.

A **theory** states how facts are related, weaving observations into insight and understanding. Sociologists use three major **theoretical approaches** to describe the operation of society.

Macro-Level Orientation
The **structural-functional approach** explores how social structures—patterns of behaviour, such as religious rituals or family life—work together to help society operate.

- Auguste Comte, Émile Durkheim, and Herbert Spencer helped develop the structural-functional approach.
- Thomas Merton pointed out that social structures have both **manifest functions** and **latent functions**; he also identified **social dysfunctions** as patterns that may disrupt the operation of society.

The **social-conflict approach** shows how inequality creates conflict and causes change.

- Karl Marx helped develop the social-conflict approach.
- The **gender-conflict approach**, linked to **feminism**, focuses on ways in which society places men in positions of power over women. Harriet Martineau is regarded as the first woman sociologist.
- The **race-conflict approach** focuses on the advantages—including higher income, more schooling, and better health—that society gives to White people over people of colour.

Micro-Level Orientation
The **symbolic-interaction approach** studies how people, in everyday interaction, construct reality.

- Max Weber's claim that people's beliefs and values shape society is the basis of the social-interaction approach.
- Social-exchange analysis states that social life is guided by what each person stands to gain or lose from an interaction.

theory a statement of how and why specific facts are related
theoretical approach a basic image of society that guides thinking and research
structural-functional approach a framework for building theory that sees society as a complex system whose parts work together to promote solidarity and stability
social structure any relatively stable pattern of social behaviour

social functions the consequences of any social pattern for the operation of society as a whole
manifest functions the recognized and intended consequences of any social pattern
latent functions the unrecognized and unintended consequences of any social pattern
social dysfunction any social pattern that may disrupt the operation of society
social-conflict approach a framework for building theory that sees society as an arena of inequality that generates conflict and change
gender-conflict approach a point of view that focuses on inequality and conflict between women and men
feminism the advocacy of social equality for women and men
race-conflict approach a point of view that focuses on inequality and conflict between people of different racial and ethnic categories
macro-level orientation a broad focus on social structures that shape society as a whole
micro-level orientation a close-up focus on social interaction in specific situations
symbolic-interaction approach a framework for building theory that sees society as the product of the everyday interactions of individuals
postmodernism an approach that is critical of modernism, with a mistrust of grand theories and ideologies, that can have either a micro or a macro orientation

Applying the Approaches: The Sociology of Sports

1.6 Apply sociology's major theoretical approaches to the topic of sports.

The Functions of Sports
The structural-functional approach looks at how sports help society function smoothly.

- Manifest functions of sports include providing recreation, a means of getting in physical shape, and a relatively harmless way to let off steam.
- Latent functions of sports include building social relationships and creating thousands of jobs.

Sports and Conflict
The social-conflict approach looks at the links between sports and social inequality.

- Historically, sports have benefitted men more than women.
- Some sports are accessible mainly to affluent people.
- Racial discrimination exists in professional sports.

Sports as Interaction
The social-interaction approach looks at the different meanings and understandings people have of sports.

- Within a team, players affect each other's understanding of the sport.
- The reaction of the public can affect how players perceive their sport.

Chapter 2
Sociological Investigation

Michael Doolittle/The Image Works

Learning Objectives

2.1 Explain how scientific evidence often challenges common sense.

2.2 Describe sociology's three research orientations.

2.3 Identify the importance of gender and ethics in sociological research.

2.4 Explain why a researcher might choose each of sociology's research methods.

The Power of Society
to influence our life chances

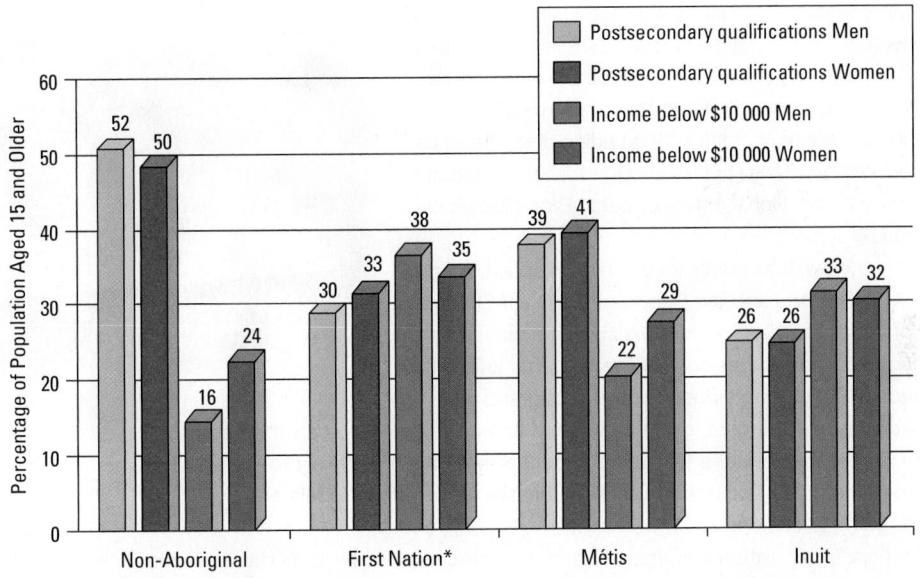

SOURCE: Compiled and calculated by L.M. Gerber based on Statistics Canada, Census 2006, Catalogue No. 97-564-XCB2006002.

Do we simply "decide" our futures? This figure suggests not. Among those born into non-Aboriginal families, half (or 50 percent) acquire postsecondary qualifications. The comparable figure for Métis men and women is 40 percent. Non-Aboriginal and Métis men and women have the highest levels of educational attainment *and* the lowest levels of poverty (or income below $10 000)—at least for men. In contrast, less than a third of First Nations and a quarter of Inuit have acquired postsecondary credentials: Consequently they experience higher levels of poverty to the point where First Nations and Inuit *men* have the highest poverty rates of all. Clearly, there is a relationship between educational attainment and income—but that is not the whole story, for ethnicity and gender are in play as well.

Chapter Overview

Having learned to use the sociological perspective and how to make use of sociological theory, it is time to learn how sociologists "do" research. This chapter explains the process of sociological investigation or how sociologists gather knowledge about the world. First, we look at science as a way of knowing and then discuss two limitations to scientific sociology that have given rise to two other approaches to knowing—interpretive sociology and critical sociology. Second, the chapter explains and illustrates four methods of data collection.

Students in Professor Gerber's political sociology course are busily engaged in *real* research. Each student is responsible for collecting census and election data for 10 of Canada's 308 federal electoral districts (ridings). By comparing notes on socio-economic characteristics and 2008 election outcomes, these students are trying to explain voting behaviour in their assigned ridings. What riding characteristics, they ask, are associated with more or less support for the candidates of the major federal parties—Conservative, Liberal, Bloc Québécois, and New Democratic?

Mike Appleton, Jennifer Becker, Kevin Bucknor, Ryan Daniels, Ryan Genoe, Amanda Ono/photo by Linda Gerber

Each student, armed with a coding sheet, collects specific items of information from the census and the Report of the Chief Electoral Officer for each of his or her 10 electoral districts. The census data are then converted into percentages so that the students know, for example, how much of each riding's population is immigrant, university-educated, francophone, bilingual, or employed full time. The students can then compare findings, asking if largely francophone Quebec ridings are the ones most likely to vote for the Bloc Québécois, or if the proportion of immigrants within Canada's ridings is related to the proportion of the vote going to the Liberals.

By looking separately at patterns in specific regions, the class begins to understand the impact of riding characteristics and region on support for specific parties. In the 2008 election, the Conservatives had their greatest support in the prairie provinces and, more generally, outside the major cities of Montreal, Toronto, and Vancouver, while the Bloc Québécois continued to dominate in Quebec. What kinds of ridings were responsible for these patterns? And what do we know about the 10 Quebec ridings that surprised everyone by electing Conservatives? Students come out of this process with a clear understanding of the ways in which 308 mini-elections, at the riding level, determine the outcome of a Canadian federal election.

Many people think that scientists work only in laboratories, carefully taking measurements using complex equipment. But, as this chapter explains, sociologists also conduct scientific research in the familiar terrain of neighbourhood streets, in homes, at workplaces, and in prisons, as well as in unfamiliar locales throughout the world—in short, wherever people can be found. The opening example illustrates the basics of scientific analysis—existing data or official statistics are used to determine the characteristics and actions of people.

There are many other approaches to sociological research, as illustrated by the work of Reginald Bibby, a professor of sociology at the University of Lethbridge. For almost 30 years, Bibby measured changes in Canadians' attitudes toward a wide range of issues. Every five years from 1975 to 1995, Bibby mailed out a self-administered questionnaire to a representative sample of about 1100 adult Canadians. These questionnaires measured changes in attitudes toward a wide range of variables, including religion, sex, family, career, the economy, intergroup relations (and intermarriage), health, and happiness. ∎

Along with his surveys of adult Canadians, Bibby has conducted a series dealing specifically with teenagers. His most recent teen survey, in the fall of 2000, involved 3500 young people, aged 15 to 19, from 150 high school classes chosen randomly throughout the country. One of his reasons for studying young people is that parents worry about their attitudes and behaviours. His research shows that many—though not

Table 2–1 Correlates of Piercings and Tattoos

	Piercings		Tattoos	
	Yes	No	Yes	No
Self-image				
I am well liked.	94%	93%	94%	93%
I am a good person.	93	96	92	96
I am good-looking.	79	76	80	76
I can do most things very well.	78	83	82	83
I have lots of confidence.	67	71	69	71
Behaviour/Values				
Engage in sex	71	45	82	45
Highly value concern for others	68	62	61	62
Use marijuana	61	33	65	33
Would return $10 in erroneous change	29	37	23	37
Attend services weekly-plus	12	23	10	23

SOURCE: Data from Bibby (2001): 73.

all—of those parental fears are unfounded. For example, Table 2–1 reveals that teens with body piercings and tattoos are similar to their peers in some respects, while different in others. Bibby finds minor differences in self-image among teens with and without piercings or tattoos; however, regardless of body ornamentation, the teens are almost equally likely to feel that they are well liked, good people, good-looking, capable, and confident. When he turns to behaviours and values, he finds that piercings and tattoos are associated with no difference in "concern for others"; but those *with* these ornamentations are more likely to engage in sex and use marijuana, and are less likely to attend religious services regularly. While this may suggest that you *can* judge a book by its cover, Bibby is careful to point out that there are many young people with piercings or tattoos who do not engage in sex or smoke marijuana (29 percent and 39 percent, respectively, compared to 49 percent and 63 percent of the national sample [Bibby, 2001]).

In this case, the individual teenager is the unit of analysis, as opposed to the electoral district in the opening example, which illustrates analysis at the aggregate or macro level; Bibby's analysis is carried out at the individual or micro level.

This chapter highlights the range of methods that sociologists use to conduct research. Along the way, we shall see that sociological research involves not just procedures for gathering information but controversies about whether that research should strive to be objective or to offer a bold prescription for change. After all, some sociological research has important policy implications. We shall tackle questions of values after addressing the basics of sociological investigation.

Basics of Sociological Investigation

2.1 Explain how scientific evidence often challenges common sense.

Sociological investigation starts with two simple requirements. The first is *Apply the sociological perspective.* This point of view reveals curious patterns of behaviour all around us that call for further study, which leads to the second requirement: *Be curious and ask questions.* These two requirements—seeing the world sociologically and asking questions—are fundamental to sociological investigation. Yet they are only the beginning. They draw us into the social world, stimulating our curiosity. But then we face the challenging task of finding answers to our questions. To understand the kind of insights sociology offers, we need to realize that there are various kinds of "truth."

Science as One Type of Truth

Saying that we "know" something can mean many things. Most members of our society, a substantial 81 percent in fact, claim to believe in the existence of God (Bibby, 1995). Few would assert that they have direct contact with God, but they are believers all the same. We call this kind of knowing "belief" or "faith."

A second kind of truth rests on the pronouncement of some recognized expert. Parents with questions about raising their children, for example, often consult child psychologists or their pediatricians about which practices are "right."

A third type of truth is based on simple agreement among ordinary people. Everyone "knows" that sex between adults and 10-year-old children is wrong.

People's "truths" differ the world over, and we often encounter "facts" at odds with our own. Imagine being a Cuso International[1] volunteer just arriving in a small, traditional village in Latin America. Assigned the job of helping the local people grow more food, you take to the fields, observing a curious practice: Farmers carefully plant seeds and then place a dead fish directly on top of each one. In response to your question, they reply that the fish is a gift to the god of the harvest. A local elder adds sternly that the harvest was poor one year when no fish were offered as gifts. From that society's point of view, using fish as gifts to the harvest god makes sense. The people believe in it, their experts endorse it, and everyone seems to agree that the system works. But, with your scientific training in agriculture, you have to shake your head and wonder. The scientific "truth" in this situation is something entirely different: The decomposing fish fertilize the ground, producing a better crop.

Science, then, represents a fourth way of knowing. **Science** is *a logical system that bases knowledge on direct, systematic observation.* Standing apart from faith, the wisdom of experts, and general agreement, scientific knowledge rests on **empirical evidence**, which is *information we can verify with our senses.*

Our Cuso example does not mean that people in traditional villages ignore what their senses tell them, or that members of technologically advanced societies reject non-scientific ways of knowing. A medical researcher using science to seek an effective treatment for cancer, for example, may still practise her religion as a matter of faith. She may turn to experts when making financial decisions, and she may derive political opinions from family and friends. In short, we all embrace various kinds of truths at the same time.

Common Sense versus Scientific Evidence

Like the sociological perspective, scientific evidence sometimes challenges our common sense. Here are six statements that many of us assume are true:

1. **"Poor people are far more likely than rich people to break the law."** Not true. If you regularly watch television shows such as *Cops,* you might think that police arrest people only from "bad" neighbourhoods. Poor people do stand out in the official arrest statistics. But research also shows that police and prosecutors treat the wealthy and powerful more leniently, as when politicians in Quebec and British Columbia were accused of shoplifting or drunk driving.

2. **"Canada is a middle-class society in which people are more or less equal."** False. In 2006, 3.5 million Canadians, or 11 percent of the population, had incomes below the poverty line (or what Statistics Canada calls the "low income cut-off"). In 2004, about 842 000 Canadians used the 250 food banks that are members of the Canadian Association of Food Banks to feed themselves and their children (CAFB, 2004). Some Canadians are clearly much better off than others.

3. **"Poor people don't want to work."** Wrong. Research suggests that this is true of some but certainly not true of all or even most of the poor. Substantial majorities of unattached people over age 65 and single parents with children are poor. *Employed* people who work for low or minimum wages (the working poor) are clearly not people who are avoiding work.

4. **"Differences in the behaviour of females and males are just 'human nature.'"** Wrong again. Much of what we call "human nature" is constructed by the society in which we live. Further, societies define "feminine" and "masculine" very differently.

5. **"People change as they grow old, losing many interests as they focus on their health."** Not really. Aging does little to change one's personality. Problems of health increase in old age but, by and large, elderly people retain their distinctive personalities and interests.

6. **"Most people marry because they are in love."** Not always. To members of our society, few statements are so obvious. Surprisingly, however, in many societies marriage has little to do with love.

These examples confirm the old saying "It's not what we don't know that gets us into trouble as much as things we *do* know that *just aren't so.*" We all have been brought up believing widely accepted "truths," being bombarded by expert advice, and feeling pressure to accept the opinions of people around us. As adults, we need to evaluate more critically what we see, read, and hear. Sociology can help us do just that.

Three Ways to Do Sociology

2.2 Describe sociology's three research orientations.

"Doing" sociology means learning more about the social world. There is more than one way to do this. Just as sociologists can use one or more theoretical approaches, they

---

[1]Cuso International began at the University of Toronto in 1960 as Canadian University Services Overseas. Its website suggests that it is now a large international organization, with its roots still firmly in Canada.

may also use different methodological orientations. The following sections describe three ways to do research: scientific sociology, interpretive sociology, and critical sociology.

Scientific Sociology

Earlier, we explained how early sociologists such as Auguste Comte and Émile Durkheim applied science to the study of society just as natural scientists investigate the physical world. **Scientific sociology**, then, is *the study of society based on systematic observation of social behaviour*. The scientific orientation to knowing, called *positivism*, assumes that an objective reality exists "out there." The student research into federal electoral districts and Bibby's findings about teenagers, discussed earlier, are both studies using the positivist approach. The job of the scientist is to discover this reality by gathering empirical evidence, facts we can verify with our senses by "seeing," "hearing," or "touching."

imageegami/Fotolia

ALCOHOL ABUSE IS COMMON AMONG MANY HOMELESS PEOPLE
But knowing that homelessness and alcohol abuse are correlated does not establish cause and effect. Can you see how abusing alcohol could lead to becoming homeless? Can you see how becoming homeless might lead people to abuse alcohol?

CONCEPTS, VARIABLES, AND MEASUREMENT   Let's take a closer look at how science works. A basic element of science is the **concept**, *a mental construct that represents some part of the world in a simplified form*. Sociologists use concepts to label aspects of social life, including "the family" and "the economy," and to categorize people in terms of their "gender," "ethnicity," or "social class."

A **variable** is *a concept whose value changes from case to case*. The familiar variable "price," for example, changes from item to item in a supermarket. Similarly, we use the concept "social class" to identify people as "upper class," "middle class," "working class," or "lower class."

The use of variables depends on **measurement,** *a procedure for determining the value of a variable in a specific case*. Some variables are easy to measure, as when you step on a scale to see how much you weigh. But measuring sociological variables can be far more difficult. For example, how would you measure a person's "social class"? You might look at clothing, listen to patterns of speech, or note a home address. Or, in an attempt to be more precise, you might ask about income, occupation, and education.

Because most variables can be measured in more than one way, sociologists often have to decide which factors to consider. For example, having a very high income might qualify a person as "upper class." But what if the income comes from selling automobiles, an occupation most people think of as "middle class"? Would having only a grade 8 education make the person "lower class"? In a case like this, sociologists usually combine three measures—income, occupation, and education—to assign social class.

Sociologists face another interesting problem in measuring variables: dealing with huge numbers of people. How, for instance, do you describe the income of all Canadian families? Reporting millions of numbers carries little meaning and tells us nothing about the people as a whole. Therefore, sociologists use statistical measures—like mode, mean, and median—to describe people or communities.

Defining Concepts   Measurement is always somewhat arbitrary because the value of any variable partly depends on how it is defined. In addition, deciding how to measure abstract concepts such as "love," "family," or "intelligence" can lead to lengthy debates.

Good research, therefore, requires that sociologists **operationalize a variable**, which means *specifying exactly what is to be measured before assigning a value to a variable*. Before measuring the concept of social class, for example, we would have to decide exactly what we were going to measure: say, income level, years of schooling,

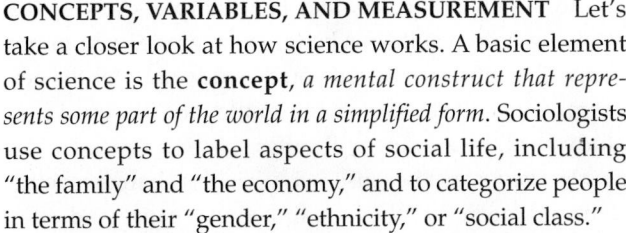

concept a mental construct that represents some aspect of the world in a simplified form

operationalize a variable specifying exactly what is to be measured before assigning a value to a variable

variable a concept whose value changes from case to case

reliability consistency in measurement

validity actually measuring exactly what you intend to measure

cause and effect a relationship in which change in one variable (the independent variable) causes change in another (the dependent variable)

independent variable the variable that causes the change

dependent variable the variable that changes

or occupational prestige. Sometimes sociologists measure several of these things; in such cases, they need to specify exactly how they plan to combine these variables into one overall score. The next time you read the results of a study, notice the way the researchers operationalize each variable. How they define terms can greatly affect the results.

The definition (or operationalization) of race and ethnicity in the Canadian census has taken some interesting turns. Until the 1980s, people were asked to note the country from which their first ancestor (on their paternal side) came to Canada. Over time, this became an inadequate measure of our multicultural and multiracial society, where individuals often have multiple origins. The census questions gradually evolved to allow for multiple responses—up to four—that respondents could identify (e.g., one might indicate a combination of German, Italian, Chinese, and Lithuanian ancestry.) People can identify themselves as Black, North American Indian, or Inuit, and, in general terms, as a visible minority. A complicating factor in achieving an accurate description of Canada's ethnic and racial diversity is the increasing choice of "Canadian/*Canadien*—and *only* Canadian/*Canadien*"— to describe one's background.

Reliability and Validity For a measurement to be useful, it must be reliable and valid. **Reliability** refers to *consistency in measurement*. A measurement is reliable if repeated measurements give the same result time after time. But consistency does not guarantee **validity**, which means *actually measuring exactly what you intend to measure*. Getting a valid measurement is sometimes tricky. For example, if you want to study how "religious" people are, you might ask the people you are studying how often they attend services. But is going to a church, temple, or mosque really the same thing as being religious? People may attend religious services because of deep personal beliefs, but they may also do so out of habit or because others pressure them to go. And what about spiritual people who avoid organized religion altogether? Even when a measurement yields consistent results (making it reliable), it still may not measure what we want it to (and therefore lack validity). We suggest that measuring religiosity should take account of not only service attendance but also a person's beliefs and the degree to which a person lives by religious convictions. In sum, careful measurement is important, but it is also often a challenge.

Relationships among Variables Once measurements are made, investigators can pursue the real payoff: seeing how variables are related. The scientific ideal is **cause and effect**, *a relationship in which change in one variable causes change in another*. Cause-and-effect relationships occur around us every day, such as when studying hard for an exam results in a high grade. *The variable that causes the change* (in this case, how much you study) is called the **independent variable**. *The variable that changes* (the exam grade) is called the **dependent variable**. The value of one variable, in other words, depends on the value of another. Why is linking variables in terms of cause and effect important? Because this kind of relationship allows us to *predict* the outcome of future events—if we know one thing, we can accurately predict another. For example, knowing that studying hard results in a better exam grade, we can predict with confidence that, if you do study hard for the next exam, you will receive a high grade, and if you do not study hard, your grade will suffer.

However, just because two variables change together does not mean that they are linked in a cause-and-effect relationship. For example, sociologists recognize that juvenile delinquency is more common among young people who live in crowded housing. Say that we operationalize the variable "juvenile delinquency" as the number of times a person under the age of 18 has been arrested and we define "crowded housing" by the number of square metres of living space per person. It turns out that these variables are related: Delinquency rates are high in densely populated neighbourhoods. But should we conclude that crowding in the home (in this case, the independent variable) causes delinquency (the dependent variable)? Not necessarily. **Correlation** is *a relationship in which two (or more) variables change together*. We know that density and delinquency are correlated because they change together, as shown in part (a) of Figure 2–1. This relationship may mean that crowding causes more delinquency, but it could also mean that some third factor is at work causing change in *both* of the variables under observation.

To identify a third variable, think about who lives in crowded housing: people with less money and few choices—the poor. Poor youngsters are also more likely to end up with police records. In reality, crowded housing and juvenile delinquency are found together because both are caused by a third factor—poverty—as shown in

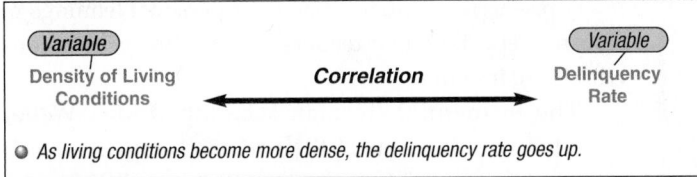

(a) If two variables increase and decrease together, they display correlation.

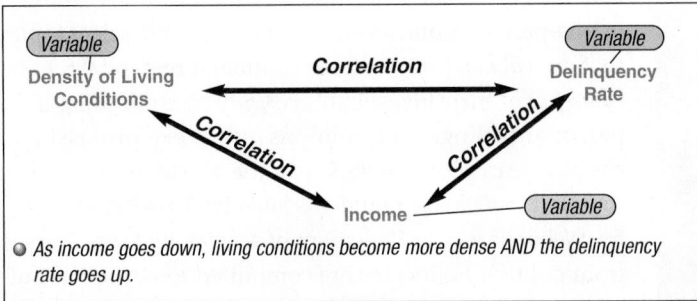

(b) Here we consider the effect of a third variable: income. Low income may cause *both* high-density living conditions *and* a high delinquency rate.

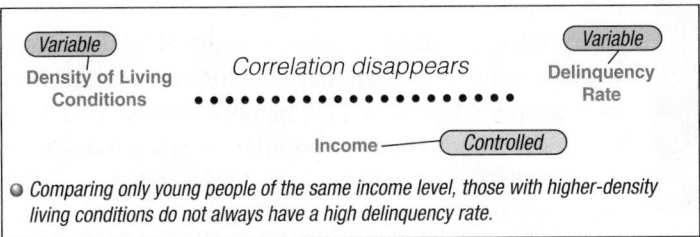

(c) When we control for income—that is, examine only young people of the same income level—we find that density of living conditions and delinquency rate no longer increase and decrease together.

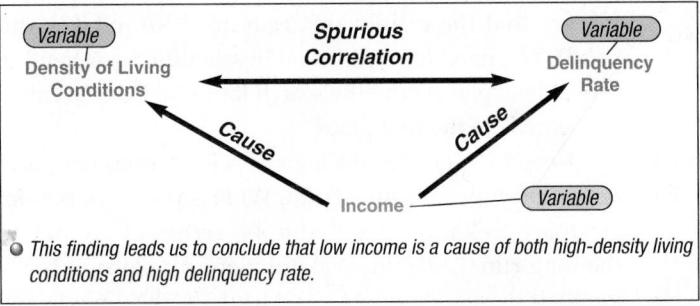

(d) Density of living conditions and delinquency rate are correlated, but their correlation is *spurious* because neither one causes the other.

Figure 2–1 Correlation and Cause: An Example
Correlation is not the same as cause. Here's why.

part (b) of Figure 2–1. In short, the apparent connection between crowding and delinquency is "explained away" by a third variable—low income—that causes them both to change. So our original connection turns out to be a **spurious correlation**, *an apparent but false relationship between two (or more) variables that is caused by some other variable.*

Exposing a correlation as spurious requires a bit of detective work, assisted by a technique called **control**—*holding constant all variables except one in order to see clearly*

the effect of that variable. In our example, we suspect that income level may be causing a spurious link between housing density and delinquency. To check whether the correlation between delinquency and crowding is spurious, we control for income—that is, we hold income constant by looking only at young people of one income level. If the correlation between density and delinquency remains—that is, if young people of the same income level living in more crowded housing show higher rates of arrest than young people in less crowded housing—we have more reason to think that crowding does, in fact, cause delinquency. But if the relationship disappears when we control for income, as shown in part (c) of Figure 2–1, then we know we were dealing with a spurious correlation. In fact, research shows that the correlation between crowding and delinquency just about disappears if income is controlled (Fischer, 1984). So we have now sorted out the relationship among the three variables, as illustrated in part (d) of the figure. Housing density and juvenile delinquency have a spurious correlation; evidence shows that both variables rise or fall according to income.

To sum up, correlation means only that two (or more) variables change together. To establish cause and effect, three requirements must be met:

1. a demonstrated correlation,
2. an independent (or causal) variable that occurs before the dependent variable, and
3. no evidence that a third variable could be causing a spurious correlation between the two.

Natural scientists usually have an easier time than social scientists in identifying cause-and-effect relationships because they work in laboratories, where they can control other variables. Carrying out research in a workplace or on the streets, however, makes control very difficult, so sociologists often have to settle for demonstrating only correlation. Also, human behaviour is highly complex, involving dozens of causal variables at any one time, so establishing all of the cause-and-effect relationships in any situation is extremely difficult.

THE IDEAL OF OBJECTIVITY Ten students are sitting around a dorm lounge discussing the dream vacation spot for the upcoming spring break. Will one place end up being everyone's clear favourite? That seems unlikely. In scientific terms, each of the 10 people probably operationalizes the concept "dream vacation" differently. For one, it might be a deserted, sunny beach in Mexico; for

Erich Schlegel/Corbis/Getty Images

ONE PRINCIPLE OF SCIENTIFIC RESEARCH IS THAT SOCI-OLOGISTS AND OTHER INVESTIGATORS SHOULD TRY TO BE OBJECTIVE IN THEIR WORK, SO THAT THEIR PERSONAL VALUES AND BELIEFS DO NOT DISTORT THEIR FINDINGS But such a detached attitude may discourage the relationship needed in order for people to open up and share information. Thus, as sociologists study human relationships, they have to decide how much to pursue objectivity and how much to show their own feelings.

another, Vancouver, a lively city with a very active social scene; for still another, hiking or skiing in the Rocky Mountains. Like so many other "bests" in life, the best vacations turn out to be a matter of individual taste.

Personal values are fine when it comes to choosing travel destinations, but they pose a challenge to scientific research. Remember, science assumes that reality is "out there." Social scientists need to study this reality without changing it in any way, and so they strive for **objectivity**—*personal neutrality in conducting research*. Objectivity means that researchers carefully hold to scientific procedures, not letting their own attitudes and beliefs influence the results. Scientific objectivity is an ideal rather than a reality, because no one can be completely neutral. Even the topic someone chooses to study reflects a personal interest of one sort or another. But the scientific ideal is to keep a professional sense of distance or detachment from the results. When conducting research, sociologists do their best to ensure that conscious or unconscious biases do not distort their findings. As an extra precaution,

many researchers openly state their personal leanings in research reports so that readers can interpret conclusions with those in mind.

The influential German sociologist Max Weber expected people to select their research topics according to personal beliefs and interests. After all, why else would one person study world hunger, another investigate the effects of racism, and still another study children in one-parent families? Knowing that people select topics that are *value-relevant,* Weber cautioned researchers to be *value-free* in their investigations. Only by controlling their personal feelings and opinions—as every professional should—can researchers study the world *as it is* rather than tell us *how they think it should be*. This detachment, for Weber, is a crucial element of science that sets it apart from politics. Politicians are committed to particular outcomes; scientists maintain open minds about the results of their investigations, whatever they may turn out to be. Weber's argument still carries much weight in sociology, although most sociologists admit that we can never be completely value free or even aware of all our biases. Keep in mind, however, that sociologists are not "average" people: Most are White, highly educated, and more politically liberal than the population as a whole (Klein & Stern, 2004). Remember that sociologists, like everyone else, are influenced by their social backgrounds.

One way to limit distortion caused by personal values is **replication**, *repetition of research by other investigators*. If other researchers repeat a study using the same procedures and obtain the same results, we gain confidence that the results are accurate (both reliable and valid). The need for replication in scientific investigation probably explains why the search for knowledge is called "re-search" in the first place.

Keep in mind that the logic of science does not guarantee objective, absolute truth. What science offers is an approach to knowledge that is *self-correcting* so that, in the long run, researchers stand a good chance of limiting their biases. Objectivity and truth lie, then, not in any one study but in the scientific process itself as it continues over time.

SOME LIMITATIONS OF SCIENTIFIC SOCIOLOGY Science is one important way of knowing. Yet, when applied to social life, science has several important limitations.

1. **Human behaviour is too complex for sociologists to predict any individual's actions precisely.** Astronomers calculate the movement of objects in the skies with remarkable precision, but comets and planets are unthinking objects. Humans have minds of their own, so no two people react to any event, whether a sports victory or a natural disaster, in exactly the same way. Sociologists, therefore, must be satisfied

with showing that *categories* of people *typically* act in one way or another. This is not a failing of sociology. It simply reflects the fact that sociologists study creative, spontaneous people.

2. **Because humans respond to their surroundings, the mere presence of a researcher may affect the behaviour being studied.** An astronomer's gaze has no effect whatever on a distant comet. But most people react to being observed. Try staring at someone for a few minutes and see for yourself. In effect, we can change people just by studying them.

3. **Social patterns change; what is true in one time or place may not hold true in another.** The same laws of physics will apply tomorrow as they do today, and they hold true all around the world. But human behaviour is so variable that there are no universal sociological laws.

4. **Because sociologists are part of the social world they study, they can never be 100 percent value-free when conducting social research.** Barring a laboratory mishap, chemists are rarely personally affected by what goes on in test tubes. But sociologists live in their "test tube," the societies they study. Therefore, social scientists may find it difficult to control—or even to recognize—personal values that may distort their work.

Interpretive Sociology

All sociologists agree that studying social behaviour scientifically presents some real challenges; others go further, suggesting that science as it is used to study the natural world misses a vital part of the social world: *meaning*. Human beings do not simply act: They engage in meaningful action. Max Weber, who pioneered this framework, incorporated that insight, arguing that the proper focus of sociology is *interpretation*, or understanding the meanings involved in everyday life. **Interpretive sociology** is *the study of society that focuses on the meanings people attach to their social world.*

Interpretive sociology differs from scientific, or positivist, sociology in three ways. First, scientific sociology focuses on action, or what people do, whereas interpretive sociology deals with the meaning attached to behaviour. Second, while scientific sociology sees an objective reality "out there," interpretive sociology sees reality as being constructed by people themselves in the course of their everyday lives. Third, while scientific sociology tends to make use of *quantitative data*, interpretive sociology relies on *qualitative data*.

In sum, the scientific or positivist approach is well suited to research in a laboratory, where investigators observe while taking careful measurements. The interpretive approach is better suited to research in a natural setting where investigators interact with people, learning how they make sense of their everyday lives.

Max Weber combined the best of both the scientific and the interpretive approaches—the positivism of Auguste Comte and the interpretive emphasis of Wilhelm Dilthey (1833–1911), who might accurately be called the founder of interpretive sociology (Bakker, 1999). Weber believed that one of the keys to the interpretive component lay in *Verstehen*—the German word for "understanding." That concept, in turn, can be attributed to Dilthey.

It is the interpretive sociologist's job not just to observe what people do but also to share in their world of meaning and come to appreciate why they act as they do. Subjective thoughts and feelings—which science tends to dismiss as "bias"—now become the focus of the researcher (Berger & Kellner, 1981; Neuman, 2000).

Interpretive Soc. Vs. Many Others
↳ Meaning of a behaviour ↗
Versthen
↳ On Quiz

...G OBSERVED AFFECTS HOW PEOPLE BEHAVE Researchers can never be certain precisely how this will occur; some people resent public attention, but others become highly animated when they think they have an audience.

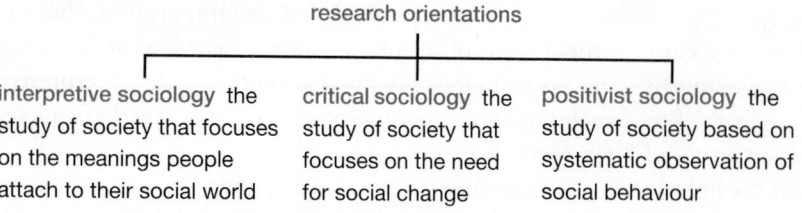

interpretive sociology the study of society that focuses on the meanings people attach to their social world

critical sociology the study of society that focuses on the need for social change

positivist sociology the study of society based on systematic observation of social behaviour

Robert Prus of the University of Waterloo argues that George Herbert Mead forged the unique interpretive tradition of *symbolic interaction*. For Mead, *language* is absolutely fundamental to the human experience, to shared symbols and understandings, and to social life and interaction. To understand group life, one must get inside the minds of the individual actors through close and sustained contact. One must achieve intimate familiarity by relying on "three sources of data: *observation, participant-observation,* and *interviews*" (Prus, 1994:21).

In an attempt to understand how Canadian university students approach studying in preparation for exams, Albas and Albas (1994) relied on interviews, observations, and logs that, over their 20 years of teaching, they had students keep. Students, they found, came to identify themselves as *aces, moderates,* or *bombers* (the terminology may differ from year to year). Their identities determined their approaches to studying, their relationships with other students in each of the categories, their friendship choices, their leisure activities, their levels of procrastination, and their expectations with respect to grades. Shared perspectives and patterns of behaviour were apparent within each of the categories, but almost all students sought to wear "the cloak of coolness"—the appearance of getting good grades with the minimum of effort. Since it is uncool to "work your butt off," serious studying—even among aces—was done out of sight or behind closed doors. Clearly, this type of interpretive understanding requires systematic analysis based on sustained personal contact with students themselves.

Critical Sociology

There is a third methodological orientation in sociology. Like the interpretive orientation, critical sociology developed in reaction to the limitations of scientific sociology. This time, however, the problem was the foremost principle of scientific research: objectivity. Scientific sociology holds that reality is "out there," and that the researcher's task is to study and document this reality. But Karl Marx, who founded the critical orientation, rejected the idea that society exists as a "natural" system with a fixed order. To assume this, he claimed, is the same as saying that society cannot be changed. Scientific sociology, from this point of view,

ends up supporting the status quo. **Critical sociology**, by contrast, is *the study of society that focuses on the need for social change.*

THE IMPORTANCE OF CHANGE

Rather than asking the scientific question "How does society work?" critical sociologists ask moral and political questions, such as "Should society exist in its present form?" Their answer to this question, typically, is that it should not. One recent account of this orientation, echoing Marx, claims that the point of sociology is "not just to research the social world but to change it in the direction of democracy and social justice" (Feagin & Hernán, 2001:1). In making value judgments about how society should be improved, critical sociology rejects Weber's goal that researchers be value-free and emphasizes instead that they should be social activists in pursuit of desirable change.

Sociologists using the critical orientation seek to change not just society but the character of research itself. They often identify personally with their research subjects and encourage them to help decide what to study and how to do the work. Typically, researchers and subjects use their findings to provide a voice for less powerful people and to advance the political goal of a more equal society (Feagin & Hernán, 2001; Hess, 1999; Perrucci, 2001).

SOCIOLOGY AS POLITICS Scientific sociologists object to taking sides in this way, charging that critical sociology—whether feminist, Marxist, or postmodern—becomes political, lacks objectivity, and cannot correct for its own biases. Critical sociologists reply that *all* research is political or biased—either it calls for change or it does not. Sociologists, they continue, have no choice about their work being political, but they can choose which positions to support. Critical sociology is an activist orientation tying knowledge to action, seeking not just to understand the world but also to improve it. Generally speaking, scientific sociology tends to appeal to researchers with non-political or conservative political views; critical sociology appeals to those whose politics range from liberal to radical left.

Research Orientations and Theory

Is there a link between research orientations and sociological theory? There is no precise connection, but each of the three methodological orientations—scientific, interpretive, and critical—does stand closer to one of the theoretical approaches presented in the chapter on The Sociological Perspective. Scientific sociology corresponds to the structural-functional approach, interpretive

SUMMING UP

Three Research Orientations in Sociology

	Positivist Sociology	Interpretive Sociology	Critical Sociology
What is reality?	Society is an orderly system. There is an objective reality "out there."	Society is ongoing interaction. People construct reality as they attach meanings to their behavior.	Society is patterns of inequality. Reality is that some categories of people dominate others.
How do we conduct research?	Using a scientific orientation, the researcher carefully observes behaviour, gathering empirical, ideally quantitative, data. Researcher tries to be a neutral observer.	Seeking to look "deeper" than outward behaviour, the researcher focuses on subjective meaning. The researcher gathers qualitative data, discovering the subjective sense people make of their world. Researcher is a participant.	Seeking to go beyond positivism's focus on studying the world as it is, the researcher is guided by politics and uses research as a strategy to bring about desired social change. Researcher is an activist.
Corresponding theoretical approach	Structural-functional approach	Symbolic-interaction approach	Social-conflict approach

sociology is related to the symbolic-interaction approach, and critical sociology is linked to the social-conflict approach. The Summing Up table provides a quick review of the differences among the three methodological orientations. Many sociologists favour one orientation over another; however, because each provides useful insights, it is a good idea to become familiar with all three.

Issues Affecting Sociological Research

2.3 Identify the importance of gender and ethics in sociological research.

Gender and Research

In recent years, sociologists have become aware that research is affected by **gender**, *the personal traits and social positions that members of a society attach to being female or male.* The Seeing Sociology in Everyday Life section offers four examples of sociology studies in which gender is integral to the research. Margrit Eichler (1988) identifies five ways in which gender can shape research:

1. **Androcentricity.** *Androcentricity* (*andro* in Greek means "male"; *centricity* means "being centred on") refers to approaching an issue from a male perspective. Sometimes researchers act as if only men's activities are important, ignoring what women do. For years, researchers studying occupations focused on the paid work of men and overlooked the housework and child care traditionally performed by women. When Matthews (1976) sought to understand the attitudes and values of three

small Newfoundland communities that were being considered for relocation, he limited his interviews to a random sample of male household heads and all of the community leaders (who were also male). Needless to say, research that seeks to understand the full range of human behaviour cannot ignore half of humanity. On the other hand, local customs may not allow a man to interview women.

Gynocentricity—seeing the world from a female perspective—can also limit good sociological investigation. While in our male-dominated society this problem arises less often, there are those who would argue that this is the main drawback of much feminist research. Feminists, in turn, would argue that gynocentricity in their work is essential to counter generations of androcentricity—in society, the media, and research.

2. **Overgeneralizing.** This problem occurs when researchers use data drawn from people of only one sex to support conclusions about "humanity" or "society." For example, in an investigation of child-rearing practices, collecting data only from women would allow researchers to draw conclusions about "motherhood" but not about the more general issue of "parenthood."

3. **Gender blindness.** Failing to consider the variable of gender at all is called *gender blindness*. As is evident throughout this text, the lives of men and women differ in countless ways. A study of growing old in Canada might suffer from gender blindness if it overlooked the fact that most elderly men live with their wives while elderly women typically live alone.

4. **Double standards.** Researchers must be careful not to distort what they study by judging men and women differently. For example, a family researcher who labels a couple as "man and wife" may define the man as the "head of household" and treat him accordingly,

Beijing Eastphoto stockimages Co.,Ltd/Alamy Stock Photo

IF YOU ASK ONLY MALE SUBJECTS ABOUT THEIR ATTITUDES OR ACTIONS, YOU MAY BE ABLE TO SUPPORT CONCLUSIONS ABOUT "MEN" BUT NOT MORE GENERALLY ABOUT "PEOPLE" What would a researcher have to do to ensure that research data support conclusions about all of society?

and may assume that the woman simply engages in family "support work."

5. **Interference.** Another way that gender can distort a study is if a subject reacts to the sex of the researcher, interfering with the research operation. While studying a small community in Sicily, for instance, Maureen Giovannini (1992) found that many men treated her as a woman rather than as a researcher. Some thought it was wrong for any single woman to speak privately with a man. Others denied her access to places they considered off limits to women.

There is nothing wrong with focusing research on one sex or the other. But all sociologists, as well as people who read their work, should be aware of the importance of gender in any investigation.

WOMEN AS METHODOLOGISTS Sociology's attention to men in the past has prompted some contemporary researchers to make special efforts to investigate the lives of women. Feminist researchers embrace two key tenets: (1) their research should focus on the condition of women in society, and (2) their research must be grounded in the assumption that women generally experience subordination. Thus, feminist research rejects Weber's value-free orientation in favour of being overtly political—doing research in pursuit of gender equality.

There is no single feminist research strategy. On the contrary, feminists employ any and all conventional scientific techniques, including all of those described in this chapter. But some go further, claiming that feminist research must transform science itself, which they see as a masculine form of knowledge. Mainstream methodology,

in the eyes of many modern feminists, is simply "malestream" methodology that supports patriarchy and the status quo (McDonald, 1994:4). Whereas traditional notions about science demand detachment, feminists seek connections: a sympathetic understanding between investigator and subject. Moreover, conventional scientists take charge of the research agenda, deciding in advance what issues to raise and how to study them. Feminist researchers, in contrast, favour a more egalitarian approach that allows participants a chance to voice their needs and interests in their own words (Nelson & Robinson, 1999).

University of Guelph professor Lynn McDonald shook up mainstream sociologists and feminists alike with her analysis of the role of women in the early development of sociology—and social science methodology in particular. McDonald argues that the feminists who reject empirical or scientific research and quantitative analysis as serving the interests of men are rejecting methodologies that women helped to develop in order to further their causes. Among the many women whose contributions are outlined in *The Women Founders of the Social Sciences* (McDonald, 1994) are Harriet Martineau (1802–1876) and Florence Nightingale (1820–1910).

Martineau made her living as a writer and an investigative journalist, producing more than 50 books and 1600 feature articles on a wide range of issues. She also dealt with methodology in "Essays on the Art of Thinking" and in an 1838 book titled *How to Observe Morals and Manners*. Her *Society in America,* which appeared in 1837, made her the first to tackle comparative analysis, applying an explicitly sociological approach. Martineau, an activist, supported the anti-slavery movement and worked for women's rights to education, divorce, occupations, the vote, and freedom from violence.

The name Florence Nightingale is familiar to all of us. She was "the lady with the lamp," the woman from a wealthy background who ministered to the needs of soldiers wounded in Crimea. McDonald (1994) reveals a Nightingale of such methodological and theoretical sophistication that one wonders if Durkheim was intellectually indebted to her. She was a "passionate statistician" who gathered data—often presented in pie charts that simultaneously compared data cross-sectionally and over time. She used her statistics to show that improved sanitation would reduce mortality in Crimean and British hospitals and would be cost-effective at the same time. Nightingale's application of statistics to more general

Sociology in Focus

Feminist Research: Critical and Interpretive Examples

How are women's lives affected by a capitalist and patriarchal social order? Canadian sociologists Dorothy Smith, Meg Luxton, and Susan Wendell have done sociological research to describe and analyze this question.

In a series of essays, Dorothy Smith (1977, 1979, 1983) notes the ways in which relations between men and women depend on economic conditions. Her argument begins with the idea that in the early homesteading period the division of labour between the sexes was fairly even. Men and women depended on one another for house building, clearing land, growing and harvesting gardens, caring for livestock, and preserving food for winter. This situation of approximate equality changed as farmers moved toward cash production. As land speculation led to increased prices and expensive mortgages on houses and machinery, families had to produce more than they themselves needed for their own subsistence. They needed profits to pay off bank loans and to buy equipment and other goods. But, legally, only men could own property and borrow money at the bank. The labour of wives earned them nothing: The benefits went to their husbands. The result was drudgery and a loss of power for the women.

As late as 1973, the powerlessness of the farm wife was underscored in court decisions regarding Irene Murdoch. She worked on the family farm for 25 years, but, when she and her husband divorced, a court decided that Murdoch had no right to any of the farm property. Women's organizations rallied to protest this injustice. Murdoch took her case to the Supreme Court of Canada—and lost. Her case, however, was important with regard to social policy. During the 1970s, province after province began to define marriage as a partnership of equals whose assets should be divided equally upon divorce (Anderson, 1991). By the late 1980s, Rosa Becker won the right to the financial assets of a 25-year common-law partnership.

Women's work is still undervalued, and women continue to play a subservient role to men in their homes and in corporations. Their services maintain the labour power of their husbands and children. Meg Luxton's book *More Than a Labour of Love* (1980) describes the process whereby women work to "re-produce" labour power for a corporation in a single-industry mining town in Flin Flon, Manitoba. She describes the way in which the lives of the women are constrained by the requirements of the corporation. The rhythms of the lives of the women and their children revolve around the husbands' need for sleep,

food, rest, and relaxation, all in the interest of maintaining their employment. Luxton also documents the ways in which the husbands' frustrations at work are carried home to be vented on the wives. In extreme cases, wives not only contend with surplus anger and frustration but also become the victims of violence, as their husbands act out their frustrations with the corporation.

Susan Wendell (1995), a woman who was suddenly stricken with a disabling chronic illness, used her own experience, along with those of other disabled individuals, to develop what she calls a "feminist theory of disability." Central to her interpretation is the assumption that disabled women are oppressed both as women in male-dominated societies and as disabled people in a world dominated by able-bodied people. But, Wendell argues, "much of what is *disabling* about our physical conditions is also a consequence of social arrangements" (p. 457). Because North American society idealizes the human body—in terms of appearance, strength, energy, and control—disabled people are marginalized. Furthermore, in a society that values independence, dependence on others is humiliating and damaging to one's self-esteem; as a result, a disabled person may experience a profound alienation from his or her own body. The physical limitations imposed by disabilities are made more problematic by the social arrangements that designate disabled persons as "other," or as marginal to normal human life; being a disabled *woman* compounds the difficulties.

Smith, Luxton, and Wendell are not concerned with the operationalization of concepts into quantitative variables. Causality is not determined mathematically on the basis of numerical measurements of variables, but instead is elicited from a subjective or interpretive analysis of the situation each one is studying. In their view, exploitation and injustice in power, gender, class, and race characterize social relations, and changes in these relations over time and place need to be explained. Since change toward justice is the ultimate goal, in this approach, interpretive sociology differs greatly from positivist sociology.

What Do You Think?

1. Should men and women share assets equally when marriages or common-law relationships fail? Why?

2. Has the relationship between women and corporations changed since Luxton wrote *More Than a Labour of Love*? If so, how?

3. In your experience, are the consequences of disability different for men and for women? How?

issues of public administration led her to "describe the laws of social science as God's laws for the right operation of the world" (p. 186). She noted that crime, suicide, mortality, accident, marriage, and poverty levels could be predicted with exact precision, despite individual free will. As an activist who believed that social and individual conditions could be changed, Nightingale sought to improve a wide range of laws, policies, and administrative practices.

Research Ethics

Like all investigators, sociologists must be aware that research can harm as well as help subjects or communities. For this reason, the American Sociological Association (1997) and Canada's Social Sciences and Humanities Research Council (Canada, 2003) have established formal guidelines for the ethical conduct of research. The prime directive is that sociologists strive to be both technically competent and fair-minded in conducting their research. Sociologists must disclose all of their findings, without omitting significant data, and they are ethically bound to make their results available to other sociologists, some of whom may wish to replicate the research.

Sociologists also must strive to ensure the safety of their subjects. Should research develop in a manner that threatens the well-being of participants, investigators must terminate their work immediately. Furthermore, professional guidelines direct researchers to protect the privacy of anyone involved in a research project. Yet this is a promise that may be difficult to keep, since researchers sometimes come under pressure (say, from the police or courts) to disclose information. Therefore, researchers must think carefully about their responsibility to protect subjects, and they should discuss this issue with those who take part in research. An important principle in ethical research is obtaining the informed consent of participants, which means that subjects understand the responsibilities and risks that the research involves and agree to take part.

Another important guideline concerns funding. Sociologists must include in their published results the sources of any and all financial support. Furthermore, sociologists must seek to avoid any conflicts of interest (or even the appearance of such conflicts) that may compromise the integrity of their work. For example, researchers must never accept funding from any organization that seeks to influence the research results for its own purposes.

Ethical concerns extend well beyond the issues raised here and address the role of sociologists as teachers, administrators, and clinical practitioners. At the broadest level, there are also global dimensions to research ethics. Before beginning research in other countries, investigators must become familiar enough with those societies to understand what people there are likely to perceive as a violation of privacy or as a source of personal danger. In a multicultural society such as ours, the same rule applies to studying people whose cultural backgrounds differ from our own. The Thinking about Diversity box on the next page offers some tips about how outsiders can effectively and sensitively study Aboriginal communities.

Research Methods

2.4 Explain why a researcher might choose each of sociology's research methods.

A **research method** is *a systematic plan for doing research.* The remainder of this chapter introduces four commonly used methods of sociological investigation: experiments, surveys, participant observation, and the use of existing data. None is better or worse than any other. Rather, in the same way that a carpenter selects a particular tool for a specific task, researchers choose a method—or mix several methods—according to whom they plan to study and what they wish to learn.

Testing a Hypothesis: The Experiment

The logic of science is most clearly found in the **experiment**, *a research method for investigating cause and effect under highly controlled conditions.* Experimental research is explanatory; that is, it asks not just what happens but why. Typically, researchers devise an experiment to test a **hypothesis**, *a statement of a possible relationship between two (or more) variables.* A hypothesis typically takes the form of an if/then statement: If one thing were to happen, then something else would result.

An experiment gathers the evidence needed to reject or not reject the hypothesis in four steps: (1) specify the *independent variable* (the "cause") as well as the *dependent variable* (the "effect"); (2) measure the initial value of the dependent variable; (3) expose the dependent variable to the independent variable (the "treatment"); and (4) measure the dependent variable to see what change, if any, took place. If the expected change did occur, the experiment supports the hypothesis; if not, the hypothesis must be rejected (or modified).

But a change in the dependent variable could be due to something other than the supposed cause. (Think back

---

research method a systematic plan for doing research

experiment a research method for investigating cause and effect under highly controlled conditions

Thinking about Diversity: Race, Class, and Gender

Conducting Research with Aboriginal Peoples

A Royal Commission on Aboriginal Peoples was announced in 1991 with a mandate to do extensive research and provide baseline data on the lives of Aboriginal peoples living in Canada. The ethical guidelines for the conduct of this research were published in the *Northern Health Research Bulletin* (Canada, 1993). As well as establishing the standard principles for the conduct of ethical research, the Royal Commission established new guidelines with respect to the benefits of research to the community—as stated under the heading "Community Benefit":

- In setting research priorities and objectives for community-based research, the Commission and the researchers it engages shall give serious and due consideration to the benefit of the community concerned.

- In assessing community benefit, regard shall be given to the widest possible range of community interest, whether the groups in question be Aboriginal or non-Aboriginal, and also to the impact of research at the local, regional, or national level. Wherever possible, conflicts between interests within the community should be identified and resolved in advance of commencing the project. Researchers should be equipped to draw on a range of problem-solving strategies to resolve such conflicts as may arise in the course of research.

- Whenever possible, research should support the transfer of skills to individuals and increase the capacity of the community to manage its own research.

The final, five-volume report of the royal commission covers every conceivable issue related to Aboriginal peoples—constitutional, political, social, medical, economic, demographic, and cultural (Canada, 1996). The report was based on the information acquired by the commission in meetings and hearings across the country, as well as from more than 400 reports prepared by various organizations and individuals (Aboriginal and non-Aboriginal); sociologists and other social scientists were among those who submitted these reports. The report is also available on cd-rom under the title *For Seven Generations: An Information Legacy of the Royal Commission on Aboriginal Peoples*. The cd-rom has an elaborate search capacity (e.g., by subject) that greatly increases access to the contents of the report. Thus, social scientists, politicians, and Aboriginal communities can do research on the report itself.

Fred Cattroll

What Do You Think?

1. Should Aboriginal peoples have the final word on research involving their communities? Why?

2. Can non-indigenous researchers do a credible job of "studying" Aboriginal communities?

3. To what extent should the report of the 1996 Royal Commission shape public policy?

---

to our discussion of spurious correlations.) To be certain that they identify the correct cause, researchers carefully control other factors that might affect the outcome of the experiment. Such control is easiest in a *laboratory*, a setting specially constructed to neutralize outside influences.

Another strategy used to gain control is dividing research subjects into an *experimental group* and a *control group*. Early in the study, the researcher measures the dependent variable for subjects in both groups but later exposes only the experimental group to the independent variable or treatment. (The control group typically gets a "placebo," a treatment that the members of the group think is the same but really has no effect on the experiment.) Then the investigator measures the subjects in both groups again. Any factor occurring during the course of the research that influences people in the experimental group (say, a news event) would do the same to those in the control group, thus controlling or "washing out" the factor. By comparing the before and after measurements of the two groups, a researcher can learn how much of the change is caused by the independent variable.

THE HAWTHORNE EFFECT Researchers need to be aware that behaviour may change because subjects are getting special attention, as one classic experiment revealed. In the late 1930s, the Western Electric Company hired researchers to investigate worker productivity in its Hawthorne factory near Chicago (Roethlisberger & Dickson, 1939). One experiment tested the hypothesis that increasing the available lighting would raise worker output. First, researchers measured worker productivity (the dependent variable). Then they increased the lighting (the independent variable) and measured output a second time. The resulting increased productivity supported the hypothesis. But when the research team later turned the lighting back down, productivity increased again. What was going on? In time, the researchers realized that the employees were working harder—even if they could not see as well—simply because people were paying attention to them and measuring their output. From this research, social scientists coined the term **Hawthorne effect** to refer to *a change in a subject's behaviour caused simply by the awareness of being studied.*

ILLUSTRATION OF AN EXPERIMENT: THE "STANFORD COUNTY PRISON" Prisons can be violent settings, but is this simply because of the "bad" people who end up there? Or, as Philip Zimbardo suspected, does the prison itself somehow generate violent behaviour? This question led Zimbardo to devise a fascinating experiment, which he called the "Stanford County Prison" (Haney et al., 1973; Zimbardo, 1972). Zimbardo thought that, once inside a prison, even emotionally healthy people are

prone to violence. Therefore, Zimbardo treated the *prison setting* as the independent variable capable of causing *violence,* the dependent variable.

To test this hypothesis, Zimbardo's research team constructed a realistic-looking "prison" in the basement of the psychology building on the campus of California's Stanford University. Then they placed an ad in the local newspaper, offering to pay young men for their help with a two-week research project. To each of the 70 men who responded they administered a series of physical and psychological tests and then selected the healthiest 24. The next step was to assign randomly half of the men to be "prisoners" and half to be "guards." The plan called for the guards and prisoners to spend the next two weeks in the mock prison. The prisoners began their part of the experiment soon afterward when the city police "arrested" them at their homes. After searching and handcuffing the men, the police drove them to the local police station, where they were fingerprinted. Then police transported their captives to the Stanford prison, where the guards locked them up. Zimbardo started his video camera rolling and watched to see what would happen next.

The experiment turned into more than anyone had bargained for. Both guards and prisoners soon became embittered and hostile toward one another. Guards humiliated the prisoners by assigning them tasks such as cleaning out toilets with their bare hands. The prisoners, for their part, resisted and insulted the guards. Within four days, the researchers removed five prisoners who displayed "extreme emotional depression, crying, rage

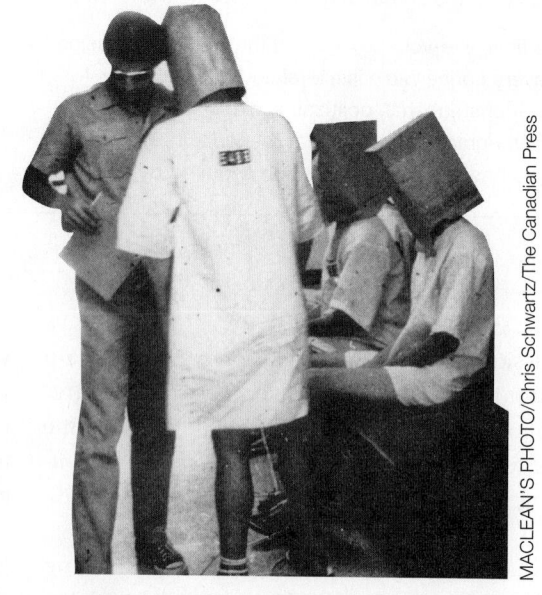

PHILIP ZIMBARDO'S RESEARCH HELPS EXPLAIN WHY VIOLENCE IS A COMMON ELEMENT IN OUR SOCIETY'S PRISONS At the same time, his work demonstrates the dangers that sociological investigation poses for subjects and the need for investigators to observe ethical standards that protect the welfare of people who participate in research.

LEFT TO RIGHT, MAXIMUM SECURITY INMATES OF THE PRISON FOR WOMEN (IN KINGSTON, ONTARIO) ELLEN YOUNG AND JOEY TWINS ARE CONCERNED ABOUT THE CLOSING OF THE FACILITY In May 1994, after a violent altercation with guards, Young and four other women spent three months in Kingston Penitentiary's Regional Treatment Centre. Young and Twins, along with 21 other women, were then moved to Kingston Penitentiary itself (a prison for men).

and acute anxiety" (Haney et al., 1973:81). Before the end of the first week, the situation had become so bad that the researchers had to cancel the experiment. Zimbardo explains:

> The ugliest, most base, pathological side of human nature surfaced. We were horrified because we saw some boys (guards) treat others as if they were despicable animals, taking pleasure in cruelty, while other boys (prisoners) became servile, dehumanized robots who thought only of escape, of their own individual survival and of their mounting hatred for the guards. (1972:4)

The events that unfolded at the "Stanford County Prison" supported Zimbardo's hypothesis that prison violence is rooted in the social character of jails themselves, not in the personalities of guards and prisoners. This finding raises questions about our society's prisons, suggesting the need for basic reform. Notice, too, that this experiment shows the potential of research to threaten the physical and mental well-being of subjects. Such dangers are not always as obvious as they were in this case. Therefore, researchers must consider carefully the potential harm to subjects at all stages of their work and end any study, as Zimbardo did, if subjects may suffer harm of any kind.

EVALUATE

In carrying out the "Stanford County Prison" study, the researchers chose to do an experiment because they were interested in testing a hypothesis. In this case, Zimbardo and his colleagues wanted to find out if the prison setting itself (rather than the personalities of individual guards and prisoners) is the cause of prison violence. The fact that the "prison" erupted in violence—involving healthy, normal people—supports their hypothesis.

CHECK YOUR LEARNING Do Zimbardo's findings help explain the abuse of Iraqi prisoners by U.S. soldiers in the Abu Ghraib prison? What about the atrocities committed by Canadian peacekeepers in Somalia?

Asking Questions: Survey Research

A **survey** is *a research method in which subjects respond to a series of statements or questions in a questionnaire or an interview*. The most widely used of all research methods, surveys are especially good for studying attitudes—such as beliefs about politics, religion, or race—since there is no way to observe directly what people think. Sometimes surveys provide clues about cause and effect, but typically they yield *descriptive* findings, painting a picture of people's views on some issue.

POPULATION AND SAMPLE A survey targets some **population**, *the people who are the focus of research*. Lois Benjamin, in a study of racism (1991), studied a select population: talented African Americans. Other surveys such as political polls that predict election results treat every adult in the country as the population.

Obviously, contacting millions of people is impossible for even the best-funded and most patient researcher. Fortunately, there is an easier way that yields accurate results. Researchers collect data from a **sample**, *a part of a population that represents the whole*. National polls typically survey a sample of about 1000 people.

How can we be sure that a sample really represents the entire population? One way is *random sampling*, in which researchers draw a sample from the population randomly so that every person in the population has an equal chance to be selected. The mathematical laws of probability dictate that a random sample is likely to represent the population as a whole. Selecting a random sample usually means listing everyone in the population and using a computer to make a random selection. Beginning researchers sometimes make the mistake of assuming that "randomly" walking up to people on a street produces a sample that is representative of the entire city. Unfortunately, this technique does not give every person an equal chance to be included in the sample. For one thing, any setting—whether a rich neighbourhood, an ethnic enclave, or a university campus—contains more of some kinds of people than others. The fact that some people are more approachable than others introduces another source of bias.

population the people who are the focus of research

sample a part of a population that represents the whole

Although constructing a good sample is no simple task, it offers considerable savings in time and expense. We are spared the tedious work of contacting everyone in a population; yet we can obtain essentially the same results.

USING QUESTIONNAIRES Selecting subjects is just the first step in carrying out a survey. Also needed is a plan for asking questions and recording answers. Most surveys use a questionnaire for this purpose. A **questionnaire** is *a series of written questions that a researcher presents to subjects*. One type of questionnaire provides not only the questions but also a selection of fixed responses (similarly to a multiple-choice examination). This *closed-ended format* makes it fairly easy to analyze the results, but, by narrowing the range of responses, it can also distort the findings. For example, Frederick Lorenz and Brent Bruton (1996) found that the number of hours per week students say they study for a college course depends on the options offered to them. When the researchers presented students with options ranging from one hour or less to nine hours or more, 75 percent said that they studied four hours or less per week. But when subjects in a comparable group were given choices ranging from four hours or less to 12 hours or longer (a higher figure that suggests students should study more), they suddenly became more studious; only 34 percent reported that they studied four hours or less each week.

A second type of questionnaire, using an *open-ended format,* allows subjects to respond freely, expressing various shades of opinion. The drawback of this approach is that the researcher has to make sense out of what can be a very wide range of answers.

The researcher must also decide how to present questions to subjects. Most often, researchers use a *self-administered survey,* mailing or emailing questionnaires to respondents and asking them to complete the form and send it back. Since no researcher is present when subjects read the questionnaire, it must be both inviting and clearly written. *Pretesting* a self-administered questionnaire with a small number of people before sending it to the entire sample can prevent the costly problem of finding out—too late—that instructions or questions are confusing.

Using the mail or email allows a researcher to contact a large number of people over a wide geographic area at minimal expense. But many people treat such questionnaires as junk mail, so typically no more than half are completed and returned. Often, researchers must send follow-up mailings to urge reluctant subjects to respond.

Finally, keep in mind that many people are not capable of completing a questionnaire on their own. Young children obviously cannot, nor can many hospital patients or a surprising number of adults who simply lack the required reading and writing skills.

Bill Keay/Vancouver Sun

MOST CENSUS DATA ARE OBTAINED FROM QUESTIONNAIRES THAT OFFICIALS SEND AND RECEIVE BACK THROUGH THE MAIL, OR DELIVER AND PICK UP BY HAND Although this strategy is generally quite efficient, it is likely to undercount the homeless or others who lack a customary street address. Olaf Solheim (*above*) was evicted from a rooming house in Vancouver's West End to make room for tourist housing for Expo '86. Less than six weeks later, he was dead. While some sociologists do research using government statistics, others are committed to research that allows voices like Solheim's to be heard.

CONDUCTING INTERVIEWS An **interview** is *a series of questions a researcher asks respondents in person*. In a closed-format design, researchers read a question or statement and then ask the subject to select a response from several that are presented. More commonly, however, interviews are open-ended, so that subjects can respond as they choose and researchers can probe with follow-up questions. In either case, the researcher must guard against influencing a subject, which is as easy as raising an eyebrow when a person begins to answer.

While subjects are more likely to complete a survey if contacted personally by the researcher, interviews have some disadvantages. Tracking people down is costly and takes time, especially if subjects do not live in the same area. Telephone interviews allow far greater "reach," but the impersonality of cold calls by telephone—and the possibility of reaching answering machines—can lower the response rate.

In both questionnaires and interviews, the wording of questions may significantly affect answers. For instance, emotionally loaded language can easily sway

survey a research method in which subjects respond to a series of statements or questions in a questionnaire or an interview

questionnaire a series of written questions a researcher presents to subjects

interview a series of questions a researcher asks respondents in person

subjects: The term *welfare mothers,* as opposed to *mothers on social assistance,* injects an emotional element into a survey and encourages respondents to answer more negatively. In still other cases, the wording of questions may hint at what other people think, thereby steering subjects. For example, people are more likely to respond positively to the question "Do you *agree* that the police force is doing a good job?" than to the almost identical question "Do you *think* that the police force is doing a good job?" Similarly, respondents are more likely to endorse a statement to "not allow" something (say, public speeches against the government) than a statement to "forbid" the same activity (Rademacher, 1992).

Conducting a good interview means standardizing the technique—thereby treating all subjects in the same way. But this, too, can lead to problems. Drawing people out requires establishing rapport, which in turn depends on responding naturally to the particular person being interviewed, as you would in a normal conversation. In the end, researchers have to decide where to strike the balance between uniformity and rapport (Lavin & Maynard, 2001).

ILLUSTRATION OF SURVEY RESEARCH: THE CASE OF ANTI-SEMITISM IN QUEBEC

On September 17, 1991, Mordecai Richler, a prominent Canadian novelist with an international reputation and a Jew, wrote an article on French-Canadian nationalism in *The New Yorker,* in which he alleged that French Canadians are anti-Semitic. His statements were the beginning of a passionately felt and argued controversy. Are French Canadians anti-Semitic? If so, are they more anti-Semitic than English Canadians? If they are more anti-Semitic, what is the explanation for this? A team of sociologists headed by Paul Sniderman attempted to answer these questions.

Sniderman used the data from an existing survey titled the *Charter of Rights Study Survey,* carried out in 1993 (Sniderman et al., 1993). The study used random-digit dialling (RDD) of a random sample (2084 people) of the 97 percent of Canadian households that have telephones. The Quebec sampling strategy was specifically designed to yield a representative sample of the province. In order to reflect the total population of both Canada and Quebec, each subsample had to include the right proportions of males and females, older and younger people, urban and rural dwellers, and so on.

The questionnaire was designed to find out whether French-speaking Quebecers or English-speaking Canadians held more anti-Semitic views (the dependent variable)—as well as to identify the specific factors (the independent variables) that account for the differences in their views.

The five questions used to measure anti-Semitism (or operationalize the variable) were as follows:

We realize no statement is true of all people in a group, but generally speaking, please tell me whether you

FOCUS GROUPS ARE A TYPE OF SURVEY IN WHICH A SMALL NUMBER OF PEOPLE REPRESENTING A TARGET POPULATION ARE ASKED FOR THEIR OPINIONS ABOUT SOME ISSUE OR PRODUCT Here a sociology professor asks students to evaluate textbooks for use in her introductory class.

agree or disagree with the following statements (Sniderman et al., 1993:247). Would you say you agree strongly, agree somewhat, disagree somewhat, or disagree with this statement?

Most Jews don't care what happens to people who aren't Jewish.

Most Jews are pushy.

Jews have made an important contribution to the cultural life of Canada.

Jews are more willing than others to use shady practices to get ahead.

Most Jews are warm and friendly people.

Note the carefully worded introduction, which was designed to make respondents feel comfortable expressing their views candidly by qualifying the responses. Given the sensitive nature of the topic, this qualification was deemed necessary in order to combat what sociologists refer to as the *social desirability effect,* whereby respondents are unwilling to commit themselves to an opinion that might place them outside the "normal" range. By acknowledging that the statements could not be applied to all Jews, the researchers allowed respondents freer rein in expressing their attitudes. Even if respondents agreed strongly with one of the negative statements, they could rest assured that they fell within "acceptable norms," since the response was not going to be taken as a blanket condemnation of all Jews.

The researchers found that French-speaking Quebecers were, in fact, more anti-Semitic than English-speaking Canadians. While the personality basis for anti-Semitism was conspicuously weak, the cultural basis for anti-Semitism was strong and related more to the high value placed on conformity in Quebec (normative conformity) than on nationalist sentiment, as had been suggested by some commentators. French-speaking Quebecers were significantly more likely than English-speaking Canadians to express support for conformity as a value: "They place a greater priority on people learning to fit in and get along with others" and on the larger society being "a unified body pursuing a common goal" (Sniderman et al., 1993:264). They are therefore more likely to distrust and dislike those whom they perceive as different or for whom cultural diversity is a more important value than cultural conformity.

The authors make the point that, while francophone Quebecers overall are more anti-Semitic than other Canadians, most are not anti-Semitic at all. Moreover, on every test but one, a majority expressed positive sentiments regarding Jews: "Quebeckers differ from other Canadians not so much in their readiness to submit to the full syndrome of anti-Semitic ideas but rather in their willingness to accept one or two negative characterizations of Jews" (Sniderman et al., 1993:265). Québécois were as tolerant as English-speaking Canadians and were as willing as anglophones to support such things as the rights of groups with unpopular points of view to hold public rallies, and the need for restrictions on the rights of Canada's security service to wiretap. Lastly, recognition of slightly more anti-Semitism in Quebec does nothing to negate its existence in the rest of Canada.

EVALUATE

Sniderman used data from an existing survey to compare levels of anti-Semitism in Quebec and the rest of Canada. The original survey, which was based on a sample that was representative of the populations of Quebec and the rest of the country, asked a wide range of questions including five measuring attitudes toward Jews. This approach allowed for the analysis of the five attitudinal questions asked of 2084 individuals from across Canada. It did not allow for any in-depth questioning about a very sensitive topic.

CHECK YOUR LEARNING What could you learn about anti-Semitism by interviewing a smaller number of people and asking open-ended questions?

In the Field: Participant Observation

Some sociological investigation takes place "in the field"—that is, where people carry on their everyday lives. The most widely used strategy for field study is **participant observation,** *a research method in which investigators systematically observe*

> **participant observation** a research method in which investigators systematically observe people while joining them in their routine activities

> **use of available data**

people while joining them in their routine activities. Participant observation allows researchers an inside look at social life in settings ranging from nightclubs to religious seminaries. Cultural anthropologists commonly use participant observation (which they call fieldwork) to study communities in other societies. They term their descriptions of unfamiliar cultures *ethnographies.* Sociologists prefer to call their accounts of people in their communities or neighbourhoods *case studies.*

At the beginning of a field study, most investigators do not have a specific hypothesis in mind. In fact, they may not yet realize what the important questions will turn out to be. Therefore, most field research is *exploratory* and *descriptive.*

As its name suggests, participant observation has two sides. On one hand, getting an insider's look depends on becoming a participant in the setting—hanging out with the research subjects, trying to act, think, and even feel the way they do. Compared to experiments and survey research, participant observation has fewer hard-and-fast rules. But it is precisely this flexibility that allows

Tim Gerard Barker/Lonely Planet Images/Getty Images

ONE PRINCIPLE OF SCIENTIFIC RESEARCH IS THAT SOCIOLOGISTS AND OTHER INVESTIGATORS SHOULD TRY TO BE OBJECTIVE IN THEIR WORK, SO THAT THEIR PERSONAL VALUES AND BELIEFS DO NOT DISTORT THEIR FINDINGS But such a detached attitude may discourage the connection needed for people to open up and share information. Thus sociologists have to decide how much to pursue objectivity and how much to show their own feelings.

investigators to explore the unfamiliar and adapt to the unexpected.

Unlike other research methods, participant observation may require that the researcher enter the setting not just for a week or two but for months or even years. At the same time, however, the researcher must maintain some distance as an "observer," mentally stepping back to record field notes and, later, to interpret them. Because the investigator must both "play the participant" to win acceptance and gain access to people's lives and "play the observer" to maintain the distance needed for thoughtful analysis, there is an inherent tension in this method. Carrying out the twin roles of insider participant and outsider observer often comes down to a series of careful compromises.

Most sociologists carry out participant observation alone, so they—and readers, too—must remember that the results depend on the work of a single person. Participant observation usually falls within interpretive sociology, yielding mostly qualitative data—the researcher's accounts of people's lives and what they think of themselves and the world around them—although researchers sometimes collect some quantitative (numerical) data. From a scientific point of view, participant observation is a "soft" method that relies heavily on personal judgment and lacks scientific rigour. Yet its personal approach is also its strength. A highly visible team of sociologists attempting to administer formal surveys would disrupt many social settings, but a single skillful participant-observer can gain a lot of insight into people's natural behaviour.

THE CLASSIC ILLUSTRATION OF PARTICIPANT OBSERVATION: *STREET CORNER SOCIETY* In the late 1930s, a young graduate student at Harvard University named William Foote Whyte (1914–2000) was fascinated by the lively street life of a nearby, rather rundown section of Boston. His curiosity led him to carry out four years of participant observation in this neighbourhood, which he called "Cornerville," and in the process to produce a sociological classic. At the time, Cornerville was home to first- and second-generation Italian immigrants, many of whom were poor. The other residents of Boston thought of Cornerville as a place to avoid: a poor slum that was home to racketeers. Unwilling to accept easy stereotypes, Whyte set out to discover for himself exactly what kind of life went on in this community. His celebrated book, *Street Corner Society* (1981; orig. 1943), describes Cornerville as a complex community with a distinctive code of values and its own social conflicts.

In beginning his investigation, Whyte considered a range of research methods. Should he take questionnaires to one of Cornerville's community centres and ask local people to fill them out? Should he invite members of the community to come to his Harvard office for interviews?

It is easy to see that such formal strategies would have gained little co-operation from the local people. Therefore, Whyte decided to set out on his own, working his way into Cornerville life in the hope of coming to understand this rather mysterious place.

Right away, Whyte discovered the challenges of getting started in field research. After all, an upper-middle-class WASP (White Anglo-Saxon Protestant) graduate student from Harvard did not exactly fit into Cornerville life. Even a friendly overture from an outsider could seem pushy and rude. One night, Whyte dropped in at a local bar, hoping to buy a woman a drink and encourage her to talk about Cornerville. Looking around the room, he could find no woman alone. But then he saw a man sitting down with two women. He walked up to them and asked, "Pardon me. Would you mind if I joined you?" Instantly, Whyte realized his mistake:

> There was a moment of silence while the man stared at me. Then he offered to throw me down the stairs. I assured him that this would not be necessary, and demonstrated as much by walking right out of there without any assistance. (1981:289)

As this incident suggests, gaining entry to a community is the difficult (and sometimes hazardous) first step in field research. "Breaking in" requires patience, quick thinking, and a little luck. Whyte's big break came when he met a young man named "Doc" at a local social service agency. Whyte explained to Doc how hard it was to make friends in Cornerville. Doc responded by taking Whyte under his wing and introducing him to others in the community. With Doc's help, Whyte soon became a neighbourhood regular.

Whyte's friendship with Doc illustrates the importance of a key informant in field research. Such people not only introduce a researcher to a community but often remain a source of information and help. But using a key informant also has its risks. Because any person has a particular circle of friends, a key informant's guidance is certain to "spin" or bias the study in one way or another. In addition, in the eyes of others, the reputation of the key informant—good or bad—usually rubs off on the investigator. So although a key informant is helpful early on, a participant-observer must soon seek a broader range of contacts.

Having entered the Cornerville world, Whyte quickly learned another lesson: A field researcher needs to know when to speak up and when to shut up. One evening, he joined a group discussing neighbourhood gambling. Wanting to get the facts straight, Whyte asked innocently, "I suppose the cops were all paid off?" In a heartbeat, Whyte reported,

> the gambler's jaw dropped. He glared at me. Then he denied vehemently that any policeman had been paid off

and immediately switched the conversation to another subject. For the rest of that evening I felt very uncomfortable. The next day, Doc offered some sound advice: "Go easy on that 'who,' 'what,' 'why,' 'when,' 'where' stuff, Bill. You ask those questions and people will clam up on you. If people accept you, you can just hang around, and you'll learn the answers in the long run without even having to ask the questions." (1981:303)

In the months and years that followed, Whyte became familiar with life in Cornerville, married a local woman, and learned that the common stereotypes were wrong. In Cornerville, most people worked hard, many were quite successful, and some boasted of sending children to college. Whyte's book remains a fascinating story of the deeds, dreams, and disappointments of immigrants and their children, containing the rich details that come from years of participant observation within an ethnic community.

EVALUATE

To study the community he called "Cornerville," William Whyte chose participant observation. This was a good choice because he had no specific hypothesis to test, nor did he know at the outset exactly what questions he would ask. By living in the community for several years, Whyte was able to paint a complex picture of its social life.

CHECK YOUR LEARNING Give examples of topics for sociological research that would be studied most appropriately through (1) an experiment, (2) a survey, and (3) participant observation.

Using Available Data: Existing Sources

Not all research requires investigators to collect their own data. Sometimes sociologists analyze existing sources—meaning data that are already collected by others—through what is often referred to as secondary analysis.

The most widely used statistics in social science are gathered by government agencies. Statistics Canada continually updates information about the Canadian population and offers much of interest to sociologists. Comparable data on the United States are available from the Bureau of the Census, while global investigations benefit from various publications of the United Nations and the World Bank. In short, a wide range of data about the world is as close as the internet. Since **use of available data**—government statistics or the findings of individual researchers—saves researchers time and money, this approach holds special appeal to sociologists with low budgets. The quality of government data is generally better than that of any data

even well-funded researchers could hope to obtain on their own. (See the Thinking Critically box on reading tables for an example of secondary analysis of Canadian census data.)

Still, despite its usefulness, secondary analysis has inherent problems. For one thing, available data may not exist in precisely the form one might wish: You may know the average income of Métis people but nothing about the income gap between Métis men and women. Furthermore, there may be questions about the meaning and accuracy of work done by others. For example, in his classic study of suicide, Émile Durkheim realized that he could not be sure that a death classified as an "accident" was not, in reality, a "suicide," and vice versa. He also knew that various agencies used different procedures and categories in collecting data, making comparisons difficult. In the end, using existing data is a little like shopping for a used car: There are plenty of bargains out there, but you have to shop carefully.

CONTENT ANALYSIS Another type of secondary analysis is called *content analysis*. This entails the counting or coding of the content of written, aural, or visual materials, such as television and radio programming, novels, magazines, and advertisements. Content analysis has a long tradition in sociology. One of the best-known early content analyses of this century in North America is *The Polish Peasant in Europe and America* by Thomas and Znaniecki (1971; orig. 1919), which used diaries and letters written to and from Polish immigrants in America to describe the adjustment processes of new American immigrants.

A 1977 study by the Montreal YWCA Women's Centre—of gender roles in 38 grade 1 readers used in Montreal's anglophone schools—is another example of the use of content analysis; this study found that gender stereotypes were mirrored in the books. Males were portrayed as central characters and as active, competitive problem solvers. Females were less often included and, when they were, tended to be portrayed in passive, domestic roles and occupations. Males were shown in 78 different occupations; most females were housewives, and those who were not were described as nurses, librarians, teachers, or cooks (Mackie, 1983).

Another intriguing example of content analysis began with a chance observation. E. Digby Baltzell (1979) made a brief visit to the library of Bowdoin College in Maine. There he saw the portraits of three famous people—Nathanial Hawthorne (author), Henry Wadsworth Longfellow (poet), and Franklin Pierce (the fourteenth president of the United States)—who had graduated from the same class in 1825! How could it be, Baltzell wondered, that this small college had graduated more famous people in *a single year* than his own,

Thinking Critically

Reading Tables: Aboriginal Employment and Income in Canada

A table provides a lot of information in a small amount of space, so learning how to interpret tables can increase your reading efficiency. When you spot a table, look first at the title to see what information it contains. The title of Table 2–2 tells you that it deals with labour-force participation and income of Aboriginal men and women. Reading across the top of the table, you see that data are presented for men and women in four categories: First Nations, Métis, Inuit, and non-Aboriginal. The research summarized here makes use of existing data—specifically, census data—for people who identify themselves as "North American Indian/First Nation," "Métis," or "Inuit" as well as for non-Aboriginal individuals. Gerber (1990) published an article titled "Indian, Métis, and Inuit Women and Men: Multiple Jeopardy in a Canadian Context," which was based on 1986 census data. The table presented here replicates one of the 1986 tables using 2006 census data, revealing some changes coupled with remarkable stability over the 15-year interval.

Reading down the left side of this complex table, you learn that, for each category (men and women), it provides data on labour-force participation rates, unemployment rates, full-time all-year employment, average employment income, and income over $50 000 per year. Notes below the table provide explanations of the measures used.

As you move from left to right across the first row of the table, you can see how Aboriginal men and women (in each category) compare on *labour-force participation* with non-Aboriginal men and women. You will notice that, except for Métis men and women—who have the highest rates—Aboriginal people have lower participation rates than non-Aboriginals. First Nations men and women have the lowest participation rates of all categories, meaning that they are least likely to be employed or "available and looking for work" (i.e., active in the labour force). The very large gaps between Métis and First Nations labour-force participation rates are largely explained by the fact that over 40 percent of the First Nations population live on reserves—where employment options may be limited— while the Métis are about 70 percent urban.

The second row reveals that, in each Aboriginal category, *unemployment rates* are higher for men than for women—especially among the Inuit, with rates of 24 and 6 percent—while non-Aboriginal men and women have very low and equal rates of unemployment at 6 percent. Métis men and women have the lowest unemployment rates among the Aboriginal categories. Note that while Inuit men have the highest unemployment rates, Inuit women's are as low as those of non-Aboriginals. Keep in mind, wherever you encounter them, that unemployment rates are based on the active labour force—those who are employed or unemployed and looking for work—rather than on the populations 15 years of age and over, as are the other measures in the table. It may seem odd to include the unemployed in the definition of the labour force but, unlike stay-at-home parents or full-time students who do not work during the school term, the "unemployed" must be *available* and *looking* for work.

Row three indicates the percentage in each category that is *employed full time, all year*. You might be surprised to learn that, among non-Aboriginal Canadians, 43 percent of men and 30 percent of women were fully employed in 2006. Other people 15 years of age and over may have been working part-time or been out of the labour force entirely as a result of retirement, disability, homemaking, attending school, or receiving welfare. In any case, full-time employment figures are lower for all Aboriginal categories than for non-Aboriginal men and women. Among the Aboriginal categories, First Nations men and women are least likely, and Métis men and women are most likely, to be employed full time, all year. In fact, Métis women almost match non-Aboriginal women on full-time employment—at 29 and 30 percent, respectively.

Table 2–2 Labour-Force Participation and Income of Aboriginal Men and Women

	First Nations*		Métis		Inuit		Non-Aboriginal	
	Men	Women	Men	Women	Men	Women	Men	Women
Participation rate**	63.2	55.0	74.1	66.2	63.9	58.9	72.5	61.7
Unemployment rate**	19.8	16.2	10.5	9.5	23.8	6.4	6.2	6.4
Full-time employment rate**	25.9	22.5	38.3	29.2	27.7	24.7	43.2	30.1
Average employment income ($)	26 536	20 812	34 785	22 626	28 220	24 726	44 273	28 272
Income over $50 000 (%)**	11.2	5.8	21.9	8.4	15.4	12.6	28.6	13.2

*In the Canadian census, "North American Indian" identity refers to First Nations (i.e., Status or Registered Indians—80%) and non-Status Indians (20%). Note that 20 percent of the people under First Nations in this table are non-status Indians who have none of the rights of First Nations or Registered Indians.

**These rates refer to percentages of populations over 15 years of age. The one exception is the unemployment rate, which is based on the number of people *in* the labour force (i.e., those who are employed or actively looking for work).

SOURCE: Compilation and calculations by LM Gerber based on Statistics Canada, Census 2006, B2020 files, Catalogue no. 97-564-XCB2006002.

(continued)

The fourth row deals with *average employment income* and reveals that the incomes of men are always higher than those of women. Non-Aboriginal incomes, for men and for women, are the highest—followed by those of Métis men and Inuit women. The lowest average employment incomes are found among First Nations men and women. The fifth row reveals the percentage of each population (15 years of age and over) with incomes greater than $50 000. Once again, non-Aboriginal men and women are *most* likely to have these high incomes; at the other extreme are First Nations men and women, who are *least* likely to have incomes over $50 000 per year. Here, as on several of the other measures, First Nations women are the most severely disadvantaged—as they have been since the census of 1986 and before.

So what have we learned from this table? We can see that, with a few exceptions, Aboriginal men and women are disadvantaged relative to their non-Aboriginal counterparts. It is also clear that First Nations men and women

fare worse than Métis and Inuit men and women. Lastly, women are consistently disadvantaged relative to men. Now that you know how to read the table, you can start thinking about what the data tell you about gender and racial or ethnic inequality in Canada. Specifically, you can see that First Nations women suffer multiple disadvantages because they are Aboriginal, First Nations, and female.

What Do You Think?

1. Why are statistical data, such as those in this table, an efficient way to convey a lot of information?

2. Looking at the table, can you determine how one is disadvantaged by being Aboriginal, First Nations, and female?

3. Do you have an explanation for the discrepancies that appear in this table? Are there identifiable social forces in play here?

much bigger University of Pennsylvania had graduated in *its entire history*? He turned to historical documents—specifically the twenty-volume *Dictionary of American Biography*—to see if New England had really produced more famous people than his native Pennsylvania.

Realizing that the longest biographies described the most famous people, Baltzell chose 75 individuals, his top achievers, from more than 13 000 profiles of outstanding men and women. New England claimed 31 of the top achievers, Pennsylvania two, and the rest of the middle Atlantic region twelve. Significantly, most of New England's great achievers had grown up in and around the city of Boston while almost no one of comparable standing came from the much larger city of Philadelphia.

What could explain this remarkable pattern? Baltzell drew inspiration from the German sociologist, Max Weber, who argued that a region's record of achievement was influenced by its major religious beliefs. In the religious differences between Boston and Philadelphia, Baltzell found the answer to his puzzle. Boston was originally a Puritan settlement, founded by people who highly valued both the pursuit of excellence and public achievement. Philadelphia, in contrast, was settled by Quakers, who believed in equality and avoided public notice. Puritanism celebrated hard work and fostered a disciplined life in which people both sought and respected achievement. Quakers believed in equality and the basic goodness of human beings. Thus rich and poor alike lived modestly and discouraged one another from standing out by seeking fame or running for public office. The two different belief systems led to different attitudes toward personal achievement, which in turn shaped the history of each region.

EVALUATE

The use of available data—in newspaper archives, historical or current census materials, books (textbooks or novels), movies, diaries, blogs, legislation, and Facebook profiles or social networks (you name it)—allows the researcher to construct socioeconomic and cultural portraits of life in particular times and places. Depending on the type of material analyzed, one could delve into beliefs, values, and the meaning of various social patterns. The internet exponentially expands the potential materials that can be studied or analyzed at minimal cost.

CHECK YOUR LEARNING Can you think of an interesting piece of research you might do with existing data?

Technology and Research

In recent decades, new information technology has changed our lives considerably, and this applies to the practice of research as well. Personal computers—which have been on the scene only since the early 1980s—now give individual sociologists remarkable technical ability to randomly select samples, perform complex statistical analysis, and prepare written reports. Today's office computer or laptop is far more powerful than even the massive mainframe devices that filled entire rooms on university campuses only a generation ago. See the Sociology and the Media box for further details.

The internet now links some 670 million people throughout the world, allowing for an unprecedented level of communication. Contemporary sociologists are capable of building networks throughout the country and around the globe, which will facilitate collaboration and prompt comparative research. Statistics Canada opened its website on the internet in 1994. Such developments—and

Sociology and the Media

From Card Punching to Cyberspace: Evolution in the Media of Research

How have technological advances changed research? One of the authors of this book began the research for her Ph.D. thesis—on out-migration from First Nations communities (Gerber, 1976)—around 1970, which in technological terms was the dinosaur era. Data collection involved laborious coding of about 80 variables for each of 600 First Nations communities. Using a keypunch machine, the data were punched onto several thousand cards that were manually fed into the University of Toronto's huge mainframe computers—every time she carried out a new piece of analysis.

Later, these cards were read onto magnetic tape, making Gerber's final analyses less labour-intensive. Her thesis was hammered out on a manual typewriter; because whiteout was not allowed, a mistake on any of the 313 pages of the final document required that the entire page in question be retyped. Subsequent papers submitted to journals for publication were produced in the same plodding way.

By the mid-1980s, the Canadian census was available on paper *and* on magnetic tape. The tapes made secondary analysis infinitely easier for anyone who analyzed census data. In addition, word processors made the typing of manuscripts a breeze. Historically, articles were submitted to journals on *paper* for consideration by reviewers. By the early 1990s, the final copy of an "accepted" paper was sent to the journal on a disk. Today, documents—including revised chapters of this text—are sent as email attachments.

Data analysis is now much less labour intensive. Those who analyze the census find their data online. The data are transferred to personal computers, where they can be recoded and subjected to all kinds of sophisticated analysis. Word processing produces "papers" that may never see anything but electronic form until they appear in journals.

Increasingly, articles in established paper-based publications are available on the internet as well, with members

FAMILIARITY WITH COMPUTERS IS FAR MORE COMMON AMONG YOUNGER MEMBERS OF OUR SOCIETY THAN AMONG OLDER GENERATIONS Today's young people will find computers a natural and indispensable part of day-to-day living.

paying for access to various papers or issues. By 1996, several new sociology journals appeared solely on the internet, with no paper copy available anywhere!

Think of the implications. One can "collect" data, conduct sophisticated analysis, write a scholarly article, submit it, and have it "published" with instantaneous access around the world. All of this can be accomplished electronically without ever putting ink or laser imprint to paper. Media theorist Marshall McLuhan would have recognized the revolutionary impact of these developments.

What Do You Think?

1. Did you experience some of this evolution or change in the way you produced papers during your high school years?
2. Do the new media of research and publication make cheating or plagiarism easier? How should colleges and universities respond?
3. Will the electronic media eventually eliminate hard-copy books and journals altogether? Why or why not?

---

other as-yet-unimagined forms of technological change—promise to transform sociological investigation throughout the current century.

The Interplay of Theory and Method

No matter how sociologists collect their data, they have to turn facts into meaning by building theory. They do this in two ways: through inductive logical thought and deductive logical thought.

Inductive logical thought is *reasoning that transforms specific observations into general theory*. In this mode, a researcher's thinking runs from the specific to the general

and goes something like this: "I have some interesting data here; I wonder what they mean?" When you read Table 2–2 and tried to determine what the data were saying, you were engaged in inductive reasoning.

A second type of logical thought moves "downward," in the opposite direction: **Deductive logical thought** is

inductive logical thought reasoning that transforms specific observations into general theory

deductive logical thought reasoning that transforms general theory into specific hypotheses suitable for testing

reasoning that transforms general theory into specific hypotheses suitable for testing. The researcher's thinking runs from the general to the specific: "I have this hunch about human behaviour; let's collect some data and put it to the test." Working deductively, the researcher first states the theory in the form of a hypothesis and then selects a method by which to test it. To the extent that the data support the hypothesis, we conclude that the theory is correct; if the data refute the hypothesis, we know that the theory needs to be revised or maybe rejected entirely.

Just as researchers may employ several methods over the course of one study, they typically use *both* kinds of logical thought. Figure 2–2 illustrates both types of reasoning: inductively building theory from observations and deductively making observations to test a theory.

Often we conclude that an argument must be true simply because there are statistics to back it up. However, we must look at statistics with a cautious eye. After all, researchers choose the data to present, interpret their statistics, and use tables and graphs to steer readers toward particular conclusions. Healthy skepticism is in order even when claims are supported with hard data.

The Summing Up table provides a quick review of the four major methods of sociological investigation.

Putting It All Together: 10 Steps in Sociological Investigation

We can summarize this chapter by outlining 10 steps in the process of carrying out sociological investigation. Each step takes the form of an important question.

1. **What is your topic?** Being curious and applying the sociological perspective can generate ideas for social

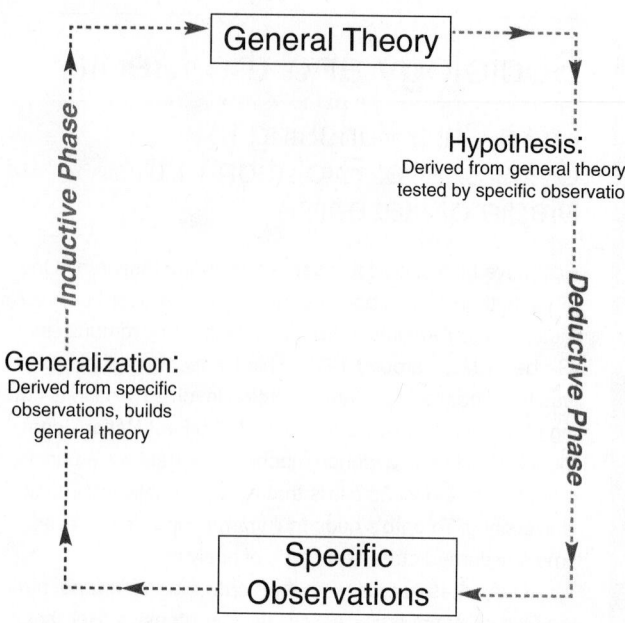

Figure 2–2 Deductive and Inductive Logical Thought
Sociologists link theory and method through both inductive and deductive logic.

research at any time and in any place. Pick a topic that you find interesting and important to study.

2. **What have others already learned?** You are probably not the first person with an interest in the issue you have selected. Review the literature to determine the theories and methods that other researchers have applied to your topic.

3. **What, exactly, are your questions?** Are you seeking to explore an unfamiliar social setting? To describe some category of people? To investigate cause and

Four Research Methods

	Experiment	Survey	Participant Observation	Secondary Analysis
Application	For explanatory research that specifies relationships between variables Generates quantitative data	For gathering information about issues that cannot be directly observed, such as attitudes and values Useful for descriptive and explanatory research Generates quantitative or qualitative data	For exploratory and descriptive study of people in a "natural" setting Generates qualitative data	For exploratory, descriptive, or explanatory research whenever suitable data are available
Advantages	Provides the greatest opportunity to specify cause-and-effect relationships Replication of research is relatively easy	Sampling, using questionnaires, allows surveys of large populations Interviews provide detailed responses	Allows study of "natural" behaviour Usually inexpensive	Saves time and expense of data collection Makes historical research possible
Limitations	Laboratory settings have an artificial quality Unless the research environment is carefully controlled, results may be biased	Questionnaires must be carefully prepared and may yield a low return rate Interviews are expensive and time-consuming	Time-consuming Replication of research is difficult Researcher must balance roles of participant and observer	Researcher has no control over possible biases in data Data may only partially fit current research needs

effect among variables? If your study is exploratory or descriptive, identify whom you wish to study, where the research will take place, and what kinds of issues you want to explore. If your study is explanatory, you also must formulate the hypothesis to be tested and operationalize each variable.

4. **What will you need to carry out research?** How much time and money are available to you? Is special equipment or training necessary? Can you do the work yourself?

5. **Are there ethical concerns?** Not all research raises serious ethical questions, but you must be sensitive to this possibility. Can the research cause harm or threaten anyone's privacy? How can you minimize the likelihood of injury? How will you ensure the anonymity of your subjects?

6. **What method(s) will you use?** Consider all major research strategies, as well as combinations of approaches. Keep in mind that the best method depends on the kinds of questions you are asking as well as the resources available to you.

7. **How will you record the data?** Your research method is a plan for data collection. Record all information accurately and in a way that will make sense later when you are doing your analysis and writing up your results.

8. **What do the data tell you?** Study the data in terms of your initial questions, and decide how to interpret the data you have collected. If your study involves a specific hypothesis, you must decide whether to confirm, reject, or modify the hypothesis. As there are several ways to look at your data, depending on which theoretical approach you use, you should consider alternate interpretations.

9. **What are your conclusions?** Prepare a final report stating your conclusions. How does your work advance sociological theory? Does it suggest ways to improve research methods? Does your study have policy implications? What would the general public find interesting in your work? Finally, evaluate your own work, noting problems that arose and questions that were left unanswered.

10. **How can you share what you've learned?** Consider sending your research paper to a campus newspaper or magazine or making a presentation to a class, a campus gathering, or perhaps a meeting of professional sociologists. The point is to share what you have learned with others and to let them respond to your work.

Seeing Sociology in Everyday Life

CHAPTER 2   Sociological Investigation

What Are Friends for?

Sociological research is the key to a deeper understanding of our everyday social world and also to knowing more about ourselves. Take friendship, for example. Everyone knows that it is fun to be surrounded by friends. But did you know that friendship has real benefits for human health? What do you think these benefits might be? Take a look at the photos below and learn more about what research has taught us about the positive effects of having friends.

> **Hint** In the first case, (*described below*) researchers defined having friends as the independent variable, and they defined longevity and health as the dependent variables. On average, those with friends (the experimental group) actually lived longer and were healthier than those without friends (the control group). In the second case (*below right*), researchers found that women with many friends were several times more likely to survive their illness than those without friends. The third case reminds us that correlation does not demonstrate cause and effect. This study covering over six years looked at more than 700 men, some with many friends (the experimental group) and also other men of comparable health (the control group) and few friends. Finding that those with friends had better heart health tells us that friendship is the independent or causal variable. In the fourth case, researchers did indeed find that the longer the people had been friends, the more positive the subject's attitude about making the climb turned out to be. Long live friendship!

Tom Grill/Corbis

ONE 10-YEAR STUDY OF OLDER PEOPLE FOUND THAT THOSE WOMEN AND MEN WHO HAD MANY FRIENDS WERE SIGNIFICANTLY LESS LIKELY TO DIE OVER THE COURSE OF THE RESEARCH THAN THOSE WITH FEW OR NO FRIENDS Other long-term research confirms that people with friends not only live longer but also healthier lives than those without friends. What are the variables in this study? What conclusion is drawn about the relationship between the variables?

Sean Justice/Corbis

ONE STUDY LOOKED AT 3000 WOMEN DIAGNOSED WITH BREAST CANCER AND COMPARED THE RATE OF SURVIVAL FOR WOMEN WITH MANY FRIENDS WITH THAT FOR WOMEN WITH FEW OR NO FRIENDS What do you think they concluded about the effect of friendship on surviving a serious illness?

PERHAPS THE REASON THAT FRIENDSHIP IMPROVES HEALTH IS THAT FRIENDS RAISE OUR SPIRITS AND GIVE US A MORE POSITIVE ATTITUDE ABOUT OUR LIVES A final study placed young college students carrying heavy backpacks at the base of a steep hill and asked them how tough it would be to climb to the top. Subjects in the company of a friend were much more optimistic that they could make the climb than those standing there alone. Would you expect to find that that the better the friend, the more positive the person's attitude?

THE "FRIENDSHIP EFFECT" IMPROVES THE HEALTH OF MEN, TOO A study of older men found that those with many friends had lower rates of heart disease than those without friends. How could you be sure of the causal direction linking these variables? That is, how can we be sure that friendship is improving health rather than good health encouraging friendship?

Stephen Derr/Getty Images

Oliver Cadeaux/Corbis

Seeing Sociology in *Your* Everyday Life

1. The research studies discussed above demonstrate that friendship means more to people than we might think. Recall Émile Durkheim's study of suicide. How did he use sociological research to uncover more about the importance of relationships? Which one of the research methods discussed in this chapter did he use in his study of suicide?

2. Observe your instructor in class one day and grade his or her teaching skills. Before you come to class, operationalize the concept "good teaching" in terms of specific traits you can observe and measure. Are there qualities of good teaching that you cannot readily observe? Overall, how easy is it to measure "good teaching"? Why?

3. As this chapter has explained, sociology involves more than a distinctive perspective and theoretical approaches. The discipline is also about learning—gaining more information about the operation of society all around us. It's possible that you will go on to study more sociology and you might even end up doing sociological research. But there is value in knowing how to carry out a sound research project even if you never do it yourself. The value of such knowledge lies in this: In a society that feeds us a steady diet of information, knowing how accurate information is gathered gives you the skills to assess what you read and enhances your critical thinking ability.

Making the Grade

CHAPTER 2 The Sociological Investigation

Basics of Sociological Investigation

2.1 Explain how scientific evidence often challenges common sense.

Two basic requirements for **sociological investigation** are
- Know how to apply the sociological perspective.
- Be curious and ready to ask questions about the world around you.

What people accept as "truth" differs around the world.
- **Science**—a logical system that bases knowledge on direct, systematic observation—is one form of truth.
- Scientific evidence gained from sociological research often challenges common sense.

> **science** a logical system that bases knowledge on direct, systematic observation
> **empirical evidence** information we can verify with our senses

Research Orientations: Three Ways to Do Sociology

2.2 Describe sociology's three research orientations.

Scientific sociology studies society by systematically observing social behaviour.

Scientific or positivist sociology
- requires carefully operationalizing variables and ensuring that measurement is both reliable and valid
- observes how variables are related and tries to establish cause and effect
- sees an objective reality "out there"
- favours quantitative data
- is well suited to research in a laboratory
- demands that researchers be objective and suspend their personal values and biases as they conduct research

Interpretive sociology focuses on the meanings that people attach to behaviour.

Interpretive sociology
- sees reality as constructed by people in the course of their everyday lives
- favours qualitative data
- is well suited to research in a natural setting

Critical sociology uses research to bring about social change.

Critical sociology
- asks moral and political questions
- focuses on inequality
- rejects the principle of objectivity, claiming that all research is political

Research Orientations and Theory
- Scientific or positivist sociology is loosely linked to the structural-functional approach.
- Interpretive sociology is related to the symbolic-interaction approach.
- Critical sociology corresponds to the social-conflict approach.

> **scientific sociology** the study of society based on systematic observation of social behaviour
> **concept** a mental construct that represents some part of the world in a simplified form
> **variable** a concept whose value changes from case to case
> **measurement** a procedure for determining the value of a variable in a specific case
> **operationalize a variable** specifying exactly what is to be measured before assigning a value to a variable
> **reliability** consistency in measurement
> **validity** actually measuring exactly what you intend to measure
> **cause and effect** a relationship in which change in one variable causes change in another (the dependent variable)
> **independent variable** the variable that causes the change
> **dependent variable** the variable that changes
> **correlation** a relationship in which two (or more) variables change together
> **spurious correlation** an apparent but false relationship between two (or more) variables that is caused by some other variable
> **control** holding constant all variables except one in order to see clearly the effect of that variable
> **objectivity** personal neutrality in conducting research
> **replication** repetition of research by other investigators
> **interpretive sociology** the study of society that focuses on the meanings people attach to their social world
> **critical sociology** the study of society that focuses on the need for social change

Issues Affecting Sociological Research

2.3 **Discuss the importance of gender and ethics in sociological research.**

Gender and Research

Gender, involving both researcher and subjects, can affect research in five ways:

- androcentricity
- overgeneralizing
- gender blindness
- double standards
- interference

There are many women who have made important contributions to sociology and research methods.

> **gender** the personal traits and social positions that members of a society attach to being female or male

Research Ethics

Researchers must

- protect the privacy of subjects
- obtain the informed consent of subjects
- indicate all sources of funding
- submit research to an institutional review board to ensure it doesn't violate ethical standards

Research Methods

2.4 **Explain why a researcher might choose each of sociology's research methods.**

The experiment allows researchers to study cause and effect between two or more variables in a controlled setting.

- Researchers conduct an experiment to test a hypothesis, a statement of a possible relationship between two (or more) variables.

Example of an experiment: Zimbardo's "Stanford County Prison"

Survey research uses questionnaires or interviews to gather subjects' responses to a series of questions.

- Surveys typically yield descriptive findings, painting a picture of people's views on some issue.

Example of a survey: Anti-Semitism in Quebec

Through participant observation, researchers join with people in a social setting for an extended period of time.

- Participant observation, also called fieldwork, allows researchers an "inside look" at a social setting. Because researchers are not attempting to test a specific hypothesis, their research is exploratory and descriptive.

Example of participant observation: Whyte's "Street Corner Society"

Sometimes researchers perform secondary analysis, using data collected by others.

- Using existing sources, especially the widely available data collected by government agencies, can save researchers time and money.
- Existing sources are the basis of historical research.

Example of using secondary analysis: "Labour-Force Participation and Income of Aboriginal Men and Women"

Researchers use both inductive and deductive logical thought.

- Using inductive logical thought, a researcher moves "upward" from the specific to the general.
- Using deductive logical thought, a researcher moves "downward" from the general to the specific.

Ten important steps in carrying out sociological research move from selecting a topic to sharing the results of research.

> **research method** a systematic plan for doing research
> **experiment** a research method for investigating cause and effect under highly controlled conditions
> **hypothesis** a statement of a possible relationship between two (or more) variables
> **Hawthorne effect** (p. 41) a change in a subject's behaviour caused simply by the awareness of being studied
> **survey** a research method in which subjects respond to a series of statements or questions on a questionnaire or in an interview
> **population** the people who are the focus of research
> **sample** a part of a population that represents the whole
> **questionnaire** a series of written questions a researcher presents to subjects
> **interview** a series of questions a researcher asks respondents in person
> **participant observation** a research method in which investigators systematically observe people while joining them in their routine activities
> **inductive logical thought** reasoning that transforms specific observations into general theory
> **deductive logical thought** reasoning that transforms general theory into specific hypotheses suitable for testing

Chapter 3
Culture

Manuel Balce Ceneta/AP Images

Learning Objectives

3.1 Explain the development of culture as a human strategy for survival.

3.2 Identify common elements of culture.

3.3 Discuss dimensions of cultural difference and cultural change.

3.4 Apply sociology's macro-level theories to gain greater understanding of culture.

3.5 Critique culture as limiting or expanding human freedom.

The Power of Society
to guide our attitudes on social issues such as abortion

Survey Question: "Please tell me whether you think abortion can always be justified, never be justified, or something in between."

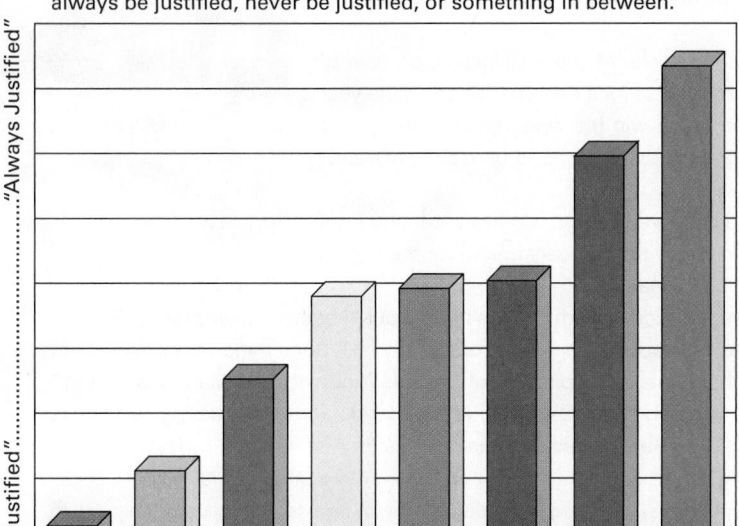

SOURCE: WVS 2010-2012 Questionnaire on http://www.worldvaluessurvey.org/index_ surveys. Used with permission.

Is how we feel about abortion as "personal" an opinion as we may think? If we compare the attitudes of people around the world, we see remarkable variation from country to country. People living in Sweden, for example, claim that abortion is almost always justified; people living in Jordan, by contrast, almost never support this procedure. For people living in Canada, Japan, and the United States, abortion is an issue on which public opinion is fairly evenly divided. By making such global comparisons, we see that society guides people's attitudes on various issues, which is part of the way of life we call culture.

Chapter Overview

This chapter focuses on the concept of "culture," which refers to a society's entire way of life. Notice that the root of the word culture is the same as that of the word *cultivate*, suggesting that people who live together actually "grow" their way of life over time.

"Mush!" the hunter cried into the wind. Through the rising vapour of a northern Manitoba February, so crisp, so dry, the snow creaked underfoot, the caribou hunter Abraham Okimasis drove his sled and team of eight grey huskies through the orange-rose–tinted dusk. His left hand gripping handlebar of sled, his right snapping moose-hide whip above his head, Abraham Okimasis was urging his huskies forward. . . .

He had sworn to his dear wife, Mariesis Okimasis, on pain of separation and divorce, unthinkable for a Roman Catholic in the year of our Lord 1951, that he would win the world championship just for her: the silver cup, that holy chalice was to be his twenty-first-anniversary gift to her. . . .

"Please, please, God in heaven, let me win this race, and I will thank you with every deed, every touch, every breath for the rest of my long life, for hallowed be thy name . . ."

"Boom," the voice went, "boom, boom." Something about "Abraham Okimasis, forty-three years old, caribou hunter, fur trapper, fisherman, boom, boom." Something about "Abraham Okimasis, musher from the Eemanapiteepitat Indian reserve, northwestern Manitoba, boom." Something having to do with "Abraham Okimasis, first Indian to win this gruelling race in its twenty-eight–year history. . . ." The syllables became one vast, rolling rumble.

Source: Extracted from *Kiss of the Fur Queen* by Tomson Highway. Copyright © Tomson Highway 1998. Reprinted by permission of Doubleday Canada. ■

The cultural differences among people around the world can delight, puzzle, disturb, and sometimes overwhelm us. Some differences in lifestyles are simply matters of convention: The Chinese, for example, wear white at funerals, while Canadians prefer black. Similarly, Chinese people associate the number four with bad luck, just as Canadians think of the number thirteen. Or consider the practice of kissing: Most Canadians may kiss in public at times, whereas most Chinese kiss only in private; the French kiss publicly twice, once on each cheek, while Belgians kiss three times, starting on either cheek. Most Nigerians don't kiss at all. At weddings, moreover, Canadian couples kiss, Koreans bow, and a Cambodian groom touches his nose to the bride's cheek. Other cultural differences are more profound. The world over, people wear much or little clothing, have many or few children, venerate or shunt aside the elderly, are peaceful or warlike, embrace different religious beliefs, and enjoy different kinds of art and music. In short, although biologically we are all the same, we have developed strikingly different ideas about what is pleasant and repulsive, polite and rude, beautiful and ugly, right and wrong. These often sometimes startling differences are the expressions of human culture.

What Is Culture?

3.1 Explain the development of culture as a human strategy for survival.

Culture refers to *the ways of thinking, the ways of acting, and the material objects that together form a people's way of life.* Thus, it includes our thoughts, our actions, and our possessions. Since culture comprises everything we create with our hands and our minds, it is both our link to the past and our guide to the future.

To fully understand culture, we must consider both thoughts and things. **Nonmaterial culture** refers to *the ideas created by members of a society,* ideas that range from art to the Canadian constitution. **Material culture**, by

culture the ways of thinking, the ways of acting, and the material objects that together form a people's way of life

nonmaterial culture the ideas created by members of a society

material culture the physical things created by members of a society

contrast, refers to *the physical things created by members of a society*, everything from beavertail doughnuts to satellites in space.

Given the extent of cultural differences in the world and people's tendency to view their own way of life as "natural," it is no wonder that travellers often find themselves feeling uneasy as they encounter an unfamiliar culture. This uneasiness is **culture shock**, *personal disorientation when experiencing an unfamiliar way of life*. People experience such disorientation when they immigrate to or visit a new country or, to a lesser extent, when they move between social environments within their own country. A young person moving from rural Newfoundland to attend university in Vancouver or Toronto knows the feeling of culture shock. More surprisingly, those who teach English in Japan for a year or more experience culture shock upon their *return* to Canada.

No way of life is "natural" to humanity, even though most people around the world view their own behaviour in that way. The co-operation that comes naturally to

HUMAN BEINGS AROUND THE GLOBE CREATE DIVERSE WAYS OF LIFE Such differences begin with outward appearance: Contrast the women shown here from Ethiopia, India, Myanmar, Tibet, and the United States and the men from Taiwan (Republic of China), Kenya, Ecuador, and Australia. Less obvious but of even greater importance are internal differences, since culture also shapes our goals in life, our sense of justice, and even our innermost personal feelings.

people in the Andes Mountains of Peru is very different from the competitive living that comes naturally to people in Toronto or New York. Such variation arises when human beings join together to create distinctive ways of life. Every other animal—from ant to zebra—behaves the same way around the world, because animal behaviour is guided by instinct, or biological programming, over which the species has no control. A few animals—notably chimpanzees and related primates—have the capacity for limited culture, as researchers have noted by observing them using tools and teaching simple skills to their offspring. But the creative power of humans is far greater than that of any other form of life and has resulted in countless ways of being "human." In short, *only humans rely on culture rather than on instinct to create a way of life and to ensure survival* (Harris, 1987). To understand how human culture came to be, we need to look at the history of our species.

Culture and Human Intelligence

Scientists estimate that this planet is 4.5 billion years old. Life appeared about 1 billion years later; fast-forward another 2 to 3 billion years and dinosaurs ruled. It was when these giant creatures disappeared—some 65 million years ago—that primates appeared. The importance of primates is that they have the largest brains relative to body size of all living creatures.

About 12 million years ago, primates began to evolve along two different lines, setting humans apart from the great apes. Then, some 3 million years ago, our distant human ancestors climbed down from the trees of central Africa to move about in the tall grasses. There, walking upright, they learned the advantages of hunting in groups and made use of fire, tools, and weapons; they built simple shelters and fashioned basic clothing. These Stone Age achievements may seem modest, but they mark the point at which our ancestors set off on a distinct evolutionary course, making culture their primary strategy for survival. By about 250 000 years ago, our own species—*Homo sapiens* (derived from the Latin meaning "thinking person")—finally emerged. Humans continued to evolve so that, by about 40 000 years ago, people who looked more or less like us roamed Earth. With larger brains, these "modern" *Homo sapiens* developed cultures rapidly, as suggested by the wide range of tools and cave art from this period.

About 12 000 years ago, the founding of permanent settlements and the creation of specialized occupations (in what are now Iraq and Egypt) marked the "birth of civilization." By then, humans no longer lived by biological instincts but by a more efficient survival scheme: *changing the natural environment to benefit themselves.* Since then, humans have made and remade their world in countless ways, resulting in today's fascinating cultural diversity.

ALL SOCIETIES CONTAIN CULTURAL DIFFERENCES THAT CAN PROVOKE A MILD CASE OF CULTURE SHOCK This woman travelling on a British subway is not sure what to make of the woman sitting next to her, who is wearing the Muslim full-face veil known as the *niqab*.

Culture, Nation, State, and Society

At this point, we pause to clarify the proper use of several similar terms: *culture, nation, state,* and *society*. Culture refers to the ideas, values, and artifacts that make up a shared way of life. Nation is commonly used to refer to a political entity—a state or country; however, it also refers to a people—or even an ethnic group—who share a culture (including language), ancestry, and history. A state is a political entity in a territory with designated borders, such as Argentina or Zimbabwe. Society refers to the organized interaction of people—within a nation, state, or other boundary—who share a culture. While Canada is a state that encompasses several nations—notably the Québécois and First Nations—when we talk of "nation building" we refer to the difficult and ongoing task of creating a sense of nationhood—at the federal or state level—that supersedes multicultural and regional loyalties.

How Many Cultures?

Globally, experts document almost 7000 languages, suggesting the existence of at least that many distinct cultures. Yet the number of languages spoken around the world is declining, and roughly half of the remaining languages are spoken by fewer than 10 000 people. Experts expect that the coming decades may see the disappearance of hundreds of these languages, from Gullah, Pennsylvania German, and Pawnee (in the United States) to Shuswap and Algonquian (in Canada), Oro (in the Amazon region of Brazil), Sardinian (on the European island of Sardinia), Aramaic (in the Middle East), Nu Shu (in southern China, the only language known to be

Thinking about Diversity: Race, Class, and Gender

Aboriginal Languages in Danger of Extinction

Of the 60 Aboriginal languages spoken throughout Canada a century ago, only four—Cree, Inuktitut, Ojibwa, and Dakota—are not on the brink of extinction today. Some of Canada's Aboriginal languages are already extinct, and six others have fewer than 10 known speakers. So serious is the linguistic hemorrhage that, in 1996, 71 percent of Aboriginal children had never spoken their native languages.

According to Ron Ignace, Canada should be declaring a state of emergency, introducing legislation, and setting aside more than $100 million to fund Aboriginal language immersion programs across the country. Ignace is the chief of the Skeetchestn Reserve in British Columbia and chair of the Committee on Aboriginal Languages (of the Assembly of First Nations). His wife, Marianne, is an associate professor of First Nations Studies at Simon Fraser University. Ignace worries because he and his wife are the only parents in their community of 400 who are still speaking Shuswap to their children. When so few people commit themselves to speaking the language of their culture, languages disappear.

"Canada is on the verge of losing precious jewels of its cultural heritage," says Ignace. "These languages represent vast reservoirs of intellectual knowledge stretching back thousands of years. The English language is an infant relative to our languages." The loss of these ancient languages, he says, is one of the world's great ecological disasters (Philp, 2000). According to Abley (2006), Canada has up to 61 indigenous languages, many of which are so radically different that they have as much in common as do English and Tibetan. Each of these indigenous tongues "embodies a unique way of understanding and responding to the world," and they may have embedded in them ancient knowledge valuable to us today. An example comes from southwestern British Columbia, where the Halkomelem word *th'alátel* refers to wild ginger but also means "a device for the heart." Only recently have medical studies revealed that, in addition to aiding digestion and reducing nausea, ginger reduces cholesterol and prevents blood clots. Science is now learning something that this indigenous community has known for thousands of years, knowledge that is built into its language.

Another important component of language is the definition of spirituality and one's relationship to a deity. A Squamish speaker (also from southwestern British Columbia) told Abley that "language and culture are an umbilical cord to the Creator." Clearly, language shapes our experience of life in the most simple and most profound ways. In short, it gives meaning to our lives. Abley asks whether the loss of language helps explain "why so many indigenous communities are now in such evident distress." The loss of Aboriginal languages in Canada can be attributed to residential schooling, English-language television and radio, migration to urban areas, and even intermarriage. The most secure languages are those spoken in the largest or most isolated communities.

The extinction of any language is a serious loss to world culture in terms of diversity and vital knowledge. North America loses irreplaceable parts of its culture when the languages that evolved on this continent and embody its rich cultural heritage disappear.

What Do You Think?

1. Does it really matter if Aboriginal languages disappear? Why?
2. What does it take to preserve these languages?
3. Is it important for people—all of us—to speak more than one language?

SOURCE: Based on Philp (2000) and Abley (2006).

used exclusively by women), and Wakka Wakka and several other Aboriginal tongues spoken in Australia. What accounts for the decline? Likely causes include electronic communication, increasing international migration, and an expanding global economy (Barovick, 2002; Hayden, 2003; Lewis, 2009; UNESCO, 2001).

The Elements of Culture

3.2 Identify common elements of culture.

Although cultures vary greatly, they all have common elements, including symbols, language, values, and norms. We begin with the element that is the basis for all the others: symbols.

Symbols

Humans not only sense the surrounding world as other creatures do, but also build a reality of meaning. Thus, humans transform elements of the world into **symbols**, *anything that carries a particular meaning recognized by people who share culture.* A whistle, a wall of graffiti, a flashing red light, and a fist raised in the air all serve as symbols. The human capacity to create and manipulate symbols is reflected in the very different meanings associated with the simple act of winking an eye: In some settings, this action conveys interest; in others, understanding; in still others, insult. We are so dependent on our culture's symbols that we take them for granted. Occasionally, however, we become keenly aware of a symbol when someone uses it in an unconventional way—as when political protesters in Brockville, Ontario, stomped on a Quebec flag in 1989. Entering an unfamiliar society also reminds us of the power of symbols: The resulting culture shock involves the inability to "read" meaning in unfamiliar surroundings. We feel lost and isolated, unsure of how to act, and sometimes frightened—a consequence of being outside the symbolic web of culture that joins individuals in meaningful social life.

Culture shock is a two-way process: It is something that the traveller experiences when encountering people whose way of life is unfamiliar, and it is also what the traveller inflicts on others by acting in ways that might offend them. For example, because North Americans consider dogs to be beloved household pets, travellers to northern regions of China may be appalled to find people roasting dogs for dinner. On the other hand, travellers may inflict culture shock on others by acting in ways that are considered inappropriate or offensive (e.g., kissing in public). Indeed, travel abroad provides endless opportunities for misunderstanding.

Symbolic meanings vary even within a single society. A fur coat, prized by one person as a luxurious symbol of success, may represent to another the inhumane treatment of animals. Similarly, the Canadian flag, which to many Canadians embodies national pride, may symbolize oppression of the Québécois to separatists. Cultural symbols also change over time. Blue jeans were created more than a century ago as sturdy, inexpensive clothing for people engaged in physical labour. In the liberal political climate of the 1960s, this working-class aura made jeans popular among affluent students— many of whom wore them simply to look "different" or to identify with working people. In the late 1970s, "designer jeans" emerged as high-priced status symbols that conveyed quite a different message. Today, everyday jeans remain as popular as ever, simply as comfortable apparel.

In sum, symbols allow people to make sense of their lives, and without them human existence would be meaningless. Manipulating symbols correctly allows us to engage others within our own cultural system. Societies create new symbols all the time. The Sociology in Focus box describes some of the cyber-symbols that have developed along with our increasing use of computers for communication.

Language

In infancy, an illness left Helen Keller (1880–1968) blind and deaf. Without these two senses, she was cut off from the symbolic world, and her social development was greatly limited. Only when her teacher, Anne Mansfield Sullivan, broke through Keller's isolation using sign language did Helen Keller begin to realize her human potential. This remarkable woman, who later became a famous educator herself, recalls the moment she first understood the concept of language:

> We walked down the path to the well-house, attracted by the smell of honeysuckle with which it was covered. Someone was drawing water, and my teacher placed my

Jacques Boissinot/The Canadian Press

PEOPLE THROUGHOUT THE WORLD COMMUNICATE NOT JUST WITH SPOKEN WORDS BUT ALSO WITH GESTURES
Because gestures vary from culture to culture, they can be the cause of misunderstandings. For instance, the commonplace "thumbs-up" gesture that we use to express "Good job!" can get a Canadian into trouble in Australia, where people take it to mean "Up yours!" Prime Minister Stephen Harper used the gesture when visiting Canadian troops in Afghanistan. While our soldiers understand it, might "thumbs-up" have an entirely different meaning for the local people?

AP Images

BEHAVIOUR THAT PEOPLE IN ONE SOCIETY CONSIDER ROUTINE CAN BE CHILLING TO MEMBERS OF ANOTHER CULTURE
In the Russian city of St. Petersburg, this young mother and her six-week-old son brave the –27°C temperature for a dip in a nearby lake To Russians, this is normal—to us, it is cruel or even dangerous.

Sociology in Focus

New Symbols in the World of Instant Messaging

Molly: gr8 to c u!
Greg: u 2
Molly: jw about next time
Greg: idk, lotta work!
Molly: no prb, xoxoxo
Greg: thanx, bcnu

The world of symbols changes all the time. One reason that people create new symbols is that we develop new ways to communicate. Today, more than 150 million people in North America communicate by "texting" using cellphones or handheld computers. Texting has become a way of life among people in their teens and twenties, more than 95 percent of whom own a cellphone. The exchange featured above shows how everyday social interaction can take place quickly and easily using instant messaging (IM) symbols. Because the symbols people use change all the time, the IM language used a year from now will differ, just as IM symbols differ from place to place. Here are some common IM symbols:

b be

bc because

b4 before

b4n 'bye for now

bbl be back later

bcnu be seeing you

brb be right back

cu see you

def definitely

g2g got to go

gal get a life

gmta great minds think alike

gr8 great

hagn have a good night

h&k hugs and kisses

idc I don't care

idt I don't think

idk I don't know

imbl it must be love

jk just kidding

jw just wondering

j4f just for fun

kc keep cool

l8r later

lmao laugh my ass off

ltnc long time no see

myob mind your own business

no prb no problem

omg oh my gosh

pcm please call me

plz please

prbly probably

qpsa ¿Qué pasa?

rt right

thanx thanks

u you

ur you are

w/ with

w/e whatever

w/o without

wan2 want to

wtf what the freak

y why

2l8 too late

? question

2 to, two
4 for, four

What Do You Think?

1. What does the creation of symbols such as those listed here suggest about culture?
2. Do you think that using such symbols is a good way to communicate? Does it lead to confusion or misunderstanding? Why or why not?
3. What other kinds of symbols can you think of that are new to your generation?

SOURCES: J. Rubin (2003), Berteau (2005), and Lenhart (2010).

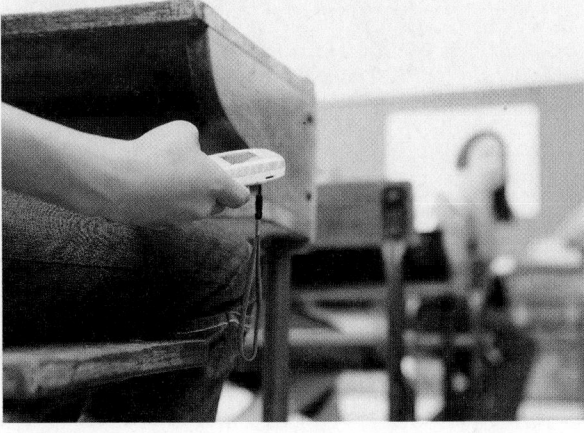

Tomas Rodriguez/Fancy/Corbis

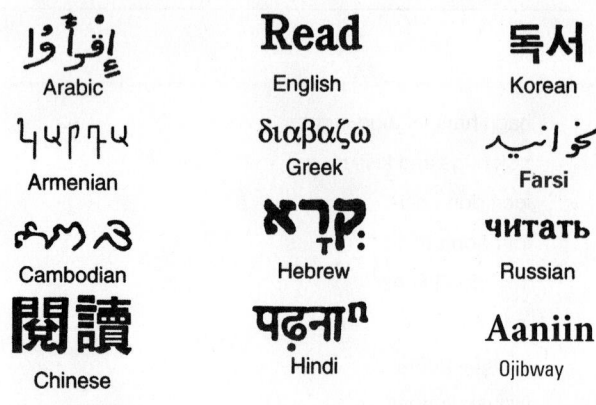

Figure 3–1 Human Languages: A Variety of Symbols

Here the single English word "*read*" is written in 12 of the hundreds of languages humans use to communicate with one another.

hand under the spout. As the cool stream gushed over one hand, she spelled into the other the word *water*, first slowly, then rapidly. I stood still, my whole attention fixed upon the motions of her fingers. Suddenly I felt a misty consciousness as of something forgotten—a thrill of returning thought; and somehow the mystery of language was revealed to me. I knew then that "w-a-t-e-r" meant the wonderful cool something that was flowing over my hand. That living word awakened my soul; gave it light, hope, joy, set it free! (Keller, 1903:24)

Language, the key to the world of culture, is *a system of symbols that allows people to communicate with one another*. Humans have created many sounds and alphabets to express the hundreds of languages we speak. Several examples are shown in Figure 3–1. Even rules for writing differ; most people in Western societies write from left to right, but people in northern Africa and western Asia write from right to left, and people in eastern Asia write from top to bottom. Global Map 3–1 shows where we find the world's three most widely spoken languages.

Language not only allows communication but also is the key to **cultural transmission**, *the process by which one generation passes culture to the next*. Just as our bodies contain the genes of our ancestors, our culture contains countless symbols of those who came before us. Language is the key that unlocks centuries of accumulated wisdom. The Thinking about Diversity box makes just such an argument with respect to Canada's Aboriginal languages, most of which are threatened with extinction.

language a system of symbols that allows people to communicate with one another

cultural transmission the process by which one generation passes culture to the next

Window on the World

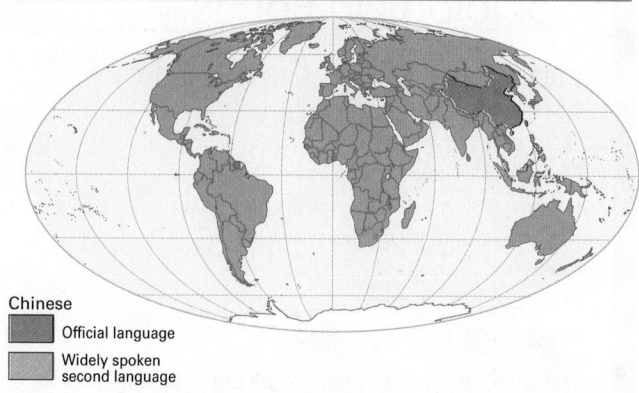

Chinese
- ☐ Official language
- ☐ Widely spoken second language

Chinese (including Mandarin, Cantonese, and dozens of other dialects) is the native tongue of one-fifth of the world's people, almost all of whom live in Asia. Although all Chinese people read and write with the same characters, they use several dozen dialects. The "official" dialect, taught in schools throughout the People's Republic of China and the Republic of Taiwan, is Mandarin (the dialect of Beijing, China's capital). Cantonese, the language of Canton, is the second most common Chinese dialect; it differs in sound from Mandarin roughly the way French differs from Spanish.

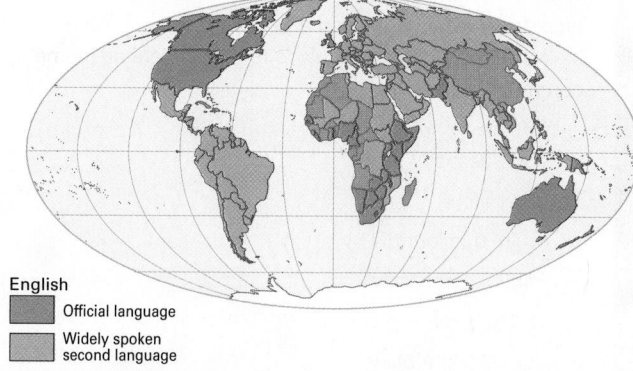

English
- ☐ Official language
- ☐ Widely spoken second language

English is the native tongue or official language in several world regions (spoken by 5 percent of humanity) and has become the preferred second language in the world. Of course, language use may vary tremendously within a single country: Whereas English and French are the official languages of Canada, in the province of Quebec—where 81 percent of the population speaks French at home—the official language is French.

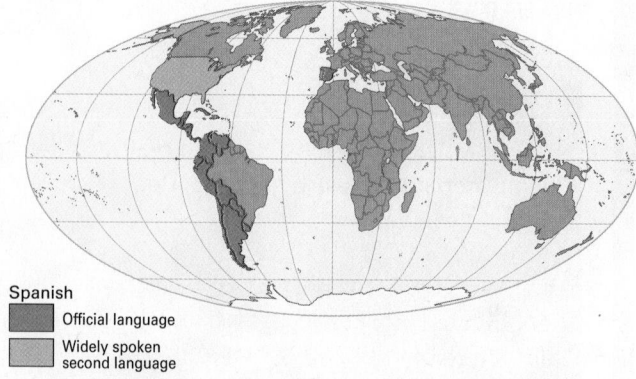

Spanish
- ☐ Official language
- ☐ Widely spoken second language

The largest concentration of Spanish speakers is in Latin America and, of course, Spain. Spanish is also the second most widely spoken language in the United States.

Global Map 3–1 Language in Global Perspective

SOURCES: Lewis (2009); *Central Intelligence Agency* (2009).

Canadians are very familiar with the importance of language to culture. Although Canada is officially bilingual, in practice it is geographically unilingual, with French-speaking majorities in Quebec and northern New Brunswick, and English predominant elsewhere. Bill 101, which regulates the use of English in Quebec and made French the only official language of that province, was an attempt to preserve the distinctive Québécois culture. To many French-speaking Quebecers, Bill 101 is essential to their survival as a nation; to some English-speaking Canadians, the law seems to be an infringement of the rights of the minority English-speaking Quebecers. The heated debates over language that characterize Canadian—and especially Quebec—politics are evidence of how strongly people feel about their languages.

Throughout human history, people have transmitted culture through speech—or the oral cultural tradition. Only as recently as 5000 years ago did humans invent writing, and, even then, just a favoured few ever learned to read and write. It was not until this century that industrial, high-income countries claimed nearly universal literacy. Nevertheless, the International Adult Literacy Survey of 2003 revealed that 42 percent of Canadians aged 16 to 65 do not have "the desired level of competence for coping with the increasing skill demands of the emerging knowledge and information economy" (Statistics Canada, 2003); furthermore, the situation has not changed since the previous literacy survey in 1994. Data on selected categories reveal that literacy levels are lower among those over 65 years of age, francophones, Aboriginal peoples, and immigrants. Among immigrants, those with French or English as their mother tongue fared better than those with other mother tongues, and there was little improvement for those who have been in this country for more than 10 years. Clearly, many Canadians face almost insurmountable barriers to opportunity in a society that increasingly demands symbolic skills.

Language skills may link us with the past, but they also spark the human imagination to connect symbols in new ways, creating an almost limitless range of future possibilities. Language sets humans apart as the only creatures who are self-conscious, aware of our limitations and ultimate mortality, yet able to dream and to hope for a future better than the present.

DOES LANGUAGE SHAPE REALITY? Do the Inuit, who think in one language (i.e., Inuktitut), experience the world differently from others who think in English, French, or Estonian? The answer is yes, since each language has its own distinct symbols serving as the building blocks of reality.

Edward Sapir (1929, 1949) and Benjamin Whorf (1956; orig. 1941), two anthropologists who specialized in linguistic studies, noted that each language has words or expressions with no precise counterparts in other languages. Further, all languages fuse symbols with distinctive emotions. Thus, as multilingual people can attest, a single idea often "feels" different if spoken in, say, French rather than in English or Chinese. For many of these reasons, jokes do not translate well from one language or culture to another.

Formally, the **Sapir-Whorf hypothesis** states that *people perceive the world through the cultural lens of language.* Using different symbolic systems, a Filipino, a Turk, a Brazilian, and, indeed, anglophone and francophone Canadians actually experience "distinct worlds, not merely the same world with different labels attached" (Sapir, 1949:162). More recently, scholars have taken issue with this thesis, arguing that, although we do fashion reality from our symbols, evidence does not support the notion that language *determines* reality the way that Sapir and Whorf claimed. For example, children understand the *idea* of "family" long before they learn the word; adults can imagine new ideas or things before naming them (Kay & Kempton, 1984; Pinker, 1994).

Values and Beliefs

What accounts for the popularity of Hollywood film characters such as James Bond, Lara Croft, and Rocky Balboa? Each is ruggedly individualistic, going it alone and relying on personal skill and savvy to challenge "the system." In admiring such characters, we are supporting certain **values**, *culturally defined standards that people use to decide what is desirable, good, and beautiful, and that serve as broad guidelines for social living.* Values are standards that people who share a culture use to make choices about how to live.

Values are broad principles that support **beliefs**, *specific statements that people hold to be true.* In other words, values are abstract standards of goodness, and beliefs are particular matters that individuals consider to be true or false. Cultural values and beliefs not only colour how we perceive our surroundings but also form the core of our personalities. We learn from families, schools, and religious organizations to think and act according to approved principles, to pursue worthy goals, and to believe a host of cultural truths while rejecting alternatives as false. Particular values and beliefs thus operate as

---

Sapir-Whorf hypothesis the idea that people see and understand the world through the cultural lens of language

values culturally defined standards that people use to decide what is desirable, good, and beautiful and that serve as broad guidelines for social living

beliefs specific ideas that people hold to be true

a form of "cultural capital" that can spark in some people the optimistic determination to pursue success and, in others, a sense of hopelessness that little will ever change (Sowell, 1996).

In a nation as large and diverse as Canada, of course, few cultural values and beliefs are shared by everyone. In fact, with a long history of immigration, Canada has become a cultural mosaic. In this regard, we stand apart from many countries, such as China or Japan, that have more homogeneous cultural values. Even so, there is a broad shape to our national life that suggests that Canadians share certain "key values." The Thinking Globally box paints a picture of North American society by comparing Canadian and American values.

VALUES: OFTEN IN HARMONY, SOMETIMES IN CONFLICT Cultural values can be inconsistent and even contradictory (Bellah et al., 1985; Lynd, 1967). Living in Canada, we sometimes find ourselves torn between the "me first" attitude of an individualistic, success-at-all-costs way of life and the opposing need to belong and contribute to some larger community. Similarly, we affirm our belief in equality of opportunity only to turn around and promote or degrade others because of their race or gender. Value inconsistency reflects the cultural diversity of Canadian society and the process of cultural change by which new trends supplant older traditions.

One tradition that continues to be central to the Canadian winter and that elusive Canadian identity is hockey. But the traditional hockey scene in Canada is being transformed by the arrival of women's hockey at the international level: Young girls now have women hockey players as role models. Hockey is so central to our identity that Canada's failure to win gold at the 1998 Winter Olympics in Nagano, Japan (a silver medal for the women and no medal at all for the men), unleashed anger, despair, and depressive slumps throughout the country. The double gold in men's and women's hockey in Salt Lake City (2002) restored our dignity and pride, but they were dashed once more when, in Turin, Italy (2006), the women won gold but the men were shut out of the medals yet again. Canadians think of themselves as co-operative rather than competitive and gentle or placid rather than violent. But, when it comes to hockey, we like things rough and aggressive—and we like to win, just as much as the Americans do. The fact that Canadian women are excelling in hockey—at both world and Olympic levels—points up value inconsistencies regarding aggressiveness, competitiveness, and even femininity.

Whether based on the ethnic mix of Canadian society or changes in our way of life, today's value inconsistencies can lead to strain and awkward balancing acts. Sometimes we pursue one value at the expense of another, supporting the principle of equal opportunity, say, while opposing the acceptance of gay people as elementary school teachers.

VALUES: A GLOBAL PERSPECTIVE Each of the thousands of cultures in the world has its own values. In general, the values that are important in higher-income countries differ somewhat from those in lower-income countries.

Societies in lower-income nations have cultures that value survival: People who are desperately poor give priority to physical safety and economic security. They worry about having enough to eat and a safe place to sleep at night. In general, lower-income societies tend

GOVERNOR GENERAL MICHAËLLE JEAN BECAME THE SUBJECT OF INTERNATIONAL CONTROVERSY WHEN SHE USED AN *ULU* (A CURVED INUIT KNIFE) TO CARVE INTO A SEAL, SUBSEQUENTLY EATING A PIECE OF RAW HEART While some Canadians cheered her actions—the *National Post* titled its lead editorial "Our G-G: Gracious and Gutsy" (2009:A14)—others, notably the European Union's Environment Commissioner, were outraged by Jean's political incorrectness. In the end, she was visiting an Inuit community, listening to local concerns, and participating in an ancient Inuit custom—exactly as a good governor general should do.

Sean Kilpatrick/The Canadian Press

Thinking Globally

Canadians and Americans: What Makes Us Different?

When asked about what it means to be Canadian or what factors contribute to a Canadian identity, the average person will shrug and say, "I don't really know." When pushed a little harder, we might admit that we know we are Canadians because we are "not American." We share many attributes and attitudes with Americans, but there are significant differences, some of which are intriguing.

Seymour Martin Lipset (1985) argued in the 1950s that the traditional differences between Canadian and American values are rooted in the past. A central feature of U.S. history was the war of independence from Great Britain. In a sense, Canada separated formally from Britain only in 1982 with the patriation of the constitution. This difference is pivotal, Lipset argues, with regard to cultural distinctions between the United States and Canada. In Lipset's view, Canada sits somewhere between the United States and Great Britain with respect to values. Americans place great value on freedom, individual initiative, achievement, and success; Canadians, on the other hand, stress conformity and obedience to the law. In the American West, outlaws such as Jesse James and Billy the Kid were heroes; in Canada, it was the Mountie—the lawman—who was admired.

Practically speaking, the Canadian tendency to emphasize the good of the collectivity over the good of the individual has resulted in social programs such as universal medical care. Until now, Americans have cherished the individual right to choose (and pay for) medical care as desired—with various sorts and levels of medical coverage for people with varying abilities to pay.

Roger Sauvé (1994), a futurist and former journalist, gathered comparable data for the early 1990s on American and Canadian characteristics and attitudes, providing us with the following insights:

- Americans believe in hell and in the devil (60% and 52%, respectively) more than Canadians do (34% and 30%).
- Canadians are more likely than Americans to say that premarital sex is okay (70% versus 54%).
- Canadians are slightly more in favour than Americans of restrictive gun laws (77% and 70%).
- Americans are more likely than Canadians to own handguns (24% versus 3%).
- The birth rate among 15- to 19-year-old girls is higher in the United States than in Canada (62 American births per 1000, compared to 27 Canadian births per 1000).
- American marriages are more likely than Canadian marriages to end in divorce (43% versus 28%).

- Americans aged 25 to 64 are more likely than Canadians of equivalent age to be university graduates (25% and 17%).

More recently, Ipsos-Reid pollsters Bricker and Wright (2005) asked Americans and Canadians a few questions of their own—once again revealing interesting differences:

- Americans are more likely than Canadians to claim that "my religious faith is very important to me in my day-to-day life" (82% versus 64%).
- Americans are more likely than Canadians to believe that same-sex marriage is "wrong and should never be lawful" (47% versus 27%).
- Americans are more likely than Canadians to support the death penalty (71% versus 42%).
- Canadians are more likely than Americans to think that decriminalizing marijuana is "a sound idea" (51% versus 36%).
- Canadians are more likely than Americans to think that Canada is a major player in world affairs (76% versus 52%).
- Canadians are much more likely than Americans to see our two countries as closest friends and allies (60% versus 18%).

Sauvé (1994) reported that 66 percent of Americans and 14 percent of Canadians are in favour of Canada becoming part of the United States. A decade later, Bricker and Wright reported that 23 percent of Canadians and 32 percent of Quebecers are in favour of a formal economic union (free trade and a common currency), while 4 percent of Canadians and 7 percent of Quebecers think that we should become part of the United States. The apparent decline in the latter measure over 10 years is complicated by the fact that two levels of union are being discussed within Canada. At either level, a quarter of us are willing to forge closer formal ties with the United States.

Bricker and Wright (2005:258) provide us with an amusing anecdote to ponder. Mavis Gallant, a famous Canadian writer who lives in France, asked Robertson Davies, a famous English author who lived in Canada: "Why don't Canadians love Canada the way the Americans love America?" His answer was: "It's not a country you love; it's a country you worry about."

What Do You Think?

1. Taking everything into account, are there more similarities or differences between Canadians and Americans?
2. Are you surprised that Canadian and American attitudes toward gun laws are so similar?
3. How do people in your extended family feel about closer economic ties between Canada and the United States?

to be traditional, with values that celebrate the past and emphasize the importance of family and religious beliefs, obedience to authority, and conformity. These nations, dominated by men, typically discourage or forbid practices such as divorce and abortion.

Societies in higher-income countries, where people take survival for granted, have cultures that value individualism and self-expression and focus on quality of life. People in these countries think about lifestyle and personal happiness. In general, these countries tend to be secular-rational, placing less emphasis on family ties and religious beliefs and more emphasis on independence and tolerance of diversity. In higher-income countries, women have social standing more equal to men, and there is widespread support for practices such as divorce and abortion (World Values Survey, 2004).

Norms

Most Canadians are eager to gossip about "who's hot" and "who's not." North American Aboriginal communities, however, typically condemn such behaviour as rude and divisive. Both patterns illustrate the operation of **norms**, *rules and expectations by which a society guides the behaviour of its members*. Some norms are *proscriptive,* stating what we should not do, as when health officials warn us to avoid casual sex. *Prescriptive* norms, on the other hand, state what we should do, as when our schools teach "safer sex" practices. The most important norms in a culture apply everywhere and at all times. For example, parents expect obedience from young children regardless of the setting. Other norms depend on the situation: In Canada, we expect the audience to applaud after a musical performance; we may applaud, although it is not expected, at the end of a classroom lecture; we do not applaud at the end of a religious sermon.

MORES AND FOLKWAYS William Graham Sumner (1959; orig. 1906), an early U.S. sociologist, recognized that some norms are more important to our lives than others. Sumner coined the term **mores** (pronounced "more-rays") to refer to *norms that are widely observed and have great moral significance*. Mores, or *taboos*, include our society's insistence that adults not engage in sexual relations with children. People pay less attention to **folkways**, *norms for routine or casual interaction*. Examples include ideas about appropriate greetings and proper dress. In short, mores distinguish between right and wrong, and folkways draw a line between right and rude. A man who does not wear a tie to a formal dinner party may raise eyebrows for violating folkways; were he to arrive wearing only a tie, he would violate cultural mores and invite a more serious response.

SOCIAL CONTROL Mores and folkways are the basic rules of everyday life. Although we sometimes resist pressures to conform, we can see that norms make our dealings with others more orderly and predictable. Observing or breaking the rules of social life prompts a response from others, in the form of reward or punishment. Sanctions—whether an approving smile or a raised eyebrow—operate as a system of **social control**, *attempts by others to regulate people's thoughts and behaviour.*

As we learn cultural norms, we gain the capacity to evaluate our own behaviour. Doing wrong (say, downloading a term paper from the internet) can cause both *shame* (the painful sense that others disapprove of our actions) and *guilt* (a negative judgment we make of ourselves). Only cultural creatures can experience shame and guilt. This is probably what Mark Twain had in mind when he remarked that people "are the only animals that blush—or need to."

Ideal and Real Culture

Societies devise values and norms as moral guidelines for their members. As such, these cultural elements do not describe actual behaviour as much as they tell us how we should behave. We must remember, then, that **ideal culture**, *social patterns mandated by cultural values and norms,* is not the same as **real culture**, *actual social patterns that only approximate cultural expectations.* To illustrate, most of us acknowledge the importance of sexual fidelity in marriage. Even so, a 1994 *Maclean's* poll indicated that about 14 percent of married men and 7 percent of married women reported being sexually unfaithful to their spouses at some point in the marriage (Maclean's/CTV, 1995). Such discrepancies occur in all societies, since no one lives up to ideal standards all the time.

Material Culture and Technology

In addition to symbolic elements such as values and norms, every culture includes a wide range of physical human creations, which sociologists call *artifacts*. The Chinese eat with chopsticks rather than knives and forks; the Japanese put mats rather than rugs on the floor; and many men and women in India prefer flowing robes to the close-fitting clothing common in North America. The

norms rules and expectations by which a society guides the behaviour of its members

mores norms that are widely observed and have great moral significance

folkways norms for routine or casual interaction

social control attempts by society to regulate people's thoughts and behaviour

material culture of a people may seem as strange to outsiders as their language, values, and norms.

A society's artifacts partly reflect underlying cultural values. The warlike Yanomamö of Venezuela and Brazil carefully craft their weapons and prize the poison tips on their arrows, while the emphasis of North Americans on individualism and independence helps to explain our love of the automobile. In Canada there are perhaps 15 million motor vehicles—one for every two people. In the United States and Canada, the sales of large sports utility vehicles and SUVs go up and down with the price of fuel. With the recent collapse of oil prices, sales of these large gas-guzzlers are increasing once again. In "good" years—as measured by fuel prices—more than half of the cars sold in the United States are those sports utility vehicles.

In addition to reflecting values, material culture also reflects a society's **technology**, *knowledge that people use to make a way of life in their surroundings*. The more complex a society's technology, the more its members are able—for better or worse—to shape the world for themselves. Advanced technology has allowed North Americans to criss-cross the continent with highways and to fill them with automobiles. At the same time, the internal combustion engines in those vehicles release carbon dioxide into the atmosphere, which contributes to air pollution and climate change. The values that push us to purchase those SUVs—or any car, for that matter—are at odds with our environmental values.

Because North Americans attach great importance to science and sophisticated technology, we tend to judge societies with simpler technology as less advanced than our own. Some facts support such an assessment. For example, life expectancy for children born in Canada today is about 80 years; the lifespan of the Yanomamö in Brazil is about 40 years (Chagnon, 1992). However, we must be careful not to make self-serving judgments about cultures that differ from our own. While our powerful and complex technology has produced work-reducing devices and seemingly miraculous forms of medical treatment, it has also contributed to unhealthy levels of stress, eroded the quality of the natural environment, and created weapons capable of destroying—in a blinding flash—everything that humankind has managed to achieve.

Finally, technology is another cultural element that varies substantially within Canada. Although many of us cannot imagine life without smartphones, televisions, and the latest computers, many members of our society cannot afford such items, and others reject them on principle.

The Old Order Mennonites, many of whom live in small farming communities across southwestern Ontario, shun most modern conveniences as a matter of religious conviction. With their traditional black garb and horse-drawn buggies, the Old Order Mennonites may seem like a curious relic of the past. Yet their communities flourish, grounded in vibrant families and individuals with a strong sense of identity and purpose. Outsiders who observe them come away with the suspicion that these simple, stable communities suggest an attractive alternative to modern materialism and competitiveness.

Technology is a very important element of culture. Some sociologists claim that a society's level of technology determines its overall way of life. Look ahead to the chapter on Society to the work of Gerhard and Jean Lenski. They argue that new technology is the trigger for societal evolution. Marshall McLuhan (discussed in the chapter on The Sociological Perspective and elsewhere) makes a similar claim for the technology of electronic or instantaneous communication.

New Information Technology and Culture

Many rich nations, including Canada, have entered a post-industrial phase based on computers and new information technology. Industrial production is centred on factories and machinery that generate material goods. In contrast,

STANDARDS OF BEAUTY—INCLUDING THE COLOUR AND DESIGN OF EVERYDAY SURROUNDINGS—VARY SIGNIFICANTLY FROM ONE CULTURE TO ANOTHER These two Ndebele women in South Africa dress in the same bright colours with which they decorate their homes. Members of North American and European societies, in contrast, make far less use of bright colours and intricate detail, so their housing appears much more subdued.

post-industrial production is based on computers and other electronic devices that create, process, store, and apply information. In this new information economy, workers need symbolic skills in place of the mechanical skills of the industrial age. Symbolic skills include the ability to speak, write, compute, design, and create images in such fields as art, advertising, entertainment, and education. In today's computer-based economy, people with creative jobs are generating new cultural ideas, images, and products all the time.

Cultural Diversity in Canada

3.3   Discuss dimensions of cultural difference and cultural change.

Canada exhibits striking cultural diversity when compared with Japan, whose historic isolation made it the most monocultural of industrial nations. Heavy immigration, over two centuries and especially the past 30 years, has made Canada the world's most multicultural country.

Figure 3–2 gives some indication of Canada's cultural diversity and reveals that patterns of immigration have changed over time. Before 1961, about 90 percent of immigrants to Canada came from Europe, especially the United Kingdom, and less than 5 percent came from

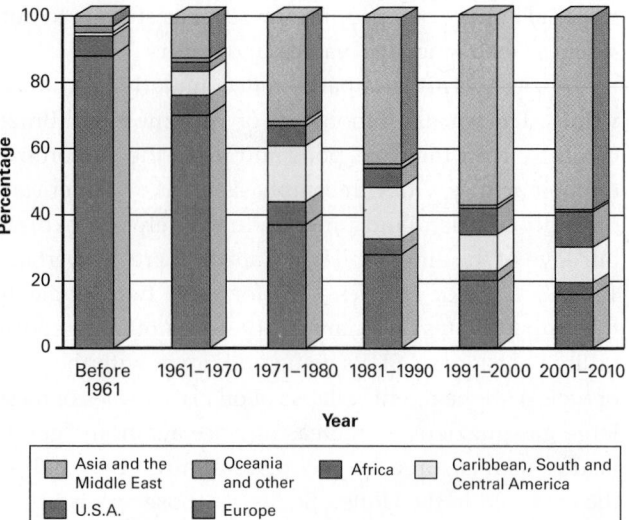

Figure 3–2 Immigrant Population by Place of Birth and Period of Immigration

SOURCE: Compilation and calculations by L.M. Gerber based on Statistics Canada, Census and NHS catalogue nos. 11-008E, 95F0359XCB2001004, 97-557-XCB2006007, and 99-010-X2011026.

countries in Asia and the Middle East. Since 1961, more and more immigrants have come from Asia and the Middle East. From 2001 to 2010, European immigrants made up only 15 percent of total immigration, while those from Asia and the Middle East made up 58 percent. Canada is experiencing increased immigration from South America, Eastern Europe, and Africa, as well. These immigration patterns, which have greatly increased the cultural diversity of our country, are the result of deliberate changes in our immigration policy. Given this diversity, sociologists refer to Canada as a *cultural mosaic*, while the United States is considered a "melting pot."

High Culture and Popular Culture

To this point cultural diversity has been linked to ethnicity and multiculturalism, but there are other dimensions of diversity. One of them is rooted in social class. In everyday conversation, we may reserve the term *culture* for sophisticated art forms such as classical literature, opera, ballet, and painting. We praise symphony conductors, Shakespearean actors, and dance choreographers as "cultured" because they presumably appreciate the "finer things in life." The term *culture* itself has the same Latin root as the word *cultivate*, suggesting that the "cultured" individual has refined tastes. In contrast, we speak less glowingly of the tastes of ordinary people, assuming that everyday cultural patterns are somehow less worthy. In more concrete terms, we are tempted to judge the music of Mozart as more "cultured" than Motown's, fine cuisine as better than fish sticks, and polo as more polished than Ping-Pong.

Photo courtesy of the Canadian Jewish Congress

ANY SOCIETY EXHIBITS COUNTLESS DIFFERENT CULTURAL PATTERNS, SOME OF WHICH MAY GIVE RISE TO A RANGE OF SOLITUDES French and English Canada were identified as "two solitudes" in a novel with that title by Hugh MacLennan (2008; orig. 1945). The relationship between the Jewish community and First Nations could also be characterized as two solitudes—that is, until David Ahenakew (former national chief of the Assembly of First Nations) engaged in anti-Semitic ranting that resulted in "unflinching condemnation" of him by both communities. This incident resulted in a trip by 20 chiefs to Israel and visits by Jewish leaders to reserve communities. "Out of this ugly situation came something quite beautiful: an unhesitating commitment by the Jewish and first nation communities to walk the journey of peace. . . ." Together, the two communities hope to combat anti-Semitism and anti-Native bigotry (Fontaine et al., 2008).

high culture cultural patterns that distinguish a society's elite

popular culture cultural patterns that are widespread among a society's population

Such judgments imply that many cultural patterns are readily accessible to some but not all members of a society (Hall & Neitz, 1993). Sociologists use the shorthand term **high culture** to refer to *cultural patterns that distinguish a society's elite*; **popular culture**, then, designates *cultural patterns that are widespread throughout society*. The book *Mondo Canuck: A Canadian Pop Culture Odyssey* (Pevere & Dymond, 1996) is a refreshing celebration of Canada's cultural creativity: The book itself is pop culture. Common sense may suggest that high culture is superior to popular culture. After all, history chronicles the lives of elites much more than those of ordinary people. But sociologists use the term *culture* to refer to all elements of a society's way of life, even as they recognize that cultural patterns vary throughout a population.

We should resist quick judgments about the merits of high culture as opposed to popular culture for two key reasons. First, neither elites nor ordinary people have uniform tastes and interests. Second, we praise high culture not because it is inherently better than popular culture, but because its supporters have more money, power, and prestige. For example, there is no difference between a violin and a fiddle; however, we refer to the instrument as a violin when it is used to produce a type of music enjoyed by the elite, and as a fiddle when the musician is playing for ordinary folk.

Subculture

The term **subculture** refers to *cultural patterns that set apart some segment of a society's population*. Teenagers, First Nations members living on reserves, homeless people, race-car drivers, jazz musicians, hockey fans, police officers, and even sociologists all display subcultural patterns. It is easy—but often inaccurate—to place people in subcultural categories. Almost everyone participates simultaneously in numerous subcultures, to which we have various levels of commitment.

In some cases, important cultural traits such as ethnicity or religion do divide people—sometimes with tragic results. Consider the former nation of Yugoslavia in southeastern Europe (now the five nations of Slovenia, Croatia, Macedonia, Bosnia and Herzegovina, and Serbia and Montenegro). The ongoing turmoil there is fuelled by astounding cultural diversity. Before its breakup, the former Yugoslavia was about the size of the Atlantic provinces, but with a population of 25 million. This one small country made use of two alphabets, professed three religions, spoke four languages, was home to five major nationalities, was divided into six political republics, and absorbed the cultural influences of seven surrounding countries.

Sociologists see Canada as a mosaic, with many nationalities contributing to a larger "Canadian" culture. But, considering the extent of our cultural diversity, how accurate is the "mosaic" description? One factor complicates this idealistic notion: Cultural diversity involves not

Installation view of Beat Nation, Art, Hip Hop and Aboriginal Culture, exhibit at the Vancouver Art Gallery, 2012, image featuring Skeena Reece, Raven: On the Colonial Fleet, 2010, performance regalia, photo: Rachel Topham, Vancouver Art Gallery

IN A BLEND OF PERFORMANCE, ART, DANCE, AND MUSIC, THE VANCOUVER ART GALLERY SHOWCASES THE "INTERSECTION OF ABORIGINAL CULTURE, CONTEMPORARY ART AND STREET CULTURE" The special four-month exhibition *Beat Nation: Art, Hip Hop and Aboriginal Culture* celebrates a blend of traditional art forms, contemporary art, and mainstream culture. Ironically, the Vancouver Art Gallery is a former courthouse—"once a symbol of government-decreed injustice" for Aboriginal people (Lederman, 2012).

Shutterstock

MANY SUBCULTURES THAT DEVELOP INVOLVE YOUNG PEOPLE One recent example is the skateboarding subculture that includes not only the sport but also a distinctive style of dress.

just variety but also hierarchy. Too often, what we view as dominant cultural patterns are those favoured by powerful segments of the population, while we relegate the lives of the disadvantaged to the realm of "subculture." Those subcultures underlie our new policy of multiculturalism.

Multiculturalism

As well as being bilingual, Canadian society is officially multicultural. **Multiculturalism** is embodied in *social policy designed to encourage ethnic or cultural heterogeneity.* Historically, our society downplayed cultural diversity, defining our way of life primarily in terms familiar to the English or French immigrants who dominated Canada socially. Historians highlighted the role of descendants of the English and French and described events from their points of view, pushing aside the perspectives and accomplishments of other immigrants and Aboriginal peoples. The European way of life was set up as an ideal to which all should aspire and by which all should be judged. Multiculturalists describe this singular pattern in Canada as **Eurocentrism**, *the dominance of European cultural patterns.* The legacy of this practice is a spirited debate over whether we should continue to stress Western European, especially French and English, cultural contributions to the exclusion of those made by Chinese, Caribbean, Ukrainian, and Indian immigrants. An interesting example of the continued presence of Eurocentric ideas in Canada was the widespread opposition to the 1990 decision to allow a Sikh, Baltej Singh Dhillon, to wear a turban as part of his RCMP uniform.

While few deny that our culture has multiple roots, multiculturalism generates controversy because it requires a rethinking of core norms and values. One area of debate involves language. Although Canada is officially bilingual, the Canadian population is actually composed of people with many different mother tongues. Table 3–1 provides the distribution of Canadians by mother tongue. Despite the significant number of languages spoken in this country, minority languages—other than French—are not officially recognized by federal law. As a result, critics charge that multiculturalism has only symbolic significance in Canada—meaning that multiculturalism allows people belonging to minorities to maintain their culture within their homes while forcing them to speak either French or English outside of it. Gradually, such people will lose the use of their mother tongues and, with them, many of their distinctive cultural

Table 3–1 Mother Tongues in Canada, 1996, 2001, 2006, and 2011

Mother Tongue	Percent of Population			
	1996	2001	2006	2011
English	59.2	58.5	58.4	58.2
French	23.2	22.6	22.3	21.5
Chinese	2.5	2.8	3.3	3.3
Italian	1.7	1.6	1.5	1.2
German	1.6	1.5	1.5	1.1
Polish	0.7	0.7	0.7	0.6
Spanish	0.7	0.8	1.2	1.2
Portuguese	0.7	0.7	0.7	0.6
Punjabi	0.7	0.9	1.2	1.3
Ukrainian	0.6	0.5	0.5	0.3
Arabic	0.5	0.7	0.9	1.0
Dutch	0.5	0.4	0.4	0.3
Tagalog (Filipino)	0.5	0.6	0.9	1.1
Greek	0.4	0.4	0.4	0.3
Vietnamese	0.4	0.4	0.5	0.5
Urdu	n/a	n/a	0.4	0.5
Persian (Farsi)	n/a	n/a	0.4	0.5
Russian	n/a	n/a	0.4	0.5
Korean	n/a	n/a	0.4	0.4
Aboriginal	n/a	n/a	n/a	0.6

SOURCE: Compilation and calculations by L.M. Gerber based on Statistics Canada, Census 2001, Catalogue no. 97F0007XCB2001009, and Census 2006, B20/20 Catalogue no. 97-555-XCB2006007 and NHS 2011 Catalogue no. 99-010-X2011034.

practices. On the other hand, some observers point out that each minority makes up a very small part of the total population of Canada. Accommodating each of the many minorities would lead to a fractured society, one with no sense of commonality or cohesiveness.

The debate rages, and important questions are left unresolved. To what extent should Canada encourage those who speak languages other than French or English to maintain their mother tongue? Should Canadian taxpayers support heritage language schools and courses? What about Aboriginal languages? How should our schools—from the early grades through university—teach about culture? It is among educators that the discussion about multiculturalism has been most intense. Four basic positions have emerged:

- First, proponents defend multiculturalism as a way to capture a more accurate picture of our past. Proposed educational reforms seek, for example, to temper the simplistic praise directed at European explorers by realistically assessing the tragic impact of the European conquest on the indigenous peoples of this hemisphere. From the point of view of North American Aboriginal peoples, contact with Europeans unleashed centuries of subordination and death

subculture cultural patterns that set apart some segment of a society's population

multiculturalism a social policy designed to encourage ethnic or cultural heterogeneity

Eurocentrism the dominance of European cultural patterns

from war and disease. Furthermore, a multicultural approach would recognize the achievements of many women and men whose cultural backgrounds have kept them on the sidelines of history.

- Second, multiculturalism allows us to come to terms with our current diversity. Children born today can expect to see immigration from African, Asian, and Hispanic countries increase even more.

- Third, proponents assert that multiculturalism is a way to strengthen the academic achievement of children of immigrants, most of whom are from visible minorities, and others who find little personal relevance in our traditional educational programs.

- Fourth, proponents see multiculturalism as worthwhile preparation for all people in Canada to live in a world that is increasingly interdependent. As various chapters of this text explain, social patterns in this country are becoming more closely linked to issues and events elsewhere in the world. Multiculturalism undermines nationalistic prejudices by pointing out global connectedness; it also makes Canadians more flexible in their international political and business dealings.

The argument most commonly voiced by opponents of multiculturalism is that any society remains cohesive only to the extent that its cultural patterns are widely shared. Multiculturalism, say critics, fuels the "politics of difference," encouraging divisiveness as individuals identify with their subcultures rather than with Canada as a whole. Opponents also charge that multiculturalism erodes the claim to common truth by maintaining that ideas should be evaluated according to the race (and gender) of those who present them. Furthermore, some ask whether multiculturalism actually benefits minorities as claimed, since multiculturalism demands precisely the kind of segregation that we deplore. For example, a heritage-centred curriculum denies children a wide range of knowledge and skills by encouraging study from a more limited point of view.

Multiculturalism is a term coined in Canada to signify formal recognition and the celebration of diversity. Other countries, such as Australia and the United States, now apply the term to themselves, but Canada is alone in enshrining the concept into law, public policy, and the structure of government. That being the case, Canada faces a very important question: Is multiculturalism a path to "unity in diversity" or to division and fragility?

Counterculture

Cultural diversity also includes outright rejection of conventional ideas or behaviour. **Counterculture** refers to

counterculture cultural patterns that strongly oppose those widely accepted within a society

cultural patterns that strongly oppose those widely accepted within a society. During the 1960s, a youth-oriented counterculture rejected mainstream culture as overly competitive, self-centred, and materialistic. Instead, hippies and other counterculturalists favoured a co-operative lifestyle in which "being" took precedence over "doing," and the capacity for personal growth—or "expanded consciousness"—was prized over material possessions such as homes and cars. They drew personal identity from long hair, headbands, and blue jeans; from peace signs instead of handshakes; from drugs; and from the energy of rock-and-roll music. Such differences—in values, behaviour, and music—led some to "drop out" of the larger society.

Some countercultures, flourishing in North America, Europe, and beyond, seek to disrupt their societies. These highly significant countercultures may involve militaristic bands of men and women who are deeply suspicious of government and are willing to resort to violence. In Canada, the Front de libération du Québec, active through the 1960s and early 1970s, resorted to bombings, kidnapping, and murder in its quest for an independent socialist Quebec.

Cultural Change

Cultural change is not only continuous, but change in one dimension is usually associated with other transformations. For example, increased labour-force participation among women occurs along with changing family patterns, including a later age at first marriage, fewer births, more divorce, and more children being raised in households without fathers. Such connections illustrate the principle of **cultural integration**, *the close relationship among various elements of a cultural system.* But all elements of a cultural system do not change at the same speed.

William Ogburn (1964) observed that technology moves quickly, generating new elements of material culture (such as test-tube babies) faster than nonmaterial culture (such as ideas about parenthood) can keep up with them. Ogburn called this inconsistency **cultural lag**, *cultural elements changing at different rates, causing various degrees of disruption in cultural systems.* In a culture with the technical ability to allow one woman to give birth to a child by using another woman's egg that has been fertilized in a laboratory with the sperm of a total stranger, how are we to apply the traditional notions of motherhood and fatherhood? What if an infertile woman has her own mother conceive by artificial insemination with her husband's sperm? The "grandmother" who bears the child would be the biological mother, and the "mother" would be a half-sister to the child. What if a man has himself cloned and implants the embryo in his wife's womb? His own parents—the child's "grandparents"—would be the child's biological mother and father. It will be decades before the social, psychological, and legal elements of our culture catch up with this technological change.

Causes of Cultural Change

Cultural change is set in motion in three ways. The first is invention, the process of creating new cultural elements. Invention has given us the telephone (1876), the airplane (1903), and the aerosol spray can (1941), all of which have had a tremendous impact on our way of life. The process of invention goes on constantly, as indicated by the number of applications submitted annually to the Canadian Patent Office.

Discovery, a second cause of cultural change, involves recognizing and understanding something not fully understood before—from a distant star to the foods of another culture and the athletic excellence of the Canadian Olympic team that brought home a record number of medals in 2006. Many discoveries result from scientific research—such as the Canadian BlackBerry. Yet discovery can also happen quite by accident, as when Marie Curie left a rock on a piece of photographic paper in 1898 and serendipitously discovered radium.

The third cause of cultural change is diffusion, the spread of cultural traits from one society to another. For example, insulin—developed first by Frederick Banting and Charles Best at the University of Toronto in the 1920s—and the telephone—conceived by Alexander Graham Bell in Brantford, Ontario, in 1874—have spread around the world. The technological ability to send information around the globe in seconds by means of radio, television, facsimile, and computer means that the level of cultural diffusion has never been greater than it is today. Certainly our own society has contributed many significant cultural elements to the world, but diffusion works the other way as well, so that much of what we assume is inherently "Canadian" actually comes from other cultures. Ralph Linton (1937) explained that many commonplace elements of our way of life—clothing and furniture, clocks, newspapers, money, and even the English language—are all derived from other cultures.

Ethnocentrism and Cultural Relativism

We think of childhood as a time of innocence and freedom from adult burdens like regular work. In poor countries throughout the world, however, families depend on income earned by children. So what people in one society think of as right and natural, people elsewhere find puzzling and even immoral. Perhaps the Chinese philosopher K'ung

Fu-tzu (Confucius) had it right when he noted that "all people are the same; it's only their habits that are different."

Just about every imaginable idea or behaviour is commonplace somewhere in the world, and this cultural variation causes travellers both excitement and distress. Australians flip light switches down to turn them on; North Americans flip them up. Japanese name city blocks; North Americans name streets. Egyptians move very close to others when in conversation; North Americans are used to maintaining considerable interpersonal space. Given that a particular culture is the basis for each person's reality, it is no wonder that people everywhere exhibit **ethnocentrism**, *the practice of judging another culture by the standards of one's own*. Some degree of ethnocentrism is necessary for people to be emotionally attached to their way of life, but ethnocentrism also generates misunderstanding and conflict.

Even terminology is culturally biased. Centuries ago, people in Europe and North America referred to China as the "Far East." But this term, unknown to the Chinese, is an ethnocentric expression for a region that is far to the east of *us*. The Chinese name for their country translates as "Central Kingdom," suggesting that they, like us, see their own society as the centre of the world. Figure 3–3 challenges our own ethnocentrism by presenting a "down under" view of the western hemisphere.

The logical alternative to ethnocentrism is **cultural relativism**, *the practice of judging a culture by its own standards*. Cultural relativism can be difficult for travellers to adopt. It requires not only openness to unfamiliar values and norms but also the ability to put aside cultural standards we have known all our lives. Even so, as people of the world come into increasing contact with one another, the importance of understanding other cultures increases. North American businesses are learning the value of marketing to culturally diverse populations. Similarly, businesses are learning that success in the global economy depends on awareness of cultural patterns around the world. For example, IBM now provides technical support for its products using websites in 22 languages (IBM, 2012).

This trend is a change from the past, when many corporations used marketing strategies that lacked sensitivity to cultural diversity. The Coors phrase "Turn It Loose" startled Spanish-speaking customers by proclaiming that the beer would cause diarrhea. Braniff Airlines translated its slogan "Fly in Leather" so carelessly into Spanish that it read "Fly Naked." Similarly, Eastern Airlines's slogan "We Earn Our Wings Daily" became "We Fly Every Day to Heaven." Even poultry giant Frank Purdue fell victim

---

ethnocentrism the practice of judging another culture by the standards of one's own culture

cultural relativism the practice of judging a culture by its own standards

judgments before grasping the perspective of the others; at the same time, we should look at our own way of life. After all, what we gain most from studying others is better insight into ourselves.

A Global Culture?

Today, more than ever before, we can observe many of the same cultural practices the world over. Walking the streets of Seoul, South Korea; Kuala Lumpur, Malaysia; Madras, India; Cairo, Egypt; and Casablanca, Morocco, we see people wearing jeans, hear familiar pop music, and read ads for many of the same products we use in this country. Recall, too, from Global Map 3–1 that English is rapidly emerging as the preferred second language around the world. Are we, therefore, witnessing the birth of a single global culture?

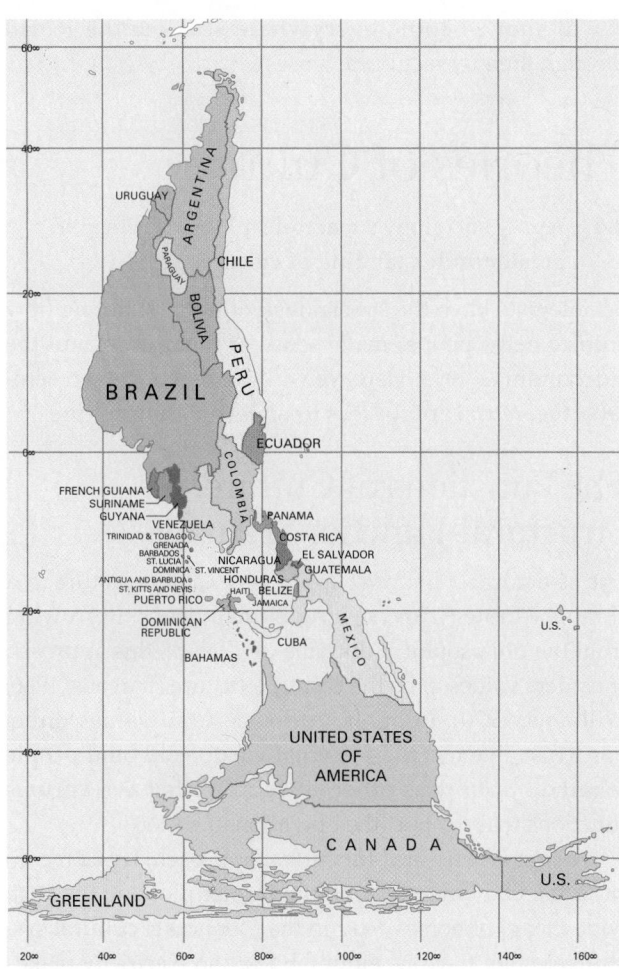

Figure 3–3 The View from "Down Under"

North America should be "up" and South America "down," right? But because we live on a globe, "up" and "down" have no meaning at all. The reason that this map of the western hemisphere looks wrong to us is not that it is geographically inaccurate; it simply violates our ethnocentric assumption that Canada and the United States should be "above" the rest of the Americas.

to poor marketing when his pitch "It Takes a Tough Man to Make a Tender Chicken" was transformed into Spanish words reading "A Sexually Excited Man Will Make a Chicken Affectionate" (Helin, 1992).

But cultural relativism introduces problems of its own. If almost any kind of behaviour is the norm somewhere in the world, does that mean that everything is equally right? Does the fact that some Indian and Moroccan families benefit from having their children work long hours justify child labour?

Since we are all members of a single species, surely there must be some universal standards of proper conduct. But what are they? And in trying to develop them, how can we avoid imposing our own standards on others? There are no simple answers. When confronting an unfamiliar cultural practice, we should not make

nik wheeler/Alamy Stock Photo

IN THE WORLD'S LOW-INCOME COUNTRIES, MOST CHILDREN MUST WORK TO PROVIDE THEIR FAMILIES WITH NEEDED INCOME This seven-year-old boy in eastern Ilam, Nepal, works long hours in a tea field. Is it ethnocentric for people living in high-income nations to condemn the practice of child labour because we think youngsters belong in school? Why or why not?

Societies now have more contact with one another than ever before, involving the flow of goods, information, and people:

1. **Global economy: The flow of goods.** International trade has never been greater. The global economy has spread many of the same consumer goods—from cars and television shows to music and fashions—throughout the world. In 2010, Canada's $818 billion ($2.3 billion each day) in imports and exports (Statistics Canada, 2012) represented tremendous movement of goods and merchandise across our borders. Note that trade with the United States alone amounted to $1.9 billion per day.

2. **Global communications: The flow of information.** Satellite-based communications enable people to experience the sights and sounds of events taking place thousands of kilometres away—often as they happen. In Marshall McLuhan's words, this has made us part of an "instantaneous happening," the "global village."

3. **Global migration: The flow of people.** Knowing about the rest of the world motivates people to move to where they imagine life will be better. In addition, today's transportation technology, especially air travel, makes relocating easier than ever before. As a result, in most countries, significant numbers of people were born elsewhere (including 6.5 million people in Canada, or 21 percent of the population).

These global links make the cultures of the world more similar. But there are three important limitations to the global culture thesis.

- First, the global flow of goods, information, and people is uneven. Generally speaking, urban areas (centres of commerce, communication, and people) have stronger ties to one another, while many rural villages remain unaffected by global movements. In addition, the greater economic and military power of North America and Western Europe means that these regions influence the rest of the world more than the rest of the world influences them.

- Second, the global culture thesis assumes that people everywhere are able to *afford* various new goods and services. Desperate poverty in much of the world deprives people of even the basic necessities of a safe and secure life.

- Third, while many cultural practices are now found throughout the world, people everywhere do not attach the same meanings to them. Do children in Tokyo draw the same insights from reading the Harry Potter books as their counterparts in Vancouver or Edinburgh? Similarly, we enjoy foods from around the world while knowing little about the lives of the people who created them.

In short, people everywhere still see the world through their own cultural lenses.

Theories of Culture

3.4 Apply sociology's macro-level theories to gain greater understanding of culture.

Sociologists have the special task of understanding how culture helps people make sense of themselves and the surrounding world. Here we will examine several macro-level theoretical approaches to understanding culture.

The Functions of Culture: Structural-Functional Analysis

The structural-functional approach explains culture as a complex strategy for meeting human needs. Borrowing from the philosophical doctrine of *idealism,* this approach considers values to be the core of a culture (Parsons, 1966; Williams, 1970). In other words, cultural values direct our lives, give meaning to what we do, and bind people together. Countless other cultural traits have various functions that support the operation of society.

Using a structural-functional approach, let us reconsider the Old Order Mennonite farmer plowing his farm with a team of horses. Within the Mennonite cultural system, rejecting tractors, automobiles, and electricity makes sense because it ensures that there is plenty of hard work. Continuous labour—usually outside of the home for men, inside the home for women—maintains the Mennonite value of discipline, which shapes their way of life. Long days of work, along with meals and recreation at home, define Old Order Mennonite culture and bind family members together. Their rejection of modern technology also has the functions of making them self-sufficient (Fretz, 1989) and minimizing the need to engage with mainstream society. Of course, cultural traits have both functional and dysfunctional consequences. The Old Order Mennonite trait of "shunning," by which people cease social contact with anyone judged to have violated Mennonite mores, generates conformity but also provokes tension and, at the extreme, can cause a serious rift in the community.

If cultures are strategies for meeting human needs, we would expect to find many common patterns around the world. The term **cultural universals** refers to *traits that are part of every known culture.* Comparing hundreds of cultures, George Murdock (1945) identified dozens of cultural universals. One common element is the family, which functions everywhere to control sexual reproduction and to oversee the care of children. Funeral rites, too, are found everywhere, because all human communities cope with the reality of death. Jokes are another cultural universal, serving as a safe means of releasing social tensions.

Three Lions/Hulton Archive/Getty Images

FOLLOWING THE STRUCTURAL-FUNCTIONAL APPROACH, WHAT DO YOU MAKE OF THE PRACTICE OF "BARN RAISING" BY AMISH OR MENNONITE COMMUNITIES, IN WHICH EVERYONE JOINS TOGETHER TO RAISE A FAMILY'S NEW BARN IN A DAY?

EVALUATE

The strength of the structural-functional approach is that it shows how culture operates to meet human needs. Yet by emphasizing a society's dominant cultural patterns, this approach largely ignores cultural diversity. Also, because this approach emphasizes cultural stability, it downplays the importance of change. In short, cultural systems are not as stable as, or subject to as much agreement as, structural functionalism leads us to believe.

CHECK YOUR LEARNING   What are the functions of sport, Canada Day celebrations, or a powwow?

Inequality and Culture: Social-Conflict Analysis

The social-conflict approach stresses the link between culture and inequality. Any cultural trait, from this theoretical point of view, benefits some members of society at the expense of others. Why do certain values dominate a society in the first place? Many conflict theorists, especially Marxists, argue that culture is shaped by a society's system of economic production. "It is not the consciousness of men that determines their being," Karl Marx proclaimed; "it is their social being that determines their consciousness" (Marx & Engels, 1978:4; orig. 1859). Social-conflict theory, then, is rooted in the philosophical doctrine of *materialism,* which holds that a society's system of material production (such as our own capitalist economy) has a powerful effect on the rest of a culture. This materialist approach contrasts with the idealist leanings of structural functionalism.

Social-conflict analysis ties our cultural values of competitiveness and material success to our country's capitalist economy, which serves the interests of the nation's wealthy elite. The culture of capitalism further teaches us to think that rich and powerful people work harder or longer than others and, therefore, deserve their wealth and privileges. It also encourages us to view capitalism as somehow "natural," discouraging us from trying to reduce economic inequality. Eventually, however, the strains of inequality erupt into movements for social change. Two examples in Canada are the women's and gay rights movements. Both seek greater equality, and both encounter opposition from defenders of the status quo.

Gender and Culture: Feminist Theory

As Marx saw it, culture is rooted in economic production. Therefore, our society's culture largely reflects the capitalist economic system. Feminists agree with Marx's claim that culture is an arena of conflict, but they see this conflict as being rooted in gender.

Gender refers to the personal traits and social positions that members of a society attach to being female or male. From a feminist point of view, gender is a crucial dimension of social inequality, a topic that the chapter on Gender Stratification examines in detail. As that chapter explains, men have greater access to the workforce than women do, and so men earn more income. Men also exercise greater political power. Except for a four-month period in 1993—the term of Kim Campbell—Canada has had only male prime ministers. Furthermore, to the dismay of feminists, after years of encouraging women to run for office, barely one-quarter of our MPs in Ottawa are women. On the level of everyday experience—though there are signs of change—men continue to exercise the most power in the typical Canadian household.

Feminists claim that our culture is "gendered." This means that our way of life reflects the ways in which our society defines what is male as more important than what is female. This inequality is evident in the language we use. We tend to say "man and wife," a phrase used in traditional wedding vows; we almost never hear the phrase "woman and husband." Similarly, the masculine word "king" conveys power and prestige, with a meaning that is almost entirely positive. The comparable feminine word "queen" has a range of meanings, few of which—Queen Elizabeth notwithstanding—connote privilege or power.

Not only does our culture define what is masculine as dominant in relation to what is feminine, but also our way of life defines this male domination as "natural." Such a system of beliefs serves to justify gender inequality by claiming it cannot be changed.

In short, cultural patterns reflect and support gender inequality. Cultural patterns also perpetuate this inequality to the extent that they carry it forward into the future.

EVALUATE

Social conflict theory suggests that cultural systems do not address human needs equally, allowing some people to dominate others. This inequity in turn generates pressure for change. Yet, by stressing the divisiveness of culture, this approach understates the ways in which cultural patterns integrate members of society. Thus, we should consider both social-conflict and structural-functional insights for a fuller understanding of culture.

CHECK YOUR LEARNING How might a social conflict-analysis of Chinatown neighbourhoods in major Canadian cities differ from a structural-functional analysis?

Evolution and Culture: Sociobiology

We know that culture is a human creation, but does human biology influence how this process unfolds? A third theoretical approach, standing with one foot in biology and one in sociology, is **sociobiology**, *a theoretical approach that explores the ways in which human biology affects how we create culture.* Sociobiology rests on the theory of evolution proposed by Charles Darwin in his book *On the Origin of Species* (1968; orig. 1859). Darwin asserted that living organisms change over long periods of time as a result of *natural selection,* a matter of four principles. First, all living things live to reproduce themselves. Second, the blueprint for reproduction is in the genes, which carry traits of one generation into the next. Third, some random variation in genes allows a species to try out new life patterns in a particular environment—allowing some organisms to survive better than others and to pass on their advantageous genes to their offspring. Finally, over thousands of generations, a species *adapts* to its environment, and dominant traits emerge as the "nature" of the organism.

Sociobiologists claim that the existence of a large number of cultural universals reflects the fact that all humans are members of a single biological species. It is our common biology that underlies, for example, the apparently universal "double standard" of sexual behaviour. Sex researcher Alfred Kinsey put it this way: "Among all people everywhere in the world, the male is more likely than the female to desire sex with a variety of partners" (quoted in Barash, 1981:49). But why?

We all know that children result from joining a woman's egg with a man's sperm. But the biological importance of a single sperm and of a single egg is quite different. For a healthy man, sperm represent a "renewable resource" produced by the testes throughout most of his life. A man releases hundreds of millions of sperm in a single ejaculation—technically, enough to fertilize every woman in North America (Barash, 1981:47). A newborn female's ovaries, however, contain her entire lifetime supply of immature eggs. A woman generally releases a single egg cell from her ovaries each month. So, while a man is biologically capable of fathering thousands, a woman can bear only a few children.

Given this biological difference, men reproduce their genes most efficiently by being promiscuous—readily engaging in sex. This scheme, however, opposes the reproductive interests of women. Each of a woman's relatively few pregnancies demands that she carry the child for nine months, give birth, and provide care for some time afterwards. Thus, efficient reproduction on the part of the woman depends on carefully selecting a mate whose qualities—beginning with the likelihood that he will stay around—will contribute to their child's survival and, later, successful reproduction.

The double standard certainly involves more than biology and is tangled up with the historical domination of women by men. But sociobiology suggests that this

USING AN EVOLUTIONARY PERSPECTIVE, SOCIOBIOLOGISTS EXPLAIN THAT DIFFERENT REPRODUCTIVE STRATEGIES GIVE RISE TO A DOUBLE STANDARD Men treat women as sexual objects more than women treat men that way. While this may be so, many sociologists counter that behaviour—such as that shown in Ruth Orkin's photograph *American Girl in Italy*—is more correctly understood as resulting from a culture of male domination.

APPLYING THEORY

Culture

	Structural-Functional Theory	Social-Conflict and Feminist Theories	Sociobiology Theory
What is the level of analysis?	Macro-level	Macro-level	Macro-level
What is culture?	Culture is a system of behavior by which members of societies cooperate to meet their needs.	Culture is a system that benefits some people and disadvantages others.	Culture is a system of behavior that is partly shaped by human biology.
What is the foundation of culture?	Cultural patterns are rooted in a society's core values and beliefs.	Marx claimed that cultural patterns are rooted in a society's system of economic production. Feminist theory says cultural conflict is rooted in gender.	Cultural patterns are rooted in humanity's biological evolution.
What core questions does the approach ask?	How does a cultural pattern help society operate? What cultural patterns are found in all societies?	How does a cultural pattern benefit some people and harm others? How does a cultural pattern support social inequality?	How does a cultural pattern help a species adapt to its environment?

cultural pattern, like many others, has an underlying "biologic." Simply put, the double standard exists around the world because biological differences lead women and men everywhere to favour distinctive reproductive strategies.

EVALUATE

Sociobiology has generated intriguing theories about the biological roots of some cultural patterns. But the approach remains controversial for two main reasons.

First, some critics fear that sociobiology may revive biological arguments from a century ago that claimed the superiority of one race or gender. But defenders counter that sociobiology rejects the past pseudoscience of racial superiority; in fact, they say, sociobiology unites all of humanity because all people share a single evolutionary history. Sociobiology does assert that men and women differ biologically in some ways that culture cannot overcome. But far from claiming that males are somehow more important than females, sociobiology emphasizes that both sexes are vital to human reproduction.

Second, say the critics, sociobiologists have little evidence to support their theories. Research to date suggests that biological forces do not determine human behaviour in any rigid sense. Rather, humans *learn* behaviour within a cultural system. The contribution of sociobiology, then, lies in explaining why some cultural patterns seem easier to learn than others (Barash, 1981).

CHECK YOUR LEARNING Using the sociobiology approach, explain why a cultural pattern such as sibling rivalry (by which children in the same family often compete and even fight with one another) is widespread.

The Applying Theory table summarizes the main lessons of each theoretical approach about culture. Because any analysis of culture requires a broad focus on the workings of society, these are all macro-level approaches. The symbolic-interaction approach, with its micro-level focus on behaviour in everyday situations, is explored in the chapter on Social Interaction in Everyday Life.

Culture and Human Freedom

3.5 Critique culture as limiting or expanding human freedom.

This entire chapter raises an important and intriguing question: To what extent are human beings, as cultural creatures, free? Does culture limit our options by binding us to each other and to the past? Or does culture enhance our capacity for individual thought and independent choices?

Culture as Constraint

As symbolic creatures, humans cannot live without culture. But the capacity for culture does have some drawbacks. We may be the only animals who name ourselves, but living in a symbolic world means that we are also the only creatures who experience alienation. In addition, culture is largely a matter of habit, which limits our choices and drives us to repeat troubling patterns, such as racial prejudice and sex discrimination, in each new generation. Our society's emphasis on competitive achievement urges us toward excellence, yet this same pattern also isolates us from one another. Material things comfort us in some ways but divert us from the security and satisfaction that come from close relationships and spiritual strength.

Culture as Freedom

For better or worse, human beings are cultural creatures, just as ants and bees are prisoners of their biology. But there is a crucial difference. Biological instincts create a ready-made world; culture, in contrast, forces us to choose as we make and remake a world for ourselves. No better evidence of this freedom exists than the cultural diversity of our own society and the even greater human diversity around the world.

Seeing Sociology in Everyday Life

CHAPTER 3   Culture

What clues do we have to a society's cultural values?

The values of any society—that is, what that society thinks is important—are reflected in various aspects of everyday life, including the things people have and the ways they behave. An interesting way to "read" our own culture's values is to look at the "superheroes" that we celebrate. Take a look at the characters in the three photos shown here and, in each case, describe what makes the character special and what each character represents in cultural terms.

Hint Superman (as well as all superheroes) defines our society as good; after all, Superman fights for "truth, justice, and the American way." Many superheroes have stories that draw on great people in our cultural history, including religious figures such as Moses and Jesus: They have mysterious origins (we never really know their true families); they are "tested" through great moral challenges; and they finally succeed in overcoming all obstacles. (Today's superheroes, however, are likely to win the day using force and often violence.) Having a "secret identity" means superheroes can lead ordinary lives (and means we ordinary people can imagine being superheroes). But to keep their focus on fighting evil, superheroes must place their work ahead of any romantic interests ("Work comes first!"). The Black Widow was orphaned as a young girl (keeping her origins somewhat mysterious), but she breaks the pattern of superheroes by occasionally pursuing a romantic interest.

Hutton Archive/Moviepix/Getty Images

SUPERMAN FIRST APPEARED IN AN *ACTION COMICS* BOOK IN 1938, AS THE UNITED STATES STRUGGLED TO CLIMB OUT OF ECONOMIC DEPRESSION AND FACED THE RISING DANGER OF WAR Since then, Superman has been featured in a television show as well as in a string of Hollywood films. One trait of most superheroes is that they have a secret identity; in this case, Superman's everyday identity is "mild-mannered news reporter" Clark Kent.

Collection Christophel/Photoshot

HEROIC HUMANS WITH SPECIAL ABILITIES AS PORTRAYED IN THE MASS MEDIA RARELY INCLUDE WOMEN The Black Widow, who first appeared in *Marvel Comics* in 1964, has appeared recently in *The Avengers* movies and in the 2016 film *Captain America: Civil War*. Interestingly, she has no super-power, but does make skillful use of high-technology equipment.

AF archive/Alamy Stock Photo

ANOTHER LONGTIME SUPERHERO IMPORTANT TO OUR CULTURE IS SPIDER-MAN In the *Spider-Man* movies, Peter Parker (who transforms into Spider-Man when he confronts evil) is secretly in love with Mary Jane Watson. Again and again the male hero rescues the female from danger. But, in true superhero style, Spider-Man does not allow himself to follow his heart, because with great power comes great responsibility, and that must come first.

Seeing Sociology in *Your* Everyday Life

1. Members of every culture, as they decide how to live their lives, look to "heroes" for role models and inspiration. In modern societies, the mass media play a big part in creating heroes. What traits define popular culture heroes such as Clint Eastwood's film character "Dirty Harry," Sylvester Stallone's film characters "Rocky" as well as "Rambo," and Arnold Schwarzenegger's character "the Terminator"?

2. Do you know someone on your campus who has lived in another country or a cultural setting different from what is familiar to you? Try to engage in conversation with someone whose way of life is significantly different from your own. Try to discover something that you accept or take for granted in one way that the other person sees in a different way, and try to understand why.

3. Go to www.sociologyinfocus.com to access the Sociology in Focus blog, where you can read the latest posts by a team of young sociologists who apply the sociological perspective to topics of popular culture.

Making the Grade

CHAPTER 3 Culture

What Is Culture?

3.1 Explain the development of culture as a human strategy for survival.

Culture is a **way of life**.

- Culture is shared by members of a society.
- Culture shapes how we act, think, and feel.

Culture is a **human trait**.

- Although several species display a limited capacity for culture, only human beings rely on culture for survival.

Culture is a **product of evolution**.

- As the human brain evolved, culture replaced biological instincts as our species' primary strategy for survival.

We experience **culture shock** when we enter an unfamiliar culture and are not able to "read" meaning in our new surroundings. We create culture shock for others when we act in ways they do not understand.

> **culture** the ways of thinking, the ways of acting, and the material objects that together from a people's way of life
>
> **nonmaterial culture** the ideas created by members of a society
> **material culture** the physical things created by members of a society
>
> **culture shock** personal disorientation when experiencing an unfamiliar way of life

The Elements of Culture

3.2 Identify common elements of culture.

Culture relies on **symbols** in the form of words, gestures, and actions to express meaning.

- The fact that different meanings can come to be associated with the same symbol (e.g., a wink of an eye) shows the human capacity to create and manipulate symbols.
- Societies create new symbols all the time (e.g., new computer technology has sparked the creation of new cyber-symbols)

Language is the symbolic system by which people in a culture communicate with one another.

- People use language—both spoken and written—to transmit culture from one generation to the next.
- Because every culture is different, each language has words or expressions not found in any other language.

Values are abstract standards of what *ought to be* (e.g., equality of opportunity).

- Values can sometimes be in conflict with one another.
- Lower-income countries have cultures that value survival; higher-income countries have cultures that value individualism and self-expression.

Beliefs are specific statements that people who share a culture hold to be true (e.g., "A qualified woman could be elected president").

Norms, rules that guide human behaviour, are of two types:

- **mores** (e.g., sexual taboos), which have great moral significance
- **folkways** (e.g., greetings or dining etiquette), which are matters of everyday politeness

Technology and Culture

- A society's **artifacts**—the wide range of physical human creations that together make up a society's material culture—reflect underlying cultural values and technology.
- The more complex a society's technology, the more its members are able to shape the world as they wish.

> **symbol** anything that carries a particular meaning recognized by people who share a culture
>
> **language** a system of symbols that allows people to communicate with one another
>
> **cultural transmission** the process by which one generation passes culture to the next
>
> **Sapir-Whorf hypothesis** the idea that people perceive the world through the cultural lens of language
>
> **values** culturally defined standards that people use to decide what is desirable, good, and beautiful, and that serve as broad guidelines for social living
>
> **beliefs** specific statements that people hold to be true
>
> **norms** rules and expectations by which a society guides the behaviour of its members
>
> **mores** norms that are widely observed and have great moral significance
>
> **folkways** norms for routine or casual interaction
>
> **social control** attempts by others to regulate people's thoughts and behaviour
>
> **ideal culture** social patterns mandated by cultural values and norms
>
> **real culture** actual social patterns that only approximate cultural expectations
>
> **technology** knowledge that people use to make a way of life in their surroundings

Cultural Diversity in Canada

3.3 Discuss dimensions of cultural difference and cultural change.

We live in a **culturally diverse society**.

- This diversity is due to our country's history of immigration.
- Sociologists call Canada a *cultural mosaic*.
- Diversity reflects regional differences.
- Diversity reflects differences in social class that set off **high culture** (available only to elites) from **popular culture** (available to average people).

A number of values are central to our way of life, but **cultural patterns** are not the same throughout our society.

Subculture is based on differences in interests and life experiences.

- First Nations, Québécois, and hockey fans are examples of subcultures.

Multiculturalism is an effort to enhance appreciation of cultural diversity.

- Multiculturalism, a term coined in Canada, developed in response to the reality of our diversity—which in turn is the result of our exceptionally high rates of immigration.

Counterculture is strongly at odds with conventional ways of life.

- The Front de libération du Québec, which sought an independent socialist Quebec, was a counterculture that was active in the 1960s and 1970s.

Cultural change results from

- **invention** (e.g., the automobile, cellphones, and the internet)
- **discovery** (e.g., the recognition that women are capable of political leadership)
- **diffusion** (e.g., the growing popularity of various ethnic foods and musical styles).

Cultural lag results when some parts of a cultural system change faster than others. How do we understand cultural differences?

- **Ethnocentrism** links people to their own societies but can cause misunderstanding and conflict between societies.
- **Cultural relativism** is increasingly important as people of the world come into contact more with each other.

high culture cultural patterns that distinguish a society's elite
popular culture cultural patterns that are widespread throughout society
subculture cultural patterns that set apart some segment of a society's population
multiculturalism a social policy designed to encourage ethnic or cultural heterogeneity
Eurocentrism the dominance of European cultural patterns
counterculture cultural patterns that strongly oppose those widely accepted within a society
cultural integration the close relationships among various elements of a cultural system
cultural lag the fact that some cultural elements change more quickly than others, disrupting a cultural system
ethnocentrism the practice of judging another culture by the standards of one's own culture
cultural relativism the practice of judging a culture by its own standards

Theories of Culture

3.4 Apply sociology's macro-level theories to gain greater understanding of culture.

The **structural-functional approach** views culture as a relatively stable system built on core values. All cultural patterns play some part in the ongoing operation of society. The **social-conflict approach** sees culture as a dynamic arena of inequality and conflict. Cultural patterns benefit some categories of people more than others.

Feminist theory highlights the ways in which culture is "gendered", dividing activities between the sexes in ways that give men greater power and privilege than women.

Sociobiology explores how the long history of evolution has shaped patterns of culture in today's world.

cultural universals traits that are part of every known culture
sociobiology a theoretical approach that explores ways in which human biology affects how we create culture

Culture and Human Freedom

3.5 Critique culture as limiting or expanding human freedom.

- **Culture can limit the choices we make.**
- As cultural creatures, we have the capacity to shape and reshape our world to meet our needs and pursue our dreams.

Chapter 4
Society

Christopher Futcher/E+/Getty Images

⌄ Learning Objectives

4.1 Describe how technological development has shaped the history of human societies.

4.2 Analyze the importance of class conflict to the historical development of human societies.

4.3 Demonstrate the importance of ideas to the development of human societies.

4.4 Contrast the social bonds typical of traditional and modern societies.

4.5 Summarize the contributions of the Lenskis, Marx, Weber, and Durkheim to our understanding of social change.

The Power of Society
to shape access to the internet

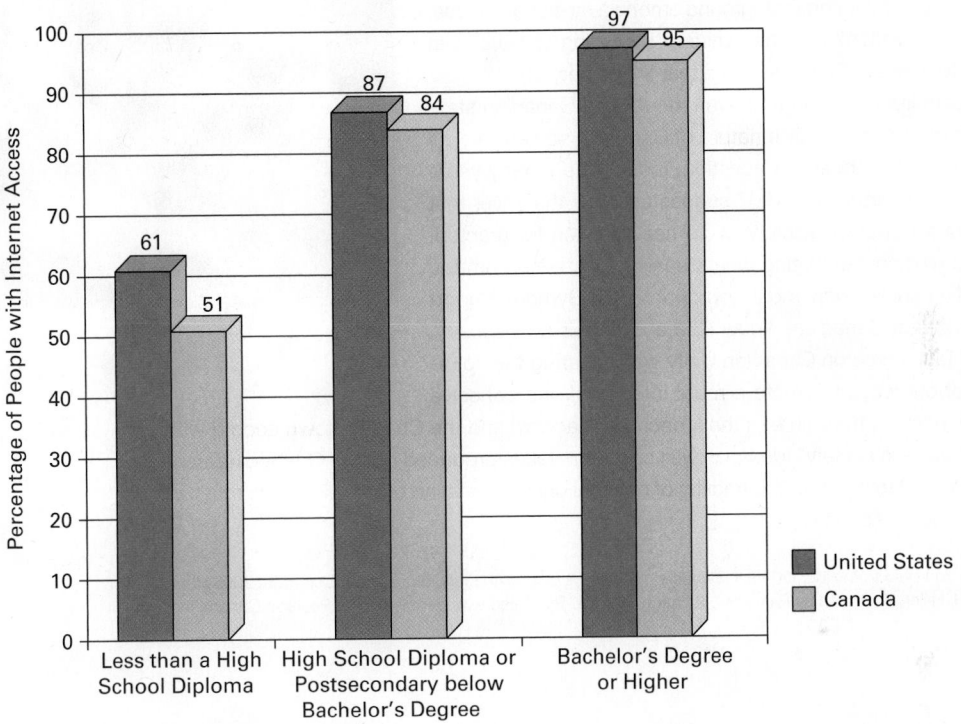

SOURCE: Pew Research Center (2012); Statistics Canada, CANSIM, tables 358-0123, 358-0124, 358-0125, and 358-0126.

Are computer technology and internet access available to everyone in North America? The data reveal that Americans—regardless of educational background—have slightly better access to the Internet than Canadians do. Almost everyone with a university degree has access, whereas this is true for only 61 and 51 percent of Americans and Canadians with no high school diploma. Substantial majorities of those with high school or postsecondary certification (below the bachelor's level) make use of the internet. Although the vast majority of North Americans are internet users, education remains a major determinant of access.

Chapter Overview

We all live in a social world. This chapter explores how societies are organized and also explains how societies have changed over the centuries. The story of human societies over time is guided by the work of one of today's leading sociologists, Gerhard Lenski, and three of sociology's founders, Karl Marx, Max Weber, and Émile Durkheim.

What is it about Canadian society that is so intriguing? Is it the dilemmas and problems of a society created by wide open spaces? Is it the reality of being a relatively young society in spite of some longevity? Is it the search for common ground among a far-flung, diverse, and changing population? Is it the sense of belonging together that persists in spite of crises that threaten to tear the society apart?

It may seem ironic indeed that even though the Canadian state is over 130 years old, the precise nature of Canadian society and its existence as an entity are still in question. In fact, the stormy years after the centennial birthday in 1967 suggested more than ever that the concept of a Canadian society could not be taken for granted. While Quebec was contemplating what degree of distance from the rest of Canadian society was most appropriate, the Symons Report was concluding that Canadians knew little about their own society, and a federal Task Force on Canadian Unity was scouring the country for clues about ways to create a more integrated and cohesive society. More recently, the failure of the Meech Lake accord and the Charlottetown accord with their "distinct Quebec society" ideas, as well as the anxieties produced by two Quebec referendums . . . continued to point up the fragility of national unity. What kind of society is this that has been problematic for so long? ■

SOURCE: Excerpted from Hiller (2006):1. *Canadian Society: A Macro Analysis*, 5th Edition. Copyright 2006 Harry H. Hiller. Published by Pearson Education Canada. Reprinted with permission by Pearson Canada Inc.

The societies that exist around the world can be quite different from our own. But what is a society? What makes societies different? How and why do they change over time?

Society refers to *people who interact in a defined territory and share a culture*. In this chapter, we discuss human societies with the help of four important sociologists. We begin with the approach of Gerhard and Jean Lenski, who describe how societies have changed over the past 10 000 years and point to the importance of technology in shaping any society. Then we turn to three of sociology's founders. Karl Marx also took a long historical view of societies, probing the roots of the social conflict that arises from the positions of owners and workers in the production of material goods. Max Weber tells a different tale, showing that the power of ideas shapes society. Weber contrasted the traditional thinking of simple societies with the rational thought that dominates complex societies today. Finally, Émile Durkheim helps us see the different ways that traditional and modern societies hang together.

All four visions of society answer a number of important questions: What makes the way of life of someone growing up among the Tuareg of the Sahara so different from your life in Canada? How and why do all societies change? What forces divide a society? What forces hold a society together? This chapter will provide answers to all of these questions as we look at the work of important sociologists.

Gerhard and Jean Lenski: Society and Technology

4.1 Describe how technological development has shaped the history of human societies.

Members of our society—who take text messaging and television, as well as schools and hospitals, for granted—must wonder at the nomads of the Sahara, who live more or less the same simple life their ancestors did centuries ago. The work of Gerhard and Jean Lenski (Lenski et al., 1995; Nolan & Lenski, 2004) helps us understand the great differences among societies that have existed throughout human history.

The Lenskis use the term **socio-cultural evolution** to mean *changes that occur as a society gains new technology*. Societies with the simplest technology have little control over nature, so they can support only a small number of people. Societies with complex technology such as cars and cellphones, while not necessarily better, support hundreds of millions of people in far more affluent ways of life.

Inventing or adopting new technology sends ripples of change throughout a society. When our ancestors first discovered how to use wind to move a boat using a sail, they created a device that would take them to new lands, greatly expand their economy, and increase their military power. In addition, the more technology a society has, the faster it changes. Technologically simple societies change very slowly, so that even today their members live more or less the life of their ancestors. How many Canadians can say that they live the way their grandparents or great-grandparents did? Modern, high-technology societies such as our own change so quickly that individuals will experience major social changes during their lives. Imagine how surprised your great-grandmother would be to hear about "Googling" and text-messaging, replacement hearts and test-tube babies, or smartphones and iPads.

Drawing on the Lenskis' work, we will describe five types of societies defined by their technology: hunting and gathering, horticultural and pastoral, agrarian, industrial, and post-industrial societies.

Hunting/Gathering Societies

In the simplest of all societies, people live by **hunting and gathering**, *the use of simple tools to hunt animals and gather vegetation*. From the time that our species appeared 3 million years ago until about 12 000 years ago, all humans were hunters and gatherers. Even in 1800, many hunter/ gatherer societies could be found around the world. But today just a few remain, such as the Aka and Baka of Central Africa, the Basarwa (or San) of Botswana, and the Batek and Semai of Malaysia. Many Aboriginal peoples in Canada, and the Aborigines of Australia, retain their hunting and gathering traditions, although they no longer rely solely on this subsistence as a way of life.

With little ability to control their environment, hunters and gatherers spend most of their time looking for game and collecting plants to eat. Only in lush areas with a lot of food do hunters and gatherers have much free

Penny Tweedie/Corbis/Getty Images

AFTER A NEARBY FOREST WAS BURNED, THESE ABORIGINAL WOMEN IN AUSTRALIA SPENT THE DAY COLLECTING ROOTS, WHICH THEY WILL USE TO MAKE DYE FOR THEIR CLOTHING Members of such societies live closely linked to nature.

time. Because it takes a large amount of land to support even a few people, hunter/gatherer societies tend to stay together in extended family groups of just a few dozen members. They must also be nomadic, moving to find new sources of vegetation or to follow migrating animals. Although they may return to favoured sites, they rarely form permanent settlements.

Hunting/gathering societies depend on the family to do many things. The family must get and distribute food, protect its members, and teach the children. Everyone's life is much the same; people spend most of their time getting their next meal. Age and gender have some effect on what individuals do. Healthy adults do most of the work, leaving the very young and the very old to help out as they can. Women gather vegetation as well as fish, small mammals, and birds—which provide most of the food—while men take on the less certain job of hunting large game. While men and women perform different tasks, most hunters and gatherers probably see the sexes as having about the same socio-economic importance (Leacock, 1978). Hunting/gathering societies usually have a shaman, or spiritual leader, who enjoys high prestige but has to work to find food like everyone else. In short, people in hunter/gatherer societies come close to being socially equal.

Hunters and gatherers use simple tools—the spear, the bow and arrow, and the bone or stone knife—but rarely as weapons to wage war. Their real enemies are

society people who interact in a defined territory and share a culture

Gerhard and Jean Lenski (society is defined by level of technology)

Karl Marx (society is defined by type of social conflict)

Max Weber (society is defined by ideas/ mode of thinking)

Émile Durkheim (society is defined by type of solidarity)

WHAT WOULD IT BE LIKE TO LIVE IN A SOCIETY WITH SIMPLE TECHNOLOGY? That's the premise of the popular television show *Survivor*. How would you manage in such a low-technology setting? What advantages do societies with simple technology afford their members? What disadvantages do you see?

the forces of nature: Storms and droughts can kill off their food supply, and there is little they can do for someone who has a serious accident or illness. Being at risk in this way encourages people to co-operate and share, a strategy that raises everyone's chances of survival. But the truth is that many die in childhood, and no more than half reach the age of 20 (Lenski et al., 1995:104).

During the past century, societies with more powerful technology have closed in on the few remaining hunters and gatherers, using their lands for other purposes and reducing their food supply. As a result, hunter/gatherer societies are disappearing from Earth. However, study of this way of life has given us valuable information about human history and our basic ties to the natural world.

Horticultural and Pastoral Societies

About 10 000 to 12 000 years ago, a new technology began to change the lives of human beings. People discovered **horticulture**, *the use of hand tools to raise crops*. Using a hoe to work the soil and a digging stick to punch holes in the ground to plant seeds may not seem like something that would change the world, but these inventions allowed people to give up gathering in favour of growing their own food. The first humans to plant gardens lived in fertile regions of the Middle East. Soon after, cultural diffusion spread this knowledge to Latin America and Asia and eventually all over the world.

Not all societies were quick to give up hunting and gathering for horticulture. Hunters and gatherers living where food was plentiful probably saw little reason to change their ways. People living in dry regions (such

as the Sahara in western Africa) or mountainous areas found little use for horticulture because they could not grow much anyway. Such people, including the Saharan Tuareg, were more likely to adopt **pastoralism**, *the domestication of animals*. Today, societies that mix horticulture and pastoralism can be found throughout South America, Africa, and Asia.

Growing plants and raising animals greatly increased food production, so populations expanded to hundreds of people in one location. Pastoralists remained nomadic, leading their herds to fresh grazing lands, but horticulturists formed settlements, moving only when the soil gave out. Joined by trade, these settlements formed societies with populations reaching into the thousands.

Once a society is capable of producing a *material surplus*—more resources are needed to support the population—not everyone has to work at providing food. Greater specialization results: Some people make crafts, while others engage in trade, cut hair, apply tattoos, or serve as priests. Compared to hunter/gatherer societies, horticultural and pastoral societies are more socially diverse. But being more productive does not make a society better. As some families produce more than others, they become richer and more powerful. Horticultural and pastoral societies have greater inequality, with elites using government power—and military force—to serve their own interests. Leaders do not have the ability to communicate or to travel over large distances, so they can control only a small number of people, rather than vast empires.

Religion also differs among types of societies. Hunters and gatherers are likely to believe that many spirits inhabit the world. Horticulturists, however, are more likely to think of one God as Creator. Pastoral societies carry this belief further, seeing God as directly involved in the well-being of the entire world. This view of God (in, for example, "The Lord is my shepherd" [Psalm 23]) is common among members of our own society because Christianity, Islam, and Judaism all began in pastoral societies of the Middle East.

Agrarian Societies

About 5000 years ago, another revolution in technology was taking place in the Middle East, one that would change the entire world. This was the development of **agriculture**, *large-scale cultivation using ploughs harnessed to animals or more powerful energy sources*. So important was the invention of the animal-drawn plough, along with other breakthroughs of the period—including irrigation, the wheel, writing, numbers, and the use of various metals—that this moment in history is often called "the dawn of civilization."

Using animal-drawn ploughs, farmers could culti-vate fields far bigger than the garden-sized plots planted by horticulturists. Ploughs have the added advantage of turning and aerating the soil, making it more fertile. As a result, farmers could work the same land for generations, encouraging the development of permanent settlements. With the ability to grow a surplus of food and to transport goods using animal-powered wagons, agrarian societies greatly expanded in size and population. About 100 CE, for example, the agrarian Roman Empire contained some 70 million people spread throughout 5.2 million square kilometres (Nolan & Lenski, 2004).

Greater production meant even more specializa-tion. Now there were dozens and dozens of distinct occupations, from farmers to builders to metalwork-ers. With so many people producing so many different things, money (or currency) was required as a common standard of exchange, and the old barter system—by which people traded one thing for another—was aban-doned. Note that this transition from barter to currency was revolutionary in many respects, opening up a tre-mendous range of options that were impossible when each individual had to produce something to trade for essentials.

Agrarian societies have extreme social inequality, typically more than in modern societies such as our own.

In most cases, a large share of the people are peasants or slaves who do most of the work. Elites therefore have time for more refined activities, including the study of philosophy, art, and literature. (This explains the histori-cal link between high culture and social privilege.)

Among hunters and gatherers and also among horti-culturists, women provide most of the food, which gives them socio-economic importance. Agriculture, however, raises men to a position of social dominance. Using the metal plough pulled by large animals, men take charge of food production in agrarian societies. Women are left with the support tasks, such as weeding and carrying water to the fields (Boulding, 1976; Fisher, 1979).

In agrarian societies, religion reinforces the power of elites by defining both loyalty and hard work as moral obligations. Many of the "wonders" of the ancient world, such as the Great Wall of China and the Great Pyramids of Egypt, were possible only because emperors and pha-raohs had almost absolute power and were able to control a large political system and order their people to work for a lifetime without pay.

Of the societies described so far, agrarian societ-ies have the most social inequality. Agrarian technology also gives people a greater range of life choices, which is the reason that agrarian societies differ more from one another than horticultural and pastoral societies do.

Koes Karnadi/Dorling Kindersley, Ltd.

AGRARIAN TECHNOLOGY ALLOWS SOCIETIES TO PRODUCE A SURPLUS—MORE FOOD THAN PEO-PLE NEED TO SURVIVE Because not everyone has to produce food, this bounty encourages a greater range of productive work. At the same time, it also increases the extent of social inequality involving class as well as gender.

Industrial Societies

Industrialism, which first took hold in the rich nations of today's world, is *the production of goods using advanced sources of energy to drive large machinery*. Until the industrial era began, the major source of energy had been the muscles of humans and the animals they tended. Around 1750, people used water power then steam boilers to operate mills and factories filled with larger and larger machines.

Industrial technology gave people such power over their environment that change took place faster than ever before. It is probably fair to say that the new industrial societies changed more in one century than they had over the course of the previous thousand years. As explained the chapter on The Sociological Perspective, change was so rapid that it sparked the birth of sociology itself. By 1900, railways crossed North America, steamships travelled the seas, and steel-framed skyscrapers reached far higher than any of the old cathedrals that symbolized the agrarian age.

But that was only the beginning. Soon after, automobiles allowed people to move quickly almost anywhere, and electricity powered homes full of modern conveniences such as refrigerators, washing machines, air conditioners, and audiovisual entertainment centres. Electronic communication—beginning with the telegraph and the telephone and followed by radio and television—gave people the ability to reach others instantly, all over the world.

Work also changed. In agrarian communities, most men and women worked in the home or in the fields nearby. Industrialization drew people away from home to factories situated near energy sources (such as coalfields) that powered their machinery. The result was that workers lost close working relationships, strong family ties, and many of the traditional values, beliefs, and customs that guided agrarian life.

With industrialization, occupational specialization became greater than ever. Today, the kind of work people do determines their standard of living, so people now size up one another in terms of their jobs rather than their family ties. Rapid change and people's tendency to move for employment also make social life more anonymous, increase cultural diversity, and promote subcultures and countercultures.

Industrial technology changed the family, too, reducing its traditional importance as the centre of social life. No longer does the family serve as the main setting for work, learning, and religious worship. Technological change also plays a part in making families more diverse, with a greater share of single people, divorced people, single-parent families, and stepfamilies.

Perhaps the greatest effect of industrialization has been to raise living standards, which increased fivefold in North America over the past century. Although at first it benefits only the elite few, industrial technology is so much more productive that incomes in general rise over time, and people throughout society have longer and more comfortable lives. Even social inequality decreases slightly, because industrial societies provide extended schooling and greater political rights. Around the world, industrialization has had the effect of increasing the demand for a greater political voice, a pattern evident in South Korea, Taiwan, the People's Republic of China, the nations of Eastern Europe and the former Soviet Union, and, since 2011, in Egypt and other nations of the Middle East.

Post-Industrial Societies

Many industrial societies, including Canada, have now entered another phase of technological development, and we can extend the Lenskis' analysis to take account of recent trends. A generation ago, sociologist Daniel Bell (1973) coined the term **post-industrialism** to refer to *technology that supports an information-based economy*. Production in industrial societies centres on factories and machinery generating material goods; today, post-industrial production relies on computers and other electronic devices that create, process, store, apply, and transmit information. Just as people in industrial societies learn mechanical skills, people in post-industrial societies develop information-based skills and carry out their work using computers and other forms of high-technology communication. A post-industrial society uses less and less of its labour force for industrial production. At the same time, more jobs become available for clerical workers, teachers, writers, sales managers, police, firefighters, and marketing representatives, all of whom process information.

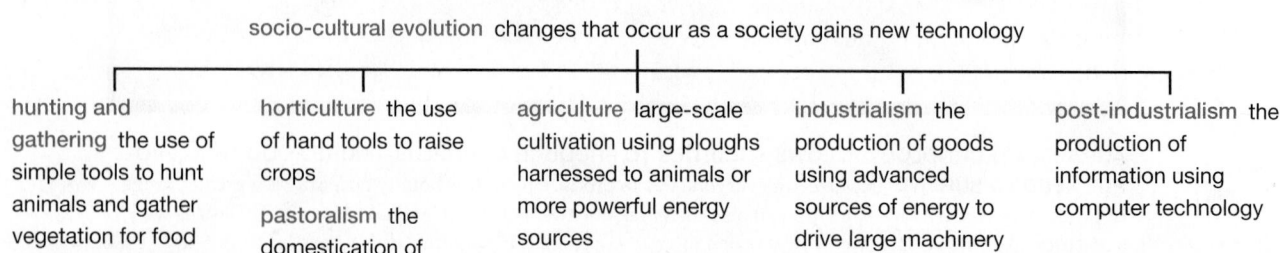

socio-cultural evolution changes that occur as a society gains new technology

hunting and gathering the use of simple tools to hunt animals and gather vegetation for food

horticulture the use of hand tools to raise crops

pastoralism the domestication of animals

agriculture large-scale cultivation using ploughs harnessed to animals or more powerful energy sources

industrialism the production of goods using advanced sources of energy to drive large machinery

post-industrialism the production of information using computer technology

SUMMING UP

Socio-Cultural Evolution

Type of Society	Historical Period	Productive Technology	Population Size	Settlement Pattern	Social Organization	Examples
Hunting and Gathering Societies	Only type of society until about 12 000 years ago; still common several centuries ago; the few examples remaining today are threatened with extinction	Primitive weapons	25–40 people	Nomadic	Family-centred; specialization limited to age and sex; little social inequality	Pygmies of Central Africa, Bushmen of southwestern Africa, Aborigines of Australia, Semai of Malaysia, Kaska Indians of Canada
Horticultural and Pastoral Societies	From about 12 000 years ago, with decreasing numbers after about 3000 BCE	Horticultural societies use hand tools for cultivating plants; pastoral societies are based on the domestication of animals	Settlements of several hundred people, connected through trading ties to form societies of several thousand people	Horticulturalists form small permanent settlements; pastoralists are nomadic	Family-centred; religious system begins to develop; moderate specialization; increased social inequality	Middle Eastern societies about 5000 BCE, various societies today in New Guinea and other Pacific islands, Yanomamö today in South America
Agrarian Societies	From about 5000 years ago, with large but decreasing numbers today	Animal-drawn plough	Millions of people	Cities become common, but they generally contain only a small proportion of the population	Family loses significance as distinct religious, political, and economic systems emerge; extensive specialization; increased social inequality	Egypt during construction of the Great Pyramids, medieval Europe, numerous predominantly agrarian societies of the world today
Industrial Societies	From about 1750 to the present	Advanced sources of energy; mechanized production	Millions of people	Cities contain most of the population	Distinct religious, political, economic, educational, and family systems; highly specialized; marked social inequality persists, lessening somewhat over time	Most societies today in Europe, North America, Australia, and Japan, which generate most of the world's industrial production
Post-Industrial Societies	Emerging in recent decades	Computers that support an information-based economy	Millions of people	Population remains concentrated in cities	Similar to industrial societies, with information processing and other service work gradually replacing industrial production	Industrial societies are now entering the post-industrial stage

The Information Revolution, which is at the heart of post-industrial society, is most evident in rich nations, yet new information technology affects the whole world. A worldwide flow of goods, people, and information now links societies and has advanced a global culture. While industrial society was the major force behind globalization, post-industrial society is now at its heart.

The Summing Up table reviews the impacts of technology on societies at different stages of socio-cultural evolution.

The Limits of Technology

More complex technology has made life better by raising productivity, reducing infectious disease, and sometimes just relieving boredom. But technology provides no quick fix for social problems. Poverty, for example, remains a reality for millions of women and men in Canada and a billion people worldwide.

Technology also creates new problems that our ancestors could hardly imagine. Industrial and post-industrial societies give us more personal freedom, but they cannot provide the sense of community that was part of pre-industrial life. Most seriously, an increasing number of the world's nations have used nuclear technology to build weapons that could send the entire world back to the Stone Age—if humanity survives at all.

Advancing technology also threatens the natural or physical environment. Each stage in socio-cultural evolution has introduced more powerful sources of energy and

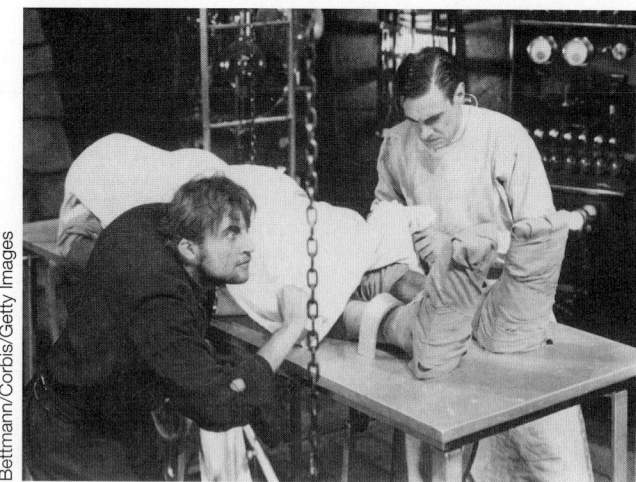

DOES ADVANCING TECHNOLOGY MAKE SOCIETY BETTER? In some ways, perhaps. However, many films and TV shows—as far back as *Frankenstein* in 1931 and as recently as the 2013 film *Iron Man 3*—have expressed the concern that new technology not only solves old problems but also creates new ones. All the sociological theorists discussed in this chapter shared this ambivalent view of the modern world.

increased the appetite for Earth's resources. Ask yourself whether we can continue to pursue material prosperity without permanently damaging our planet.

Technological advances have improved life and brought the world's people closer. But establishing peace, ensuring justice, and protecting the environment are problems that technology alone cannot solve.

Karl Marx: Society and Conflict

4.2 **Analyze the importance of class conflict to the historical development of human societies.**

The first of our classic visions of society comes from Karl Marx (1818–1883), an early giant in the field of sociology whose influence continues today. A keen observer of how the Industrial Revolution changed Europe, Marx spent most of his adult life in London, the capital of what was then the vast British Empire. He was awed by the size and productive power of the new factories going up all over Britain. Along with other industrial nations, Great Britain was producing more goods than ever before, drawing resources from around the world and churning out products at a dizzying rate.

What astounded Marx even more was how the riches produced by this new technology ended up in the hands of only a few people. As he walked around London, he could see for himself how a handful of aristocrats and industrialists lived in fabulous mansions staffed by servants, where they enjoyed both luxury and

privilege. At the same time, most people laboured long hours for low wages and lived in slums. Some even slept in the streets, where they were likely to die young from diseases brought on by cold and poor nutrition. Marx saw his society in terms of a basic contradiction: In a country so rich, how could so many people be so poor? Just as importantly, he asked, how can this situation be changed? Many people think that Karl Marx set out to tear societies apart. But he was motivated by compassion and wanted to help a badly divided society create a new and just social order.

At the heart of Marx's thinking is the idea of **social conflict**, *the struggle between segments of society over valued resources.* Social conflict can take many forms: Individuals quarrel, colleges have long-standing sports rivalries, and nations go to war. For Marx, however, the most important type of social conflict was class conflict arising from the way a society produces material goods.

Society and Production

Living in the nineteenth century, Marx observed the early decades of industrial capitalism in Europe. This economic system, Marx explained, turned a small part of the population into **capitalists**, *people who own and operate factories and other businesses in pursuit of profits.* A capitalist tries to make a profit by selling a product for more than it costs to produce. Capitalism turns most of the population into industrial workers, whom Marx called **proletarians**, *people who sell their labour for wages.* To Marx, a system of capitalist production always ends up creating conflict between capitalists and workers. To keep profits high, capitalists keep wages low. But workers want higher wages. Since profits and wages come from the same pool of funds, the result is conflict. As Marx saw it, this conflict could end only with the end of capitalism itself.

All societies are composed of **social institutions**, *the major spheres of social life, or societal subsystems, organized to meet human needs.* Examples of social institutions include the economy, political systems, family, religion, and education. In his analysis of society, Marx argued that one institution—the economy—dominates all others and defines the true nature of a society. Drawing on the philosophical approach called *materialism,* which states that the means by which humans produce material goods shape their experiences, Marx believed that the other social institutions all operate in a way that supports a society's economy. The Lenskis focused on how technology moulds a society, but Marx argued that the economy is a society's "real foundation" (1959:43; orig. 1859).

Marx viewed the economic system as society's *infrastructure* (*infra* is Latin, meaning "below"). Other social institutions, including the family, political systems, and religion, are built on this foundation, form society's *superstructure,* and support the economy. Marx's theory is illustrated in Figure 4–1. For example, under capitalism, the legal system protects capitalists' wealth just as the family allows capitalists to pass their property from one generation to the next.

Note that this focus on social institutions and the relationships among them is central to sociology as practised by a large majority of scholars in the field. A glance at the table of contents of this text reveals that a cluster of chapters is grouped under Social Institutions: the economy and work, politics and government, family, religion, education, and health and medicine. For Marx, the economy in the industrial/capitalist societies trumps all of the other social institutions that support it.

At the same time, Marx was well aware that most people living in industrial/capitalist societies do not see how capitalism shapes the entire operation of their society. For example, the right to own private property or pass it on to children is seen as natural. In the same way, many of us tend to see rich people as having earned their money through long years of schooling and hard work; we might see the poor, on the other hand, as lacking skills and the personal drive to make more of themselves. Marx rejected this type of thinking, calling it **false**

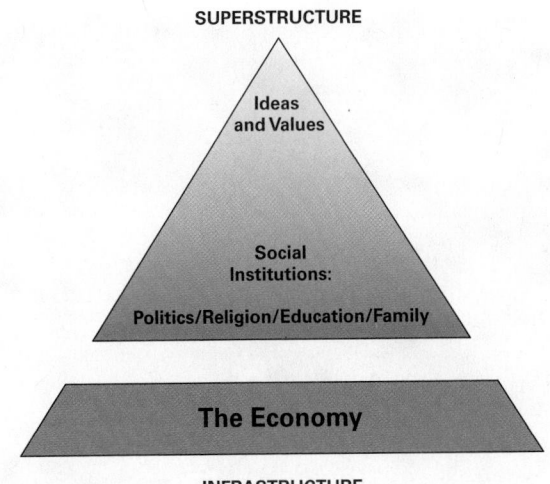

Figure 4–1 Karl Marx's Model of Society
This diagram illustrates Marx's materialist view that the system of economic production shapes the entire society. Economic production involves both technology and social relationships—for capitalism, the relationships involve the capitalists, who own the factories and businesses, and the workers, who are the source of labour. On this infrastructure, or foundation, rests society's superstructure, which includes its major social institutions as well as core cultural values and ideas. Marx maintained that every part of a society supports the economic system.

consciousness, *explanations of social problems as the shortcomings of individuals rather than as the flaws of society.* Marx was saying, in effect, that it is the system of capitalist production, and not people, that makes society so unequal. False consciousness, he continued, hurts people by hiding the real cause of their problems.

Conflict and History

For Marx, conflict is the engine that drives social change. While some societies change at slow, *evolutionary* rates, others erupt in rapid, *revolutionary change.* To Marx, early hunters and gatherers formed primitive communist societies. *Communism* is a system by which people commonly own and equally share the food and other things they produce. People in hunting and gathering societies do not have much, but they share what they have. In addition, because everyone does the same kind of work, there is little chance of social conflict.

---

social conflict the struggle between segments of society over valued resources

capitalists people who own and operate factories and other businesses in pursuit of profits

proletarians people who sell their labour for wages

social institutions the major spheres of social life, or societal subsystems, organized to meet human needs

KARL MARX WAS SURELY THE PIONEERING SOCIOLOGIST WITH THE GREATEST INFLUENCE ON THE WORLD AS A WHOLE Through the second half of the twentieth century, 1 billion people—nearly one-fifth of humanity—lived in societies organized on Marxist principles.

With technological advance comes social inequality. Among horticultural, pastoral, and early agrarian societies—which Marx lumped together as the "ancient world"—warfare was frequent, and the victors made their captives slaves. Agriculture brings still more wealth to a society's elite but does little for most other people, who labour as serfs and are barely better off than slaves. As Marx saw it, the state supported the feudal system, in which the elite or nobility had all of the power, assisted by the church, which claimed that this arrangement was God's will. This is why Marx thought that feudalism was simply "exploitation, veiled by religious and political illusions" (Marx & Engels, 1972:337; orig. 1848).

Gradually, new productive forces started to break down the feudal order. As trade steadily increased, cities grew, and merchants and others skilled in various crafts formed the new capitalist class, or bourgeoisie (a French word meaning "people of the town"). After 1800, the bourgeoisie also controlled factories, becoming richer and richer so that they soon rivalled the ancient landowning nobility. For their part, the nobles looked down their noses at this upstart commercial class, but, in time, these capitalists took control of European societies. To Marx's way of thinking, then, new technology was only part of the Industrial Revolution; it also served as a class revolution in which capitalists overthrew the old agrarian elite.

Industrialization also led to the growth of the proletariat. English landowners converted fields once ploughed by serfs into grazing land for sheep to produce wool for the textile mills. Forced from the land, millions of people migrated to cities to work in factories. Marx envisioned these workers one day joining together to form a revolutionary class that would overthrow the capitalist system.

Take a look at the Sociology in Focus box for a look at the development of Quebec as a "distinct society" within Canada. The roots of Quebec's alienation from the larger Canadian society lie in history, ethnic conflict, distinct social institutions, and capitalism.

Capitalism and Class Conflict

"The history of all hitherto existing society is the history of class struggles": With these words, Marx and his collaborator, Friedrich Engels, began their best-known statement, the *Manifesto of the Communist Party* (1972:335; orig. 1848). Industrial capitalism, like earlier types of society, contains two major social classes—the ruling class, whose members (capitalists or bourgeoisie) own productive property, and the oppressed (proletarians), who sell their labour—reflecting the two basic positions in the productive system. Like masters and slaves in the ancient world, and like nobles and serfs in feudal systems, capitalists and proletarians are engaged in class conflict today. Currently, as in the past, one class controls the other as productive property. Marx used the term **class conflict** (and sometimes class struggle) to refer to *conflict between entire classes over the distribution of a society's wealth and power.*

Class conflict is nothing new. However, as Marx pointed out, conflict in capitalist society is distinguished by the extent to which it is out in the open. Agrarian nobles and serfs, for all of their differences, were bound together by traditions and mutual obligations. Industrial capitalism dissolved those ties so that loyalty and honour were replaced by naked self-interest. Because the proletarians had no personal ties to the capitalists, Marx saw no reason for them to put up with their oppression. Marx knew that revolution still would not come easily. First, workers must become aware of their oppression and see capitalism as its true cause. Second, they must organize and act to address their problems. This means that false consciousness must be replaced with **class consciousness**, *workers' recognition of themselves as a class unified in opposition to capitalists and ultimately to capitalism itself.* Because the inhumanity of early capitalism was plain for him to see, Marx concluded that industrial workers would soon rise up to destroy this economic system.

How would the capitalists react? Their wealth made them strong. But Marx saw a weakness in the capitalist armour. Motivated by a desire for personal gain, capitalists feared competition with other capitalists. Marx

Sociology in Focus

What Makes Quebec a "Distinct Society" within Canada?

In order to place the notion of a distinct Quebec society in context, one needs to understand that "Canadian society" is problematic and not to be taken for granted. This is the message of the opening vignette of this chapter. After more than 140 years, we still have not developed a cohesive Canadian identity or sense of national unity. Our population is spread, often sparsely, across the second largest country in the world. We are divided into 10 provinces and three territories, each with distinctive socio-economic traits and regional cultures. Though officially bilingual, Canada is in fact a multicultural and multilingual country. Regionalism and even separatism (not only in Quebec) pose constant challenges to the building and sustaining of Canadian society.

Canadian writers frequently introduce these themes as they deal with the tensions within our society—even in the installation speeches of our governors general. On October 7, 1999, Adrienne Clarkson underlined the complexity of the Canadian state with a quote from her husband, John Ralston Saul: We are a "permanently incomplete experiment built on a triangular foundation—aboriginal, francophone and anglophone" (Clarkson, 2001:11). Our newly minted governor general had no way of knowing that, six years later (on September 27, 2005), a second visible minority woman, francophone immigrant Michaëlle Jean, would be giving her own installation speech as governor general.

If any country is ripe for the emergence of "distinct" societies within it, that country is Canada. Quebec is the largest and most significant society to fight for recognition and accommodation within the Canadian state. So what does it take to qualify as a society? From a sociological perspective, "a human society must possess the following characteristics: locality, organization, durability, and self-identification" (Hiller, 2006). The members of a society must live in a common territory (locality); a society must have its own organizations and social institutions to draw together its members in interaction "for their mutual benefit" (organization); its interactive organization must be "relatively permanent and durable" (durability); and "a society must be aware of itself as a unique and independent entity" (self-identity).

Clearly, Canada meets these basic requirements, though there are cracks in the structures, interactions, and identities that hold us together. It is equally clear that Quebec meets these criteria—better than our country as a whole. Quebec is much less culturally diverse:

Some 60 percent of Quebecers claim *Canadien* roots (meaning French going back to the 1600s), while another 30 percent claim French origins, and a mere 2 percent claim Québécois origins (Statistics Canada, 2011): People in each of these categories are predominantly francophone. The residents of Quebec are a "people" or a "nation" in

Christopher Morris/Corbis/Getty Images

SUPPORTERS OF THE NOTION OF A "DISTINCT SOCIETY" WERE DEVASTATED WHEN THEIR DREAM WAS CRUSHED AFTER A REFERENDUM ON OCTOBER 30, 1995 Those seeking independence for Quebec lost by less than one percentage point.

the sense that they share a common heritage (language, ethnicity, religion, culture, and history). Quebec is our only officially unilingual province, and its language is French. Thus, its self-identity is much stronger than that of Canada as a whole. In fact, Canada rarely appears on the radar of the majority of Quebeckers as they live their lives in French.

Quebec has a full range of organizations and social institutions that provide a framework for interaction and meet the needs of its residents. Like the other provinces, Quebec has its own legislature and political parties—including the sovereigntist (i.e., separatist) Parti Québécois. *Unlike* any other province, it has a party (the Bloc Québécois) that represents it in the Parliament of Canada, in order to protect Quebec's interests and promote the separatist cause. Quebec's legal system is different as well, being a blend of English common law and French civil law. Although it has lost its hold on Quebec society, the Catholic Church still predominates. The French-language media (television, radio, newspapers, and magazines) are robust and committed to promoting Quebec culture. French-language schooling is compulsory for almost all youngsters and available through to the university level. Professional and voluntary associations are specific to Quebec, as are its health care

(continued)

and child-care systems. Of all the provincial governments, Quebec's is the most actively involved in the economy, through investment and regulation (e.g., Quebec developed and still owns its massive hydroelectric industry).

In 1608, Champlain established "Canada's" first permanent settlement, with 28 settlers, at what is now Quebec City. Over the next 50 years, the population of New France grew to roughly 3000 (along the north shore of the St. Lawrence from Quebec City to Montreal). Until it lost interest in favour of Louisiana, France supported the colony of New France and encouraged more settlers to move there. Long before France ceded its North American claims (in the Treaty of Paris, 1763), all migration had stopped: Future growth of the francophone population depended on the high fertility rate of Quebec's settlers and their dependants. Today, there are 7.4 million people in Quebec; among them, 83 percent speak French at home—and 73 percent speak French exclusively. Clearly, durability characterizes this distinct society in the heart of Canada, making it a permanent fixture in North America.

When Quebec joined Confederation in 1867, the province stretched along the north and south shores of the St. Lawrence River. A year later, the Hudson's Bay Company surrendered Rupert's Land for inclusion in Canada: In two phases—in 1898 and 1912—Quebec was expanded to its current northern borders. (Quebec's border with Labrador is disputed to this day.) One can make the argument that, in the event of Quebec's separation from Canada, only the parts of the province that voted for separation should be included in an independent Quebec (Gerber, 1992; Reid, 1992) and that the right of self-determination of the Aboriginal peoples of Quebec means that they cannot be forcibly included in a sovereign Quebec (Grand Council of the Crees, 1995). While the borders of an *independent* Quebec would be hotly contested, those of the *province* are secure (the dispute with Labrador notwithstanding). Thus, Quebec society meets the criterion of locality (or territory).

Quebec—as a society meeting the criteria of self-identity, organization, durability, and locality—has fought

for recognition as a "distinct society." The province lost special rights (e.g., a veto on constitutional change) when we patriated (or "brought home") our constitution from Great Britain in 1982. Quebec had hoped to gain recognition as a distinct society through the Meech Lake Accord of 1987 and the Charlottetown Accord of 1992, but Meech Lake failed because it was not approved (or ratified) by all 10 provinces, and Charlottetown was rejected by Canadians in a referendum. These two failures precipitated Quebec's second referendum on separation in 1995, which brought Canadians to within one percentage point of losing our country.

In November 2007, Prime Minister Stephen Harper surprised Canadians—Conservatives don't do such things!—by introducing and passing a motion to recognize the Québécois as a *nation* within Canada. At first glance, you might conclude that this is better than recognition as a distinct society. Think again. The term *distinct society* applies to the *province* of Quebec or to an entity that could separate from Canada. Highly significant is the fact that Harper's motion recognized the Québécois **people** as a nation. Recall the definition of *nation*: "Nation" is commonly used to refer to a political entity, but also refers to *a people* who share a culture, ancestry, and history. A people or an ethnic group does not have the characteristics of a society and, in their absence, cannot declare independence. It remains to be seen if recognition of the Québécois as a nation satisfies the desire for recognition of Quebec as a distinct society.

What Do You Think?

1. Will Quebec eventually remove its "distinct society" from Confederation?

2. Why does a distinct society have the potential to separate when a nation does not?

3. What, in your opinion, are the defining characteristics of the Canadian identity?

---

predicted, therefore, that capitalists would be slow to band together despite their common interests. In addition, he reasoned, capitalists kept employees' wages low in order to maximize profits, which made the workers' misery grow ever greater. In the long run, Marx believed, capitalists would bring about their own undoing.

Capitalism and Alienation

Marx also condemned capitalist society for producing **alienation**, *the experience of isolation and misery resulting from powerlessness*. To the capitalists, workers are nothing more than a source of labour, to be hired and fired at will.

---

false consciousness explanations of social problems as the shortcomings of individuals rather than as the flaws of society

class conflict conflict between entire classes over the distribution of a society's wealth and power

class consciousness workers' recognition of themselves as a class unified in opposition to capitalists and ultimately to capitalism itself

alienation the experience of isolation and misery resulting from powerlessness

Dehumanized by their jobs (i.e., repetitive factory work in the past and processing orders on a computer today), workers find little satisfaction and feel unable to improve their situation. Here we see another contradiction of capitalist society: As people develop technology to gain power over the world, the capitalist economy gains more control over people.

Marx noted four ways in which capitalism alienates workers:

1. *Alienation from the act of working.* Ideally, people work to meet their needs and to develop their personal potential. Capitalism, however, denies workers a say in what they make or how they make it. Further, much of the work is a constant repetition of routine tasks. The fact that today we replace workers with machines whenever possible would not have surprised Marx. As far as he was concerned, capitalism turned human beings into machines long ago.

2. *Alienation from the product of work.* The product of work belongs not to workers but to capitalists, who sell it for profit. Thus, Marx reasoned, the more of themselves that workers invest in their work, the more they lose.

3. *Alienation from other workers.* Through work, Marx claimed, people build bonds of community. Industrial capitalism, however, makes work competitive rather than co-operative, setting each person apart from everyone else and offering little chance for human companionship.

4. *Alienation from human potential.* Industrial capitalism alienates workers from their human potential. Marx argued that a worker "does not fulfill himself in his work but denies himself, has feelings of misery rather than well-being, does not freely develop his physical and mental energies, but is physically exhausted and mentally debased. The worker, therefore, feels himself to be at home only during his leisure time, whereas at work he feels homeless" (1964:124–125; orig. 1844). In short, industrial capitalism turns an activity that should express the best qualities in human beings into a dull and dehumanizing experience.

Marx viewed alienation, in its various forms, as a barrier to social change. But he hoped that industrial workers would overcome their alienation by uniting into a true social class, aware of the cause of their problems and ready to change society.

Revolution

The only way out of the trap of capitalism, argued Marx, is to remake society. He imagined a system of production that could provide for the social needs of all people. He called this system *socialism*. Although Marx knew that

THE 2004 FILM *THE MOTORCYCLE DIARIES* TELLS THE STORY OF CHE GUEVARA'S MOTORCYCLE JOURNEY THROUGH SOUTH AMERICA Seeing such desperate poverty inspired Guevara to become a Marxist and fight for revolutionary change. He went on to play an important role in the Cuban Revolution.

such a dramatic change would not come easily, he must have been disappointed that he did not live to see workers in England rise up. Still, convinced that capitalism was a social evil, he believed that in time the working majority would realize that they held the key to a better future. This change would certainly be revolutionary and perhaps even violent. Marx believed that a socialist society would bring class conflict to an end.

The chapter on Social Stratification explains more about changes in industrial-capitalist societies since Marx's time and why the revolution he wanted never took place. In addition, Marx failed to foresee that the revolution he imagined could take the form of repressive regimes—such as Stalin's government in the Soviet Union—that would end up killing tens of millions of people (Hamilton, 2001). But in his own time, Marx looked toward the future with hope: "The proletarians have nothing to lose but their chains. They have a world to win" (Marx & Engels, 1972:362; orig. 1848).

Max Weber: The Rationalization of Society

4.3 Demonstrate the importance of ideas to the development of human societies.

With a wide knowledge of law, economics, religion, and history, Max Weber (1864–1920) produced what many experts regard as the greatest individual contribution to sociology. This scholar, born to a prosperous family in Germany, had much to say about how modern society differs from earlier types of social organization.

A COMMON FEAR AMONG THINKERS IN THE EARLY INDUSTRIAL ERA WAS THAT PEOPLE—NOW SLAVES TO THE NEW MACHINES—WOULD BE STRIPPED OF THEIR HUMANITY No one better captured this idea than the comic actor Charlie Chaplin, who starred in the 1936 film *Modern Times.*

Weber understood the power of technology, and he shared many of Marx's ideas about social conflict. But he disagreed with Marx's philosophy of materialism. Weber's philosophical approach, called *idealism,* emphasized how human ideas—especially beliefs and values—shape society. He argued that societies differ not in terms of how people produce things but in how people think about the world. In Weber's view, modern society was the product of a new way of thinking.

Weber compared societies in different times and places. To make the comparisons, he relied on the **ideal type,** *an abstract statement of the essential characteristics of any social phenomenon.* Following Weber's approach, for example, we might speak of pre-industrial and industrial societies as ideal types. The use of the word "ideal" does not mean that one or the other is good or better. Nor does an ideal type refer to any actual society. Rather, think of an "ideal" type as a way of defining a type of society in its pure form. We have already used ideal types in comparing hunting and gathering societies with industrial societies, and capitalism with socialism.

Two World Views: Tradition and Rationality

Rather than categorizing societies according to their technology or productive systems, Weber focused on ways that people think about their world: Members of pre-industrial societies are bound by tradition, and people in industrial-capitalist societies are guided by *rationality.*

By **tradition,** Weber meant *values and beliefs passed from generation to generation.* In other words, traditional people are guided by the past. They consider particular actions right and proper mostly because they have been accepted for so long.

People in modern societies, however, favour **rationality,** *a way of thinking that emphasizes deliberate, matter-of-fact calculation of the most efficient way to accomplish a particular task.* Sentimental ties to the past have no place in a rational world view, and tradition becomes simply one kind of information. Typically, modern people think and act on the basis of what they see as the present and future consequences of their choices. They evaluate jobs, schooling, and even relationships in terms of what they put into them and what they expect to receive in return.

Weber viewed both the Industrial Revolution and the development of capitalism as evidence of modern rationality. Such changes are all part of the **rationalization of society,** *the historical change from tradition to rationality as the main mode of human thought.* Weber went on to describe modern society as "disenchanted" because scientific thinking has swept away most of people's sentimental ties to the past.

The willingness to adopt the latest technology is one strong indicator of how rationalized a society is. To illustrate the global pattern of rationalization, Global Map 4–1 shows where personal computers are found in the world. In general, computer use in the high-income countries of North America and Europe is highest, and it is rare in low-income nations.

Why are some societies more eager than others to adopt new technology, such as personal computers? Those with a more rational world view might consider new computer or medical technology a breakthrough, but those with a very traditional culture might reject such devices as a threat to their way of life. The Tuareg nomads of northern Mali shrug off the idea of using telephones; similarly, Canada's Old Order Mennonites do not embrace the telephone because of its potential to disrupt their traditional way of life. In Weber's view, the amount of technological innovation depends on how a society's people understand their world. Many people throughout history have had the opportunity to adopt new technology, but only in the rational cultural climate of Western

ideal type an abstract statement of the essential characteristics of any social phenomenon

tradition values and beliefs passed from generation to generation

rationality a way of thinking that emphasizes deliberate, matter-of-fact calculation of the most efficient way to accomplish a particular task

rationalization of society the historical change from tradition to rationality as the main type of human thought

Window on the World

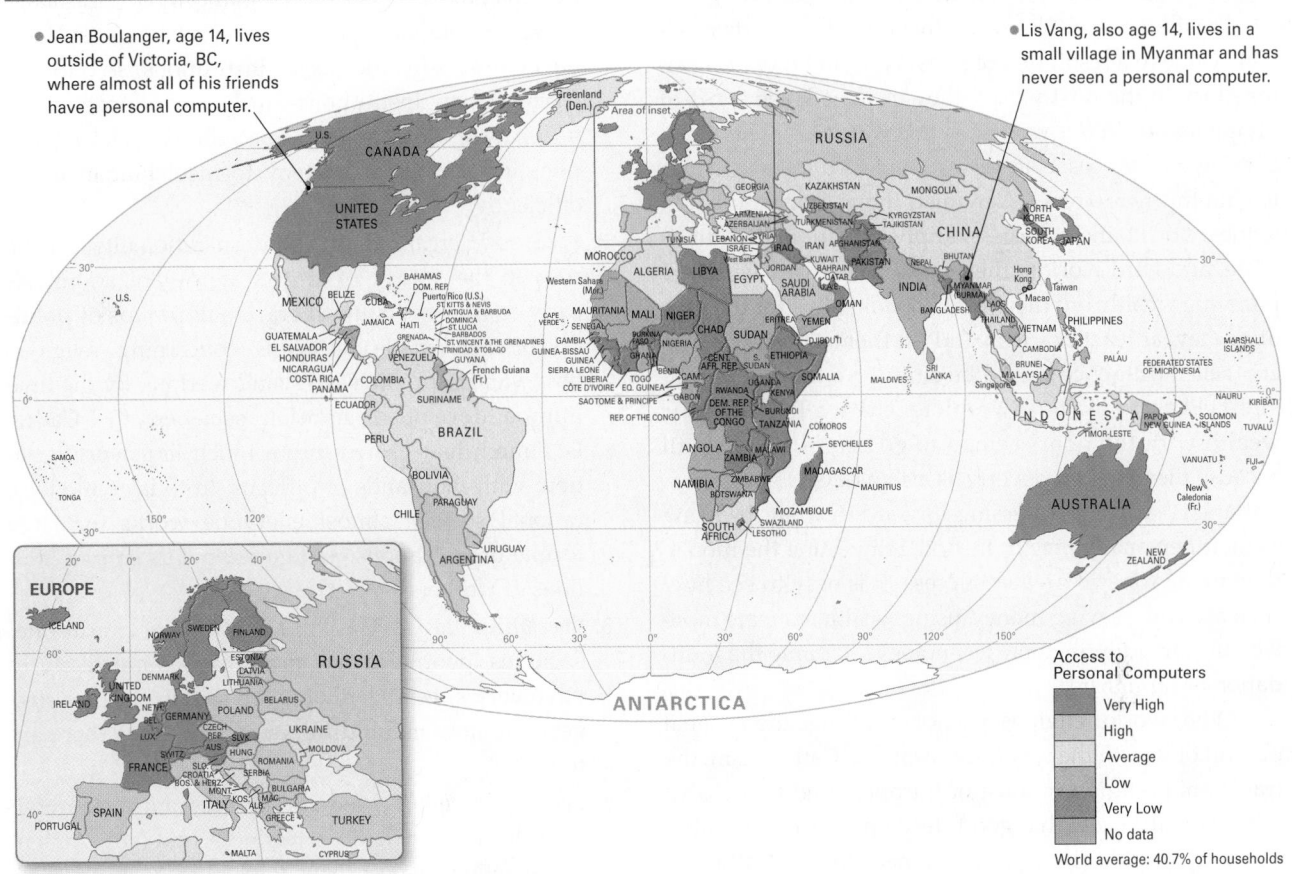

● Jean Boulanger, age 14, lives outside of Victoria, BC, where almost all of his friends have a personal computer.

● Lis Vang, also age 14, lives in a small village in Myanmar and has never seen a personal computer.

Access to Personal Computers

- Very High
- High
- Average
- Low
- Very Low
- No data

World average: 40.7% of households

Global Map 4–1 High Technology in Global Perspective

Countries with traditional cultures cannot afford, choose to ignore, or even intentionally resist new technology that nations with highly rationalized ways of life quickly embrace. Personal computers, central to today's high technology, are commonplace in high-income countries such as Canada. In low-income nations, by contrast, they are unknown to most people.

SOURCE: United Nations (2010).

Europe did people exploit scientific discoveries to spark the Industrial Revolution (Weber, 1958; orig. 1904–05).

Is Capitalism Rational?

Is industrial capitalism a rational economic system? Here again, Weber and Marx came down on different sides. Weber considered industrial capitalism to be highly rational because capitalists try to make money in any way they can. Marx, however, thought capitalism irrational because it fails to meet the basic needs of most of the people (Gerth & Mills, 1946:49).

Weber's Great Thesis: Protestantism and Capitalism

Weber spent many years considering how and why industrial capitalism developed in the first place. Why did it emerge in parts of Western Europe during the eighteenth and nineteenth centuries?

Weber claimed that the key to the birth of industrial capitalism lay in the Protestant Reformation. Specifically, he saw industrial capitalism as the major outcome of Calvinism, a Christian religious movement founded by John Calvin (1509–1564). Calvinists approached life in a formal and rational way that Weber characterized as *inner-worldly asceticism*. This mindset leads people to deny themselves worldly pleasures in favour of a highly disciplined focus on economic pursuits. In practice, Calvinism encouraged people to put their time and energy into their work; in modern terms, we might say that such people become good businesspeople or entrepreneurs (Berger, 2009).

Another of Calvin's most important ideas was *predestination*, the belief that an all-knowing and all-powerful God had predestined some people for salvation and others for damnation. Believing that everyone's fate was set before birth, early Calvinists thought that people could only guess at what their destiny was and that, in any case, they could do nothing to change it. So Calvinists swung between hopeful visions of spiritual salvation and anxious fears of eternal damnation.

Frustrated at not knowing their fate, Calvinists gradually came to a resolution of sorts. Wouldn't those chosen for glory in the next world, they reasoned, see signs of divine favour in *this* world? In this way, Calvinists came to see worldly prosperity as a sign of God's grace. Eager to gain this reassurance, Calvinists threw themselves into a quest for business success, applying rationality, discipline, and hard work to their tasks. They were certainly pursuing wealth, but they were not doing this for the sake of money, at least not to spend on themselves, because any self-indulgence would be sinful. Neither were Calvinists likely to use their wealth for charity. To share their wealth with the poor seemed to go against God's will because they viewed poverty as a sign of God's rejection. Calvinists' duty was pressing forward in what they saw as their personal *calling* from God, reinvesting the money they made for still greater success. It is easy to see how such activity—saving money, using wealth to create more wealth, and adopting new technology—became the foundation of capitalism.

Other world religions did not encourage the rational pursuit of wealth the way Calvinism did. Catholicism, the traditional religion in most of Europe, taught a passive otherworldly view, that good deeds performed humbly on Earth would bring rewards in heaven. For Catholics, making money had none of the spiritual significance it had for Calvinists. Weber concluded that this was the reason that industrial capitalism developed primarily in areas of Europe where Calvinism was strong.

Weber's study of Calvinism provides striking evidence of the power of ideas to shape society. Not one to accept simple explanations, Weber knew that industrial capitalism had many causes. But by stressing the importance of ideas, Weber tried to counter Marx's strictly economic explanation of modern society.

As the decades passed, later generations of Calvinists lost much of their early religious enthusiasm. But their drive for success and personal discipline remained, and slowly a religious ethic was transformed into a work ethic. In this sense, industrial capitalism can be seen as disenchanted religion, with wealth now valued for its own sake. This trend is seen in the fact that the practice of accounting—which, to early Calvinists, meant keeping a daily record of moral deeds—before long came to mean simply keeping track of money.

Rational Social Organization

According to Weber, rationality is the basis of modern society, giving rise to both the Industrial Revolution and capitalism. He identified seven characteristics of rational social organization:

1. *Distinctive social institutions.* In hunter/gatherer societies, the family is the centre of all activity. Gradually, however, religious, political, and economic systems develop as separate social institutions. In modern societies, new institutions—including education and health care—also appear. Specialized social institutions are a rational strategy to meet human needs efficiently.

2. *Large-scale organizations.* Modern rationality can be seen in the spread of large-scale organizations. As early as the horticultural era, small groups of political officials made decisions concerning religious observances, public works, and warfare. By the time Europe developed agrarian societies, the Catholic church had grown into a much larger organization, with thousands of officials. In today's modern, rational society, almost everyone works for large formal organizations, and governments employ millions of workers.

3. *Specialized tasks.* Unlike members of traditional societies, people in modern societies are likely to have very specialized jobs. Job search engines suggest just how many different occupations there are today.

4. *Personal discipline.* Modern societies put a premium on self-discipline. Most business and government organizations expect their workers to be disciplined, and discipline is also encouraged by our cultural values of achievement and success.

5. *Awareness of time.* In traditional societies, people measure time according to the rhythm of the sun and seasons. Modern people, by contrast, schedule events precisely by the hour and even the minute. Clocks began appearing in European cities some 500 years ago, about the same time commerce began to expand. Soon people began to think (to borrow Benjamin Franklin's phrase) that "time is money."

6. *Technical competence.* Members of traditional societies size up one another on the basis of who they are—their family ties. Modern rationality leads us to judge people according to what they are, with an eye toward their education, skills, and abilities. Most workers have to keep up with the latest skills and knowledge in their field to be successful.

7. *Impersonality.* In a rational society, technical competence is the basis for hiring, so the world becomes impersonal. People interact as specialists concerned with particular tasks, rather than as individuals concerned with one another as people. Because showing your feelings can threaten personal discipline, modern people tend to devalue emotion.

All of these characteristics can be found in one important expression of modern rationality: bureaucracy.

George Tooker, Landscape with Figures, 1963, Egg tempera on gesso panel, 26 x 30 inches. Private collection. Reproduction courtesy DC Moore Gallery, NYC

MAX WEBER AGREED WITH KARL MARX THAT MODERN SOCIETY IS ALIENATING TO THE INDIVIDUAL, BUT THEY IDENTIFIED DIFFERENT CAUSES OF THIS PROBLEM For Marx, economic inequality is the reason; for Weber, the issue is widespread and dehumanizing bureaucracy. George Tooker's painting *Landscape with Figures* echoes Weber's sentiments.

RATIONALITY, BUREAUCRACY, AND SCIENCE Weber considered the growth of large, rational organizations to be one of the defining traits of modern societies. Another term for this type of organization is *bureaucracy*. Weber believed that bureaucracy has much in common with capitalism—another key factor in modern social life:

> Today, it is primarily the capitalist market economy which demands that the official business of public administration be discharged precisely, unambiguously, continuously, and with as much speed as possible. Normally, the very large capitalist enterprises are themselves unequalled models of strict bureaucratic organization. (1978:974; orig. 1921)

We can find aspects of bureaucracy in today's businesses, government agencies, labour unions, and universities. Weber considered bureaucracy highly rational because its elements—offices, duties, and policies—help achieve specific goals as efficiently as possible. Weber saw that capitalism, bureaucracy, and also science—the highly disciplined pursuit of knowledge—are all expressions of the same underlying factor: rationality.

RATIONALITY AND ALIENATION Max Weber agreed with Karl Marx that industrial capitalism was highly productive. Weber also agreed with Marx that modern society generates widespread alienation, although his reasons were different. Marx thought alienation was caused by economic inequality. Weber blamed alienation on bureaucracy's countless rules and regulations. Bureaucracies, Weber warned, treat a human being as a "number" or a

"case" rather than as a unique individual. In addition, working for large organizations demands highly specialized and often tedious routines. In the end, Weber saw modern society as a vast and growing system of rules trying to regulate everything, and he feared that modern society would end up crushing the human spirit.

Like Marx, Weber found it ironic that modern society—meant to serve humanity—turns on its creators and enslaves them. Just as Marx described the dehumanizing effects of industrial capitalism, Weber portrayed the modern individual as "only a small cog in a ceaselessly moving mechanism that prescribes to him an endlessly fixed routine of march" (1978:988; orig. 1921). Although Weber could see the advantages of modern society, he was deeply pessimistic about the future. He feared that, in the end, the rationalization of society would reduce human beings to robots.

Émile Durkheim: Society and Function

4.4 Contrast the social bonds typical of traditional and modern societies.

"To love society is to love something beyond us and something in ourselves" (Durkheim, 1974:55; orig. 1924). These are the words of French sociologist Émile Durkheim (1858–1917), another of the discipline's founders. In Durkheim's ideas we find another important vision of human society.

Structure: Society beyond Ourselves

Émile Durkheim's great insight was recognizing that society exists beyond ourselves. Society is more than the individuals who compose it. Society was here long before we were born; it shapes us while we live; and it will remain long after we are gone. Patterns of human behaviour—cultural norms, values, and beliefs—exist as established structures, or *social facts*, that have an objective reality beyond the lives of individuals.

Because society is bigger than any one of us, it has the power to guide our thoughts and actions. This is why studying individuals alone (as psychologists or biologists do) can never capture the heart of the social experience. A classroom of students taking a math exam, a family gathered around a table sharing a meal, people quietly waiting their turn in a doctor's office—all are examples of the countless situations that have a familiar organization apart from any particular individual who has ever been part of them.

Once created by people, Durkheim claimed, society takes on a life of its own and demands a measure of obedience from its creators. We experience the power of society when we see lives falling into common patterns or when we feel the tug of morality during a moment of temptation.

Function: Society as System

Having established that society has structure, Durkheim turned to the concept of *function*. The significance of a social fact, he explained, is that it is greater than the sum of individual experience: Social facts contribute to the operation of society as a whole.

Consider crime. As victims of crime, individuals experience pain and loss. By taking a broader view, Durkheim saw that crime is vital to the ongoing life of society itself. Only by defining acts as wrong do people construct and defend morality, which gives direction and meaning to our collective lives. For this reason, Durkheim rejected the common view of crime as abnormal; on the contrary, he concluded, crime is "normal" for the most basic of reasons: A society could not exist without it (1964a; orig. 1895; 1964b; orig. 1893).

Personality: Society in Ourselves

Durkheim said that society is not only "beyond ourselves" but also "in ourselves," helping to form our personalities. Our actions, thoughts, and feelings are derived from the society that nurtures us. Society shapes us in another way, as well—by providing the moral discipline that guides our behaviour and controls our desires. Durkheim believed that humans need the restraint of society because, as creatures who want more and more, we are in constant danger of being overpowered by our own desires: "The more one has, the more one wants, since satisfactions received only stimulate instead of filling needs" (Durkheim, 1966:248; orig. 1897).

Nowhere is the need for societal regulation better illustrated than in Durkheim's study of suicide (1966; orig. 1897). Why is it that rock stars—from Janis Joplin to Jimi Hendrix, Kurt Cobain, and Michael Jackson—seem so prone to self-destruction? Durkheim had the answer long before the invention of the electric guitar: Now, as then, the *highest* suicide rates are found among categories of people with the lowest level of societal integration. In short, the enormous freedom of the young, rich, and famous carries a high price in terms of the risk of suicide.

Modernity and Anomie

Compared to traditional societies, modern societies impose fewer restrictions on everyone. Durkheim acknowledged the advantages of modern-day freedom, but he warned of increased **anomie**, or normlessness, *a condition in which norms and values are so weak and inconsistent that society provides little moral guidance to individuals*. The pattern by which many celebrities are "destroyed by fame" well illustrates the destructive effects of anomie. Sudden fame tears people from their families and familiar routines, disrupts established values and norms, and breaks down society's support and regulation of an individual—sometimes with fatal results. Thus, Durkheim explained, an individual's desires must be balanced by the claims and guidance of society—a balance that is sometimes difficult to achieve in the modern world. Durkheim would not have been surprised to see a rising suicide rate in modern societies such as Canada.

Evolving Societies: The Division of Labour

Like Marx and Weber, Durkheim lived through rapid social change in Europe during the nineteenth century. But Durkheim offered different reasons for this change.

In pre-industrial societies, he explained, tradition operates as the social cement that binds people together. In fact, what he termed the *collective conscience* is so strong that the community moves quickly to punish anyone who dares to challenge conventional ways of life. Durkheim used the term **mechanical solidarity** to refer to *strong social bonds, based on common sentiments and shared moral values, among members of pre-industrial societies*. In practice, mechanical solidarity is based on likeness. Durkheim called these bonds "mechanical" because people are linked together in lockstep, with a more or less automatic sense of belonging together and acting alike.

With industrialization, Durkheim continued, mechanical solidarity becomes weaker and weaker, and people are much less bound by tradition. But this does not mean that society dissolves. Modern life creates a new type of solidarity. Durkheim called this new social integration **organic solidarity**, defined as *social bonds based on specialization and interdependence that are strong among members of industrial societies*. The solidarity that was once rooted in likeness is now based on *differences* among

---

anomie a condition in which society provides little moral guidance to individuals

mechanical solidarity social bonds, based on common sentiments and shared moral values, that are strong among members of pre-industrial societies

organic solidarity social bonds, based on specialization and interdependence, that are strong among members of industrial societies

division of labour specialized economic activity

DURKHEIM'S OBSERVATION THAT PEOPLE WITH WEAK SOCIAL BONDS ARE PRONE TO SELF-DESTRUCTIVE BEHAVIOUR STANDS AS STARK EVIDENCE OF THE POWER OF SOCIETY TO SHAPE INDIVIDUAL LIVES When rock-and-roll singers become famous, they are wrenched out of familiar life patterns and existing relationships, sometimes with deadly results. The history of rock-and-roll contains many tragic stories of this kind, including (*from left*) Janis Joplin's and Jimi Hendrix's deaths by drug overdose (both 1970), Kurt Cobain's suicide (1994), the drugs-induced death of Michael Jackson (2009), and the death of Whitney Houston attributed to cocaine use and drowning (2012).

people who find that their specialized work—as plumbers, students, midwives, or sociology instructors—makes them rely on other people for most of their daily needs.

For Durkheim, then, the key to change in a society is an expanding **division of labour**, or *specialized economic activity*. Weber said that modern societies specialize to become more efficient, and Durkheim filled out the picture by showing that members of modern societies count on tens of thousands of others—most of them strangers—for the goods and services needed every day. As members of modern societies, we depend more and more on people we trust less and less. Why do we look to people we hardly know and whose beliefs may well differ from our own? Durkheim's answer was "because we can't live without them."

So, for Durkheim, modern society rests far less on *moral consensus* and far more on *functional interdependence*.

Herein lies what we might call "Durkheim's dilemma": The technological power and greater personal freedom of modern society come at the cost of declining morality and the rising risk of anomie.

Like Marx and Weber, Durkheim worried about the direction society was taking. But of the three, Durkheim was the most optimistic. He saw that large, anonymous societies—despite their impersonality—had the positive effect of giving people more freedom and privacy than small towns did. Anomie remains a danger, but Durkheim hoped we would be able to create laws and other norms to regulate our behaviour.

How can we apply Durkheim's views to the Information Revolution? The Sociology and the Media box suggests that Durkheim, Weber, and Marx would have had much to say about today's new computer technology.

IN TRADITIONAL SOCIETIES, PEOPLE DRESS THE SAME AND EVERYONE DOES MUCH THE SAME WORK These societies are held together by strong moral beliefs. Modern societies, illustrated by urban areas in this country, are held together by a system of production in which people perform specialized work and rely on one another for all the things they cannot do for themselves.

Sociology and the Media

The Information Revolution: What Would Durkheim, Weber, and Marx Have Thought?

New technology is changing our society at a dizzying pace. Were they alive today, the three founding sociologists would be eager observers of the current scene. Imagine for a moment the kinds of questions that Émile Durkheim, Max Weber, and Karl Marx might ask about the effects of computer technology on society.

Durkheim, who emphasized the increasing division of labour in modern society, would probably wonder if new information technology is pushing specialization even further. There is good reason to think that it is. Because electronic communication (say, a website) gives anyone a vast market (already, several billion people use the internet), people can specialize far more than if they were trying to make a living in a small geographic area.

For example, while most small-town lawyers have a general practice, an attorney in the information age living anywhere can provide specialized guidance on, say, prenuptial agreements or electronic copyright law. As we move into the electronic age, the number of highly specialized small businesses—some of which become very large—in all fields is increasing rapidly.

Durkheim might also point out that the internet threatens to increase the problem of anomie. Using computers has a tendency to isolate people from personal relationships with others. In addition, although the internet offers a flood of information, it provides little in the way of moral guidance about what is wise or good or worth knowing.

Weber believed that modern societies are distinctive because their members share a rational world view, and nothing illustrates this world view better than bureaucracy. But will bureaucracy be as important during the twenty-first century? Here is one reason to think it may not: While

organizations will probably continue to regulate workers performing the kinds of routine tasks that were common in the industrial era, much work in the post-industrial era involves imagination. Consider the work of creating animation sequences for film, designing ergonomic furniture, or writing software; such creative work cannot be regulated in the same way as putting together automobiles as they move down an assembly line. Perhaps this is the reason many high-technology companies have done away with dress codes and time clocks.

Finally, what might Marx make of the Information Revolution? Since Marx considered the earlier Industrial Revolution a *class* revolution that allowed the owners of industry to dominate society, he would probably be concerned about the emergence of a new symbolic elite. Some analysts point out that film and television writers, producers, and performers now enjoy vast wealth, international prestige, and enormous power (Lichter et al., 1990). Just as people without industrial skills stayed at the bottom of the class system in past decades, so people without symbolic skills may well become the "underclass" of the twenty-first century.

Durkheim, Weber, and Marx greatly improved our understanding of industrial societies. As we continue into the post-industrial age, there is plenty of room for new generations of sociologists to carry on.

What Do You Think?

1. Is computer technology likely to continue to increase specialization? Why?
2. Can you think of examples of creative businesses that are less bureaucratic than industrial companies are? Why would you expect this to be the case?
3. What effect will the increased importance of symbolic skills have on the earning power of college or university education?

Critical Review: Four Visions of Society

4.5   Summarize the contributions of the Lenskis, Marx, Weber, and Durkheim to our understanding of social change.

This chapter opened with several important questions about society. We will conclude by summarizing how each of the four visions of society answers these questions.

What Holds Societies Together?

How is something as complex as society possible? The Lenskis claim that members of a society are united by a shared culture, and that cultural patterns become more diverse as a society gains more complex technology. They also point out that, as technology becomes more complex, inequality divides a society more and more, although industrialization reduces inequality somewhat.

Marx saw in society not unity but social division based on class. From his point of view, elites may force an uneasy peace, but true social unity can occur only if production becomes a co-operative process. To Weber, the members of a society share a world view. Just as tradition joined people together in the past, modern societies have created rational, large-scale organizations that connect people's lives. Finally, Durkheim made solidarity the focus of his work. He contrasted the mechanical solidarity of pre-industrial societies, which is based on shared morality, with modern society's organic solidarity, which is based on specialization.

How Have Societies Changed?

According to the Lenskis' model of socio-cultural evolution, societies differ mostly in terms of changing technology. Modern society stands out from past societies in terms of its enormous productive power. Marx, too, noted historical differences in productivity, yet pointed to continuing social conflict, except perhaps among egalitarian hunter/gatherers; for Marx, modern society is distinctive mostly because it brings that conflict out into the open. Weber considered the question of change from the perspective of how people look at the world. Members of pre-industrial societies have a traditional outlook; modern people have a rational world view. For Durkheim, traditional societies are characterized by mechanical solidarity based on moral cohesion. In industrial societies, mechanical solidarity gives way to organic solidarity based on productive specialization.

Why Do Societies Change?

As the Lenskis see it, social change comes about through technological innovation that, over time, transforms an entire society. Marx's materialist approach highlights the struggle between classes as the engine of change, pushing societies toward revolution. Weber, by contrast, pointed out that ideas contribute to social change. He demonstrated how a particular world view—Calvinism—set in motion the Industrial Revolution, which reshaped all of society. Durkheim pointed to an expanding division of labour as the key dimension of social change.

The fact that these four approaches are so different does not mean that any one of them is right or wrong. Society is exceedingly complex, and our understanding of society benefits from applying all four visions.

Seeing Sociology in Everyday Life

CHAPTER 4   Society

Does having advanced technology make a society better?

The four thinkers discussed in this chapter all had their doubts. Here's a chance for you to do some thinking about the pros and cons of computer technology in terms of its effect on our everyday lives. For each of the three photos shown here, answer these questions: What do you see as the advantages of this technology for our everyday lives? What are the disadvantages?

> **Hint** In the first case, being linked to the internet allows us to stay in touch with the office, and this may help our careers. At the same time, being "connected" in this way blurs the line between work and play, as it may allow work to come into our lives at home. In addition, employers may expect us to be on call 24/7.
>
> In the second case, cellphones allow us to talk with others and to send and receive messages. We all know that cellphones and cars don't add up to safe driving. In addition, doesn't using cellphones in public end up reducing our privacy? And what about the other people around us? How do you feel about having to listen to the personal conversations of people sitting nearby?
>
> In the third case, computer gaming can certainly be fun, and it may develop various sensory-motor skills. At the same time, the rise of computer gaming discourages physical play and plays a part in the alarming increase of obesity, which now affects more than one in five children. Also, computers (and iPods) have the effect of isolating individuals, not only from the natural world but also from other people.

I love images/Fotolia

MARK RECENTLY STARTED A NEW JOB, AND HE DECIDED TO CARRY A LAPTOP SO THAT HE CAN ACCESS THE INTERNET AND RECEIVE EMAIL—EVEN OUT ON THE LAKE What advantages and disadvantages do you think this technology provides to Mark?

Gijsbert Hanekroot/Alamy Stock Photo

ANDY'S PARENTS HAVE LEARNED THAT LETTING HIM PLAY VIDEO GAMES ON A COMPUTER TABLET ENSURES THAT THEY'LL BE ABLE TO ENJOY A DISTRACTION-FREE RESTAURANT MEAL Assess the use of computer technology as a form of recreation.

London Ent/Splash News/Newscom

WHETHER WE'RE COLLEGE STUDENTS OR FAMOUS ACTRESSES, MOST OF US HAVE BECOME ACCUSTOMED TO STAYING IN TOUCH WITH FRIENDS AS WE RIDE IN A CAR, WAIT FOR OUR DINNER IN A RESTAURANT, OR PASS THE TIME DURING A BREAK IN A SPORTING EVENT What advantages and disadvantages do you see in cell phone technology?

Seeing Sociology in *Your* Everyday Life

1. The defining trait of a post-industrial society is computer technology. Spend a few minutes walking around your apartment, dorm room, or home trying to identify every device that has a computer chip in it. How many did you find? Were you surprised by the number?

2. Over the next few days, be alert for everyday evidence of these concepts: Marx's alienation, Weber's alienation, and Durkheim's anomie. So that you can identify everyday examples of these concepts, answer this question now: What type of behaviour

or social pattern qualifies as an example of each in action? How are they different?

3. Is modern society good for us? This chapter makes clear that the founders of sociology were aware that modern societies provide many benefits, but all of them were also critical of modern society.

4. Based on what you have read in this chapter, list three ways in which you would argue that modern society is better than traditional societies. Also point to three ways in which you think traditional societies are better than modern societies.

Making the Grade

CHAPTER 4 Society

Four Visions of Society

Gerhard and Jean Lenski: Society and Technology

4.1 Describe how technological development has shaped the history of human societies.

The Lenskis point to the importance of **technology** in shaping any society. They use the term **socio-cultural evolution** to mean changes that occur as a society gains new technology.

In **hunting/gathering societies**, men use simple tools to hunt animals and women gather vegetation.

Hunting/gathering societies

- have only a few dozen members and are nomadic
- are built around the family
- consider men and women roughly equal in social importance

Horticultural and pastoral societies developed some 12 000 years ago as people began to use hand tools to raise crops and shifted to raising animals for food instead of hunting them.

Horticultural and pastoral societies

- are able to produce more food, so populations expand to hundreds
- show greater specialization of work
- show increasing levels of social inequality

Agrarian societies developed 5000 years ago as the use of ploughs harnessed to animals or more powerful energy sources enabled large-scale cultivation.

Agrarian societies

- may expand into vast empires
- show even greater specialization, with dozens of distinct occupations
- have extreme social inequality
- reduce the importance of women

Industrial societies, which developed first in Europe 250 years ago, use advanced sources of energy to drive large machinery.

Industrialization

- moves work from home to factory
- reduces the traditional importance of the family
- raises living standards

Post-industrial societies represent the most recent stage of technological development—namely, technology that supports an information-based economy.

Post-industrialization

- shifts production from heavy machinery making material things to computers processing information
- requires a population with information-based skills
- is the driving force behind the Information Revolution, a worldwide flow of information that now links societies with an emerging global culture

society people who interact in a defined territory and share a culture
socio-cultural evolution Gerhard and Jean Lenski's term for the changes that occur as a society gains new technology
hunting and gathering the use of simple tools to hunt animals and gather vegetation
horticulture the use of hand tools to raise crops
pastoralism the domestication of animals
agriculture large-scale cultivation using ploughs harnessed to animals or more powerful energy sources
industrialism the production of goods using advanced sources of energy to drive large machinery
post-industrialism technology that supports an information-based economy

Karl Marx: Society and Conflict

4.2 Analyze the importance of class conflict to the historical development of human societies.

Karl Marx's **materialist approach** claims that societies are defined by their economic systems: How humans produce material goods shapes their experiences.

Conflict and History
Class conflict is the conflict between entire classes over the distribution of a society's wealth and power.

Marx traced conflict between social classes in societies as the source of social change throughout history:

- In "ancient" societies, masters dominated slaves.
- In agrarian societies, nobles dominated serfs.
- In industrial-capitalist societies, capitalists dominate proletarians.

Capitalism
Marx focused on the role of **capitalism** in creating inequality and class conflict in modern societies.

- Under capitalism, the ruling class (capitalists, who own the means of production) oppresses the working class (proletarians, who sell their labour).
- Capitalism alienates workers from the act of working, from the products of work, from other workers, and from their own potential.

- Marx predicted that a workers' revolution would eventually overthrow capitalism and replace it with socialism, a system of production that would provide for the social needs of all.

> **social conflict** the struggle between segments of society over valued resources
> **capitalists** people who own and operate factories and other businesses in pursuit of profits
> **proletarians** people who sell their labour for wages
> **social institutions** the major spheres of social life, or societal subsystems, organized to meet human needs
> **false consciousness** explanations of social problems as the short-comings of individuals rather than as the flaws of society
> **class conflict** conflict between entire classes over the distribution of a society's wealth and power
> **class consciousness** workers' recognition of themselves as a class unified in opposition to capitalists and ultimately to capitalism itself
> **alienation** the experience of isolation and misery resulting from powerlessness

Max Weber: The Rationalization of Society

4.3 **Demonstrate the importance of ideas to the development of human societies.**

Max Weber's **idealist approach** emphasizes the power of ideas to shape society.

Ideas and History

Weber traced the ideas—especially beliefs and values—that have shaped societies throughout history.

- Members of pre-industrial societies are bound by **tradition**, the beliefs and values passed from generation to generation.
- Members of industrial-capitalist societies are guided by **rationality**, a way of thinking that emphasizes deliberate, matter-of-fact calculation of the most efficient way to accomplish a particular task.

The Rise of Rationality

Weber focused on the growth of large, rational organizations as the defining characteristic of modern societies.

- Increasing rationality gave rise to both the Industrial Revolution and capitalism.
- Protestantism (specifically, Calvinism) encouraged the rational pursuit of wealth, laying the groundwork for the rise of industrial-capitalism.
- Weber feared that excessive rationality, while promoting efficiency, would stifle human creativity.

> **ideal type** an abstract statement of the essential characteristics of any social phenomenon
> **tradition** values and beliefs passed from generation to generation
> **rationality** a way of thinking that emphasizes deliberate, matter-of-fact calculation of the most efficient way to accomplish a particular task
> **rationalization of society** historical change from tradition to rationality as the main mode of human thought

Émile Durkheim: Society and Function

4.4 **Contrast the social bonds typical of traditional and modern societies.**

Émile Durkheim claimed that society has an objective existence apart from its individual members.

Structure and Function

Durkheim believed that because society is bigger than any one of us, it dictates how we are expected to act in any given social situation.

- He pointed out that social elements (such as crime) have functions that help society operate.
- Society also shapes our personalities and provides the moral discipline that guides our behaviour and controls our desires.

Evolving Societies

Durkheim traced the evolution of social change by describing the different ways societies throughout history have guided the lives of their members.

- In pre-industrial societies, **mechanical solidarity**, or social bonds based on common sentiments and shared moral values, guides the social life of individuals.
- Industrialization and the **division of labour** weaken traditional bonds, so that social life in modern societies is characterized by **organic solidarity**, social bonds based on specialization and interdependence.
- Durkheim warned of increased **anomie** in modern societies, as society provides little moral guidance to individuals.

> **anomie** Durkheim's term for a condition in which norms and values are so weak and inconsistent that society provides little moral guidance to individuals
> **mechanical solidarity** Durkheim's term for social bonds, based on common sentiments and shared moral values, that are strong among members of pre-industrial societies
> **organic solidarity** Durkheim's term for social bonds, based on specialization and interdependence, that are strong among members of industrial societies
> **division of labour** specialized economic activity

Critical Review: Four Visions of Society

4.5 **Summarize the contributions of the Lenskis, Marx, Weber, and Durkheim to our understanding of social change.**

- All four see modern societies as distinct from societies of the past.
- Each thinker highlights a different dimension of change. For the Lenskis, it is technology; for Marx it is social conflict; for Weber it is ideas; for Durkheim it is the increasing degree of specialization.

Chapter 5
Socialization

Radius Images/Alamy Stock Photo

⌄ Learning Objectives

5.1 Describe how social interaction is the foundation of personality.

5.2 Explain six major theories of socialization.

5.3 Analyze how the family, school, peer groups, and the mass media guide the socialization process.

5.4 Discuss how our society organizes human experience into distinctive stages of life.

5.5 Characterize the operation of total institutions.

The Power of Society
to shape how much television we watch

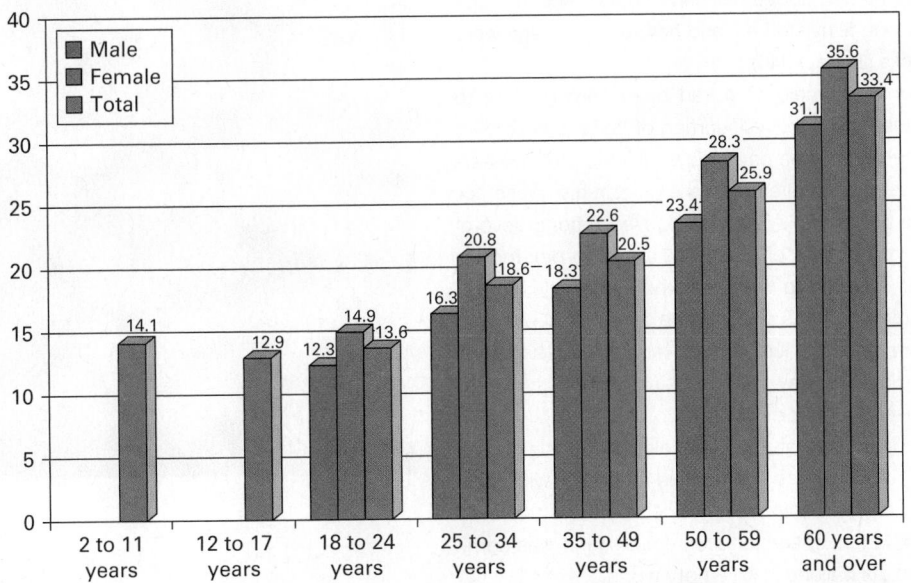

SOURCE: Compilation and calculation by LM Gerber based on Statistics Canada, CANSIM tables 502-0002 and 502-0003.

How conscious is the decision to spend time watching television? Is time spent watching TV determined by factors other than personal choice? Here we see that the number of hours per week spent watching television increases steadily with age—from 14 hours per week for children to 33 hours per week for people 60 years of age and over. But that is not the whole story. Among those 18 years of age and over, women watch two or three hours more television than men—in each age category. Related analyses suggest that people who have not graduated from high school watch twice as much television as those with bachelor's degrees. Patterns like these suggest that forces beyond the individual are in play.

Chapter Overview

Having completed two macro-level chapters, Culture and Society, exploring our social world, we turn now to a micro-level look at how individuals become members of society through the process of socialization.

On a cold winter day in 1938, a social worker walked quickly to the door of a rural Pennsylvania farmhouse. Investigating a case of possible child abuse, the social worker entered the home and soon discovered a five-year-old girl hidden in a second-floor storage room. The child, whose name was Anna, was wedged into an old chair with her arms tied above her head so that she couldn't move. She was wearing filthy clothes, and her arms and legs were as thin as matchsticks (Davis, 1940).

Anna's situation was tragic. She had been born in 1932 to an unmarried and mentally impaired woman of 26 who lived with her strict father. Angry about his daughter's "illegitimate" motherhood, the grandfather did not even want the child in his house; for the first six months of her life, Anna was passed among several welfare agencies. But her mother could not afford to pay for her care, and Anna was returned to the hostile home of her grandfather. To lessen the grandfather's anger, Anna's mother kept her in the storage room and gave her just enough milk to keep her alive. There she stayed—day after day, month after month, with almost no human contact—enduring for five years.

Learning of the discovery of Anna, sociologist Kingsley Davis (1940, 1947) immediately went to see her. He found her with local officials at a county home. Davis was stunned by the emaciated child, who could not laugh, speak, or even smile. Anna was completely unresponsive, as if alone in an empty world. ∎

Ariel Skelley/Blend Images/Alamy Stock Photo

Social Experience: The Key to Our Humanity

5.1 Describe how social interaction is the foundation of personality.

Socialization is so basic to human development that we sometimes overlook its importance. But here, in the terrible case of an isolated child, we can see what humans would be like without social contact. Although physically alive, Anna hardly seemed to have been human. We can see that, without social experience, a child is not able to act or communicate in a meaningful way and seems to be as much an *object* as a *person*.

Sociologists use the term **socialization** to refer to *the lifelong social experience by which people develop their human potential and learn culture*. Unlike other living species, whose behaviour is biologically set, humans need social experience to learn their culture and to survive. Social experience is also the foundation of **personality**, *a person's fairly consistent patterns of acting, thinking, and feeling*. We build a personality by internalizing (taking in) our surroundings. But without social experience, as Anna's case shows, personality hardly develops at all.

Human Development: Nature and Nurture

Anna's case makes clear that humans depend on others to provide the care and nurture needed not only for physical growth but also for personality to develop. A century ago, however, people mistakenly believed that humans were born with instincts that determined their personality and behaviour.

THE BIOLOGICAL SCIENCES: THE ROLE OF NATURE Charles Darwin's 1859 groundbreaking study of evolution led people to think that human behaviour was instinctive, simply our *nature*. Such ideas led to claims that the North American economic system reflects "instinctive human competitiveness," that some people are "born criminals," or that women are "naturally" emotional while men are "naturally" rational.

People trying to understand cultural diversity also misunderstood Darwin's thinking. From centuries of

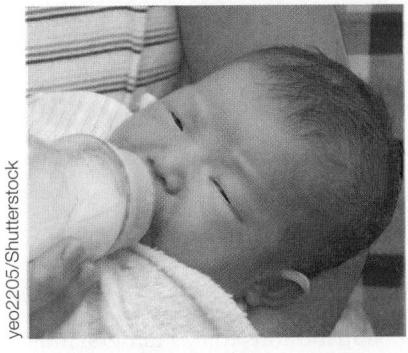 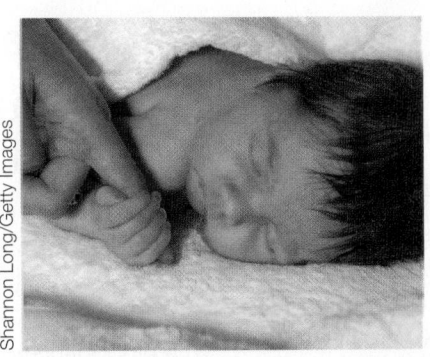 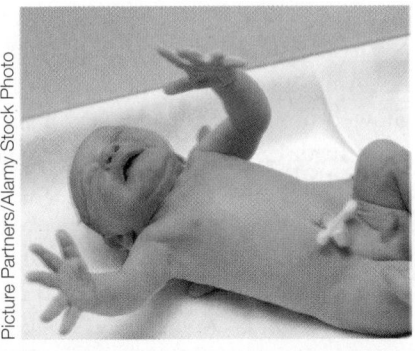

HUMAN INFANTS DISPLAY VARIOUS REFLEXES—BIOLOGICALLY BASED BEHAVIOUR PATTERNS THAT ENHANCE SURVIVAL
The sucking reflex, which actually begins before birth, enables the infant to obtain nourishment. The grasping reflex, triggered by placing a finger on the infant's palm causing the hand to close, helps the infant to maintain contact with a parent and, later, to grasp objects. The Moro reflex, activated by startling the infant, has the infant swinging both arms outward and then bringing them together across the chest. This action, which disappears after several months of life, probably developed among our evolutionary ancestors so that a falling infant could grasp the body of a parent.

world exploration, Western Europeans knew that people around the world behaved quite differently from one another. But Europeans linked these differences to biology rather than to culture. It was an easy, although incorrect and very damaging, step to claim that members of technologically simple societies were biologically less evolved and therefore less human. This ethnocentric view helped to justify colonialism: Why not take advantage of those who do not seem to be human in the same sense that you are?

THE SOCIAL SCIENCES: THE ROLE OF NURTURE In the twentieth century, biological explanations of human behaviour came under fire. Psychologist John B. Watson (1878–1958) developed a theory called *behaviourism,* which holds that behaviour is not instinctive but learned. Thus, people everywhere are equally human, differing only in their cultural patterns. In short, Watson rooted human behaviour not in nature but in *nurture.*

Social scientists today are cautious about describing *any* human behaviour as instinctive; however, this does not mean that biology plays no part. Human life, after all, depends on the functioning of the body. We also know that children often share biological traits (such as height and hair colour) with their parents and that heredity plays a part in intelligence, musical and artistic talent, and personality (such as how you react to frustration). However, whether you develop your inherited potential depends on how you are raised. For example, unless children are stimulated to use their brains early in life, the brain does not develop fully (Begley, 1995; Goldsmith, 1983).

Without denying the importance of nature, then, we can correctly say that nurture matters more in shaping human behaviour. More precisely, *nurture is our nature.*

Social Isolation

As the story of Anna shows, cutting people off from the social world is very harmful. For ethical reasons,

researchers can never place human beings in total isolation to study what happens. But, in the past, they have studied the effects of social isolation on non-human primates.

RESEARCH WITH MONKEYS In a classic study, psychologists Harry and Margaret Harlow (1962) placed rhesus monkeys—whose behaviour is in some ways surprisingly similar to that of humans—in various conditions of social isolation. They found that complete isolation with adequate nutrition for even six months seriously disturbed the monkeys' development. When returned to their group, these monkeys were passive, anxious, and fearful.

The Harlows then placed infant rhesus monkeys in cages with an artificial "mother" made of wire mesh with a wooden head and the nipple of a feeding tube where the breast would be. These monkeys also survived but were unable to interact with others when placed in a group.

But monkeys in a third category, isolated with an artificial wire mesh "mother" covered with soft terry cloth, did better. Each of these monkeys would cling to its "mother" closely. Because these monkeys showed less developmental damage than earlier groups, the Harlows concluded that the monkeys benefited from this closeness. The experiment confirmed how important it is that adults cradle infants affectionately.

The Harlows discovered that infant monkeys could recover from about three months of isolation. However, by about six months, isolation caused irreversible emotional and behavioural damage. This research and the case studies that follow put the query—"Have you hugged your child today?"—that appears on Canadian bumper stickers in a whole new light. Affectionate physical contact is crucial for the healthy development of monkeys *and* humans.

STUDIES OF ISOLATED CHILDREN Tragic cases of children isolated by abusive family members show the damage caused by depriving human beings of social experience. We will review three such cases.

Anna: The Rest of the Story The rest of Anna's story squares with the Harlows' findings. After her discovery, Anna received extensive medical attention and soon showed improvement. When Kingsley Davis visited her after 10 days, he found her more alert and even smiling—perhaps for the first time in her life! Over the next year, Anna made slow but steady progress, showing more interest in other people and gradually learning to walk. After a year and a half, she could feed herself and play with toys. But, as the Harlows might have predicted, five years of social isolation had caused permanent damage. At age eight, her mental development was less than that of a two-year-old. Not until she was almost 10 did she begin to use words. Because Anna's mother was mentally impaired, perhaps Anna was also. The riddle was never solved, because Anna died at age 10 from a blood disorder, possibly related to the years of abuse she suffered (Davis, 1940, 1947).

Isabelle: Another Case A second case involves another girl, Isabelle, found at about the same time as Anna and under similar circumstances. After more than six years of virtual isolation, this girl displayed the same lack of responsiveness as Anna. But Isabelle had the benefit of an intensive learning program directed by psychologists. Within a week, she was trying to speak and, a year and a half later, she knew some 2000 words. The psychologists concluded that intensive effort had pushed Isabelle through six years of normal development in only two years. By the time she was 14, Isabelle was attending grade 6 classes, damaged by her early ordeal but on her way to a relatively normal life (Davis, 1947).

Genie: A Third Case A more recent case of childhood isolation involves a California girl abused by her parents (Curtiss, 1977; Rymer, 1994). From the time she was two, Genie was tied to a potty chair in a dark garage. In 1970, when she was rescued at age 13, Genie weighed only 27 kilograms (59 pounds) and had the mental development of a one-year-old. With intensive treatment, she became physically healthy, but her language ability remains that of a young child. Today, Genie lives in a home for developmentally disabled adults.

EVALUATE

All evidence points to the crucial importance of social experience in personality development. Humans can recover from abuse and short-term isolation. But there is a point—precisely when is unclear from the small number of cases studied—at which isolation in early childhood causes permanent developmental damage.

CHECK YOUR LEARNING What do studies of isolated children teach us about the importance of social experience?

Understanding Socialization

5.2 Explain six major theories of socialization.

Socialization is a complex, lifelong process. The following discussions highlight the work of six researchers—Sigmund Freud, Jean Piaget, Lawrence Kohlberg, Carol Gilligan, George Herbert Mead, and Erik H. Erikson—who have made lasting contributions to our understanding of human development.

Sigmund Freud's Elements of Personality

Sigmund Freud (1856–1939) lived in Vienna at a time when most Europeans considered human behaviour to be biologically fixed. Trained as a physician, Freud gradually turned to the study of personality and mental disorders and eventually developed the celebrated theory of psychoanalysis.

BASIC HUMAN NEEDS Freud claimed that biology plays a major part in human development, although not in terms of specific instincts, as is the case in other species. Rather, he theorized that humans have two basic needs or drives that are present at birth. First is a need for sexual and emotional bonding, which he called the "life instinct" or *eros* (from the Greek god of love). Second, we share an aggressive drive he called the "death instinct" or *thanatos* (from the Greek, meaning "death"). These opposing forces, operating at an unconscious level, create deep inner tensions.

FREUD'S MODEL OF PERSONALITY Freud combined basic needs and the influence of society into a model of personality with three parts: id, ego, and superego. The **id** (the Latin word for "it") represents *the human's basic drives*, which are unconscious and demand immediate satisfaction. Rooted in biology, the id is present at birth, making a newborn a bundle of demands for attention, touching, and food. But society opposes the self-centred id, which is why one of the first words a child typically learns is "no".

To avoid frustration, a child must learn to approach the world realistically. This is done through the **ego** (Latin for "I"), which is *a person's conscious efforts to balance innate pleasure-seeking drives with the demands of society*. The ego develops as we become aware of ourselves and at the same time realize that we cannot have everything we want.

In the human personality, **superego** (Latin meaning "above" or "beyond" the ego) refers to *the cultural values and norms internalized by an individual*. The superego operates as our conscience, telling us why we cannot have everything we want. The superego begins to form as a

Bradley Secker/The Washington Post/Getty Images

THE PERSONALITIES WE DEVELOP DEPEND LARGELY ON THE ENVIRONMENT IN WHICH WE LIVE When a child's world is shredded by violence, the damage can be profound and lasting. This drawing was made by a child living through the daily violence of the civil war in Syria. What are the likely effects of such experiences on a young person's self-confidence and capacity to trust others?

child becomes aware of parental demands, and it matures as the child comes to understand that everyone's behaviour should take account of cultural norms.

PERSONALITY DEVELOPMENT To the id-centred child, the world is a bewildering assortment of physical sensations that bring either pleasure or pain. As the superego develops, however, the child learns the moral concepts of right and wrong. Initially, in other words, children can feel good only in a physical way (such as by being held and cuddled), but after three or four years, they feel good or bad according to how they judge their behaviour against cultural norms (doing the right thing).

The id and superego remain in conflict, but, in a well-adjusted person, the ego manages these two opposing forces. If conflicts are not resolved during childhood, Freud claimed, they may surface as personality disorders later on.

Culture, in the form of the superego, *represses* selfish demands, forcing people to look beyond their own desires. Often the competing demands of self and society result in a compromise that Freud called *sublimation*. Sublimation redirects selfish drives into socially acceptable behaviour: Marriage makes the satisfaction of sexual urges socially acceptable, for example, and competitive sports are an outlet for aggression.

In Freud's time, few people were ready to accept sex as a basic human drive. More recent critics have charged that Freud's work presents humans in male terms and devalues women (Donovan & Littenberg, 1982). Freud's theories are also difficult to test scientifically. However, Freud influenced everyone who later studied human personality. Of special importance to sociology are his ideas that we internalize social norms and that childhood experiences have a lasting impact on our personalities.

CHECK YOUR LEARNING What are the three elements in **Freud's model of personality**? Explain how each one operates.

Jean Piaget's Theory of Cognitive Development

Swiss psychologist Jean Piaget (1896–1980) studied human *cognition*, how people think and understand. As Piaget watched his own three children grow, he wondered about not just *what* they knew but *how* they made sense of the world. Piaget went on to identify four stages of cognitive development.

THE SENSORIMOTOR STAGE Stage one is the **sensorimotor stage,** *the level of human development at which individuals experience the world only through their senses.* For about the first two years of life, the infant knows the world only through the five senses: touching, tasting, smelling, looking, and listening. "Knowing" to young children amounts to what their senses tell them.

THE PRE-OPERATIONAL STAGE At about age two, children enter the **pre-operational stage,** *the level of human development at which individuals first use language and other symbols.* Here, children begin to think about the world mentally and use imagination. But "pre-op" children between about two and six still attach meaning only to specific experiences and objects. They can identify a toy as their favourite but cannot explain what kinds of toys they like.

Lacking abstract concepts, a child also cannot judge size, weight, or volume. In one of his best-known experiments, Piaget placed two identical glasses containing equal amounts of water on a table. He asked several children aged five and six if the amount in each glass was the same. They nodded that it was. The children then watched Piaget take one of the glasses and pour its contents into a taller, narrower glass so that the level of the water in the glass was higher. Asked again if each glass held the same amount, the five- and six-year-olds insisted that the taller glass held more water. By about age seven, children are able to think abstractly and realize that the amount of water stays the same.

THE CONCRETE OPERATIONAL STAGE Next comes the **concrete operational stage,** *the level of human development at*

Freud's Model of Personality

id basic human drives	ego a person's conscious efforts to balance innate pleasure-seeking drives with the demands of society	superego the cultural values and norms internalized by an individual

Piaget's Stages of Development

sensorimotor stage the level of human development at which individuals experience the world only through their senses	**pre-operational stage** the level of human development at which individuals first use language and other symbols	**concrete operational stage** the level of human development at which individuals first see causal connections in their surroundings	**formal operational stage** the level of human development at which individuals think abstractly and critically

which individuals first see causal connections in their surroundings. Between the ages of seven and eleven, children focus on how and why things happen. In addition, children attach more than one symbol to a particular event or object. If, for example, you say to a child of five, "Today is Wednesday," she might respond, "No, it's my birthday!" indicating that she can use just one symbol at a time. But a ten-year-old at the concrete operational stage would be able to respond, "Yes, and it's also my birthday!"

THE FORMAL OPERATIONAL STAGE   The last stage in Piaget's model is the **formal operational stage**, *the level of human development at which individuals think abstractly and critically.* At about age twelve, young people begin to reason abstractly rather than thinking only of concrete situations. If, for example, you were to ask a seven-year-old, "What would you like to be when you grow up?" you might receive a concrete response such as "a teacher." But most teenagers can think more abstractly and might reply, "I would like a job that helps others." As they gain the capacity for abstract thought, young people also learn to understand metaphors. Hearing the phrase "A penny for your thoughts" might lead a child to ask for a coin, but a teenager will recognize a gentle invitation to confide.

EVALUATE

Freud saw humans as torn by opposing forces of biology and culture. Piaget saw the mind as active and creative. He saw an ability to engage the world unfolding in stages as the result of both biological maturation and social experience. But do people in all societies pass through all four of Piaget's stages? Living in a traditional society that changes slowly probably limits a person's capacity for abstract and critical thought. Even in North America, perhaps 30 percent of people never reach the formal operational stage (Kohlberg & Gilligan, 1971).

CHECK YOUR LEARNING   What are Piaget's four stages of cognitive development? What does his theory teach us about socialization?

Lawrence Kohlberg's Theory of Moral Development

Lawrence Kohlberg (1981) built on Piaget's work to study *moral reasoning*, how individuals judge situations as right or wrong. Here again, development occurs in stages. Young children who experience the world in terms of pain and pleasure (Piaget's sensorimotor stage) are at the

preconventional level of moral development. At this early stage, in other words, "rightness" amounts to "what feels good to me." For example, a young child may simply reach for something on a table that looks shiny, which is the reason why parents of young children have to child-proof their homes.

The *conventional* level, Kohlberg's second stage, appears by the teen years (corresponding to Piaget's final, formal operational stage). At this point, young people lose some of their selfishness as they learn to define right and wrong in terms of what pleases parents and conforms to cultural norms. Individuals at this stage also begin to assess intention in reaching moral judgments instead of simply looking at what people do. For example, they understand that stealing to feed one's hungry children is not the same as stealing an iPod to sell for pocket change.

In Kohlberg's final stage of moral development, the *post-conventional* level, people move beyond their society's norms to consider abstract ethical principles. Here, they think about liberty, freedom, or justice, perhaps arguing that what is legal still may not be right. When African-American activist Rosa Parks refused to give up her seat on a bus in Montgomery, Alabama, in 1955, she violated that city's segregation laws to call attention to the racial injustice of the law.

EVALUATE

Like the work of Piaget, Kohlberg's model explains moral development in terms of distinct stages. But whether this model applies to people in all societies remains unclear. Further, many people never reach the post-conventional level of moral reasoning, although exactly why is still an open question. Another problem with Kohlberg's research is that his subjects were all boys. He committed a common research error by generalizing the results of male subjects to all people. This problem led a colleague, Carol Gilligan, to investigate how gender affects moral reasoning.

CHECK YOUR LEARNING   What are Kohlberg's three stages of moral development? What does his theory teach us about socialization?

Carol Gilligan's Theory of Gender and Moral Development

Carol Gilligan compared the moral development of girls and boys, and concluded that the two genders use different standards of rightness.

Amy Mikler/Alamy Stock Photo

CHILDHOOD IS A TIME TO LEARN PRINCIPLES OF RIGHT AND WRONG According to Carol Gilligan, however, boys and girls define what is "right" in different ways. After reading about her theory, can you suggest what these two might be arguing about?

Boys, Gilligan (1982, 1990) claims, have a *justice perspective*, meaning that they rely on formal rules to define right and wrong. Girls, in contrast, have a *care and responsibility perspective*, judging a situation with an eye toward personal relationships. For example, as boys see it, stealing is wrong because it breaks the law. Girls are more likely to wonder why one would steal and to sympathize with someone stealing to feed her family.

Kohlberg treats rule-based male reasoning as superior to the person-based female approach. Gilligan notes that impersonal rules dominate men's lives in the workplace, but personal relationships are more relevant to women's lives as mothers and caregivers. Why, then, Gilligan asks, should our society accept male standards as the norms by which we judge everyone?

Gilligan also studied the effect of gender on self-esteem. Her research team interviewed more than 2000 girls, aged 6 to 18, over a five-year period. She found a clear pattern: Young girls start out eager and confident, but their self-esteem slips away as they pass through adolescence. Why? Gilligan claims that the answer lies in our society's socialization of females: The ideal woman is calm, controlled, and eager to please. Then, too, as girls move from the elementary grades to secondary school,

they have fewer women teachers and find that most authority figures are men. As a result, by their late teens, girls struggle to regain the personal strength they had a decade earlier.

EVALUATE

Gilligan's work sharpens our understanding of both human development and gender issues in research. Yet the question remains: Does *nature* or *nurture* account for the differences between females and males? Gilligan's view, that cultural conditioning is at work, finds support in other research. Nancy Chodorow (1994) claims that children grow up in homes in which, typically, mothers do much more nurturing than fathers. As girls identify with their mothers, they become more concerned with care and responsibility to others. In contrast, boys become more like fathers, who are often detached from the home, and develop the same formal and detached personalities. Perhaps the moral reasoning of women and men will become more similar as women increasingly organize their lives around the workplace.

CHECK YOUR LEARNING According to Gilligan, how do boys and girls differ in their approach to understanding right and wrong?

George Herbert Mead's Theory of the Social Self

George Herbert Mead (1863–1931) developed a theory of *social behaviourism* to explain how social experience develops an individual's personality (1962; orig. 1934).

THE SELF Mead's central concept is the **self**, *the part of an individual's personality composed of self-awareness and self-image*. Mead's genius was in seeing the self as the product of social experience.

First, said Mead, *the self is not there at birth: It develops*. The self is not part of the body, nor does it exist at birth. Mead rejected the idea that personality is guided by biological drives (as Freud asserted) or biological maturation (as Piaget claimed).

Second, Mead explained, *the self develops only with social experience*, as the individual interacts with others. Without interaction, as we see from the cases of isolated children, the body grows but no self emerges.

Third, Mead continued, *social experience is the exchange of symbols*. Only people use words, a wave of the hand, or a smile to create meaning. We can train a dog using reward and praise, but the dog attaches no meaning to its actions. Humans, in contrast, find meaning in almost every action.

Fourth, Mead stated that *seeking meaning leads us to imagine the intentions of others*. Thus, we draw conclusions from the actions of others by imagining their underlying intentions. A dog responds to *what you do*; a human responds to *what you have in your mind* when you do it.

Fifth, Mead explained that *understanding intention requires imagining the situation from the other's point of view.* Using symbols, we imagine ourselves "in another person's shoes" and see ourselves as that person does. We can therefore anticipate how others will respond to us even before we act. A simple toss of a ball requires stepping outside ourselves to imagine how another will catch our throw. All social interaction involves seeing ourselves as others see us—a process that Mead termed *taking the role of the other.*

THE LOOKING-GLASS SELF   In effect, others are a mirror (once called a "looking glass") in which we can see ourselves. What we think of ourselves, then, depends on how we think others see us. For example, if we think that others see us as clever, we will think of ourselves in the same way. But if we feel that they think of us as clumsy, then that is how we will see ourselves. Charles Horton Cooley (1864–1929) used the phrase **looking-glass self** to mean *a self-image based on how we think others see us* (1964; orig. 1902).

THE I AND THE ME   Mead's sixth point is that, *by taking the role of the other, we become self-aware.* Another way of saying this is that the self has two parts. One part of the self operates as subject, being active and spontaneous. Mead called the active side of the self the *I* (the subjective form of the personal pronoun). The other part of the self-works as an object, the way we imagine others see us. Mead called the objective side of the self the *me* (the objective form of the personal pronoun). All social experience has both components: We initiate an action (the I-phase, or subject side, of self) and then we continue the action based on how others respond to us (the me-phase, or object side, of self).

DEVELOPMENT OF THE SELF   According to Mead, the key to developing the self is learning to take the role of the other. With limited social experience, infants can do this only through *imitation.* They mimic behaviour without understanding underlying intentions and so, at this point, they have no self.

As children learn to use language and other symbols, the self emerges in the form of *play.* Play involves assuming roles modelled on **significant others,** *such as*

parents, who have special importance for socialization. Playing "mommy and daddy"—often putting themselves literally in the shoes of a parent—helps young children imagine the world from a parent's point of view.

Gradually, children learn to take the roles of several others at once. This skill lets them move from simple play (say, playing catch) with one other person to complex *games* (such as baseball) involving many others. By about age seven, most children have the social experience needed to engage in team sports. Figure 5–1 charts the progression from imitation to play to games.

But there is a final stage in the development of the self. A game involves taking the role of specific people in just one situation. Everyday life demands that we see ourselves in terms of cultural norms as *any* member of our society might. Mead used the term **generalized other** to refer to *widespread cultural norms and values we use as a reference in evaluating ourselves.*

As life goes on, the self continues to change along with our social experiences. But no matter how much the world shapes us, we always remain creative beings, able to act back toward the world. Thus, Mead concluded, we play a key role in our own socialization.

EVALUATE

Mead's work explores the character of social experience itself. In the symbolic interaction of human beings, he believed that he had found the root of both self and society. Mead's view is completely social, allowing no biological element at all. This is a problem for critics who stand with Freud (who said our general drives are rooted in the body) and Piaget (whose stages of development are tied to biological maturity).

Be careful not to confuse Mead's concepts of the I and the me with Freud's id and superego. For Freud, the id originates in our biology, but Mead rejected any biological element of the self, although he never clearly spelled out the origin of the I. In addition, the id and the superego are locked in continual combat, but the I and the me work co-operatively together (Meltzer, 1978).

CHECK YOUR LEARNING   Explain the meaning and importance of Mead's concepts of the I and the me. What did Mead mean by "taking the role of the other"? Why is this process so important to socialization?

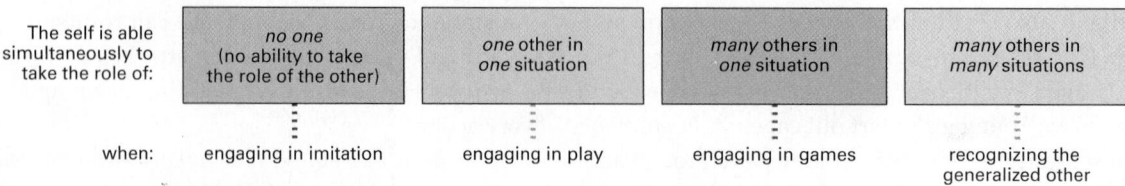

The self is able simultaneously to take the role of:	*no one* (no ability to take the role of the other)	*one* other in *one* situation	*many* others in *one* situation	*many* others in *many* situations
when:	engaging in imitation	engaging in play	engaging in games	recognizing the generalized other

Figure 5–1 Building on Social Experience

George Herbert Mead described the development of the self as a process of gaining social experience. That is, the self develops as we expand our capacity to take the role of the other.

Erik H. Erikson's Eight Stages of Development

While some analysts, including Freud, point to childhood as the crucial time when personality takes shape, Erik H. Erikson (1902–1994) took a broader view of socialization. He explained that we face challenges throughout the life course (Erikson, 1963; orig. 1950).

Stage 1—Infancy: the challenge of trust (versus mistrust). Between birth and about 18 months, infants face the first of life's challenges: to establish a sense of trust that their world is a safe place. Family members play a key part in how any infant meets this challenge.

Stage 2—Toddlerhood: the challenge of autonomy (versus doubt and shame). The next challenge, up to age three, is to learn skills to cope with the world in a confident way. Failing to gain self-control leads children to doubt their abilities.

Stage 3—Preschool: the challenge of initiative (versus guilt). Four- and five-year-olds must learn to engage their surroundings, including people outside the family, or experience guilt at failing to meet the expectations of parents and others.

Stage 4—Pre-adolescence: the challenge of industriousness (versus inferiority). Between ages six and thirteen, children enter school, make friends, and strike out on their own more and more. They either feel proud of their accomplishments or fear that they do not measure up.

Stage 5—Adolescence: the challenge of gaining identity (versus confusion). During the teen years, young people struggle to establish their own identity. In part, teenagers identify with others, but they also want to be unique. Almost all teens experience some confusion as they struggle to establish an identity.

Stage 6—Young adulthood: the challenge of intimacy (versus isolation). The challenge for young adults is to form and maintain intimate relationships with others. Falling in love or making close friends involves balancing the need to bond with the need to have a separate identity.

Stage 7—Middle adulthood: the challenge of making a difference (versus self-absorption). The challenge of middle age is contributing to the lives of others in the family, at work, and in the larger world. Failing at this, people become self-centred, caught up in their own limited concerns.

Stage 8—Old age: the challenge of integrity (versus despair). Near the end of our lives, Erikson explains, people hope to look back on what they have accomplished with a sense of integrity and satisfaction. For those who have been self-absorbed, old age brings only a sense of despair over missed opportunities.

EVALUATE

Erikson's theory views personality formation as a lifelong process, with success at one stage (say, as an infant gaining trust) preparing us to meet the next challenge. However, not everyone faces these challenges in the exact order presented by Erikson. Nor is it clear that failure to meet the challenge of one stage of life means that a person is doomed to fail later on. A broader question, raised earlier in our discussion of Piaget's ideas, is whether people in other cultures and in other times in history would define a successful life in Erikson's terms.

In sum, Erikson's model points out how many factors—including the family and school—shape our personalities. In the next section, we will take a close look at these important agents of socialization.

CHECK YOUR LEARNING In what ways does Erikson take a broader view of socialization than other thinkers discussed in this chapter?

Agents of Socialization

5.3 Analyze how the family, school, peer groups, and the mass media guide the socialization process.

Every social experience we have affects us in at least a small way. However, several familiar settings have special importance in the socialization process.

The Family

The family affects socialization in many ways. For most people, in fact, the family is the most important socialization agent of all.

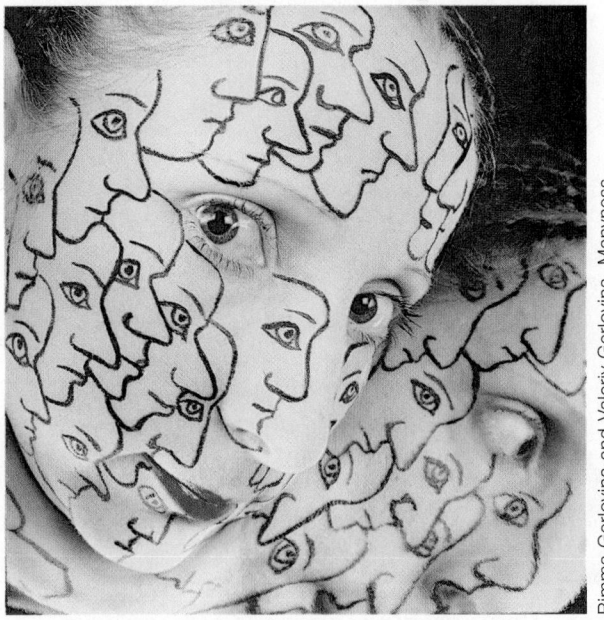

Rimma Gerlovina and Valeriy Gerlovin, *Manyness*, photograph © 1990 gerlovin.com

GEORGE HERBERT MEAD WROTE, "NO HARD-AND-FAST LINE CAN BE DRAWN BETWEEN OUR OWN SELVES AND THE SELVES OF OTHERS" The painting *Manyness* by Rimma Gerlovina and Valeriy Gerlovin conveys this important truth. While we tend to think of ourselves as unique individuals, each person's characteristics develop in an ongoing process of interaction with others.

Infants are almost totally dependent on others, and the responsibility of meeting their needs almost always falls on parents and other family members. At least until the onset of schooling, the family also shoulders the task of teaching children cultural values and attitudes about themselves and others. Overall, research suggests that nothing is more likely to produce a happy, well-adjusted child than being in a loving family (Gibbs, 2001).

Not all family learning is the result of intentional teaching by parents. Children also learn from the environment adults create for them. Whether children learn to think of themselves as strong or weak, smart or stupid, loved or simply tolerated—and, as Erikson suggests, whether they believe the world to be trustworthy or dangerous—depends largely on the quality of the surroundings provided by parents and other caregivers.

The most profound impact of the family is on gender socialization. What is the first question we ask about a new baby—or even an unborn child? "Is it a boy or a girl?" The answer to that question is the basis for different treatment from birth onward. Baby girls and boys are handled differently (boys more roughly), dressed in different colours, and later given different kinds of toys. Within the family, children learn what it means to be a boy or a girl and to be masculine or feminine in tastes, values, emotions, behaviour, and aspirations. The family also confers social position on children—that is, parents not only bring children into the physical world but also place them in society in terms of race, ethnicity, religion, and class. In time, all of these elements become part of a child's self-concept. Of course, some aspects of social position may change later on, but social standing at birth affects us throughout our lives.

Interestingly, children are aware from a very early age of the accessories of class. Canadian sociologists Bernd Baldus and Verna Tribe (1978) presented children in grades 1, 3, and 6 with sets of pictures of two men (one who was well dressed and one who was casually dressed), two houses (one from a high-income area of the city), two dining rooms, and two cars (both reflecting expensive taste and less expensive taste). Regardless of gender, school environment, or class background, the children's ability to match person and appropriate taste level increased with grade level. Furthermore, the children were able to give "character" descriptions of the two men: The well-dressed man was described as cheerful, nice, smart, and likeable, while the casually dressed man was described as tough, lazy, and likely to swear, steal, drink, or be uncaring about his family. Clearly, when children learn about class, they are actually learning to assign different values to different people. This ability, in return, can have an effect on how they value themselves—in short, on their self-esteem.

In addition, research shows that class position affects not just how much money parents spend on their children but also what parents expect of them (Ellison et al., 1996). When asked to pick from a list of traits most desirable in a child, those with lower social standing favoured obedience and conformity; in contrast, affluent people chose good judgment and creativity (NORC, 2007). Why the difference? Melvin Kohn (1977) explains that people of lower social standing usually have limited education and perform routine jobs under close supervision. Expecting that their children will hold similar positions, they encourage obedience and may even use physical punishment, such as spanking, to get it. Because well-off parents have had more schooling, they usually have jobs that demand imagination and creativity, so they try to inspire the same qualities in their children. Consciously or not, all parents act in ways that encourage their children to follow in their footsteps.

Affluent parents typically provide their children with an extensive program of leisure activities, including sports, travel, and music or dance lessons. These enrichment activities—far less available to children growing up in low-income families—represent important *cultural capital* that advances learning and creates a sense of confidence in these children that they will succeed later in life (Lareau, 2002).

Linda Gerber

SOCIOLOGICAL RESEARCH INDICATES THAT AFFLUENT PARENTS TEND TO ENCOURAGE CREATIVITY IN THEIR CHILDREN, WHILE POOR PARENTS FOSTER CONFORMITY While this general difference may be valid, parents at all class levels can and do provide loving support and guidance by simply involving themselves in their children's lives. Here a father and daughter add a little fun to a practice session at a week-long Suzuki Institute workshop.

The ethnic or racial background of families also contributes to the development of social identity, placing individuals within the cultural mosaic or the "rainbow" class structure—as visible minorities increasingly find themselves unemployed and poor (Frideres, 2005). One's ethnic or racial background has profound effects on the development of self and identity, particularly if one is an immigrant, or the child of immigrants, and lives in a cohesive ethnic community.

Race also affects how we see ourselves and how we see others. Many people think of race as something obvious, a category based on a physical trait such as skin color. Osagie Obasogie (2013) interviewed people who have been blind since birth to discover that they think about race in very much the same terms as sighted people. This finding suggests that, rather than "seeing" race with our eyes, we learn to "see" race as a result of the ways our society defines various categories of people. The Thinking about Diversity box reveals the complexity of ethnic or racial socialization resulting from the arrival of new immigrants (renewal of diversity) and ethnic or racial intermarriage (dilution of diversity).

Thinking about Diversity: Race, Class, and Gender

Ethnic and Racial Identities: Evidence of Renewal and Dilution

Our multiculturalism policy frames Canada's response to the diversity created by a history of immigration. We celebrate diversity—rather than force assimilation—and encourage each ethnic community to pass on its heritage and values to generations of Canadian-born children. Nonetheless, the colourful cultural mosaic has developed blurred edges as a result of interethnic and interracial marriages (or relationships). Over time, an ever-larger proportion of Canadians claims multiple origins, thereby diluting the impacts of ethnic socialization. This dilution process is less advanced in the communities that experience renewal in the form of continuing immigration.

Census a and Census 2006 provide wonderful data that illustrate cultural dilution and renewal by asking about (1) the ethnic group(s)—up to four—to which one's ancestors belonged and (2) one's racial identity—White, Black, Chinese, South Asian, Latin American, and so forth. A census respondent who claimed to be anything but "White" on this question was classified as a member of a visible minority. Thus, for each individual, we know ethnic background (up to four ethnicities) and visible minority status.

Table 5–1 reveals the number of Canadians with selected ethnic backgrounds. For example, 4.7 million

Table 5–1 Ethnic and Racial Identities: Immigration and Intermarriage* (2001 and 2006)

	Population		Immigrant (%)		Multiple Origins (%)	
	2006	Visible Minority (%)	2001	2006	2001	2006
Canadian/*Canadien***	10 066 290	0	0.0	1.1	42.2	42.9
French	5 000 350	0	3.0	3.4	77.3	74.9
Irish	4 354 155	1	5.1	5.0	87.0	88.7
Scottish	4 719 850	1	5.9	5.5	85.4	88.0
English	6 570 015	2	9.1	8.0	75.2	79.2
German	3 179 425	1	11.5	10.8	74.3	78.9
Finnish	131 045	0	13.9	11.5	72.2	77.0
Italian	1 445 330	2	28.4	25.1	42.8	48.7
Japanese	98 905	89	34.4	26.1	37.7	42.9
Lebanese	165 150	50	48.8	45.5	34.6	37.1
Jamaican	231 110	90	53.1	47.9	34.7	41.9
Haitian	102 430	97	56.8	53.6	14.2	21.0
Somali	37 790	99	61.4	58.3	8.6	10.0
Egyptian	54 875	63	63.9	60.9	36.8	39.5
East Indian	962 670	97	66.6	66.4	18.5	19.0
Filipino	436 195	97	69.9	67.6	18.7	26.3
Chinese	1 346 510	98	72.0	69.8	14.5	15.7

*Intermarriage is measured by the proportion of each ethnic category claiming multiple origins.

**Francophones in Quebec are likely to claim *Canadien* rather than French or Québécois origins, meaning that they trace their origins back to the original French settlers in New France. Outside Quebec, Canadian origins are claimed by people whose ancestors have been in Canada for many generations, by those who identify simply as Canadian, and by those who have too many origins (six or eight or more) to list.

SOURCE: Calculations by L.M. Gerber based on Statistics Canada, Census 2001 and Census 2006, Catalogue nos. 97F0010XCB2001040 and 97-564-XCB2006007.

(continued)

people claim some Scottish ancestry; among them are those who are Scottish on both paternal and maternal sides and those who include at least one Scottish ancestor in their list of four. The former are single-origin, the latter multiple-origin. The two columns at the far right of the table indicate that, in 2001, 85 percent of the people claiming Scottish heritage had multiple origins and, therefore, might be only one-quarter Scottish—or less if there are additional ancestral origins that could not be listed on the census questionnaire. Note that, by 2006, the proportion with multiple origins increased to 88 percent. Since the early Scottish settlers arrived in what we now call Canada, they have formed families and produced children with Aboriginal, French, English, German, and Japanese partners—to name a few possibilities. Over the years—except in isolated pockets—Scottish cultural influences and Scottish identity have been diluted.

The profile of the Somali people contrasts sharply with that of the Scots in that only 8.6 and 10 percent claimed multiple origins (in 2001 and 2006, respectively). Being newcomers to Canada, the Somalis have not been here long enough to produce new generations with blended ancestries. The fact that about 60 percent of the Somali population consists of immigrants means that the Somali culture is sustained and renewed by the steady flow of people from their homeland. A vibrant culture provides some protection against intermarriage.

Table 5–1 contains data that allow us to examine relationships among the variables introduced above: From left to right, the columns indicate ethnicity, population, percent visible minority, percent immigrant (in 2001 and 2006), and percent with multiple origins (2001 and 2006).

The third column indicates the percentage of people in each ethnic category who self-identify as members of a visible minority. Looking back at Figure 3–2 you will see that, increasingly since 1970, immigrants to Canada have come not from Europe but from Asia, Africa, and the Caribbean. Relatively recent waves of immigration from these countries mean that relatively few are Canadian-born, most belong to a visible minority, and intermarriage has not yet increased the multiple-origin components. In other words, in Table 5–1, where the percentage of immigrants is large, so, too, is the percentage of visible minority; in contrast, the proportion with multiple origins is small. In the language of scientific sociology we can observe a positive relationship between percent immigrant and percent visible minority—and, although the relationship is less clear, a negative relationship between each of these and percent multiple-origin.

The fourth and fifth columns are used to rank the ethnic categories, French to Chinese, from low to high on percentage immigrant. The "newer" ethnic communities (e.g., Filipino) have higher proportions of immigrants. In contrast, older communities (e.g., French and English) are composed of very few immigrants. Note that, between 2001 and 2006, all but one of the ethnic groups (from Finnish down) dropped from 2 to 8 points on percent immigrant. This means that the growth of ethnic populations is due more to births in Canada than to immigration. With the exception of East Indians, the groups from Japanese down increased

their proportions with multiple origins by 1 to 7 percentage points—through inter-ethnic marriage.

Among the long-established categories of European origin (French to Finnish), Table 5–1 shows very large multiple-origin components (more than 70 percent), indicating a great deal of inter-ethnic marriage. The Italian and Japanese communities have slightly larger immigrant components and smaller multiple-origin components. From Lebanese to Chinese, we see larger immigrant components—meaning that these communities experience continuing cultural renewal. While people who report Haitian or East Indian ancestry are unlikely to report multiple origins, this is especially true of Somalis and Chinese. Imagine being part of Vancouver's Chinese community, and compare that to having *some* Scottish ancestry. In which case would ethnic background frame one's life and shape one's identity?

You may have noticed the "Canadian" ethnic category. This is used mainly, but not exclusively, by people whose ancestors came to Canada many generations ago and who probably have very complicated—and possibly unknown—ancestral histories. The speed at which one's ancestral record can become unmanageable is illustrated by the family history of your author, Linda Gerber. Her mother, Elsie, was born near Winnipeg of Finnish immigrant parents; she married a recent immigrant from Finland and had three children, who would describe themselves on the census as single-origin Finnish. Linda then married a German immigrant, so her children would report Finnish and German origins—and would appear in four places in Table 5–1 (i.e., Finnish origin, German origin, Finnish multiple-origin, and German multiple-origin). Linda's daughter married a man of English and Irish ancestry—so *their* daughter, Grace, would fill in all four spaces in the census with Finnish, German, English, and Irish, thereby appearing in eight places in the table. If Grace were to marry a man with an equally diverse ancestry—perhaps Italian, Jamaican, Scottish, and Japanese—*her* daughter would have too many distinct ancestries to report. How would she decide which of her eight ancestries to include in the four allotted spaces? Her surname and inherited racial characteristics might help her choose. On the other hand, if her parents and grandparents were all Canadian-born, she might report—despite eight distinct ancestries and diverse cultural influences—that she belongs to a visible minority and is a single-origin Canadian.

The speed with which ethnic and racial boundaries can be blurred is illustrated by Jamaicans; their percent with multiple-origin increased seven points to 42 percent between 2001 and 2006. If that change resulted from births to parents of differing ethnicity or race, the youngest members of the group should have higher multiple-origin levels than the older ones. In fact, among Jamaicans 15 years of age and older, 33 percent have multiple origins. The comparable figure, for zero- to 14-year-olds, is an astounding *63 percent*—almost double that of older Jamaicans.

Postscript

Note that the Canadian/*Canadien* category includes an unexpectedly low multiple-origin level of 43 percent. The main reason is that this category *already includes multiple ancestries*—as outlined in the story of Grace and her imaginary daughter (the great grandchild of author Linda Gerber).

Note also that the children of German and Italian parents have inter-ethnic but *not* interracial origins. The same is true of the children of Jamaican and Haitian parents. Only when the children have German and Japanese, Jamaican and East Indian, or Somali and Scottish parentage do we have inter-ethnic *and* interracial ancestry.

What Do You Think?

1. How does a family get from such diversity to "Canadian" identities (or values), as described here?

2. If you were filling in the census, how would you report your own ancestry?

3. Has your life or identity been shaped by socialization involving cultural influences from the country or countries of origin of your ancestors?

The School

Schooling enlarges the social world of children to include people with backgrounds different from their own. It is only as they encounter people who differ from themselves that children come to understand the importance of factors such as race and social class. As they do, they are likely to cluster in playgroups made up of one class, race, and gender (Finkelstein & Haskins, 1983; Lever, 1978).

Schools join with families in socializing children into gender roles. Studies show that, at school, boys engage in more physical activities and spend more time outdoors, whereas girls are more likely to help teachers with various housekeeping chores. Boys also engage in more aggressive behaviour in the classroom, while girls are typically quieter and better behaved (Best, 1983; Jordan & Cowan, 1995). While there has been considerable improvement on this front, schools contribute to the gender stereotyping that affects course choices and, ultimately, career aspirations—so that fewer girls prepare for advanced study in mathematics, engineering, or the physical sciences.

Schooling is not the same for children living in rich and poor communities. Children from well-off families typically have a far better experience in school than do those whose families are poor.

For all children, the lessons learned in school include more than the formal lesson plans. Schools informally teach many things, which together might be called the *hidden curriculum*. Activities such as spelling bees teach children not only how to spell but also how society divides people into "winners" and "losers." Moving beyond the personal web of family life, children discover that evaluation of skills, such as in reading and arithmetic, is based on impersonal standardized tests. Here, the emphasis shifts from who they are to *how* they perform. Organized sports help students develop strength and skills and teach them important lessons in co-operation and competition.

For most children, school provides their first experience with bureaucracy. The school day is based on impersonal rules and a strict time schedule. Not surprisingly, these are also the traits of the large organizations that will employ most of them later in life.

The Peer Group

By the time they enter school, children have discovered the **peer group**, *a social group whose members have interests, social position, and age in common*. Unlike the family and the school, the peer group lets children escape the direct supervision of adults. Among peers, children learn to form relationships on their own. Peer groups also offer the chance to discuss interests that adults may not share with their children (such as clothing and popular music) or permit (such as drugs and sex).

Not surprisingly, parents express concern about their children's friends. In a rapidly changing society, peer groups have tremendous influence and contribute to the generation gap. Peer group influence typically peaks during adolescence, when young people begin to break away from their families and think of themselves as adults. Even during adolescence, however, parental influence on children remains strong. Peers may affect short-term interests, such as music or films, but parents have greater influence on long-term goals, such as going to university or college (Davies & Kandel, 1981).

Any neighbourhood or school is made up of many peer groups. Individuals tend to view their own groups in positive terms and put down other groups. In addition, people are influenced by peer groups they would like to join, a process sociologists call **anticipatory socialization**, *learning that helps a person achieve a desired position*. In school, for example, young people may copy the styles and slang of a group they hope will accept them. Later in life, a young lawyer who hopes to become a partner in a law firm may conform to the attitudes and behaviour of the firm's partners in order to be accepted.

The Mass Media

The **mass media** are *the means for delivering impersonal communications directed to a vast audience*. The term *media* (the plural of *medium*) comes from Latin meaning "middle," suggesting that the media function to connect people. Mass media arise as communications technologies—first newspapers, then radio and television, and now the internet—disseminate information on a broad

Global Snapshot

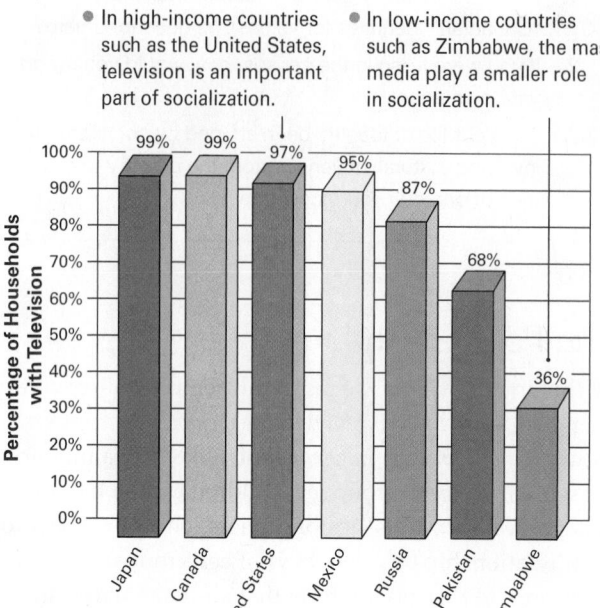

- In high-income countries such as the United States, television is an important part of socialization.
- In low-income countries such as Zimbabwe, the mass media play a smaller role in socialization.

Figure 5–2 Television Ownership in Global Perspective

Television is popular in high- and middle-income countries, where almost every household owns at least one TV set.

SOURCES: International Telecommunication Union (2014).

scale. See Figure 5–2 for the extent of television ownership worldwide.

Since the mass media have enormous effects on our attitudes and behaviour, they are important contributors to the socialization process. Television, broadcast on a regular basis in North America since the 1950s, has rapidly become the dominant medium in Canada. By 2001, 99.2 percent of Canadian households had colour televisions, 91.5 percent had VCRs, 19.8 had DVD players, and 68.3 had cable television (Statistics Canada, 2002b). Furthermore, rental spending on videos and DVDs was expected to reach $1.7 billion by 2007 (PricewaterhouseCoopers, 2003). Unfortunately, the vast majority of these expenditures will be on non-Canadian cultural products.

Just how "glued" to the television are we? The average Canadian watches 22 hours of television per week (see the Power of Society figure at the beginning of this chapter). Years before children learn to read, watching television becomes a regular routine—as they grow up, young girls and boys spend about 14 hours per week in front of a television. Indeed, television consumes as much of a child's time as interacting with parents. The extent of television viewing during childhood concerns researchers, who have found that television renders children more passive and less likely to use their imaginations (American Psychological Association, 1993; Fellman, 1995).

TELEVISION AND POLITICS Comedian Fred Allen once quipped that we call television a "medium" because it is rarely well done. For a variety of reasons, television has provoked plenty of criticism. Some cite biases in television programming: Liberal (or left-leaning) critics maintain that television shows mirror our society's patterns of inequality and rarely challenge the status quo. That is, television shows have traditionally portrayed men and women according to cultural stereotypes, placing men in positions of power and relegating women to the roles of mothers or subordinates. Moreover, television shows have long portrayed well-to-do people favourably, while depicting less affluent individuals—Archie Bunker of *All in the Family* is the classic example—as ignorant and wrongheaded. And, although visible minority populations are increasing rapidly, until recently they have been all but absent from North American. The Sociology and the Media box deals with change in the characterization of minorities on television in North America and in Canada where the portrayal of minorities—and Aboriginal peoples—has improved substantially over the years. On the other hand, the majority of programs watched by Canadians continue to be of foreign, mostly U.S., origin, with roughly 40 percent originating in Canada (Statistics Canada, 2002a). The Canadian Radio-television and Telecommunications Commission (CRTC) requires 60 percent of the programming on television between 6 A.M. and midnight be Canadian. Of course, television producers can provide Canadian content, but the viewer operates the remote control.

Television played an important role in the last two Canadian elections. In 2011, Jack Layton's NDP swept across Quebec like an orange tidal wave and achieved opposition party status for the first time – largely on the charismatic appeal of the leader. By 2016, television and the social media turned Justin Trudeau into a celebrity, not only in Canada but abroad. The second wave of Trudeaumania—this time for the son of Pierre Trudeau—was fuelled by his good looks, his telegenic family, his apparent rapport with ordinary folks and world leaders alike, and his complete ease in front of the TV cameras.

On the other side of the fence, conservative critics charge that the television and film industries are dominated by a cultural elite that is far more liberal than the population as a whole. Especially in recent years, they maintain, the media have become increasingly "politically correct," advancing various socially liberal causes, including feminism and gay rights (Goldberg, 2002; Rothman et al., 1993). The increasing popularity of Fox News—home to Sean Hannity, Bill O'Reilly, Brit Hume, and other more conservative commentators—suggests that Americans can now find programming with "spin" from both sides of the political spectrum. Fox News was approved for digital cable in Canada by the CRTC in November 2004.

Sociology and the Media

How Do the Media Portray Minorities?

In an old *Saturday Night Live* sketch, Ron Howard tells comedian Eddie Murphy about a new film, *Night Shift*, in which two mortuary workers decide to open their own sideline business, a prostitution ring. Murphy asks whether any Black actors are in the film; Howard shakes his head no. Murphy then thunders: "A story about two pimps and there wasn't no brothers in it? I don't know whether to thank you or punch you in the mouth, man!"

Murphy's ambivalence points up twin criticisms of the mass media. The first is that films and television exclude minorities altogether; the second is that minorities are portrayed in stereotypical fashion (Press, 1993). Certainly, in the 1950s, minorities were almost nowhere to be found on television and in films. Even the wildly successful 1950s comedy *I Love Lucy* was originally turned down by every major television studio because it featured Desi Arnaz, a Cuban, in a starring role. While the early Westerns presented stereotypical images of cowboys and "Indians," at least one of them starred an authentic Canadian Aboriginal actor: Six Nations' Jay Silverheels as Tonto (loyal sidekick of the Lone Ranger). Since then, the media have steadily included more minorities, so that the issue of exclusion has declined in importance. Since a majority of the programming watched by Canadians is of U.S. origin, changes there have an immediate impact here.

But the second issue—*how* the media portray minorities—is just as important. The few African Americans who managed to break into television in the 1950s (e.g., the infamous Amos and Andy, and Jack Benny's butler, Rochester) were confined to stereotypical roles portraying uneducated people of lowly status. More recently, many television shows feature Black stars: Some are situation comedies replete with crude humour and bumbling characters; others, though humorous, depict upper-status Black families. Several soap operas (e.g., *The Young and the Restless* and *As the World Turns*) revealed Blacks as young professionals—among them, physicians, hospital administrators, lawyers, fashion photographers, successful models, and corporate vice-presidents. Oprah Winfrey, until recently the host of her own talk show, is very successful, very wealthy, and in a position of power or authority relative to that of her guests.

The portrayal of Aboriginal peoples has changed from the days when made-up White actors played "Indians" to American cowboys. Two Aboriginal performers from Canada, Chief Dan George (British Columbia) and Graham Greene (Ontario), helped redefine the role of the "Indian" in the major U.S. films *Little Big Man* and *Dances with Wolves*, respectively. Greene continues to appear in a wide range of film and television roles. In the meantime, singer/actor Buffy Sainte-Marie (Saskatchewan) provided early exposure to youngsters through her long-term involvement with *Sesame Street*. The popular Canadian production *North of 60* depicted Aboriginal peoples in the whole range of roles common to northern communities. Inuit singer Susan Aglukark (Nunavut) has expanded the range of "Canadian" music, just as Shania Twain (whose name means "on my way" in Ojibwa and who was raised for a time by an Ojibwa stepfather) has changed the sound of country music.

Perhaps the best indicator of the stature of Aboriginal programming is the creation of the Aboriginal Peoples Television Network, which is broadcast to every Canadian home via cable or satellite (Richards, 2006). Notably, Carla Robinson (Haisla/Heitsuk), with university degrees in mass communication and journalism, is a broadcast journalist with CBC Television: over the years, she hosted the weekly CBC show *Absolutely Canadian*—devoted to First Peoples' news—replaced Knowlton Nash as host of the monthly education program *News in Review,* and anchored CBC Newsworld's evening news. She is also the founder and president of Carla Robinson Media Productions.

But Aboriginal people are not the only subjects of specialty programing. Little Mosque on the Prairie—the creation of Zarqa Nawaz—is a successful sitcom that ran as a TV series from 2007–2012. The episodes track the experience of a tiny Muslim community in a small prairie town.

Overall, significant change has taken place in news reporting on the CBC and other television channels. Representation of social diversity today is greater than it was even a decade ago. In large measure, this stems from deliberate policies—responding to demands for greater minority representation as well as the need to appeal to and connect with diverse audiences. Increasingly, the news is conveyed to us by women, by members of visible minorities, and, in Canada, by people with names that are neither English nor French. Even such exclusively "White male" areas as sports, stock market coverage, business analysis, and war zone activity are reported more frequently by women and visible minorities.

While *equal* representation is a distant goal, the mass media in Canada and the United States can boast of improvement in the portrayal of minorities. The perpetuation of former stereotypes has given way to depiction of minority individuals in a wide range of occupations and social classes. Some critics argue that the portrayal of minorities in high-status positions is unrealistic, as it masks the fact that minorities continue to face major barriers to full participation. On the other hand, apart from providing role models for minority youth, such representation reflects the fact that visible minorities, as well as women, are found in the *real* world across the socio-economic spectrum.

(continued)

What Do You Think?

1. Do you think that the mass media still present stereotypical images based on race, ethnicity, and gender?

2. What images of Aboriginal peoples have you acquired from the mass media?

3. Is Oprah Winfrey a token African-American woman placed in the spotlight in the interests of political correctness—or is hers a genuine success story based on her talents?

TELEVISION AND VIOLENCE In 1996, the American Medical Association issued the startling statement that violence in television and film had reached such a high level that it posed a hazard to health. For example, there is a strong link between aggressive behaviour and the amount of time elementary schoolchildren spend watching television and using video games. The public is concerned about this issue: Three-quarters of American adults report having walked out of a movie or turned off the television because of too much violence. Almost two-thirds of television programs contain violence and, in most such scenes, violent characters show no remorse and are not punished (Wilson, 1998). Canadians have the same concerns and their own measures for dealing with media violence.

Two similar neighbouring towns in British Columbia provided a unique opportunity to study the impact of television violence, as one of the towns received television before the other. By measuring the level of aggressive behaviour in children in both communities, initially and two years after the arrival of television in the second town, Williams (1986) was able to demonstrate that, after the arrival of television, the children caught up—in terms of aggressiveness—to those in the neighbouring community who had had longer exposure.

The federal government turned its attention to the impact of television violence on the behaviour of children through a House of Commons committee. The committee concluded that the evidence of a link was inconclusive and contradictory; nonetheless, it recommended implementation of legislation to control extremely violent forms of entertainment and a classification system to help parents protect their children from exposure to television violence (Canada, 1993). The 1990s witnessed sustained activity on the part of the CRTC regarding television violence. Two studies commissioned by the CRTC, reported in 1992, concluded that there is a link between violence on television and violence in society, though it is not one of direct cause and effect. The Action Group for Violence on Television was set up with representatives from advertisers, producers, broadcasters, and cable companies. This committee developed classification guidelines and worked with other groups to regulate programming and broadcasting. Members have worked closely with American legislators and producers on regulation and in the development of the V-chip, which allows parents to block unduly violent programming from their televisions. The Canadian Association of Broadcasters, deciding that *Mighty Morphin Power Rangers* violated its violence code, was instrumental in getting YTV and Global to remove the program from their schedules in 1994. As a result, most of the students currently in Canada's colleges and universities have had no exposure to the show.

Television and other mass media have enriched our lives, generating a wide range of entertaining and educational programming. Moreover, the media increase our understanding of diverse cultures and provoke discussion of current issues. Note that television and radio have become highly interactive in recent years, asking people to call, email, or tweet with their responses and reactions to current events or a range of issues. Even children

Damian Dovarganes/AP Images

CONCERN WITH VIOLENCE AND THE MASS MEDIA EXTENDS TO THE WORLD OF VIDEO GAMES, ESPECIALLY THOSE POPULAR WITH YOUNG BOYS Among the most controversial games, which include high levels of violence, is "Call of Duty." Do you think that the current rating codes are sufficient to guide parents and children who buy video games, or would you support greater restrictions on game content?

participate. At the same time, the power of the media—especially television—to shape how we think continues to fuel controversy on many fronts. Computers and the internet complicate the picture further because governments have great difficulty censoring or otherwise controlling the flow of information into or out of their countries.

EVALUATE

This section shows that socialization is complex, with many different factors shaping our personalities as we grow. These factors do not always work together. For instance, children learn certain things from peer groups and the mass media that may conflict with what they learn at home. Beyond family, school, peer group, and the media, other spheres of life also play a part in social learning. These include the workplace, religious organizations, the military, and social clubs. In the end, socialization proves to be not a simple matter of learning but a complex balancing act as we absorb information from

a variety of sources. In the process of sorting and weighing all the information we receive, we form our own distinctive personalities.

CHECK YOUR LEARNING Identify all the major agents of socialization discussed in this section of the chapter. What are some of the unique ways that each helps us develop our individual personalities?

Socialization and the Life Course

5.4 **Discuss how our society organizes human experience into distinctive stages of life.**

While childhood has special importance in the socialization process, learning continues throughout our lives. An overview of the life course reveals that our society

Window on the World

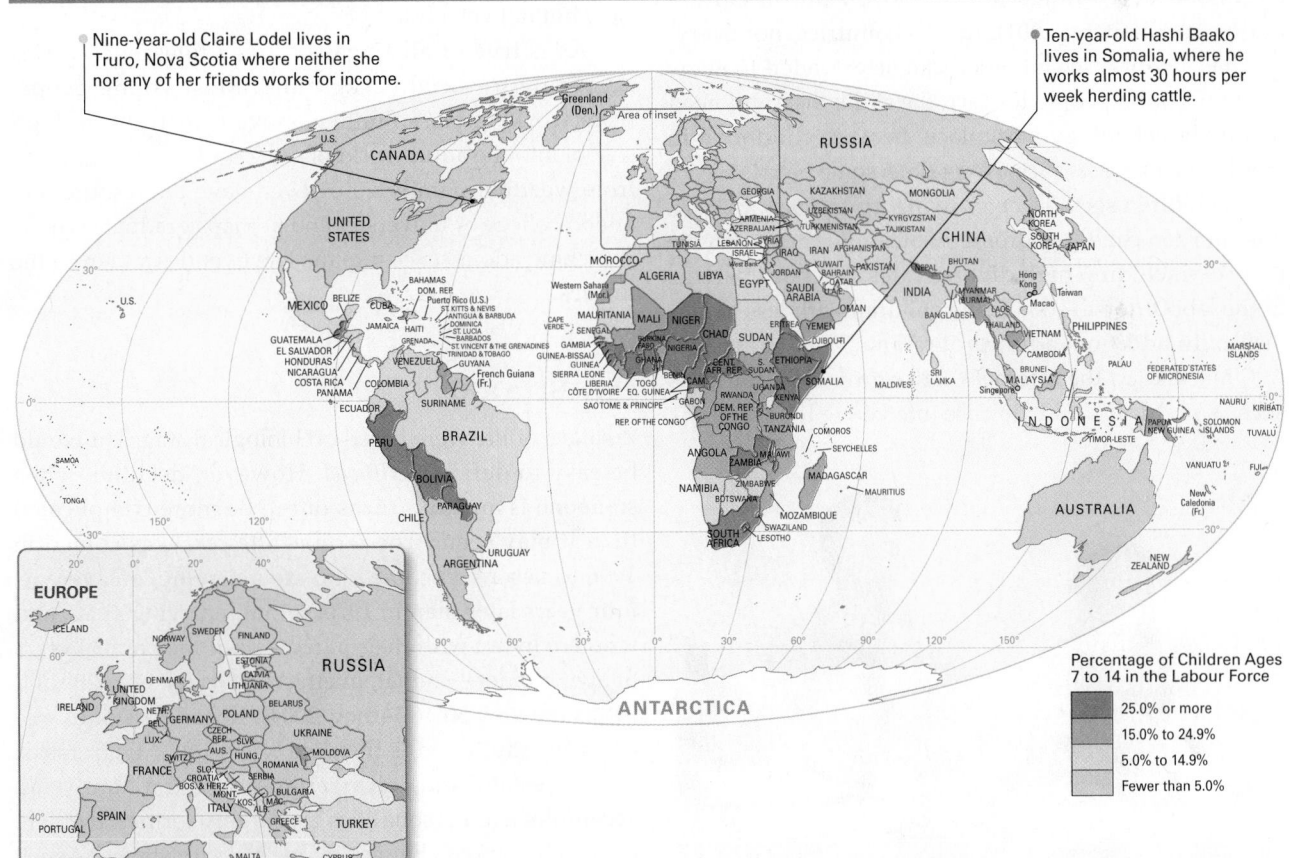

Nine-year-old Claire Lodel lives in Truro, Nova Scotia where neither she nor any of her friends works for income.

Ten-year-old Hashi Baako lives in Somalia, where he works almost 30 hours per week herding cattle.

Percentage of Children Ages 7 to 14 in the Labour Force

- 25.0% or more
- 15.0% to 24.9%
- 5.0% to 14.9%
- Fewer than 5.0%

Global Map 5-1 Child Labour in Global Perspective

Because industrialization extends childhood and discourages children from working and other activities considered suitable only for adults, child labour is uncommon in Canada and other high-income countries. In less economically developed nations of the world, however, children are a vital economic asset, and they typically begin working as soon as they are able. How would childhood in, say, the African nation of Chad or Sudan differ from that in North America?

SOURCES: UNICEF (2010) and World Bank (2010).

organizes human experience according to age: childhood, adolescence, adulthood, and old age.

Childhood

A few years ago, Nike Corporation, the maker of popular athletic shoes, came under attack. Its shoes are made in Taiwan and Indonesia—in many cases by children who work in factories instead of going to school. Some 250 million of the world's children work, half of them full-time, earning about $0.50 an hour (Human Rights Watch, 2004). Criticism of Nike springs from the fact that most North Americans think of *childhood*—roughly the first 12 years of life—as a carefree time for learning and play. Yet, as historian Philippe Ariès (1965) explains, that notion of childhood is fairly new. During the Middle Ages, children of four or five were treated like adults, expected to fend for themselves.

Today we defend our idea of childhood because children are biologically immature. But a look back in time and around the world shows that the concept of childhood is grounded not in biology but in culture (LaRossa & Reitzes, 2001). In rich countries, not everyone has to work, so childhood can be extended to allow time for young people to learn the skills they will need in a high-technology workplace. Because childhood in North America lasts such a long time, some people worry when children seem to be growing up too fast. In part, this "hurried child" syndrome results from changes in the family—including high divorce rates and both parents in the labour force—that leave children with less supervision. In addition, adult programming on television, in films, and on the internet carries grown-up concerns such as sex, drugs, and violence into young lives. Today's

10- to 12-year-olds, says one executive of a children's television channel, have interests and experiences typical of 12- to 14-year-olds a generation ago (Hymowitz, 1998). Perhaps this is why today's children, when compared to kids 50 years ago, have higher levels of stress and anxiety (Gorman, 2000).

Adolescence

At the same time that industrialization created childhood as a distinct stage of life, adolescence emerged as a buffer between childhood and adulthood. We generally link *adolescence*, or the teenage years, with emotional and social turmoil as young people struggle to develop their own identities. Again, we are tempted to attribute teenage rebelliousness and confusion to the biological changes of puberty, but it correctly reflects cultural inconsistency; for example, the mass media glorify sex, and schools hand out condoms, even as parents urge restraint. Consider, too, that an 18-year-old can go off to war but lacks the adult right to drink a beer. In short, adolescence is a time of social contradictions, when people are no longer children but not yet adults.

As is true of all stages of life, adolescence varies according to social background. Most young people from working-class families move directly from high school into the adult world of work and parenting. Teens from wealthier families, however, have the resources to attend college or university and perhaps graduate school, stretching adolescence into the late twenties and even the thirties.

Adulthood

If stages of life were based on biological stages, it would be easy to define *adulthood*. However, deciding when someone is an adult turns out to be more complicated than it may seem. The term *adultescent* was coined in 1996 to describe people who are marrying, on average, four years later than in 1970, or not marrying at all, and who are living with their parents until they are 30 years of age or older—so that, in effect, "30 is the new 20" and "40 is the new 30" (Tierney, 2004). Regardless of its age of onset, adulthood is the time when life's major tasks, such as establishing a career and raising a family, are accomplished. Personalities are largely formed by then, although marked changes in one's circumstances—such as marriage, parenthood, unemployment, divorce, disability, or serious illness—cause significant changes to the self.

During early adulthood—until about age 40—young adults learn to manage day-to-day affairs for themselves, often juggling conflicting priorities: parents, partner, children, schooling, and work. Women are especially likely to

Randy Holmes/Getty Images

IN RECENT DECADES, SOME PEOPLE HAVE BECOME CONCERNED THAT SOCIETY IS SHORTENING CHILDHOOD, PUSHING CHILDREN TO GROW UP FASTER AND FASTER

In the television show *Pretty Little Liars*, this young woman in high school is having an affair with her teacher. Do television programs and films like this contribute to a "hurried child syndrome"? Do you see this as a problem or not? Why?

try to "do it all," because our culture gives them the major responsibility for child rearing and housework even if they have demanding jobs outside the home.

In middle adulthood—roughly ages 40 to 60—one's life circumstances are pretty well set. People become more aware of the fragility of health, which the young typically take for granted. Women who have spent many years raising a family find middle adulthood to be emotionally trying. Children grow up and require less attention, and husbands become absorbed in their careers, leaving some women with spaces in their lives that are difficult to fill. Many women who divorce also face serious financial problems (Weitzman, 1985, 1996). For all of these reasons, an increasing number of women in middle adulthood return to school and seek new careers.

For everyone, growing older means facing physical decline, a prospect that our culture makes especially painful for women. Because good looks are important for women, wrinkles and greying hair can be traumatic. Men have their own particular difficulties as they get older, perhaps worrying about the loss of hair or virility. Some must admit that they are never going to reach their career goals; others realize that the price of career success has been neglect of family, friends, and health.

Old Age

Old age comprises the later years of adulthood and the final stage of life itself, beginning in about the mid-sixties. Here again, societies attach different meanings to a time of life. Pre-industrial people typically grant elders great influence and prestige. Traditional societies confer on older people control of most of the land and other wealth; moreover, since their societies change slowly, older people amass a lifetime of wisdom, which earns them great respect (Hareven, 1982; Sheehan, 1976). In industrial societies, however, younger people work apart from the family, becoming more independent of their elders. Rapid change and our society's youth orientation combine to define anyone older as obsolete or even unimportant. To younger people, then, elderly people may be dismissed as old-fashioned and irrelevant. No doubt, however, this anti-elderly bias will diminish as the proportion of older people increases. The proportion of our population older than age 65 has tripled since the beginning of the twentieth century, and life expectancy is still increasing. Most men and women in their mid-sixties (the "young" elderly) can look forward to decades more of life. Statistics Canada reports that the population aged 80 years old had increased to 1.3 million by 2011, representing an increase of 43 percent from 2001 (Statistics Canada, 2011). The 4.9 million people aged 65 and older account for 14.8 percent of the Canadian population: The 1.3 million

Newscom

A COHORT IS A CATEGORY OF SIMILAR-AGE PEOPLE WHO SHARE COMMON LIFE EXPERIENCES Just as audiences at Rolling Stones concerts in the 1960s were mainly young people, so many of the group's fans today are the same people, now over age 60.

80 years of age and over make up 4.0 percent. The comparable figures for 2006 were 13.7 and 3.7 percent.

Old age differs in an important way from earlier stages. Growing up typically means entering new roles and assuming new responsibilities; growing old, in contrast, involves leaving roles that provided satisfaction and social identity. Retirement may turn out to be restful or rewarding, but it may mean the loss of valued activity, sometimes resulting in outright boredom. As another life transition, retirement demands learning new and different patterns while unlearning familiar routines, such as those associated with work.

Death and Dying

Through most of human history, death caused by disease or accident came at any age because of low living standards and primitive medical technology. In Canada today, however, the average lifespan is 79 years (76 for males, 83 for females). Therefore, while most senior citizens can look forward to more than another decade of life, growing old cannot be separated from eventual physical decline and, ultimately, death.

After observing many dying people, psychologist Elisabeth Kübler-Ross (1969) described death as an orderly transition involving five distinct stages. Typically, a person first faces death with *denial*, perhaps out of fear and perhaps because our culture largely ignores the reality of death. The second phase is *anger*, when a person facing death sees it as a gross injustice. Third, anger gives way to *negotiation* as the person imagines avoiding death by striking a bargain with God. The fourth response, *resignation*, is often accompanied by psychological depression. Finally, a complete adjustment to death requires *acceptance*. At this point, no longer paralyzed by fear and anxiety, the person whose life is ending finds peace and makes the most of whatever time remains.

As the proportion of older women and men increases in our society, we can expect our culture to become more comfortable with the idea of death. In recent years, we have started talking about death more openly and, increasingly, viewing dying as natural—and better than painful or prolonged suffering. More married couples now prepare for death with legal and financial planning, which may ease the pain of the surviving spouse who, most often, is a woman.

The Life Course: Patterns and Variations

This brief look at the life course points to two major conclusions. While each stage of life is linked to the biological process of aging, the life course is largely a social construction. For this reason, people in other societies may experience a stage of life quite differently or, for that matter, not at all. Next, in any society, the stages of the life course present certain problems and transitions that involve learning new routines and unlearning established routines.

Societies organize the life course according to age, but other forces—such as class, race, ethnicity, religion, and gender—also shape people's lives. This means that the general patterns described in this chapter apply differently to various categories of people within any society. Life experiences also vary depending on when, in the history of the society, people are born. A **cohort** is *a category of people with something in common, usually their age*. Because age cohorts are generally influenced by the same economic and cultural trends, they tend to have similar attitudes and values. Women and men born in the 1940s and 1950s, for example, grew up during a time of economic expansion that gave them a sense of optimism. Today's young people, who have grown up in an age of economic uncertainty, are less confident of the future.

Resocialization: Total Institutions

5.5 Characterize the operation of total institutions.

A final type of socialization involves being confined—usually against one's will—in prisons or psychiatric hospitals. This is the **total institution**, *a setting in which people are isolated from the rest of society and manipulated by an administrative staff*. According to Erving Goffman (1961), total institutions have three important characteristics. First, staff members supervise all aspects of daily life, including where residents (or inmates) eat, sleep, and work. Second, life in a total institution is controlled and standardized, with the same food, uniforms, and activities for everyone. And lastly, formal rules dictate when, where, and how inmates perform their daily routines.

The purpose of such rigid routines is **resocialization**, *efforts to effect radical change in an inmate's personality by carefully controlling the environment*. Prisons and psychiatric hospitals physically isolate inmates behind fences, barred windows, and locked doors and limit their access to the telephone, mail, and visitors. The institution becomes their entire world, making it easier for the staff to bring about personality change—or at least obedience—in the inmate.

Resocialization is a two-part process. The staff breaks down the new inmate's existing identity. For example, an inmate must give up personal possessions, including clothing and grooming articles used to maintain a distinctive appearance; in their place, the staff provides standard-issue clothes so that everyone looks alike. In prisons, the staff subjects new inmates to "mortifications of the self," which can include searches, head shaving, medical examinations, fingerprinting, and assignment of a serial number. Once inside the walls of a prison or psychiatric hospital, individuals also give up their privacy as guards or staff routinely inspect their living quarters.

In the second part of the resocialization process, the staff tries to build a new self in the inmate through a system of rewards and punishments. Having a book to read, watching television, or making a telephone call may seem like minor pleasures to the outsider, but, in the rigid environment of the total institution, gaining such simple privileges as these can be a powerful motivation to conform. The length of confinement or the condition of the patient typically depends on how well the inmate co-operates with the staff.

Total institutions affect people in different ways. Some inmates end up "rehabilitated" or "recovered," but others change little, and still others become hostile and bitter or increasingly withdrawn. Over a long period of time, living in a rigidly controlled environment can leave some *institutionalized*, without the capacity for independent living. The Controversy and Debate box takes a look at the effects on young offenders of short-term confinement in an Ontario strict-discipline facility or boot camp.

Controversy and Debate

Ontario's First Boot Camp as a Total Institution: 1997–2003

Resocialization in a total institution can actually change one's personality, or so the theory goes. The rebuilding of the self is extremely difficult, however, and no two people are likely to respond to any program in precisely the same way. Resocialization is the goal of prisons, psychiatric hospitals, and, in this case, Project Turnaround (1997–2003)—otherwise known as "boot camp." The key to the operation of a total institution such as a boot camp is complete control of the environment so that only desired behaviours are permitted.

Staff members with a background in the military or social work maintain discipline but are expected to treat inmates (called cadets) with respect. In return, the cadets are expected to refer to staff as "sir" or "ma'am"—and are made to do push-ups if they forget. The atmosphere is stern but not brutal: Cadets do not experience physical punishment or abuse.

On arrival, young offenders get military-style brush cuts and learn to make their beds and tie their shoes in the required way. They are introduced to discipline and plenty of it! Up at 6 A.M., lights out at 10 P.M., tidiness in austere surroundings, and a lot of marching to wherever they otherwise might have sauntered. Other detention centres may allow inmates to watch television; play Ping-Pong, pool, or video games; and even select their own food—idle moments are also part of an inmate's day. However, none of these is on the agenda at Project Turnaround. Instead, plenty of marching on the tarmac, more marching to and from various activities, calisthenics and some outdoor basketball and volleyball, three hours of school plus home-work, and meals fill up the typical day. Toward the end of their term, the cadets build cedar canoes—no mean achievement—and take them on a wilderness adventure, under staff supervision.

The program is designed, ultimately, to change cadet behaviour, attitudes, and values as well as to foster respect for themselves and for others. "Chins up. Look proud," they are told, in hopes that looking proud will make them feel proud. Those running the program believe that young people who respect themselves will be less inclined to return to a life of crime.

Postscript

Project Turnaround was created in 1997, during the period when Ontario Premier Mike Harris privatized a number of

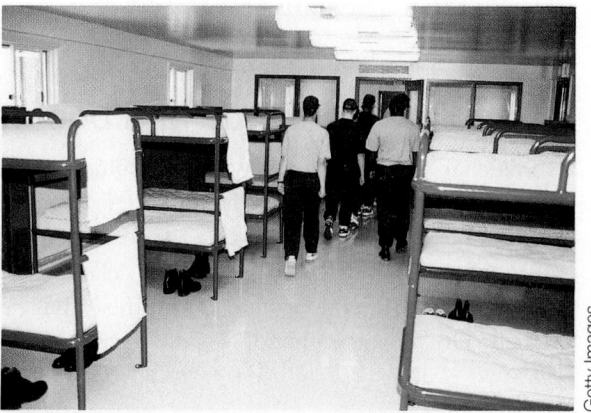

Getty Images

NEWLY ARRIVED CADETS, IN BLACK, MARCH IN FRONT OF THEIR GUARDS AT PROJECT TURNAROUND, A STRICT DISCIPLINE FACILITY IN COTTAGE COUNTRY NEAR ORILLIA, ONTARIO The staff hopes that, by the time inmates leave in four to six months, they will have learned to respect discipline and structure. In theory, the 32 repeat offenders will leave the facility with greater self-esteem, new attitudes and values, and a reduced likelihood of returning to crime.

public services, in part to achieve cost reductions. This new facility cost 33 percent less per inmate per day to run and achieved a recidivism (reoffending) rate that was 17 percent lower than for other youth detention facilities. Nonetheless, when Dalton McGuinty's Liberals defeated the Conservative government, his government cancelled Project Turnaround (in 2003)—partly in response to union demands. The local MPP, Garfield Dunlop (2003:236), brought the project story into the Ontario legislature, point-ing up its achievements (in cost and recidivism) and the loss of jobs in the Orillia area resulting from its cancellation.

What Do You Think?

1. Why did incarceration at Project Turnaround result in a recidivism rate 17 percent lower than for other youth detention facilities? What is it about their experience that made the inmates less likely to reoffend?

2. Does the "punishment fit the crime" or is boot camp "cruel and unusual punishment"?

3. If you were to be convicted of a crime, would you pre-fer to be sent to boot camp or to a conventional youth detention centre (or secure-custody facility)? Why?

Source: Based in part on Edwards (1997).

Seeing Sociology in Everyday Life

CHAPTER 5 Socialization

When do we grow up and become adults?

As this chapter explains, many factors come into play as we move from one stage of the life course to another. In global perspective, what makes our society unusual is that there is no one event that clearly tells everyone (and us, too) that the milestone of adulthood has been reached. On the other hand, we do have important events to say, for example, when someone completes high school (graduation ceremony) or becomes married (wedding ceremony). Look at the photos shown here. In each case, what do we learn about how the society defines the transition from one stage of life to another?

Hint Societies differ in how they structure the life course, including which stages of life are defined as important, what years of life various stages correspond to, and how clearly movement from one stage to another is marked. Given our cultural emphasis on individual choice and freedom, many people tend to say "You're only as old as you feel" and let people decide these things for themselves. When it comes to reaching adulthood, our society is not very clear, because so many factors are involved in the transition to adulthood. So we have no widely recognized "adult ritual," as seen in these photos. Keep in mind that, for us, class matters a lot in this process, with young people from more affluent families staying in school and delaying full adulthood until well into their twenties or even their thirties. Finally, in these tough economic times, the share of young people in their twenties living with parents goes way up and contributes to the blurring of boundaries between youth and adulthood.

Remi Benali/Corbis

AMONG THE HAMER PEOPLE IN THE OMO VALLEY OF ETHIOPIA, YOUNG BOYS MUST UNDERGO A TEST TO MARK THEIR TRANSITION TO MANHOOD Usually the event is triggered by the boy's expressing a desire to marry. In this ritual, witnessed by everyone in his society, the boy must jump over a line of bulls selected by the girl's family. If he succeeds in doing this three times, he is declared a man and the wedding can take place (marking the girl's transition to womanhood). Does our society have any ceremony or event similar to this to mark the transition to adulthood?

THESE YOUNG MEN AND WOMEN IN SEOUL, SOUTH KOREA, ARE PARTICIPATING IN A CONFUCIAN CEREMONY TO MARK THEIR BECOMING ADULTS This ritual, which takes place on the twentieth birthday, defines young people as full members of the community and also reminds them of all the responsibilities they are now expected to fulfill. If we had such a ritual in Canada, at what age would it take place? Would a person's social class affect the timing of this ritual?

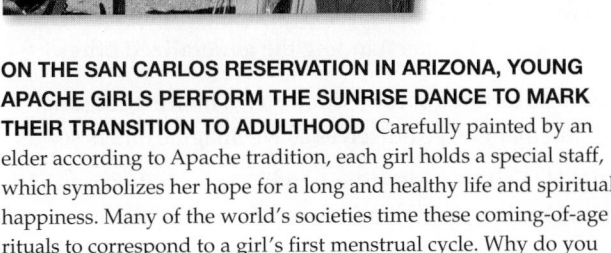

ON THE SAN CARLOS RESERVATION IN ARIZONA, YOUNG APACHE GIRLS PERFORM THE SUNRISE DANCE TO MARK THEIR TRANSITION TO ADULTHOOD Carefully painted by an elder according to Apache tradition, each girl holds a special staff, which symbolizes her hope for a long and healthy life and spiritual happiness. Many of the world's societies time these coming-of-age rituals to correspond to a girl's first menstrual cycle. Why do you think this is so?

Seeing Sociology in *Your* Everyday Life

1. Across Canada, many families plan elaborate parties to celebrate a young person's graduation from high school. In what respects is this event a ritual that symbolizes a person reaching adulthood? How does social class affect whether or not people define high school graduation as an achievement that marks the beginning of adulthood?

2. When does the stage of life we call "old age" begin? Is there an event that marks the transition to old age? Has the meaning of old age, and the age at which it begins, changed over the last several generations? Does social class play a part in defining this stage of life? If so, how?

3. In what sense are human beings free? After reading through this chapter, develop a personal statement of the extent to which you think you are able to guide your own life. Notice that some of the thinkers discussed in this chapter (such as Sigmund Freud) argued that there are sharp limits on our ability to act freely; by contrast, others (especially George Herbert Mead) claimed that human beings have significant ability to be creative. What is your personal statement about the extent of human freedom?

Making the Grade

CHAPTER 5 Socialization

Social Experience: The Key to Our Humanity

5.1 Describe how social interaction is the foundation of personality.

Socialization is a **lifelong process**.

- Socialization develops our humanity as well as our particular personalities.
- The importance of socialization is seen in the fact that extended periods of social isolation result in permanent damage (as in the cases of Anna, Isabelle, and Genie).

Socialization is a matter of **nurture** rather than **nature**.

- A century ago, most people thought human behaviour resulted from biological instinct.
- For us as human beings, it is our nature to nurture.

socialization the lifelong social experience by which people develop their human potential and learn culture
personality a person's fairly consistent patterns of acting, thinking, and feeling

Understanding Socialization

5.2 Explain six major theories of socialization.

Sigmund Freud's model of the human personality has three parts:

- **id:** innate, pleasure-seeking human drives
- **superego:** the demands of society in the form of internalized values and norms
- **ego:** our efforts to balance innate, pleasure-seeking drives and the demands of society

Jean Piaget believed that human development involves both biological maturation and gaining social experience. He identified four stages of cognitive development:

- The **sensorimotor stage** involves knowing the world only through the senses.
- The **pre-operational stage** involves starting to use language and other symbols.
- The **concrete operational stage** allows individuals to understand causal connections.
- The **formal operational stage** involves abstract and critical thought.

Lawrence Kohlberg applied Piaget's approach to stages of moral development:

- We first judge rightness in **preconventional** terms, according to our individual needs.

- Next, **conventional** moral reasoning takes account of parental attitudes and cultural norms.
- Finally, **postconventional** reasoning allows us to criticize society itself.

Carol Gilligan found that gender plays an important part in moral development, with males relying more on abstract standards of rightness and females relying more on the effects of actions on relationships.

To **George Herbert Mead**

- The **self** is part of our personality and includes self-awareness and self-image.
- The self develops only as a result of social experience.
- Social experience involves the exchange of symbols.
- Social interaction depends on understanding the intention of another, which requires taking the role of the other.
- Human action is partly spontaneous (the I) and partly in response to others (the me).
- We gain social experience through imitation, play, games, and understanding the **generalized other**.

Charles Horton Cooley used the term **looking-glass self** to explain that we see ourselves as we imagine others see us.

Erik H. Erikson identified challenges that individuals face at each stage of life from infancy to old age.

id Freud's term for the human being's basic drives
ego Freud's term for a person's conscious efforts to balance innate pleasure-seeking drives with the demands of society
superego Freud's term for the cultural values and norms internalized by an individual
sensorimotor stage Piaget's term for the level of human development at which individuals experience the world only through their senses
pre-operational stage Piaget's term for the level of human development at which individuals first use language and other symbols
concrete operational stage Piaget's term for the level of human development at which individuals first see causal connections in their surroundings
formal operational stage Piaget's term for the level of human development at which individuals think abstractly and critically
self George Herbert Mead's term for the part of an individual's personality composed of self-awareness and self-image
looking-glass self Cooley's term for a self-image based on how we think others see us
significant others people, such as parents, who have special importance for socialization
generalized other George Herbert Mead's term for widespread cultural norms and values we use as references in evaluating ourselves

Agents of Socialization

5.3 **Analyze how the family, school, peer groups, and the mass media guide the socialization process.**

The **family** is usually the first setting of socialization.

- Family has the greatest impact on attitudes and behaviour.
- A family's social position, including race and social class, shapes a child's personality.
- Ideas about gender are learned first in the family.

Schools give most children their first experience with bureaucracy and impersonal evaluation.

- Schools teach knowledge and skills needed for later life.
- Schools expose children to greater social diversity.
- Schools reinforce ideas about gender.

The **peer group** helps shape attitudes and behaviour.

- The peer group takes on great importance during adolescence.
- The peer group frees young people from adult supervision.

The **mass media** have a huge impact on socialization in modern, high-income societies.

- The average North American child spends as much time watching television and videos as attending school and interacting with parents.
- The mass media often reinforce stereotypes about gender and race.
- The mass media expose people to a great deal of violence.

> **peer group** a social group whose members have interests, social position, and age in common
> **anticipatory socialization** learning that helps a person achieve a desired position
> **mass media** the means for delivering impersonal communications to a vast audience

Socialization and the Life Course

5.4 **Discuss how our society organizes human experience into distinctive stages of life.**

The concept of **childhood** is grounded not in biology but in culture. In high-income countries, childhood is extended.

The emotional and social turmoil of **adolescence** results from cultural inconsistency in defining people who are not children but not yet adults. Adolescence varies by social class.

Adulthood is the stage of life when most accomplishments take place. Although personality is now formed, it continues to change with new life experiences.

Old age is defined as much by culture as biology.

- Traditional societies give power and respect to elders.
- Industrial societies define elders as unimportant and out of touch.

Acceptance of **death and dying** is part of socialization for the elderly. This process typically involves five stages: denial, anger, negotiation, resignation, and acceptance.

> **cohort** a category of people with something in common, usually their age

Resocialization: Total Institutions

5.5 **Characterize the operation of total institutions.**

Total institutions include prisons, psychiatric hospitals, and monasteries.

- Staff members supervise all aspects of life.
- Life is standardized, with all inmates following set rules and routines.

Resocialization is a two-part process:

- breaking down inmates' existing identity
- building a new self through a system of rewards and punishments

> **total institution** a setting in which people are isolated from the rest of society and controlled by an administrative staff
> **resocialization** efforts to effect radical change in an inmate's personality by carefully controlling the environment

Chapter 6
Social Interaction in Everyday Life

David J. Green/Alamy Stock Photo

Learning Objectives

6.1 Explain how social structure helps us to make sense of everyday situations.

6.2 State the importance of status to social organization.

6.3 State the importance of role to social organization.

6.4 Describe how we socially construct reality.

6.5 Apply Goffman's analysis to several familiar situations.

6.6 Construct a sociological analysis of three aspects of everyday life: emotions, language, and humor.

The Power of Society
to guide the way we do social networking

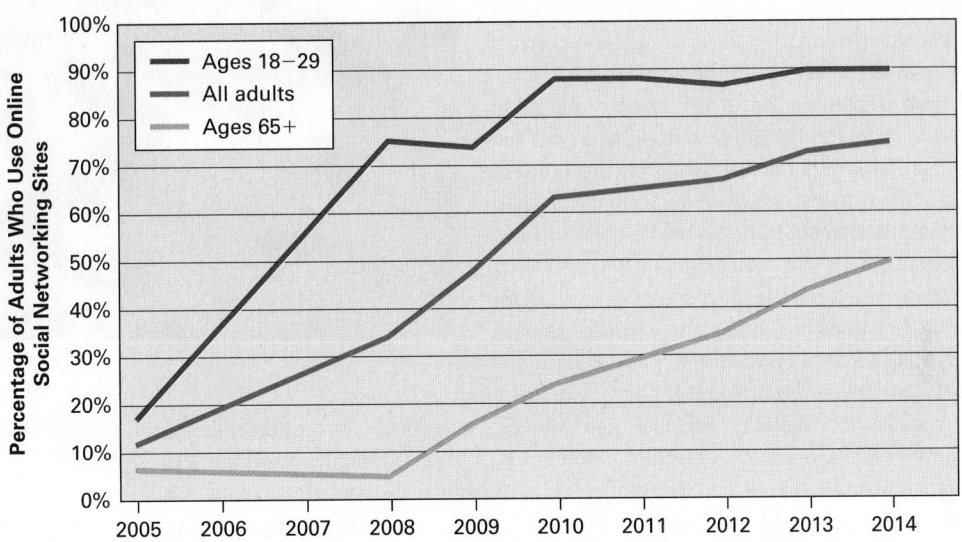

SOURCE: Pew Research Center, Internet and American Life Project. "Social Media Use by Age Group Over Time." 2014. Available at http://www.pewinternet.org/data-trend/social-media/social-media-use-by-age-group.

Is our use of social networking sites as much of a personal choice as we may think? This study of American adults suggests not. Overall, rates of social networking increased from 10 to 74 percent over the nine-year period between 2005 and 2014. But age is a powerful predictor of social media use—resulting in vastly different patterns of adoption by young adults and their older counterparts. Young adults (aged 18 to 29)—perhaps in response to peer pressure or the need to belong—exhibit massive social change in the first three years by increasing their social networking from 15 to 75 percent. In comparison, older adults (aged 65 and over) are laggards whose use of such sites stalled at around 5 percent over the initial three-year period—before increasing steadily to 50 percent by 2014. But by that time a phenomenal 89 percent of young adults were immersed in social networking!

Chapter Overview

This chapter takes a "micro-level" look at society, examining patterns of everyday social interaction. First, the chapter identifies important social structures, including status and role. Then it explains how we construct reality through social interaction. Finally, it applies the lessons learned to everyday experiences involving emotion, gender, and humour.

Matt and Dianne are on their way to visit friends in an unfamiliar section of Calgary. They are now late because, for the last 20 minutes, they have been going in circles looking for Riverview Drive. Matt, gripping the wheel ever more tightly, is doing a slow burn. Dianne, sitting next to him, looks straight ahead, afraid to utter a word. Both realize that the evening is off to a bad start.

Here we have a simple case of two people unable to locate the home of some friends. But Matt and Dianne are lost in more ways than one, failing to see why they are growing more and more angry with their situation and with each other.

Consider the predicament from the man's point of view. Matt cannot tolerate getting lost—the longer he drives around, the more incompetent he feels. Dianne is seething, too, but for a different reason. She does not understand why Matt refuses to pull over and ask for directions. If she were driving, she fumes to herself, they would be comfortably settled with their friends by now.

Why don't men ask for directions? Because men value their independence, they are uncomfortable asking for help—and are also reluctant to accept it. To men, asking for assistance is an admission of inadequacy, a sure sign that others know something they do not. So what if it takes Matt a few more minutes to find Riverview Drive on his own, keeping his self-respect in the process?

Women are more in tune with others and strive for connectedness. From Dianne's point of view, asking for help from others is the right course of action—and it gets the job done. Asking for directions seems as natural to her as finding the street himself is to Matt. Because neither of them understands the other's point of view, getting lost is sure to result in conflict. ■

Such everyday experiences are the focus of this chapter. The central concept is **social interaction**, *the process by which people act and react in relation to others*. We begin by presenting several important sociological concepts that describe the building blocks of common experience and then explore the almost magical way that face-to-face interaction creates the reality in which we live.

Social Structure: A Guide to Everyday Living

6.1 Explain how social structure helps us to make sense of everyday situations.

Imagine yourself and your young family on vacation, arriving in Ho Chi Minh City, Vietnam. As you leave the docks, security officers wave you through heavy metal gates. Pressed along the fence are dozens of men who operate cyclos (bicycles with small carriages attached to the front), the Vietnamese version of taxicabs. You wave them off and spend the next 20 minutes shaking your heads at several drivers who pedal alongside, pleading for your business. The pressure is uncomfortable. You decide to cross the street but realize that there are no stop signs or traffic lights—and the street is an unbroken stream of bicycles, cyclos, motorbikes, and small trucks. The locals don't bat an eye; they just walk at a steady pace across the street, parting waves of vehicles that immediately close in again behind them. Walk right into traffic? With small children on your backs? Yup, you do it; that's the way it works in Vietnam.

Members of every society rely on social structure to make sense of everyday situations and frame their lives. The world can be confusing—even frightening—when society's rules are unclear. We now take a closer look at the ways societies set the rules of everyday life.

Fred Chartrand/The Canadian Press

FORMER GOVERNOR GENERAL MICHAËLLE JEAN, ONCE COMMANDER-IN-CHIEF OF CANADIAN FORCES, IS REVIEWING TROOPS IN THIS PHOTO In any rigidly ranked setting, no interaction can proceed until people assess each other's social standing; thus, military personnel wear clear insignia to designate their level of authority. Don't we size up one another in much the same way in routine interaction, noting a person's rough age, quality of clothing, and manner for clues about social position?

Frank Gunn/The Canadian Press

MIKE MYERS POSES WITH LORNE MICHAELS AFTER THE TWO UNVEILED THEIR STARS ON CANADA'S WALK OF FAME IN TORONTO IN 2003 Are there qualities that make Mike Myers a role model for young people?

Status

6.2 State the importance of status to social organization.

In every society, one of the building blocks of everyday life is **status**, *a social position that a person holds*. In general use, the word status means "prestige," in the sense that a university president is of higher status than a newly hired assistant professor. But sociologically speaking, "president," "professor," and "student" are statuses within the university organization. Status is part of social identity and helps define our relationships to others. As Georg Simmel (1950; orig. 1902), one of the founders of sociology, once pointed out, before we can deal with anyone, we need to know who the person is.

Status Set

Each of us holds many statuses at once. The term **status set** refers to *all of the statuses that a person holds at a given time*. A teenage girl is a daughter to her parents, a sister to her brother, a student at school, and a goalie on her hockey team. Status sets change over the life course. A

child grows up to become a parent, a student graduates to become a lawyer, and a single person marries to become a husband or wife, sometimes becoming single again as a result of death or divorce. Joining an organization or finding a job enlarges our status set; withdrawing from activities makes it smaller. Over a lifetime, people gain and lose dozens of statuses.

Ascribed and Achieved Status

Sociologists classify statuses in terms of how people obtain them. An **ascribed status** is *a social position that someone receives at birth or assumes involuntarily later in life*. Examples of statuses that are generally ascribed include being a daughter, an Aboriginal person, a teenager, or a widower. Ascribed statuses are matters about which people have little or no choice. In contrast, an **achieved status** refers to *a social position that someone assumes voluntarily and that reflects personal ability and effort*. Among achieved statuses are being an honour student, an Olympic athlete, a spouse, a computer programmer, a Rhodes Scholar, or a thief. In each case, the individual has at least some choice in the matter.

In practice, most statuses involve some combination of ascription and achievement. That is, ascribed status affects achieved status. Adults who achieve the status of lawyer, for example, are likely to share the ascribed trait of being born into relatively privileged families. And any person of privileged sex, race, ethnicity, or age has far more opportunity to realize desirable achieved statuses than does someone without such advantages. In contrast, less desirable statuses, such as criminal, drug addict, or welfare recipient, are more easily acquired by people born into poverty.

---

status a social position that a person holds

ascribed status a social position a person receives at birth or takes on involuntarily later in life

achieved status a social position a person takes on voluntarily that reflects personal ability and effort

status set all the statuses a person holds at a given time

master status a status that has special importance for social identity, often shaping a person's entire life

Master Status

Some statuses matter more than others. A **master status** is *a status that has exceptional importance for social identity, often shaping a person's entire life.* For many people, occupation is a master status, because it conveys a great deal about social background, education, and income. Family of birth or marriage can function this way, too. Being an Eaton, a McCain, a Trudeau, a Mulroney, or a Stronach is enough by itself to push an individual into the limelight. Most societies of the world also limit the opportunities of women, whatever their abilities, making gender, too, a master status.

In a negative sense, serious disease also operates as a master status. Sometimes even lifelong friends avoid people with cancer, AIDS, or mental illness—simply because of the illness. In part, this is because we do not know what to say or how to act. We sometimes dehumanize people with physical disabilities by perceiving them only in terms of their disability. Although it is not a disability in the same sense, being too tall (e.g., a 6'4" woman), too fat, or too thin can act as a master status that gets in the way of normal social interaction.

Role

6.3 State the importance of role to social organization.

A second important component of social structure is **role**, *behaviour expected of someone who holds a particular status.* A person holds a status and performs a role (Linton, 1937). For example, holding the status of student leads you to perform the roles of attending classes and completing assignments.

Statuses and roles vary by culture. In North America, the status of "uncle" refers to the brother of either your mother or your father, and the role of your maternal and paternal uncles might be much the same. In Vietnam, however, the word for "uncle" is different on the mother's and father's sides of the family and implies different responsibilities. In every society, actual role performance varies according to an individual's unique personality, although some societies permit more individual expression of a role than others.

Role Set

Because we hold many statuses at once—a status set—everyday life is a mix of multiple roles. Robert Merton

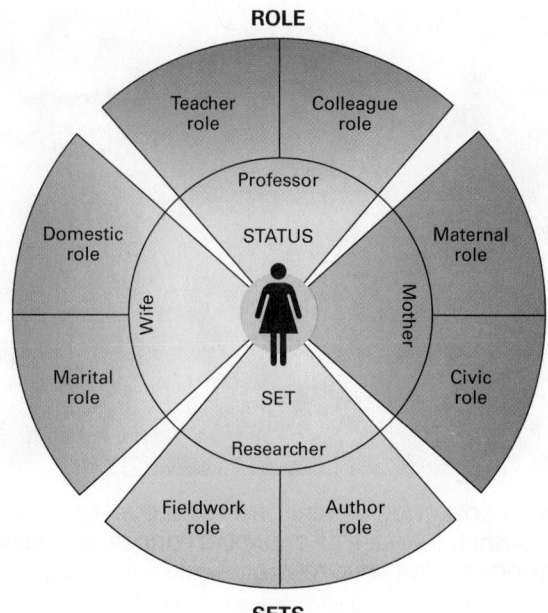

ROLE

Teacher role / Colleague role / Professor / STATUS / Domestic role / Maternal role / Wife / Mother / Marital role / Civic role / SET / Researcher / Fieldwork role / Author role

SETS

Figure 6–1 Status Set and Role Set

A status set includes the statuses a person holds at a given time. Because each status usually involves more than one role, a role set is even larger.

SOURCE: Created by John J. Macionis.

(1968) introduced the term **role set** to identify *a number of roles attached to a single status.*

Figure 6–1 shows four statuses of one person, each status linked to a different role set. First, in her status as a professor, this woman interacts with students (teacher role) and with other academics (colleague role). Second, in her status as a researcher, she gathers and analyzes data (fieldwork role) that she uses in her publications (author role). Third, the woman occupies the status of wife, with a marital role (such as confidante and sexual partner) toward her husband, with whom she shares household duties (domestic role). Fourth, she holds the status of mother, with routine responsibilities for her children (maternal role), as well as toward their school and other organizations in her community (civic role).

A global perspective shows that the roles people use to define their lives differ from society to society. In general, in low-income countries, people spend fewer years as students, and family roles are often very important to social identity. In high-income nations, people spend more years as students, and family roles typically are less important to social identity. Another dimension of difference involves housework. As Global Map 6–1 shows, especially in poor countries, housework falls heavily on women.

Role Conflict and Role Strain

People in modern, high-income nations juggle many responsibilities demanded by their various statuses and

Window on the World

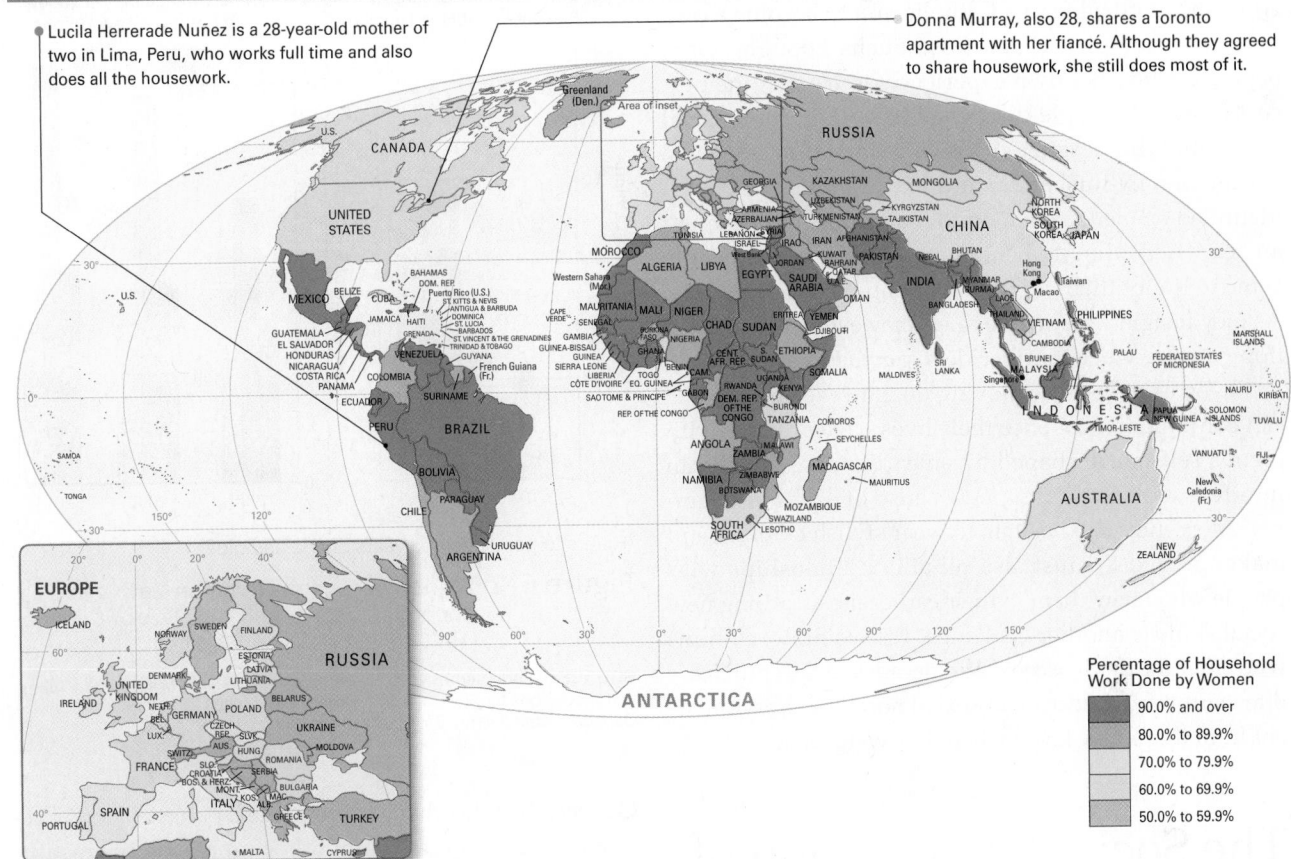

Lucila Herrerade Nuñez is a 28-year-old mother of two in Lima, Peru, who works full time and also does all the housework.

Donna Murray, also 28, shares a Toronto apartment with her fiancé. Although they agreed to share housework, she still does most of it.

Percentage of Household Work Done by Women

- 90.0% and over
- 80.0% to 89.9%
- 70.0% to 79.9%
- 60.0% to 69.9%
- 50.0% to 59.9%

Global Map 6–1 Housework in Global Perspective

Throughout the world, housework is a major part of women's routines and identities. This is especially true in poor nations of Latin America, Africa, and Asia, where the social position of women is far below that of men. But our society also defines housework and child care as "feminine" activities, even though women and men have the same legal rights and most women work outside the home.

SOURCE: United Nations (2010).

---

roles. As most mothers—and more and more fathers—can testify, the combination of parenting and working outside the home is physically and emotionally draining. Sociologists therefore recognize **role conflict** as *conflict among the roles connected to two or more statuses.* We experience role conflict when we find ourselves pulled in various directions as we try to respond to the many statuses we hold. One response to role conflict is deciding that something has to go. More than one politician, for example, has decided not to run for office because of the conflicting demands of a hectic campaign schedule and family life. In other cases, people put off having children in order to stay on the fast track for career success.

Even roles linked to a single status may make competing demands on us. **Role strain** refers to *tension among the roles connected to a single status.* A professor may enjoy being friendly with students; at the same time, however, she must maintain the personal distance needed in order

to evaluate students fairly. In short, performing the various roles attached to even one status can be something of a balancing act.

One strategy for minimizing role conflict is separating parts of our lives so that we perform roles for one status at one time, and place and carry out roles connected to another status in a completely different setting. A familiar example is leaving the job at work before heading home to one's family. People who work from their homes—full-time or part of the time, like most of your professors—often have considerable difficulty separating job and family life.

Role conflict and role strain are easy to confuse, unless you remember that it takes two to have conflict. Therefore, role conflict arises among roles linked to separate statuses, while role strain is tension arising among roles linked to a single status. Applying these concepts to your own life can help you keep them straight.

Role Exit

After she left the life of a Catholic nun to become a university sociologist, Helen Rose Fuchs Ebaugh (1988) began to study her own experience of *role exit*, the process by which people disengage from important social roles. Studying a range of "exes"—including ex-nuns, ex-doctors, ex-husbands, and ex-alcoholics—Ebaugh identified elements common to the process of becoming an "ex." According to her, the process begins as people come to doubt their ability to continue in a certain role. As they imagine alternative roles, they eventually reach a tipping point when they decide to pursue a new life.

Even as people are moving on, however, a past role can continue to influence their lives. "Exes" carry with them a self-image shaped by an earlier role, which can interfere with building a new sense of self. For example, an ex-nun may hesitate to wear stylish clothing and makeup. "Exes" must also rebuild relationships with people who knew them in their earlier life. Learning new social skills is another challenge. For example, ex-nuns who enter the dating scene after decades in the church are often surprised to learn that sexual norms are very different from those they knew when they were teenagers.

The Social Construction of Reality

6.4 Describe how we socially construct reality.

While behaviour is guided by status and role, each human has considerable ability to shape what happens moment to moment. "Reality," in other words, is not as fixed as we may think. The phrase **social construction of reality** identifies *the process by which people creatively shape reality through social interaction*. This is the foundation of sociology's symbolic-interaction paradigm, as described in earlier chapters. It means that social interaction amounts to negotiating reality.

One area in which personal decisions have restructured social reality is that of family formation. Figure 6–2(a) reveals that, in the 25-year period between 1970 and 1995, the proportion of *first unions* that were common-law increased dramatically—from 17 to 57 percent across Canada and from 21 to an astounding 80 percent in Quebec. Think about it: As Quebec couples negotiated the terms of their first unions, *8 out of 10* chose to cohabit rather than marry. Figure 6–2(b) reveals that Quebec's lead in the formation of common-law unions persisted to Census 2011. Over 15 years (1996 to 2011) the proportion of Quebecers (15 and older) living common-law increased from about 14 to 21 percent; among Canadians outside

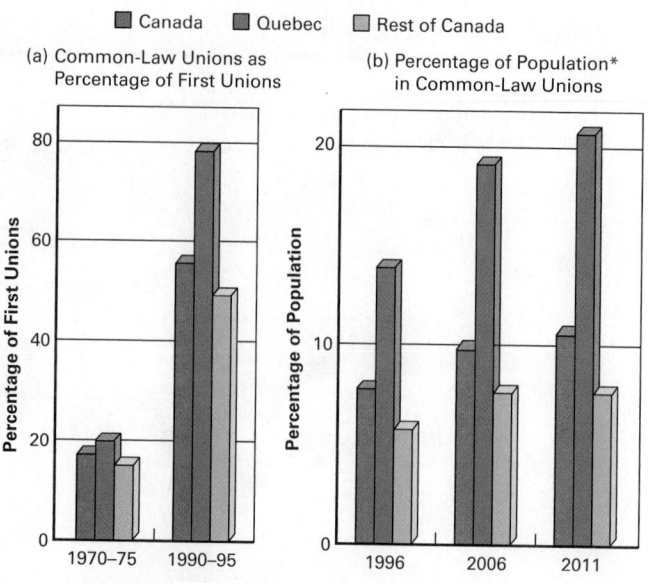

■ Canada   ■ Quebec   ■ Rest of Canada

(a) Common-Law Unions as Percentage of First Unions

(b) Percentage of Population* in Common-Law Unions

*Refers to population 15 years of age and older.

Figure 6–2 The Prevalence of Common-Law Unions in Canada, Quebec, and the Rest of Canada (1970 to 2011)

SOURCE: (a) Adapted by L.M. Gerber from Turcotte and Bélanger (2000); (b) Calculations for 2011 by L.M. Gerber from Census 2011 Statistics Canada, Catalogue no. 98-312-X2011044.

Quebec, the rates changed from 6 to 8 percent. The collective impact of these common-law unions on the institution of marriage is far greater than that of the gays and lesbians who benefit from the redefinition of marriage to include same-sex couples. For the symbolic interactionist, the important elements in this restructuring of social life are the personal decisions made by the roughly 3 million Canadians who chose cohabitation, thereby creating a new social reality.

For another example of the social construction of reality, consider how this excerpt from "True Trash," a short story by Margaret Atwood, illustrates one way that names and clothing styles construct a certain type of person.

> Eleven years later Donny is walking along Yorkville Avenue, in Toronto, in the summer heat. He's no longer Donny. At some point, which even he can't remember exactly, he has changed into Don. He's wearing sandals, and a white Indian-style shirt over his cut-off jeans. He has longish hair and a beard. The beard has come out yellow, whereas the hair is brown. He likes the effect: wasp Jesus or Hollywood Viking, depending on his mood. He has a string of wooden beads around his neck.
>
> This is how he dresses on Saturdays, to go to Yorkville; to go there and just hang around, with the crowds of others who are doing the same. Sometimes he gets high, on the pot that circulates as freely as cigarettes did once. He thinks he should be enjoying this experience more than he actually does.

During the rest of the week he has a job in his father's law office. He can get away with the beard there, just barely, as long as he balances it with a suit. (But even the older guys are growing their sideburns and wearing coloured shirts, and using words like "creative" more than they used to.) He doesn't tell the people he meets in Yorkville about this job, just as he doesn't tell the law office about his friends' acid trips. He's leading a double life. It feels precarious, and brave. (Atwood, 1991:30–31)

This situation reveals the drama by which humans create reality. Not everyone enters a negotiation with equal standing. The fact that Donny was the son of the lawyer in whose office he was working likely helped him bridge the two realities.

Don's narrative illustrates the fact that "reality" is not as fixed as you may think. Today, people use internet sites such as Facebook and YouTube to present themselves to others, thereby creating a "reality" that may bear little resemblance to the reality constructed through face-to-face interaction.

The Thomas Theorem

Donny's impression management allowed him to be part of the Yorkville scene and his father's law office. W.I. Thomas (1966:301; orig. 1931) succinctly explained this phenomenon in what has come to be known as the **Thomas theorem**: *Situations we define as real become real in their consequences.* Applied to social interaction, Thomas's insight means that, although reality is "soft" as it is socially constructed, it can become "hard" in its effects. Donny, having succeeded as a member of two very different groups, is able to lead a double life.

Ethnomethodology

Most of the time, we take social reality for granted. To help us understand the world we create, Harold Garfinkel (1967) developed the approach called **ethnomethodology**, *the study of the way people make sense of their everyday surroundings.* This approach begins by pointing out that everyday behaviour rests on a number of assumptions. When you ask someone the simple question "How are you?" you usually want to know how the person is doing in general, but you might really be wondering how the person is dealing with a specific physical, mental, spiritual, or financial challenge. However,

Ron Chapple/Taxi/Getty Images

FLIRTING IS AN EVERYDAY EXPERIENCE IN REALITY CONSTRUCTION Each person offers information to the other and hints at romantic interest. Yet the interaction proceeds with a tentative and often humorous air so that either individual can withdraw at any time without further obligation.

the person being asked probably assumes that you are not really interested in details about any of these things, and that you are just being polite.

Staton R. Winter/The New York Times/Redux Pictures

PEOPLE BUILD REALITY FROM THEIR SURROUNDING CULTURE Yet, because cultural systems are marked by diversity and even outright conflict, reality construction always involves tensions and choices. Turkey is a nation with a mostly Muslim population, but it is also a country that has embraced Western culture. Here, women confront starkly different definitions of what is "feminine."

One good way to uncover the assumptions we make about reality is to purposely *break the rules*. For example, the next time someone greets you by saying "How're you doing?" offer details from your last physical examination, or explain all of the good and bad things that have happened since you woke up that morning, and see how the person reacts. To test assumptions about how closely people should stand to each other while talking, slowly move closer to another person during a conversation. What happens if you face the back of the elevator, or—if you are a woman—you take your boyfriend or partner's hand from the front?

The results are predictable, because we all have some idea of what the "rules" of everyday interaction are. Witnesses to your rule breaking will most likely become confused or irritated by your unexpected behaviour, a reaction that helps us see not only what the "rules" are but also how important they are to everyday reality.

Reality Building: Class and Culture

People do not build everyday experience out of thin air. In part, how we act or what we see in our surroundings depends on our interests. Gazing at the sky on a starry night, for example, lovers discover romance and scientists see hydrogen atoms fusing into helium. Social background also affects what we see: For this reason, residents of affluent Westmount in Montreal experience the city differently from those living in the city's east end, where the unemployment rate is one of the highest in Canada.

In global perspective, reality construction is even more variable. Consider these everyday situations: People waiting for their luggage in a Swedish airport stand behind a yellow line about 3 metres from the conveyor belt that carries the bags and step forward only when they see their bags passing by; in Canada, we push right up to the conveyor system and lean forward looking for our bags. People waiting for a bus in London, England, typically queue in a straight line; people in Montreal wait in a much less orderly fashion. Constraints on women in Saudi Arabia—for example, they are not allowed to drive cars—would be incomprehensible here. In Canada, we assume that "a short walk" means a few blocks; in the Andes Mountains of Peru, "a short walk" may mean several kilometres.

The point is that people construct reality in the contexts of their cultures. The chapter on, Culture explains that people the world over find different meanings in specific gestures, so that inexperienced travellers using a gesture such as "thumbs up" can find themselves building an unexpected and unwelcome reality. Similarly, in a study of popular culture, Shively (1992) screened "westerns" to men of European descent and to Aboriginal men. The men in both categories claimed to enjoy the films, but

for very different reasons. The men of European descent interpreted the films as praising rugged people striking out for the West and conquering the forces of nature. The Aboriginal men saw in the same films a celebration of land and nature. It is as if the people in the two groups saw two different films.

Films can also have an effect on the reality we all experience. The film *Ray*, about the life of musician Ray Charles, who overcame the challenge of blindness, and *Adam*, about a man who lives with Asperger's syndrome, are the latest in a series of films that have changed the public's awareness of disabilities. (See the Sociology and the Media box.)

Dramaturgical Analysis: The "Presentation of Self"

6.5 Apply Goffman's analysis to several familiar situations.

Erving Goffman is another sociologist who studied social interaction, explaining how people live their lives much like actors performing on a stage. If we imagine ourselves as directors observing what goes on in the theatre of everyday life, we are doing what Goffman called **dramaturgical analysis**, *the study of social interaction in terms of theatrical performance*.

Dramaturgical analysis offers a fresh look at the concepts of "status" and "role." A status is like a part in a play, and a role serves as a script, supplying dialogue and action for the characters. Goffman described each individual's "performance" as the **presentation of self**, *a person's efforts to create specific impressions in the minds of others*. This process, sometimes called impression management, begins with the idea of personal performance (Goffman, 1959, 1967). The Sociology and the Media box invites you to try your hand at dramaturgical analysis by taking a look at presentation of self and performance in the context of master status based on disability—in the context of major Hollywood films.

To make sure that you understand Goffman's dramaturgical analysis, try applying the technique to a lecture, a rock concert, a job interview, or a church service. Wherever people manage the presentation of self, you can analyze social interaction in terms of a theatrical performance. Think of stage (and backstage), costume, script, role, rehearsal, and, ultimately, performance.

Performances

As we present ourselves in everyday situations, we reveal information—consciously and unconsciously—to others. Our performance includes the way we dress (costume),

Sociology and the Media

Disease and Disability in Hollywood Film: 20 Years of Change

Jamie Foxx won an Oscar (for best actor) for his brilliant portrayal of the blind musician Ray Charles. The film, *Ray*, is part of a series that has raised public awareness of the challenges faced—and frequently overcome—by people with disabilities. This is good news for people with disabilities and for the people who help them. Most importantly, people with disabilities are being portrayed with greater accuracy and realism, so that the public learns what it means to live with a specific illness or disability. These films give human faces to various conditions and remove some of the fear that comes with lack of knowledge or unfamiliarity. They also illustrate the powerful grip of a master status defined by disability as well as the consequences of these disabilities for presentation of self and the performances of everyday life.

The first of these influential movies, *The Miracle Worker*, came out in 1962, telling the story of Helen Keller who, though both deaf and blind, was taught to communicate by her persistent tutor, Annie Sullivan. The Helen Keller National Center for Deaf-Blind Youths and Adults is still reaping the benefits of that film more than 50 years later.

In the past two decades, people with a wide range of disabilities have been the subjects of perhaps 15 major motion pictures. So important are these films that it seems one cannot win an Oscar or a nomination for best actor without playing a severely troubled or challenged character. Dustin Hoffman portrays a man with autism in *Rain Man;* Anthony Hopkins plays a man who is criminally insane in *The Silence of the Lambs;* and Al Pacino portrays blindness in *Scent of a Woman.* Tom Hanks has AIDS in *Philadelphia* and is developmentally challenged in *Forrest Gump.* In *Leaving Las Vegas,* Nicholas Cage portrays an alcoholic, while Jack Nicholson plays someone with obsessive-compulsive disorder in *As Good as It Gets.* Leonardo DiCaprio portrays a developmentally challenged younger brother, Arnie, in *What's Eating Gilbert Grape*—and later plays the disturbed and reclusive Howard Hughes in *The Aviator.*

Each of these powerful films takes us into a previously unknown world and allows us to identify with someone who faces seemingly insurmountable physical and psychological challenges. These films destigmatize disabilities and encourage donations to meaningful causes. At the very least, after viewing them, we should be more sensitive to and empathetic with the disabled people we encounter. In addition, we might be more willing to donate time or money to the organizations that do research and provide services for people with a range of disabilities. Often the actors themselves take up the cause, using their clout to raise funds, as did Tom Hanks after filming *Philadelphia*.

Among the films that depict the triumph of talent or genius over the adversity of physical or psychological disability are *My Left Foot,* in which Daniel Day-Lewis portrays Irish writer/artist Christy Brown, whose cerebral palsy leaves him in total control of only his left foot; *Shine,* in which Geoffrey Rush portrays Australian concert pianist David Helfgott, whose early career is ruined by a nervous breakdown; and *A Beautiful Mind,* in which Russell Crowe assumes the role of John Nash, mathematical genius and Nobel Laureate who suffers from paranoid schizophrenia. In a recent film (2009), Hugh Dancy portrays *Adam*—a man who has Asperger's syndrome.

Each story, embellished though it is by Hollywood, is based on a true story and on the life of a real—and inspiring—individual. In each case, the individual achieves greatness despite the overarching master status defined by his disability. In these films, we see performances—or presentation of self—at two levels: those of the characters portrayed in the films and those of the brilliant actors who portray them.

What Do You Think?

1. Can you point to specific lessons about disabilities that we can learn from films?

2. Have you seen any of the films mentioned in this box? Why did you choose to see them and what were your reactions?

3. Can you apply dramaturgical analysis to these films? Can you do so at the two levels noted above?

SOURCE: Based, in part, on Haberman (2005).

---

the objects we carry (props), and our tone of voice and gestures (manner). In addition, we vary our performances according to where we are (the set). We may joke loudly in a restaurant, for example, but lower our voices when entering a church or other place of worship. People also design settings, such as homes or offices, to bring about desired reactions in others.

AN APPLICATION: THE DOCTOR'S OFFICE Consider how a physician uses an office to convey particular information to the audience of patients. The fact that physicians enjoy high prestige and power is clear on entering a doctor's office. First, the doctor is nowhere to be seen. Instead, in what Goffman describes as the "front region" of the setting, each patient encounters a receptionist, or gatekeeper, who decides whether and when the patient can meet the doctor. A simple glance around the doctor's waiting room, with patients—often impatiently—waiting to be invited into the inner sanctum, leaves little doubt that the doctor and the staff are in charge.

David Sipress/The New Yorker Collection/The Cartoon Bank

The "back region" of the setting is composed of the examination room plus the doctor's private office. Once inside the office, a patient can see a wide range of props, such as medical books and framed degrees, that give the impression that the doctor has the specialized knowledge necessary to call the shots. The doctor is often seated behind a desk—the larger the desk, the greater the statement of power—and a patient is given only a chair.

The doctor's appearance and manner offer still more information. The white lab coat (costume) may have the practical function of keeping clothes from becoming dirty, but its social function is to let others know at a glance the physician's status. A stethoscope around the neck, and a medical chart in hand (more props), have the same purpose. A doctor uses highly technical language that is often mystifying to a patient, again emphasizing that the doctor is in charge. A patient usually uses the title "Doctor," but the doctor often addresses a patient by his or her first name, which further shows the doctor's dominant position. The overall message of a doctor's performance is clear: "I will help you, but you must allow me to take charge."

Non-Verbal Communication

Novelist William Sansom describes a fictional Mr. Preedy, an English vacationer on a beach in Spain:

> He took care to avoid catching anyone's eye. First, he had to make it clear to those potential companions of his holiday that they were of no concern to him whatsoever. He stared through them, round them, over them—eyes lost in space. The beach might have been empty. If by chance a ball was thrown his way, he looked surprised; then let a smile of amusement light his face (Kindly Preedy), looked around dazed to see that there were people on the beach, tossed it back with a smile to himself and not a smile at the people. . . .
>
> [He] then gathered together his beach-wrap and bag into a neat sand-resistant pile (Methodical and Sensible Preedy), rose slowly to stretch his huge frame (Big-Cat Preedy), and tossed aside his sandals (Carefree Preedy, after all).

Without saying a single word, Mr. Preedy offers a great deal of information about himself to anyone watching him. This is the process of **non-verbal communication**, *communication using body movements, gestures, and facial expressions rather than speech.*

People use many parts of the body to convey information to others through body language. Facial expressions are the most important type of *body language*. Smiling, for instance, shows pleasure, although we distinguish among

Paul W Liebhardt

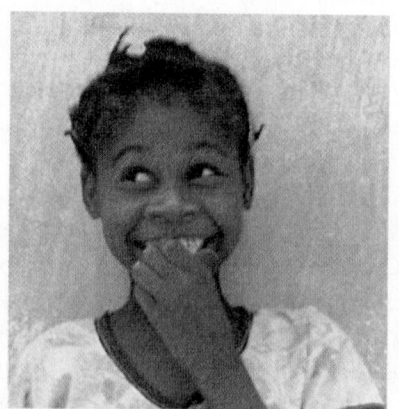

Paul W Liebhardt

Hisham Ibrahim/Photodisc/Getty Images

HAND GESTURES VARY WIDELY FROM ONE CULTURE TO ANOTHER Yet people everywhere chuckle, grin, or smirk to indicate that they don't take another person's performance seriously. Therefore, the world over, people who cannot restrain their mirth tactfully cover their faces.

the deliberate smile of Kindly Preedy on the beach, a spontaneous smile of joy at seeing a friend, a pained smile of embarrassment after spilling a cup of coffee, and the full unrestrained smile of self-satisfaction we often associate with winning some important contest.

Eye contact is another key element of non-verbal communication. Generally, we use eye contact to invite social interaction. Someone across the room "catches your eye," sparking a conversation. Avoiding another's eyes, in contrast, discourages communication. Hands, too, speak for us. Common hand gestures in our society convey, among other things, an insult, a request for a ride, an invitation for someone to join us, or a demand that others stop in their tracks. Gestures also supplement spoken words; for example, pointing at someone in a threatening way gives greater emphasis to a word of warning, just as shrugging the shoulders adds an air of indifference to the phrase "I don't know," and rapidly waving the arms adds urgency to the single word "Hurry!"

BODY LANGUAGE AND DECEPTION   As any actor knows, it is very difficult to pull off a perfect performance. In everyday performances, unintended body language can contradict our planned meaning: A teenage boy offers an explanation for getting home late, for example, but his mother doubts his words because he avoids looking her in the eye. The movie star on a television talk show claims that her recent flop at the box office is "no big deal," but the nervous swing of her leg suggests otherwise. Because non-verbal communication is hard to control, it offers clues to deception, in much the same way that changes in breathing, pulse rate, perspiration, and blood pressure recorded on a lie detector indicate that a person is lying.

Can you tell an honest smile from a phoney one? Detecting phoney performances is difficult, because no one bodily gesture tells us that someone is lying. But because any performance involves so much body language, few people can lie without some slip-up, raising the suspicions of a careful observer. The key to detecting lies is to view the whole performance with an eye to inconsistencies.

Gender and Performances

Because women are socialized to respond to others, they tend to be more sensitive than men to non-verbal communication. In fact, gender is a central element in personal performances, particularly with regard to demeanour, personal space, facial expression, and touching.

DEMEANOUR   *Demeanour*—the way we act and carry ourselves—is a clue to social power. Simply put, powerful people enjoy more freedom in how they act. Off-colour remarks, swearing, or putting one's feet on the desk may be acceptable for the boss but rarely for employees.

Similarly, powerful people can interrupt others, while less powerful people are expected to show respect through silence (Henley, Hamilton, & Thorne, 1992; Johnson, 1994; Smith-Lovin & Brody, 1989).

Because women generally occupy positions of less power, demeanour is a gender issue as well. Close to half of all working women in Canada hold clerical or service jobs under the control of supervisors who are usually men. Women, then, learn to craft their personal performances more carefully than men and to defer to men more often in everyday interaction.

USE OF SPACE   How much space does a personal performance require? Power plays a key role here; the more power you have, the more space you use. Men typically command more space than women, whether pacing back and forth before an audience or casually sitting on a bench. Why? Our culture traditionally has measured femininity by how *little* space women occupy with the standard of "daintiness"—and masculinity by how *much* territory a man controls with the standard of "turf" (Henley et al., 1992).

For both sexes, the concept of **personal space** refers to *the surrounding area over which a person makes some claim to privacy*. In Canada, people typically position themselves some distance apart when speaking, though this distance varies depending on how well the speakers know each other; throughout the Middle East, in contrast, people stand much closer when conversing. Just about everywhere, men—with their greater social power—often intrude into women's personal space. If a woman moves into a man's personal space, however, her movement is likely to be interpreted as a sign of sexual interest.

STARING, SMILING, AND TOUCHING   For most North Americans, eye contact encourages interaction. In conversations, women hold eye contact more than men. But men have their own brand of eye contact: staring. When men stare at women, they are claiming social dominance and defining women as sexual objects. While it often shows pleasure, smiling can also be a sign of trying to please someone or of submission. In a male-dominated world, it is not surprising that women smile more than men (Henley et al., 1992). Note, however, that most Aboriginal cultures have quite different patterns of eye contact; for men and women, staring is discourteous and eye contact is made only fleetingly, perhaps in greeting or to check to see if someone else has finished speaking.

Mutual touching suggests intimacy and caring. Apart from close relationships, touching is generally something men do to women but, in North American culture, rarely do to other men. A male physician touches the shoulder of his female nurse as they examine a report, a young man touches the back of his woman friend as he guides her across the street, or a male skiing instructor touches young women as he teaches them to ski. In such examples, the intent of touching may be harmless and may bring little response, but it amounts to a subtle ritual by which men claim dominance over women.

The Thinking Critically box moves social interaction from physical space to cyberspace. Note that we socially construct and reconstruct reality through online interaction—just as we do through face-to-face contact.

Idealization

People behave the way they do for many, often complex, reasons. Even so, Goffman suggests, we construct performances to *idealize* our intentions. That is, we try to convince others, and perhaps ourselves, that what we do reflects ideal cultural standards rather than selfish motives. Idealization is easily illustrated by returning to

Thinking Critically

Social Interaction: Life, Work, and Leisure in Cyberspace

Any technology tends to create a new human environment. . . . Technological environments are not merely passive containers of people but are active processes that reshape people and other technologies alike. In our time the sudden shift from the mechanical technology of the wheel to the technology of electric circuitry represents one of the major shifts of all historical time. (McLuhan, 1969)

When Alexander Graham Bell invented the telephone in 1874 and made the first long-distance call between Brantford and Paris, Ontario, people were astounded as he talked to others who were far away. People reeled in amazement once again when Guglielmo Marconi received the first transatlantic wireless (radio) message on a hilltop at St. John's, Newfoundland, (1901) and when the first television signal was broadcast (1928).

Is today's new information technology once again restructuring reality? Absolutely. Computers and other information technologies have already altered the Canadian economy: The manufacture of material goods (paper, steel, and cars) has been overshadowed in the post-industrial era by the creation of ideas and images. This changes the nature of work, the skills needed for employment, our legal definition of property, as well as our social and work relationships or interactions.

Whereas technology traditionally merely sustained human relationships already formed from face-to-face contact, an internet relationship can be initiated technologically. Because they are so disembodied, so devoid of physical presence . . . divisions between man and woman, old and young, strong and weak, sick and healthy, cool dude and nerd begin to be bridged as in few other ways. (Goyder, 1997:186)

This "disembodiment" through modern technology allows the creation of completely new online relationships, identities, and patterns of social interaction. Film director Atom Egoyan argues that social schizophrenia is a common result of the differences between Facebook profiles

and those of the real people involved. In *Adoration*, Egoyan explores the far-reaching consequences—for a young teenage boy's identity and pubescent sense of self—of creating a false persona online (Monk, 2009). As dramatic as this film may be, it reflects the experience of ordinary people who engage in fanciful or embellished presentation of self online.

Just as new information technology disembodies us, it erodes the importance of place in our lives. Bell's telephone was able to "reshape people"—to borrow McLuhan's phrase—by greatly extending the "reach" of their ears. At that time, because sound travelled along wires, Bell knew exactly where the call was going. A century later, cellular technology allows us to reach someone anywhere on Earth—or even in flight. Similarly, technological advances are reconstructing the workplace so that "the new factory" is now any place with a computer terminal and internet connection—including one's home. Even the centuries-old concepts of "national boundaries" and "citizenship" have grown fuzzy under the influence of recent technology. Consider an employee who logs on to a computer terminal in Vancouver and connects to a U.S. bank in Manhattan (her employer), where she processes transactions throughout the day. Is this "electronic migrant" part of the workforce of Canada or the United States?

More than 30 years ago, Canadian media theorist Marshall McLuhan predicted that nations and their boundaries would be unable to survive the new electronic technologies with their power of "totally involving all people in all other people." He would argue that, under the influence of border-jumping technologies such as the internet, our borders and our Canadian identity are challenged. In effect, instantaneous communication catapults us into McLuhan's "global village."

The BlackBerry (a Canadian invention) revolutionized the conduct of business by facilitating instant communication among those who are wired 24/7; in effect, it is a pocket-sized office that allows for the transmission of voice, visual images, email messages, and even attachments—to almost any location on Earth. As a result of such technologies, corporate or home offices have escaped the confines of physical space or place.

There is no more basic foundation for our sense of reality than that reflected in the timeless adage "Seeing is believing." So advanced is our technology that digital imagery allows photographers to combine and manipulate pictures to show almost anything. Computer animation enables movie producers to have humans interact with lifelike dinosaurs, and the technology of "virtual reality" means that, when connected to computers, we can see, hear, and even feel the "touch" of another person thousands of kilometres away.

New information technology is also reshaping the university and college scene. Historically, publishers have produced textbooks that augment the instruction of a classroom teacher. But books are becoming a smaller and smaller part of publishers' offerings, as we witness a proliferation of images on tape, film, disk, and online. In the years to come, textbooks themselves may gradually be replaced by digital texts. In a world of interactive, computer-based instruction, will students still need to travel to classrooms to learn? When even science can be taught with animated computer graphics (simulating a laboratory experiment, for example), might the university or college campus eventually become obsolete?

What Do You Think?

1. Have you embellished or added false information to the personal profiles you "publish" online? Will you someday regret intimate revelations posted on Facebook or Twitter?

2. As the "electronic age" unfolds further, what changes would you predict in our everyday interactions involving family, friends, school, recreation, entertainment, work, and the economy?

3. Do you think that virtual learning and virtual universities or colleges will eliminate the campus as we know it today?

---

the world of doctors and patients. In a hospital, doctors engage in a performance commonly described as "making rounds." Entering the room of a patient, the doctor often stops at the foot of the bed and silently reads the patient's chart. Afterwards, doctor and patient talk briefly. In ideal terms, this routine involves a doctor making a personal visit to check on a patient's condition. In reality, the picture is not so perfect. A doctor may see several dozen patients a day and remember little about many of them. Reading the chart is a chance to recall the patient's name and medical problems, but revealing the impersonality of medical care would undermine the cultural ideal of the doctor as being deeply concerned about the welfare of others.

Doctors, professors, and other professionals typically idealize their motives for entering their chosen careers. They describe their work as "making a contribution to science," "helping others," "serving the community," or even "answering a calling from God." Rarely do they admit the more common, less honourable, motives: the income, power, prestige, and leisure time that these occupations provide.

We all use idealization to some degree. When was the last time you smiled and spoke politely to someone you do not like? Such little deceptions help us get through everyday life. Even when we suspect that others are putting on an act, we are unlikely to challenge their performances, for reasons we shall examine next.

Embarrassment and Tact

The famous speaker keeps mispronouncing the dean's name; the visiting ambassador rises from the table to speak, unaware of the napkin still hanging from her neck; the president becomes ill at a state dinner. As carefully as individuals may craft their performances, slip-ups of all kinds occur. The result is *embarrassment*, discomfort following a spoiled performance. Goffman describes embarrassment as "losing face"—that is, temporarily losing some of the prestige associated with a status. Embarrassment is an ever-present danger because idealized performances usually contain some deception. In addition, most performances involve juggling so many elements that one thoughtless moment can shatter the intended impression.

A curious fact is that an audience often overlooks flaws in a performance, allowing an actor to avoid embarrassment. If we do point out a misstep—"Excuse me, but your fly is open"—we do it quietly and only to help someone avoid even greater loss of face. In Hans Christian Andersen's classic fable "The Emperor's New Clothes," the child who blurts out the truth—that the emperor is parading about naked—is scolded for being rude.

Often, members of an audience actually help the performer recover a flawed performance. *Tact,* then, amounts to helping someone "save face." After hearing a supposed expert make an embarrassingly inaccurate remark, for example, people may tactfully ignore the comment, as if it had never been spoken, or treat what was said as a joke, perhaps with mild laughter. Or they may simply respond, "I'm sure you didn't mean that," hearing the statement but not allowing it to destroy the actor's performance. With this in mind, we can understand Abraham Lincoln's comment: "Tact is the ability to describe others the way they see themselves." Tact is so common because embarrassment creates discomfort for the actor and for everyone else. Just as a theatre audience feels uneasy when an actor forgets a line, people who observe awkward behaviour are reminded of how fragile their own performances are. Socially constructed reality thus functions like a dam holding back a sea of chaos. When one person's

Barbara Penoyar/Photodisc/Getty Images

Iko/Fotolia

George Hunter/SuperStock

Lucian Coman/Shutterstock

Ajay Bhaskar/Getty Images

Jon Schulte/Getty Images

TO MOST OF US, THESE EXPRESSIONS CONVEY ANGER, FEAR, DISGUST, HAPPINESS, SURPRISE, AND SADNESS But do people elsewhere in the world define them in the same way? Research suggests that all humans experience the same basic emotions and display them to others in the same basic ways. But culture plays a part by specifying the situations that trigger one emotion or another.

performance springs a leak, others tactfully help make repairs. Everyone, after all, lends a hand in building reality, and no one wants it suddenly swept away.

In sum, Goffman's research shows that, although behaviour is spontaneous in some respects, it is more patterned than it appears on the surface. Four centuries ago, Shakespeare captured this idea in memorable lines that still ring true:

> All the world's a stage,
> And all the men and women merely players:
> They have their exits and their entrances;
> And one man in his time plays many parts.
>
> (*As You Like It*, act 2, scene 7)

Interaction in Everyday Life: Three Applications

6.6   Construct a sociological analysis of three aspects of everyday life: emotions, language, and humour.

The final sections of this chapter illustrate the major elements of social interaction by focusing on three dimensions of everyday life: emotions, language, and humour.

Emotions: The Social Construction of Feeling

Emotions, more commonly called *feelings*, are an important element of human social life. In truth, what we *do* often matters less than how we *feel* about it. Emotions seem very personal because they are private. Even so, just as society guides our behaviour, it guides our emotional life.

THE BIOLOGICAL SIDE OF EMOTIONS   Studying people all over the world, Paul Ekman (1980a, 1980b) reports that people everywhere recognize and express six basic emotions: happiness, sadness, anger, fear, disgust, and surprise. In addition, he found that people everywhere use the same facial expressions to show these emotions. Some emotional responses are "wired" into humans—that is, they are biologically programmed in our facial features, muscles, and central nervous system. Why? From an evolutionary perspective, emotions have biological roots, but they also serve a social purpose: supporting group life. Emotions are powerful forces that allow us to overcome our self-centredness and build connections with others. Thus, the capacity for emotion arose in our ancestors along with the capacity for culture (Turner, 2000).

THE CULTURAL SIDE OF EMOTIONS Culture, however, does play an important role in guiding human emotions. As Ekman explains, culture determines the *trigger* for emotion. Whether a specific event is defined as joyous (causing happiness), insulting (arousing anger), a loss (producing sadness), or mystical (provoking surprise and awe), it is a function of culture. Culture also provides rules or contexts for the *display* of emotions. For example, most of us express emotions more freely with family members than we do with workplace colleagues. Similarly, we expect children to express emotions to parents, but parents to hide their emotions from children. Furthermore, culture guides how we value emotions. Some societies encourage the expression of emotion; others expect members to control their feelings and maintain a "stiff upper lip." Gender also plays a part; traditionally, many cultures expect women to show emotions, but consider emotional expression by men to be a sign of weakness. In some cultures this pattern is less pronounced or even reversed.

EMOTIONS ON THE JOB Most people are freer to express their feelings at home than on the job. The reason, as Hochschild (1979, 1983) explains, is that the typical company tries to regulate the behaviour and emotions of its employees. Take the case of an airline flight attendant who offers passengers a meal and a smile. While this smile may convey real pleasure at serving the customer, Hochschild's study points to a different conclusion: The smile is an emotional script demanded by the airline as the right way to do the job. Therefore, we see that the "presentation of self" described by Erving Goffman can involve not just surface acting but also the "deep acting" of emotions. Thus, we socially construct our emotions as part of everyday reality, a process sociologists call *emotion management*.

Language: The Social Construction of Gender

Language is the thread that weaves members of a society into the symbolic web we call culture. Language communicates not only a surface reality but also deeper levels of meaning. One such level involves gender. Language defines men and women differently in terms of both power and value (Henley et al., 1992; Thorne et al., 1983).

LANGUAGE AND POWER A young man proudly rides his new motorcycle up his friend's driveway and boasts, "Isn't she a beauty?" On the surface, the question has little to do with gender. Yet why does he use the pronoun *she* to refer to his prized possession? The answer is that men often use language to establish control over their surroundings. In Roman and medieval Europe, a woman was legally the possession of a man (her father, brother, spouse, or guardian)—a situation that has changed in law only in recent years. But everyday language retains this concept when a man attaches a female pronoun to a motorcycle or boat or car, because it reflects the power of ownership.

Perhaps this is also why, in North America and elsewhere, a woman who marries usually takes the last name of her husband. When Joe Clark became Canada's prime minister in 1979, he encountered hostility and resistance from some quarters because his wife, Maureen McTeer, had retained her birth name; the attitude seemed to reflect the idea that if a man cannot control his wife, how can he possibly run the country? Stephen Harper, leader of Canada's Conservative Party, is married to Laureen Teskey, who also kept her unmarried name; on her husband becoming prime minister, she seems to have become Laureen Harper. On the other hand, in Quebec, women are not merely encouraged to retain their birth names; the law actually requires them to do so.

LANGUAGE AND VALUE Typically, the English language treats as masculine whatever has great value, force, or significance. For instance, the word *virtuous* (meaning "morally worthy" or "excellent") comes from the Latin word *vir,* meaning "man." On the other hand, the adjective *hysterical* (meaning "emotionally out of control") is taken from the Greek word *hystera,* meaning "uterus." In many familiar ways, language also confers different value on the two sexes. Traditional masculine terms such as *king* and *lord* have a positive meaning, while comparable feminine terms, such as *queen, madam,* and *dame,* can have negative meanings. Similarly, use of the suffixes *-ette* and *-ess* to denote femininity usually devalues the words to which they are added. For example, a *major* has higher standing than a *majorette,* as does a *host* in relation to a *hostess,* or a *master* in relation to a *mistress.* Language both mirrors social attitudes and helps perpetuate them.

LANGUAGE AND ATTENTION Language also shapes reality by directing greater attention to masculine endeavours. Consider our use of personal pronouns. In the English language, the plural pronoun *they* is neutral, as it refers to both sexes. But the corresponding singular pronouns *he* and *she* specify gender. Formerly, it was grammatical practice to use *he, his,* and *him* to refer to all people. Accordingly, readers were to assume that the bit of wisdom "He who hesitates is lost" refers to women as well as to men. But this practice also reflected the traditional cultural pattern of ignoring the lives of women. This factual statement is a classic example: "Man, like other mammals, breast-feeds his young."

The English language has no gender-neutral, third-person-singular personal pronoun. Recently, however, the plural pronouns *they* and *them* have gained currency as singular pronouns in speech (e.g., "A person should do as they please"). This usage remains controversial—because it violates grammatical rules—but spoken English is now evolving to accept such gender-neutral constructions.

Even as the English language changes in response to social imperatives, gender is likely to remain a source of miscommunication between women and men. A booklet titled *Words That Count Women Out/In* (Ontario, 1992) examines some of the most common assumptions and barriers that have made the transition to gender-inclusive language troublesome. The authors point out that sexist language can even be found in the one piece of music that all Canadians hear and sing so frequently:

> O Canada! Our home and native land!
> True patriot love in all thy sons command.

Our national anthem, the symbol of our democratic spirit, excludes half of the population—women—as well as immigrants who are not native to Canada. Despite considerable controversy, the introduction of several bills, and a promised parliamentary review, the words of our national anthem remained unchanged. With the new Liberal-majority government in power, Liberal MP Mauri Bélanger reintroduced a bill in late January, 2016.

Reality Play: The Social Construction of Humour

Humour plays an important part in everyday life. Everyone laughs at a joke, but few people think about what makes something funny. We can apply many of the ideas developed in this chapter to explain how, by using humour, we "play with reality" (Macionis, 1987).

THE FOUNDATION OF HUMOUR Humour is produced by the social construction of reality; it arises as people create and contrast two different realities. Generally, one reality is *conventional*—that is, what people in a specific situation expect. The other reality is *unconventional,* an unexpected violation of cultural patterns. Humour therefore arises from contradiction, ambiguity, and double meanings found in differing definitions of the same situation.

There are countless ways to mix realities and generate humour. Contrasting realities are found in statements that contradict themselves, such as "Nostalgia is not what it used to be"; statements that repeat themselves, such as

Yogi Berra's line "It's *déjà vu* all over again"; or statements that mix up words, such as Oscar Wilde's quip "Work is the curse of the drinking class." Even switching around syllables does the trick, as in the case of the country song "I'd Rather Have a Bottle in Front of Me than a Frontal Lobotomy."

Of course, a joke can be built the other way around, so that the audience is led to expect an unconventional answer and then receives a very ordinary one. When a reporter asked the famous criminal Willy Sutton why he robbed banks, for example, he replied dryly, "Because that's where the money is." However a joke is constructed, the greater the opposition or difference between two definitions of reality, the greater the humour.

When telling jokes, a comedian uses various strategies to strengthen this opposition and make the joke funnier. One common technique is to present the first, or conventional, remark in conversation with another actor, then to turn toward the audience (or the camera) to deliver the second, unexpected, line. In a Marx Brothers film, Groucho remarks, "Outside of a dog, a book is a man's best friend"; then, raising his voice and turning to the camera, he adds, "And *inside* of a dog, it's too dark to read!" Such "changing channels" emphasizes the difference between the two realities. Following the same logic, stand-up comedians may "reset" the audience to conventional expectations by interjecting the phrase "But seriously, folks" between jokes.

People who like to tell jokes pay careful attention to their performance—the precise words they use and the timing of their delivery. A joke is well told if the teller creates the sharpest possible opposition between the realities; in a careless performance, the joke falls flat. Because the key to humour lies in the collision of realities, we can see why the climax of a joke is termed the *punch* line.

THE DYNAMICS OF HUMOUR: "GETTING IT" After someone tells you a joke, have you ever had to say, "I don't get it"? To "get" humour, you must understand both the conventional and the unconventional realities well enough to appreciate their difference. Someone telling a joke may make getting it harder by leaving out some important information. In such cases, listeners must pay attention to the stated elements of the joke and then fill in the missing pieces on their own. A simple example is the comment made by the movie producer Hal Roach on his hundredth birthday: "If I had known I would live to be one hundred, I would have taken better care of myself!" Here, getting the joke depends on realizing that Roach must have taken pretty good care of himself to make it to 100. Or take one of W.C. Fields's lines: "Some weasel took the cork out of my lunch." Here is an even more complex joke: "What do you get if you cross an insomniac, a dyslexic, and an agnostic? Answer: A person who stays up all night wondering if there is a dog." To get this joke, you must know that insomnia is an inability to sleep, that dyslexia can cause a person to reverse the letters in words, and that an agnostic doubts the existence of God.

The *Globe and Mail*, under "Your Morning Smile," published a submission by Torontonian Poly O'Keefe: "What was the name of the first sociologist to study the impact of new communications technology on society? Answer: E-mail Durkheim" (1997:A1). Getting this joke requires some knowledge of sociology. Needless to say, your recognition chuckle would have been more spontaneous had you encountered this tidbit out of context in the newspaper.

Why would someone telling a joke want the hearer to make this sort of effort to understand it? Our enjoyment of a joke is increased by the pleasure of figuring out all of the pieces needed to "get it." In addition, getting the joke makes you an "insider" compared to those who don't "get it." We have all experienced the frustration of not getting a joke: fear of being judged stupid, along with a sense of being excluded from shared pleasure. People may tactfully explain a joke so that no one feels left out, but, as the old saying goes, if a joke has to be explained, it isn't very funny.

THE TOPICS OF HUMOUR   All over the world, people smile and laugh, making humour a universal element of human culture. But, because people live in different cultures, humour rarely travels well. This travel journal entry provides an illustration:

> **October 1, Kobe, Japan.** Can you share a joke with people who live halfway around the world? At dinner, I ask two Japanese college women to tell me a joke. "You know 'crayon'?" Asako asks. I nod. "How do you ask for a crayon in Japanese?" I respond that I have no idea. She laughs out loud as she says what sounds like "crayon crayon." Her companion Mayumi laughs too. My wife and I sit awkwardly, straight-faced. Asako relieves some of our embarrassment by explaining that the Japanese word for "give me" is *kureyo*, which sounds like "crayon." I force a smile. [John J. Macionis]

What is humorous to the Japanese may be lost on Chinese, Iraqis, or Canadians. Even the social diversity of this country means that different types of people will find humour in different situations. Newfoundlanders, Québécois, Inuit, and Albertans have their own brands of humour, as do Canadians of Italian or Jamaican origin. Teenage girls, middle-aged men, Bay Street brokers, and rodeo riders will have specific kinds of jokes that they find funny. But for everyone, topics that lend themselves to double meanings or controversy generate humour. The first jokes many of us learned as children concerned bodily functions that kids are not supposed to talk about. The mere mention of "unmentionable acts" or even certain parts of the body can dissolve young faces in laughter.

Are there jokes that do break through the culture barrier? Yes, but they must touch on universal human experiences such as, for example, turning on a friend:

> I think of a number of jokes, but none seems likely to work in this cross-cultural setting. Is there something more universal? Inspiration: "Two fellows are walking in the woods and come upon a huge bear. One guy leans over and tightens up the laces on his running shoes. 'Jake,' says the other, 'what are you doing? You can't outrun this bear!' 'I don't have to outrun the bear,' responds Jake. 'I just have to outrun you!'" Smiles all around. [John J. Macionis]

The controversy found in humour often walks a fine line between what is funny and what is "sick." Before and during the Middle Ages, people used the word *humours* (derived from the Latin *humidus*, meaning "moist") to refer to four bodily fluids that were thought to regulate a person's temperament and, therefore, their health. Researchers today document the power of humour to reduce stress and improve health, confirming the old saying that "Laughter is the best medicine" (Bakalar, 2005; Haig, 1988).

Then, too, every social group considers certain topics too sensitive for humorous treatment. Of course, you can still joke about them, but doing so risks criticism for telling a "sick" joke, or being labelled "sick" yourself. People's religious beliefs, tragic accidents, or appalling crimes are the stuff of "sick" jokes or jokes without humour. Even all these years later, no one jokes about the terrorist attacks of September 11, 2001.

THE FUNCTIONS OF HUMOUR   Humour is found everywhere because it works as a safety valve for potentially disruptive sentiments. Put another way, it provides an acceptable way to discuss sensitive topics without appearing to be serious. Having said something controversial, people can use humour to defuse the situation by simply stating, "I didn't mean anything—it was just a joke!" People also use humour to relieve tension in uncomfortable situations. One study of medical examinations found that most patients try to joke with doctors to ease their own nervousness (Baker et al., 1997).

As Canadians, we use humour to express our common identity. By laughing at ourselves or putting ourselves down, we reinforce a sense of our common bond. In a panel discussion called "Why Are Canadians So Funny?" moderator Michael J. Fox noted that *Maclean's* asked its readers to fill in the blank at the end of the phrase "As Canadian as…" to counterbalance the motto "As American as apple pie." According to Fox, the winning entry was "As Canadian as possible under the circumstances" (Vowell, 1999).

Or Canada's idea of a joke is debating a constitutional accord as a matter of life and death, and then changing the subject. "Canada is a nation without a punch line." These jokes play on Canadian insecurity about who we are. In the midst of the deep divisions caused by the constitutional discussions of the 1980s and 1990s, the second joke reminds us that we have a common national identity. We are "insiders" to the joke, not only because we

are familiar with the debate but also because we recognize a pattern that characterizes our country. Because anglophones share constitutional angst with the Québécois, this joke should be funny in French. Would Americans find the joke funny? Further analysis of Canadian humour appears in the Sociology in Focus box.

Sociology in Focus

The Social Construction of Reality: Reflections on Canadian Humour

One could argue that humour, or comedy, is one of Canada's most successful cultural exports. Among the Canadian comedians who "made it big" in the United States are Dan Aykroyd, John Candy, Jim Carrey, Tom Green, Rich Little, Lorne Michaels, Mike Myers, Leslie Nielsen, and Martin Short. Does Canada produce more comedians per capita than the United States? Perhaps. If so, what is it about Canada that nurtures the comic spirit or talent?

Canadian humour often plays on insecurities regarding our common "identity" or our place on the world stage. For example, in 2007 the *National Post* ran a contest where people were asked to come up with the new unofficial Canadian motto, in six words or less. All of those entries say something about our Canadian identity—many of them are self-deprecating or poke fun at Canadians, and many of them are funny. Together, the 75 published entries (*National Post*, 2007), provide a panoramic view of Canadian culture with thoughtful insights —brilliant little pinpricks—into what makes Canada tick.

John Robert Colombo began collecting Canadian jokes in 1967 and compiled them into a book, *The Penguin Book of Canadian Jokes* (2001). In his preface, he quotes Jan Morris, who observed that the "genius of Canada remains essentially a deflationary genius" and that it is "part of the Canadian genius . . . to reduce the heroic to the banal" (2001:x). Morris is noting the propensity of Canadians to put themselves down—as illustrated in the *National Post* excerpts.

When Marshall McLuhan was asked if there is a Canadian identity, he said, "No, there is no Canadian identity. Canadians are the only people in the world who have learned to live without a national identity" (2001:1). Our weak or non-existent identity is illustrated by a long list of definitions of a Canadian (pp. 2, 3), including this small sample:

A Canadian is someone who. . .

thinks an income tax refund is a gift from the government.

doesn't know anyone who owns a flag.

is convinced that democracy involves keeping your opinions to yourself.

says "Sorry" when you accidentally bump into him.

spends an inordinate amount of time trying to define what a Canadian is.

What other kinds of jokes did Colombo gather in his 30-odd year search? He found that many people were required to change light bulbs and many chickens crossed the road. There are jokes about beavers, the maple leaf, Mounties, kayaks, and canoes—as well as many places known to Canadians (e.g., Toronto, Barrie, Kamloops, Moose Jaw, Shawinigan). There are jokes about body parts and functions—including the sexual— and ones dealing with various occupations (e.g., farmer, lawyer, travelling salesman, soldier, evangelist, Montreal taxi driver, businessman). There are also a number of jokes by and about famous people, such as Stephen Leacock, Marshall McLuhan, Wayne Gretzky (and other hockey greats), early feminist Nellie McClung, and Ottawa's late mayor Charlotte Whitton. Albertans, Quebecers, and Newfies are fair game—and Newfies tell the best Newfie jokes—but there are few jokes about specific religious or ethnic groups in Colombo's collection. French Canadians and "Indians" are notable exceptions to this rule, but then they make up "founding nations" rather than ordinary ethnic groups.

And *many* of the included jokes deal with politics: Canada's federal and provincial politicians, including whole sections on Pierre Elliott Trudeau and Brian Mulroney; government programs or policies, such as multiculturalism, welfare, and separatism; and political ideologies and parties. In fact, Colombo claims that we have "a preference for political humour over all other kinds" (2001:132)—our favourite targets being prime ministers, premiers, other politicians, and our unelected senators. Clearly, putting down powerful people is uniquely satisfying.

Anyone who doubts the Canadian appetite for political humour need only watch the CBC comedies *This Hour Has 22 Minutes, The Rick Mercer Report,* and *Royal Canadian*

Air Farce (which ran on CBC radio, television, or both for 35 years—until December 31, 2008). All three shows cover the news and have their own recurring characters, but inevitably they tend to make fun of our politicians: The actors on *Air Farce* parodied Jean Chrétien, Paul Martin, Lucien Bouchard, Preston Manning, Belinda Stronach, and Stephen Harper with uncanny skill. These shows are so popular and influential that our politicians respond positively to invitations to appear on them—in the flesh, so to speak. By allowing the comedians to poke fun at them in person, the politicians reveal their vulnerable human selves, stripped of the trappings of power.

When Canadians tell and respond to jokes, they are involved in the social construction of reality—often turning conventional definitions of social situations and relationships upside down. They forge bonds with people who "get it" on the basis of shared understandings or a common identity, sharpen the boundaries between "us" and "them," and deal with tensions and hostilities through the safety valve of humour. Humour, more often than not, is lost in translation from one language to another. Even when told in the same language, a joke told in one social setting or cultural milieu can fall flat in another when listeners fail to "get it." It takes shared understanding and meaning to make our jokes funny to our fellow Canadians.

What Do You Think?

1. How do you feel when someone tells a joke and you "get it"? How do you feel when you *don't* "get it"?

2. Have you ever thought about what makes a joke funny or which jokes make you laugh the hardest?

3. Why can jokes serve as icebreakers to diffuse tensions between individuals or groups of people?

HUMOUR AND CONFLICT Humour may be a source of pleasure, but it can also be used to put down others. Men who tell jokes about women, for example, typically are expressing some measure of hostility toward them (Benokraitis & Feagin, 1995; Powell & Paton, 1988). Similarly, jokes about gay people reveal tensions about sexual orientation. Real conflict can be masked by humour in situations where one or both parties choose not to bring the conflict out into the open (Primeggia & Varacalli, 1990).

"Put-down" jokes make one category of people feel good at the expense of another. After collecting and analyzing jokes from many societies, Christie Davies (1990) confirmed that ethnic conflict is one driving force behind humour in most of the world. The typical ethnic joke makes fun of some disadvantaged category of people, at the same time making the joke teller feel superior. Given the Anglo-Saxon and French traditions of Canadian society, ethnic and racial minorities have long been the butt of jokes, as have Newfoundlanders ("Newfies") in eastern Canada, Irish in England, Sikhs in India, Turks in Germany, and Kurds in Iraq.

At times, people belonging to cultural minorities turn the joke on themselves. Peter Berger (1997) points out that Jews are so good at this that their jokes have become part of the larger American repertoire. This kind of humour illustrates that "jokes can summarize an often complex situation in wondrously economical ways, simplifying and illuminating and definitely providing some cognitive benefit" (p. 137). One of Berger's examples reveals the feelings of the Québécois, who believe that they exist on an island of French in an English-speaking ocean.

In a village in Quebec a little girl goes out to collect mushrooms when the Virgin Mary appears to her. The little girl sinks to her knees and says: "Ah, vous êtes Notre Dame! Vous êtes si belle. Vous êtes magnifique. Je vous adore. Je vous aime." And the Virgin Mary replies: "I'm sorry. I don't speak French."

Aboriginal Canadians also create this kind of humour. Many Aboriginal comedians have become popular with Aboriginal and non-Aboriginal audiences. Actor Graham Greene has been featured often on the CBC's *Royal Canadian Air Farce*. And the CBC radio program *Dead Dog Café* (1997–2000) had the effect of illuminating Aboriginal culture: It was corny, satirical, and right on!

Disadvantaged people also make fun of the powerful, as well as themselves, although they usually do so discreetly. Women routinely joke about men, and poor people poke fun at the rich. Throughout the world, people target their leaders with humour, and officials in some countries take such jokes seriously enough to vigorously repress them. Political jokes are "subversive by definition" (Berger, 1997).

In sum, the significance of humour is much greater than first impressions suggest. Humour amounts to a means of mental escape from a conventional world that is not entirely to our liking (Flaherty, 1984, 1990; Yoels & Clair, 1995). With that in mind, it makes sense that a disproportionate number of North America's comedians come from among the ranks of oppressed people, including Jews and Blacks. They also come, disproportionately, from Canada. As long as we maintain a sense of humour, we assert our freedom and are no longer prisoners of reality; in doing so, we change the world and ourselves just a little.

Seeing Sociology in Everyday Life

CHAPTER 6 Social Interaction in Everyday Life

How do we construct the reality we experience?

This chapter suggests that Shakespeare may have had it right when he said, "All the world's a stage." And if so, then the internet may be the latest and greatest stage so far. When we use websites such as Facebook, as Goffman explains, we present ourselves as we want others to see us. Everything we write about ourselves as well as how we arrange our pages creates an impression in the mind of anyone interested in "checking us out." Take a

look at the Facebook page below, paying careful attention to all the details. What is the young man explicitly saying about himself? What can you read "between the lines"? That is, what information can you identify that he may be trying to conceal, or at least purposely not be mentioning? How honest do you think his "presentation of self" is? Why? Do a similar analysis of the young woman's Facebook profile shown on the next page.

Hint Just about every element of a presentation conveys information about us to others, so all the information found on a website like this one is significant. Some information is intentional—for example, what people write about themselves and the photos they choose to post. Other information may be unintentional but is nevertheless picked up by the careful viewer who may be noting such things as these:

- The length and tone of the person's profile. Is it a long-winded list of talents and accomplishments or humorous and modest?
- The language used. Poor grammar may be a clue to educational level.
- What hour of the day or night the person wrote the material. A person creating his profile at 11 p.m. on a Saturday night may not be quite the party person he describes himself to be.

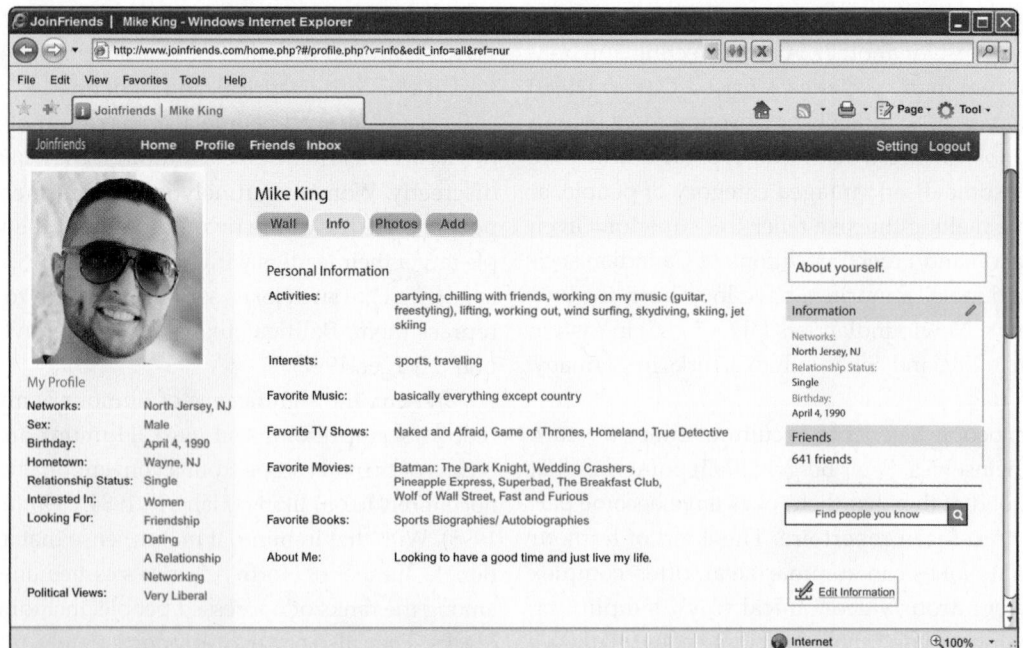

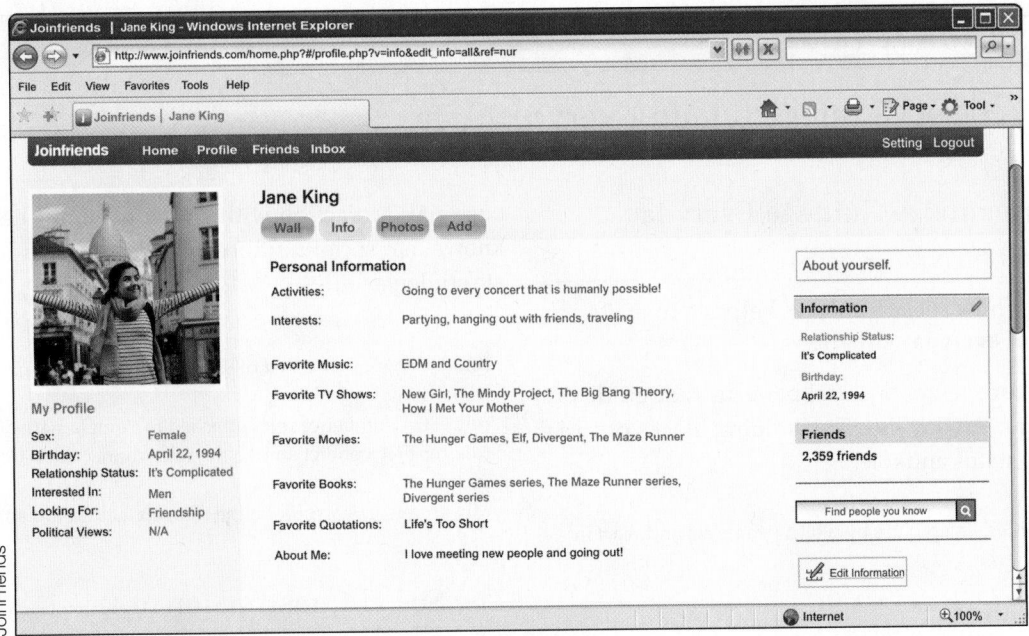

Seeing Sociology in *Your* Everyday Life

1. Identify five important ways in which you "present yourself" to others including, for example, the way you decorate your dorm room, apartment, or house; the way you dress; and the way you behave in the classroom. In each case, think about what you are trying to say about yourself. Do you present a different self to various others, such as friends, professors, and parents? If so, how do you account for the differences?

2. During one full day, every time somebody asks, "How are you?" or "How's it goin'?" stop and try to actually give a complete, truthful answer. What happens when you respond to a polite question in an honest way? Listen to how people respond, and also watch their body language. What can you conclude?

3. This chapter has explained that we all engage in a process called the social construction of reality. What that means is that each of us plays a part in shaping the reality we experience. Let's apply this idea to the issue of personal freedom. To what extent does the material presented in this chapter support a claim that humans are free to shape their own lives?

Making the Grade

CHAPTER 6 Social Interaction in Everyday Life

Social Structure: A Guide to Everyday Living

6.1 **Explain how social structure helps us to make sense of everyday situations.**

Social structure refers to social patterns that guide our behaviour in everyday life. The building blocks of social structure are status and role.

> **social interaction** the process by which people act and react in relation to others

Status

6.2 **State the importance of status to social organization.**

Status is a social position that is part of our social identity and that defines our relationships to others.

A status can be either an

- **ascribed status**, which is involuntary (e.g., being a teenager, an orphan, or a Mexican American), or an
- **achieved status**, which is earned (e.g., being an honours student, a pilot, or a thief).

A master status, which can be either ascribed or achieved, has special importance for a person's identity (e.g., being blind, a doctor, or a Trudeau).

> **status** a social position that a person holds
> **status set** all the statuses a person holds at a given time
> **ascribed status** a social position a person receives at birth or takes on involuntarily later in life
> **achieved status** a social position a person takes on voluntarily that reflects personal ability and effort
> **master status** a status that has special importance for social identity, often shaping a person's entire life

Role

6.3 **State the importance of role to social organization.**

Role refers to the behaviour expected of someone who holds a particular status.

Role conflict results from tension among roles linked to two or more statuses (e.g., a woman who juggles her responsibilities as a mother and a corporate CEO).

Role strain results from tension among roles linked to a single status (e.g., the college professor who enjoys personal interaction with students but at the same time knows that social distance is necessary in order to evaluate students fairly).

> **role** behaviour expected of someone who holds a particular status
> **role set** a number of roles attached to a single status
> **role conflict** conflict among the roles connected to two or more statuses
> **role strain** tension among the roles connected to a single status

The Social Construction of Reality

6.4 **Describe how we socially construct reality.**

Through **social interaction**, we construct the reality we experience.

- For example, two people interacting both try to shape the reality of their situation.

The **Thomas theorem** says that the reality people construct in their interaction has real consequences for the future.

- For example, a teacher who believes a certain student to be intellectually gifted may well encourage exceptional academic performance.

Ethnomethodology is a strategy to reveal the assumptions people have about their social world.

- We can expose these assumptions by intentionally breaking the "rules" of social interaction and observing the reactions of other people.

Both **culture** and **social class** shape the reality people construct.

- For example, a "short walk" for a Calgarian might be a few city blocks, but for a peasant in Latin America, it could be a few miles.

The expansion of social media has dramatically changed how people interact.

- The social construction of reality no longer requires people to have face-to-face interaction.

> **social construction of reality** the process by which people creatively shape reality through social interaction
> **Thomas theorem** W.I. Thomas's claim that situations defined as real are real in their consequences
> **ethnomethodology** Harold Garfinkel's term for the study of the way people make sense of their everyday surroundings

Dramaturgical Analysis: The "Presentation of Self"

6.5 Apply Goffman's analysis to several familiar situations.

Dramaturgical analysis explores social interaction in terms of theatrical performance: A status operates as a part in a play, and a role is a script.

Performances are the way we present ourselves to others.

- Performances are both conscious (intentional action) and unconscious (non-verbal communication).
- Performances include costume (the way we dress), props (objects we carry), and demeanor (tone of voice and the way we carry ourselves).

Gender affects performances because men typically have greater social power than women. Gender differences involve *demeanour, use of space,* and *smiling, staring,* and *touching.*

- **Demeanour**—With greater social power, men have more freedom in how they act.
- **Use of space**—Men typically command more space than women.
- **Staring** and **touching** are generally done by men to women.
- **Smiling,** as a way to please another, is more commonly done by women.

Idealization of performances means we try to convince others that our actions reflect ideal culture rather than selfish motives.

Embarrassment is the "loss of face" in a performance. People use **tact** to help others "save face."

> **dramaturgical analysis** Erving Goffman's term for the study of social interaction in terms of theatrical performance
> **presentation of self** Erving Goffman's term for a person's efforts to create specific impressions in the minds of others
> **nonverbal communication** communication using body movements, gestures, and facial expressions rather than speech
> **personal space** the surrounding area over which a person makes some claim to privacy

Interaction in Everyday Life: Three Applications

6.6 Construct a sociological analysis of three aspects of everyday life: emotions, language, and humour.

Emotions: The Social Construction of **Feeling**

The same basic emotions are biologically programmed into all human beings, but culture guides what triggers emotions, how people display emotions, and how people value emotions. In everyday life, the presentation of self involves managing emotions as well as behaviour.

Language: The Social Construction of **Gender**

Gender is an important element of everyday interaction. Language defines women and men as different types of people, reflecting the fact that society attaches greater power and value to what is viewed as masculine.

Reality Play: The Social Construction of **Humour**

Humour results from the difference between conventional and unconventional definitions of a situation. Because humour is a part of culture, people around the world find different situations funny.

Chapter 7
Groups and Organizations

Paul Bradbury/OJO Images/Getty Images

⌄ Learning Objectives

7.1 Explain the importance of various types of groups to social life.

7.2 Describe the operation of large, formal organizations.

7.3 Summarize the changes to formal organizations over the course of the past century.

The Power of Society
to link people into groups

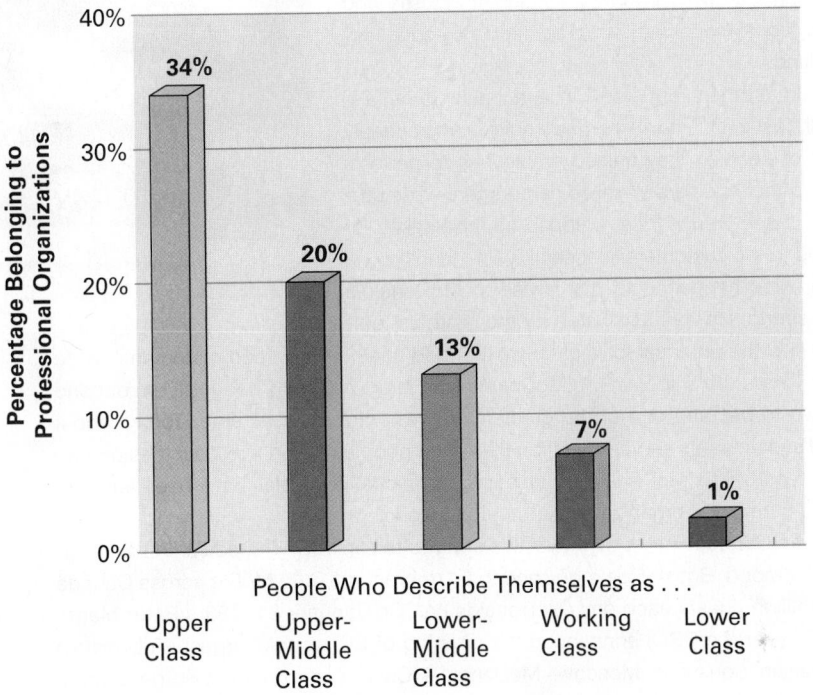

SOURCE: World Values Survey (2015).

Does your social class influence which groups and organizations you join? Professional organizations include people who work as physicians, lawyers, engineers, and nurses. Look at how social class affects membership in such organizations—people who identified themselves as being "upper class" were five times more likely to be members of professional organizations than people who said they were "working class"—the latter being more likely to belong to unions instead. Membership in organizations—such as professional associations or unions—is not simply a matter of choice; in many cases membership is compulsory. In effect, groups and organizations reflect the ways in which societies are organized and regulated.

Chapter Overview

We spend much of our lives within the collectivities that sociologists call social groups and formal organizations. This chapter begins by analyzing social groups, both small and large, highlighting the differences between them. Then the focus shifts to the formal organizations that carry out various tasks in modern society.

In 1948, the opening of a new restaurant in Pasadena, California, attracted little attention. Yet this seemingly insignificant small business, owned and operated by Maurice and Richard McDonald, would eventually spark a revolution in the restaurant industry and provide an organizational model that would be copied by countless businesses of all kinds.

The McDonald brothers put into place a basic formula—which we now call "fast food"—to serve meals quickly and cheaply to large numbers of people. They trained employees to perform specialized jobs, so that one person grilled hamburgers while others dressed them, made French fries, whipped up milkshakes, or presented the food to the customers in assembly-line fashion.

In 1954, Ray Kroc happened to pay a visit to McDonald's while on a business trip. He was fascinated by the brothers' efficient system and saw the potential for a greatly expanded chain of fast-food restaurants. Kroc launched his plans in partnership with the McDonald brothers—but soon bought them out and set out on his own to become one of the greatest success stories of all time. Today, about 36 000 McDonald's restaurants serve more than 69 million people daily in 119 countries around the world. So successful was McDonald's that its organizational principles have been adopted by businesses and other large organizations around the world.

But McDonald's Canada has its own success story to tell. In 1967 Canada's first McDonald's opened in Richmond, British Columbia, and today more than 1400 McD's across Canada serve close to 3 million guests each day (McDonalds.ca). On January 31, 1990, Peter Mansbridge (news anchor for the CBC) announced the opening of the world's largest McDonald's restaurant on Pushkin Square in Moscow. McDonald's Canada president, George Cohon, made his initial proposal to Soviet officials at the 1976 Olympics in Montreal and invested $50 million in the project. Fourteen years later, the new restaurant broke two opening-day records—for highest sales and the most customers served. CBC reporter Don Murray covered the story, finding a wide range of reactions to the unfamiliar food and the friendly, smiling servers (CBC, 2012). ■

We begin this chapter with an examination of *social groups,* the clusters of people with whom we interact in our daily lives. As you will learn, the scope of group life in Canada expanded greatly during the twentieth century. From a world of families, local neighbourhoods, and small businesses, our society now turns on the operation of huge corporations and other bureaucracies (e.g., government) that sociologists describe as *formal organizations.* Understanding this expanding scale of social life and appreciating what it means for us as individuals are the main objectives of this chapter.

Social Groups

7.1 Explain the importance of various types of groups to social life.

Almost everyone wants a sense of belonging, which is the essence of group life. A **social group** is *two or more people who identify with and interact with one another.* Humans come together in couples, families, circles of friends, churches, clubs, businesses, neighbourhoods, and large organizations. Whatever its form, a group is made up of

> **social group** two or more people who identify with and interact with one another
>
> **primary group** a small social group whose members share personal and lasting relationships
>
> **secondary group** a large and impersonal social group whose members pursue a specific goal or activity

people with shared experiences, loyalties, and interests. In short, while keeping their individuality, members of social groups also think of themselves as a special "us."

Not every collection of individuals forms a group. People all over the country with a status in common, such as women, homeowners, soldiers, millionaires, university graduates, and Roman Catholics, are not a group but a *category*. While they know that others hold the same status, most are strangers to one another. Similarly, students sitting in a large stadium interact to a very limited extent. Such a loosely formed collection of people in one place is a crowd rather than a group.

However, the right circumstances can quickly turn a crowd into a group. Unexpected events, from power failures to terrorist attacks, can make strangers bond quickly with strangers. As Ontarians learned during the massive power failure that occurred in August 2003, people rapidly become keenly aware of their common plight and begin to help one another. Such extraordinary experiences sometimes become the basis for lasting relationships.

Primary and Secondary Groups

People often greet one another with a smile and the simple phrase, "Hi! How are you?" The response usually is, "Fine, thanks. How about you?" This answer is often more scripted than truthful. Explaining how one is *really* doing would make most strangers or casual acquaintances feel so awkward that they would beat a hasty retreat. Friends, however, might genuinely want to hear a fuller response.

Social groups fall into one of two types, depending on their members' degree of personal concern for one another. According to Charles Horton Cooley (1864–1929), a **primary group** is *a small social group whose members share personal and lasting relationships*. People joined in primary relationships spend a great deal of time together, engage in a wide range of activities, and feel that they know one another well. In short, they show real concern for one another. In every society, the family is the most important primary group.

Groups based on lasting friendships are also primary groups.

Cooley called personal and tightly integrated groups "primary" because they are among the first groups we experience in life. In addition, the family and early play groups have primary importance in the socialization process, shaping attitudes, behaviour, and social identity. Members of primary groups help one another in many ways, but they generally think of the group as an end in itself rather than as a means to some goal. In other words, we prefer to think that family and friendship link people who belong together. Members of a primary group also tend to view each other as unique and irreplaceable. Especially in the family, we are bound to others by emotion and loyalty. Brothers and sisters may not always get along, but they always remain "family."

In contrast to the primary group, the **secondary group** is *a large and impersonal social group whose members pursue a specific goal or activity*. In most respects, secondary groups have characteristics opposite to those of primary groups. Secondary relationships involve weak emotional ties and little personal knowledge of one another. Most secondary groups are short term, beginning and ending without particular significance. Students in a college course, who interact but may not see one another after the semester ends, are one example of a secondary group.

Secondary groups include many more people than primary groups. For example, dozens or even hundreds of people may work together in the same company, yet most of them pay only passing attention to one another. In some cases, time may transform a group from secondary to primary, as with co-workers who share an office for many years and develop closer relationships. But, generally, members of a secondary group do not think of

Alex Charlton, Andrew Edelman, Noah Forster, Martin Gerber, Chris Golda/photo by Linda Gerber

AROUND THE WORLD, FAMILIES ARE THE MOST IMPORTANT PRIMARY GROUP In industrialized societies, numerous friendship groups stand with families, joining individuals on the basis of shared interests rather than kinship.

SUMMING UP

Primary Groups and Secondary Groups

	Primary Group	Secondary Group
Quality of relationships	Personal orientation	Goal orientation
Duration of relationships	Usually long term	Variable, often short term
Breadth of relationships	Broad, usually involving many activities	Narrow, usually involving few activities
Perception of relationships	Ends in themselves	Means to an end
Examples	Families, circles of friends	Co-workers, political organizations

themselves as "us." Secondary ties need not be hostile or cold, of course. Interactions among students, co-workers, and business associates are often quite pleasant, even if they are impersonal.

Unlike members of primary groups, who display a *personal orientation*, people in secondary groups have a *goal orientation*. Primary group members define each other according to *who* they are in terms of family ties or personal qualities, but people in secondary groups look to one another for *what* they are—that is, what they can do for each other. In secondary groups, we tend to "keep score," aware of what we give others and what we receive in return. This goal orientation means that secondary-group members usually remain formal and polite. In a secondary relationship, therefore, we ask the question "How are you?" without expecting a truthful answer.

The Summing Up table reviews the characteristics of primary and secondary groups. Keep in mind that these traits define two types of groups in general terms; most real groups contain elements of both. For example, a women's group on a university campus may be quite large (and therefore secondary), but its members may identify strongly with one another and provide a lot of mutual support (making it seem primary). The Sociology in Focus box deals with the world of the club DJ, where primary and secondary groups coexist.

Many people think that small towns and rural areas have mostly primary relationships and that large cities are characterized by more secondary ties. This generalization is partly true, but some urban neighbourhoods—especially those populated by people of a single ethnic or religious category, or by long-time residents—can be very tightly knit.

Group Leadership

One important element of group dynamics, or behaviour, is leadership. While a small circle of friends may have no leader at all, most large secondary groups place leaders in a formal chain of command.

TWO LEADERSHIP ROLES Groups typically benefit from two kinds of leadership. **Instrumental leadership** refers to *group leadership that focuses on the completion of tasks*. Members look to instrumental leaders to make plans, give orders, and get things done. **Expressive leadership**, by contrast, is *group leadership that focuses on the group's well-being*. Expressive leaders take less interest in achieving goals than in raising group morale and minimizing tension and conflict among members.

Because they concentrate on performance, instrumental leaders usually have formal secondary relationships with other members; these leaders give orders and reward or punish members according to how much the members contribute to the group's efforts. Expressive leaders build more personal primary ties; they offer sympathy to a member going through tough times, keep the group united, and lighten serious moments with humour. Typically, successful instrumental leaders enjoy more *respect* from members, and expressive leaders generally receive more personal *affection*.

THREE LEADERSHIP STYLES Sociologists also describe leadership in terms of decision-making style: *Authoritarian leadership* focuses on instrumental concerns, takes personal charge of decision making, and demands that group members obey orders. While this leadership style may win little affection from the group, a fast-acting authoritarian leader is appreciated in a crisis. *Democratic leadership* is more expressive and makes a point of including everyone in the decision-making process. Although less successful in a crisis situation, democratic leaders generally draw on the ideas of all members to develop creative solutions to problems. *Laissez-faire leadership* allows the group to function more or less on its own. (*Laissez-faire* is French for "leave it alone.") Typically, this style is the least effective in promoting group goals (Ridgeway, 1983; White & Lippitt, 1953).

Take a look at the Sociology in Focus box and ask yourself what kind of leadership is most likely to emerge in the DJ subculture.

Group Conformity

Canadians throughout the country were shocked by news from Vancouver Island in November 1997. A group of

Sociology in Focus

The Club DJ: Local Musician, Global Ties

A father–son team set out to understand the social world of club DJs from a symbolic-interactionist perspective—using the interpretive approach. The father is University of Guelph professor Hans Bakker; the son is Theo Bakker, otherwise known as DJ Krinjah of Montreal. Together they attempted to make sense of the DJ scene. The father provided the analytical framework, while the son acted as participant observer and informant. They recently published a paper titled "The Club DJ: A Semiotic and Interactionist Analysis." You already know that we are dealing here with micro-level analysis, the everyday social interaction of individuals, the *social construction of reality,* and *meaning.*

In determining "meaningful signs in the world of popular music," the Bakkers identified the most important as the beat and the turntable. Variation of the beat from one song to the next is "the real thing": The ability to do this requires "listening to music of one tempo in one ear and then adjusting another song until it is the right tempo in the other ear" in a process called "beat matching." The turntable techniques of scratching and juggling constitute the "grammar of dubbing." When reggae DJs spin records (and that's old-tech vinyl record albums), they don't just play them: "They are dubbing, adding another layer of interpretation, the additional 'dub' of meaning." The reputation of DJs among their peers is determined by their skills in this fine art.

The roots of club DJing lie in the reggae music of Jamaica and are reflected in the continued use of Jamaican patois by DJs. While DJ Krinjah did most of his empirical work in Montreal, he also had extensive discussions with about 300 DJs, over a six-year period, throughout North America and Europe. Because of the spatial or geographic scope of the study, the Bakker team argues that some of its claims can apply to "club DJs throughout the Western world." The global network of reggae club DJs spreads beyond the Western world. Obviously, no individual has contact with all of the others in the network, but the ties that bind them are strong because of their shared techniques and meanings. When they do meet, they speak the same international language.

Changes in technology gave rise to two different kinds of DJs—some of whom use turntables, while others use digital media. The former continue to perfect their skills on the turntable, while the latter have turned to the digital media, which are cheaper and allow new options, without the requirement of learning turntable techniques. One of the measures of prestige—in this world of turntables, the beat, and dubbing—is the DJ's collection of records, which is so important that the collector may forgo eating in order to purchase them. Without vinyl, the DJ cannot display the valued skill: "Ability to manipulate vinyl is a technical skill that is highly respected and that differentiates DJs among themselves."

Once again, we come back to the beat, and beat-matching. It is through the beat of the music—more than the melody—that club DJs "speak" to the audience and earn the respect of their peers. Engaged in symbolic communication and meaning-making, they shape the social world of the reggae DJ, and of the audiences who understand and respond to the language and grammar of the beat.

What Do You Think?

1. To what extent are club DJs and their audiences in a world of their own making?
2. How do primary and secondary groups function within the world of the club DJ?
3. Why did the researchers use symbolic-interactionism to frame this study?

Source: Bakker and Bakker (2006).

---

teenagers on a riverbank had brutally beaten 14-year-old Reena Virk, whose body was found in the water a week later. Perhaps the most shocking element in this story was the fact that the teenagers who viciously attacked their classmate were, with one exception, girls. An incident that began with accusations that Reena had been spreading rumours about one of the girls escalated into brutal violence after the girl stubbed out a cigarette on Reena's forehead. Seven girls and one boy proceeded to assault Reena, while 10 others watched and did nothing to intervene; the boy and one girl returned after the others left and pushed the unconscious Reena into the river. Actions that would not have been contemplated individually by the people involved became possible in the group context—in fact, the actions became part of the process of belonging to the group or conforming to group expectations.

The fact that teens are anxious to fit in surprises no one, although many people might be amazed at the lengths to which some will go to gain acceptance. Social scientists confirm the power of group pressure to shape human behaviour and report that it remains strong into adulthood. Thus, groups influence the behaviour of their members by promoting conformity. Fitting in provides a secure feeling of belonging but, in the extreme, group pressure can be unpleasant and even dangerous. As experiments by Solomon Asch and Stanley Milgram showed, even strangers can encourage conformity.

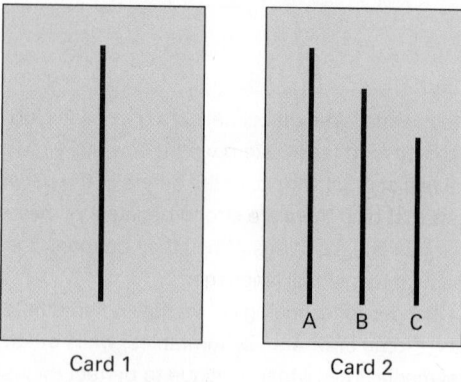

Card 1   Card 2

Figure 7–1 Cards Used in Asch's Experiment in Group Conformity

In Asch's experiment, subjects were asked to match the line on Card 1 to one of the lines on Card 2. Most subjects agreed with the wrong answers given by others in their group.

SOURCE: Asch (1952).

ASCH'S RESEARCH   Solomon Asch (1952) recruited students, supposedly to study visual perception. Before the experiment began, he explained to all but one member of a small group that their real purpose was to put pressure on the remaining person. Arranging six to eight students around a table, Asch showed them a standard line, as drawn on Card 1 in Figure 7–1, and asked them to match it to one of three lines on Card 2. Anyone with normal vision could easily see that the line marked "A" on Card 2 is the correct choice.

At the beginning of the experiment, everyone made the matches correctly. But then Asch's secret accomplices began answering incorrectly, leaving the naive subject—seated at the table so as to answer next to last—bewildered and uncomfortable. What happened? Asch found that one-third of all subjects chose to conform by answering incorrectly. Apparently, many of us are willing to compromise our own judgment to avoid the discomfort of being seen as different, even from people we do not know.

MILGRAM'S RESEARCH   Stanley Milgram, a former student of Solomon Asch's, conducted conformity experiments of his own (1963, 1965; Miller, 1986). In Milgram's controversial study (1963), a researcher explained to male recruits that they would be taking part in a study of how punishment affects learning. One by one, he assigned the subjects to the role of "teacher" and placed another person—actually an accomplice of Milgram's—in a connecting room to pose as a "learner."

The "teacher" watched as the "learner" was seated in what looked like an electric chair. The researcher applied electrode paste to one wrist of the "learner," explaining that this would "prevent blisters and burns." The researcher then attached an electrode to the wrist and secured leather straps, explaining that these would "prevent excessive movement while the learner was being

shocked." The researcher assured the "teacher" that, although the shocks would be painful, they would cause "no permanent tissue damage."

The researcher then led the "teacher" back to the next room, explaining that the "electric chair" was connected to a "shock generator"—actually a phoney but realistic-looking piece of equipment with a label that read "Shock Generator, Type ZLB, Dyson Instrument Company, Waltham, Mass." On the front was a dial that appeared to regulate electric current from 15 volts (labelled "Slight Shock") to 300 volts (marked "Intense Shock") to 450 volts (marked "Danger: Severe Shock"). Seated in front of the "shock generator," the "teacher" was told to read aloud pairs of words. Then the "teacher" was to repeat the first word of each pair and wait for the "learner" to recall the second word. Whenever the "learner" failed to answer correctly, the "teacher" was told to apply an electric shock.

The researcher, dressed in the white lab coat of a scientist, directed the "teacher" to begin at the lowest level (15 volts) and to increase the shock by another 15 volts every time the learner made a mistake. And so the "teacher" did. At 75, 90, and 105 volts, the "teacher" heard moans from the "learner"; at 120 volts, shouts of pain; at 270 volts, screams; at 315 volts, pounding on the wall; after that, deadly silence. None of 40 subjects assigned to the role of "teacher" during the initial research even questioned the procedure before reaching 300 volts, and 26 of the subjects—almost two-thirds—went all the way to 450 volts. Even Milgram was surprised at how readily people obeyed authority figures.

Milgram (1964) then modified his research to see if groups of ordinary people—not authority figures—could pressure others to administer electrical shocks, as Asch's groups had pressured individuals to match lines incorrectly.

This time, Milgram formed a group of three "teachers," two of whom were his accomplices. Each of the three "teachers" was to suggest a shock level when the "learner" made an error; the rule was that the group would then administer the lowest of the three suggested levels. This arrangement gave the naive subject the power to deliver a lesser shock regardless of what the others said.

The accomplices suggested increasing the shock level with each error, putting pressure on the third member to do the same. The subjects in these groups applied voltages three to four times higher than the levels applied by subjects acting alone. Thus, Milgram's research suggests that people are likely to follow the lead of not only legitimate authority figures but also groups of ordinary individuals, even when it means harming another person. Recall that Canadian peacekeepers tortured and brutally murdered a Somali civilian under the influence of their peers.

JANIS'S "GROUPTHINK" Experts also cave in to group pressure, says Irving L. Janis (1972, 1989). Janis argues that a number of U.S. foreign policy errors—including the failure to foresee Japan's attack on Pearl Harbor during World War II and the ill-fated involvement in the Vietnam War—resulted from group conformity among the highest-ranking political leaders. Common sense tells us that group discussion improves decision making. Janis counters that group members often seek agreement that closes off other points of view. Janis called this process **groupthink**, *the tendency of group members to conform, resulting in a narrow view of some issue.*

A Canadian illustration of the groupthink phenomenon was the inability of the federalists, who were on the "no" side of the 1995 Quebec sovereignty referendum, to see that they were in difficulty. Assuming that Quebecers would vote against sovereignty, Prime Minister Chrétien and his strategists had no "Plan B" for dealing with a victory by the "yes" side. (How would the break-up of Canada be negotiated? Could a prime minister from Quebec be the one to negotiate on behalf of the rest of Canada?) The dramatic takeover of the "yes" supporters by Bloc Québécois leader Lucien Bouchard, which took federal strategists by surprise, contributed to a razor-thin "no" victory (50.4 percent). Embarrassment and discomfort in the wake of the referendum led to attempts to assign or apportion blame. The Quebec Liberal leader and head of the provincial "no" campaign, Daniel Johnson, became the convenient scapegoat. By implication, federal leaders and strategists were not at fault.

More recently, the same-sex marriage debate provided another illustration of groupthink. As we contemplated changing the definition of marriage (from the union of a man and a women to the union of two persons), the Liberals and Conservatives found themselves on opposite sides of the debate. The Liberals supported the change in definition while the Conservatives opposed it. *Both* parties believed that they were on the "right" side of the fence on the issue and *both* believed that they were on the "winning" side in public opinion polls. Clearly, *both* parties on opposite sides of a controversial issue cannot be "right" and "winning" at the same time. Nonetheless, each party believed it—because it had engaged in groupthink; the opinion-leaders and decision-makers in each party had turned inward and listened only to those who agreed with them.

Reference Groups

How do we assess our own attitudes and behaviour? Frequently, we use a **reference group**, *a social group that serves as a point of reference in making evaluations and decisions.* A young man who imagines his family's response to a woman he is dating is using his family as a reference group. A supervisor who tries to predict her employees' reaction to a new vacation policy is using them in the same way. As these examples suggest, reference groups can be primary or secondary. In either case, our need to conform shows how others' attitudes affect us. We also use groups that we do not belong to for reference. Being well prepared for a job interview means showing up dressed the way people in that company dress for work. Conforming to groups we do not belong to is a strategy to win acceptance and illustrates the process of *anticipatory socialization*.

STOUFFER'S RESEARCH Samuel A. Stouffer and his colleagues (1949) conducted a classic study of reference group dynamics during World War II. Among many other things, the researchers asked soldiers to rate their own or any competent soldier's chances of promotion in their army unit. You might guess that soldiers serving in outfits with a high promotion rate would be optimistic about advancement. Yet the Stouffer research pointed to the opposite conclusion: Soldiers in army units with low promotion rates were actually more positive about their chances to move ahead.

The key to understanding the Stouffer results lies in the groups against which soldiers measured themselves. Those assigned to units with lower promotion rates looked around them and saw people making no more headway than they were. That is, although they had not been promoted, neither had many others, so they did not feel deprived. However, soldiers in units with a higher promotion rate could easily think of people who had been promoted sooner or more often than they had been. With such people in mind, even soldiers who had been promoted were likely to feel shortchanged.

The point is that we do not make judgments about ourselves in isolation, nor do we compare ourselves with just anyone. Regardless of our situation in *absolute* terms, we form a subjective sense of our well-being by looking at ourselves in relation to specific reference groups.

In-Groups and Out-Groups

Each of us favours some groups over others, because of political outlook, social prestige, or just manner of dress. On campus, for example, left-leaning student activists may look down on fraternity members, whom they consider too conservative; fraternity members, in turn, may snub the computer nerds who work too hard. People in just about every social setting make positive and negative evaluations of members of other groups.

Such judgments illustrate another important element of group dynamics: the opposition of in-groups and out-groups. An **in-group** is *a social group toward which a member feels respect and loyalty.* An in-group exists in relation to an **out-group**, *a social group toward which a person feels a sense of competition or opposition.* Many social groups

in-group a social group toward which a member feels respect and loyalty

out-group a social group toward which a person feels a sense of competition or opposition

follow this pattern. A sports team, the Montreal Canadiens, for example, is both an in-group to its members and an out-group for members of opposing teams, such as the Calgary Flames. A town's active New Democrats are likely to think of themselves as an in-group in relation to the local Tories. Pairs of universities, such as the universities of Guelph and Western Ontario, may have long-standing rivalries. Whatever the boundaries, in-groups and out-groups work on the principle that "we" have valued characteristics that "they" lack.

Tensions between groups sharpen the groups' boundaries and give people a clearer social identity. However, members of in-groups generally hold overly positive views of themselves and unfairly negative views of various out-groups.

Power also plays a part in intergroup relations. A powerful in-group can define others as lower-status out-groups. Historically, in countless Canadian towns and cities, those of English heritage viewed a wide range of others as out-groups, subordinating them socially, politically, and economically. The subordinated out-groups included the French and the Irish, Ukrainians and the Japanese—both interned in Canadian concentration camps—the Chinese, Jews, early Black communities (especially in Halifax), and a steady stream of the most recent immigrants. No other category experienced the systematic and legally sanctioned subordination extended to the First Nations (through the *Indian Act* and the department responsible for "Indian affairs"). Minorities often internalize the negative attitudes of the powerful or dominant in-group and pull together in their struggle to overcome negative self-images. In this way, in-groups and out-groups foster internal loyalty while also generating conflict (Bobo & Hutchings, 1996; Tajfel, 1982).

Group Size

The next time you go to a party, try to arrive first. If you do, you will be able to watch some fascinating group dynamics. Until about six people enter the room, every person who arrives contributes to a single conversation. As more people arrive, the group divides into two clusters, and it divides again and again as the party grows. Size plays an important role in how group members interact.

To understand why, note the mathematical number of relationships among two to seven people. As shown in Figure 7–2, two people form a single relationship; adding a third person results in three relationships; adding a fourth person yields six. Increasing the number of people one at a time, then, expands the number of relationships

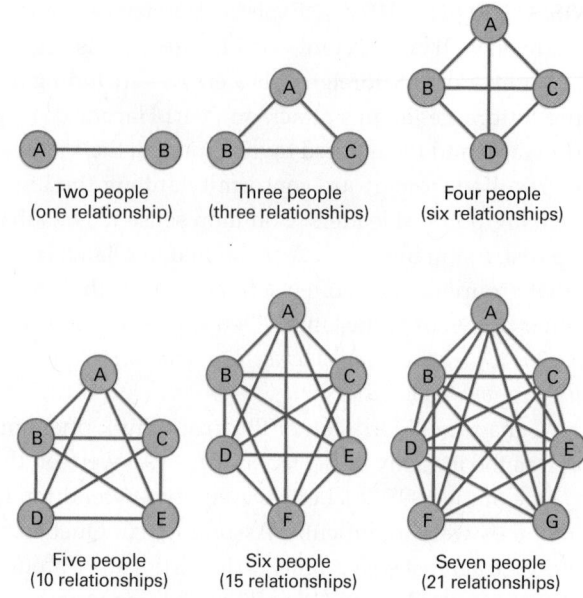

Figure 7–2 Group Size and Relationships

As the number of people in a group increases, the number of relationships that link them increases even faster. By the time six or seven people share a conversation, the group usually divides into two.

SOURCE: Created by John J. Macionis.

much more rapidly since every new individual can interact with everyone already there. Thus, by the time seven people join one conversation, 21 "channels" connect them. With so many open channels, some people begin to feel left out, and the group usually divides.

THE DYAD German sociologist Georg Simmel (1858–1918) studied social dynamics in the smallest groups. Simmel (1950; orig. 1902) used the term **dyad** to designate *a social group with two members*. Simmel explained that social interaction in a dyad is typically more intense than in larger groups because neither member shares the other's attention with anyone else. In North America, love affairs, marriages, and the closest friendships are dyadic. But like a stool with only two legs, dyads are unstable. Both members of a dyad must work to keep the relationship going; if either withdraws, the group collapses. Because the stability of marriages is important to society, the marital dyad is supported by legal, economic, and often religious ties.

THE TRIAD Simmel also studied the **triad**, *a social group with three members*, which contains three relationships, each uniting two of the three people. A triad is more stable than a dyad because one member can act as a mediator should the relationship between the other two become strained. Such group dynamics help explain why members of a dyad (say, a married couple) might seek out a third person (such as a counsellor) to discuss tensions between them. On the other hand, two of the three can pair up to press their views on the third, or two may

Jonathan Green. Collection of Patric McCoy

THE TRIAD, ILLUSTRATED BY JONATHAN GREEN'S PAINTING
***FRIENDS*, INCLUDES THREE PEOPLE** A triad is more stable than
a dyad because conflict between any two persons can be mediated
by the third member. Even so, should the relationship between any
two become more intense in a positive sense, those two are likely to
exclude the third.

Jonathan Green, *Friends*, 1992. Oil on masonite, 14 in. × 11 in. © Jonathan
Green, Naples, Florida. Collection of Patric McCoy.

intensify their relationship, leaving the other feeling left
out. For example, when two of the three develop a romantic interest in each other, they will come to understand the
old saying, "Two's company; three's a crowd."

As groups grow beyond three people, they become
more stable and capable of withstanding the loss of one
or more members. At the same time, increases in group
size reduce the intense personal interaction possible only
in the smallest groups. This is why larger groups are
based less on personal attachment and more on formal
rules and regulations.

Social Diversity: Race, Class, and Gender

Race, ethnicity, class, and gender each play a part in
group dynamics. Peter Blau (1977; Blau et al., 1982; South
& Messner, 1986) points out three ways in which social
diversity influences intergroup contact:

- **Large groups turn inward.** Blau explains that the
  larger a group, the more likely its members are to

maintain relationships exclusively among themselves. University of Toronto sociologist Raymond
Breton (1964) studied this phenomenon among urban
minorities, coining the term *institutional completeness*
to account for the abilities of larger groups to meet
their members' needs from within their own boundaries. Given large populations and institutional completeness, ethnic minorities are able to retain their
members. In contrast, members of smaller groups
reach beyond their immediate social circles. Note that
efforts to promote diversity (through multicultural
programs and policies) may have the unintended
effect of promoting separatism.

- **Heterogeneous groups turn outward.** The more
  internally diverse the group, the more likely its members are to interact with outsiders.
  Members of campus groups that include students of
  both sexes and various social backgrounds typically
  have more intergroup contact than those with members of one social category (e.g., sororities or frater-
  nities). Similarly, minorities that are economically
  integrated (in terms of occupation and income) are
  more likely to be socially integrated with the larger
  community as well.

- **Physical boundaries create social boundaries.** To
  the extent that a social group is physically segregated
  from others, its members are less likely to interact
  with other people. For example, First Nations people
  living on reserves have more limited contact with
  non-Aboriginal people than do their urban relatives.
  On the other hand, building a limited access, multi-
  lane highway (a physical barrier) through a pre-existing community effectively destroys old patterns of

Deborah Baic/The Globe and Mail/The Canadian Press

**TODAY'S COLLEGES AND UNIVERSITIES ENCOURAGE
SOCIAL DIVERSITY** One of the resulting challenges is ensuring
that all categories of students are fully integrated into campus life.
This is not always easy. Following Blau's theory of group dynamics,
as students from minorities increase in numbers, they tend to form
groups of their own and interact less with others.

Sociology in Focus

The Tattoo and Social Organization

In her fourth-year honours thesis, Monika Semma (2012) traced the movement of tattooing from its ancient origins to the tattoo parlours of today—through the process of cultural diffusion. Although archeological evidence dates tattooing to the Late Pleistocene period (about 12 000 BCE), the most widely agreed upon place of origin is Egypt (the Pacific Islands are close contenders). Semma argues that early Egyptian tattoos were *utilitarian*—reserved for women to ensure health or fertility—and that tattoos as an *art form* likely originated in the Pacific Islands.

Intriguingly, the frozen body of Otzi the Iceman (found in 1991, 3210 metres above sea level in the Italian Alps) is so well preserved that his skin—with 57 tattoos—was intact. Otzi's remains date back about 5000 years, giving us a glimpse into the Stone Age. Through cultural diffusion, the practice of tattooing may have spread from Egypt to Italy (where Otzi was found), Persia, Arabia, China, Japan, and the Pacific Islands.

Tattoos served many different purposes: marking puberty and readiness for child-bearing or other rites of passage, record-keeping (a social registry), recording lineage, and indicating social status or group membership. For many cultures, tattoos had religious or spiritual significance. In a practice that continues to this day, the Ramnaamis of India tattooed the name of their God, Ram, on every square inch of their bodies—including the tongue and inside the lips—as a sign of religious devotion. The elaborate facial tattoos of the Maori in New Zealand ensured the safe passage of their souls to the next world.

On the other hand, war tattoos act as symbols of status or machismo—and help to build solidarity among warriors. They have also been used to record the number of people killed by a warrior (like notches on a gun). In fact, members of some criminal gangs carry on the practice today as a "living tally for murder" that serves as a "readable history of criminality" (Semma, 2012:30).

For centuries, tattoos were associated with criminality. However, during the American Civil War, tattooing was acceptable for soldiers, and in the 1880s, in England and America, it gained popularity among the upper classes. Tattoos from foreign countries were symbols of worldliness—so much so that King George travelled to Japan for a dragon tattoo on his chest.

A single individual, James F. O'Connell, is credited with introducing the tattoo to North America. In 1826, the whaling ship on which O'Connell was a crew member crashed into a reef in the Pacific Islands. The entire crew made it into four lifeboats, but they became separated overnight. After three days and four nights at sea, the lifeboat carrying O'Connell and five comrades made it to shore. The natives, who were initially hostile, eventually accepted them into their society. O'Connell and one other

Monica Semma

TATTOOS ARE OFTEN SYMBOLS OF TRUE LOVE; GROUP MEMBERSHIP; ALLEGIANCE TO A BAND, SUCH AS THE GRATEFUL DEAD; OR AN OCCUPATION, SUCH AS SAILOR This one, which translates as "love without regret," is in German to reflect the wearer's ethnic origins.

man were taken to another island by a visiting chief and were adopted as full members of the community. They soon learned that acceptance meant they would be subjected to ink and a mallet (a piece of wood with embedded thorns) in the process of having their bodies tattooed. All adult men in the island society were similarly tattooed—in artwork that functioned as a social registry.

After nine years on the island, O'Connell was rescued by a passing schooner and eventually made his way to New York City. There, women and children ran away from him in fear, and pregnant women were told not to look at him or his markings would be transferred to their unborn children. In the end, O'Connell made his living touring North America with a circus—as an exhibit. His memoirs make fascinating reading.

Today, we associate tattoos not with circuses but with sailors and biker gangs who rely on group solidarity for their survival. But tattoos are found throughout Canadian society—in all social classes and on the bodies of men and women of all ages and ethnic backgrounds. Most tattoos are tiny flowers or hearts. Nonetheless, large and full-body tattoos serve as very obvious symbols that indicate where the wearer fits into our social structure.

What Do You Think?

1. Do you have a tattoo, or two, or more? If so, do your tattoos somehow symbolize your connection to other individuals or groups?

2. If you don't have a tattoo, have you contemplated getting one?

3. How accepted are tattoos among your friends and family? Can you explain their attitudes in terms of the information in this box?

interaction and creates new social boundaries. Civil engineers who design and build Canada's highways are now required to do social, economic, and environmental impact assessments for their projects.

Networks

A **network** is *a web of weak social ties*. Think of a network as a "fuzzy" group containing people who come into occasional contact but who lack a sense of boundaries and belonging. If a group is a circle of friends, then a network might be described as a "social web" expanding outward, often reaching great distances and including large numbers of people. Some networks come close to being groups, as is the case with classmates who stay in touch after graduation through class newsletters and reunions. More commonly, however, a network includes people we *know of*—or who *know of us*—but with whom we interact rarely, if at all.

It is almost certain that your contacts on Facebook form a network (a web of weak social ties) rather than a group; in fact, Facebook is a social networking service that has created the largest social network in the world – though one could argue that the World Wide Web itself is the largest of them all. With any of the social media there is a tendency to develop ties that extend far beyond the boundaries of people you know personally. How widespread are the contacts that you have established through the social media? The likelihood that you "know" all of the people in your network is extremely small.

Network ties often give us the sense that we live in a "small" world. In a classic experiment, Stanley Milgram (1967; Watts, 1999) gave letters to subjects in Kansas and Nebraska intended for a few specific people in Boston who were unknown to the original subjects. No addresses were supplied, and the subjects in the study were told to send the letters to others they knew personally who might know the target people. Milgram found that the target people received the letters with, on average, six subjects passing them on. This result led Milgram to conclude that just about everyone is connected to everyone else by "six degrees of separation." Later research, however, has cast doubt on Milgram's conclusions. Examining Milgram's original data, Judith Kleinfeld (Wildavsky, 2002) points out that most of Milgram's letters (240 out of 300) never arrived at all. Those that did were typically given to subjects who were wealthy, a fact that led Kleinfeld to conclude that rich people are far better connected throughout the United States than are ordinary women and men.

Illustrating this assertion, convicted swindler Bernard Madoff was able to recruit more than 5000 clients entirely through his extensive business networks, with one new client encouraging others to sign up. In the end, these people and organizations lost some \$50 billion in the largest Ponzi pyramid scheme of all time (Lewis, 2010).

Network ties may be weak, but they can be a powerful resource. For immigrants trying to become established in a new community, businesspeople seeking to expand their operations (e.g., through LinkedIn), or anyone looking for a job, *who you know* is often as important as *what you know* (Hagan, 1998; Petersen et al., 2000).

Networks may be based on schools, clubs, neighbourhoods, political parties, and personal interests. Obviously, some networks contain people with considerably more wealth, power, and prestige than others; that explains the importance of being "well" connected. The networks of more privileged categories of people—such as the members of an expensive country club—are a valuable form of social "capital," which is more likely to lead people to higher-paying jobs (Green et al., 1999; Lin et al., 2001).

Some people have denser networks than others; that is, they are connected to more people. Typically, the largest social networks include people who are young, well educated, and living in large cities. Networks are also dynamic. Research suggests that about half of the individuals in a person's social network change over a period of about seven years (Fernandez & Weinberg, 1997; Mollenhorst, 2009; Podolny & Baron, 1997).

Gender also shapes networks. While the networks of men and women are typically the same size, women include more relatives (and more women) in their networks, and men include more co-workers (and more men). In the end, women's ties do not carry quite the same clout as typical "old boy" networks. It is also the case that, as gender equality increases, the networks of women and men are becoming more alike (Reskin & McBrier, 2000; Torres & Huffman, 2002).

In a study of "intimate networks," Wellman (1999) found that almost everyone could name one to six intimates outside the home, only half of whom were kin. While most of their intimate contacts lived within Metropolitan Toronto, only 13 percent lived in their neighbourhood; in other words, Wellman's respondents felt close to people who were widely dispersed. Neither weak-tie networks nor the intimate variety are geographically bound. More recently, Wellman has turned his attention to internet-based social networks—as revealed in the Sociology and the Media box. Although new information technology has generated a global network of unprecedented size—in the form of the internet—the Web has not yet linked the entire world. Global Map 7–1 shows that internet use is high in rich countries and far less common in poor nations.

Sociology and the Media

Virtual Community: Building Networks through Cyberspace

A decade or two ago, young people turned to ICQ or MSN Messenger for intensive "conversation" with a network of friends and acquaintances—most often the classmates they had left at school an hour or two beforehand. More recently, Facebook and other social media have taken over. Students with laptops may well be on Facebook during lectures, but they are not alone in combining "work" with Facebook activity. Employees of some corporations communicate on Facebook, especially if co-workers are geographically dispersed. Broadcasters on CNN or the CBC regularly refer to their Facebook or Twitter messages. Even presidents and prime ministers tweet and blog these days. Add YouTube and LinkedIn to the mix and it is clear that social networking has taken off in ways that were unimaginable in the days of ICQ and MSN Messenger.

Barry Wellman, a University of Toronto sociologist, and other prominent scholars have dedicated their careers to studying social networks and their role in the creation of community. Every new technology—such as the telegraph, telephone, automobile, and airplane—that lifted the individual from a geographically defined community or neighbourhood has raised concerns about the demise of community. When social ties extend beyond the neighbourhood, sociologists have argued, surely they will be less meaningful and supportive.

Wellman and Gulia (1999) argue that, instead of being "lost in cyberspace," people who establish contact over the internet are able to build meaningful relationships and a sense of community. They found that online relationships mimic those of the face-to-face world in many ways: Some relationships are weak while others are strong and broadly supportive. Some are short-lived while others become more personal and intimate over time. In many cases, online contact complements and enhances face-to-face relationships or maintains ties among relatives or long-time friends separated by distance.

Wellman and Gulia conclude that the lack of social and physical cues allows individuals "to control the timing and content of self-disclosure" (1999:352) and, thus, the development of *intimacy*. Further, the internet fosters community diversity across the boundaries of geography, social class,

Martin Gerber/photo by Linda Gerber

gender, and race or ethnicity, so that "cyberlinks between people become social links between groups that otherwise would be socially and physically dispersed" (p. 356).

On the basis of recent research into email use, reported by Mahoney (2006a) in the *Globe and Mail,* Wellman points out that the sky hasn't fallen as predicted. Rather than destroying community, the internet and email actually expand and strengthen relationships. Email *supplements* communication with others—we continue to have telephone and face-to-face contact—rather than replaces it. The bulk of email contact appears to be with people in close physical proximity to us. On the other hand, as a medium that is more convenient and cheaper than letters or long-distance telephone calls, email helps make us part of McLuhan's "global village."

What Do You Think?

1. Why would anyone send an email or a Facebook message to someone a few blocks—or three offices—away?

2. Do you and your family keep in touch with distant friends and relatives through email? Are some of these people in other countries, and is contact more frequent than it would be by mail or telephone?

3. Are you part of a network that is sustained by the internet? If so, how would you describe your relationships in sociological terms?

Formal Organizations

7.2 Describe the operation of large, formal organizations.

A century ago, most people lived in small groups of family, friends, and neighbours. Today, most North Americans' lives revolve more and more around **formal organizations**, *large secondary groups organized to achieve*

their goals efficiently. Formal organizations, such as business corporations and government agencies, differ from families and neighbourhoods in their impersonal and formally planned atmosphere.

Organizing a society with 35 million members is a remarkable feat. Countless tasks are involved, from collecting taxes to delivering the mail. To meet most of these responsibilities, we rely on large, formal organizations.

Window on the World

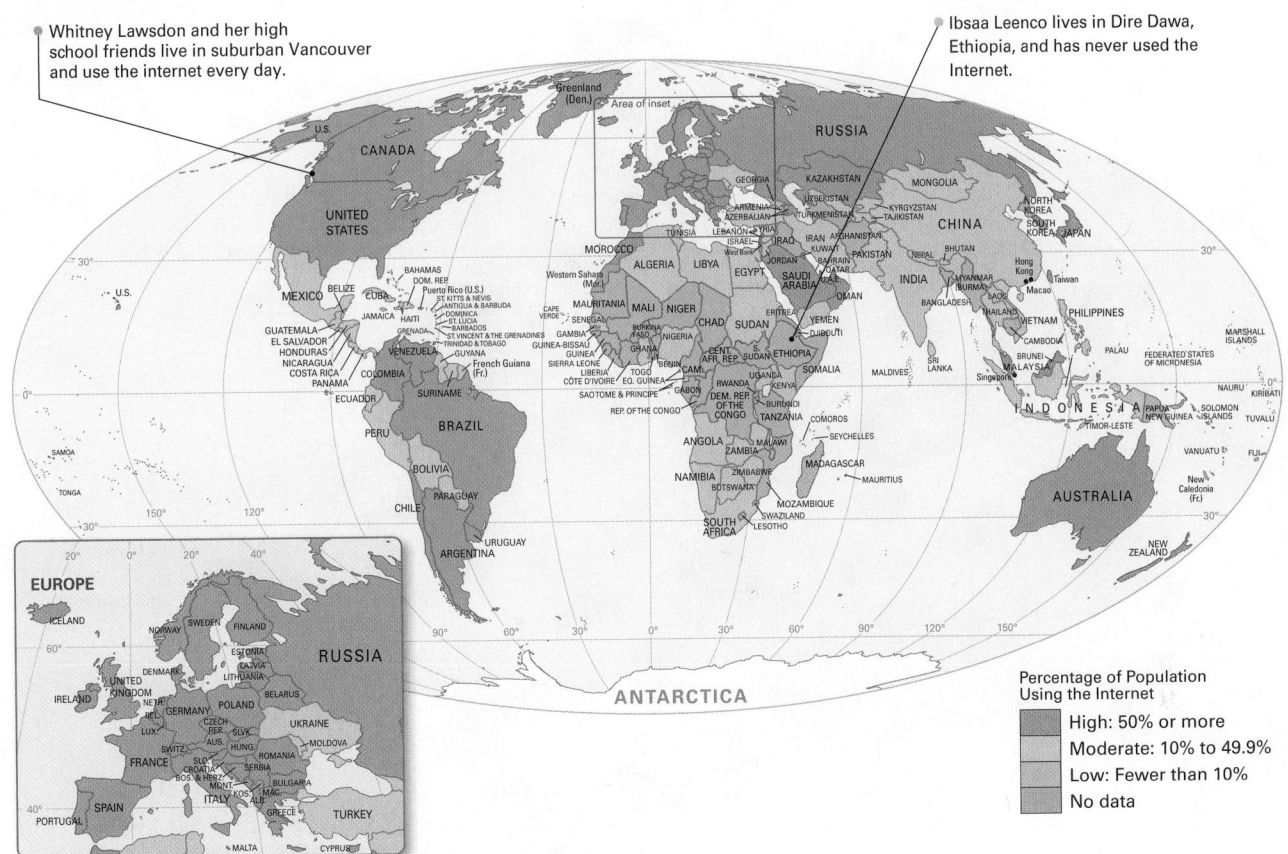

Whitney Lawsdon and her high school friends live in suburban Vancouver and use the internet every day.

Ibsaa Leenco lives in Dire Dawa, Ethiopia, and has never used the Internet.

Percentage of Population Using the Internet

High: 50% or more
Moderate: 10% to 49.9%
Low: Fewer than 10%
No data

Global Map 7–1 Internet Users in Global Perspective

This map shows how the Information Revolution has affected countries around the world. In most high-income nations, at least half of the population uses the internet. By contrast, only a small share of people in low-income nations does so. What effect does this pattern have on people's access to information? What does this mean for the future in terms of global inequality?

SOURCE: Based on International Telecommunications Union (2015).

Government, Canada's largest formal organization, employs about 1 million people in federal, provincial/territorial, regional, and municipal administration, and in police, military, and intelligence services. Such vast organizations develop lives and cultures of their own, so that, as members come and go, the statuses they fill and the roles they perform remain relatively unchanged.

Canada Map 7–1 illustrates the extent to which government bureaucracy permeates Canadian society. While 7.2 percent of Canada's labour force is employed in public administration (federal, provincial/territorial, and municipal), regional variation is clearly evident—with levels ranging from 6.2 percent in Alberta and British Columbia to a remarkable high of 32.8 percent in Nunavut.

Types of Formal Organizations

Amitai Etzioni (1975) identified three types of formal organizations, distinguished by the reasons people participate in them: utilitarian organizations, normative organizations, and coercive organizations.

UTILITARIAN ORGANIZATIONS Just about everyone who works for a regular paycheque belongs to a *utilitarian organization*, one that pays people for their efforts. Large businesses, for example, generate profits for their owners and income for their employees. Joining a utilitarian organization is usually a matter of individual choice, although most people must join one or another such organization to make a living. As noted above, government is Canada's largest employer.

NORMATIVE ORGANIZATIONS People join *normative organizations* not for income but to pursue some goal they think is morally worthwhile. Sometimes called *voluntary associations*, these include community service groups (such as the Lions Club or Kiwanis, and the Red Cross) as well as political parties and religious organizations. In global perspective, people living in Canada and other high-income nations with relatively democratic political systems are likely to join voluntary associations. Recent studies have found that 82 percent of first-year college students in the United States claimed to have participated in some

Seeing Ourselves

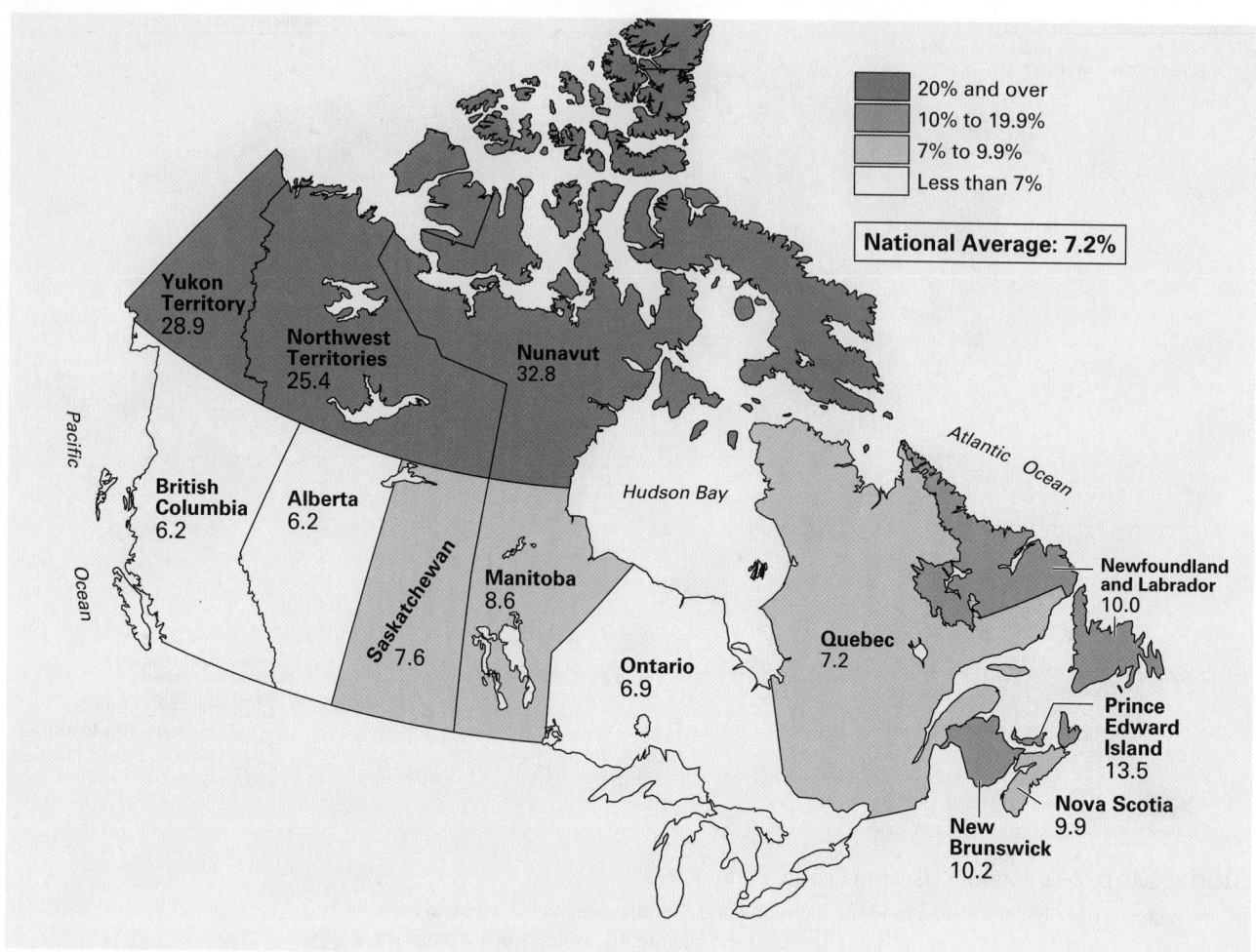

Canada Map 7–1   Employment in Government Service for Canada, the Provinces, and Territories, 2011

Government is a major employer in the territories (25.4 to 32.8 percent of the labour force) because these sparsely populated areas still require a full range of government services. Alberta, British Columbia, and Ontario, with their more diversified economies, have the lowest levels of government employment.

SOURCE: Compilation and calculations by L.M. Gerber based on Statistics Canada, NHS 2011, Catalogue no. 99-010-X2011047.

volunteer activity within the past year (Curtis et al., 2001; Hurtado et al., 2004; Schofer & Fourcade-Gourinchas, 2001). Canadian students are increasingly involved in volunteering, at high school and post-secondary levels, and can join people of all ages in matching themselves with appropriate volunteering opportunities through Volunteer Canada.

COERCIVE ORGANIZATIONS   *Coercive organizations* have involuntary memberships. People are forced to join these organizations as a form of punishment (i.e., prisons) or treatment (i.e., some psychiatric hospitals). Coercive organizations have special physical features, such as locked doors and barred windows, and are supervised by security personnel. They isolate people, whom they label "inmates" or "patients," for a period of time in order to radically change their attitudes and behaviour.

It is possible for a single organization to fall into *all* of these categories. For example, a psychiatric hospital serves as a coercive organization for the patient, a utilitarian organization for the psychiatrist, and a normative organization for the hospital volunteer.

Origins of Formal Organizations

Formal organizations date back thousands of years. Elites that controlled early empires relied on government officials to collect taxes, undertake military campaigns, and build monumental structures, such as the Great Wall of China and the pyramids of Egypt. However, early organizations had two limitations. They lacked the technology to let people travel over long distances, to communicate quickly, and to collect and store information. In addition,

SUMMING UP

Small Groups and Formal Organizations

	Small Groups	Formal Organizations
Activities	Much the same for all members	Distinct and highly specialized
Hierarchy	Often informal or non-existent	Clearly defined according to position
Norms	General norms, informally applied	Clearly defined rules and regulations
Membership criteria	Variable, often based on personal affection or kinship	Technical competence to carry out assigned tasks
Relationships	Variable and typically primary	Typically secondary, with selective primary ties
Communications	Typically casual and face to face	Typically formal and in writing
Focus	Person-oriented	Task-oriented

these pre-industrial societies had traditional cultures, so for the most part ruling organizations tried to preserve cultural systems, not change them. But during the past few centuries, what Max Weber called a "rational" world view emerged in parts of the world. In Europe and North America, the Industrial Revolution ushered in a new structure for formal organizations concerned with efficiency that Weber called "bureaucracy."

Characteristics of Bureaucracy

Bureaucracy is *an organizational model rationally designed to perform tasks efficiently.* Bureaucratic officials regularly create and revise policy to increase efficiency. To appreciate the power and scope of bureaucratic organization, consider that any one of more than 300 million telephones in North America can connect you within seconds to any other phone in a home, business, automobile, or even a hiker's backpack on a remote mountain trail in the Rockies. Such instant communication was inconceivable in the early to mid-1900s.

Our telephone system depends on technology such as electricity, fibre optics, and computers. But the system could not exist without the bureaucracy that keeps track of every telephone call—noting which telephone calls which other telephone, when, and for how long—and then presents only the relevant bits of this information to each of millions of telephone users in the form of a monthly bill.

What specific traits promote organizational efficiency? Max Weber (1978; orig. 1921) identified six key elements of the ideal bureaucratic organization:

1. *Specialization.* Our ancestors spent most of their time looking for food and shelter. Bureaucracy, in contrast, assigns individuals highly specialized jobs and compensates them so that they can pay other people for food and shelter.
2. *Hierarchy of positions.* Bureaucracies arrange personnel in a vertical ranking. Each person is supervised by higher-ups in the organization, while in turn supervising others in lower positions. Usually, with few people at the top and many at the bottom, bureaucratic organizations take the form of a pyramid.

3. *Rules and regulations.* Cultural tradition counts for little in a bureaucracy. Instead, rationally enacted rules and regulations guide its operation. Ideally, a bureaucracy operates in a completely predictable way.
4. *Technical competence.* Bureaucratic officials and staff have the technical competence to carry out their duties. Bureaucracies typically hire new members according to set standards and regularly monitor their performance. Such impersonal evaluation contrasts with the custom of nepotism, favouring relatives, whatever their talents, over strangers.
5. *Impersonality.* Bureaucracy puts rules ahead of personal whim, so that both clients and workers are treated in the same way. From this impersonal approach comes the idea of the "faceless" bureaucrat.
6. *Formal, written communications.* Someone once said that the heart of bureaucracy is not people but paperwork. Rather than casual, face-to-face talk, bureaucracy relies on formal, written memos and reports, which accumulate in vast files.

Bureaucratic organization promotes efficiency by carefully hiring workers and limiting the edictable effects of personal taste and opinion. The Summing Up table

WEBER DESCRIBED THE OPERATION OF THE IDEAL BUREAUCRACY AS RATIONAL AND HIGHLY EFFICIENT In real life, however, organizations often operate very differently than Weber's model, as can be seen in the television show *The Mindy Project.*

Jordin Althaus/Fox/Everett Collection

reviews the differences between small social groups and large bureaucratic organizations.

Organizational Environment

No organization operates in a vacuum. The performance of any organization depends not only on its own goals and policies but also on the **organizational environment**, *factors outside an organization that affect its operation.* These factors include technology, economic and political trends, current events, the available workforce, and other organizations.

- Modern organizations are shaped by the *technology* of computers, telephone systems, and personal digital assistants. Computers give employees access to more information and people than ever before. At the same time, computer technology allows managers to monitor closely the activities of workers (Markoff, 1991).

- *Economic and political trends* affect organizations. All organizations are helped or hurt by periodic economic growth or recession. Most industries also face competition as well as changes in laws, such as new environmental standards.

- *Current events* can have significant effects on organizations that are far removed from the location of the events themselves. The terrorist attacks in the United States on September 11, 2001, for example, were followed by an economic slowdown and an increase in security at the U.S.–Canada border that affects many businesses in Canada.

- *Population patterns,* such as the size and composition of the surrounding population, also affect organizations. The average age, typical education, and social diversity of a local community determine the available workforce and sometimes the market for an organization's products or services.

- *Other organizations* also contribute to the organizational environment. To be competitive, a hospital must be responsive to the insurance industry and to organizations representing doctors, nurses, and other health care workers. It must also be aware of the equipment and procedures available at nearby facilities, as well as their prices.

The Informal Side of Bureaucracy

Weber's ideal bureaucracy deliberately regulates every activity. In actual organizations, however, human beings are creative—and

Merrick Morton/picture alliance/dpa/Newscom

THE 2010 FILM *THE SOCIAL NETWORK* DEPICTS THE BIRTH OF FACEBOOK, NOW ONE OF THE LARGEST SOCIAL NETWORKING SITES IN THE WORLD In what ways have internet-based social networks changed social life in Canada?

stubborn—enough to resist bureaucratic regulation. Informality may amount to simply cutting corners on your job, but it can also provide the flexibility needed to adapt and prosper.

In part, informality comes from the personalities of organizational leaders. Studies reveal that the qualities and quirks of individuals—including personal charisma, interpersonal skills, and the willingness to recognize problems—can greatly affect organizational outcomes (Baron et al., 1999; Halberstam, 1986). Authoritarian, democratic, and laissez-faire types of leadership (described earlier in this chapter) reflect individual personality as

GEORGE TOOKER'S PAINTING *GOVERNMENT BUREAU* IS A POWERFUL STATEMENT ABOUT THE HUMAN COSTS OF BUREAUCRACY The artist paints members of the public in a drab sameness—reduced from humans to mere "cases" to be disposed of as quickly as possible. Set apart from others by their positions, officials are "faceless bureaucrats" concerned more with numbers than with providing genuine assistance. (Notice that the artist places the fingers of the officials on calculators.)

George Tooker, Government Bureau, 1956, egg tempera on gesso panel, 19 5/8 × 29 5/8 in. George A. Hearn Fund, Reproduction courtesy DC Moore Gallery, NYC.

much as any organizational plan. In actual organizations, leaders sometimes seek to benefit personally by abusing organizational power. High-profile examples include corporate scandals in such companies as Enron, Conrad Black's Hollinger International, and Bernard Ebbers's WorldCom. More commonly, leaders take credit for the efforts of the people who work for them; for example, the authority and responsibilities of many executive assistants are far greater than their official job titles and salaries suggest.

Communication offers another example of organizational informality. Memos and other written communications are the formal way to spread information throughout an organization. Typically, however, individuals also create informal networks, or grapevines, that spread information quickly, if not always accurately. Grapevines, using both word of mouth and email, are particularly important to rank-and-file workers because higher-ups often try to keep important information from them. The spread of email has flattened organizations somewhat, allowing even the lowest-ranking employee to bypass immediate superiors and communicate directly with the organization's leader or with all fellow employees at once. Some organizations object to open-channel communication and, therefore, limit the use of email. Microsoft Corporation has developed screens that filter out messages from everyone except certain approved people (Gwynne & Dickerson, 1997).

Using new information technology as well as age-old human ingenuity, members of organizations often try to break free of rigid rules in order to personalize procedures and surroundings. Such efforts suggest that we should take a closer look at some of the problems of bureaucracy.

Problems of Bureaucracy

We rely on bureaucracy to manage everyday life efficiently, but many people are uneasy about large organizations. Bureaucracy can dehumanize and manipulate us, and some say it poses a threat to political democracy.

BUREAUCRATIC ALIENATION Max Weber held up bureaucracy as a model of productivity. However, Weber was keenly aware of bureaucracy's ability to *dehumanize* the people it is supposed to serve. The same impersonality that fosters efficiency also keeps officials and clients from responding to one another's unique personal needs. Officials in large government and corporate agencies must treat each client impersonally, as a standard "case."

Formal organizations cause *alienation*, according to Weber, by reducing the human to "a small cog in a ceaselessly moving mechanism" (1978:988; orig. 1921). While formal organizations are intended to benefit humanity, Weber feared that humanity might well end up serving formal organizations.

BUREAUCRATIC INEFFICIENCY AND RITUAL- ISM *Inefficiency*, the failure of an organization to carry out the work that it exists to perform, is a familiar problem. You may recall that, in September 2005, when the people of New Orleans were struggling to survive in the wake of Hurricane Katrina, officials in the U.S. Federal Emergency Management Agency (FEMA) failed to coordinate the rescue efforts of hundreds or thousands of firefighters and others who went to New Orleans to offer help. In Canada, First Nations communities have waited decades to have their land claims processed, despite the existence of land claims commissions devoted to the task. Refugees wait many years to have their claims considered, so that by the time their cases are heard, many of them have married and had children in Canada. Once refugees have settled, it is much more difficult to justify sending them back to their countries of origin.

The problem of inefficiency is captured in the concept of *red tape*, a term that refers to the red tape used by eighteenth-century English administrators to wrap official parcels and records (Shipley, 1985). To Robert Merton (1968), red tape amounts to a new twist on the already familiar concept of group conformity. He coined the term **bureaucratic ritualism** to describe *a focus on rules and regulations to the point of undermining an organization's goals*. After the terrorist attacks of September 11, 2001, for example, the U.S. Postal Service continued to help deliver mail addressed to Osama bin Laden to a post office in Afghanistan, despite the objections of the FBI. It took an act of Congress to change the policy (Bedard, 2002).

BUREAUCRATIC INERTIA If bureaucrats sometimes have little reason to work especially hard, they have every reason to protect their jobs. Officials typically work to keep an organization going, as Weber observed, even after its original goal has been realized: "Once fully established, bureaucracy is among the social structures which are hardest to destroy" (1978:987; orig. 1921). **Bureaucratic inertia** refers to *the tendency of bureaucratic organizations to perpetuate themselves*. Formal organizations tend to take on a life of their own beyond their formal objectives; for example, as the need for service to veterans declined, War Amputations of Canada turned its attention to the needs of child amputees. Bureaucratic inertia usually leads formal organizations to devise new justifications for themselves after they have outlived their original purpose.

The discussion of oligarchy suggests that the most serious problem with bureaucracy may not be inefficiency but weakened democracy and overly powerful elites.

Oligarchy

Early in the twentieth century, Robert Michels (1876–1936) pointed out the link between bureaucracy and political **oligarchy**, *the rule of the many by the few* (1949; orig.

1911). According to Michels's "iron law of oligarchy," the pyramidal shape of bureaucracy places a few leaders in charge of the resources of the entire organization.

Max Weber credited a strict hierarchy of responsibility with high organizational efficiency. But Michels countered that this hierarchical structure also concentrates power and, thus, threatens democracy because executives can and often do use their access to information, resources, and the media to promote their personal interests.

Furthermore, bureaucracy helps distance executives from the public, as in the case of the corporate president or public official who is "unavailable for comment" to the local press, or of the Canadian prime minister who withholds documents from Parliament or the public for security reasons. Oligarchy, then, thrives in the hierarchical structure of bureaucracy and reduces the accountability of leaders to other personnel or citizens (Tolson, 1995).

Canada Map 7–1 illustrates the extent to which government bureaucracy permeates Canadian society. While 7.2 percent of Canada's labour force is employed in public administration (federal, provincial/territorial, and municipal), regional variation is clearly evident—with levels ranging from 6.2 percent in Alberta to 32.8 percent in Nunavut.

The Evolution of Formal Organizations

7.3 **Summarize the changes to formal organizations over the course of the past century.**

The problems of bureaucracy—especially the alienation it produces and its tendency toward oligarchy—stem from two organizational traits: hierarchy and rigidity. To Weber, bureaucracy is a top-down system: Rules and regulations made at the top guide every aspect of work down the chain of command. A century ago, Weber's ideas took hold in an organizational model called *scientific management*. We begin with a look at this model, then examine three challenges over the course of the twentieth century that gradually led to a new model, the *flexible organization*.

Scientific Management

Frederick Winslow Taylor (1911) had a simple message: Most businesses in the United States were sadly inefficient. Managers had little idea of how to increase their businesses' output, and workers relied on the same tired skills of earlier generations. To increase efficiency, Taylor explained, business should apply the principles of science. **Scientific management**, then, is *the application of scientific principles to the operation of a business or other large organization.*

Scientific management involves three steps. First, managers carefully observe the task performed by each worker, identifying all of the operations involved and measuring the time needed for each. Second, managers analyze their data, trying to discover ways for workers to perform each job more efficiently. Third, management provides guidance and incentives for workers to do their jobs more quickly. Taylor concluded that, if scientific principles were applied in this way, companies would become more profitable, workers would earn higher wages, and consumers would pay lower prices.

The principles of scientific management suggested that workplace power should reside with owners and executives, who paid little attention to the ideas or needs of their workers. As the decades passed, formal organizations faced important challenges, involving race and gender, rising competition, and the changing nature of work. We now take a brief look at each of these challenges.

The First Challenge: Race and Gender

In the 1960s, critics pointed out that big businesses and other organizations engaged in unfair hiring practices. Rather than hiring on the basis of competence as Weber had proposed, they excluded women and minorities, especially from positions of power. Hiring on the basis of competence is partly a matter of fairness; it is also a matter of increasing the source of talent to promote efficiency.

PATTERNS OF PRIVILEGE AND EXCLUSION Excluding women and minorities from the workplace ignores the talents of more than half of the population and leaves underrepresented people in an organization feeling like socially isolated out-groups—uncomfortably visible, taken less seriously, and given fewer chances for promotion. Understandably, minority individuals may conclude that they must work twice as hard as those in dominant categories to maintain their present positions, let alone advance to higher ones (Kanter, 1977; Kanter & Stein, 1979). Bassett (1985) found a similar belief among Canadian career women and refers to this requirement as one of society's double standards.[1]

Opening up an organization so that change and advancement happen more often, Kanter claims, motivates employees, turning them into "fast-trackers" with higher aspirations, greater self-esteem, and stronger commitment to the organization. In an open organization, leaders value the input of subordinates, thereby bolstering their morale and well-being. This, in turn, improves decision making.

THE "FEMALE ADVANTAGE" Some organizational researchers argue that women bring special management

---

[1] Charlotte Whitton, the late mayor of Ottawa, put it as follows: "A woman has to be twice as good as a man to get ahead—fortunately, it's not difficult" (cited in Bassett, 1985:45).

skills that strengthen an organization. According to Deborah Tannen (1994), women have a greater "information focus" and more readily ask questions in order to understand an issue. Men, on the other hand, have an "image focus" that makes them wonder how asking questions in a particular situation will affect their reputations.

In another study of women executives, Sally Helgesen (1990) found three other gender-linked patterns. First, women place greater value on communication skills than men and share information more than men do. Second, women are more flexible leaders who typically give their employees greater freedom. Third, compared to men, women tend to emphasize the interconnectedness of all organizational operations. In these ways, women bring a *female advantage* to companies striving to be more flexible and democratic. In sum, one challenge to conventional bureaucracy is to become more open and flexible in order to take advantage of the experience, ideas, and creativity of everyone, regardless of race or gender. The result goes right to the bottom line: greater profits.

The Second Challenge: The Japanese Work Organization

In 1980, the corporate world was shaken by the discovery that the most popular automobile model sold in the United States was not a Chevrolet, Ford, or Plymouth but the Honda Accord, made in Japan. As late as the 1950s, the label "Made in Japan" generally was found on products that were cheap and poorly made. But times had changed. The success of the Japanese auto industry, as well as companies making cameras and a range of electronic products, drew attention to the "Japanese work organization."

Japanese organizations reflect that country's strong collective spirit. In contrast to the North American emphasis on individualism, the Japanese value co-operation. In effect, formal organizations in Japan are more like large primary groups. A generation ago, William Ouchi (1981) highlighted five differences between formal organizations in Japan and those in North America. First, Japanese companies hired new workers in groups, giving everyone the same salary and responsibilities. Second, many Japanese companies hired workers for life, fostering a strong sense of loyalty. Third, with employees spending their entire careers there, many Japanese companies trained workers in all phases of their operations. Fourth, although Japanese corporate leaders took final responsibility for organizational performance, they involved workers in "quality circles" to discuss decisions that affected them. Fifth, Japanese companies played a large role in the lives of workers, providing home mortgages, sponsoring recreational activities, and scheduling social events. These policies encourage much greater loyalty in Japanese organizations than is typical in North America.

Manufacturing plants operated in Canada by Honda and Toyota (in Alliston, Ontario, and Cambridge, Ontario) achieved the same degree of efficiency and quality that won these companies praise in Japan. However, these plants struggled to win support for Japanese practices such as broad worker participation. Our corporate culture, with its rigid hierarchy and history of labour–management conflict, makes enhanced worker participation highly controversial. Workers fear that it increases their workload by making them responsible for quality control, unit costs, and overall company efficiency—while requiring them to learn new skills. Union leaders fear the undermining of union strength. Managers are reluctant to share with employees the power to direct production and schedule vacations.

Other Canadian firms have adopted Japanese management practices. "Total Quality Management" was adopted at Culinar (Montreal), Cadet Uniform Services (Toronto), Reimer Express Lines (Winnipeg), and General Electric (Bromont, Quebec). The second approach, "Continuous Improvement," was responsible for a major comeback at the Schneider food-processing plant in Kitchener, Ontario; the plant experienced improved efficiency, reduced waste, had less absenteeism, and saw a dramatic increase in profits (Fife, 1992; Florida & Kenny, 1991; Hoerr, 1989; Scott, 1992).

While Canadian businesses were adopting Japanese management principles to their benefit, Japan reeled from the effects of a prolonged recession in the 1990s and again after the American-led economic crisis of 2008. Japan is experiencing reduced competitiveness and efficiency, downsizing, unprecedented levels of unemployment, an aging population, and currency devaluation. The notion of lifelong bonds and loyalty between corporations and their employees suffered strain in some organizations and was abandoned in others. Despite what seemed to be superior business practices, Japan has joined the rest of the industrialized world in undergoing economic restructuring.

The Third Challenge: The Changing Nature of Work

Beyond rising global competition and the need to provide equal opportunity for all, pressure to modify conventional organizations is coming from changes in the nature of work itself—specifically the shift from industrial to post-industrial production. Rather than working in factories using heavy machinery to make *things,* more and more people are using computers and other electronic technology to create or process *information.* The post-industrial society, then, is characterized by information-based organizations.

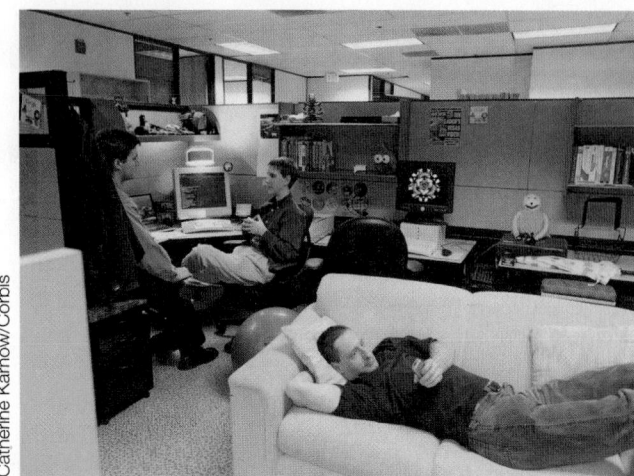

Catherine Karnow/Corbis

George Frey/Bloomberg/Getty Images

THE BEST OF TODAY'S INFORMATION-AGE JOBS—INCLUDING WORKING AT THE POPULAR SEARCH-ENGINE WEBSITE GOOGLE—ALLOW PEOPLE A LOT OF PERSONAL FREEDOM AS LONG AS THEY PRODUCE GOOD IDEAS At the same time, many other jobs—such as working the counter at McDonald's—involve the same routines and strict supervision found in factories a century ago.

Frederick Taylor developed his concept of scientific management at a time when jobs involved routine—often back-breaking—tasks. Workers shovelled coal, poured liquid iron into moulds, welded body panels to automobiles on an assembly line, or shot hot rivets into steel girders to build skyscrapers. In addition, many of the industrial workers in Taylor's day were immigrants, most of whom had little schooling and many of whom knew little English. The routine nature of industrial jobs, coupled with the limited skills of the labour force, led Taylor to treat work as a series of fixed tasks, set down by management and followed by employees.

Many of today's information age jobs are very different. The work of designers, artists, writers, composers, programmers, and entrepreneurs now demands individual creativity and imagination. Here are several ways in which today's organizations differ from those of a century ago:

1. **Creative freedom.** One Hewlett-Packard executive remarked that "From their first day of work here, people are given important responsibilities and are encouraged to grow" (cited in Brooks, 2000:128). Today's organizations treat employees with information-age skills as a vital resource. Executives can set production goals but cannot dictate how a worker is to accomplish tasks that require imagination and discovery. This gives highly skilled workers *creative freedom,* which means less supervision as they generate ideas.

2. **Competitive work teams.** Organizations typically give several groups of employees the freedom to work on a problem, offering the greatest rewards to those who come up with the best solution. Competitive work teams, a strategy first used by Japanese organizations, draw out the creative contributions of everyone and at the same time reduce the alienation

often found in conventional organizations (Maddox, 1994; Yeatts, 1994).

3. **A flatter organization.** By spreading responsibility for creative problem solving throughout the workforce, organizations take on a flatter shape. That is, the pyramidal shape of conventional bureaucracy is replaced by an organizational form with fewer levels in the chain of command, as shown in Figure 7–3.

4. **Greater flexibility.** The typical industrial organization was a rigid structure guided from the top. Such organizations may accomplish a large amount of work, but they are not especially creative or able to respond quickly to changes in the larger environment. The ideal model in the information age is a more open, flexible organization that both generates new ideas and, in a rapidly changing global marketplace, adapts quickly.

Keep in mind, however, that many of today's jobs do not involve creative work at all. More correctly, the post-industrial economy has created two very different types of work: high-skill creative work and low-skill service work. Work in the fast-food industry, for example, is routine and highly supervised and, thus, has much more in common with the factory work of a century ago than with the creative teamwork typical of today's information organizations. Therefore, at the same time that some organizations have taken on a flexible, flatter form, others continue to use the rigid chain of command.

The "McDonaldization" of Society

McDonald's has enjoyed enormous success. Expanding from a single restaurant in 1948, McDonald's now operates more than 36 000 restaurants around the world. Japan has more than 3700 Golden Arches, and the

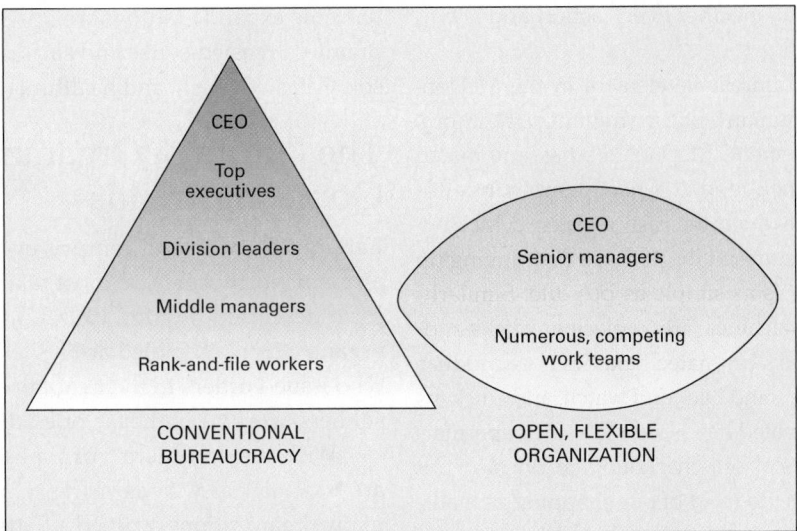

Figure 7–3 Two Organizational Models

The conventional model of bureaucratic organizations has a pyramidal shape (*left*), with a clear chain of command. Orders flow from the top down, and reports of performance flow from the base up. Such organizations have extensive rules and regulations, and their workers have highly specialized jobs. More open and flexible organizations have a flatter shape (*right*), more like a football. With fewer levels in the hierarchy, responsibility for generating ideas and making decisions is shared throughout the organization. Many workers do their jobs in teams and have a broad knowledge of the entire organization's operation.

SOURCE: Created by John J. Macionis.

world's largest McDonald's is located in Beijing. Today, McDonald's Restaurants of Canada operates more than 1400 outlets in Canada. It was the Canadian branch that ventured into Moscow just as the Soviet Union crumbled, and its restaurant in Pushkin Square may still be the busiest McDonald's restaurant in the world.

McDonald's has become a symbol of the North American way of life. When you consider that children are exposed to Ronald McDonald daily or weekly, the gleeful clown is as much a celebrity as Santa Claus, who is relevant to children only once a year. More importantly, the organizational principles that underlie McDonald's are beginning to dominate our entire society. Our culture is heavily influenced by "McDonaldization"[2]—meaning that we model many aspects of our lives on the famous restaurant chain. Canadians, who love doughnuts, indulge their cravings at Tim Hortons or Country Style Donuts, where they know exactly what they'll get because those outlets follow the McDonald's model. We buy our household and automotive supplies at Canadian Tire, where inventory is continuously monitored for just-in-time replacement. More vacations take the form of resort and tour packages, and television presents the news in 10-second sound bites. The list goes on.

FOUR PRINCIPLES What do all of these developments have in common? According to George Ritzer (1993), the McDonaldization of society rests on four organizational principles:

1. **Efficiency.** Ray Kroc, the marketing genius behind the expansion of McDonald's, set out to serve a hamburger, french fries, and a milkshake to a customer in 50 seconds. Today, one of the company's most popular items is the Egg McMuffin, an entire breakfast in a single sandwich. In the restaurant, customers dispose of their trash and stack their own trays as they walk out the door or, better still, drive away from the pickup window taking whatever mess they make with them. Such efficiency is now central to our way of life.

2. **Predictability.** An efficient organization wants to make everything it does as predictable as possible. McDonald's prepares all food using set formulas. Company policies guide the performance of each job.

3. **Uniformity.** The first McDonald's operating manual set the weight of a regular raw hamburger at 1.6 ounces (45.36 grams), its diameter at 3.875 inches (9.84 centimetres), and its fat content at 19 percent. A slice of cheese weighs exactly half an ounce (14.2 grams). Fries are cut precisely 9/32 of an inch (7 millimetres) thick. Almost anywhere in the world, one can walk into McDonald's and receive the same sandwiches, drinks, and desserts prepared in precisely the same way. Uniformity results from a highly

---

[2] The term *McDonaldization* was coined by Jim Hightower (1975); much of this discussion is based on Ritzer (1993, 1998, 2000) and Schlosser (2002).

rational system that specifies every action and leaves nothing to chance.[3]

4. **Control.** The most unreliable element in the McDonald's system is the human being. To minimize the unpredictable human element, McDonald's has automated its equipment to cook food at a fixed temperature for a set length of time. Even the cash register at McDonald's is keyed to pictures of the items so that ringing up a customer's order is as simple as possible. Similarly, automatic teller machines are replacing bricks-and-mortar banks, highly automated bakeries now produce bread while people stand back and watch, and chickens emerge from automated hatcheries. In some supermarkets, laser scanners at self-checkouts are phasing out human cashiers. We do most of our shopping in malls, where everything from temperature and humidity to the kinds of stores and products are carefully controlled and supervised (Ide & Cordell, 1994).

CAN RATIONALITY BE IRRATIONAL? There is no doubt about the popularity or efficiency of McDonald's. But there is another side to the story. Max Weber was alarmed at the increasing rationalization of the world, fearing that formal organizations would cage our imaginations and crush the human spirit. As Weber saw it, rational systems were efficient but dehumanizing. "McDonaldization" bears him out. Each of the four principles just discussed limits human creativity, choice, and freedom. Echoing Weber, Ritzer states that "the ultimate irrationality of McDonaldization is that people could lose control over the system and it would come to control us" (1993:145). Perhaps even McDonald's understands this: The company

has now expanded into more upscale offerings to include premium roasted coffee and salad selections that are more sophisticated, fresh, and healthful (Philadelphia, 2002).

The Future of Organizations: Opposing Trends

Early in the twentieth century, ever-larger organizations arose in North America, most taking on the bureaucratic form described by Max Weber. In many respects, these organizations resembled armies led by powerful generals who issued orders to their captains and lieutenants. Foot soldiers, working in the factories, did what they were told.

With the emergence of a post-industrial economy around 1950, as well as rising competition from abroad, many organizations evolved a flatter, more flexible model that prizes communication and creativity. Such "intelligent organizations" (Brooks, 2000; Pinchot & Pinchot, 1993) have become more productive than ever. Just as importantly, for highly skilled people who now enjoy creative freedom, these organizations cause less of the alienation that so worried Max Weber.

But this is only half of the story. Although the post-industrial economy has created many highly skilled jobs, it has created even more routine service jobs, such as those offered by McDonald's. Fast-food companies now represent the largest pool of low-wage labour, aside from migrant workers (Schlosser, 2002). Work of this kind, which Ritzer terms "McJobs," offers few of the benefits that today's highly skilled workers enjoy. On the contrary, the automated routines that define work in the fast-food industry, telemarketing, and similar fields are very much the same as those that Frederick Taylor described a century ago.

Today, the organizational flexibility that gives highly skilled and creative workers more freedom carries, for rank-and-file employees, the ever-present threat of "downsizing" and job loss. Organizations facing global competition seek creative employees, but they are also eager to cut costs by eliminating as many routine jobs as possible. The net result is that some people are better off than ever, while others worry about holding on to their jobs and struggle to make ends meet.

---

[3] As McDonald's has "gone global," a few products have been added or changed to accommodate local tastes. For example, in Uruguay, customers enjoy the McHuevo (hamburger with poached egg on top); Norwegians can buy McLaks (grilled salmon sandwiches); the Dutch favour the Groenteburger (vegetable burger); in Thailand, McDonald's serves Samurai pork burgers (pork burgers with teriyaki sauce); the Japanese can purchase a Chicken Tatsuta Sandwich (chicken seasoned with soy and ginger); Filipinos eat McSpaghetti (spaghetti with tomato sauce and bits of hot dogs); and in India, where Hindus eat no beef, McDonald's sells a vegetarian Maharaja Mac (Sullivan, 1995). In Quebec, McDonald's serves poutine.

Thinking Critically

Computer Technology, Large Organizations, and the Assault on Privacy

Late for a meeting with a new client, Sarah drives her car through a yellow light as it turns red at a main intersection. A computer linked to a pair of cameras notes the violation and takes one picture of her licence plate and another of

her sitting in the driver's seat. In seven days, she receives a summons to appear in traffic court (Hamilton, 2001).

Julio looks through his mail and finds a letter from a data services company in Vancouver, British Columbia, telling him that he is one of about 145 000 people whose name, address, social insurance number, and credit file have recently been sold to criminals in Toronto, posing as business people. With this information, other people can obtain credit cards or take out loans in his name (O'Harrow, 2005).

Today's large organizations—which know more about us than ever before and more than most of us realize—pose a growing threat to personal privacy. These organizations are required in our modern society, but their large databases lay the groundwork for rising identity theft and declining personal privacy.

In the past, small-town life gave people little privacy—but at least if people knew something about you, you were just as likely to know something about them. Today, as a result of our complex computer technology, unknown people can access information about each of us at any time. Every email you send and every website you visit leaves a record in one or more computers that can be retrieved by numerous people, including employers and other public officials.

Today's loss of privacy reflects the number and size of formal organizations that treat people impersonally and have huge appetites for information. Mix large organizations with ever more complex computer technology and we have every reason to wonder what others know and what they are doing with our personal information.

Consider some of the obvious ways in which organizations compile personal information. As they issue driver's licences, for example, provincial/territorial departments generate files that they can dispatch to police or other officials at the touch of a button. In Canada, driver's licences—and address changes on those licences—are used to create and modify permanent voters' lists in provincial/territorial and federal ridings. Similarly, our customs and tax departments, health care system, welfare system, and government programs benefitting veterans, students, the poor, and the unemployed all collect extensive information.

Businesses compile information on our tastes and preferences—and our whereabouts—every time we use a credit card or purchase something online. Most people consider the use of credit cards a great convenience—North Americans now average more than five such cards per adult. But few people stop to think that credit card purchases automatically generate electronic records that can end up almost anywhere.

We also experience the erosion of privacy through the surveillance cameras that monitor more and more public places, along main streets, in shopping malls, and even across campuses. And then there is the escalating amount of junk mail. Mailing lists for this material grow exponentially as one company sells names and addresses to others. Many video stores keep records of the movie preferences of customers (X-rated videos?) and pass them along to other businesses, whose advertising soon arrives by mail or email.

Of particular concern to Canadians is the information stored in connection with our social insurance numbers (SINs). The amount of personal information associated with one's SIN, the multiple uses of the number, and the possibility of merging massive files are particularly troublesome. Access by one government department or agency, such as the Canada Customs and Revenue Agency or the RCMP, to SIN-related data or Statistics Canada files also contributes to the invasion of privacy. It is possible, as well, for unauthorized users—from anywhere in the world, in fact—to gain access to and link the various files containing personal information about us. Identity theft based on such personal files can have incalculable consequences. In the spring of 2000, Human Resources Development Canada came under fire for compiling, into single files, data on individual Canadians from a variety of sources. The department was storing up to 2000 items of information about every adult Canadian. The public's reaction to the discovery of this practice was so extreme that the department was forced to destroy the files.

Similar concerns arise from the proliferation of multipurpose smart cards. Simpler ones—debit cards, for example—act as cash and allow access to all of our accounts. Potentially, a single card—with a fingerprint—could act as a driver's licence, cash card, health card, insurance record, and so on. The potential for information abuse here is high. Now that Canadians and Americans require passports—or some other secure identification—to enter or return to the United States, Canada has considered developing cards containing biometric data (i.e., fingerprints or iris scans) that can take the place of costly passports.

Concern about the erosion of privacy runs high. In response, privacy legislation has been enacted in Canada by the provinces and territories, and by the federal government. The federal *Privacy Act* (1978; amended in 1982) permits citizens to examine and correct information contained about them in government files. Canadians also have access to information (e.g., consultants' reports) that contributes to the making of government decisions and policy. The *Personal Information Protection and Electronic Documents Act* (2001) outlines corporate responsibilities and consumer rights when companies and other organizations collect information about individuals. But so many organizations now have information about us that current laws simply cannot address the scope of the problem.

What Do You Think?

1. Which do you think represents a larger threat to personal privacy: government or business? Why?

2. Internet search engines such as Yahoo! Canada and Google have "people search" programs that let you locate almost anyone. Do you think such programs are, on balance, helpful or threatening to the public?

3. Have you checked your credit history recently? Do you know how to reduce the chances of someone stealing your identity?

Seeing Sociology in Everyday Life

CHAPTER 7 Groups and Organizations

What have we learned about the way modern society is organized?

This chapter explains that, since the opening of the first McDonald's restaurant in 1948, the principles that underlie the fast-food industry—efficiency, predictability, uniformity, and control—have spread to many aspects of our everyday lives. Here is a chance to identify aspects of McDonaldization in several familiar routines. In each of the two photos on the facing page below, can you identify specific elements of McDonaldization? That is, in what ways does the organizational pattern or the technology involved increase efficiency, predictability, uniformity, and control? In the photo below, what elements do you see that are clearly not McDonaldization? Why?

Hint This process, which is described as the "McDonaldization of society," has made our lives easier in some ways, but it has also made our society ever more impersonal, gradually diminishing our range of human contact. Also, although this organizational pattern is intended to serve human needs, it may end up doing the opposite by forcing people to live according to the demands of machines. Max Weber feared that our future would be an overly rational world in which we all might lose much of our humanity.

Lisa F. Young/Shutterstock

SMALL NEIGHBOURHOOD BUSINESSES LIKE THIS ONE WERE ONCE THE RULE But the number of "mom and pop" businesses is declining as "big box" discount stores and fast-food chains expand. Why are small stores disappearing? What social qualities of these stores are we losing in the process?

B Christopher/Alamy Stock Photo

AUTOMATED TELLER MACHINES HAVE BEEN WITH US SINCE THE 1970S Today, a customer with an electronic identification card can complete certain banking operations (such as withdrawing cash and paying bills) without having to deal with a human bank teller. What makes the ATM one example of McDonaldization? Do you enjoy using an ATM? Why or why not?

Robert Harbison

AT CHECKOUT COUNTERS IN MANY GROCERY STORES, CUSTOMERS MOVE EACH PRODUCT THROUGH A LASER SCANNER—WHICH IS LINKED TO A COMPUTER THAT IDENTIFIES THE PRODUCT AND ITS COST The customer then inserts a credit or debit card to pay for the purchases.

Seeing Sociology in *Your* Everyday Life

1. Have colleges and universities been affected by the process called McDonaldization? Do large, anonymous lecture courses qualify as an example? Why? What other examples of McDonaldization can you identify on your campus?

2. Visit any large public building with an elevator. Observe groups of people, as they approach the elevator, and enter the elevator with them. Watch their behaviour: What happens to conversations as the elevator doors close? Where do people fix their eyes? Can you explain these patterns?

3. What experiences do you have that are similar to using an ATM or a self-checkout at a grocery store? Identify several examples and explain ways that you benefit from using them. In what ways might you be harmed by using these devices?

Making the Grade

CHAPTER 7 Groups and Organizations

What Are Social Groups?

7.1 Explain the importance of various types of groups to social life.

Social groups are two or more people who identify with and interact with one another.

- **A primary group** is small, personal, and lasting (examples include family and close friends).
- **A secondary group** is large, impersonal and goal-oriented, and often of shorter duration (examples include a college class or a corporation).

Elements of Group Dynamics
Group leadership

- **Instrumental leadership** focuses on completing tasks.
- **Expressive leadership** focuses on a group's well-being.
- *Authoritarian leadership* is a "take charge" style that demands obedience; *democratic leadership* includes everyone in decision making; *laissez-faire leadership* lets the group function mostly on its own.

Group conformity

- The Asch, Milgram, and Janis research shows that group members often seek agreement and may pressure one another toward conformity.
- Individuals use **reference groups**—including both **in-groups** and **out-groups**—to form attitudes and make evaluations.

Group size and diversity

- Georg Simmel described the **dyad** as intense but unstable; the **triad**, he said, is more stable but can dissolve into a dyad by excluding one member.
- Peter Blau claimed that larger groups turn inward, socially diverse groups turn outward, and physically segregated groups turn inward.

Networks are relational webs that link people with little common identity and limited interaction. Being "well connected" in networks is a valuable type of social capital.

- **Social media** based on computer technology have involved people in more and larger social networks that extend around the world.

social group two or more people who identify with and interact with one another
primary group a small social group whose members share personal and lasting relationships

secondary group a large and impersonal social group whose members pursue a specific goal or activity
instrumental leadership group leadership that focuses on the completion of tasks
expressive leadership group leadership that focuses on the group's well-being
groupthink the tendency of group members to conform, resulting in a narrow view of some issue
reference group a social group that serves as a point of reference in making evaluations and decisions
in-group a social group toward which a member feels respect and loyalty
out-group a social group toward which a person feels a sense of competition or opposition
dyad a social group with two members
triad a social group with three members
network a web of weak social ties

What Are Formal Organizations?

7.2 Describe the operation of large, formal organizations.

Formal organizations are large secondary groups organized to achieve their goals efficiently.

- **Utilitarian organizations** pay people for their efforts (examples include a business or government agency).
- **Normative organizations** have goals people consider worthwhile (examples include voluntary associations such as the PTA).
- **Coercive organizations** are organizations people are forced to join (examples include prisons and mental hospitals).

All formal organizations operate in an **organizational environment**, which is influenced by

- technology
- political and economic trends
- current events
- population patterns
- other organizations

Modern Formal Organizations: Bureaucracy
Bureaucracy, which Max Weber saw as the dominant type of organization in modern societies, is based on

- specialization
- hierarchy of positions
- rules and regulations
- technical competence
- impersonality
- formal, written communications

Problems of bureaucracy include

- bureaucratic alienation
- bureaucratic inefficiency and ritualism
- **bureaucratic inertia**
- **oligarchy**

formal organization a large secondary group organized to achieve its goals efficiently

bureaucracy an organizational model rationally designed to perform tasks efficiently

organizational environment factors outside an organization that affect its operation

bureaucratic ritualism a focus on rules and regulations to the point of undermining an organization's goals

bureaucratic inertia the tendency of bureaucratic organizations to perpetuate themselves

oligarchy the rule of the many by the few

The Evolution of Formal Organizations

7.3 **Summarize the changes to formal organizations over the course of the past century.**

Conventional Bureaucracy

- In the early 1900s, Frederick Taylor's **scientific management** applied scientific principles to increase productivity.

The Changing Nature of Work

Recently, the rise of a post-industrial economy has created two very different types of work:

- highly skilled and creative work (examples include designers, consultants, programmers, and executives)
- low-skilled service work associated with the "McDonaldization" of society, based on efficiency, uniformity, and control (examples include jobs in fast-food restaurants and telemarketing)

The Future of Organizations: Opposing Trends

- In our postindustrial society, many organizations are evolving toward a "flatter", more flexible model that encourages worker creativity.
- At the same time, other organizations that provide services require more workers to perform "McJobs." which describes low-wage, routine work.

scientific management Frederick Taylor's term for the application of scientific principles to the operation of a business or other large organization

Chapter 8
Sexuality and Society

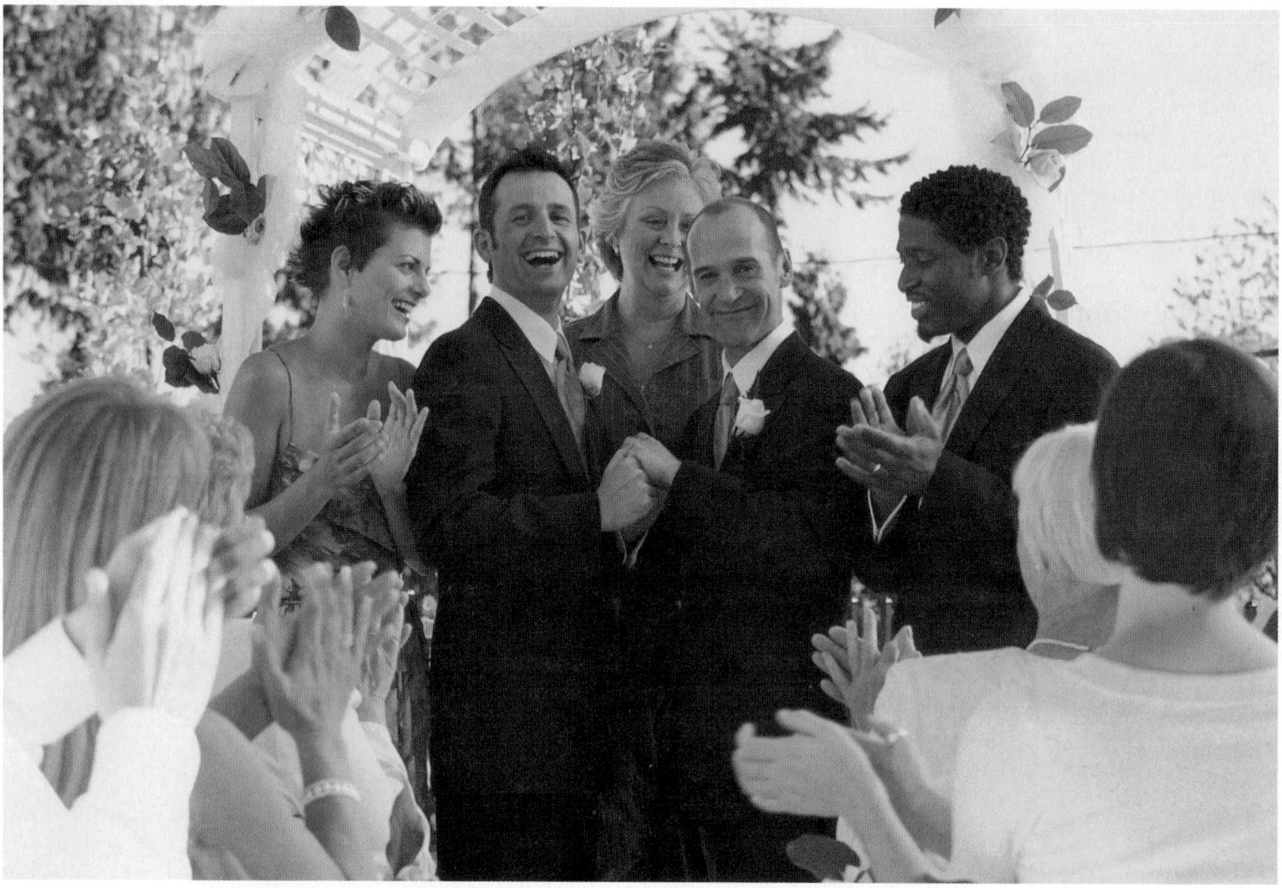

Rob Melnychuk/Photodisc/Getty Images

Learning Objectives

8.1 Describe how sexuality is both a biological and a cultural issue.

8.2 Explain changes in sexual attitudes in Canada and elsewhere.

8.3 Analyze factors that shape sexual orientation.

8.4 Discuss several current controversies involving sexuality.

8.5 Apply sociology's major theories to the topic of sexuality.

The Power of Society

to shape our attitudes on social issues involving sexuality

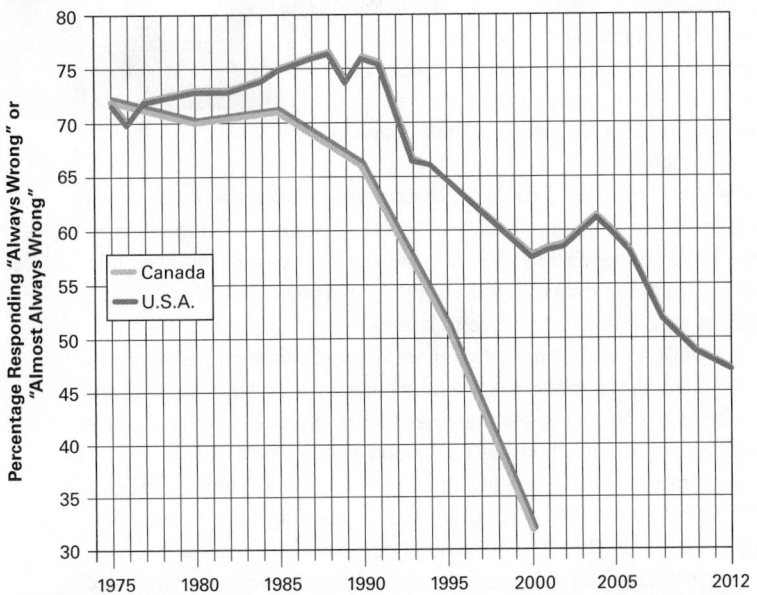

SOURCE: Bibby, Reginald W. The Bibby Report: Social Trends Canadian Style. Toronto: Stoddart, 1995. 2. Bibby, Reginald W. Restless Gods: The Renaissance of Religion in Canada. Toronto: Novalis, 2004b. 3. NORC 2013.

Does society shape our attitudes on issues involving sexuality? Back in 1970, about three-fourths of Canadians and Americans felt that sexual relations between two people of the same sex were always or almost always wrong. But something happened around 1990: The proportions on both sides of the border saying that same-sex relations were wrong declined sharply—most rapidly in Canada. By 2000, one-third of Canadians and more than half of Americans still viewed such relations negatively. While it is legal in Canada and some U.S. states, majorities in both countries now support same-sex marriage. These changes reveal the impacts of larger social trends on our personal attitudes.

Chapter Overview

Sex—no one can doubt that it is an important dimension of our lives. But, as this chapter explains, sex is far more than a simple biological process linked to reproduction. It is society, including culture and patterns of inequality, that shapes human sexuality and gives meaning to its expression in our everyday lives.

Sergeant Sylvia Durand, seen here in a leopard-skin jacket and long auburn hair, is a symbol of profound change in the Canadian military. Until 1998, she was Sergeant Sylvain Durand, a male communications specialist at the Department of National Defence in Ottawa. Her sex reassignment is significant enough in itself, but it is also a historic event: Sylvia Durand was the "first transsexual soldier who transitioned (M to F) while still serving in the Canadian Forces" (Cousens & Durand, 2012). The military was not just tolerant of her transition, it actually paid her medical expenses at a Quebec clinic that draws clients from throughout North America.

Durand's partner, Cynthia Cousens, is a former police officer. As Peter Cousens, he put in 28 years of service in downtown Toronto's tough 14 Division—and went to his retirement party dressed as a woman. Cousens had been a married man who loved his wife deeply and had two children; yet, because he felt compelled to deal with this deeply rooted yearning within him, he, too, went through the process of transitioning from male to female.

Durand and Cousens met while they were undergoing counselling and treatment prior to their operations, and they went on to form a relationship that defies easy classification. They are not, as Sergeant Durand explains, in a traditional lesbian relationship. Nor are they gay. At the time, they were two transsexuals in transition who were very much in love (Peritz, 2000).

Both Durand and Cousens realized, at about age five, that they were not like other little boys and felt that they were in the wrong bodies. According to Durand, her surgery was a miracle that left her feeling at peace with herself. Durand's metamorphosis from he to she is a tribute to Canadian open-mindedness. Although she was the first soldier in the world to undergo sex reassignment while serving in the military, her transition was accepted by her colleagues without ridicule or discrimination. This speaks volumes about changing attitudes among Canadians in general as well as in the Canadian Forces (Peritz, 2000).

Since then, Cousens and Durand have been active as invited speakers, teachers, advisors, and expert witnesses in the area of Gender Identity Disorder (GID)—for colleges and universities, federal and provincial governments, a variety of commissions, and an Ontario Human Rights Commission tribunal trial. Cousens represents the Ontario Police Liaison Committee in policing educational institutions, while Durand serves a spiritual guide for First Nations, Métis, and Inuit peoples and, most importantly for her own Huron nation, the Wendats of Wendake (Cousens & Durand, 2012). ■

This chapter examines sex and sexuality as important aspects of social life. As you will see, sexual attitudes vary widely around the world and, in North America specifically, beliefs about sex have changed dramatically over the past century. While many issues involving sexuality appear to be resolved—for example, same-sex marriage—Canadians across the country continue the debate on gay rights, teen pregnancy, prostitution, date rape, abortion, and sexual abuse (particularly when it involves children).

Understanding Sexuality

8.1 Describe how sexuality is both a biological and a cultural issue.

To what extent do your everyday thoughts and actions involve sexuality? If you are like most people, your answer would have to be "quite a lot," because sexuality is about much more than having sex. Sexuality is a theme found almost everywhere—in sports, on campus, in the workplace, and especially in the mass media. And, of course, religion has a great deal to say about sexuality. There are also sex industries—multibillion-dollar businesses—that deal in pornography and prostitution. The bottom line is that sexuality is an important part of how we think about ourselves as well as how others think about us. For this reason, there are few areas of everyday life in which sexuality does not play some part.

Despite the fact that sexuality permeates our culture and our social lives, many people treat sex as taboo and avoid talking about it. As a result, although sex can produce much pleasure, it also causes confusion, anxiety, and sometimes outright fear. Even scientists long considered sex to be off limits as a topic of research. It was not until the middle of the twentieth century that researchers turned their attention to this vital dimension of social life. Since then, we have discovered a great deal about human sexuality.

Sex: A Biological Issue

Sex refers to *the biological distinction between females and males*. From a biological point of view, sex is the way that humans reproduce. A female ovum and a male sperm—each containing 23 pairs of chromosomes (i.e., biological codes that guide physical development)—combine to form a fertilized embryo. To one of these pairs, which determines the child's sex, the mother contributes an X chromosome and the father contributes either an X or a Y. An X from the father produces a female (XX) embryo; a Y from the father produces a male (XY) embryo. In this way, a child's sex is determined biologically at the moment of conception.

The sex of an embryo guides its development. If the embryo is male, testicular tissue starts to produce large amounts of testosterone, a hormone that triggers the development of male genitals, or sex organs. If little testosterone is present, the embryo develops female genitals. Interestingly, about 105 boys are born for every 100 girls, but a higher death rate among males makes females a slight majority by the time people reach their mid-thirties (Mathews & Hamilton, 2005).

SEX AND THE BODY Some differences in the body set males and females apart. Right from birth, the two sexes have different **primary sex characteristics**—namely, *the genitals, organs used for reproduction*. At puberty, as people reach sexual maturity, additional sex differentiation takes place. At this point, people develop **secondary sex characteristics**, *bodily development, apart from the genitals, that distinguishes biologically mature females and males*. Mature females have wider hips for giving birth, milk-producing breasts for nurturing infants, and deposits of soft, fatty tissue that provide a reserve supply of nutrition during pregnancy and breastfeeding. Mature males typically develop more muscle in the upper body, more extensive body hair, and deeper voices. Of course, these are general differences; some males are smaller and have less body hair and higher voices than some females.

It has been apparent for 20 years or more that girls are reaching puberty at earlier ages than did previous generations. Only recently have we become aware of the fact that boys, too, are reaching puberty at younger ages—sometimes as early as grade 5! In a *Globe and Mail* article titled "Is it time to have that talk a little earlier?" Weeks (2012) points out that if parents are going to explain the bodily changes of puberty to their sons and daughters, they need to be aware of subtle changes that suggest when the timing might be right to do so.

Keep in mind that sex is not the same thing as gender. *Gender* is an element of culture that refers to the personal traits and patterns of behaviour, including responsibilities, opportunities, and privileges, that a culture attaches to being female or male. *Gender identity* involves the incorporation of these cultural definitions and expectations into personality.

Intersexual People Sex is not always as clear-cut as we have just described. The term **intersexual people** refers to *people whose bodies, including genitals, have both female and male characteristics*. Another term for intersexual people is *hermaphrodites* (derived from Hermaphroditus, the child of the mythological Greek gods Hermes and Aphrodite, who embodied both sexes). A true hermaphrodite has both a female ovary and a male testis. However, our culture demands sex to be clear cut, a fact evident in the requirement that parents record the sex of their new child at birth as either female or male. (Your passport and driver's licence have the same requirement.) In North America, people respond to hermaphrodites with confusion or fear. But attitudes in other cultures are quite different: Pokot people in eastern Africa, for example, pay little attention to what they consider a simple biological error, and Dinee (or Navajo) look on intersexual people with awe, seeing in them the full potential of both the female and the male (Geertz, 1975).

Transsexuals **Transsexuals** are *people who feel they are one sex even though biologically they are the other*. Estimates suggest that one or two out of every 1000 people who are born experience the feeling of being trapped in a body of the wrong sex and a desire to be the other sex.

---

primary sex characteristics
the genitals, organs used for
reproduction

secondary sex characteristics
bodily development, apart from
the genitals, that distinguishes
biologically mature females and
males

Some people, like Sylvain and Peter in the chapter opener, respond to this feeling by undergoing *sex reassignment,* surgical alteration of their genitals and breasts, usually accompanied by hormone treatments. This medical procedure is complex and takes months or even years, but it helps many people gain the joyful sense of finally becoming on the outside the person that they feel they are on the inside (Gagné et al., 1997; Olyslager & Conway, 2007; Tewksbury & Gagné, 1996).

The Sociology and the Media box deals with a unique and involuntary case of sex reassignment and eventual reversal. This case tests the assumption that gender identity—the social construct—is infinitely malleable.

Sociology and the Media
The Boy Who Was Raised as a Girl

In 1963, a physician in a Canadian prairie town was performing routine circumcisions on seven-month-old identical twin boys. While using electrocautery (surgery with a heated needle), the physician accidentally burned off the penis of one of the boys. Understandably, the parents were horrified. After consulting with Dr. John Money of Johns Hopkins University, they decided to surgically change the boy's sex and raise him as a girl.

The parents dressed "Joan" as a girl, let her hair grow long, and treated her according to cultural definitions of femininity. Meanwhile, the twin brother was raised as a boy. The researchers initially reported that, because of their different socialization, each child adopted a distinctive **gender identity**, *traits that females and males, guided by their culture, incorporate into their personalities*. In this extraordinary case, it was reported, one child learned to think of himself in masculine terms, while the other child—despite beginning life as a male—soon began to think of herself as feminine.

The girl's development did not proceed smoothly, however, suggesting that some biological forces were coming into play. While feminine in some respects, later researchers reported that she began to display some masculine traits, including a desire to gain dominance among her peers. As she reached adolescence, she was showing signs of resisting her feminine gender identity (Diamond, 1982). By the spring of 1997, the gender reassignment appeared much less successful than previously reported. By age 14, "Joan," who had been teased mercilessly by other children for her boyish looks and behaviour, was suicidal and refused to continue living as a girl. When the father broke down and told "Joan" the truth, she was relieved to finally understand herself. "Joan" became "John," undergoing a mastectomy, hormone treatment, and surgical reconstruction of male genitalia. Happy as a man, John married and adopted his wife's children (Angier, 1997). This complex case reveals that, while gender, a social construct, is the product of the social environment, cultural conditioning is limited by biology.

Joan/John (whose real name was David Reimer) was featured in a *Fifth Estate* documentary on gender reassignment, in which he talked about the painful childhood he

Winnipeg Free Press/The Canadian Press

DAVID REIMER IS THE MAN FEATURED IN THE BOOK *AS NATURE MADE HIM: THE BOY WHO WAS RAISED AS A GIRL* (2000) Author John Colapinto convinced Reimer that his story needed to be told.

had endured because of rejection by his peers. His mother told of their experience from her perspective and, essentially, contradicted the researchers concerning the "feminine" qualities of her child. Several years later, reporter John Colapinto travelled to Winnipeg to learn more about David Reimer. He convinced Reimer that it was time to put his experience into book form—but only if he was ready to reveal his true identity. The book, written by Colapinto with Reimer's co-operation, tells the story of David's struggle against his imposed girlhood, challenging Dr. Money's contention that gender identity is determined by cultural conditioning rather than by genes.

Sadly, David Reimer took his own life in 2004.

What Do You Think?

1. What should his parents have done when Reimer's penis was destroyed through a botched circumcision?
2. Who has the right to "choose" the gender of a baby with damaged sex organs or indeterminate sex characteristics?
3. Is infant male circumcision genital mutilation? Since it is done without the infant's consent, is it a violation of basic human rights?

JENNA TALACKOVA OF VANCOUVER MADE IT TO THE FINALS OF THE MISS UNIVERSE CANADA PAGEANT BEFORE BEING DISQUALIFIED The reason: She is not a "natural born" female, even though she has considered herself to be female since she was four years old. The issues of sex/gender definition are so problematic that one might ask if it is really necessary to know everyone's sex. "Is the desire for such information a residue of an era in which women were excluded from a wide range of roles and positions, and thus denied the privileges that go with them"? (Singer & Sagan, 2012).

Sex: A Cultural Issue

Sexuality has a biological foundation. But like all elements of human behaviour, sexuality is also very much a cultural issue. Biology may explain some animals' mating rituals, but humans have no similar biological program. While there is a biological "sex drive" in the sense that people find sex pleasurable and may want to engage in sexual activity, our biology does not dictate any specific ways of being sexual any more than our desire to eat dictates any particular foods to consume or our table manners.

CULTURAL VARIATION   Almost every sexual practice shows considerable variation from one society to another. In his pioneering study of sexuality in the United States, Alfred Kinsey (1948) found that most heterosexual couples reported having intercourse in a single position—face to face, with the woman under the man. Halfway around the world, in the South Seas, most couples never have sex in this way. In fact, when the people of the South Seas learned of this practice from Western missionaries, they poked fun at it as the strange "missionary position."

Even the simple practice of showing affection varies from society to society. Most of us kiss in public, but the Chinese kiss only in private. The French kiss publicly (once on each cheek) and the Belgians kiss three times (starting on either cheek). The Maoris of New Zealand rub noses, and most people in Nigeria don't kiss at all.

Modesty, too, is culturally variable. If a woman stepping into a bath is interrupted, what body parts do you think she will cover? Helen Colton (1983) reports that an Islamic woman covers her face, a Laotian woman covers her breasts, a Samoan woman covers her navel, a Sumatran woman covers her knees, and a European woman covers her breasts with one hand and her genital area with the other.

Around the world, some societies restrict sexuality, and others are more permissive. In China, for example, norms closely regulate sexuality so that few people have sexual intercourse before they marry. In Canada—at least in recent decades—intercourse prior to marriage has become the norm, and many choose to have sex without strong commitment.

THE INCEST TABOO   When it comes to sex, do all societies agree on anything? The answer is yes. One *cultural universal*—an element found in every society the world over—is the **incest taboo**, *a norm forbidding sexual relations or marriage between certain relatives.* In Canada, both law and cultural mores prohibit close relatives—including brothers and sisters, parents and children—from having sex or marrying. The incest taboo varies from state to state in the United States, where 24 states outlaw marriage between first cousins and 26 do not. In Canada, first-cousin marriage is permitted.

Some societies, such as the Dinee (or Navajo), apply incest taboos only to the mother and others on her side of the family. There are also societies on record, including those in ancient Peru and Egypt, that have approved brother/sister marriages among the nobility to keep power within a single family (Murdock, 1965; orig. 1949).

Why does some form of incest taboo exist everywhere? Part of the reason is biology: Reproduction between close relatives of any species raises the odds of producing offspring with genetic diseases. But why, of all living species, do only humans observe an incest taboo? This fact suggests that controlling sexuality among close relatives is a necessary element of *social* organization. For one thing, the incest taboo limits sexual competition in families by restricting sex to spouses—ruling out, for example, sex between parent and child. Because family ties define people's rights and obligations toward one another, reproduction between close relatives would hopelessly confuse kinship; if a mother and son had a daughter, would the child consider the son to be her father or brother? Requiring marriage outside immediate families, the incest taboo integrates the larger society as people look beyond their close kin to form new families.

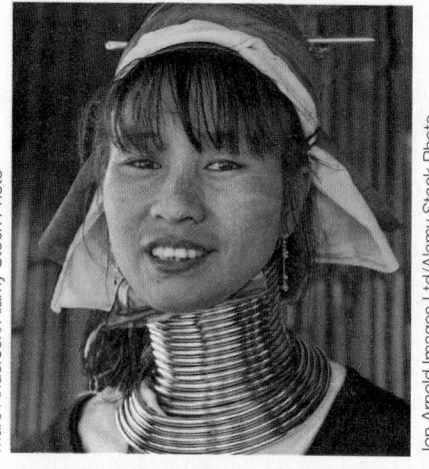
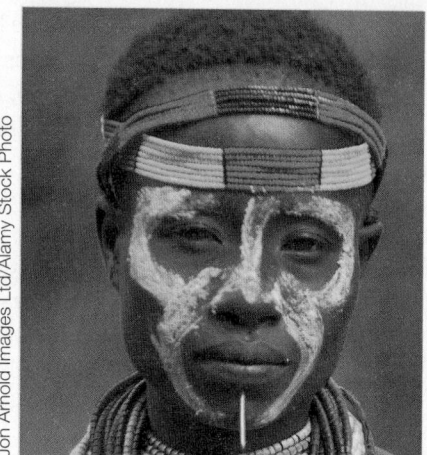
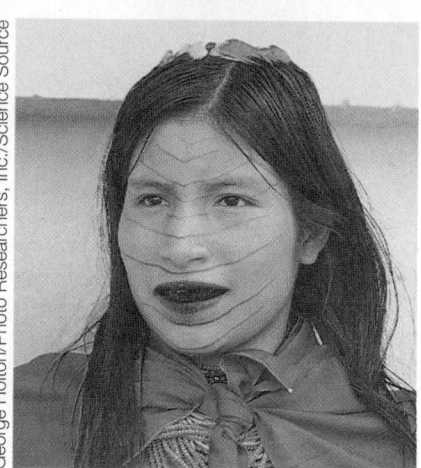

WE CLAIM THAT "BEAUTY IS IN THE EYE OF THE BEHOLDER," WHICH SUGGESTS THE IMPORTANCE OF CULTURE IN SETTING STANDARDS OF ATTRACTIVENESS All of the people pictured here—(*from top left*) from Kenya, Arizona, Saudi Arabia, Thailand, Ethiopia, and Ecuador—are beautiful to members of their own society. At the same time, sociobiologists point out that, in every society on Earth, people are attracted to youthfulness. The reason is that, as sociobiologists see it, attractiveness underlies our choices about reproduction, which is accomplished most readily in early adulthood.

Sexual Attitudes

8.2 Explain changes in sexual attitudes in Canada and elsewhere.

What do North Americans think about sex? Our cultural orientation toward sexuality has always been something of a contradiction. Most European immigrants arrived with rigid ideas about "correct" sexual conduct, typically limiting sex to reproduction within marriage. The early Puritan settlers of New England demanded strict conformity in attitudes and behaviour, and imposed severe penalties for what they perceived as sexual misconduct.

Regulation of sexuality has continued ever since. As late as the 1960s in the United States, several states legally banned the sale of condoms in stores; until 2003, thirteen states had laws forbidding sexual acts between partners of the same sex; and "fornication" laws are still on the books in eight states. In Canada, it was not until 1969 that birth control and homosexual acts, in private between consenting adults, were removed from the *Criminal Code*. Being a prescription drug, use of the "pill" was controlled by physicians, who initially would prescribe it to married women only. Teenage girls had to wait until the late 1980s before doctors could prescribe oral contraceptives without parental consent, and many secondary schools still refuse to install condom vending machines. In 2012, a Catholic university (Saint Paul University) in Ottawa prevented its student union from offering free condoms on campus (CBC News, 2010). The regulation of sexuality continues into the present.

On the other hand, since our culture is individualistic, many of us believe we should be free to do what we wish as long as we cause no direct harm to others. The idea that actions in the privacy of one's home are "my own business" makes sex a matter of individual freedom and personal choice. What, one may ask, has happened to our tendency to control or condemn various kinds of sexual behaviour?

IN DECEMBER 1967, PRIME MINISTER PIERRE ELLIOTT TRUDEAU SHOCKED CONSERVATIVE CANADA WITH THE RADICAL STATEMENT THAT "THE STATE HAS NO PLACE IN THE BEDROOMS OF THE NATION" As justice minister, he had proposed the decriminalization of homosexual acts carried out in private by two consenting adults—at a time when police actions and public opinion were still highly punitive of homosexuality (Kinsman, 1996).

Table 8–1 Canadian Attitudes toward Non-Marital Sex, Extramarital Sex, and Homosexuality, 1975–1995

	Distribution of Responses (%)				
	1975	1980	1985	1990	1995
Non-Marital sex					
Not wrong at all	39	46	50	55	57
Sometimes wrong	29	28	27	25	23
Almost always wrong	13	10	8	7	7
Always wrong	19	16	15	13	13
Extramarital sex					
Not wrong at all	5	4	3	3	3
Sometimes wrong	17	17	16	13	12
Almost always wrong	28	26	26	22	25
Always wrong	50	53	55	62	60
Homosexuality					
Not wrong at all	14	16	16	21	32
Sometimes wrong	14	14	13	13	16
Almost always wrong	10	8	9	7	7
Always wrong	62	62	62	59	45

SOURCE: Adapted by L.M. Gerber from Bibby (1995:69, 72, 75).

When it comes to sexuality, are Canadians restrictive or permissive? The answer is both. Many of us still see sexual conduct in terms of personal morality. But sex is strongly promoted by the mass media—even to children as young as 10 or 12—as if to say "anything goes." Table 8–1 shows the change in our attitudes between 1975 and 1995 toward non-marital sex (sex outside marriage), extramarital sex (adultery), and homosexuality. Bibby (1995) asked respondents to classify each of these categories as "not wrong at all," "sometimes wrong," "almost always wrong," or "always wrong." He found that Canadians became more accepting of non-marital sex and homosexuality over time; conversely, we have increasingly viewed extramarital sex as "always wrong" (from 50 to 60 percent). In other words, we are more permissive with respect to non-marital sex and homosexuality, but more restrictive when it comes to extramarital sex. Have a a close look at the table to make sure you understand how these conclusions are supported by the data.

In a survey of boomers (as well as pre-boomers and post-boomers), Bibby (2006:19) asked the question about approval of premarital (or non-marital) sex. Combining "not wrong at all" and "sometimes wrong," he was able to track changes on "approval" from 1975 to 2005. Canadian approval of premarital sex increased from 67 to 80 percent in the interval. He found that people aged 35 to 54 were increasingly likely to approve of premarital sex (63 and 87 percent in 1975 and 2005). The same was true of people over 55 years of age (40 to 75 percent). On the other hand, approval of premarital sex among younger people (18 to 34 years old) *declined* from 90 to 77 percent over the 30-year period. In effect, *young people are less likely to approve of premarital sex than those in their parents' generation!*

The Sexual Revolution

Over the past century, we saw profound changes in sexual attitudes and practices. The first indications of change came in the 1920s as people left farms and small towns for rapidly growing cities. There, away from their families and meeting new friends, young people enjoyed considerable sexual freedom during the "Roaring Twenties." In the 1930s and 1940s, the Great Depression and World War II slowed the rate of change. But in the postwar period, Alfred Kinsey helped to set the stage for the Sexual Revolution. Kinsey and his colleagues published their first study of sexuality in the United States in 1948,

4FR/E+/Getty Images

Bettmann/Corbis

OVER THE COURSE OF THE PAST CENTURY, SOCIAL ATTITUDES HAVE BECOME MORE ACCEPTING OF HUMAN SEXUALITY
What do you see as some of the benefits of this greater openness? What are some of the negative consequences?

and it raised eyebrows everywhere. While he presented startling results, the national uproar resulted not so much from what he said as from the fact that scientists were actually studying sex. Kinsey's two books (1948, 1953) became bestsellers partly because they revealed that Americans, on average, were far less conventional in sexual matters than most had thought. These books encouraged a new openness toward sexuality.

In the late 1960s, the Sexual Revolution truly came of age. Youth culture dominated public life, and such expressions as "if it feels good, do it" and "sex, drugs, and rock 'n' roll" summed up a new, freer attitude toward sex. The baby boom generation, born between 1946 and 1964, became the first cohort to grow up with the idea that sex was part of life—with or without marriage.

Technology also played a part in the Sexual Revolution. The birth control pill, introduced in 1960, not only prevented pregnancy but also made sex more convenient. Unlike a condom or a diaphragm, which must be applied before or at the time of intercourse, the pill could be taken at any time during the day. With it, women could engage in sex spontaneously without specific preparation.

Historically, women were subject to greater sexual regulation than men, so the Sexual Revolution had special significance for them. Society's sexual "double standard" allows—and even encourages—men to be sexually active but expects women to be virgins until marriage and faithful to their husbands afterwards. The survey data in Figure 8–1 show the narrowing of the double standard. Among people born between 1933 and 1942 (i.e., people who are in their sixties and seventies today), 56 percent of men but just 16 percent of women report having had two or more sexual partners by the time they reached age 20. Compare this wide gap to the pattern among the baby boomers born between 1953 and 1962 (people now in their forties and fifties), who came of age after the

Diversity Snapshot

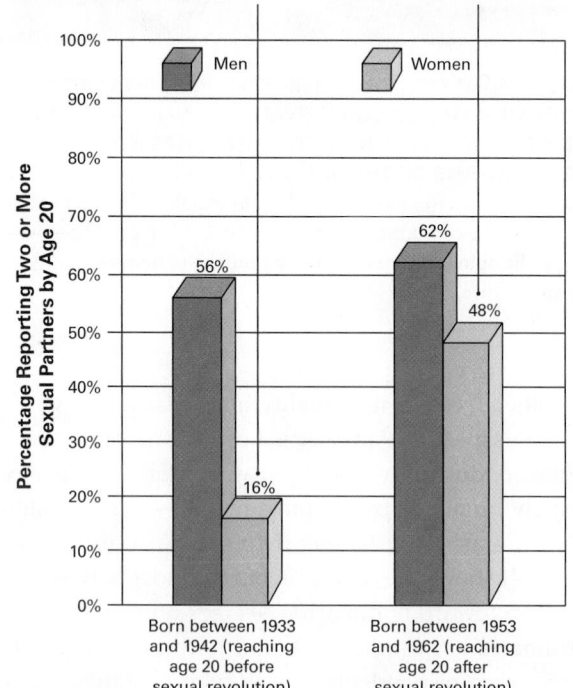

- Nancy Houck, now 76 years old, has lived most of her life in a social world where men have had much more sexual freedom than women.
- Sarah Roholt, 56, is a baby boomer who feels that she and her women friends have pretty much the same sexual freedom as men.

Figure 8–1 The Sexual Revolution: Closing the Double Standard

Diversity Snapshot

A larger share of men than women report having two or more sexual partners by age 20, but the Sexual Revolution greatly reduced the gender gap. In other words, the Sexual Revolution affected women more than it did men.

SOURCE: Laumann et al. (1994:198).

Window on the World

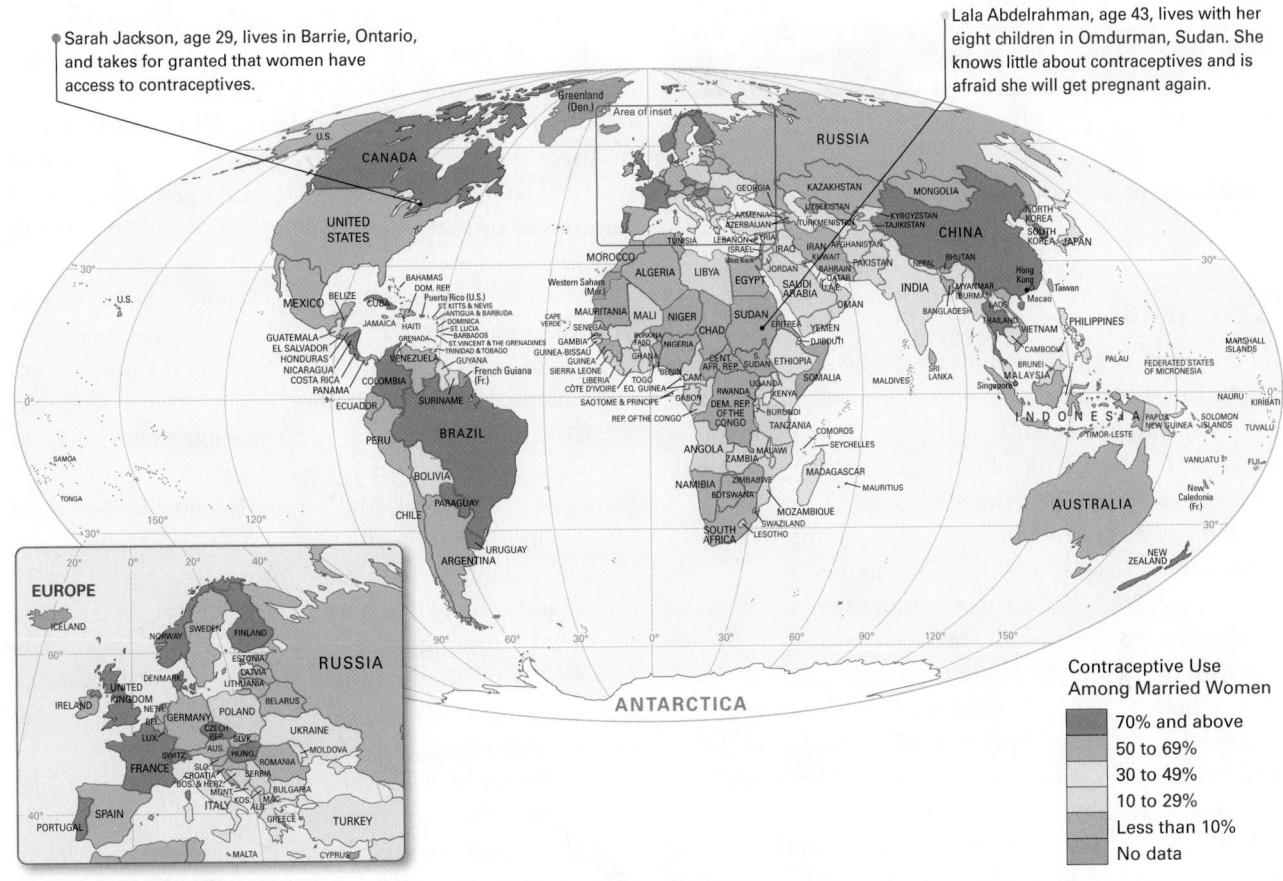

Sarah Jackson, age 29, lives in Barrie, Ontario, and takes for granted that women have access to contraceptives.

Lala Abdelrahman, age 43, lives with her eight children in Omdurman, Sudan. She knows little about contraceptives and is afraid she will get pregnant again.

Contraceptive Use Among Married Women

- 70% and above
- 50 to 69%
- 30 to 49%
- 10 to 29%
- Less than 10%
- No data

Global Map 8–1 Contraceptive Use in Global Perspective

The map shows the percentage of married women using modern contraceptive methods (such as barrier methods, contraceptive pill, implants, injectables, intrauterine devices, or sterilization). In general, how do high-income nations differ from low-income nations? Can you explain this difference?

SOURCES: Data from United Nations (2008) and Population Reference Bureau (2010).

Sexual Revolution; in this category, 62 percent of men and 48 percent of women say that they had two or more sexual partners by age 20 (Laumann et al., 1994:198). The Sexual Revolution increased sexual activity overall, but it changed the behaviour of women much more than that of men.

Greater openness about sexuality develops as societies become richer and the opportunities for women increase. With these facts in mind, look for a pattern in the global use of birth control shown in Global Map 8–1.

The Sexual Counter-Revolution

The Sexual Revolution made sex a topic of everyday discussion and sexual activity more a matter of individual choice. However, by 1980, the climate of sexual freedom that had marked the late 1960s and 1970s was criticized by some as evidence of moral decline, and the *sexual counter-revolution* began.

Politically speaking, this was a conservative call for a return to "family values" and a change from sexual freedom back to what critics saw as the sexual responsibility valued by earlier generations. Critics of the Sexual Revolution objected not just to the idea of free love but to trends such as cohabitation (living together) and childbearing by unmarried couples or single women.

The sexual counter-revolution did not turn back the tide: Under most circumstances, people still decide for themselves when and with whom to have sexual relationships. But, for reasons of morality or concern about sexually transmitted diseases, more people are limiting the number of sexual partners or choosing not to have sex at all.

Is the Sexual Revolution over? Is it true that many people are making more careful decisions about sexuality? Whatever the verdict on the impacts of the sexual counter-revolution in Canada, it has not diminished our acceptance of premarital sex or our tolerance for same-sex relationships.

Table 8–2 How Canadians and Americans View Premarital Sex

	Canada		United States	
	1975	1995	1998	2012
"Always wrong"	19%	13%	25%	21%
"Not wrong at all"	39%	57%	42%	54%

SOURCES: Bibby (1995) and NORC (1999, 2013).

Premarital Sex

In light of the Sexual Revolution and the sexual counter-revolution, how much has sexual behaviour in North America really changed? One interesting trend involves premarital sex—the likelihood that young people will have sexual intercourse before marriage.

Table 8–2 shows attitudes toward premarital sex in Canada for 1975 and 1995, as well as in the United States for 1998 and 2012. In Canada, attitudes toward premarital sex changed dramatically between 1975 and 1995—in step with the Sexual Revolution. The proportion of Canadians who felt that premarital sex is "not wrong at all" increased from 39 to 57 percent, while the belief that it is "always wrong" decreased from 19 to 13 percent. Premarital sex, within Canada, clearly gained in approval over this 20-year period (Bibby, 1995:69). Americans have been and continue to be less liberal than their Canadian counterparts. In fact, in 2012 the proportion of Americans saying that premarital sex is "always wrong" is almost identical to the proportion of Canadians with the same opinion almost 40 years earlier (19 and 21 percent in 1975 and 2012). At the other end of the continuum are those who feel that premarital sex is "not wrong at all": In this case, Americans come close to matching Canadian tolerance—but not until 17 years later (57 and 54 percent in 1995 and 2012).

In his latest book, Bibby (2009:46) reveals very interesting trends in teenage sexual attitudes. When asked about sex before marriage when the individuals involved *love* one another, 80, 87, and 82 percent of respondents in 1984, 1992, and 2000, respectively, approved. Note that the level of approval dropped between 1992 and 2000. When asked about premarital sex between people who *like* one another, 64 and 58 percent of teenaged respondents in 1992 and 2000, respectively, approved. Thus, levels of approval were *much* lower when sexually involved individuals were said to *like* rather than *love* one another; furthermore, in this case, approval ratings dropped over time—by a rather dramatic 24 percentage points (from 82 to 68 percent).

Now let's look at what young people actually *do*. For women, there has been marked change over time. The Kinsey studies (1948, 1953) report that, among people born in the early 1900s, about 50 percent of men but only 6 percent of women had had premarital sexual intercourse before age 19. Studies of baby boomers born after World War II show a slight increase in premarital intercourse among men but a large increase—to about one-third—among women. Recent studies, targeting men and women born in the 1970s, show that 76 percent of men and 66 percent of women had had premarital sexual intercourse by their senior year in high school (Laumann et al., 1994:323–324).

Statistics Canada published a report detailing trends in sexual activity and condom use among young people aged 15 to 18 (Rotermann, 2008). Some of the findings are very interesting indeed. In the decade between 1996 and 2005, the proportion of 15- to 19-year-olds who reported having sexual intercourse at least once actually *declined*—from 47 to 43 percent. Males reported no change, while females indicated a decline from 51 to 43 percent. When the respondents were divided into groups aged 15 to 17 and 18 to 19 the pattern of decline over time was apparent in both: Among those aged 15 to 17, the proportions reporting that they had had intercourse at least once dropped from 32 to 29 percent; among the older teens, the rates dropped from 70 to 65 percent.

Furthermore, *among those who were sexually active,* one-third reported having had multiple partners in the past year. Involvement with multiple partners was more likely among males than females (40 and 27 percent, respectively) and more likely among the older teens than the younger ones (36 and 29 percent, respectively). Among the sexually active teens, 75 percent claimed to have used a condom the last time they had intercourse—with 81 percent of the younger ones making that claim. In both cases the rates represent slight *increases* over time (Rotermann, 2008).

A comparison of provinces reveals that the proportion of teenagers saying they had had sexual intercourse at least once was *lowest* in Ontario and *highest* in Quebec (37 and 58 percent, respectively). Condom use among sexually active teenagers was highest in Nova Scotia and second lowest in Manitoba. Quebec stands out because its teenagers are *most likely* to report having had intercourse at least once and *least likely* to have used a condom the last time they did so (66 percent): Ontario teenagers who reported the lowest levels of sexual intercourse were average with respect to condom use (77 percent).

But what about that old double standard? Although the notion that "guys should and gals shouldn't" has been challenged, male/female differences in the meaning attached to sex persist among Canadian university students. Among anglophone students, males are more likely than females (36.4 and 19.7 percent, respectively) to endorse the recreational or fun aspect of sex. Women, in contrast, adhere to a love aspect more than men do

(48.9 and 39.1 percent, respectively). While the gender difference persists, francophone men and women are more likely to endorse the fun aspect (51.9 and 37.1 percent, respectively) than are their anglophone peers; at the same time, francophone men are slightly less likely (33.9 percent) to embrace the love aspect (Nelson & Robinson, 1999:354). Keep in mind that—in the late 1990s—39 percent of the male university students in Canada endorsed the "love" aspect of sexual relations.

Sex between Adults

Judging from the media, Americans are very active sexually. But do popular images reflect reality? The study by Laumann and his colleagues (1994), the largest study of sexuality since Kinsey's groundbreaking research, found that frequency of sexual activity varies widely among Americans. One-third of adults have sex with a partner a few times a year or not at all, another third once or several times a month, and the remainder two or more times a week.

And how do Canadians compare? Bibby (1995:65–67) also found considerable variation in the frequency of sexual activity in Canada. The pattern breaks down as follows: 24 percent report sexual activity rarely or never; 23 percent are active one to three times per month; and 53 percent of Canadian adults have sex at least once a week. Quebecers report higher levels of sexual activity than Canadians on the whole, and activity peaks among 30- to 39-year-olds for both men and women, decreasing gradually into old age. It appears that Canadian adults are more sexually active than American adults.

More recently, Laumann was involved in a study of subjective sexual well-being in 29 countries (Mahoney, 2006b)—which revealed that Canadians claim to be more sexually satisfied than Americans, though not by much. This study is the first of its kind—since it looks at sexual behaviour and satisfaction among people over 40 years of age—finding greater contentment in countries with gender equality. A ranking of countries by the percentage of people reporting sexual satisfaction reveals the following: Austria ranks first at 71 percent; Canada ranks third at 66 percent; the United States is fifth at 64 percent; and Sweden ranks ninth at 61 percent. Among the lowest five are Thailand, China, and Japan at 36, 35, and 26 percent, respectively. Professor Edward Herold at the University of Guelph notes that this study of sexuality in the second half of life is "quite an achievement" and is the result of a revitalized attitude toward sexuality among aging baby boomers (reported in Mahoney, 2006b).

Despite our openness to the notion that people over 40 are having sex (witness the ads for Viagra or Cialis), it will be a long time before we conduct surveys of sexual activity and satisfaction among the elderly (including those in their eighties and nineties). Nonetheless, elderly people do find love, sex, and even marriage—often to the dismay of their adult children. Imagine your reaction if, on a visit to the nursing home, you were to come upon your mother or father engaged in sexual activity with another resident. What if you questioned your parent's judgment because of dementia or Alzheimer's disease (Hennenberger, 2008)? The question of what to do about sexuality in nursing homes troubles many families and probably every nursing home. This issue even found its way into the world of Canadian film—in the 2006 movie *Away from Her*, starring Julie Christie and Gordon Pinsent.

EXTRAMARITAL SEX   What about sex outside of marriage? Adultery, or extramarital sex, is widely condemned: More than 85 and 90 percent, respectively, of Canadian and American adults consider extramarital sex to be "almost always wrong" or "always wrong." Thus, the norm of sexual fidelity within marriage has been and remains strongly supported in North American culture. In fact, this is one area in which we have become less liberal over the past few decades: The proportion of Canadians saying that extramarital sex is "always wrong" increased from 50 to 60 percent between 1975 and 1995 (see Table 8–1).

Cultural ideals often differ from real life—so that, predictably, extramarital sex is more common than it *should* be. Among Americans, about 25 percent of married men and 10 percent of married women have had at least one extramarital sexual experience (Laumann et al., 1994:214; NORC, 2003:1227).

Bricker and Wright (2005:214–217), of the polling firm Ipsos Reid, report some interesting findings regarding cheating on one's partner (whether married or not): 10 percent of men and 5 percent of women say they would cheat on their partners if there were no chance of getting caught—with those in British Columbia and Ontario being slightly more likely to stray—while 33 and 35 percent of men and women report a partner who cheated. Once again, note the discrepancy between the ideal and real. Somewhat surprisingly, 39 percent of Canadians believe that even "happily married people" have affairs, and 53 percent of married people would forgive an affair. On the other hand, 63 percent of divorces can be attributed to extramarital affairs.

Sexual Orientation

8.3   **Analyze factors that shape sexual orientation.**

In recent decades, public opinion about sexual orientation has changed remarkably. **Sexual orientation** refers to *a person's romantic and emotional attraction to another person*. **Heterosexuality** (*hetero* is a Greek word meaning

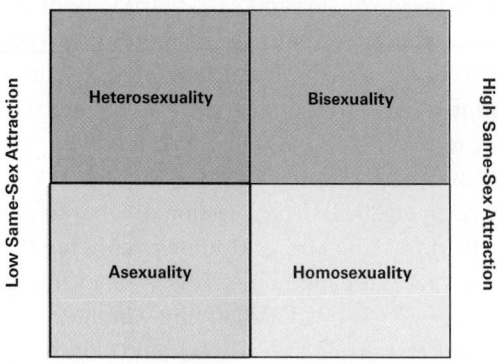

High Opposite-Sex Attraction

Heterosexuality	Bisexuality
Asexuality	Homosexuality

Low Opposite-Sex Attraction

Figure 8–2 Four Sexual Orientations

A person's levels of same-sex attraction and opposite-sex attraction are two distinct dimensions that combine in various ways to produce four major sexual orientations.

SOURCE: Adapted by J.J. Macionis from Storms (1980).

"the other of two") means *sexual attraction to someone of the* other *sex*, whereas **homosexuality** (*homo* is the Greek word for "the same") means *sexual attraction to someone of the* same *sex*. Keep in mind that people do not necessarily fall into just one of these categories; they may have varying degrees of attraction to both sexes. The idea that sexual orientation is not clear-cut is confirmed by the existence of a third category: **bisexuality**, or *sexual attraction to people of both sexes*. Some bisexual people are equally attracted to males and females; many others are more attracted to one sex than to the other. Finally, **asexuality** refers to *a lack of sexual attraction to people of either sex*. Figure 8–2 describes each of these sexual orientations in relation to the others.

It is important to remember that sexual *attraction* is not the same thing as sexual *behaviour*. Many people, perhaps even most people, have experienced attraction to someone of the same sex, but far fewer engage in same-sex sexual behaviour. This is in large part because our culture discourages such actions.

While heterosexuality is the norm almost everywhere, most societies tolerate homosexuality. Among the ancient Greeks, upper-class men considered homosexuality to be the highest form of relationship, partly because they looked down on women as intellectually inferior;

as these men saw it, heterosexuality was necessary only so they could have children, and "real" men preferred homosexual relations (Ford & Beach, 1951; Greenberg, 1988; Kluckhohn, 1948).

The acronym pertaining to the wide range of sexual orientations is LGBTTIQ2SA—lesbian, gay, bisexual, transgendered, transexual, intersex, queer/questioning, two-spirited, and asexual.

What Gives Us a Sexual Orientation?

The question of *how* people develop sexual orientation in the first place is vigorously debated. The arguments cluster into two general positions: sexual orientation as a product of society and sexual orientation as a product of biology.

SEXUAL ORIENTATION: A PRODUCT OF SOCIETY This approach argues that people in any society attach meanings to sexual activity, and these meanings differ from place to place and over time. Michel Foucault (1990; orig. 1978) points out, for example, that there was no distinct category of people called "homosexuals" until a century ago, when scientists and eventually the public as a whole began defining people that way. Throughout history, many people no doubt had what we would call "homosexual experiences," but neither they nor others saw in this behaviour the basis for any special identity.

Anthropological studies show that patterns of homosexuality differ from one society to another. In Siberia, for example, Chukchee homosexual males have a practice in which one man dresses like a female and does a woman's work. Sambia, who dwell in the Eastern Highlands of New Guinea, have a ritual in which young boys perform oral sex on older men in the belief that ingesting semen will enhance their masculinity. The existence of such diverse patterns in societies around the world indicates that human sexual expression is socially constructed (Blackwood & Wieringa, 1999; Murray & Roscoe, 1998).

SEXUAL ORIENTATION: A PRODUCT OF BIOLOGY A growing body of evidence suggests that sexual orientation is innate or biological. Arguing this position, LeVay (1993) links sexual orientation to the structure of a person's brain, finding a small but important difference in

---

sexual orientation a person's romantic and emotional attraction to another person

heterosexuality sexual attraction to someone of the other sex	**homosexuality** sexual attraction to someone of the same sex	**bisexuality** sexual attraction to people of both sexes	**asexuality** a lack of sexual attraction to people of either sex

the size of the hypothalamus, a part of the brain that regulates hormones. This anatomical difference may play a part in shaping sexual orientation.

Genetics also may influence sexual orientation. One study of 44 pairs of brothers, all homosexual, found that 33 pairs had a distinctive genetic pattern involving the X chromosome. The gay brothers also had an unusually high number of gay male relatives—but only on their mother's side. Such evidence leads some researchers to think there may be a "gay" gene located on the X chromosome (Hamer & Copeland, 1994).

EVALUATE

Mounting evidence supports the conclusion that sexual orientation is rooted in biology, although the best guess at present is that both nature and nurture play a part. Remember that sexual orientation is not a matter of neat categories. Many who think of themselves as homosexual have had heterosexual experiences, just as many heterosexuals have had homosexual experiences.

There is also a political issue here, with great importance for gay men and lesbians. To the extent that sexual orientation is based in biology, homosexuals have no more choice about their sexual orientation than they do about their skin colour. If this is so, shouldn't gay men and lesbians expect the same rights and legal protection as visible minorities?

CHECK YOUR LEARNING What evidence supports the position that sexual behaviour is constructed by society? What evidence supports the position that sexual orientation is rooted in biology?

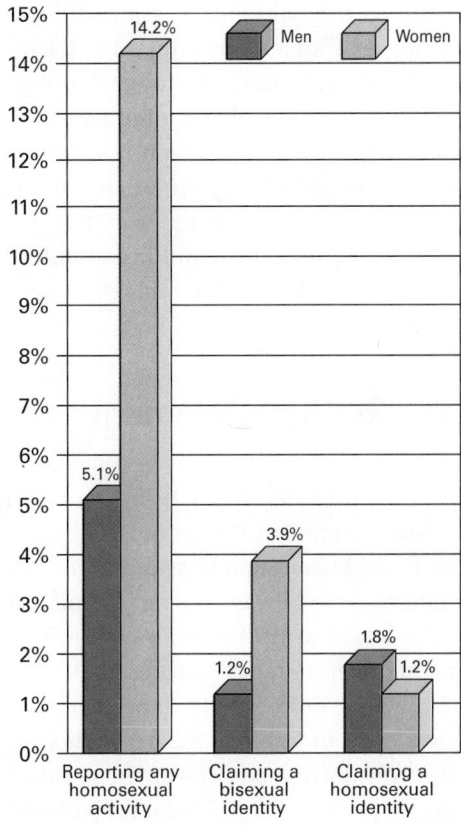

Figure 8–3 Share of the Population that Is Bisexual or Homosexual

Although more women than men report having had a homosexual experience, more men than women claim to have a homosexual identity.

SOURCE: Centers for Disease Control and Prevention (2014).

How Many Gay People Are There?

What share of our population is homosexual, or gay? This is a difficult question to answer because, as we have explained, sexual orientation is not a matter of neat categories. In addition, not all people are willing to reveal their sexuality to strangers or even to family members. Pioneering sex researcher Alfred Kinsey (1948, 1953) estimated that about 4 percent of males and 2 percent of females have an exclusively same-sex orientation, although he pointed out that most people experience same-sex attraction at some point in their lives.

As Figure 8–3 shows, about 5 percent of men and 14 percent of women report homosexual activity *at some time in their lives*, but few claim either bisexual or homosexual identities. Women are much more likely than men to claim bisexual identities (4 and 1 percent respectively) while the opposite is true of homosexual identity: Men are more likely than women (2 and 1 percent) to see themselves as homosexuals. Note that these figures are lower than those of Kinsey (above).

Kinsey treated sexual orientation as an either/or trait, but same-sex and other-sex attractions can operate independently. Bisexual people (less than 1 percent

of adults) feel a strong attraction to people of both sexes, and asexual people experience little sexual attraction to those of either sex.

For the first time, in 2001, the Canadian census asked individuals in common-law relationships to

HALIFAX, TORONTO, AND VANCOUVER ARE AMONG THE NORTH AMERICAN AND EUROPEAN CITIES THAT HOLD ANNUAL GAY PRIDE PARADES, LIKE THE ONE ATTENDED BY THIS COUPLE.

indicate whether they are same-sex couples, because by then same-sex coupleswere entitled to the same benefits as heterosexual common-law partners. The 2011 National Household Survey counted 64 575 same-sex couples, 43 560 of them in common-law unions. Same-sex couples represent 0.8 percent of all Canadian couples, 0.3 percent of married couples and 2.8 percent of common-law couples. The Thinking about Diversity box looks more deeply into the topic of same-sex marriage in Canada.

The Gay Rights Movement

In recent decades, the public has become increasingly accepting of homosexuality. In 1975—as shown in the Power of Society figure in the opening of this chapter—72 percent of Americans and Canadians felt that homosexual relations were "always wrong" or "almost always wrong." From 1975 to 1990, Americans became slightly more intolerant before rapidly changing their attitudes, to the point where, in 1995, only 66 percent disapproved of homosexuality. In Canada, the proportion of people who disapproved dropped off sooner, so that by 1995, only 51 percent of Canadians claimed that homosexuality is "always wrong" or "almost always wrong" (Bibby, 1995:72). By 2000, 32 percent of Canadians and 57 percent of Americans felt that homosexuality was wrong. By 2010, the proportion of Americans believing that homosexual relations were wrong had declined to *47 percent*—a full 10 years after it had dropped to *32 percent* in Canada. The overall trend in attitudes is very similar in the United States and Canada; both countries registered 72 percent disapproval in 1975, with levels declining rapidly after 1990. Nonetheless, Americans continue to lag behind Canadians in acceptance and approval of same-sex relations.

Bibby (2001) reveals increasing approval of homosexuality among teenagers—26, 38, and 54 percent of teenaged respondents in 1984, 1992, and 2000, respectively, approved of or accepted same-sex relations. The level in 2000 is almost identical to that for teenage approval of premarital sex among people who *like* (as opposed to *love*) each other, as discussed earlier. Bibby found that baby boomers are more likely to approve of homosexuality than their parents and grandparents. Approval among this group increased from 43 to 66 percent between 1975 and 2000; in fact, boomer approval was greater than that of teenagers in 2000 (66 versus 54 percent).

In large measure, these changes came about through the gay rights movement that arose in the 1960s (Chauncey, 1994). At that time, most people did not discuss homosexuality, and it was common for organizations—including companies, the federal government and the military—to fire anyone who was thought to be gay. Mental health professionals, too, took a hard line, describing homosexuals as "sick" and sometimes placing them in mental hospitals, where, presumably, they might be cured.

In this climate of intolerance, most lesbians and gay men remained "in the closet"—closely guarding their secret. The gay rights movement strengthened during the 1960s and, in 1969, Canada removed homosexual activity in private between consenting adults (aged 21 or older) from the *Criminal Code*. This limited reform passed in the context of heated debate, including talk of "gross indecency," "horror," and "sickness" (Kinsman, 1996). In 1974, the American Psychological Association declared that homosexuality was not an illness but simply a form of "sexual behaviour."

By 1998, Canada had extended some benefits (e.g., pensions) to partners in same-sex relationships, but was careful to reiterate that "marriage" was defined as the union of a man and a woman. This definition was affirmed in Bill C-23, which, in June 2000, extended to same-sex couples in committed relationships both the *benefits* and the *obligations* of other unions. In June 2003, after the marriage laws were struck down by courts in Ontario, British Columbia, and Quebec, the federal government announced that it would submit legislation allowing same-sex marriages to the Supreme Court of Canada for review. On July 20, 2005, the *Civil Marriage Act*—passed by Paul Martin's Liberal government—made same-sex marriage legal throughout the country.

The United States is also dealing with pressure to recognize "gay marriage" in law. In 2004, a number of cities and towns began to allow gay couples to marry, although these unions were later declared illegal. But gay marriage became legal in Massachusetts in 2004, and is now also legal in Connecticut (2008), Vermont (2009), Iowa (2009), Maine (2009), New Hampshire (2009), New York (2011), Washington (2012), Maryland (2012), Maine (2012), Delaware (2013), Rhode Island (2013), Minnesota (2013), and California (briefly in 2008, then in 2013). A number of other states recognize either "domestic partnerships" or "civil unions," which provide most or all of the benefits of marriage. At the same time, a majority of the states have enacted laws that forbid gay marriage and prohibit recognizing gay marriages performed elsewhere (National Conference of State Legislatures, 2015).

In May 2012, U.S. President Barack Obama took a courageous stand by declaring his support for same-sex marriage: "Same-sex couples should be able to get married." He explained that his views on gay marriage had changed and credited "friends, his wife and his daughters for shaping his current view." In fact, his views are consistent with a "growing majority of Americans" and likely energized his political base in his bid for reelection (Verma, 2012).

The gay rights movement began using the term **homophobia** to describe *the dread of close personal*

Thinking about Diversity: Race, Class, and Gender

Same-Sex Marriage in Canada

On January 14, 2001, Toronto made history by witnessing the world's first legal homosexual marriage since the Middle Ages—an event that attracted reporters from around the world. In Canada, legal marriage can be arranged through two routes: The first is through application for a marriage licence; the second involves the Christian tradition of the publication of banns on three Sundays prior to the marriage. Applications for marriage licences made by homosexual couples had, until that point, been refused throughout Canada, but Toronto's Metropolitan Community Church published banns for Joe Varnell and Kevin Bourassa and for Anne and Elaine Vantour. Even though the Ontario government refused to register these marriages, they were legal (Humphreys, 2001).

In a judgment in June 2003 making same-sex marriage legal in Ontario, the province's Court of Appeal said that the "exclusion of gays from the institution of marriage is illogical, offensive, and unjustifiable" (Makin, 2003). In doing so, the Ontario court joined those of British Columbia and Quebec in striking down marriage laws. But, unlike the courts in British Columbia and Quebec, the Ontario court did not give the province a grace period to bring its laws into conformity with the Canadian Charter of Rights and Freedoms. As a result, Ontario immediately began to give out marriage licences to gays and lesbians—the first among them being Joe Varnell and Kevin Bourassa, one of the two couples married by the Metropolitan Community Church in 2001.

Over the past decade or two, Canadians have become more tolerant and supportive of the alternative lifestyles of lesbians and gays. The extension of spousal rights—similar to those of heterosexual common-law couples—to same-sex couples was accepted by a majority of Canadians as just. A poll reported in the *Globe and Mail* (Makin, 2003) suggests that young adults 18 to 24 years of age are most supportive of same-sex marriage (61.2 percent of males, 69.2 percent of females); among those 35 to 54 years old, support comes in at 55 percent among males and 62.2 percent among females. Among those over 55 years of age, support limps along at 24.6 percent for males and 37.6 percent for females. Thus, a majority of Canadians—especially younger adults—was in favour of extending the right to marry to same-sex couples.

While these figures reveal substantial support for same-sex marriage in principle, they do not reveal the extent of support for changing the *definition* of marriage. As recently as 1999, a motion to reaffirm the definition of marriage "as a union of one man and one woman to the exclusion of all others" was passed in Parliament with 216 votes for and 55 against (Lunman, 2003). A repeat motion to that effect, in the fall of 2003, was defeated by a very narrow margin. Whatever the values and beliefs of our parliamentarians, court rulings stating that existing laws were discriminatory meant that the government could no

Linda Gerber

IN AUGUST 2002, FRIENDS AND FAMILY GATHERED ON ALGONQUIN ISLAND, SET AGAINST THE TORONTO SKY-LINE, FOR A COMMITMENT CEREMONY CELEBRATING THE LOVE OF THIS SAME-SEX COUPLE On the first anniversary of this ceremony, the two women were able to marry legally, as the Court of Appeal had made same-sex marriage legal in Ontario.

longer avoid dealing with this issue. Justice Canada presented draft legislation defining marriage as a union of two persons—rather than one man and one woman—to the Supreme Court of Canada for its opinion. It was then presented to the House of Commons for debate and approval, and was passed on July 20, 2005.

Canada joined the Netherlands (in 2001) and Belgium (in 2002) as the first countries to allow same-sex marriage. Because they rushed to have their marriage of January 2001 registered "legally" on June 11, 2003, Joe Varnell and Kevin Bourassa became the first gays to marry—not just in Canada but in the world.

POSTSCRIPT According to Census 2011, there are 64 575 same-sex couples in Canada—including 43 560 common-law and 21 018 married couples (triple the number in 2006). Thus, of all our same-sex couples, 33 percent are married (up from 17 percent in 2006). Whereas 10 percent of all same-sex couples have children, this is true of 9 and 15 percent of common-law and married same-sex couples, respectively. Not surprisingly, *women* in same-sex relationships, common-law and married are most likely to have children—at 15 and 21 percent (Statistics Canada, 2011a and b).

What Do You Think?

1. Are you aware that a number of American states have legalized same-sex marriage and that President Obama declared his support for same-sex marriage?

2. Are you gay or lesbian or are there gays or lesbians in your family? If so, did your family adjust to this reality easily or with difficulty?

3. We know that, as of 2011, 33 percent of same-sex couples in Canada are married. Do you think this proportion will grow? Keep in mind that growing numbers of heterosexuals are choosing the common-law option.

interaction with people thought to be gay, lesbian, or bisexual (Weinberg, 1973). The concept of "homophobia" (literally, "fear of sameness") turns the tables on society; instead of asking "What's wrong with gay people?" the question becomes "What's wrong with people who cannot accept a different sexual orientation?" Can you see the tension between these two approaches in the political manoeuvrings regarding same-sex marriage?

TRANSGENDER As the gay rights movement gained acceptance for gay, lesbian, and bisexual people, we have seen greater tolerance of people who challenge conventional gender patterns. *Transgender* is a broad concept that applies to people who challenge the conventional cultural norms defining male or female appearance and behaviour. People in the transgender community do not think of themselves or express their sexuality according to conventional standards. In other words, transgender people disregard conventional ideas about femininity or masculinity in favour of combining feminine and masculine traits or perhaps embodying something entirely different.

Transgender is not a sexual orientation. Transgender people may think of themselves as gay or lesbian, heterosexual, bisexual, asexual, as some combination of these categories, or in entirely different terms.

Researchers estimate that about three in every 1000 adults have transgender identities—which is why we commonly refer to the lesbian, gay, bisexual, and transgender (LGBT) population. Because someone may identify with more than one of these categories, no exact number can be placed on the size of the LGBT population. But estimates suggest that almost 4 percent of adults belong to the LGBT community (Gates, 2011). As noted earlier, the most inclusive acronym pertaining to sexual orientation is LGBTTIQ2SA—lesbian, gay, bisexual, transgendered, transsexual, intersex, queer/questioning, two-spirited, and asexual.

Transgender people are at high risk of rejection and discrimination, as well as physical or sexual violence—which all too often cause them to consider or attempt suicide (Hass et al., 2014). On the home front, in May 2016, transgender Canadians and human rights activists cheered "as the Liberal government introduced legislation that would make it against the law to discriminate on the basis of gender identity or expression" (Press, 2016). If passed, Bill C-16 would amend both the *Canadian Human Rights Act* and the *Criminal Code* (which would prohibit hate speech based on gender identity and expression). There have been earlier attempts to pass such legislation, including one in 2015 that was scuttled by the Senate. As we wait to see what happens to Bill C-16, we will continue to put out local brush fires as schools and other public venues sort out questions about the use of washrooms or locker rooms by transgendered people.

Sexual Issues and Controversies

8.4 Discuss several current controversies involving sexuality.

Sexuality lies at the heart of a number of controversies in North America today. Here we take a look at four key issues: teen pregnancy, pornography, prostitution, and sexual assault.

Teen Pregnancy

Sexual activity—especially intercourse—demands a high level of responsibility, since pregnancy can result. Teenagers who may be biologically, but not socially, mature might fail to appreciate the consequences of their actions. Surveys show that there are some 768 000 teen pregnancies in the United States each year, most of them unplanned. The American rate of births to teens is higher than that of all other high-income countries and is twice the rate in Canada (Alan Guttmacher Institute, 2006; Ventura et al., 2009).

Concern about high rates of teenage pregnancy led to sex education in schools, but to some extent the focus in Canada has changed to concern about the problems of female-headed single-parent families—including those of teenage mothers. This is largely because Canada's rate of teen pregnancy dropped from 50 pregnancies per 1000 women aged 15 to 19 in the early 1990s to 43 per 1000 by 1997. In 1995, there were 19 724 babies born to teenage mothers and an additional 21 233 pregnancies that ended in **abortion**, *the deliberate termination of a pregnancy*; in other words, more than half of Canada's teen pregnancies end in abortion. (The Controversy and Debate box looks at the issue of abortion generally.)

Interestingly, between 1961 and 1991, the proportion of births to unmarried mothers that involved teens dropped from 38 to 19 percent because *older* women, in growing numbers, began to have children out of wedlock (Belle & McQuillan, 2000; Dryburgh, 2003). The teen pregnancy rate has continued to drop in recent years so that, by 2002, there were 34 pregnancies per 1000 women aged 15 to 19 (Society of Obstetricians and Gynaecologists of Canada, 2006). In fact, within a single decade, Canada's teen pregnancy rate dropped from 50 to 34 per 1000 teenage women. The teenage pregnancy rate dipped even lower to 28/1000 before taking off in New Brunswick (40/100) and Newfoundland and Labrador (36/1000 by 2010). Experts point to tough economic times as the main factor leading to those increases—saying that better access to contraception as well as optimism about their educational and employment future are required to bring teen pregnancy rates down again (Bielski, 2013).

Controversy and Debate

The Abortion Controversy

A van pulls up in front of a storefront in a busy section of the city. Two women get out of the front seat and cautiously scan the sidewalk. After a moment, one nods to the other and opens the rear door to let a third woman out of the van. Standing to the right and left of their charge, the two quickly whisk her inside the building. They are escorting a woman who has decided to have an abortion. Why should they be so cautious? There have been heated confrontations at abortion clinics across North America, and some doctors who perform abortions have been targeted and killed.

About 850 000 abortions are performed in the United States each year, compared to 105 000 in Canada. A quick calculation reveals that in both countries the rate is 3 abortions per 1000 population. Most therapeutic abortions in Canada are performed in hospitals, while others take place in doctors' offices or in private clinics like those run by Dr. Henry Morgentaler, an advocate who performed illegal abortions long before the liberalization of Canada's laws. (During the 1970s and 1980s, Dr. Morgentaler was arrested, tried, acquitted, and eventually convicted for his illegal activities. In 2008, the ongoing abortion debate intensified when Morgentaler was honoured with the Order of Canada for his commitment to the health care rights of women.)

Abortion was illegal until the mid-1900s, driving abortion underground, where many women, especially the poor, had little choice but to seek help from unlicensed abortionists, sometimes with tragic results.

In 1969, under Pierre Trudeau's Liberal government, Canada's laws were liberalized to allow abortion in cases where three physicians certified that the mother's life or health was endangered. The law was not applied evenly across provinces or between large cities and rural areas—because the definition of "danger" to the mother's life or health was not specified. If hospitals, many of them Catholic, simply refused to perform abortions, women were forced to turn elsewhere. In 1973, the U.S. Supreme Court rendered a landmark decision striking down all state laws banning abortion—in effect, establishing a woman's legal access to abortion. In 1988, the Supreme Court of Canada left Canadians *without* an abortion law by declaring the existing legislation unconstitutional.

While North American women now have legal access to abortion, the controversy has not abated. On one side are people, describing themselves as "pro-choice," who support a woman's right to choose; some of them are feminists who argue that women should have complete control of their sexuality and their bodies. On the other side are those, calling themselves "pro-life," who oppose abortion as morally wrong and defend life from the very moment of conception. Because of his support of the pro-life

perspective, Stephen Harper in the 2006 federal election campaign and as prime minister had to assure Canadians that his government would not reopen the abortion debate.

How strong is the support for each side of the abortion controversy? About 40 percent of Canadians and Americans feel that women should have access to abortion, whatever their reasons for seeking one. The vast majority of Americans and Canadians are in favour of abortion if a woman's health is in danger, and would allow abortion if there is a serious defect in the baby or if the pregnancy is the result of sexual assault. Only about 5 percent would prohibit abortion under any circumstances. Pro-life proponents feel that abortion amounts to killing unborn children. Pro-choice advocates see the abortion debate in terms of the standing of women in society, arguing that women must control their own sexuality. If pregnancy dictates the course of women's lives, they will never be able to compete with men on equal terms. For pro-choice supporters, legal and safe abortion is a necessary condition for the full participation of women in society.

One of the newer abortion controversies in Canada raises serious issues for the pro-choicers who insist that women have the right to control their own bodies. Now that the sex of a child can be determined early on in pregnancy, some women are aborting fetuses on the basis of sex. This became an issue when physicians noticed that women in one or two Asian-Canadian communities were targeting female fetuses. If pro-choice supporters tell these women that they do *not* have the right to abort female fetuses, the implication would be that their choice is politically incorrect. The message is that women have the right to control their own bodies through abortion—but *only* if their "choice" is acceptable to pro-choice supporters. The question is: Do women have the right to control their own bodies or not?

Canada may be the only country in the developed world with no abortion law whatsoever. Some European countries, for example, limit abortions to the first two trimesters to avoid the termination of pregnancies involving a viable fetus. In theory, an abortion can take place in Canada at any time during a normal pregnancy. Many of the people who are pressing for some kind of abortion law in Canada are concerned not with abortions that take place in the first few weeks of pregnancy but with later-stage abortions where the fetus would be able to survive outside the womb. Others point out that our abortion rates are unnecessarily high because some women use abortion as a means of birth control. Considering the grey areas involving very sensitive issues, you may understand why our parliamentarians are not anxious to revisit this contentious and divisive debate.

It is very difficult to get an accurate count of abortions performed in Canada—for the simple reason that

(continued)

reporting them is not compulsory. Providers are encouraged to report all abortions but have become increasingly brazen in their non-compliance. Nevertheless, Johnston (2014) has compiled abortion statistics from 1970 to the present. The number of recorded abortions increased from 11 451 in 1970 to a high of 112 002 in 1997 and then dropped to 82 903 in 2013. The abortion ratio—abortions per 1000 live births—followed a similar path from 120 in 1971 to roughly 320 between 1997 and 2002 before declining to 215 in 2013. (As a point of comparison, the number of births per year peaked between 1956 and 1964, when the numbers remained in the 450 000 to 480 000 range. The all-time high was 479 275—almost half a million—in 1959.)

What Do You Think?

1. More conservative people (who generally do not support abortion) see abortion as a moral issue, while more liberal people (who generally support abortion) see it as a power issue. Where do you stand?

2. Surveys show that men and women have almost the same opinions about abortion. Does this surprise you? Why?

3. Why is the abortion controversy so bitter that Canadians have been unable to find middle ground?

SOURCES: Bibby (1995), Jonas (2012), Johnston (2014), Luker (1984), MacKenzie (1990), Nelson and Robinson (1999), Tannahill (1992), and Wente (2008).

Pornography

In general terms, **pornography** refers to *sexually explicit material that causes sexual arousal*. But what, exactly, is or is not pornographic has long been a matter of debate. In Canada, pornography is legal, while *obscenity*, which involves undue exploitation of sex and violation of community standards, is illegal. Much of the debate about material featuring adults deals with the point at which pornography crosses the line from erotica to obscenity. Sex combined with bestiality, the

Window on the World

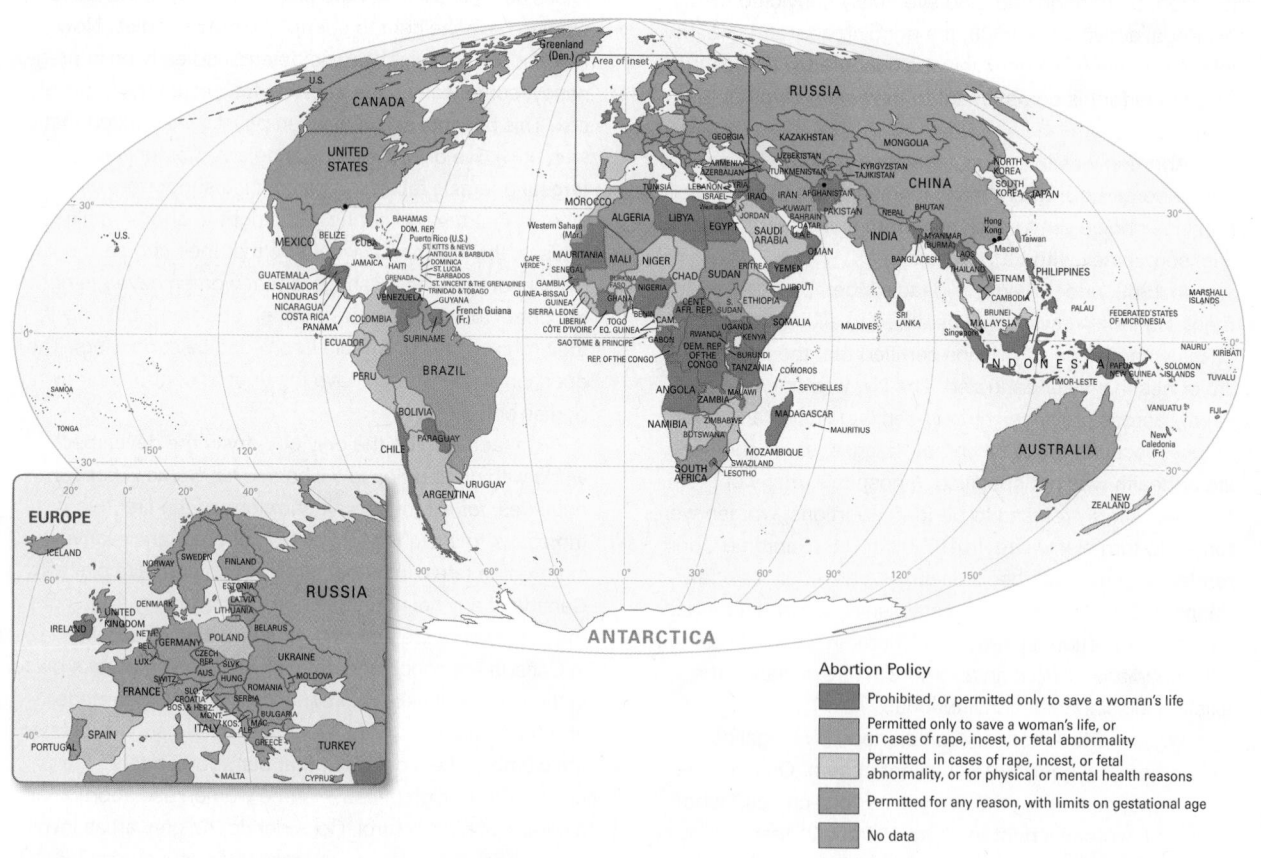

Abortion Policy

- Prohibited, or permitted only to save a woman's life
- Permitted only to save a woman's life, or in cases of rape, incest, or fetal abnormality
- Permitted in cases of rape, incest, or fetal abnormality, or for physical or mental health reasons
- Permitted for any reason, with limits on gestational age
- No data

Global Map 8–2 Women's Access to Abortion in Global Perspective

In global perspective, just 68 nations permit a woman to obtain an abortion for a wide variety of reasons. Generally, these are high-income nations, including many countries in Europe and North America. What pattern do you see involving countries that place the greatest restriction on abortion?

SOURCE: Population Reference Bureau (2012).

degradation or humiliation of women, and/or violence—even murder (i.e., in "snuff" films)—qualifies as obscenity. But where, in the continuum from *Playboy* to "snuff," is that line crossed? Child pornography, especially pictures transmitted over the internet, has elicited a lot of reaction recently: This is one area where the line is *not* fuzzy.

Definitions aside, pornography is popular in North America: X-rated videos, 1-900 telephone numbers for sexual conversations, and a host of sexually explicit movies and magazines together constitute an industry that generates US$10 billion a year. The figure is rising as people have gained access to pornography from thousands of sites on the internet.

Traditionally, people have criticized pornography on moral grounds. Today, however, pornography is also seen as a power issue because it depicts women as the sexual playthings of men (Nelson & Fleras, 1998). Pornography may also cause violence against women. While it is difficult to document a scientific cause-and-effect relationship between viewing and acting, research suggests that pornography is a *power* issue because it degrades women by portraying them as the sexual playthings of men—and because it encourages sexual assault or rape (NORC, 2013:424). These concerns, among others, inform Canada's obscenity legislation.

While people everywhere object to sexual material they find offensive, many also value free speech and want to protect artistic expression. Therefore, when we propose censorship of pornography in Canada, we need to balance our demands against the constitutionally protected rights of free expression.

Prostitution

Prostitution is *the selling of sexual services*. Often called the "oldest profession," prostitution has always been widespread. Even so, since people think of sex as interpersonal intimacy, many find the idea of sex performed for money disturbing. As a result, prostitution is against the law in the United States. In Canada, prostitution itself is not a crime; instead, the *Criminal Code* prohibits "those activities related to prostitution that are considered threatening to public order or offensive to public decency"—activities such as soliciting or communicating for the purposes of prostitution in a public place (Wolff & Geissel, 2000).

TYPES OF PROSTITUTION Most—but not all—prostitutes are women. Prostitutes—or sex workers, as they prefer to be called—fall into different categories. *Call girls* are elite prostitutes, typically women who are young, attractive, and well educated, and who arrange to meet clients by telephone. The classified pages of any large city newspaper contain numerous ads for escort services, by

which women (and sometimes men) offer both companionship and sex for a fee.

Members of a middle category of prostitutes work in massage parlours or brothels under the control of managers. These sex workers have less choice in clients, receive less money for their services, and keep only half of their earnings.

At the bottom of the sex-worker hierarchy are *streetwalkers*, women and men who "work the streets" of large cities. Female streetwalkers are often under the control of male managers, or *pimps*, who take most of their earnings. Many street prostitutes fall victim to violence from pimps and clients (Davidson, 1998; Estes, 2001; Gordon & Snyder, 1989).

A VICTIMLESS CRIME? Whereas prostitution itself is not illegal in Canada, associated activities—like keeping a brothel or "common bawdy house" or communicating for the purposes of prostitution—were illegal until very recently. Whatever the technicalities, many people consider prostitution to be a victimless crime, because the clients are unharmed and fail to see themselves as victims.

Is it true that selling sex hurts no one? Certainly, those who assume a "live and let live" attitude toward prostitution think so. But they ignore the fact that prostitutes are subjected to abuse and violence and play a part in spreading sexually transmitted diseases, including AIDS. Also, many poor women, trapped in a life of selling sex, put their own lives at risk. Canadian homicide statistics highlight the dangers associated with prostitution. In 1991 and 1992, 22 prostitutes were murdered in Canada, and constituted 5 percent of all female murder victims aged 16 or older; four of the murdered women were 16 or 17 years of age (Wolff & Geissel, 2000).

Through 2002 and 2003, the most extensive murder probe in Canadian history looked into the disappearance since the mid-1990s of 63 women from Vancouver's skid row, most of whom were drug-addicted prostitutes. Hundreds of investigators, including 52 forensic anthropologists, searched every part of Robert Pickton's pig farm and a nearby piece of land along a highway close to Mission, British Columbia. As a result, evidence of 15 of the missing women was initially found and identified, and Pickton was charged with 15 counts of first-degree murder (Armstrong, 2003). By 2006, Pickton stood charged with the murder of at least 26 women. In 2007, he was tried for the murder of six of the women after the judge decided that there were too many victims to be considered at a single trial. Pickton was found guilty of second-degree murder of the six women and was sentenced to life in prison with no possibility of parole for 25 years. Unfortunately, it took the disappearance of many prostitutes and pressure by their families and social activists

Victor R. Caivano/AP Images

EXPERTS AGREE THAT ONE FACTOR CONTRIBUTING TO THE PROBLEM OF SEXUAL VIOLENCE ON CAMPUS IS THE WIDESPREAD USE OF ALCOHOL What policies are in force on your campus to discourage the kind of drinking that leads to one person imposing sex on another?

before the police would investigate the possibility of serial murder.

In September 2010, the Ontario Superior Court of Justice overturned Canada's anti-prostitution laws—on the basis of the Canadian Charter of Rights and Freedoms—in a ruling that put the safety and security of sex workers first. Because brothels are now legal in Ontario, sex workers are able to move off the streets to a safer environment where they can screen clients and even hire bodyguards. Theoretically, they are no longer easy pickings for the likes of Robert Picton.

Sexual Assault

Ideally, sexual activity occurs within a loving relationship. In reality, sex can be twisted by hate and violence. In Canada, rape is officially recorded as *sexual assault*. Between 2001 and 2005, there were, on average, 75 *reported* incidents per 100 000 population (Statistics Canada, 2009a), but be aware that the number of unreported incidents is much higher. Victimization surveys in Canada lead to tremendous variation in estimates of sexual assault rates—for example, estimates vary from 600 to 2900 per 100 000 women, with only a fraction of cases showing up in official statistics (Johnson, 1996). Sexual assault statistics include only victims who are women, but men are also raped, accounting for perhaps 10 percent of all cases. Most men who rape men are heterosexual, motivated not by a desire for sex but by the urge to dominate. Keep in mind, too, that sexual assault is not necessarily perpetrated by strangers; often, it occurs in situations characterized by trust, including marriage. For a detailed discussion of date, or acquaintance, rape, see the Sociology in Focus box.

Theories of Sexuality

8.5 Apply sociology's major theories to the topic of sexuality.

Applying sociology's various theoretical approaches gives us a better understanding of human sexuality. The following sections discuss the three major approaches, and the Applying Theory table highlights the key insights of each approach.

Structural-Functional Analysis

The structural-functional approach highlights the contribution of any social pattern to the overall operation of society. Because sexuality can have such important consequences, it is regulated by society.

THE NEED TO REGULATE SEXUALITY From a biological point of view, sex allows our species to reproduce. But culture and social institutions regulate *with whom* and *when* people reproduce. For example, most societies condemn people for extramarital sex. To allow sexual passion to go unchecked would threaten family life, especially the raising of children. The fact that the incest taboo exists everywhere shows that no society permits completely free choice in sexual partners. Reproduction by family members other than married partners would break down the system of kinship and hopelessly confuse human relationships.

Historically, the social control of sexuality was strong because sex led to childbirth. We see these controls at work in the traditional distinction between legitimate reproduction (i.e., within marriage) and illegitimate reproduction (i.e., outside marriage). Once a society develops birth control, it becomes more permissive—to the point where sex moves beyond its basic reproductive function and becomes accepted as a form of intimacy and even recreation (Giddens, 1992).

LATENT FUNCTIONS: THE CASE OF PROSTITUTION It is easy to see that prostitution is harmful because it spreads disease and exploits women, but it takes latent functions to explain why prostitution is so widespread. According to Kingsley Davis (1971), prostitution performs several useful functions. It is one way to meet the sexual needs of a large number of people who may not have ready access to sex, including soldiers, travellers, people who are not physically attractive, or people who are too poor to attract a marriage partner. Some people favour prostitutes because they want sex without the "trouble" of a relationship: "Men don't pay for sex; they pay so they can leave" (Miracle et al., 2003:421).

Sociology in Focus

Rape and Date Rape: Exposing Dangerous Myths

When is it appropriate to have sexual intercourse? How well should you know the other person? If your date says "no," and you press on with your sexual advances, are you simply persistent or guilty of sexual assault? If you are both drunk, is your behaviour justified?

Legitimate sexual activity must involve clear statements of consent by both participants. In other words, giving consent differentiates "having sex" from being raped.

In recent years, the issue of date rape has been widely discussed on campus—where the open environment encourages trust and communication but also invites alarming levels of sexual violence. While 12 percent of Canadian women (aged 18 and older) have experienced sexual assault by a date or boyfriend, this is true of 17 percent of female students (Johnson, 1996). Thus, being a student *increases* the likelihood of sexual violence. Equally disturbing is the observation that university men who abuse their dates do so, quite often, with the support of male friends who encourage and legitimize female victimization (DeKeseredy and Hinch, 1991).

If you *have* been raped and file a report, will the authorities take you seriously? Can you prosecute in the absence of bruises and torn clothes? Is it worth filing a report? So reluctant are victims to come forward that, in Canada, "somewhere between 60 and 90 percent of rapes go unreported" (DeKeseredy and Hinch, 1991:94).

When women do report sexual attacks, police judgment as to whether a crime has occurred depends on the victim's reputation. Certain women are almost certain to have their claims dismissed as unfounded. Police claimed that "these women were prostitutes, known alcoholics, women who were drinking at the time of the offence, drug users, women on welfare, and unemployed women as well as women noted in police reports as 'idle'" (DeKeseredy and Hinch, 1991:66–67). Small wonder that women are reluctant to report a sexual assault—particularly if their attacker is known to them or if they had been partying. In fact, "rape by a stranger is more likely to be defined as a criminal act and reported to authorities" than is rape by an acquaintance or intimate partner (Nelson, 2010:317).

To clear up confusion about sexual assault, or rape, we look at four false notions that are so common they qualify as "rape myths":

Myth #1: *Rape involves strangers.* This is the exception rather than the rule. Experts report that only one in five sexual assaults involves a stranger. Most sexual assaults, in fact, are *acquaintance rape* or, more simply, *date rape.*

Myth #2: *Women provoke their attackers.* The woman claiming sexual assault must have done *something* to lead on her attacker. Didn't she agree to have dinner with him and willingly admit him to her room? These questions may paralyze victims, but either action is no more a woman's statement of consent to have sex than it is an invitation to have him beat her with a club.

Myth #3: *Rape is simply sex.* If there is no knife held to a woman's throat, how can sex be a crime? The answer is that, under the law, forcing a woman to have sex *without her consent* is a violent crime. "Having sex" implies intimacy, caring, and communication—none of which is present in cases of sexual assault.

Myth #4: *Only women are raped.* Over 40 percent of young men tell researchers that they have experienced "pressured or forced sexual contact" with a woman. In fact, "Canadian sexual assault laws recognize both males and females as potential offenders *and* victims" (Nelson, 2010:317).

To eliminate sexual violence or address the crisis of acquaintance or date rape in particular, everyone needs to understand two simple truths: Forcing sex without explicit consent is sexual assault (a crime in Canada) and, when someone says "no", she (or he) means just that.

What Do You Think?

1. Is sexual assault a serious problem on your campus? Is there a program to walk students safely to a car or bus from late-night classes or events?

2. Have you heard of cases of date rape among your peers? How did the victim handle the situation? Was it reported and, if so, what was the outcome?

3. Do you think that the boundary between consensual sex and date rape is confusing? Why?

EVALUATE

The structural-functional approach helps us see the important part that sexuality plays in the organization of society. The incest taboo and other cultural norms also suggest that society has always paid attention to who has sex with whom and, especially, to who reproduces with whom. But functionalist analysis sometimes ignores gender; when Kingsley Davis wrote of the benefits of prostitution for society, he was really talking about the benefits to *men.* In addition, the fact that sexual patterns change over time and differ in remarkable ways around the world gets little attention when using the functionalist approach.

CHECK YOUR LEARNING Compared to traditional societies, why do modern societies give people more choice about matters involving sexuality?

Symbolic-Interaction Analysis

The symbolic-interaction approach highlights the construction of everyday reality. Because people construct very different realities regarding sexuality, they vary from context to context and change over time.

THE SOCIAL CONSTRUCTION OF SEXUALITY Social patterns involving sexuality changed considerably during the twentieth century. Take virginity as an example. A century ago, women were expected to be virgins until marriage, mainly because there was no effective birth control and virginity was a man's only assurance that his bride-to-be was not carrying another man's child. Today, with sex largely separated from reproduction, the virginity norm has weakened. Not surprisingly, premarital sex has increased dramatically in Canada—revealing a doubling of sexual activity levels among youth since the 1970s (Nelson & Robinson, 1999:354). Among single adults who have never been married, 87 percent say that they engage in sex—half of them at least weekly (Bibby, 1995:66). Very few, it seems, adhere to the norm of virginity until marriage.

Another example of our society's construction of sexuality involves children. A century ago, childhood was a time of innocence in sexual matters. In recent decades, however, our thinking has changed. Though we expect them to refrain from sex, we believe children should be educated about sex so they can make intelligent choices as they grow older.

GLOBAL COMPARISONS Around the world, different meanings are attached to sexuality. Ruth Benedict (1938), who spent years learning the ways of life of the Melanesian peoples of southeastern New Guinea, reported that adults paid little attention when young children engaged in sexual experimentation with one another. Parents shrugged off such activity because, before puberty, sex cannot lead to reproduction. Sexual practices vary from culture to culture. *Male circumcision* of infant boys (the practice of removing all or part of the foreskin of the penis) is common in North America but rare in many other parts of the world. A practice sometimes referred to incorrectly as *female circumcision* (the removal of the clitoris) is prohibited here but is common in parts of Africa and the Middle East (Crossette, 1995; Huffman, 2000).

EVALUATE

The strength of the symbolic-interaction approach lies in revealing the constructed character of familiar social patterns. Knowing that people "construct" sexuality helps us understand the variety of sexual practices found over time and in different societies. One limitation of this approach, however, is that not all sexual practices are so variable. For example, throughout our own history—and around the world—men are more likely to see women in sexual terms than the other way around. Some

broader social structure must be at work in a pattern that is this widespread.

CHECK YOUR LEARNING What evidence can you provide that human sexuality is socially constructed?

Social-Conflict and Feminist Analysis

As you have seen in earlier chapters, the social-conflict approach—particularly the gender-conflict or feminist approach—highlights dimensions of inequality. This approach shows how sexuality both reflects patterns of social inequality and helps perpetuate them.

SEXUALITY: REFLECTING SOCIAL INEQUALITY Societal response to prostitution varies considerably throughout North America, but, whatever the nature of prostitution laws, enforcement is uneven at best—especially when it comes to who is and is not likely to be arrested. While two people are involved, the record shows that police are far more likely to arrest (less powerful) female prostitutes than (more powerful) male clients. Similarly, of all women engaged in prostitution, streetwalkers—women with the least income and those most likely to be visible minorities—face the highest risk

Richard Lord/The Image Works

FROM A SOCIAL-CONFLICT POINT OF VIEW, SEXUALITY IS NOT SO MUCH A "NATURAL" PART OF OUR HUMANITY AS IT IS A SOCIALLY CONSTRUCTED PATTERN OF BEHAVIOUR Sexuality plays an important part in social inequality: By defining women in sexual terms, men devalue them as objects. Would you consider the behaviour shown here to be "natural" or socially directed? Why?

akg-images

THE CONTROL OF WOMEN'S SEXUALITY IS A COMMON THEME IN HUMAN HISTORY During the Middle Ages, wealthy European men devised the "chastity belt"—a metal device locked about a woman's groin that prevented sexual intercourse and probably interfered with other bodily functions as well. While such devices are all but unknown today, the social control of sexuality continues. Can you point to examples?

of arrest. And it is poverty that drives many women into prostitution in the first place.

SEXUALITY: CREATING SOCIAL INEQUALITY Social-conflict theorists, especially feminists, point to sexuality as the root of inequality between women and men. Defining women in sexual terms amounts to devaluing them from full human beings into objects of men's interest and attention. Is it any wonder that the word *pornography* comes from the Greek word *porne,* meaning "a man's sexual slave"? If men define women in sexual terms, it is easy to see pornography—almost all of which is consumed by males—as a power issue. Because it typically shows women pleasing men, pornography supports the idea that men have power over women.

Some radical critics doubt that the element of power can ever be removed from heterosexual relations (Dworkin, 1987). Our culture often describes sexuality in terms of sport (men "scoring" with women) and violence ("slamming," "banging," and "hitting on"). Most social-conflict theorists do not reject heterosexuality but do agree that sexuality can and does degrade women.

QUEER THEORY Finally, social-conflict theory has taken aim not only at the domination of women by men but also at heterosexuals dominating homosexuals. In recent years, as many lesbians and gay men have sought public acceptance, a gay voice has arisen in sociology. The term **queer theory** refers to *a growing body of research findings that challenges the heterosexual bias in Western society.* Queer theory begins with the claim that our society is characterized by **heterosexism**, *a view that labels anyone who is not heterosexual as "queer."* Our heterosexual culture victimizes a wide range of people, including gay men, lesbians, and bisexual, intersexual, transsexual, and even asexual people. While most people agree that bias against women (sexism) and visible minorities (racism) is wrong, heterosexism is widely tolerated and often well within the law.

EVALUATE

The social-conflict approach shows that sexuality is both a cause and an effect of inequality. In particular, it helps us understand men's power over women and the domination of heterosexual people over homosexual people. At the same time, this approach overlooks the fact that many people do not see sexuality as a power issue; on the contrary, many couples enjoy a vital sexual relationship that deepens their commitment to one another. In addition, the social-conflict approach pays little attention to steps taken by society to reduce inequality, the treatment of women as sex objects, and sexual harassment in the workplace—or the success of the gay rights movement in securing greater opportunities and social acceptance for gays and lesbians.

CHECK YOUR LEARNING How does sexuality play a part in creating social inequality?

APPLYING THEORY

Sexuality

	Structural-Functional Approach	Symbolic-Interaction Approach	Social Conflict/Feminist Approach
What is the level of analysis?	Macro-level	Micro-level	Macro-level
What is the importance of sexuality for society?	Society depends on sexuality for reproduction. Society uses the incest taboo and other norms to control sexuality in order to maintain social order.	Sexual practices vary among the many cultures of the world. Some societies allow individuals more freedom than others in matters of sexual behaviour.	Sexuality is linked to social inequality. Society regulates women's sexuality more than men's, which is part of the larger pattern of men dominating women.
Has sexuality changed over time? How?	Yes. As advances in birth control technology separate sex from reproduction, societies relax some controls on sexuality.	Yes. The meanings people attach to virginity and other sexual matters are all socially constructed and subject to change.	Yes and no. Some sexual standards have relaxed, but society still defines women in sexual terms, just as homosexual people are harmed by society's heterosexual bias.

Seeing Sociology in Everyday Life

CHAPTER 8 Sexuality and Society

How do the mass media play into society's views of human sexuality?

Far from human sexuality being a "natural" or simply "biological" concept, cultures around the world attach all sorts of meanings to it. The magazine covers presented here show how the mass media—in this case, popular magazines—reflect our own culture's ideas about sexuality. In each case, can you "decode" the magazine cover and explain its messages? To what extent do you think the messages are true?

> **Hint** The messages we get from mass media sources like these not only tell us about sexuality but also tell us what sort of people we ought to be. There is a lot of importance attached to sexuality for women, placing pressure on women to look good to men and to define life success in terms of attracting men with their sexuality. Similarly, being masculine means being successful, sophisticated, in charge, and able to attract desirable women. When the mass media endorse sexuality, it is almost always according to the norm of heterosexuality.

MAGAZINES LIKE THIS ONE ARE FOUND AT THE CHECKOUT LINES OF JUST ABOUT EVERY GROCERY STORE Looking just at the cover, what can you conclude about women's sexuality in our society?

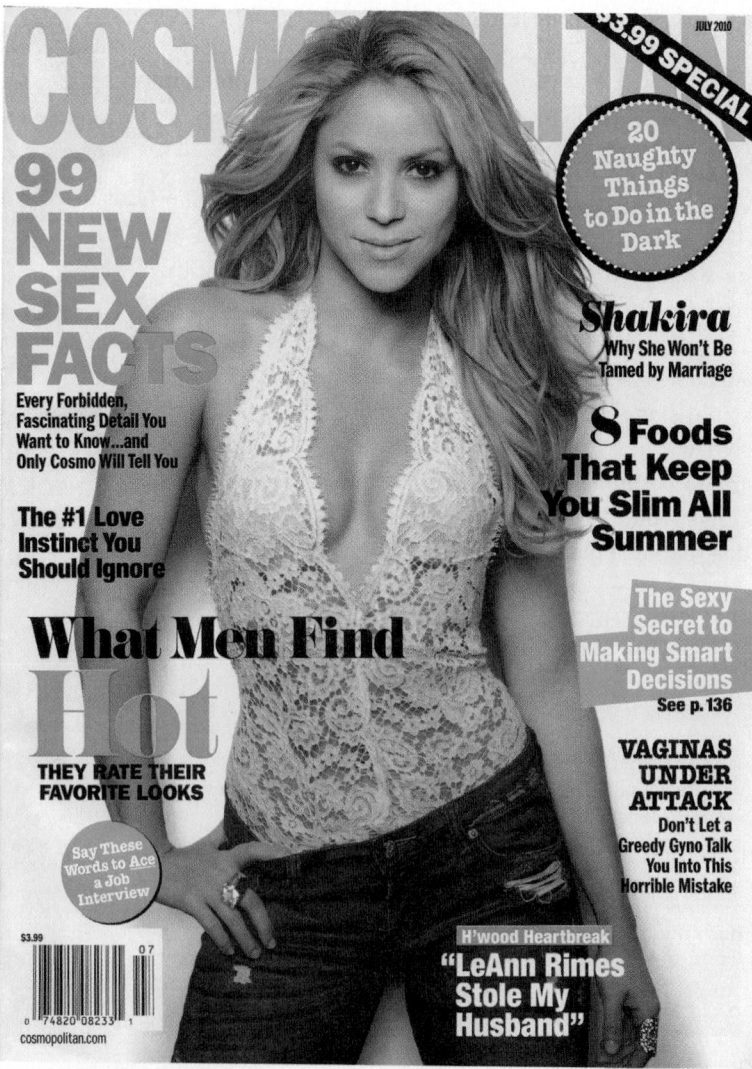

Bill Aron/PhotoEdit, Inc.

MESSAGES ABOUT SEXUALITY ARE DIRECTED TO MEN AS WELL AS TO WOMEN Here is a recent issue of *GQ*. What messages about masculinity can you find? Do you see any evidence of heterosexual bias?

Seeing Sociology in *Your* Everyday Life

1. Looking at the *Cosmopolitan* cover, what evidence of heterosexual bias do you see? Explain.

2. Contact student services and ask for information about the extent of sexual violence on your campus. Do people typically report such crimes? What policies and procedures does your school have to respond to sexual violence?

3. Based on what you have read in this chapter, what evidence supports the argument that sexuality is constructed by society?

Making the Grade

CHAPTER 8 Sexuality and Society

Understanding Sexuality

8.1 Describe how sexuality is both a biological and a cultural issue.

Sex is biological, referring to bodily differences between females and males.

Gender is cultural, referring to the behaviour, power, and privileges a society attaches to being female or male.

Sexuality is a **biological issue**.

- Sex is determined at conception as a male sperm joins a female ovum.
- Males and females have different genitals *(primary sex characteristics)* and bodily development *(secondary sex characteristics)*.
- *Intersexual people (hermaphrodites)* have some combination of male and female genitalia.
- *Transsexual people* feel they are one sex although biologically they are the other.

Sexuality is a **cultural issue**.

- For humans, sex is a matter of cultural meaning and personal choice rather than biological programming.
- Sexual practices vary considerably from one society to another (examples include kissing, ideas about modesty, and standards of beauty).
- The *incest taboo* exists in all societies because regulating sexuality, especially reproduction, is a necessary element of social organization. Specific taboos vary from one society to another.

> **sex** the biological distinction between females and males
> **primary sex characteristics** the genitals, organs used for reproduction
> **secondary sex characteristics** bodily development, apart from the genitals, that distinguishes biologically mature females and males
> **intersexual people** people whose bodies, including genitals, have both female and male characteristics
> **transsexuals** people who feel they are one sex even though biologically they are the other
> **gender identity** traits that females or males, guided by their culture, incorporate into their personalities
> **incest taboo** a norm forbidding sexual relations or marriage between certain relatives

Sexual Attitudes

8.2 Explain changes in sexual attitudes in Canada and elsewhere.

The Sexual Revolution, which peaked in the 1960s and 1970s, drew sexuality out into the open. Baby boomers were the first generation to grow up with the idea that sex is a normal part of social life.

The sexual counterrevolution, which began around 1980, aimed criticism at "permissiveness" and urged a return to more traditional "family values."

Beginning with the work of Alfred Kinsey, researchers have studied sexual behaviour and reached many interesting conclusions:

- Premarital sexual intercourse became more common during the twentieth century.
- About three-fourths of young men and two-thirds of young women have had sexual intercourse by their senior year in high school.
- Among Canadian adults, sexual activity varies: A quarter report having sex with a partner a few times a year or not at all; another quarter have sex one to three times a month; the remaining half have sex one or more times a week.
- Extramarital sex is widely condemned, with 85 percent of Canadians saying it is always or almost always wrong. While 10 and 5 percent of men and women, respectively, say they would cheat on their partners, 33 and 35 percent claim that their partners have cheated.

Sexual Orientation

8.3 Analyze factors that shape sexual orientation.

Sexual orientation is a person's romantic or emotional attraction to another person. Four sexual orientations are

- heterosexuality
- homosexuality
- bisexuality
- asexuality

Most research supports the claim that sexual orientation is rooted in biology in much the same way as is being right-handed or left-handed.

Sexual orientation is not a matter of neat categories, because many people who think of themselves as heterosexual have homosexual experiences; the reverse is also true.

- The share of our population that is homosexual depends on how you define "homosexuality."
- Among American adults, about 5 percent of men and 14 percent of women report engaging in some homosexual activity; 1.8 percent of men and 1.2 percent of women consider themselves homosexual. Canadian estimates of the gay or lesbian identity range from 1 to 10 percent, while only 0.5 percent of those living common-law claim to be same-sex couples.

The gay rights movement helped change public attitudes toward greater acceptance of homosexuality. Still, almost half of Americans and a third of Canadians say that homosexuality is always or almost always wrong.

> **sexual orientation** a person's romantic and emotional attraction to another person
> **heterosexuality** sexual attraction to someone of the *other* sex
> **homosexuality** sexual attraction to someone of the *same* sex
> **bisexuality** sexual attraction to people of both sexes
> **asexuality** a lack of sexual attraction to people of either sex
> **homophobia** the dread of close personal interaction with people thought to be gay, lesbian, or bisexual

Sexual Issues and Controversies

8.4 Discuss several current controversies involving sexuality.

Teen Pregnancy In Canada, about 20 000 babies are born each year to teenage mothers (15 to 19 years old). On the other hand, in a single decade the teen pregnancy rate dropped from 50 to 43 per 1000 teenage women.

Pornography In Canada, pornography is legal, while obscenity (which involves undue exploitation and violation of community standards) is not. Traditionally, pornography was condemned on moral grounds; today, pornography is viewed as a power issue, and is condemned as demeaning to women.

Prostitution The selling of sexual services is not illegal in Canada but, until recently, soliciting or communicating for the purposes of prostitution and running a brothel were against the law. Many people view prostitution as a victimless crime, but it victimizes women and spreads sexually transmitted diseases. In Canada, many prostitutes have been murdered.

Sexual Assault From 2001 to 2005, sexual assault rates in Canada averaged 75 reported incidents per 100 000 population, but victimization surveys estimate actual levels that vary between 600 and 2900 per 100 000 population. Rapes are violent crimes in which victims and offenders typically know one another.

Abortion Canada may be the only country in the developed world with no abortion law whatsoever. However, abortion is the subject of continuous debate and controversy. Those who are pro-life argue that abortion should be allowed under very limited circumstances or not at all. Those who are pro-choice argue that women must have control over their own bodies.

> **abortion** the deliberate termination of a pregnancy
> **pornography** sexually explicit material that causes sexual arousal
> **prostitution** the selling of sexual services

Theories of Sexuality

8.5 Apply sociology's major theories to the topic of sexuality.

The **structural-functional approach** highlights society's need to regulate sexual activity, especially reproduction. One universal norm is the incest taboo, which keeps family relations clear.

The **symbolic-interaction approach** emphasizes the various meanings people attach to sexuality. The social construction of sexuality can be seen in sexual differences between societies and in changing sexual patterns over time.

The **social-conflict approach** links sexuality to social inequality. Feminist theory claims that men dominate women by devaluing them to the level of sexual objects. Queer theory claims our society has a heterosexual bias, defining anything different as "queer."

> **queer theory** a growing body of research findings that challenges the heterosexual bias in Western society
> **heterosexism** a view that labels anyone who is not heterosexual as "queer"

Chapter 9
Deviance

Michael Matthews - Police Images/Alamy Stock Photo

Learning Objectives

9.1 Explain how sociology addresses the limitations of a biological or psychological approach to deviance.

9.2 Apply structural-functional theories to the topic of deviance.

9.3 Apply symbolic-interaction theories to the topic of deviance.

9.4 Apply social-conflict theories to the topic of deviance.

9.5 Apply race-conflict and feminist theories to the topic of deviance.

9.6 Identify patterns of crime in Canada and around the world.

9.7 Analyze the operation of the criminal justice system.

The Power of Society
to affect the odds of being incarcerated

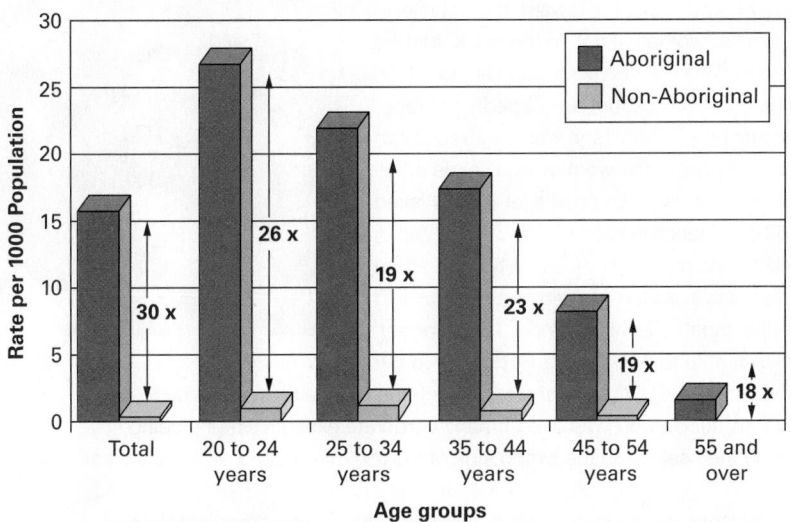

Incarceration Rate on Census Day, by Age Groups, Saskatchewan, May 16, 2006

SOURCE: Adapted from Statistics Canada, Canadian Centre for Justice Statistics, Integrated Correctional Services Survey and 2006 Census of Population. Statistics Canada, Juristat no. 85-002-X. July 2009.

Does everyone—regardless of race or age—run the same risk of being incarcerated? The picture revealed by incarceration rates in Saskatchewan's provincial prison system suggests that imprisonment is much more likely—indeed 26 times more likely—if you are an Aboriginal, 20 to 24 years of age. Whatever the age, Aboriginals are much more likely to be incarcerated than non-Aboriginals. For the province as a whole, Aboriginal people of all ages are 30 times more likely to be incarcerated than their non-Aboriginal counterparts. Although incarceration rates drop off rapidly with increasing age, Aboriginal people 55 years of age and over are still 18 times more likely to be imprisoned than their non-Aboriginal age-mates.

Chapter Overview

Common sense may suggest that some things are simply "right" and some things are simply "wrong." We also tend to think—or hope—that most of us, at least most of the time, know the difference. But the line between "good" and "bad" is constructed by society in a way that is far from simple. This chapter investigates how and why society encourages both conformity and deviance. This chapter also introduces the concept of crime and surveys the operation of the criminal justice system.

The black SUV rolled through the gates of the federal women's prison in Alderson, West Virginia, threading its way among the sea of news reporters, many of whom leaned toward the vehicle to catch a glimpse of the famous woman sitting in the back. Martha Stewart had just been released from jail. Stewart was sent to prison in 2004 after being convicted of lying about an allegedly improper stock deal. After five months behind bars, she was eager to return home. Soon after leaving the prison, the woman who made a fortune explaining how to live well boarded a private jet that whisked her to her 62-hectare (153-acre) ranch in Katonah, New York. Within three days, she reported to her probation officer, who placed an electronic monitor on her ankle and explained that she would have to spend the next five months at home under house arrest. Released from prison in March 2005, Martha Stewart resumed her

AP Images

active life—writing books, hosting her TV show, and expanding the Martha Stewart brand to cover new products (e.g., house paint). Stewart was one of many corporate executives—including several Canadians—who found themselves on the wrong side of the law for engaging in what we call "white collar" crime.

This chapter explores issues involving crime and criminals, asking why some categories of people are at higher risk of being offenders—and victims—than others. In addition, the chapter explains how our criminal justice system handles offenders and also how it tackles the broader question of why societies develop standards of right and wrong in the first place. As you will see, law is simply one part of a complex system of social control: Society teaches us all to conform to countless rules, at least most of the time. We begin our investigation by defining several basic concepts. ∎

What Is Deviance?

9.1 **Explain how sociology addresses the limitations of a biological or psychological approach to deviance.**

Deviance is *the recognized violation of cultural norms.* Norms guide almost all human activities, so the concept of deviance is quite broad. One category of deviance is **crime**, *the violation of a society's formally enacted criminal law.* Even criminal deviance spans a wide range of behaviour, from minor traffic violations to sexual assault and murder.

Most familiar examples of nonconformity are negative instances of rule breaking, such as stealing from a campus bookstore, assaulting a fellow student, or driving while intoxicated. But we also define especially righteous people—for example, students who speak up too much in class or computer "geeks"—as deviant, even if we give them a measure of respect. What deviant actions or attitudes, whether negative or positive, have in common is some element of *difference* that causes us to think of another person as an "outsider" (Becker, 1966).

Social Control

All of us are subject to **social control**, *attempts by others to regulate people's thoughts and behaviour.* Often this process is informal, as when parents praise or scold their children or when friends make fun of a classmate's unusual choice of music. Cases of serious deviance, however, may

---

deviance the recognized violation of cultural norms

crime the violation of a society's formally enacted criminal law

involve the **criminal justice system**, *the organizations— police, courts, and prison officials—that respond to alleged violations of the law.*

How a society defines deviance, *who* is branded as deviant, and *what* people decide to do about deviance all have to do with the way in which society is organized. Only gradually, however, have people recognized that deviance is much more than a matter of individual choice in that its roots are to be found deep in society.

The Biological Context

A century ago, most people understood—or, more correctly, misunderstood—human behaviour to be the result of biological instincts. Early interest in criminality therefore focused on biological causes. In 1876, Cesare Lombroso (1835–1909), an Italian physician who worked in prisons, theorized that criminals stand out physically, with low foreheads, prominent jaws and cheekbones, hairiness, and unusually long arms. Had he looked more carefully, he would have found the physical features he linked to criminality throughout the entire population. We now know that no physical traits distinguish criminals from non-criminals.

In the middle of the twentieth century, William Sheldon suggested that body structure might predict criminality (Sheldon et al., 1949). Checking hundreds of young men for body type and criminal history, he linked criminality to muscular, athletic builds. Glueck and Glueck (1950) cautioned that a powerful build does not necessarily cause criminality: Parents tend to be distant with powerfully built sons, and general expectations about muscular boys may lead to self-fulfilling prophecies.

Today, genetics research seeks possible links between biology and crime. In 2003, scientists reported results of a 25-year study of crime among 400 boys. They collected DNA samples and noted any trouble with the law. The researchers concluded that genetic factors (i.e., defective genes) *together with* environmental factors (e.g., abuse early in life) were strong predictors of adult crime and violence (Lemonick, 2003; Pinker, 2003).

EVALUATE

Biological theories offer a limited explanation of crime. The best guess at present is that biological traits in combination with environmental factors explain some serious crime—most acts we call "deviant" are carried out by people who are biologically

normal. Because a biological approach offers no insight into the process by which certain behaviours are defined as deviant in the first place, current research puts greater emphasis on social influences.

CHECK YOUR LEARNING What does biological research add to our understanding of crime? What are the limitations of this approach?

Personality Factors

Like biological theories, psychological explanations of deviance focus on abnormality in the individual personality. Some personality traits are inherited, but most psychologists think that personality is shaped primarily by social experience. Deviance, then, is viewed as the result of "unsuccessful" socialization.

Classic research by Walter Reckless and Simon Dinitz (1967) illustrates the psychological approach. Reckless and Dinitz began by asking a number of teachers to categorize 12-year-old male students as either likely or unlikely to get into trouble with the law. They then interviewed both the boys and their mothers to assess each boy's self-concept and how he related to others. Analyzing their results, Reckless and Dinitz found that the "good boys" displayed a strong conscience (what Freud called *superego*), could handle frustration, and identified with conventional cultural norms and values. The "bad boys," by contrast, had a weaker conscience, displayed little tolerance of frustration, and felt out of step with conventional culture.

Melissa Moore/The Image Works

DEVIANCE IS ALWAYS A MATTER OF DIFFERENCE Deviance emerges in everyday life as we encounter people whose appearance or behaviour differs from what we consider to be "right." Who is the "deviant" in this photograph? From whose point of view?

---

social control attempts by others to regulate people's thoughts and behaviour

criminal justice system the organizations—police, courts, and prison officials—that respond to alleged violations of the law

As we might expect, the "good boys" went on to have fewer run-ins with the police than the "bad boys." Because all the boys lived in an area where delinquency was widespread, the investigators attributed staying out of trouble to a personality that controlled deviant impulses. Based on this conclusion, Reckless and Dinitz called their analysis *containment theory*.

In a more recent study, researchers followed 500 non-identical twin boys from birth until they reached the age of 32. Twins were used so that researchers could compare each of the twins to his brother controlling for social class and family environment. Observing the boys when they were young, parents, teachers, and the researchers assessed their level of self-control, ability to withstand frustration, and ability to delay gratification. Echoing the earlier conclusions of Reckless and Dinitz, the researchers found that the brother who had lower scores on these measures in childhood almost always went on to get into more trouble, including criminal activity (Moffitt et al., 2011).

EVALUATE

Psychologists have shown that personality patterns have some connection to deviance. Some serious criminals are psychopaths who do not feel guilt or shame, have no fear of punishment, and have little sympathy for the people they harm (Herpertz & Sass, 2000). However, most serious crimes are committed by people whose psychological profiles are normal.

Both the biological and the psychological approaches view deviance as a trait of individuals, but wrongdoing is largely a function of society. We now turn to a sociological approach to look at the source of ideas of right and wrong, the labelling of some rule breakers as deviant, and the role of power in this process.

WHY IS IT THAT STREET-CORNER GAMBLING IS USUALLY AGAINST THE LAW BUT PLAYING THE SAME GAMES IN A FANCY CASINO IS NOT?

Jim Cole/AP Images

CHECK YOUR LEARNING Why do biological and psychological analyses not explain deviance very well?

The Social Foundations of Deviance

While we view deviance as the free choice or personal failing of individuals, all behaviour—deviance as well as conformity—is shaped by society. Three social foundations of deviance identified here will be discussed later in this chapter:

1. **Deviance varies according to cultural norms.** No thought or action is inherently deviant; it becomes deviant only in relation to particular norms. The life patterns of rural Albertans, residents of Newfoundland fishing villages, and West Vancouverites differ in highly significant ways. As a result, their values and behavioural standards are different. Laws, too, differ from place to place. Quebecers can drink at a younger age than Ontarians and are able to purchase wine and beer at corner stores. Casinos are now legal in Ontario and Saskatchewan, even for First Nations; they are also legal in Manitoba, but definitely not on reserves. In other words, what is deviant or even criminal is not uniform throughout the country. Around the world, deviance is even more diverse: Albania outlaws any public display of religious faith (such as crossing oneself); Cuba and Vietnam can prosecute citizens for meeting with foreigners; Malaysia prohibits tight-fitting jeans on women; and Iran outlaws women wearing makeup.

2. **People become deviant as others define them that way.** Everyone violates cultural norms at one time or another. Have you ever laughed in public by yourself or taken a pen from your workplace without intending to return it? Whether such behaviour defines us as mentally ill or criminal depends on how others perceive, define, and respond to it.

3. **Both norms and the way in which people define rule breaking involve social power.** The law, declared Karl Marx, is the means by which powerful people protect their interests. A homeless person who stands on a street corner speaking out against the government risks arrest for disturbing the peace; a mayoral candidate during an election campaign does exactly the same thing and gets police protection. In short, norms and their application reflect social inequality.

The Functions of Deviance: Structural-Functional Theories

9.2 Apply structural-functional theories to the topic of deviance.

The key insight of the structural-functional approach is that deviance is a necessary part of social organization. This point was made a century ago by Émile Durkheim.

Durkheim's Basic Insight

In his pioneering study of deviance, Émile Durkheim (1964a; orig. 1895, 1964b; orig. 1893) made the surprising statement that there is nothing abnormal about deviance. In fact, it performs four essential functions:

1. **Deviance affirms cultural values and norms.** Any definition of virtue rests on an opposing idea of vice: There can be no good without evil and no justice without crime. Deviance draws the limits of acceptable behaviour.

2. **Responding to deviance clarifies moral boundaries.** By defining some individuals as deviant, people draw a boundary between right and wrong. For example, there's a line between academic honesty and cheating, and students who cross it are punished.

3. **Responding to serious deviance brings people together.** People typically react to serious deviance with shared outrage. In doing so, Durkheim explained, they reaffirm the moral ties that bind them. For example, the murder of 14 female engineering students at Montreal's École Polytechnique on December 6, 1989, was met with reactions of horror, profound grief, and a sense of solidarity throughout Canada. For many years, Take Back the Night marches were held each fall in remembrance of the Montreal Massacre.

4. **Deviance encourages social change.** Deviant people push a society's moral boundaries, suggesting alternatives to the status quo and encouraging change. Today's deviance, declared Durkheim, can become tomorrow's morality (1964b:71; orig. 1893). For example, rock 'n' roll, condemned as immoral in the 1950s, became a multibillion-dollar mainstream industry a few years later. In recent years hip-hop music followed the same path toward respectability.

Aboriginal suicide has been attributed to the effects of rapid social change and damages to social solidarity brought on by the residential school system. The Thinking about Diversity box looks more closely at the social context of suicide among Aboriginal peoples in Canada.

AN ILLUSTRATION: THE PURITANS OF MASSACHUSETTS BAY Kai Erikson's (2005a; orig. 1966) classic study of the Puritans of Massachusetts Bay brings Durkheim's theory to life. Even the Puritans, a disciplined and highly religious group, created deviance to clarify their moral boundaries. In fact, Durkheim might well have had the Puritans in mind when he wrote,

> Imagine a society of saints, a perfect cloister of exemplary individuals. Crimes, properly so called, will there be unknown; but faults which appear [insignificant] to the layman will create there the same scandal that the ordinary offence does in ordinary consciousness. . . . For the same reason, the perfect and upright man judges his smallest failings with a severity that the majority reserve for acts more truly in the nature of an offence. (1964b:68–69; orig. 1893)

Deviance is thus not a matter of a few "bad apples" but a necessary condition of "good" social living.

Deviance may be found in every society, but the *kind* of deviance people generate depends on the moral issues they seek to clarify. The Puritans, for example, experienced a number of crime waves, including the infamous outbreak of witchcraft in 1692. With each response, the Puritans defined the range of proper beliefs by condemning some of their members as deviant. While the offences changed, the proportion of people the Puritans defined as deviant remained steady over time—confirming Durkheim's claim that society creates deviants to mark its changing moral boundaries.

Merton's Strain Theory

Some deviance may be necessary for a society to function, but Robert Merton (1938, 1968) argued that society can be set up in a way that encourages too much deviance. Specifically, the extent and type of deviance people engage in depend on whether a society provides the *means* (such as schooling and job opportunities) to achieve cultural *goals* (such as financial success). Merton's strain theory is illustrated in Figure 9–1.

Conformity lies in pursuing cultural goals through approved means. Thus, the North American success story is someone who gains wealth and prestige through talent, schooling, and hard work. But not everyone who wants conventional success has the opportunity to attain it. According to Merton, the strain generated by our culture's emphasis on wealth and the lack of opportunities to get rich encourage some people to engage in stealing, drug dealing, or other forms of crime. Merton called this type of deviance *innovation*—using unconventional means (i.e., street crime) to achieve a culturally approved goal (e.g., wealth).

In some respects, a notorious gangster such as Al Capone was quite conventional: He pursued the

Thinking about Diversity: Race, Class, and Gender

Suicide among Aboriginal People

So serious is the problem of suicide among Aboriginal people—among youth in particular—that the Royal Commission on Aboriginal Peoples felt compelled to conduct a study of the problem (Canada, 1995). The commission felt that suicide is a crucial issue not only because it is a matter of life and death but also because it is an expression of collective anguish based on "the cumulative effect of three hundred years of colonial history: lands occupied, resources seized, beliefs and cultures ridiculed, children taken away, power concentrated in distant capitals, hopes for honourable coexistence dashed over and over again." Note the emphasis on social conditions as causes of suicide.

The report points out that, year after year, Aboriginal suicide rates are two to three times higher than those of non-Aboriginal Canadians; rates among Aboriginal *youth* are five to six times higher than among their non-Aboriginal peers. The problem is compounded by the ripple effect, whereby copycat suicides occur in related families and communities.

Looking for causes, the commission identifies four contributors: (1) psycho-biological factors, (2) life history or situational factors, (3) socio-economic factors, and (4) cultural stress. Once again, social conditions loom large, particularly with respect to the last two categories. Cultural stress applies to "societies that have undergone massive, imposed or uncontrollable change" (Canada, 1995).

The solutions suggested by the commission are varied. But among them are a number that relate to community solidarity or social integration: community development, self-government or community control, cultural and spiritual revitalization, strengthened bonds of family and community, holistic health and healing programs, and involvement of the whole community.

In his analysis of suicide, Émile Durkheim concluded that the degree of *social integration* is the key to understanding suicide. The cultural and social dislocation experienced by Aboriginal people is the result of their colonial history—a history based on government paternalism and compulsory residential schooling—compounded by the phenomenal rate of social and economic change in recent decades. This report contains insights that mirror those of Durkheim's pioneering sociological analysis a century ago.

What Do You Think?

1. How would Durkheim account for the high rates of suicide among Aboriginal people?

2. How would you enhance social integration among Aboriginal people?

3. In school, what did you learn about the history of Aboriginal/non-Aboriginal relations in Canada?

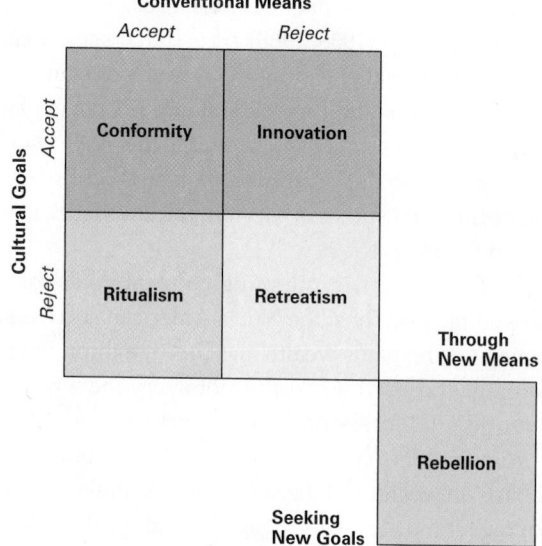

Figure 9–1 Merton's Strain Theory of Deviance

Combining a person's view of cultural goals and the conventional means to obtain them allowed Robert Merton to identify various types of deviants.

SOURCE: Merton (1968).

American dream of fame and fortune. But, finding the usual doors to success closed to members of a minority, blazed his own trail to the top. A Canadian with close ties to Capone established a parallel career. In 1918, when Prohibition outlawed the sale of liquor in Canada, Rocco Perri saw an opportunity to augment his income by selling bootleg liquor at the back of his grocery store in Hamilton, Ontario. By the time Prohibition was adopted in the United States, in 1920, Perri had "the organization and experience to take quick advantage of the opportunity.... Before long, he was a major supplier to gangsters like Al Capone" (Carrigan, 1991:174). Perri had become "King of the Bootleggers." In the wake of Prohibition, Rocco Perri's "formidable criminal organization" expanded its links to U.S. gangs through a wide range of activities, including gambling, prostitution, and extortion. Like Capone, Canada's innovator acquired wealth and power but never attained prestige in the larger society.

Figure 9–1 shows that innovation involves accepting a cultural goal (e.g., financial success) but rejecting the conventional means of obtaining it (e.g., hard work at a legal job) in favour of unconventional means (e.g., crime).

Deviant Subcultures

Richard Cloward and Lloyd Ohlin (1966) extended Merton's theory, proposing that crime results not simply from limited legitimate (legal) opportunity but also from readily accessible illegitimate (illegal) opportunity. In short, deviance or conformity arises from the *relative opportunity structure* that frames a person's life.

The lives of Al Capone and Rocco Perri show how an ambitious person denied legitimate opportunity by the barriers of poverty and ethnic prejudice can organize a criminal empire to meet the demand for alcohol during Prohibition. In other words, illegal opportunities foster the development of *criminal subcultures* that offer the knowledge, skills, and other resources needed to succeed in unconventional ways. Indeed, gangs such as Hells Angels specialize in one or another form of criminality according to available opportunities and resources (Carrigan, 1991; Sheley et al., 1995).

But what happens when people cannot identify *any* kind of opportunity, legal or illegal? Then deviance may take the form of *conflict subcultures* (e.g., armed street gangs), where violence is ignited by frustration and a desire for respect, or *retreatist subcultures* (e.g., skid rows), in which deviants drop out and perhaps abuse alcohol or other drugs.

Albert Cohen (1971; orig. 1955) suggests that *delinquency* (minor crime) is most common among lower-class youths because they have the least opportunity to achieve conventional success. Neglected by society, they seek self-respect by creating a delinquent subculture that defines as worthy the traits these youths do have. Being feared on the street may satisfy a young person's desire to be "somebody" in the local neighbourhood.

Elijah Anderson (1994, 2002) explains that, in poor urban neighbourhoods, most people manage to conform to conventional values. Yet faced with neighbourhood crime and violence, indifference or even hostility from police, and sometimes even neglect by their own parents, some young men decide to live by the "street code." To show that they can survive on the street, young men display nerve, a willingness to stand up to any threat. The risk of ending up in jail—or worse—is very high for these young men, who have been pushed to the margins of our society. The same argument can be applied to Aboriginal people—among whom young adult males are many times more likely to end up in jail than their non-Aboriginal counterparts. Justice—when it comes to the treatment of Aboriginal people—is not blind (MacDonald, 2016).

Paul Chiasson/stf/The Canadian Press

MANY GANGS CONSTITUTE A PEER GROUP IN WHICH VIOLENCE, DRUG USE, AND TRAFFICKING ARE "NORMAL" In Montreal, members of the Hells Angels, identifiable by their motorcycles and clothing, attend a funeral of one of their compatriots.

The inability to reach a cultural goal may also prompt another type of deviance, which Merton calls *ritualism*. For example, many people believe that they cannot achieve the cultural goal of becoming rich; therefore, they rigidly stick to the conventional means (the rules) in order to at least feel respectable. In essence, they embrace the rules to the point where they lose sight of their larger goals. Thus, lower-level bureaucrats may succumb to ritualism to maintain their self-respect.

A third response to the inability to succeed is *retreatism*—the rejection of both cultural goals and means, so that a person in effect "drops out." Some alcoholics, drug addicts, and street people are retreatists. The deviance of retreatists lies in their unconventional lifestyle and in what seems to be their willingness to live this way.

The fourth response to failure is *rebellion*. Like retreatists, rebels (such as radical "survivalists") reject both the cultural definition of success and the conventional means of achieving it, but they go one step further by forming a counterculture that supports alternatives to the existing social order. Many of us applaud rebels, whom we might admire, but do not emulate in their breaking of rules or laws. The popularity of rebellion is evident from the number of movies and novels about it.

EVALUATE

Durkheim made an important contribution by pointing out the functions of deviance. However, there is evidence that a community does not always come together in reaction to crime;

IN WINNIPEG, A BORN-AGAIN CHRISTIAN GIVES VISIBLE EXPRESSION TO HIS FAITH When city council warned him that his signs violated civic bylaws, the man vowed to challenge any charges in court.

sometimes fear of crime causes people to withdraw from public life (Liska & Warner, 1991; Warr & Ellison, 2000).

Merton's strain theory has been criticized for explaining some kinds of deviance (stealing) better than others (crimes of passion). In addition, not everyone seeks success in the conventional terms of wealth, as strain theory suggests.

Furthermore, the theory that deviance reflects the opportunity structure of society falls short by assuming that everyone shares the same cultural standards for judging right and wrong. If we define crime as not just burglary and auto theft but also as corporate or white-collar crime, then more high-income people, like Martha Stewart and Conrad Black, will be counted among criminals.

All structural-functional theories suggest that everyone who breaks important rules will be labelled deviant. However, becoming deviant is actually a highly complex process, as the next section explains.

CHECK YOUR LEARNING Why do the previous theories imply that crime is more common among people of lower social standing?

Labelling Theory

The main contribution of symbolic-interaction analysis is **labelling theory**, *the idea that deviance and conformity result not so much from what people do as from how others respond to those actions.* Labelling theory stresses the relativity of deviance, the idea that people may define the same behaviour in any number of ways. Consider these situations: A university student takes an article of clothing from a roommate's drawer; a married woman attending a convention has sex with a former boyfriend; a mayor gives a big city contract to a major campaign contributor. The consequences in each case depend on detection and then labelling the behaviour as deviant or criminal.

PRIMARY AND SECONDARY DEVIANCE Edwin Lemert (1951, 1972) observed that some norm violations—say, skipping school or underage drinking—provoke slight reaction from others and have little effect on a person's self-concept. Lemert calls such passing episodes *primary deviance.*

But what happens if other people notice someone's deviance and make something of it? For example, if friends describe a young man as an "alcohol abuser" and exclude him from their group, he may become bitter, drink even more, and seek the company of others who approve of his behaviour. The response to primary deviance sets in motion *secondary deviance*, by which a person repeatedly violates a norm and begins to take on a deviant identity. Thus, a situation that is defined as real becomes real in its consequences.

An old saying goes, "Sticks and stones can break my bones, but names can never hurt me." From the labelling theory perspective, names (or labels) *can* hurt—to the point of changing one's self-concept and even the course of one's life.

Labelling Deviance: Symbolic-Interaction Theories

9.3 Apply symbolic-interaction theories to the topic of deviance.

The symbolic-interaction approach explains how people define deviance in everyday situations. From this point of view, definitions of deviance and conformity are surprisingly flexible.

labelling theory the idea that deviance and conformity result not so much from what people do as from how others respond to those actions

stigma a powerfully negative label that greatly changes a person's self-concept and social identity

medicalization of deviance the transformation of moral and legal deviance into a medical condition

STIGMA Secondary deviance marks the start of what Erving Goffman (1963) called a deviant career. As people develop a stronger commitment to deviant behaviour, they typically acquire a **stigma**, *a powerfully negative label that greatly changes a person's self-concept and social identity.* A stigma operates as a master status, overpowering other aspects of social identity, so that a person is discredited in the minds of others and becomes socially isolated. Cigarette smokers, for example, have become stigmatized in North America. Sometimes an entire community formally stigmatizes an individual through what Harold Garfinkel (1956) called a *degradation ceremony*—such as a criminal trial.

RETROSPECTIVE AND PROJECTIVE LABELLING Once people stigmatize an individual, they may engage in *retrospective labelling*, interpreting someone's past in light of present deviance (Scheff, 1984). For example, after discovering that a priest has sexually molested a child, others rethink his past, noting that he liked to be around children. In *projective labelling*, a deviant identity is used to predict future action, such as repeated molestation. Either type of labelling increases the likelihood of further deviance.

Figure 9–2 presents the consequences of being observed—or not—in the first or *primary* deviant act. If primary deviance is *not* observed, there is no reaction from others, no labelling, and no internalization of a deviant identity. In this case, the deviant act may or may not be repeated.

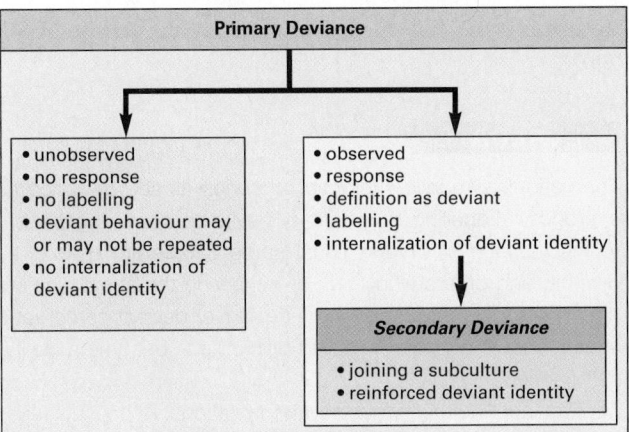

Figure 9–2 Labelling Theory: Linking Primary and Secondary Deviance

If primary deviance is *not* observed, there is no reaction from others, no labelling, and no internalization of a deviant identity. In this case, the deviant act may or may not be repeated. If the primary deviant act *is* observed and there is a response from others, the individual may be defined as deviant and labelled as such. This leads to the internalization of a deviant identity and involvement in secondary deviance.

SOURCE: Created by L.M. Gerber (2012).

On the other hand, if the primary deviant act *is* observed and there is a response from others, the individual may be defined as deviant and labelled as such. This leads to the internalization of a deviant identity and involvement in *secondary* deviance. At this point, the individual might join a subculture that, in turn, reinforces her identity.

LABELLING DIFFERENCE AS DEVIANCE Is a homeless man who refuses to allow police to take him to a city shelter on a cold night behaving independently or "insanely"? Behaviour that irritates or threatens us is labelled not just as "different" but as deviance or mental illness.

The psychiatrist Thomas Szasz (1961, 1970; orig. 1961, 2003, 2004) charges that people are too quick to apply the label of mental illness to conditions that simply amount to a difference we do not like. The only way to avoid this troubling practice, Szasz said, is to abandon the idea of mental illness entirely. The world is full of people whose differences in thought or action may annoy us, but such differences are no grounds for defining them as mentally ill.

Most mental health care professionals believe that mental illness exists, but agree that it is important to think critically about how we define difference. People who are mentally ill are no more to blame for their condition than are people who suffer from cancer or arthritis. Therefore, neither mental nor physical illness is grounds for being labelled deviant. Such labelling, Szasz claimed, is merely the exercise of power by those in a position to enforce conformity.

The Medicalization of Deviance

Labelling theory helps explain an important shift in the way our society understands deviance. Over the past 50 years, the growing influence of psychiatry and medicine has led to the **medicalization of deviance**, *the transformation of moral and legal deviance into a medical condition.*

Medicalization amounts to swapping one set of labels for another. In moral terms, we evaluate people or their behaviour as "bad" or "good." However, the scientific objectivity of medicine passes no moral judgment, instead applying a clinical diagnosis—such as "sick."

To illustrate, until the mid-twentieth century, people generally viewed alcoholics as morally weak people easily tempted by the pleasure of drink. Gradually, however, medical specialists redefined alcoholism so that most people now consider it to be a condition that renders people "sick" rather than "bad." In the same way, obesity, drug addiction, child abuse, sexual promiscuity, and other behaviours that used to be strictly moral matters are widely defined today as illnesses for which people need help rather than punishment.

In contrast, behaviours that used to be defined as criminal—such as smoking marijuana—may be seen later on as a form of treatment. At this point, it is legal to possess, consume, and grow marijuana for medicinal purposes under regulations adopted by Health Canada in June 2015. Medical marijuana is also legal in a number of U.S. states.

THE DIFFERENCE LABELS MAKE Whether we define deviance as a moral or a medical issue has three consequences. First, it affects *who responds* to deviance. An offence against common morality usually brings about a reaction from members of the community or the police. A medical label, however, places the situation under the control of clinical specialists, including counsellors, psychiatrists, and doctors. A second difference is *how people respond* to deviance. A moral approach defines deviants as offenders subject to punishment; medically, they are patients who need treatment. Punishment is designed to fit the crime, treatment to fit the patient.

Most importantly, the two labels differ on the *personal competence of the deviant person*. From a moral standpoint, whether we are right or wrong, at least we take responsibility for our own behaviour. Once defined as sick, however, a deviant is seen as unable to control—or, if "mentally ill," even to understand—his or her actions. People who are labelled incompetent are in turn subjected to treatment, often against their will. Therefore, defining deviance in medical terms should be done with caution.

Sutherland's Differential Association Theory

Learning any behavioural pattern, whether conventional or deviant, is a process that takes place in groups. According to Edwin Sutherland (1940), a person's tendency toward conformity or deviance depends on the amount of contact with others who encourage—or reject—conventional behaviour. This is Sutherland's theory of *differential association*.

Several studies confirm the idea that young people are more likely to engage in delinquency if they believe that members of their peer groups encourage such activity (Akers et al., 1979; Miller & Matthews, 2001). One recent investigation focused on sexual activity among grade 8 students. Two strong predictors of such behaviour for young girls were having a boyfriend who encouraged sexual relations and having girlfriends who approved. Similarly, boys were encouraged to become sexually active by friends who rewarded them with high status in the peer group (Little & Rankin, 2001).

Hirschi's Control Theory

The sociologist Travis Hirschi (1969; Gottfredson & Hirschi, 1995) developed *control theory*, which states that social control depends on people anticipating the consequences of their behaviour. Hirschi assumed that everyone finds at least some deviance tempting. But the thought of a ruined life or career keeps most people from breaking the rules; for some, just imagining the reactions of family and friends is enough. On the other hand, individuals who feel that they have little to lose by deviance are likely to become rule breakers.

Specifically, Hirschi links conformity to four different types of social control:

1. *Attachment.* Strong social attachments encourage conformity. Weak family, peer, and school relationships leave people freer to engage in deviance.
2. *Opportunity.* The greater one's access to legitimate opportunity, the greater the advantages of conformity. It follows that someone with limited opportunities and little confidence in future success will drift more readily toward deviance.
3. *Involvement.* Extensive involvement in legitimate activities—such as holding a job, going to school, or playing sports—inhibits deviance (Langbein & Bess, 2002). In contrast, people who simply "hang out" waiting for something to happen have time and energy to engage in deviant activity.
4. *Belief.* Strong belief in conventional morality and respect for authority figures restrain tendencies toward deviance. Someone with a weak conscience is more open to temptation (Stack et al., 2004).

Hirschi's analysis combines a number of earlier ideas about the causes of deviant behaviour. Note that social privilege, as well as family and community environment, determine the risk of deviant behaviour (Hope et al., 2003).

EVALUATE

The various symbolic-interaction theories all see deviance as a process. Labelling theory links deviance not to *action* but to the *reaction* of others. Thus, some people are defined as deviant, and others who think or behave in the same way are not. The concepts of secondary deviance, deviant career, and stigma show how being labelled deviant can become a lasting self-concept.

Yet labelling theory has several limitations. Because it takes a relative view of deviance, it ignores the fact that some kinds of behaviour—such as murder—are condemned just about everywhere. Therefore, labelling theory is most usefully applied to less serious issues, such as sexual promiscuity or theft. Also, research reveals that deviant labelling may encourage or discourage further deviance (Sherman & Smith, 1992; Smith & Gartin, 1989). Lastly, not everyone resists being labelled deviant; some people actively seek it out (Vold & Bernard, 1986). For example, people take part in civil disobedience and willingly subject themselves to arrest in order to call attention to social or environmental injustice.

Deviance and Inequality: Social-Conflict Analysis

9.4 Apply social-conflict theories to the topic of deviance.

The social-conflict approach links deviance to social inequality—that is, *who* or *what* is labelled "deviant" depends on who holds power.

Deviance and Power

Alexander Liazos (1972) pointed out that the people we call deviant—those we dismiss as "nuts" and "sluts"—are typically powerless. Bag ladies (not corporate polluters) and panhandlers (not international arms dealers) carry the stigma of deviance.

Social-conflict theory explains this pattern in three ways. First, all norms and especially the laws of any society generally reflect the interests of the rich and powerful. Those who threaten the wealthy, either by taking their property or by advocating a more egalitarian society, are defined as "common thieves" or "political radicals." Karl Marx argued that the law and all other social institutions support the interests of the rich. Richard Quinney observed that "Capitalist justice is by the capitalist class, for the capitalist class, and against the working class" (1977:3).

Second, even if their behaviour is called into question, the powerful have the resources to resist deviant labels. The majority of the executives involved in recent corporate scandals have yet to be arrested; very few have gone to jail.

Third, the widespread belief that norms and laws are natural and good masks their political character. For this reason, although we may condemn the *unequal application* of the law, we give little thought to whether or not the *laws themselves* are fair.

Deviance and Capitalism

In the Marxist tradition, Steven Spitzer (1980) argued that deviant labels are applied to people who interfere with the operation of capitalism. Since capitalism is based on private control of wealth, people who threaten the property of others—especially the poor who steal from the rich—are prime candidates for being labelled deviant. Conversely, the rich who take advantage of the poor are less likely to be labelled deviant. For example, landlords who charge poor tenants high rents and evict those who cannot pay are not considered criminals; they are simply doing business.

Capitalism depends on productive labour. People who cannot or will not work risk being labelled deviant. Many people think that someone out of work is necessarily deviant. Similarly, capitalism depends on respect for authority figures, so people who resist authority are called deviant. Examples are children who skip school or talk back to teachers, and adults who play Solitaire on their computers at work. Those who directly challenge the capitalist status quo—labour organizers, radical environmentalists, and antiwar activists—are likely to be defined as deviant.

On the other side of the coin, society labels positively behaviour that supports the operation of capitalism. For example, winning athletes enjoy celebrity status because they express the values of individual achievement and competition, both vital to capitalism. Also, Spitzer noted, we condemn using drugs of escape as deviant (such as marijuana, psychedelics, heroin, and crack) but encourage drugs consistent with the status quo (such as alcohol and caffeine). The capitalist system also tries to control people who don't fit into the system. The elderly, people with mental or physical disabilities, and Robert Merton's retreatists (people addicted to alcohol or other drugs) are a "costly yet relatively harmless burden" on society. Such people, claimed Spitzer, are subject to control by social welfare agencies. But people who openly challenge the capitalist system, including the inner-city underclass and revolutionaries—Merton's innovators and rebels—are controlled by the criminal justice system.

Note that both the social welfare system and the criminal justice system blame individuals, not the system, for social problems. Welfare recipients are considered unworthy freeloaders; poor people who express rage at their plight are labelled rioters; anyone who challenges the government is branded a radical, and those who try to gain illegally what they will never get legally are rounded up as criminals.

The Applying Theory table summarizes the treatment of deviance from the structural-functional, symbolic-interaction, and social conflict perspectives.

White-Collar Crime

Reputable Canadians have long been known to circumvent the law when doing so is likely to be immensely profitable (Carrigan, 1991:113–165). For example, during World War II, when consumer goods were rationed, big and small businesses and government officials were caught up in wartime racketeering, supplying illegal goods through the black market. More recently, Canada has had its share of stock and real estate fraud, bid-rigging, and tax evasion—activities that have cost taxpayers and consumers billions of dollars. Many of these perpetrators are never charged or convicted of their crimes.

APPLYING THEORY

Deviance				
	Structural-Functional Theory	**Symbolic-Interaction Theory**	**Social-Conflict Theory**	**Race-Conflict and Feminist Theories**
What is the level of analysis?	Macro-level	Micro-level	Macro-level	Macro-level
What is deviance? **What part does it play in society?**	Deviance is a basic part of social organization. By defining deviance, society sets its moral boundaries.	Deviance is part of socially constructed reality that emerges in interaction. Deviance comes into being as individuals label something deviant.	Deviance results from social inequality. Norms, including laws, reflect the interests of powerful members of society.	Deviance reflects racial and gender inequality. Deviant labels are more readily applied to women and other minorities.
What is important about deviance?	Deviance is universal: It exists in all societies.	Deviance is variable: Any act or person may or may not be labeled deviant.	Deviance is political: People with little power are at high risk of being labeled deviant.	Deviance is a means of control: Dominant categories of people discredit others as a means to dominate them.

The cases described in the Sociology and the Media box exemplify **white-collar crime**, defined by Edwin Sutherland in 1940 as *crime committed by persons of high social position in the course of their occupations* (Sutherland & Cressey, 1978:44). White-collar crime rarely involves uniformed police converging on a scene with drawn guns; much less dramatically, white-collar crimes involve powerful people making use of their occupational position to enrich themselves or others illegally, often causing significant public harm in the process (Hagan & Parker, 1985; Vold & Bernard, 1986). Crime in government offices and corporate boardrooms is *crime in the suites* rather than *crime in the streets*.

The public harm wreaked by false advertising, marketing of unsafe products, embezzlement, and bribery of public officials is more extensive than most people realize—possibly greater than the more visible street crime (Reiman, 1990). The marketing of unsafe products and the failure to implement workplace safety regulations are responsible for many deaths. Immeasurable sums of money are stolen every year through fraud. Since much of it goes undetected, and overburdened fraud units are unable to prosecute all known cases, it is difficult to estimate the dollar value of white-collar crime.

Until recently, such deviance rarely resulted in criminal labelling of powerful people. Even when their actions lead to extensive public harm, officials are rarely prosecuted. And in the event that white-collar criminals do face the music, the odds are that they will not go to jail. The public is less concerned about white-collar crime than street crime, because corporate crime victimizes everyone and thus no one.

Corporate Crime

Sometimes whole companies, not just individuals, break the law. **Corporate crime** refers to *the illegal actions of a corporation or people acting on its behalf*. Corporate crime ranges from knowingly selling faulty or dangerous products to deliberately polluting the environment (Derber, 2004). The collapse of the Enron Corporation in 2001 followed extensive violations of business and accounting laws, and resulted in losses to shareholders and others exceeding US$50 billion (Lavelle, 2002). Keep in mind that shareholders of Canadian and American companies can be anywhere in the world: When they collectively lose billions of dollars to corporate crime, Canadians, Canadian pension plans, and perhaps your own family are among those affected.

As with white-collar crime, most cases of corporate crime go unpunished, and many are never even known to the public. In addition, the cost of corporate crime goes beyond dollars. The collapse of Enron and other corporations in recent years cost tens of thousands of people their jobs and their pensions. Even more seriously, for decades, coal-mining companies have knowingly put miners at risk from inhaling coal dust, and hundreds of people die annually of "black lung" disease; miners realized only recently that their cancers are related to decades of work in the mines. Canadian uranium mines are even more deadly: Effluent from the uranium processing plants contaminates large areas, often devastating Aboriginal lands and communities. The U.S. death toll from all job-related hazards exceeds 100 000 annually (Carroll, 1999; Jones, 1999). The proportionate figure for Canada, with its smaller population base, would be about 11 000.

Organized Crime

Organized crime is *a business that supplies illegal goods or services*. Sometimes criminal

white-collar crime crime committed by people of high social position in the course of their occupations

corporate crime the illegal actions of a corporation or people acting on its behalf

organized crime a business supplying illegal goods or services

Sociology and the Media

Crime in High Places

Over the past two decades, North America witnessed an escalating wave of scandals involving politicians, corporate executives, and other powerful individuals who broke the law. In some cases, the scandals were made public by the media, forcing governments or the police to take action. Thereafter, the media kept us informed of investigations, inquiries, arrests, and trials involving influential people, political parties, and corporations.

One notorious example, Alberta's Bre-X case, may be the greatest gold hoax of all time (Francis, 1997). Investors, big and small alike, were scammed to the tune of more than $3 billion by an upstart company that tampered with ore samples to fake a massive gold find in Indonesia. The apparent suicide of the chief geologist and the complete collapse of Bre-X share prices brought the scam to an end.

More recent American examples—Enron, World-Com, and ImClone—brought corporate and white-collar crime into the limelight. The energy trading company Enron deceived its investors and employees by falsifying its accounts in order to enhance the value of its shares. The investigations and trials that followed Enron's bankruptcy were played out in the media. Canada's CIBC aided Enron's deception by lending it money (US$205 million) while aware that it was concealing US$22 billion in debt (Howlett et al., 2003). Executives at telecommunications giant WorldCom, including Canadian-born CEO Bernard Ebbers, were accused of securities fraud when the company fell US$41 billion in debt. At the time, WorldCom and Enron were the biggest American companies to have filed for bankruptcy protection—in the wake of large-scale financial fraud (Waldie & Howlett, 2003). ImClone was a simpler case of insider trading: Company executives and friends sold their shares before bad news became common knowledge. ImClone's CEO was imprisoned. The trial of his friend Martha Stewart, for obstruction of justice by lying about a timely stock trade, resulted in a prison sentence followed by a lengthy period of house arrest.

Financial scandals in the Canadian political system have been with us since the days of Sir John A. Macdonald, who solicited money from businesspeople in exchange for contracts to build the Canadian National Railway. Nonetheless, no previous incident had the public exposure of our recent sponsorship scandal, Adscam. After almost losing the Quebec sovereignty referendum in 1995, Prime Minister Jean Chrétien created a sponsorship program with the intention of promoting Canada in a variety of Quebec venues. Millions of dollars went to Liberal-friendly ad agencies. In some cases, the money was accepted but no work was done; in another, the money found its way illegally—via brown paper envelope—into the coffers of the Quebec wing of the federal Liberal Party.

CONRAD BLACK.

When Paul Martin took over as prime minister in December 2003, he created the *televised* Gomery inquiry to investigate the mismanagement of public funds. He had no way of knowing what Justice Gomery would reveal or that the public, especially Quebecers, would be mesmerized by television coverage showing how "every rule in the book" had been broken. Heads rolled: Senior civil servants and executives lost their jobs, and several people were tried and convicted of offences. But the most significant result was the fall of Martin's Liberal government in January 2006, when Quebecers realized that the sponsorship program had been an attempt to "buy" their votes. Stephen Harper's Conservatives won an astounding 10 seats in Quebec as a direct result of Adscam and the televised Gomery inquiry.

Over the same period, Canadians watched the downfall of Conrad Black, former CEO of the newspaper conglomerate Hollinger International. Born in Montreal, Black made his fortune in the newspaper business, assumed a lavish lifestyle, and gave up his Canadian citizenship in 2001 in order to become Baron Black of Crossharbour, in England. In 2004, the U.S. Securities and Exchange Commission filed a civil fraud lawsuit against Black, alleging that he had diverted millions of shareholder dollars to himself and others. In 2006, he was charged with failure to pay taxes. Black vehemently denied any wrongdoing, countersued, was convicted, served time in an American jail, and unsuccessfully applied for bail while his appeal was being heard. He was eventually released from prison (though not allowed to leave the United States) but was resentenced and returned to prison in September 2011.

While in prison, Black wrote regularly for the *National Post* (which he founded in 1998) and published

(continued)

his prison memoir, *A Matter of Principle*. "During his 37 months as a guest of the U.S. Federal Bureau of Prisons, Lord Black ... became an impassioned advocate for prison reform" and a harsh critic of Canada's new crime policies, calling them "sadistic and malicious" (Wente, 2012). Upon his release from prison (in May 2012), Black returned to Toronto, where he would reapply for Canadian citizenship. He was welcomed home by his wife, Barbara Amiel, as well as many friends and admirers, but others were openly hostile to his return—saying that he should not be allowed to resume his life here and that he should be stripped of his Order of Canada (Chase & Waldie, 2012).

The rich and well-connected still retain their influence and prestige when they break the rules, but—in large part because of the media—infractions by the powerful are on our radar.

What Do You Think?

1. Does the average Canadian suffer as a result of white-collar crime? If so, how?
2. Are powerful people now more likely to be caught and punished for their crimes?
3. How have the media turned investigative journalism into investigative policing?

---

organizations force people to do business with them, as when a gang extorts money from shopkeepers for "protection." In most cases, however, organized crime involves the sale of illegal goods and services—including sex, drugs, and gambling—to willing buyers. Organized crime expanded among immigrants, who found that society was not always willing to share its opportunities with them. Some ambitious individuals (such as Capone and Perri) made their own success, especially during Prohibition, as described earlier. The Italian Mafia is a well-known example of organized crime. But other criminal organizations in North America involve Blacks, Chinese, Colombians, Cubans, Haitians, Nigerians, Russians, and others of almost every racial and ethnic category—and motorcycle gangs, such as Hells Angels. Today, organized crime involves a wide range of activities: selling drugs, sex, fraudulent credit cards, and counterfeit passports (Valdez, 1997).

EVALUATE

According to social-conflict theory, a capitalist society's inequality in wealth and power shapes its laws and their application. The criminal justice and social welfare systems act as political agents, controlling categories of people who are a threat to the capitalist system.

Like other approaches to deviance, social-conflict theory has its critics. It implies that laws and other cultural norms are created directly by the rich and powerful to promote their own interests. This is oversimplification, as laws also protect human rights, workers, consumers, and the environment—often at the expense of corporations and the rich.

Social-conflict analysis argues that criminality is the result of inequality. However, as Durkheim noted, deviance exists in all societies, whatever the economic system. It also appears in all social strata, as white-collar crime so clearly reveals.

The sociological explanations for crime and other types of deviance we have discussed are summarized in the Applying Theory table.

CHECK YOUR LEARNING Define white-collar crime, corporate crime, and organized crime.

Deviance, Race, and Gender: Race-Conflict and Feminist Theories

9.5 Apply race-conflict and feminist theories to the topic of deviance.

What is considered deviant reflects the relative power and privilege of different categories of people. The following sections offer two examples: Hate crimes motivated by race or ethnicity and the link between gender and deviance.

Hate Crimes

A **hate crime** is *a criminal act against a person or a person's property by an offender motivated by racial or other bias.* Hate crimes, which may refer to race, religion, ancestry, sexual orientation, or physical disability, are common in all societies, but rates vary dramatically across countries, over time, and in response to crises like war or recession.

A survey of 12 major Canadian police forces collected data on hate crimes for 2001 and 2002, finding 928 reported hate crimes over the two years. A full quarter of these hate crimes were directed against Jewish people or institutions. Anti-Semitism, it appears, is firmly embedded in Canadian culture. At that time, 57 percent of hate crimes were motivated by ethnicity and race, targeting mainly Blacks and Asians, while 43 percent targeted religion, mainly Jewish and Muslim. A relatively small 9 percent targeted gays and lesbians.

A *Juristat* study (Statistics Canada, 2012a) reported that Ontario had the highest rate of hate crimes in 2010, at 5.7 per 100 000 population, followed by Manitoba (4.6) and British Columbia (4.0). Among metropolitan areas, Guelph and Ottawa topped the rates at 15 and 14 incidents per 100 000 population, respectively, and the first eight metropolitan areas were in Ontario—Toronto registered a rate of 6 per 100 000, which is roughly one-third the Guelph rate.

What a difference a decade makes! Whereas 2001 and 2002 combined witnessed 928 incidents of hate crime, 2013 had almost as many—909—in a *single* year. The targets also changed. In the first instance, a quarter of hate crimes targeted Jews, while 17 and 9 percent targeted Blacks and gays or lesbians respectively. By 2013, Blacks were the prime target (at 28 percent) followed by gays and lesbians (21 percent) and Jews (20 percent). The most dramatic shift was in the percentage of hate crimes motivated by sexual orientation—a move from 9 to 21 percent in 11 years (see Figure 9–3).

Both Canada and the United States have hate crime laws that protect multiple categories of people. A given crime (e.g., arson or homicide) is treated more harshly if it is motivated by hatred.

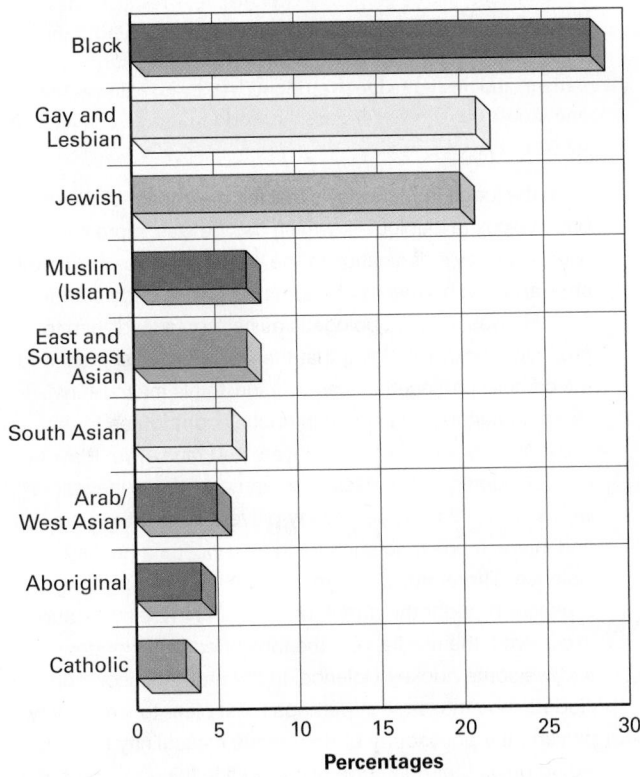

Figure 9–3 Incidence of Hate Crimes Motivated by Race, Ethnicity, Religion, and Sexual Orientation, Canada, 2013

SOURCE: Adapted by LM Gerber from Statistics Canada, Juristat, no. 85-002-X, 2015.

The Feminist Perspective: Deviance and Gender

Virtually every society in the world applies stricter normative controls to women than to men, usually centring the lives of women on the home. Women's opportunities in the workplace, in politics, in athletics, and in the military are more limited than those of men; those who test the limits are deviants. In Saudi Arabia, women cannot vote or drive; in Iran, women who dare to expose their hair in public can be whipped; a Nigerian court convicted a divorced woman of bearing a child out of wedlock and sentenced her to death by stoning (Eboh, 2002). In 2009, several women in Sudan were convicted of "dressing indecently." The punishment was imprisonment and, in several cases, 10 lashes. The crime was wearing trousers (BBC, 2009).

Gender also figures in the theories of deviance discussed earlier. Robert Merton's strain theory, for example, defines cultural goals in terms of financial success. Traditionally, at least, this goal has had more to do with the lives of men because women have been taught to define success in terms of relationships, particularly marriage and motherhood (Leonard, 1982). A more clearly woman-focused theory might recognize the strain that results from the cultural ideal of equality clashing with the reality of gender-based inequality.

According to labelling theory, deviance derives from the different standards applied to women and men. Further, because society puts men in positions of power over women, men often escape direct responsibility for actions that victimize women. In the past, at least, men who sexually harassed or assaulted women were labelled as only mildly deviant and escaped punishment entirely. In contrast, women who are victimized may have to convince others—even members of a jury—that they were not to blame for sexual assault. The trial of Jian Ghomeshi illustrates this pattern very well: "It's a familiar plot: the evisceration of the witness, the questioning of details adjacent to but not directly associated with the charge. The primary plot lines revolved around a yellow Volkswagen bug, hair extensions, and by day two, flirtatious emails ..." (Kingston, 2016) In the end, research confirms an important truth: The definition of deviance depends on the gender of audience and actor (King & Clayson, 1988).

Despite its focus on social inequality, much social-conflict analysis fails to address the issue of gender. If economic disadvantage is a primary cause of crime, as conflict theory suggests, why do women commit far *fewer* crimes than men? Why are men more violent in general? The Sociology in Focus box illustrates the role of culture by taking a look at the link between masculinity and violence in hockey.

Sociology in Focus

Dangerous Masculinity: Violence and Crime in Hockey

When is assault criminal and when is it just part of the game? To what extent is violence in men's hockey part of the culture of the game—that is, normal and therefore not criminal? How do the law, the NHL, the players, the media, and the fans react in the face of serious on-ice assault?

Michael Atkinson immersed himself in the hockey world in an attempt to understand the responses of various parties when, in a game on February 21, 2000, Marty McSorley viciously assaulted opposing player Donald Brashear. Atkinson's approach to understanding this event is interpretive—consistent with symbolic-interactionist participant observation.

Atkinson (2007) reported that McSorley clipped Brashear from behind "with a two-handed stick slash to the right temple" that dropped him to the ice, unconscious. Brashear's head hit the ice, blood poured from his nose, and he lay motionless except for the periodic seizure. Clearly, what Atkinson calls the *dangerous masculinity* of ice hockey allowed McSorley to make a vicious assault that would be judged as criminal had the incident occurred *off* the ice.

The police got involved, and McSorley was found guilty of assault with a weapon under the *Criminal Code*. He was sentenced to 18 months of probation (i.e., conditional discharge) and ordered never to play against Brashear again. As a result, McSorley has no criminal record and is able to cross international boundaries freely. The NHL punished McSorley by suspending him for the rest of season.

This incident, Atkinson argued, illustrates the embedding of social constructions of masculinity in the interpretation of on-ice violence—or viewing violence in hockey through "the lens of dangerous masculinity." Through that lens, we see hockey as a game that includes fights, violence, and *explicit consent,* on the part of the players, to the risk of on-ice contact and injury. Being a hockey player, Brashear had given his consent to the assault. Atkinson observed that dangerous masculinity requires hockey players to intimidate opponents and endure pain and injury while managing their emotions. Since this is central to hockey and hockey culture, which Brashear embraced, he was *not* the victim of a random vicious attack or subject to criminal victimization.

Brashear, we are told, was asking for it, by taunting McSorley and refusing to fight. Media commentator Don Cherry's assessment of the situation was "You should never ridicule and humiliate a warrior.... You play with the bull, and you're gonna get the horns." The general public was horrified, but the media, the fans, and the justice system—like Don Cherry—were sympathetic and even protective of McSorley. The NHL defended its authority to deal with on-ice behaviour without intervention by the police or courts.

Courtesy of Michael Atkinson

MICHAEL ATKINSON CONDUCTS RESEARCH ON VIOLENCE AND AGGRESSION IN SPORTS CULTURES (E.G., ICE HOCKEY, ANIMAL BLOOD SPORTS), RADICAL BODY MODIFICATION (E.G., TATTOOING, COSMETIC SURGERY), AND YOUTH SUBCULTURES SUCH AS STRAIGHT-EDGE He engages in participant observation by becoming a full member of the groups he explores. As a result, he has participated in the social world as a ticket scalper, endurance athlete, hockey player, tattoo enthusiast, cosmetic surgery patient, and Straightedge practitioner. Atkinson believes that one should actively experience the world rather than imagine it theoretically.

Even the judge in McSorley's trial felt the impact of dangerous masculine ideologies, writing that he was impressed with McSorley's dedication to the game, diligence, and bravery—and that his *inability* to admit his guilt is understandable. He was almost apologetic as he "sentenced" him to probation, acknowledging that the league's punishment and the criminal prosecution were a "blow to his masculinity."

The culture of violence in hockey contributes to the excitement of the game for players and fans alike. Players are considered to be masculine warriors whose inevitable wounds will heal. Since hockey players consent to pain and injury, there is no such thing as a victim in hockey violence. Therefore, we blame the victim, implying that Brashear brought the attack on himself. NHL players and executives, the media, and the fans effectively condone and welcome hockey violence. In the end, Atkinson concluded, "the message is perhaps most clear to ice hockey players; the philosophy of dangerous masculinity is a privileging but brutalizing code of conduct within the world of professional sport."

POSTSCRIPT: When Sidney Crosby of the Pittsburgh Penguins collapsed on the ice after a blow to the head in 2011, the debate about hockey violence became more intense. Concerns about the long-term effects of concussions increased public pressure to the point that the NHL took steps to bring violence under control. Nonetheless, violence seems to be escalating—at least it was in the 2012 playoff season. Ratings normally increase during playoffs, but some argue that the controversy regarding violence resulting in head injuries and concussion has intensified interest in the game among less ardent fans (Houpt & Ladurantaye, 2012). As Atkinson pointed out, violence adds to the excitement of the game. The fans love it.

The suicides of Wade Belak, Rick Rupien, and Derek Boogard highlighted the long-term effects of multiple concussions and the importance of preventing head injuries. In this light, some people want to eliminate fighting altogether; others such as Don Cherry argue that there is no need to do this because *only* eight NHL players have committed suicide since 1999. Hockey is meant to be "tough, passionate and gritty. Fighting is a big part of that passion, and it's what makes hockey great" (Kline, 2011).

What Do You Think?

1. Is the level of violence in hockey acceptable or out of control?

2. Why was the condition of Brashear, the victim, ignored while the media, fans, and justice system were protective of McSorley?

3. What does the concept of hockey as a display of dangerous masculinity mean for women's hockey in Canada? Do those Olympic gold medals make a difference?

SOURCE: Adapted, in part, from Atkinson (2007) and from Atkinson himself.

Crime

9.6   Identify patterns of crime in Canada and around the world.

Crime is the violation of criminal law enacted by the federal government. Nonetheless, implementation of Canada's *Criminal Code* may vary among provincial and territorial jurisdictions. All crimes are composed of two elements: The act itself (or, sometimes, the failure to act) and criminal intent—in legal terminology, the *mens rea* ("guilty mind"). Intent is a matter of degree, ranging from negligence to willful conduct; someone who is negligent does not deliberately set out to hurt anyone but acts, or fails to act, in a way that results in harm. Prosecutors weigh the degree of intent in deciding whether, for example, to charge someone with first-degree murder, second-degree murder, or manslaughter. Alternatively, they may consider a killing justifiable, as in self-defence.

Types of Crime

In Canada, information on criminal offences is obtained from the Uniform Crime Reporting system and reported in a Statistics Canada publication called *Canadian Crime Statistics*. Violent crime and property crime are recorded separately. **Violent crimes**, *crimes against people that involve violence or the threat of violence,* include murder, manslaughter, infanticide, assault, sexual assault, abduction, and robbery. **Property crimes**, *crimes that involve theft of property belonging to others,* include breaking and entering, motor vehicle theft, theft over $5000, theft of $5000 and under, possession of stolen goods, and fraud.

A third category of offences includes **victimless crimes**, *violations of law in which there are no obvious victims,* such as prostitution and gambling. There is also a separate category of offences under the *Narcotic Control Act* regarding the use of illegal drugs, including cannabis or marijuana. However, "victimless crime" is often a misnomer. How victimless is a crime when a young runaway is lured into prostitution? Or if a young pregnant woman using crack causes death or permanent injury to her baby? Or if a spouse spends the family's savings on gambling losses? Generally, a person who commits such a crime is both offender and victim.

Criminal Statistics

Canada's crime statistics show steady increases in both violent and property crime rates from 1962 to the late 1990s followed by declines through to 2012. Figure 9–4 illustrates these trends in violent and property crimes over the period in question. Note that violent and property crime rates in the United States also peaked in the 1990s and then declined.

Canada Map 9–1 suggests that homicide rates differ not only between countries, but also between our own provinces and territories. In fact, the variation within Canada is greater than that between Canada and the United States. Nunavut's homicide rate is 21 times that of Prince Edward Island, while the American rate is three to four times that of Canada. Homicide rates in Canada generally increase from east to west and again to the north. For the country

violent crimes *crimes against people* that direct violence or the threat of violence against others

property crimes *crimes against property* that involve theft of money or property belonging to others

victimless crimes violations of law in which there are no obvious victims

"YOU LOOK LIKE THIS SKETCH OF SOMEONE WHO'S THINKING ABOUT COMMITTING A CRIME." © The New Yorker Collection 2000, David Sipress from cartoonbank.com. All rights reserved.

crimes, especially when losses are minor. And reported sexual assault—which includes date rape—still grossly understates the extent of these crimes.

One way to evaluate official crime statistics is through a *victimization survey*, in which a representative sample is asked about its experience with crime. People do not always respond fully or truthfully to such surveys, but the results indicate that actual crime occurs at substantially higher rates than stated by official reports. Canada's first national survey on violence against women, in 1993, found that half of Canadian women have experienced physical or sexual violence at least once since turning 16. Among those who have been married or lived common-law, 29 percent have been physically or sexually

as a whole, homicide rates have dropped from a high of 2.7 per 100 000 population in 1992 to 2.1 in 1996 to 1.8 in 2006 and 1.6 in the 2010–2014 period. The average rates (2010 to 2014) that appear on Canada Map 9–1 have declined almost everywhere in Canada except Nunavut, where the rate has increased (from a previous 12 to 15 per 100 000). Importantly, in 2014, Canada registered its lowest homicide rate in 40 years at 1.45 per 100 000 population. If nothing else, this map should be reassuring: The likelihood of being murdered in Canada is very, very small.

Always read crime statistics with caution, since they include only crimes known to the police. The police learn about almost all homicides, but assaults—especially among acquaintances—are far less likely to be reported. The police record an even smaller proportion of property

assaulted by their partners. Victimization remained stable between 1988 and 1993, with 24 percent of the female population experiencing at least one instance of criminal victimization (Statistics Canada, 1994a).

The most recent study of criminal victimization in Canada reported that sexual assault rates remained constant between 1999 and 2014—at about 20 incidents per 1000 population. The overall rate of violent victimization dropped in 2014 mainly because physical assault, which affects men more than women, declined sharply from about 80/1000 to 43/1000 in 2014. The victims of violent crime are more likely to be women than men and likely to be between 15 and 29 years of age where the victimization rate is 150/1000 or higher. Victimization is linked to drug use (256/1000), alcohol consumption (127/1000),

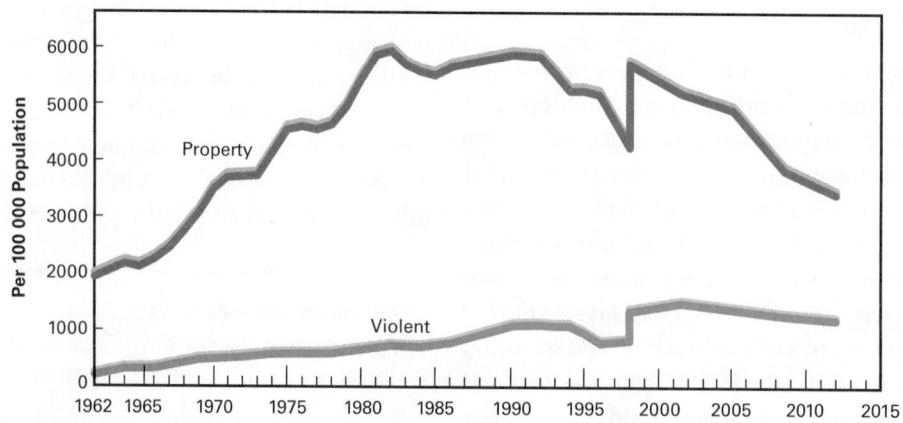

Figure 9–4 Violent and Property Crime Rates in Canada, 1962–2012

SOURCE: Compilation and calculations by L.M. Gerber based on data from Statistics Canada. Catalogue nos. 85-205 and 85-002 and Statistics Canada 2016, CANSIM table 252-0051.

Seeing Ourselves

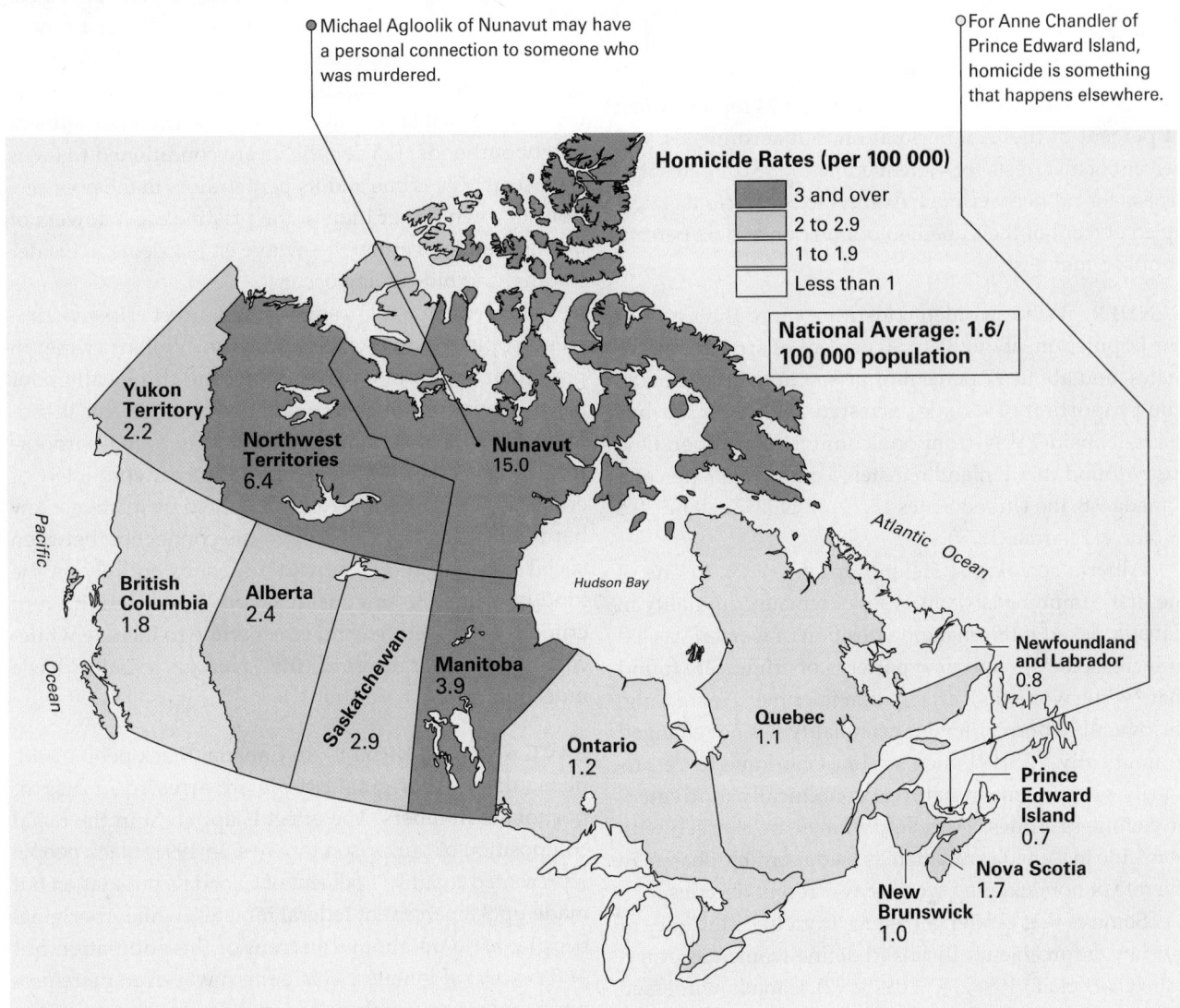

Michael Agloolik of Nunavut may have a personal connection to someone who was murdered.

For Anne Chandler of Prince Edward Island, homicide is something that happens elsewhere.

Homicide Rates (per 100 000)

- 3 and over
- 2 to 2.9
- 1 to 1.9
- Less than 1

National Average: 1.6/ 100 000 population

Yukon Territory 2.2

Northwest Territories 6.4

Nunavut 15.0

British Columbia 1.8

Alberta 2.4

Saskatchewan 2.9

Manitoba 3.9

Ontario 1.2

Quebec 1.1

Newfoundland and Labrador 0.8

Prince Edward Island 0.7

Nova Scotia 1.7

New Brunswick 1.0

Pacific Ocean

Atlantic Ocean

Hudson Bay

Canada Map 9–1 Homicide Rates for Canada, Provinces, and Territories, 2010 to 2014 (Five-Year Averages, Rates per 100 000 People)*

*Averages are calculated to even out the impacts of large variations from year to year for relatively small populations—specifically those of Yukon, Northwest Territories, and Nunavut.

SOURCE: Compilation and calculation by LM Gerber from Statistics Canada (2015), CANSIM table 253-0001.

and involvement in more than 20 evening activities per month (127/1000 victimizations). Of course, victimization varies with the type of evening activity: Spending more than 10 evenings per month in a bar or pub dramatically increases the likelihood of victimization (Statistics Canada, 2015).

The initial study in 1993 involved a "single-gender victimization survey" (Lupri, 2002), which implies that only women are subject to domestic abuse and ignores the fact that more than 30 studies in the 1970s and 1980s found "equal rates of assault by men and women." While more women report physical injury, both abused men and women suffer low levels of self-esteem,

embarrassment, and shame. Whatever the direction of the abuse, Lupri argues, the impacts on children in the home are the same—behavioural effects such as "aggression and delinquency," or psychological effects including "anxiety, depression, and low self-esteem." By focusing on the abuse of women and ignoring the abuse of men, society acknowledges only part of the problem.

The Street Criminal: A Profile

Official statistics paint a broad-brush picture of people arrested for violent and property crimes. Here we examine the breakdown of these arrest statistics by age, gender, social class, race, and ethnicity.

AGE Official crime rates rise sharply during adolescence, peak in the late teens, and then fall as people get older. People between the ages of 15 and 24 represent just 14 percent of the U.S. population, but account for 39.3 percent of all arrests for violent crimes and 46.8 percent of arrests for property crimes. Twenty- to 34-year-olds make up 25 percent of the Canadian population and 62 percent of prison inmates.

GENDER While women constitute more than half of our population, about 85 to 90 percent of arrests involve males, and about 97 percent of prison inmates are male. The proportion of females arrested is always low but varies considerably from one country to another. One study found that Finland registered a low of 6.7 percent, Canada 9.8, the United States 13.7, and New Zealand 20.5 (Simon & Sharma, 1979).

Alberta sociologist Helen Boritch (1997), in one of the first comprehensive analyses of female criminality in Canada, asked if the changing position of women has led to increased rates and new patterns of crime. She found that "while women's participation in crime is increasing, the overall pattern of female criminality has not changed dramatically. . . . [W]omen's crimes continue to be primarily non-violent in nature, economically motivated, or victimless crimes." Very few women are charged with homicide in Canada, and there is no discernible change in the rate of homicides by women over recent decades.

Some of this gender gap stems from the reluctance of our law enforcement officials to define women as criminals (Cluff et al., 1998; H. Scott, 1992). Canada witnessed this reluctance to assume the worst about women as it watched the Bernardo–Homolka murder case unfold. Initially, the justice system and the public were ready to believe that Karla Homolka was an unwilling accomplice—a victim, in effect—forced to participate in abduction, rape, and murder by a husband she feared. Before the incriminating videotapes, which revealed her to be an enthusiastic participant, were found, Homolka was allowed to **plea bargain**, *a legal negotiation in which the prosecution reduces a defendant's charge in exchange for a guilty plea*. She received a manslaughter conviction and a 12-year sentence in exchange for giving evidence against Paul Bernardo. In 2005, Homolka was released from prison, to media scrutiny, public outrage, and fears for public safety in neighbourhoods where she might have settled.

SOCIAL CLASS While people commonly associate criminality with poverty, sociological research suggests that rich and poor alike commit crimes, albeit somewhat different kinds of offences. People arrested for violent and property crimes, in North America and elsewhere, disproportionately have low social standing (Thornberry

& Farnsworth, 1982; Wolfgang et al., 1987). In part, this pattern reflects the historical tendency to view poor people as less worthy than those whose wealth and power confer apparent respectability (Elias, 1986; Tittle et al., 1978). Strain theory, discussed earlier, contributes to the expectation that law breakers will come from less affluent neighbourhoods. Police officers are conditioned to focus their search for crime and its perpetrators in the poor sections of town rather than in the pristine office towers of business and government—where embezzlement, insider trading, and bid-rigging occur.

The evidence also suggests that street crime victimizes people of lower social position. Violent crime, in particular, is commonplace among the chronically poor people living in inner-city neighbourhoods—or in isolated Aboriginal communities. But only a small proportion of less advantaged people are ever convicted of crimes, since most crimes are committed by relatively few hard-core offenders. Moreover, the connection between social standing and criminality depends entirely on the kind of crime under consideration. If the definition of crime is expanded beyond street crime to include white-collar and corporate crime, the "average" criminal has a much higher social position.

RACE AND ETHNICITY In Canada, Black people and, particularly, Aboriginal people are arrested in disproportionate numbers. The effect is apparent in the racial composition of our prison inmates: In 1991, Black people represented roughly 1 percent of Canada's population but made up 3.8 percent of federal inmates, while Aboriginal people made up about 2 percent of the population but 11.3 percent of inmates. This pattern was even more pronounced among female prisoners, where 8.8 percent were Black and 15.4 percent were Aboriginal. More disturbing is the fact that, in the prairie provinces, Aboriginal people make up about 6 percent of the population but 36 percent of male inmates and 47 percent of female inmates in federal prisons. By 1999, despite programs designed to divert them from prison, the proportion of Aboriginal inmates in federal prisons had increased to 17.2 percent (Canada, 2006a): The figures for Aboriginal women and men were 21 and 17 percent, respectively.

Not only are Aboriginal women grossly overrepresented in Canadian prisons, they are also more likely to be "over-classified," which means that they end up in maximum security prisons. Fiorillo (2012) explains this phenomenon in terms of Canada's colonial history and the *Indian Act*—which led to the establishment of reserves, residential schools, and band councils along with the exclusion of women from voting or running for office (as chiefs or band councillors). They were denied any meaningful participation in leadership or decision-making, lost their Indian status (upon intermarriage), and were left without rights in the case of divorce. The result is that Aboriginal women—and First Nations or status Indian women in particular—are doubly disadvantaged and the poorest of the poor in Canadian society. It is poverty and the lack of other opportunities that account for the over-representation of Aboriginal women in prostitution and drug use. This in turn brings them into conflict with the criminal justice system.

The report of the Commission on Systemic Racism in the Ontario Criminal Justice System (Ontario, 1996) reveals that the imprisonment of Black people increased by 204 percent between 1986 and 1994, while the comparable figure for White people was 23 percent. The report argues that, at every stage of their contact with the justice system—from arrest through trial to imprisonment—Black people are treated more harshly. Frideres and Gadacz note that members of minority groups are 7 to 16 times more likely than other Canadians to be imprisoned, and that "Aboriginals are disproportionately suspects for homicides in every major city in Canada" (2008:139–140).

To the degree that prejudice related to race prompts police to arrest Aboriginal and Black people more readily than others, these two groups are overly criminalized. In similar situations, Aboriginal people are more likely than non-Aboriginal people to be arrested, charged with an offence, and denied bail. Once involved in the criminal justice system, they find themselves in the "revolving door syndrome": Many are "admitted to a prison several times in their lifetime and it is estimated that 90 percent of all adult male Natives have been in jail at least once" (Frideres & Gadacz, 2008:143).

Race in Canada closely relates to social standing (Fleras, 2010:117–138; Kallen, 2003:46–47; Li, 2003:104–114), which, as we have already shown, affects the likelihood of engaging in street crimes. Several researchers claim that membership in lower-class gangs promotes criminality. American sociologists Judith and Peter Blau (1982) take a different tack, suggesting that criminality—especially violent crime—is promoted by the sting of poverty in the midst of affluence. Suffering the hardships of poverty in a rich society encourages some people to perceive society as unjust and to disregard its laws.

Crime: Canadian, American, and Global Perspectives

By world standards, the United States has a lot of crime. The U.S. homicide rate stands at four times higher than Canada's and five times higher than Europe's, while its rape (sexual assault) rate is 2.6 times higher than Canada's and seven times higher than Europe's (Kalish, 1988). New York City led American cities, with 1182 murders in 1995—dropping to 575 in 2002. In comparison, Canada as a whole (with almost four times the population of New York City) had 732 murders in 1995, 582 in 2002, and 622 in 2004 (Messing, 2003; Statistics Canada, 2003a).

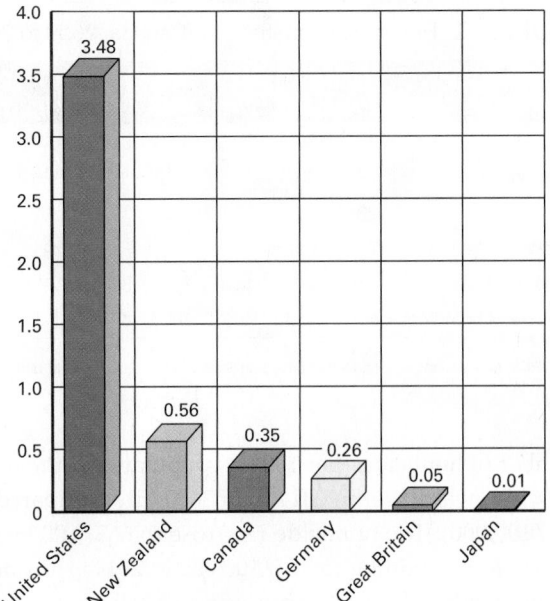

Figure 9–5 Handgun Deaths (Rate per 100 000 Population) in Selected Countries

SOURCE: Adapted by L.M. Gerber from Handgun Control Inc. (1998).

Why are U.S. crime rates so high? Elliot Currie (1985) blames that country's cultural emphasis on personal economic success—at the expense of family and community. Unlike European nations, the United States does not guarantee minimum income, medical care, or other social services—and has high levels of unemployment and underemployment. The key to reducing crime, then, lies in social change, not in hiring more police and building more prisons. Canada falls between Europe and the United States in the provision of social services and income support but, in recent years, our "safety nets" have become increasingly frayed. According to Currie's reasoning, we should have experienced rising crime rates. Instead, crime rates—including violent crime rates—have declined in Canada and the United States.

Another factor contributing to the relatively high level of violence in the United States is the widespread private ownership of guns. In any given year, roughly two-thirds of murder victims die from shootings. (In Canada, about one-third of murder victims die in this way.) The fact that the number of guns in the United States is equal to the American population helps to account for its runaway leadership in handgun deaths among industrial nations (see Figure 9–5).

Table 9–1 provides statistics for Canadian homicide, by method, for 2000 to 2014. Note that the proportion of murders by stabbing *increased* from 27.3 to 36.6 percent, while the proportion of murders by shooting *declined* during that period, from 33.7 to 30.2 percent. Homicide by beating and strangulation declined as proportions of the total, leaving stabbing as the most common method of homicide. It is worth noting as well that the

Table 9–1 Homicide by Method for Canada, 2000 to 2014

Method	2000 (%)	2001 (%)	2003 (%)	2005 (%)	2007 (%)	2010 (%)	2014 (%)
Shooting	33.7	30.9	29.3	33.6	31.6	30.7	30.2
Stabbing	27.3	30.9	25.9	29.9	32.0	29.6	36.6
Beating	23.4	22.1	22.0	21.7	19.5	21.1	18.4
Strangulation	7.1	8.5	11.7	7.1	8.4	7.4	6.0
Other methods	8.5	7.6	11.1	7.7	8.4	7.6	8.7
Number of homicides	546	553	549	663	594	554	516

SOURCE: Calculations by L.M. Gerber based on Statistics Canada, CANSIM table 253-0002.

number of homicides per 100 000 population—the murder rate—was lower in 2014 than 2000 (516 compared to 546/100 000). The homicide rate rose to 663/100 000 in 2005 before declining to 516/100 000 in 2014. Thus both the homicide rate and the proportion attributed to guns declined over the past decade.

Gun control legislation was enacted in Canada in the fall of 1995. Public interest groups, such as Canadians Against Violence Everywhere Advocating Its Termination, were instrumental in persuading the government to prohibit certain kinds of weapons and require the registration of others. As of 2000, all guns had to be registered, and licences had to be shown to purchase ammunition.

Collectors and rural people, including Aboriginal people, mounted significant resistance to the new regulations. Costs for the gun registry ballooned to well over $1 billion as a result of technical problems and public resistance. Registration "deadlines" have been moved several times. By 2015, registration of non-restricted firearms had been dropped across Canada and the registry records were destroyed.

The Controversy and Debate box deals with contribution of guns to homicide in Toronto in the first half of 2012—and leads to some surprising conclusions.

Globalization is increasing on many fronts, including crime. Some types of crime have always been multinational, including terrorism, espionage, and arms dealing (Martin & Romano, 1992). Since the terrorist attacks on New York's World Trade Center and the Pentagon on September 11, 2001, the United States and Canada have become partners in the war on terror. However reluctantly, Canada has modified its approach to border and airport security in response to American fears. We even toyed, temporarily, with national identity cards that would include biometric data, such as fingerprints or iris scans, but have held off on implementation because of privacy concerns.

Another multinational crime is the illegal drug trade. In part, the proliferation of illegal drugs in North America stems from demand: There is a very profitable

Controversy and Debate

Homicide in Toronto by Method and Region: Surprising Findings

In the wake of the fatal shooting at Toronto's Eaton Centre on June 2, 2012, the *Globe and Mail* published a map of that city that indicated the locations of all homicides (by method) and non-fatal shootings occurring in the first half of 2012 (Davis & Mamak, 2012). The statistics in Table 9–2 were compiled by dividing the city into areas and counting the colour-coded dots. The resulting table reveals some surprising findings.

The map also marked the location of each of Toronto's eight gangs. Many of you will have seen or heard references to the Jane and Finch area, which is considered to be a particularly dangerous part of Toronto. But take a close look at the table. The Jane and Finch area is in the northwest area of the city, where three of Toronto's eight gangs are engaged in turf wars. No one was killed in the area, despite 29 non-fatal shootings. Another observation, perhaps not as surprising, is that 55 percent of the homicides involved guns—while this is true of only 30.7 percent of homicides nationally (see Table 9–1). Since the 30 percent involving stabbing is identical to the national statistic, homicides that would have been carried out by "other" means can be attributed to guns in Toronto.

The article accompanying the homicide map made the claim that the City of Toronto "is safer than it's been in decades" (Paperny, 2012). That city, which is home to 16.7 percent of Canada's population, will have seen 6.7 percent of its homicides by the end of the year (assuming that 20 homicides occur in the second half). Converting these numbers to homicide rates per 100 000, Toronto's rate is much lower than that of the country as a whole (0.7 and 1.8, respectively). In fact, Toronto's rate is less than half of Canada's. Toronto is not only safer than in the past, but it is safer than the rest of the country. Look again at Canada Map 9–1; homicide rates are much higher in the provinces to the west of Ontario—and highest in the Territories.

What Do You Think?

1. How do the media contribute to the perception that Toronto is a very dangerous place?

2. Are you surprised to learn that close to half of the homicides in Toronto *did not involve guns?*

3. Note that non-fatal shootings (85 in the first half of 2012) are still a major concern, since any one of them could have increased Toronto's homicide rate. Is the conclusion that Toronto is a relatively safe place unwarranted in the long term?

Table 9–2 Homicide by Method and Non-Fatal Shootings in Toronto, January to June 2012

| | Homicide by Method | | | | |
	Shooting	Stabbing	Other	Total Homicides	Non-Fatal Shooting
Northeast*	3	2	0	5	8
Northwest*	0	0	0	0	29
Southeast*	2	1	1	4	10
Southwest*	4	1	2	7	25
Central*	2	2	0	4	13
Total Toronto	11	6	3	20	85
Method %	55	30	15	100	

*The boundaries of the areas of Toronto are as follows:

Northeast = north of the 401 and east of Bathurst

Northwest = north of the 401 and west of Bathurst

Southeast = south of the 401 and east of the Don Valley Parkway

Southwest = south of the 401 and west of Bathurst

Central = south of the 401 between Bathurst and the Don Valley Parkway

SOURCE: Compiled by L.M. Gerber from a Toronto map in the *Globe and Mail* (Davis & Mamak, 2012).

market—Hells Angels, or "Les Hells," are involved in murderous wars with other gangs as they manoeuvre for international domination of the illegal drug trade—much of which passes through Canada on its way to the United States. Furthermore, Americans are concerned about the flow from Canada of marijuana—which organized crime grows in large amounts here, often in empty houses or warehouses in rural areas with power tapped illegally from hydro lines. It remains to be seen if the legalization of medical marijuana in a number of U.S. states serves to disrupt the illegal drug trade to any extent.

The Criminal Justice System

9.7 **Analyze the operation of the criminal justice system.**

The criminal justice system is a society's formal response to crime. In some countries, military police keep a tight rein on everyone; in others, including Canada, police have more limited powers to respond to specific violations of criminal law. We will briefly introduce the key elements of this scheme: police, the courts, and punishment.

Police

The police are the primary point of contact between society and the criminal justice system. In principle, the police maintain public order by uniformly enforcing the law. Since Canada's police officers (1 per 523 people in 1995) cannot effectively monitor the activities of 30 million people, the police exercise considerable discretion about which situations warrant their attention and how to handle them.

How, then, do police carry out their duties? A study of police behaviour in five U.S. cities (Smith & Visher, 1981; Smith, 1987) concluded that, because they must respond swiftly, police make several quick assessments that guide their actions. They are more likely to make an arrest if the crime is serious, if the suspect is uncooperative, if the suspect has been arrested before, if there are bystanders present, and if the suspect is of a visible minority.

Factors affecting police discretion have been examined in Ontario as well (Schellenberg, 1995). Police officers are more likely to apply the rules regarding traffic offences, leaving less room for leniency, when their actions are being recorded by mobile video camera. More generally, when the police are considering arrests, they are less likely to check an individual's record—even when they have computer access to such records in their patrol cars—if they know the person or feel that he or she is trustworthy. Race and class can easily enter into the decision-making process at this point, raising the issue of racial profiling.

In Canada, visible minorities are arrested and imprisoned in disproportionate numbers, but this observation does not apply equally to all visible minorities. While Black and Aboriginal people are imprisoned at five and three times, respectively, the rate for White people, people of Arabic, East Indian, and Asian origin are imprisoned at two-thirds to half the rate for White people (Ontario, 1996).

Kayte Deioma/PhotoEdit, Inc.

POLICE MUST BE ALLOWED DISCRETION IF THEY ARE TO HANDLE EFFECTIVELY THE MANY DIFFERENT SITUATIONS THEY FACE EVERY DAY At the same time, it is important that the police treat people fairly. Here we see a police officer deciding whether to charge a young woman for driving while intoxicated.

A greater number of police relative to population are found in areas with two key characteristics: High concentrations of minorities and large income disparities between rich and poor (Jacobs, 1979). As a result, the Northwest Territories and the Yukon had both the highest rates of violent crime, as indicated by homicide rates, and the largest numbers of police officers relative to population (1 officer per 275 and 266 residents, respectively, in 1995). See Canada Map 9–1. The higher crime rates in these areas may be related, in part, to alcohol consumption and poverty or social disruption; they may also reflect bias in police surveillance, arrests, and convictions, as well as an emphasis on crime control and law enforcement rather than on crime prevention (Depew, 1992; LaPrairie, 1988, 2002).

The Sociology in Focus box provides insight into police officers as people with self-images and role definitions (or role constructs) that contrast sharply with the reality of their working lives. The disconnect between ideal and real allows for the application of Merton's strain theory to explain police deviance.

Courts

After a person's arrest, a court determines guilt or innocence. In principle, courts in Canada rely on an adversarial process involving attorneys in the presence of a judge who ensures adherence to legal procedures. In practice, however, a large percentage of criminal cases are resolved prior to court appearance through plea bargaining. Getting a reduced sentence by pleading guilty is a widespread practice because it spares the judicial system the time and expense of a court trial. Also, a trial is unnecessary if there is little disagreement about the facts of the case. By selectively trying only a small proportion of cases, the courts can channel resources into the most important ones (Reid, 1991).

But this process pressures defendants, who are presumed innocent, to plead guilty, thereby undercutting their rights. Defendants who have little understanding of the criminal justice system, as well as those unable to afford a good lawyer, are likely to suffer from what has been called "bargain-counter justice" (Blumberg, 1970). On the other hand, Canadians who felt that Karla Homolka got off too lightly asked to have her plea bargain reassessed. Her case was not reopened, though, because doing so would have threatened the plea-bargaining system.

Punishment

Ever since differences in power and authority began to emerge in human groups, punishment has been a means of discipline or control. Punishment may range from a "time out" or the spanking of children to imprisonment or capital punishment for the most serious of crimes.

The use of the death penalty differs across time and countries. In 1831, the officials in an English town hanged a nine-year-old boy who was found guilty of setting fire to a house (Kittrie, 1971:103). Canadians today would be appalled by this outcome for several reasons. As shown on Global Map 9–1, the global trend now is toward abolition of the death penalty. According to Amnesty International (2005), since 1980, more than 30 nations have ended this practice. The United States still has the death penalty, though several states have abolished it. Canada last conducted an execution in 1962 and abolished the death penalty in 1976.

Canadians have also decided that young people have a lower capacity for crime and deserve the special protections of the *Youth Criminal Justice Act*. Clearly, approaches to punishment have changed over time and vary from country to country. Debate about the appropriateness of specific punishments as applied to adults and juvenile offenders raises the question of how and why society should punish its wrongdoers. This leads us to consider four justifications for punishment.

Sociology in Focus

Cops Are People, Too! Reconciling Role Constructs with the Reality of Police Work and Explaining Police Deviance

In conducting research for her MA thesis, Sonya Buffone (2011) carried out in-depth, semi-structured interviews with male and female officers in an urban police department on the outskirts of Toronto. Her goal was to understand how officers defined their role and what happens when role definitions (or role constructs) are at odds with the reality of their day-to-day work.

The police officers were very clear in describing their role—which was to enforce the law, protect the public, and maintain social order. Social order depends on their enforcement of the law and, without the police, the "good guys" would be victimized by the "bad guys" and society would run amok and fall into a state of mayhem and violence. People couldn't walk down the street without fear of assault or robbery.

Of course, if you are maintaining law and order by chasing down the "bad guys," it goes without saying that your job is *dangerous*. The adrenaline factor was liked by many of the officers in Buffone's study. One canine officer referred to dangerous calls as the "best" calls or the ones where the dogs go: "We'll go out to high-risk stuff, pursuits, foot chases, bank robberies, shootings, we go to all of those" (Buffone, 2011:73). Note that this image of police work is reinforced and promoted by "cop shows" on TV.

But what is it that police actually *do*? Buffone points out that "most calls for service do not encompass any form of law enforcement and rarely involve catching bad guys" (p. 78). Instead, officers are sorting out people's problems or acting as marriage counsellors, social workers, and "amateur psychiatrists." One female officer admitted that roughly 80 percent of her calls are domestic disputes for which she has to solve problems or act as a referee: "[I]t has nothing to do with policing like I wanna go lights and sirens to something" (p. 80). Officers often spend their days solving problems but don't see that as part of their job description even though it is what the public *expects* of them. For these officers, problem-solving is not *real* police work, and they are *not* social workers.

When officers aren't problem solving, they sit behind a desk and deal with the reams of paperwork and report-writing that are required to be fully accountable for everything they do. They can spend anywhere from 50 to 80 percent of their day dealing with paperwork: "We can't even pee without writing it down" (Buffone, 2011:108). That is another disconnect between the officers' role construction and the reality of their work: No new recruit is drawn to a career in law enforcement because of the excitement of paperwork; in fact, the disconnect between ideal and real is one reason for high turnover in policing.

Since officers see their role as noble, increasing demands for accountability damage their role construct. Accountability is linked to increased surveillance or scrutiny of police actions—to the point that they feel so constrained they cannot exercise the discretionary power that is required to deal with unpredictability. Discretion, in essence, is the power to choose. By undermining their freedom to make decisions in response to the unexpected, accountability makes them feel powerless.

Another demoralizing aspect of police work is related to the difficulty of securing a conviction in court. Investigation is hampered by the fact that "it's a high mountain to climb to meet the threshold to get a conviction." The amount of detailed paperwork required to present evidence for a credible case is daunting—and "there's no use in laying a charge if you can't get a conviction" (Buffone, 2011:120). The police officer feels that his credibility is in question in the courtroom and that defence lawyers are "out to get him" and make him look "foolish and incompetent" (pp. 122–23). It's hard to be an effective crime fighter under these conditions.

Stop and think about this: Police officers see themselves as crime fighters, charged with the tasks of enforcing the law, protecting the public, and maintaining social order—while facing danger at any moment. The media reinforce that image, but demands for problem solving from the public, blocked convictions by the courts, and mountains of paperwork (in the interests of accountability) get in the way. The disconnect between ideal self images and the reality of their day-to-day lives has to be stressful.

Look again at Figure 9–1. Merton's basic argument is that deviance depends on the extent to which society provides the *means* to achieve cultural *goals*. Parnaby and Leyden (2011) explain *police deviance* in terms of Merton's model—starting with the media image (or construction) of policing as a "non-stop adrenaline rush," where good and evil are relatively clearly defined and the cops almost always get their man. Our society's value system "equates successful policing with fighting crime," and, as described by Buffone, this is how officers define or construct their role. In other words, whereas the cultural goal of the officer is successful crime fighting, numerous structural impediments make it impossible for police officers to meet that goal.

Parnaby and Leyden identify innovation, rebellion, ritualism, and retreatism as the deviant responses of police officers to the lack of fit between goals and means. The *innovator* finds unethical or malicious means to achieve his goal. The beating or threatening of suspects to acquire evidence, deception aimed at getting confessions, the planting of narcotics, and unlawful searches are among the innovative "means" used to reach the "goal" of successful crime fighting. The *rebel* adopts new means to reach new goals. When, knowing that a conviction is impossible, an

(continued)

officer changes the goal to "street justice," he or she inflicts his or her own just punishment. Thus, Neil Stonechild, a 17-year-old Aboriginal man, was dropped at the outskirts of Saskatoon to sober up—and *die*—while walking home in a temperature of –28.1 degrees Celsius. The *ritualist* rejects the goal while accepting the means. One police officer might reject the *normal goal* of aggressive or violent crime fighting and substitute the *unaccepted goal* of problem solving or "social work," while another might go overboard and strictly observe the formal regulations and standardized procedures (the means), modifying the goal of crime-fighting itself in favour of one based on appearances (i.e., that she or he not be seen as soft on crime or a pushover). The *retreatist* is the officer who is unable to sustain "the crime fighter persona" and withdraws from co-workers, friends, and family into substance abuse and stress-related illness, thereby giving up on both goals and means.

Combining two very different approaches to understanding police officers provides a glimpse into the social construction of the officer role, the factors that prevent them from fulfilling that role, and the deviant responses that arise when goals and means are out of sync.

What Do You Think?

1. Does this box give you greater insight into the lives of police officers?

2. Does the application of Merton's typology, based on the fit between goals and means, help you understand deviance in other contexts?

3. What impact might this analysis have on the likelihood of you applying to become a police officer?

Window on the World

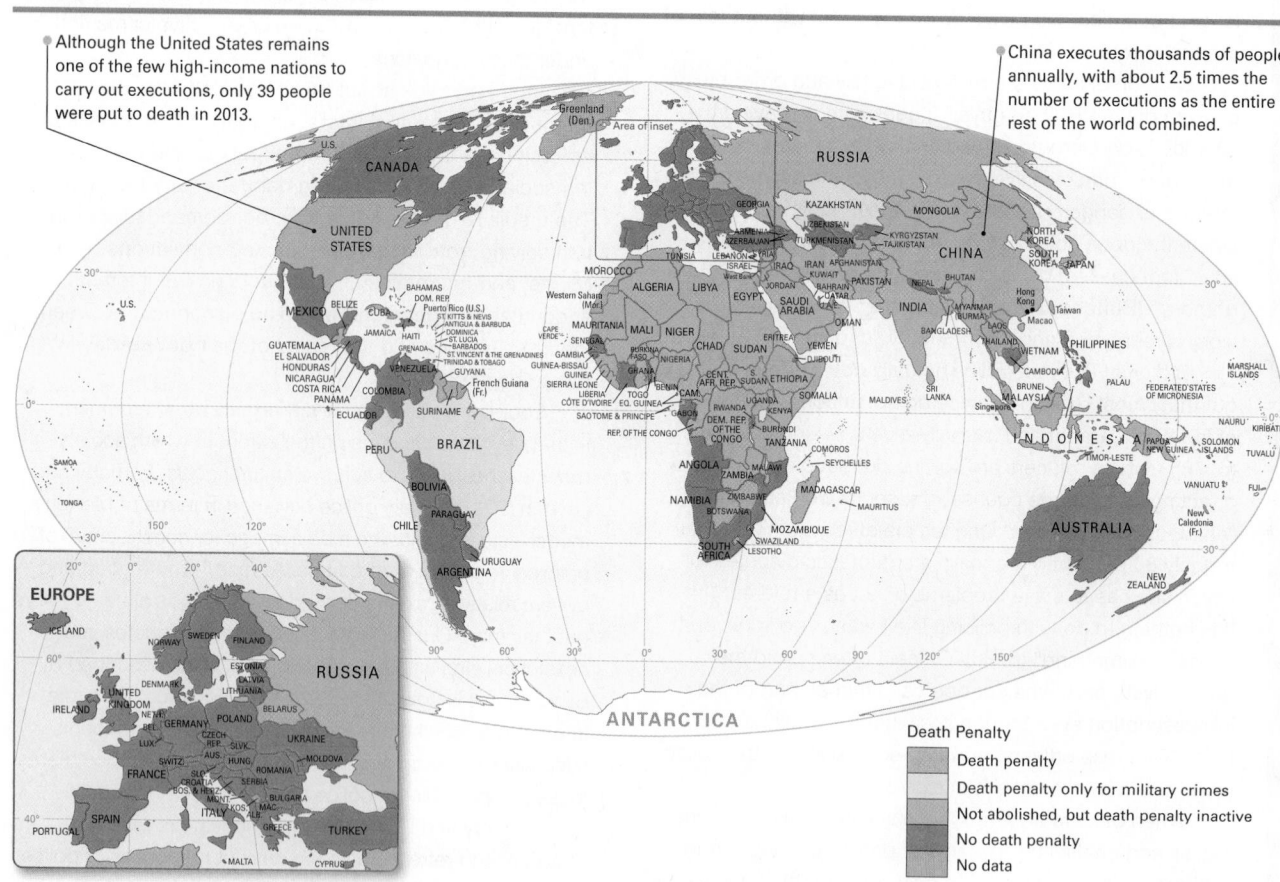

Global Map 9–1 Capital Punishment in Global Perspective

The map identifies 58 countries in which the law allows the death penalty for ordinary crimes; in seven more, the death penalty is reserved for exceptional crimes under military law or during times of war. The death penalty does not exist in 98 countries; in 35 more, although the death penalty remains in law, no execution has taken place in more than ten years. Compare rich and poor nations: What general pattern do you see? In what way are the United States and Japan exceptions to this pattern?

SOURCE: Amnesty International (2014).

retribution an act of moral vengeance by which society makes the offender suffer as much as the suffering caused by the crime	deterrence the attempt to discourage criminality through punishment	rehabilitation a program for reforming the offender to preclude subsequent offences	societal protection rendering an offender incapable of further offences either temporarily through incarceration or permanently by execution

RETRIBUTION The oldest justification for punishment is to satisfy people's need for **retribution**, *an act of moral vengeance by which society makes the offender suffer as much as the suffering caused by the crime*. Retribution assumes that society maintains a moral order, supported by punishment in equal measure.

A Toronto case illustrates the importance of the perceived appropriateness of judicial response. In October 1997, Gordon Stuckless, the equipment manager at Maple Leaf Gardens, was sentenced to two years less a day for the sexual abuse of young boys over a period of more than 20 years. Stuckless had traded sexual favours for tickets to hockey games or opportunities to meet players. After Martin Kruse came forward with allegations of sexual abuse, police received calls from many other men who had had similar experiences. Shortly after Stuckless was sentenced, Kruse committed suicide. His family felt that the light sentence—which did not fit the crime—was one of the reasons for his suicide.

DETERRENCE A second justification for punishment, **deterrence**, amounts to *the attempt to discourage criminality through punishment*. Deterrence reflects the notion from the eighteenth-century Enlightenment that, as calculating and rational creatures, humans will forgo deviance if they perceive that the pain of punishment outweighs the pleasure of mischief.

Deterrence emerged as an alternative to harsh punishment based on retribution. Why put someone to death for stealing, critics asked, if theft can be discouraged with a prison sentence? Punishment may deter crime in two ways: *Specific deterrence* demonstrates to an offender that crime does not pay, and through *general deterrence*, the punishment of one person serves as an example to others.

REHABILITATION The third justification for punishment is **rehabilitation**, *a program for reforming the offender to preclude subsequent offences*. If people learn deviance in environments marked by poverty or a lack of parental supervision, they can also learn to obey the rules—the key being control of the environment. *Reformatories* or *houses of correction* served as a controlled setting to help people learn proper behaviour. (Recall the description of total institutions and boot camp.) Rehabilitation resembles deterrence in that both motivate the offender toward conformity. But rehabilitation emphasizes constructive improvement, while deterrence, like retribution, inflicts

suffering on an offender. Whereas retribution demands that the punishment fit the crime, rehabilitation tailors treatment to the offender.

SOCIETAL PROTECTION A final justification for punishment, **societal protection**, refers to *rendering an offender incapable of further offences, either temporarily through incarceration or permanently by execution*. One of the concerns expressed by the Canadian public is that dangerous offenders are given "life" sentences and then released on parole. After the murder of her daughter Nina in Burlington, Ontario, Priscilla de Villiers founded Canadians Against Violence Everywhere Advocating Its Termination and involved herself in a massive campaign to restrict parole and bail for dangerous offenders. Her campaign touched a responsive chord in an apprehensive public that feels inadequately protected at present. When a dangerous man such as Clifford Olson is granted early release and kills 11 young people, as he did in British Columbia in 1980–1981, people question the level of protection afforded them.

EVALUATE

The Summing Up table summarizes four justifications for punishment; however, an accurate assessment of the consequences of punishment is no simple task.

The value of retribution lies in Durkheim's claim that punishing the deviant individual increases society's moral awareness. To accomplish this objective, punishment was traditionally a public event. Public executions occurred in England until 1868, whereas the last public execution in the United States took place in Kentucky in 1937. Even today, the American mass media ensure public awareness of executions carried out inside prison walls (Kittrie, 1971). Though executions no longer occur in Canada, we have television coverage when criminals convicted of sensational crimes, such as Paul Bernardo, are taken away to prison.

North Americans can agree that punishment deters crime (Wright, 1994), yet we see high rates of **criminal recidivism**, *subsequent offences by people previously convicted of crimes*. Various studies of people released from prison show that substantial percentages are rearrested and returned to prison within a few years, raising questions about the extent to which punishment actually deters crime. Then, too, only about one-third of all crimes are known to police and, of these, only about one in five results in an arrest. Most crimes go unpunished, so the old saying that "crime doesn't pay" rings hollow.

Prisons accomplish short-term societal protection by keeping offenders off the streets, but they do little to reshape attitudes or behaviour (Wright, 1994). Rehabilitation may be an unrealistic expectation, since, according to Sutherland's theory

SUMMING UP

Four Justifications for Punishment

Retribution	The oldest justification for punishment. Punishment is society's revenge for a moral wrong. In principle, punishment should be equal in severity to the crime itself.
Deterrence	An early modern approach. Crime is considered social disruption, which society acts to control. People are viewed as rational and self-interested; deterrence works because the pain of punishment outweighs the pleasure of crime.
Rehabilitation	A modern strategy linked to the development of social sciences. Crime and other deviance are viewed as the result of social problems (such as poverty) or personal problems (such as mental illness). Social conditions are improved; treatment is tailored to the offender's condition.
Societal protection	A modern approach easier to carry out than rehabilitation. Even if society is unable or unwilling to rehabilitate offenders or reform social conditions, people are protected by the imprisonment or execution of the offender.

of differential association, locking someone up among criminals for months or years strengthens criminal attitudes and skills. And, according to Hirschi's control theory, incarceration severs whatever social ties inmates may have, making them prone to further crime upon release.

CHECK YOUR LEARNING What are society's four justifications for punishment? Does sending offenders to prison accomplish each of them? Why?

Community-Based Corrections

Prisons keep convicted criminals off the streets. But evidence suggests that prisons do little to rehabilitate most offenders. Furthermore, prisons are expensive because of the annual cost of supporting each inmate and the initial costs of building the facilities. One alternative to traditional prison is **community-based corrections**, *correctional programs operating within society at large rather than behind prison walls*. Community-based corrections have three main advantages—reducing costs, reducing overcrowding in prisons, and allowing for supervision of convicts—and eliminate the hardships and stigma of imprisonment. Since the aim of community-based corrections is not to punish but to reform, such programs are usually offered to those who have committed less serious offences (Inciardi, 2000).

PROBATION One form of community-based corrections is probation, a policy that permits a convicted offender to remain in the community under the regular supervision of a probation officer. Courts may require, for example, that a probationer receive counselling, attend a drug treatment program, hold a job, or avoid associating with known criminals. Should the probationer commit a new offence or fail to live up to the conditions set, the court may revoke probation in favour of imprisonment.

PAROLE Parole is a policy of releasing inmates from prison to serve the remainder of their sentences in the local community under the supervision of parole officers. While some sentences specifically deny the possibility of parole, most inmates become eligible for parole after serving a certain portion of their sentences. At that time, a parole board evaluates the risks and benefits of each inmate's early release from prison. If parole is granted, the parole board monitors the parolee's conduct until the sentence is completed. Should the offender be arrested for another crime or not comply with the conditions of parole, the board can revoke parole and return the offender to prison to complete the sentence.

SENTENCING CIRCLES Canada has been experimenting with a unique form of community-based corrections for Aboriginal offenders, who may choose to submit to a *sentencing circle* to determine a suitable punishment. Sentencing circles—which may include the accused, the victim, their families, and other community members—are intended to start the healing process in the accused, the victim, and the community at large (Frideres & Gadacz, 2008; LaPrairie & Roberts, 1997).

EVALUATE

Evaluations of probation and parole are mixed. There is little question that these programs are much less expensive than conventional imprisonment and that they free up room in prisons for individuals who commit more serious crimes. Yet research suggests that, although probation does seem to work for some people, it does not significantly reduce recidivism. Parole is also useful to prison officials as a means to encourage good behaviour among inmates. It is too early to evaluate the impacts of sentencing circles on recidivism rates but, if Hirshi is to be believed, they should be effective.

CHECK YOUR LEARNING What three types of community-based corrections are applied in Canada? What are the advantages of each?

Seeing Sociology in Everyday Life

CHAPTER 9 Deviance

Why do most of us—at least most of the time—obey the rules?

As this chapter has explained, every society is a system of social control that encourages conformity to certain norms and discourages deviance or norm breaking. One way society does this is through the construction of heroes and villains. Heroes are people we are supposed to "look up to" and use as role models. Villains are people whom we "look down on" and whose example we reject, allowing them to become "anti-heroes" who point us in the opposite direction. Organizations of all types create heroes and villains that serve as guides to everyday behaviour. In each case that follows, who is being made into a hero? Why? What are the values or behaviours that we are encouraged to copy in our own lives?

> **Hint** A society without heroes and villains would be one in which no one cared what people thought or how they acted. Societies create heroes as role models—think of Wayne Gretzky, The Great One—who should inspire us to be more like them. Societies create heroes by emphasizing one aspect of someone's life and ignoring lots of other things. For example, Babe Ruth was a great ball player, but his private life was sometimes less than inspiring.

Charlie Campbell/The Star-Democrat/AP Images

COLLEGES AND UNIVERSITIES CREATE HEROES IN VARIOUS WAYS Here we see the president of Washington College (Maryland) awarding the Sophie Kerr Prize at a recent graduation ceremony. This prize, which included a cheque for more than $50 000, recognized English major Claire Tompkins's ability to write outstanding short stories. What is heroic in this case? What does graduating with honours or a Latin phrase (*cum laude* and so on) define as heroic? What about villains—how do colleges and universities create them, too?

RELIGIOUS ORGANIZATIONS, TOO, USE HEROES TO
ENCOURAGE CERTAIN BEHAVIOUR AND BELIEFS The Roman
Catholic Church has defined the Virgin Mary and more than 10 000
other men and women as "saints." For what reasons might someone be honoured in this way? What do saints do for the rest of us?

MOST SPORTS HAVE A "HALL OF FAME" A larger-than-life-size
statue of the legendary slugger Babe Ruth attracts these New York
City children on their visit to the Baseball Hall of Fame in
Cooperstown, New York. What are the qualities that make an athlete "legendary"? Isn't it more than just how far someone hits a ball?

Seeing Sociology in *Your* Everyday Life

1. Identity theft is a new type of crime that victimizes
as many as 10 million North Americans each year.
Research this phenomenon and explain how this
offence differs from property crime that takes place
"on the street." (Consider differences in the crime,
the offenders, and the victims.)

2. Watch an episode of any real-action police show such
as *Cops*. Based on what you see, how would you
profile the people who commit street crimes? What
types of crimes do you typically *not* see on police
reality shows?

3. Based on the material presented in this chapter, we
might say that "Deviance is a difference that makes
a difference." That is, deviance is constructed
as part of social life because, as Émile Durkheim
argued, it is a necessary part of society. Make a
(private) list of 10 negative traits that have been
directed at you (or that you have directed at yourself). Then look at your list and try to determine
what it says about the society we live in. Why, in
other words, do these differences make a difference
to members of our society?

Making the Grade

CHAPTER 9 Deviance

What Is Deviance?

9.1 **Explain how sociology addresses the limitations of a biological or psychological approach to deviance.**

Deviance refers to norm violations ranging from minor infractions, such as bad manners, to major infractions, such as serious violence.

Theories of Deviance

Biological theories

- focus on individual abnormality
- explain human behaviour as the result of biological instincts

Lombroso claimed that criminals have apelike physical traits; later research links criminal behaviour to certain body types and genetics.

Psychological theories

- focus on individual abnormality
- see deviance as the result of "unsuccessful socialization"

Reckless and Dinitz's *containment theory* links delinquency to weak conscience.

Sociological theories view all behaviour—deviance as well as conformity—as products of society. Sociologists point out that

- what is deviant varies from place to place according to cultural norms
- behaviour and individuals become deviant as others define them that way
- what and who a society defines as deviant reflect who has and does not have social power

> **deviance** the recognized violation of cultural norms
> **crime** the violation of a society's formally enacted criminal law
> **social control** attempts by others to regulate people's thoughts and behaviour
> **criminal justice system** the organizations—police, courts, and prison officials—that respond to alleged violations of the law

The Functions of Deviance: Structural-Functional Theories

9.2 **Apply structural-functional theories to the topic of deviance.**

Durkheim claimed that deviance is a normal element of society that

- affirms cultural norms and values
- clarifies moral boundaries

- brings people together
- encourages social change

Merton's **strain theory** explains deviance in terms of a society's cultural goals and the means available to achieve them.

Deviant subcultures are discussed by Cloward and Ohlin, Cohen, Miller, and Anderson.

Labelling Deviance: Symbolic-Interaction Theories

9.3 **Apply symbolic interaction theories to the topic of deviance.**

Labelling theory claims that deviance depends less on what someone does than on how others react to that behaviour. If people respond to primary deviance by stigmatizing a person, secondary deviance and a deviant career may result.

The **medicalization of deviance** is the transformation of moral and legal deviance into a medical condition. In practice, this means a change in labels, replacing "good" and "bad" with "sick" and "well."

Sutherland's **differential association theory** links deviance to how much others encourage or discourage such behaviour.

Hirschi's **control theory** states that imagining the possible consequences of deviance often discourages such behaviour. People who are well integrated into society are less likely to engage in deviant behaviour.

> **labelling theory** the idea that deviance and conformity result not so much from what people do as from how others respond to those actions
> **stigma** a powerfully negative label that greatly changes a person's self-concept and social identity
> **medicalization of deviance** the transformation of moral and legal deviance into a medical condition

Deviance and Inequality: Social-Conflict Theory

9.4 **Apply social-conflict theories to the topic of deviance.**

Based on Karl Marx's ideas, social-conflict theory holds that laws and other norms operate to protect the interests of powerful members of any society.

- **White-collar offences** are committed by people of high social position as part of their jobs. Sutherland claimed that such offences are rarely prosecuted and are most likely to end up in civil rather than criminal court.
- **Corporate crime** refers to illegal actions by a corporation or people acting on its behalf. Although corporate crimes cause considerable public harm, most cases of corporate crime go unpunished.
- **Organized crime** has a long history in North America, especially among categories of people with few legitimate opportunities.

Deviance, Race, and Gender: Race-Conflict and Feminist Theories

9.5 Apply race-conflict and feminist theories to the topic of deviance.

- Race-conflict theory and feminist theory argue that what people consider to be deviant reflects the relative power and privilege of different categories of people.
- **Hate crimes** are crimes motivated by racial, religious, or other bias; they target people who are already disadvantaged based on race, gender, or sexual orientation.
- Around the world, societies control the behaviour of women more closely than that of men.

> **white-collar crime** crime committed by people of high social position in the course of their occupations
> **corporate crime** the illegal actions of a corporation or people acting on its behalf
> **organized crime** a business supplying illegal goods or services
> **hate crime** a criminal act against a person or a person's property by an offender motivated by racial or other bias

Crime

9.6 Identify patterns of crime in Canada and around the world.

Crime is the violation of criminal laws enacted by the federal government. There are two major categories of serious crime:

- Crimes against the person (violent crime), including murder, aggravated assault, forcible rape, and robbery.
- Crimes against property (property crime), including burglary, larceny-theft, auto theft, and arson.

Official statistics show the following:

- Arrest rates peak in late adolescence and drop steadily with age.
- About 85 percent to 90 percent of arrests involve males.
- Street crime is more common among people of lower social position. Including white-collar and corporate crime makes class differences in criminality smaller.

- Black people and particularly Aboriginal people are arrested and imprisoned in disproportionate numbers.

> **violent crimes** *crimes against people* that direct violence or the threat of violence against others
> **property crimes** *crimes against property* that involve theft of property belonging to others
> **victimless crimes** violations of law in which there are no obvious victims
> **plea bargain** a legal negotiation in which the prosecution reduces a defendant's charge in exchange for a guilty plea

The Criminal Justice System

9.7 Analyze the operation of the criminal justice system.

The police maintain public order by enforcing the law.

- Police use personal discretion in deciding whether and how to handle a situation.
- Research suggests that police are more likely to make an arrest if the offence is serious, if bystanders are present, or if the suspect is of a visible minority or Aboriginal.

Courts rely on an adversarial process in which attorneys—one representing the defendant and one representing the Crown—present their cases in the presence of a judge who monitors legal procedures.

- In practice, courts resolve most cases through plea bargaining. Though efficient, this method puts less powerful people at a disadvantage.

There are four justifications for punishment:

- retribution
- deterrence
- rehabilitation
- societal protection

Community-based corrections include probation, parole, and sentencing circles. These programs lower the cost of supervising people convicted of crimes and reduce prison overcrowding, but they have not been shown to reduce recidivism.

> **retribution** an act of moral vengeance by which society makes the offender suffer as much as the suffering caused by the crime
> **deterrence** the attempt to discourage criminality through punishment
> **rehabilitation** a program for reforming the offender to preclude subsequent offences
> **societal protection** rendering an offender incapable of further offences, either temporarily through incarceration or permanently by execution
> **criminal recidivism** subsequent offences by people previously convicted of crimes
> **community-based corrections** correctional programs operating within society at large rather than behind prison walls

Chapter 10
Social Stratification

David Pearson/Alamy Stock Photo

Learning Objectives

10.1 Identify four principles that underlie social stratification.

10.2 Apply the concepts of caste, class, and meritocracy to societies around the world.

10.3 Explain how cultural beliefs justify social inequality.

10.4 Apply sociology's major theories to the topic of social inequality.

10.5 Analyze the link between a society's technology and its social stratification.

The Power of Society
to affect life expectancy

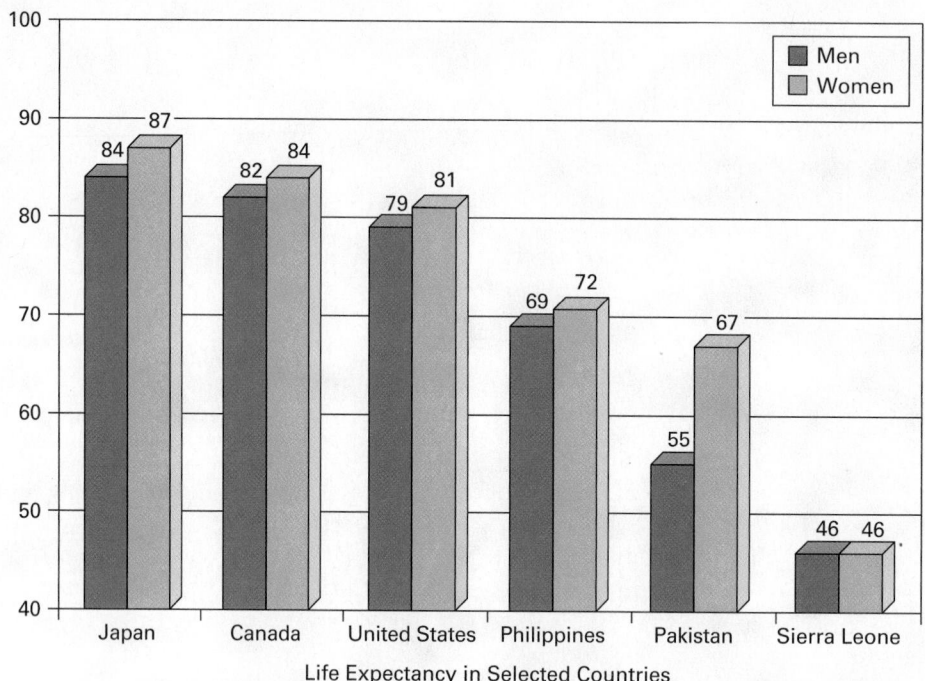

Life Expectancy in Selected Countries

SOURCE: Data from United Nations, 2014. World Population Prospects, The 2015 Revision. Population Division. Department of Economic and Social Affairs.

Does where we live affect our chances of living to a ripe old age? Men and women in Japan live *much* longer than their counterparts in Sierra Leone; in fact, the difference is a phenomenal 38 years for men and 41 years for women. Life expectancy in Canada is lower than that of Japan yet higher than that of the United States. Nonetheless, people in all three countries live longer than those from the Philippines, Pakistan, and especially Sierra Leone. What explains these dramatic differences? On one hand, we have affluent, postindustrial countries where income and education levels are high, advanced medical care is available, and both food and shelter contribute to good health and wellbeing. On the other, we have widespread poverty—as in Sierra Leone where most people live on a dollar or two a day—inadequate food supply, poor sanitation, limited education and employment, and minimal medical care (or immunization). Growing up under such vastly different circumstances shapes ones opportunities, health, and ultimately the quality and length of life.

Chapter Overview

This chapter introduces the central concept of social stratification which, to a greater or lesser extent, informs most sociological analysis and the remaining chapters of the text. Social stratification is extremely important because social standing affects almost everything in our lives.

On April 10, 1912, the ocean liner *Titanic* slipped away from the docks of Southampton, England, on its first voyage. After stops in France and Ireland, it would cross the northern Atlantic to New York. A proud symbol of the new industrial age, the towering ship carried 2300 passengers, some enjoying more luxury than most travellers today could imagine. Poor passengers crowded the lower decks, journeying to what they hoped would be a better life in North America.

Enno Kleinert/dieKleinert/Alamy Stock Photo

Two days out, the crew received radio warnings of icebergs in the area but paid little notice. Then, near midnight, as the ship steamed swiftly westward, a lookout was stunned to see a massive shape rising out of the dark ocean directly ahead. Moments later, the *Titanic* collided with a huge iceberg, its tip almost as tall as the ship itself, which split open its starboard side as if the grand vessel were nothing more than a giant tin can.

Sea water surged into the ship's lower levels as passengers rushed for the lifeboats. By 2 a.m., the bow of the *Titanic* was submerged and the stern reared high above the water. Clinging to the deck, observed by those in the lifeboats, hundreds of helpless passengers solemnly passed their final minutes before the ship disappeared into the frigid Atlantic Ocean (Lord, 1976). ∎

The tragic loss of more than 1600 lives made news around the world. Looking back dispassionately at this terrible accident with a sociological eye, however, we see that some categories of passengers had much better odds of survival than others. In an age of conventional gallantry, women and children boarded the lifeboats first, so that 80 percent of the casualties were men. Class, too, was at work. Of people holding first-class tickets, more than 60 percent were saved, primarily because they were on the upper decks, where warnings were sounded first and lifeboats were available. Only 36 percent of the second-class passengers survived and only 24 percent of the third-class passengers on the lower decks escaped drowning. On board the *Titanic*, class turned out to mean much more than the quality of accommodations—it was a matter of life or death.

The hundredth anniversary of the sinking of the *Titanic* generated tremendous media coverage, as well as the re-release of James Cameron's *Titanic*—in 3D. Why are we so captivated by this story when there have been other maritime disasters involving many more deaths? What about the massive explosion of a munitions ship that levelled much of Halifax in 1917? One explanation for our fascination with the *Titanic* is that it was a technological marvel, the fastest passenger liner ever built, and it was considered unsinkable. On top of that, it was sunk not by an enemy torpedo but by a big chunk of ice. The sinking of the unsinkable *Titanic* signalled the end of the "old

social order, the class system" as it was known then. High society with its ostentation, glamourous women, men in white tie, and many servants was central to the tragedy: "How could something that beautiful—something so exquisitely crafted, so refined and so solid—be cast down to the depths of the Atlantic" (Geiger, 2012)?

The fate of those aboard the *Titanic* dramatically illustrates how social inequality affects the way people live—and often the way they die. In effect, to the core of our being, we are all products of social stratification. This chapter is a detailed exploration of the important concept of social stratification—its roots, its shape in different societies, its ideological underpinnings, and its consequences. In addition, it applies sociological theories to enhance our understanding of stratification.

What Is Social Stratification?

10.1 Identify four principles that underlie social stratification.

For tens of thousands of years, humans lived in small societies of hunter/gatherers. While members of these bands might have singled out one person as swifter, stronger, or more skillful in collecting food, everyone had roughly the same social standing. As societies became more complex, a

Thinking About Diversity: Race, Class, and Gender

Titanic: Personal and Canadian Connections

In the spring of 1912, Maria Panula set off from Lapua, Finland, with five sons, aged 13 months to 16 years. They boarded the magnificent new ship *Titanic* on its maiden voyage to the United States, where they were to join Juha Panula, who had gone on ahead to get established in America. Before leaving, Maria Panula had given an American silver dollar to her five-year-old godson and cousin Viljo Kojola—the father of author Linda Gerber. The Panulas were among the third-class passengers, 76 percent of whom perished in the icy waters of the northern Atlantic. They must have been on the upper decks at the time disaster struck, for Maria made it onto a lifeboat with her infant son Eino. Survivors told her husband that, when she realized her other children did not have places in the lifeboat, she got out again with Eino in her arms to face certain death with the rest of her children.

ROGERIO BARBOSA/AFP/Getty Images

THE GRAVE OF THE UNKNOWN CHILD IN HALIFAX, IDENTIFIED INITIALLY AS EINO PANULA OF FINLAND (2002) AND LATER AS SYDNEY GOODWIN OF ENGLAND (2011).

After the shipwreck, the crew of the *Mackay-Bennett,* a Canadian ship, spotted a number of bodies floating in the water. Among them was "a young child, his blond hair and blue eyes poking through a grey coat trimmed with fur" (Humphreys, 2001). When no one claimed the child's body, the sailors resolved that he would have a proper burial. As a result, in a Halifax cemetery, you could find a tombstone that reads:

> Erected to the memory of an unknown child whose remains were recovered after the disaster to the 'Titanic' April 15th 1912.

In the mid-1990s, Ryan Parr, a professor at Lakehead University in Thunder Bay, and Alan Ruffman, a Halifax oceanographer and historian, pulled together an international team of researchers who would use archives, genealogy, and cutting-edge DNA testing to determine the identity of the Unknown Child. Since there were six children of approximately the right age who went down with the *Titanic,* they had to track down each family, get blood samples from relatives on the maternal side, and match the mitochondrial DNA from the women with that of the tiny exhumed body. By early November 2002, the researchers had identified the child as Eino Panula.

The news hit the papers all over the world, but nowhere with as much impact as in Finland and Canada. Relatives had lived for 90 years with the story of Maria Panula, her children, and the *Titanic* tucked away in their memory banks. No one could have imagined that one day a nameless child buried in Halifax would be identified as one of their own kin. Unfortunately for the Panula clan, the story does not end there. A pair of shoes, saved by a Halifax police sergeant when the child was buried, were too big for the 13-month-old Eino. The research team renewed its efforts and by 2011 found a rare difference in mitochondrial DNA that identified the child—with 98 percent certainty—as Sydney Goodwin of England.

What Do You Think?

1. How do life and death on the *Titanic* reflect the class structure of modern societies?
2. Were you aware of the power of modern genealogical research?
3. Are you curious about your family history and genealogy? Does your family keep records? Are there rags-to-riches stories, major achievements, or fascinating tales in your background?

SOURCE: Based on Humphreys (2002), Parry (2011), and personal knowledge of the author, Linda Gerber.

major change came about. Societies began to elevate specific categories of people above others, giving some parts of the population more power, wealth, and prestige than others. **Social stratification**, *a system by which a society ranks categories of people in a hierarchy*, is based on four basic principles:

1. **Social stratification is a trait of society, not simply a reflection of individual differences.** Many of us think of social standing in terms of personal talent and effort and, as a result, we often exaggerate the extent to which we control our own fate. Did a higher percentage of the first-class passengers on the *Titanic* survive because they were better swimmers than second- and third-class passengers? No. They did better because of their privileged position on the ship, which gave them first access to the lifeboats. Similarly, children born into wealthy families are more likely than children born into poverty to enjoy good health, do well in school, succeed in a career, and live a long life. Neither the rich nor the poor created social stratification, yet this system shapes the lives of us all.

2. **Social stratification carries over from generation to generation.** We have to look only at how parents pass their social position on to their children to see that stratification is a trait of societies rather than individuals.

   Some individuals, especially in high-income societies, do experience **social mobility**, *a change in position within the social hierarchy*. Social mobility may be upward or downward. Our society celebrates the achievements of a Jean Chrétien, a Céline Dion, a Jim Carrey, or a Wayne Gretzky, all of whom rose to prominence from modest beginnings. We also acknowledge that people move downward as a result of business setbacks, unemployment, or illness. More often, people move *horizontally*, exchanging one occupation for another at a comparable level. The social standing of most people remains much the same over their individual lifetimes.

3. **Social stratification is universal but variable.** Social stratification is found everywhere. Yet *what* is distributed unequally and the extent of inequality vary from one society to another. In some societies, inequality is mostly a matter of prestige; in others, wealth or power is the key element of difference. In addition, some societies contain more inequality than others. The Thinking about Diversity box picks up the theme of the *Titanic* tragedy opener—that social class can be a matter of life and death.

4. **Social stratification involves not just inequality but beliefs as well.** Any system of inequality not only gives some people more than others but also defines these arrangements as fair. Like the *what* of inequality, the explanation of *why* people should be unequal differs from society to society.

Caste and Class Systems

10.2 Apply the concepts of caste, class, and meritocracy to societies around the world.

Sociologists distinguish between *closed systems*, which allow for little change in social position, and *open systems*, which permit much more social mobility (Tumin, 1985). The *caste system* is closed, and the class system is more open.

The Caste System

A **caste system** is *social stratification based on ascription, or birth*. A pure caste system is closed because birth alone determines a person's entire future, allowing little or no social mobility based on individual effort. People live out their lives in the rigid categories assigned to them, without the possibility of change for the better or worse. Many of the world's societies, most of them agrarian, are caste systems. In India, for example, much of the population still lives in traditional villages where the caste system persists more than 60 years after being formally outlawed.

THE PERSONAL EXPERIENCE OF POVERTY IS CLEAR IN THIS PHOTOGRAPH OF MEALTIME IN A HOMELESS SHELTER The main sociological insight is that although we feel the effects of social stratification personally, our social standing is largely the result of the way society (or a world of societies) structures opportunity and reward. To the core of our being, we are all products of social stratification.

Viviane Moos/Corbis News/Corbis

AN ILLUSTRATION: INDIA The Indian system identifies four major castes (or *varna*, a Sanskrit word that means "colour"): Brahman, Kshatriya, Vaishya, and Shudra. On the local level, each of these is composed of hundreds of subcaste groups (or *jati*). From birth, a caste system determines the direction of a person's life:

- First, with the exception of farming, which is open to everyone, families in each caste perform one type of work, as priests, soldiers, barbers, leather workers, sweepers, and so on.

- Second, a caste system demands that people marry others of the same ranking. If people were to have "mixed" marriages with members of other castes, what rank would their children hold? Sociologists call this pattern of marrying within a social category *endogamous* marriage (*endo* stems from the Greek, meaning "within"). According to tradition—this practice is now rare and found only in remote rural areas—Indian parents select their children's marriage partners, often before the children reach their teens.

- Third, caste guides everyday life by keeping people in the company of "their own kind." Norms reinforce this practice by teaching, for example, that a "purer" person of a higher caste is "polluted" by contact with someone of lower standing.

- Fourth, caste systems rest on powerful cultural beliefs. Indian culture is built on the Hindu tradition that doing the caste's life work and accepting an arranged marriage are moral duties.

CASTE AND AGRARIAN LIFE Caste systems are typical of agrarian societies because agriculture demands a lifelong routine of hard work. By teaching a sense of moral duty, a caste system ensures that people are disciplined

caste system social stratification based on ascription, or birth

class system social stratification based on both birth and individual achievement

meritocracy social stratification based on personal merit

for a lifetime of work and are willing to perform the same jobs as their parents. Thus, the caste system persists in rural areas of India. Although caste still matters, people living in the country's industrial cities have many more choices about work and marriage partners than do people in rural areas.

The Class System

Because a modern economy must attract people to work in many occupations other than farming, it depends on developing people's talents in many diverse fields. This gives rise to a **class system**, *social stratification based on both birth and individual achievement.* Class systems are more open than caste systems, so people who gain schooling and skills may experience social mobility. As a result, class distinctions become blurred, and even blood relatives may have different social standings. Categorizing people according to their colour, sex, or social background comes to be seen as wrong in modern societies as all people gain political rights and, in principle, equal standing before the law. In addition, work is no longer fixed at birth but involves some personal choice. Greater individuality also translates into more freedom in selecting a marriage partner.

Meritocracy

The concept of **meritocracy** refers to *social stratification based on personal merit.* Because industrial societies need to

IN RURAL INDIA, THE TRADITIONAL CASTE SYSTEM STILL SHAPES PEOPLE'S LIVES This girl (on the left) is a member of the "untouchables," a category below the four basic castes. She and her family are clothes washers, people who clean material "polluted" by blood or human waste. Such work is defined as unclean for people of higher caste position.

William Albert Allard/National Geographic Stock

Gurinder Osan/AP Images

develop a broad range of abilities beyond farming, stratification is based not just on the accident of birth but also on *merit* (from a Latin word meaning "worthy of praise"), which includes a person's knowledge, abilities, and effort. A rough measure of merit is a person's job and how well it is done. To increase meritocracy, industrial societies expand equality of opportunity and teach people to expect inequality of rewards based on individual performance.

In a pure meritocracy, social position would depend entirely on a person's ability and effort. Such a system would have ongoing social mobility, blurring social categories as individuals continuously move up or down in the system, depending on their latest performance.

Caste societies define "merit" in terms of loyalty to the system—that is, dutifully performing whatever job comes with a person's birth. Caste systems waste human potential, but they are very orderly. A need for order is the reason that industrial societies keep some elements of caste—such as letting wealth pass from generation to generation—rather than becoming complete meritocracies. A pure meritocracy would weaken families and other social groupings. After all, economic performance is not everything: Would we want to evaluate our family members solely on how successful they are in their jobs outside the home? Probably not. Class systems in industrial societies move toward meritocracy—to promote productivity and efficiency—but keep caste elements, such as family, to maintain order and social unity.

Status Consistency

Status consistency is *the degree of consistency in a person's social standing across various dimensions of social inequality.* A caste system has limited social mobility and high status consistency, so the typical person has the same relative ranking with regard to wealth, power, and prestige. The greater mobility of class systems produces less status consistency. In Canada, for example, most university professors with advanced academic degrees (a Ph.D. and, in many fields, additional years of post-doctoral study) enjoy high social prestige but earn less than the average lawyer or dentist. Low status consistency means that classes are much harder to define than *castes*.

Caste and Class: The United Kingdom

The mix of caste and meritocracy in class systems is well illustrated by the United Kingdom (Great Britain—consisting of England, Wales, Scotland, and Northern Ireland), an industrial nation with a long agrarian history.

ARISTOCRATIC ENGLAND In the Middle Ages, England had a caste-like system of aristocracy. The aristocracy included the leading members of the church, who were

thought to speak with the authority of God. Some clergy were local priests, who were not members of the aristocracy and who lived simple lives. But the highest church officials lived in palaces and presided over an organization that owned much land, which was the major source of wealth. Church leaders, typically referred to as the *first estate* in France and other European countries, also had a great deal of power to shape the political events of the day.

The rest of the aristocracy, which in France and other European countries was known as the *second estate,* was a hereditary nobility that made up barely 5 percent of the population. The royal family—the king and queen at the top of the power structure—as well as lesser nobles (including several hundred families headed by men titled as dukes, earls, and barons) together owned most of the nation's land. Most of the men and women within the aristocracy were wealthy due to their landholdings, and they had many servants for their homes as well as ordinary farmers or serfs to work their fields. With all of their work done for them by others, members of the aristocracy had no occupations and came to believe that engaging in a trade or any other work for income was beneath them. Aristocrats used their leisure time to develop skills in horseback riding and warfare and to cultivate refined tastes in art, music, and literature.

To prevent their vast landholdings from being divided by heirs when they died, aristocrats devised the law of primogeniture (from the Latin meaning "first-born"), which required that all property pass to the oldest son or other male relation. Younger sons had to find other means of support. Some of these men became leaders in the church—where they would live as well as they were accustomed to—and helped tie together the church and the state by having members of the same families running both. Other younger sons within the aristocracy became military officers or judges or took up other professions considered honourable for gentlemen. In an age when no woman could inherit her father's property and few women had the opportunity to earn a living on their own, a noble daughter depended for her security on marrying well.

Below the high clergy and the rest of the aristocracy, the vast majority of men and women were simply called *commoners* or, in France and other European countries, the *third estate*. Most commoners were serfs working land owned by nobles or the church. Unlike members of the aristocracy, most commoners had little schooling and were illiterate.

As the Industrial Revolution expanded England's economy, some commoners living in cities made enough money to challenge the nobility. More emphasis on meritocracy, the growing importance of money, and the expansion of schooling and legal rights eventually blurred the difference between aristocrats and commoners and gave rise to a class system.

newsphoto/Alamy Stock Photo

FOLLOWING THE CENTURIES-OLD PRACTICE AMONG ARISTOCRATIC MEN IN ENGLAND, PRINCE HARRY COMPLETED MILITARY TRAINING AS PART OF HIS STUDIES AT ETON He is a member of a royal family that traces its ancestry back for more than 1000 years—an element of caste that remains in the British class system.

Splash News/WUF/Newscom

IN 2011, PRINCE WILLIAM, SECOND IN LINE TO THE BRITISH THRONE, MARRIED COMMONER CATHERINE MIDDLETON, WHO THEN TOOK THE TITLE, "HER ROYAL HIGHNESS THE DUCHESS OF CAMBRIDGE" They were expected to produce an heir to the throne—and because of changes to succession laws in 2011 their first-born, *either* son or daughter, would have equal right to the throne. As it happened, Prince George was born before his sister Princess Charlotte.

Perhaps it is a sign of the times that, these days, traditional titles are put up for sale by aristocrats who need money. In 1996, for example, Earl Spencer—the brother of Princess Diana—sold one of his titles, Lord of Wimbledon, to raise the $300 000 he needed to redo the plumbing in one of his large homes (McKee, 1996).

THE UNITED KINGDOM TODAY The United Kingdom has a class system, but caste elements from England's aristocratic past are still evident. A small number of British families still holds considerable inherited wealth and enjoys high prestige, schooling at excellent universities, and substantial political influence. A traditional monarch, Queen Elizabeth II, is the United Kingdom's head of state, and Parliament's House of Lords is composed of "peers," about half of whom are aristocrats of noble birth. However, control of government now rests with commoners—specifically, members of Parliament's House of Commons—where the prime minister and other leaders reach their positions by achievement (winning an election) rather than by birth.

Lower in the class hierarchy, roughly one-fourth of the British people form the middle class. Many earn comfortable incomes from professions and business and are likely to have investments in the form of stocks and bonds. Below the middle class, perhaps half of all Britons think of themselves as "working class," earning modest incomes through manual labour. The remaining one-fourth of the British people make up the lower class, the poor who lack steady work or who work full-time but are paid too little to live comfortably. Most lower-class Britons live in the nation's northern and western regions, which have been further impoverished by the closings of mines and factories.

Today's British class system has a mix of caste elements and meritocracy, producing a highly stratified society with some opportunity to move upward or downward. One result of centuries of aristocracy is that social mobility occurs less often in the United Kingdom than it does in North America. The more rigid system of inequality in the United Kingdom is reflected in the importance attached to accent. Distinctive patterns of speech develop in any society when people are set off from one another over many generations. Accent is a mark of social class, with upper-class people speaking "the Queen's English" but most people speaking "like commoners." So different are these two accents that the British seem to be, as the saying goes, "a single people divided by a common language."

Another Example: Japan

Social stratification in Japan also mixes caste and meritocracy. Japan is both the world's oldest continuously operating monarchy and a modern society where wealth follows individual achievement.

ARISTOCRATIC JAPAN   By the fifth century CE, Japan was an agrarian society with a rigid caste system in which an imperial family ruled over nobles and commoners. The emperor ruled by divine right (meaning that he claimed that God intended him to rule), and his shogun (military leader) enforced the emperor's rule with the help of regional nobles or warlords.

Below the nobility were the *samurai*, a warrior caste whose name means "to serve." This second rank of Japanese society was made up of soldiers who learned martial arts and who lived by a code of honour based on absolute loyalty to their leaders.

As in Great Britain, most people in Japan at this time in history were commoners who worked very hard to live from day to day. Unlike their European counterparts, however, Japanese commoners were not lowest in rank; below them were the *burakumin* (outcasts), looked down on by both lord and commoner. Like the lowest caste in India, these outcasts lived apart from others, performed the most distasteful work, and could not change their social standing.

MODERN JAPAN   By the 1860s, the Japanese nobles had realized that their traditional caste system would prevent the country from entering the modern industrial era. Besides, as in Britain, some nobles were happy to have their children marry wealthy commoners who had more money than they did. As Japan opened up to the larger world, the traditional caste system weakened. In 1871, the Japanese legally banned the social category of outcast, although today some people still look down on those whose ancestors held this rank. After Japan's defeat in World War II, the nobility lost their privileges; only the emperor remains as a symbol of Japan's traditions, and he has little real power.

Social stratification in Japan is much different from the rigid caste system of centuries ago. Today, Japanese society consists of upper, upper-middle, lower-middle, and lower classes; the exact lines between these classes are unclear to most Japanese, and many people do move between classes over time. But because Japanese culture tends to respect tradition, family background is never far from the surface when sizing up someone's social standing. Officially, everyone is equal before the law but, in reality, many people still look at one another through the centuries-old lens of caste.

Traditional ideas about gender continue to shape Japanese society. Legally, the two sexes are equal, but men dominate women in many ways. Because Japanese parents are more likely to send sons than daughters to university, there is a significant gender gap in education. With the recent economic downturn in Japan, many more women have entered the labour force. But most working women fill lower-level support positions in the corporate world, only rarely assuming leadership roles. In short, individual achievement in Japan's modern class system operates in the shadow of centuries of traditional male privilege (Brinton, 1988; French, 2002; Norbeck, 1983; OECD, 2009).

Classless Societies? The Former Soviet Union

Nowhere in the world do we find a society without some degree of social inequality. Yet some nations, such as Russia, have claimed to be classless.

THE RUSSIAN REVOLUTION   The former Union of Soviet Socialist Republics (USSR) was born out of a revolution in Russia in 1917. The Russian Revolution ended the feudal aristocracy, in which the nobility ruled, and transferred farms, factories, and other productive property from private ownership to state control.

The Russian Revolution was guided by the ideas of Karl Marx, who observed that private ownership of productive property is the basis of social classes. When the state took control of the economy, Soviet officials boasted that they had created the first modern classless society.

DEA PICTURE LIBRARY/De Agostini Picture Library/Getty Images

ONE OF THE MAJOR EVENTS OF THE TWENTIETH CENTURY WAS THE SOCIALIST REVOLUTION IN RUSSIA, WHICH LED TO THE CREATION OF THE SOVIET UNION Following the ideas of Karl Marx, the popular uprising overthrew a feudal aristocracy, as depicted in the 1920 painting *Bolshevik* by Boris Mikhailovich Kustodiev.

Critics, however, pointed out that, based on their jobs, the Soviet people actually were stratified into four unequal categories. At the top were high government officials known as *apparatchiks*. Next came the Soviet intelligentsia, including lower government officials, professors, scientists, physicians, and engineers. Below them were manual workers and, at the lowest level, the rural peasantry.

In reality, the Soviet Union was not classless at all. But putting factories, farms, universities, and hospitals under state control did create more economic equality—although with sharp differences in power—than found in capitalist societies.

THE MODERN RUSSIAN FEDERATION   In 1985, Mikhail Gorbachev came to power in the Soviet Union with a new economic program known as *perestroika* (restructuring). Gorbachev saw that, while the Soviet system had reduced economic inequality, living standards were far behind those of other industrial nations. Gorbachev tried to generate economic growth by reducing the inefficient centralized control of the economy.

Gorbachev's economic reforms turned into one of the most dramatic social movements in history. People in the Soviet Union and in other socialist countries of Eastern Europe blamed their poverty and lack of basic freedoms on the repressive ruling class of Communist party officials. Beginning in 1989, people throughout Eastern Europe toppled their socialist governments and, in 1991, the Soviet Union itself collapsed, remaking itself as the Russian Federation.

The Soviet Union's story shows that social inequality involves more than economic resources. Soviet society did not have the extremes of wealth and poverty found in the United Kingdom, Japan, and the United States. But an elite class existed all the same, one based on political power rather than on wealth.

What about social mobility in so-called classless societies? During the twentieth century, there was as much upward social mobility in the Soviet Union as in North America. Rapidly expanding industry and government drew many poor rural peasants into factories and offices. This trend illustrates what sociologists call **structural social mobility**, *a shift in the social position of large numbers of people owing more to changes in society itself than to individual efforts.*

During the 1990s, the forces of structural social mobility in the new Russian Federation turned downward. One indicator is that the average lifespan for Russian men dropped by eight years and for women by two years. Many factors are involved in this decline, including Russia's poor health care system, but the Russian

Imaginechina/AP Images

CHINA HAS THE FASTEST-GROWING ECONOMY OF ALL THE MAJOR NATIONS AND CURRENTLY MANUFACTURES MORE PRODUCTS THAN EVEN THE UNITED STATES With more and more money to spend, the Chinese are now a major consumer of automobiles—a fact that probably saved the Buick brand from extinction.

people clearly suffered in the turbulent period of economic change that began in 1991 (Gerber & Hout, 1998; Mason, 2004; World Bank, 2012).

The hope was that, in the long run, closing inefficient state industries would improve the nation's economic performance. The economy has expanded, but for many Russians, living standards have fallen, and millions face hard times. The few people who made huge fortunes have seen much of their new wealth vanish in the recent recession. This fact, along with more government control over the Russian economy, has caused economic inequality to decline. At the same time, however, many people wonder what a return to a more socialist society will mean for their living standards and political freedoms (Wendle, 2009; World Bank, 2012; Zuckerman, 2006).

China: Emerging Social Classes

Sweeping political and economic change has affected not just the former Soviet Union but also the People's Republic of China. After the Communist revolution in 1949, the state took control of all productive property. Communist party leader Mao Zedong declared all types of work to be equally important, so that, officially, social classes no longer existed.

The new program greatly reduced economic inequality. But, as in the Soviet Union, social differences remained. The country was ruled by a political elite with enormous power and considerable privilege; below them were managers of large factories as well as skilled professionals; next came industrial workers; and, at the bottom, were rural peasants, who were not allowed to leave their villages and migrate to cities.

Further economic change came in 1978 when Mao died and Deng Xiaoping became China's leader. The state gradually loosened its hold on the economy, allowing a new class of business owners to emerge. Communist party leaders remain in control of the country, and some have prospered as they have joined the ranks of the small but wealthy elite who control new privately run industries. China's economy has experienced rapid growth—in economic output, the country is now second only to the United States—and China has joined the ranks of "middle-income nations." But much of this new economic growth has been concentrated in cities, especially in coastal areas, where living standards have soared far above those in China's rural interior. A sign of the times is that the luxury automobile producer Bentley now sells more of its cars in China than in its home nation, Great Britain (Richberg, 2011; United Nations, 2014).

Since the late 1990s, the booming cities along China's coast have become home to many thousands of people made rich by the expanding economy. In addition, these cities have attracted more than 100 million young migrants from rural areas in search of better jobs and a better life. Many more have wanted to move to the booming cities, but the government still restricts movement, which has the effect of slowing upward social mobility. For those who have been able to move, the jobs that are available are generally better than the work that people knew before. But many of these new jobs are dangerous, and most pay wages that barely meet the higher costs of living in the city, so the majority of the migrants remain poor.

A new category in China's social hierarchy consists of the *hai gui*, a term derived from words meaning "returned from overseas" or "sea turtles." The ranks of the "sea turtles" are increasing by tens of thousands each year as young women and men return from education in other countries, in many cases from college and university campuses in Canada and the United States. These young people, most of whom were from privileged families to begin with, typically return to China to find many opportunities and soon become very influential (Liu & Hewitt, 2008).

In China, a new class system is emerging, a mix of the old political hierarchy and a new business hierarchy. Economic inequality in China has increased as members of the new business elite have become millionaires and even billionaires. As Figure 10–1 shows, economic inequality in China is now about the same as it is in the United States. With so much change in China, that country's social stratification is likely to remain dynamic for some time to come (Bian, 2002; Johnson, 2012).

Global Snapshot

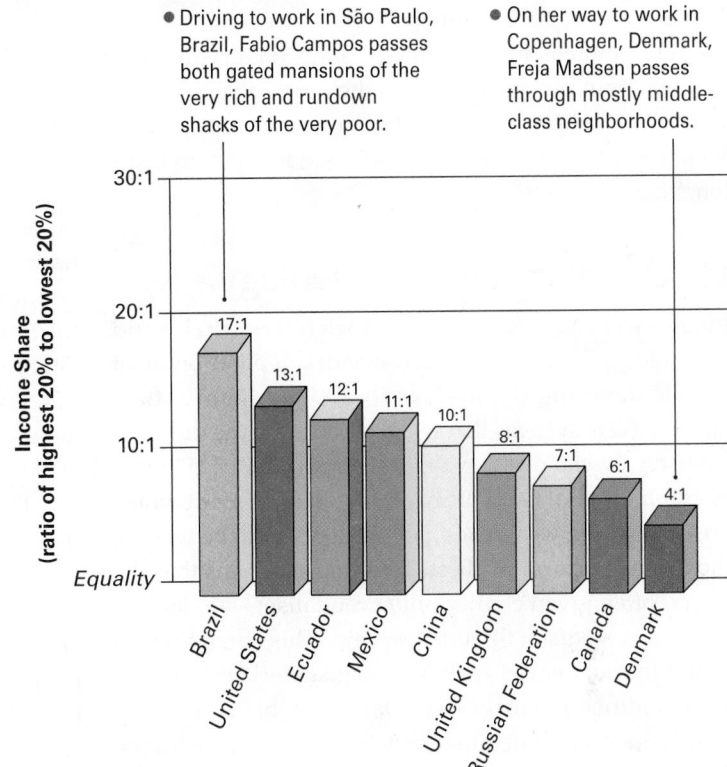

Figure 10–1 Economic Inequality in Selected Countries, 2014

Many low- and middle-income countries have greater economic inequality than the United States. But the United States has more economic inequality than most high-income nations—and substantially more than Canada.

SOURCE: Data from U.S. Census Bureau (2014) and World Bank (2015).

Ideology: Supporting Stratification

10.3 Explain how cultural beliefs justify social inequality.

How do societies persist without sharing resources more equitably? The highly stratified British estate system and Japanese caste system each survived for centuries and, for 2000 years, people in India accepted the idea that they should be privileged or poor based on the accident of birth.

A major reason that social hierarchies endure is **ideology**, *cultural beliefs that justify particular social arrangements, including patterns of inequality*. A belief—for example, the idea that rich people are smart and poor people are lazy—is ideological to the extent that it supports inequality by defining it as fair.

Plato and Marx on Ideology

According to the Ancient Greek philosopher Plato (427–347 CE), every culture considers some type of inequality to be fair. Although Karl Marx understood this, he was far more critical of inequality than was Plato. Marx criticized capitalist societies for defending wealth and power in the hands of a few as "a law of the marketplace." Capitalist law, he continued, defines the right to own property and ensures that money stays within the same families from one generation to the next. In short, Marx concluded, culture and institutions combine to support a society's elite, which is why established hierarchies last a long time.

Historical Patterns of Ideology

Ideology changes along with a society's economy and technology. Because agrarian societies depend on most people devoting themselves to lifelong labour, they develop caste systems that make performing the duties of a person's social position a moral responsibility. With the rise of industrial capitalism, an ideology of meritocracy arises, defining wealth and power as prizes to be won by those who perform the best. This change means that the poor—often given charity under feudalism—are looked down on as personally undeserving. This harsh view is found in the ideas of early sociologist Herbert Spencer, who modified the theories of Darwin on biological evolution; Spencer argued that society is a "jungle" with the "fittest" people rising to wealth and the "failures" sinking into miserable poverty.

History shows how difficult it is to change social stratification. However, challenges to the status quo always arise. The traditional idea that a woman's place is in the home, for example, has given way to increased economic opportunities for women in many societies today. The continuing progress toward racial equality in South Africa demonstrates widespread rejection of the ideology of apartheid. The popular uprisings against political dictatorship across the Middle East that began in 2011 show that the process of challenging entrenched social stratification continues.

Theories of Social Inequality

10.4 Apply sociology's major theories to the topic of social inequality.

Why does social stratification exist at all? Sociological theories provide several different insights into the causes and consequences of social inequality. We present three theoretical approaches—structural-functional theory, social-conflict theory, and symbolic-interaction theory. We begin with the structural-functional approach, which claims that social inequality plays a vital part in the smooth operation of society. This argument was set forth more than 60 years ago by Kingsley Davis and Wilbert Moore (1945).

Structural-Functional Theory: The Davis-Moore Thesis

The **Davis-Moore thesis** states that *social stratification has beneficial consequences for the operation of a society.* How else, asked Davis and Moore, can we explain the fact that some form of social stratification has been found in every society? Davis and Moore noted that modern societies have hundreds of occupational positions of varying importance. Certain jobs—say, washing windows, cutting grass, or answering a telephone—are fairly easy and can be performed by almost anyone. Other jobs—such as designing new generations of computers or transplanting human organs—are difficult and demand the scarce talents of people with extensive and expensive training.

Therefore, Davis and Moore explained, the greater the functional importance of a position, the more rewards a society attaches to it. This strategy promotes productivity and efficiency because rewarding important work with income, prestige, power, and leisure encourages people to do these jobs and to work better, longer, and harder. In short, unequal rewards—the essence of social stratification—benefit society as a whole.

Davis and Moore claimed that any society could be egalitarian, but only to the extent that people are willing to let anyone perform any job. Equality would also demand that someone who carries out a job poorly be rewarded the same as someone who performs it well. Such a system clearly would offer little incentive for people to try their best, reducing a society's productive efficiency.

The Davis-Moore thesis suggests the reason for stratification; it does not state precisely what rewards a society should give to any occupational position or just how unequal rewards should be. It merely points out that the socio-economic positions a society considers more important must carry enough reward to draw talented people away from less important work.

EVALUATE

Although the Davis-Moore thesis is an important contribution to understanding social stratification, it has provoked criticism. Melvin Tumin (1953) wondered, first, how we assess the importance of a particular occupation. Perhaps the high rewards our society gives to physicians results partly from deliberate efforts by the medical profession to limit the supply of physicians and, thereby, increase the demand for their services. In Canada, the Canadian Medical Association controls the certification of physicians, but provincial governments control the number of positions in medical schools and the availability of residencies. Knowing the compensation of Canada's most highly paid CEOs, can we argue that rewards actually reflect the contribution someone makes to society? Take a look at the Sociology in Focus box for more on the topic of fair remuneration.

Sociology in Focus

Salaries: Are the Rich Worth What They Earn?

According to the Davis-Moore thesis, rewards reflect an occupation's value to society. But are the talents of Julia Louis-Dreyfus, who earned about US$13 million a year as a sidekick on *Seinfeld,* worth almost as much as the efforts of all 100 U.S. senators? Is Blue Jays outfielder, Jose Bautista, worth as much as 95 family physicians? In short, do earnings reflect the social importance of work? Salaries in industrial/capitalist societies such as Canada are the product of market forces. Defenders of the laws of supply and demand claim that the market impartially evaluates worth, rewarding each worker according to the supply of the talent in question and the public demand for it. Thus, movie and television stars, top athletes, skilled professionals, and many business executives have rare talents that are much in demand; therefore, they may earn hundreds of times more than the typical worker.

According to the census of 2006, the average Canadian worker—employed full-time, all year—earned $58 537 (men) and $41 331 (women); professionals with university degrees and further specialist training earned two to four times as much. Heavy equipment operators, plumbers, and motor vehicle mechanics earned $40 000 to $50 000 (men) and $35 000 to $40 000 (women). And, near the bottom of the income scale, early-childhood educators, farm workers, and cashiers earned $23 000 to $26 500 (men) and $20 000 to $21 000 (women). High-end professionals earn ten times more than cashiers, musicians, or famers (Statistics Canada, 2006).

American celebrity salaries are the highest. Barry Bonds, with a 2006 salary of US$20 million, garnered more than US$40 000 per hour playing baseball for the San Francisco Giants. And what about the US$100 000 or more that Jim Carrey earns for every hour he spends

CÉLINE DION IS A MULTIMILLIONAIRE WHO EARNED US$78 MILLION IN 2006 BY PERFORMING IN LAS VEGAS.

making movies? At the same time, Oprah Winfrey was earning about US$200 000 for each hour she spent chatting with guests in front of the television cameras, while the six actors in *Friends* were being paid US$1.2 million per episode. Is it any wonder that many Canadians—among them Jim Carrey, Michael J. Fox, Mike Myers, Pamela Anderson, William Shatner, Tom Green, and Céline Dion—have gone to the United States in search of more lucrative opportunities?.

Our Members of Parliament, in 2014, earned $163 000 while the Prime Minister earned $327 000. Starting in 2016, Prime Minister Trudeau earns $340 800. As high as these salaries might be, they pale in comparison with those of Canada's corporate executives. In order to get the whole picture one needs to combine their base salaries with other compensation. The five highest-paid CEOs in Canada are (Scott, 2016):

• John Chen	Blackberry Ltd.	$89 715 019
• Donald Walker	Magna International Inc.	$23 417 274
• Gerald Schwartz	Onex Corporation	$21 135 946
• Hunter Harrison	Canadian Pacific Railway	$17 632 169
• Mark Thierer	Catamaran Corporation	$16 330 467

Some critics claim that the market is not a good evaluator of occupational importance. The economy, they argue, is dominated by a small number of people who manipulate the system for their own benefit. In the 1980s, 32 of Canada's wealthiest families played "monopoly with the money of average Canadians" (Francis, 1986). Peter C. Newman (1998) argues that this "old" establishment—based on inherited wealth, private schools, club contacts, and intermarriage—has been pushed aside by the "new" establishment (which anyone can join), composed of hard-driving risk-takers whose global networks are maintained through their BlackBerrys rather than posh country clubs. In this new world, you can be nobody one day and a very big somebody the next—think Mark Zuckerberg—and reverse the process just as quickly. Again, it is the rare individual who can tolerate this stressful lifestyle. Most of us take holidays for granted, but these new business titans do not take *real* holidays at all. If they do travel for pleasure, it is with BlackBerry and computer in hand as they *must* remain connected.

A second problem with the idea that the market measures people's contributions to society is that many who make clear and significant contributions receive surprisingly little money. Tens of thousands of teachers, firefighters, and health care workers enhance the welfare of others every day for relatively small salaries. The average high school teacher would have to work for 365 years to earn as much as Gerald Schwartz of Onex Corporation received in 2015. John Chen, CEO of Blackberry, earns 275 times more than our prime minister; is this really a measure of his worth to society? Using earnings to measure social worth works only to the extent that market forces actually gauge one's societal contribution. Some people view market forces as the most accurate measure of occupational worth; others contend that lucrative activities may or may not be socially valuable. Thus, the market system remains controversial.

What Do You Think?

1. Do highly paid athletes and celebrities deserve their salaries? Why?

2. Given the skills needed to pull off a "Bill Gates," would you be willing to assume his stressful lifestyle?

3. Is it easy to become a millionaire in Canada? What about a billionaire?

Second, Tumin claimed that Davis and Moore ignored how caste elements of social stratification can *prevent* the development of individual talent. Born to privilege, rich children have opportunities to develop their abilities, which is something that many gifted poor children never have.

Third, living in a society that places so much emphasis on money, we tend to overestimate the importance of high-paying work. For example, how much does someone who trades international currencies contribute to society? For the same reason, it is difficult for us to see the value of work that is not oriented toward making money, such as parenting, creative writing, playing music in a symphony, or just being a good friend to someone in need.

By suggesting that social stratification benefits all of society, the Davis-Moore thesis ignores the role of social inequality in promoting conflict and even revolution. This criticism leads us to the social-conflict approach, which provides a very different explanation for social inequality.

CHECK YOUR LEARNING State the Davis-Moore thesis in your own words. What are Tumin's criticisms of this thesis?

Social Conflict Theories: Karl Marx and Max Weber

Social-conflict analysis argues that, rather than benefiting society as a whole, social stratification benefits some people and disadvantages others. This analysis draws heavily on the ideas of Karl Marx, with contributions from Max Weber.

KARL MARX: CLASS CONFLICT Karl Marx explained that most people have one of two basic relationships to the means of economic production: They either own productive property or labour for others. Different productive roles arise from different social classes. In medieval Europe, the nobility and church officials owned the land on which peasants laboured as farmers. In industrial class systems, the capitalists (or the bourgeoisie) own the factories, which use the labour of workers (the proletarians).

Marx lived during the nineteenth century, a time when a few industrialists in the United States were amassing great fortunes. Andrew Carnegie, J.P. Morgan, John D. Rockefeller, and John Jacob Astor (one of the few very rich passengers to die on the *Titanic*) lived in fabulous mansions staffed by dozens of servants. Even by today's standards, their incomes were staggering. For example, Andrew Carnegie earned about US$20 million a year in 1900 (more than US$100 million in today's dollars) at a time when the average American worker earned roughly US$500 a year (Baltzell, 1964; Williamson, 2012).

Marx explained that capitalist society *reproduces the class structure in each new generation*. This happens as families gain wealth and pass it down from generation to generation. But, he predicted, oppression and misery would eventually drive the working majority to come together to overthrow capitalism.

EVALUATE

Marx has had enormous influence on sociological thinking. But his revolutionary ideas—calling for the overthrow of capitalist society—also make his work highly controversial.

One of the strongest criticisms of Marxism is that it denies a central idea of the Davis-Moore thesis: that a system of unequal rewards is necessary to place talented people in the right jobs and to motivate them to work hard. Marx separated reward from performance; his egalitarian ideal was based on the principle "from each according to his ability; to each according to his needs" (Marx & Engels, 1972:388; orig. 1848). However, failure to reward individual performance may be precisely what caused the low productivity of the former Soviet Union and other socialist economies around the world. Defenders of Marxism respond to such criticism by asking why it is assumed that humanity is inherently selfish rather than social; individual rewards are not the only way to motivate people to perform their social roles (Clark, 1991).

A second problem is that the revolutionary change Marx predicted did not occur, at least not in advanced capitalist societies.

CHECK YOUR LEARNING How does Marx's view of social stratification differ from the Davis-Moore thesis?

WHY NO MARXIST REVOLUTION? Despite Marx's prediction, capitalism is still thriving. Why have industrial workers not overthrown capitalism? Ralf Dahrendorf (1959) suggested four reasons:

- *The fragmentation of the capitalist class.* Today, millions of shareholders, rather than single families, own most large companies. Day-to-day corporate operations are in the hands of a large class of managers, who may or may not be major shareholders. With stock widely held—about 50 percent of North American adults own stocks, some in the form of pension funds—more and more people have a direct stake in the capitalist system.

- *A higher standard of living.* A century ago, most workers were in factories or on farms employed in **blue-collar occupations**, *lower-prestige jobs that involve mostly manual labour.* Today, most workers are engaged in **white-collar occupations**, *higher-prestige jobs that involve mostly mental activity.* These jobs are in sales, management, teaching, and other service fields. Most of today's white-collar workers do not think of themselves as "industrial proletariats." Just as importantly, the average income in North America rose almost tenfold over the course of the twentieth century, even allowing for inflation, and the number of hours in the workweek decreased. In short, most workers today are far better off than workers were a century ago, as a result of structural social mobility. One outcome of this rising standard of living is that more people are content with the status quo.

- *More worker organizations.* Workers today have the right to form labour unions that make demands of management and to back up their demands with threats of work slowdowns and strikes. As a result, labour disputes are settled without threatening the capitalist system.

- *Greater legal protections.* Over the past century, the government passed laws to make workplaces safer. In addition, pensions, employment insurance, disability protection, and social security now provide workers with greater financial security.

A COUNTERPOINT These developments suggest that we have smoothed many of capitalism's rough edges. Advocates of social-conflict analysis, however, counter that Marx's analysis of capitalism is still largely valid (Brym, 1985; Clement, 1990; Matthews, 1983; Smith, 1987; Wotherspoon & Satzewich, 1993). They offer the following counterpoint:

1. **Wealth remains highly concentrated.** As Marx contended, wealth remains in the hands of the few. In the mid-1980s, Canada had 6 billionaire families, and another 22 worth $100 million or more, who controlled an inordinate amount of the country's wealth (Francis, 1986). In 2003, Canada's Thomson family ranked number 13 on *Forbes* magazine's list of the world's wealthiest people, with an estimated worth of more than US$14 billion; by 2006, *Forbes*

listed the Thomsons as the ninth wealthiest in the world, worth US$19.6 billion. In particular, the concentration of wealth and ownership of newspapers, cable television, and other media by the Asper and Rogers families is a source of tremendous concern to critics of capitalist industrial society. Conrad Black sold his creation, the *National Post,* to Asper's Can-West Global Communications—which also owns *The Gazette* (Montreal), the *Ottawa Citizen,* the *Calgary Herald,* and the *Vancouver Sun,* among other Canadian newspapers. Rogers got its start in radio, but is now a major player in cable television, as well as internet, cellphone, and BlackBerry service; Rogers also owns *Maclean's* magazine. These three families have a large part of Canadian communications under their control.

2. **White-collar work offers little to workers.** As contemporary Marxists see it, the white-collar revolution delivered little in the way of higher income or better working conditions over the factory jobs of a century ago. On the contrary, much white-collar work remains monotonous and routine, especially the low-level clerical jobs commonly held by women.

3. **Progress requires struggle.** Labour organizations may have advanced the interests of workers over the past half-century, but regular and often acrimonious negotiation between workers and management hardly signals the end of social conflict. In fact, many of the concessions won by workers came about precisely through the class conflict Marx described. Moreover, workers still strive to gain concessions from capitalists and struggle to hold on to the advances already achieved.

4. **The law still favours the rich.** Workers have gained some legal protections over the course of the past century. Even so, the law still defends the overall distribution of wealth in Canada and the United States. Just as importantly, people with an average income cannot use the legal system to the same advantage as do the rich.

In sum, according to social-conflict theory, the fact that no socialist revolution has taken place in Canada or the United States hardly invalidates Marx's analysis of capitalism. Pronounced social inequality persists, as does social conflict—albeit less overtly and violently than in the nineteenth century.

Some defenders of capitalism cite the collapse of communist regimes in Eastern Europe and the former Soviet Union as proof of the superiority of capitalism over socialism. Most analysts agree that socialism failed to meet the needs of the people it purported to serve, either in terms of raising living standards or ensuring personal freedoms. But, to be fair, socialism's failings do

MOST NORTH AMERICAN WORKERS TODAY (ABOUT 75 PERCENT) HAVE SERVICE JOBS; INSTEAD OF FARMING OR WORKING IN A FACTORY, THEY WORK WITH OTHER PEOPLE Some analysts say that the spread of service work has made many people feel that they are "getting ahead" and, thereby, has reduced class conflict; others claim that many service jobs actually provide lower pay, fewer benefits, and less job security than factory jobs of the past. Which argument do you think is more correct? Why?

not excuse flaws in capitalism. Many critics maintain that capitalism in North America has yet to demonstrate its ability to address problems of public education and desperate poverty, especially among the urban underclass and Aboriginal peoples.

MAX WEBER: CLASS, STATUS, AND POWER Max Weber agreed with Karl Marx that social stratification causes social conflict, but he viewed Marx's economics-based model as simplistic. Instead, he claimed that social stratification involves three distinct dimensions of inequality. The first dimension is economic inequality—the issue so important to Marx—which Weber termed class position; Weber did not think of classes as well-defined categories but as a continuum ranging from high to low. Weber's second dimension is status, or social prestige, and the third is power.

Weber's Socioeconomic Status Hierarchy Marx viewed social prestige and power as simple reflections of economic position and did not treat them as distinct dimensions of inequality. But Weber noted that status consistency in modern societies is often quite low: A local official might exercise great power yet have little wealth or social prestige.

Weber, then, portrayed social stratification in industrial societies as a multi-dimensional ranking rather than a hierarchy of clearly defined classes. In line with Weber's

thinking, sociologists use the term **socio-economic status** to refer to *a composite ranking based on various dimensions of social inequality.*

Inequality in History Weber claimed that each of his three dimensions of social inequality stands out at different points in the evolution of human societies. Status, or social prestige, is the main difference in agrarian societies, taking the form of honour. Members of these societies—whether nobles or servants—gain status by conforming to cultural norms that correspond to their rank. Industrialization and the development of capitalism eliminate traditional rankings based on birth but create striking financial inequality. Thus, in an industrial society, the crucial difference between people is the economic dimension of class. Over time, industrial societies witness the growth of a bureaucratic state. Bigger government and the spread of all types of other organizations make power more important in the stratification system. Especially in socialist societies, where government regulates many aspects of life, high-ranking officials become the new ruling elite.

THE EXTENT OF SOCIAL INEQUALITY IN AGRARIAN SYSTEMS IS GREATER THAN THAT FOUND IN INDUSTRIAL SOCIETIES
One indication of the unchallenged power of rulers is the monumental structures built over years with the unpaid labour of common people. Although the Taj Mahal in India is among the world's most beautiful buildings, it is in fact the tomb of a single individual.

This historical analysis points to a final difference between Weber and Marx. Marx thought that societies could eliminate social stratification by abolishing the private ownership of productive property that is the basis of capitalism. Weber doubted that overthrowing capitalism would significantly lessen social stratification. It might reduce economic differences, he reasoned, but socialism would increase inequality by expanding government and concentrating power in the hands of a political elite. Popular uprisings against socialist bureaucracies in Eastern Europe and the former Soviet Union support Weber's position.

EVALUATE

Weber's multi-dimensional view of social stratification has influenced sociologists greatly. But critics—particularly those who favour Marx's ideas—argue that, while social class boundaries may have blurred, industrial and post-industrial societies still show striking patterns of social inequality.

Income inequality characterizes our society. While some people still favour Weber's multi-dimensional hierarchy, others think that Marx's view of the rich versus the poor is closer to the truth.

CHECK YOUR LEARNING What are Weber's three dimensions of social inequality? Which one, according to Weber, is most important to North Americans? Would his assessment be the same for Canada and the United States?

Symbolic-Interaction Theory: Stratification in Everyday Life

Because social stratification has to do with the way an entire society is organized, sociologists—including Marx and Weber—typically treat it as a macro-level issue. But a micro-level analysis of social stratification is also important because people's social standing affects their everyday interactions.

In most communities, people socialize primarily with others of more or less the same social standing. To some extent, this is because we tend to live near others like ourselves. In any public setting, such as a downtown shopping area, if you watch people for even a few minutes, you will see that couples or groups tend to contain individuals whose appearance and shopping habits are similar. People with very different social standing commonly keep their distance from one another. Well-dressed people walking down the street on their way to an expensive restaurant, for example, might move across the sidewalk or even cross the street to avoid getting close to others who appear to be homeless people.

Just about everyone realizes that the way we dress, the car we drive or the bus we ride, and even the food and drink we order at the campus snack bar say something about our budget and personal tastes. Sociologists use the term **conspicuous consumption** to refer to *buying and using products because of the "statements" they make about social position.* Ignoring the water fountain in favour of paying for bottled water tells people you have extra money to spend. No one needs a $100 000 automobile to get around, of course, but being seen in such a vehicle says "I have arrived" in more ways than one. In a *National Post* article about the 12 priciest residences in the United States, Vallis (2006) described homes that sell in the range of $10 million to $60 million. One of these is the three-storey penthouse apartment in New York's "legendary Pierre Hotel": The asking price is US$70 million for a home with a living room of 300 square metres (3200 square feet) that was once the hotel's *ballroom.*

The Applying Theory table summarizes the contributions of the three theoretical approaches to social stratification.

APPLYING THEORY

Social Stratification

	Structural-Functional Approach	Social-Conflict Approach	Symbolic-Interaction Approach
What is the level of analysis?	Macro level	Macro level	Micro level
What is social stratification?	Stratification is a system of unequal rewards that benefits society as a whole.	Stratification is a division of a society's resources that benefits some and harms others.	Stratification is a factor that guides people's interactions in everyday life.
What is the reason for our social position?	Social position reflects personal talents and abilities in a competitive economy.	Social position reflects the way in which society divides resources.	The products we consume all make a "statement" about social position.
Are unequal rewards fair?	Yes. Unequal rewards boost economic production by encouraging people to work harder and try new ideas. Linking greater rewards to more important work is widely accepted.	No. Unequal rewards serve only to divide society, creating "haves" and "have-nots." There is widespread opposition to social inequality.	Maybe. People may or may not define inequality as fair. People may view their social position as a measure of self-worth, justifying inequality in terms of personal differences.

Social Stratification and Technology: A Global Perspective

10.5   Analyze the link between a society's technology and its social stratification.

We can weave together a number of observations made in this chapter to show that a society's technology affects its type of social stratification. This analysis draws on Gerhard and Jean Lenski's model of socio-cultural evolution.

- *Hunter/gatherer societies.* With simple technology, hunter/gatherers produce only what is necessary for day-to-day living. Some people may produce more than others, but the group's survival depends on all sharing what they have. Thus, no categories of people are better off than others.

- *Horticultural, pastoral, and agrarian societies.* As technological advances create a surplus, social inequality increases. In horticultural and pastoral societies, a small elite controls most of the surplus. Large-scale agriculture is more productive still, and striking inequality—as great as at any time in history—places the nobility in an almost godlike position over the masses.

- *Industrial societies.* Industrialization turns the tide, pushing inequality downward. Prompted by the need to develop individual talents, meritocracy takes hold and weakens the power of the traditional elites. Industrial productivity also raises the standard of living of the historically poor majority. Specialized work demands schooling for all, sharply reducing illiteracy. A literate population, in turn, presses for a greater voice in political decision making, reducing inequality and lessening men's domination of women.

Over time, even wealth becomes somewhat less concentrated (contradicting Marx's prediction). In the 1920s, the richest 1 percent of the U.S. population owned about 40 percent of all wealth, a figure that fell to 30 percent by the 1980s (Beeghley, 1989; Williamson & Lindert, 1980). Such trends help explain why Marxist revolutions occurred in *agrarian* societies—such as Russia (1917), Cuba (1959), and Nicaragua (1979)—where social inequality is most pronounced, rather than in industrial societies as Marx had predicted. However, in the United States, wealth inequality increased after 1990 and is once again about the same as it was in the 1920s (Keister & Moller, 2000). While at one time Canada appeared to have more billionaire families per capita than the United States—6 compared to 12 (Francis, 1986)—it is likely that our overall pattern in the control of wealth is similar to that of the

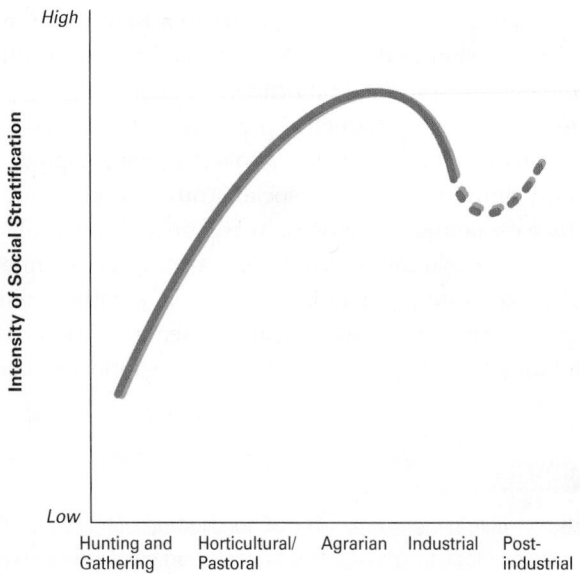

Figure 10–2 Social Stratification and Technological Development: The Kuznets Curve

The Kuznets curve shows that greater technological sophistication generally is accompanied by more pronounced social stratification. The trend reverses itself as industrial societies relax rigid, caste-like distinctions in favour of greater opportunity and equality under the law. Political rights are more widely extended, and there is even some levelling of economic differences. However, the emergence of post-industrial society has brought an upturn in economic inequality, as indicated by the broken line added by author John Macionis.

SOURCE: Created by John J. Macionis, based on Kuznets (1955) and Lenski (1966).

United States, though the gap between rich and poor is not as extreme.

The Kuznets Curve

In human history, then, technological advances first increase but then moderate the extent of social stratification. Greater inequality is functional for agrarian societies, but industrial societies benefit from a less inequitable system. This historical trend, recognized by Simon Kuznets (1955, 1966), the Harvard economist who was awarded a Nobel Prize in 1971, is illustrated by the Kuznets curve, shown in Figure 10–2. Social inequality around the world generally supports the Kuznets curve. Global Map 10–1 shows that high-income nations that have passed through the industrial era (including the United States, Canada, and the nations of Western Europe) have somewhat less income inequality than nations in which a larger share of the labour force remains in farming (as is common in Latin America and Africa). Income inequality reflects not just technological development but also political and economic priorities. Of all high-income nations, the United States has the greatest income inequality.

Window on the World

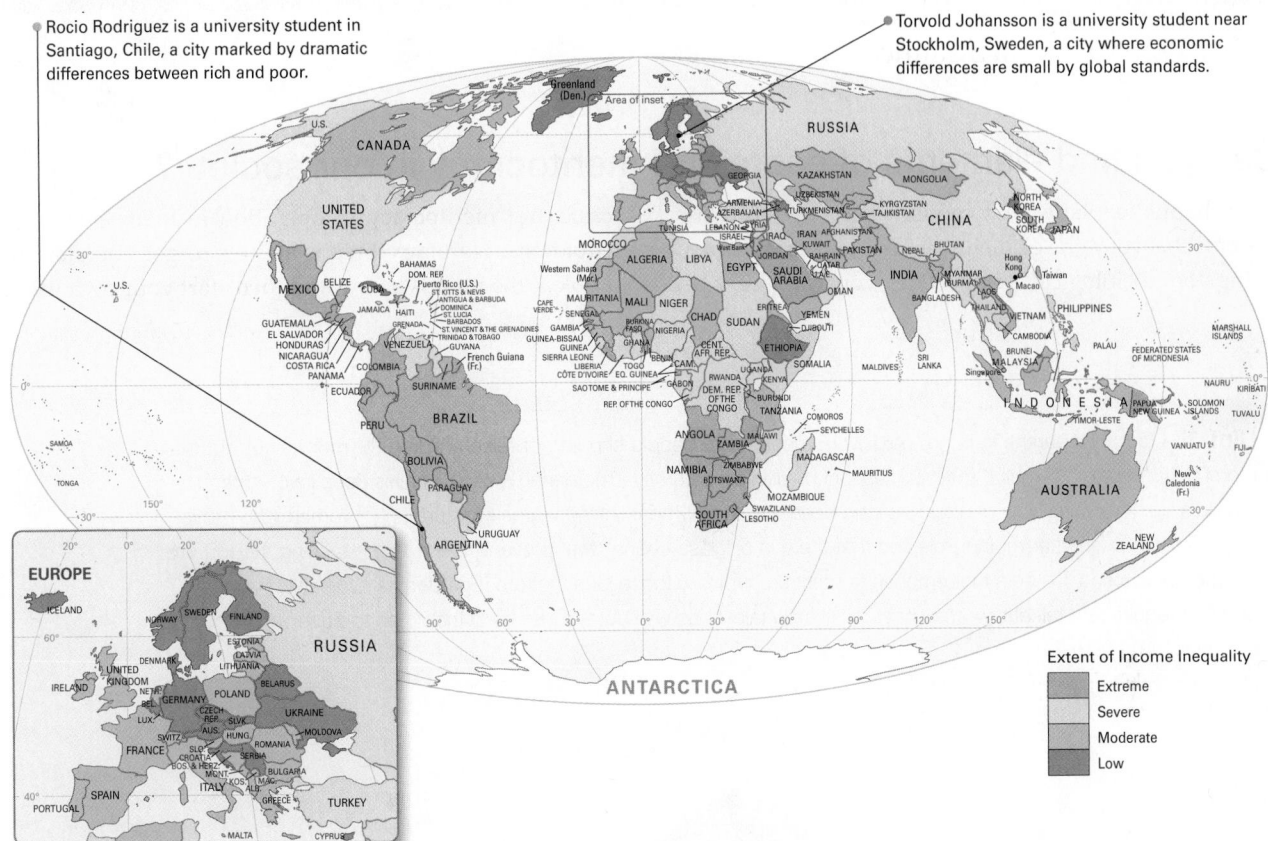

Rocio Rodriguez is a university student in Santiago, Chile, a city marked by dramatic differences between rich and poor.

Torvold Johansson is a university student near Stockholm, Sweden, a city where economic differences are small by global standards.

Extent of Income Inequality

- Extreme
- Severe
- Moderate
- Low

Global Map 10–1   Income Inequality in Global Perspective

Societies throughout the world differ in the rigidity and extent of their social stratification and their overall standard of living. This map highlights income inequality. Generally speaking, the United States stands out among high-income nations, such as Great Britain, Sweden, Japan, and Australia, as having greater income inequality. The less economically developed countries of Latin America and Africa, including Colombia, Brazil, and the Central African Republic, as well as much of the Arab world, exhibit the most pronounced inequality of income. Is this pattern consistent with the Kuznets curve?

SOURCE: Based on Gini coefficients obtained from the World Bank (2015).

Seeing Sociology in Everyday Life

CHAPTER 10 Social Stratification

Can you find elements of caste and meritocracy in our society?

This chapter explains that modern societies are class systems that combine elements of caste and meritocracy. Using the sociological perspective, you can see both caste and meritocracy in operation in many everyday situations. Here are three examples to get you started. Look at the photos below and then start your own list.

> **Hint** The fact that parenting is not paid work means that people should not raise children for money but out of moral duty. "Fathering a child" may suggest only biological paternity; "mothering a child" implies deep involvement in a child's life, indicating how gender has long been a caste element linking women to nurturing. Women who move beyond the homemaker/mother role find that there is a "glass ceiling" that prevents them from reaching the top in most organizations. Careers that emphasize merit are typically those jobs that are regarded as especially important and that require rare talents; women have those rare talents as well but are less likely than men to be rewarded with success.

Dex Images, Inc./Flirt/Corbis

ONE OF THE MOST DEMANDING JOBS YOU CAN HAVE IS BEING A PARENT And traditionally at least, most parenting is performed by women, with gender operating as a caste element. Why do you think our society does not pay parents for their work? What difference in meaning can you see between the phrases "fathering a child" and "mothering a child"?

Jonathan Hayward/The Canadian Press

BEVERLEY MCLACHLIN IS THE FIRST WOMAN TO BE NAMED CHIEF JUSTICE OF CANADA How many women do you think have served on the Supreme Court of Canada, and when was the first woman appointed?

Marc Nader/ZUMA Press/Newscom

JUSTIN BIEBER IS A CANADIAN SINGER WHO WAS BORN TO A SINGLE TEEN MOTHER WHO RAISED HER SON IN LOW-INCOME HOUSING After his first record went platinum in the United States, he became one of the highest-paid entertainers in the world—an example of a "rags to riches" move upward in social standing.

Seeing Sociology in *Your* Everyday Life

1. The "seven deadly sins," the human failings recognized by the Roman Catholic Church during the Middle Ages, were pride, greed, envy, anger, lust, gluttony, and sloth. Why are these traits dangerous to an agrarian caste system? Are they a threat to today's capitalist class system? Why or why not?

2. Sit down with parents, grandparents, or other relatives, and talk about how your family's social position changed over the last three generations. Has social mobility taken place? If so, describe the change. Was it caused by the effort of individuals or changes in society itself?

3. Identify three ways in which social stratification is evident in the everyday lives of students on your campus. In each case, explain exactly what is unequal and what difference it makes. Do you think individual talent or family background is more important in creating these social differences?

Making the Grade

CHAPTER 10 Social Stratification

What Is Social Stratification?

10.1 Identify four principles that underlie social stratification.

Social stratification

- is a trait of society, not simply a reflection of individual differences
- is found in all societies but varies according to *what* is unequal and *how* unequal it is
- carries over from one generation to the next
- is supported by a system of cultural beliefs that defines certain kinds of inequality as just
- takes two general forms: caste systems and class systems

> **social stratification** system by which a society ranks categories of people in a hierarchy
> **social mobility** a change in position within the social hierarchy

Caste and Class Systems

10.2 Apply the concepts of caste, class, and meritocracy to societies around the world.

Caste Systems

- are based on birth (ascription)
- permit little or no social mobility
- shape a person's entire life, including occupation and marriage
- are common in traditional, agrarian societies

An Illustration: India

Although the caste system is formally outlawed in India, it is still observed in rural areas, where agriculture demands a lifetime of hard work and discipline.

- In traditional villages, people's caste determines the type of work they perform.
- People must interact with and marry others of the same ranking.
- Powerful cultural beliefs make observing caste rules a moral duty.

Class Systems

- are based on both birth (ascription) and meritocracy (individual achievement)
- permit some social mobility based on individual achievement
- are common in modern industrial and post-industrial societies

- include elements of both caste and meritocracy
- advance meritocracy to promote specialization, productivity, and efficiency
- keep caste elements, such as family, to maintain order and social unity

Status consistency in class systems is low due to increased social mobility.

Caste and Class: The United Kingdom

- In the Middle Ages, England had a caste-like aristocracy, including the leading clergy and a hereditary nobility. The vast majority of people were commoners.
- Today's British class system mixes caste and meritocracy, producing a highly stratified society with some social mobility.

Caste and Class: Japan

- In the Middle Ages, Japan had a rigid caste system in which an imperial family ruled over nobles and commoners.
- Today's Japanese class system still places great importance on family background and traditional gender roles.

> **caste system** social stratification based on ascription, or birth
> **class system** social stratification based on both birth and individual achievement
> **meritocracy** social stratification based on personal merit
> **status consistency** the degree of consistency in a person's social standing across various dimensions of social inequality
> **structural social mobility** a shift in the social position of large numbers of people owing more to changes in society itself than to individual efforts

Classless Societies? The Former Soviet Union

- Although the Russian Revolution in 1917 attempted to abolish social classes, the new Soviet Union was still stratified based on unequal job categories and the concentration of power in the new political elite. Economic development created new types of jobs, which resulted in **structural social mobility**.
- Since the collapse of the Soviet Union in the early 1990s, the forces of structural social mobility have turned downward and the gap between rich and poor has increased.

China: Emerging Social Classes

- Economic reforms introduced after the Communist revolution in 1949—including state control of factories and productive property—greatly reduced economic inequality, although social differences remained.

- In the past 30 years, China's government has loosened control of the economy, causing the emergence of a new class of business owners and an increase in economic inequality.

> **ideology** cultural beliefs that justify particular social arrangements, including patterns of inequality

Ideology: Supporting Stratification

10.3 Explain how cultural beliefs justify social inequality.

- Cultural beliefs justify patterns of inequality.
- Ideology reflects both a society's economic system and its level of technology.

Theories of Social Inequality

10.4 Apply sociology's major theories to the topic of social inequality.

Structural-functional theory points to ways social stratification helps society operate.

- The **Davis-Moore thesis** states that social stratification is universal because of its functional consequences.
- In caste systems, people are rewarded for performing the duties of their position at birth.
- In class systems, unequal rewards attract the ablest people to the most important jobs and encourage effort.

Social-conflict theory claims that stratification divides societies in classes, benefiting some categories of people at the expense of others and causing social conflict.

- Karl Marx claimed that capitalism places economic production under the ownership of capitalists, who exploit the proletarians who sell their labour for wages.
- Max Weber identified three distinct dimensions of social stratification: economic class, social status or prestige, and power. Conflict exists between people at various positions on a multi-dimensional hierarchy of **socio-economic status** (SES).

Symbolic-interaction theory, a micro-level analysis, explains that we size up people by looking for clues to their social standing.

- **Conspicuous consumption** refers to buying and displaying products that make a "statement" about social class.
- People's attitudes about social inequality reflect not just facts but also politics and values concerning how a society should be organized.

> **Davis-Moore thesis** the functional analysis claiming that social stratification has beneficial consequences for the operation of a society
> **blue-collar occupations** lower-prestige jobs that involve mostly manual labour
> **white-collar occupations** higher-prestige jobs that involve mostly mental activity
> **socio-economic status** a composite ranking based on various dimensions of social inequality
> **conspicuous consumption** buying and using products because of the "statements" they make about social position

Social Stratification and Technology: A Global Perspective

10.5 Analyze the link between a society's technology and its social stratification.

- Gerhard and Jean Lenski identify five types of societies defined by their productive technology: hunting and gathering, horticultural and pastoral, agrarian, industrial, and postindustrial societies.
- The Lenskis explained that advancing technology initially increases social stratification, which is most intense in agrarian societies.
- Industrialization reverses the trend, reducing social stratification.
- In post-industrial societies, social stratification again increases.

Chapter 11
Social Class in Canada

IMAGE SOLUTIONS/Alamy Stock Photo

Learning Objectives

11.1 Describe the distribution of income and wealth in Canada.

11.2 Explain how one's position at birth affects social stranding later in life.

11.3 Describe the various social class positions in Canadian society.

11.4 Analyze the impacts of social class position on health, values, and family life.

11.5 Assess the extent of social mobility in Canada.

11.6 Discuss patterns and explanations of poverty among Canadians.

The Power of Society
to shape our chances of living in poverty

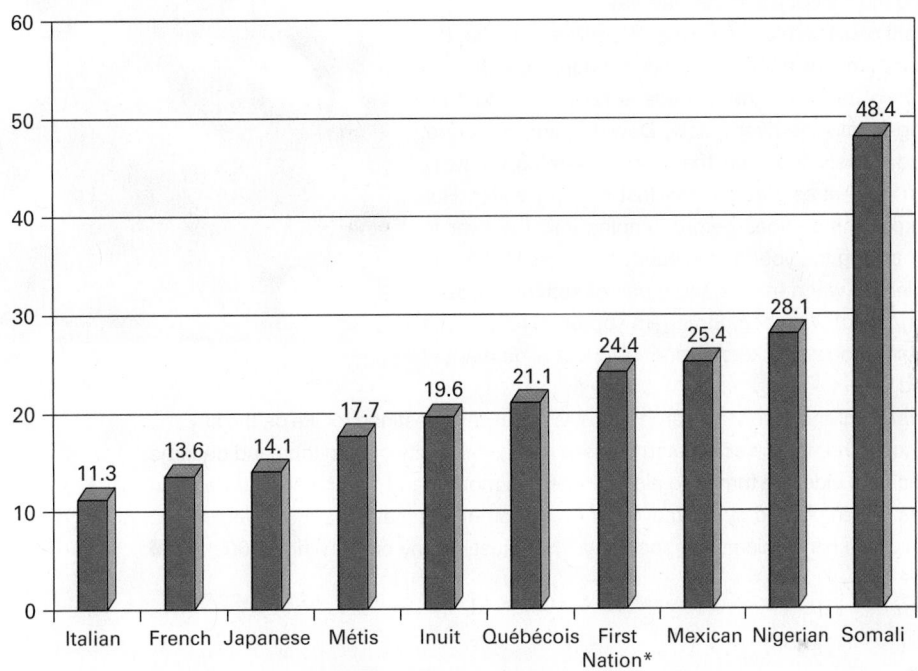

*First Nation here refers to Registered Indian (First Nation) and non-status Indians combined.

SOURCE: Compilation by L.M. Gerber based on Statistics Canada, National Household Survey 2011, Catalogue no. 99-010-X2011036.

Do the ethnic origins of Canadians affect the likelihood of living in poverty—or falling below the "low-income cutoff"? The answer to this question is a resounding "yes"! If your roots are Italian (or English, German, or Dutch, for that matter), you are among those least likely (one in ten) to live in poverty. French, Japanese, or Métis ancestry substantially increases your chances of living in poverty. So far, everything makes sense, but the fact that Inuit and Québécois are *almost equally* likely to fall below the poverty line (one in five) probably requires some explanation. The Quebecers who claim Québécois roots trace their ancestry back to the early days of French settlement in Canada. Compared with other Quebecers, they tend to be more rural and to have lower levels of education, employment, and income. Roughly one in four First Nations, Mexican, and Nigerian people live with poverty, These figures are alarming—until you find out that almost *half of the Somali population is poor*. From left to right in this figure, poverty increases from one in *ten* to one-half. There is no doubt whatsoever that the position of an ethnic group within Canadian society determines the odds of its members experiencing poverty.

Chapter Overview

This chapter deals with stratification, or social inequality, in Canada, beginning with a look at important measures of inequality. Inequality in our country is multi-dimensional and much greater than most of us imagine.

Winnipeg's homeless hero, Faron Hall, made a split-second decision that turned him into a celebrity—and left every politician in town, including the mayor, wanting to shake his hand. On a Sunday morning in early May, he jumped into the chilly waters of the Red River to rescue a teenager who had fallen from a bridge through the gap separating the car deck and the walkway.

Hall made light of his heroic act, saying, "People ignore me. But I don't ignore them. We look after each other out here." Bystanders had seen the look of terror on the teenager's face as he lost his footing and plunged into the river below. Downstream, on shore, Hall heard a loud splash and then the teen screaming for help. Seeing the youth 40 metres away in the fast-moving water, Hall took off his backpack and shoes before jumping into the river to rescue him. After pulling the young man safely to shore, Hall found himself the recipient of warm thanks and a pair of season baseball tickets from the mayor of Winnipeg. Strangers approached him with congratulations, and social workers arranged to put a permanent roof over his head.

A self-described chronic alcoholic, Faron Hall was not always destined for life on the streets. Though raised in foster homes, he completed courses at the University of Manitoba and became a high school teacher's aide. He turned to alcohol after his mother and sister were murdered in separate incidents. When praised by the mayor for doing something that few others would have done, Hall made light of his heroism by responding, "No, I just did my best" (White, 2009). ∎

Canadians tend to think of Canada as a middle-class society, but in fact our society is highly stratified. The rich not only control most of the money but also benefit from more schooling, enjoy better health, and consume a greater share of almost all goods and services than others do. On the other end of the socio-economic spectrum, poor families struggle from day to day simply to make ends meet. This chapter will explain that the popular perception of Canada as a society with a bulging middle class and a uniformly high standard of living does not square with many important facts.

Dimensions of Social Inequality

11.1 Describe the distribution of income and wealth in Canada.

Canada's egalitarian values suggest that we experience equality of opportunity and widespread upward mobility and that, at the very least, we provide a broad social safety net that catches those who fall through the cracks.

We fail to recognize that, in reality, birth confers advantages and opportunities on some people that others who are less fortunate could never imagine.

Social inequality in Canada is not easily recognized because our primary groups—including families, neighbours, and friends—typically have the same social standing as we do. At work, we mix with others like ourselves. In effect, most of our daily interaction involves a narrow stratum of society, with only brief and impersonal encounters with people very different from ourselves. The mass media, even in their ads, project a largely middle-class picture of our social world, and Canada is known to have one of the highest standards of living in the world. The effect of these images of homogeneity is that the very rich and the very poor are largely invisible to the rest of us.

When people do acknowledge their differences, they often talk of inequality as if it were determined by a single factor such as money. More accurately, however, social class in Canada has several dimensions. *Socio-economic status* amounts to a composite measure of social position that encompasses not only money but also power, occupational prestige, and schooling.

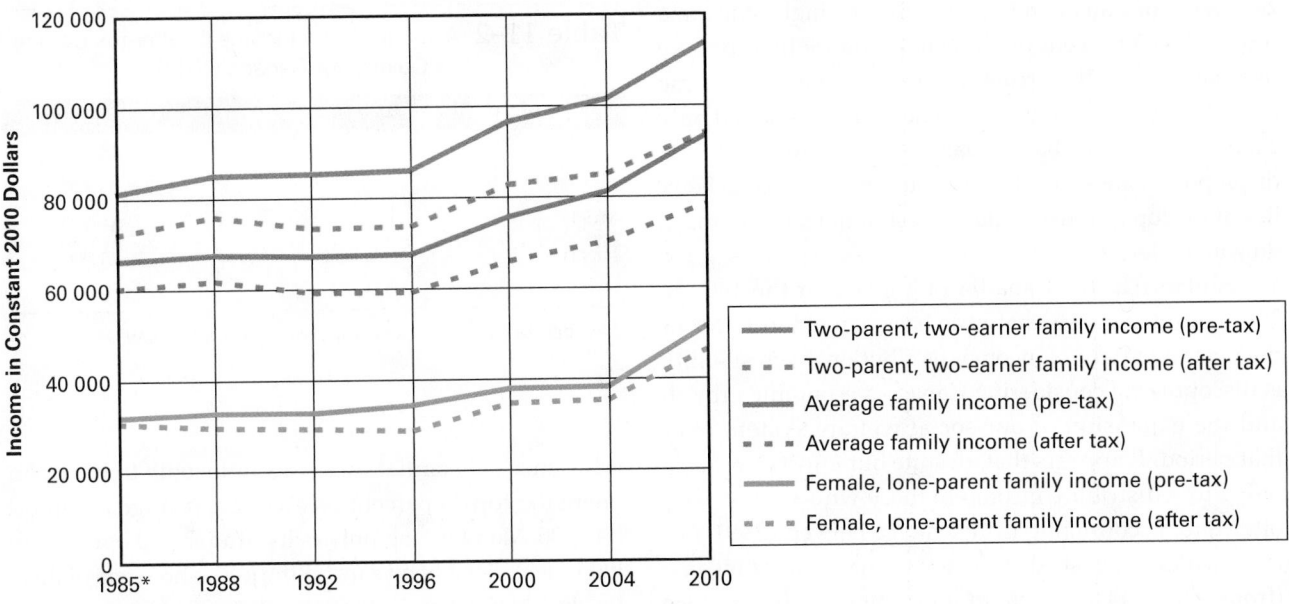

*Prior to 1985, incomes rose steadily. In 1961, 1971, and 1985 average income
(in constant 2010 dollars) was $43 816, $65 155, and $72 196 respectively.

Figure 11–1 Pre- and After-Tax Income by Family Structure in Canada, 1985 to 2010 (in constant 2010* dollars)

SOURCE: Created by L.M. Gerber based on data from Statistics Canada, Catalogue no. 75-202-XIE and the National Household Survey 2011, Table 99-014-X2011038.

Income

One important dimension of inequality involves **income**, *occupational wages or salaries, earnings from investments, and government transfer payments (e.g., welfare).*

As revealed in Figure 11–1, average family income in Canada rose substantially between 1985 and 2010 (from $72 196 to $94 000 in constant 2010 dollars) Not shown in the figure is the rise in real income over the preceding 25 years (i.e., from $43 816 to $72 196 in 2010 dollars.) Since all dollar values have been converted to 2010 dollars—to account for inflation—the increases you see indicate real growth in buying power.

Note that Figure 11–1 provides very detailed information about the economic well-being of Canadian families—depicting pre- and after-tax income over time for three kinds of families. Note that two-parent, two-earner families have substantially higher incomes (pre- and after-tax) than average families, and that the rise after 1996 was even sharper for them. An important contributor to rising income for the average family was the increase in dual-income families that began in the 1960s and 1970s. The sharper rise in the 1996 to 2010 period can be explained by movement of the women in two-earner families into better-paid and often professional jobs. The effect, in many cases, was the transformation of dual-income families into *dual-career* families.

Taking a very different approach, Table 11–1 deals with the distribution of income by quintiles (by fifths or groups of 20 percent). With 2011 as the point of reference, the

Table 11–1 Distribution of Income by Quintile for Canada (1961 to 2011) and the United States (1990 to 2011)

Quintile*	Canada						United States		
	1961	1971	1981	1991	2001	2011	1990	2000	2011
Lowest	6.6	5.6	6.4	6.4	5.2	4.8	3.9	4.3	3.8
Second	13.5	12.6	12.9	12.2	11.3	10.6	9.6	9.8	9.3
Middle	18.3	18.0	18.3	17.6	16.7	16.3	15.9	15.5	15.1
Fourth	23.4	23.7	24.1	23.9	23.3	24.1	24.0	22.3	23.0
Highest	38.4	40.0	38.4	40.0	43.6	44.3	46.6	47.4	48.8
Total	100	100	100	100	100	100	100	100	100

*Quintiles divide families into five equal categories (20 percent of families in each quintile). Distribution refers to the percentage of total income (in Canada or the US) that goes to each quintile.

SOURCES: Fréshette (1988); Statistics Canada, Catalogue no. 13-207; Statistics Canada, CANSIM Table 202-0701; and U.S. Census Bureau (2011).

20 percent of Canadian families with the highest income received 44.3 percent of all income—more than double their share (i.e., 20 percent) assuming complete income equality—while the lowest-income quintile received only 4.8 percent, or less than a quarter of its share. In short, a disproportionate share of the nation's income goes to families in the top quintile while the rest of the families make do with far less.

A glance at the Canadian figures over the 1961 to 2011 period suggests that little has changed in terms of the overall pattern of income distribution. Such stability is discouraging considering Canada's economic growth and the expansion of our social welfare system over that period. It appears that, despite our efforts, we have failed to redistribute income to those who are less well off. More discouraging is the change between 1991 and 2011, which suggests that the top quintile *gained* income (from 40.0 to 44.3 percent of all income) at the expense of the poorest quintile (whose share dropped from 6.4 to 4.8 percent). This short period—two decades—supports the argument that Canadians are experiencing greater inequality; in other words the rich got richer while the poor got poorer.

A comparison of the Canadian and American figures (Table 11–1) suggests that, until recently, Canada's income was more equally distributed than that of the United States. Initially, the lowest income quintile in Canada had about 6 percent of the income pie compared to 4 percent in the United States, but lately the Canadian record is looking more like the American. In 1990–1991, the top income quintiles had 40 and 47 percent of total income in Canada and the U.S., respectively. By 2011, that gap had closed, however slightly, to 44 and 49 percent. All one can safely say on the basis of this table is that, despite recent increases here, income inequality remains greater in the United States than in Canada.

Canadians are well aware of the concern expressed by the media, politicians, and other opinion leaders about increasing inequality. Complaints about the top 1 or 0.1 percent and plans to increase their taxes—by President Obama (or presidential candidate Hillary Clinton) and Prime Minister Trudeau—are music to the ears of many taxpayers. When you look at the top 1, 5, or 10 percent of the population, the evidence is clear. There is very real inequality in Canada. It shows up in Table 11–2—but in a more dramatic way.

Let's see what Table 11–2 reveals. Here we see the average family income of each quintile (or 20 percent of the population). Families in the first or lowest quintile make do with income averaging $15 000. Think of it! One in five families lives on this low level of income. Families in the second quintile, on average, have more than twice the income of the lowest. There are no further doublings, but families in the third, fourth, and fifth quintiles

Table 11–2 Average Family Income (in after-tax dollars) by Quintile for Canada (2011)

Quintile*	
Lowest	$ 15 100
Second	$ 33 400
Middle	$ 51 200
Fourth	$ 75 900
Highest	$139 400

SOURCE: Compiled by L.M. Gerber from Statistics Canada 2011, CANSIM Table 202-0701.

experience substantial increases in income to the point where the top 20 percent receives an average of almost $140 000. Many young university graduates hope to earn that much after a few years on the job—and some of them do—but in most cases that average of $140 000 is based on two incomes in a dual-career household. In the bottom quintile you have many single parents—overwhelmingly single mothers—and even people working full time in minimum-wage jobs. In the top quintile, you find many dual earners, one or both of whom are in relatively well-paid professions. If there is any comfort to be had, it is in the fact that the tax bite is bigger for the two-parent, two-earner family—as seen in the pre-tax/after-tax income data of Figure 11–1.

Another aspect of income distribution is presented on Canada Map 11–1, which shows average family income for Canada, the provinces, and the territories. In 2010, New Brunswick families had the lowest average income ($76 500)—followed closely by the other eastern provinces. You may be surprised to learn that family income in Ontario is only slightly higher than the Canadian average—while that of the Northwest Territories is the highest (at $127 500). In fact, in terms of family income, Alberta and the three territories are ahead of the rest of Canada. Nunavut—once among the poorest in Canada—had an average family income of $104 500 by 2010. The higher incomes in the northern territories can be attributed to high levels of government employment, professionals who work for the mining industries, and isolation pay. Prior to the recent collapse of oil prices—through 2015—Alberta ranked second on average family income. When the results of the 2016 census are released, we will know the extent to which the oil-based crash of the Alberta economy has affected the well-being of its families.

Wealth

Income is but one component of **wealth**, *the total amount of money and other assets, minus outstanding debts*. Wealth in the form of stocks, bonds, real estate, and other

Seeing Ourselves

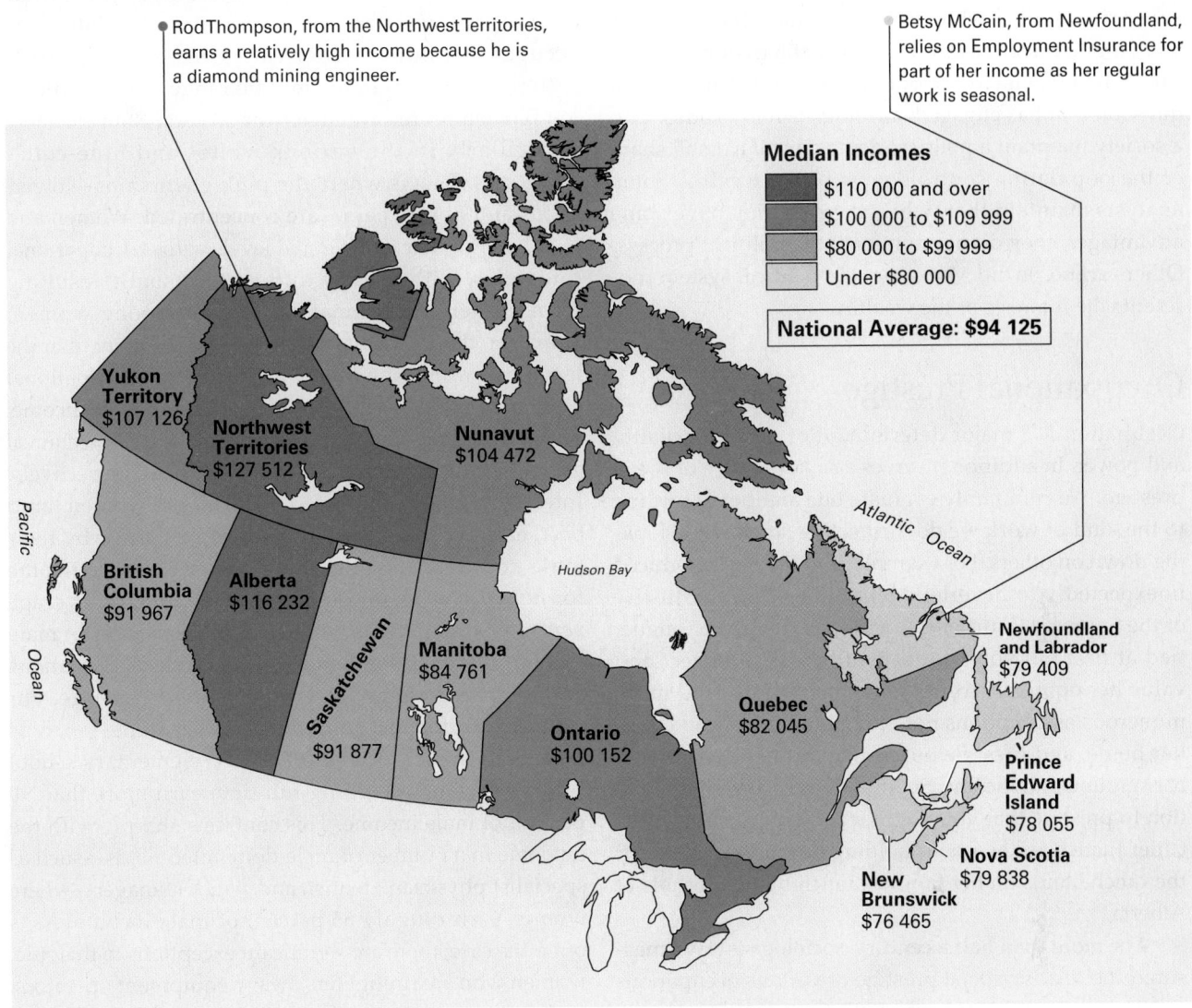

Rod Thompson, from the Northwest Territories, earns a relatively high income because he is a diamond mining engineer.

Betsy McCain, from Newfoundland, relies on Employment Insurance for part of her income as her regular work is seasonal.

Median Incomes

- $110 000 and over
- $100 000 to $109 999
- $80 000 to $99 999
- Under $80 000

National Average: $94 125

Yukon Territory $107 126

Northwest Territories $127 512

Nunavut $104 472

British Columbia $91 967

Alberta $116 232

Saskatchewan $91 877

Manitoba $84 761

Ontario $100 152

Quebec $82 045

Newfoundland and Labrador $79 409

Prince Edward Island $78 055

Nova Scotia $79 838

New Brunswick $76 465

Pacific Ocean

Atlantic Ocean

Hudson Bay

Canada Map 11–1   Average Family Income* for Canada, the Provinces and Territories (2010).

*Income refers to income from all sources, including employment, government transfers, and investment.

SOURCE: Created by L.M. Gerber, based on Statistics Canada, 2011 National Household Survey, Catalogue no. 99-014-X2011038.

privately owned property is distributed even less evenly than income. Alain Bellemare, CEO of Bombardier, for example, has to declare his *income* to the Canada Revenue Agency, but not the value of his mansions or business holdings. It is the control of these kinds of assets that really sets the wealthy apart from the rest of us. When the political left talks of establishing a wealth tax and an inheritance tax, it is this component of wealth that it seeks to redistribute. Canada does not measure or tax wealth, but the United States does. The most recent American figures (for 2011) reveal that the richest 20 percent of families receive 49 percent of all income and own an astounding 89 percent of all wealth (Macionis, 2014:303). In all likelihood, Canada's disparities in the distribution of wealth—though not as extreme—differ little from those of the United States.

Power

In Canadian society, as elsewhere, wealth stands as an important source of power. Wealth is not earned income, but rather one's assets—such as stocks, bonds, real estate, and other property. Major owners of corporate stock, for example, make decisions that create jobs

income occupational wages or salaries, earnings from investments, and government transfer payments (e.g., welfare)

wealth the total amount of money and other assets, minus outstanding debts

for ordinary people or, conversely scale back operations and throw people out of work. More broadly, the super-rich families who own most of the nation's wealth have a great deal of influence over the national political agenda (Clement, 1975; Francis, 1986). This raises a question that has engaged sociologists for decades: Can a society maintain a political democracy if a small share of the population controls most of the wealth? Some analysts maintain that, while the rich may have some advantages, they do not dominate the political process. Others argue, as did Marx, that the political system represents the interests of the wealthy.

Occupational Prestige

Occupation is a major determinant of income, wealth, and power. In addition it serves as a key source of social prestige. We commonly evaluate one another according to the kind of work we do, respecting some while looking down on others. For example, if you were introduced unexpectedly to Beverley McLachlin—as Chief Justice of the Supreme Court of Canada—you might be tongue-tied at first but you would treat her with respect and value her opinions. At the same time, you would make numerous assumptions not only about her social circle, her home, and lifestyle but also about her educational background and income. So important is current occupation to prestige that you might react with surprise if the Chief Justice talked about helping her mother cook for the ranch hands on her family's ranch in the foothills of Alberta.

For more than half a century, sociologists have measured the relative social prestige of various occupations (Blishen, 1958; Blishen et al., 1987; Counts, 1925; Hodge et al., 1966). Surveys asking respondents to rate occupations in terms of prestige produce a ranking that reflects both income and education. Physicians, lawyers, and engineers—all high on income and education—are ranked near the top on prestige, while cashiers and janitors are ranked near the bottom. In fact, occupational prestige rankings tend to be roughly the same in all industrial, high-income societies (Lin & Xie, 1988)—including the United States, where physicians score 86 on the prestige scale and shoe shiners score 9 (Macionis, 2014:304). Almost everywhere, white-collar work that involves mental activity free from extensive supervision confers greater prestige than do blue-collar occupations that require supervised, manual labour. There are exceptions to this pattern, however; for example, a blue-collar aircraft mechanic enjoys greater social prestige than a white-collar filing clerk.

Another study (Creese et al., 1991) ranked various occupational categories in Canada, applying the Blishen scale to data from the General Social Survey of 1986.

In a ranking of 514 census occupations, physicians and surgeons came out at the top, with a score of 101.3, while newspaper carriers and vendors scored 17.8. Collapsing occupations into broader categories makes certain patterns apparent. In the middle range of occupations, the Blishen scores are lower for women than for men, particularly in the various white- and blue-collar categories. This is where the pink ghetto jobs—lower-status and poorly paid—are concentrated. Women and men have similar educational levels across occupational categories, with the few differences usually resulting from higher educational attainment among women. However, the 1986 data reveal marked differences in the income of women and men: In most of the occupational categories, women earn about 60 percent of male income, but in the professional and semi-professional/technical categories, the figures are 72 and 84 percent, respectively. Interestingly, self-employed professional women fared best, earning 88 percent of the income earned by their male counterparts. Research focused upon income for *full-time* work in Canada, reveals that, on average across all occupations, women earn 71 percent of male income. On the other hand, when selected occupations are compared, some intriguing patterns emerge. For example, in female-dominated occupations—such as registered nurse, social worker, and elementary school teacher—women working full time earn more than 90 percent of male income. This contrasts sharply with the outcome in a number of male-dominated fields—such as specialist physician, dentist, and senior manager—where women earn roughly 65 percent of male income. As is often the case, there are significant exceptions to this rule; women who are firefighters, heavy equipment operators, and motor vehicle mechanics (where women make up less than 3 percent of the workers) earn 85 percent of male income. Your author, Linda Gerber, expands on her research into the complexities underlying the income gender gap in the chapter on Gender Stratification. Although prestige is tied to occupation and/or income, the three measures are not always correlated—as illustrated by this study into variations in prestige over time. In 2000, University of Waterloo professor John Goyder replicated a study of occupational prestige that was conducted in the Kitchener-Waterloo area of Ontario a quarter of a century earlier. Noting that occupational prestige ratings done through the 1960s to 1980s were highly correlated (usually at the 0.99 level), Goyder (2005) decided to replicate the 1975 study to measure changes that intuition told him must have occurred. Both studies asked people, in face-to-face interviews, to rank a wide range of occupations. Because of changes in the economy between the studies, 13 obsolete job titles were dropped and 10 new ones were added; but 80 occupational categories were common to both studies.

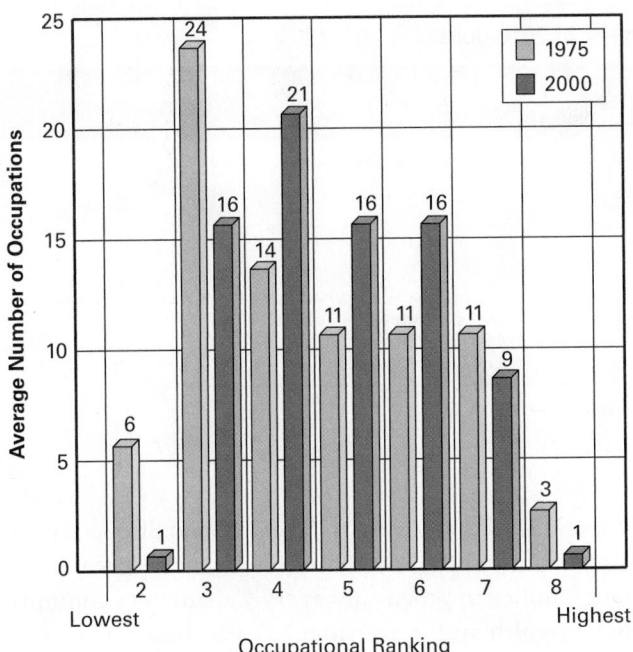

Figure 11–2 Distribution of Occupational Prestige, 1975 and 2000*

*Number of occupation titles rated at each level of prestige, from surveys of Kitchener-Waterloo, Ontario, 1975 and 2000.

SOURCE: Goyder, John, "The Dynamics of Occupational Prestige: 1975-2000," The Canadian Review of Sociology and Anthropology, Vol. 42, No. 1 (2005): 1, 23. Used with permission.

Figure 11–2 reveals Goyder's findings that the distribution of rankings changed dramatically. Fewer occupations are given either very low or very high rankings. By 2000, many more occupations were ranked in the middle ranges. The following examples illustrate the changes that underlie the graph: Tool and die makers and auto workers are up 12 points; firefighters, police officers, and registered nurses are up 23, 13, and 10 points, respectively; lawyers, members of Parliament, and physicists are down 15, 13, and 11 points, respectively. Physicians held up remarkably well, dropping less than one point from 93.6 to 92.7, while university professors dropped 5 points. Throughout the 1975 to 2000 period, many low- to moderate-prestige jobs came to require added skills because of computers: Truck drivers, farmers, secretaries, and nurses have to deal with new technology on the job. At the upper end of the scale, computers had a different effect: "Internet and software packages help transform the common man and woman into instant experts with access to the latest research knowledge. The professions may have less prestige nowadays because the Internet has demystified their secret knowledge" (Goyder, 2005). Marshall McLuhan would have agreed with Goyder's analysis.

The Kitchener-Waterloo studies of 1975 and 2000 both addressed the gender dimension of occupational prestige.

In each survey, random thirds were asked to rate job titles described as male-specified (e.g., "male accountant"), female-specified (e.g., "female accountant"), and gender-neutral (e.g., "accountant") (Goyder et al., 2003; Goyder, 2005). In 1975, there was a tendency to assign different rankings to male accountants and female accountants, for example, with greater prestige accruing to male workers. By 2000, that gender gap had disappeared (Goyder et al., 2003).

Schooling

Education is an important determinant of labour force participation, occupation, and income, so it is highly valued in industrial societies. While industrial societies generally define schooling as everyone's right, the opportunity for formal education is not always equal. Clearly, Aboriginal people face barriers to education as, to a lesser extent, do the residents of other geographically isolated communities. Poverty, wherever it occurs—in rural, urban, or even large metropolitan areas—makes the pursuit of higher education much more difficult if not impossible. Whereas, in the past, Canadian women did not pursue formal education as far as their male counterparts, in recent years the majority of bachelor's and master's degrees—but not doctorates—have been earned by women.

Schooling not only promotes personal development but also affects an individual's occupation and income. Individuals with higher levels of schooling are more likely to be in the labour force, to be employed (especially full time) rather than unemployed, and to earn higher incomes. Advanced education is required for a number of highly paid occupations, including those of physician, dentist, senior manager, pharmacist, or university professor. Police officers, registered nurses, teachers, and social workers may not earn as much but they too need post-graduate certification. Plumbers, electricians, oil or gas drillers, and tool and die makers—many of whom are very well paid—require specialized training and the right credentials. Those without a high-school diploma or some kind of specialized skill are severely disadvantaged in the search for steady employment with adequate income.

Table 11–3 deals with the effect of educational attainment on income—in this case median and average income (pre-tax and after-tax). Whichever column one examines, several things are clear: First, income increases with each additional level of educational attainment; second, college or CJEP graduates have a relatively small income boost over those with apprenticeship or trades certification; and third, postgraduate credentials are associated with roughly three times the income of those who lack high school diplomas.

Table 11–3 Income by Highest Level of Educational Attainment (in 2010 dollars)

Educational Certification	Median income (pre-tax)	Median income (after-tax)	Average Income (pre-tax)	Average income (after-tax)
None	18 075	17 772	23 739	21 371
High school	23 192	21 834	31 082	26 839
Apprenticeship or trades	33 285	30 045	40 003	33 959
College or CGEP	35 559	31 863	42 152	35 559
Bachelor's	46 898	40 648	58 807	47 215
Postgraduate	56 769	48 175	73 624	57 482

SOURCE: Compiled by L.M. Gerber from Statistics Canada, 2011 National Household Survey, 99-014-X2011038.

It is also worth noting that median incomes are substantially lower than average incomes. The reason is that the median is the point at which half of the people have income above that level while the other half falls below. Unlike average income, median income is not affected by the high-fliers. The $73 624 average income of those with postgraduate qualifications includes a large number of people who have much higher income than the rest. Another thing that shows up clearly in this table is that the tax bite is much larger at higher average income levels. The tax man claims about $2500 from those without certification (10.5 percent) and $16 200 from those with postgraduate qualifications (22 percent). In the end, the effect of taxation is to *reduce the gap* in average income—between the lowest and highest educational attainment levels—from $50 000 to $36 000.

Canadian Stratification: Merit and Caste

11.2 Explain how one's position at birth affects social standing later in life.

The Canadian class system is partly a meritocracy in that social position reflects individual talent and effort. But it also has caste elements, because birth plays a part in what we become later in life.

Ancestry

Nothing affects social standing in Canada as much as our birth into a particular family, an event over which we have no control. Ancestry determines our point of entry into the system of social inequality. Some Canadian families, including the Reichmanns, Blacks, Aspers, Thomsons, Irvings, Nygards, and Stronachs, are known around the world. On a more modest scale, certain families in practically every Canadian community have wealth and power that have become well established over several generations. Being born to privilege or poverty sets the stage for future schooling, occupation, and income. While there are numerous rags-to-riches stories in Canada (e.g., Peter Nygard, Paul Demarais, and Frank Stronach), many of the richest individuals—those

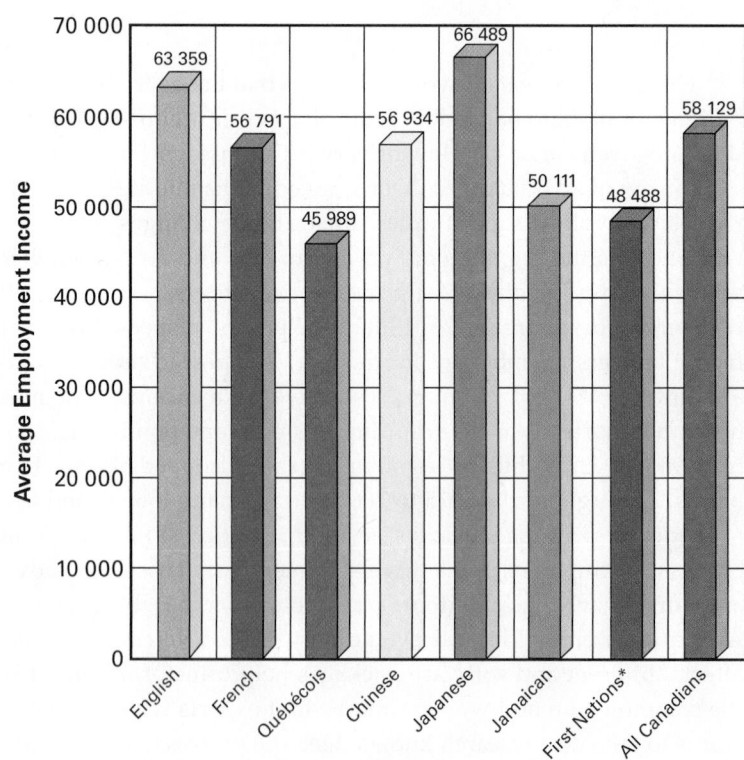

*Note that, for present purposes, the term *First Nations* refers to registered and non-status Indians combined.

Figure 11–3 Average Employment Income in Canada for Selected Categories, 2010

SOURCE: Compiled by L.M. Gerber from Statistics Canada, 2011 National Household Survey, Catalogue number 99-010-X2011036.

with hundreds of millions or even billions of dollars in wealth—are likely to have derived their fortunes primarily through inheritance. By the same token, the legacy of poverty and the lack of opportunity that goes with it just as surely shape the future of those in need. The family, in short, transmits property, power, prestige, and possibilities from one generation to the next, contributing to the persistence of social stratification.

Race and Ethnicity

While we think that Canadian society is largely egalitarian, race and ethnicity remain important determinants of social position—though not always with the expected results. Canadians of Chinese and Japanese origins are more likely to have university degrees and even postgraduate certification than those of English or French origin; Aboriginal people—and First Nations in particular—lag behind in terms of educational attainment and employment. Figures 11–3 and 11–4 suggest that race and ethnicity have a bearing on income, as well.

As has been the case for many a census, Canadians of Japanese origin have the highest average employment income—$66 500—of all the selected categories in Figure 11–3. Those of English origins have ranked second in terms of employment income. In 2010, Quebecers who claim French origins earn almost the same income as Chinese Canadians—at almost $57 000. The surprise here is that Canadians of Jamaican origins and First Nations have higher employment income than the Quebecers who identify as Québécois. How can that be? The Québécois trace their lineage back to the original settlers, the *habitant*, who came to the shores of the St. Lawrence River from France. They tend to be rural, relatively poorly educated, unilingual French, and poor.

Figure 11–4 presents income differences based on another measure. The bars in the graph indicate the proportion of the population aged 15 years and over in each category with income—from employment, investments, and government transfers—of $80 000 or more. Note that, on this measure, Canadians of English origin fare a little better than Japanese Canadians (by a single percentage point). As in Figure 11–3, people of French and Chinese origins are fairly evenly matched. Similarly, Jamaicans are slightly more likely than Québécois and First Nations to have income above $80 000. The pattern observed in Figure 11–3 is repeated here; on either measure—employment income or percentage with income above $80 000—Québécois and First Nations have the lowest income among the selected categories. It's worth noting that both populations tend to live in rural, sometimes isolated areas and to have lower levels of education and employment. In sharp contrast, Japanese Canadians live in urban areas and have high levels of educational attainment.

Together, Figures 11–3 and 11–4 suggest that, while income is only one dimension of social class, race and ethnicity are clearly associated with differential placement in the socio-economic hierarchy of Canada. On the other hand, it is clear that racism and discrimination are only a partial explanation for economic inequality. The Thinking about Diversity box takes a look at social class distinctions *within* the Aboriginal community, thereby providing a very different perspective on inequality.

Gender

Women born into families of high social standing draw on many more social resources than men born into disadvantaged families. Yet, on average, women earn lower income, accumulate less wealth, enjoy lower occupational prestige, and are less likely to have advanced degrees in math, science, and engineering. It is also the case that, among single-parent families, those headed by women are more than twice as likely to be poor than those headed by men.

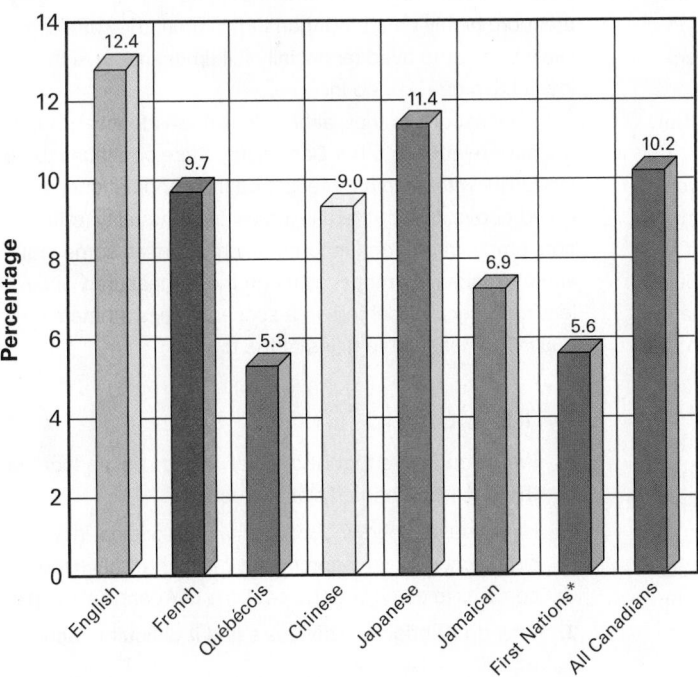

*Note that these percentages are based on populations 15 years of age and over.
*For present purposes, the term *First Nations* refers to registered and non-status Indians combined.

Figure 11–4 Percentage with Income of $80 000 or More for Selected Categories, 2010*

SOURCE: Compilation and calculations by L.M. Gerber from Statistics Canada, 2011 National Household Survey, Catalogue number 99-010-X2011036.

Thinking About Diversity: Race, Class, and Gender

Social Class and Aboriginal Peoples

Many scholars and observers of the Canadian scene have characterized Aboriginal peoples as suffering from cultural dislocation, substance abuse, suicide, and poverty. Furthermore, the figures and tables throughout this text suggest that Aboriginal people lag behind the rest of us in terms of education, labour force participation, and income. In other words, the general belief is that Aboriginal people—First Nations, non-status Indians, Métis, and Inuit—live in relative poverty.

These observations apply to Aboriginal peoples in the *aggregate*. Indeed, Aboriginal peoples—on average—do fare poorly on a wide range of measures of social, economic, and physical health. Yet in an early publication, based on her analysis of 600 First Nations communities, Gerber (1979) pointed out the diversity among them. That diversity led her to develop a typology of reserve-based communities: Inert, Pluralistic, Municipal, and Integrative communities reveal very different responses to changing socio-economic circumstances. Underlying this diversity are real differences in economic well-being. Where communities have acquired wealth, there is also individual diversity, as some individuals benefit more than others.

Wotherspoon and Satzewich (1993) observe the situation of Aboriginal people from a Marxist—or, rather, neo-Marxist—perspective, noting that race, class, and gender relations enter into the picture. These variables, they argue, "intersect in complex ways to structure the social position of groups." The authors are quick to point out that, collectively, Aboriginal peoples "occupy disadvantaged positions within social and economic structures of Canada" and that, because they "share a structurally similar position," the assumption is that race and class converge—in other words, race equals class. While the aggregate statistics support this assumption, Wotherspoon and Satzewich counter it with evidence that, in fact, Aboriginal people "are distributed across the range of class sites" (pp. 42–43). Some of that evidence comes from Gerber (1990), who provides an occupational breakdown for Indian,* Métis, and Inuit peoples.

Aboriginal people are found in each of the Marxist categories of proletariat, reserve army of labour, working class, petit bourgeoisie, and bourgeoisie. Thus, they span the range from street people to capitalists. However, while the media and the literature provide substantial analysis of Aboriginal communities and populations, they rarely focus on the Aboriginal capitalists (the petit bourgeoisie and the bourgeoisie)—the people with large sums of private capital or those who control large sums of communal capital (Wotherspoon & Satzewich, 1993:64).

As expected, some Aboriginal-owned businesses are based on crafts, tourism, natural resources, construction, hunting, fishing, and farming; but others offer services in consulting and multimedia communications. Businesses are located on reserves and in major urban centres. The start-up capital for these ventures comes from land claim settlements, special funds from Indian and Northern Affairs Canada (INAC), or banks, some of which specifically serve Aboriginal people and businesses. Aboriginal businesses are newer and generally smaller than their mainstream counterparts, but many are multimillion-dollar ventures. In fact, executive incomes put many Aboriginal individuals in Canada's upper-income categories. The federal government provides services for Aboriginal businesses through INAC as well as through Industry Canada.

In her comparison of 2001 and 2006 census data, Gerber (2014) found that Aboriginal people continue to trail behind non-Aboriginals in terms of education, employment (particularly full time), and income. Although Aboriginals have lower levels of postsecondary certification than non-Aboriginals, there is one measure on which both men and women excel—and that is apprenticeship or trades certification. The Inuit lag farthest behind on the educational front and match Indian* men and women at the lowest level of full-time employment; however, they do very well when it comes to *income* from full-time employment and income over $80 000. In fact, by 2005, Inuit women *surpassed* non-Aboriginal women on both income measures.

Two important findings are highlighted in this study (Gerber, 2014). The first is that Indian women—particularly First Nations women living on reserve—suffer multiple layers of disadvantage. They are disadvantaged as Aboriginals, as Indians, and as women. Despite the fact that they are more highly educated than Indian men, they are less likely to be employed (especially full time) and have the lowest average earned income.

The second is that, although all three identity groups are poor relative to other Canadians, there continues to be inequality *within* Indian, Métis, and Inuit populations, as noted above. In fact there is increasing inequality (education, employment, and income polarization) as some individuals make substantial gains on these measures while leaving others far behind. In a sense, there is a bittersweet quality to measurable gains at the top.

What Do You Think?

1. Were you aware that Aboriginal individuals are located throughout Canada's class structure?

2. Have you had personal contact with Aboriginal individuals in school or your community? If so, how have those contacts affected your perceptions of Aboriginal people?

3. Why do Aboriginal individuals find it difficult to achieve equality in Canada?

* These people, who identified as North American Indian on Census 2001 and 2006, are roughly 80 percent registered Indian (First Nations) and 20 percent non-status Indian. The latter are not subject to the *Indian Act*, are not the responsibility of Aboriginal and Northern Affairs Canada, and are not represented by the Assembly of First Nations. To complicate matters even more, 10 percent of the people who identify as Métis and 2 percent of Inuit are registered Indians and thus First Nations.

Social Classes in Canada

11.3 Describe the various social class positions in Canadian society.

Assessing someone's social position in a relatively fluid class system—as opposed to a rigid caste system—poses a number of challenges. Consider the joke about the fellow who orders a pizza, asking that it be cut into six slices because he isn't hungry enough to eat eight. Sociologists do the same thing with social class; some slice the population into more slices than others. At one extreme, people find as many as six or even seven social classes; at the other, some follow Karl Marx in seeing two major classes—capitalist and proletarian. Still others side with Max Weber, claiming that stratification creates not clear-cut classes but a multidimensional status hierarchy.

Defining classes in Canada is difficult owing to the relatively low level of status consistency. Especially toward the middle of the hierarchy, an individual's social standing on one dimension often contradicts his or her position on another (Gilbert & Kahl, 1987; Tepperman, 1979). A government official, for example, may control a multimillion-dollar budget yet earn a modest income. Similarly, members of the clergy typically enjoy ample prestige while possessing only moderate power and earning low pay. Or consider a lucky professional gambler or a gangster who may win little respect despite considerable wealth. The social mobility typical of class systems means that social position often changes during one's lifetime, further blurring the lines between social classes.

Despite these problems of definition, it is useful to think of four general social classes in Canada: the upper class, the middle class, the working class, and the lower class. As we shall explain, however, some categories are more clear-cut than others.

In a society in which economic development is focused on knowledge-based industries, computer technology is being applied very widely, even in underground mining. Computer literacy increasingly distinguishes the highly employable from those who face multiple barriers to satisfactory employment. If the children of the affluent have more exposure to computers at school, and that exposure is augmented by the presence of computers in the home, they are likely to perpetuate their parents' social class position. See the Sociology and the Media box for a closer look at the link between computers and social class.

Sociology and the Media

Computers and Social Class

In the past decade or so, Canada ceased to be an industrial society and moved to the post-industrial phase. This means that the service sector has expanded to include a high proportion of knowledge-based industries, which in turn means that Canadians increasingly rely on information technology in a wide range of work environments. If computer literacy, in particular, is becoming the key to opportunity in Canada, then the question of who is comfortable with the technology is of considerable importance.

Schools throughout Canada—in rural or urban, affluent or poor communities—are gradually introducing computers into the classroom from the earliest grades; where available, special school networks and the internet have expanded horizons and revolutionized the learning process. But the number of computers available is usually limited, so that individual students often have little opportunity to put new skills into practice. The most aggressive students—often the boys—tend to monopolize the equipment, while the more reticent students watch from the sidelines. As long as the supply of computers in the school is limited, additional exposure to computers in the home environment will play an important role in skill development. It is here that social class background has an impact.

John Goyder (1997) examined patterns of technology diffusion in Canada, comparing the presence of telephones in 1911 and personal computers (PCs) in 1994 in the homes of people in various occupational categories. Note that both of these technologies started off in offices and were later adopted in homes.

Goyder found that more affluent homes were the first to have both telephones and computers. Home telephone subscribers in 1911, in Kingston, Ontario, were overwhelmingly in the professional and managerial categories: 96 percent of professionals had telephones at home, compared with 3 percent of those in skilled and semi-skilled trades. In 1994, PCs were more evenly distributed in the homes of various occupational categories. Among professionals (employed and self-employed), 61 percent had computers at home, compared with 24 percent of unskilled craft and farm labourers. Considering the expense of computers, the fact that about 25 percent of households in the four lowest occupational categories have PCs is remarkable and indicative of the centrality of computers in modern Canadian life. The absence of computers in the homes of

(continued)

39 percent of professionals may be a function of age, as some older professionals have not adopted computers either in the office or at home.

Statistics Canada tracks changes in internet use by education and age of household head, specifying location of access (e.g., home, work, or school). Between 1997 and 2003, the proportion of households with home access headed by those with less than high school education increased from 3.9 to 31.6 percent. Among households with heads having university degrees, home access increased from 37.6 to 87.8 percent. The effect of the age of the household head has a similarly dramatic impact. Among households with heads under 35 years of age, internet access at home increased from 37.3 to 79.5 percent in the same five-year period. Among households with heads 65 years of age and over, home access increased from 5.3 to 24.9 percent. Clearly, both education and age of household head have dramatic effects on internet access at home (Statistics Canada, 2006).

By 2012, roughly 90 percent of Canadians were internet users—more or less depending on age, education, and household income. Among people 16 to 44 years of age, 95 percent were users, compared to 89 percent of those aged 65 and over. Education is also a factor; 87 percent of those with high school or less used computers, whereas this was true of 98 percent of those with at least a bachelor's degree (an 11-point spread). If household income had been measured in quintiles or deciles it might have been a better predictor of internet use. As it is, 88 percent of people in the lowest income quartile and 96 percent in the highest were using the internet (Statistics Canada, 2011). Almost all Canadians (90 percent) are internet users, with minor variation related to age, household income, and most clearly education.

What Do You Think?

1. How important are computers in the home for preparing young people to succeed in school?

2. What differences have you observed between families with computers and those without?

3. Do primary and secondary schools have enough computers to meet the educational needs of their students?

The Upper Class

The upper class, roughly 5 percent of the Canadian population, derives much of its income from inherited wealth—in the form of stocks and bonds, real estate, and other investments—or from the founding and management of incredibly successful business enterprises (such as Uber). In January 1996, *Financial Post* magazine profiled 50 of the richest individuals and families in Canada, each of them with a minimum net worth of $145 million and *eight* of them worth at least $1 billion. By 2015, there were 39 Canadians on *Forbes'* 2015 list of the world's billionaires (Pelley, 2015) but there are many more.

On top of the ranking produced by *Canadian Business* (2015) is the Thomson family, with a net worth of $36.76 billion. Second on the list is Galen Weston, whose net worth is $13.67 billion. In third place there is a newcomer to the list of wealthy Canadians—namely Calgarian Garret Camp, the co-founder of Uber, who has built a net worth of $9.18 billion in less than a decade. The Rogers Family takes fourth place, with a net worth of $8.86 billion, followed by the Irving Family at $7.50 billion. With the exception of Garret Camp, these individuals and families have been at or near the top ranks of the richest Canadians for many years. Along with 85 other billionaires and 10 multi-millionaires, Canada's richest members of the upper class comprise what Karl Marx called capitalists, those who own or control most of the nation's productive property.

Apart from such immense wealth, many members of the upper class work as top executives in large corporations, often earning annual salaries in the millions. A ranking of executive compensation in Canada's largest companies (McFarland, 2011) reveals that *salaries* rarely exceed $1.5 million—however, including bonuses and stock options, annual executive compensation ranges from $185 000 to over $10 million, with roughly three-quarters coming in at over $2 million. Very few of these executives are members of Canada's wealthiest families—in other words, like Garret Camp, they made it to the upper class (and to the top 0.1 or 0.01 percent of tax filers) through their own efforts and *without* the benefit of inherited wealth. These extremely well-paid individuals are joined in the upper class by a wide range of professionals, entrepreneurs, senior-level politicians, and celebrities who have the power to shape events in Canada and sometimes even the world.

Members of the upper class also attain the highest levels of education, typically in the most expensive and highly regarded schools. Of the 50 most wealthy Canadian families or individuals, about half were of British origin and the rest were a mix of Jewish, French, other European, and one Asian. Over the next few decades, we can expect to find an increasing number of people of Asian ancestry represented in this highly select group.

UPPER-UPPERS The *upper-upper class,* often described as "high society" or "bluebloods," includes less than 1 percent of the Canadian population. Membership is usually the result of ascription, or birth, as suggested by the old quip that the easiest way to break into "society" is to be born there. These families possess enormous wealth, primarily inherited rather than earned. For this reason, members of the upper-upper class are said to have *old money*. Set apart by their wealth, members of the upper-upper class live in a world of exclusive affiliations. They inhabit elite neighbourhoods, such as Forest Hill in Toronto or Westmount in Montreal. Schools extend this privileged environment. Their children typically attend private schools such as Upper Canada College with others of similar background and complete their formal education at high-prestige universities such as Cambridge, Oxford, or Harvard. In the historical pattern of European aristocrats, they study liberal arts rather than vocationally directed subjects.

Women of the upper-upper class often maintain a full schedule of volunteer work for charitable organizations. For example, women from Toronto's upper-crust neighbourhoods are the backbone of the Toronto Symphony and the National Ballet; old-money families support these organizations, offering their time as well as funds. While helping the larger community, such charitable activities also build networks that put these families at the centre of the nation's power elite.

LOWER-UPPERS   The remaining 2 to 4 percent of the population that makes up the upper class falls into the *lower-upper class*. From the point of view of the average Canadian, such people seem every bit as privileged as the upper-upper class. The major difference, however, is that "lower-uppers" are the "working rich" who depend on earnings rather than wealth as their primary source of income. Few people in this category inherit a vast fortune from their parents, although the majority does inherit some wealth.

Especially in the eyes of members of "society," those in the lower-upper class are merely the *nouveaux riches*, people who can never savour the highest levels of prestige enjoyed by those with rich and famous grandparents. Thus, while the new rich typically live in expensive homes and own cottages on the most exclusive lakes, they often find themselves excluded from the most prestigious clubs and associations maintained by families with old money.

Historically, the dream of great success has meant joining the ranks of the lower-upper class through exceptional accomplishment. The entrepreneurial individual who makes the right business moves with split-second timing, the athlete who accepts a million-dollar contract to play in the big leagues, the computer whiz who designs a new program that sets a standard for the industry—these are the lucky and talented achievers who reach the level of the lower-upper class. Their success stories fascinate us because this kind of upward social mobility has long stood as a goal that, however unlikely, is still within the realm of the possible. A dual-earner family in which both wife and husband are professionals can make it into this lower-upper stratum of society. Members of the upper-upper class, in contrast, move in rarefied circles far from the everyday reality of the rest of us.

Check out Table 11–4 to assess your chances of making it into the lower-upper class.

The Middle Class

Encompassing about 40 to 50 percent of the Canadian population, the middle class exerts tremendous influence on our culture. Television and other mass media usually

PEOPLE OFTEN DISTINGUISH BETWEEN THE "NEW RICH" AND FAMILIES WITH "OLD MONEY" Men and women who suddenly begin to earn high incomes tend to spend their money on status symbols because they enjoy the new thrill of high-roller living and they want others to know of their success. Those who grow up surrounded by wealth, by contrast, are used to a privileged way of life and are more quiet about it. Thus the conspicuous consumption of the lower-upper class can differ dramatically from the more private pursuits and understatement of the upper-upper class.

Table 11–4 You Are Richer Than You Think

	Income by Tax Filer			
	Canada		United States	
	2006	2012	2006	2012
Top 5%	$ 89 000	$ 98 000	$165 000	$184 000
Top 1%	$181 000	$203 000	$393 000	$438 000
Top 0.01%	$2.8 million	$3.1 million	$9.4 million	$10.5 million

It is *much* easier to make it onto the "top income-tax filer" list in Canada than in the United States. Most established Canadian professionals earn salaries of $95 000 or more, as do many unionized blue-collar workers. A family with two top filers might be ranked in the top 2 or 3 percent in terms of family income.

*Canadian and American constant dollar calculators were used to convert 2006 dollars to 2012 dollars.

SOURCE: Adapted by L.M. Gerber from Report on Business, *Globe and Mail*, December 2007:32.

portray middle-class people, and most commercial advertising is directed at the "average" consumer. The middle class encompasses far more racial and ethnic diversity than the upper class. While many upper-class people—especially upper-uppers—know each other personally, such exclusiveness and familiarity do not characterize the middle class.

UPPER-MIDDLES The top half of this large category is often termed the *upper-middle class*, Higher income allows families in the upper-middle class to accumulate

FOR DECADES, FARM FAMILIES WHO WORKED HARD COULD EXPECT TO FALL WITHIN THE MIDDLE CLASS But the trend toward large-scale agribusiness has put the future of the small family farm in doubt. While many young people in rural areas are turning away from farming toward other careers, some carry on, incorporating high technology into their farm management in a determined effort to succeed.

considerable property—a comfortable house in a fairly expensive area, several automobiles, and some investments. Virtually all people in the upper-middle class receive university educations, and postgraduate degrees are common. Many go on to a high-prestige occupation (e.g., physician, engineer, lawyer, accountant, or business executive). Lacking the power of the upper class to influence national or international events, the upper-middle class often plays an important role in local political affairs.

AVERAGE-MIDDLES The rest of the middle class falls near the centre of our class structure. People in the *average-middle class* typically work in less prestigious white-collar occupations (as bank tellers, middle managers, and sales clerks) or in highly skilled blue-collar jobs (including electrical work and carpentry). Family income is sufficient to provide a secure, if modest, standard of living. Average-middle-class Canadians generally accumulate a small amount of wealth over the course of their working lives, and most will own a house. Average-middle-class men and women are likely to be high school graduates. If they do send their children to university, it is more likely to be the one closest to home to save on accommodation expenses.

The Working Class

Including about one-third of the population, the *working class* (sometimes called the *lower-middle class*) refers to people who have lower incomes than those in the middle class and little or no accumulated wealth. In Marxist terms, the working class forms the core of the industrial proletariat. The blue-collar occupations of the working class generally yield a family income that is somewhat below the national average, although unionized blue-collar workers can contribute to family incomes that are well above that level.

Many working-class jobs provide little personal satisfaction, requiring discipline but rarely imagination, and subject workers to continual supervision. These jobs also provide fewer benefits, such as dental insurance and pension plans. University is less likely to be part of the experience of children of working-class parents. The many working-class families who own their own homes are likely to own them in lower-cost neighbourhoods.

The Lower Class

The 20 percent of our population with the lowest family income makes up the *lower class*. For these people, a lack of work and little income render life unstable and insecure. About 15 percent of the Canadian population is classified as poor—meaning that their income falls below the

Greg Locke/Stray Light Media

THE LIFE OF THIS NEWFOUNDLAND FISHER HAS BEEN CHANGED DRASTICALLY BY THE MORATORIUM ON COD FISHING How do you think different classes are affected by this type of change in the local economy?

poverty line or more accurately below the official "low income cut-off" (calculated on the basis of family size and the cost of food, clothing, and shelter). While some of these people are supported entirely by social benefits, others are among the *working poor*—those whose incomes from full-time jobs or multiple part-time jobs fall short of what is required to cover the necessities of food, shelter, and clothing. The working poor have low-prestige jobs that provide minimal income and little intrinsic satisfaction. Some have managed to complete high school, but university degrees and college diplomas are relatively rare. In fact, many lower-class men and women are functionally illiterate.

Lower-class families find themselves segregated into specific, less-desirable neighbourhoods—some of which are ethnically or racially distinct (Michelson, 1988:93). While there are many poor people in small towns and rural areas where resource-based industries have collapsed or plants have closed, physical segregation of the poor is most starkly apparent in cities, where large numbers of poor people live in rental housing that is avoided by others.

Lower-class children quickly learn that others consider them to be only marginal members of society. Observing their parents and other lower-status adults, they may conclude that their own futures hold little hope for breaking the cycle of poverty. Lower-class life, then, can generate self-defeating resignation among those cut off from the resources of an affluent society; welfare dependency, as a lifestyle, can be passed from one generation to the next. Some of the poor simply give up, but others—the working poor—go to great lengths to avoid going on welfare, often working at two or three jobs to make ends meet.

In the mid-1990s, the policies of Conservative governments in Alberta and Ontario led to reductions in

Russell Lee/Corbis

COMPARED TO HIGH-INCOME PEOPLE, LOW-INCOME PEOPLE ARE HALF AS LIKELY TO REPORT GOOD HEALTH AND, ON AVERAGE, LIVE ABOUT SEVEN FEWER YEARS The toll of low income—played out in inadequate nutrition, little medical care, and high stress—is easy to see on the faces of the poor, who look old before their time.

welfare payments and tighter eligibility requirements. Soon there were fewer people on welfare, but studies have yet to identify where the missing welfare recipients went or how they are managing to survive. Relatively low unemployment rates during that period may account for some of the decline in welfare dependency.

The Difference Class Makes

11.4 **Analyze the impacts of social class position on health, values, and family life.**

Social stratification affects nearly every dimension of our lives. We will briefly examine some of the ways in which social standing is linked to our health, values, and family life.

Health

Health is closely related to social standing. Children born into poor families are three times more likely to die from disease, neglect, accidents, or violence during their first years of life than children born into privileged families. Among adults, people with above-average incomes are almost twice as likely as low-income people to describe their health as excellent. In addition, richer people live, on average, seven years longer because they eat more nutritious food, live and work in safer and less stressful environments, and get the medical care they need (Singh, 2010; Adams et al., 2012). Canadians who grow up in poverty will have difficulty maintaining a healthy diet and may rely on walk-in clinics—or the emergency room—for basic health care. Without a family doctor, they are less likely to be referred to a specialist.

Values and Attitudes

Some cultural values vary from class to class. People with old money have an unusually strong sense of family history because their social position is based on wealth passed from generation to generation. Secure in their birthright privileges, people from the upper-upper class also favour understated manners and tastes; many *nouveaux riches* engage in conspicuous consumption, using homes, cars, and even airplanes as status symbols to make a statement about their social position.

Affluent people with greater education and financial security are also more tolerant of controversial behaviour such as homosexuality. Working-class people, who grow up in an atmosphere of greater supervision and discipline, and who are less likely to attend university or college, tend to be less tolerant (Lareau, 2002).

Furthermore, social class has a great deal to do with self-concept. People with higher social standing experience more confidence in everyday interaction for the simple reason that others tend to view them as being important. In contrast, people who grow up in poverty will see themselves in less positive light and will face the world with less confidence.

Family and Gender

Social class also shapes family life. Generally, lower-class families are somewhat larger than middle-class families because of earlier marriage and less career orientation on the part of women. Labour force participation encourages women to limit family size. Also, working-class parents encourage children to conform to conventional norms and to respect authority figures. Parents of higher social standing pass on different cultural capital to their children, teaching them to express their individuality and imagination more freely. In both cases, parents are looking to the future; the odds are that less privileged children will have jobs that require them to follow rules

and that more privileged children will have careers that require more creativity (Kohn, 1977; Lareau, 2002; McLeod, 1995).

The more money a family has, the more parents can develop their children's talents and abilities. It costs a great deal to raise children—with music lessons, sports activity, and higher education—which is another reason to limit family size. The bottom line is that privilege leads to privilege as family life reproduces the class structure in each new generation.

Class also shapes our world of relationships. In a classic study of married life, Elizabeth Bott (1971; orig. 1957) found that most working-class couples divide their responsibilities according to gender roles; middle-class couples, in contrast, are more egalitarian, sharing more activities and expressing greater intimacy. Karen Walker (1995) discovered that working-class friendships typically serve as sources of material assistance; among those with higher incomes, friendships are likely to involve shared interests and leisure pursuits instead.

Social Mobility

11.5 Assess the extent of social mobility in Canada.

Canadians have a dynamic society marked by significant social movement. Earning a university degree, landing a higher-paying job, or marrying someone who earns a good income contributes to *upward social mobility*; dropping out of school, losing a job, or becoming divorced (especially for women) may result in *downward social mobility*.

Over the long term, social mobility is not so much a matter of changes in individuals as changes in society itself. In the first half of the twentieth century, for example, industrialization expanded the North American economy, pushing up living standards. Even people who were not good swimmers rode the rising tide of prosperity. More recently, *structural social mobility* in a downward direction has dealt many people economic setbacks.

Sociologists distinguish between shorter- and longer-term changes in social position. **Intragenerational social mobility** is *a change in social position occurring during a person's lifetime* (*intra* is Latin for "within"). **Intergenerational social mobility**, *upward or downward social mobility of children in relation to their parents*, is important because it usually reveals long-term changes in society, such as industrialization, that affect everyone.

intragenerational social mobility a change in social position occurring during a person's lifetime

intergenerational social mobility upward or downward social mobility of children in relation to their parents

Social Mobility in Canada

While the American dream may be attributed to people south of the border, Canadians share, to some extent, the belief that those who apply themselves can get ahead and that each new generation will do better than the last. Clearly, that is the hope of most of our immigrants. But how much social mobility is there in Canada?

Data from the 1986 General Social Survey revealed that Canadians have been a little more likely to experience upward rather than downward mobility (Creese et al., 1991). Compared with their fathers, 48 percent of women moved upward, while 40 percent moved downward; the comparable figures for men are 39 and 36 percent, respectively. Only 12 percent of women and 26 percent of men experienced no mobility at all, meaning that they ended up in the same occupational category as their fathers. Occupational inheritance (following in Dad's footsteps) occurs most commonly among men whose fathers are in the professional, white-collar, and farming categories. Specific occupational inheritance has been less common for women because of the types of occupations traditionally available to them.

While overall educational levels are increasing, class background continues to affect educational attainment: The higher the level of education and occupation of one's father, the more years of schooling one is likely to complete. Furthermore, a person's first job is *principally* affected by his or her level of education. Therefore, parental education and occupation have an impact on occupational status, not directly but through their effects on the educational attainment of the younger generation. Thus, a physician passes the occupation on to a son or daughter *if* he or she inspires that child to jump the educational hurdles required to gain admission to and complete medical school. *Education* is the key to occupational mobility in Canada. If family background has an impact, it is through its effect on schooling. Many parents have learned that one cannot impose education upon children—not if the son or daughter has no interest in preparing for medical or law school. Others have also noted a general lack of occupational inheritance in Canada. In a study of occupational mobility over four generations, Goyder and Curtis (1979) found that the occupations of great-grandfathers had no bearing whatsoever on those of their great-grandsons. Occupationally speaking, the descendants were all over the map. On the basis of their findings and those of others who have studied the extreme upper and lower ends of the spectrum, Goyder and Curtis concluded that the "two types of processes may well occur together: high overall three-generation mobility in the general population along with low three-generation mobility in poverty and elite groups" (p. 229). In other words, those at the very top and bottom of the socio-economic ladder may experience substantial occupational inheritance, while those in the middle do not.

Research points to the conclusion that marriage has an important effect on social standing. In a study of women and men in their forties, Jay Zagorsky (2006) found that people who marry and stay married accumulate about twice as much wealth as people who remain single or who divorce. Reasons for this difference include the fact that couples who live together typically enjoy double incomes and also pay roughly half the bills they would have if they were single and living in separate households.

It is also likely that, compared to single people, married men and women work harder in their jobs and save more money. Why? The main reason is that they are working not just for themselves but also to support others who are counting on them.

Just as marriage pushes social standing upward, divorce usually makes social position go down. Couples who divorce take on the financial burden of supporting two households. After divorce, women are hurt more than men because it is typically the man who earns more. Many women who divorce lose not only most of their income but also benefits such as health care, pension, and insurance coverage (Weitzman, 1996).

Poverty in Canada

11.6 Discuss patterns and explanations of poverty in the Canadian population.

Social stratification simultaneously creates haves and have-nots. Poverty, therefore, inevitably exists within all systems of social inequality. Sociologists employ the concept of poverty in two different ways, however. **Relative poverty**, which is by definition universal and inevitable, refers to *the deprivation of some people in relation to those who have more*. The richest and most egalitarian of societies have some members who live in relative poverty. Much more serious is **absolute poverty**, or *a deprivation of resources that is life-threatening*. Defined in this way, poverty is a pressing, but solvable, human problem. The global dimensions of absolute poverty place the lives of perhaps 1.3 billion people—one in five of the earth's population—at risk. Even in affluent Canada, with its social safety net, families go hungry, live in inadequate housing, and endure poor health because of wrenching poverty.

relative poverty the deprivation of some people in relation to those who have more

absolute poverty a deprivation of resources that is life-threatening

The Extent of Canadian Poverty

Poverty statistics are based on the "poverty line," also known as the "low income cut-off." People who spend at least 55 percent of their pre-tax income on food, clothing, and shelter are considered to be below the poverty line. By that measure, a recent high of 15.7 percent of the population fell below the poverty line in 1995—in a recession period. By 2004, the proportion had dropped, fairly steadily, to 11.2 percent. This drop in the proportion of the population below the poverty line gave rise to a little excitement at the *Globe and Mail*, where an editorial on April 1, 2006, claimed that "The poor, it seems, do not always get poorer. The number of low-income families actually declined in 2004. And child poverty, despite alarming bulletins from the activists, isn't getting worse either" (p. A22). The editorial followed up on front-page coverage of the issue—"Growth spurs decline in poverty" (Scoffield, 2006)—and a major analytical article with dramatic graphs (Mahoney, 2006c) *published on the previous day*. Alas, the proportion of Canada's population falling below the low-income cutoff climbed to 12.9 percent by 2011 (Statistics Canada, 2011).

In the past, Canada's lack of progress in eliminating poverty prompted a United Nations committee to sharply criticize the Canadian government "for allowing poverty and homelessness to persist at disturbing levels in one of the world's richest countries" (York, 1993:A1). At the time, about half of Canada's single mothers and a million children lived in poverty, and many Canadians depended on food banks to deal with hunger. By 2009, poverty levels had declined so that 21.5 percent of children in female lone-parent families lived below the poverty line—down from 60 percent in 1985. In 2010, 43 percent of female lone-parent families with children under 18 fell below the poverty line; with children under 6, the percentage jumps to 59.3, which is right back where it was in 1985. Whatever the precise numbers, poverty means *hunger*, and many people at lower income levels are forced to rely on food banks and soup kitchens, both of which are run by charitable organizations in Canada. The demand for food banks has increased substantially over the past few years to a point where, today, there are more than 650 food banks that feed more than 850 000 people each month (Food Banks Canada, 2016).

A 1998 United Nations report also criticized Canada for its poor response in dealing with poverty. Canada placed tenth among 17 industrialized nations—behind Sweden, the Netherlands, Germany, Norway, Italy, Finland, France, Japan, and Denmark—in "spreading around the wealth," reducing social inequality, and avoiding the immense social costs of impoverishment (Duffy & Mandell, 2001:79). The fact that so many people continue to resort to food banks, which function only because some people volunteer to staff them while others donate food, is particularly distressing in a country where we have the resources to alleviate poverty, if only we have the political will.

Who Are the Poor?

While no single description covers all poor people, poverty is pronounced within certain segments of our population. Women, children, some visible minorities, and people living in rural areas are all at higher risk of being poor—as are Aboriginal people. Regional disparities in economic development and income are also in evidence, in that poverty is a particularly acute problem in the Atlantic provinces and rural areas across the country.

AGE The burden of poverty falls heavily on Canadian children. Child poverty rates rose from a low of 11.7 percent in 1989 to a high of 17.5 in 1995, before dropping to 11.7 percent in 2005—mainly because of "the federal government's child tax benefit, which has been rising steadily over the past decade" (Scoffield, 2006). By 2011, 13.3 percent of children under 18 years of age were living in poverty (Statistics Canada, 2011). Canada has taken steps to eradicate child poverty—something that the Liberal party vowed to do during the federal elections of 1993, 1997, and 2000. The Conservative government's payment of $1200 per year per child under age six was another attempt to eradicate child poverty. And, most recently, the 2016 budget of the new Liberal government targets child poverty once again. Yet, despite our best efforts, child poverty persists—notably among Aboriginals and in lone-parent families headed by women.

A generation ago, the elderly were at the greatest risk of poverty. In 1985, the poverty rates for women and men aged 65 and over were 19.3 and 8.4 percent, respectively; by 2004, the rates had dropped to 7.3 and 3.5 percent. Yet by 2011, the poverty rates for women and men aged 65 years of age and over had increased again to 13.9 and 8.4 percent (Statistics Canada, 2011). Older women and men *in economic families* have poverty rates of 2.8 and 4.0 percent, while *unattached* women and men 65 and over experience much higher rates of poverty—at 34.0 and 27.0 percent respectively (Statistics Canada, 2011). Better pension support from the government and employers was supposed to reduce poverty among the elderly but, at least on the surface, there is little evidence of such reduction. This is particularly discouraging at a time when the movement of baby boomers into their retirement years means increases in the number and proportion of elderly among us.

EDUCATION Education is another factor that determines the likelihood of having an income below the poverty line. People who have higher levels of education are less likely to be unemployed and more likely to be employed full-time, to earn higher incomes, and to remain above the poverty line. In other words, the incidence of poverty drops with each added level of education. Looking back at Table 11–3, we see that median income (after tax) for those with no certification whatsoever or with only a high-school diploma approaches $18 000 and $22 000 respectively. Imagine trying to support a family with two children on that income. Since the low-income cutoff takes family size into account, it is very likely that these families will fall below the poverty line—especially if they are supported by a single wage-earner.

RACE AND ETHNICITY   The likelihood of experiencing poverty is related to race and ethnicity in Canada, but the ranking of various categories is not necessarily what we might expect. A study based on 1986 census data offered some surprising results. Those of English origin are not all at the top of the income hierarchy; in fact, in a ranking of 60 ethnic and racial categories—by average male income for those employed full-time, all year—those of English origin ranked twenty-fifth (Gerber, 1990:79). The French, too, were near the middle. Canadians of Welsh and Scottish background appeared in the top 15, along with those of Jewish and Japanese descent.

In the lowest 15 categories we find Black, West Indian, and Latin American people, some people of Asian origins, and Aboriginal peoples. The only categories that rank below Aboriginal peoples are groups that tend to be recent immigrants and refugees (Chileans and other Latin Americans, Vietnamese, Haitians, Laotians, and Cambodians). While male income for those employed full time is only one indicator of economic well-being, the rank-ordering by race or ethnicity is suggestive. We would expect to find that, at the time, more of the individuals or families in the lowest 15 categories had incomes below the poverty line.

The Power of Society figure that opens this chapter suggests that ethnic inequality persists today. The proportions below the low income cut-off in 2010 ranged from 11 or 14 percent for those of Italian, French, and Japanese origins to 24 or 28 percent for First Nations, Mexican, and Nigerian people—and an astounding 48 percent for Canadians with Somali origins. There is no doubt whatsoever that, despite Canada's social safety net, ethnicity is a powerful predictor of poverty levels.

Figure 11–5 illustrates the fact that immigrants who arrived in Canada prior to 1961 or 1970 had higher average income (in 2005) than those who arrived more recently. As you move left to right—from the immigrants who have been here for 45 years or more to the most recent arrivals—income drops off steadily for all immigrants (the lower line on the graph) as well for immigrants who have at least bachelor's degrees (the upper line on the graph) The most dramatic—almost precipitous—decline in income occurs among immigrants with university degrees. In order to make sense of this graph, you need to know that it usually takes up to 15 years for immigrants to settle in and reach their peak earning power. It took immigrants—highly educated or not—that long to catch up to or surpass their Canadian-born counterparts. The immigrants who arrived here prior to 1970 had 35 *years* to acquire that 2005 income. For obvious reasons, it would be impossible for those who arrived after 2000 to reach full earning potential by 2005.

Let's look at the other side of the coin. In the year 1990—15 years prior to 2005—one would expect to see higher incomes for both categories of immigrants. The income gap between immigrants with university degrees and all immigrants should be wider. The economic climate in Canada has changed for all immigrants, one of the main reasons being that Canada has become a highly credentialed country. A physician arriving from India or Egypt has

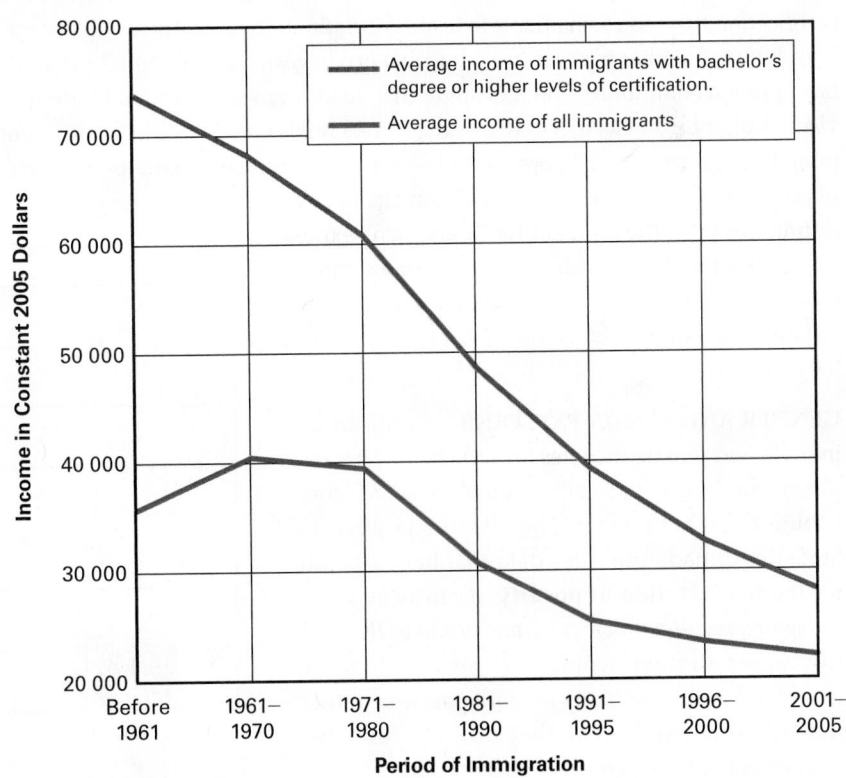

Figure 11–5   Average Income of Immigrants (in Constant 2005 Dollars) by Period of Immigration and Educational Achievement

SOURCE: Data were compiled and incorporated into this figure by L.M. Gerber from Statistics Canada, 2006 Census, Catalogue no. 97-563-XCB2006006.

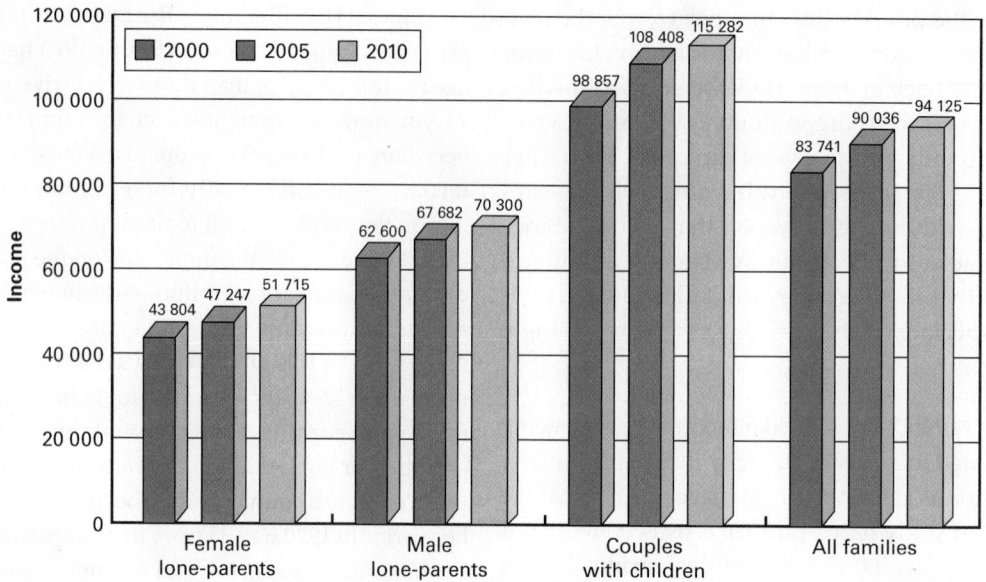

Figure 11–6 Average Family Income* by Family Structure, 2000, 2005, and 2010

*Incomes are in constant 2010 dollars, meaning that inflation is taken into account.

SOURCES: Compiled from Statistics Canada, 2006 Census, catalogue no. 97-563-XCB2006006

to overcome many barriers in order to practise in Canada. She must retrain, pass exams, find a residency (which is difficult even for Canadian medical school graduates), and get certification from the Canadian Medical Association. Then, in order to set up her practice (with hospital privileges), she has to find a community and a hospital that needs her services. A plumber or electrician with foreign credentials must jump through a series of hoops as well—with no guarantee of acquiring Canadian certification. Then again, any immigrant faces the demand for "Canadian" experience. It is much more difficult, today, for an immigrant to find employment and get established in the Canadian labour market. Figure 11–5 tells this side of the story too.

GENDER AND FAMILY PATTERNS The disparity in male and female incomes and the fact that lone-parent families are normally headed by women contribute to higher rates of poverty among women. Statistics Canada provides data that help account for the **feminization of poverty**, *the trend by which women represent an increasing proportion of the poor.* Compared to men, women are less likely to be employed and more likely to work part time rather than full time. And, when they do work full time, women get only 71 percent of male income.

Lone-parent families headed by men or women have lower income than two-parent families. Female lone-parent families have the lowest average income, as shown in Figure 11–6, and

have the largest percentage falling below the low income cut-off (see Figure 11–7). To top it off, an astounding 59 percent of female lone-parent families with children under six years of age live in poverty. (This is down from 67 percent in 2005.) Single mothers with children under 18 are less likely to live in poverty (at 43 percent). Male lone-parent families experience roughly half of the females' poverty rates.

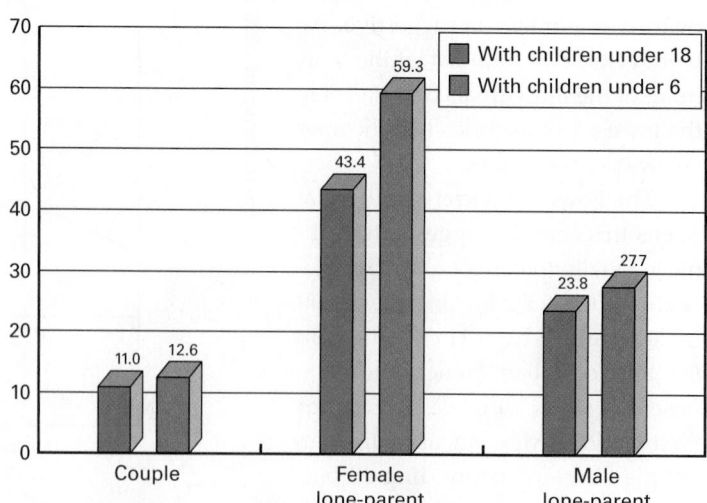

Figure 11–7 Prevalence of Low Income by Family Structure, 2010

SOURCE: Compiled by L.M. Gerber from Statistics Canada, 2006 Census, Catalogue no. 97-563-XCB2006019 and 2011 National Household Survey, Catalogue no. 99-014-X2011038.

The real winners here are two-parent families who have low-income rates of 11 and 13 percent, depending on the ages of their children. In addition, the average 2010 income of two-parent families is more than double than of the single-mother family—$115 000 and $52 000 respectively.

It is clear, then, that lone-parent families have substantially lower incomes than two-parent families, and that female lone-parent families are the most disadvantaged. Issues of pay equity, employment equity, family structure, and age of children combine to increase the incidence of poverty among women, thereby contributing to the feminization of poverty.

Explaining Poverty

The presence of 4.8 million poor people in one of the world's most affluent societies raises serious social and moral concerns. It also sparks considerable controversy within Canada—and from abroad. Many Canadians concur with the UN committees mentioned earlier, arguing that our government should take a much more active role in eradicating poverty. Others feel that the poor must bear responsibility for themselves. It is also possible to argue that *both* governments and the poor themselves need to contribute to the solution. The arguments underlying these approaches to the problem of poverty together frame a lively and pressing political debate.

ONE VIEW: BLAME THE POOR   Proponents on this side of the issue hold the view that *the poor are primarily responsible for their own poverty.* In this land of immigration and once seemingly unlimited resources and opportunities, we have embraced the notion that people are largely responsible for their own social standing. This approach assumes that our society offers considerable opportunity for anyone able and willing to take advantage of it. The poor, then, are those with fewer skills, less schooling, lower motivation, or, perhaps, a debilitating drug addiction—in sum, people who are somehow undeserving.

Anthropologist Oscar Lewis (1961) illustrates this approach in his studies of Latin American poverty. Lewis claims that the poor become trapped in a *culture of poverty* that fosters resignation to one's plight. Socialized in this environment, children come to believe that there is little point in aspiring to a better life. The result is a self-perpetuating cycle of poverty. Edward Banfield (1974) adds the contention that, where there is intense poverty, there exists a distinctive lower-class subculture that denigrates and erodes personal achievement. One element of this subculture encourages living for the moment, rather than looking toward the future by engaging in hard work, saving, and other behaviour likely to promote upward social mobility. In Banfield's view, poor people who live largely for the moment perpetuate their own poverty; he defines this kind of behaviour as basically irresponsible,

AFRICAN-AMERICAN ARTIST HENRY OSSAWA TANNER CAPTURED THE HUMILITY AND HUMANITY OF IMPOVERISHED PEOPLE IN HIS PAINTING *THE THANKFUL POOR*   This insight is important in a society that tends to define poor people as morally unworthy and deserving of their bitter plight.

Henry Ossawa Tanner (1859–1937)/Art Resource, NY

and he concludes that the poor reap more or less what they deserve.

COUNTERPOINT: BLAME SOCIETY   The other view of the issue is that *society is primarily responsible for poverty.* This alternative position, argued by William Ryan (1976), holds that society—not the poor—is responsible for poverty because of the way resources are distributed. In global context, societies that distribute wealth very disproportionately face a significant poverty problem. Societies that strive for more equality (such as Sweden and Japan) lack such extremes of social stratification. Poverty, Ryan insists, is not inevitable: The problem is simply a matter of low income, not personal deficiencies. Ryan interprets any lack of ambition on the part of poor people as a *consequence* rather than a *cause* of their lack of opportunity. He therefore dismisses Banfield's analysis as little more than "blaming the victims" for their own suffering. In Ryan's view, social policies that empower the poor would give them real economic opportunity, and this should yield greater equality.

EVALUATE

Each of these explanations of poverty has won its share of public support, and each has advocates among government policy-makers. Some, particularly those on the right of the political spectrum, believe that society should strive to encourage equality of opportunity, but should otherwise adopt a laissez-faire attitude toward the poor. Others, those on the political left, hold that society should actively reduce poverty by redistributing income more proportionately, providing a comprehensive daycare program like that of Quebec, or ensuring a guaranteed minimum income for every family.

Since the heads of many low-income families do not have jobs, their poverty is attributed to *not holding a job*. But the reasons that people do not work are a reflection on society as much as on the individuals concerned. Middle-class women combine working and child rearing, but doing so is much harder for poor women who cannot afford child care. Quebec is the exception with respect to child care, which is available at the phenomenal rate of $7 per day—to those who are accepted to the limited number of spaces. In the rest of Canada, few employers provide child-care programs for their employees, and few low-income workers can afford to buy this service from the private sector. Where child-care subsidies are provided, parents may still find that, when all costs are considered, it is cheaper to stay at home and take care of one's own children. The federal government currently provides $1200 per child annually to parents of children under age six, with the intention of supporting choice in child care. Among those choices is that of one parent staying at home to care for young children.

Most poor men report that either there are no jobs to be found, illness or disability has sidelined them, or, in the case of the elderly, they have retired. Overall, poor adults are poor not by choice, but because they know of no alternatives. These people may be among those for whom welfare (or social assistance) is a lifeline. See the Thinking Critically box for a discussion of Canada's welfare dilemma.

CHECK YOUR LEARNING Explain the view that the poor should take responsibility for poverty and the view that society is responsible. Which is closer to your own view?

Thinking Critically

The Welfare Dilemma: Canadian Perspectives

There is a remarkable consensus in this country regarding welfare: Nobody likes it. The political left criticizes it as an inadequate response to poverty; those on the right charge that it is hurting the people it allegedly helps and driving the country to bankruptcy; and the poor themselves find welfare to be a complex, confusing, and often degrading program.

Critics on *the political right* contend that welfare has actually *worsened* the problem of poverty for two reasons. First, it has eroded the traditional family by making it economically beneficial for women to have children outside of marriage and by contributing to the rapid rise in out-of-wedlock births among poor people. Second, government assistance undermines self-reliance among the poor and fosters dependency. Clearly, from the perspective of the right, welfare has strayed far from its original purpose of helping non-working women with children make the transition to self-sufficiency—typically, after divorce or the death of a husband. Instead, trapped in dependency, poor women raise children who will become poor adults.

The *political left* points to a double standard for assessing government social programs. Why, it asks, is there so much outrage at the thought of the government transferring money to poor mothers and children when most "welfare" goes to relatively rich people? From the perspective of the left, the amounts spent on welfare, while not negligible, pale in comparison with the tax write-offs received by more affluent people for the registered retirement savings plans (RRSPs) they buy each year. And what about the billions of dollars in tax write-offs for corporations, many of which are enjoying record profits? As the left sees it, "wealthfare" costs the country a great deal more than "welfare," even though public opinion supports the opposite view.

Critics claim that the political right—and much public opinion—distorts our understanding of the functions of social assistance. Images of irresponsible "welfare bums" mask the fact that most poor families who turn to public assistance are truly needy. Throughout Canada in recent years, the trend has been to slash welfare or social assistance rates as a deficit-reduction measure. Whatever the merits of social assistance, the political left faults it as a band-aid approach to the growing social problems of unemployment and poverty in Canada.

As for the charge that social assistance undermines families, the political left concedes that the proportion of single-parent families is rising, but disputes the argument that welfare is to blame. Rather, single parenting is a widespread cultural trend found at all class levels in most industrial societies. Therefore, leftist critics conclude, welfare or social assistance programs are attacked not because they have failed, but because they benefit poor people, a segment of the population long scorned as "undeserving." Our cultural tradition of equating wealth with virtue, and poverty with vice, allows rich people to display privilege as an indicator of ability—while poverty carries a negative stigma.

Many on the political right believe that welfare should be limited. Those on the left, in contrast, want to both improve and expand social assistance. Are there areas of common ground in this debate? In the mid-1990s, Conservative governments in Ontario and Alberta introduced reforms amounting to "workfare." Ontario's workfare program, called Ontario Works, still exists despite the fact that Dalton McGuinty took over as Ontario's Liberal premier in 2003, followed by Kathleen Wynne in 2013. Is this an indicator of "common ground" between left and right?

What Do You Think?

1. Should provinces and territories slash their welfare budgets while allowing tax writeoffs for the purchase of RRSPs?

2. Do you think welfare has become a way of life for many people?

3. Would an expanded welfare program lessen the extent of poverty in Canada? Why?

The Working Poor

Not all poor people are jobless. At various points in this chapter, tables and figures refer to salaries of people who work full time, all year. Many of these salaries—for women, for certain occupations, and for people belonging to specific ethnic and racial categories—are low relative to the official poverty line. If these people, working full-time, have incomes that are below the poverty line for individuals, what happens if they are single parents with two or three children? The working poor include the men and women who labour for at least 50 weeks of the year and yet cannot escape poverty; many people who involuntarily work part-time are also included among the working poor. Such "working poverty" places the poor in a bind: Their jobs provide low wages that barely allow them to make ends meet, but consume the time and energy needed to obtain training or schooling that might open new doors. People in this situation are often reluctant or simply unable to risk the jobs they do have in hopes of finding something better. Even with minimum hourly wages of $9.27 in Yukon to $11 in Nunavut (in 2012), a full-time worker could not support a family above the official poverty line.

Individual ability and initiative play a part in shaping everyone's social position. On balance, though, the weight of sociological evidence points to society—not to individual character traits—as the primary cause of poverty. This is because the poor are categories of people who contend with special barriers and limited opportunities.

Homelessness

As a society, we have failed to ensure an adequate supply of affordable housing, so many low-income people

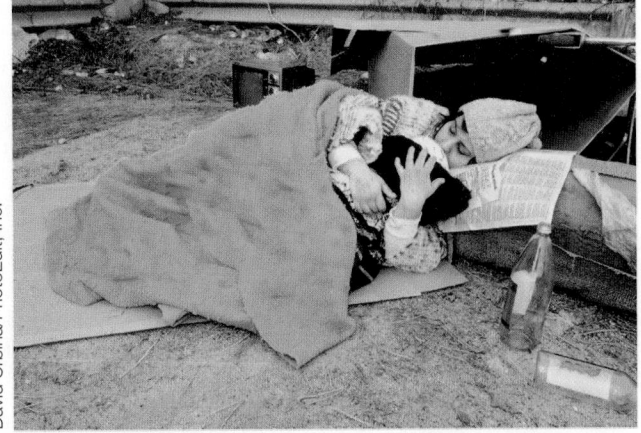

David Urbina/PhotoEdit, Inc.

SOCIAL SCIENTISTS DEBATE THE CAUSES OF POVERTY
Some cite the failings of individuals (lack of initiative or drug abuse), while others point to flaws in society, including minimum-wage levels that do not allow a full-time worker to support a family. One of the most disturbing patterns to emerge in recent years is the presence of young families among the homeless in Canada's largest cities.

in Canada cannot afford even basic housing. In light of the enormous wealth of our country—and its purported commitment to providing opportunity and/or social safety nets for everyone—homelessness may be fairly described as a societal scar that demands an effective response.

Throughout Canada, thousands of people live on the streets, in various often temporary shelters, and even in our jails. The familiar stereotypes of homeless people—men sleeping in doorways and women carrying everything they own in a shopping bag—have been undermined by the reality of the "new" homeless: those thrown out of work by plant closings; people forced out of apartments by rising rents, condominium conversions, or "gentrification" (e.g., converting rooming houses into expensive single-family homes); and people unable to meet mortgage or rent payments because they must work for low wages. Clearly, no stereotype paints a complete picture of the homeless. But virtually all homeless people have one thing in common: poverty.

For that reason, the explanations of poverty already offered also apply to homelessness. One side of the debate places responsibility on personal traits of the homeless themselves. Perhaps one-third of homeless people are mentally ill; others are addicted to alcohol or other drugs. Some, for whatever reason, seem unable to cope in a complex and highly competitive society (Bassuk, 1984; Whitman, 1989). On the other side, advocates assert that homelessness results from *societal* factors, including a lack of low-income housing and the economic transition toward low-paying jobs (Bohannon, 1991; Kaufman, 2004). Fully one-third of all homeless people are now entire families, and children are the fastest-growing category of the homeless.

No one disputes that a large proportion of homeless people have personal difficulties to some degree, although how much is cause and how much is effect is difficult to untangle. But structural changes in the Canadian economy coupled with declining government support for lower-income people have all contributed to homelessness. In the winter of 1995–1996, the Toronto churches that provide emergency overnight accommodation for the homeless found that more *families* were appearing on their doorsteps. Some of these families were evicted by landlords when reduced welfare payments could no longer cover their rent. In the same winter (a record-setting one for cold in Toronto), at least two homeless people froze to death while huddled in their makeshift shelters. One man, who died under a highway ramp, did not even have shoes on his feet.

A comprehensive response to homelessness must consider both personal and societal dimensions of the problem. Increasing the supply of low-income housing (other than shelters) is one important step. In addition, low-income people must have the opportunity to earn the income necessary to pay for housing. Homelessness, however, is not only a housing problem—it is also a human problem. People who endure months or years of insecure living come to need various types of social services.

The Sociology and the Media box provides insight into an attempt to produce a census of the homeless in Toronto.

Social stratification extends far beyond the borders of Canada. In fact, as noted in the chapter on Global Stratification, the most striking social inequality is found not within any one nation but in the different living standards from nation to nation around the world.

Sociology and the Media

Counting the Homeless in Toronto

The census of Canada, which counts and assesses the characteristics of our population, is carried out in the years ending in 1 (i.e., 1981 or 2001) and 6 (i.e., 1976 or 2006). Since almost all census forms are mailed to home addresses, homeless people fall through the cracks—just as they do for the General Social Survey, which asks much more detailed questions relating to overall well-being. As a result, we know very little about the numbers and characteristics of the homeless anywhere in Canada.

For the first time, on May 19, 2006, Toronto undertook a census of its homeless population—involving 1600 volunteers and 400 paid team leaders (earning $100 each), who covered the downtown core and outlying areas. *National Post* journalist James Cowan (2006) reported on the survey, its methodology, and general reactions to the survey itself. A number of people—including some at the Scott Mission, which feeds the poor and homeless—were cynical about the whole process. While the volunteers generally were greeted warmly by the homeless themselves, some treated the project "with a mixture of skepticism and curiosity." For many of the homeless, though, it was the first time they had ever been asked, formally, about their opinions, needs, or identities.

The survey itself—which cost $90 000—was conducted as follows: "Working in three to four-person groups, half of the teams were assigned to blanket the downtown core. Additional teams were sent to spots in Etobicoke, Scarborough, and North York where homeless people are believed to live, as well as 100 randomly selected locations" and 60 Toronto shelters (Cowan, 2006). High-risk areas—such as the Don Valley and underneath bridges or the elevated Gardiner Expressway—were covered by city staff instead of volunteers. Cowan noted one other thing: "Each homeless person who completed the survey received a $5 gift certificate for Tim Hortons, McDonald's, Pizza Pizza, or Country Style."

Other *National Post* journalists were at work that night. Peter Kuitenbrouwer (2006) sat through the night with Dave, Bonnie, and Cheryle, homeless people settled down at the corner of Bathurst and Queen Street West. He heard their life stories and found out what Dave—father of four and a drywaller who became homeless after tearing the rotator cuff in his shoulder—thought of the census: "I think it's a crock of s_____." The obvious solution, according to Dave and Bonnie, is more affordable housing. The three were in plain view and were clearly homeless, with Cheryle lying on a blue sleeping bag fighting pneumonia, but they "never saw hide nor hair of a census-taker." Kuitenbrouwer therefore titled his story "The Uncounted Ones."

In the meantime, Jacob Richler (2006) looked at the problem of overcounting. By posing as a homeless person himself, he answered the survey questions several times over: "'Have you already been interviewed tonight by someone wearing a name tag like this?' 'No,' I say, discretely patting the pocketful of $5 meal coupons I've been collecting at the rate of one per chat all night." Clearly, some homeless people were missed by the census-takers and others were interviewed numerous times. The attempt to count every homeless person—once each—clearly was flawed in execution.

What Do You Think?

1. Do you feel that this city census of the homeless was worthwhile or a waste of $90 000?

2. What kinds of questions would you have asked the homeless if you were coordinating these interviews?

3. Under what circumstances might you find yourself among the homeless? Can homelessness happen to anyone?

Seeing Sociology in Everyday Life

CHAPTER 11   Social Class in Canada

How do we understand inequality in our society?

This chapter sketches the class structure of Canada and explains how factors such as race and ethnicity are linked to social standing. You know, for example, that poverty rates are higher among Black and Aboriginal people as well as among new immigrants. Unattached elders and single-parent families headed by women are also very likely to be poor. How accurately do the mass media—that is, the American television shows we watch—reflect the reality of inequality in our society? Look at the three photos of television shows, one from back in the 1950s and the other two from today. What messages about social standing, and how we get there, does each show convey?

> **Hint** In general, the mass media present social standing as a reflection of an individual's personal traits and sometimes sheer luck. In *The Millionaire*, wealth was visited on some people for no apparent reason at all. In *The Bachelor*, women try to gain the approval of a man. In *America's Next Top Model*, the key to success is good looks and personal style. But social structure is also involved in ways that we easily overlook. Is there any significance to the fact that (as of 2011) all the bachelors on that show have been White? Do "good looks" matter as much to men they do to women? Is becoming a millionaire really a matter of luck? Does social standing result from personal competition as much as television shows suggest?

IN *THE MILLIONAIRE*, A POPULAR TELEVISION SHOW THAT RAN FROM 1955 UNTIL 1960, A VERY RICH MAN (WHO WAS NEVER FULLY SHOWN ON CAMERA) HAD THE CURIOUS HOBBY OF GIVING AWAY $1 MILLION TO OTHER PEOPLE HE HAD NEVER EVEN MET Each week, he gave his personal assistant, Michael Anthony, a cheque to pass along to "the next millionaire." Anthony tracked down the person and handed over the money, and the story went on to reveal how such great wealth from out of nowhere changed someone's life for better (or sometimes for worse). What does this story line seem to suggest about social class position?

IN THE TV SHOW *THE BACHELOR*, FIRST AIRED IN 2002, A YOUNG BACHELOR WORKS HIS WAY THROUGH A COLLECTION OF 25 ATTRACTIVE YOUNG WOMEN, BEGINNING WITH GROUP DATES, MOVING ON TO OVERNIGHT VISITS WITH THREE "FINALISTS," AND (IN MOST CASES) PROPOSING TO HIS "FINAL SELECTION" Much of the interaction takes place in a lavish, 697-square-metre (7500-square-foot) home somewhere in southern California. What does this show suggest is the key to social position? What message does it promote about the importance of marriage for women?

Lauren Browdy/Alamy Stock Photo

PROJECT RUNWAY, WHICH BEGAN IN 2004, PLACES TWELVE OR MORE FASHION DESIGNERS IN COMPETITION, GRADUALLY ELIMINATING THEM UNTIL ONLY ONE "WINNER" REMAINS
What messages about social position and achieving success does this show present to young people?

Seeing Sociology in *Your* Everyday Life

1. During an evening of television viewing, assess the social class level of the characters you see on various shows. In each case, explain why you assign someone a particular social position. Do you find many clearly upper-class people? Middle-class people? Working-class people? Poor people? Describe the patterns you find.

2. Develop several questions that together will let you measure social class position. The trick is to decide what you think social class really means. Then try your questions on several adults, refining the questions as you proceed.

3. Social stratification involves how a society distributes resources. It also has a relational dimension—social inequality guides *with whom* we do and do not interact and also *how* we interact with people. Can you give examples of how social class differences guide social interaction in your everyday life?

Making the Grade

CHAPTER 11 Social Class in Canada

Dimensions of Social Inequality

11.1 Describe the distribution of income and wealth in Canada.

Social stratification involves many dimensions:

- *Income*—Earnings from work and investments are unequal. In Canada, the poorest 20 percent of families receive a quarter (i.e., roughly 4.8 percent of the total income pie) of what they "should" if income were equally distributed. The richest 20 percent earn double their "fair share" of the income pie (i.e., 44.3 percent of the income pie).
- *Wealth*—The total value of all assets minus debts (i.e., wealth) is distributed even more unequally than income. In Canada, we do not report our assets or wealth annually, but we can be sure that the richest 20 percent of families have many times more (perhaps four times more) the real estate, stocks, businesses, private aircraft, expensive cars, and savings of the poorest 20 percent.
- *Power*—Income and wealth are important sources of power.
- *Occupational prestige*—Work generates not only income but also prestige. White-collar jobs (especially professional occupations) generally offer more income and prestige than blue-collar jobs. Many lower-prestige jobs are performed by women, visible minorities, or recent immigrants.
- *Schooling*—Schooling affects both occupation and income. Some categories of people have greater opportunities for schooling than others.

> **income** occupational wages or salaries, earnings from investments, and government transfer payments (e.g., welfare)
> **wealth** the total amount of money and other assets, minus outstanding debts

Stratification in Canada: Merit and Caste

11.2 Explain how one's position at birth affects social stranding later in life.

Although Canada is a meritocracy, social position in this country involves some caste elements:

- *Ancestry*—Being born into a particular family affects a person's opportunities for schooling, occupation, and income.
- *Race and Ethnicity*—Families of European ancestry enjoy high social standing based on income and

wealth. In contrast, Aboriginal and most visible minority families are disadvantaged.
- *Gender*—On average, women have less income, wealth, and occupational prestige than men.

Social Classes in Canada

11.3 Describe the various social class positions in Canadian society.

Defining **social classes** in Canada is difficult because of low status consistency and relatively high social mobility. But we can describe four general rankings:

- the upper class
- the middle class
- the working class
- the lower class

Upper Class—5 percent of the population. Most members of the upper-upper class, or "high society," inherited their wealth; the lower-upper class, or "working rich," work at high-paying jobs.

Middle Class—40 to 50 percent of the population. People in the upper-middle class have significant wealth and almost all attend university; average-middles have less prestige, do white-collar work, and are likely to be high school graduates.

Working Class—30 to 35 percent of the population. People in the lower-middle class do blue-collar work; their children are less likely to attend university.

Lower Class—20 percent of the population. Most people in the lower class lack financial security due to low income; many live below the poverty line; some complete high school but university and college attendance is relatively rare.

The Difference Class Makes

11.4 Analyze the impacts of social class position on health, values, and family life.

Health

- Rich people, on average, live longer and receive better health care than poor people.

Values and Attitudes

- Affluent people, with greater education and financial security, display greater tolerance than working-class people.

- Affluent people tend to be more conservative on economic issues and more liberal on social issues than poor people.
- Affluent people, who are better served by the political system, are more likely to vote than poor people.

Family and Gender

- Affluent families pass on advantages in the form of "cultural capital" to their children.
- Class also shapes the division of family responsibilities, with lower-class people maintaining more traditional gender roles.

Social Mobility

11.5 Assess the extent of social mobility in Canada.

- Social mobility is common in Canada, as it is in other high-income countries, but typically only small changes occur from one generation to the next.
- Historically, Aboriginal people, visible minorities, and women have had less opportunity for upward mobility than others in Canada.
- The expectation of upward social mobility is deeply rooted in our culture. Although high-income families are earning more and more, many average families are struggling to hold on to what they have.
- Marriage encourages upward social mobility. Divorce lowers social standing.
- The global reorganization of work has created upward social mobility for educated people but has hurt average workers, whose factory jobs have moved overseas and who are forced to take low-wage service work.

intragenerational social mobility a change in social position occurring during a person's lifetime
intergenerational social mobility upward or downward social mobility of children in relation to their parents

Poverty in Canada

11.6 Discuss patterns and explanations of poverty among Canadians.

Poverty Profile

- In 2011, 12.9 percent of Canada's population was classified as poor or falling below the low income cut-off.
- Children under age 18 are overrepresented among the poor—especially if they are in female lone-parent families.
- Aboriginal individuals and members of visible minorities are more likely to be poor than other Canadians.
- The **feminization of poverty** means that more poor families are headed by women.
- Many heads of poor families are among the "working poor" who work part-time or full-time but do not earn enough to lift a family of four above the poverty line.
- Thousands of people live on the streets across Canada. Recently, the proportion of families among the homeless has increased.

Explanations of Poverty

- Blame individuals: The *culture of poverty* thesis states that poverty is caused by shortcomings in the poor themselves (Lewis, 1961).
- Blame society: Poverty is caused by society's unequal distribution of wealth and lack of good jobs (William Julius Wilson).

relative poverty the deprivation of some people in relation to those who have more
absolute poverty a deprivation of resources that is life-threatening
feminization of poverty the trend by which women represent an increasing proportion of the poor

Chapter 12
Global Stratification

Odell Mitchell Jr. Photography/PhotoEdit, Inc.

∨ Learning Objectives

12.1 Describe the division of the world into high-, middle-, and low-income countries.

12.2 Discuss patterns and explanations of poverty around the world

12.3 Apply sociological theories to the topic of global inequality.

The Power of Society
to determine a child's chance of survival to age five

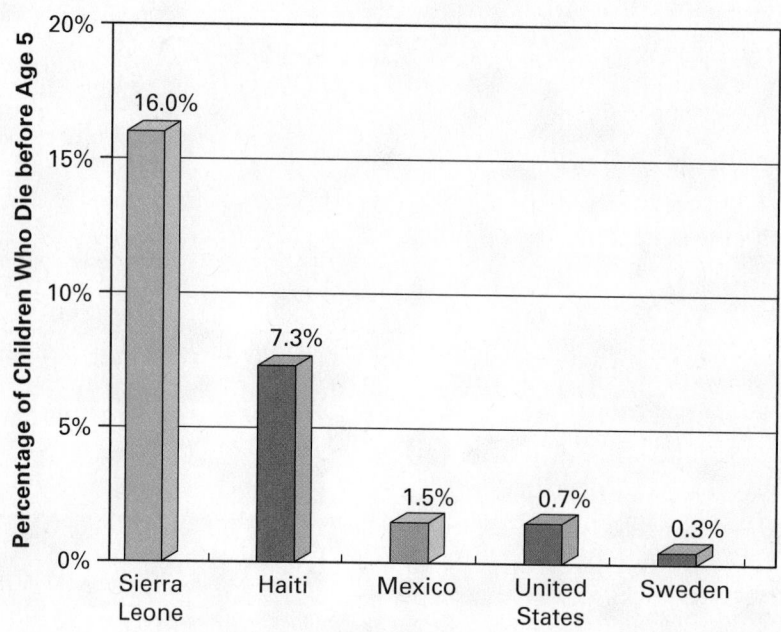

SOURCE: UNICEF. "ChildInfo Statistics by Area: Child Survival and Health." 2012. Available at http://www.childinfo.org/.

In a world of unequal economic development, how does a child's country of birth affect the chances of survival? Of all children born in Sierra Leone, a low-income nation on Africa's western coast, 16 percent die before reaching the age of five. In Haiti, another low-income nation, 7 percent of children suffer this fate. In high-income nations, the share is much lower. In the United States, less than 1 percent of children will die so early in life. In nations, including Sweden, with more extensive social welfare systems, the share is even lower.

Chapter Overview

Social stratification involves not just people within a single country; it is also a worldwide pattern of inequality among nations. This chapter shifts the focus from inequality within Canada to inequality in the world as a whole. The chapter begins by describing global inequality and then provides two theoretical models that explain global stratification.

More than a thousand workers were busily sewing together polo shirts on the fourth floor of the garment factory in Narsingdi, a small town about 48 kilometres (30 miles) northeast of Bangladesh's capital city of Dhaka. The thumping of hundreds of sewing machines combined to produce a steady roar that never stopped throughout the long working day.

But in an instant everything changed. An electric gun that a worker used to shoot spot remover gave off a spark, which ignited the flammable liquid. Suddenly, a work table burst into flames. Nearby workers rushed to smother the fire with shirts, but there was no stopping the blaze; in a room filled with combustible materials, the flames spread quickly.

The workers scrambled toward the narrow staircase that led to the street. At the bottom, however, the human wave pouring down the steep steps collided with a folding metal gate across the doorway that was kept locked to prevent workers from leaving during work hours. Panicked, the people turned, only to be pushed back by the hundreds behind them. In a single terrifying minute of screaming voices, thrusting legs, and pounding hearts, dozens were crushed and trampled. By the time the gates were opened and the fire put out, 52 garment workers lay dead.

Andrew Biraj/REUTERS/Newscom

Deadly fires such as this one occur regularly in Asian garment factories, where safety standards do not adequately protect workers. In recent years, almost 100 garment workers have perished annually in such fires in Bangladesh. Garment factories like this one are big business in Bangladesh, where clothing makes up 78 percent of the country's total economic exports. One quarter of these garments end up in clothing stores across North America. The reason so much of the clothing we buy is made in poor countries like Bangladesh is simple economics: Bangladeshi garment workers labour for close to 12 hours a day, typically seven days a week, earning less than $2 an hour.

Tanveer Chowdhury manages the garment factory owned by his family where this fire took place. Speaking to reporters, he complained bitterly about the tragedy: "This fire has cost me $586 373, and that does not include $70 000 for machinery and $20 000 for furniture. I made commitments to meet deadlines, and I still have the deadlines. I am now paying for air freight at $10 a dozen when I should be shipping by sea at 87 cents a dozen."

There was one other cost Chowdhury did not mention. To compensate families for the loss of their loved ones in the fire, he eventually agreed to pay $1952 per person. In Bangladesh, life—like labour—is cheap (based on Bearak, 2001; Bangladesh Garment Manufacturers & Exporters Association, 2012; Hossain, 2011; World Bank, 2012). ■

Garment workers in Bangladesh are among the roughly 1.4 billion of the world's people who work hard every day and yet remain poor (Chen & Ravallion, 2008). As this chapter explains, although poverty is a reality in Canada and other nations, the greatest social inequality is not *within* nations but *between* them (Goesling, 2001). We can understand the full dimensions of poverty only by exploring **global stratification**, *patterns of social inequality in the world as a whole.*

Global Stratification: An Overview

12.1 Describe the division of the world into high-, middle-, and low-income countries.

In a global perspective, social inequality is far greater than anything we experience in Canada. Figure 12–1 divides the world's total income by fifths of the population. The richest 20 percent of Canadian families receive 44 percent of national income. The richest 20 percent of global population, however, receives about 77 percent of total world income. The poorest 20 percent of the Canadian population earns roughly 5 percent of our total national income, while the poorest fifth of the world's people struggles to survive on just 2 percent of total world income. Canadians with income below the government's poverty line (i.e., the low income cut-off) live far better than the majority of the earth's people. People who earn an average income in a rich nation like Canada are extremely well-off by world standards.

In terms of wealth, as the pie chart on the right in Figure 12–1 shows, global inequality is even greater. The richest 20 percent of the world's adult population still owns about 95 percent of the planet's wealth. About half of all wealth is owned by about 1 percent the world's adult population. On the other hand, the poorest half of the world's adults own less than 1 percent of all global wealth. In terms of dollars, about half the world's families have less than $3641 in total wealth, , far less than the $81 200 in wealth for the typical family in the United States, for example (Bricker et al., 2014; Davies et al., 2014).

Look at it this way. Any one of the world's richest people (in 2015, the world's three richest *people*—Carlos Slim Helé in Mexico and Bill Gates and Warren Buffett in the United States—were *each* worth more than $472 billion) has personal wealth that exceeds the total economic output of more than 100 of the world's *countries* (World Bank, 2015; Forbes, 2015).

A Word about Terminology

Classifying the world's 195 nations into categories ignores many striking differences. These nations have rich and varied histories, speak different languages, and take pride in distinctive cultures. However, various models have been developed that help distinguish countries on the basis of global stratification.

One such model, developed after World War II, labelled the rich industrial countries the "First World," less industrialized socialist countries the "Second World," and non-industrialized poor countries the "Third World." But the "three worlds" model is now less useful. For one thing, it was a product of Cold War politics by which the capitalist West (the First World) faced off against the socialist East (the Second World), while other nations (the Third World) remained more or less on the sidelines. But the sweeping changes in Eastern Europe and the collapse of the former Soviet Union mean that a distinctive Second World no longer exists.

A second problem is that the "three worlds" model lumped together more than 100 countries as the Third World. In reality, some relatively better-off nations of the Third World (such as Chile) have industrialized enough

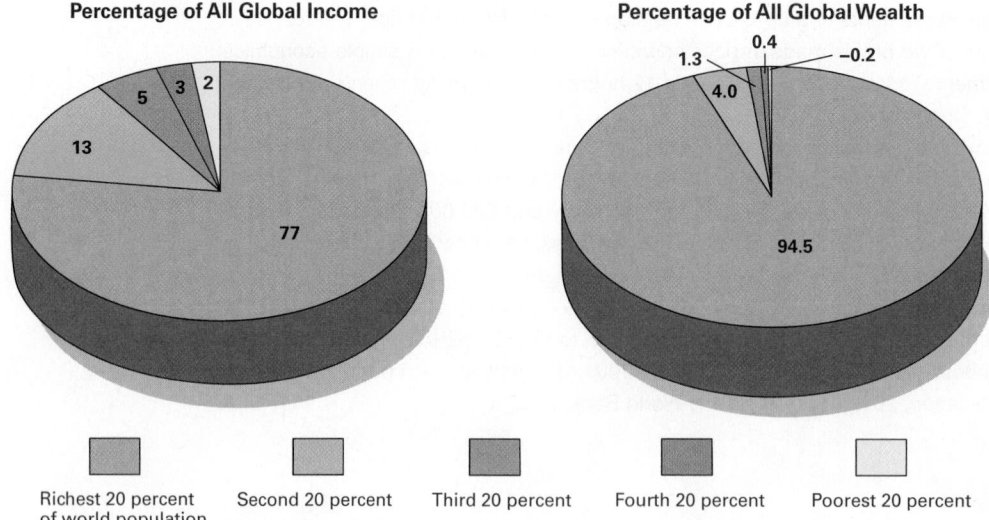

Figure 12–1 Distribution of Global Income and Wealth

Global income is very unequal, with the richest 20 percent of the world's people earning almost 50 times as much as the poorest 20 percent. Global wealth is even more unequally divided, with the richest 20 percent owning 95 percent of private wealth and the poorest half of the world's people having barely anything at all.

SOURCES: Based on Milanovic (2009, 2011) and Davies, Lluberas, and Shorrocks (2014).

global stratification patterns of social inequality in the world as a whole

high-income countries	middle-income countries	low-income countries
the nations with the highest overall standards of living	nations with a standard of living about average for the world as a whole	nations with a low standard of living in which most people are poor

that they have 15 times the per-person productivity of the poorest countries of the world (including Ethiopia).

These facts call for a revised system of classification. The 72 **high-income countries** are defined as *the nations with the highest overall standards of living*. These nations have a per capita gross domestic product (GDP) greater than $12 500. The world's 70 **middle-income countries** are not as rich; they are *nations with a standard of living about average for the world as a whole*. Their per capita GDP is less than $12 500 but greater than $2500. The remaining 53 **low-income countries** are *nations with a low standard of living in which most people are poor*. In these nations, per capita GDP is less than $2500 (United Nations Development Programme, 2012; World Bank, 2012).

This model has two advantages over the older "three worlds" system. First, it focuses on economic development rather than whether societies are capitalist or socialist. Second, it gives a better picture of the relative economic development of various countries because it does not lump together all lower-income nations into a single "Third World."

When ranking countries, keep in mind that *there is social stratification within every nation*. In Bangladesh, for example, members of the Chowdhury family, who own the garment factory where fire took the lives of 52 workers, earn as much as $1 million per year, which is several thousand times more than their workers earn. Of course, the full extent of global inequality is even greater, because the wealthiest people in rich countries like Canada live worlds apart from the poorest people in low-income nations such as Bangladesh, Haiti, or Sudan.

High-Income Countries

In nations where the Industrial Revolution first took place more than two centuries ago, productivity increased more than a hundredfold. To understand the power of industrial and computer technology, consider that one small European nation, the Netherlands, is more productive than all of the African nations south of the Sahara.

Global Map 12–1 shows that the high-income nations of the world include Canada, the United States, Mexico, Argentina, Chile, the nations of Western Europe, Israel, Saudi Arabia, Singapore, Hong Kong (part of the People's

THE UNITED STATES IS AMONG THE WORLD'S HIGH-INCOME COUNTRIES, IN WHICH INDUSTRIAL TECHNOLOGY AND ECONOMIC EXPANSION HAVE PRODUCED MATERIAL PROSPERITY
The presence of market forces is evident in this view of New York City (above, left). India has recently become one of the world's middle-income countries (above, right). An increasing number of motor vehicles fill city streets. Mali (left) is among the world's low-income countries. As the photograph suggests, these nations have limited economic development as well as rapidly increasing populations. The result is widespread poverty.

Window on the World

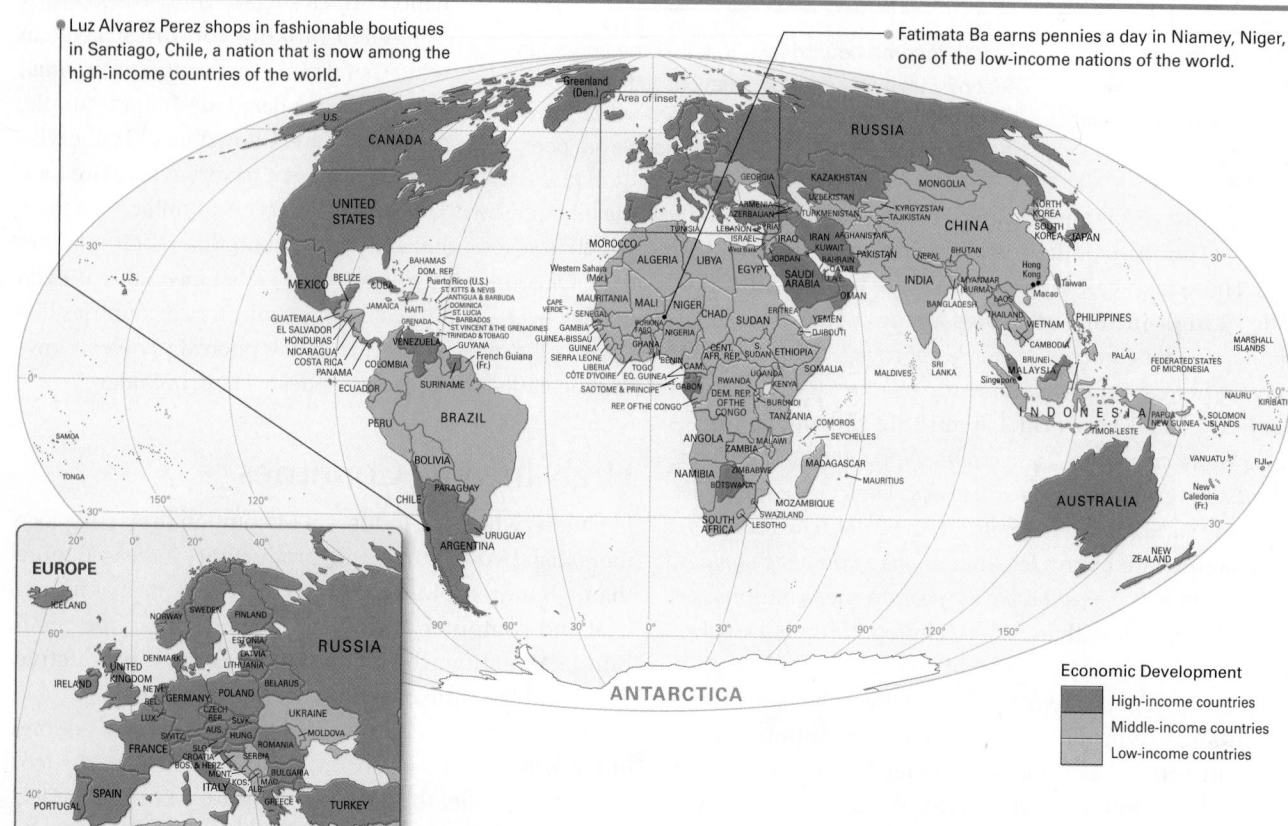

Luz Alvarez Perez shops in fashionable boutiques in Santiago, Chile, a nation that is now among the high-income countries of the world.

Fatimata Ba earns pennies a day in Niamey, Niger, one of the low-income nations of the world.

Economic Development

- High-income countries
- Middle-income countries
- Low-income countries

Global Map 12–1 Economic Development in Global Perspective

In *high-income countries*—including Canada, the United States, Mexico, Chile, Argentina, the nations of Western Europe, Israel, Saudi Arabia, Singapore, Hong Kong, South Korea, Malaysia, Australia, the Russian Federation, Japan, and New Zealand—a highly productive economy provides people, on average, with material plenty. *Middle-income countries*—including most of Latin America and Asia—are less economically productive, with a standard of living about average for the world as a whole. These nations also have a significant share of poor people who are barely able to feed and house themselves. In the *low-income countries* of the world (mainly in Africa), poverty is severe and widespread. Although small numbers of elites live very well in the poorest nations, most people struggle to survive on a small fraction of the income common in high-income countries.

Note: Data for this map are provided by the United Nations and the World Bank. Each country's economic productivity is measured in terms of its gross national income (GNI), which is the total value of all the goods and services produced by a country's economy within its borders in a given year, plus net compensation and property income from abroad. Dividing each country's GNI by the country's population gives us the per capita (per-person) GNI and allows us to compare the economic performance of countries of different population sizes. High-income countries have a per capita GNI of more than $15 000. Many are far richer than this, however; the figure for the United States exceeds $53 000. Middle-income countries have a per capita GNI ranging from $3500 to $14 999. Low-income countries have a per capita GNI of less than $3500. Figures used here reflect the World Bank's "purchasing power parities" system, which is an estimate of what people can buy using their income in the local economy.

SOURCES: Data from United Nations Development Programme (2014) and the World Bank (2014).

Republic of China), Japan, South Korea, the Russian Federation, Malaysia, Australia, and New Zealand.

These countries cover roughly 47 percent of Earth's land area, including parts of five continents, and they lie mostly in the northern hemisphere. In 2014, the total population of these nations was about 1.8 billion, or about 24 percent of the world's people. Close to three-fourths of the people in high-income countries live in or near cities (Population Reference Bureau, 2014; World Bank, 2014).

Significant cultural differences exist among high-income countries; for example, the nations of Europe recognize more than 30 official languages. But these societies all produce enough economic goods and services to enable their people to lead comfortable lives. Per capita income (i.e., average income per person per year) ranges from about $15 000 annually (in Botswana, Bulgaria, and Iran) to more than $50 000 annually (in Canada, the United States, Singapore, and Norway).

In fact, people in high-income countries enjoy 59 percent of the world's total income.

Keep in mind that high-income countries have many low-income people. The residents of the poorest communities in Canada (e.g., some of the Fist Nations) are still better off than about half the world's people, but they represent a striking contrast to what most members of high-income nations take for granted.

Middle-Income Countries

Middle-income countries have a per capita income of between $2500 and $12 500, close to the median (about $8350) for the world's nations. About 52 percent of the people in middle-income countries live in or near cities, and industrial jobs are common. The remaining 48 percent of people live in rural areas, where most are poor and lack access to schools, medical care, adequate housing, and even safe drinking water.

Looking at Global Map 12–1, we see that 70 of the world's nations fall into the middle-income category. At the high end are Venezuela (Latin America), Bulgaria (Europe), and Kazakhstan (Asia), where annual income is about $11 000. At the low end are Nicaragua (Latin America), Cape Verde (Africa), and Vietnam (Asia), with roughly $3000 annually in per capita income.

One cluster of middle-income countries used to be part of the Second World. These countries, found in Eastern Europe and Western Asia, had mostly socialist economies until popular revolts between 1989 and 1991 swept their governments aside. Since then, these nations have introduced more free-market systems. These middle-income countries include Ukraine, Uzbekistan, Georgia, and Turkmenistan.

Other middle-income nations include Peru and Brazil in South America and Namibia and South Africa in Africa. Both India and the People's Republic of China have entered the middle-income category, which now includes most of Asia.

Taken together, middle-income countries span roughly 36 percent of Earth's land area and are home to about 4.5 billion people, or about 60 percent of humanity. Some very large countries (such as China) are far less crowded than other smaller nations (such as El Salvador), but compared to high-income countries, these societies are densely populated.

Low-Income Countries

Low-income countries, where most people are very poor, are mostly agrarian societies with some industry. Fifty-three low-income countries, identified in Global Map 12–1, are spread across Central and East Africa and Asia. Low-income countries cover 17 percent of the planet's land area and are home to about 990 million people, or 14 percent of humanity. Population density is generally high, although it is greater in Asian countries (such as Bangladesh) than in Central African nations (such as Chad and the Democratic Republic of the Congo).

In poor countries, one-third of the people live in cities; most inhabit villages and farms as their ancestors have done for centuries. In fact, half the world's people are farmers, most of whom follow cultural traditions. With limited industrial technology, they cannot be very productive, one reason that many suffer severe poverty. Hunger, disease, and unsafe housing shape the lives of the world's poorest people.

Those of us who live in the world's richest nations find it hard to understand the scope of human need in much of the world. From time to time, televised pictures of famine in very poor countries such as Ethiopia and Bangladesh or the struggle with the Ebola outbreak in Sierra Leone and Liberia give us shocking glimpses of the poverty that makes every day a life-and-death battle. Behind these

IN GENERAL, WHEN NATURAL DISASTERS STRIKE HIGH-INCOME NATIONS, PROPERTY DAMAGE MAY BE GREAT, BUT LOSS OF LIFE IS LOW Hurricane Sandy, which was characterized as a "superstorm" (left), struck the East Coast of the United States in 2012, resulting in more than $60 billion in damage and 72 deaths. The earthquake that hit Haiti (right) in 2010, by contrast, resulted in more than 300 000 deaths.

images lie cultural, historical, and economic forces that we will explore in the remainder of this chapter.

Global Wealth and Poverty

12.2 **Discuss patterns and explanations of poverty around the world.**

October 14, Manila, Philippines. What caught my eye was how clean she was—a girl no more than seven or eight years old. She was wearing a freshly laundered dress, and her hair was carefully combed. She stopped to watch us, following us with her eyes: camera-toting Americans stand out in this, one of the poorest neighbourhoods in the entire world.

Fed by methane from decomposing garbage, the fires never go out on Smokey Mountain, the vast garbage dump on the north side of Manila. Smoke covers the hills of refuse like a thick fog. But Smokey Mountain is more than a dump; it is a neighbourhood that is home to thousands of people. It is hard to imagine a setting more hostile to human life. Amid the smoke and the squalor, men and women do what they can to survive. They pick plastic bags from the garbage and wash them in the river, and they collect cardboard boxes or anything else they can sell. What chance do their children have, coming from families that earn only a few hundred dollars a year, with hardly any opportunity for schooling, year after year breathing this foul air? Against this backdrop of human tragedy, one lovely little girl had put on a fresh dress and gone out to play.

Now our taxi driver threads his way through heavy traffic as we head for the other side of Manila. The change is amazing: The smoke and smell of the dump give way to neighbourhoods that could be in Miami or Los Angeles. A cluster of yachts floats on the bay in the distance. No more rutted streets; now we glide quietly along wide boulevards lined with trees and filled with expensive Japanese cars. We pass shopping plazas, upscale hotels, and high-rise office buildings. Every block or so we see the gated entrance to another exclusive residential community, with security guards standing watch. Here, in large, air-conditioned homes, the rich of Manila live—and many of the poor work. [John J. Macionis]

Low-income nations are home to a few rich and *many* poor people. People who live with incomes of just a few hundred dollars a year suffer a greater burden of poverty than the poor of North America. This is not to suggest that poverty in Canada and the United States is a minor problem. In our rich countries, too little food, substandard housing, and limited access to the best medical care amount to a national tragedy. The discovery—by the media—of contaminated drinking water in about 150 First Nations communities reveals another dimension in the gap between rich and poor.

The Severity of Poverty

Poverty in poor countries is more severe than it is in rich countries. A key reason that the quality of life differs so much around the world is that economic productivity is lowest in precisely the regions where population growth

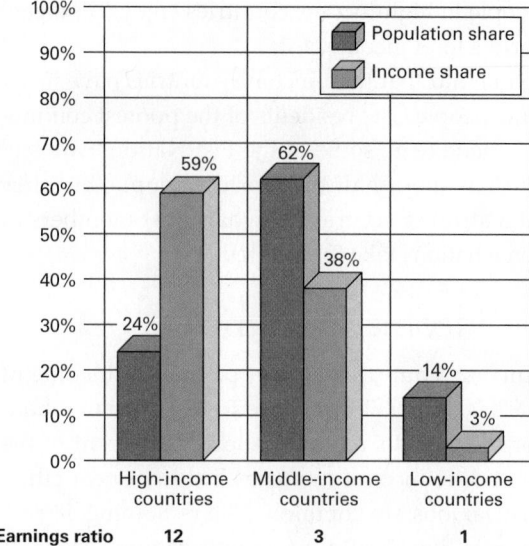

Figure 12–2 The Relative Share of Income and Population by Level of Economic Development

For every dollar earned by people in low-income countries, people in high-income countries earn $12.

SOURCES: Based on Population Reference Bureau (2014) and World Bank (2014).

is highest. Figure 12–2 shows the proportion of world population and global income for countries at each level of economic development. High-income countries are by far the most advantaged, with 64 percent of global income supporting just 23 percent of humanity. In middle-income nations, 60 percent of the world's people earn 33 percent of global income. This leaves 17 percent of the planet's population with just 3 percent of global income. In short, for every dollar received by individuals in a low-income country, someone in a high-income country takes home $12.

Table 12–1 shows the extent of wealth and well-being in selected countries from around the world. The first column of figures gives gross national income (GNI) for a number of high-, middle-, and low-income countries. The United States, a large and highly productive nation, had a 2014 GNI of $15 trillion; Japan's GNI was $4.8 trillion; Canada's was 1.5 trillion. A comparison of GNI figures shows that the world's richest nations are thousands of times more productive than the poorest countries.

The second column of figures in Table 12–1 divides GNI, or Gross National Income, by population to give an estimate of what people can buy with their income in the local economy. The per capita GNI for rich countries like Canada, the United States, and Sweden is very high, exceeding $40 000. For middle-income countries, the figures range from about $5350 in India to almost $15 000 in Brazil. In the low-income countries included here, per capita GNI is just one or two thousand dollars. In Niger

Table 12–1 Wealth and Well-Being in Global Perspective, 2014

Country	Gross National Income ($ billions)	GNI per Capita (PPP US$)*	Quality of Life Index
High-Income			
Norway	338	66 520	.944
Australia	982	42 450	.933
United States	16 992	53 750	.914
Canada	1498	42 610	.902
Sweden	448	46 680	.898
United Kingdom	2446	38 160	.892
South Korea	1679	33 440	.891
Japan	4812	37 790	.890
Middle-Income			
Eastern Europe			
Serbia	89	12 480	.745
Ukraine	408	8970	.734
Albania	29	10 400	.716
Latin America			
Costa Rica	66	13 570	.763
Brazil	2956	14 750	.744
Ecuador	169	10 720	.711
Asia			
Thailand	900	13 430	.722
China	16 085	11 850	.719
India	6700	5350	.586
Middle East			
Egypt	885	10 790	.682
Iraq	499	14 930	.642
Africa			
Algeria	513	13 070	.717
Namibia	22	9490	.624
Low-Income			
Latin America			
Haiti	18	1720	.471
Asia			
Cambodia	44	2890	.584
Bangladesh	499	3190	.558
Papua New Guinea	18	2430	.492
Africa			
Kenya	123	2780	.535
Ethiopia	130	1380	.435
Mali	24	1540	.407
Guinea	14	1160	.392
Democratic Republic of the Congo	50	740	.338

*These data are purchasing power parity (PPP) calculations, which avoid currency rate distortion by showing the local purchasing power of each domestic currency.

SOURCES: Based on United Nations Development Programme (2014), World Bank (2014).

or Mali, for example, a typical person labours all year to earn the average weekly wage in North America.

The last column of Table 12–1 is a measure of the *quality of life* in the various nations. This index, calculated by the United Nations (2014), is based on income, education (extent of adult literacy and average years of schooling), and longevity (how long people typically live). Index values are decimals that fall between extremes of 1 (highest) and 0 (lowest). By this calculation, Norwegians enjoy the highest quality of life (.944), with Australians, Americans, and Canadians close behind at .933 and .914, and .902 respectively. At the other extreme, people in the African nation of the Democratic Republic of the Congo have the lowest quality of life (.338).

A little history lesson is in order here. While Jean Chrétien was our prime minister (1993–2003), Canada was in a nine-year run as Number One on the UN Quality of Life Index. Chrétien never lost an opportunity to boast of Canada's rank as the world's best country in which to live. Since then, Norway moved into first place and Canada found itself in fourth place and even lower.

RELATIVE VERSUS ABSOLUTE POVERTY The distinction between relative and absolute poverty has an important application to global inequality. People living in rich countries generally focus on *relative poverty,* meaning that some people lack resources that are taken for granted by others. By definition, relative poverty exists in every society, rich or poor.

More important in global perspective, however, is *absolute poverty,* a lack of resources that is life-threatening. Human beings in absolute poverty lack the nutrition necessary for health and long-term survival. To be sure, some absolute poverty exists in North America. But such immediately life-threatening poverty strikes only a very small proportion of our population, such as the homeless. In low-income countries, in contrast, almost one half of the people live on about $1.25 a day and are in desperate need.

Because absolute poverty is deadly, people in low-income nations face an elevated risk of dying young. Global Map 12–2 lets us explore this pattern by presenting the odds of living to the age of 65 that are typical for the nations of the world. In rich societies, more than 85 percent of people reach this age. In the world poorest countries, however, the odds of living to age 65 are less than one in three, and one in ten children does not survive to the age of five (United Nations, 2013).

The Extent of Poverty

Poverty in poor countries is more widespread than it is in North America. The National Household Survey revealed that, in 2010, 14.9 percent of the population lived in poverty—whereas in low-income countries the majority lives no better than or far worse than the poorest in Canada. As Global Map 12–2 shows, the low odds of living to the age of 65 in the countries of sub-Saharan Africa indicate that absolute poverty is greatest there, where more than one-fourth of the population is malnourished. In the world

Window on the World

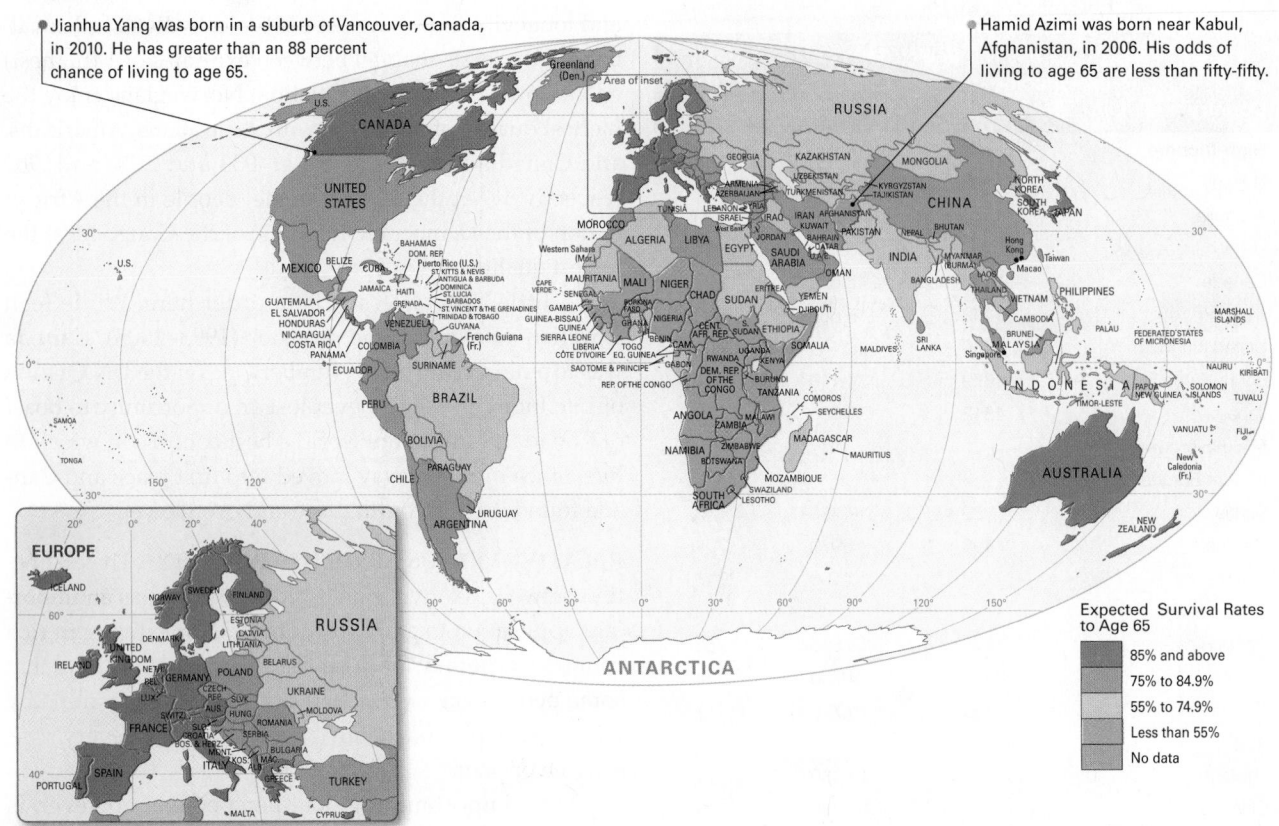

Jianhua Yang was born in a suburb of Vancouver, Canada, in 2010. He has greater than an 88 percent chance of living to age 65.

Hamid Azimi was born near Kabul, Afghanistan, in 2006. His odds of living to age 65 are less than fifty-fifty.

Expected Survival Rates to Age 65

- 85% and above
- 75% to 84.9%
- 55% to 74.9%
- Less than 55%
- No data

Global Map 12–2 The Odds of Surviving to the Age of 65 in Global Perspective

This map identifies expected survival rates to the age of 65 for nations around the world. In high-income countries, more than 85 percent of people live to this age. But in low-income nations, death often comes early, with just one-third of people reaching the age of 65.

SOURCE: Based on United Nations (2013).

as a whole, at any given time, 13 percent of the people—about 868 million—suffer from chronic hunger, which leaves them less able to work and puts them at high risk of disease (United Nations Food and Agriculture Organization, 2014).

The typical adult in a rich nation like Canada consumes about 3750 calories a day, an excess that contributes to widespread obesity and related health problems. The typical adult in a low-income country not only does more physical labour but consumes just 2350 calories a day. The result is undernourishment: too little food or not enough of the right kinds of food (United Nations Food and Agriculture Organization, 2014).

In the 10 minutes it takes to read this section of the chapter, about 100 people in the world who are sick and weakened from hunger will die. This number amounts to about 25 000 people a day, or 9 million people each year. Clearly, easing world hunger is one of the most serious responsibilities facing humanity today (United Nations Development Programme, 2014).

Poverty and Children

Death comes early in poor societies, where families lack adequate food, safe water, secure housing, and access to medical care. In the world's low- and middle-income nations, one-quarter of all children do not receive enough nutrition to be healthy (World Bank, 2014).

Poor children live in poor families and share in the struggle to get through each day. Organizations fighting child poverty estimate that at least 100 million children living in cities in poor countries beg, steal, sell sex, or work for drug gangs to provide income for their families. Such a life almost always means dropping out of school and puts children at high risk of disease and violence. Many girls, with little or no access to medical assistance, become pregnant; thus children who cannot support themselves are having children of their own.

Analysts estimate that tens of millions of the world's children are orphaned or have left their families altogether, sleeping and living on the streets as best they can. Roughly

TENS OF MILLIONS OF CHILDREN FEND FOR THEMSELVES EVERY DAY ON THE STREETS OF POOR CITIES, WHERE MANY FALL VICTIM TO DISEASE, DRUG ABUSE, AND VIOLENCE What do you think should be done to ensure that children like these in Bangalore, India, receive adequate nutrition and a quality education?

half of the world's street children are found in Latin American cities, such as Mexico City and Rio de Janeiro, where half of all children grow up in poverty. Many of us know these cities as exotic travel destinations, but they are also home to thousands of street children living in makeshift huts, under bridges, or in alleyways (Consortium for Street Children, 2011; Leopold, 2007; Levinson & Bassett, 2007).

Poverty and Women

In rich societies, much of the work women do is undervalued, underpaid, or overlooked entirely. In poor societies, women face even greater disadvantages. Most of the people who work in sweatshops (like the one described in the opening to this chapter) are women.

To make matters worse, tradition keeps women out of many jobs in low-income nations. In Bangladesh, for example, women work in garment factories because that society's conservative religious norms bar them from most other paid work and limit their opportunity for advanced schooling (Bearak, 2001). At the same time, traditional norms in poor societies give women primary responsibility for child rearing and maintaining the household. Analysts estimate that in poor countries, although women produce about 70 percent of the food, men own 90 percent of the land. This gender disparity in wealth is far greater than that found in high-income nations. Furthermore, about 70 percent of the world's 1 billion people living at or near absolute poverty are women (Landesa Center for Women's Land Rights, 2011; United Nations, 2010; World Bank, 2008).

Finally, most women in poor countries receive little or no reproductive health care. Limited access to birth control keeps women at home with their children, keeps the birth rate high, and limits the economic production

Global Snapshot

- Compared to a woman in Canada, an Ethiopian woman is far less likely to give birth with the help of medical professionals and is much more likely to die in childbirth.

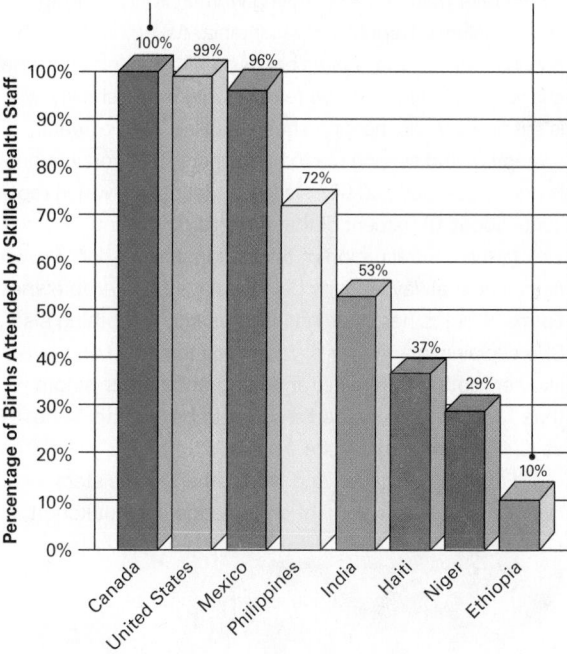

Figure 12–3 Percentage of Births Attended by Skilled Health Staff

In the Canada, most women give birth with the help of medical professionals, but this is usually not the case in low-income nations.

SOURCE: Data from World Bank (2015).

of the country. In addition, the world's poorest women typically give birth without help from trained health care personnel. Figure 12–3 draws a stark difference between low- and high-income countries in this regard.

Almost every woman in Canada gives birth with the help of medical professionals, but this is not the case in low-income countries.

Slavery

Poor societies have many problems in addition to hunger, including illiteracy, warfare, and even slavery. Upper Canada banned slavery in 1793, the British Empire in 1833, and the United States in 1865. But according to Anti-Slavery International, as many as 20 million men, women, and children (about 3 percent of humanity) live in conditions that amount to slavery (International Labour Organization, 2012).

Anti-Slavery International describes five types of slavery. The first is *chattel slavery*, in which one person owns another. In spite of the fact that this practice is against the law almost everywhere in the world, several million people fall into this category. The buying and selling

Thinking Globally

"God Made Me to Be a Slave"

Fatma Mint Mamadou is a young woman living in North Africa's Islamic Republic of Mauritania. Asked her age, she pauses, smiles, and shakes her head. She has no idea when she was born. Nor can she read or write. What she knows is tending camels, herding sheep, hauling bags of water, sweeping, and serving tea to her owners. This young woman is one of perhaps 500 000 slaves in Mauritania, which represents about 18 percent of that nation's population.

In the central region of this nation, having dark brown skin almost always means being a slave to an Arab owner. Fatma accepts her situation; she has known nothing else. She explains in a matter-of-fact voice that she is a slave like her mother before her and her grandmother before that. "Just as God created a camel to be a camel," she says, "he created me to be a slave."

Fatma, her mother, and her brothers and sisters live in a squatter settlement on the edge of Nouakchott,

Malcolm Linton/Hulton Archive/Getty Images

HUMAN SLAVERY CONTINUES TO EXIST IN THE TWENTY-FIRST CENTURY.

Mauritania's capital city. Their home is a hut measuring 3 × 4 metres (9 × 12 feet) that they built from wood scraps and other materials found at construction sites. The roof is nothing more than a piece of cloth; there is no plumbing or furniture. The nearest water comes from a well a long way down the road.

In this region, slavery began 500 years ago. As Arab and Berber tribes raided local villages, they made slaves of the people, and so it has been for dozens of generations ever since. In 1905, the French colonial rulers of Mauritania banned slavery. After the nation gained independence in 1961, the new government reaffirmed the ban. However, slavery was not officially abolished until 1981, and even then, it was not made a crime. In 2007, the nation passed legislation making the practice of slavery an offence punishable by up to 10 years in prison, and the government now provides monetary compensation to victims of slavery. But such proclamations have done little to change strong traditions. Indeed, people like Fatma have no idea what "freedom to choose" means.

The next question is more personal: "Are you and other girls ever raped?" Again, Fatma hesitates. With no hint of emotion, she responds, "Of course, in the night the men come to breed us. Is that what you mean by 'rape'?"

What Do You Think?

1. How does tradition play a part in keeping some people in slavery?

2. Why do you think the world still tolerates slavery?

3. Explain the connection between slavery and poverty.

SOURCE: Based on Anti-Slavery International (2015); Burkett (1997); and Fisher (2011).

---

of slaves—generally people of one ethnic or caste group enslaving members of another—still takes place in many countries throughout Asia, the Middle East, and especially Africa. The Thinking Globally box (p. 318) describes the reality of one slave's life in the African nation of Mauritania.

A second type of bondage is *slavery imposed by the state*. In this case, a government imposes forced labour on people convicted of crime or on others simply because the government needs their labour. In China, for example, people who are addicted to drugs, who engage in prostitution or other crimes, or who are involved in political dissent are subject to forced labour. In North Korea, the government can force people to work for almost any reason at all.

A third and common form of bondage is *child slavery*, in which desperately poor families send their children out into the streets to beg or steal or do whatever they can to survive. Probably tens of millions of children—many in the poorest countries of Latin America and Africa—fall

into this category. In addition, an estimated 10 million children are forced to labour daily in the production of tobacco, sugarcane, cotton, coffee, or chocolate in more than 70 nations.

Fourth, *debt bondage* is the practice by which an employer pays wages to workers that are less than what the employer charges the workers for company-provided food and housing. Under such an arrangement, workers can never pay their debts so, for practical purposes, workers are enslaved. Many sweatshop workers in low-income nations fall into this category.

Fifth, *servile forms of marriage* may also amount to slavery. In India, Thailand, and some African nations, families marry off women against their will. Many end up as slaves working for their husband's family; some are forced into prostitution.

An additional form of slavery involves *human trafficking*—moving men, women, and children from one place to another for the purposes of forced labour. Women or men are brought to a new country with the promise of a job and then forced to become prostitutes or farm labourers, or "parents" adopt children from another country and then force them to work in sweatshops. Such activity is big business: Next to trading in guns and drugs, trading in people brings the greatest profit to organized crime around the world (Anti-Slavery International, 2015; International Labour Organization, 2013; Orhant, 2002).

In 1948, the United Nations issued its Universal Declaration of Human Rights, which states, "No one shall be held in slavery or servitude; slavery and the slave trade shall be prohibited in all their forms." Unfortunately, more than six decades later, this social evil still exists.

Explanations of Global Poverty

What accounts for the severe and extensive poverty throughout much of the world? The rest of this chapter weaves together explanations from the following facts about poor societies:

- *Technology.* About one-quarter of people in low-income countries farm the land using human muscle or animal power. With limited energy sources, economic production is modest.

- *Population growth.* The countries that cannot feed their children adequately—the poorest ones—have the world's highest birth rates. Despite the death toll from poverty, the populations of many poor countries in Africa, for example, double every 25 years. In sub-Saharan Africa, 43 percent of the people are under the age of 15. With so many people entering their child-bearing years, the wave of population growth will roll into the future. For example, the population of Uganda has swelled by more than 5 percent annually in recent years, so even with economic development, living standards there have fallen. This is far from an isolated case. Globally, just about all future population increase will be in low-income countries (Population Reference Bureau, 2012).

1. *Cultural patterns.* Poor societies are usually traditional. Holding on to long-established ways of life means resisting change—even change that promises a higher standard of living.

2. *Social stratification.* Low-income societies distribute whatever wealth they have wealth very unequally. Social inequality is greater in agrarian than industrial societies for the simple reason that land is the major productive asset. In Brazil, for example, 75 percent of all farmland is owned by 4 percent of the people (Frayssinet, 2009; Galano, 1998; IGBE, 2006).

3. *Gender inequality.* Gender inequality in poor and traditional societies denies women education and pre-

vents them from holding jobs. Add lack of access to effective birth control and women will have more children. An expanding population, in turn, slows economic development. Many analysts conclude that raising living standards in much of the world depends on improving the social standing of women.

4. *Global power relationships.* A final cause of global poverty lies in the relationships among the nations of the world. Historically, wealth flowed from poor societies to rich nations through **colonialism**, *the process by which some nations enrich themselves through political and economic control of other nations.* The countries of Western Europe colonized much of Latin America beginning roughly 500 years ago. Such global exploitation allowed some nations to develop economically at the expense of others.

Although 130 former colonies gained their independence during the twentieth century, exploitation continues through **neocolonialism** (*neo* is Greek for "new"), *a new form of global power relationships that involves not direct political control but economic exploitation by multinational corporations.* A **multinational corporation** is *a very large business that operates in many countries.* Corporate leaders often impose their will on countries where they do business to create favourable economic conditions for their corporations, just as colonizers did in the past (Bonanno et al., 2000).

Theories of Global Stratification

12.3 Apply sociological theories to the topic of global inequality.

There are two major explanations for the unequal distribution of the world's wealth and power: *modernization theory* and *dependency theory.* Each theory suggests a different solution to the suffering of hungry people in much of the world.

Modernization Theory

Modernization theory is *a model of economic and social development that explains global inequality in terms of technological and cultural differences between nations.* Modernization theory emerged in the 1950s, a time when we were fascinated by new developments in technology. To

---

colonialism the process by which some nations enrich themselves through political and economic control of other nations

neocolonialism a new form of global power relationships that involves not direct political control but economic exploitation by multinational corporations

showcase the power of productive technology and also to counter the growing influence of the Soviet Union, U.S. policy-makers drafted a market-based foreign policy that persists to this day (Bauer, 1981; Berger, 1986; Firebaugh, 1996; Firebaugh & Sandu, 1998; Rostow, 1960, 1978).

HISTORICAL PERSPECTIVE Until a few centuries ago, the entire world was poor. Because poverty has been the norm throughout human history, modernization theory claims that it is *affluence* that demands an explanation. Affluence came into being in Western Europe during the late Middle Ages as world exploration and trade expanded. Once the Industrial Revolution was under way, Western Europe and then North America were transformed. Industrial technology coupled with the spirit of capitalism created new wealth as never before. At first, this new wealth benefited only a few. But industrial technology was so productive that, gradually, the living standard of even the poorest people began to improve. Absolute poverty, which had plagued humanity throughout history, was finally in decline.

In high-income countries, where the Industrial Revolution began in the late 1700s or early 1800s, the standard of living jumped at least fourfold during the twentieth century. As middle-income nations in Asia and Latin America have industrialized, they, too, have become richer. But with limited industrial technology, low-income countries have changed much less.

THE IMPORTANCE OF CULTURE Why didn't the Industrial Revolution sweep away poverty the world over? Modernization theory points out that not every society wants to adopt new technology. Doing so requires a cultural environment that emphasizes the benefits of material wealth and new ideas.

Modernization theory identifies *tradition* as the greatest barrier to economic development. In some societies, strong family systems and a reverence for the past discourage people from adopting new technologies that would raise their living standards. Even today, many people—from the North American Amish and Mennonite people to Islamic people in rural regions of the Middle East and Asia and the Semai of Malaysia—oppose technological advances as a threat to their family relationships, customs, and religious beliefs.

Max Weber (1958; orig. 1904–1905) found that at the end of the Middle Ages, Western Europe's cultural environment favoured change. The Protestant Reformation reshaped traditional Christian beliefs to generate a progress-oriented way of life. Wealth—regarded with suspicion by the Catholic Church—became a sign of personal virtue, and the growing importance of individualism steadily replaced the traditional emphasis on family and community. Taken together, these new cultural patterns nurtured the Industrial Revolution.

ROSTOW'S STAGES OF MODERNIZATION Modernization theory holds that the door to affluence is open to all. As technological advances spread around the world, all societies should gradually industrialize. According to Walt W. Rostow (1960, 1978), modernization occurs in four stages:

1. *Traditional stage.* Socialized to honour the past, people in traditional societies cannot easily imagine that life could or should be any different. Therefore, they build their lives around families and local communities, following well-worn paths that allow for little individual freedom or change. Life is often spiritually rich but lacking in material goods. A century ago, much of the world was in this initial stage of economic development. Nations such as Bangladesh, Niger, and Somalia are still at the traditional stage and remain poor.

2. *Takeoff stage.* As a society shakes off the grip of tradition, people start to use their talents and imagination, sparking economic growth. A market emerges as people produce goods not just for their own use but to trade with others for profit. Greater individualism, a willingness to take risks, and a desire for material

IN RICH NATIONS, MOST PARENTS EXPECT THEIR CHILDREN TO ENJOY YEARS OF CHILDHOOD, LARGELY FREE FROM THE RESPONSIBILITIES OF ADULT LIFE This is not the case in poor nations across Latin America, Africa, and Asia. Poor families depend on whatever income their children can earn, and many children as young as six or seven work full days weaving or performing other kinds of manual labour. Child labour lies behind the low prices of many products imported for sale in this country.

goods also take hold, often at the expense of family ties and time-honoured norms and values. Great Britain reached takeoff by about 1800, the United States by 1820. Takeoff in Canada occurred between 1890 and 1914 (Pomfret, 1981). Thailand, a middle-income country in eastern Asia, is now at this stage. Rich nations can help poor countries reach the takeoff stage by supplying foreign aid, advanced technology, investment capital, and opportunities for schooling abroad.

The danger in the latter is that once students are educated abroad they may be reluctant to return to their own countries. For many years, Canada insisted that international students were required to go back to their countries of origin as soon as they graduated. The tide has turned so that, in recent years, Canada has been encouraging its international students to remain in Canada after graduation. In effect, we are promoting "brain drain" from lower-income countries to Canada. At the same time we complain about the "brain drain" that takes highly educated Canadians to the United States.

3. *Drive to technological maturity.* During this stage, economic growth is a widely accepted idea that fuels a society's pursuit of higher living standards. A diversified economy drives a population eager to enjoy the benefits of industrial technology. At the same time, however, people begin to realize—and sometimes regret—that industrialization is eroding traditional family and local community life. Great Britain reached this stage in about 1840, the United States by 1860, and Canada between 1914 and 1950. Mexico, Puerto Rico, and South Korea are among the nations now driving to technological maturity.

At this stage of development, absolute poverty is greatly reduced. Cities swell with people who leave rural villages in search of economic opportunity. Specialization greatly expands the range of jobs, and the increasing focus on work makes relationships less personal. Growing individualism generates social movements demanding greater political rights. Societies approaching technological maturity also provide basic schooling for all of their people and advanced training for some; the newly educated consider tradition to be "backward" and push for further change. The social position of women gradually approaches that of men.

4. *High mass consumption.* Economic development steadily raises living standards as mass production stimulates mass consumption. Simply put, people soon learn to "need" the expanding array of goods that their society produces. The United States, Japan, and other rich nations moved into this stage by 1900. Canada followed a few years later. Now entering this level of economic development are two former British colonies that are prosperous small societies of Asia: Hong Kong

(part of the People's Republic of China since 1997) and Singapore (independent since 1965).

THE ROLE OF RICH NATIONS Modernization theory claims that high-income countries play four important roles in global economic development:

1. *Controlling population.* Since population growth is greatest in the poorest societies, rising population can overtake economic advances. Rich nations can help limit population growth by exporting birth control technology and promoting its use. Once economic development is under way, birth rates should decline, as they have in industrialized nations—because children are no longer an economic asset.

2. *Increasing food production.* Rich nations can export high-tech farming methods to poor nations to increase agricultural yields. Such techniques—collectively referred to as the Green Revolution—include new hybrid seeds, modern irrigation methods, chemical fertilizers, and pesticides for insect control. See the Thinking Globally box (p. 322) for Canada's contribution to food security.

3. *Introducing industrial technology.* Rich nations can encourage economic growth in poor societies by introducing machinery and information technology, which raise productivity. Industrialization also shifts the labour force from farming to skilled industrial and service jobs.

4. *Providing foreign aid.* Investment capital from rich nations can boost the prospects of poor societies trying to reach Rostow's takeoff stage. Foreign aid can raise farm output by helping poor countries buy more fertilizer and build irrigation projects. In the same way, financial and technical assistance can help build power plants and factories to improve industrial output. Each year, the United States provides more than $35 billion in foreign aid to developing countries, while Canada gives about CAD$5 billion. In fact, Canada's foreign aid spending has declined recently from CAD$5.7 billion in 2011 to CAD$4.9 billion in 2014. Neither country approaches the 0.7 percent of GDP that the United Nations—and some vocal celebrities—would like to see. Canada is spending 0.24 percent of GDP on foreign aid.

EVALUATE

Modernization theory has many influential supporters among social scientists (Bauer, 1981; Berger, 1986; Firebaugh, 1996, 1999; Firebaugh & Beck, 1994; Firebaugh & Sandu, 1998; Moore, 1977, 1979; Parsons, 1966). For decades, it has shaped the foreign policies of Canada, the United States, and other rich nations. Supporters point to rapid economic development in Asia—including South Korea, Taiwan, Singapore, and Hong Kong—as proof that the affluence that accompanied industrialization in Western Europe and North America is within reach of other countries.

Thinking Globally

Canadian Contributions to Livelihood and Food Security in Isolated Communities of Latin America and India

Sociologists and anthropologists at the University of Guelph are studying and working with farmers in isolated and mountainous regions of the world—with funding from the former Canadian International Development Agency (CIDA) and the Social Sciences and Humanities Research Council (SSHRC). Two of these individuals are introduced here.

Sally Humphries has devoted her career to enhancing sustainable agricultural development in the fragile tropical environments of Latin America. Some of her research (1993) involved farmers of Mexico's Yucatán region, who had switched from traditional agriculture to intensive horticultural production for outside markets. Is it possible, Humphries asked, to maintain traditional systems in the face of market integration?

Traditional farming, which was sustainable, came under pressure when improved *transportation links* allowed a switch to delicate perishable crops and opened northern Yucatán to Mexican and world markets. At this time, *profit* rather than *subsistence* became the goal—and, in the pursuit of profit, soils were depleted by repeated use. Crop specialization, in tomatoes, left farmers vulnerable to losses owing to poor weather, pest attack, and plant diseases. The use of chemical fertilizers and pesticides to deal with these new problems ultimately led to environmental damage. Humphries points to the "difficulty of achieving the twin goal of economic and environmental sustainability" and suggests that, whatever the outcome, more attention must be paid to the "decision-making and livelihood strategies" of the farmers themselves (Humphries, 1993:100).

Elizabeth Finnis, who studies farming communities in the Kolli Hills of India (2006, 2009), found that improved roads contribute to dramatic changes—both good and bad. Traditionally, people in these communities grew millets or coarse grains that are both tasty and nutritious. Lately, they have been cultivating cassava (tapioca) as a cash crop replacing millets. Finnis wanted to understand the reasons for this transition. She soon learned that, despite some regrets, women eagerly supported the shift from millets to cassava. Planting, harvesting, and preparing millet for consumption was the responsibility of women, who would get up very early in the morning and spend much of the day processing millet for their daily food. Cassava production—tubers dug up and thrown into a truck for processing in the lowlands—provided cash income that could be used to buy televisions or food from outside sources. More importantly, it gave women

leisure time; they did not want to grow millet again because "now is an easy life." Millet meant hours of hard physical labour.

Cultivating cassava almost exclusively represents "negative nutritional change"—cutting down fruit-bearing trees, depletion of soils, heavy use of chemical fertilizers, and failure to grow bananas, pineapple, or other cash crops that maintain agricultural diversity. Finnis argues that, in order to understand change in the Kolli Hills, researchers must consider "local-level agriculture decision making" or "conscious decisions based on individual and household aspirations" (2006:363).

As part of a larger group (Classen et al., 2008), Humphries has been engaged in "community-driven development," or "participatory" agricultural initiatives on remote hillsides in Honduras, far from roads and consequently neglected by former sector researchers who prefer to work with farmers in more accessible locations. The goal is to train poor and marginal community members as researchers who test, as well as breed, their own new crop varieties and techniques. Whereas male dominance loomed large as a potential problem—because of the *machismo* embedded in local cultures—40 percent of the participants were women. The farmer research teams carried out real experiments on their own farms, assessing soil conservation techniques and the suitability of a variety of new crops to local growing conditions. Participatory research led to improvements in the cultivation of cash crops and greater food security in local communities. It also led to bonding among participants, greater confidence, development of leadership skills, and interest in planning for the future. In other words, participants experienced "growth of human, social, and financial capital."

Note that, in each of the above cases, access to transportation played an important role in development, especially with respect to cash crops and market integration. Furthermore, "development" was not a top-down process but the result of decisions made by farmers themselves—and many of the farmers were women. And lastly, in each case, development had consequences for food security, the environment, sustainability, and livelihood or financial security.

What Do You Think?

1. What lessons should we take from this box regarding the relationship between economic and environmental concerns?

2. Is it possible to change farming practices in marginal communities without affecting the health of both people and the environment?

3. Is intervention by researchers in traditional farming communities positive or negative?

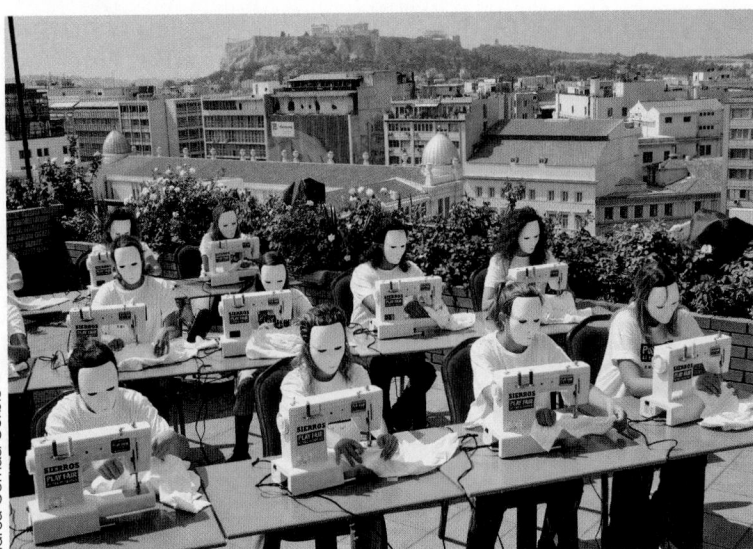

Andrea Comas/Corbis

MODERNIZATION THEORY CLAIMS THAT CORPORATIONS THAT BUILD FACTORIES IN LOW-INCOME NATIONS HELP PEOPLE BY PROVIDING THEM WITH JOBS AND HIGHER WAGES THAN THEY HAD BEFORE; DEPENDENCY THEORY VIEWS THESE FACTORIES AS "SWEATSHOPS" THAT EXPLOIT WORKERS In response to the Olympic Games selling sports clothing produced by sweatshops, these women staged a protest in Athens, Greece; they are wearing white masks to symbolize the "faceless" workers who make much of what we wear. Is any of the clothing you wear made in sweatshop factories?

But modernization theory comes under fire from socialist countries (and left-leaning analysts in the West) as little more than a defence of capitalism. Its most serious flaw, according to critics, is that modernization simply has not occurred in many poor countries. The United Nations reported that living standards in a number of nations—including Haiti and Nicaragua in Latin America, and Sudan, Ghana, and Rwanda in Africa—are little changed, and in some cases are worse than in the 1960s (United Nations Development Programme, 2008).

A second criticism of modernization theory is that it fails to recognize how rich nations, which benefit from the status quo, block paths to development for poor countries. Centuries ago, critics charge, rich countries industrialized from a position of global strength. Can we expect poor countries today to do so from a position of global weakness?

Third, modernization theory treats rich and poor societies as separate worlds, ignoring the ways in which international relations have affected all nations. Many countries in Latin America and Asia are still struggling to overcome the harm caused by colonialism, which boosted the fortunes of Europe.

Fourth, modernization theory holds up the world's most economically developed countries as the standard for judging the rest of humanity, revealing an ethnocentric bias. We should remember that our Western idea of "progress" has caused us to rush headlong into a competitive, materialistic way of life, which uses up the world's scarce resources and pollutes the natural environment.

Fifth, and finally, modernization theory suggests that the causes of global poverty lie almost entirely in the poor societies themselves. Critics see this analysis as little more than blaming the victims for their own problems. Instead, these critics argue, an analysis of global inequality should focus just as much on the behaviour of rich nations as it does on the behaviour of poor ones.

Concerns such as these reflect a second major approach to understanding global inequality: dependency theory.

CHECK YOUR LEARNING State the important ideas of modernization theory, including Rostow's four stages of economic development. Point to several strengths and weaknesses of this theory.

Dependency Theory

Dependency theory is *a model of economic and social development that explains global inequality in terms of the historical exploitation of poor nations by rich ones.* This analysis, which follows the social conflict approach, puts the main responsibility for global poverty on rich nations, which for centuries have systematically impoverished low-income countries and made them dependent on the rich ones. This destructive process continues today.

HISTORICAL PERSPECTIVE Everyone agrees that, before the Industrial Revolution, there was little affluence in the world. Dependency theory asserts, however, that people living in poor countries were actually better off economically in the past than their descendants are now. André Gunder Frank (1975), a noted supporter of this theory, argues that the colonial process that helped develop rich nations also led to the *under* development of poor societies.

Dependency theory is based on the idea that the economic positions of rich and poor nations of the world are linked and cannot be understood apart from each other. From this perspective, poor nations do not simply lag behind rich ones on the "path of progress"; rather, some nations became rich only because they impoverished others. Both are products of the global commerce that began five centuries ago.

THE IMPORTANCE OF COLONIALISM Late in the fifteenth century, Europeans began exploring the Americas to the west, Africa to the south, and Asia to the east in order to establish colonies. They were so successful that a century ago, Great Britain controlled about one-fourth of the world's land, boasting that "the sun never sets on the British Empire." The United States, itself originally a collection of small British colonies on the eastern seaboard

modernization theory a model of economic and social development that explains global inequality in terms of technological and cultural differences between nations

dependency theory a model of economic and social development that explains global inequality in terms of the historical exploitation of poor nations by rich ones

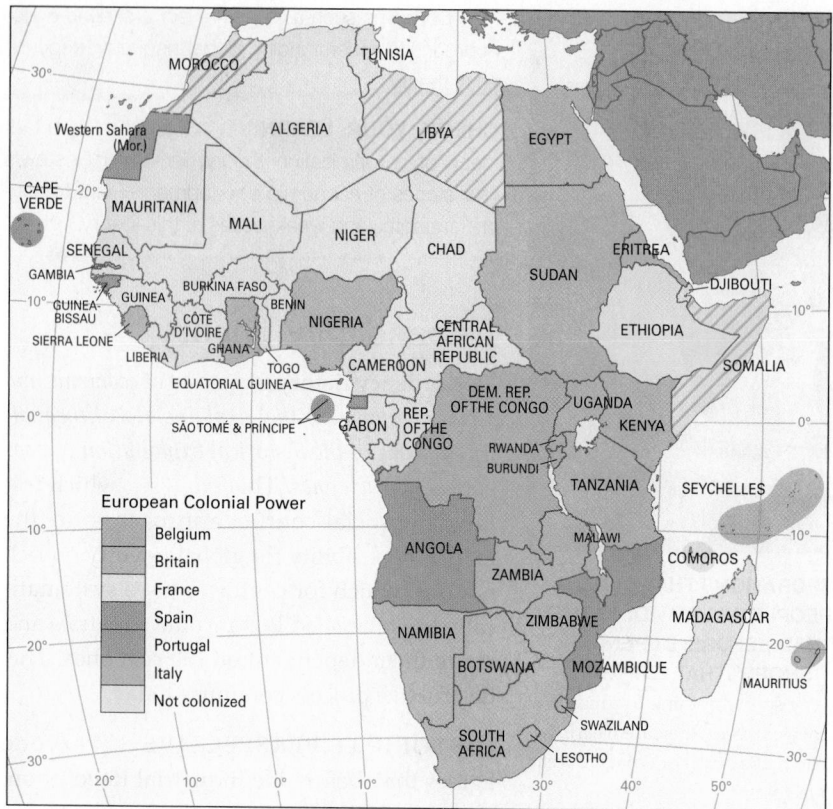

Figure 12–4 Africa's Colonial History

For more than a century, most of Africa was colonized by European nations, with France dominating in the northwest region of the continent and Great Britain dominating in the east and south.

of North America, soon pushed across the continent, purchased Alaska, and gained control of Haiti, Puerto Rico, Guam, the Philippines, the Hawaiian Islands, part of Panama, and Guantanamo Bay in Cuba.

As colonialism spread, there emerged a brutal form of human exploitation—the international slave trade—beginning about 1500 and continuing until 1850. Even as the world was turning away from slavery, Europeans took control of most of the African continent, as Figure 12–4 shows, and dominated most of the continent until the early 1960s.

Formal colonialism has almost disappeared from the world. However, according to dependency theory, political liberation has not translated into economic independence. Far from it—the economic relationship between poor and rich nations continues the colonial pattern of domination. This neocolonialism is the heart of the capitalist world economy.

WALLERSTEIN'S CAPITALIST WORLD ECONOMY Immanuel Wallerstein (1974, 1979, 1983, and 1984) explains global stratification using a model of the "capitalist world economy." Wallerstein's term *world economy* suggests that the prosperity of some nations and the poverty and dependency of other countries result from a global economic system. He traces the roots of the global economy to the beginning of colonization 500 years ago, when Europeans began gathering wealth from the rest of the world. Because the world economy is based in the high-income countries, it is capitalist in character.

Wallerstein calls the rich nations the *core* of the world economy. Colonialism enriched this core by funnelling raw materials from around the world to Western Europe, where they fuelled the Industrial Revolution. Today, multinational corporations operate profitably worldwide, channelling wealth to North America, Western Europe, Australia, and Japan.

Low-income countries, on the other hand, represent the *periphery* of the world economy. Drawn into the world economy by colonial exploitation, poor nations continue to support rich ones by providing inexpensive labour and a vast market for industrial products. The remaining countries—the *semiperiphery* of the world economy—include middle-income nations, such as India and Brazil, that have closer ties to the global economic core.

According to Wallerstein, the world economy benefits rich societies by generating profits and harms the rest of the world by causing poverty. The world economy thus makes poor nations dependent on rich ones. This dependency involves three factors:

1. *Narrow, export-oriented economies.* Poor nations produce only a few crops for export to rich countries. Examples include coffee and fruit from Latin American nations, oil from Nigeria, hardwoods from the Philippines, and palm oil from Malaysia. Today's multinational corporations purchase raw materials cheaply in poor societies and transport them to core nations, where factories process them for profitable sale. As a result, poor nations develop few industries of their own.

2. *Lack of industrial capacity.* Without an industrial base, poor societies face a double bind: They count on rich nations to buy their inexpensive raw materials and try to buy from them whatever expensive manufactured goods they can afford. In a classic example of this dependency, British colonial officials encouraged the people of India to raise cotton but prevented them from weaving their own cloth. Instead, the British shipped Indian cotton to their own textile mills in Birmingham and Manchester, manufactured the cloth, and shipped finished goods back to India, where the very people who harvested the cotton bought the garments.

Dependency theorists claim that the Green Revolution—widely praised by modernization theorists—works in the same way. Poor countries sell cheap raw materials to rich nations and then try to buy expensive fertilizers, pesticides, and machinery in return. Rich countries profit from this exchange more than poor nations do.

3. *Foreign debt.* Unequal trade patterns have plunged poor countries into debt to the core nations. Collectively, the poor nations of the world owe rich countries some US$4 trillion. Such staggering debt paralyzes a country, causing high unemployment and rampant inflation (World Bank, 2012).

THE ROLE OF RICH NATIONS Modernization theory and dependency theory assign very different roles to rich nations. Modernization theory holds that rich countries *produce wealth* through capital investment and new technology. Dependency theory views global inequality in terms of how countries *distribute wealth,* arguing that rich nations have overdeveloped themselves as they have *under*developed the rest of the world.

Dependency theorists dismiss the idea that programs developed by rich countries to control population and to boost agricultural and industrial output raise living standards in poor countries. Instead, they claim, such programs actually benefit rich nations and the ruling elites, not the poor majority, in low-income countries (Kentor, 2001).

Hunger activists Frances Moore Lappé and Joseph Collins (1986; Lappé et al., 1998) maintain that capitalist culture encourages people to think of poverty as somehow inevitable. In this line of reasoning, poverty results from "natural" processes, including having too many children and experiencing disasters such as droughts. But global poverty is far from inevitable; in their view, it results from deliberate policies. Lappé and Collins point out that the world already produces enough food to allow every person on the planet to become quite fat. Moreover, India and most of Africa actually export food, even though many of their own people go hungry. See the Thinking Globally box (p. 327) to learn about the contribution of Canadian researchers to food security in such countries.

According to Lappé and Collins, the contradiction of poverty amid plenty stems from rich nations' policy of producing food for profits, not people. That is, corporations in rich nations co-operate with elites in poor countries to grow and export profitable crops, such as coffee, thereby using land that could otherwise produce basics, such as beans and corn for local families. Governments of poor countries support the practice of growing for export because they need food profits to repay foreign debt. For Lappé and Collins, the capitalist corporate structure of the global economy is at the core of this vicious cycle.

EVALUATE

The main idea of dependency theory is that no nation becomes rich or poor in isolation because a single global economy shapes the destiny of all nations. Pointing to continuing poverty in Latin America, Africa, and Asia, dependency theorists claim that development simply cannot proceed under the constraints now imposed by rich countries; rather, they call for radical reform of the entire world economy so that it operates in the interests of the majority of people.

Critics charge that dependency theory wrongly treats wealth as if no one gets richer without someone else getting poorer. Corporations, small business owners, and farmers can and do create new wealth through hard work and imaginative use of new technology. After all, they point out, the entire world's wealth has increased sixfold since 1950.

Second, dependency theory is wrong in blaming rich nations for global poverty because many of the world's poorest countries (e.g., Ethiopia) have had little contact with rich nations. On the contrary, a long history of trade with rich countries has dramatically improved the economies of many nations, including Sri Lanka, Singapore, and Hong Kong (all former British colonies), as well as South Korea and Japan. In short, say the critics, most evidence shows that foreign investment by rich nations encourages economic growth, as modernization theory claims, not economic decline, as dependency theorists claim (Firebaugh, 1992; Vogel, 1991).

Jan Sochor/Alamy Stock Photo

ALTHOUGH THE WORLD CONTINUES TO GROW RICHER, BILLIONS OF PEOPLE ARE BEING LEFT BEHIND This shantytown of Cité Soleil, Haiti, is typical of many cities in low-income countries. What can you say about the quality of life in such a place?

Third, critics call dependency theory simplistic for pointing the finger at a single factor—capitalism—as the cause of global inequality (Worsley, 1990). Dependency theory views poor societies as passive victims and ignores factors inside these countries that contribute to their economic problems. Sociologists have long recognized the vital role of culture in shaping people's willingness to embrace or resist change. Under the rule of the ultra-traditional Muslim Taliban, for example, Afghanistan became economically isolated, and its living standards sank to among the lowest in the world. Is it reasonable to blame capitalist nations for that country's stagnation?

Nor can rich societies be held responsible for the reckless behaviour of foreign leaders whose corruption and militaristic campaigns impoverish their countries. Examples include the regimes of Ferdinand Marcos in the Philippines, François Duvalier in Haiti, Manuel Noriega in Panama, Mobutu Sese Seko in Zaire (now Democratic Republic of the Congo), Robert Mugabe in Zimbabwe, Saddam Hussein in Iraq, Hosni Mubarak in Egypt, and Muammar el-Qaddafi in Libya. Some leaders even use food supplies as weapons in internal political struggles, leaving the masses starving, as in the African nations of Ethiopia, Sudan, and Somalia. Likewise, many countries throughout the world have done little to improve the status of women or to control population growth.

Fourth, critics say that dependency theory is wrong to claim that global trade always makes rich nations richer and poor nations poorer. For example, in 2011, the United States had a trade deficit of US$738 billion, meaning that it imported three-quarters of a trillion dollars more than it sold abroad. In the same year, Canada had a trade deficit of CAD$144 billion; in other words, we imported $143 billion more than we exported to other countries (Statistics Canada, 2011; U.S. Census Bureau, 2012). Prior to the recent collapse of oil prices, a large proportion—up to 80 percent—of our exports (traditionally natural resources including oil and gas) went to the United States—but our imports come from all over the world. In fact, rich countries like Canada and the United States import more than they export—to the benefit of other countries, many if not most of which are poor.

Fifth, critics fault dependency theory for offering only vague solutions to global poverty. Most dependency theorists urge poor nations to end all contact with rich countries, and some call for nationalizing foreign-owned industries. In other words, they charge, dependency theory is really an argument for some sort of world socialism. In light of the difficulties that socialist societies—even better-off socialist countries like Russia—have had in meeting the needs of their own people, critics ask, should we really expect such a system to rescue the entire world from poverty?

The Applying Theory table summarizes the main arguments of modernization theory and dependency theory.

CHECK YOUR LEARNING   State the main ideas of dependency theory. What are several of its strengths and weaknesses?

CANADA AND LOW-INCOME COUNTRIES   Canada's approach to development in low-income countries reveals tension between the modernization and dependency models on which it is based. In 1995, Canada spent $2.2 billion on aid to developing countries (0.3 percent of gross national product [GNP]), down from $3.2 billion (0.5 percent of GNP) in 1992. The 2003 federal budget called for increasing aid spending to $3.2 billion (0.3 percent of GDP) in 2003 and set a goal of increasing this to $8 billion (0.4 percent of GDP) by 2015 (Partridge, 2003). We fell far short of the mark; in 2014 Canada spent only CAD$4.9 billion.

Most Canadian aid was distributed through the Canadian International Development Agency (CIDA). Initially CIDA—which has effectively been disbanded—concentrated on encouraging industrial development Later on it emphasized self-sufficiency and improvement of the lives of the poor through enhancement of health care, housing, education, and agricultural methods, and made the involvement of women a high priority.

Canadians were shaken when—on December 26, 2004—an earthquake in the Indian Ocean gave rise to a tsunami with disastrous consequences, including the loss of more than 150 000 lives, throughout coastal Asia. The Americans were there relatively quickly with hospital ships, aircraft carriers, and helicopters. Canada's official response was slower. But the outpouring of generosity by the Canadian people was phenomenal: Individuals, businesses, schools, and other organizations

APPLYING THEORY

Global Poverty

	Modernization Theory	Dependency Theory
Which theoretical approach is applied?	Structural-functional approach	Social-conflict approach
How did global poverty come about?	The whole world was poor until some countries developed industrial technology, which allowed mass production and created affluence.	Colonialism moved wealth from some countries to others, making some nations poor as it made other nations rich.
What are the main causes of global poverty today?	Traditional culture and a lack of productive technology.	Neocolonialism—the operation of multinational corporations in the global, capitalist economy.
Are rich countries part of the problem or part of the solution?	Rich countries are part of the solution, contributing new technology, advanced schooling, and foreign aid.	Rich countries are part of the problem, making poor countries economically dependent and in debt.

donated tens of millions of dollars, much of which was eventually matched by the federal government. The flood of donations was so great that many organizations, such as *Médecins sans frontiers*, received more money than they could deploy (Gregg, 2005). Eight months later, when Hurricane Katrina hit New Orleans, Canadians responded with generosity once again. In these days of instantaneous electronic communication—within Marshall McLuhan's global village—we see the images of disaster and respond. In the absence of such dramatic images, though, Canadians seem content that our government contributes only a small amount of foreign aid (roughly 0.3 percent of GDP), despite the fact that "something like 12 million people a year continue to die from treatable, preventable diseases" associated with poverty (Gregg, 2005).

In the mid-1980s, Canada responded to changing conditions in low-income countries "with increasingly sophisticated social, cultural, and economic programs for human development and self-reliance" (Tomlinson, 1991). But tension remains between the goals of eliminating poverty and creating an environment conducive to private-sector development and debt reduction through "economic structural adjustment" policies (Canada, 1987). Despite its humanitarian goals, much of Canada's aid continues to be linked to trade or the perceived potential for trade (i.e., "tied aid"). While in this sense Canada's role is similar to that of the United States, some low-income countries are more comfortable accepting aid from Canada, which does not have the superpower status of the United States.

Nonetheless, aid from Canada is sometimes mixed with peacekeeping or military activity. Canada's involvement in Afghanistan is, in effect, aid delivered through military force. Canada contemplated stretching its commitments to intervene in Sudan to help the people of Darfur, who faced what was widely recognized as genocide. This was another situation in which aid could not be delivered without military intervention. People who were opposed to Western military intervention everywhere else pressed Canada and other countries to help Darfur (Wente, 2006). Even though it was already involved in Darfur—helping to negotiate a fragile peace—the Canadian government was under pressure to do more (Galloway, 2006).

Most recently, our attention has turned to the growing threat of ISIS, the crisis in Syria, and the plight of the massive wave of refugees escaping to Europe. Canada responded with a new form of "foreign aid" based on the incredible generosity of its people, welcoming people from a war-torn country rather than having them receive aid in Syrian or Turkish refugee camps. By the end of March 2016, 26 000 Syrian refugees had arrived in Canada. Many of the Syrian refugees have been sponsored by families, community groups, or churches whose actions are those "of the people" rather than the Canadian government.

Some individuals go great lengths to help the Syrian refugees. Sam Jirsi, a father of four who has successful clothing store in Mississauga and teaches graphic design part-time, put all of that on the back burner in order to devote himself to helping the refugees get settled. He started Syrian Active Volunteers (SAV) and soon had more than 600 volunteers, a toll-free Arabic hotline, and warehouse full of clothes, baby supplies, and food staples. When new groups of refugees arrived, the volunteers would meet them and help them deal with the unfamiliar surroundings. SAV also places government-sponsored families in local homes (Smyth, 2016). This is a unique form of "foreign aid"—one that undoubtedly contributes to easier and more rapid adjustment of these newcomers.

In addition to its aid and trade involvements with low-income countries, Canada plays an active role in the generation and dissemination of knowledge in those societies. Several Canadian universities are involved in overseas research and development projects, and most are involved in teaching international students who take their knowledge home or stay to apply it here in Canada. In 2010, Canada was host to 218 245 international students at all levels of education, from elementary to graduate school; roughly half were attending university. The doubling of the number of international students, since 2000, is attributable to economic growth in some of the countries the students came from and active recruitment on the part of our government (Canada, 2016). Most of our foreign students—roughly 55 percent—come from South Korea, China, Japan, France, and Malaysia—countries that, one might say, are beneficiaries of Canada's educational activism.

Another Canadian initiative involves the promotion of a model for the democratic coexistence of diverse groups based on multiculturalism. In September 2007, the Canadian Ethnic Studies Association held a special conference on Ethnicity, Civil Society, and Public Policy: Engaging Cultures in a Globalizing World—and published a special issue of its journal under the same title. The conference was a response to the "pressing issues of governance and ethnic and minority inclusion in a globalizing world" (Aponiuk, 2007). The conference organizers wanted to gain insights into "ethnic inclusion in the global context" and to use those insights "to ensure that ethnic and minority inclusion is fully achieved in Canada."

The Thinking Globally box (p. 327) describes one example of Canadian research and activism in the Yucatán region of Mexico and the Kolli Hills of India.

The Future of Global Stratification

Among the most important economic trends in recent decades is the development of a global economy. In North America, rising production and sales abroad bring profits to many corporations and their shareholders, especially those who already have substantial wealth. People who support the global economy claim that the expansion of trade results in benefits for all countries involved. For this reason, they endorse policies such as the North American Free Trade Agreement (NAFTA), signed by Canada, the United States, and Mexico. They would also encourage Canada to ratify the Trans-Pacific Partnership—which involves 12 Pacific Rim countries, namely the United States, Japan, Malaysia, Vietnam, Singapore, Brunei, Australia, New Zealand, Canada, Mexico, Chile, and Peru. Critics of expanding globalization make other claims: Factory jobs are lost in North America, as more manufacturing now takes place abroad where workers are underpaid and few laws ensure their safety in the workplace. In addition, expanding globalization places ever greater stress on the natural environment—often in low-income countries.

But perhaps the greatest concern is the vast economic inequality that exists among the world's countries. The concentration of wealth in high-income countries, coupled with the grinding poverty in low-income nations, may well be the biggest problem facing humanity in the twenty-first century.

Both modernization theory and dependency theory offer some understanding of this urgent problem. In evaluating these theories, we must consider empirical evidence. Over the course of the twentieth century, living standards rose in most of the world. Even the economic output of the poorest 25 percent of the world's people almost tripled during those 100 years. As a result, the share of the world's population living on less than $1.25 a day fell from about 52 percent in 1981 to about 43 percent in 1990 and to about 22 percent in 2008 (Chen & Ravallion, 2012). The greatest reduction in poverty has taken place in Asia, a region generally regarded as an economic success story. In 1981, almost 77 percent of the population of East Asia was living on less than $1.25 per day. By, 2008, however, that share had declined dramatically to about 14 percent. In 2005, two very large Asian countries—India and China—joined the ranks of the middle-income nations (Bussollo et al., 2007; Chen & Ravallion, 2012; Davies et al., 2008; Sala-i-Martin, 2002; World Bank, 2015).

During the 1970s, Latin America enjoyed significant economic growth, which pushed the share of its population living on $1.25 down to 12 percent by 1981. During the 1980s and 1990s, however, there was little overall improvement until after 2005. By 2008, the share of people living in such poverty was about 7 percent (Chen & Ravallion, 2012).

Sub-Saharan Africa represents the greatest challenge in humanity's efforts to reduce poverty. By 2008, for the first time, less than half of the people of this region were living on $1.25 or less per day. This poverty rate is still well above that of other world regions. Yet analysts are optimistic about Africa's future, pointing out that it has enjoyed average economic growth of more than 5 percent a year over the past decade. In addition, six of the ten fastest developing countries in the world are now in southern Africa (Chen & Ravillion, 2012; Perry, 2012; Sala-i-Martin, 2002).

Looking at the world as a whole, the good news is that, in absolute terms, living standards are rising. Over the course of the past century, economic output has increased for both rich and poor nations. But the troubling trend is that living standards in rich and poor countries are not rising at the same rate. As a result, the relative gap between the rich and the poor in the world is increasing and, in 2013, this divide was nearly five times larger than it was back in 1900. Figure 12–5

Global Snapshot

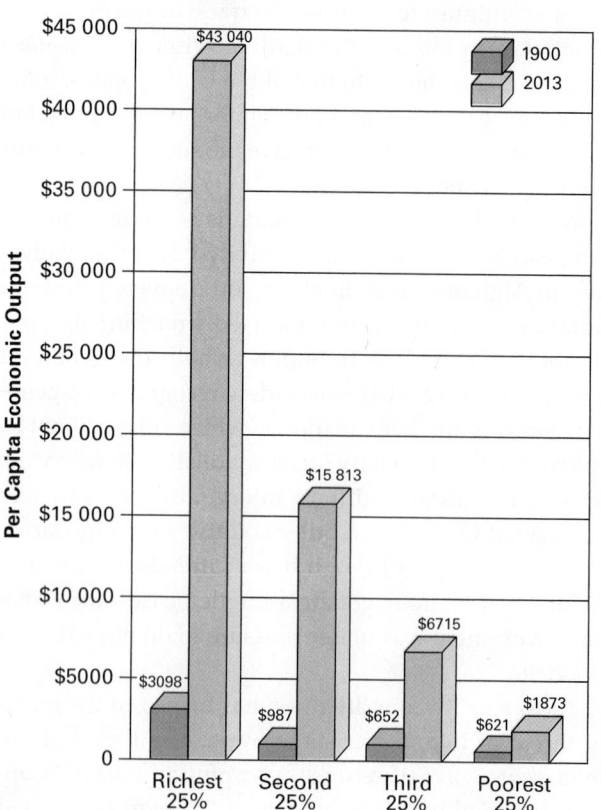

Figure 12–5 The World's Increasing Economic Inequality

The gap between the richest and poorest people in the world in 2013 was more than five times bigger than it was in 1900.

SOURCE: Based on World Bank (2014).

shows that the lower-income people in the world are being left behind.

Recent trends suggest the need to look critically at both modernization and dependency theories. The fact that governments have played a large role in the economic growth that has occurred in Asia and elsewhere challenges modernization theory and its free-market approach to development. On the other hand, since the upheavals in the former Soviet Union and Eastern Europe, a global re-evaluation of socialism has been taking place. Because some socialist nations have a record of decades of poor economic performance and political repression, many low-income nations are unwilling to follow the advice of dependency theory and place economic development entirely under government control.

Although the world's future is uncertain, we have learned a great deal about global stratification. One insight offered by modernization theory is that poverty is partly a problem of technology. A higher standard of living for a surging world population depends on the ability of poor nations to raise their agricultural and industrial productivity. A second insight, derived from dependency theory, is that global inequality is also a political issue. Even with higher productivity, the human community must address crucial questions concerning how resources are distributed, both within societies and around the globe.

Although economic development raises living standards, it also places greater strains on the natural environment. As nations such as India and China—with a combined population of 2.7 billion—become more affluent, their people will consume more energy and other resources. (China has recently passed Japan to become the second-largest consumer of oil, behind the United States.) Richer nations also produce more solid waste and create more pollution.

Finally, the vast gulf that separates the world's richest and poorest people puts everyone at greater risk of war and terrorism as the poorest people challenge the social arrangements that threaten their existence (Lindauer & Weerapana, 2002). In the long run, we can achieve peace on this planet only by ensuring that all people enjoy a significant measure of dignity and security.

Seeing Sociology in Everyday Life

CHAPTER 12   Global Stratification

How much social inequality can we find if we look around the world?

This chapter explains that a global perspective reveals even more social stratification than we find here in North America. Around the world, an increasing number of people in lower-income countries are travelling to higher-income nations in search of jobs. As "guest workers," they perform low-wage work that the country's own more well-off citizens do not wish to do. In such cases, the rich and poor truly live "worlds apart."

> **Hint** Dubai's recent building boom has been accomplished using the labour of about 1 million guest workers, who actually make up about 85 percent of the population of the United Arab Emirates. Recent years have seen a rising level of social unrest, including labour strikes, which has led to some improvements in working and living conditions and better health care. But guest workers have no legal rights to form labour unions, nor do they have any chance to gain citizenship.

MANY GUEST WORKERS COME TO DUBAI FROM INDIA TO TAKE JOBS BUILDING THAT COUNTRY'S NEW HIGH-RISE HOTELS AND BUSINESS TOWERS With very little income, they often sleep six to a small room. How do you think living in a strange country, with few legal rights, affects these workers' ability to improve their working conditions?

Kamran Jebreili/AP Images

GUEST WORKERS IN DUBAI LABOUR ABOUT 12 HOURS A DAY BUT EARN ONLY BETWEEN $50 AND $175 A MONTH Do you think the chance to take a job like this in a foreign country is an opportunity (income is typically twice what people can earn at home), or is it a form of exploitation?

KAMRAN JEBREILI/AP Images

OIL WEALTH HAS MADE SOME OF THE PEOPLE OF DUBAI, IN THE UNITED ARAB EMIRATES, AMONG THE RICHEST IN THE WORLD Dubai's wealthiest people can afford to ski on snow—in one of the hottest regions of the world—on enormous indoor ski slopes like this one. Is there anything about this picture that makes you uncomfortable? Explain your reaction.

Seeing Sociology in *Your* Everyday Life

1. What comparisons can you make between the pattern of guest workers coming to places like Dubai in the Middle East and workers coming to Canada from the Caribbean or to Germany from Turkey?

2. Page through several issues of any current newsmagazine or travel magazine to find any stories or advertising mentioning lower-income countries (selling, say, coffee from Colombia or exotic vacations to India). What picture of life in low-income countries does the advertising present? In light of what you have learned in this chapter, how accurate does this image seem to you?

3. Have you ever travelled in a low-income nation? Do you think people from high-income countries should feel guilty when seeing the daily struggles of the world's poorest people? Why or why not?

Making the Grade

CHAPTER 12 Global Stratification

Global Stratification: An Overview

12.1 Describe the division of the world into high-, middle-, and low-income countries.

High-income countries

- contain 24 percent of the world's people
- receive 59 percent of global income
- have a high standard of living based on advanced technology
- produce enough economic goods to enable their people to lead comfortable lives
- include 74 nations, among them Canada, the United States, Mexico, Argentina, Chile, the nations of Western Europe, Israel, Saudi Arabia, the Russian Federation, Japan, South Korea, Malaysia, and Australia

Middle-income countries

- contain 62 percent of the world's people
- receive 38 percent of global income
- have a standard of living about average for the world as a whole
- include 72 nations, among them the nations of Eastern Europe, Peru, Brazil, Namibia, Egypt, Indonesia, India, and the People's Republic of China

Low-income countries

- contain 14 percent of the world's people
- receive 3 percent of global income
- have a low standard of living
- include 49 nations, generally in Central and East Africa and Asia, among them Chad, the Democratic Republic of the Congo, Ethiopia, and Bangladesh.

> **global stratification** patterns of social inequality in the world as a whole
> **high-income countries** the nations with the highest overall standards of living
> **middle-income countries** nations with a standard of living about average for the world as a whole
> **low-income countries** nations with a low standard of living in which most people are poor

Global Wealth and Poverty

12.2 Discuss patterns and explanations of poverty around the world.

All societies contain relative poverty, but low-income nations face widespread absolute poverty that is life-threatening.

- Worldwide, about 868 million people are at risk due to poor nutrition.
- About 9 million people each year die from diseases caused by poverty.
- Throughout the world, women are more likely than men to be poor. Gender bias is strongest in poor societies.
- As many as 20 million men, women, and children live in conditions that can be described as slavery.

Factors Causing Poverty

- Lack of technology limits production.
- High birth rates produce rapid population increase.
- Traditional cultural patterns make people resist change.
- Extreme social inequality distributes wealth very unequally.
- Extreme gender inequality limits the opportunities of women.
- Colonialism allowed some nations to exploit other nations; neocolonialism continues today.

> **colonialism** the process by which some nations enrich themselves through political and economic control of other nations
> **neocolonialism** a new form of global power relationships that involves not direct political control but economic exploitation by multinational corporations
> **multinational corporation** a large business that operates in many countries

Global Stratification: Applying Theory

12.3 Apply sociological theories to the topic of global inequality.

Modernization theory maintains that nations achieve affluence by developing advanced technology. This process depends on a culture that encourages innovation and change toward higher living standards.

Walt Rostow identified four stages of development:

- *Traditional stage*—People's lives are built around families and local communities. (Example: Democratic Republic of the Congo)
- *Takeoff stage*—A market emerges as people produce goods not just for their own use but also to trade with others for profit. (Example: Thailand)
- *Drive to technological maturity*—Economic growth and higher livings standards are goals; schooling is widely available; the social standing of women improves. (Example: Mexico)

- *High mass consumption*—Advanced technology fuels mass production and mass consumption as people now "need" countless goods. (Example: Canada)

Modernization theory claims . . .

- Rich nations can help poor nations by providing technology to control population size, increase food production, and expand industrial and information economy output and by providing foreign aid to pay for new economic development.
- Rapid economic development in Asia shows that affluence is within reach of other nations.

Critics claim . . .

- Rich nations do little to help poor countries and benefit from the status quo. Low living standards in much of Africa and South America result from the policies of rich nations.
- Because rich nations, including the United States, control the global economy, many poor nations struggle to support their people and cannot follow the path to development taken by rich countries centuries ago.

Dependency theory maintains that global wealth and poverty were created by the colonial process beginning 500 years ago that developed rich nations and underdeveloped poor nations. This capitalist process continues today in the form of neocolonialism—economic exploitation of poor nations by multinational corporations.

Immanuel Wallerstein's model of the capitalist world economy identified three categories of nations:

- *Core*—the world's high-income countries, which are home to multinational corporations
- *Semiperiphery*—the world's middle-income countries, with ties to core nations
- *Periphery*—the world's low-income countries, which provide low-cost labour and a vast market for industrial products

Dependency theory claims . . .

- Three key factors—export-oriented economies, a lack of industrial capacity, and foreign debt—make poor countries dependent on rich nations and prevent their economic development.
- Radical reform of the entire world economy is needed so that it operates in the interests of the majority of people.

Critics claim . . .

- Dependency theory overlooks the tenfold increase in global wealth since 1950 and the fact that the world's poorest countries have had weak, not strong, ties to rich countries.
- Rich nations are not responsible for cultural patterns and political corruption that block economic development in many poor nations.

> **modernization theory** a model of economic and social development that explains global inequality in terms of technological and cultural differences between nations
>
> **dependency theory** a model of economic and social development that explains global inequality in terms of the historical exploitation of poor nations by rich ones

The Future of Global Stratification

- Global stratification is partly a matter of global differences in productive technology and partly a political matter involving the ways in which economic resources are distributed among nations and within nations.
- Although all regions of the world have made economic gains in absolute terms, the gap between rich and poor nations is more than five times larger than it was a century ago.

Chapter 13
Gender Stratification

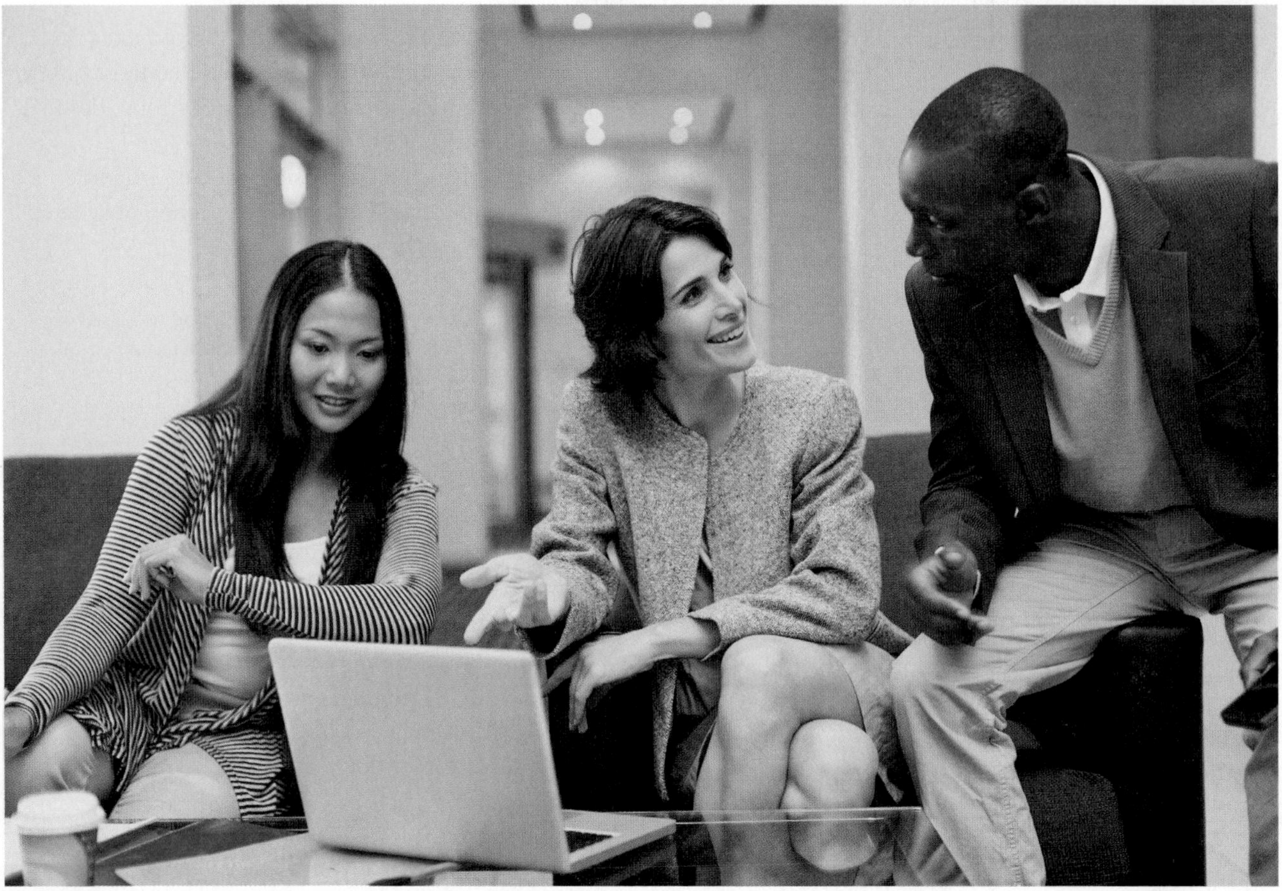

Hybrid Images/Cultura Creative/Alamy Stock Photo

Learning Objectives

13.1 Describe the ways in which society creates gender stratification.

13.2 Explain the importance of gender to socialization.

13.3 Analyze the extent of gender inequality in various social institutions.

13.4 Apply sociology's major theories to gender stratification.

13.5 Contrast liberal, radical, and socialist feminism.

The Power of Society
to guide our life choices

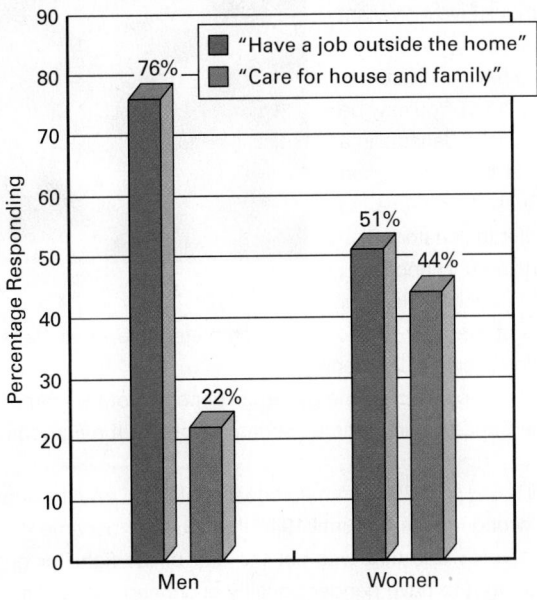

Survey Question: "If you were free to do either, would you prefer to have a job outside the home, or would you prefer to stay at home and take care of the house and family?"

SOURCE: Based on Gallup (2012).

A recent survey asked this question and got different answers from men and women. Among men it was no contest; a large majority (three-quarters) chose a job outside the home, with 22 percent preferring "to stay at home and take care of the house and family." Among women, one-half chose a job outside the home and almost as many (44 percent) chose to stay at home to care for house and children. Not surprisingly, women were twice as likely to choose home over an outside job. These differences between men and women show the power of society to shape our most personal of choices. But they also illustrate the power of society to change our responses over time. If this question was asked in the 1950s, would we have found that *almost a quarter of men preferred to stay at home*? That seems unlikely; however, the significant words in the question are "if you were free to do either." In the real world—for any number of reasons—men may not feel free to make that choice.

Chapter Overview

We live in a world organized around not only differences of social class but also around the concepts of feminine and masculine, which sociologists call "gender." This chapter examines gender, explores the meaning societies attach to being female or male, and explains how gender is an important dimension of social stratification.

In 1927, five women—each a well-known activist at the time—asked the Supreme Court of Canada to recognize women as "persons" so that they could be eligible for appointment to the Senate. The case is known as the *Persons Case,* and the women were Henrietta Muir Edwards, Nellie Mooney McClung, Louise Crummy McKinney, Emily Ferguson Murphy, and Irene Marryat Parlby. Collectively known as The Famous Five (or Valiant Five), they have statues erected in their honour in Calgary and on Parliament Hill in Ottawa and have their stories told in *100 Canadian Heroines* (Forster, 2004). You may be surprised to learn that the Supreme Court of Canada, in a unanimous ruling, declared in 1927 that the word *person* did *not* refer to women. After all, the *British North America Act* used the word *he* exclusively to refer to senators. The five women then went to London, England, to appeal to the Judicial Committee of the Privy Council—the final court of appeal for the British Empire at the time; in 1929, the Committee ruled that Canadian women *are* persons who could, therefore, serve in the Senate.

Barrett&MacKay Photo

As a result, in 1930, Cairine Wilson was called by the governor-general (not the prime minister, as is the case today) to become Canada's first woman senator. None of the Famous Five was made a senator.

If you think that the Privy Council ruling of 1929 confirmed equal rights for Canadian women in the broader sense, you would be wrong. It was not until 1940 that Quebec became the last province to grant women the right to vote—and that was not the end of the fight for gender equality. Astonishingly, women had to fight to have gender equality enshrined in the *Canadian Charter of Rights and Freedoms* in 1982. At a time when Prime Minister Trudeau and other politicians were willing to grant equality on the basis of race, ethnicity, age, disability, and religion, there were some who thought it would be unwise or even dangerous to add sex to the list, fearing demands for equal pay and abortion rights. The Advisory Council on the Status of Women was thwarted by the Liberals—specifically by Lloyd Axworthy, the minister responsible for the status of women—in its attempt to hold a national conference on the proposed charter. Regional conferences were preferred by the government.

In defiance, through networking—on parliamentary telephones—three women (Doris Anderson, Pauline Jewett, and Flora MacDonald) were able to arrange for 1300 women from across Canada to gather in Ottawa for an ad hoc conference in February 1981. The women's conference was instrumental in having sexual equality enshrined in our constitution—just as American women saw their Equal Rights Amendment go down to defeat (McKenzie, 1999: 123–125). Subsection 15(1) of the *Canadian Charter of Rights and Freedoms* (Canada, 1982) now provides that "Every individual is equal before and under the law and has the right to the equal protection and equal benefit of the law without discrimination based on race, national or ethnic origin, colour, religion, sex, age, or mental or physical disability." ∎

While sexual equality is now guaranteed by the *Canadian Charter of Rights and Freedoms,* women and men still lead different lives in Canada and throughout the world; in most respects, men are still in charge. In this chapter, we explore the importance of gender as a major dimension of social stratification.

Gender and Inequality

13.1 Describe the ways in which society creates gender stratification.

Sex refers to the biological differences that divide the human population into the categories of female and male. **Gender**, on the other hand, refers to *the personal traits and social positions that members of a society attach to being female or male.* Gender operates as a dimension of social organization, shaping how we interact with others and how we think about ourselves. More importantly, gender also involves hierarchy, ranking men and women differently in terms of power, wealth, and other resources. This is why sociologists speak of **gender stratification**, *the unequal distribution of wealth, power, and privilege between men and women.* Gender, in short, affects the opportunities and constraints we face throughout our lives.

Male/Female Differences

Many people think there is something "natural" about gender distinctions because the sexes do have biological differences. But we must be careful not to think of social differences in biological terms. Until recently—1918 in Canada—women were denied the vote because it was assumed that women did not have enough intelligence or interest in politics to warrant enfranchisement. Such attitudes had nothing to do with biology; they reflected the cultural patterns of that time and place.

Another example is athletic performance. In 1925, most people—both women and men—believed that the best women runners could never compete with men in a marathon. Today, as Figure 13–1 shows, the gender gap has greatly narrowed, and the fastest women routinely post better times than the fastest men of decades past. Here again, most of the differences between men and women turn out to be socially constructed.

Nonetheless, differences in physical ability between the sexes do exist. On average, males are 10 percent taller, 20 percent heavier, and 30 percent stronger, especially in their upper body (Ehrenreich, 1999). On the other hand, women outperform men in the ultimate game of life itself: Life expectancies for women and men in Canada are 83 and 79 years, respectively (compared to 81 and 76 years in the United States).

In adolescence, males do a bit better in mathematics, and females show stronger writing skills, differences that

---

gender the personal traits and social positions that members of a society attach to being female or male

gender stratification the unequal distribution of wealth, power, and privilege between men and women

---

Diversity Snapshot

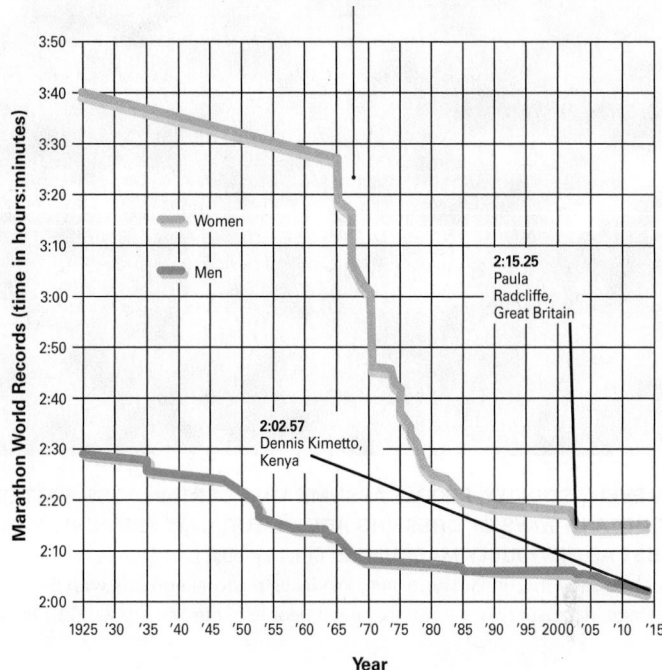

● The women's movement of the 1960s encouraged women to show their true abilities.

Figure 13–1 Men's and Women's Athletic Performance

Do men naturally outperform women in athletic competition? The answer is not obvious. Early in the twentieth century, men outpaced women by more than an hour in marathon races. But as opportunities for women in athletics have increased, women have been closing the performance gap. Only twelve and one-half minutes separate the current world marathon records for women (set in 2003) and for men (set in 2014).

SOURCE: Marathonguide.com (2015).

---

reflect both biology and socialization (Lewin, 2008). However, research does not point to any difference in overall intelligence between males and females.

Biologically, then, men and women differ in limited ways; neither is naturally superior. But culture can define the two sexes very differently, as the global study of gender in the next section shows.

Gender in Global Perspective

The best way to see the cultural foundation of gender is by comparing one society to another. Three important studies highlight just how different "masculine" and "feminine" can be.

THE ISRAELI KIBBUTZ In Israel, collective settlements are called *kibbutzim.* The *kibbutz* (the singular form of the word) is an important setting for research because gender equality is one of its stated goals; men and women share in both work and decision making. In kibbutzim, both sexes share most everyday jobs: Both men and women

Carol Beckwith/Robert Estall photo agency/Alamy Stock Photo

IN EVERY SOCIETY, PEOPLE ASSUME THAT CERTAIN JOBS, PATTERNS OF BEHAV-IOUR, AND WAYS OF DRESSING ARE "NATURALLY" FEMININE WHILE OTHERS ARE JUST AS OBVIOUSLY MASCULINE But, in global perspective, we see remarkable variety in such social definitions. These men, Wodaabe pastoral nomads who live in Niger, are proud to engage in a display of beauty that most people in our society would consider feminine.

take care of children, cook and clean, repair buildings, and make day-to-day decisions concerning life in the kibbutz. Girls and boys are raised in the same way and, from the first weeks of life, children live together in dormitories. Women and men in kibbutzim have achieved remarkable—although not complete—social equality, evidence that cultures define what is feminine and what is masculine.

MARGARET MEAD'S RESEARCH Anthropologist Margaret Mead carried out groundbreaking research on gender. If gender is based on biological differences between men and women, she reasoned, people everywhere should define "feminine" and "masculine" in the same way; if gender is cultural, these conceptions should vary.

Mead (1963; orig. 1935) studied three societies in New Guinea. In the mountainous home of the Arapesh, she observed men and women with remarkably similar attitudes and behaviour. Both sexes, she reported, were co-operative and sensitive to others—in short, what North American culture would label "feminine."

Moving south, Mead then studied the Mundugumor, whose headhunting and cannibalism stood in striking contrast to the gentle ways of the Arapesh. In this culture, both sexes were typically selfish and aggressive, traits that North Americans define as more "masculine."

Travelling west to the Tchambuli, Mead discovered a culture that, like our own, defines females and males differently. But, she reported, the Tchambuli *reversed* many of our notions of gender: Females were dominant

and rational, and males were submissive, emotional, and nurturing toward children. Based on her observations, Mead concluded that culture is the key to gender differences, because what one society defines as masculine another may see as feminine.

Some critics view Mead's findings as "too neat," as if she saw in these three societies just the patterns she was looking for. Deborah Gewertz (1981) challenged what she called Mead's "reversal hypothesis," pointing out that Tchambuli males are really the more aggressive sex. Gewertz explained that Mead visited the Tchambuli during the 1930s, after they had lost much of their property in tribal wars; Mead had observed men rebuilding their homes: a temporary role only.

GEORGE MURDOCK'S RESEARCH In a broader study of more than 200 pre-industrial societies, George Murdock (1937) found some global agreement about which tasks are feminine and which are masculine. Hunting and warfare, Murdock concluded, generally fall to men, and home-centred tasks such as cooking and child care tend to be women's work. With their simple technology, pre-industrial societies apparently assign roles reflecting men's and women's physical characteristics. With greater size and strength, men hunt game and protect the group; because women bear children, they do most of the work in the home.

But beyond this general pattern, Murdock found much variety. Consider agriculture: Women did the farming in about the same number of societies as men; in most farming societies, the two sexes shared this work. When it came to many other tasks—from building shelters to tattooing the body—Murdock found that various societies were as likely to turn to one sex as the other.

EVALUATE

Global comparisons show that, overall, societies do not consistently define tasks as either feminine or masculine. With industrialization, the importance of muscle power declines, further reducing gender differences (Nolan & Lenski, 2007). In sum, gender is too variable across cultures to be a simple expression of biology; what it means to be female and male is mostly a creation of society.

CHECK YOUR LEARNING By comparing many cultures, what do we learn about the origin of gender differences?

Patriarchy and Sexism

Although conceptions of gender vary, everywhere in the world we find some degree of **patriarchy** (literally, "the rule of fathers"), *a form of social organization in which males dominate females.* Despite mythical tales of societies run by female Amazons, **matriarchy**, *a form of social organization in which females dominate males,* has only rarely been documented in human history.

The pattern found almost everywhere in the world is patriarchy. Global Map 13–1 shows the great variation in the relative power and privilege of women that exists from country to country. According to the United Nations, the Netherlands, Denmark, and Sweden give women the highest social standing; by contrast, women in the nations of Niger, Democratic Republic of Congo, and Yemen have the lowest social standing in comparison to men (United Nations Development Programme, 2010).

The justification for patriarchy is **sexism**, *the belief that one sex is innately superior to the other.* Sexism is not just a

patriarchy a form of social organization in which males dominate females

matriarchy a form of social organization in which females dominate males

sexism the belief that one sex is innately superior to the other

matter of individual attitudes; it is built into the institutions of society. *Institutional sexism* is found throughout the economy, with women concentrated in low-paying jobs. Similarly, the legal system has long excused violence against women, especially on the part of boyfriends, husbands, and fathers.

THE COSTS OF SEXISM Sexism limits the talents and ambitions of the half of the human population who are women. While men benefit in some respects from sexism, their privilege comes at a high price. Masculinity in our culture encourages men to engage in many high-risk

Window on the World

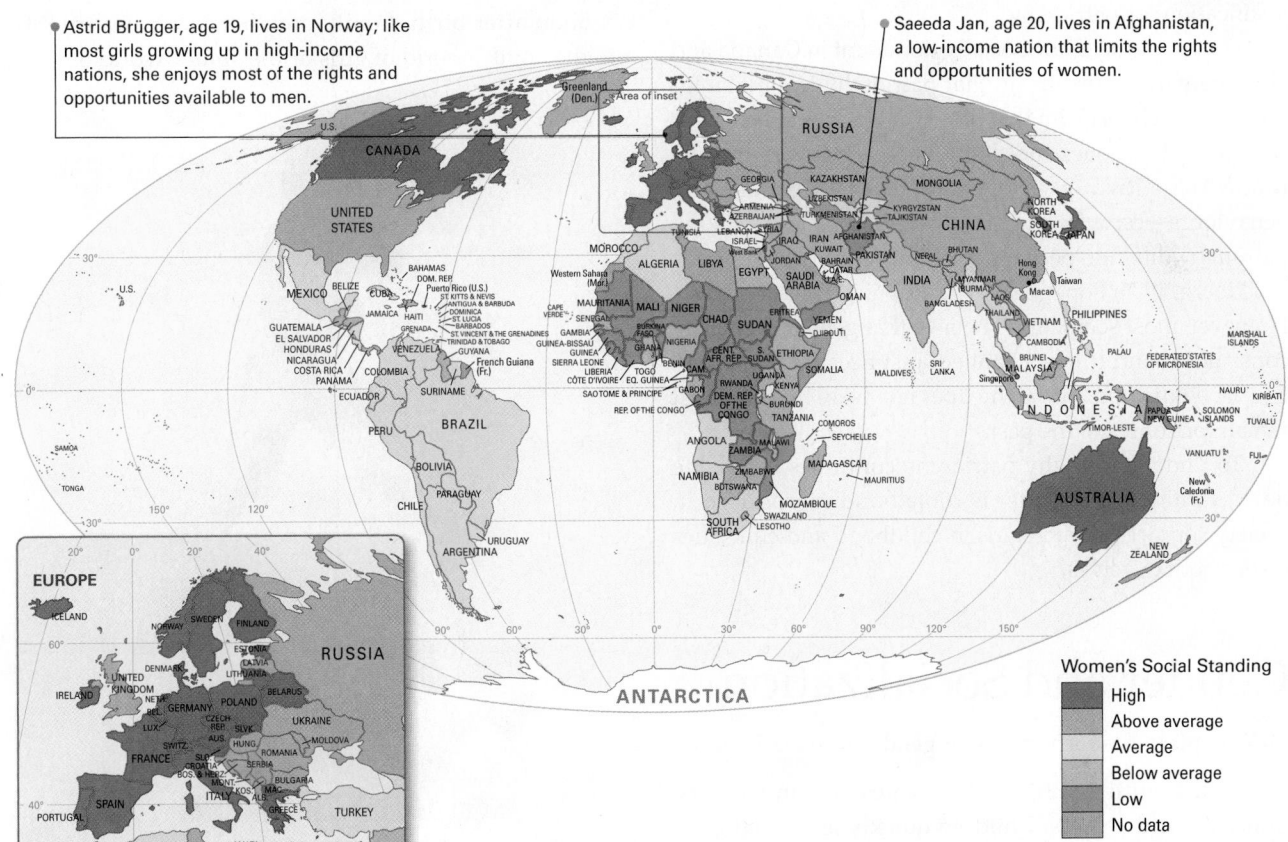

Global Map 13–1 Women's Power in Global Perspective

Women's social standing in relation to men's varies around the world. In general, women live better in rich countries than in poor countries. Even so, some nations stand out: In the Netherlands, Sweden, Slovenia, and Switzerland women come closest to social equality with men.

SOURCE: Data from United Nations Development Programme (2014).

behaviours: using tobacco and alcohol, playing dangerous sports, and driving recklessly. As Marilyn French (1985) argued, patriarchy leads men to seek control, not only of women but also of themselves and their world. This is why masculinity is closely linked not only to accidents but also to suicide, violence, and stress-related diseases. The *Type A personality* (marked by chronic impatience, driving ambition, competitiveness, and free-floating hostility) is a recipe for heart disease and almost perfectly matches the behaviour that our culture considers masculine (Ehrenreich, 1983).

Finally, as men seek control over others, they lose opportunities for intimacy and trust. As one analyst put it, competition is supposed to "separate the men from the boys"; in practice, however, it separates men from men and everyone else (Raphael, 1988).

IS PATRIARCHY INEVITABLE?   In pre-industrial societies, women have little control over pregnancy and childbirth, which limits the scope of their lives. In those same societies, men's greater height and physical strength are highly valued resources. But industrialization and birth-control technology give people real choices in life—so that in modern societies biological differences offer little justification for patriarchy.

However, males are socially dominant in Canada and elsewhere. Does this mean that patriarchy is inevitable? Some researchers claim that biological factors such as differences in hormones and slight differences in brain structure wire the two sexes with different motivations and behaviours—especially aggressiveness in males—making patriarchy difficult, perhaps even impossible, to eliminate (Goldberg, 1974; Popenoe, 1993b; Rossi, 1985; Udry, 2000). However, most sociologists believe that gender is socially constructed and can be changed. Just because no society has yet eliminated patriarchy does not mean that we must remain prisoners of the past.

To understand why patriarchy continues today, we next examine how gender is rooted and reproduced in society, a process that begins in childhood and continues throughout our lives.

Gender and Socialization

13.2 Explain the importance of gender to socialization.

From birth until death, gender shapes human feelings, thoughts, and actions. Children quickly learn that their society considers females and males to be different kinds of people; by about age three, they begin to think of themselves in these terms.

In the past, women were described using such terms as *emotional, passive,* and *co-operative;* in contrast, men were described in opposing terms, such as *rational, active,*

and *competitive.* We have been taught to think of gender in terms of opposition—one sex being the opposite of the other—despite the fact that women and men have much in common and that most young people develop personalities that are a mix of feminine and masculine traits (Bem, 1993).

Just as gender affects how we think of ourselves, so it teaches us how to behave. **Gender roles** (or **sex roles**) are *attitudes and activities that a society links to each sex.* A culture that defines males as ambitious and competitive encourages them to seek out positions of leadership and play team sports. To the extent that females are defined as deferential and emotional, they are expected to be supportive helpers and quick to show their feelings.

Gender and the Family

The first question people usually ask about a newborn—Is it a boy or a girl?—has great importance because the answer involves not just sex but the likely direction of the child's life. In fact, gender is at work even before the birth of a child because, especially in low-income nations, parents hope their first-born will be a boy rather than a girl (Pappas, 2011).

Soon after birth, family members welcome infants into the "pink" world of girls or the "blue" world of boys

Biddiboo/The Image Bank/Getty Images

SEX IS A BIOLOGICAL DISTINCTION THAT DEVELOPS PRIOR TO BIRTH Gender is the meaning that a society attaches to being female or male. Gender differences are a matter of power, because what is defined as masculine typically has more importance than what is defined as feminine. Infants begin to learn the importance of gender by the way parents treat them. Do you think this child is a girl or a boy? Why?

(Bernard, 1981). Parents even send gender messages in the way they handle infants. One researcher at an English university presented an infant dressed as either a boy or a girl to a number of women; her subjects handled the "female" child tenderly, with frequent hugs and caresses, and treated the "male" child more roughly, often lifting him up high in the air or bouncing him on the knee (Bonner, 1984; Tavris & Wade, 2001). The lesson to children is clear: The female world revolves around co-operation and emotion, and the male world puts a premium on independence and action.

Gender and the Peer Group

About the time they enter school, children begin to move outside the family and make friends with others of the same age. Considerable research shows that young children tend to form single-sex play groups (Martin & Fabes, 2001).

Peer groups teach additional lessons about gender. After spending a year observing children at play, Janet Lever (1978) concluded that boys favour team sports that have complex rules and clear objectives such as scoring runs or making touchdowns. Such games nearly always have winners and losers, reinforcing masculine traits of aggression and control.

Girls, too, play team sports. But, Lever explains, girls also play hopscotch, jump rope, or simply talk, sing, or dance. These activities have few rules, and rarely is

"victory" the ultimate goal. Instead of teaching girls to be competitive, Lever explains, female peer groups promote the interpersonal skills of communication and co-operation, presumably the basis for girls' future roles as wives and mothers.

Gender and Schooling

Even before children enter school, their reading tends to promote gender distinctions. More than a generation ago, the Royal Commission on the Status of Women (Canada, 1970) analyzed a selection of children's texts and found that "versatile characters who have adventures are invariably males" (Mackie, 1983:185). Even math books represented males and females differently; for example, a problem focusing on the number of words typed per minute in 45 minutes referred to the typist as female. The royal commission concluded that "a woman's creative and intellectual potential is either underplayed or ignored in the education of children from their earliest years" (Canada, 1970:175). More recently, a growing awareness among authors, publishers, and teachers of the limiting effects of gender stereotypes on young people has led to changes. Today's books for children portray females and males in more balanced ways.

Through primary and secondary school, despite many efforts at change, classroom curricula may still encourage children to embrace traditional gender patterns. Young women are expected to excel in languages and social studies, young men in mathematics and sciences. In university, the pattern continues, with men and women tending toward different majors. Men are disproportionately represented in mathematics and the sciences, including physics, chemistry, and biology. Women cluster in the humanities (such as English), the fine arts (painting, music, dance, and drama), education courses, and the social sciences (including anthropology and sociology). New areas of study are also likely to be gender-typed: Computer science, with its grounding in engineering, logic, and mathematics, attracts mostly men, while courses in gender studies tend to attract mostly women.

Gender and the Mass Media

Since television first captured the public imagination in the 1950s, White males have held centre stage. Racial and ethnic minorities were all but absent from television until the early 1970s; only in the past few decades have programs featured women in prominent roles. Even when both sexes appear on camera, men generally play the brilliant detectives, fearless explorers, and skilled surgeons. Women, in contrast, play the less-capable characters, often unnecessary except for the sexual interest they add to the story.

IN OUR SOCIETY, THE MASS MEDIA HAVE ENORMOUS INFLUENCE ON OUR ATTITUDES AND BEHAVIOR, AND WHAT WE SEE SHAPES OUR VIEW OF GENDER In the 2012 film *Hunger Games*, we see Jennifer Lawrence playing Katniss Everdeen, a take-charge, female lead character. Such a portrayal is an exception to the conventional pattern by which active males play against more passive females. In your opinion, how much can the mass media change conventional ideas about gender? Why?

Murray Close/Lionsgate/Everett Collection

Historically, advertisements have shown women in the home, cheerfully using cleaning products, serving foods, and trying out new appliances. Men, on the other hand, predominate in ads for cars, travel, banking services, industrial companies, and alcoholic beverages. The authoritative "voice-over" (the voice that promotes products on television and radio) is almost always male (Coltrane & Messineo, 2000; Davis, 1993; Messineo, 2008; Statista, 2015).

A careful study of gender in advertising reveals that men usually appear taller than women, implying male superiority. Women are more frequently presented lying down (on sofas and beds) or, like children, seated on the floor. Men's facial expressions and behaviour give an air of competence and imply dominance; women often appear childlike, submissive, and sexual. Men focus on the products being advertised; women direct their interest to men, conveying support and submission (Cortese, 1999; Goffman, 1979).

Gender and Social Stratification

13.3 **Analyze the extent of gender inequality in various social institutions.**

Gender involves more than thought and action. It also determines one's place in the social hierarchy. The reality of gender stratification can be seen most clearly in the world of work.

Working Women and Men

In 1901, women made up 13 percent of Canada's paid workforce and earned half of men's income. Figure 13–2 reveals that, in 1971, women (15 years of age and over) had an employment rate of 36 percent; by 2011, this rate had risen to 57 percent, up 21 percentage points. Over the same period, the male employment rate—always higher—actually dropped by 6 percentage points (from 71 to 65 percent). Note that the population aged 15 years and over includes people who are too *young* or too *old* to be working as well as those pursuing their education full time. Luckily, it is possible to examine employment rates by age.

By examining employment in the prime working years (i.e., 35 to 44 years of age), we can minimize the contaminating effects of prolonged schooling, child-bearing and caring for preschool children, disability, or retirement. If in your lifetime you are ever going to be working, it is in that age range. Figure 13–3 shows that male employment rates in those prime working

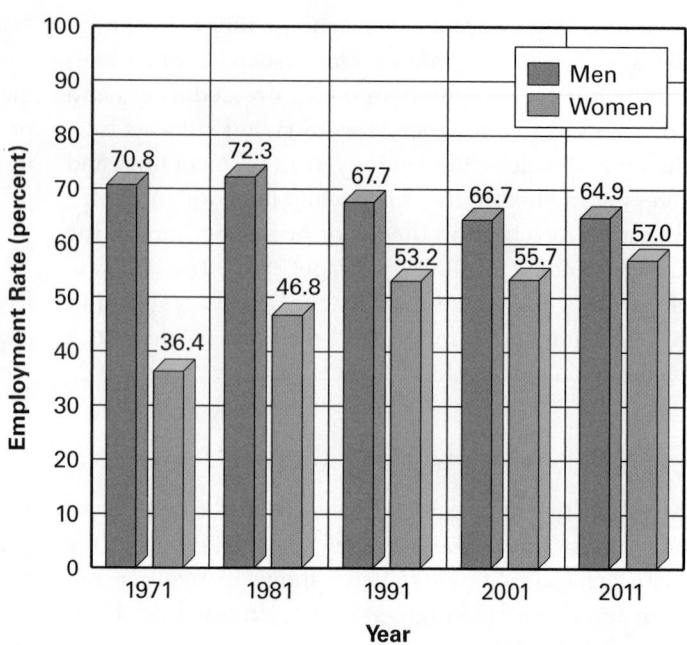

Figure 13–2 Employment Rates of Men and Women (15 Years of Age and Over) in Canada, 1971 to 2011

SOURCE: Compiled by L.M. Gerber from Statistics Canada, NHS 2011, Catalogue no. 99-010-X2011036.

years are consistently high: 89 dropping to 86 percent by 2011. In sharp contrast, employment rates for women 35 to 44 years of age increased by *36 points* between 1971 and 2011—from 41 to 77 percent. In other words, in

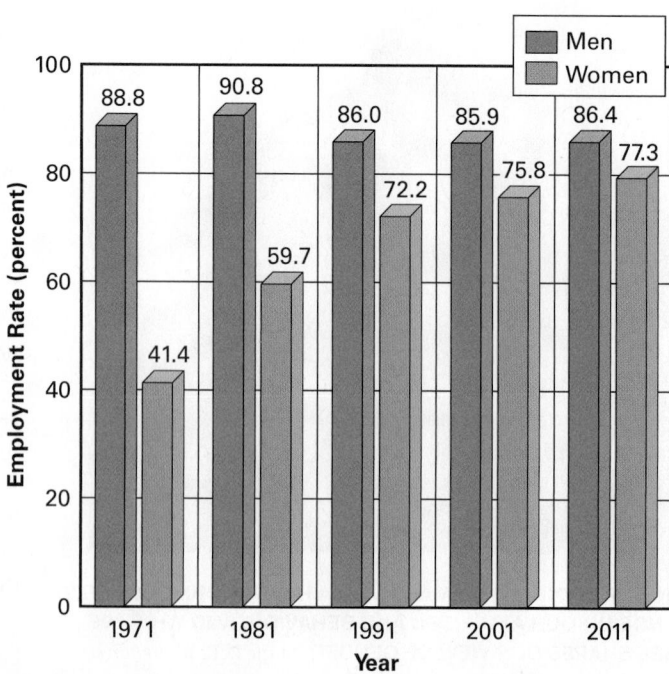

Figure 13–3 Employment Rates of Men and Women (35 to 44 Years of Age) in Canada, 1971 to 2011

SOURCE: Compiled by L.M. Gerber from Statistics Canada, NHS 2011, Catalogue no. 99-010-X2011036.

1971, only a minority of women were employed—even in their prime working years. By 2011, three-quarters of prime-working-age women were employed—a dramatic increase by any measure.

Factors that changed Canada's employment rates include the decline of farming, the growth of cities, the post-industrial economy, increasing education, shrinking family size, and a rising divorce rate—and the fact that 65 percent of married couples depend on two incomes (*Statistics Canada* 1995:65). Women working for income today are the rule rather than the exception, for they now represent almost half (48 percent in 2011) of our paid labour force; among those who are employed, 62 and 52 percent of men and women have full-time jobs. In the past, mothers with young children stayed at home; today, they are very likely to continue working when parental leave ends. In fact, many career women fail to take advantage of the full year of parental leave to which they are entitled. (*Parental leave* used to be called *maternity leave*; the term was changed when men began to leave work to care for infants.)

Gender, Occupations, and Income

In the past, many jobs were done mainly by women—with others done mainly by men. During the past few decades, we have seen considerable blurring of the distinctions between men's work and women's work. In unprecedented numbers, women are moving into business, finance, engineering, the sciences, medicine, and veterinary medicine—while a visit to a hospital or a nursing home reveals the presence of male nurses, who now make up 7 percent of the total. In 1982 and 1994, respectively, clerical occupations employed 34 and 27 percent of all working women; by 2001, the figure had dropped to 14 percent. In this category are secretaries, typists, stenographers, and others whose efforts typically support those of men. Not surprisingly, while in 1994 more than 80 percent of all such "pink-collar" job-holders were women, by 2001, the figure had dropped to 73 percent. The second-largest category is service work, performed by more than 17 percent of employed women. These jobs include waiting tables, hairdressing, house- or office-cleaning, *and* early childhood education. Both categories of jobs—clerical and service—lie at the low end of the pay scale and offer limited opportunities for advancement.

Overall, gender stratification permeates the workplace, where men tend to hold occupational positions that confer more wealth and power than those typically held by women. On the other hand, change is occurring, however slowly. The Sociology in Focus box takes a closer look at the complex interactions of gender, occupation, and income and deals with some of the factors that—along with discrimination and the "glass ceiling"—give rise to the gender gap in income.

Housework: Women's "Second Shift"

In North America, we have always been of two minds about housework: We claim that it is essential to family life, but people get little reward for doing it. Here, as around the world, taking care of the home and children has always been considered "women's work." With women's entry into the labour force, the amount of housework women do has decreased, but women continue to do more than men. Men do support the idea of women entering the paid labour force, and most count on the money that women earn, but most resist taking on a more equal share of household duties—because our society gives men no support or encouragement for doing more housework (Nelson & Robinson, 1999:299). The result is that married men with children do 3.2 hours of housework per day while their wives do 4.8—despite the fact that both partners are employed full time (p. 293).

Recent analysis done for Statistics Canada (Milan et al., 2010) presents what can only be described as discouraging findings. In dual-earner households—where the woman works *full time*—she does 14 hours of domestic work per week (or 2 hours per day) while the man does 8.6 per week (or 1.2 hours per day). Whereas men do a little more than half of the domestic work (2010), this falls short of the share reported for the 1990s in the previous paragraph. And we have only considered domestic chores. The statistics on hours spent in child care support the claim that women work a *second shift* at home. Women in dual-earner families, who work full time, put in another 50 hours per week (7 hours/day) on child care—something that clearly qualifies as a second job! In the meantime, the man in that dual-earner family puts in 27 hours (almost 4 per day) to the woman's 50—which is a little more than half of her work load. That said, men are making significant—though far from equal—contributions to domestic work and child care. However, the real eye-opener is the fact that women put 50 hours per week into child care along with 14 more into household chores. That is 64 hours in total—a very hefty second shift indeed.

Gender and Education

In the past, our society considered schooling to be more necessary for men than women because they worked outside the home. But times have changed. In Canada, in every year from 1999 to 2003, women earned more than 58 percent of all degrees, diplomas, and certificates granted throughout the country. Of the larger provinces,

Sociology in Focus

Understanding the Gender Gap in Occupation and Income and All the Fuss about Women as Breadwinners

Among people employed full time, all year, women earn 71 percent of male income. Generally speaking, we hear six explanations for this fact:

- Women choose occupations that are poorly paid (i.e., cashier rather than motor vehicle assembler).
- Women take time out from their jobs or careers to have children.
- Women are more likely to work part time.
- Women are shut out of traditional male occupations, such as engineering.
- If women make it into these occupations at all, employers choose to pay them less.
- Women are less likely to be promoted.

Note that the last three explanations imply gender discrimination.

In an attempt to assess the merits of these six explanations, we can look at occupational and income data for women and men. We deal here with 43 of the several hundred occupations in Canada, ranging from upper to lower income; these occupations are ranked by male income (in 2005) and include a number that might be of interest to you. Useful comparative statistics are presented in Table 13–1. The table may be difficult to read, but it contains a wealth of information extracted from Statistics Canada's massive census databases—a medium greatly underused but available to everyone via the internet. (Do a Google search for "Statistics Canada census.")

Before doing any analysis, we must determine the nature of the data in each of the columns of Table 13–1, noting first that we are dealing exclusively with workers who are employed full time, all year. The first column lists selected occupations (from specialist physicians and web designers to taxi or limousine drivers) ranked by male income in 2005. Halfway down that column, the row labelled "ALL OCCUPATIONS" refers to average income earned by full-time workers in all of the (perhaps 1000) occupations listed in the census. All occupations above this point provide above-average incomes for *men*; occupations with below-average male incomes (for full-time work) appear below it.

The second and third columns list average incomes for males and females who work full time in the selected occupations. Average incomes (for all occupations) appear in bold about halfway into the table. The reason for ranking occupations by male income is that it is the basis for calculating female/male income ratios. Keep in mind that male and female rankings are not identical. For example, secretaries rank twenty-seventh on the male list and thirty-first on the female list. Whereas only 2 percent of secretaries are men (see column five), they are *very* well paid relative to women ($55 929 versus $33 538).

The fourth column includes the female/male income ratio—otherwise known as the "gender gap" in income. A glance at the ratio for ALL OCCUPATIONS reveals that women who work full time earn 71 percent of the income earned by men. At the low end, female tool and die makers earn 56 percent of male income, rising to 60 percent for senior managers, auditors and accountants, and secretaries. At the top end, female actors and comedians or taxi and limousine drivers earn *more* than their male counterparts for full-time work. Notice that some of the income ratios, namely those above 0.85, or 85 percent, appear in *bold italics*. These refer to occupations for which female income is most equal to that of men.

What about the concentration of men and women in different occupations? The fifth column indicates the percentage of each occupation that is female, with levels of 80 percent or more appearing in *bold italics*. Less than 2 percent of plumbers and motor vehicle mechanics are women—as are 3 or 4 percent of heavy equipment operators, miners and oil or gas drillers, firefighters, and tool and die makers. At the other extreme, registered nurses, early childhood educators, and secretaries are between 94 and 98 percent female. These occupations are commonly referred to as "pink ghetto" jobs.

The 43 occupations listed in Table 13–1 are not a random sample of the hundreds included in the census. Instead, specific jobs were chosen because they might be of interest to students. Nonetheless, it is worth noting some interesting patterns.

The top six occupations are between 25 and 40 percent female but, while these levels may be low, they do indicate that women are moving into high-income fields. Close to 40 percent of family physicians and lawyers are women. On the other hand, there is only one occupation (that of court judges) in which women are well-paid relative to men. *One* of the explanations is that, as newcomers, women have less seniority, less experience, and (among physicians, lawyers, and dentists) less time to have established their practices.

The next four occupations—from pharmacists to veterinarians—are 40 to 60 percent female and, with the exception of auditors and accountants, have above average female/male income ratios. With the exception of human resources managers, the next five occupations—engineers through firefighters—include very few women (3 to 20 percent), but they close the gender gap in income, especially among police officers, where the ratio is 0.86. (Pay equity is most apparent among police officers, miners and gas or oil drillers, and firefighters, but women are not drawn to these typically dangerous jobs that include shift work.)

Table 13–1 Average Income for Full-Time Work (2005), the Gender Gap, and Percentage Female in Selected Occupations

	Male income ($)	Female income ($)	Female/male income ratio	Percentage female
Specialist physician	225 613	151 286	0.67	33.8
Judge	198 031	178 351	*0.90*	24.6
Family physician	163 640	118 264	0.72	38.5
Lawyer	161 942	106 671	0.66	38.6
Dentist	158 094	100 047	0.63	31.2
Senior manager	154 521	92 588	0.60	23.8
Pharmacist	112 702	85 299	0.76	59.4
University professor	96 281	78 798	0.82	38.9
Auditor and accountant	95 523	57 600	0.60	49.4
Veterinarian	83 149	66 514	0.80	50.3
Engineer	82 165	62 480	0.76	11.4
Human resources manager	79 330	58 206	0.73	63.9
Police officer	75 064	64 792	*0.86*	20.4
Miner and oil or gas driller	73 348	59 999	0.82	3.1
Firefighter	69 596	58 176	0.84	3.0
Physiotherapist	62 173	55 916	*0.90*	*80.0*
Probation and parole officer	61 671	56 043	*0.91*	59.2
Secondary school teacher	60 964	55 121	*0.90*	57.3
Registered nurse	60 889	58 750	*0.96*	*93.8*
Librarian	59 931	53 670	*0.90*	*82.6*
Chiropractor	59 908	45 802	0.76	30.1
Tool and die maker	59 734	33 277	0.56	4.4
Elementary school teacher	59 122	54 048	*0.91*	*83.6*
ALL OCCUPATIONS	**58 537**	**41 331**	**0.71**	**47.3**
Motor vehicle assembler	57 558	42 345	0.74	32.1
Journalist	56 860	50 356	*0.89*	45.1
Secretary	55 929	33 538	0.60	*97.9*
Social worker	54 244	50 627	*0.93*	*81.6*
Editor	52 890	46 997	*0.89*	59.3
Heavy equipment operator	50 447	42 972	*0.85*	2.8
Plumber	48 007	33 532	0.70	1.9
Author and writer	44 692	41 675	*0.93*	52.9
Web designer and developer	43 344	40 404	*0.93*	34.1
Truck driver	42 635	33 217	0.78	3.6
Motor vehicle mechanic	41 404	35 607	*0.86*	1.7
Chef	31 693	25 503	0.80	22.4
Dancer	29 836	23 263	0.78	*86.3*
Actor and comedian	27 281	29 765	*1.09*	45.0
Early childhood educator	26 559	20 999	0.79	*96.4*
Farm worker	24 576	16 994	0.69	33.0
Musician and singer	24 180	21 660	*0.90*	51.8
Cashier	23 387	19 614	0.84	*85.2*
Farmer and farm manager	22 116	17 875	0.81	25.4
Taxi and limousine driver	19 599	20 603	*1.05*	8.0

SOURCE: Compilations and calculations by L.M. Gerber based on Statistics Canada, 2006 Census of Population, Catalogue no. 97-564-XCB2006005.

(continued)

The last of the occupations with above-average incomes—from physiotherapists to elementary school teachers—stand in sharp contrast to those in the higher income categories. With the exception of chiropractors and tool and die makers, percentage female varies from almost 60 to 94 percent. And, most significantly, all the occupations dominated by women have income ratios of 0.90 or more (0.96 among registered nurses).

The jobs appearing below ALL OCCUPATIONS in terms of average income are a mixed bag of proportion female, but are remarkably consistent in terms of pay equity. The representation of women is *very* low among heavy equipment operators, plumbers, truck drivers, and motor vehicle mechanics—but they are well paid, relative to men, in these occupations (with ratios of 0.85 and 0.86, respectively). At the other extreme, women comprise 81 to 98 percent of those employed full time as secretaries, social workers, dancers, early childhood educators, and cashiers. Unfortunately, the only occupation among them that stands out in terms of pay equity is social work (which requires a bachelor's degree and a master's in social work), with a ratio of 0.93. The lowest equity score among these female-dominated occupations is that of secretaries. Men represent a mere 2 percent of secretaries and are probably employed in highly unusual settings (wherever a male secretary is a status symbol). The 4 percent of men among early childhood educators may find themselves promoted to supervisory roles.

Women who are employed as journalists, editors, authors/writers, and web designers (35 to 60 percent) are consistently well-paid relative to their male counterparts, with equity ratios of 0.89 to 0.93. Might it be that each of these occupations requires language and symbolic skills? Note that, traditionally, women were presumed to excel in this area rather than at mathematics and the hard sciences.

Lastly, the two occupational categories in which women are paid slightly more than men (at 1.09 and 1.05, or 109 and 105 percent) are actors and comedians and taxi or limousine drivers.

Now that you know how to interpret the data in the table, look closely at the six explanations for the gender gap in income.

The first is that women choose jobs that are poorly paid. In 2005, women made up 80 to 98 percent of full-time cashiers, early childhood educators, dancers, social workers, secretaries, elementary school teachers, librarians, registered nurses, and physiotherapists. Significantly, none of these occupations appears among the top 15 in the table—four are above average and five are below average in income. On the basis of Table 13–1, one could argue that, whatever the decision-making process, women are indeed choosing to enter low-paying jobs, or at least choosing not to prepare for high-paying jobs. Why, *in the past,* were women more likely to choose nurses' training, while men went to medical school? Part of the answer lies in socialization. Girls learned that they were not "capable" of mastering the mathematics and science needed to get into medical

school. Also, since most hoped to get married and raise families, it made little sense to pursue 12 or more years of post-secondary education. But things are changing. For at least the past 15 years, the majority of medical students in Canada have been women, and many men have become nurses (making up 6 percent of the full-time nursing workforce). The data are not included in this table, but, between 1995 and 2005, the proportion of women among human resources managers increased by 20 percentage points, 14 points among university professors, and 13 points among secondary school teachers. This suggests that, although historically women have been employed in poorly paid pink ghetto jobs, currently they are preparing for and making inroads into top-end occupations.

The second explanation for the gender gap is that women take time off work or interrupt their careers to have children. If a young lawyer leaves her firm for six to 10 years to have three children and raise them to school age, what happens to her career? Even if she leaves work for only three years of parental leave, she still takes a hit in terms of career continuity, client base, and promotion. As career-oriented women calculate the "costs" of having children, many decide to forgo motherhood altogether or to have only one child. Women in highly paid occupations, such as senior managers or lawyers, incur greater costs on this front than do early childhood educators or social workers.

The third explanation is that women are more likely to work part time. This is true, but part-time work does not contribute to the gender differences in income shown in the table—for the simple reason that the data refer to women and men who are employed *full time*. Thus, we are comparing apples and apples. When full- and part-time employment are *combined,* women earn 63 percent of men's income (compared to 71 percent among full-time workers).

The fourth basis for the gender gap is that gatekeepers exclude women from certain occupations. Steelworkers and truck drivers (now 3.6 percent female) undoubtedly reacted with skepticism or even hostility when women first had the audacity to compete for their jobs; those in other male-dominated occupations undoubtedly resisted as well. In this light, it is surprising to learn that 32 percent of motor vehicle assemblers are women! Although many of the women working in male-dominated fields are younger and lack the seniority or the experience that secures a high income, female motor vehicle assemblers earn 74 percent of male income. Since the doors of engineering schools, medical schools, and veterinary colleges are wide open to women—and many such programs are 50 to 80 percent female—it seems that women are no longer being excluded from occupations that were traditionally dominated by men.

The fifth explanation is that employers choose to pay women less. Perhaps the best way to poke a small hole in this argument is to look at the income ratio for specialist physicians. In that prestigious occupation, women earned 67 percent of male income in 2005 (for full-time employment). How could this be? Note that doctors in Canada do not have employers; more than 95 percent are in private practice (i.e., self-employed), so there is no employer to pay women less. The vast majority of physicians earn income, and pay office expenses, by billing the government on a fee-for-service basis—every time they operate, deliver a baby, or take a blood pressure. Women now make up one-third of specialist physicians, but the *new or younger* specialists are disproportionately *female*. They have had only a short time to establish their practices and gain the reputations that bring them referrals from local family doctors. The point is that women specialists earn two-thirds the income of their male colleagues, in part because of their choice of specialties (brain surgeons earn more than pediatricians), but it has nothing to do with the actions of employers.

Income in many, if not most, other occupations is related to years of service; if women have recently increased their representation, they are *by definition* young relative to their male counterparts. There is no doubt that some employers pay women (in the same occupation) less if they can get away with it, but we cannot discount or wish away the influence of age or seniority. To the extent that women are new to their professions, they will be paid much less than men who have been working for 15 years or more.

The last explanation is that women do not get promoted. The occupational category that most clearly reflects the results of promotion is senior management. The proportion of women among senior managers increased from 18 to 24 percent between 1995 and 2005—meaning that women now make up a quarter of Canada's senior managers. It is important to keep in mind that these women are relatively new to the organizations that they lead. Women encounter the "glass ceiling" and discrimination in their quest for promotion, but the situation is changing, in part because there is a larger cadre of talented, career-oriented women from which to draw. These women must put in time before they qualify for promotion. Think for a moment about engineering firms, which have been criticized for a lack of female executives. Only recently have women entered engineering schools in significant numbers. If it takes men 15 years to move through the ranks to senior management levels, how long will it be before there is a pool of female engineers qualified for promotion to the top ranks? The point is that discrimination—which accounts for about one-third of the gender gap in income (Fuller & Schoenberger, 1991)—is not the only explanation for the lack of women in the highest corporate ranks.

Warren Farrell, in *Why Men Earn More: The Startling Truth behind the Pay Gap—and What Women Can Do about It* (2005), gives the following advice. If, as a woman, higher pay is your goal—which is not the case for many—you should "choose a field in technology or the hard sciences, not the arts or social sciences." Know that, in high-paying fields, women cannot "psychologically check out at the end of the day." They need to be willing to take risks, assume new and bigger responsibilities, work very long hours, put in more years of uninterrupted work with their current employer, relocate, and travel extensively

on the job. More women today are willing to make these commitments and sacrifices—often forgoing marriage and children altogether. As women make these decisions and commitments, we will see more of them in the highest income brackets and at the top of the corporate world. But, argues Farrell, dreams of gender equality notwithstanding, women may never equal men in their willingness to do what it takes to make it to the top.

"Women Make the Grade, but Not the Money" is the title of a *Globe and Mail* article (Morrow & Alphonso, 2010) that contends that women are outperforming men at all educational levels, "but they fall starkly behind on the bottom line—in their paycheques." This, in part, is the result of biases *and* the tendency of women to choose "less lucrative occupations than men—social work, say, rather than engineering." However, the authors argue, it does not explain why Canada's record on pay equity lags behind the 30 countries in the Organisation for Economic Co-operation and Development. The question centres around why women make these choices. High on the list of reasons are responsibility for children and more part-time work.

Even though, *on average,* women trail behind men on earned income, there is an increasingly large number of women who are incredibly successful in terms of education, employment, occupation, and income. The Thinking about Diversity box tells the stories of a number of women, but there are hundreds of thousands of others—physicians, lawyers, CEOs, bankers, provincial premiers, university presidents, and owners of successful businesses—whose incomes are two or three times those of the men in their lives. It is not easy for a successful, high-profile woman to meet eligible men at her level.

A *Maclean's* article (Gulli, 2012) titled "The Richer Sex: One-Third of Women Now Earn More Than Their Husbands, and Not Everyone Is Happy" deals with authors in the United Kingdom and the United States who have written books about the phenomenal increase in the proportion of women earning more than their husbands (31 percent in the United Kingdom and over 40 percent in the United States). The American book *The Richer Sex: How the New Majority of Female Breadwinners Is Transforming Sex, Love and Family* (Mundy, 2012) deals with the tremendous adjustments that women and men must make as they negotiate their relationships through uncharted territory in a period of unprecedented social change. Mundy (2012, 26) explains that, in the early 1800s, "the prevailing view was that woman's sphere was the home and that she should be made as uncomfortable as possible in the workplace." Because women were paid less than men, when they *did* enter the workplace, men complained of "ruinous competition"—competition that prevented them from securing the "family wage" required of the breadwinner. Men and women "occupied not merely separate roles, but separate spheres" and, in order to ensure that women stayed at home, they needed to be completely dependent on men for food and shelter. Tradition, religion, the law, and culture reinforced the gender inequality that persists to this day.

(continued)

Table 13–1 suggests that the higher levels of education acquired by women are beginning to chip away at the old order. Although incomes are far from equal, women are moving into traditionally male occupations, where they will gradually gain experience, expertise, clientele, and seniority. At another level, if a women leaves her job as a cashier and signs on as a motor vehicle assembler, her income more than doubles. The female physician, police officer, or motor vehicle assembler may have a higher income than her male partner. Once this happens—and it *is* happening—couples negotiate very different kinds of relationships. Mundy has a vision of gender relations that goes beyond equality or a 50–50 sharing of responsibilities. "Something has to give" in order for women to assume the breadwinner role and succeed in their chosen careers, especially if there are children involved. Women who thrive in their work "will be valued for their earnings and achievements" and will be "supported by men who understand just what they have won in the bargain: Emotional lives that are richer and life trajectories that are more varied than men's once were" (2012:222). This revolutionary change, which turns the traditional order upside down, is global (touching even Japan). York University women's studies professor Andrea

O'Reilly recognizes the "rise of women" phenomenon, while University of Guelph business professor Sean Lyons points out that couples are questioning the desirability of the male breadwinner model and suggests that "gender equality norms are changing" (cited in Gulli, 2012). No one argues that renegotiating or reconstructing gender roles is easy or that all couples will survive the process intact—but change is clearly under way.

What Do You Think?

1. What does Table 13–1 reveal about gender equality or inequality and changes in gender relations? Are there positive messages in the statistics?

2. Farrell points out that jobs with higher pay are often less fulfilling or emotionally satisfying (e.g., engineer versus child-care professional). Are you willing to give up fulfillment for higher pay? Does your gender affect your answer to this question?

3. Does the "female breadwinner" or "rise of women" phenomenon make sense to you? Do you know couples with female breadwinners? If so, how have they adjusted to this relatively new state of affairs?

the only one that stood out was British Columbia, which started off below average (at 57.8 percent female in 1999) and took the lead in 2003 (at 60.6 percent female).

Table 13–2 deals with educational attainment—in 2006 and 2011—by men and women 15 years of age and over (the standard measure) and between 35 and 44 years of age. Data for the age range of 35 to 44 years are significant because they better reflect recent changes in gender attainment patterns. Also, by 35 years of age, almost everyone has completed his or her education—even through medical or graduate school. The first row in the table reveals that, in either year, roughly a quarter of the adult population will have completed high school at least,

even though 15- to 18-year-olds are included in the population. Trades or apprenticeship certification is acquired by 14 percent of men but only 7 percent of women.

Recent changes in patterns of attainment rarely make a dent in the record of the population aged 15 and over, but you can see that women are more likely than men to earn bachelor's degrees and that the gender gap—in favour of women—increased ever so slightly in the 2006–2011 interval. As far as postgraduate certification is concerned, it's worth noting that, in this huge population (15 to 100+ years in age), master's degrees are the most common—a little more so among men than women. Furthermore, women are half as likely to have Ph.D.s as men.

Table 13–2 Educational Certification by Sex and Age in Canada, 2006 and 2011

	15 Years of Age and Over				35 to 44 Years of Age			
	2006 Men	2011 Men	2006 Women	2011 Women	2006 Men	2011 Men	2006 Women	2011 Women
High school	24.1	24.9	23.4	26.2	14.1	21.5	11.1	19.3
Trades/Apprenticeship	14.3	14.5	7.6	7.3	15.8	14.7	9.7	8.2
College or CEGEP	15.3	15.9	19.2	20.4	19.4	20.0	24.9	25.7
Bachelor's degree	11.1	12.4	12.2	14.3	15.0	17.4	16.9	21.2
Medical degree*	0.7	0.7	0.4	0.5	0.7	0.8	0.7	0.8
Master's degree	3.7	4.1	3.1	3.8	5.2	6.1	4.4	6.0
Doctorate (Ph.D.)	1.0	1.0	0.4	0.5	1.2	1.2	0.6	0.9

*Refers to degrees in medicine, dentistry, veterinary medicine, or optometry.

SOURCES: Compilation and Calculations by L.M. Gerber, based on Statistics Canada, Census 2006, Catalogue no. 97-559-XCB2006028 and NHS 2011, Catalogue no. 99-012-X2011040.

Courtesy Canadian Forces

IN MAY 2006, CAPTAIN NICOLA GODDARD, AGE 26, WAS KILLED IN A BATTLE WITH THE TALIBAN NEAR KANDAHAR Knowing the risks of deployment to Afghanistan, she was eager to take on the job for which she had been training for eight years. Women, who make up 15 percent of the armed forces, have been fully integrated in Canada's armed forces since gender equality was guaranteed by the *Canadian Charter of Rights and Freedoms* in 1982. Unlike the United Kingdom and the United States, Canada allows women to serve in combat zones.

Among people aged 35 to 44—the ones who have more recently completed their education—women stand out with more college diplomas and bachelor's degrees than men. In addition, the effect of women earning the majority of bachelor's degrees in recent years shows up quite clearly here. While men gained 2 percentage points in the attainment of bachelor's degrees between 2006 and 2011, women gained 4 points. Thus the gap between men and women increased. In this smaller cohort, we find that women are equal to men in the attainment of medical certification (broadly defined as medicine, dentistry, veterinary medicine, or optometry) and earn almost half of the doctorates or Ph.D.s—albeit in the social and behavioural sciences or education rather than engineering, mathematics, physics, and computer sciences. Clearly, women are gaining on men and even surpassing them at some levels (such as the bachelor's degree), but it may be some time

before we see added education opening doors to equal employment opportunities (including promotions) and higher income.

Field of study also factors into the educational attainment picture because men and women predominate in different disciplines of study. Although women are making inroads, men still lead in engineering and the hard sciences (e.g., mathematics, physics, computer science). Note that women are slower to move into engineering than hard sciences. Women predominate most clearly in the health professions and education, but also in fine arts, the natural sciences (e.g., biology, nutrition), the humanities, and the social sciences. Recently, women are as likely as men to study commerce or business administration and the law. The fact that women make up more than two-thirds of those who study sociology will not surprise you.

Gender and Politics

Before 1918, women could not vote in federal elections. Until 1919, no women were allowed to sit in the House of Commons, and until 1929, no women were allowed to sit in the Senate of Canada. It was not until 1940 that women could vote in all provincial elections (Quebec was the holdout), and not until 1982 that were women granted equal protection and equal benefit of the law in the *Canadian Charter of Rights and Freedoms*. Table 13–3 cites benchmarks in women's gradual movement into Canadian politics and public life.

Today, women are involved in all levels of politics in Canada. Still, the largest proportion of women politicians is found in the municipal arena. Women are also well represented on local school boards, where they can act on their normative and institutionalized "responsibility" for their children. Women face many barriers to participation in federal politics, especially if they have young families at home and live in different time zones from Ottawa, where they must spend a major portion of each year, or most of the year if they are Cabinet ministers.

There are, however, signs of change. An increasing proportion of members of Parliament (MPs) are women. The Canadian Advisory Council on the Status of Women stated that, if the number of women in the House of Commons continued to increase at the rate it did between the 1984 and 1988 elections, in nine elections (or approximately 45 years), there would be equal numbers of men and women in the House. While, by 1997, 20.6 percent of MPs were women, there was essentially no change through the 2000, 2004, and 2006 elections, suggesting that the expected increase in female representation had stalled. The 2006 election, which resulted in a Conservative minority government under Stephen Harper, left us with the same level of representation by women, rather than a drop as some had expected. In 2008, Canada

Table 13–3 Benchmarks for Women in Canadian Politics and Public Life

Year	Benchmark
1916	Women in Manitoba, Alberta, and Saskatchewan gain right to vote in provincial elections.
1917	Women with property permitted to hold office in Saskatchewan. Women in British Columbia and Ontario gain right to vote in provincial elections.
1918	Most women gain right to vote in federal elections.* Women in Nova Scotia gain right to vote in provincial elections.
1919	Women in New Brunswick gain right to vote in provincial elections.
1920	Uniform franchise established through the *Dominion Election Act*, making permanent the right of women to be elected to Parliament.
1921	Agnes Macphail is the first woman elected to the Canadian Parliament.
1922	Women in Prince Edward Island gain right to vote and to hold elected office.
1925	Women over age 25 gain right to vote in Newfoundland.
1929	Women are deemed "persons" and can therefore be appointed to Senate after the British Privy Council overturns Supreme Court of Canada's 1928 *Persons Case* decision.
1930	First woman, Cairine Wilson, is appointed to the Senate.
1940	Women in Quebec gain right to vote in provincial elections, completing enfranchisement of most women in Canada.*
1957	Ellen Fairclough becomes the first woman federal Cabinet minister.
1982	Activists Doris Anderson, Pauline Jewett, and Floral MacDonald help secure—for women—equal protection benefit of the law under the Charter.
1983	*Canadian Human Rights Act* amended to prohibit sexual harassment and to ban discrimination on the basis of pregnancy and family or marital status.
1984	Jean Sauvé is the first woman to be appointed as governor-general.
1989	Audrey McLaughlin becomes the first woman to lead a federal Canadian political party.
1993	Kim Campbell becomes Canada's first woman prime minister.
1999	Adrienne Clarkson becomes the first governor-general to belong to a visible minority (and the second woman).
2000	Beverley McLachlin is the first woman to be sworn in as Chief Justice of the Supreme Court of Canada.
2004	Ruby Dhalla and Yasmin Ratansi are the first Sikh woman and the first Muslim woman, respectively, to be elected as members of Parliament.
2004	Louise Arbor, a Supreme Court of Canada Justice, is appointed United Nations High Commissioner for Human Rights.

*Exceptions are Chinese, Indo-Canadian, Japanese, Inuit, and First Nations women, who were excluded because of their race or ethnicity, rather than because they were women. Canadians of Chinese and Indian origins were enfranchised in 1947, and those of Japanese origin by 1948. Inuit men and women gained the right to vote in 1950, and First Nations men and women became enfranchised without losing their Treaty status in 1960.

SOURCE: Adapted from the Statistics Canada publication "Canada Year Book," Catalogue no. 11-402, 1992; *Canadian Global Almanac* (2005), McKenzie (1999).

elected 69 women (22.1 percent of MPs) and, in 2011, set a record by electing 76 women to the House of Commons (24.6 percent of the members). The majority of female MPs (40 of the 76) were elected under the NDP banner—27 of them in Quebec (Fitzpatrick, 2011). The federal election of 2015—which resulted in a Liberal majority government led by Prime Minister Justin Trudeau—elected 88 female MPs or 26 percent of the total. This is a record high that might have been higher still had the NDP not collapsed (Anderssen, 2015).

In 1989, the New Democratic Party (NDP) became the first of Canada's major federal political parties to elect a woman leader: Audrey McLaughlin. In June 1993, Kim Campbell became Canada's first female prime minister by winning the leadership of the Progressive Conservative party when Brian Mulroney stepped down. From 1997 to 2003, Alexa McDonough was the only female party leader in the House of Commons. In the Liberal party, Sheila Copps was a star member of the federal cabinet, deputy prime minister for a term, and several times

a contender for leadership of her party. Belinda Stronach was instrumental in uniting the right—the Canadian Alliance and the Progressive Conservatives. In 2011, Elizabeth May—the only female federal party leader in the House of Commons—was the first Green Party candidate to be elected (Fitzpatrick, 2011). Elizabeth May was re-elected in 2015 and joined Rona Ambrose, interim leader of the Conservative Party of Canada, as one of two female party leaders.

Are Women a Minority?

A **minority** is *any category of people distinguished by physical or cultural difference that a society sets apart and subordinates.* Given the economic disadvantage of being a woman in our society, it seems reasonable to say that Canadian women are a minority even though they outnumber men.

Subjectively speaking, most White women do not think of themselves as members of a minority (Lengermann & Wallace, 1985). This is partly because,

BELINDA STRONACH, FORMER CEO AND PRESIDENT OF MAGNA INTERNATIONAL—THE AUTO-PARTS MANUFAC-TURER WITH MORE THAN US$12 BILLION IN ANNUAL REV-ENUES—WAS NAMED BY *FORTUNE* **AS THE SECOND MOST POWERFUL WOMAN IN BUSINESS OUTSIDE THE UNITED STATES** This influential woman facilitated the merger of the Canadian Alliance and the Progressive Conservatives in the fall of 2003—a move that would dramatically change Canada's political landscape (Dubé, 2003). Stronach switched to politics, first as a Conservative, then as a Liberal Cabinet minister. In 2007, she announced that she would not seek re-election because she had breast cancer. Currently, she is a vocal advocate of breast cancer research and treatment.

unlike racial and ethnic minorities, White women are well represented at all levels of the class structure, including the very top. Bear in mind, however, that, at every class level, women typically have less income, wealth, education, and power than men. Patriarchy makes women dependent on men—first on their fathers and later on their husbands—for their social standing (Bernard, 1981). The Thinking about Diversity box tells the stories of powerful Canadian women who overcame the barriers associated with their minority position in society.

Violence against Women

Perhaps the most wrenching kind of suffering that our society imposes on women is violence. Official statistics paint criminal violence as overwhelmingly the actions of men—hardly surprising, since aggressiveness is a trait our culture defines as masculine. Furthermore, a great deal of "manly" violence is directed against women, which we also might expect because North American society devalues what is culturally defined as feminine.

A 1993 Statistics Canada survey found that 51 percent of Canadian women had experienced at least one instance of sexual or physical violence; about 25 percent of women were subject to violence at the hands of an intimate partner (Statistics Canada, 1994b). The most common location for gender-linked violence is the home. Another study by Statistics Canada (2005a) found that an "estimated 7 percent of women and 6 percent of men in a current or previous spousal relationship encountered spousal violence" in the previous five years. Richard Gelles (cited in Roesch, 1984) argues that, with the exception of the police and the military, the family is the most violent organization in the United States; there is no reason to think that the picture is any different in Canada. Both sexes suffer from family violence, but in most cases women sustain more serious injuries than men (Gelles & Cornell, 1990; Lupri, 2002; Shupe et al., 1987; Smolowe, 1994; Straus & Gelles, 1986). Spousal homicide rates have declined since the 1970s—for women *and* for men. However, "the rate of spousal homicide against women has been 3 to 5 times higher than against males" (Nelson, 2010:365).

Violence against women also occurs in casual relationships. Most sexual assaults (specifically rapes) involve not strangers but men known to—and often trusted by—women. Dianne F. Herman (2001) argues that the extent of abuse suggests that sexual violence is built into our way of life. All forms of violence against women—from the wolf whistles that intimidate women on city streets to a pinch in a crowded subway and physical assaults that occur at home—express what she calls a "rape culture" by which men try to dominate women. Sexual violence, then, is fundamentally about power rather than about sex and should, therefore, be understood as a dimension of gender stratification (Nelson, 2010).

In global perspective, violence against women is built into diverse cultures in different ways. One case in point is the practice of female genital mutilation, a painful and often dangerous surgical procedure performed in more than 40 countries and known to occur in Canada and the United States. Among some members of highly patriarchal societies, husbands demand that their wives be virgins at marriage and remain sexually faithful thereafter. The point of female genital mutilation (i.e., *clitoridectomy*) is to eliminate sexual feeling, which, people assume, makes a girl less likely to violate sexual norms and thus be more desirable to men. In about one-fifth of all cases, an even more severe procedure, called *infibulation,* is performed, in which the entire external genital area is removed and the surfaces are stitched together, leaving only a small hole for urination. Before marriage, a husband retains the right to open the wound and ensure

Thinking About Diversity: Race, Class, and Gender

Powerful Canadian Women

Most of us are vaguely aware of powerful or influential Canadian women in our collective past and present. Some of them are historical figures, such as the Famous Five, or Molly Brant, Emily Carr, Pauline Johnson, Agnes Macphail, Lucy Maud Montgomery, Laura Secord, and Harriet Tubman (Forster, 2004; Merritt, 1993). More recently, political activist Pauline Jewett joined the list of trailblazers (McKenzie, 1999).

Financial Post recognizes Canada's most influential women by publishing, annually, "The Power 50" and the Women's Executive Network's list 100 of "Canada's Most Powerful Women" (Jeffrey, 2011). Francis (2003) points out that any list of influential women is arbitrary and subjective. How do you choose 50 or 100 when there is such a "wealth of talented Canadian women"? So much that is written about women in the workplace or gender stratification emphasizes the negative, focusing on the barriers faced by women—the effects of patriarchy, poverty, and the "glass ceiling." Here we will do an about-face and look at some of the stellar achievements of the women around us.

Chief Justice for Canada Beverley McLachlin, in addition to her legal training, has acquired an impressive number of honourary degrees "granted to acknowledge the incredible academic feats of a rancher's daughter who eventually reached the pinnacle of the Canadian judiciary system." On the other hand, her climb to the top was not always easy. Grateful to have come on the scene when our legal institutions were looking for female talent, she concedes that, at times, she was discouraged because "you felt you had to work harder with less opportunity and recognition" (Pratt, 2003).

There are many women who are the presidents, CEOs, or senior executives of major corporations, such as Linda Hasenfratz, CEO of Linamar Corp; Sherry Cooper, executive vice-president and global economic strategist of BMO Financial Group (until her retirement in 2013); Annette Verschuren, president of Home Depot Canada (1996–2011); Belinda Stronach, former president and CEO of Magna International; Anna Porter, co-founder, publisher, and CEO of Key Porter Books (until 2004); Heather Reisman, founder of Indigo and current owner of Indigo, Chapters, and Coles; Kathy Sendall, former senior vice-president of Petro-Canada, with multiple awards and board memberships, teaching fellow and director of the Manning Foundation for Innovation; Bobbie Brooks, CEO and president of Hudson's Bay Company (until 2014); Betty Devita, former president of MasterCard Canada, currently chief commercial officer of MasterCard Labs (global research and development); Mandy Shapansky, CEO and president of Xerox Canada until her retirement in 2014; and Lisa de Wilde, CEO of TVOntario since 2005. It is worth noting

CHIEF JUSTICE FOR CANADA BEVERLEY MCLACHLIN, THE ELDEST OF FIVE CHILDREN, GREW UP ON A RANCH IN THE FOOTHILLS OF THE ALBERTA ROCKIES, WHERE SHE HELPED HER MOTHER COOK FOR THE RANCH HANDS As Chief Justice of the Supreme Court of Canada (since 2000), she is arguably the most influential woman—if not person—in the country.

that several of these companies are in such distinctly "masculine" fields as auto parts, oil and gas, and home improvement.

One of the most unlikely stories is that of Catherine McLeod-Seltzer and Eira Thomas, founders of Vancouver-based Stornoway Ventures. These women already had "formidable reputations" in the prospecting world before they discovered two diamond-bearing rock formations on a remote tip of land in northern Nunavut. "'Exploration is in my blood,' Thomas says. 'It really is the thrill of the chase that I find rewarding'" (quoted in Hasselback, 2003). McLeod-Seltzer is equally in love with her work—and that is prospecting and mining we are talking about. She is also a board member at Kinross Gold Corporation.

Then there are those women who change our way of thinking about the world around us. Margaret Atwood has written more than 50 books, many of which have won international awards, that shake up our perceptions of the world around us. Roberta Jamieson (CEO and president of the National Aboriginal Achievement Foundation since 2004 and a member of the Order of Canada) has provided scholarships to over 11 000 Aboriginal students and showcased the outstanding achievements of Aboriginal people in the arts, science, business, communications, and other fields. Wanda Wuttunee (professor and director of the Aboriginal Business Education Program at the University of Manitoba) taught us about the interaction of Aboriginal and capitalist values and helped students bridge the gap. Jane Jacobs came to Canada from the United States, where she had written the influential book *The Death and Life of Great American Cities.* Jacobs played a key role in stopping the Spadina Expressway, which many felt would have had a devastating effect on downtown Toronto, and was an "urban planning activist" until her death in 2006. Her goal was to make cities livable, and she had tremendous influence on local planners and politicians—making fans of former Toronto mayor David Miller and late NDP leader Jack Layton in the process (Evans, 2003).

Sheila Fraser, auditor-general of Canada (2001–2010), has had immeasurable influence on the Canadian political scene. Most notably, she uncovered and reported the mismanagement of funds in the Quebec sponsorship program (or Adscam). The Gomery inquiry into the sponsorship program, which was televised in English and French, led to trials and convictions as well as the downfall of the Liberal government. The success of Harper's Conservative government in heartland Quebec (in the 2006 election) is directly attributable to Adscam. More recently, Fraser discovered serious problems with Canada's gun registry—in the areas of cost overruns and the quality and accuracy of registry information.

If we turn to the university scene, we find that at least four of Canada's major universities are, or have recently been, headed by women: Heather Munroe-Blum, former principal and vice-chancellor of McGill; Indira Samarasekera, former president and vice-chancellor of the University of Alberta (2005–2015); Martha Piper, former president of the University of British Columbia; and Lorna Marsden (sociologist), former senator and former president of York University. Each of these women has credentials galore, along with awards and honours for outstanding achievement. And each is incredibly influential in university affairs and in the broader realm of public policy.

Canada has had three women governors-general—all in the past 30 years. Each was chosen for her accomplishments. Jeanne Sauvé, a successful journalist, then parliamentarian and first woman Speaker of the House, was the first woman to be appointed to this position in 1984. Adrienne Clarkson (1999–2005) and Michaëlle Jean (2005–2010) have some things in common. Clarkson came to Canada as a refugee from China and made her name in broadcasting. As governor-general, she spent Christmas or New Year's with our troops in Kosovo, the Persian Gulf, or Afghanistan, and she travelled extensively throughout Canada, giving people in the smallest and most remote communities a sense that they are special. Jean was born in Haiti and raised by a single mother in Montreal, and also made her name in broadcasting. She is keenly interested in immigrants, visible minorities, and the poor, wherever they are to be found in Canada. Like Clarkson, Jean has strong ties to Aboriginal peoples.

In 2012, Canada had a record number of women premiers—Eva Aariak (Nunavut), Christie Clark (British Columbia), Kathy Dunderdale (Newfoundland and Labrador), and Alison Redford (Alberta). At a time when 25 percent of our members of Parliament were women, 31 percent of our premiers were women. This reveals a dramatic shift in Canada's political culture and an unprecedented change in the power relations among men and women.

Without doubt, the most notable mayor in Canada is Hazel McCallion. At 91 years old, McCallion had been mayor of Mississauga, Ontario, for 34 years. So frequent were the requests for her to drop the puck at hockey games that she kept a pair of skates in her trunk. McCallion was the most popular mayor of the 15 largest cities in Canada, and had been elected mayor 12 times. Three months after her retirement—in 2015 *at the age of 94*—she had found a new job as special advisor to the principal of the University of Toronto Mississauga, where in addition she is developing a course to teach people how to participate in public office (Bascaramurty, 2012; 2015; O'Toole, 2012).

The global economic crisis of 2008 led to the collapse of banks and other financial institutions in the United States and around the world. Canadian banks remained stable throughout—and the reason for that stability is Julie Dickson, Canada's superintendent of financial institutions. This position made Dickson "Canada's top cop when it comes to ensuring that financial institutions are playing safe" or "the most powerful woman in Canadian banking" (Perkins, 2009). Not only did she determine public policy relating to Canada's banking practices, but she also advised G7 leaders on reforming the international banking system.

These are only a few of the truly remarkable women who have made their marks on this country. They stand as role models for all Canadians, but particularly for Canadian women.

What Do You Think?

1. Did you have any idea that there are hundreds of women like these in Canada?

2. How do you feel reading about these highly successful women? Does your gender affect your reaction to this reading?

3. What is it that sets these women apart: special qualities or special circumstances? Why?

Window on the World

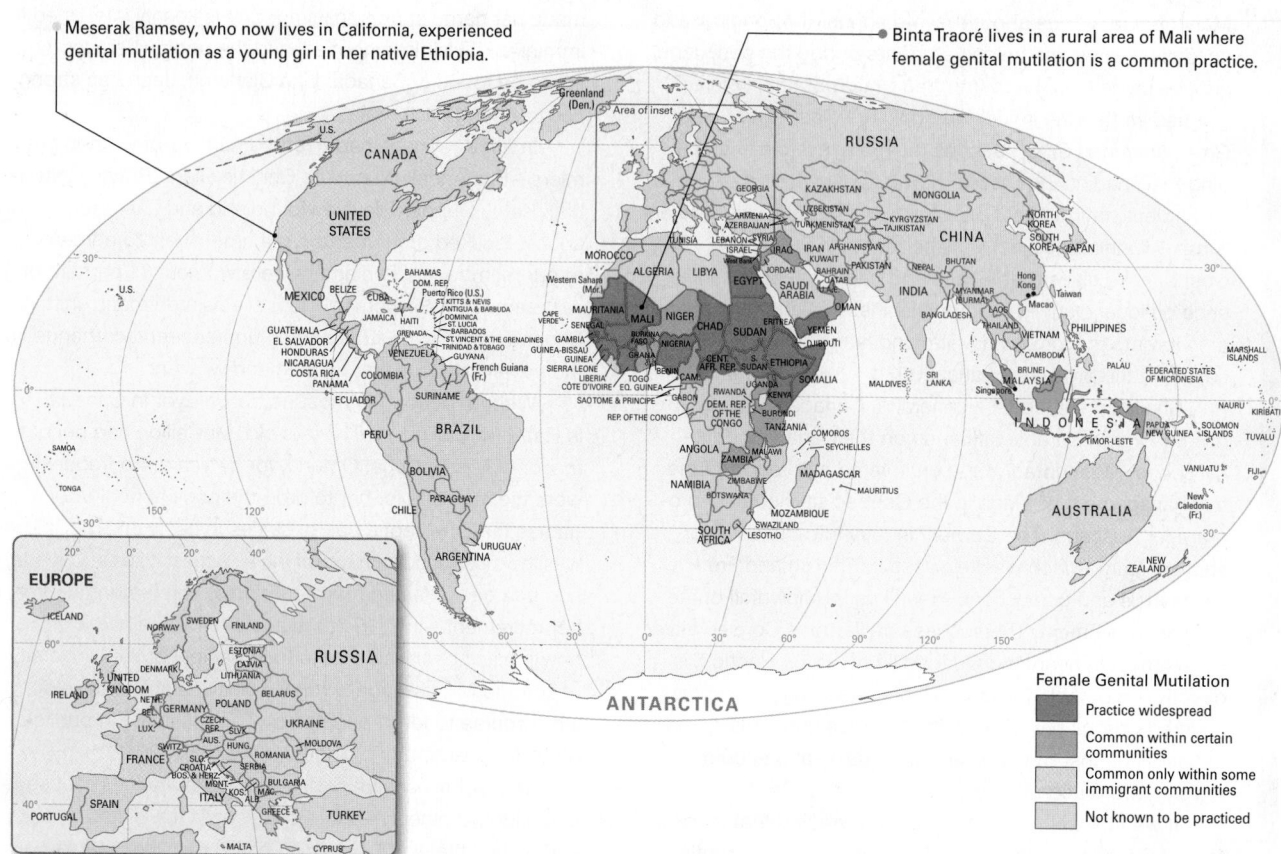

Meserak Ramsey, who now lives in California, experienced genital mutilation as a young girl in her native Ethiopia.

Binta Traoré lives in a rural area of Mali where female genital mutilation is a common practice.

Female Genital Mutilation

- Practice widespread
- Common within certain communities
- Common only within some immigrant communities
- Not known to be practiced

Global Map 13–2 Female Genital Mutilation in Global Perspective

Female genital mutilation is known to be performed in at least 29 countries around the world. Across Africa, the practice is common and affects a majority of girls in the eastern African nations of Sudan, Ethiopia, and Somalia. In several Asian nations, the practice is limited to a few ethnic minorities. In the United States, Canada, several European nations, and Australia, there are reports of the practice among some immigrants.

SOURCES: Population Reference Bureau. "Female Genital Mutilation/Cutting: Data and Trends: Update 2010." 2010. Available at http://www.prb.org/pdf10/fgm-wallchart2010.pdf; United Nations, 2012; World Health Organization (2015).

himself of his bride's virginity. Global Map 13–2 shows the distribution of countries where genital mutilation is widely practised and where it is practised only among certain immigrant communities.

How many women have undergone genital mutilation? Worldwide, estimates place the number at 135 million. In the United States, hundreds or even thousands of such procedures are performed every year; in Canada, there might be several hundred cases. Often, immigrant mothers and grandmothers who have themselves been mutilated insist that young girls in their family follow their example. Indeed, many immigrant women demand the procedure *because* their daughters now live in North America, where sexual mores are more lax.

VIOLENCE BY WOMEN Generally speaking, violence by women is off our radar screen—except when we are

confronted with violent behaviour by gangs of girls (as in the 1997 murder of Reena Virk) or serial murder (as perpetrated by Karla Homolka and her husband, Paul Bernardo). We are equally unaware of the fact that spousal abuse is committed by women against men (Lupri, 2002). Recently, the residents of Melfort, Saskatchewan (population 5500), learned that its girls are not gentler than its boys: "It's the teenaged girls who start the majority of the fistfights, swarmings, and beatings." While members of Melfort's girl gangs report that "violence had become an ordinary part of their social scene," a national study reveals that, among 12- to 15-year-olds, for every nine boys who engage in violent delinquency, two girls do (Smith, 2004).

VIOLENCE AGAINST MEN If our way of life encourages violence against women, it may encourage even more violence against men. In more than 80 percent of cases in which police make an arrest for a violent crime, including murder, robbery, and assault, the offender is a male. In addition, men are twice as likely as women to suffer serious assault, and three times more likely to fall victim to homicide.

Our culture tends to define masculinity in terms of aggression and violence—or "dangerous masculinity" (Atkinson, 2007). "Real men" work and play hard (especially on the hockey rink), speed on the highways, and let nothing stand in their way. A higher crime rate is one result. But even when no laws are broken, men's lives involve more stress and isolation than women's lives do, which is one reason that the suicide rate for men is four times higher than it is for women. In addition, as noted earlier, men live, on average, about five fewer years than women do.

If genital mutilation is violence against women, what is male circumcision? In some cultures, young boys are circumcised in public before they reach puberty; while in Canada, many baby boys are circumcised soon after birth. A practice that is religious in origin (Muslim and Jewish) is often carried out today in the interests of hygiene or other health benefits. Young boys or babies are circumcised *without their consent* by a procedure that changes their bodies for life. A procedure that is essentially a violation of human rights is assumed to be normal in our society. (Is there an echo here? Canadian men have their baby sons circumcised because they themselves were circumcised.) Estimates of neonatal circumcision rates in Canada vary dramatically, but it is clear that they have been declining since the 1970s. Note that, despite the reputed health benefits, circumcision is no longer covered by Canada's provincial or territorial health insurance plans.

Violence is not simply a matter of choices made by individuals. It is built into our culture or way of life, with resulting harm to both men and women. In short, the way any culture constructs gender plays an important part in how violent or peaceful a society will be.

Sexual Harassment

Sexual harassment refers to *comments, gestures, or physical contact of a sexual nature that is deliberate, repeated, and unwelcome.* During the 1990s, sexual harassment became an issue of national importance that rewrote the rules for workplace interaction between women and men. Most, but not all, victims of sexual harassment are women, for two main reasons. First, our culture encourages men to be sexually assertive and to see women in sexual terms. As a result, social interaction in the workplace, on campus, and elsewhere can easily take on sexual overtones. Second, most people in positions of power—including business executives, doctors, bureau chiefs, assembly-line supervisors, professors, and military officers—are men who oversee the work of women. Surveys carried out in very different work settings show that half of women respondents receive unwanted sexual attention (NORC, 2003).

Canadians had been alerted—by the media and the 2015 Deschamps report—to the fact that sexual harassment is very much part of military life. An official response had been slow in coming, but the Canadian Armed Forces now has a "sexual misconduct response centre that has fielded more than 100 complaints of sexual harassment since it opened" (four months earlier), eight of which resulted in formal investigations. "The fact that people are calling the centre is a tremendous—great—step forward" are the words of Lt.-Gen. Christine Whitecross, Canada's top female general. Gen. Jonathan Vance, chief of the defence staff, was instrumental in the creation of the centre and is happy to see large numbers of complaints. "I'm actually pleased that the numbers have come up because when numbers go up we can actually start to address the problem" (Tasker, 2016). Considering the subculture of the military, these steps by the Canadian armed forces are quite remarkable.

Sexual harassment is sometimes obvious and direct—as when a supervisor asks for sexual favours while making threats about the consequences of non-compliance. But more often than not it is a matter of subtle behaviour—sexual teasing, off-colour jokes, the display of nudes—that may not even be *intended* to harass anyone. Nonetheless, the *effect* of such actions is the creation of a *hostile environment* in which women may feel uncomfortable or threatened. Incidents of this kind are far more complex because they involve different perceptions of the same behaviour. For example, a man may think that, by repeatedly complimenting a co-worker on her appearance, he is simply being friendly. The co-worker may believe that the man is thinking of her in sexual terms and not taking her work seriously, an attitude that could harm her job performance and prospects for advancement.

Pornography

Pornography is defined as sexually explicit material that causes sexual arousal. It also underlies sexual violence. Defining pornography has long challenged scholars and lawmakers alike. Unable to set a single, specific standard to distinguish what is, and what is not, pornographic, the Supreme Court of Canada allows provinces, territories, and municipalities to decide what violates "community standards" of decency and lacks "any redeeming social value."

Traditionally, people have raised concerns about pornography as a *moral* issue. But pornography also plays a part in gender stratification. From this point of view, pornography is really a *power* issue because most pornography dehumanizes women, depicting them as the playthings of men. That is, pornography is really a power issue because it fosters the notion that men should control both sexuality and women (Nelson & Robinson, 1999:355). In addition, there is widespread concern that pornography promotes violence against women by portraying them as weak and undeserving of respect. Surveys show that about half of American adults think that pornography encourages men to commit rape (Smith et al., 2013:424).

Like sexual harassment, pornography raises complex and conflicting issues. Despite the fact that some material may offend just about everybody, many support the rights of free speech and artistic expression. Pressure to restrict pornography has increased in recent decades, reflecting both the long-standing concern that pornography weakens morality as well as more recent concerns that it is demeaning and threatening to women.

Theories of Gender

13.4 Apply sociology's major theories to gender stratification.

Why does gender exist in all known societies? Sociology's macro-level approaches—the structural-functional and social-conflict approaches—address the central place of gender in social organization. In addition, the symbolic-interaction approach helps us to see the importance of gender in everyday life. The Applying Theory table summarizes the important insights of each of these approaches.

Structural-Functional Theory

The structural-functional approach views society as a complex system of many separate but integrated parts. From this point of view, gender serves as a means to organize social life. Members of hunter/gatherer societies had little power over the forces of biology. Lacking effective birth control, women were frequently pregnant, and the responsibilities of child care kept them close to home. At the same time, men's greater strength made them more suited for warfare and hunting game. Over the centuries, this sexual division of labour became institutionalized and largely taken for granted (Freedman, 2002; Lengermann & Wallace, 1985).

Industrial technology opens up a much greater range of cultural possibilities. With human muscles no longer the main energy source, the physical strength of men becomes less important. In addition, the ability to control reproduction gives women greater choices about how to live. Modern societies relax traditional gender roles as they become more meritocratic, because such rigid roles waste an enormous amount of human talent. Yet because gender is deeply rooted in culture, change comes slowly.

GENDER AND SOCIAL INTEGRATION Talcott Parsons (1942, 1954, 1964; orig. 1951) argued that keeping some gender differences helps integrate society, at least in its traditional form. Gender forms a *complementary* set of roles that links men and women into family units and gives each sex responsibility for important tasks. Women take the lead in managing the household and raising children. Men connect the family to the larger world as they participate in the labour force.

Therefore, gender plays an important part in socialization. Society teaches boys—presumably destined for the labour force—to be rational, self-assured, and competitive. Parsons called this complex of traits *instrumental* qualities. To prepare girls for child rearing, their socialization stresses *expressive* qualities, such as emotional responsiveness and sensitivity to others.

APPLYING THEORY

Gender

	Structural-Functional Theory	Symbolic-Interaction Theory	Social-Conflict and Intersection Theories
What is the level of analysis?	Macro-level	Micro-level	Macro-level
What does gender mean?	Parsons described gender in terms of two complementary patterns of behaviour: masculine and feminine.	Numerous sociologists have shown that gender is part of the reality that guides social interaction in everyday situations.	Engels described gender in terms of the power of one sex over the other. Gender interacts with class, race, and ethnicity to create various levels of disadvantage.
Is gender helpful or harmful?	Helpful. Gender gives men and women distinctive roles and responsibilities that help society operate smoothly. Gender builds social unity as men and women come together to form families.	Hard to say; gender is both helpful and harmful. In everyday life, gender is one of the factors that help us relate to one another. At the same time, gender shapes human behaviour, placing men in control of social situations. Men tend to initiate most interactions, while women typically act in a more deferential manner.	Harmful. Gender limits people's personal development. Gender divides society by giving power to men to control the lives of women. Intersection theory explains that minority women face multiple disadvantages.

Society encourages gender conformity by instilling in men and women a fear that straying too far from accepted standards of masculinity or femininity will cause rejection by the other sex. In simple terms, women learn to reject non-masculine men as sexually unattractive, and men learn to reject unfeminine women. In sum, gender-based expectations integrate society both structurally (in terms of what we do) and morally (in terms of what we believe).

EVALUATE

Influential in the 1950s, this approach has lost much of its standing today. First, functionalism assumes a singular vision of society that is not shared by everyone. Historically, many women have worked outside the home because of economic need, a fact not reflected in Parsons's conventional, middle-class view of family life. Second, Parsons's analysis ignores the personal strains and social costs of rigid, traditional gender roles. Third, in the eyes of those seeking sexual equality, Parsons's gender "complementarity" amounts to little more than women submitting to male domination.

CHECK YOUR LEARNING   In Parsons's analysis, what functions does gender perform for society?

Symbolic-Interaction Theory

The symbolic-interaction approach takes a micro-level view of society, focusing on face-to-face interaction in everyday life. Gender, as it turns out, affects everyday interaction in a number of ways.

GENDER AND EVERYDAY LIFE   If you watch women and men interacting, you will probably notice that women typically engage in more eye contact than men do. Why? Holding eye contact is a way of encouraging the conversation to continue; in addition, looking directly at someone clearly shows the other person that you are paying attention.

This pattern is an example of sex roles, defined as the way a society defines how women and men should think and behave. To understand such patterns, consider the fact that people with more power tend to take charge of social encounters. When men and women engage one another, as they do in families and in the workplace, it is men who typically initiate the interaction. That is, men speak first, set the topics of discussion, and control the outcomes. With less power, women are expected to be more *deferential,* meaning that they show respect for others of higher social position. In many cases, this means that women (just like children or others with less power) spend more time being silent and also encouraging men (or others with more power) not just with eye contact but by smiling or nodding in agreement. As a technique to control a conversation, men often interrupt others and feel less need to ask the opinions of other people, especially those with less power (Henley et al., 1992; Ridgeway & Smith-Lovin, 1999; Tannen, 1990, 1994).

Gender and Reality Construction   If a woman is planning to marry a man, should she take his last name or keep her own? This decision is about more than how she will sign a cheque: It also affects how employers will see her and even her future pay.

In North America today, at least 10 percent of women who marry men keep their own name. This is a decline from the 1990s, when the share peaked at about 23 percent. Research shows that women who marry in their thirties (after they have started a career) are much more likely to keep their own name than women who marry in their early twenties. Research also shows that subjects asked to assess women's personal traits typically perceive those who take their husband's last name as more caring, dependent, and emotional (traditional feminine qualities). By contrast, they assess women who keep their maiden names as more ambitious, talented, and capable (more competitive against others, including men). Data on salaries reveal a significant difference in pay: Married women who keep their own name end up earning about 40 percent more than those who adopt their husband's name (Gooding & Kreider, 2010; Shellenbarger, 2011).

IN THE 1950S, TALCOTT PARSONS PROPOSED THAT SOCIOLOGISTS INTERPRET GENDER AS A MATTER OF *DIFFERENCES* As he saw it, masculine men and feminine women formed strong families and made for an orderly society. In recent decades, however, social-conflict theory has reinterpreted gender as a matter of *inequality.* From this point of view, North American society places men in a position of dominance over women.

FPG/Archive Photos/Getty Images

Such patterns demonstrate how gender shapes the reality we experience in everyday life. They also suggest that women who face a decision about surnames when they marry may consider the choice they make will carry particular meaning to others and have important consequences.

EVALUATE

The strength of the symbolic-interaction approach is helping us see how gender plays a part in shaping almost all our everyday experiences. Our society defines men (and everything we consider to be masculine) as having more value than women (and what is defined as feminine). For this reason, just about every familiar social encounter is "gendered," so that men and women interact in distinctive and unequal ways.

The symbolic-interaction approach suggests that individuals socially construct the reality they experience as they interact every day, using gender-linked traits such as clothing and demeanour (and, for women, also last name) as elements of their personal "performances" that shape ongoing reality.

Gender plays a part in the reality we experience. Yet, as a structural dimension of society, gender is at least largely beyond the immediate control of any of us as individuals as it gives some people power over others. In other words, patterns of everyday social interaction reflect our society's gender stratification. Everyday interaction also helps reinforce this inequality. For example, to the extent that fathers take the lead in dinner table discussions, the entire family learns to expect men to "display leadership" and "show their wisdom." As mothers do the laundry, children learn that women are expected to do household chores.

A limitation of the symbolic-interaction approach is that by focusing on situational social experience, it says little about the broad patterns of inequality that set the rules for our everyday lives. To understand the roots of gender stratification, we have to "kick it up a level" to see more closely how society makes men and women unequal. We will do this using the social-conflict approach.

CHECK YOUR LEARNING   Point to several ways that gender shapes the everyday face-to-face interactions of individuals.

Social-Conflict Theory

From a social-conflict point of view, gender involves much more than differences in behaviour—gender is a structural system of power that provides privilege to some and disadvantage to others. Consider the striking similarity between the way traditional ideas about gender benefit men and harm women and the way ideas about race benefit Whites and disadvantage racial and ethnic minorities. Conventional ideas about gender do not make society operate smoothly, as a structural-functional analysis suggests. On the contrary, gender is a societal structure that creates division and tension, with men seeking to protect their privileges as women challenge the status quo.

The social-conflict approach draws heavily on the ideas of Karl Marx; yet, as far as gender is concerned, Marx was a product of his time, and his writings focused almost entirely on men. His friend and collaborator Friedrich Engels, however, did develop a theory of gender stratification.

GENDER AND CLASS INEQUALITY   Looking back through history, Engels saw that, in hunter/gatherer societies, the activities of women and men, although different, had the same importance. A successful hunt brought men great prestige, but the vegetation gathered by women provided most of a group's food supply. As technological advances led to a productive surplus, however, social equality and communal sharing gave way to private property and, ultimately, a class hierarchy. With the rise of agriculture, men gained significant power over women. With surplus wealth to pass on to their heirs, upper-class men wanted to be sure who their sons were, which led them to control the sexuality of women. The desire to control property brought about monogamous marriage and the family. Women were taught to remain virgins until marriage, to remain faithful to their husbands thereafter, and to build their lives around bearing and raising one man's children. Family law ensured that property is transmitted within families from one generation for the next, keeping the class system intact.

According to Engels (1902; orig. 1884), capitalism makes male domination even stronger. First, capitalism creates more wealth, which gives greater power to men as income earners and owners of property. Second, an expanding capitalist economy depends on turning people, especially women, into consumers who seek personal fulfillment through buying and using products. Third, society assigns women the task of maintaining the home to free men to work in factories. The double exploitation of capitalism, as Engels saw it, lies in paying men low wages for their labour and paying women no wages at all.

EVALUATE

Social-conflict analysis is strongly critical of conventional ideas about gender, claiming that society would be better off if we minimized or even did away with this dimension of social structure. Thus, this approach regards conventional families—supported by traditionalists as personally and socially positive—as a social evil. A problem with social-conflict analysis, then, is that it minimizes the extent to which women and men live together co-operatively, and often happily, in families. A second problem lies in the assertion that capitalism is the basis of gender stratification. In fact, agrarian societies are typically more patriarchal than industrial-capitalist societies. Although socialist nations—including the People's Republic of China and the former Soviet Union—did move women into the workforce, by and large they provided women with very low pay in sex-segregated jobs (Haney, 2002; Rosendahl, 1997).

CHECK YOUR LEARNING   According to Friedrich Engels, how does gender support social inequality in a capitalist class system?

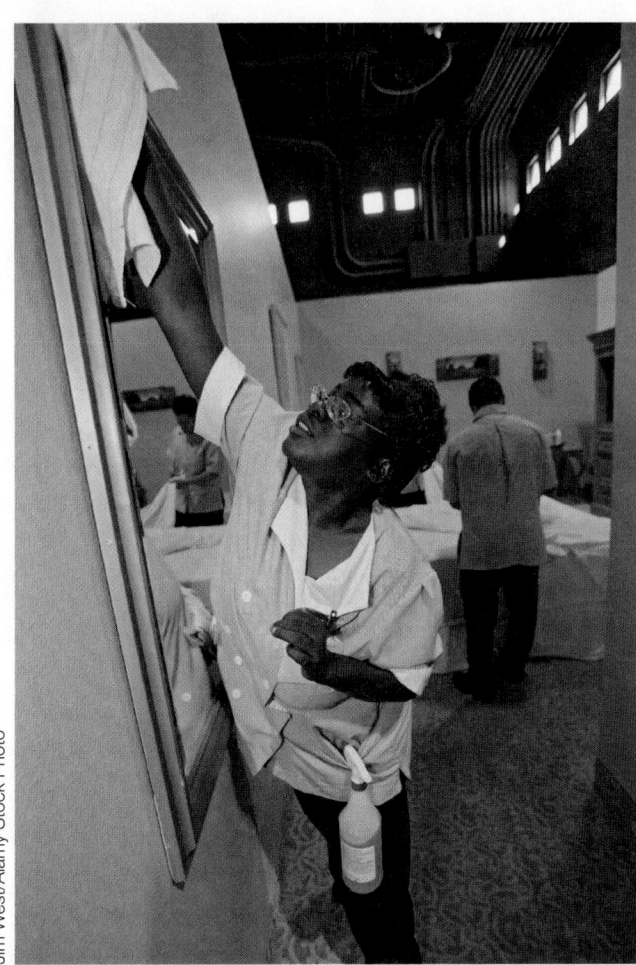

Jim West/Alamy Stock Photo

THE BASIC INSIGHT OF INTERSECTION THEORY IS THAT VARIOUS DIMENSIONS OF SOCIAL STRATIFICATION—INCLUDING RACE AND GENDER—CAN ADD UP TO GREAT DISADVANTAGES FOR SOME CATEGORIES OF PEOPLE Just as workers from visible minorities earn less than White workers, women earn less than men. Thus, women belonging to a visible minority confront a "double disadvantage" or experience "double jeopardy," ending up in low-paying jobs like this one.

Intersection Theory

If women are defined as a minority, what about minority women? Are they doubly handicapped? This question lies at the heart of **intersection theory**, *analysis of the interplay of race, class, and gender, often resulting in multiple dimensions of disadvantage*. Research shows that disadvantages linked to gender and race often combine to produce especially low social standing (Ovadia, 2001; Wotherspoon & Satzewich, 1993). A First Nations woman, for example, is female, of a minority race, and subject to the *Indian Act*—which results in multiple jeopardy (Gerber, 1990). Compared to the general Canadian population, as well as to Inuit and Métis women and men, First Nations women have had the lowest income from the 1980s to the present day (Gerber, 2014). Today, multiple jeopardy is called intersectionality—especially by women doing feminist intersectional analysis (Stasiulis, 1999). Intersection theory "incorporates

the inseparability and simultaneity of race, ethnicity, class, and gender as interlocking and overlapping expressions of inequality (Fleras, 2012:167). Or, more simply, race, gender, ethnicity, and class combined create multiple disadvantages.

To explore the "intersections" of various dimensions of inequality, we find that some categories of women experience greater disadvantages. African-American women earn 63 percent of the income of non-Hispanic white men, and Hispanic women earn 56 percent (U.S. Census Bureau, 2014). These differences reflect minority women's lower positions in the occupational and educational hierarchies.

Intersection theory helps us to see that although gender has a powerful effect on our lives, it does not operate alone. Class position, race and ethnicity, gender, and sexual orientation form a multilayered system of disadvantage for some and privilege for others (St. Jean & Feagin, 1998).

Feminism

13.5 Contrast liberal, radical and socialist feminism.

Feminism is *the advocacy of social equality for women and men, in opposition to patriarchy and sexism*. The first wave of the feminist movement in Canada began in the mid-1800s as Canadian women were influenced by writing such as Mary Wollstonecraft's *A Vindication of the Rights of Women* (1792) and John Stuart Mill's *The Subjection of Women* (1869). The primary objective of the early women's movement was securing the right to vote, which was achieved for federal elections in Canada by 1918 with the passage of the *Women's Franchise Act*. But other disadvantages persisted, prompting the rise of a second wave of feminism in the 1960s, which continues today.

Basic Feminist Ideas

Feminism views the personal experiences of women and men through the lens of gender. How we think of ourselves (*gender identity*), how we act (*gender roles*), and our sex's social standing (*gender stratification*) are all rooted in the operation of society. Although feminists disagree about many things, most support five general principles:

1. *Working to increase equality.* Feminist thinking is strongly political; it links ideas to action. Feminism is critical of the status quo, pushing for change toward social equality for women and men. Many feminists are also guided by intersection theory to seek equality based on race and class as well as gender.

2. *Expanding human choice.* Feminists argue that cultural conceptions of gender divide the full range of human

John Bazemore/AP Images

NASCAR RACING HAS ALWAYS BEEN A MASCULINE WORLD But Danica Patrick has made a name for herself as an outstanding driver. At the same time, she has made much of her income from trading on her good looks, including the 2009 *Sports Illustrated* swimsuit edition. Are men as likely to do the same? Why or why not?

qualities into two opposing and limiting spheres: the female world of emotions and co-operation, and the male world of rationality and competition. As an alternative, feminists propose a "reintegration of humanity" by which all individuals can develop all human traits (French, 1985).

3. *Eliminating gender stratification.* Feminism opposes laws and cultural norms that limit the education, income, and job opportunities of women. For this reason, American feminists have long supported passage of the Equal Rights Amendment to the U.S. Constitution, which has yet to become law. In Canada, gender equality was guaranteed in the *Canadian Charter of Rights and Freedoms* (Canada, 1982) after a modern-day struggle over women's rights (outlined in the opener to this chapter).

4. *Ending sexual violence.* Today's women's movement seeks to eliminate sexual violence. Feminists argue that patriarchy distorts the relationships between women and men, encouraging violence against women in the form of sexual assault (including rape),

domestic abuse, sexual harassment, and pornography (Dworkin, 1987; Freedman, 2002).

5. *Promoting sexual freedom.* Feminism supports women's control over their sexuality and reproduction. Feminists support the free availability of birth control information.

As Figure 13–4 shows, about three-quarters of Canadian women of child-bearing age use contraception; the use of contraceptives is far less common in many low-income nations. In Canada, while information about birth control circulated from the early 1930s onward, birth control became legal only in 1969 (Bishop, 1988). Most feminists also support a woman's right to choose whether to bear children or end a pregnancy, rather than allowing men—husbands, physicians, and legislators—to control their reproduction. And many feminists support gay people's efforts to end prejudice and discrimination in a mostly heterosexual culture (Armstrong, 2002; Ferree & Hess, 1995).

Global Snapshot

● Achen Eke, age 24 and mother of three, lives in Uganda, where most women do not have access to contraception.

● Chen-chi Bai, age 31 and the mother of one boy, lives in China, where contraception is encouraged and widely practiced.

Percentage of Married Women of Childbearing Age Who Use Contraception

Country	Percentage
China	84%
Canada	72%
United States	68%
Egypt	58%
India	48%
Guatemala	44%
Philippines	37%
Uganda	26%

Figure 13–4 Use of Contraception by Married Women of Childbearing Age

In Canada, most married women of child-bearing age use contraception. In many lower-income countries, however, most women do not have the opportunity to make this choice.

SOURCE: Population Reference Bureau (2014).

Types of Feminism

Feminists agree on the importance of gender equality, but they disagree on how to achieve it: through liberal feminism, socialist feminism, or radical feminism (Armstrong, 2002; Ferree & Hess, 1995; Freedman, 2002; Stacey, 1983; Vogel, 1983).

Liberal Feminism   Liberal feminism is rooted in the classic liberal thinking that individuals should be free to develop their own talents and pursue their own interests. Liberal feminism accepts the basic organization of our society but seeks to expand the equality rights and opportunities of women. Liberal feminists also support reproductive freedom for all women. They respect the family as a social institution but seek changes, including more widely available parental leave and child care for parents who work. Given their belief in the rights of individuals, liberal feminists think that women should advance according to their own efforts, rather than working collectively for change. Both women and men, through their individual achievement, are capable of improving their lives—as long as society removes legal and cultural barriers.

Socialist Feminism   Socialist feminism evolved from the ideas of Karl Marx and Friedrich Engels. From this point of view, capitalism strengthens patriarchy by concentrating wealth and power in the hands of a small number of men. Socialist feminists do not think the reforms supported by liberal feminism go far enough. The family form created by capitalism must change if we are to replace "domestic slavery" with some collective means of carrying out housework and community-run child care. Replacing the traditional family can come about only through a socialist revolution that creates a state-centred economy to meet the needs of all. Such a basic transformation of society requires that women and men pursue their personal liberation not individually, as liberal feminists propose, but collectively.

Radical Feminism   Like socialist feminism, radical feminism finds liberal feminism inadequate. Radical feminists believe that patriarchy is so deeply rooted in society that even a socialist revolution would not end it. Instead, reaching the goal of gender equality means that society must eliminate gender itself. One possible way to achieve this goal is to use new reproductive technology (see the chapter on Family) to separate women's bodies from the process of child-bearing. With an end to motherhood, radical feminists reason, society could leave behind the entire family system, liberating women, men, and children from the oppression of family, gender, and sex itself (Dworkin, 1987). Thus, radical feminism envisions an egalitarian and gender-free society, a revolution more sweeping than the one sought by Marx.

The Applying Theory table that follows summarizes the main arguments of liberal, socialist, and radical feminism.

CULTURAL AND POSTMODERN FEMINISM   Canadian sociologists Nelson and Robinson (1999:101–111) identify several other variants of feminism that differ from the liberal, socialist, and radical approaches we have outlined.

Marxist feminism argues that one's position with respect to economic production determines all other aspects of social life. Therefore, the entire structure of society must be changed to achieve gender equality.

Cultural feminism identifies "the suppression of distinctive or different female qualities, experiences, and values as the primary cause of women's subordination." Inclusive feminists reject a privileged White middle-class feminism that ignores the "experiences of differently raced, abled, and classed women."

And, lastly, *postmodern feminism* "rejects all statements of claim made by other branches of feminist thought," arguing that any theory "claiming to be fully explanatory is necessarily assuming a dominant and oppressive stance."

All of the feminist approaches overlap to some extent, so specific authors may move among these approaches or blend them in one way or another.

Public Reaction to Feminism

Feminism provokes criticism and resistance from both men and women who hold conventional ideas about

APPLYING THEORY

Feminism

	Liberal Feminism	Socialist Feminism	Radical Feminism
Does it accept the basic order of society?	Yes. Liberal feminism seeks change only to ensure equality of opportunity.	No. Socialist feminism supports an end to social classes and to family gender roles that encourage "domestic slavery."	No. Radical feminism supports an end to the family system.
How do women improve their social standing?	Individually, according to personal ability and effort.	Collectively, through socialist revolution.	Collectively, by working to eliminate gender itself.

gender. Some men oppose sexual equality for the same reason that many White people have historically opposed social equality for people from visible minorities: They do not want to give up their privileges. Other men and women, including those who are neither rich nor powerful, distrust a social movement—especially its radical expressions—that attacks the traditional family and rejects patterns that have guided male/female relations for centuries.

Men who have been socialized to value strength and dominance feel uneasy about feminist ideas of men as gentle and warm (Doyle, 1983). Similarly, some women whose lives centre on their husbands and children may think that feminism does not value the social roles that give meaning to their lives. In general, resistance to feminism is strongest among women who have the least education and those who do not work outside the home (CBS News, 2005; Ferree & Hess, 1995; Marshall, 1985).

Resistance to feminism is also found within academic circles. Some sociologists charge that feminism ignores a growing body of evidence that men and women do think and act in different ways, which may make complete gender equality impossible. Furthermore, say critics, with its drive to increase women's presence in the workplace, feminism undervalues the crucial and unique contribution women make to the development of children, especially in the first years of life (Baydar & Brooks-Gunn, 1991; Gibbs, 2001; Popenoe, 1993).

And there is the question of how women should go about improving their social standing. Although a large majority of Canadians believes that women should have equal rights, most also believe that women should advance individually according to their abilities rather than through collective action.

Opposition to feminism is primarily directed at its socialist and radical variants; otherwise, there is widespread support for the principles of liberal feminism. Moreover, we are seeing an unmistakable trend toward greater gender equality. In 1942, during World War II, when a Gallup poll asked Canadians, "If women take the place of men in industry, should they be paid the same wages as men?" 89 percent of women and 78 percent of men agreed. By 1995, the idea of equal pay for equal work was supported by 98 percent of a representative sample of Canadians (Bibby, 1995:4).

Gender: Looking Ahead

Predictions about the future are always a matter of informed guesswork. Just as economists disagree about what the inflation rate will be a year from now, sociologists can offer only general observations about the likely future of gender and society.

Change so far has been remarkable. A century ago, women were second-class citizens, without access to many jobs, barred from political office, and with no right to vote. While women remain socially disadvantaged, the movement toward equality has surged ahead. Two-thirds of those entering the workforce during the 1990s were women and, in most couples, both partners work. Today's economy depends on the earnings of women and, for a growing number of couples, women are breadwinners with higher incomes than their partners.

Many factors have contributed to these changes. Perhaps most importantly, industrialization and recent advances in computer technology have shifted the nature of work from physically demanding tasks that favour male strength to jobs that require thought and imagination. This change puts women and men on a more even footing. Also, because birth control technology has given us greater control over reproduction, women's lives are less constrained by unwanted pregnancies.

Many women and men deliberately pursue social equality. For example, sexual harassment complaints in the workplace are now taken much more seriously than they were a generation ago. Women are achieving higher levels of education than men and are making inroads into occupations, including hockey (see the Thinking about Diversity box), that were previously dominated by men. In some occupations, but not all, the gender gap in income is decreasing. As more women compete in fields dominated by men, and assume positions of power in the corporate and political worlds, we can anticipate continuing social change in the twenty-first century.

Thinking About Diversity: Race, Class, and Gender

Canadian Women in Hockey: Going for Gold

At the turn of the century, Canadian women were involved in hockey, doing battle in long, flowing skirts that made them look like sisters of the cloth rather than members of a hockey team. In the 1930s, the Preston Rivulettes, from what is now part of Cambridge, Ontario, recorded an incredible record of 348 wins to two losses! But World War II intervened, draining attention and energy away from hockey so that by the 1950s women's hockey had died. The struggle to re-establish women's hockey—to get ice time, good equipment, sponsorships, public acceptance and support, media coverage, the attention of Don Cherry, and Olympic status—consumed the next 40 to 50 years. In 1998, in Nagano, Japan, women's hockey was an official Olympic sport for the first time, and the world of Canadian women's hockey changed forever.

THE CANADIAN WOMEN'S HOCKEY TEAM WON GOLD—FOR THE THIRD TIME—AT THE 2010 WINTER OLYMPIC GAMES IN VANCOUVER.

Canada won the silver medal in Nagano (1998), losing to the American team, but went on to win gold in the Olympics of 2002 (Salt Lake City), 2006 (Turin, Italy), and 2010 (Vancouver). The game that originated in Canada had become part of our collective identity, continues to be our most popular sport, and is now played by women—legitimately and successfully! Many of the women on Team Canada grew up playing on boys' teams; at least two, Manon Rheaume and Hayley Wickenheiser, have played in professional male leagues. With the decision to prohibit bodychecking in women's hockey, parents in large numbers are willing to enroll their young daughters in girls' hockey leagues. Girls' teams—which often play against boys' teams—are springing up throughout Canada, and girls' participation in hockey has taken off to the point that more than 80 000 girls and women are registered hockey players.

Without doubt, the image of girls and women as hockey players is inconsistent with our societal expectations of femininity. Off the ice, most of these women—some of whom are mothers—conform to our cultural standards of feminine behaviour, dress, and makeup; however, when they don their protective hockey uniforms and helmets and step onto the ice, they enter a world in which they exhibit aggression, speed, and impressive skill. Power skating, agility, and adroit handling of stick and puck become their tools.

This transformation from "woman" to "athlete" in a traditionally male or macho sport is not easy for the women themselves, nor is it easy for all members of the general public to accept. There are still people who feel strongly that women should stick to ballet, gymnastics, and synchronized swimming (another Canadian sporting development). But when the women's and men's hockey teams both won gold at the 2002 Olympics in Salt Lake City, celebrations erupted throughout the country.

Olympic publicity has changed the lives of the women who play hockey for Team Canada. The quest for public awareness and support is over. Don Cherry's active support of women's hockey is now part of the public record. Major media in Canada all provide extensive coverage of the exploits and victories of Team Canada, women's style. The team members have agents and contracts for product endorsements. Sports Canada helps cover their expenses, and employers are willing to give the athletes time off to prepare for championship or Olympic competition. These young women are now accustomed to being recognized on the street and being the subject of sometimes overwhelming media attention. The dramatic change in the status of women's hockey is exciting for female players across the country and for the Canadian public as a whole. In their own way, these women have stretched the limits of and changed the definition of femininity.

Cassie Campbell-Pascall is the face of women's hockey in Canada. She was the captain of Team Canada

(continued)

from 2001 until she retired in 2006—after leading her team to two Olympic gold medals, in 2002 and 2006. She is the longest-serving team captain and the only one—man or woman—to lead a team to two Olympic gold medals. She still "lives and breathes hockey," watches an average of 15 games a week, and is a commentator for *Hockey Night in Canada*. She is also the first female hockey player to be inducted into Canada's Sports Hall of Fame. She loves her job with *Hockey Night in Canada,* but the birth of her first child, Brooke, turned her life around once again. Family, meaning Brooke, her husband, Brad, and their child, is now the focal point of Cassie's life.

Postscript: On January 16, 1998, as women's hockey was played for the first time at the Olympics, the CBC ran a full-length edition of *The National* about women's hockey in Canada and our Olympic team. Among other guests, two of the women who had played for the Preston Rivulettes in the 1930s shared their thoughts on the dramatic changes in the world of women's hockey.

What Do You Think?

1. Did you know girls who played hockey when you were in high school? Did they seem like ordinary girls or were they different?

2. Would you encourage your daughter to play hockey?

3. Read the Sociology in Focus box about violence and crime in hockey in the chapter on Deviance. How does the link between hockey and "dangerous masculinity" reflect on Canada's support of women's hockey? Do you think women's hockey lacks appeal because of the absence of violence?

SOURCES: CBC (1998), Smith (1997a, 1997b), and Hampson (2012).

Seeing Sociology in Everyday Life

CHAPTER 13 Gender Stratification

Can you spot "gender messages" in the world around you?

As this chapter makes clear, gender is one of the basic organizing principles of everyday life. Most of the places we go and most of the activities we engage in as part of our daily routines are "gendered," meaning that they are defined as either more masculine or more feminine.

Understanding this fact, corporations keep gender in mind when they market products to the public. Take a look at the ads below. In each case, can you explain how gender is at work in selling these products?

> **Hint** Looking for "gender messages" in ads is a process that involves several levels of analysis. Start on the surface by noting everything obvious in the ad, including the setting, the background, and especially the people. Then notice how the people are shown—what they are doing, how they are situated, their facial expressions, how they are dressed, and how they appear to relate to each other. Finally, state what you think is the message of the ad, based on both the ad itself and also what you know about the surrounding society.

THERE IS A LOT OF GENDER DYNAMICS GOING ON IN THIS AD What do you see?

GENERALLY, OUR SOCIETY DEFINES COSMETICS AS FEMININE BECAUSE MOST COSMETICS ARE MARKETED TOWARD WOMEN How and why is this ad different?

PHCP Incorporated

The Advertising Archives

WHAT GENDER MESSAGES DO YOU SEE IN THIS AD?

Seeing Sociology in *Your* Everyday Life

1. Look through some recent magazines and select three advertisements that involve gender. In each case, provide analysis of how gender is used in the ad.

2. Watch several hours of children's television programming on a Saturday morning. Notice the advertising, which mostly sells toys and breakfast cereal. Keep track of the toys that are "gendered" (i.e., aimed at one sex or the other). What traits do you associate with toys intended for boys and those intended for girls?

3. To what extent does being a male or a female affect your field of study and your career aspirations? Which do you think will be more important to you: family life or earning a high income? How will you balance those aspects of your life?

Making the Grade

CHAPTER 13 Gender Stratification

Gender and Inequality

13.1 Describe the ways in which society creates gender stratification.

Gender refers to the meaning a culture attaches to being female or male.

- Evidence that gender is rooted in culture includes global comparisons by Margaret Mead and others showing how societies define what is feminine and masculine in various ways.
- Gender is not only about difference: Because societies give more power and other resources to men than to women, gender is an important dimension of social stratification. Sexism is built into the operation of social institutions.
- Although some degree of patriarchy is found almost everywhere, it varies throughout history and from society to society.

gender the personal traits and social positions that members of a society attach to being female or male
gender stratification the unequal distribution of wealth, power, and privilege between men and women
patriarchy a form of social organization in which males dominate females
matriarchy a form of social organization in which females dominate males
sexism the belief that one sex is innately superior to the other

Gender and Socialization

13.2 Explain the importance of gender to socialization.

Through the socialization process, gender becomes part of our personalities (gender identity) and our actions (gender roles). All the major agents of socialization—family, peer groups, schools, and the mass media—reinforce cultural definitions of what is feminine and masculine.

gender roles (sex roles) attitudes and activities that a society links to each sex

Gender and Social Stratification

13.3 Analyze the extent of gender inequality in various social institutions.

Gender stratification shapes **the workplace**:

- A majority of women are now in the paid labour force, but 30 percent hold clerical or service jobs.

- Comparing full-time workers, women earn 71 percent of male income.
- This gender difference in earnings results from differences in jobs, differences in family responsibilities, and discrimination.

Gender stratification shapes **family life**:

- Most unpaid housework is performed by women, whether or not they hold jobs outside the home.
- Pregnancy and raising small children keep many women out of the labour force at a time when their male peers are making important career gains.

Gender stratification shapes **education**:

- Women now earn the majority of all degrees, diplomas, and certificates granted across Canada.
- Canadian women make up the majority of recent medical school graduates and are an increasing share of graduates in professions traditionally dominated by men, such as engineering and business administration.

Gender stratification shapes **politics**:

- Until 90 years ago, no women were elected to the Canadian Parliament.
- In recent decades, the number of women in politics has increased significantly.
- Even so, 74 percent of our members of Parliament are men.
- In 2012, four out of thirteen premiers were women.

Violence against women and men is a widespread problem that is linked to a society's definition of gender. Related issues include

- **sexual harassment**, which mostly victimizes women because our culture encourages men to be assertive and to see women in sexual terms.
- **pornography**, which portrays women as sexual objects. Many see pornography as a moral issue; because pornography dehumanizes women, it is also a power issue.

minority any category of people distinguished by physical or cultural difference that a society sets apart and subordinates
sexual harassment comments, gestures, or physical contact of a sexual nature that is deliberate, repeated, and unwelcome
intersection theory analysis of the interplay of race, class, and gender, often resulting in multiple dimensions of disadvantage

Theories of Gender

13.4 Apply sociology's major theories to gender stratification.

Structural-functional theory suggests that

- in pre-industrial societies, distinctive roles for males and females reflect biological differences between the sexes.
- in industrial societies, marked gender inequality becomes dysfunctional and gradually decreases.

Talcott Parsons described gender differences in terms of complementary roles that promote the social integration of families and society as a whole.

Symbolic-interaction theory suggests that

- individuals use gender as one element of their personal performances as they socially construct reality through everyday interactions.
- gender plays a part in shaping almost all our everyday experiences.

Because our society defines men as having more value than women, the sex roles that define how women and men should behave place men in control of social situations; women play a more deferential role.

Social-conflict theory suggests that

- gender is an important dimension of social inequality and social conflict.
- gender inequality benefits men and disadvantages women.

Friedrich Engels tied gender stratification to the rise of private property and a class hierarchy. Marriage and the family are strategies by which men control their property through control of the sexuality of women. Capitalism exploits everyone by paying men low wages and assigning women the task of maintaining the home.

Intersection theory investigates the factors of race, class, and gender, which combine to cause multiple disadvantages for some categories of people.

- Visible minority women are disadvantaged in terms of race and gender.
- Because all women have a distinctive social identity and are disadvantaged, they are a minority, although most White women do not think of themselves this way.

Feminism

13.5 Contrast liberal, radical, and socialist feminism.

Feminism

- endorses the social equality of women and men and opposes patriarchy and sexism.
- seeks to eliminate violence against women.
- advocates giving women control over their reproduction.

There are three types of feminism:

- *Liberal feminism* seeks equal opportunity for both sexes within the existing society.
- *Socialist feminism* claims that gender equality will come about by replacing capitalism with socialism.
- *Radical feminism* seeks to eliminate the concept of gender itself and to create an egalitarian and gender-free society.

Most opposition to feminism is directed toward socialist and radical feminism. Support for liberal feminism is widespread.

---

feminism the advocacy of social equality for women and men, in opposition to patriarchy and sexism

Chapter 14
Race and Ethnicity

Jim West/Alamy Stock Photo

 Learning Objectives

14.1 Explain the social construction of race and ethnicity.

14.2 Describe the extent and causes of prejudice.

14.3 Distinguish discrimination from prejudice.

14.4 Identify examples of pluralism, assimilation, segregation, and genocide.

14.5 Assess the social standing of racial and ethnic categories in Canadian society.

The Power of Society
to determine the choice between marriage and common-law union

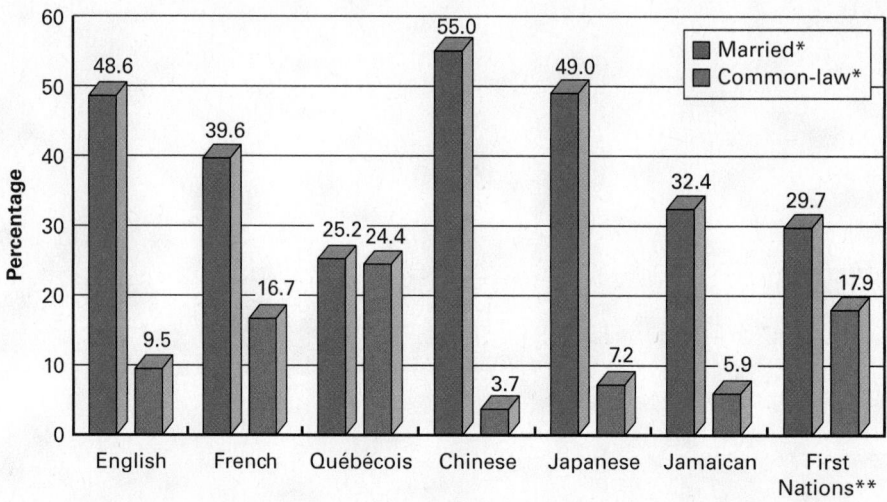

*Percentages married or in common-law relationships are based on populations 15 years of age and over.
**Note that, for present purposes, the term First Nations refers to registered and non-status Indians combined.
SOURCE: Compiled by L.M. Gerber from Statistics Canada, 2011 National Household Survey, Catalogue number 99-010-X2011036.

The decision to get married or live common-law is a private matter, right? Why would anyone or anything else determine your choice? The fact is that social forces beyond your control nudge you and your partner in one direction or another. The result of subtle and no-so-subtle influences is variation among ethnic groups that is anything but random. In this case, we are comparing ethnic populations—15 years of age and over—on rates of marriage and cohabitation. Three ethnic categories stand out with relatively high levels of common-law union. The Québécois are the most likely to live common-law—at 24 percent—followed by the French and First Nations. At the lower end of the continuum, we find Chinese Canadians with 4 percent in common-law unions and 55 percent married—at 59 percent they are the most likely live as couples. Jamaicans, Japanese, and the English all have cohabitation rates below 10 percent. These differences are significant—as is one other fact. The low rate of cohabitation among Jamaican Canadians (6 percent) is coupled with a relatively low marriage rate. Jamaicans, in effect, are least likely to live in couples.

Chapter Overview

Canada is arguably the most racially and ethnically diverse of all societies. Traditional heritage—a source of pride—accounts for many of the racial and ethnic differences we observe. This chapter explains how race and ethnicity are created by society. Both race and ethnicity are not only matters of difference but also dimensions of social inequality.

"When you're brought up with discrimination," says **Barbara Carter of Dresden, Ontario, "you know what you can do and what you can't do.** So you just abide by the rules and it's not that bad. We knew we couldn't go into the restaurants with our White girlfriends after school, so we just didn't go. I never understood, however, why there were two churches. There were two Baptist churches in town. One for the Whites and one for the Blacks."

"It was different for me," says Bruce. "I was a very bitter person when I was a teenager. At one time there was not one restaurant in town where I could get a cup of coffee. Towards the end of the war we had German prisoners of war around here. They were working in the sugar-beet fields under guard. The prisoners of war could go into the restaurants, but a Negro soldier in a Canadian army uniform couldn't. It was pretty bad. My aunt taught in a segregated school. The last one closed in the sixties.

Library of Congress Prints and Photographs Division [Shahn, Ben, 1898–1969/LC-DIG-fsa-8a17588]

"We went to Disney World a while ago," says Bruce. "We went to the Canadian pavilion. They have a movie about Canada there. It's a tremendous movie—all in the round. But do you know what? There is not one Black person in the whole movie. I was watching it and I thought, 'Wait a minute, where am I?' So I sat through it a second time to make sure. It's like we're a non-people. We weren't even in the crowd scenes." ■

SOURCE: From *Welcome Home: Travels in Small-Town Canada* by Stuart McLean. Copyright © Stuart McLean, permission of Penguin Group (Canada), a Division of Pearson Penguin Canada Inc.

This chapter examines the meaning of race and ethnicity, explains how these social constructs have shaped human history, and suggests why they continue to play such a central part in the global community today. We will also explore Canada's unique blend of race, ethnic, and Aboriginal dynamics (Fleras, 2010).

The Social Meaning of Race and Ethnicity

14.1 Explain the social construction of race and ethnicity.

The terms *race* and *ethnicity* are often used imprecisely and interchangeably. For this reason, we begin with some definitions.

Race

A **race** is *a socially constructed category of people who share biologically transmitted traits that members of a society consider important.* People may classify one another racially based on physical characteristics such as skin colour, facial features, hair texture, and body shape. Physical diversity appeared among our human ancestors as the result of living in different geographic regions of the world. In regions of intense heat, for example, humans developed darker skin, from the natural pigment melanin, as protection from the sun; in regions with moderate climates, people have lighter skin. Such differences are literally only skin-deep, since we are members of a single biological species.

The striking variety of physical traits found today is also the product of migration; physical characteristics once common to a single place (such as light skin or curly

THE RANGE OF BIOLOGICAL VARIATION IN HUMANS IS FAR GREATER THAN ANY SYSTEM OF RACIAL CLASSIFICATION ALLOWS This fact is made obvious by trying to place all of the people pictured here into simple racial categories.

hair) are now found in many lands. Mixture is especially pronounced in the Middle East, historically a crossroads of human migration. Greater physical uniformity characterizes more isolated people, such as the island-dwelling Japanese. But every population has some genetic mixture, and increasing contact among the world's people ensures even more blending of physical characteristics in the future.

Although we think of race in terms of biological elements, race is a socially constructed concept. At one level, different categories of people "see" physical traits differently; for example, research shows that White people rate Black subjects as darker in skin tone than Black people do (Hill, 2002). Also, some people—especially biracial and multiracial people—define themselves and are defined by others differently, depending on the setting (Harris & Sim, 2002). More broadly, entire societies define physical traits differently. Typically, Canadians "see" fewer racial categories—commonly, Black, White, and Asian—than do Brazilians, who distinguish between *branca* (white), *parda* (brown), *morena* (brunette), *mulata* (mulatto), *preta* (black), and *amarela* (yellow) (Inciardi et al., 2000). To allow for a range of self-definitions, the Canadian census allows people to describe themselves using any number of racial or ethnic terms—writing in up to four choices.

RACIAL AND ETHNIC CATEGORIES Scientists invented the concept of "race" in the nineteenth century as they tried to organize the world's physical diversity, identifying three racial types. They called people with relatively light skin and fine hair *Caucasoid,* people with darker skin and coarse hair *Negroid,* and people with yellow or brown skin and distinctive folds on the eyelids *Mongoloid.* Sociologists consider such terms misleading at best and harmful at worst. For one thing, no society contains biologically "pure" people. The skin colour of people we might call "Caucasoid" (or "Indo-European," "Caucasian," or, more commonly, "White") ranges from very light (typical in Scandinavia) to very dark (in southern India). The same variation exists among so-called "Negroid" ("African" or, more commonly, "Black") people and "Mongoloid" (that is, "Asian") people. Across all humans, about 0.1% of DNA varies (Jorde & Wooding, 2004). Of that 0.1%, the three racial categories differ in only 6 percent of their genes, meaning there is less than the genetic variation *within* each category than *between* categories (American Sociological Association, 2003; Harris & Sim, 2002). Nonetheless, "superficial physical traits are regarded as logical grounds for classifying people into racial groups" (Li, 1999).

Why, then, do people make so much of race? Such categories imply hierarchical ranking, which allows some people to feel that they are inherently better than others. Because racial ranking shapes access to wealth and prestige, societies may construct racial categories in extreme ways. Throughout much of the twentieth century, for example, many states in the American South labelled as "coloured" anyone with as little as 1/32 African ancestry (i.e., one African-American great-great-great-grandparent). Today, U.S. law leaves it up to parents to decide the race of a child.

Aboriginal peoples have unique positions in Canadian society. Status, registered, or treaty Indians (i.e., First Nations) fall under the *Indian Act*, are administered by Aboriginal and Northern Affairs Canada, belong to one of about 630 First Nations, and are represented federally by their chiefs through the Assembly of First Nations. At the same time, First Nations, non-status Indian, Inuit, and Métis peoples have special rights and protections under the Canadian Charter of Rights and Freedoms. We identify racial groups of immigrant background—but not Aboriginals—as visible minorities and, officially at least, celebrate multiculturalism and racial diversity as part of our Canadian identity.

Whereas the United States has measured race—and ignored ethnicity—throughout its history, Canada has taken the opposite approach. While Canada has a long-standing interest in its ethnic composition, it was only in the 1996 census that an attempt was made to determine racial identification. In the past, attempts to determine the size of our visible minority population were based on declared country of origin (or ancestry) and self-definition. If someone claimed to be of Jamaican origin, for example, it was assumed (often incorrectly) that he or she was Black. Similarly, and equally incorrectly at times, someone who declared British or U.S. origins was assumed to be White. Even First Nations individuals are of mixed racial and ethnic ancestry—the result being that there are registered Indians or members of First Nations with blond hair and blue eyes.

A TREND TOWARD MIXTURE Over many generations and throughout the Americas, the genetic traits from around the world have become mixed. Many dark- and light-skinned people have multiracial ancestry. Today, people are more willing to define themselves as multiracial. When completing their 2010 census forms, 2.2 percent of Americans checked two or more racial categories, and 4 percent of children under five were listed as multiracial. In Canada (2011), where we blend ethnic and racial categories, 42 percent of the total population claims multiple origins. This is the case for 19 percent of those with Chinese background, 21 percent of East Indians, 62 percent of North American Indians (First Nations and non-status Indians combined), 44 percent of Jamaicans, and 29 percent of Vietnamese. People of British or northern European background have been in Canada for many generations—have intermarried—and are much more likely to claim multiple origins: English 80 percent, Irish 89 percent, French 77 percent, German 81 percent, Danish 85 percent, and Swedish 92 percent (see Table 14–1). The emergence of these multi-ethnicities, or multi-ethnic identities, is the result of intermarriage or mixed unions among ethnic groups (Li, 1999:6). At one point, the Canadian census measured ethnic composition on the basis of the country of origin of one's first male ancestor to arrive in Canada. Today, the census allows us to write in up to four ethnic origins; it is this change that allows us to see the effects of mixed unions.

When reading Table 14–1, it is important to understand that the first column indicates the number of people in Canada who claim each ethnic origin—either singly or as one of up to four origins. The percentages in the second column refer to the proportion of Canada's population claiming each identity; thus, the 5 million people claiming French origins make up 15 percent of Canada's total population. The next two columns refer to the number of people claiming each ethnicity as a single origin and the *percentage* of each ethnic category claiming that specific single origin. Thus, 19 percent of those with German origins claim to have *only* German ancestry, whereas 81 percent of Chinese Canadians claim only Chinese ancestry. The last two columns provide the numbers and percentages in each ethnic category claiming *multiple* origins. Ethnic categories that have large proportions claiming multiple origins (e.g., Scottish, Norwegian, or Austrian) are normally those that have been established in Canada for generations. Categories with *small* percentages claiming multiple origins (e.g., Chinese, East Indian, or Vietnamese) are largely immigrant, so they have had little or no opportunity for intermarriage. As a general rule, old, established ethnic groups have experienced the most ethnic or racial blending, and their descendants are the most likely to call themselves Canadian or—if they are old-stock Quebecers—*Canadien*.

When you looked at the data for French and English, did the percentages claiming these origins seem very low to you? Aren't French and English the founding groups that settled here in the 1700s and 1800s? In fact, people whose French origins are in the distant past now call themselves French, Acadian, Québécois, *Canadien*, and maybe even Métis. English- and French-origin Canadians have much in common—1.3 and 1.7 million people claim single origins while 80 and 77 percent claim mixed ancestry—effectively assuming Canadian or *Canadien* identities.

Perhaps the best evidence for the blending of ethnic—and, to a large extent, racial—identities is the fact that, in 17 of the 30 ethnic groups included in Table 14–1, 75 percent or more claim multiple origins (indicated in bold). On the other hand, only eight of the 30 claim more

Table 14–1 The Top 30 Ethnic Origins in Canada: Single- and Multiple-Origin Responses, 2011

Population	Total Origins*	%	Single Origin*	%	Multiple Origins*	%
	32 852 320		19 036 295		13 816 025	
Canadian/*Canadien***	10 563 805	32.2	5 834 535	**55.2**	4 729 265	44.8
English	6 509 500	19.8	1 312 570	20.2	5 196 930	**79.8**
French	5 065 690	15.4	1 165 465	23.0	3 900 225	**77.0**
Scottish	4 714 970	14.4	544 440	11.5	4 170 530	**88.5**
Irish	4 544 870	13.8	506 445	11.1	4 038 425	**88.9**
German	3 203 330	9.8	608 520	19.0	2 594 805	**81.0**
Italian	1 488 425	4.5	700 845	47.1	787 580	52.9
Chinese	1 487 580	4.5	1 210 945	**81.4**	276 635	18.6
NA Indian***	1 369 115	4.2	517 550	37.8	851 565	62.2
Ukrainian	1 251 170	3.8	276 055	22.1	975 110	**77.9**
East Indian	1 165 145	3.5	919 155	**78.9**	245 985	21.1
Dutch	1 067 245	3.2	297 885	27.9	769 355	72.1
Polish	1 010 705	3.1	255 135	25.2	755 565	**74.8**
Filipino	662 600	2.0	506 545	**76.4**	156 060	23.6
Russian	550 520	1.7	107 300	19.5	443 220	**80.5**
Welsh	458 705	1.4	28 785	6.3	429 915	**93.7**
Norwegian	452 705	1.4	44 075	9.7	408 630	**90.3**
Métis	447 655	1.4	68 205	15.2	379 445	**84.8**
Portuguese	429 850	1.3	250 320	**58.2**	179 530	41.8
American	372 575	1.1	32 935	8.8	339 640	**91.2**
Spanish	368 305	1.1	66 575	18.1	301 730	**81.9**
Swedish	341 845	1.0	26 080	7.6	315 770	**92.4**
Hungarian	316 765	1.0	80 540	25.4	236 220	**74.6**
Jewish	309 650	0.9	115 640	37.3	194 010	62.7
Jamaican	256 915	0.8	142 870	**55.6**	114 040	44.4
Greek	252 960	0.8	141 755	**56.0**	111 205	44.0
Vietnamese	220 425	0.7	157 450	**71.4**	62 970	28.6
Romanian	204 625	0.6	82 995	40.6	121 635	59.4
Danish	203 080	0.6	31 370	15.4	171 705	**84.6**
Austrian	197 990	0.6	22 945	11.6	175 040	**88.4**

*In 1996, for the first time, the census question allowed people to write in up to four ethnic or cultural origins. Thus, the first column, Total Origins, includes people who claim a Single Origin (e.g., Hungarian) or Multiple Origins (e.g., Greek, Italian, and Jamaican).

**Census 1996 also provided a list of examples of ethnicities, which included the category "Canadian"—or *Canadien* in the French version. The structure of this question produced a sevenfold increase in the number of people who identified themselves as single-origin "Canadian" or "*Canadien*." *Canadien* in Quebec refers to descendants of the original French settlers. The number indicating Canadian/*Canadien* roots increased from 765 095 in 1991 to 5,326 995 in 1996.

***Strictly speaking, the term North American Indian cannot be used interchangeably with First Nation(s). The reason is that only 42 percent of the 1.4 million people claiming Indian ancestry are Registered Indians (or First Nations) or self-identify as Indian. It makes no sense to call someone with one Indian grandparent, who does not self-identify as Indian, a member of one of Canada's 630 First Nations.

SOURCE: Compilation and calculations by L.M. Gerber based on Statistics Canada, NHS 2011, Catalogue no. 91-010-X2011028.

than 70 percent single origins. Racial blending is clear among North American Indians, Jamaicans, and Métis (with 62, 44, and 85 percent respectively claiming mixed origins); on the other hand, among Chinese, East Indian, Filipino, and Vietnamese Canadians, only 19 to 29 percent claim multiple origins. Since racial groups are themselves multi-ethnic; ethnic intermarriage is not always racial intermarriage. Nonetheless, the overall pattern suggests that, as new generations of ethnic groups grow up in Canada, ethnically and racially mixed parentage become more common.

Ethnicity

Ethnicity is *a shared cultural heritage*. People define themselves or others as members of an *ethnic category* based on common ancestry, language, or religion that gives them a

race a socially constructed category of people who share biologically transmitted traits that members of a society consider important

ethnicity a shared cultural heritage

distinctive social identity. For certain purposes, as in dealing with ethnic categories that are undergoing change, it is important to distinguish between *objective* and *subjective* criteria (Isajiw, 1985). Objective criteria are traits such as ancestry, cultural practices, dress, religion, and language. Subjective criteria involve the internalization of a distinctive social identity, whereby people identify themselves or are perceived by others as belonging to a different group. Subjective ethnic identities may persist despite cultural assimilation, sometimes over many generations, without perpetuation of traditional ethnic culture (the objective components). For example, Canadian-born Finns continue to see themselves as "Finnish" though they do not speak the language, dance, sing, prepare foods, or go to sauna according to Finnish tradition. Whatever the degree of assimilation, ethnicity remains an important basis of social differentiation in Canada.

Roughly 6.6 million Canadians—or 20 percent of the population—claim languages other than French or English as their mother tongues. About half of them speak those non-official languages at home. Furthermore, there are now more Catholics than Protestants in Canada, as Catholic French Canadians have been joined by immigrants from such traditionally Catholic areas as Italy, Poland, and Latin America. Canada's Jewish population traces its ancestral ties to various countries, as do Eastern Orthodox and Muslim Canadians. In fact, churches help perpetuate ethnicity: In the 1970s, our major churches—Roman Catholic, United, Anglican, Presbyterian, Lutheran, and Baptist combined—held services in 74 minority languages (Ujimoto, 1999:256).

Like race, the concept of "ethnicity" is socially constructed, becoming important only when society defines it that way. Sometimes the two go hand in hand. Japanese Canadians, for example, have distinctive physical traits and, for those who maintain their traditions, cultural attributes as well. But ethnic distinctiveness should not be viewed as racial. Jews may be described as a race but they are distinctive only in their religious beliefs and their history of persecution.

People can *change* their ethnicities by adopting a different way of life. Polish immigrants who discard their cultural background over time may cease to have a particular ethnicity. Someone of British ancestry might marry a German and become "more German" than his or her partner. People of mixed Aboriginal and non-Aboriginal heritage may have blended into the dominant francophone or anglophone populations of their respective provinces or territories to the point where many are unaware of their mixed ancestry. From time to time, people actually renew ethnic ties and identities after two or three generations, making serious efforts to return to their roots, be they Polish, Jewish, or Aboriginal. The latter illustrates the "returning or rediscovery" pattern of ethnic identity

maintenance, which "is not for day-to-day survival but for more symbolic reasons" (Ujimoto, 1999:258).

Minorities

A **minority** is *any category of people distinguished by physical or cultural difference that a society sets apart and subordinates.* Minority standing can be based on race, ethnicity, or both. In recent years, the breadth of the term *minority* has expanded in meaning to include not only people with particular racial and ethnic traits but also people with physical disabilities and, as the previous chapter explained, women. Elderly people, gays, and lesbians can also be considered minorities.

Minorities have two major characteristics. One trait is that they share a *distinctive identity*. Because race is highly visible—and virtually impossible for a person to change—most minority men and women are keenly aware of their physical differences. The significance of ethnicity—which people can change—is more variable. In Canada, some people downplay their historic ethnicity, while others maintain their cultural traditions and live in distinctive ethnic neighbourhoods. Some go so far as to insulate themselves from outside influences: Hasidic Jews in Montreal have been particularly successful in nurturing a lifestyle that separates them from their neighbours. The Hutterite people of Alberta and Saskatchewan, who live in communal agricultural communities (or colonies), manage to minimize contact with the "outside" even more effectively.

Sean Kilpatrick/The Canadian Press

IN 2010, DAVID JOHNSTON WAS APPOINTED BY QUEEN ELIZABETH II TO REPLACE MICHAËLLE JEAN AS GOVERNOR GENERAL As always, new governors general are appointed on the recommendation of the prime minister. Accordingly, the governor general reads the throne speech at the opening of each new Parliament, confers royal assent on all laws passed, is commander-in-chief of the armed forces, and officiates at ceremonial occasions, such as awarding the Order of Canada. Furthermore, when the prime minister wishes to have an election—or when a minority government is defeated—the governor general decides whether or not an election will be held.

A second characteristic of minorities is *subordination*. Minorities in Canada tend to have lower income and less occupational prestige than their counterparts of British or French origin, even if—as in the case of Chinese Canadians—their levels of educational attainment are as high or higher. Thus, class, race, and ethnicity, as well as gender, are overlapping and reinforcing dimensions of social stratification.

Of course, not all members of any minority are disadvantaged. But even the greatest success rarely allows individuals to transcend their minority standing; that is, race or ethnicity often serves as a master status (described in the chapter on Social Interaction in Everyday Life) that overshadows personal accomplishments.

The term *minority* suggests that these categories of people constitute a small proportion of a society's population. But this is not always the case. Black South Africans are disadvantaged even though they are a numerical majority. In Canada, women represent more than half of the population but are still struggling to gain opportunities and privileges long enjoyed by men.

Prejudice and Stereotypes

14.2 Describe the extent and causes of prejudice.

Prejudice is *a rigid and unfair generalization about an entire category of people.* Prejudice is unfair because all people in some category are assumed to be the same—with little or no direct evidence. Prejudice may target a particular social class, sex, sexual orientation, age, physical ability, religion, political affiliation, race, or ethnicity.

Prejudices are *prejudgments* that may be positive or negative. Our positive prejudices tend to exaggerate the virtues of people like ourselves, while our negative prejudices condemn those who differ from us. Negative prejudice runs along a continuum, ranging from mild aversion to outright hostility. Because attitudes are rooted in our culture, everyone has at least some measure of prejudice.

Prejudice often takes the form of a **stereotype** (*stereo* is derived from Greek, meaning "hard" or "solid"), *a simplified description applied to every person in some category.* Many White people hold stereotypes of visible minorities—which can be especially harmful to minorities in the workplace. If company officials see workers in stereotypical terms, they will make assumptions about their abilities and limit their access to better opportunities (Kaufman, 2002). In 1986, the Canadian government passed the *Employment Equity Act* to ensure a more inclusive environment by encouraging the employment and

---

prejudice a rigid and unfair generalization about an entire category of people

stereotype a simplified description applied to every person in some category

---

promotion of targeted minorities; "however, the results of this social engineering are modest at best, and dismal at worst" in that the "gap between the haves and the have-nots is widening" (Fleras, 2010:117, 125). In particular, recent—that is, visible minority—immigrants earn less than the predominantly White immigrants who arrived in earlier periods. An examination of unemployment rates for immigrants from Latin America, Africa, Asia, Europe, and North America—while controlling for period of immigration—reveals that "race" affects levels of unemployment (Fleras, 2010:129).

RACISM   A powerful and destructive form of prejudice, **racism** refers to *the belief that one racial category is innately superior or inferior to another.* Racism pervades world history. The ancient Greeks, the peoples of India, and the Chinese were among the first to view people unlike themselves as inferior. Racism has also been widespread in Canadian history. At one point, the enslavement of people of African descent or of Aboriginal peoples (called *Panis* in New France) was supported by notions of their innate inferiority—as was the placement of Indian nations on reserves under paternalistic administration by British colonial officials.

Historically, the assertion that certain categories of people are *innately* inferior has provided a powerful justification for subjugation and the establishment of vast colonial empires. Canada never acquired external colonies, being one itself, but it did establish a system of *internal* colonialism involving "Indian" reserves.

Stanley Barrett, an anthropologist who did field research among various White supremacists in Canada, notes that:

> Racism constitutes an elaborate and systematic ideology; it acts as a conceptual tool to rationalize the division of the world's population into the privileged and the deprived. It is inherently a political phenomenon. It emerged with the advent of the colonization of the Third World by European nations, and thus coincided too with the development of capitalism. (1987:5–6)

While some think of racism in Canada as a thing of the past, Fleras argues that it is an everyday reality for many Canadians: "a moving target that is difficult to pin down or control." Racism is simultaneously elusive and pervasive, and defies definition because Whites and minorities do not perceive it in the same way. Whites may think of racism as an "irrational aberration" in an otherwise benevolent society. Minorities experience a system in which "patterns of power and privilege are reproduced" so that they perpetuate "a racialized status quo" (2001:81–82).

Although Canadians are by no means devoid of prejudice or racism, there is evidence that we are more tolerant of racial and ethnic minorities than our American neighbours (Lipset, 1991:112). The peaceful transformation of the once staunchly anglocentric cities of Toronto and Vancouver into "vibrant, cosmopolitan centres" is a positive indicator of our tolerance (Fleras, 2010:53–54). Between 1975 and 1995, Canadians became more aware of discrimination affecting minorities (up about 10 points). Over the same period, acceptance of interracial and interfaith marriage increased by a similar amount: More than 80 percent approve of interracial marriage, and 90 percent approve of interfaith marriage (Bibby, 1995:52–54).

Overt ("in-your-face") racism in this country has subsided to some extent because of a more egalitarian culture and is "checked by the state in order to preserve social harmony and order" (Li, 1988:49). Racism persists, though, in less open and direct forms—and research continues to document the injury, humiliation, and inequality caused by racism (Fleras, 2010; Li, 2003; Wotherspoon & Satzewich, 1993).

More recently, racial conflict has intensified in Britain and Western European societies as Whites confront millions of immigrants from former colonies and refugees from strife-torn Eastern Europe. Several terrorist attacks in Europe served to exacerbate racial conflict. Similarly, in Canada, one can observe signs of increasing racial tensions during tough economic times and in response to political events abroad. Racism—in thought and deed—remains a serious social problem here and elsewhere.

Theories of Prejudice

Where does prejudice come from? Social scientists provide several answers to this question, focusing on frustration, personality, culture, and social conflict.

SCAPEGOAT THEORY *Scapegoat theory* holds that prejudice springs from frustration among people who are themselves disadvantaged (Dollard et al., 1939). Take the case of a White woman frustrated by her low-paying job in a textile factory. Directing hostility at the powerful factory owners carries the obvious risk of being fired; therefore, she may blame her low pay on the presence of minority co-workers. Her prejudice does not improve her situation, but it is a relatively safe way to express anger, and it may give her the comforting feeling that at least she is superior to someone.

A **scapegoat**, then, is *a person or category of people, typically with little power, whom people unfairly blame for their own troubles.* Because they have little power and thus are usually "safe targets," minorities often are used as scapegoats.

AUTHORITARIAN PERSONALITY THEORY T.W. Adorno and colleagues (1950) considered extreme prejudice to be a personality trait of certain individuals. This conclusion is supported by research showing that people who express strong prejudice toward one minority typically do so toward all minorities. These *authoritarian personalities* rigidly conform to conventional cultural values and see moral issues as clear-cut matters of right and wrong. People with authoritarian personalities also view society as naturally competitive and hierarchical, with "better" people—like themselves—inevitably dominating those who are weaker, including all minorities.

Adorno also found that people tolerant toward one minority are likely to be accepting of all. They tend to be more flexible in their moral judgments and treat all people as equals. Adorno thought that people with little schooling and those raised by cold and demanding parents tend to develop authoritarian personalities. Filled with anger and anxiety as children, they grow into hostile, aggressive adults who seek out scapegoats.

CULTURE THEORY A third theory contends that, while extreme prejudice may be characteristic of certain people, some prejudice is found in everyone because it is embedded in culture. Belief in the social superiority of some categories of people—for example, the British and French or the hard-working and reliable people of northern and western European roots—still colours Canadian culture, despite Canada's multicultural policies and programs.

Emory Bogardus (1968) studied the effects of culturally rooted prejudices on interpersonal relationships, devising the concept of *social distance* to assess how close or distant people feel in relation to members of various racial and ethnic categories. When Canadians were asked to rank various racial and ethnic categories on the Bogardus scale (Mackie, 1974), the ranking was very similar to that of Americans.

A critical perspective on research into social distance is provided by Peter Li (2003:175). By asking people how close to or how comfortable they are with various social groups, researchers "unwittingly encourage respondents to rank order social groups on the basis of origin and skin colour." In turn, this leads to "racializing immigrants and minority groups by accepting the legitimacy of placing social value on race or colour." In other words, the academic exercise itself contributes to social distance.

CONFLICT THEORY A fourth analysis views prejudice as the product of social conflict. According to this theory, powerful people use prejudice to justify their oppression of minorities. Canadians certainly did this with the Chinese labourers who were allowed to come to Canada to work—under appalling conditions—on the Canadian Pacific Railway in the 1870s and 1880s. Similarly, all elites benefit when prejudice divides workers along racial and ethnic lines and discourages them from working together to advance their common interests (Geschwender, 1978; Olzak, 1989).

A different conflict-based argument, advanced by Shelby Steele (1990), is that minorities themselves cultivate a climate of race consciousness in order to win greater power and privileges. In raising *race consciousness*, Steele explains, minorities argue that they are victims and that dominant groups are their victimizers. Because of their historic disadvantage, minorities claim that they are entitled to special considerations based on their race. While this strategy may yield short-term gains, such policies are likely to spark a backlash from those who condemn "special treatment"—such as that mandated by Canada's *Employment Equity Act*—for anyone on the basis of race or ethnicity. Critics have argued that "affirmative action was unnecessary ... because the ethnic inequality implied by the vertical mosaic was exaggerated" (Lautard & Guppy, 1999:222). Others claim that "this exercise in preferential hiring is nothing less than '*reverse*' discrimination against white males" (Fleras, 2010:118).

The Québécois made their claims on the basis of past injustices and the threat of assimilation in an English-speaking North America. Some non-Quebecers feel that the wrongs of the past have now been redressed and that entrenching special status (i.e., recognition as a "distinct society") in Canada's constitution is going too far. In part because the Charlottetown Accord of 1992 proposed distinct society status for Quebec, it was rejected by Canadians in a referendum.

Discrimination

14.3 Distinguish discrimination from prejudice.

Closely related to prejudice is **discrimination**, *unequal treatment of various categories of people. Prejudice* refers to *attitudes,* but *discrimination* is a matter of *action.* Like prejudice, discrimination can be either positive (providing special advantages) or negative (creating obstacles) and ranges from subtle to blatant.

Institutional Prejudice and Discrimination

We typically think of prejudice and discrimination as the hateful ideas or actions of specific people. But Stokely Carmichael and Charles Hamilton (1967) pointed out that far greater harm results from **institutional prejudice and discrimination**, *bias built into the operation of society's institutions, including schools, hospitals, the police, and the workplace.* For example, researchers have found that banks reject home mortgage applications from minorities at a higher rate than those from White people, even

when income and quality of neighbourhood are held constant (Gotham, 1998). Anderson and Frideres (1981:208) describe the process within the Department of Indian Affairs as follows: When an Aboriginal person asked to be hired by the department, the minister responded that only those belonging to a particular union—and having seniority in the union—could be hired. If an Aboriginal applicant without these qualifications was hired, the union would strike.

Prejudice and Discrimination: The Vicious Circle

Prejudice and discrimination reinforce each other. The Thomas theorem, discussed in the chapter on Social Interaction in Everyday Life, offers a simple explanation of this fact: Situations that are defined as real become real in their consequences (Thomas, 1966:301; orig. 1931). As Thomas recognized, stereotypes become real to people who believe them and sometimes even to those who are victimized by them. Prejudice on the part of White people toward people belonging to visible minorities does not produce innate inferiority, but it can produce social inferiority—pushing minorities into low-paying jobs, inferior schools, and racially segregated housing. Then, as White people see social disadvantage as evidence that minorities do not measure up, they begin a new round of prejudice and discrimination, giving rise to a vicious circle in which each perpetuates the other, as shown in Figure 14–1.

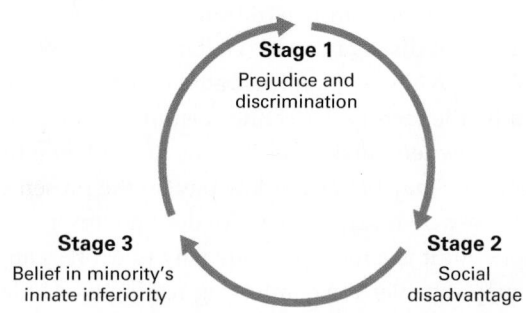

Stage 1: Prejudice and discrimination begin, often as an expression of ethnocentrism or an attempt to justify economic exploitation.

Stage 2: As a result of prejudice and discrimination, a minority is socially disadvantaged, occupying a low position in the system of social stratification.

Stage 3: This social disadvantage is then interpreted not as the result of earlier prejudice and discrimination but as evidence that the minority is innately inferior, unleashing renewed prejudice and discrimination by which the cycle repeats itself.

Figure 14–1 Prejudice and Discrimination: The Vicious Circle

Prejudice and discrimination can form a vicious, self-perpetuating circle.

---

discrimination unequal treatment of various categories of people

institutional prejudice and discrimination bias built into the operation of society's institutions

Majority and Minority: Patterns of Interaction

14.4 Identify examples of pluralism, assimilation, segregation, and genocide.

Sociologists describe patterns of interaction among racial and ethnic categories in a society in terms of four models: pluralism, assimilation, segregation, and genocide.

Pluralism and Multiculturalism

Pluralism is *a state in which racial and ethnic minorities are distinct but have social parity.* In a pluralist society, categories of people are different but share resources more or less equally. The relationship between Quebec and the rest of Canada provides an example of pluralism in action. Aboriginal peoples, too, would like to acquire social and political parity or equality. While the United States considers itself to be pluralist—recently even multicultural—Canada has an official policy of fostering multiculturalism, as discussed in the chapter on Culture.

Social diversity has long been a source of pride in Canada. Some argue that multiculturalism not only acknowledges but also actually celebrates our differences and encourages the perpetuation of countless "ethnic villages," communities where people proudly maintain their cultural traditions. These ethnic communities—the components of our cultural mosaic—add variety and colour to our social landscape. The viability of these communities is affected by their levels of **institutional completeness**, *the complexity of community organizations that meet the needs of members.* Where communities are institutionally complete, members are able to live, shop, pray, and sometimes work within the boundaries of their culture. They might also have their own welfare and mutual aid societies, credit unions, newspapers, and radio stations. Raymond Breton (1964), who coined the term *institutional completeness*, points out that the presence of these formal organizations maintains "in-group" boundaries and minimizes "out-group" contact.

Canada embraces the ideal of multiculturalism, recognition of cultural heterogeneity, and mutual respect among culturally diverse groups. Through policies of multiculturalism, Canada encourages people to participate fully in all aspects of Canadian life without giving up ethnic identities and cultural practices. The aim of multiculturalism is to promote unity through diversity and to enhance a Canadian identity that embraces differences. Canada adopted multiculturalism as government policy in 1971. The *Canadian Multiculturalism Act* of 1988 sought "to recognize all Canadians as full and equal partners in Canadian society," and in 1991 the Department of Multiculturalism and Citizenship (now Heritage Canada)

was created. Multicultural programs provide education, consultative support, and funding for a wide range of activities, including heritage-language training, race relations and cross-cultural understanding programs, the ethnic press, ethnic celebrations, policing and justice, and family violence programs.

Not everyone approves of the official goal of multiculturalism. Critics argue that it discourages immigrant adaptation and is divisive and detrimental to a shared and coherent Canadian identity. While Canadians prefer our cultural mosaic to the American melting pot and more than 80 percent approve of interracial marriage, 85 percent feel that immigrants have an obligation to learn Canadian ways (Bibby, 1995). Writer Neil Bissoondath, who feels that continued ethnic identification weakens the social fabric of Canada, met with hostility and caught the attention of the media when he made a plea to be accepted as an unhyphenated Canadian. Criticism of multiculturalism by this member of a visible minority led to cries of "traitor" or "sellout" from minority members and anger from mainstream defenders of the policy. Bissoondath (1994:5) feels that these reactions have "more than a little to do with the psychology of the True Believer, who sees Canada's multicultural policy as the only one possible."

In November 2004, Theo Van Gogh was murdered in the Netherlands for producing a film, *Submission, Part I*, that dealt with the mistreatment of women in the name of Islam. Van Gogh's co-producer, Ayaan Hirsi Ali—who had herself received death threats—came to Toronto a year after his death to help fight the adoption of sharia in Ontario. Sharia is a body of laws, based on Islamic teachings, for handling family matters. The Ontario government considered the adoption of sharia to deal with matters of family law in the Muslim community in that province. This articulate, passionate, former Muslim woman argued that Ontario's adoption of sharia would effectively authorize discrimination against and mistreatment of women (Fulford, 2005). In the end, Ontario did not give legal recognition to sharia.

Augie Fleras (2010:112) argues that few societies could survive multiculturalism at its extreme—"competing groups with clearly demarcated political boundaries, separate power bases, and parallel institutions." As a result, Canada endorses only "pretend pluralism" involving the "symbols of differences at personal or private levels."

Questions about the impact of multiculturalism can be raised from other perspectives as well. Although their aim was not to criticize multicultural policy, Reitz and Breton (1994) point out that Canada's cultural mosaic and the American melting pot result in only minimal differences in assimilation, economic integration, intermarriage, or tolerance of ethnic distinctiveness. The perception that

John Felstead/The Canadian Press

LINCOLN MACCAULEY ALEXANDER WAS BORN TO IMMI-GRANT PARENTS IN 1922 AND GREW UP IN HAMILTON, ONTARIO With a B.A. from McMaster University and a law degree from Osgoode Hall, Alexander practised law before entering federal politics as Canada's first Black MP. He was lieutenant-governor of Ontario from 1985 to 1991 and chancellor of the University of Guelph from 1991 to 2007. He was appointed a Companion of the Order of Canada and received honourary degrees from five universities and numerous outstanding-citizen awards. Hamilton's Lincoln Alexander Expressway is affectionately known as "The Linc." Throughout his career—which ended with his death in October 2012—Alexander sustained his interest in multicultural affairs.

Canada's minorities retain their cultural identities more than American minorities do is largely an illusion.

Assimilation

Assimilation is *the process by which minorities gradually adopt patterns of the dominant culture, thereby becoming more similar to the dominant group.* Assimilation involves changing modes of dress, values, religion, language, and friends. While the United States has been seen as a *melting pot* in which different nationalities fuse into a new way of life, this characterization is misleading. Rather than "melting" into some new cultural pattern, minorities have adopted the traits—the dress, the accent, and sometimes even the names—of the dominant culture established by the earliest settlers. Why? Assimilation is the avenue to upward social mobility and to escape from the prejudice and discrimination often directed at people perceived to be foreigners.

Although our *cultural mosaic* is supposed to perpetuate diversity, Canadian and American minority experience is very similar. In both countries, the Germans and Irish have "melted" more than the Italians, and the Japanese

more than the Chinese or Koreans. Vibrant ethnic enclaves exist in both countries, despite assimilation. Immigrants learn to function in English and French in Canada, and in English and Spanish in the United States, as they acquire a set of shared attitudes and values that can only be called Canadian or American. Despite our melting pot and mosaic ideals, the dynamics of assimilation and ethnic viability are similar in the United States and Canada (Reitz & Breton, 1994).

Segregation

Segregation refers to *the physical and social separation of categories of people.* Some minorities, especially religious orders such as the Hutterites, voluntarily segregate themselves. The concentration of various ethnic and racial groups in Canada's cities results, at least in part, from voluntary action (i.e., people want to live near people like themselves). Mostly, however, majorities segregate minorities involuntarily by excluding them. Residential neighbourhoods, schools, workplaces, hospitals, and even cemeteries may be segregated. While pluralism and multiculturalism foster distinctiveness without disadvantage, segregation enforces separation to the detriment of the minority.

In the United States, too, racial segregation has a long history, beginning with slavery and evolving into racially separated housing, schooling, buses, and trains. Court decisions have reduced overt and lawful discrimination in the United States, but countless segregated neighbourhoods exist to this day.

Although Canadians might not admit that we practise segregation, we have done so historically and still do today. Early Black migrants—Loyalists in Nova Scotia and those brought via the Underground Railroad to Ontario—found themselves living in Africville (part of Halifax) or in small rural communities such as Buxton and Dawn in Ontario. As a general rule, people in these communities did not receive the same kinds of land grants as other immigrants. They often attended segregated schools and were denied access to local services. Residential and social segregation were very real. The Thinking about Diversity box deals with the experience of slavery in Canada's past.

The clearest example of segregation in Canada is found in our treatment of Aboriginal peoples, through the system of reserves for Status Indians (or First Nations) administered by Aboriginal and Northern Affairs Canada. The overall effect has been one of extreme physical and social segregation, especially when reserves are located in remote areas. Prior to the late 1960s, most of the education of status Indian or First Nations children took place in distant residential schools (far from their parents) or on their reserves. The physical and social segregation of the reserve

Thinking About Diversity: Race, Class, and Gender

Black Citizens of Canada: A History Ignored

When the average Canadian thinks about slavery, the image that comes to mind is likely that of plantation slavery in the Deep South. Few of us are aware that Canada has its own history of slavery and that about 3500 freed slaves came to Nova Scotia and New Brunswick as United Empire Loyalists. They had fought on the side of the British during the American Revolution as members of the Black Pioneers (also known as the Black Loyalists). We are also largely unaware of the 30 000 to 40 000 slaves who escaped and made it to Canada via the Underground Railroad between 1840 and 1865, when slavery was abolished in the United States.

Slaves were on the scene in the earliest settlements of New France. Olivier Le Jeune, who was brought here directly from Africa, was later sold in the first recorded slave sale in 1629. By 1759, there were 3604 slaves in New France: 1132 Black people and the rest Aboriginal people. In 1793, under the leadership of John Graves Simcoe, Upper Canada became the first British colony to legislate the abolition of slavery.[1] While slavery remained legal in the rest of Canada until it was abolished throughout the British Empire in 1833, it had effectively died out by about 1810. Slavery was essentially unsuited to Canadian agriculture.

Fugitive slaves arrived in Ontario between the 1790s and 1860s. From about 1840, they used the Underground Railroad, an informal system of people and safe houses bringing escaped slaves to freedom in the northern United States and Canada. These former slaves formed scattered rural settlements across southern Ontario from Windsor to Barrie, where some farmed their own land while others hired themselves out as farm labourers. Some Black settlements, such as Buxton and Dawn, were thriving communities with their own schools, blacksmith shops, and other businesses.[2] Most of the residents of these communities and their descendants eventually abandoned their rural homes and moved to the cities. Some, however, stayed behind. Descendants of the residents of Dawn still live in Dresden, Ontario.

Freed from slavery, Black people in Canada experienced economic hardship as well as prejudice and discrimination—suggesting that, despite our smugness, Canadians are not much more tolerant than Americans. Nevertheless, immigration from many parts of the world,

HARRIET TUBMAN, KNOWN AS "MOSES," WAS ASSISTED IN HER ESCAPE FROM SLAVERY BY WORKERS ON THE UNDERGROUND RAILROAD She returned to Maryland a year later, in 1850, to free members of her family and then became one of the most active "conductors" on the Railroad, repeatedly risking her life to guide more than 300 slaves to freedom—many of them to Ontario, where she provided shelter for refugees in a rented house in St. Catharines.

including the Caribbean, has added to Canada's Black population, now comprising 945 665 individuals living mainly in southern Ontario and Montreal. At this time (Statistics Canada, 2011), there are three urban centres with significant Black populations: Halifax (4 percent), Montreal (6 percent), and Toronto (7 percent).

More than half of the Nova Scotians who belong to visible minorities identify themselves as Black and are descendants of Black Loyalists who came north at the time of the American Revolution. Most live in Halifax, where they have experienced their share of prejudice and discrimination. Nonetheless, since they are "old stock" Canadians rather than immigrants, their concerns and interests differ from those of Black people in other parts of the country.

The Black communities of Montreal are made up of immigrants and descendants who come from French-speaking countries such as Algeria and Haiti. But shared language has not resulted in easy or painless social and economic integration. Racism and discrimination are as likely to appear in Montreal as in Toronto, where many Black people encounter the combined barriers associated with recent immigration and visible minority status. Despite continued disadvantages, Black people have made important contributions to Canada's economic and cultural life. Former Governor-General Michaëlle Jean was born in Haiti and had established a highly successful career in broadcasting before assuming her political position.

What Do You Think?

1. Were you aware that we have so much slavery in our history?

2. How many examples of successful Black Canadians—in politics, music, athletics, or business—can you recall?

3. When you encounter Black Canadians, do you automatically think of them as immigrants?

SOURCES: Ducharme (1985), McClain (1979), Merrit (1993), Nader et al. (1992), Walker (1980), and Winks (1988).

---

[1] When Governor Simcoe had dinner at the home of Mohawk leader and Loyalist Joseph Brant (Thayendanegea) in 1793, he was served by Brant's "Black slaves resplendent in scarlet uniforms with white ruffles, and with silver buckles on their shoes" (Walker, 1980:21).

[2] Dawn was founded in 1842 by Hiram Wilson and Josiah Henson. The latter, a "conductor" on the Underground Railroad who brought about a hundred slaves to freedom, is thought to be the model for Harriet Beecher Stowe's Uncle Tom in her anti-slavery novel *Uncle Tom's Cabin*.

Patterns of Majority and Minority Interaction

pluralism a state in which people of all races and ethnicities are distinct but have equal social standing

assimilation the process by which minorities gradually adopt patterns of the dominant culture

segregation the physical and social separation of categories of people

genocide the systematic killing of one category of people by another

system created barriers to integration with the mainstream—above and beyond those experienced by other Aboriginal peoples (non-status Indians, Métis, and Inuit).

Genocide

Genocide is *the systematic killing of one category of people by another.* This deadly form of racism and ethnocentrism violates nearly every recognized moral standard, yet it has occurred time and time again in human history. Genocide figured prominently in centuries of contact between Europeans and the original inhabitants of the Americas. From the sixteenth century onward, as the Spanish, Portuguese, English, French, and Dutch forcibly established vast colonial empires, they decimated the Aboriginal populations of North, Central, and South America. Some Aboriginal peoples fell victim to calculated killing sprees, but most succumbed to diseases brought by Europeans to which they had no natural immunities (Butterworth & Chance, 1981; Cottrell, 1979; Dickason, 1997; Matthiessen, 1984; Sale, 1990). The Beothuk (in what is now Newfoundland and Labrador), who experienced the earliest contact with Europeans, disappeared completely by 1829. Feuding and open hunting season against the Beothuk, as well as tuberculosis, took their toll (Dickason, 1997).

Genocide also occurred in the twentieth century. During World War I, at least 1 million Armenians in Eastern Europe perished under the rule of the Ottoman Empire. During Adolf Hitler's reign of terror, known as the Holocaust, the Nazis exterminated more than 6 million Jewish men, women, and children—along with gays, Gypsies (now called Roma), and people with handicaps. Soviet dictator Josef Stalin murdered his country's people on an even greater scale, killing perhaps 28 million real and imagined enemies in the 1930s. Between 1975 and 1980, Pol Pot's Communist regime in Cambodia butchered all "capitalists," a category that included anyone who could speak a Western language. In all, some 2 million people (one-quarter of the population) perished in Cambodian "killing fields."

The breakup of Yugoslavia resulted in conflict between ethnic Serbians and Albanians based on 600 years of feuding. During the spring of 1999, an estimated 10 000 ethnic Albanians were victims of "ethnic cleansing," or mass murder, by their Serbian neighbours. This is one of many trouble spots to which Canadian Erin Mooney

travelled for her United Nations research into the experience of internal refugees (Mooney, 1995). In the winter of 2002, Canadian commander General Romeo Dallaire led UN troops to prevent the genocide of Tutsis at the hands of Hutus in Rwanda. Unable to get the number of troops needed for the job—and defying UN orders to withdraw from Rwanda—Dallaire witnessed the slaughter of 800 000 Tutsis in a 100-day reign of terror (Allen, 2002).

These four patterns of minority/majority interaction coexist in our society. We proudly point to patterns of pluralism (multiculturalism) and assimilation but only reluctantly acknowledge that our society has been built on segregation and genocide. The remainder of this chapter examines how these four patterns have shaped the history and present social standing of major racial and ethnic categories in Canada.

Race and Ethnicity in Canada

14.5 Assess the social standing of racial and ethnic categories in Canadian society.

Thousands of years ago, the people we now call Aboriginal appeared on this continent. One theory is that they came over a land bridge that may have connected Alaska and Siberia. Of course, they might have come by sea. The first European explorers and settlers were met by more than 50 "founding" nations. The French and then the British established permanent settlements in the 1600s and 1700s, conveniently ignoring the Aboriginal nations and declaring themselves the two founding nations. Successive waves of immigration brought northern and then southern and eastern European people to our shores. More recently, in part as a result of changes in immigration laws, new Canadians have come from Asia, Africa, and the Caribbean. In addition, refugees have come to Canada in unprecedented numbers over the past decade. These inflows have completely transformed our sociocultural landscape, giving rise to what we now call "visible minorities" (Li, 2003:33) and making Canada one of the most—if not *the* most—diverse countries in the world.

Recall from our discussion of Table 14–1 that, as the waves of immigrants established themselves in Canada over several generations, mixed ethnic and racial unions became commonplace. As a result, 42 percent of Canadians (in 2011) claimed *multiple* origins or ancestries. Since 1996, our census has allowed us to record up to four origins—but many people have more than four. If you had six ancestries (perhaps Métis, French, English, German, Ukrainian, and Jamaican), which four would you indicate on the census? Would you include the *same* four on the next census? One of the options for dealing with such complexity is to say that you are single-origin "Canadian." During the 1990s, there was a dramatic increase in people claiming "Canadian/*Canadien*" ancestry—increasing from 3 percent in 1991 to 31 percent in 1996, a high of *39 percent* in 2001, before *dropping* to 32 percent by 2011. People *choose* to describe their origins in one way or another as they complete each census. In effect, if circumstances vary, people are free to change their minds and report origins that differ from the previous census. An individual who learns that her great-grandmother was Métis may well incorporate that new knowledge as she fills out the next census form.

Not surprisingly, considering their early settlement of this country, the largest ethnic categories in Canada (after those reporting Canadian/*Canadien* ancestry) are English and French (6.5 and 5.1 million, respectively), followed by Scottish, Irish, and German (at 4.7, 4.5, and 3.2 million each). People with Italian, Chinese, North American Indian, Ukrainian, East Indian, Dutch, and Polish roots

number more than 1 million each. Other ethnic categories among the top 30 drop off quickly in size—down to 197 990 people of Austrian origin. Overall, Table 14–1 portrays Canada as dominated by people of English and French origins, but otherwise of remarkable diversity.

Canada's censuses in 1996 and 2001 attempted to measure the status of visible minorities (as distinct from ethnic or Aboriginal origins) to assess compliance with the *Employment Equity Act*. Respondents were asked to identify as White, Chinese, South Asian, Black, Arab/West Asian, Filipino, Southeast Asian, Latin American, Japanese, Korean, or "Other." Black appeared as a choice among *ethnic* categories in the 1991 census, but now is part of a more direct question aimed at identifying visible minority populations. Figure 14–2 illustrates the fact that visible minorities are not evenly distributed across Canada, which is 19.1 percent visible minority. A number of provinces and territories—namely Newfoundland and Labrador, Prince Edward Island, New Brunswick, and Nunavut—are less than 5 percent. Visible minorities make up 11 to 18 percent of the populations of Quebec, Manitoba, and Alberta but they don't hold a candle to Ontario and British Columbia (at 26 and 27 percent or more than a quarter visible minority).

The Thinking about Diversity box shines a spotlight on visible minorities in Toronto, Vancouver, and Montreal.

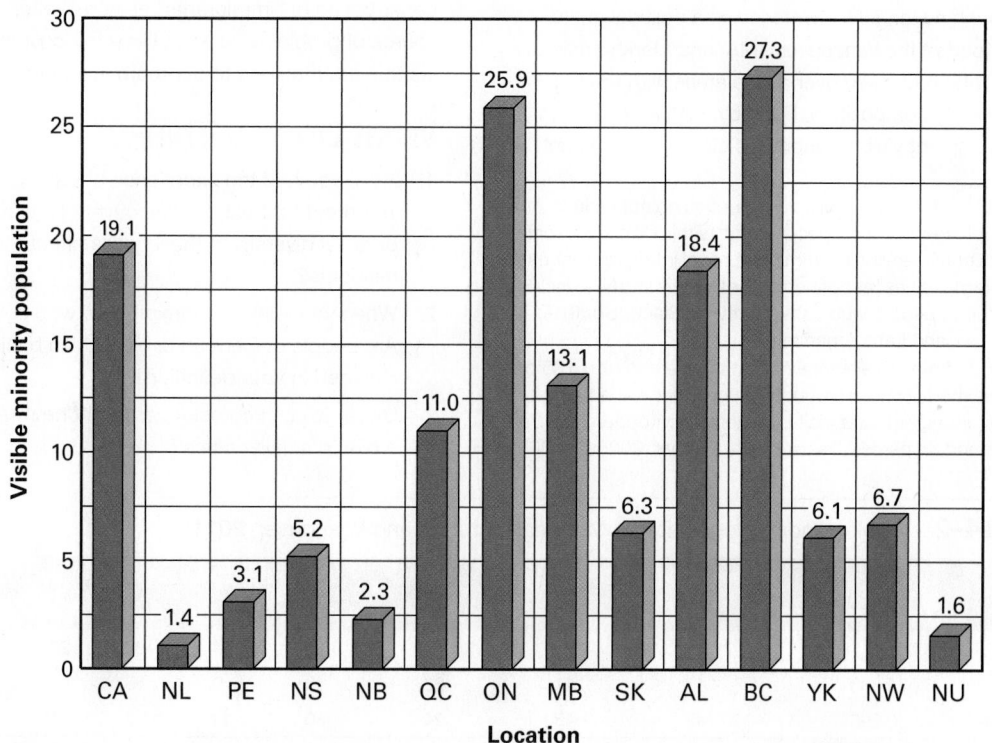

Figure 14–2 Visible Minority Population of Canada, Provinces, and Territories, 2011

SOURCE: Compilation and Calculations by L.M. Gerber based on Statistics Canada, NHS 2011. Catalogue no. 99-010- X2011029.

Thinking About Diversity: Race, Class, and Gender

Visible Minorities: Toronto, Vancouver, and Montreal

The National Household Survey (NHS) of 2011 reveals that 6.3 million people (19 percent of Canada's population) identify as members of visible minorities.[3] Although the majority of these individuals are immigrants, increasing proportions are Canadian-born. Three census metropolitan areas (CMAs)—Toronto, Vancouver, and Montreal—have attracted more than three-quarters of Canada's visible minority population. The mix of visible minorities is different in each city. Toronto is the most diverse: 47 percent of its population is composed of visible minorities—more than half of whom are from South Asia (including India) and China, while another 15 percent self-identifies as Black. Vancouver's visible minority population (45 percent of its total) is almost entirely South Asian, Chinese, and Filipino. Montreal has the smallest visible minority component (20 percent), which is largely Black, Arab, and Latin American (Table 14–2).

Not only do our major metropolitan areas attract very different visible minorities but certain minorities tend to settle in specific neighbourhoods. By going to neighbourhoods where relatives or friends have already located, they contribute to different concentrations of minorities in various parts of each CMA. Prior to the amalgamation of several municipalities into a larger Toronto (i.e., at the time of the 1991 census), Scarborough had the largest visible minority population (at 52 percent) in the country.[4] By 2001, with Scarborough no longer in existence as a political entity, Burnaby (part of the Vancouver CMA) and Markham (in the Toronto CMA) had taken over as the areas with the largest visible minority composition. Burnaby, with a population that is 49 percent visible minority, is close to 40 percent

Warren Toda/EPA/Newscom

TORONTO IS THE DIVERSITY CAPITAL OF CANADA, WITH 41 PERCENT OF THE COUNTRY'S VISIBLE MINORITY POPULATION.

Asian. Similarly, Markham (at 56 percent visible minority) is at least 45 percent Asian and 4 percent Black. Montréal Nord (24 percent visible minority) is 15 percent Black.

The fact that about 80 percent of Canada's immigrants in recent years have come from Asia, the Middle East, Africa, and the Caribbean has changed our understanding of the term *immigrant* (Li, 2003:44–45). While formally the term refers to anyone who came to Canada from another country, the "folk version" now tends to refer to people who appear foreign-looking—or to those of different racial backgrounds. Even if they are born in Canada, members of visible minorities are likely to be labelled immigrants—and assumed to be the cause of urban problems. This social construction of "immigrants" as non-White, and as the source of problems, is most likely to occur in the major cities that are magnets to our more recent immigrants.

What Do You Think?

1. Have you had the experience of visiting—or living in—Toronto, Montreal, or Vancouver? How does the ethnic or racial diversity in those cities affect the lives of their residents?

2. When you think of "immigrants," who come to mind? Are people of German or Hungarian background included in your definition?

3. Under what circumstances might new immigrants move to smaller cities?

[3]Note that the statistics for visible minorities do not include Aboriginal peoples—who hold special status within Canadian society and are not considered to be immigrants or of immigrant ancestry. The "visible minorities" as defined by the Census and NHS include, among others, people who self-identify as Black, South Asian, Filipino, Arab, and Latin American.

[4]The five Scarborough electoral districts range from 43 to 85 percent visible minority. Scarborough Rouge River is the riding with the largest immigrant and visible minority components in Canada, at 67 and 85 percent, respectively (Gerber, 2006a, 2006b).

Table 14–2   Visible Minority Population of Montreal, Toronto, and Vancouver, 2011

	Total Population	Percent Visible Minority*		Percentage of Visible Minority**					
		2006	2011	South Asian	Chinese	Filipino	Black	Arab	Latin American
Montreal	3 752 475	17	20	10	10	4	28	20	13
Toronto	5 521 235	43	47	32	20	9	15	3	5
Vancouver	2 280 695	42	45	24	40	11	2	1	3

*These figures refer to the percentage of each city's population that self-identifies as visible minority.

**These figures refer to the composition of the visible minority population in each city. For example, 28 percent of Montreal's visible minority population self-identifies as Black, whereas 40 percent of Vancouver's visible minority population is Chinese.

SOURCE: Compiled by L.M. Gerber from Statistics Canada, 2011 National Household Survey, Catalogue number 99-010-X2011036.

Social Standing

A great deal has been written about ethnic and racial inequality in Canada and its causes (Driedger & Church, 1974; Fleras, 2010; Frideres, 2011; Frideres & Gadacz, 2012; Gerber, 1983, 1990, 1995, 2014; Lautard & Guppy, 1999; Li, 2003; McAll, 1990; Porter, 1965; Ramcharan, 1982; Wotherspoon & Satzewich, 1993). The general consensus seems to be that the workings of our capitalist economy, along with racism, prejudice, and discrimination, contribute to socio-economic inequality, with recent immigrants and visible minorities at the bottom of the scale. For a number of reasons, including a system of internal colonialism, Aboriginal peoples are the most severely disadvantaged in this regard.

Table 14–3 compares selected ethnic categories— English, French, Québécois, Chinese, Japanese, Jamaican, and First Nations—on a number of socio-economic dimensions. Japanese Canadians are least likely and First Nations most likely to lack even high school certification (at 3 and 26 percent, respectively). Chinese and Japanese Canadians lead with respect to the attainment of university degrees (at 44 percent) while First Nations fall far behind (at 13 percent). Although educational attainment varies dramatically, employment levels in 2010 do not. The gap in full-time employment rates is not as wide as it has been in the past, but the pattern is intriguing nonetheless. More than a third (35 percent) of English, French, and Jamaican Canadians were employed full time in 2010. Of those three categories, Jamaicans are least likely to have university degrees, yet they match the French and English in terms of full-time employment. But working full time does not ensure equality of income—as illustrated by the fact that average income is $10 000 lower for Jamaicans than for those of English origin. If there is any consistency here it applies to First Nations people, who lag behind their counterparts in both educational attainment *and* income.

Lautard and Guppy (1999:223) argue that, when it comes to educational attainment, "clear evidence exists that British dominance has eroded." The data in Table 14–3 are consistent with other research findings: Some visible minorities are in the top ranks of those who have post-secondary credentials. In Canada, those of Chinese and Japanese origins—who are far ahead of French- and even English-Canadians—are more than twice as likely to have university degrees as the Québécois or Jamaicans (and more than three times as likely as First Nations). Unfortunately, as already noted, "when it comes to translating education into occupational position and income," visible minorities are likely to come up against "ethnic penalties." For the Chinese in particular, educational attainment has not resulted in higher income as their median income is on par with that of First Nations. In other words, the Chinese encounter "ethnic penalties" but the Japanese do not. In sharp contrast, the Japanese—who excel on both measures of educational attainment—have an average income second only to the English (and a median income surpassed by only the French and English).

Why are Canadians of Japanese and Chinese origins, whose educational attainment levels are almost identical, so far apart in terms of average income? First, the Japanese have been here much longer than the Chinese—so that 36 percent of the Japanese are immigrants or first-generation Canadians whereas this is the case with 71 percent of the Chinese. Another third of Japanese Canadians have been on this soil for *three generations or more*—and 70 percent of them report mixed origins, mainly as a result of intermarriage. On this basis, one can argue that there are many factors that mitigate the impacts of those "ethnic penalties."

Explaining income disparities is not easy, as a variety of factors come into play, but both racism and discrimination play a part. Many immigrants enter the Canadian

Table 14–3 Education, Employment, and Income among Selected Ethnic Categories, 2011

	Less Than High School %**	University Degree or Higher %**	Employed in 2010 %***	Employed Full Time in 2010 %***	Average Income in 2010 $****	Median Income in 2010 $****
English	13	32	61	35	**44 414**	**32 609**
French	12	24	**62**	**35**	40 223	30 777
Québécois	19	18	60	33	33 096	26 100
Chinese	11	**44**	57	31	34 598	21 916
Japanese	3	44	60	31	42 263	28 645
Jamaican	10	19	61	35	34 448	26 528
First Nations*	**26**	**13**	**54**	**29**	30 254	**21 268**

*Note that, for present purposes, the term *First Nations* refers to registered and non-status Indians combined.
**Educational attainment figures are based on populations aged 25 to 64.
***Employment figures for 2010 are based on populations aged 15 and over.
****Average and median incomes refer to total income—e.g., from employment, investment, and government transfers—in 2010.
SOURCE: Compilation and Calculations by L.M. Gerber based on Statistics Canada, NHS 2011. Catalogue no. 99-010- X2011029.

labour market at a lower entrance status than they occupied in their countries of origin (Li, 2003; Reitz, 1980; Ujimoto, 1979) and, like the Chinese, are not rewarded for high educational attainment. Aboriginal people face numerous but different barriers—in achieving higher education, in securing employment, and in earning a decent income. To the extent that there is socio-economic stratification in Canada based on race and ethnicity (Li, 1988, 2003; McAll, 1990), Aboriginal people are most severely disadvantaged (Frideres & Gadacz, 2012; Gerber, 1990, 2014).

Keep in mind the fact that average income provides only partial information because the data do not reveal the proportions in each category with very high incomes. Just as there are many rich or well-to-do French and English people, there are many Chinese, Japanese, Black, and Aboriginal people who earn very high incomes—and who are very well educated, firmly established in professions or business, and living in expensive neighbourhoods.

Special Status Societies

On historical grounds, one might argue that people of British ancestry have special status within Canada. We have a British parliamentary system; the majority of Canadians speak English; and the dominant culture is Anglo-Saxon. In the past, admission to Canada itself, to the economic elite, and to the most exclusive clubs was controlled, for the most part, by Canadians of British descent. It could also be argued that the policy of multiculturalism gives special status to all of the ethnic and cultural minorities that contribute to the Canadian mosaic. Nonetheless, two categories stand out because they have unique relationships with the federal government and with other Canadians: Aboriginal peoples and Québécois.

ABORIGINAL PEOPLES "Aboriginal peoples" refers collectively to 55 or more sovereign peoples who occupied the North American continent before the arrival of European explorers and settlers. Aboriginal peoples include registered or status Indians (First Nations comprising individuals of Cree, Ojibwa, Micmac, Blackfoot, Six Nations, Haida, and other origins), non-status Indians, Métis, and Inuit. Until 2011, the census classified status and non-status Indians as North American Indian. Now the census and the NHS classify status and non-status Indians as First Nations even though the latter are not subject to the *Indian Act* nor are they members of any of the roughly 630 First Nations represented by their chiefs in the Assembly of First Nations. The Métis are a sociocultural category of biracial descent—usually French and Indian. The Inuit include the western Arctic Inuvialuit as well as three eastern Arctic Inuit cultures.

Registered or status Indians, now called First Nations, are registered with Indian and Northern Affairs Canada—now Aboriginal Affairs and Northern Development Canada (or Indigenous and Northern Affairs Canada)—which has responsibility for them under the *Indian Act*. In addition, there are many people who are biologically and culturally Indian[5] but are not legally recognized as such because their ancestors, for whatever reasons, did not enter into agreements with the Crown; they are referred to as non-status or non-registered Indians (Frideres & Gadacz, 2008:25–31). Many individuals lost or gave up Indian status by acquiring a university education (in the early 1900s), in order to vote (prior to 1960, when status Indians were granted the franchise), or by marriage (when a woman with Indian status married a man without such status). In 1985, Bill C-31 allowed people who had lost Indian status to reclaim it. More than 100 000 people, most of them women who had lost Treaty status by marrying out, took advantage of this opportunity.

The 2011 NHS identifies 1.8 million individuals who claim Aboriginal ancestry. Among them are 73 000 Inuit, 452 000 Métis, and 1.4 million North American Indians (now called First Nations) Since not all people acknowledge or are aware of their Aboriginal ancestors, these figures probably underestimate the number of people with Aboriginal ancestry. It is likely that more than 2.5 million Canadians have Aboriginal roots.

Registered Indians who live on reserves or settlements are the special responsibility of Aboriginal Affairs and Northern Development Canada (AANDC). Over the years, their relationship with Ottawa has been characterized as paternalistic and bureaucratic. For example, until the 1980s, children could be removed from their reserves and taken to boarding schools, where they were punished for "talking Indian" among themselves, forced to speak English, and taught that their own languages and cultures were of no value. Removed from their homes and communities for 10 months of the year and deprived of parent/child relationships, these children were not prepared to live effectively in either the Aboriginal or the non-Aboriginal worlds. Christianity was imposed on communities and on children in boarding schools, and education beyond the level required for farming or raising livestock was discouraged. The effect of these measures was an erosion of the social, economic, and cultural fabric of Aboriginal community life. In January 1998, the federal government took the long overdue step of

---

[5]A note about terminology: Many of you are aware that use of the term *Indian* may be offensive to Aboriginal people. *Native*, *Aboriginal*, and *Indigenous* are useful collective terms—except when you need to differentiate among Indian, Métis, and Inuit. The term *First Nations* applies only to those who are status or registered Indians under the *Indian Act*. Likewise, the Assembly of First Nations includes only the chiefs of status-Indian communities. Non-registered Indians are neither represented by the assembly nor the responsibility of Indian and Northern Affairs Canada (now AANDC).

Nathan Denette/The Canadian Press

CANADA'S ABORIGINAL PEOPLES HAVE SOUGHT SELF-DETERMINATION FOR A VERY LONG TIME—OFTEN IN WAYS THAT LEAD TO SUSTAINED MEDIA COVERAGE Here, protestors between Six Nations and Caledonia (southwest of Hamilton, Ontario) are trying to prevent the building of a subdivision on lands that Six Nations says it has never relinquished. They first occupied the land, with partially completed houses, in 2006. Six years later, in 2012, the residents of the town of Caledonia were urging the government to negotiate a resolution to the conflict with the Six Nations community.

formally apologizing for the residential school experiences of Aboriginal youth, which often included physical and sexual abuse. In 2005, Ottawa finally announced $2 billion in compensation for individuals who had attended residential schools. An initial sum of $10 000 plus an additional $3000 per year will be paid to approximately 86 000 eligible people (CBC, 2005).

Recently, the Truth and Reconciliation Commission (2015) released its eight-volume report on the terrible abuses—psychological, physical, and sexual—suffered by Aboriginal children within Canada's residential school system. After years of research, consultation, and listening to the survivors of the residential schools, the commission was in a position to issue a long list of recommendations for continuing the healing process that began when survivors found the courage to come forth and tell their stories.

Because non-status Indians, the Métis, and the Inuit did not have reserves, they have escaped some of the negative effects of reserve life. Living in Canada's Arctic, the Inuit have not felt the same population pressures as Aboriginal peoples in the rest of the country. Because they have been pushed out of their hunting territories relatively recently, they have experienced the disruption of their traditional patterns of life very abruptly. Oil, gas, and uranium companies have degraded the fragile northern environment and reduced the game supply.

Inuit families have moved into permanent settlements, both for employment and to meet the legal requirement of school attendance for their children. Consequently, extended families no longer establish year-round camps in traditional hunting grounds or teach their children the old survival skills that used to foster a sense of self-worth.

It is important to realize that there is a great deal of diversity among Aboriginal communities. Gerber (1979) developed a typology of reserve communities—labelled Inert, Pluralistic, Integrative, and Communal—that exhibit very different patterns of adaptation to mainstream society, just as there are among individuals (Wotherspoon & Satzewich, 1993). Nonetheless, there is a tendency to lump all of these communities and individuals together as problematic. Where government policy once was based on the assumption that the "Indian problem" would solve itself through urban migration and assimilation, it is now recognized that communities on reserves and elsewhere are not only surviving but growing (Gerber, 1984). In addition, such high-profile Aboriginal leaders as Ovid Mercredi, Matthew Coon Come, Phil Fontaine, Roberta Jamieson, Paul Okalik, and Shawn Atleo have been effective in articulating their demands and thereby have gained public support for greater self-determination. National organizations such as the Assembly of First Nations, Inuit Tapiriit Kanatami, Native Council of Canada (now the Congress of Aboriginal Peoples), and Métis National Council were instrumental in negotiating recognition of the inherent right to self-government in the Charlottetown Accord—which was rejected in the 1992 federal referendum.

One dramatic result of the Aboriginal quest for self-government was the creation in 1999 of a new territory, Nunavut, which was carved out of the Northwest Territories. The new territorial government is controlled by the Inuit majority, with support from an established system of co-operatives and the Inuit Broadcasting Corporation. Political and administrative positions are bringing new employment prospects, potentially stimulating greater educational achievement and enhancing pride. Returning control of Inuit communities to Inuit hands will not alleviate problems overnight; the hope on the part of Inuit leaders, however, is that it will be one meaningful step toward dealing with a wide range of serious social problems. The Sociology and the Media box introduces you to the Aboriginal Peoples Television Network, which is available to all Canadians with cable or satellite service. It has tremendous potential to empower the Aboriginal community by providing it with the ability to communicate effectively with its members, wherever they live in Canada.

Sociology and the Media

The Aboriginal Peoples Television Network

Aboriginal peoples of Canada have something that has no parallel anywhere else in the world. They have their own television channel—the Aboriginal Peoples Television Network (APTN)—that reaches every Canadian home with satellite or cable access. Importantly, the APTN does not have to rely on government grants or advertising for its survival; because of "mandatory carriage," it receives $0.25 per month—or somewhat more by now—from the satellite and cable fees of all Canadian subscribers. Thus, you and I enhance the network's independence (or autonomy) by subsidizing the APTN.

Karen Richards (2006), a graduate student at the University of Guelph, carried out an extensive study of the APTN—including its history, mandate, policies, and programming—framed by a postmodern orientation and analysis of empowerment. She also travelled to the APTN headquarters in Winnipeg to conduct semi-structured interviews with 24 staff members. These interviews were recorded on tape and then transcribed to print in a laborious, time-consuming process. The next stage involved content analysis in which Richards essentially counted the number of times that certain concepts came up in the interviews. Then she recorded APTN broadcasts to get a sample of its programs through the week in all time slots—and did further content analysis based on the programming.

The staff at the APTN, Richards found, is very enthusiastic and feels empowered. Here are Aboriginal people making decisions about the content of newscasts and *Contact* (which deals with current issues)—or about coverage of the Ipperwash inquiry, elections, and the land dispute by Six Nations at Caledonia. Documentaries, children's shows, movies, and plays are all vetted and aired on a schedule determined by the staff. While most programs are in English, others in French and Aboriginal languages are also included (about 5 percent of census participants who identify as Aboriginal speak Aboriginal languages at home). The staff at the APTN is largely Aboriginal, the few exceptions being experts with broadcasting experience brought in to mentor and train Aboriginal people to replace them.

One can make the argument that the APTN empowers both its staff and the Aboriginal community as a whole. There are hundreds of Aboriginal communities in Canada and more than 2 million people in total who acknowledge some Aboriginal heritage. Among the latter, only 20 percent

Courtesy of APTN

live on reserves. Others live in non-reserve, Métis, or Inuit settlements or in Canada's towns, cities, and metropolitan areas with the rest of us. In other words, the Aboriginal population is anything but homogeneous. Tremendous cultural diversity—stemming from 50 or more distinct linguistic and cultural heritages—and rural, small-town, and urban residence mean that Aboriginal people differ among themselves just as other Canadians do. The power of broadcasting allows the APTN, potentially, to communicate with all of the Aboriginal individuals and communities in Canada. It also allows the APTN to change the way in which Aboriginal peoples are portrayed by the broadcasting medium as a whole. The APTN website (www.aptn.ca) encourages Aboriginal peoples and Canadians in general to respond to and comment on programs or issues of concern, so that communication goes both ways.

Think, for a moment, of media theorist Marshall McLuhan, and try to imagine the impact of instant electronic communication—in this case, APTN broadcasting—on the diverse and scattered Aboriginal population in Canada. McLuhan taught us that "the instantaneous world of electronic information media involves all of us, all at once" in a "global village" or "instantaneous happening." This instant awareness explodes local boundaries, which cease to exist, making each of us part of the global village. At the same time, the world implodes or collapses in on us as instantaneous communication comes at us from everywhere. Explosion and implosion occur simultaneously. Can you see how the APTN might explode the local boundaries that separate Cree, Ojibwa, Haida, Inuit, and Métis peoples? Being part of every other Aboriginal person's business draws people into a mini–global village as the larger pan-Aboriginal world collapses in on them. The transformation that McLuhan describes so graphically does not require every Aboriginal person to watch APTN; after all, the internet and the information age shape your grandmother's world—even if she herself knows nothing about computers.

On June 5, 2006, the APTN *National News* reported that former prime minister Paul Martin had tabled a private

(continued)

member's bill in the House of Commons in an attempt to get some of the elements of the Kelowna Accord onto the new Conservative government's agenda. Martin had negotiated the accord with Aboriginal leaders before his government was defeated. The newscast that evening also covered developments in the Six Nations land dispute near Caledonia. Neither of those stories made it onto the CBC *National* that night. Without the APTN, Aboriginal peoples would have been deprived of news that is vital to their interests. With the APTN, Aboriginal peoples are empowered by access to information. As Sir Francis Bacon once said, "Knowledge is power."

What Do You Think?

1. Have you ever watched anything on the Aboriginal Peoples Television Network?

2. How do you think the existence of the APTN affects the lives of Aboriginal individuals?

3. How do you feel about the fact that your cable fees support APTN?

SOURCE: Inspired by Richards (2006).

Various tables and graphs in this text that compare Aboriginal people to others—in terms of education, employment, and income—cast them in an unfavourable light. It is very important to understand that average and, to a greater extent, median incomes can be very deceiving. In fact, there are many Aboriginal people, First Nation/Indian, Métis, and Inuit who are very well educated, established in business or professions, and earning more than $80 000 a year. In fact, there is polarization *within* each category, because those at the top are closing the gaps between themselves and non-Aboriginals while conditions at the lower end of the hierarchy are stagnating or getting worse. For example, between 2001 and 2006, levels of high school completion or certification did not improve among First Nation and Inuit people. On the other hand, in 2006, there were over 16 000 people of Aboriginal ancestry with master's degrees and doctorates (Gerber, 2014).

THE QUÉBÉCOIS: FROM NEW FRANCE TO THE QUIET REVOLUTION AND BEYOND The French presence in what is now Canada goes back to 1608, when the first permanent settlement in New France was established at Quebec City by Samuel de Champlain with 28 settlers—only eight of whom survived the first winter. France claimed a vast territory that extended west of the thirteen colonies and down to Louisiana, encompassing most of southern Ontario and the Great Lakes region. But New France grew slowly because of a lack of interest on the part of France in supporting the tiny settlement or in sending more settlers to the area. The population grew from eight in 1609 to just over 3000 in 1663—spread among Quebec City, Trois-Rivières, and Montreal—mainly because of an "extraordinary rate of child bearing" (Beaujot & McQuillan, 1982:4). Two centuries later, at the time of Confederation, the French formed 31 percent of Canada's population of 3.5 million people. As a result of the size of the French population and its concentration in Quebec, the *British North America Act*, 1867, recognized the province's civil law tradition, Catholic schools, and language. Confederation was based on bilingualism and assumed that anglophone and francophone communities would

coexist. English and French were to be the legislative and judicial languages in federal and Quebec institutions. Bilingualism was later strengthened and expanded by the *Official Languages Act*, 1969, which declared the equality of the two languages in Parliament and in the Canadian public service.

At Confederation in 1867, Quebec encompassed a traditional society based on the seigneurial system of land tenure, in which *habitants* (tenant farmers) worked the lands of the seigneurs (landowners). In the political vacuum left by an ineffective provincial government, the Catholic Church took on itself the task of administering many aspects of Quebec society, including education, health care, and social welfare. The Catholic Church, which long dominated Quebec's major institutions, resisted change:

> Uninterested in questioning the established authorities and the excesses of industrialization, and wary of new ideas, the Quebec church was more concerned with maintaining its privileged position than with helping Quebecers enter the twentieth century. It extolled the virtues of rural life, cautioned against the evils of the city and the dangers of education, and preached the need to accept one's lot in life. (Latouche, 1988:1801)

Up to the 1980s, a British economic and industrial elite based in Montreal dominated the provincial economy. A clear linguistic class structure had developed with the unilingual English at the top, the unilingual French at the bottom, and bilingual people in the middle in supervisory positions. The unilingual French had few opportunities to better their social or financial standing, and even French-origin bilingual people could rise only so far. Individuals who moved to the cities to seek employment found that a linguistic ceiling restricted upward mobility.

Quebec's Quiet Revolution of the 1960s greatly diminished the political power and social influence of the Catholic Church and began to challenge the economic domination of the British elites. Newly elected premier Jean Lesage chose to expand the role of the state in the economic, social, and cultural life of the province. The

Lesage government established a department of education, encouraging the study of engineering, math, sciences, and business, especially by Catholics; nationalized Hydro-Québec to attract industry with the promise of cheap electricity; and took over the administration of Quebec's pension funds. These and other changes served to integrate Quebec into the North American economic structure (Coleman, 1984). Quebec was characterized by a rapidly growing working class, a declining birth rate—eliminating "the revenge of the cradle" as a tool for maintaining or improving the linguistic balance in Canada—and a decline in the influence of the Church.

French-Canadian society was becoming more like the rest of North America: urban, secular, and industrialized. As a result, language became the primary defining characteristic of Québécois society, and francophone Quebecers became even more aware of the relative numbers of French-speaking and English-speaking people. They also realized that the continued existence of the small francophone minorities outside Quebec was threatened by assimilation. Reaching the conclusion that French language and culture could be protected only in the province of Quebec, many rejected their Canadian or French-Canadian identities and began to think of themselves as Québécois only. The desire to protect their distinct language and culture led them to seek institutional dominance in Quebec—with profound implications for federal/provincial relations. Quebec is in a position to challenge the status quo with "the society-busting demands of ethnic nationalism" (Fleras, 2010:112).

The Growing Demand for Sovereignty The logical extension of a demand for institutional control was the demand for sovereignty. The late 1960s and 1970s saw an increase in Québécois nationalism and in support for the separatist movement. The sentiments that gave rise to the radical terrorist group Front de libération du Québec (FLQ) became more widespread and eventually paved the way for the 1976 election of the separatist Parti Québécois, led by René Lévesque. One of the first acts of this new government was to introduce Bill 101, making French the only official language of Quebec, including in business and education. Francophones were no longer excluded from the economic elite. In addition, the children of immigrants from other countries or other provinces would be educated in French and assimilated into francophone culture (and eventually integrated into Québécois society).

In response to the election of a separatist government and the language laws, many anglophones and businesses, both large and small, left the province. From 1976 to 1981, Quebec's net loss through interprovincial migration was 156 000 people, double that of the previous five-year period.

In a 1980 referendum on Quebec's "sovereignty association" with Canada, 60 percent of Quebecers voted

"no." The debate leading up to the referendum was often divisive, especially in Montreal. There, as elsewhere in the province, the referendum revealed a general pattern of increased support for sovereignty the farther east one moved from Ontario (Gerber, 1992).

In 1982, under the Liberal government of Pierre Trudeau, Canada patriated its constitution and incorporated the *Canadian Charter of Rights and Freedoms*. The provincial government of Quebec did not agree to the conditions of patriation and did not sign the constitution at that point. Brian Mulroney and the Progressive Conservative party won the 1984 federal election with massive support in Quebec, in part because they promised amendments that would overcome Quebec's objections to the constitution.

For complex political reasons, the Meech Lake Accord of 1987, which included recognition of Quebec as a "distinct society," was not ratified by all provincial legislatures (specifically, Manitoba and Newfoundland) before its 1990 deadline. Among the reasons for public disenchantment with Meech was Quebec's 1988 sign law, which banned English from outdoor signs altogether. Anglophone Canadians perceived the sign law as a slap in the face. In turn, Quebecers saw the failure of the Meech Lake Accord as a symbol of rejection by English Canada. Such symbols, as Breton (1992) points out, can have a powerful political impact. Among other things, the failure of Meech spawned the separatist Bloc Québécois, a political party working at the federal level to promote the cause of separation.

The failure of Meech was followed by the rejection of the Charlottetown Accord by Canadians (including 55 percent of Quebecers) in the referendum of October 26, 1992. Support for the separatist Bloc Québécois and Parti Québécois grew, at least in part because of the repeated failures in constitutional accommodation as well as the economic pain associated with a prolonged recession. The success of the two separatist parties clearly reveals that the politics surrounding the quest for special status and related powers continued to have potentially explosive consequences for Canada. On October 30, 1995, Canadians were stunned by the razor-thin victory for the "no" side in Quebec's most recent referendum on sovereignty: 50.6 percent of Quebecers voted "no" and 49.4 percent voted "yes." Quebecers came dangerously close to giving its leaders the go-ahead to negotiate separation, which would have had incalculable costs for the country as a whole. The 1995 referendum alarm wakened federalist forces in Ottawa and Quebec City, reactivated the unity agenda, and again raised the question of what could be done to keep Canada whole (see the Sociology in Focus box dealing with national unity). The Quebec election of 2003 produced a Liberal government under Jean Charest. Unlike his Parti Québécois predecessors, Charest reduced

Sociology in Focus

Distinct Societies and National Unity

Pluralism and diversity are so central to Canadian identity that they are enshrined in our constitution. The French language (official bilingualism and minority language rights), civil law (in Quebec), Catholic or denominational schooling, existing Aboriginal and Treaty rights, and the right to preserve and enhance our multicultural heritage are guaranteed by our constitution in the *Canadian Charter of Rights and Freedoms* (Canada, 1982). Freedom from the pressures of assimilation could be taken for granted in this country, yet some of us, anxious to ensure the viability of our own cultures, demand constitutional recognition as distinct societies.

The unwillingness or inability of Canadians throughout the country to respond positively to demands for such recognition by Quebec threatens the stability of our federation—as we learned so painfully on referendum day in October 1995, when the Québécois came within a hair's breadth of voting for sovereignty and separation. Because status as a distinct society is significant for both Quebec and Canada, the debate surrounding it receives a great deal of media attention. The concept or symbol of a "distinct society" could have explosive consequences (Breton, 1992). Applying the concept to Quebec, people elsewhere in Canada say, "But *of course* Quebec is a distinct society. It has its own language, legal system, political parties, and a vibrant French culture." Quebec leaders want to know why, if we accept Quebec's distinctiveness, we cannot agree to include that recognition in our constitution. The answer lies, in part, with the controversy surrounding the label itself.

Let's look at this concept. At one level, it implies that Quebec is *different*—and few would argue with that. (Aboriginal societies are different, too.) The controversy emerges with the argument that different or distinct implies *special* status. The notion that Quebec is not only different but also perhaps *special* raises the issue of two classes of Canadians, one having special rights. It is this interpretation that raises the hackles of many Canadians and some provinces.

If we assume that the label "distinct society" is purely symbolic and merely implies the recognition of existing social and cultural differences, then putting it into the constitution would not have any significant effect. One way to restrict its potential impact on the constitution would be to define it carefully, so that the distinction implies no new powers, or no powers that substantially differentiate Quebec from the other provinces. However, to be acceptable to Quebec, "distinct society" must imply special powers, for it is through those powers that the Québécois hope to become "masters in their own house." To preserve and protect the small island of francophone culture, Quebec sovereigntists want unquestioned control over language (in business, education, social discourse, and government), immigration, employment, trade, natural resources, the economy, population policy and mobility, social services, and more. Since other provinces do not want all of these powers, mainly because of funding concerns, granting them to Quebec would give that province special status.

Another aspect of Quebec's relationship with the rest of the country is threatening to other provinces. Many Québécois see Confederation as joining together *two founding nations,* while other Canadians see it as joining *equal provinces*. Is Quebec now one of 10 equal partners, or one of only two? Clearly, these are serious and potentially catastrophic clashes of vision.

In another attempt to circumvent the "distinct society" problem, Canada's premiers proposed constitutional recognition of Quebec's "unique characteristics" in the Calgary declaration of September 1997. Whatever words are used to describe different, special, or distinct status to imply enhanced autonomy, the impact is not neutral. The process itself is controversial and divisive and, even if we were able to deliver distinct society status, its implementation would generate its own strains.

In 2006, Parliament passed a motion to recognize the Québécois as a "nation" within Canada. This *should* satisfy Quebec's demand for distinct society status—or does it? Recall that other definition of "nation," which refers to "a people" sharing a common heritage. Prime Minister Harper did *not* say that *Quebec,* the province, is a nation; he *did* say that the *Québécois people* are a nation. It remains to be seen, in the long run, if those who seek distinct society status for Quebec will be satisfied with Harper's recognition of the Québécois as a nation. With Quebec MP Thomas Mulcair as the NDP leader of the Official Opposition this seemed highly unlikely. The 2012 student protest against tuition increases, which turned into a broader social movement opposed to Quebec's Liberal government and capitalism, indicates that there continues to be a great deal of social unrest in the province.

This discussion is complicated by the less vocal but equally valid claim to status as distinct societies by Aboriginal communities. The heated debate that erupts periodically around this powerful concept is both inevitable and justifiable in the context of Canada's multi-dimensional, and not entirely equitable, pluralism.

What Do You Think?

1. How might francophones in Ontario or Saskatchewan react to the granting of "distinct society" status to Quebec or "nation" status to the Québécois?

2. Aboriginal peoples claim distinctiveness and the right to self-determination as well. What are the implications of granting "distinct society" status to Quebec for the Aboriginal peoples in that province?

3. Should Canada grant special status to both Quebec and Aboriginal peoples?

interprovincial tensions—at least initially—because of his willingness to work with the other premiers in a Canadian framework.

Immigration to Canada: A Hundred-Year Perspective

Canada has been—and will remain—a land of immigrants. The 10-year period from 1905 to 1914 saw the arrival of 2.5 million people, making it the peak decade for Canadian immigration. (See Figure 14–3, which details our immigration history from 1885 to 2009.) At the height of immigration to Canada, in 1913, one in every 17 people was a newcomer—not just an immigrant, but someone who had arrived within the past year. In contrast, we now admit about 225 000 immigrants per year into a population of about 33 million: One in every 300 people today is a newly arrived immigrant in the current year. Knowing the numbers of immigrants absorbed by the tiny Canadian population of the early 1900s should give us encouragement regarding Canada's ability to absorb the numbers arriving today. Immigration increased between 1990 and

1994 and has continued at a rate of more than 1 million immigrants in each of the five-year periods since then.

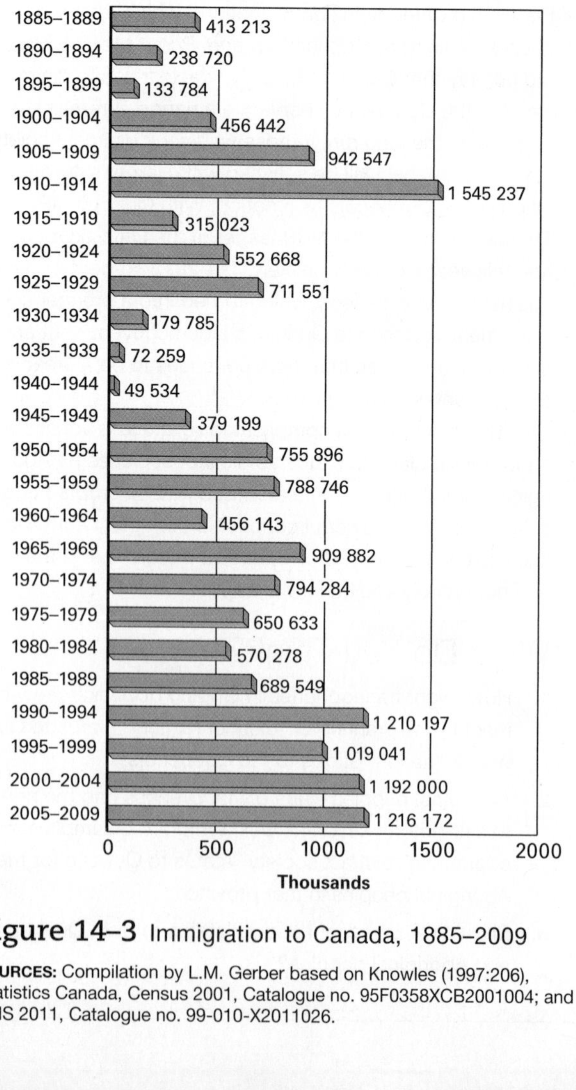

Race and ethnicity retain their significance in part because of the continuous flow of immigrants into our country. The first wave of immigration after Confederation was driven by the desire to populate western Canada and to provide workers for the growing economy. This trend was encouraged by the controversial policies of Clifford Sifton, minister of the interior at about the turn of the twentieth century (Hiller, 2006).

During the Sifton years, Canada was still trying to promote immigration from Britain—in part out of political necessity. English Canadians assumed that the government would do everything it could to retain the British character of the country (Knowles, 1997). By setting up an immigration office in London, England, Sifton was able to increase the flow from Britain to the point where, by 1905, about a third of our immigrants came from there. But because Sifton was primarily interested in attracting good farmers to populate western Canada, he also started a trickle of Ukrainian immigration that would peak in 1913, when 22 363 individuals arrived from that country. These Ukrainians, along with a trickle of Doukhobors, Finns, Germans, and Scandinavians, were seen by many politicians and ordinary Canadians as ignorant, unassimilable aliens who would do irreparable damage to Canada (Knowles, 1997).

In the early 1900s, policy severely restricted immigration to Canada to White people of Anglo-Saxon origin. Southern and eastern Europeans, as well as Chinese, Japanese, and African-American peoples, were discouraged from entering; for example, the *Chinese Immigration Act, 1923*, barred all but a select few Chinese from entering Canada. Despite these efforts, immigration soared—in part because politicians and businessmen believed that economic prosperity depended on continued population growth. Immigration fell during World War I (1914–1918), the Great Depression (1929–1939), and World War II (1939–1945). During a short boom in the 1920s, immigrants from Britain and Europe were admitted along with some Jews and Russian Mennonites. By 1931, however, Canada would close her doors to refugees—especially Jewish refugees, in part because of widespread anti-Semitism.

After World War II there was mounting pressure to open the doors once again and accept large numbers of refugees. Once again, "old" Commonwealth countries and the United States were the initial source of regular immigrants (i.e., not refugees) required to meet labour needs, settle unpopulated areas, and expand the internal market for goods. However, by the 1950s, Germany, Italy, and the Netherlands had become important sources of immigrants, and immigration laws had been liberalized to allow more Asians, as well as Palestinian and

Period	Thousands
1885–1889	413 213
1890–1894	238 720
1895–1899	133 784
1900–1904	456 442
1905–1909	942 547
1910–1914	1 545 237
1915–1919	315 023
1920–1924	552 668
1925–1929	711 551
1930–1934	179 785
1935–1939	72 259
1940–1944	49 534
1945–1949	379 199
1950–1954	755 896
1955–1959	788 746
1960–1964	456 143
1965–1969	909 882
1970–1974	794 284
1975–1979	650 633
1980–1984	570 278
1985–1989	689 549
1990–1994	1 210 197
1995–1999	1 019 041
2000–2004	1 192 000
2005–2009	1 216 172

Figure 14–3 Immigration to Canada, 1885–2009

SOURCES: Compilation by L.M. Gerber based on Knowles (1997:206), Statistics Canada, Census 2001, Catalogue no. 95F0358XCB2001004; and NHS 2011, Catalogue no. 99-010-X2011026.

Hungarian refugees. Further liberalization would occur under the Conservative government of John Diefenbaker, who foresaw a population of 40 million in the near future and argued that "Canada must populate or perish" (Knowles, 1997:146).

It was not until 1962 that Ellen Fairclough, Canada's first woman federal Cabinet minister, put an end to our White Canada immigration policy. Education, occupation, and language skills, replaced race or national origin as the criteria of admission. After the 1965 election, the Liberals formalized the selection criteria through what we call the points system, which allocates points to education, occupation, facility in English or French, age, and the demand for the applicant's skills in the Canadian labour market. The points system reduces reliance on the judgment of the individual immigration officer. More recently, Canada has experienced waves of immigration from the Caribbean and Asia in the 1970s, from Central and South America in the 1980s, and from China and India in the 1990s. Hiller points out that "these repeated waves of immigration reinvigorated ethnic groups already resident in Canada, and reminded residents of their own ethnicity" (1991:173).

The *Immigration Act*, 1976, recognized three classes of people as eligible for landed immigrant status: *family class* (immediate family and dependent children, parents, and grandparents of Canadian citizens or landed immigrants), *humanitarian class* (refugees or persecuted and displaced persons), and *independent class* (those who apply as individuals and are admitted on the basis of the points system). These changes altered the countries of origin of the applicants, stimulated a greatly expanded flow of refugees, and increased applications by family members, who now outnumber independent applicants. In recent years, Canada has made a concerted effort to attract people who are experienced in business or who have significant amounts of money to invest.

Table 14–4 indicates place of birth for immigrants arriving in Canada from 2006 to 2011. China and India, which ranked first and second for at least two decades as countries of origin, have fallen to second and third place behind the Philippines which accounts for 13 percent of our immigrants between 2006 and 2011. The United States is the place of birth of 4 percent of our immigrants—followed by Pakistan, the United Kingdom, Iran, South Korea, Colombia, and Mexico, each as the birthplace of 2 to 3 percent of our immigrants. There are more than 190 countries around the world – the exact number changes from year to year—yet the ten top countries of birth in Table 14-4 account for 53 percent of our immigrants over the five-year period. It is not by accident that one-third of our immigrants come from three countries and more than one-half from ten. Patterns of migration around the world are the product of social forces, not the result of random

Table 14–4 The Top 25 Places of Birth for Immigrants Arriving in Canada from 2006 to 2011

Total Immigrants	Number 1 162 915	% 100
Philippines	152 270	13.1
China	122 090	10.5
India	121 420	10.4
United States	45 015	3.9
Pakistan	35 040	3.0
United Kingdom	32 965	2.8
Iran	30 290	2.6
South Korea	27 670	2.4
Columbia	27 555	2.4
Mexico	22 310	1.9
Sri Lanka	21 430	1.8
Algeria	21 240	1.8
France	20 380	1.8
Morocco	20 295	1.7
Haiti	19 305	1.7
Russian Federation	17 100	1.5
Iraq	16 915	1.5
Bangladesh	14 110	1.2
Romania	13 365	1.1
Nigeria	13 035	1.1
Lebanon	12 420	1.1
Ukraine	12 385	1.1
Vietnam	11 280	1.0
Egypt	11 105	1.0
Germany	10 455	0.9
Other countries	311 470	26.8

SOURCE: Compilation and calculations by L.M. Gerber based on Statistics Canada, NHS 2011, Catalogue no. 99-010-X2011026.

or idiosyncratic decisions made by individuals. Once again we see the power of societies or some larger global system to guide the behaviour of individuals.

Most of the immigrants who came to Canada in recent decades moved to Ontario and British Columbia and, secondly, to Alberta and Manitoba. (See Canada Map 14–1.) In comparison, the Atlantic provinces, Saskatchewan, Nunavut, and the Northwest Territories have not been as able to attract immigrants. As one would expect, the metropolitan areas of Toronto and Vancouver have the largest immigrant components, with visible minorities making up 47 and 45 percent of their respective populations. In Quebec, Montreal has attracted a significant immigrant component, whereas Quebec City has not. Recent immigration has clearly touched some parts of Canada more than others.

Race and Ethnicity: Looking Ahead

Immigration has contributed to the development of a country which—though it started out Aboriginal, British,

Seeing Ourselves

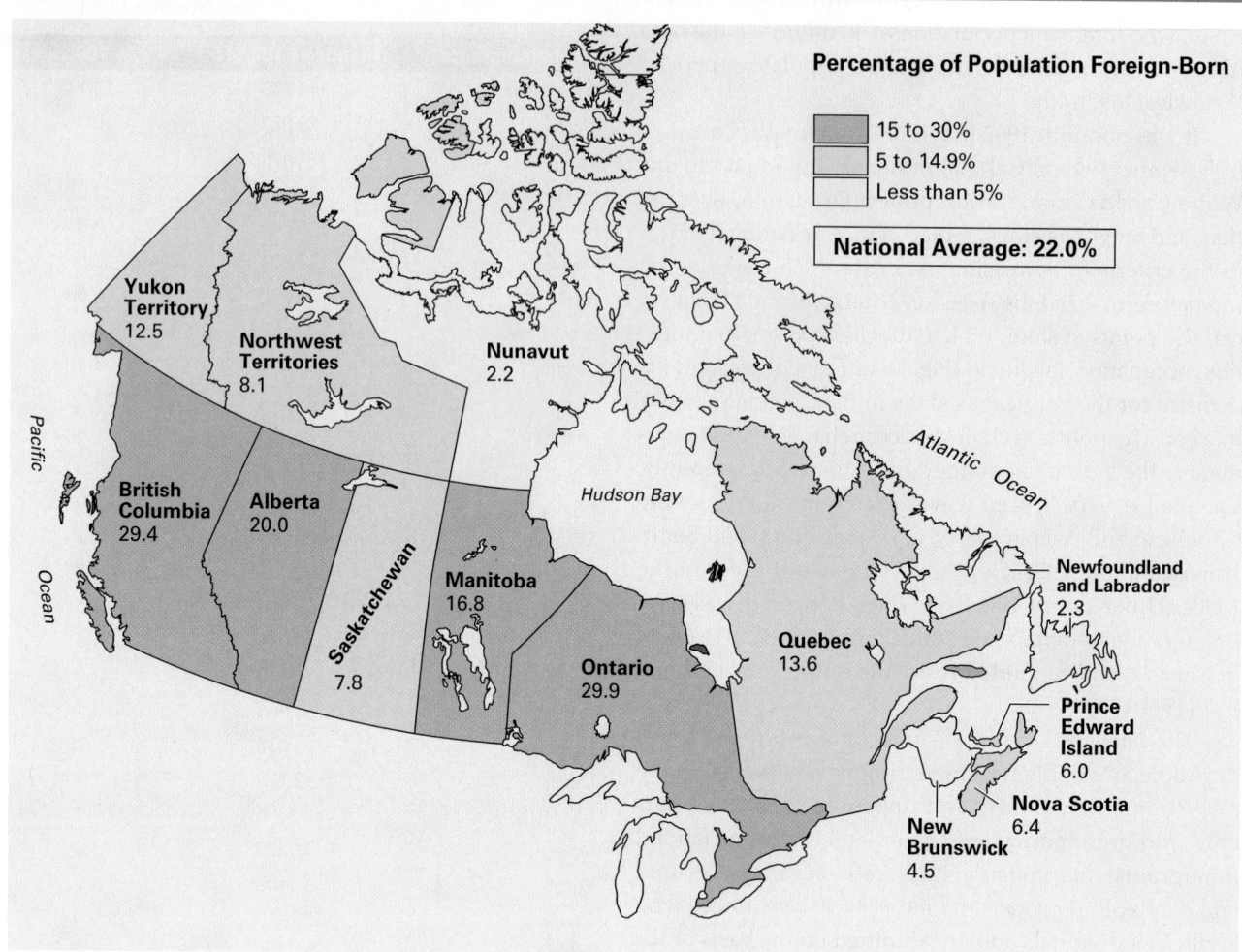

Percentage of Population Foreign-Born

- 15 to 30%
- 5 to 14.9%
- Less than 5%

National Average: 22.0%

Yukon Territory 12.5

Northwest Territories 8.1

Nunavut 2.2

British Columbia 29.4

Alberta 20.0

Saskatchewan 7.8

Manitoba 16.8

Ontario 29.9

Quebec 13.6

Newfoundland and Labrador 2.3

Prince Edward Island 6.0

Nova Scotia 6.4

New Brunswick 4.5

Hudson Bay

Pacific Ocean

Atlantic Ocean

Canada Map 14–1 Percentage of Foreign-Born Population for Canada, the Provinces, and Territories, 2011

SOURCE: Compilation and Calculations by L.M. Gerber based on Statistics Canada, NHS 2011. Catalogue no. 99-010- X2011029.

and French at Confederation in 1867—is now quite rightly called multicultural. The characteristics of the newcomers have stimulated the continued, and often uneasy, awareness of race and ethnicity among Canadians. Their geographic distribution has contributed to regional diversity, as people with different backgrounds have found themselves drawn to various parts of the country and to different cities, thereby giving substance to the vision of Canada that former prime minister Joe Clark called a "community of communities."

Canada is an experiment in multi-layered pluralism—multi-layered because the British, French, and Aboriginal

peoples and other ethnic and racial minorities have different kinds of relationships with one another and with society as a whole. Each new wave of immigration—including that of the Syrians who are arriving today in large numbers—adds to the complexity of the mosaic. Newly articulated demands and expectations on the part of the Québécois and the various Aboriginal peoples will contribute, along with immigrant aspirations, to the definition and redefinition of our unique country. Our survival depends on our success in forging a Canadian identity out of our diversity.

Seeing Sociology in Everyday Life

CHAPTER 14   Race and Ethnicity

Do race and ethnicity still affect people's social standing?

Is our society becoming more tolerant and accepting of social diversity based on race and ethnicity? How do we react to racially mixed couples? And to what extent does our society provide equal opportunities for education, employment, income, and leisure pursuits to Canadians of all backgrounds—including Aboriginal?

Aurora Photos

VISIBLE MINORITIES ARE OVERREPRESENTED IN DOWNTOWN TORONTO AND VANCOUVER AS WELL AS IN SOME SUBURBAN AREAS Both cities have Chinatowns and other neighbourhoods in which ethnic and racial groups predominate. Even in a large city—where half of the population consists of visible minorities—diversity will not be apparent at a symphony concert or the opera. What about restaurants? Those of you who are skiers might stop to observe the level of diversity apparent on ski slopes across the country.

CANADA CAN BE SEEN AS A *VERTICAL* MOSAIC IN WHICH THE COLOURFUL TILES ARE ARRANGED IN A HIERARCHY OF SOCIAL STANDING Ethnic and racial categories are not on equal footing and, *on average,* recent immigrants and Aboriginal people face multiple barriers to success. You can certainly find evidence, in many urban neighbourhoods, of poverty disproportionately involving visible minorities. But you will also come across professors, physicians, engineers, celebrities, politicians, and successful business people who are members of visible minorities. These people have achieved the comfortable, upper-middle-class lifestyle to which many of us aspire.

Seeing Sociology in *Your* Everyday Life

1. Does your college or university take account of race and ethnicity in its admissions policies? Ask to speak with an admissions officer to see what you can learn about your school's policies and the reasons for them.

2. Give several of your friends or family members a quick quiz, asking them what proportion of the Canadian population is British, French, Polish, German, Chinese, East Indian or Aboriginal (refer to Table 14–1 for the correct figures). Most people overestimate the minority share of the population. Why do you think that is?

3. Talk to immigrants on your campus or in your local community about their homelands and their experiences since arriving in Canada. Were they surprised by their experiences in this country? If so, why?

Making the Grade

CHAPTER 14 Race and Ethnicity

The Social Meaning of Race and Ethnicity

14.1 Explain the social construction of race and ethnicity.

Race refers to socially constructed categories based on biological traits a society defines as important.

- The meaning and importance of race vary from place to place and over time.
- Societies use racial categories to rank people in a hierarchy, giving some people more money, power, and prestige than others.
- In the past, scientists created three broad categories—Caucasoids, Mongoloids, and Negroids—but there are no biologically pure races.

Ethnicity refers to socially constructed categories based on cultural traits a society defines as important.

- Ethnicity reflects common ancestors, language, and religion.
- The importance of ethnicity varies from place to place and over time.
- People choose to play up or play down their ethnicity.
- Societies may or may not set categories of people apart based on differences in ethnicity.

> **race** a socially constructed category of people who share biologically transmitted traits that members of a society consider important
> **ethnicity** a shared cultural heritage
> **minority** any category of people distinguished by physical or cultural difference that a society sets apart and subordinates

Prejudice and Stereotypes

14.2 Describe the extent and causes of prejudice.

Prejudice is a rigid and unfair generalization about a category of people.

- The social distance scale is one measure of prejudice.
- One type of prejudice is the stereotype, an exaggerated description applied to every person in some category.
- Racism, a very destructive type of prejudice, asserts that one race is innately superior or inferior to another.

There are four theories of prejudice:

- Scapegoat theory claims that prejudice results from frustration among people who are disadvantaged.
- Authoritarian personality theory (Adorno) claims that prejudice is a personality trait of certain individuals, especially those with little education and those raised by cold and demanding parents.
- Culture theory (Bogardus) claims that prejudice is rooted in culture; we learn to feel greater social distance from some categories of people.
- Conflict theory claims that prejudice is a tool used by powerful people to divide and control the population.

> **prejudice** a rigid and unfair generalization about an entire category of people
> **stereotype** a simplified description applied to every person in some category
> **racism** the belief that one racial category is innately superior or inferior to another
> **scapegoat** a person or category of people, typically with little power, whom people unfairly blame for their own troubles

Discrimination

14.3 Distinguish discrimination from prejudice.

Discrimination refers to actions by which a person treats various categories of people unequally.

- *Prejudice* refers to *attitudes*; *discrimination* involves *actions*.
- Institutional prejudice and discrimination are biases built into the operation of society's institutions, including schools, hospitals, the police, and the workplace.
- Prejudice and discrimination perpetuate themselves in a vicious circle, resulting in social disadvantage that fuels additional prejudice and discrimination.

> **discrimination** unequal treatment of various categories of people
> **institutional prejudice and discrimination** bias built into the operation of society's institutions

Majority and Minority: Patterns of Interaction

14.4 Identify examples of pluralism, assimilation, segregation, and genocide.

Pluralism means that racial and ethnic categories, although distinct, have roughly equal social standing.

- Canadian society is pluralistic in that all people, regardless of race or ethnicity, have equal standing under the law.
- Canadian society is not pluralistic in that all racial and ethnic categories do not have equal social standing.

Assimilation is a process by which minorities gradually adopt the patterns of the dominant culture.

- Assimilation involves changes in dress, language, religion, values, and friends.
- Assimilation is a strategy to escape prejudice and discrimination and to achieve upward social mobility.
- Some categories of people have assimilated more than others.

Segregation is the physical and social separation of categories of people.

- Although some segregation is voluntary (e.g., the Hutterites), majorities usually segregate minorities by excluding them from neighbourhoods, schools, and occupations.
- Extreme segregation means having little social contact with people beyond the local community. An important Canadian example is the First Nations reserve system.

Genocide is the systematic killing of one category of people by another.

- Historical examples of genocide include the extermination of Jews by the Nazis and the killing of Western-leaning people in Cambodia by Pol Pot.
- Recent examples of genocide include Hutus killing Tutsis in the African nation of Rwanda, Serbs killing Bosnians in the Balkans of Eastern Europe, and systematic killing in the Darfur region of Sudan.

---

pluralism a state in which racial and ethnic minorities are distinct but have social parity

institutional completeness the complexity of community organizations that meet the needs of members

assimilation the process by which minorities gradually adopt patterns of the dominant culture, thereby becoming more similar to the dominant group

segregation the physical and social separation of categories of people

genocide the systematic killing of one category of people by another

---

Race and Ethnicity in Canada

14.5 Assess the social standing of racial and ethnic categories in Canadian society.

Aboriginal people, the earliest human inhabitants of what is now Canada, have endured genocide, segregation, and forced assimilation.

The various **Aboriginal peoples** in Canada have unique relationships with federal and provincial governments. They are unique in a global perspective because they have their own Aboriginal Peoples Television Network (APTN). One of their goals is to establish their right to self-government.

Upper Canada, with its own history of slavery, was the first British colony to legislate the abolition of slavery (in 1793). Fugitive slaves from the American South came to Ontario through the Underground Railroad to establish the communities of Dawn and Buxton—and to experience further segregation and discrimination. Today, despite *Charter* protection, Blacks are still disadvantaged

Ethnic and racial minorities differ on social standing, measured in terms of education, employment, and income. Aboriginal people are disadvantaged on all three measures.

At Confederation, **the French** made up more than a third of the Canadian population; since then, they have been trying to ensure their continuing existence and to maximize their powers relative to the federal government. There is also a serious social movement aimed at sovereignty through separation from Canada.

Canada is a country that relies heavily on **immigration** for its growth. Recent immigration flows have contributed to the ethnic and racial composition we see today—in Canada, its regions, and its cities. **In recent years,** Canada has admitted around 225 000 immigrants yearly, primarily from Asia. In the period 1910 to 1914, Canada absorbed 1.5 million immigrants, something that has not been matched in any five-year period since then.

Chapter 15
Aging and the Elderly

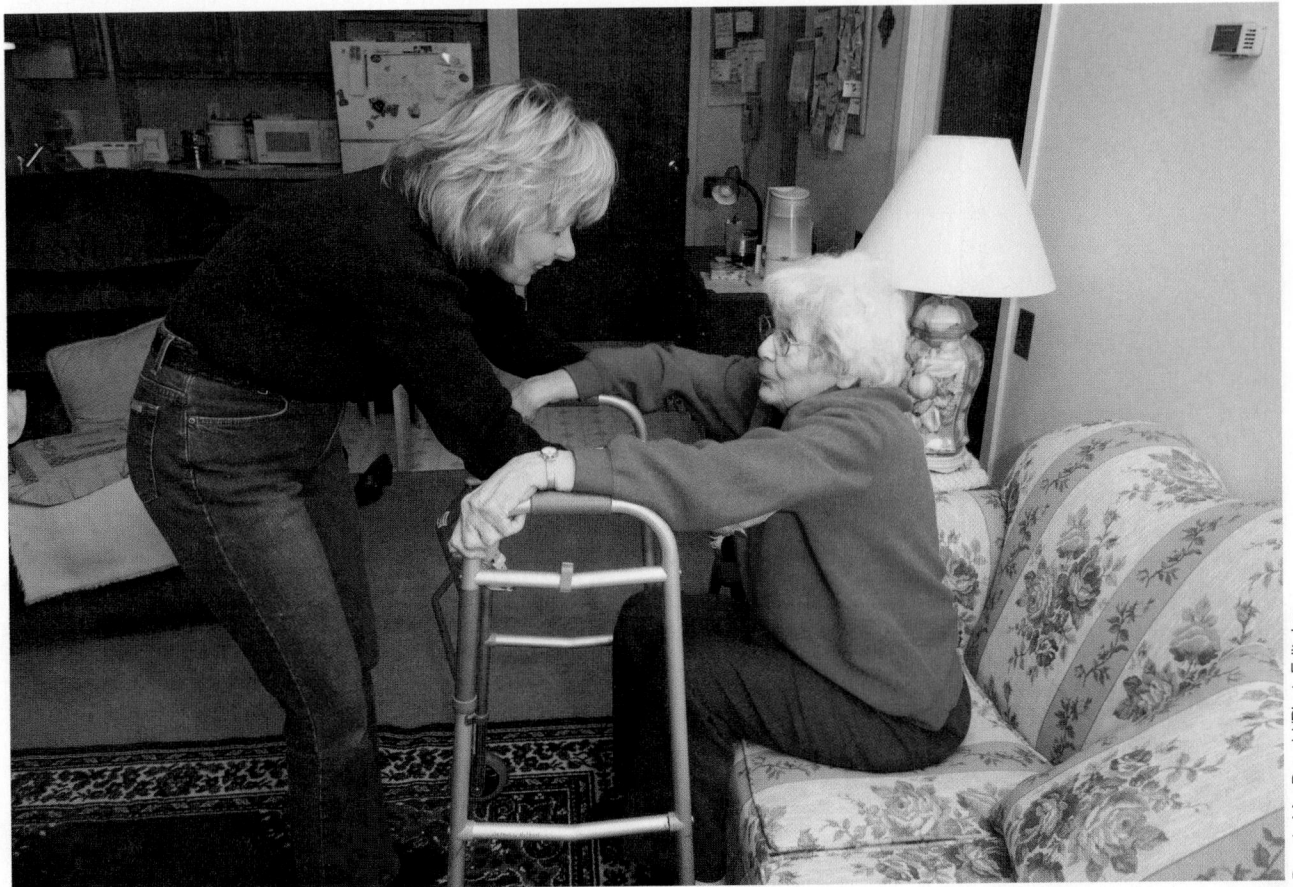

Dennis MacDonald/PhotoEdit, Inc.

⌄ Learning Objectives

15.1 Explain the increasing share of elderly people in modern societies.

15.2 Describe age stratification in global context.

15.3 Discuss problems related to aging.

15.4 Apply sociology's major theories to the topic of aging.

15.5 Analyze changing attitudes about the end of life.

The Power of Society
to shape emotional support for elderly people

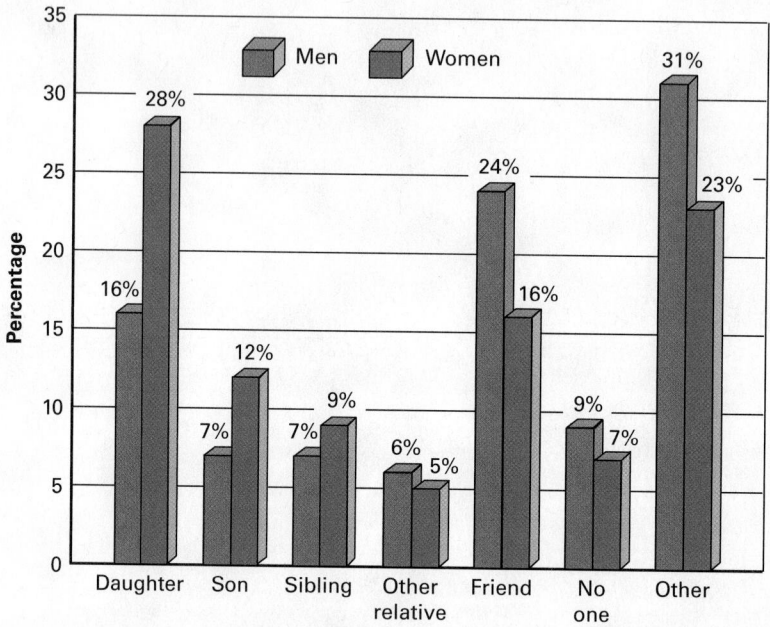

SOURCE: Adapted from the Statistics Canada publication General Social Survey analysis series, catalogue no. 89F00133, May 2003.

Emotional support is important at any stage of life, but there are no guarantees that it will be available to the elderly. When asked who gives them support, few elders say "no one," while the rest report major differences based on gender. Women are most likely to report their daughters, whereas men claim that "others" and "friends"—rather than family—are their source of emotional support. Women are more likely than men to have the support of daughters, sons, or siblings. Men are more likely to rely on the support of friends and others, although those are still significant for women. "Others" may be health-care workers, staff in a retirement residence or nursing home, or volunteers of one kind or another. Nonetheless, the most striking thing about the data is the pattern of gender differences revealed.

Chapter Overview

For all of us, life is a process of growing older. This chapter explores the consequences of growing old and explains why aging is a dimension of social stratification. The importance of understanding aging is increasing along with the elderly share of our population.

Gladys Powers, who died at age 109 on August 15, 2008, in Abbotsford, British Columbia, may have been the last living female veteran of World War I. She was described as follows in the *Globe and Mail*: "Born in London as a subject of Queen Victoria, she has lived in three centuries, survived two world wars and outlasted four husbands" (Hawthorn, 2006).

Gladys Winifred Stokes was born to a wealthy British family and, as a child, lived in the Ottoman Empire for four years with her family. By the time she was 14 years old, she had lost both parents and her family fortune to her stepmother, ending up in the care of Church of England nuns. At age 18, she joined the war effort, ending up in the Women's Royal Air Force. As the war was ending, she met a tall, handsome soldier and moved with him to Canada as a war bride. When she and her husband decided to move from Calgary to Vancouver in 1914, they walked the railway tracks due to lack of funds. On their month-long journey, they encountered a cougar; Gladys assured her husband that it would not attack because they were too skinny.

All of her years were eventful ones. After her fourth husband died, she lived alone in her home—until she was 103. After moving into the Valhaven Home, she continued to be active as a regular in the daily exercise class. Although she used a walker, that didn't stop her from taking advantage of any opportunity to dance, thereby indulging one of her passions. Asked why she loved to dance, Powers replied, "You've got to have happiness in this world." ■

Jean Konda-Witte/Abbotsford Times

You have just been introduced to one of several fascinating elders you will meet in this chapter. Through their lives and as they aged these individuals were survivors—overcoming a range of challenges life threw at them. In their later years, they were among those who learned that social stratification is not just about class, gender, and race—it is also about age. While they overwhelmingly report that they are happy, older people face a number of disadvantages, including lower income, prejudice, and sometimes even abuse. These factors, along with deterioration in health, mean that, as Canada's population ages, increasing numbers of people face threats to their quality of life.

The Greying of Canada

15.1 Explain the increasing share of elderly people in modern societies.

A quiet but powerful revolution is reshaping Canada: The number of elderly people—women and men aged 65 and over—is increasing more than twice as fast as the population as a whole. The "greying" of Canada (or population aging) is clearly apparent. The 2011 census reveals that, in Canada, people older than 65 make up 14.8 percent of our population. By 2041, elderly people will make up almost a quarter—23.8 percent—of all Canadians (McPherson, 2004:6). Another way of measuring the aging of the Canadian population is by its median age, which has risen from 29.6 in 1981 to 40.6 in 2011 (39.6 for men, 41.5 for women).

In just over a century, the life expectancy of Canadians has doubled, while the average number of children has declined by half. The result is population aging, which shows up clearly in the age/sex pyramids of Figure 15–1. The pyramids for 1951, 1981, and 2011 are based on the percentages of males (*left*) and females (*right*) in each five-year age category. The pyramids show and will continue to demonstrate dramatic shape changes—with the tops becoming wider and the bottoms becoming narrower. These changes are the result of baby boomers moving up through the age categories of the pyramids.

Canada Map 15–1 shows the percentage of the population older than 65 by province and territory. The national average increased from 13 to 14.8 percent in the five years between 2006 and 2011, which is consistent with our increasing life expectancies. Note that the provinces with the largest populations of elderly people are all on the east coast, where 16 percent or more are 65 and older. In Quebec 15.9 percent of the population is elderly. In effect, the "oldest" provinces are on the east coast (i.e., the four Atlantic Provinces)—with Quebec and British Columbia following

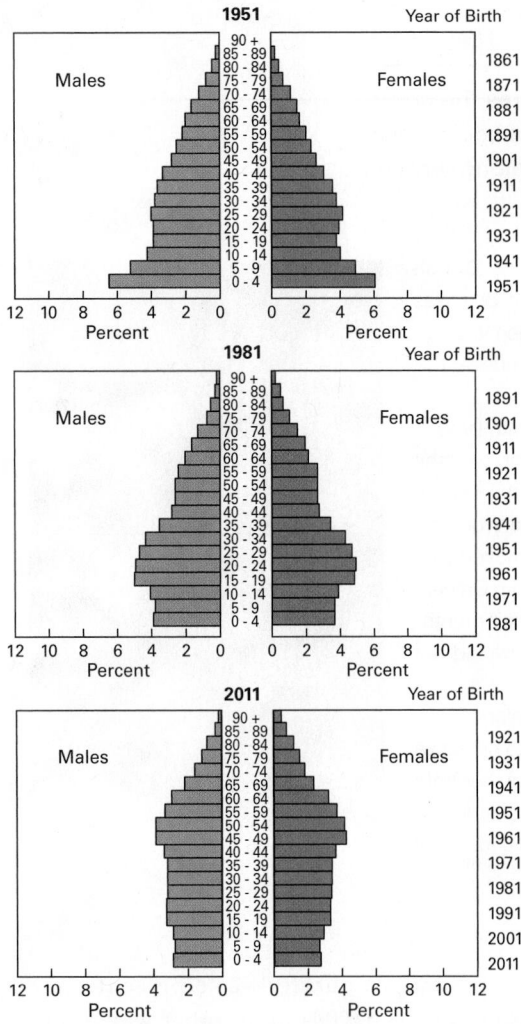

Figure 15–1 Age Pyramids of Canada for 1951, 1981, and 2011

SOURCES: Adapted from the Statistics Canada publication "Report on the Demographic Situations in Canada," Catalogue no. 91-209, 1992. Compilation and calculations for the 2011 pyramid by L.M. Gerber based on Statistics Canada, Census 2011, Catalogue no. 98-311-XCB2011018.

very closely behind. Ontario, Manitoba, and Saskatchewan are slightly younger. Alberta, at least in 2011, was the youngest of the provinces, mainly because it attracted younger workers from other parts of Canada to take advantage of its booming economy. Among the territories—all of which are younger than the provinces—Yukon is the "oldest," Nunavut the "youngest." Birth rates, life expectancies, and migration of young people in particular—from the east coast to Alberta, Yukon, and the Northwest Territories—determine the age structure of each province or territory.

Population aging characterizes some parts of Canada more than others. Nunavut's relative youth is easy to explain; the Inuit—85 percent of the population—have very high birth rates. Both Yukon and Northwest Territories have substantial Aboriginal populations with relatively high birth rates and, in addition, have healthy economies (and the highest median incomes in Canada) that attract young workers and their families from

elsewhere. British Columbia has a less vibrant economy and, more importantly, is a powerful magnet for people of "retirement age." Until the crash in oil prices, Alberta had a booming economy and a shortage of workers, so it actively recruited young adults from the rest of the country and from abroad. The central provinces (Ontario, Manitoba, and Saskatchewan) have moderately healthy economies that are reflected in average proportions of seniors. All of the provinces east of Ontario lose young people to Alberta and other points west. Their own economies have stagnated; that, in turn, makes it difficult for them to retain their own young people or attract immigrants.

What is prompting the aging of Canadian society? Two factors stand out. The first is the baby boom that began in the late 1940s. After World War II, men and women enthusiastically settled into family life and child-bearing. After 1965, the birth rate took a sharp turn downturn (see the 1981 pyramid in Figure 15–1), creating the so-called baby bust; as a result, our population will become increasingly top heavy in the coming decades. As these trends continue, there comes a point at which population *decline* becomes a threat. Japan and several European countries already worry about the prospect of falling population counts. Canada, which faces the same problem, promotes increased immigration as the solution.

Birth Rate: Going Down

The birth rate in Canada, in all but the baby boom years, has been falling for more than a century, as it does when societies industrialize. Since children are more likely to survive into adulthood in industrialized countries, couples bear fewer children. In addition, although children are an economic asset to farming families, they are an economic liability to families in industrial centres. In other words, children no longer add to their family's financial well-being but instead are a major expense.

As more women achieve higher education, work outside the home, and commit to careers, they choose to have fewer children. This choice is made possible by advances in birth control technology during the past century.

Life Expectancy: Going Up

Canada experienced a remarkable 30-year increase in life expectancy over the twentieth century. Females born in 1900 lived 50 years; males lived 47 years. In contrast, women born between 2007 and 2009 look forward to 83 years of life, men to 79 years (Statistics Canada, 2012b). Our longer lifespans are mainly the result of medical advances that virtually eliminated infectious diseases such as smallpox, diphtheria, and measles, which killed many young people in the past. More recent medical strides fend off cancer and heart disease, afflictions common to

Seeing Ourselves

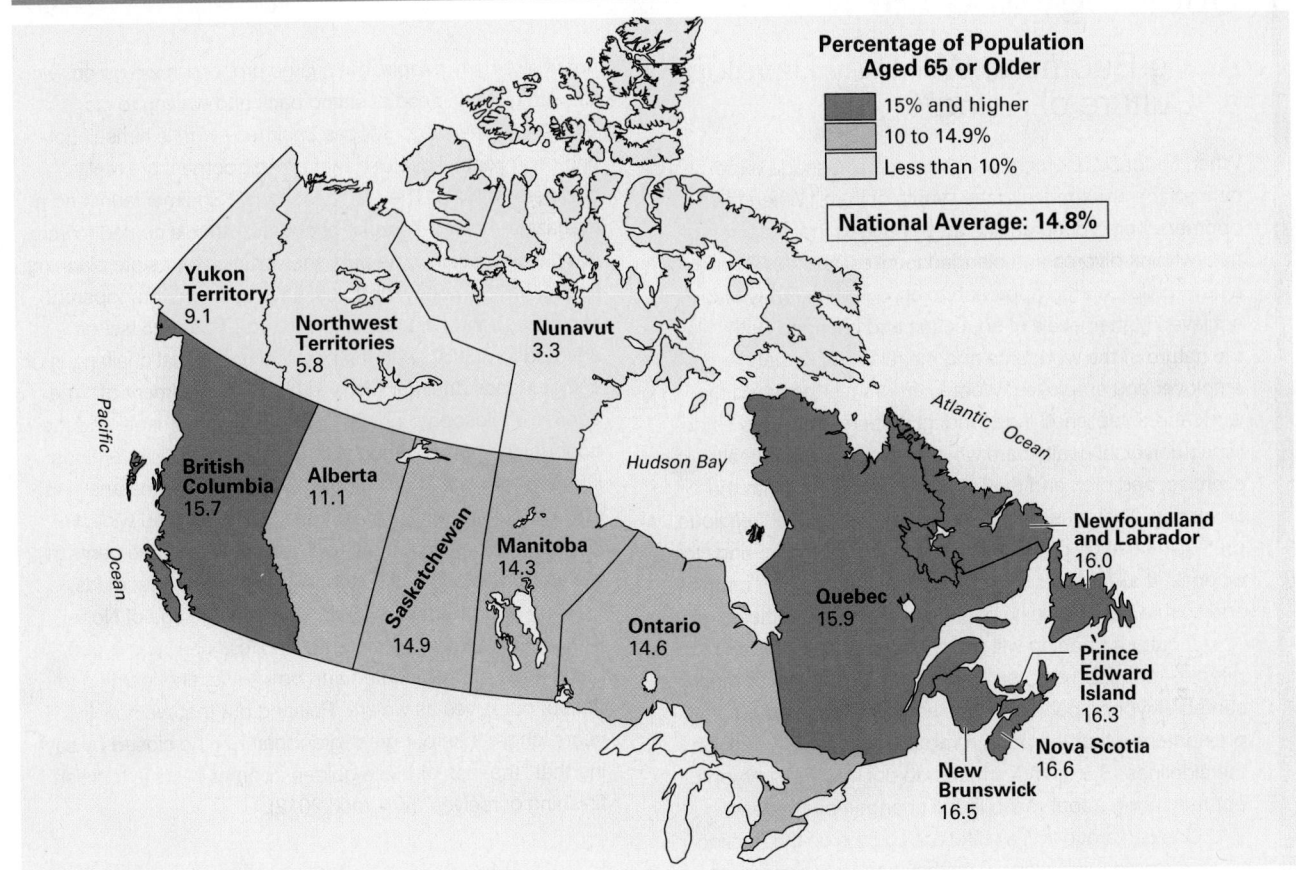

Canada Map 15–1 Percentage of the Population Aged 65 and Older for Canada, 2011

SOURCE: Compilation and calculations by L.M. Gerber, based on Statistics Canada, Census 2011, Catalogue no. 98-311-XCB2011018.

elderly people. One clear indication of this change is that the fastest-growing segment of the population is people older than 85, who are already more than 20 times more numerous than they were at the beginning of the twentieth century. Note that the 2001 census "counted 3795 Canadians aged 100 or older ... with women centenarians outnumbering men four to one" (McPherson, 2004:5–6). The figures for 2011 show 5825 people over 100 years of age—4870 women and 955 men. This means women centenarians now outnumber men five to one.

The Consequences of Population Aging for Canada

We can only begin to imagine the consequences of this massive increase in the elderly population. As elderly people retire from the labour force, they will add to the proportion of non-working adults—which is already about 10 times greater than it was in 1900. The expanding elderly population will generate ever-greater demands for health care and other social services. Importantly, the ratio of elderly people to working-age adults—which

analysts call the *old-age dependency ratio*—will almost double in the next 50 years. Pointing to "periodic fear-mongering by politicians and the media," McPherson argues that "we should not fear population aging, nor view it as a crisis." Instead, population aging should be viewed as a significant, but manageable, challenge (2004:9).

On the other hand, today's adults, especially women, differ in many important ways from previous generations. They will not be exactly like the people who are older than 65 today. Elderly people of the future will tend to have higher levels of education, fewer family responsibilities, better work experiences, more savings, and better health. Thus, predicting the use of social services (such as health care) on the basis of current use is very difficult (Statistics Canada, 1992:144). In recent years, Canada has made tremendous advances in alleviating poverty among elderly people. This, in turn, means that the elderly of the future will be less dependent on social services.

In recent years, older people have drawn heavily on the health care system. One study indicates that health care spending is 4.5 times greater for Canadians over 65, and 6.5 times greater for those over 75, than for those

Sociology and the Media

Aging Boomers: Will They Develop a "Culture of Aging"?

When the baby boomers were teenagers, Canada experienced the emergence of the "youth culture." When the boomers were young adults, they changed the definition of family (think divorce and blended families) and developed a new, child-centred approach to child rearing. They also achieved higher levels of education and changed both the nature of the workforce and the relationship between employer and employee. Women embraced the world of work and established independent careers. Boomers established universal health care while obsessing about health, exercise, and diet, and they infected our society with the travel bug. They questioned all authority—political, religious, professional (e.g., physicians), economic, scientific, and "traditional." If all this falls short of qualifying for a new "middle-age culture," the meaning of cultural change is unclear.

A culture of aging will never encompass all elderly people—nor should it, for "youth culture" has never represented all young people. It was essentially a middle-class phenomenon that left poor, rural, and immigrant youth on the sidelines. Social movements do not involve everyone, but they bring about real cultural change nonetheless.

One can argue that a culture of aging is on the horizon because tomorrow's elders—the baby boomer generation now entering retirement age—will be totally unlike their predecessors. Many of them will delay retirement, and others will shed their old lives to pursue entirely new careers. They will stay physically and socially active, volunteer, travel, take up new causes (like the environment) or ballroom dancing, go back to school, and run marathons. They will be healthier for much longer and will not look or dress their age (within reason)—and they will not give up on sex. This description will not fit all elderly people, but a large proportion will go on living life with gusto instead of sitting back and waiting to die.

A few years ago, Moses Znaimer—who is himself getting on in years—decided that aging boomers are really boomers with zip. They are "Zoomers"! Znaimer launched a magazine—called *Zoomer,* of course—that is geared toward people over 50. In it, he publishes articles on estate planning, health, travel, money, hobbies, entertainment, grandparenting, philosophy, "vitality," and "attitude." After 25 issues devoted to dealing with the physical and social challenges of aging, Moses Znaimer focused his 26th installment of "The Zoomer Philosophy" on the "age of enlightenment" and the good things that go along with aging. Typing "What things improve with age?" on Google, Znaimer got some answers: cheese, guitars, violins, cast iron skillets, and red wine. He went on to compile a more relevant set of improvements in the areas of wisdom, life stories, body image, grandkids, mastery of profession, serenity, the average age of Nobel Prize winners, being *less* cranky and *less* narrow-minded, being more future-oriented and optimistic, and learning to accept ourselves as we are. Pointing out that we now live 34 years longer than our great-grandparents, he closed by saying that "the task of these golden Zoomer years is to finish finishing ourselves" (Znaimer, 2012).

What Do You Think?

1. Is there a culture of aging emerging in Canada? Can you see differences between your parents and your grandparents in their attitudes toward getting older?
2. Have you given any thought to the kind of old age you would like to experience?
3. Is this box "for real"? Or does it look at the aging through rose-coloured glasses?

under 65 (Canada, 1991). Older Canadians make the greatest use of physicians, hospitals, and prescription drugs. The costs of medical care have grown in recent years, a trend that shows no evidence of slowing. Unless steps are taken to address the real medical needs of millions of additional older people, at prices that Canadian taxpayers can afford, our society will face a monumental health care crisis in the coming years. While this is a widespread concern, some analysts argue that the situation is not as dismal as it seems, pointing out that today's seniors are healthier than any previous generation (Foot, 1998).

An Aging Society: Cultural Change

As the share of Canada's population that is older than 65 pushes upward, our way of life will change. In coming decades, interacting with elderly people will become commonplace. As the proportion of our population over 65 increases from 14.8 percent today to 17 percent by 2020 (or one for every six people) younger generations will inevitably have more contact with older people (Foot, 1998)—especially if the elderly are healthier and more active in the workplace or their communities. Reduced age segregation, in turn, will lead to greater familiarity, shared understandings, and fewer negative stereotypes.

Will a "culture of aging" ever emerge? Probably not, one might argue, for one key reason: Elderly people collectively are too diverse. After all, older Canadians represent an open category in which all of us, if we are lucky, end up. Thus, elderly people in Canada represent not just the two sexes but all cultures, classes, and races. The Sociology and the Media box argues that a culture of aging is already emerging and that tomorrow's seniors will live longer, healthier, and more active lives.

The "Young" Old and the "Old" Old

Analysts sometimes distinguish between two cohorts of elderly people. The "younger" elderly, who are between 65 and 75 years of age, are typically autonomous, enjoy good health and financial security, and are likely to be living as couples. The "older" elderly, who have passed the age of 75, are more likely to be dependent on others because of health and money problems. Women outnumber men in both cohorts owing to their greater longevity, a discrepancy that increases with advancing age.

While there are good reasons to be alert to population aging in Canada, some scholars argue that we have pressed the panic button 15 years too early. Susan McDaniel, a demographer, and David Foot, economics professor and author of *Boom, Bust, and Echo*, agree that we have started worrying too early about the social costs of an elderly population—those costs are growing at a rate slower than anticipated. Foot notes that when "all the surviving boomers are over 65, Canada's elderly as a percentage of its population will be about 22 percent, a level that will match, not exceed, the rest of the developed world" (1998:275). The implication is that other countries—mainly those of northern Europe—have already dealt with the issues that are causing panic here in Canada.

Growing Old: Biology and Culture

15.2 Describe age stratification in global context.

Studying the greying of a society's population is the focus of **gerontology** (derived from the Greek word *geron*, meaning "an old person"), *the study of aging and elderly people.* Gerontologists—who work in many disciplines, including medicine, psychology, and sociology—investigate not only how people change as they grow old but also the different ways in which societies around the world define old age.

Biological Changes

Aging consists of gradual, ongoing changes. How we experience life's transitions—whether we welcome biological maturity or bemoan physical decline—depends largely on how our cultural system defines the various stages of life. Canada's youth-oriented culture defines the changes in early life as positive: Through childhood and adolescence, we grow up, or mature, and gain expanded opportunities and responsibilities.

But our culture takes a dimmer view of the biological changes that unfold later in life. Few people receive congratulations for getting old—at least not until they reach 85 or 90 years of age. Rather, we sympathize with friends as they turn 40, 50, or 60 and make jokes to avoid facing the fact that advancing age puts us on a slippery slope of physical and mental decline. "Happy 39th Birthday—again!" We assume that, by about 50, people cease growing *up* and begin growing *down*.

Growing old brings predictable changes: grey hair, wrinkles, loss of height and weight, and an overall decline in strength and vitality. After the age of 50, bones become more brittle, so injuries take longer to heal, and the odds of suffering from chronic illnesses (such as arthritis and diabetes) as well as life-threatening conditions (such as heart disease and cancer) rise steadily. The sensory abilities—taste, sight, touch, smell, and especially hearing—also become less keen with age (Segall & Chappell, 2000; Treas, 1995).

One of the most troublesome problems of old age is a group of illnesses called *dementias,* which are characterized by progressive cognitive impairment, including the loss of abilities such as attention span, concentration, orientation, and memory. While dementias can result from several diseases that affect the brain, Alzheimer's disease is the best-known and most common form of dementia (about 50 percent of dementia is Alzheimer's). Dementia is a serious and prevalent health problem among elderly Canadians, affecting between 5 and 10 percent of those older than 65, and approximately 20 percent of those over 80. The apparent increase in Alzheimer's disease is, almost entirely, the result of more people living past the age of 80 and more people living longer with the symptoms (McPherson, 2004:425).

While health becomes more fragile with advancing age, the vast majority of older Canadians are neither discouraged nor disabled by their physical condition. Only about one in 10 seniors report trouble walking, and fewer than one in 20 require intensive care in a hospital or nursing home. No more than 1 percent of the elderly are bedridden. In a 1990 survey, less than 25 percent of people over the age of 55 characterized their health as "fair" or "poor," while about 75 percent described their overall condition as "good" or "excellent" (Keith & Landry, 1994:134). Not only are older Canadians in better health these days, but they are spending fewer days in the hospital as well. If these trends continue, older people will not be the drain on medical resources suggested by "apocalyptic demography" (Carrière, 2000).

Psychological Changes

We tend to overstate the physical problems and to exaggerate the psychological changes that accompany growing old. Looking at intelligence over the life course, the conventional wisdom can be summed up in the simple rule "What goes up must come down" (Baltes & Schaie, 1974). If we measure skills such as sensorimotor coordination (e.g., the ability to arrange objects to match a drawing),

John Mahler/Toronto Star/Getty Images

JACKRABBIT (HERMAN SMITH) JOHANNSEN WAS BORN IN NORWAY IN 1875 Along with his skis, he left "an indelible mark on Canada: many kilometres of cross-country ski trails and jumps are directly attributable to him, and so are the thousands of skiers who have been inspired by his spirit of adventure and love for the Canadian winter." He promoted cross-country skiing throughout Quebec, Ontario, and parts of the United States. He was also responsible for introducing skiing to the Cree in northern Ontario—from whom he learned their language (his eighth) and who honoured him with the title Chief Jackrabbit. The Jackrabbit part stuck so well that many people never knew his Christian name. When asked, at age 105, about his skiing, he said, "I'm steadier on skis with two poles to hold me up. But I'm not as good a skier as I was 100 years ago" (Norton, 1997). Johannsen died in 1987 at age 112.

we do find a steady decline after midlife. The ability to learn new material and to think quickly also decline, although not until around age 70. But the ability to apply familiar ideas holds steady with advancing age, and the capacity for thoughtful reflection actually increases (Baltes & Schaie, 1974; Cortez, 2008; Metz & Miner, 1998).

We all wonder if we will think or feel differently as we get older. Gerontologists assure us that the answer is usually no. The only common personality change with advancing age is becoming more introspective. That is, people become more engaged with their own thoughts and emotions, and become less materialistic. Generally, therefore, two elderly people who were childhood friends would recognize in each other many of the same personality traits that distinguished them as youngsters (Neugarten, 1977; Wolfe, 1994).

Not surprisingly, Canadian studies reveal that happiness among elders is related to health: "Senior men in good health living with a partner in good health were the most likely to report feeling happy," but at the same time, regardless of their partner's health, "over 90 percent of

healthy senior men and women reported that they were happy" (Crompton & Kemeny, 2000). Of course, wealthier people can afford much more preventive medical care and are healthier. It turns out that happiness levels also depend on income. In one survey, 56 percent of men and 49 percent of women (over age 55) reported being very happy. Few happy men (4 percent) or women (9 percent) had incomes of less than $10 000. The greatest proportion of very happy people fell into the highest income category (Keith & Landry, 1994:134).

Aging and Culture

November 1, Kandy, Sri Lanka. Our little van struggles up the steep mountain incline. Breaks in the lush vegetation offer spectacular views that interrupt our conversation about growing old. "Then there are no old-age homes in your country?" I ask. "In Colombo and other cities, I am sure," our driver responds, "but not many. We are not like you Americans." "And how is that?" I counter, stiffening a bit. His eyes remain fixed on the road: "We would not leave our fathers and mothers to live alone." [John J. Macionis]

THE REALITY OF GROWING OLD IS AS MUCH A MATTER OF CULTURE AS IT IS OF BIOLOGY
In North America, being elderly often means being inactive; yet in many other countries, elders continue familiar and productive routines.

When do people grow old? How do younger people regard society's oldest members? How do elderly people view themselves? The answers people give to these questions vary from society to society, showing that, although aging is a biological process, it is also a matter of culture.

How long and how well people live depend, first, on a society's technology and standard of living. Through most of human history, as English philosopher Thomas Hobbes (1588–1679) put it, people's lives were "nasty, brutish, and short"—although Hobbes himself made it to the ripe old age of 91. In his day, most people married and had children as teenagers, became middle-aged in their twenties, and died from various illnesses in their thirties and forties.

Many great men and women never reached what we would call old age at all. The English poet Keats died at age 26; Mozart, the Austrian composer, died at 35. Among famous writers, none of the three Brontë sisters lived to the end of her thirties; Edgar Allan Poe died at 40, Henry David Thoreau at 45, Oscar Wilde at 46, and William Shakespeare at 52.

By about 1900, however, rising living standards and advancing medical technology in North America and Western Europe had extended longevity to about age 50. As Global Map 15–1 shows, this is still the figure in many low-income countries today. In high-income nations, however, increasing affluence has added almost 30 more years to the average lifespan.

Just as significant as longevity is the importance that societies attach to their older members. Most industrial societies push their elderly to the margins, as we will discuss shortly. Canada, as a whole, is no exception. On the other hand, Aboriginal elders are highly respected, as revealed in the Thinking about Diversity box.

Age Stratification: A Global Survey

Like race, ethnicity, and gender, age is a basis for social ranking. **Age stratification** is *the unequal distribution of wealth, power, and privilege among people at different stages of the life course.* Age stratification varies according to a society's level of technological development.

HUNTER/GATHERER SOCIETIES Without the technology to produce a surplus of food, hunters and gatherers must be nomadic. This means that survival depends on physical strength and stamina. As members of these societies grow old (in this case, about age 30), they become less active and may even be considered an economic burden and, when food is in short supply, abandoned (Sheehan, 1976).

PASTORAL, HORTICULTURAL, AND AGRARIAN SOCIETIES Once societies develop the technology to raise their own crops and animals, they produce a surplus. In such societies, some individuals build up considerable wealth over a lifetime. Of all age categories, the most privileged are typically older people, a pattern called **gerontocracy**, *a form of social organization in which older people have the most wealth, power, and prestige.* Old people, particularly men, are honoured and sometimes feared by their families, and they remain active leaders of society until they die. This respect for elders also explains the widespread practice of ancestor worship in agrarian societies.

age stratification the unequal distribution of wealth, power, and privilege among people at different stages of the life course

gerontocracy a form of social organization in which older people have the most wealth, power, and prestige

Window on the World

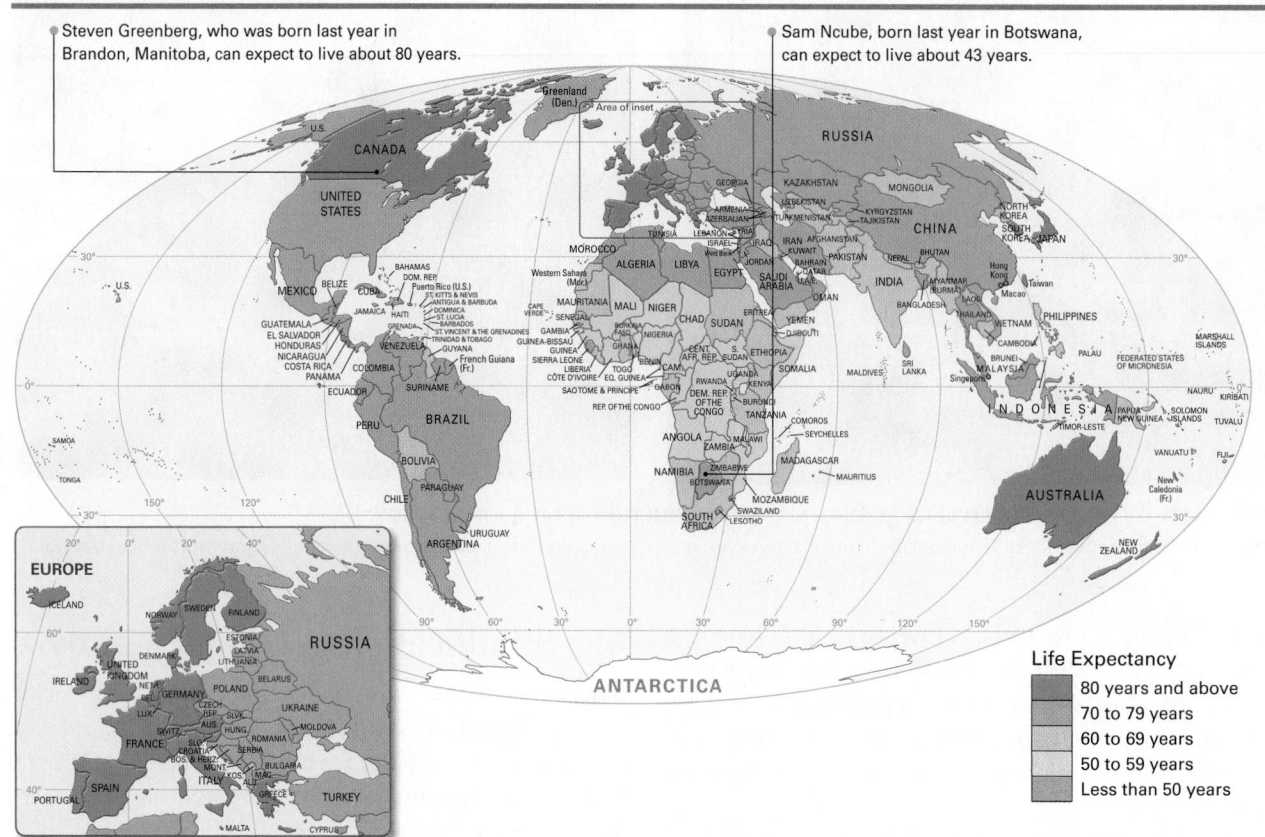

Steven Greenberg, who was born last year in Brandon, Manitoba, can expect to live about 80 years.

Sam Ncube, born last year in Botswana, can expect to live about 43 years.

Life Expectancy
- 80 years and above
- 70 to 79 years
- 60 to 69 years
- 50 to 59 years
- Less than 50 years

Global Map 15–1 Life Expectancy in Global Perspective

Life expectancy shot up during the twentieth century in high-income countries, including Canada, the United States, Western Europe, Japan, and Australia. A newborn in Canada can now expect to live about 80 years and would live even longer were it not for the high risk of death among infants born into poverty. Because poverty is the rule in much of the world, lives are correspondingly shorter, especially in parts of Africa, where life expectancy may be less than 60 years.

SOURCE: Based on Population Reference Bureau (2014).

INDUSTRIAL AND POST-INDUSTRIAL SOCIETIES

Industrialization pushes living standards upward and advances medical technology, both of which increase human life expectancy. But although industrialization adds to the *quantity* of life, it can harm the *quality* of life for older people. Contrary to the practice in traditional societies, industrial societies give little power and prestige to elderly people. The reason is that, with industrialization, the prime source of wealth shifts from land—typically controlled by the oldest members of society—to businesses and other goods—usually owned and managed by younger people. For all low-income nations, 76 percent of men and 44 percent of women over age 65 remain in the labour force; in high-income countries, these percentages are far smaller: 23 percent of men and 16 percent of women. The fact that older people move out of the paid labour force is one reason that the peak earning year among Canadian workers is about age 50, after which earnings decline.

In high-income countries, younger people move away from their parents to pursue their careers, depending less on their parents and more on their own earning power. In addition, because industrial, urban societies change rapidly, the skills, traditions, and life experiences that served the old may seem unimportant to the young. The tremendous productivity of industrial nations means that not all members of a society need to work, so most of the very old and the very young play nonproductive roles.

The long-term effect of all of these factors transforms *elders* (a word with positive connotations) into the *elderly* (a term that carries far less prestige and turns people into a category). In post-industrial societies such as Canada and the United States, economic and political leaders are usually people between the ages of 40 and 60 who combine experience with up-to-date skills. In Canada, the "old establishment" is replaced by the "new establishment" of business Titans, who are invariably younger

Thinking About Diversity: Race, Class, and Gender

Aboriginal Elders: Cultural Custodians

For thousands of years, Aboriginal cultures have survived on Turtle Island (the Aboriginal name for North America), for the most part without written records. Their values, skills, knowledge, laws, and histories have been passed on orally from generation to generation—and elders play a pivotal role in that transmission. The result is that, wherever Aboriginal peoples strive to maintain cultural traditions, elders are held in high esteem.

Cathie Archbould/The Whitehorse Star

SARAH ABEL LIVED IN THE ISOLATED VILLAGE OF OLD CROW ABOVE THE ARCTIC CIRCLE IN THE NORTHERN TIP OF THE YUKON Only at 100 years of age did she move out of the home in which she had raised 17 children—on her own after her husband died of tuberculosis. She drove a dog sled, hunted moose and muskrat, and tanned her own hides; in other words, she did whatever had to be done. She had vivid memories of the past and told stories in person or on the CBC in her native tongue (Vuntut Gwitchin). As someone who had never touched alcohol, she worried a great deal about the social costs of alcohol abuse in her community (Brend, 1997). Sarah Abel died in August 1998 at age 102.

The 1993 Royal Commission on Aboriginal Peoples, in a massive report, published its findings on the social conditions of Aboriginal peoples throughout Canada. The following are some of the descriptions in the report that together define the position of elders—men and women—in Aboriginal societies and traditions. The Elders or Old Ones

- Teach the "ancient wisdom about how to live, how to relate to the Creator, and how to coexist [with] brothers and sisters of the plant and animal world"
- Have insight, wisdom, and authority
- Have already walked a great distance on the path of life
- Have received "the gifts of experience and knowledge"
- "Live their lives by example, according to the laws of the Creator"
- Will recount stories and legends
- Are good listeners
- Apply spiritual understanding to community and family life
- Are "a contemporary link to traditional knowledge"
- See life as a sacred ceremony
- "Play a critical role in the retention, renewal and celebration of Aboriginal languages"
- Are the guardians of Aboriginal cultures
- Can make important contributions in the classroom
- Are teachers of the ethics of traditional justice
- Mediate when conflicts arise
- Lead the struggle for self-government
- Take a holistic and spiritual approach to healing
- Help youth find pride and strength in their Aboriginal identity

What Do You Think?

1. Could the rest of us learn something from the Aboriginal tradition of respect for the elderly?
2. Do you remember hearing stories of the old days from your grandparents and great-grandparents?
3. Do you think that older people can help youth deal with their problems?

SOURCE: Based on the Royal Commission on Aboriginal Peoples (Canada, 1996a:107–143).

(Newman, 1998). In rapidly changing sectors of the economy, especially the high-tech fields, many key executives are younger still, sometimes barely out of college or university. Industrial societies often give older people only marginal participation in the economy because they lack the knowledge and training demanded in a fast-changing marketplace.

Despite overall trends, some occupations are dominated by older people. The average farmer is 55, and more than one-third of today's farmers are over the age of 65. Older people also predominate in other traditional occupations, working as barbers, tailors, and shop clerks, and in jobs that involve minimal physical activity, such as night security guards (Yudelman & Kealy, 2000).

JAPAN: AN EXCEPTIONAL CASE Throughout the past century, Japan stood out as an exception to the rule that industrialization lowers the social standing of older people. Not only is the share of older people in Japan increasing as fast as anywhere in the world, but Japan's more traditional culture gives elders great importance. Most elders in Japan live with an adult daughter or son and play a significant role in family life. Elderly men in Japan are also more likely than their North American counterparts to stay in the labour force, and in many Japanese corporations the oldest employees enjoy the greatest respect.

But Japan is becoming more like other industrial nations, where growing old means giving up some measure of social importance. In addition, a long economic downturn has left Japanese families less able to care for their older members, which may further weaken the traditional importance of elders (Lah, 2008; Ogawa & Retherford, 1997).

Transitions and Challenges of Aging

15.3 Discuss problems related to aging.

We confront change at each stage of life. Old age has its rewards but, of all stages of the life course, it presents the greatest challenges. Physical decline in old age is less serious than most younger people think. But even so, older people endure pain, limit their activities, increase their dependency on others, lose dear friends and relatives, and face up to their own mortality. Because our culture places such a high value on youthfulness, aging often leads to fear and self-doubt. One retired psychologist commented about old age: "Don't let the current hype about the joys of retirement fool you. They are not the best of times. It's just that the alternative is even worse" (Rubenstein, 1991).

Finding Meaning

Erik Erikson (1963; orig. 1950, 1980) argued that elderly people must resolve the tension between "integrity" and "despair." No matter how much they still may be learning and achieving, older people recognize that their lives are nearing an end. As a result, elderly people spend more time reflecting on their past, remembering disappointments as well as accomplishments. Integrity, to Erikson, means assessing your life realistically; without such honesty, this stage of life may turn into a time of despair—a dead end with little positive meaning.

Negative myths about the health, happiness, and sexuality of older people abound (McPherson, 1990). Some elderly people share this dim view of their plight,

Table 15–1 Happiness Reported by Senior Men and Women by Health of Self and Spouse

	Percentage Who Are Happy	
	Older Men	Older Women
In good health		
Spouse in good health	96	90
Spouse in poor health	88	94
In poor health		
Spouse in good health	77	64
Spouse in poor health	64	60

SOURCE: Data from L.M. Gerber from Crompton and Kemeny (2000:48).

but most have a more positive outlook. As Table 15–1 indicates, a large majority of senior men and women consider themselves to be happy—especially if they and their partners are in good health. Those most likely to report happiness (96 percent) are men in good health with partners in good health; those least likely to report happiness (60 percent) are women in poor health with partners in poor health. Married elders have advantages over single ones in a number of areas, including morbidity (their rate of illness), mortality, and psychological well-being. Marriage appears to be particularly advantageous for elderly males because it unites them with a network of other people more easily than singlehood does (Nett, 1993).

Overall, research suggests that, while personal adjustments are necessary, the experience of growing old may provide cause for joy. However, a person's view does vary based on individual personality, family circumstances, social class, and financial position. People who adapt successfully to changes earlier in life can confidently look forward to deriving satisfaction and meaning from their lives later on. As Neugarten (1971) sees it, the key to successful aging lies in maintaining personal dignity and self-confidence while accepting growing old. She found that people with *integrated personalities* cope best with the challenges of growing old. Many books, magazines (e.g., *Zoomer*), and websites try to help older people—especially the retired—answer questions about the meaning of life. Some help elders achieve spiritual goals, while others stress making a continuing contribution to society—through volunteering or otherwise staying active and making a difference. With the proper outlook, old age provides the opportunity to develop wisdom, balance, gratitude, and self-awareness (Todd, 2003).

Social Isolation

Being alone may provoke anxiety in people of any age; isolation, however, is most common among elderly people. Retirement closes off workplace social interaction; physical problems may limit mobility; and negative

Table 15–2 Living Arrangements of Seniors*
in Canada, 2011

	Over 65 Years		Over 75 Years	
	Men (%)	Women (%)	Men (%)	Women (%)
Living with spouse or partner	76.2	48.7	71.7	34.1
Living with relatives	4.9	14.5	6.5	19.1
Living with non-relatives	2.1	1.8	1.8	1.6
Living alone	16.9	35.0	20.1	45.3
Total	2 081 800	2 470 105	825 810	1 106 635

* The percentages refer to seniors who are living in private households rather than
retirement residences or nursing homes.

SOURCE: Compilation and calculations by L.M. Gerber based on Statistics Canada,
Census 2011, Catalogue no. 98-312-XCB2011030.

stereotypes depicting elderly people as "over the hill" may discourage younger people from maintaining close social contact with their elders.

The greatest cause of social isolation, however, is the inevitable death of significant others. Few human experiences affect people as profoundly as the death of a spouse. One study found that almost three-quarters of widows and widowers cited loneliness as their most serious problem (Lund, 1989). Table 15–2 reveals that—among seniors living in private households rather than retirement residences or nursing homes—three-quarters of men aged 65 and over live with a spouse or partner, while this is true of only 49 percent of women. Among those 65 years of age and older, 17 and 35 percent of men and women, respectively, live alone. These gender gaps only become wider in the population 75 years of age and older. Once again, many more men than women live with a spouse or common-law partner—with advancing age, the level for men drops by 4 percentage points, while that for women drops by 14 points. The proportions living *alone* increase by 3 points for men and 10 points for women. So what is going on here? Men are very likely to live with wives or partners regardless of advanced age. There are several reasons for this, including the fact that widowed men have a tendency to remarry and, as we know, women outlive men. As women move into the "old elderly" years, they are more likely than men to live with relatives or to live alone. An astounding 45 percent of women, aged 75 and older, live alone and are at most risk of social isolation.

While some studies have found that elderly women suffer more mental health problems as a result of isolation (Nett, 1993), others have found that half of elderly widows choose to live in the homes they once shared with their husbands; in doing so, they rely on a wider range of social supports than men do (McDaniel, 1994). Elderly women tend to have close emotional ties to neighbours as

well as to friends, other relatives, and their adult children, particularly their daughters (Bess, 2000). On the other hand, living alone—a valued dimension of autonomy—presumes the financial means to do so.

It may surprise you to learn that women who are widowed later in life (i.e., between the ages of 65 and 74) are three times more likely to live by themselves than women who were widowed before they were 65 (Bess, 2000:167). One reason may be that younger widows move in with their children to help raise their grandchildren. Older widows may not be needed in child rearing and may not feel that they have the energy. On the other hand, older widows who have grown accustomed to an empty nest and have created new lives for themselves without their adult children might be more reluctant to give up their independence by moving into a three-generation household. The formation of three-generation households is related to ethnicity, as well. Recent immigrants, from Asia in particular, are more likely than other Canadians to have their parents or widowed mothers live in their homes (Che-Alford & Hamm, 2000; Gerber, 1983). Chinese Canadians between 80 and 85 years of age are four times more likely to live with their adult children than are their non-Asian counterparts (McPherson, 2004:216).

Some elderly people opt to live in housing specifically for them. Residences for older Canadians range from retirement communities offering many amenities and leisure activities to low-rent apartments for seniors, retirement homes (with dining rooms and housekeeping services), and nursing homes with full-time medical staff (McPherson, 2004:219). The Sociology in Focus box looks at some issues related to these residence options.

Retirement

Beyond earnings, work provides an important part of our personal identities. Therefore, retirement means not only a reduction in income but also less social prestige and perhaps some loss of purpose in life. Some organizations help ease this transition. Universities, for example, confer the title "professor emeritus" (*emeritus* is from the Latin, meaning "fully earned") or "professor emerita" (for women) on retired faculty members, who maintain many university privileges and often continue to publish and teach the occasional course. These highly experienced faculty members can be a valuable resource not only to students but also to younger professors (Parini, 2001).

Because seniors are socially diverse, there is no single formula for successful retirement. Part-time work occupies many people entering old age and provides some extra cash as well. Grandparenting is an enormous source of pleasure for many elders. Volunteer work is another path to rewarding activity, especially for those who have saved enough so that they do not have to work. This is

Sociology in Focus

Aging in Retirement Residences and Nursing Homes with a Little Sex on the Side

The aging of Canada's population has led to the rapid proliferation of retirement homes (some of them opulent) and nursing homes—or even whole towns, like Elliott Lake in northern Ontario, that reshape themselves into retirement communities. In each, older people live in settings designed to meet their special physical, social, and medical needs.

Retirement homes, with assisted living options, are of particular interest because they are a relatively new phenomenon. They differ from nursing homes in many ways—most significantly in their lack of public subsidy. In other words, the resident pays the full cost of his or her accommodation, meals, social activities, housekeeping, and nursing care. Physicians' services, on or off the premises, are covered by provincial health care plans. The cost of residence in a retirement home *with assisted living* may range from $3000 to $5000 per month or much more, making it accessible only to more affluent seniors.

Note that most Canadians move into retirement residences before they need assistance with such daily living activities as eating, bathing, or getting out of bed; only a portion of residents require fully assisted living. Residents live as individuals or couples in rooms, and share common areas (e.g., lounges, dining room, crafts room, library, gardens, exercise room). Accommodation costs may include meals, housekeeping, and transportation to, for example, concerts, wine country tours, or shopping at the mall. Seniors are encouraged to participate as much as possible in a wide range of activities.

In an article for the *New York Times* titled "Under One Roof, Aging Together Yet Alone," Jane Gross described the assisted living setting as a "dignified alternative" to the nursing home. She looked at a relatively posh assisted living facility called Atria Stratford in Stratford, Connecticut, finding that

> Everyone complains about the food. Nobody wants to sit with the misfits. There are leaders and followers, social butterflies and loners, goody-goodies and troublemakers. Friendships are intense and so are rivalries. Everybody knows everybody else's business.

She quoted public health professor Dr. Catherine Hawes, who described it as "high school all over again, without the expectations."

Life for the residents—overwhelmingly women with an average age of 85—is a humbling experience, involving loss of control, fear for the future, and loneliness in a group setting. People who are most impaired are ostracized by those who fear what they themselves may soon become. Complaints about food are commonplace, and memory

John Mahoney/The Gazette 2001.

loss leads to widespread suspicion. On the other hand, there is laughter, social interaction, friendship and, for some, love and marriage.

The situation in Canada's nursing homes is very similar, except for higher levels of physical and mental impairment. The newer nursing homes are anything but dark and dreary. Wings or floors are limited to 28 residents, who share common areas (e.g., lounges and dining rooms) and their own staff. You may be surprised to learn that this aspect of health care is provided mainly by private enterprise, and that a number of Ontario's nursing homes are owned by a Mennonite firm. Others cater to specific ethnic communities, though they must accept anyone who signs on to their waiting lists. Nursing homes are tightly regulated and subsidized by provincial governments to the point where anyone with a Canadian pension can afford the cost. Universal healthcare covers visits to physicians (on site or off) as well as prescription costs—as it does for all seniors. It may take up to two years on a waiting list to get into the nursing home of one's choice.

It may come as a surprise to some students that people over 30 have sex—and so do people over 65. In a full-page article in the *National Post* titled "Old People F—ing," Melinda Hennenberger wrote about sex in nursing homes and about the reactions of the adult son who came upon his 95-year-old father engaged in sex. Older people *do* form intense relationships in nursing homes, and sometimes those relationships involve sex. "Gerontologists recommend sex for the elderly because it improves mood and overall physical function, but the legal issues are complicated: Can someone with dementia give informed consent? How do caregivers balance safety and privacy concerns? When families object to a demented person being sexually active, are nursing homes responsible for

(continued)

chaperoning?" At a more general level, one might ask if older people have the right to a sex life.

There's a modern dilemma facing retirement and nursing homes in Canada. In "Home for the Grey and Gay," Jo-Anne MacDonald looked into the housing experiences of aging gays and lesbians. Not long ago, gays feared growing old because they felt they had to go back into the closet in order to fit into a nursing home environment. Nursing homes were doing nothing to accommodate them. Recently, two of ten city-owned nursing homes in Toronto opened their doors to gay residents. They have changed their definition of "family members," added gay-themed movies to their film collections, given sensitivity training to staff and residents, encouraged conjugal visits, and declared themselves safe havens for "elderly gays, lesbians, bisexuals, and transgendered." Privately owned nursing homes are also seeking guidance in becoming gay-friendly. Soon, retirement homes—and some nursing homes—will have same-sex couples moving into single rooms or suites.

There are some 600 000 gays and lesbians in Canada who are over 45 years of age, with 80 000 of them living in Toronto. A condominium is coming on stream in Toronto to cater to this older gay community. MacDonald's article does not point it out, but this would be an ideal setting for one floor designed as a retirement home (with shared dining room and other facilities) with assisted living possibilities. Ideally, gays and lesbians—anywhere in Canada—will have a range of choices for accommodation and care as they age, where they are free to be themselves without risk of rejection, discrimination, or abuse. Some elderly gays, who grew up at a time when their relationships were illegal, must find this an astounding proposition.

What Do You Think?

1. Would you consider living in a retirement home, with assisted living options, before making the move to a nursing home? What are the advantages and disadvantages of doing so?

2. Do you think that elders living in nursing homes have the right to a sex life? What if the elder involved is your mother or father?

3. Why is it so important for retirement and nursing homes to rethink their approaches to gay residents?

SOURCES: Gross (2005), Hennenberger (2008), and MacDonald (2005).

one reason why volunteerism is increasing more among older people than in any other age category (Gardyn, 2000; Savishinsky, 2000; Shapiro, 2001).

Although retirement is a familiar idea, the concept developed only within the past century or so in high-income countries. High-income societies are so productive that not everyone needs to work; in addition, advanced technology places a premium on up-to-date skills. Therefore, retirement emerged as a strategy to permit younger workers—presumably, those with the most current knowledge and training—to have the largest presence in the labour force. Whereas, a decade or so ago, it was common for Canadians to retire at age 65, many now consider early retirement. In high-income countries, private and public pension programs make it financially possible for older people to retire; that opportunity does not exist in low-income nations.

In Canada, the "normal" retirement age of 65 is closely tied to the development of pension plans and, until recently, to mandatory retirement legislation. In July 2009, Nova Scotia became the last province to end mandatory retirement. In the past, about half of the Canadian workforce was subject to mandatory retirement regulations, but a study found that only about 1 percent of the workforce would continue to work past age 65 if given the choice (Tindale, 1991). Recall from the Sociology and the Media box that zoomers (boomers with zip) may well feel fit and energetic enough to put off retirement beyond age 65—sometimes retiring from a long-term job and embarking on an entirely new career. As the baby boomer generation moves into "normal" retirement age, we will have a much better picture of its retirement patterns.

In recent decades, with rapid transitions in the Canadian economy resulting from global economic restructuring, free trade agreements, and a general move to the political right, more and more people are being forced out of work or encouraged to take early retirement. Many of those who have been given the "golden handshake" are embarking on brand-new careers, sometimes using severance packages as the initial investment for their new ventures (Lipovenko, 1996). In the past few years, with increasing threats of labour and skills shortages, we have reduced the emphasis on early retirement.

Clearly, the retirement decision is based on the state of the economy. In good times, people can afford to retire early if they wish. However, the economic downturn that began in 2007 has had the opposite effect, forcing seniors to confront the hard reality that their retirement "nest eggs" have been cracked by the sinking stock market and disappearing pensions. With so much wealth suddenly gone, many find that they must continue to work. Others, who had already retired, are being forced back into paid work.

Aging and Income

On the whole, the image of elderly people as poverty-stricken is unfounded: The poverty rate among older Canadians has declined substantially since 1990 to the point where the poverty rate among seniors is lower than that among Canada's children. Table 15–3 shows that while 14 percent of all persons fall below the low-income cutoff, the poverty rate for children (under 18 years) is 16 percent, for seniors it is 12 percent. But one's family situation makes all the difference in the world. The poverty rate for children in two-parent families is 8 percent compared to 30 percent in female lone-parent families. In similar vein, only 6 percent of elders living in families are poor while 29 percent of unattached seniors live in poverty. Recall that senior women are much more likely to live alone than are men. In fact, 45 percent of women over 75 years of age are "unattached" (i.e., living alone) and therefore much more likely to be poor. Table 15–4 notes that 4.5 percent of senior men but only 1.3 percent of senior women have income of over $100 000 per year. Furthermore, median and average incomes of senior women are about two-thirds those of senior men. Lower income and living alone ensure higher poverty levels for women.

For most Canadians, retirement leads to a significant decline in income. For many, home mortgages and children's university expenses are paid off; yet the expenses for medical and dental care, household help, and home utilities typically rise. Many elderly people lack sufficient savings or pension benefits to be self-supporting; for this reason, various pension programs, including the Canada Pension Plan, are their greatest source of income. Because many retirees live with a fixed income, inflation tends to affect them more severely than it does younger working people. Women and members of visible minorities are especially likely to find that growing old means growing poorer.

Poverty among the elderly is often hidden from view. Because of personal pride and a desire to maintain the dignity of independent living, many older people conceal financial problems even from their own families. It

IT IS COMMON FOR BUSINESSES TO OFFER A "SENIORS' DISCOUNT" TO PEOPLE OVER AGE 65 (OR SOMETIMES EVEN AGE 55) What is the reason for this practice? Would you prefer a policy of offering discounts to single parents with children, a category of people at higher risk of poverty? Why is that an unlikely move by businesses?

is difficult for people who have supported their children for years to admit that they can no longer provide for themselves.

Caregiving

In an aging society, the need for caregiving is bound to increase. **Caregiving** refers to *informal and unpaid care provided to a dependent person by family members, other relatives, or friends.* While parents provide caregiving to children, the term is more often applied to the needs of elderly men and women. Indeed, today's middle-aged adults are called the "sandwich generation" because many will spend as much time caring for their aging parents as for their own children. Nelson and Robinson (1999:466) point out that, more accurately, we should refer to the "sandwich phase" since it applies only to those who have caregiving responsibility for their children and their parents simultaneously, and the situation is temporary.

Table 15–3 Low Income After Tax by Age and Family Status, 2012

	Percent with Low Income
All persons	13.8
Persons under 18 years	16.3
In two-parent families	8.4
In female lone-parent families	30.2
Persons 18 to 64 years	13.3
Persons 65 years and over	12.1
In families	6.2
Unattached individuals	28.5

SOURCE: Compiled by L.M. Gerber from Statistics Canada, CANSIM Table 206-0003.

Table 15–4 Income among Canadian Seniors by Sex, 2011

	Males	Females
Population age 65 and over	2 083 895	2 467 635
Income over $100 000 (%)	4.5	1.3
Median income ($)	30 553	19 961
Average income ($)	42 967	27 129

SOURCE: Compilation and calculations by L.M. Gerber based on Statistics Canada, NHS 2011, Catalogue no. 99-010-X2011047.

WHO ARE THE CAREGIVERS? Surveys show that 80 percent of caregiving to elders is provided by family members, in most cases by one person. Most caregivers live nearby. In addition, 75 percent of all caregiving is provided by women, most often daughters and wives. The gender norm is so strong that daughters-in-law are more likely than sons to care for an aging parent: "Research consistently finds that primary caregivers are most likely to be women, in their roles as wives, daughters, or daughters-in-law" (Nelson & Robinson, 1999:467). Also, "elderly women, especially widows and divorcees, tend to be the recipients of more social support than men" (McPherson, 2004:367).

About two-thirds of caregivers are married, and one-third are also responsible for young children. When we add the fact that half of all caregivers also have a part-time or full-time job, it is clear that caregiving is a responsibility over and above what most people already consider to be a full day's work. Half of all primary caregivers spend more than 20 hours per week providing elder care and, although caregiving is not considered onerous, women are twice as likely as men to report negative effects on their health. Men are less likely to feel burdened because women face our cultural expectation that caregiving is "an integral part of the female role in our society" (Nelson & Robinson 1999:468).

ELDER ABUSE In Canada, we seem to awaken to social problems in stages: We became aware of child abuse in the 1960s, spousal abuse in the 1970s, and elder abuse in the 1980s. Abuse of older people takes many forms, from passive neglect to active torment, and includes verbal, emotional, financial, and physical harm. Most elderly people suffer from none of these. But, when it does occur, elder abuse tends to go unreported because victims are reluctant to talk about their plight (as is the case with other forms of family violence).

The Canadian Network for the Prevention of Elder Abuse defines elder abuse as harm to an older adult—that is, doing something that causes harm or distress or not doing something that is one's duty (such as providing food or medication). Most abuse occurs in relationships of trust linking the older person to family or service providers (e.g., lawyers, accountants, or nursing home staff). It can occur in the home or in institutions. Abuse, in the community or in institutions, is most likely to occur if caregiving tasks are difficult and the caregiver is otherwise stressed or lacks appropriate support from others.

In Ontario, in recent years, hospital stays have been shortened by diverting patients (many of them elderly) to home care, either in the patient's own home or in the home of a relative. While home care programs provide nursing and housekeeping support, "responsibility" for overall care is placed in the hands of family members. As a result of social policy, some caregivers who lack the resources and skills required to cope are made responsible for the care of their frail and sometimes desperately ill relatives. In some cases, the caregivers have to give up their jobs in order to assume their new responsibilities. These and other accumulated stresses may set the scene for neglect if not outright abuse.

Ageism

In earlier chapters, we explained how ideology—including racism and sexism—serves to justify the social disadvantages of minorities. In a similar way, sociologists use the term **ageism** for *prejudice and discrimination against older people.* Elderly people are the primary targets of ageism, although middle-aged people can suffer as well. Examples of ageism include passing over qualified older job applicants in favour of younger workers or firing older workers first.

Like racism and sexism, ageism can be blatant (as when a university decides not to hire a 60-year-old professor because of her age) or subtle (as when nurses speak to elderly patients in a condescending tone, as if they were children). Also like racism and sexism, ageism builds physical traits into stereotypes. In the case of elderly people, some people consider grey hair, wrinkled skin, and stooped posture to be signs of personal incompetence. Negative stereotypes portray older people as helpless, confused, unable to deal with change, and generally unhappy. Even "positive" images of sweet little old ladies and eccentric old gentlemen are stereotypes that gloss over individuality and ignore years of experience and accomplishment (Butler, 1975; Cohen, 2001).

Sometimes ageism contains a bit of truth. Statistically speaking, older people are more likely than younger people to be mentally and physically impaired. But we slip into ageism when we make unfair generalizations about an entire category of people.

Betty Friedan (1993), a pioneer of the modern feminist movement, argues that ageism is deeply rooted in our culture. She points out that few elderly people appear in the mass media; only a small percentage of television shows, for example, feature main characters over age 60. More generally, when most of us think about older people, it is often in negative terms. This older man *lacks* a job, that older woman has *lost* her vitality, and seniors *look back* to their youth. In short, says Friedan, we often treat being old as if it were a disease, marked by decline and deterioration, for which there is no cure.

Even so, Friedan believes that older women and men are discovering that they still have a great deal to contribute. Advising small business owners, designing housing for the poor, teaching children to read—there are countless ways in which older people can help others and at the same time enhance their own lives.

The Elderly: A Minority?

Elderly people in Canada face social disadvantages. Does that mean that the elderly constitute a minority in the same way as, say, Aboriginal people or women do?

Elderly Canadians appear to meet the definition of a minority because they have a clear social identity based on their age, and they are subject to prejudice and discrimination. But Gordon Streib (1968) argues that we should not think of elderly people as a minority, because minority status is usually both permanent and exclusive. That is, a person is an Aboriginal person or a woman *for life* and can never be part of the dominant category of White men. But being elderly is an *open* status because people are elderly for only part of their lives, and everyone who has the good fortune to live long enough grows old.

Also, the elders at highest risk of being poor or otherwise disadvantaged fall into specific categories of people—women, Aboriginal peoples—who are at highest risk of being poor throughout their lives. As Streib sees it, it is not so much that the old grow poor as that the poor grow old.

If so, older people are not a minority in the same sense as other categories. It might be better to say that elderly people are a part of our population that faces special challenges based on age.

Theories of Aging

15.4 Apply sociology's major theories to the topic of aging.

Let us now apply sociology's theoretical approaches to gain insight into how society shapes the lives of the elderly. We will consider the structural-functional, symbolic-interaction, and social-conflict approaches in turn.

Structural-Functional Analysis: Aging and Disengagement

Drawing on the ideas of Talcott Parsons, an architect of the structural-functional approach, Elaine Cumming and William Henry (1961) explain that the physical decline and death that accompany aging can disrupt society. In response, society disengages elderly people, gradually transferring statuses and roles from older to younger people so that tasks are performed with minimal interruption. **Disengagement theory** is *the idea that society functions in an orderly way by disengaging people from* *positions of responsibility as they reach old age.* Based on both a developmental and a functionalist perspective, disengagement theory assumes that change and adaptation are necessary for both the older individual and society (McPherson, 2004:139).

Disengagement ensures the orderly operation of society by removing aging people from productive roles before they are no longer able to perform them. Another benefit of disengagement in a rapidly changing society is that it makes room for young workers, who typically have the most up-to-date skills and training. Disengagement provides benefits to aging people as well. Although most 60-year-olds wish to keep working, they may begin to think about retirement and perhaps cutting back a bit on their workloads. Exactly when people begin to disengage from their careers, of course, depends on their health, enjoyment of the job, and financial circumstances.

Retiring does not mean being inactive. Some people start new careers or different jobs, while others pursue hobbies or engage in volunteer work. In general, people in their sixties start to think less about what they *have been doing* and begin to think more about what they *want to do* with the rest of their lives (Palmore, 1979; Schultz & Heckhausen, 1996).

EVALUATE

Disengagement theory explains why rapidly changing high-income societies tend to define their oldest members as socially marginal. But there are several limitations to this approach.

DISENGAGEMENT THEORY SUGGESTS THAT SOCIETY GRADUALLY REMOVES RESPONSIBILITIES FROM PEOPLE AS THEY GROW OLD Activity theory counters that, like people at any stage of life, elders find life worthwhile to the extent that they stay active. As a result, many older men and women seek out new jobs, hobbies, and social activities.

Assembly/Digital Vision/Getty Images

First, especially in recent years, many workers have found that they cannot disengage from paid work because they need the income. Second, some elderly people, rich or poor, do not want to disengage from work they enjoy. Disengagement may also mean losing friends and social prestige. Third, it is not clear that the societal benefits of disengagement outweigh its social costs, which include the loss of human resources and the need to take care of people who might otherwise be unable to support themselves. As the number of elderly people swells, finding ways to help them remain independent is a high priority. Fourth, any rigid system of disengagement does not take account of the widely differing abilities of the elderly. This concern leads us to the symbolic-interaction approach.

CHECK YOUR LEARNING State clearly the basic idea behind disengagement theory. How does disengagement benefit the aging individual? How does it benefit society?

Symbolic-Interaction Analysis: Aging and Activity

Drawing on the symbolic-interaction approach, **activity theory** is *the idea that a high level of activity increases personal satisfaction in old age.* Because everyone bases social identity on many roles, disengagement is bound to reduce satisfaction and meaning in the lives of older people. What aging people need is not to be pushed out of roles but to have many productive or recreational options. The importance of having choices is especially great for those aged 65 today, who can look forward to about 20 more years of life (Smart, 2001; Walsh, 2001).

Activity theory does not reject the idea of job disengagement; it simply says that people need to find new roles to replace those they leave behind. Research confirms that elderly people who maintain a high activity level find the most satisfaction in their lives.

Activity theory also recognizes that elderly people are diverse, with highly variable interests, needs, and physical abilities. For this reason, the activities that people choose, and the pace at which they pursue them, are always an individual matter (Moen et al., 1992; Neugarten, 1977).

EVALUATE

Activity theory shifts the focus of analysis from the needs of society—as stated in disengagement theory—to the needs of elderly people themselves. It emphasizes the social diversity of aging and older people and highlights the importance of choice in any government policy.

A limitation of this approach is that it assumes that elders are both healthy and competent, which may not consistently be the case. Another problem with this approach is that it ignores the fact that many of the problems older people face, such as poverty, have more to do with society than with themselves. We turn now to the point of view of social-conflict theory.

CHECK YOUR LEARNING Explain what activity theory says about aging. How does this approach challenge disengagement theory?

Social-Conflict Analysis: Aging and Inequality

Social-conflict analysis assumes that access to opportunities and social resources varies for people of different ages. Thus, age is a dimension of social stratification. In our society, middle-aged people enjoy the greatest power and the most opportunities and privileges, and the elderly and young people under the age of 25 have a higher risk of poverty. Employers who replace senior workers with younger men and women in order to keep wages low may not intend to harm older people. However, such actions amount to discrimination.

The social-conflict approach claims that our industrial-capitalist economy creates an age-based hierarchy. In line with Marxist thought, Steven Spitzer (1980) points out that a profit-oriented society devalues any category of people that is less productive. To the extent that older people do not work, our society labels them as mildly deviant.

Social-conflict analysis also draws attention to various dimensions of social inequality within the elderly population. Differences of class, race, ethnicity, and gender divide older people as they do everyone else. For this reason, some seniors have far greater economic security and more options for personal satisfaction than others. Elderly White people typically enjoy advantages denied to minority elders, while women—an increasing majority as people age—suffer the social and economic disadvantages of both sexism and ageism.

EVALUATE

The social-conflict approach adds to our understanding of the aging process by highlighting age-based inequality and explaining how capitalism devalues elderly people who are considered to be less productive. But critics claim that the real culprit is *industrialization.* As evidence they point to the fact that the elderly are not better off under a socialist system, as a Marxist analysis implies. Furthermore, the idea that either industrialization or capitalism necessarily causes the elderly to suffer is challenged by the long-term rise in income and well-being experienced by seniors in North America.

CHECK YOUR LEARNING What does Marxist theory teach us about aging in a capitalist society?

disengagement theory the idea that society functions in an orderly way by removing people from positions of responsibility as they reach old age

activity theory the idea that a high level of activity increases personal satisfaction in old age

	Structural-Functional Approach	Symbolic-Interaction Approach	Social-Conflict Approach
What is the level of analysis?	Macro level	Micro level	Macro level
How do we understand growing old?	The fact that people grow old and eventually die can disrupt the operation of society. Therefore, societies disengage the elderly from important tasks and other responsibilities as they reach old age.	Aging is one dimension of social stratification. Generally, middle-aged people have the most wealth and power. Poor people, women, and other minorities face the greatest disadvantages as they grow old.	For elders, like everyone else, being active encourages both health and happiness. Therefore, elders strive to maintain a high activity level, replacing roles they leave with new roles.

The Applying Theory table summarizes what we learn from each of the theoretical perspectives.

Death and Dying

15.5 Analyze changing attitudes about the end of life.

> To every thing there is a season,
> And a time for every purpose under heaven:
> A time to be born and a time to die....

These well-known lines from the biblical book of Ecclesiastes state two basic truths about human existence: the fact of birth and the inevitability of death. Just as life varies throughout history and around the world, death has many faces. Death may occur at any age and be unexpected, but we conclude this chapter with a brief look at the changing character of death as the final stage in the process of growing old.

Historical Patterns of Death

In the past, death was a familiar part of life. Many children died soon after birth, a fact that led many parents to delay naming children until they were one or two years old. For those fortunate enough to survive infancy, illness, accidents, and natural catastrophes made life uncertain at best.

Sometimes food shortages forced societies to protect the majority by sacrificing the least productive members: *Infanticide* is the killing of newborn infants, and *geronticide* is the killing of the elderly. Because death was commonplace, it was readily accepted.

As industrializing societies gradually learned more about health and medicine, death became less of an everyday experience. Fewer children died at birth, and accidents and disease took a smaller toll among adults. As a result, most people living in high-income societies today view dying as extraordinary, something that happens to the very old or to younger people in rare and tragic cases.

In 1900, about one-third of all deaths in North America occurred before the age of five and fully two-thirds before the age of 55. Today, by contrast, 85 percent of our population dies after the age of 55. Death and old age are closely linked in our culture.

The Modern Separation of Life and Death

Now removed from everyday experience, death somehow seems unnatural. Social conditions prepared our ancestors to accept death, but modern society's youth culture and aggressive medical technology foster a desire for eternal youth and immortality. Death has become separated from our lives. Death is also *physically* removed from everyday activities. The clearest evidence of this is that few of us have ever seen a person die. Our ancestors typically died at home in the presence of family and friends, but most deaths today occur in impersonal settings such as hospitals and nursing homes. Even in hospitals, dying patients occupy a special part of the building, and hospital morgues are located well out of sight of patients and visitors alike (Ariès, 1974; Lee, 2002).

Chris Rainier/Corbis/Getty Images

IN MANY TRADITIONAL SOCIETIES, PEOPLE EXPRESS GREAT RESPECT NOT ONLY FOR ELDERS BUT ALSO FOR THEIR ANCESTORS Dani villagers in New Guinea mummified the body of this elder in a sitting position so that they could continue to honour him and feel his presence in their daily lives.

Ethical Issues: Confronting Death

In a society in which technology gives us the power to prolong life—or, conversely, to prolong the process of dying (McPherson, 2004:434)—moral questions about when and how people should die are more pressing than ever. For example, the debate in 2005 surrounding the death of American Terri Schiavo, who had been kept alive by mechanical means for 15 years, was not just about the fate of one woman; many people feel that we need a better understanding of what the right to die should be.

WHEN DOES DEATH OCCUR?   Perhaps the most basic question is the most difficult: Exactly how do we define death? Common sense suggests that life ceases when breathing and heartbeat stop. But the ability of medical personnel to resuscitate someone after a heart attack and artificially sustain breathing makes such definitions of death obsolete. Medical and legal experts continue to debate the meaning of death, but many now consider death an *irreversible* state involving no response to stimulation, no movement or breathing, no reflexes, and no indication of brain activity (Jones, 1998; Wall, 1980).

THE RIGHT-TO-DIE DEBATE   Terri Schiavo remained alive without evidence of being conscious or responsive to her surroundings for 15 years following a heart attack that cut off blood to her brain. Debate surrounding this case, which ended when her feeding tube was removed in 2005, reveals that many people are less afraid of death than of the prospect of being kept alive at all costs. In other words, medical technology that can sustain life also threatens personal freedom by letting doctors or others rather than the dying person decide when life is to end. In response, people who support a movement for the right to die now seek control over their deaths just as they seek control over their lives (Ogden, 2001). After thoughtful discussion, patients, families, and physicians may decide not to take "heroic measures" to keep a person alive. Physicians and family members may decide to issue a "do not resuscitate" order, which will allow a patient to die. Living wills—documents stating which medical procedures an individual wants and does not want under specific conditions—are now widely used in Canada and the United States.

A more difficult issue involves mercy killing, or **euthanasia**—*assisting in the death of a person suffering from an incurable disease.* Euthanasia (from the Greek, meaning "a good death") poses an ethical dilemma because it involves not just refusing treatment but actively taking steps to end life. Some people see euthanasia as an act of kindness, while others consider it a form of murder. In Canada and the United States, euthanasia is illegal—even physician-assisted suicide for the elderly and those who are terminally ill—but the issue continues to be hotly debated. One country, the Netherlands, settled the issue for itself and enacted the most permissive euthanasia law in the world.

Canadians did their own soul-searching about euthanasia in the early 1990s. Sue Rodrigues was diagnosed with the terminal illness amyotrophic lateral sclerosis (ALS, or Lou Gehrig's disease), which would lead to increasing disability and pain followed eventually by her death. Her situation was the subject of widespread media coverage because she applied to the courts—right up to the Supreme Court of Canada—for permission to have assistance in committing suicide. The Supreme Court turned her down. Less than a year later, in February 1994, Rodrigues arranged for assisted suicide with her friend, a Canadian member of parliament, Svend Robinson, at her side. Robinson had supported her through her court appeals and made it clear that he would be with her when she ended her life. The nature of the assistance Rodrigues required was never revealed, and Robinson was not charged with a crime.

Should Canada hold the line on euthanasia or follow the lead of the Netherlands? Right-to-die advocates maintain that, faced with unbearable suffering, an individual should be able to choose to live or die. And, if death is the choice, medical assistance should help people achieve a pain-free death (or death with dignity). On the other side of the debate, opponents fear that laws allowing physician-assisted suicide invite abuse. Pointing to the Netherlands, critics cite surveys indicating that, in most cases, the five conditions for physician-assisted suicide are not met. In particular, most physicians do not consult another doctor or even report the euthanasia to authorities. Of greater concern is the fact that, in about one-fifth of all physician-assisted suicides, the patient never explicitly asks to die. This is so even though half of these patients are conscious and capable of making decisions for themselves (Gillon, 1999). Such facts lead opponents to argue that legalizing physician-assisted suicide puts a nation on a slippery slope toward more and more euthanasia. How can we be sure, they ask, that ill people won't be pushed into accepting death by doctors who consider suicide to be the right choice for the terminally ill, or by family members who are weary of caring for them?

However the right-to-die debate turns out, Canadian society has entered a new era when it comes to dying. More often, individuals, family members, and medical personnel must face death not as a medical fact but as a negotiated outcome. Quebec is the first province to pass assisted-dying legislation. Theoretically, with certification by two physicians, patients can arrange for medically assisted suicide. Gone are the days when Quebec doctors risked criminal or civil prosecution for medically assisting death. Although the general public and physicians may agree—however reluctantly—with assisted death *in principle*, finding doctors willing to carry out the procedure is another matter. The Quebec experience has taught us that when there are few doctors willing to assist in the process of dying, finding them when they are needed is complicated (*CBC News*, 2016). In all likelihood, the passage of time will increase patient access to willing practitioners.

The Supreme Court of Canada struck down the law prohibiting assisted suicide on February 6, 2015 *without indicating* that "doctor-prescribed suicide and doctor-administered death would be limited to those who are diagnosed with a terminal illness." Canada's new Liberal government, which supports assisted dying in principle and practice, will be setting up special travelling teams "to deliver physician-assisted death to the country's remote regions to guarantee that patients can have their lives ended" (Patients Rights Council, 2016). These actions, combined with the example set by Quebec, take the right-to-die debate in Canada into new, as yet uncharted, territory.

Bereavement

Elisabeth Kübler-Ross (1969) found that most people confront their own death in stages. Initially, individuals react with *denial*, followed by *anger*; then they try *negotiation*, hoping for divine intervention. Gradually, they fall into *resignation* and finally reach *acceptance*.

According to some researchers, bereavement follows the same pattern of stages. Those close to a dying person, for instance, may initially deny the reality of impending death and then, with time, gradually reach a point of acceptance. Other investigators, however, question any "linear stage" theory, arguing that bereavement is a personal and unpredictable process (Cutcliffe, 1998; Lund, 1989; Lund et al., 1986). What experts do agree on, however, is the fact that how family and friends view an impending death has an effect on the person who is dying. By accepting an approaching death, others help the dying person do the same; denying death isolates the dying person, who is unable to share feelings and experiences with others.

Many dying people find support in the *hospice movement*. Unlike a hospital, which is designed to cure disease, a hospice helps people have a good death. These care centres for dying people try to minimize pain and suffering—either at the centre or at home—and encourage family members to stay close by. Most hospices also provide social support for family members experiencing bereavement (Foliart & Clausen, 2001).

Under the best of circumstances, bereavement involves profound grief. Research documents show that bereavement is less intense for someone who accepts the death of a loved one and has brought satisfactory closure to the relationship. Such closure also allows family and friends to better comfort one another after death occurs.

Reaching closure is not possible when a death is unexpected. Especially in such cases, social disorientation may be profound and may last for years. One study of

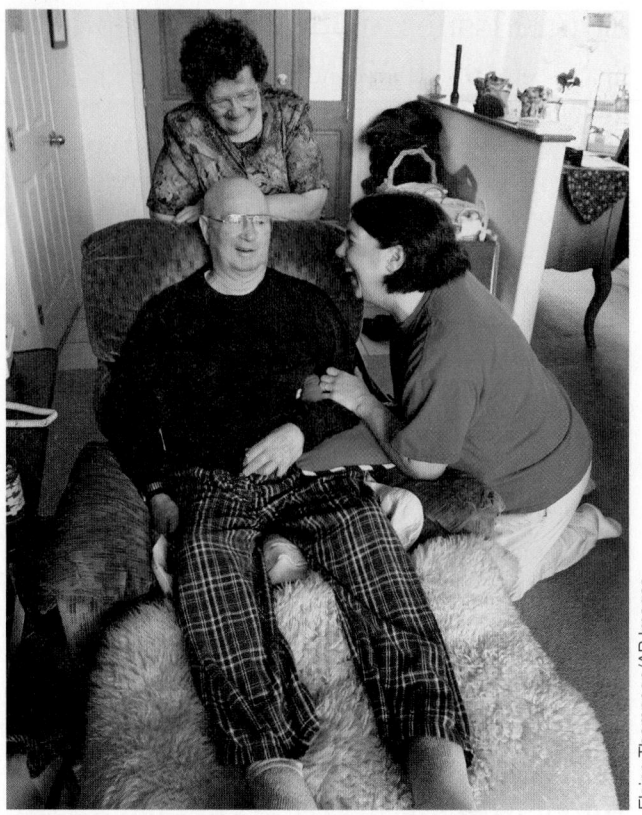

UNLIKE A HOSPITAL, WHICH TRIES TO SAVE AND EXTEND LIFE, A HOSPICE TRIES TO GIVE DYING PEOPLE GREATER COMFORT
The setting is, as much as possible, personal, and the dying person can have the companionship and support of family members.

middle-aged women who had recently experienced the death of their husbands found that many felt they had lost not only a spouse but also their reason for living. In such circumstances, dealing successfully with bereavement requires the time and social support necessary to form a new sense of self and to recognize new life options (Atchley, 1983; Danforth & Glass, 2001). With the number of older people increasing so fast, understanding death and dying is taking on greater importance.

Aging: Looking Ahead

This chapter has explored the greying of Canada and other high-income nations. By 2050, the elderly population of this country will exceed the population of the entire country in 1900—and one-quarter of our seniors will be older than 85. In decades to come, then, Canadian society's oldest members will gain a far greater voice in everyday life. Younger people will find that careers relating to gerontology (the study of elderly people) are increasingly important.

With more elderly people living longer and longer, will our society have the support services necessary to sustain them? Remember that, as the needs of elderly people increase, a smaller share of younger people will be there to respond and to pay the bills for social

Controversy and Debate

Setting Limits: Must We "Pull the Plug" on Old Age?

As our elderly population grows, as new technology gives us more power to prolong life, and as medical care becomes increasingly expensive, many wonder just how much old age we can afford. Currently, about half of the average person's lifetime spending on medical care occurs during the final years of life, and the share is rising. Against the spiralling costs of prolonging life, we well may ask if what is medically possible is morally desirable. In the decades to come, warns gerontologist Daniel Callahan (1987), a population of elderly people ready and eager to extend their lives will eventually force society either to pull the plug on old age or to shortchange everyone else.

Just raising this issue, Callahan admits, seems cold and heartless. But consider that the bill for health care of older people is doubling or quadrupling over time. This dramatic increase reflects the current policy of directing more and more medical resources to studying and treating the diseases and disabilities of old age. Callahan is writing about the American situation, but Canada must make similar decisions. The fact that almost all health care is publicly funded makes the problem here more acute: Taxpayers have to pay the whole bill, with no help from private wealth.

So Callahan makes the case for limits. First, the more we spend on the elderly, the less we can provide for others. With so many other demands, including child poverty, can we afford to spend more and more on the oldest members of our society?

Second, a *longer* life does not necessarily mean a *better* life. Cost aside, does heart surgery that prolongs the life of an 84-year-old woman for a year or two necessarily improve the quality of her life? Cost considered, would those resources yield more "quality of life" if used, say, to give a 10-year-old child a kidney transplant or to provide basic care and comfort to hundreds of low-income seniors?

Third, we need to reconsider our view of death as an enemy to be conquered at all costs. Rather, Callahan suggests, a more realistic position for an aging society is to treat death as a natural end to the life course. If we cannot make peace with death for our own well-being, then a society with limited resources must do it for the benefit of others.

But not everyone agrees. Shouldn't people who have worked all of their lives and made our society what it is enjoy our generosity in their final years? Is it right to deny medical care to aging people?

Today, we face questions that few would have imagined even 50 years ago. Is peak longevity good for everyone? Is it even *possible* for everyone?

What Do You Think?

1. Should doctors and hospitals use a double standard, offering more complete care to younger people and more limited care to the elderly? Why or why not?

2. Do you think that a goal of the medical establishment should be to extend life at all costs? Explain your position.

3. How should society balance the health care needs of elderly people with the needs of the rest of society (such as education, roads, public transit, clean water, and electricity), all of which are funded by the taxpayer?

SOURCE: Based on Callahan, 1987.

---

services with their taxes. What about the spiralling medical costs of an aging society? As the baby boomers enter old age, some analysts paint a doomsday picture, with desperate and dying elderly people everywhere (Longino, 1994). In contrast, David Foot (1998:275) argues that Europe has already learned to cope with proportions of elders greater than the 22 percent we expect to reach in Canada.

But there is also good news. For one thing, the health of tomorrow's elderly people (i.e., today's middle-aged adults) is better than ever. Smoking and alcohol consumption are down and, as more people become aware of the national problem of obesity, they are eating more healthfully. Such trends suggest that tomorrow's older Canadians may well be more vigorous and independent (as discussed in the Sociology and the Media box at the beginning of the chapter). They also will enjoy the benefits of steadily advancing medical technology—although, as the Controversy and Debate box explains, the question of how much of a country's medical resources older people can claim is already being hotly debated.

Another positive sign is the growing financial security of elderly people. While recent years have been stressful, it is likely that tomorrow's elders—not all of them, of course—will be more affluent than ever before. The baby boomer generation is the first with women who have been in the labour force for most of their lives and have substantial savings and pensions. At the same time, younger adults will face mounting responsibility to care for aging parents. A falling birth rate coupled with a growing elderly population means that middle-aged people will provide more elder care.

Most of us need to learn more about caring for aging parents, which includes far more than meeting physical needs. More important lessons involve communicating, expressing love, and facing up to eventual death. In caring for our parents, we will also teach important lessons to our children, including the skills they will need, one day, to care for us.

Seeing Sociology in Everyday Life

CHAPTER 15   Aging and the Elderly

How are older adults changing today's society?

A lot has been said about the baby boomers—the women and men born between 1945 and 1964—who were the driving force behind many of the changes that took place in the 1960s and 1970s. Women's rights and gay rights reflect just two of the social movements they invented or carried on. Now, as this cohort begins to enter old age, it is rewriting the rules once again, this time about what it means to be old.

> **Hint** The baby boomers have been a cohort making change, and as they have aged they have redefined every stage of life. As elders, they appear determined to maintain active lives well beyond the traditional time of retirement. The celebrities pictured here also suggest that older people can be sexy—and the generation that brought sex out into the open for young people is defining sex as a part of growing old. The social justice values that defined the boomers as young people still seem to drive them as seniors. Most of all, they appear determined that their political voice will be heard.

Ryan Remiorz/AP Images

MICK JAGGER AND KEITH RICHARDS LAUNCHED THE ROLLING STONES ALMOST 50 YEARS AGO AND THEY CONTINUE TO PERFORM AS THEY REACH THEIR LATE SIXTIES What do these stars of popular culture say about older men?

James Devaney/WireImage/Getty Images

A MUCH YOUNGER PAUL MCCARTNEY WROTE THE LYRICS TO "WHEN I'M SIXTY-FOUR," PROBABLY NEVER IMAGINING THAT HE WOULD STILL BE WRITING MUSIC AND PERFORMING TODAY—HE REACHED AGE 70 IN 2012 In what ways is he a role model for elders?

Toronto Star/Getty Images

NOVA SCOTIA–BORN ANNE MURRAY, WHOSE EARLY SONG "SNOWBIRD" HIT NUMBER ONE ON BOTH CANADIAN AND AMERICAN CHARTS, IS STILL PERFORMING AND RECORDING IN HER LATE SIXTIES, ADDING TO HER MANY ALBUMS, WHICH HAVE SOLD OVER 54 MILLION COPIES.

Seeing Sociology in *Your* Everyday Life

1. Ask several faculty members nearing retirement about the practices and policies of your college or university for helping older faculty ease into retirement. Based on what you learn, decide whether retiring from an academic career is harder or easier than retiring from other kinds of work, and explain why.

2. Look through an issue of a popular magazine—say, *Maclean's* or *People*—and note pictures of men and women in news stories and advertising. What share of the pictures show elderly people? In what types of advertising are they featured?

3. Obtain a copy of a living will (through an online search) and try to respond to all of the questions it asks. How does filling out this form affect your thinking about death?

Making the Grade

CHAPTER 15 Aging and the Elderly

The Greying of Canada

15.1 Explain the increasing share of elderly people in modern societies.

The "greying of Canada" means that the average age of our population is steadily going up.

- The elderly population is increasing more than twice as fast as the population as a whole.
- In 2011, the median age was 40.6 and elderly people made up 14.8 of the population.

In high-income countries like Canada, the share of elderly people has been increasing for two reasons:

- Birth rates have been falling as families choose to have fewer children.
- Life expectancy has been rising as living standards improve and medical advances reduce deaths from infectious diseases.

As our population ages, cultural patterns are likely to change, with elderly people becoming more evident in everyday life.

Growing Old: Biology and Culture

15.2 Describe age stratification in global context.

Biological and psychological changes are associated with aging.

- Although people's health becomes more fragile with advancing age, affluent elderly people experience fewer health problems than poor people.
- Psychological research confirms that growing old does not result in overall loss of intelligence or major changes in personality.

Although aging is a biological process, how elderly people are regarded by society is a matter of **culture**.

The age at which people are defined as old varies:

- Until several centuries ago, old age began as early as 30.
- In poor societies today, where life expectancy is low, people become old at 50 or even 40.

Age Stratification: A Global Survey

- In hunting/gathering societies, where survival depends on physical stamina, both the very young and the very old contribute less to society.
- In agrarian societies, elders are typically the most privileged and respected members of society, a pattern known as **gerontocracy**.

- In industrial and post-industrial societies, the social standing of the elderly is low because the fast pace of social change is dominated by the young.

> **gerontology** the study of aging and the elderly
> **age stratification** the unequal distribution of wealth, power, and privilege among people at different stages of the life course
> **gerontocracy** a form of social organization in which older people have the most wealth, power, and prestige

Transitions and Challenges of Aging

15.3 Describe problems related to aging.

Personal challenges that elderly people face include

- the realization that one's life is nearing an end
- social isolation caused by the death of friends or a spouse, physical disability, or retirement from one's job
- reduced social prestige and a loss of purpose in life due to retirement

A person's risk of **poverty** rises after midlife but, since 1985, the poverty rate for the elderly has fallen steadily to the point that it is now below the poverty rate (or low-income rate) for the Canadian population as a whole.

- The aged poor include categories of people—such as single women and visible minorities—who are at high risk of poverty at any age.
- Some retired people have had to return to work as a result of the recent economic downturn.

The need for **caregiving** is increasing in our aging society.

- Most caregiving for the elderly is performed by family members, typically women.
- Unknown numbers of elderly people are victims of **elder abuse** each year.

Ageism—prejudice and discrimination against older people—is used to justify age stratification.

- Like racism and sexism, ageism builds physical traits into stereotypes that make unfair generalizations about all elderly people.

The fact that the elderly include men and women of all races, ethnicities, and social classes suggests that older people do not constitute a minority.

> **caregiving** informal and unpaid care provided to a dependent person by family members, other relatives, or friends
> **ageism** prejudice and discrimination against older people

Theories of Aging

15.4 Apply sociology's major theories to the topic of aging.

The **structural-functional approach** points to the role that aging plays in the orderly operation of society.

- **Disengagement theory** suggests that society helps the elderly disengage from positions of social responsibility before the onset of disability or death.
- The process of disengagement provides for the orderly transfer of statuses and roles from the older to the younger generation.

The **symbolic-interaction approach** focuses on the meanings that people attach to growing old.

- **Activity theory** claims that a high level of activity increases people's personal satisfaction in old age.
- People must find new roles in old age to replace the ones they left behind.

The **social-conflict approach** highlights the inequalities in opportunities and social resources available to people in different age categories.

- A capitalist society's emphasis on economic efficiency leads to the devaluation of those who are less productive, including the elderly.
- Some categories of elderly people—namely, women and other minorities—have less economic security, less access to quality medical care, and fewer options for personal satisfaction in old age than others.

disengagement theory the idea that society functions in an orderly way by disengaging people from positions of responsibility as they reach old age

activity theory the idea that a high level of activity increases personal satisfaction in old age

Death and Dying

15.5 Analyze changing attitudes about the end of life.

Historical perspective

- In the past, death was a familiar part of everyday life and was accepted as a natural event that might occur at any age.
- Modern society has set death physically apart from everyday activities, and advances in medical technology have resulted in people's inability or unwillingness to accept death.
- This avoidance of death also reflects the fact that most people in high-income societies die in old age.

Ethical issues: confronting death

- Our society's power to prolong life has sparked a debate as to the circumstances under which a dying person should be kept alive by medical means.
- People who support a person's right to die seek control over the process of their own dying.
- **Euthanasia** poses an ethical dilemma because it involves not just refusing treatment but actively taking steps to end a person's life;

Bereavement

- Some researchers believe that the process of bereavement follows the same pattern of stages as a dying person coming to accept approaching death: denial, anger, negotiation, resignation, and acceptance.
- The **hospice movement** offers support to dying people and their families.

euthanasia assisting in the death of a person suffering from an incurable disease; also known as mercy killing

Chapter 16
The Economy and Work

Monkey Business Images/Shutterstock

∨ Learning Objectives

16.1 Summarize historical changes to the economy.

16.2 Assess the operation of capitalist and socialist economies.

16.3 Analyze patterns of employment and unemployment in Canada.

16.4 Discuss the importance of corporations to the Canadian economy.

The Power of Society
to shape your choices in jobs

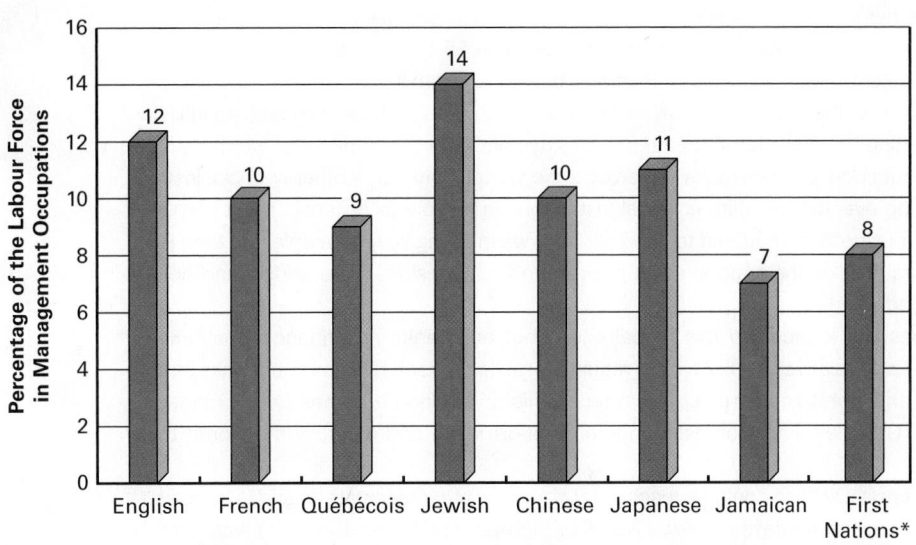

*First Nations combines First Nations (status Indians) and non-status Indians.

SOURCE: Compilation and calculations by LM Gerber based on Statistics Canada, NHS 2011, Catalogue no. 99-010-X2011036.

Will the jobs you have throughout your life reflect choices you make based on your personal abilities and interests? To some extent, yes. But the work we do has a lot to do with our position in society and the fact that society distributes opportunity unequally. In Canada, ethnic origins affect your chances of working in management. People claiming Jewish origins are twice as likely to be managers as those of Jamaican ancestry. People of English ancestry are also overrepresented among managers, whereas people of First Nations or Québécois roots clearly are not. The effects of ethnicity on occupation would be stronger still if each category were not a mix of ethnicities and races. Francophone Quebecers—namely French, Québécois, and *Canadien* (not included here)—as well as all but the Chinese, tend to report multiple ancestries (the census or NHS allows four). The most remarkable thing is that, *despite* ethnic and racial mixing, the effects of ethnic ancestry on life chances—in this case occupation—are still clearly apparent.

Chapter Overview

This chapter begins a survey of the major social institutions. We begin with the economy, which is the institution widely regarded as having the greatest impact on society as a whole. The chapter explores the operation of the economy and also explains how revolutionary changes in economic production have reshaped society.

Courtesy of the OSFI

"The most powerful woman in Canadian banking" may be called quiet, low-key, or unassuming, but "when she speaks, bank CEOs across the land take notes." From 2007 to 2014, Julie Dickson headed the Office of the Superintendent of Financial Institutions (OSFI)—that is, Canada's financial regulator. It was her job, as the "top cop," to ensure that our financial institutions were not taking undue risks. Dickson oversaw the management of some $5 trillion in assets, while advising G7 leaders "on potential reforms to the international banking system."

The meltdown in the global economy began in 2007, just as Dickson was settling into her new job and putting her own stamp on our financial system. The economic crisis started in the United States, but soon had repercussions around the world: Banks and other financial institutions were folding everywhere. With financial institutions in trouble or collapsing, big corporations and small businesses struggled to keep afloat. It wasn't long before people lost their jobs and the crisis was felt on the streets; stock prices tumbled; pensions were at risk; and house prices plummeted.

Canada was not immune to this global crisis, but our banks and financial institutions weathered the storm relatively well. As chief regulator, "Julie Dickson has kept our banks stable through one of the worst economic crises in recent history." When it comes to risk management, she kept Canada's financial institutions on a short leash and carefully monitored their annual reports.

During the crisis, Dickson could be reached by government representatives and bank executives 24 hours a day, seven days a week. Like other high-powered executives, she was permanently wired. She has been called the saviour of Canada's banking system, but doesn't like being put on a pedestal. When asked about the wild ride of the global crisis, Dickson replied with dry understatement, "The job has been more interesting than I anticipated" (Perkins, 2009). ■

This chapter examines the economy, widely considered to be the most influential of all social institutions. It also explores the character of work and explains some of the consequences of the emerging global marketplace for Canadians. We will see that a good deal of the conventional wisdom about economic life no longer applies in the face of sweeping global changes. The global economic upheaval described above gave rise to the second recession experienced by Canadians since the early 1990s. In periods of economic stability or upheaval, sociologists debate how the economy operates, whose interests it serves, the nature of work, and what jobs mean to us.

The Economy: Historical Overview

16.1 Summarize historical changes to the economy.

The **economy** is *the social institution that organizes a society's production, distribution, and consumption of goods and services.* As an institution, the economy operates in a

generally predictable manner. Goods are commodities ranging from necessities (food, clothing, shelter) to luxury items (cars, swimming pools, yachts). Services are activities that benefit others (e.g., the work of priests, physicians, teachers, couriers, and software specialists). In Canada, more than in the United States, governments are involved in the distribution of a number of these services.

We value goods and services because they ensure survival or because they make life easier or more interesting. Also, what people produce as workers and what they buy as consumers are important parts of social identity, as when we say, "He's a steelworker," or "She drives a Mercedes." The distribution of goods and services, then, shapes the lives of everyone in basic ways.

The economies of modern high-income nations are the result of centuries of social change. We turn now to three technological revolutions that reorganized production and, in the process, transformed social life.

The Agricultural Revolution

The earliest human societies were made up of hunters and gatherers living off the land. In these technologically simple societies, there was no distinct economy. Rather, production and consumption took place within the family. When people harnessed animals to ploughs some 5000 years ago, a new agricultural economy was created that was 50 times more productive than hunting and gathering. The resulting surplus meant that not everyone had to produce food, so many took on specialized work: making tools, raising animals, or building homes. Soon towns sprang up, linked by networks of traders dealing in food, animals, and other goods. These four factors—agricultural technology, job specialization, permanent settlements, and trade—made the economy a distinct social institution.

The Industrial Revolution

By the mid-eighteenth century, a second technological revolution was under way, first in England and then in North America: the Industrial Revolution. The development of industry was even more powerful than that of agriculture in bringing change to the economy. Industrialization changed the economy in five fundamental ways:

1. **New sources of energy.** Throughout history, "energy" meant the muscle power of people or animals. But in 1765, English inventor James Watt introduced the steam engine, so that steam engines—a hundred times stronger than muscle power—soon drove heavy machinery.

2. **Centralization of work in factories.** Steam-powered machines soon moved work from homes to factories, the centralized and impersonal workplaces that housed the machines.

3. **Manufacturing and mass production.** Before the Industrial Revolution, most people grew or gathered

THE RISE OF A GLOBAL ECONOMY MEANS THAT MORE AND MORE PRODUCTS ORIGINALLY PRODUCED IN ONE COUNTRY—E.G., COCA-COLA—ARE NOW MADE AND CONSUMED AROUND THE WORLD What do you see as some of the good consequences of globalization? What about harmful consequences?

Sven-Olof Lindblad/Photo Researchers, Inc./Science Source

raw materials such as grain, wood, or wool. In an industrial economy, the focus shifts so that most people work to turn raw materials into a wide range of finished products such as furniture and clothing.

4. **Specialization.** Before industrialization, people worked at home as artisans, making products from start to finish. In the factory, a worker repeats a single task over and over, making only a small contribution to the finished product. Such specialization raises productivity but lowers the skill level of the average worker.

5. **Wage labour.** Instead of working for themselves, factory workers became wage labourers working for strangers, who often cared less for them than for the machines they operated.

The Industrial Revolution gradually raised the standard of living as countless new products and services fuelled an expanding marketplace. Yet the benefits of industrial technology were shared very unequally, especially at the beginning. Some factory owners made vast fortunes, while the majority of industrial workers lived close to poverty. Women working in factories were among the most poorly paid; children, too, worked in factories or in coal mines for pennies a day. The Thinking about Diversity box looks at the experience of francophone Canadians in an American textile factory.

The Information Revolution and Post-Industrial Society

By the middle of the twentieth century, the nature of production was changing once again. Canada was becoming a **post-industrial economy**, *a productive system based on service work and high technology*. Automated machinery—and, more recently, robotics—reduced the role of human labour in factory production and expanded the ranks of clerical workers and managers.

Driving this change is a third technological breakthrough: the computer. Just as the Industrial Revolution did two-and-a-half centuries ago, the Information Revolution has introduced new kinds of products and new forms of communication and has altered the character of work. In general, there have been three significant changes:

1. **From tangible products to ideas.** The industrial era was defined by the production of goods; in the post-industrial era, people work with symbols. Computer programmers, graphic designers, financial analysts, advertising executives, architects, editors, and all sorts of consultants make up the labour force of the information age.

2. **From mechanical skills to literacy skills.** The Industrial Revolution required mechanical skills, but the Information Revolution requires literacy skills:

Thinking About Diversity: Race, Class, and Gender

The French Canadians of Manchester, New Hampshire

In the 1870s, French-Canadian immigrants who had been forced out of impoverished farming areas by a scarcity of land found their way, in substantial numbers, from rural Quebec to the Amoskeag mills in Manchester, New Hampshire. The mill owners soon concluded that French Canadians were the ideal labour force, and Amoskeag proceeded

11450—"Picking the cloth" after weaving, scene in a modern silk mill, Paterson, N.J.   © Underwood & Underwood, U-139766

Library of Congress Prints and Photographs Division [LC-USZ62-7316]

THE AMOSKEAG MANUFACTURING COMPANY, ONCE THE LARGEST TEXTILE FACTORY IN THE WORLD, WAS THE PILLAR OF ECONOMIC LIFE IN MANCHESTER, NEW HAMPSHIRE From its founding in 1837 to its closing in 1935, the Amoskeag plant provided the major source of employment in Manchester and controlled the development of the city as a whole. When the company was initially founded, a community of young women from rural New England worked at the factory, living together in boarding houses with a 10 p.m. curfew and compulsory church attendance. Irish immigrant families, who were willing to work for lower wages, eventually replaced the mill girls.

to recruit them actively. Mill agents scanned the Quebec countryside for possible recruits, and advertisements in Quebec newspapers extolled the virtues of Amoskeag and Manchester.

French-Canadian workers were ideal in part because they had large families. Entire families, including children, were brought into the mills and could be counted on to draw kinfolk with their own large families. So numerous did they become that the mill bosses were forced to learn a little French. This large group was appreciated by management because it proved to be a "docile," "industrious," and "stable" labour force with a family-based structure that discouraged union involvement. Despite their numbers, however, not one French Canadian was promoted into the supervisory ranks. These positions were filled by native-born Americans or immigrants of British and northern European stock.

Migration from Quebec to Manchester—a convenient stop on the railway linking Montreal and Boston—was so substantial that, by 1910, French Canadians made up 35 percent of the Amoskeag labour force and 38 percent of the population of Manchester. Some of the families that migrated to Manchester stayed only long enough to save some money before returning to their farms in Quebec. Others put down permanent roots and contributed a French flavour to life in the section of Manchester that is still called Little Canada.

What Do You Think?

1. What would have happened if the French Canadians who moved to Manchester and elsewhere in New England had gone to Ontario instead? What would Ontario look like today if, from the beginning, francophone migrants had gone west instead of south?

2. Why was Amoskeag so anxious to recruit workers from Quebec?

3. What does this story tell you about the migration patterns of families?

SOURCE: Based on Hareven and Langenbach (1978).

speaking and writing well and, of course, knowing how to use a computer. People able to communicate effectively enjoy new opportunities; people without these skills face fewer opportunities.

3. **From factories to almost anywhere.** Industrial technology drew workers into factories located near power sources, but computer technology allows people to work almost anywhere. Laptop and wireless computers, cellphones, and especially smartphones now turn the home, a car, or even an airplane into a

"virtual" office. In short, new information technology blurs the line between work and home life.

Sectors of the Economy

The three revolutions just described reflect a shifting balance among the three sectors of the economy. The **primary sector** is *the part of the economy that draws raw materials from the natural environment.* The primary sector—agriculture, raising animals, fishing, forestry, and

● In high-income nations such as Canada, three out of four jobs are in the tertiary or service sector of the economy.

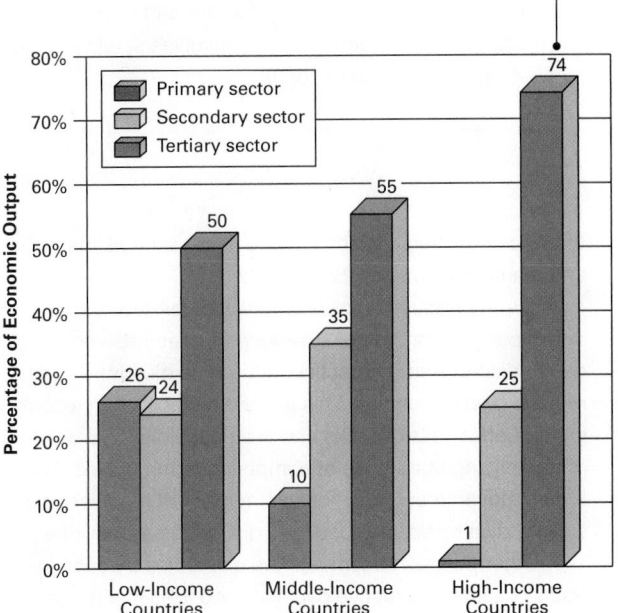

Figure 16–1 The Size of Economic Sectors, by Income Level of Country

As countries become richer, the primary sector becomes a smaller part of the economy and the tertiary or service sector becomes larger.

SOURCE: Estimates based on World Bank (2015).

quickly as societies industrialize, includes operations such as refining petroleum into gasoline and turning metals into tools and automobiles. The globalization of industry means that just about all of the world's countries have a significant share of their workers in the secondary sector. Canada's secondary sector (see Figure 16–2) is small by world standards, but has remained fairly stable since 1871. Despite concerns about the effects of globalization, our manufacturing, or goods-producing, sector did not drop below 20 percent until the census of 2006. By 2011, it had dropped to a new low of 17 percent. Unfortunately, our secondary sector is smaller than that of other countries—regardless of income level (see Figure 16–1). Canada has lost manufacturing jobs to lower-wage countries in response to globalization—the result being that, despite the growth of new manufacturing industries, our secondary sector has suffered unprecedented setbacks.

The Thinking Critically box looks at the distribution of secondary sector employment—in terms of the percentage of the labour force employed in manufacturing—across Canada's provinces and territories.

The **tertiary sector** is *the part of the economy that involves services rather than goods.* Accounting for percent of the labour force in low-income countries, the tertiary sector grows with industrialization and dominates the economies of middle- and high-income countries (59 and 72 percent, respectively). More than three-quarters of the

mining or oil and gas extraction—is largest in low-income nations. Figure 16–1 shows that 26 percent of the labour force is employed in the primary sector in low-income countries, compared to 10 percent in middle-income nations and just 1 percent in high-income countries. Figure 16–2 traces the decline of the primary sector in Canada from 41 percent of the labour force in 1871 to 4.0 percent in 2011. Note that the primary sector was larger in Canada in 1871, 1961, and 2011 than in the low-, middle-, and high-income countries depicted in Figure 16–1. In earlier years, this reflected the importance of farming; more recently, it reflects the continuing importance of oil, mining, and forestry. In Alberta, the primary sector, at 9.5 percent, is more than double the Canadian average of 4.0 percent. However, as a result of the collapse in oil prices, Alberta's primary sector will be much smaller when the outcome of Census 2016 is known.

The **secondary sector** is *the part of the economy that transforms raw materials into manufactured goods.* This sector, which grows

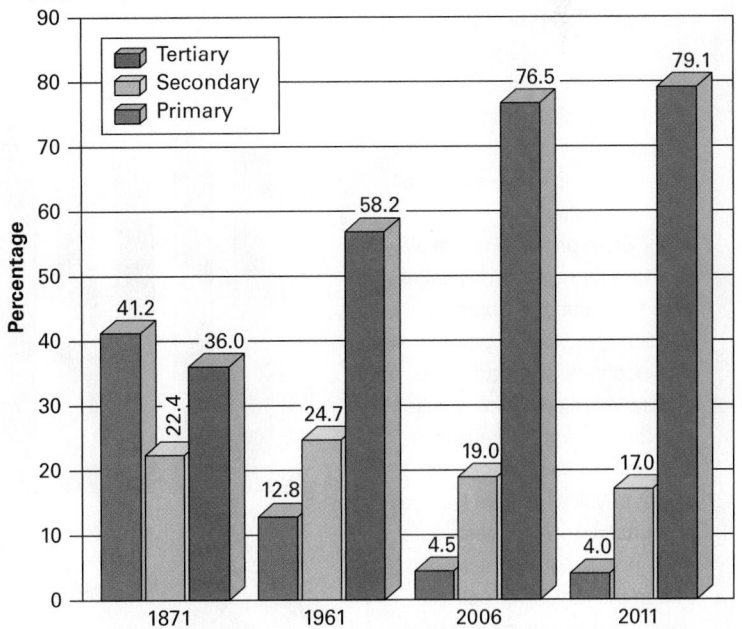

Figure 16–2 The Canadian Economic Structure, 1871–2011 (Percentages)

SOURCE: Adapted by LM Gerber from Watson (1988) and Statistics Canada, NHS 2011, Catalogue no. 99-010-X2011036.

Sectors of the Economy

primary sector the part of the economy that draws raw materials from the natural environment

secondary sector the part of the economy that transforms raw materials into manufactured goods

tertiary sector the part of the economy that involves services rather than goods

Thinking Critically

Regional Economic Disparities

Manufacturing industries are considered by some to be the real wealth-creating engine of our economy. Figure 16–3 shows the variation in the percentage of the Canadian labour force employed in manufacturing industries for different regions of Canada. Although one can debate the definition of "region" (Brodie, 1989), there is some justification for defining regions of Canada as units with political boundaries (Breton, 1981; Matthews, 1983). Since measuring regional disparities is easier if data are collected regularly for the units in question, regions are defined here in terms of provinces and territories.

Despite consistent official efforts to promote regional development and to spread the manufacturing base more evenly throughout Canada, Ontario and Quebec remain the manufacturing core of the Canadian economy, with 18 percent of their workers involved. Another way of looking at the manufacturing clout of Ontario and Quebec is to note that the two provinces have 65 percent of Canada's manufacturing jobs. Saskatchewan has the smallest manufacturing base of all of the provinces—just above the level in the three territories. As recently as in 2011, the manufacturing gap between British Columbia and Ontario or Quebec was 3 percentage points. Even Alberta's manufacturing sector is smaller than that of Canada on the whole—in part because its primary sector (oil and gas extraction) is so large.

Brym provides two explanations for regional disparities: the "mainstream" approach and the "radical" or political economy approach. The mainstream approach focuses on the geographic causes of diversity: distance from markets, physical barriers (such as mountains), natural resources, and population characteristics. From the radical, or political economy, perspective, inequities derive from human actions rather than nature, in that confederation allowed "powerful central Canadian economic interests to drain wealth from

the weak peripheral or hinterland regions" such as the prairie and maritime provinces (Brym, 1986:8).

Some policies of federal, provincial/territorial, and municipal governments are designed to decrease economic disparities by attracting industry to disadvantaged regions or communities. This is done by facilitating rezoning and offering tax breaks and even subsidies that are more enticing than those of competing communities. The federal government has moved a number of its offices outside Ottawa to reduce economic disparities even further.

Other policies accentuate the disparities by concentrating capital, productive capacity, and jobs in a particular region. Not long ago, the western provinces—Alberta in particular—were facing a desperate shortage of workers even though migrants were arriving in large numbers from other provinces and countries (including the United States). The population flow to Alberta translated into economic growth and ultimately political power (i.e., increased representation in Parliament in the form of several new electoral districts), resulting in new polices that favoured the West. With the collapse of oil prices, population has been flowing out of Alberta, but the increased number of electoral districts and MPs remains in place. Until Alberta recovers from

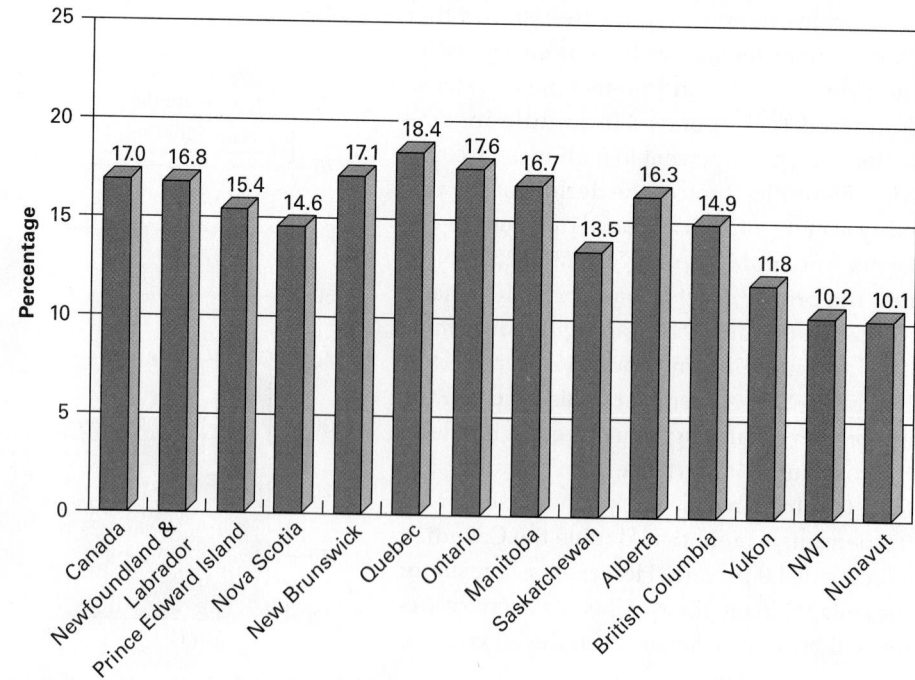

Figure 16–3 Percentage of Labour Force Employed in Manufacturing Industries (the Secondary Sector) in Canada, 2011

SOURCE: Compilation and calculations by LM Gerber, based on Statistics Canada NHS 2011, Catalogue no. 99-010-X2011036.

this setback it may be overrepresented in Ottawa relative to its population and the size of its economy.

What Do You Think?

1. Should governments take steps to reduce economic disparities throughout Canada, through subsidies or tax breaks?

2. Why is it important, for regional economies, that manufacturing be spread more evenly throughout the country?

3. Should we allow economic and political clout to flow to Alberta and other western provinces?

Canadian labour force—a full 79 percent—is involved in service work, including secretarial and clerical work, food services, sales, web design, law, health care, law enforcement, advertising, public administration, and teaching from preschool to university. This dramatic increase in the Canadian service sector was a result of the shift in labour from the primary (extraction) sector more than from the secondary (manufacturing) sector. Note that our tertiary sector is larger than that of other high-income countries.

The Global Economy

As Marshall McLuhan predicted, new information technology is drawing people around the world closer together and creating a **global economy**, *economic activity that crosses national borders*. The development of a global economy has five major consequences.

- First, we see a global division of labour. Different regions of the world specialize in one sector of economic activity. As Global Map 16–1 shows,

Window on the World

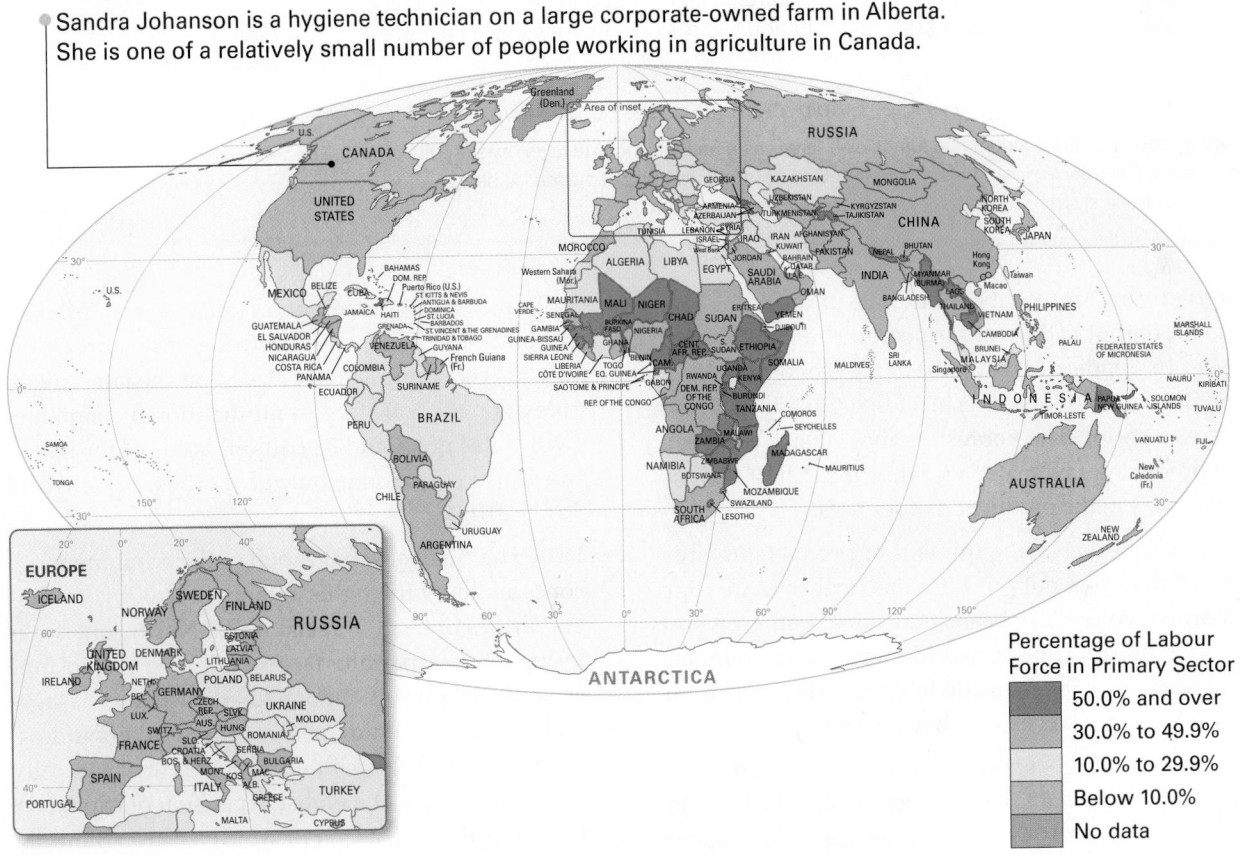

Sandra Johanson is a hygiene technician on a large corporate-owned farm in Alberta. She is one of a relatively small number of people working in agriculture in Canada.

Percentage of Labour Force in Primary Sector
- 50.0% and over
- 30.0% to 49.9%
- 10.0% to 29.9%
- Below 10.0%
- No data

Global Map 16–1 Agricultural Employment in Global Perspective

The primary sector of the economy is largest in the nations that are least developed. Thus in the poor countries of Africa and Asia, up to half of all workers are farmers. This picture is altogether different in the world's most economically developed countries—including the United States, Canada, Great Britain, and Australia—which have only about 1 percent of their labor force in agriculture.

SOURCE: Data from International Labour Organization (2014).

Window on the World

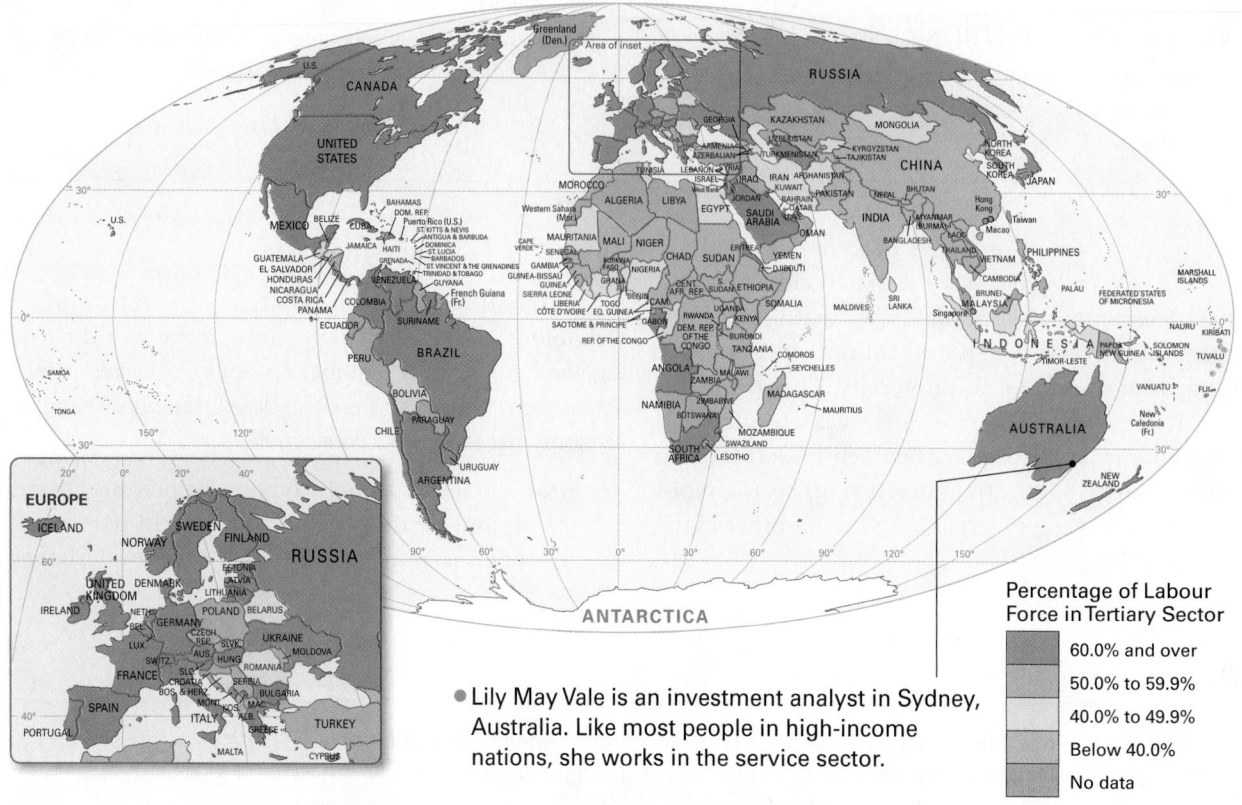

Percentage of Labour
Force in Tertiary Sector

60.0% and over
50.0% to 59.9%
40.0% to 49.9%
Below 40.0%
No data

● Lily May Vale is an investment analyst in Sydney, Australia. Like most people in high-income nations, she works in the service sector.

Global Map 16–2 Service-Sector Employment in Global Perspective

The tertiary sector of the economy becomes ever larger as a nation's income level rises. In the United States, Canada, the countries of Western Europe, much of South America, Australia, and Japan, about three-quarters of the labor force performs service work.

SOURCE: Data from International Labour Organization (2014).

agriculture represents about half of the total economic output of the world's poorest countries. Global Map 16–2 indicates that most of the economic output of high-income countries, including Canada, is in the service sector. The poorest nations, then, specialize in producing raw materials, while the richest nations specialize in the production of services.

- Second, an increasing number of products involve more than one nation. Look no further than your morning coffee: The beans may have been grown in Colombia and transported to Canada on a freighter registered in Liberia, made in Japan using steel from Korea, and fuelled by oil from Venezuela.

- Third, national governments no longer control the economic activity that takes place within their borders. In fact, governments cannot even regulate the value of their national currencies because dollars, euros, pounds sterling, and yen are traded around the clock in financial markets in Toronto, New York, Tokyo, and elsewhere. Global markets are a network using satellite communications to link the world's businesses and markets.

- Fourth, a small number of businesses, operating internationally, now control a vast share of the world's economic activity. Based on the latest available data, the 2000 largest multinational companies (with sales of about $38 trillion) account for half of the world's economic output (Forbes, 2014; World Bank, 2015).

- Fifth, and finally, globalization of the economy raises concerns about the rights and opportunities of workers. Critics of this trend claim that North America is losing jobs—especially factory jobs—to low-income nations. As a result, workers here face lower wages and higher unemployment, while workers in low-income nations are paid extremely low wages. As a result, say critics, the global expansion of capitalism threatens the well-being of workers throughout the world.

The world is still divided into 194 politically distinct nations. But increasing international economic activity makes "nationhood" less significant than it was even a decade ago.

Economic Systems: Paths to Justice

16.2 Assess the operation of capitalist and socialist economies.

Every society's economic system makes a statement about justice by determining who is entitled to what. Two general economic models are capitalism and socialism. No nation anywhere in the world has an economy that is completely one or the other; capitalism and socialism represent two ends of a continuum along which all real-world economies can be located. We now look, in turn, at these two models.

Capitalism

Capitalism is *an economic system in which natural resources and the means of producing goods and services are privately owned.* An ideal capitalist economy has three distinctive features:

1. **Private ownership of property.** In a capitalist economy, individuals can own almost anything. The more capitalistic an economy is, the more private ownership there is of wealth-producing property such as factories, real estate, and natural resources.
2. **Pursuit of personal profit.** A capitalist society seeks to create profit and wealth. The profit motive inspires people to open new businesses, modernize for greater efficiency, or improve their products. Scottish philosopher Adam Smith (1723–1790) claimed that, when individuals pursue their self-interest, the entire society prospers (1937; orig. 1776).
3. **Competition and consumer choice.** A purely capitalist economy is a free-market system with no government interference (sometimes called a *laissez-faire economy,* from the French words meaning "leave it alone"). Adam Smith stated that a freely competitive economy regulates itself by the "invisible hand" of the law of supply and demand.

    Consumers regulate a free-market economy, Smith explained, by selecting the goods and services offering the greatest value. As producers compete for the customer's business, they provide the highest-quality goods at the lowest possible prices. In Smith's time-honoured phrase, from narrow self-interest comes the "greatest good for the greatest number of people." Government control of an economy distorts market forces driven by supply and demand.

To supporters of capitalist enterprise, justice is freedom of the marketplace—where one can produce, invest, and buy according to individual self-interest. Tim Horton can create a chain of doughnut shops; Grandma can invest in Nortel; and shoppers can spend at The Bay or on eBay.

While Canada is a capitalist society, government plays an extensive role in economic affairs—making ours a capitalist system with socialist leanings. Through taxation and various regulatory agencies, governments influence what companies produce, the quality and cost of merchandise, the products that are imported and exported, and how we consume or conserve natural resources. In the past, our government was able to define and determine the extent of "Canadian content" and more generally what we saw on television or heard on the radio. The rise of social media and the increased capacity of the internet to provide information and entertainment have weakened government control of broadcasting. Nonetheless, governments own and operate a number of businesses, including the Canadian Broadcasting Corporation, VIA Rail, Atomic Energy of Canada, and Hydro-Québec. Our governments regulate securities, step in to prevent the collapse of businesses (as in loans to General Motors or Bombardier), mandate minimum wages, enforce workplace safety standards, regulate corporate mergers, provide farm price supports, and administer employment insurance, welfare, and pensions. Not surprisingly, federal, provincial/territorial, and municipal governments employ 7.2 percent of Canada's labour force in public administration.

Socialism

Socialism is *an economic system in which natural resources and the means of producing goods and services are collectively owned.* In its ideal form, a socialist economy rejects each of the three characteristics of capitalism just described in favour of three opposite features:

1. **Collective ownership of property.** A socialist economy limits rights to private property, especially property used to generate income. Government controls such property and makes housing and other goods available to all, not just to the people with the most money.
2. **Pursuit of collective goals.** The individualistic pursuit of profit goes against the collective orientation of socialism. What capitalism celebrates as the "entrepreneurial spirit," socialism condemns as greed; individuals are urged to work for the common good of all.
3. **Government control of the economy.** Socialism rejects capitalism's laissez-faire approach in favour of a *centrally controlled* or *command economy* operated by the government. Commercial advertising therefore has only a small role in socialist economies.

Justice in a socialist context means not competing to gain wealth but meeting everyone's basic needs in a roughly equal manner. From a socialist point of view, the

CAPITALISM STILL THRIVES IN HONG KONG (*LEFT*), EVIDENT IN STREETS CHOKED WITH ADVERTISING AND SHOPPERS
Socialism is more the rule in China's capital, Beijing (*right*), a city dominated by government buildings rather than a downtown business district.

common capitalist practice of giving workers as little in pay and benefits as possible, to boost company earnings, is putting profits before people and is unjust.

Venezuela, Cuba, North Korea, the People's Republic of China, and more than two dozen other nations in Asia, Africa, and Latin America model their economies on socialism, placing almost all wealth-generating property under state control (*The Wall Street Journal*/Heritage Foundation, 2015). The extent of world socialism declined during the 1990s as most of the countries in Eastern Europe and the former Soviet Union geared their economies toward a market system. More recently, however, voters in Bolivia, Venezuela, Ecuador, and other nations in South America have elected leaders who have moved the national economies in a socialist direction.

Socialism and Communism

Many people think of *socialism* and *communism* as the same thing, but they are not. **Communism** is *a hypothetical economic and political system in which all members of a society are socially equal.* Karl Marx viewed socialism as one important step on the path toward the ideal of a communist society that abolishes all class divisions. In many socialist societies today, the dominant political party describes itself as communist, but the communist goal has not been achieved in any country.

Why? For one thing, social stratification involves differences in power as well as wealth. Socialist societies have reduced economic differences by regulating people's range of choices. In the process, government did not "wither away," as Marx imagined it would; rather, government has grown, giving socialist political elites enormous power and privilege.

Marx might have agreed that a communist society is a utopia (from Greek words meaning "no place"), an ideal society. Yet Marx considered communism a worthy goal

and might well have criticized so-called Marxist societies such as North Korea, China, and Cuba for falling short of the promise of communism.

Welfare Capitalism and State Capitalism

Many nations of Western Europe, including Sweden, Finland, France, and Italy, have market-based economies but also offer broad social welfare programs. Analysts call this third type of economic system **welfare capitalism**, *an economic and political system that combines a mostly market-based economy with extensive social welfare programs.* Canada falls between Europe and the United States in its embrace of these programs. Under welfare capitalism, the government owns some of the largest industries and services, such as transportation, the mass media, and health care. In Greece, France, and Sweden, almost half of economic production is "nationalized," or state-controlled. Most industry is left in private hands, although it is subject to extensive government regulation. High taxation—aimed especially at the rich—funds a wide range of social welfare programs, including universal health care and child care. In Sweden, for example, social services represent one-third of all economic output. The Thinking Globally box takes a look at taxation in countries characterized by different levels of welfare capitalism.

capitalism an economic system in which natural resources and the means of producing goods and services are privately owned	socialism an economic system in which natural resources and the means of producing goods and services are collectively owned	communism a hypothetical economic and political system in which all members of a society are socially equal

Thinking Globally

Taxes and Tax Freedom Day

Governments pay for roads, airports, waste disposal, water treatment, welfare, national and provincial parks, libraries, art galleries, subways, commuter trains, police and firefighters, employment insurance, education (kindergarten to postgraduate), health care, and many other social services—from funds acquired by personal, corporate, and other forms of taxation (e.g., the HST and specific taxes on imports, gasoline, cigarettes, and alcohol). Canada falls between the United States and Europe in its embrace of welfare capitalism—and in its level of taxation: The more extensive the social welfare net, the higher the taxes. A method of comparing countries on their taxation levels is discussed here.

On Tax Freedom Day, you "stop working for the government" and start working for yourself. Put less bluntly, it is the first day in the year that the earnings of the average Canadian family are sufficient to pay the taxes imposed by governments at federal, provincial, and municipal levels.

In 2015, the average Canadian family paid 43.7 percent of its income in taxes. As a result, we worked for the government for 43.7 percent of the year (until June 10, 2015). In Alberta, Tax Freedom Day arrived on May 19, making it the province with the lowest taxation rate. In Newfoundland and Labrador, the province with the highest taxes, freedom day was June 21.

In the United States, people pay 31 percent of their income in taxes, so American Tax Freedom Day arrives earlier—on April 24—than in Canada—on June 10 (see Table 16–1). Note that American taxation levels have increased since 2011, whereas in Canada they have levelled off.

Table 16–1 Tax Freedom Days in Canada and the United States, 2000–2016

	Canada	United States
2016	June 10	April 24
2012	June 11	April 17
2011	June 10	April 12
2010	June 5	April 9
2009	June 6	April 8
2008	June 9	
2000	June 24*	

*The latest Tax Freedom Day in Canadian history.

In the European Union, taxation levels vary from a high of 59 percent in Belgium to a low of 16 percent in Switzerland. Germany, Norway, and France are taxed at rates of roughly 55 percent—making Tax Freedom Day in late July. Note that Germany and France are the economic heavy hitters of the European Union and prime examples of welfare capitalist countries.

What Do You Think?

1. To what extent does welfare capitalism deliver social justice?
2. Would you prefer lower taxes and fewer social programs or higher taxes and a wider social safety net?
3. Except in Quebec, tuition covers about 20 percent of the cost of university education. Is that fair? Or should the taxpayer bear the whole cost?

SOURCE: Fraser Institute (2016) and Wikipedia (2016).

Yet another blend of capitalism and socialism is **state capitalism**, *an economic and political system in which companies are privately owned but co-operate closely with the government.* State capitalism is the rule among the nations along the Pacific Rim. Japan, South Korea, and Singapore are all capitalist countries, but their governments work in partnership with large companies, supplying financial assistance and controlling foreign imports to help their businesses compete in world markets (Gerlach, 1992).

Relative Advantages of Capitalism and Socialism

Which economic system works best? Comparing economic models is difficult because all countries mix capitalism and socialism to varying degrees. In addition, nations differ in cultural attitudes toward work, access to natural resources, levels of technological development, and patterns of trade. Despite such complicating factors, some crude comparisons are revealing.

ECONOMIC PRODUCTIVITY One key dimension of economic performance is productivity. A commonly used measure of economic output is *gross domestic product* (GDP), the total value of all goods and services produced annually. Per capita (per person) GDP allows us to compare the economic performance of nations of different population sizes.

The output of mostly capitalist countries at the end of the 1980s—before the fall of the socialist systems in

welfare capitalism an economic and political system that combines a mostly market-based economy with extensive social welfare programs

state capitalism an economic and political system in which companies are privately owned but co-operate closely with the government

the Soviet Union and Eastern Europe—varied somewhat but averaged about $13 500 per person. The comparable figure for the mostly socialist former Soviet Union and nations of Eastern Europe was about $5000. This means that the capitalist countries outproduced the socialist nations by a ratio of 2.7 to 1 (United Nations Development Programme, 1990). A recent comparison of socialist North Korea (per capita GDP of $1800) and capitalist South Korea ($24 156) provides an even sharper contrast (World Bank, 2015).

ECONOMIC EQUALITY The distribution of resources within a population is another important measure of how well an economic system works. A comparative study of Europe in the mid-1970s, when that region was split between mostly capitalist and mostly socialist countries, compared the earnings of the richest 5 percent of the population and the poorest 5 percent (Wiles, 1977). Societies with mostly capitalist economies had a ratio of 10 to 1; the ratio for socialist countries was about 5 to 1. In other words, capitalist economies support a higher overall standard of living, but with greater income inequality. Alternatively, socialist economies create more economic equality but with a lower overall living standard.

PERSONAL FREEDOM One additional consideration in evaluating capitalism and socialism is the personal freedom that each system gives its people. Capitalism emphasizes *freedom to pursue self-interest* and depends on the ability of producers and consumers to interact, with little interference by the state. Socialism, in contrast, emphasizes *freedom from basic want*. The goal of equality requires the state to regulate the economy, which in turn limits the personal choices and opportunities for citizens.

Can a single society offer both political freedom and economic equality? In the capitalist United States, the political system guarantees many personal freedoms, but these freedoms are not worth as much to a poor person as to a rich one. In contrast, China or Cuba has more economic equality, but people do not have as much freedom to speak out or to travel within or outside the country. Perhaps the closest any country has come to "having it all" is Denmark, where welfare capitalism combines a market economy with broad government programs that provide for the welfare of all citizens.

Changes in Socialist Countries

In 1989 and 1990, the nations of Eastern Europe, which had been seized by the Soviet Union at the end of World War II, overthrew their socialist regimes. These nations— including the former German Democratic Republic (reunited with Germany), the Czech Republic, Hungary, Romania, and Bulgaria—are moving toward capitalist market systems after decades of state-controlled economies. In 1991, the Soviet Union itself formally dissolved, and the new Russian Federation has introduced some free-market principles. Within a decade, three-quarters of former Soviet government enterprises were partly or entirely in private hands (Montaigne, 2001).

There were many reasons for these sweeping changes. First, the capitalist economies far outproduced their socialist counterparts. The socialist economies were successful in achieving economic equality, but living standards were low compared to those of Western Europe. Second, Soviet socialism was heavy-handed, rigidly controlling the media and restricting individual freedoms. In short, socialism did away with *economic* elites, as Karl Marx predicted, but, as Max Weber foresaw, socialism increased the power of *political* elites.

So far, the market reforms in Eastern Europe have proceeded unevenly. Some nations, such as Azerbaijan, Uzbekistan, and Turkmenistan, all with extensive oil and natural gas reserves, did well even during the recent global recession. Other nations, including Lithuania, Latvia, and Ukraine, have seen their economies shrink and have faced rising unemployment. In just about every formerly socialist nation, the introduction of a market economy has brought with it an increase in economic inequality (Ignatius, 2008; World Bank, 2012).

A number of other countries have recently begun moving toward

NASA

DIRECTLY COMPARING THE ECONOMIC PERFORMANCE OF CAPITALISM AND SOCIALISM IS DIFFICULT BECAUSE NATIONS DIFFER IN MANY WAYS But a satellite image of socialist North Korea and capitalist South Korea at night shows the dramatically different electrical output of the two nations, one indication of economic activity.

more socialist economies. In 2005, the people of Bolivia elected Evo Morales, a former farmer, union leader, and activist, as their new president, over a wealthy business leader who was educated in the United States. This election placed Bolivia in a group of nations—including Ecuador, Venezuela, Brazil, Chile, and Uruguay—that are moving toward more socialist economies. The reasons for this shift toward socialism vary from country to country, but a common element is economic inequality. In Bolivia, for example, economic production has increased in recent decades, but most of the benefits have gone to the wealthy business elite. In contrast, more than half of the country's people remain very poor (Howden, 2005).

Work in Canada's Post-Industrial Economy

16.3 Analyze patterns of employment and unemployment in Canada.

Economic change is not restricted to the socialist world; the economy of Canada has also changed dramatically during the past century. The Industrial Revolution transformed our workforce a century ago, and further changes are taking place today. In 2011, 18 million Canadians were in the labour force, representing two-thirds of those over age 15. As has been the case historically, a larger proportion of men (70.6 percent) than women (61.6 percent) are employed in Canada. But the gender gap in labour force participation has diminished in recent decades: The figure for males has increased very little since 1980, but the female rate has risen substantially. It is important to note that the labour force includes those who are employed as well as those who are looking for work—in other words, the unemployed.

According to the 2011 NHS, labour force involvement varies relatively little by ethnic origins. For example, labour force participation varies from a low of 63 percent among First Nations to a high of 68 percent among those of Jewish and Jamaican ancestry (see Figure 16–4). Knowing that prejudice and discrimination affect the likelihood that visible minorities find employment, you might be surprised that Jamaican labour force participation is that high. On the other hand, though Canadians

of Jamaican origin are very likely to be employed full time, their *overall* employment rate falls below their Jewish counterparts. Employment rates are highest among Jewish- and French-origin populations—at 63 and 62 percent respectively. The lowest employment rates are found among those of Chinese and First Nations origins (at 57 and 54 percent).

Unemployment rates (Figure 16–4)—unlike participation and employment rates—are *not* calculated on the basis of populations 15 years of age and over. Instead, they refer to percentages of the labour force. Labour-force participation, as already noted, involves both those who are employed and those who are unemployed but available and actively looking for work. The highest unemployment rates are found among First Nations and Jamaicans (14 and 11 percent) At the other end of the continuum, French-, Chinese-, and Japanese-origin Canadians share a very low level of unemployment (at 7 percent of the labour force.).

The Decline of Agricultural Work

In 1900, about 35 percent of the Canadian labour force was engaged in farming. By 1961, this proportion had fallen to almost 13 percent and, by 2011, to less than 2 percent. Still, because today's agriculture involves more machinery and fewer people, it is more productive than ever. A century ago, a typical farmer could feed five people; today, one farmer feeds 75. The average Canadian farm has more

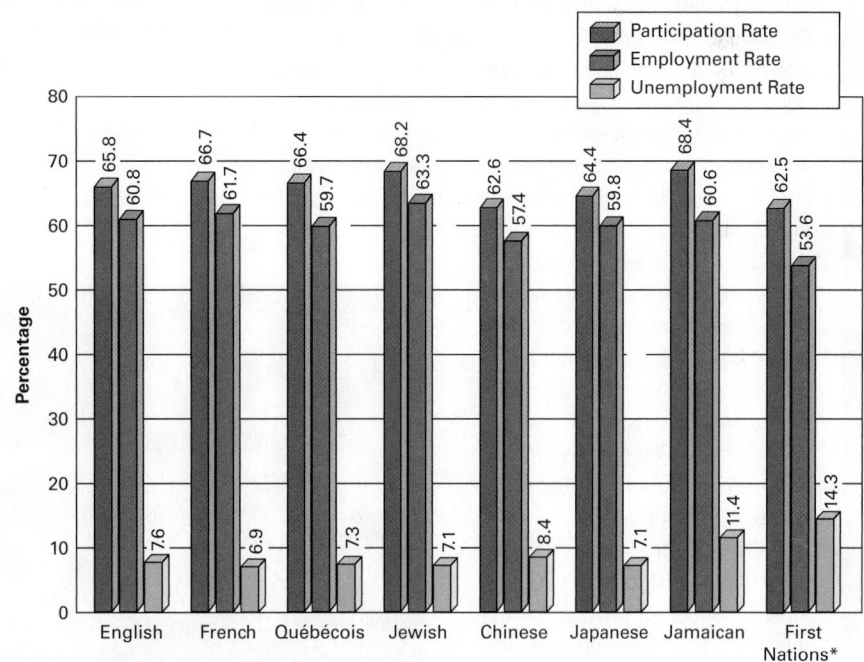

Figure 16–4 Employment Status of Populations 15 Years of Age and Over for Selected Categories, 2011

*First Nations combines First Nations (status Indians) and non-status Indians.

SOURCE: Compilation by LM Gerber based on Statistics Canada, NHS 2011, Catalogue no. 99-010-X2011036.

Sociology in Focus

Migrant Workers: Exploitation in Canadian Agriculture

As societies industrialize, a smaller share of the labour force works in agriculture. In Canada, much of the agricultural work that remains is performed by immigrants from lower-income nations.

There are a number of academics who study the history and current situation of migrant workers employed in Canadian agriculture. One of the researchers is Kerry Preibisch (of the University of Guelph), who points out that the Canadian state has been involved in supplying cheap seasonal labour to farms since Confederation in 1867. Much has changed since then but, to this day, Canadian agriculture depends on "foreign" workers, especially during the harvest season. In fact, without this source of cheap labour, Canadian agriculture would not be competitive (Preibisch, 2007, 2011).

It is important to know that migrant labour is required because few Canadians are willing to work long days at often back-breaking tasks (e.g., picking apples, berries, or tobacco). When the going gets tough, local workers can "walk with their feet" or quit. In this context, you may be able to understand the farmer's need for a "captive" workforce that is willing and often eager to put in long hours. Foreign workers are in Canada to make as much money as they can to support their families back home in developing countries where jobs are scarce or non-existent.

In the late 1960s, the Seasonal Agricultural Workers Program (SAWP) provided the framework for employing international migrants through a series of tightly managed agreements. The first agreement with Jamaica (1966) brought 264 migrant workers to Canada. Agreements with other Caribbean countries—and eventually Mexico (1974)—bring "some 25 000 migrants from these countries into Canada each year and, following the completion of their six-week to eight-month contracts, returns an estimated 98 percent of them home" (Preibisch, 2011:66). Note that their contracts *require* them to return home after a specified length of time. These workers do not have the right to remain in Canada or to apply for landed immigrant status.

Workers (or a group of workers) are recruited to work for a specific farmer for the duration of their contracts. The employer usually subsidizes travel costs, pays a minimum hourly wage, and provides housing (often hidden away from the road) with cooking facilities. Workers are expected to put in long hours

and to do everything they are asked to do by the employer. They are not to "make trouble" by talking back, organizing protests, or leaving the farm to mingle with the local people. The migrant workers pay employment insurance (which they can never claim) and may have a portion of their pay held back until they actually return home. Another method of ensuring that they leave is to hold on to their passports and work visas until their contract is up. The captive migrant workers are completely at the mercy of their employer, who is in a position to exploit and even abuse them.

With such complete control over their workers, farmers can require them to work faster and faster. He or she might measure each worker's productivity (e.g., by the number of baskets of beans picked each day), demand increasing levels of productivity, and threaten to send the less productive workers home. Migrants are under tremendous pressure to be "good" workers (i.e., hardworking, obedient, with the physical and emotional stamina to complete their contracts). Furthermore, "good" workers do not "question employment practices or housing conditions" (Preibisch, 2007:24). Jamaican workers are threatened with replacement by Mexicans who, because of their lack of facility in English, are especially vulnerable and thus docile. There is always the threat that, if workers are slow or cause trouble, they will not be invited back the following year. In fact, whole groups of Jamaicans might be replaced by Mexicans the following year.

The position of migrant workers is more precarious today than ever. In 2007, there were 75 different countries (under many different kinds of agreements) competing to have their citizens chosen for low-level agricultural jobs in Canada. It is important for these countries to place workers in Canada because they send home, or come back with, "hard" currency—which is injected into the local economy. With so many options, employers can chose among workers with a variety of distinct ethnic and cultural

Chris Thomaidis/The Image Bank/Getty Images

backgrounds. And they talk among themselves—if they agree that Thai migrants are the most reliable and hard-working, Jamaican and Mexican workers are at risk of displacement. Not only do individual workers compete among themselves for favourable work evaluations, but Jamaicans are pitted against workers from Mexico, Thailand, Philippines, or Guatemala. If they misbehave or slow in productivity, they might not be invited to return in the future.

No matter how carefully migrant workers are controlled, there are always a few who take their chances as undocumented workers. Jamaicans are more likely to leave farms than many others because often they have relatives in nearby cities (such as Toronto). Once this became a pattern, the Jamaican government began to recruit more of its workers from rural areas (where people would be better suited to agricultural work and have fewer relatives in Canadian cities).

The fact that migrant workers are bound to a single farm and employer—and are escorted out of the country when their contracts expire—makes them vulnerable to exploitation. Workers need money; sending countries need hard currency; and farmers could not survive without cheap foreign labour. As agricultural production expands in Canada, increasing proportions of farm workers are migrants from some 75 other countries. Thus, migrant workers will make up an ever-larger tile in a colour-coded vertical mosaic based on blatant racism.

What Do You Think?

1. Should Canada employ migrant workers? If not, what other options are available to farmers?

2. Should immigrants be recruited for farm work rather than temporary or seasonal workers?

3. Why does Canada offer no meaningful safeguards or employment standards to migrant workers, who have become an increasingly large component of our essential workforce?

---

than doubled in size from about 100 hectares (250 acres) in 1950 to about 240 hectares (600 acres) today.

This process signalled the eclipse of "family" farms, which declined in number and produce only a small part of our agricultural yield; more and more production is carried out by corporate agribusinesses (Bakker & Winson, 1993; Winson, 1993). But, more productive or not, this transformation has brought painful adjustments for farming communities throughout Canada, as a way of life is lost. The rest of us are affected indirectly by this change: Prices have generally been kept low by the rising productivity of agribusiness, although a growing proportion of people are concerned about the effect of widespread use of pesticides and chemicals on crops. One of the goals of genetic modification is to limit the need for such chemicals. Organic farming, which is increasing in production and in popularity with consumers, is a response to both pesticide proliferation and genetic modification.

From Factory Work to Service Work

A century ago, industrialization swelled the ranks of blue-collar workers. By 1950, however, a white-collar revolution had moved a majority of workers into service occupations. By 2011, 79 percent of the Canadian labour force worked in the service sector, and the vast majority of new jobs were being created here.

The expansion of service work is one reason for the perception of Canada as a middle-class society. But much service work—including sales and clerical positions and jobs in hospitals and restaurants—pays much less than former factory jobs. This means that many of the jobs in today's post-industrial society provide only a modest standard of living. Women and other minorities, as well as many young people just starting their working careers, are the most likely to have jobs doing low-paying service work (Greenhouse, 2006; Kalleberg et al., 2000). That said, other jobs in the service sector pay *very* well. Physicians, lawyers, professors, teachers, members of parliament, and corporate executives have salaries that are far above average.

The expansion of the service or tertiary sector of the economy has created many more employment opportunities for women. With this development in mind, one might predict increasing labour-force participation rates among women. Over a period of 110 years—that is between 1901 and 2011—women's labour-force participation *increased* from 14 to 62 percent. Over the same period, men's participation rates *decreased* from 78 percent in 1901 to 68 percent in 2006 (Nelson, 2010:224)—before climbing back to 71 percent in 2011.

The Dual Labour Market

Sociologists see the jobs in today's economy as falling into two categories. The **primary labour market** offers *jobs that provide extensive benefits to workers.* This segment of the labour market includes professions such as medicine, engineering, and law, as well as upper-management positions. These are jobs that people think of as careers, interesting work that provides high income, job security, and opportunity for advancement.

Few of these advantages apply to work in the **secondary labour market**, *jobs that provide minimal benefits to workers.* This segment of the labour force is employed on low-skilled, blue-collar assembly lines (where workers are not unionized) and in low-level service-sector jobs, including clerical positions. Workers in the secondary

primary labour market jobs
that provide extensive benefits
to workers

secondary labour market
jobs that provide minimal
benefits to workers

labour market receive lower income, have less job security and fewer benefits, and find less satisfaction in their work. Women and other minorities are overly represented in the secondary labour market workforce (Kalleberg et al., 2000; Nelson, 1994). Another term used to describe some of these workers is the *reserve army of labour,* the part of the labour force that is last hired during expansion and first fired when the economy contracts. These problems are especially serious for women, other minorities, and particularly Aboriginal workers, who tend to be overrepresented in this segment of the labour force (Gerber, 1990; Wotherspoon & Satzewich, 1993). Frideres and Gadacz (2012) point out that Aboriginal people often work in seasonal and part-time jobs with little security. Even highly skilled Aboriginal workers employed by mining exploration companies face discrimination, lower wages, and relatively poor working conditions.

Labour Unions

Labour unions are *worker organizations that seek to improve wages and working conditions through various strategies, including negotiations and strikes.* In Canada, union membership was remarkably stable over the 1980s and 1990s at just over one-third of the labour force. The involvement of women increased slightly, so that women constitute half of the union membership in Canada. On the other hand, the involvement of Canadian workers in international unions has dropped dramatically (Glenday, 2001:18–19). The highest level of union membership is found in government or public administration, at more than 70 percent; the manufacturing and service sectors are both at about the one-third mark, while mining and the trades lag behind. Most of the new service-sector jobs being created today are not unionized. As a result, union membership has declined—from 38 percent in 1981 to 31 percent in 2004 (Statistics Canada, 2009b).

Historically, there has been substantial interprovincial variation in levels of unionization. In the late 1980s, 55 percent of the labour force in Newfoundland and Labrador was unionized; at the other end of the spectrum, Alberta's labour force was 27 percent unionized (Statistics Canada, 1990). The other relatively highly unionized provinces were British Columbia, Ontario, and Quebec. The differences are not entirely the result of the economic structures of the various provinces, for even within the same industry there can be substantial variation. The level of unionization within the construction industry, for example, varied from 81 percent in Quebec to 25 percent

in Prince Edward Island. By 2011, Canada's level of unionization had decreased to 30 percent. Newfoundland and Labrador, Quebec, Manitoba, and Saskatchewan (in that order) were the provinces with the highest levels of unionization in 2011, at 35 percent or more. Ontario and Alberta were the least unionized (at 27 and 22 percent, respectively). This means that unionization in specific provinces declined by 5 to 15 percent over two decades (Statistics Canada, 2012c).

In global perspective, union membership in industrialized countries also varies substantially—from a low of 12 percent of the workforce in the United States to 18 percent in Japan, 30 percent in Canada, between 15 to 40 percent in much of Europe, and a high of 68 percent in Sweden (Visser, 2006). Clearly, some cultures are more receptive to unions; those with social-democratic values tend to have higher levels of unionization. The United States, with its pro-capitalist values, has never been particularly supportive of the union movement, but President Obama's administration proposed new laws that made it easier for American workers to form unions.

In the twenty-first century, Canadian unions face new challenges from the realities of flatter organizational structures (i.e., less room for promotion), downsizing, and outsourcing as corporations attempt to remain competitive in a global environment. Instead of focusing on wage increases, unions now struggle to ensure job security. Trade unions continue to negotiate for reductions in working time, restrictions on overtime, voluntary early retirement, improved training for job transfer, and an end to subcontracting (Glenday, 2001:33). As one might expect, current economic conditions are increasing the tensions between employers—some of whom are facing bankruptcy—and workers seeking job and pension security in turbulent times.

The problem is especially acute in the United States. In 2011, the nation's attention was drawn to efforts by several states to limit the power of government employee unions. On one side of the debate were people who claim that high wages and generous benefits for public employees threaten to bankrupt state treasuries. On the other side are people who claim some political leaders are trying to destroy the union movement.

Professions

All kinds of jobs today are called *professional*—we hear of professional tennis players, professional dancers, and even professional sanitation engineers. The difference between an *amateur*—from the Latin for "lover," meaning someone who acts out of love for the activity itself—and a professional is that the latter engages in a particular activity *in order to make a living.* When a young man leaves the local ice rink to join the NHL, his days of competing in amateur sport are over for, at that point, he becomes a professional hockey player. Thus, in everyday language, "profession" refers to paid employment.

Strictly speaking, a **profession** is *a prestigious, white-collar occupation that requires extensive formal education.* People performing this kind of work make a profession (a public declaration) of their willingness to work according to certain principles. Professions include medicine, dentistry, law, architecture, and engineering. For decades, sociologists studying professions have assumed that an occupation is a profession to the extent that it demonstrates the following four characteristics (Goode, 1960; Ritzer & Walczak, 1990):

- **Theoretical knowledge.** Professionals have a theoretical understanding of their field rather than mere technical training. Anyone can master first-aid skills, for example, but physicians have a theoretical understanding of human physiology, health, and disease. In this sense, tennis or hockey players, house cleaners, and exterminators do not qualify as professionals.

- **Self-regulating practice.** Many professionals, such as physicians and lawyers, are self-employed, "in private practice," or quite simply "in business." Professionals oversee their own work, observe a code of ethics, and belong to associations that determine educational qualifications, license members to practise, and set standards.

- **Authority over clients.** Because of their expertise, professionals are sought out by clients, who value their advice and follow their directions.

- **Community orientation rather than self-interest.** The traditional professing of duty states an intention to serve others rather than merely to seek income.

In almost all cases, professional work requires not just a bachelor's degree but also a graduate degree (or degrees). But graduate education itself does not make a professional. Your professors have bachelor's degrees, master's degrees, and doctorates. But, in terms of the criteria set out here, they are not professionals. Certainly, they have theoretical knowledge and they are often committed to serving the larger community and helping to create a better world. However, theirs is not a *self-regulating practice.* Professors may have considerable "academic freedom" in defining and pursuing their research interests or in designing their courses, but there is no professional association that grants them licences to put their theoretical knowledge into practice. And they are not sought out by clients for their expertise. The right, or licence, to practise as a professor (in a specific province and discipline) is not granted by a professional association. Whether or not a woman with a Ph.D. becomes a professor of sociology is determined, quite simply, by a university's hiring decision.

Many occupations that do not qualify as *true* professions nonetheless seek to professionalize their services. Claiming professional standing often begins by renaming the work to suggest special theoretical knowledge, thereby raising the reputation or image of the field. Stockroom workers become "inventory supply managers," and garbage collectors are reborn as "sanitation engineers."

Professional associations often refer to themselves as "colleges"—for example, the College of Physicians and Surgeons of Ontario or the Ontario College of Nurses. (Note that such professional associations are always provincial.) In any case, a recent move to claim professional status comes from the Ontario College of Trades (2012). Its stated aim is ground-breaking and broad in scope: "Never before have skilled tradespersons and their employers created a membership-based association to regulate and promote the skilled trades." The college will "set standards for training and certification of more than 150 trades" and "put skilled trades on equal footing with other professional occupations such as nurses, teachers and engineers." Note the references to training, certification, and other professions in light of the criteria for professions outlined above.

Because there is such confusion regarding "professions," Adams (2010) set out to study the legislation regulating professions—in Nova Scotia, Quebec, Ontario, Saskatchewan, and British Columbia—from Confederation (1867) to 1961. Her first task was to *identify* professional groups—to her surprise, a review of over 1000 pieces of legislation revealed 36 distinct regulated professions. She found two things that set "professions" apart from other regulated occupations: "(1) the establishment of a regulatory body, at least partially composed of practitioners, to govern the profession; and (2) the limitation of the right to practice or to utilize a restricted title to those with a demonstrated level of competence" (p. 56). There are other regulated *occupations* (such as private detectives and real estate agents) with systems of licensing, but they lack separate regulatory bodies and competency requirements. Furthermore, she points out, there are "many well-respected occupations, such as scientists, university professors, and managers" that are not professions (p. 66). They lack the required regulatory bodies as well as the power to control the right to practise through licensing.

In everyday conversation, we will continue to refer to prestigious, white-collar occupations as professions. Salaried hockey players and dance instructors are called professionals as well because they make their living in hockey or dance. However, when it comes to the sociological analysis of professions, it is helpful to see them as "organized occupations with status whose relations

Christopher Morris

D'ARCY MOSES, OF CREE AND DENE DESCENT, IS FROM THE DEH CHO REGION OF THE NORTHWEST TERRITORIES Incorporating Aboriginal themes and issues into his carvings and fashion creations—many in fur and hide—Moses is a popular and highly successful designer working out of Montreal.

with the state, the public, and other professional groups are structured and regulated" (Adams, 2010:66). Then we no longer need to obsess about whether nurses or dental technicians are professionals; that is determined by the way they are regulated (by the province in question) and by the power of their associations to self-regulate and license practitioners.

Because of Canada's proximity to the United States, it faces the loss of its professional—loosely or strictly defined—and otherwise highly educated workforce in a process referred to as the *brain drain*. As the Sociology and the Media box explains, we have only recently countered this trend with *brain gain*.

Self-Employment

Self-employment—*earning a living without working for a large organization*—was once commonplace in North America. Families owned and operated farms, and self-employed workers in the cities owned shops and other small businesses or sold their skills on the open market. C. Wright Mills (1951) estimated that, in the early nineteenth century, about 80 percent of the American labour force was self-employed; with the onset of the Industrial Revolution, that picture changed dramatically. Self-employment plummeted to one-third, one-fifth, and lower in both Canada and the United States.

Sociology and the Media

Brain Drain: Brain Gain

Columnist and author Jeffrey Simpson applied sociological methods to his work when he prepared his book *Star-Spangled Canadians: Canadians Living the American Dream* (2000). His research involved historical and statistical analyses and, most importantly, in-depth interviews with Canadians who live and work in the United States. His book appeared at a time of increasing concern about the so-called brain drain.

Simpson (2000) points out that emigration to the United States is nothing new for Canadians. In fact, historical flows were much larger than the relative trickle today: "Canada's population of 30 million might today be 40 or 50 million had so many Canadians not migrated to the United States, or had so many immigrants to Canada stayed put rather than passing through Canada en route to their eventual destination: the United States" (p. 2). The current concern about the brain drain stems from the fact that today's minor flow, facilitated by the North American Free Trade Agreement (NAFTA), consists of highly skilled and educated people lured south by the promise of expanded opportunities and higher incomes: "They are, in a sense, NAFTA's children" (p. 142).

Interviews that Simpson conducted across the country revealed that the overwhelming reason for moving to the United States was opportunity—not higher income or lower taxes. For some, such as the 2000 to 5000 nurses who have left Canada each year since 1992, it is simply a matter of finding employment. That many others left for the same reason can be deduced from the fact that, for university graduates (in 1997), unemployment rates were 2 and 4.6 percent for the United States and Canada, respectively. With the U.S. economy growing much faster than Canada's, there were simply more and better jobs south of the border. In fact, during the 1990s, many American corporations—most notably Microsoft—began aggressively recruiting on Canadian campuses, especially at the University of Waterloo. The current economic crisis and President Trump's plan to renegotiate NAFTA may result in a reversal of this pattern.

For other Canadian expatriates, opportunity meant better research facilities, state-of-the-art equipment, the ability to work at the "cutting edge" of one's field, greater challenges, larger audiences, a greater critical mass of colleagues, or, more simply, a range and scale of options that cannot be matched in Canada. We are losing our innovators and our entrepreneurs in part because American culture celebrates success while ours does not. Those interviewed by Simpson sense that "Americans recognize, honour, and thrive on success, whereas Canadians are more likely to think that a successful person, economically speaking, got there by mysterious means, might have a skeleton or two lurking in the closet, or somehow doesn't quite deserve to be there" (p. 156).

In summary, the brain drain numbers are not large when one compares today's migration to historic levels or even to the already reduced levels of the 1950s and 1960s. The important distinction is that recent emigrants do not come from all walks of life, as did their earlier counterparts; the emigrant of the 1990s was more highly skilled and educated, and more likely to be a professional—specifically, part of the knowledge-based economy.

Although 250 000 or more immigrants reach Canada each year—many of them highly educated and holding professional credentials—they cannot necessarily step into the shoes of those who have left for the United States, some of whom were recruited by American companies and universities precisely because they excel in their fields. The ideal, according to Simpson, is to create an environment that continues to attract immigrants (including Americans) while simultaneously slowing the brain drain to the south. In an effort to do just that, the federal government established a program to create up to 2000 Canada Research Chairs that would allow our universities to attract and retain internationally renowned researchers.

More recently, Canada has succeeded in attracting highly qualified people from the United States. Saskatchewan had been losing about 20 000 people a year—"many of them young and recently educated"—but managed a unique brain gain in the fall of 2004. Ingrid Pickering and Graham George, professors of molecular environmental science and geological science, moved with their children from sunny California to snowy Saskatoon: "Both were offered prestigious Canada Research Chairs at the University of Saskatchewan and came to Saskatoon specifically to continue their research using the new $174-million synchrotron light source that has been built on the edge of the university campus" (MacGregor, 2004). The extravagant tool, which is essential to their work, is the "most modern light-beam in the world." Other key players came to Saskatoon from Chicago and Grenoble, France. A top-notch facility with cutting-edge technology is attracting top-notch people. Equally significant, in terms of attracting the brightest scientific minds, is the Institute for Quantum Computing at the University of Waterloo (Janigan, 2006).

A front-page story in *The Globe and Mail* proclaimed that the University of British Columbia "scored a major academic coup, snagging an American Nobel Prize winner with a promise to pump $12 million over the next five years towards the professor's passion to improve the teaching of science" (Matas, 2006). Professor Carl Weiman, who is leaving the University of Colorado at Boulder, is a Nobel laureate (in 2001) as part of a team proving "the existence of a form of matter predicted by Albert Einstein called the Bose-Einstein condensate." He is now most interested in educational reform, and the University of British Columbia gave him the opportunity to pursue that passion.

Canada has created Canada Research Chairs, the Canadian Institutes of Health Research with a budget of $700 million, and the Canadian Foundation for Innovation to allow for the purchase of the latest in research equipment. As a result, more talented people are staying or moving here: "For the first time in 30 years, more doctors are returning to Canada than leaving the country for so-called greener pastures in the United States or overseas" (Ubelacker, 2005). The Canadian Institute for Health Information reported that, in 2004, for the first time since it began collecting data in 1969, more physicians returned to Canada (317) than left (262). Despite a gradual decline in the number leaving since the mid-1960s and despite a gradual increase in the total number of doctors throughout Canada, it is no easier to find a family doctor or get access to specialists. Population growth has kept pace with the supply of physicians. To complicate matters, physicians who have experienced burnout are opting for reduced hours and others are retiring—while medical schools are graduating fewer doctors than in the past. As a result, meeting the health care demands of an aging population will be a challenge.

On the whole, more Canadians and Americans are moving back and forth across the border these days. Nonetheless, "the number of people relocating south of the border remains significantly higher than the number heading north" (Greenaway, 2006a). The number of Canadians moving to the United States reached a high of 21 900 in 2005, while more than 8000 Americans moved north to Canada. Clearly, migrants are following opportunities in both directions, but 60 percent of Canadians move south under the employment category while 57 percent of Americans moving to Canada come under the family class. The global economic crisis will change these patterns, with more Canadians staying at home. Whatever the impact, it seems that Canada is no longer losing out in terms of excellence. We have moderated the brain drain with brain gain.

What Do You Think?

1. Do you know anyone who has moved to the United States because of job opportunities there?

2. Would you consider moving to the United States if the right job became available? Why?

3. What additional steps do you think Canada could take to keep highly qualified Canadians here and to attract more well-educated immigrants from the United States and elsewhere?

SOURCES: Based mainly on Simpson (2000); also Greenaway (2006a), Janigan (2006), Matas (2006), MacGregor (2004), and Ubelacker (2005).

In 2001 and 2006, close to 11.7 percent of Canada's workers were self-employed (compared to 7.5 percent of American workers), with the highest levels of self-employment found in fishing, trapping, and agriculture. Both censuses revealed that 14.6 and 8.5 of male and female workers, respectively, were self-employed. Among those who were self-employed, 39.2 percent reported paid help. A gender gap is apparent: 42.7 and 32.5 percent of self-employed men and women, respectively, had paid help. In other words, men are more likely to have larger businesses that require hired help—or male entrepreneurs are more likely than their female counterparts to be employers. The 2011 NHS reveals a slight drop in self-employment levels to 13.4 and 8.3 percent for men and women respectively—from 14.6 and 8.5 in 2006. A brief glance at ethnic origins as a factor determining self-employment levels reveals that those of English origins are very slightly above the Canadian average on this measure. The levels for those of Jewish origins are very high—26.6 and 14.8 percent for men and women—whereas the rates for First Nations men and women are exceptionally low—at 8.5 and 6.2 percent. Once again, there are social forces in play producing these dramatic variations.

Professionals such as lawyers, physicians, architects, and dentists have always been well represented among the self-employed—and, when you think of it, are quite likely to have employees. But most self-employed workers in Canada are small business owners, plumbers, carpenters, freelance writers, editors, artists, and long-distance truck drivers. Increasingly, women are joining the ranks of the self-employed—mainly, though not exclusively, in white-collar or professional occupations and small business (Gardner, 2000). However, more than 60 percent of self-employed Canadians today are men.

Analysis of enumeration areas in Burlington, Ontario (Gerber, 1991), revealed that, in one-quarter of the enumeration areas, 15 to 18 percent of working men—but only 6 percent of women—were self-employed. The areas where larger proportions of men and women were self-employed tended to have higher levels of at-home work, home ownership, university degrees, and incomes—and more people who were married. By and large, self-employed people in Burlington were not marginal to the mainstream economy: They are numerous, well educated, and relatively affluent. Undoubtedly, computers have facilitated the move to self-employment by allowing people to work from home offices. This trend (computer-driven as it is) to self-employment and working from home offices will undoubtedly increase in well-to-do neighbourhoods across Canada.

Historically, our society has painted an appealing or romanticized picture of working independently or establishing a small business: no time clocks to punch and no one looking over your shoulder. For those excluded from organizations by prejudice or discrimination, self-employment serves as a strategy to increase economic opportunity (Evans, 1989). Furthermore, self-employment holds the potential for earning a great deal of money. But, for all of its advantages, self-employment presents workers with special problems. Many are vulnerable to fluctuations in the economy; for example, during recessions such as that of the early 1990s, small businesses file for bankruptcy in alarming numbers. Another common problem is that, unless they buy expensive insurance, self-employed people lack the pension, employment insurance, parental leave, and health care benefits provided to employees of large organizations. Furthermore, self-employed people who work from home offices are isolated from meaningful contact with co-workers.

Underemployment

Underemployment is employment that uses less than a person's full credentials, talents, or abilities. It is a serious problem in Canada that affects many categories of workers and is increasingly recognized as the "gap between usable knowledge and its actual use in employment" (Livingstone, 2001:144). Many part-time workers are in that position involuntarily because full-time employment is unavailable to them. Younger workers, many of whom have university degrees, are underemployed, as "almost 50 percent of university graduates in Canada find themselves in jobs that do not require university-level credentials" (Côté & Allahar, 2001:258; Kelly et al., 2000). Women who hit the "glass ceiling" and immigrants whose credentials are not recognized in Canada are also among the underemployed. For every person who is underemployed, Canada loses the potential value of his or her human capital. As a society, we do not take full advantage of the skills and knowledge of our citizens.

Although people with higher levels of education are, by definition, more susceptible to underemployment, it is important to keep in mind that level of education is a major predictor of employment itself. Table 16–2 shows that, among Canadians 25 to 64 years of age, employment rates tend to increase for both women and men with higher levels of educational attainment. The employment rates of men increase from 65 percent among those with no certification to 86 percent for those with bachelor's degrees, whereas for women the increase is from 46 to 80 percent—or 34 percentage points compared to 21 for men. When it comes to *employment*—not necessarily full-time employment—advanced education makes the most difference for women. Note that acquiring a master's degree does not increase the likelihood of employment over the bachelor's degree, although it might affect the balance between part-time and full-time employment as well as employment income.

Table 16–2 Employment among Canadians 25 to 64 Years of Age by Sex and Educational Attainment, 2011 (Percentage Employed)

	Both Sexes %	Men %	Women %
Total	75.3	79.8	71.0
No certification	55.8	64.5	45.9
High school diploma	71.4	78.1	65.3
Trade certificate*	77.8	80.8	72.4
College or CEGEP	80.6	84.4	77.7
Bachelor's degree	82.4	85.9	79.5
Medical degree**	85.9	89.1	82.3
Master's degree	81.9	84.6	79.3
Earned doctorate	85.6	87.2	83.2

*Refers to apprenticeship or trade certification.

**Includes degrees in medicine, dentistry, veterinary medicine, or optometry.

SOURCE: Compilation and calculations by LM Gerber based on Statistics Canada, NHS 2011, Catalogue numbers 99-012-X2011035 and 99-012-X2011040.

Employment rates for men and women—and specifically for men—are highest for those with medical degrees (in medicine, dentistry, veterinary medicine, or optometry) and earned doctorates (or PhDs). Although people with bachelor's degrees and university certification beyond the bachelor's level are the most likely to be employed, these data do not preclude underemployment—employment that is only part time or that fails to use the individual's full credentials.

UNEMPLOYMENT Every society has some unemployment. Few young people entering the labour force find a job right away; workers may leave their jobs to seek new work or stay at home raising children; others may be on strike or suffer from long-term illnesses; still others lack the skills to perform useful work.

Although people may be quick to blame themselves if they find themselves out of work, unemployment is not just a personal problem; it is also a product of the economy itself. Capable and willing workers lose their jobs when economic recession occurs, if occupations become obsolete, or as factories close in the face of rising foreign competition. Mergers and downsizing can also lead to the dismissal of employees from all levels of an organization. The emerging post-industrial economy has shattered the job security of workers in many traditional blue-collar occupations as well (Kasarda, 1983). Stelco, Canada's largest steel producer, based in Hamilton, Ontario, was in danger of collapse in 2003; in 2009, General Motors and Chrysler (based in Windsor and Oshawa, Ontario) needed government assistance to stay afloat. Many workers were laid off while these companies floundered.

In capitalist societies such as Canada, the unemployment rate rarely dips below 5 percent of the labour force. Public officials view this level of unemployment as natural, and sometimes even describe it as "full" employment; unemployment becomes a publicly acknowledged problem only when the unemployment rate exceeds 7 or 8 percent (Albrecht, 1983). In principle, predominantly socialist societies consider work to be each person's right and obligation, so the government may create jobs to keep the unemployment rate low. In practice, however, unemployment is as great a problem in these societies.

Canada's unemployment rate rose to more than 11 percent in 1992 and 1993, before dropping to 9.5 percent in 1995 and to 8.1 percent by December 1997. By 2000 and 2005, our unemployment rate had dropped further to 7.4 and 6.6 percent, respectively. In response to the global economic crisis, Canada's unemployment rate reached 8.4 percent in May 2009—the highest rate in 11 years. In May and June 2012, Canada's unemployment rate was 7.3 percent.

While there were substantial gains in the numbers employed after the recession of the early 1990s, economic restructuring meant that hundreds of thousands of old jobs were lost as new ones were created. Many people who failed to make the transition from old to new jobs were casualties of this employment shift.

Part-time work accounts for 18 percent of all employment, a rate that was consistent for 2001, 2005, and 2008. In each of those years, 11 percent of male workers and 27 percent of female workers engaged in part-time work. In other words, the rate of part-time employment is stable over time, as is the higher rate for women. Some women, even physicians and other professionals, work part time by choice for a wide range of reasons (including family

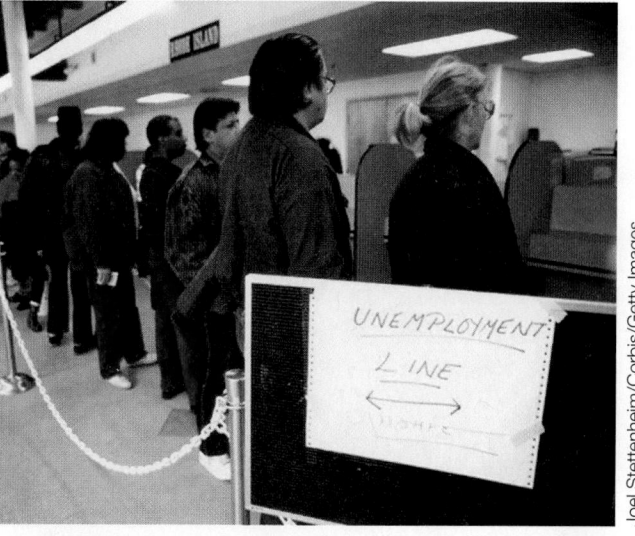

UNEMPLOYMENT MEANS NOT HAVING A JOB AND THE INCOME IT PROVIDES But it also means not having the respect that comes from being self-reliant in a society that expects people to take care of themselves. How does the sociological perspective help us understand being out of work as more than a personal problem?

Joel Stettenheim/Corbis/Getty Images

responsibilities), but others do so involuntarily. Thus, some, but not all, of this part-time work can be classified as underemployment. In 1994, 5.4 percent of all workers (compared to 2.3 percent in 1981) were "involuntary part-timers," or people who have been unable to find full-time employment (Wells, 1996). It is probable that this type of underemployment is also consistent over time.

The national unemployment rate tells only part of the story, for unemployment in provinces such as Prince Edward Island and Newfoundland and Labrador is known to approach three times the national rate. Canada Map 16–1 reveals the regional pattern in unemployment rates at the time of the 2011 census and National Household Survey. Canada, as a whole, had an unemployment rate of 7.8 percent—up from 6.6 percent in 2006. In fact, every province and territory except Newfoundland and Labrador posted higher rates of unemployment in 2011 than in 2006. The decline in unemployment in Newfoundland and Labrador (from 18.6 to 14.6) was countered by unusually large increases in Alberta and Ontario (from 4.3 to 5.8 and 6.4 to 8.3 percent respectively). Ontario continues to experience higher unemployment rates than the three prairie provinces but the surprise is that Ontario's unemployment rate is *above* the national average and substantially *higher* than Quebec's. That said, unemployment rates in Nunavut and Newfoundland and Labrador—despite their four-point improvement over 2006—are the highest in Canada. Prince Edward Island, Nova Scotia and New Brunswick share the next rung with the Northwest Territories—with unemployment rates from 10 to 13.9 percent. Quebec, Ontario, British Columbia, and the Yukon experienced 7.2 to 9.8 percent unemployment—compared to 6 percent in the prairies. A great deal has happened since 2011. The collapse in oil prices is hitting Alberta and Newfoundland and Labrador (with its reliance on offshore oil) the hardest. The 2016 census will yield very different unemployment rates for these two provinces.

Seeing Ourselves

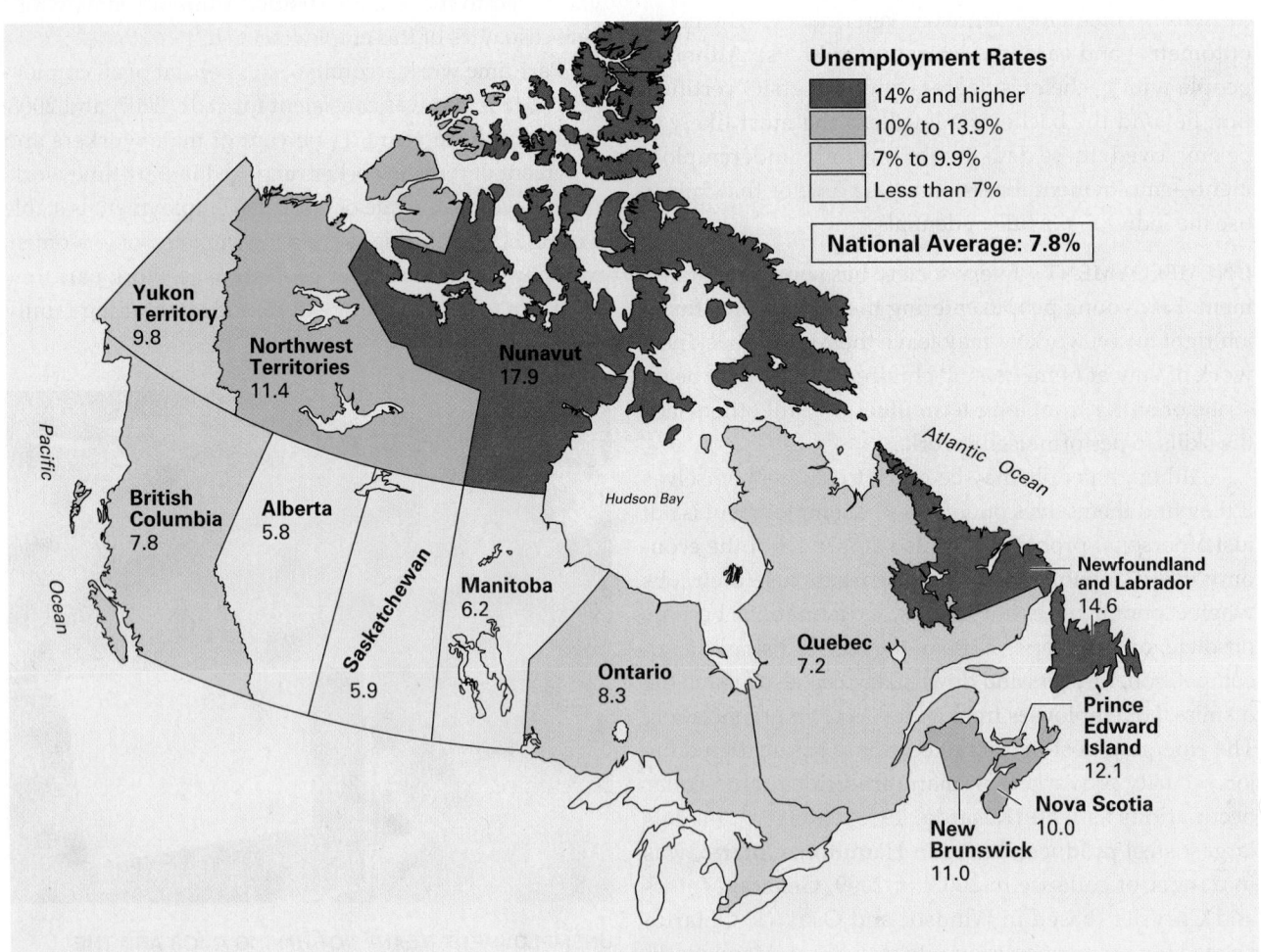

Canada Map 16-1 Unemployment Rates for Canada, the Provinces, and Territories, 2011

SOURCE: Compilation by LM Gerber based on Statistics Canada, NHS 2011, Catalogue no. 99-010-X2011036.

It is important to understand the numbers that are reported regularly in the media. Some people are *not in the labour force* at all, for reasons of disability, age, school attendance, child rearing, or even elder care. The labour force is defined in terms of people who are working or available and looking for work. The percentage of the labour force that is available and looking for work is used to calculate the official unemployment rate. In other words, the base does not include full-time students, aged grandparents, or stay-at-home parents.

Unemployment rates vary dramatically across the country, but they also differ among various segments of the population. In 2011, the lowest unemployment rates were found among those of Japanese and Jewish origins (7.1 percent), the highest among those with Jamaican and First Nations ancestry (11.4 and 14.3 percent respectively). In effect, unemployment rates vary with area of residence, ancestry, age—think youth unemployment—education, and gender.

Official unemployment statistics, based on monthly national surveys, generally understate unemployment for two reasons. First, to be counted among the unemployed, a person must be actively seeking work. Especially during economic recessions, many people become discouraged after failing to find a job and stop looking; these "discouraged" workers are not counted among the unemployed. Further, many people who are unable to find jobs for which they are qualified take "lesser" employment while seeking new positions in their fields. Such people are included among the employed, although they, too, might better be described as underemployed. Official statistics also overlook the fact that some people who are out of work receive income from odd jobs, unreported work, or illegal activity—parts of the "underground economy."

The Underground Economy

Government requires all businesses and individuals to report annually on their economic activity, especially earnings. Not reporting income received makes a transaction part of the **underground economy**, which refers to *economic activity involving income or the exchange of goods and services that is not reported to the government as required by law.* On a small scale, evidence of the underground economy can be found everywhere: Teenagers babysit for neighbours; a family makes some extra money by holding a garage sale without reporting the income to the government. Far more of the underground economy is attributable to criminal activity such as illegal drug sales, prostitution, bribery, theft, illegal gambling, and loan sharking.

However, the single largest segment of the underground economy involves "honest" people who fail to report their legally obtained income accurately on income

tax forms. Self-employed people, such as various tradespeople or owners of small businesses, may understate their incomes; waiters, waitresses, taxi drivers, and other service workers may not report the full amount of their tips received in cash. Even relatively small omissions and misrepresentations on individual income tax returns add up to billions of dollars in the underground economy (Dalglish, 1993; Simon & Witte, 1982).

In Canada, the underground economy accounted for some 15 to 20 percent of economic activity in 1990, up from about 10 percent a decade earlier (Dalglish, 1993:20), while another source pegged the rate at 15 or 16 percent of GDP (Hill, 2002). A survey by the Canadian Home Builders' Association estimated that 55 percent of all renovations in 1992 were done "under the table," with cash payment that was undeclared as income. Statistics Canada suggests that underground activity accounts for only 3.5 percent of GDP. In other words, because it is the "underground" or hidden economy, estimates of the magnitude of the problem vary widely.

This sudden increase in underground economic activity has been attributed to high tax levels in general and, in particular, to the imposition of the Goods and Services Tax (GST) in 1991. The effect of taxing *services*, for the first time, was to increase greatly the demand for cash payments for under-the-table services. One indication of this trend is a 57 percent increase, between 1991 and 1992, in the use of hard cash rather than credit cards or cheques (Dalglish, 1993). It is important to understand that *both* parties to "under-the-table" or cash payments of this type are breaking the law—the worker because the income will not be reported at tax time, and the person paying for the service should be aware that he or she is participating in fraud when the cost is lower if the worker does not tack on the appropriate GST.

New Information Technology and Work

Another workplace issue is the increasing role of computers and other new information technology. The Information Revolution is changing what people do in a number of ways (Rule & Brantley, 1992; Vallas & Beck, 1996):

1. **Computers are deskilling labour.** Just as industrial machinery replaced the craft and trade masters of an earlier era, computers now threaten the skills of managers. More business operations are based not on executive decisions but on computer modelling. In other words, a machine decides whether to place an order, stock a dress in a certain size and colour, or approve a loan application.

2. **Computers are making work more abstract.** Most industrial workers have a hands-on relationship with their products. Post-industrial workers use symbols

to perform abstract tasks, such as making a company more profitable or making software more user-friendly.

3. **Computers limit workplace interaction.** As workers spend more time at computer terminals, they become increasingly isolated from other workers.

4. **Computers increase employers' control of workers.** Computers allow supervisors to monitor employees' output continuously, whether they work at computer terminals or on assembly lines.

5. **Computers allow companies to relocate work.** Because computer technology allows information to flow almost anywhere instantly, the symbolic work in today's economy may not take place where we might think. We have all had the experience of calling a business (say, a hotel or a toy store) located in our own town only to find that we are talking to a person at a computer workstation or call centre thousands of kilometres away, perhaps in another country. (See the Sociology and the Media box for further insight on this issue.)

IN TODAY'S CORPORATE WORLD, COMPUTERS ARE CHANGING THE NATURE OF WORK JUST AS FACTORIES DID MORE THAN A CENTURY AGO In what ways is computer-based work different from factory work? In what ways is it the same?

Such changes remind us that technology is not socially neutral. Rather, it changes the relationships between people in the workplace, shapes the way we work, and often alters the balance of power between

Sociology and the Media

Working through Cyberspace

The 1998 Winter Olympic Games in Nagano, Japan, gave IBM an opportunity to showcase its latest technology by transmitting, worldwide, millions of megabytes of data from the games to television viewers, radio listeners, newspaper readers, and internet surfers. Now, IBM (1998) makes the same technology available to business organizations that are involved in "e-business" or internet-based commerce.

Business has become increasingly dependent on computers linked by intranets, extranets, and the World Wide Web. The number of people connected to the internet had increased to 1.5 billion by 2008 (Computer Industry Almanac, 2009). In Canada alone, private and public sales online increased from $14 billion in 2001 to $63 billion in 2008 (Statistics Canada, 2008a). But the Web is not limited to commercial transactions. Employees of a Vancouver firm can work—on data analysis, design, reports, or problem solving as part of an interactive group—from a home office in Winnipeg, Munich, or Helsinki. Work has invaded cyberspace—the McLuhanesque world that is free of the limitations of time and space.

Inco's Stobie mine in Sudbury, Ontario, took miners out of the underground tunnels and seated them at surface computer terminals from which they run automated drill rigs and scoop trams in various locations (Robinson, 1998). Robo-operator Stan Holloway, who spent 15 years in Inco's dangerous, dreary, diesel-fumed tunnels, is comfortably seated, operating million-dollar scoop trams with a joystick and foot pedals and observing the otherwise back-breaking job through miniature cameras and microphones mounted on the machines. Inco turned to this kind of high-tech mining to remain competitive at this particular mine, which has 30 to 40 years' worth of low-grade ore left at the site. To remain in operation, Stobie must compete with mines that have high-grade ore and low labour costs. In Russia, a miner makes about $850 per year; Sudbury miners are employed at $85 000 to $100 000 per year (in 1998). Robo-trams and drill rigs do a lot of dangerous and dirty work but displace large numbers of highly paid miners. Only a few miners will make the transition from hard manual labour to robo-operator.

Finance Canada (Canada, 1997) points out that many Canadian industries—beyond software, electronics, and aviation—are leaders in the development and adoption of new technology. New methods of inventory management are changing retailing and the skills needed by personnel, and satellite-generated images are used in resource exploration and development. So pervasive is this change that knowledge-based technology is now the major stimulus to economic growth and job creation. In the past decade, employment growth has been closely linked to intensity of information technology:

- employment has increased substantially (12 percent) in areas of high information-technology intensity
- employment has increased moderately (8 percent) in areas of medium intensity
- employment has declined (–9 percent) in sectors that make minimal use of information technology (Statistics Canada, 2003b)

Canada's Research In Motion made staying connected much easier for today's busy executive with its invention of the BlackBerry. Newman's Titans (or "new" establishment) are connected at all hours with their counterparts around the world. Unlike the family dynasties of the "old" establishment—bound by private school, country club, and intermarriage—the "Titans of the Info Age are joined more by their cellphones than by any sense of belonging" (Newman, 1998:4). Their networks need to be aggressively managed, and the BlackBerry or other smartphones (the pocket offices) make it possible to phone, transmit email, and even read attached documents while on the go—even on rare extended weekends or holidays.

It might surprise you to learn that a number of corporations (including Pearson Canada, the publisher of this textbook) use Facebook to keep their employees—who are spread across Canada, North America, or the globe—in constant communication.

What Do You Think?

1. Is your future work likely to be confined to a nine-to-five weekday schedule, or will you be continuously connected to the "office" and co-workers by cellphone, smartphone, laptop, or BlackBerry?

2. Do you know people whose jobs have been transformed by the new technology? What kinds of jobs were involved?

3. How has the Information Revolution affected family life in Canada?

---

employers and employees. Understandably, then, people welcome some aspects of the Information Revolution and oppose others.

General Electric, which files an average of five patents per day, has developed a "culture of risk" that informs its "talent management process." Susan Peters (vice-president, executive development, and chief learning officer at General Electric) describes her company's guiding principles as follows (Peters, 2012):

- external focus (collaboration with customers, government agencies, and others)
- inclusiveness (recognition of diversity as essential to team-building)
- clear thinking (requiring "agility, decisiveness, and strategic commitment")
- expertise (indicating "a deep knowledge base and a passion to develop others")
- imagination and courage

The last point underlines the fact that innovators are risk takers who must face the possibility of failure. The people who are nurtured here are not the assembly-line workers at GE but the creative thinkers and dreamers who come up with five patentable ideas per day. GE is not alone in promoting innovation and creativity among its employees, but this change in corporate culture is revolutionary—unthinkable as recently as 15 years ago.

Corporations

16.4 Discuss the importance of corporations to the Canadian economy.

At the core of today's capitalist economies lies the **corporation**, *an organization with a legal existence including rights and liabilities apart from those of its members.* By

HOANG DINH NAM/AFP/Getty Images

WHILE THE INFORMATION REVOLUTION IS CENTRED IN HIGH-INCOME COUNTRIES SUCH AS CANADA, THE EFFECTS OF HIGH TECHNOLOGY ARE BECOMING EVIDENT EVEN IN LOW-INCOME NATIONS Do you think that the expansion of information technology will change the lives of rural people such as this peasant in Vietnam? If so, how?

incorporating, an organization becomes a legal entity, able to enter into contracts and own property. Incorporation, which arose about a century ago, protects the personal wealth of owners and top executives from lawsuits that might arise from business debts or harm to consumers. Most large corporations operating in Canada are public—that is, owned by potentially thousands of shareholders, including other corporations—rather than private, where ownership is limited to a single person or family. This dispersion of corporate ownership has spread wealth by making more people small-scale capitalists.

Ralf Dahrendorf (1959) notes that the day-to-day operation of a public corporation is the task of white-collar executives who are responsible to the shareholders. Nonetheless, a great deal of corporate stock is owned by a small number of the corporation's top executives and directors, who, in Canada, have typically been members of a very small number of families (Clement, 1975; Francis, 1986); these major shareholders make up a small economic elite, which owns and operates the richest and most powerful Canadian businesses. Although a "new" establishment has taken over from the old family dynasties (Newman, 1998) and a significant proportion of the population now owns stock—often in retirement savings plans or pension funds—Canada still has an economic elite (the top 1 percent). Ultimately, the proliferation of corporations has not substantially changed how large businesses operate or affected the distribution of wealth in Canada.

Economic Concentration

Profit-making corporations range in size from one-person businesses to veritable giants, such as Loblaw Companies (134 000 employees) and Onex Corp. (138 000 employees) (*Globe and Mail*, 2006b:66). Many of Canada's corporations are small, with less than $100 000 in assets, but the largest corporations dominate the Canadian economy and periodically expand their empires through mergers and buyouts of smaller firms. In a pattern that differs from that of the United States, Canada's banks and other financial institutions are well represented among the top corporations in terms of revenue and profits. The attempted merger, announced in January 1998, of the Royal Bank and the Bank of Montreal would have enhanced the position of the new bank within Canada—and placed it among the top 25 banks in the world. The companies' hopes were dashed when the federal government failed to approve the merger for fear that it would reduce competition in service to the public.

Canada's problem of corporate concentration stems from

- the inordinate wealth and power of specific individuals, families, and corporations

- interlocking directorships that bind otherwise diverse corporations
- geographic centralization of investment in Ontario and Quebec
- the tendency of corporations to expand or diversify by merging or buying existing firms instead of developing new productive capacity

This last problem was exacerbated by the 1989 free trade agreement with the United States, as evidenced by a $20-billion boom in acquisitions and mergers in the first few months of that year (Bronson, 1993:204). This trend has been referred to as "paper entrepreneurship," which does nothing to contribute to Canada's wealth: "The pie remains the same size, but the pieces are cut differently" (Francis, 1986:229).

Conglomerates and Corporate Linkages

The largest businesses are **conglomerates**, *giant corporations composed of many smaller corporations.* A conglomerate emerges as a corporation enters new markets, spins off new companies, or takes over other companies. Forging a conglomerate is also a way to diversify a company, so that new products can provide a hedge against declining profits in the original market. Sometimes these mergers are extremely diverse, as illustrated by New Brunswick's Irving empire (Francis, 1986:16). The Irving group of companies is big by anybody's standards. It includes the country's largest shipyard and dry dock facilities. Irving Oil is one of Canada's 10 largest oil companies, with 3000 service stations in Atlantic Canada and the Ottawa Valley; it has the country's largest refinery, as well as untold holdings in oil and gas discoveries in western Canada. Irving's forestry business is world-scale, including half a dozen pulp and paper mills and sawmills, and title to 0.6 million hectares (1.5 million acres) of timberlands in New Brunswick and Maine, an area equivalent to the size of Prince Edward Island. Included as well are fleets of ships, trucks, buses, and railway cars; most of the media in New Brunswick; stores selling cars, food, hardware, drugs, and construction materials; and factories producing everything from prefabricated housing to concrete, steel, and hundreds more products. It is hard to get an exact picture of the scope of the Irving

corporation an organization with a legal existence including rights and liabilities separate from that of its members

conglomerate a giant corporation composed of many smaller corporations

empire. None of the companies is publicly owned, and the Irvings fiercely protect their privacy through a complicated and impenetrable corporate structure.

In the 1980s, Beatrice Foods, then a Canadian company, was another corporate umbrella, containing more than 50 smaller corporations that manufacture such well-known products as Hunt's foods, Tropicana fruit juices, La Choy foods, Orville Redenbacher popcorn, Max Factor cosmetics, Playtex clothing, and Samsonite luggage. But Beatrice has long since been purchased by Parmalat of Milan, Italy, and lost its diversified umbrella function. Toronto-based George Weston Limited is another corporate umbrella but more clearly in the food sector, as it owns, among other companies, Loblaws, Zehrs, Provigo, Fortinos, and Interbake Foods (which supplies most of the Girl Guide cookies to Canada and the United States).

Corporations are linked not only in conglomerates, but also through interlocking directorates, social networks of people serving simultaneously on the boards of directors of many corporations. These connections give corporations access to insider information about each other's products and marketing strategies (Clement, 1975; Herman, 1981; Marlios, 1975; Scott & Griff, 1985). Peter Bentley of Vancouver-based Canfor Corporation, for example, sat on more than a dozen "blue ribbon boards," had "titled Europeans on his boards and has served on theirs," and "entered into countless partnerships with English and German firms" (Francis, 1986:193–194).

Corporations are also linked by owning each other's stock. For example, in today's global economy, many companies invest heavily in other corporations commonly regarded as their competitors. In the automobile industry, Ford owns a significant share of Mazda, General Motors is a major investor in Isuzu, and DaimlerChrysler is part owner of Mitsubishi. Corporations are also linked by extremely wealthy families who own their stock (Clement, 1975). Among the Canadian families who have had large and varied corporate holdings in Canada are the Belzberg, Bentley, Bronfman, Desmarais, Eaton, Irving, Mannix, McCain, Molson, Richardson, Steinberg, Thomson, and Weston families. With business interests in common, these families know each other and interact socially. Gwen Moore (1979) has described how social networks informally link members of the corporate elite. In other words, corporate executives travel in many of the same social circles, allowing them to exchange valuable information. Such networks not only enhance the economic clout of big businesses, but also expand the influence of corporate leaders in political, social, and charitable organizations (Clement, 1975; Francis, 1986; Useem, 1979).

Peter C. Newman, columnist and author, argues that the picture just outlined is outdated. Some of the families named are not just "old" establishment: They go back further to the "Jurassic Canadian Establishment." In his third volume on the Canadian establishment, *Titans: How the New Canadian Establishment Seized Power* (1998), Newman argues that Canada's economy is in the hands of a new breed of entrepreneurs. Gone are the days of old family control through family dynasties based on exclusive club memberships, inherited wealth, interlocking directorships, contacts, and intermarriage. The new establishment, a meritocracy, is based on "what one can do" rather than on "whom one knows." The vertical structure of Canadian business has been transformed into a broader one "where nobody really can prevent someone popping up almost anywhere in the scene" (Newman, quoting John Evans, p. 18).

Whereas the "old" establishment was linked by club membership, the new one is based on networks that are sustained by cell phones, the internet, smartphones, and transcontinental flights. The creative spark that gives birth to great enterprises is "hard to define and impossible to reproduce," Newman states; no longer can "the essential life force that creates and sustains family fortune … be passed on to the eldest son through genes" (p. 24). The result is that control of Canada's corporate world is slipping away from the old dynasties into the hands of an aggressive global elite.

Corporations and the Global Economy

Corporations have grown so large that they now account for most of the world's economic output. The largest corporations, centred in the United States, Canada, Japan, and Western Europe, have spilled across national borders and now view the entire world as one vast marketplace. Such *multinational corporations* produce and market products in many different nations. Nortel (prior to its collapse in 2009), BlackBerry, Magna International, Goldcorp, and all of our major banks are among hundreds of huge Canadian corporations that earn much—and, in some cases, most—of their profits beyond our borders.

For many years, Tim Hortons (based in Oakville, Ontario) has been expanding its operations in the United States; as part of that thrust, it opened up in Times Square with plans to expand to 100 stores throughout New York City (Vieira, 2009; Whitman, 2009). As of August 2014, Tim Hortons and Burger King merged to form the world's third largest quick service restaurant company, with 18 000 restaurants in 100 countries and roughly $23 billion in sales. This transaction moves the Tim Hortons brand beyond North America into the global marketplace (Tim Hortons, 2016).

There is another corporation that is woven into our history; the Hudson's Bay Company goes back to 1670, when its involvement in the fur trade gave it a central role in opening up what is now Canada to exploration and settlement. Once a simple collection of isolated trading posts, this quintessential cultural icon is now a multinational corporation. The Hudson's Bay Company—which owns Lord & Taylor, Saks Fifth Avenue, and several other retailers—is firmly established in the American market and parts of the European Union. But it is also changing the Canadian retail scene, for example, by bringing Saks Fifth Avenue to Ontario by way of the Toronto Eaton Centre and Sherway Gardens (*Toronto Star*, 2015).

Because most of the planet's resources and people are found in low-income countries, multinationals spread their operations around the world to gain access to raw materials, inexpensive labour, and vast markets. Multinational corporations recognize that poor countries contain most of the world's resources and people, who will work for attractively low wages. A manufacturing worker in Mexico, whose average hourly wage is $6.82, labours for a week to earn what a worker in Canada, the United States, or Japan earns in a single day.

The impact of multinationals on poor countries is controversial. Modernization theorists claim that, by unleashing the great productive power of capitalism, multinationals raise living standards in poor nations, offering them tax revenue, new jobs, and advanced technology that together accelerate economic growth (Berger, 1986; Firebaugh & Beck, 1994; Firebaugh & Sandu, 1998).

Dependency theorists counter that multinationals make global inequality worse, blocking the development of local industries and pushing poor countries to make goods for export, rather than food and other products for local people. From this standpoint, multinationals make poor nations poorer and increasingly dependent on rich nations (Dixon & Boswell, 1996; Kentor, 1998; Wallerstein, 1979; Walton & Ragin, 1990).

Modernization theory hails the market as the key to progress and affluence for all of the world's people, and dependency theory calls for replacing market systems with government-based economic policies. The Thinking Critically box takes a closer look at the issue of market versus government economies.

The Economy: Looking Ahead

Social institutions are a society's way of meeting the people's needs. But, as we have seen, the Canadian economy only partly succeeds in this respect. Though highly productive, our economy distributes its products in a highly unequal fashion. Moreover, as we move into the new century, economic transformations in our society and the world present us with new opportunities and challenges.

One important factor that underlies change in the economy is the Information Revolution. In the post-industrial era, the share of the Canadian labour force involved in the service (or tertiary) sector has increased dramatically to 79 percent. Increasingly, the broad range of workers involved in this sector—for example, hairdressers, physicians, researchers, tax consultants, computer programmers—are highly skilled and educated people. Most of them (such as teachers from primary to university levels) find that, with each passing year, information technology is more integral to their work. Canada must face up to the challenge of providing its people with the language and computer skills they need to succeed in the new economy.

A second transformation of recent years is the expansion of the global economy. Two centuries ago, the ups and downs of a local economy reflected events and trends within a single town. One century ago, local communities throughout the country had become interconnected, so prosperity in once place depended on producing goods demanded by people elsewhere. We have entered this century with powerful economic connections on the global level. It now makes little sense to speak of a national economy, as what Saskatchewan farmers produce and sell may be affected more by what transpires in the wheat-growing region of Russia than by events in their own provincial capital. In short, Canadian workers and business owners are not only generating new products and services but are doing so in response to factors and forces that are distant and unseen.

Change is causing analysts around the world to rethink conventional economic models. The emerging global system shows that socialist economies are less productive than their capitalist counterparts, one important reason for the collapse of socialist regimes in Eastern Europe and the former Soviet Union. But capitalism, too, has seen marked changes, especially an increasing involvement of government in the economy. Moreover, productive enterprises have outgrown national boundaries with the emergence of multinational corporations. The world's societies are becoming increasingly interconnected, as illustrated by the European Union and the NAFTA.

The on-going pressure to expand global trade agreements resulted in the yet-to-be-ratified Trans-Pacific Partnership (TPP). On February 4, 2016, the TPP agreement was signed by twelve Pacific Rim countries, including Canada, with the understanding that the citizens of each country will be consulted before the very complex agreement is ratified. To that end, Global Affairs Canada has created an informative TPP website (still a work in progress) which provides a summary of the agreement under 27 headings, a portrait of each of our potential partners (including data on Canada's exports to each one),

Thinking Critically

The Free Market or Government Intervention?

The free market or government intervention? Each is a means of economic decision making, determining what products and services companies produce and what people will consume. So important is this process that the degree to which the market or government directs the economy affects how nations define themselves, choose their allies, and identify their enemies.

Historically, the United States has relied on the market—the "invisible hand" of supply and demand—for most economic decisions. Canada has a tradition of greater government involvement in the economy in terms of both control and ownership. The North American Free Trade Agreement (NAFTA) pushes Canada in the direction of reduced government interference in the economy.

Nevertheless, for the most part, both Canada and the United States allow the market to move prices for products upward or downward according to the supply of sellers and the demand of buyers. The market thus coordinates the efforts of countless people, each of whom—to return to Adam Smith's insight—is motivated only by self-interest.

Defenders also praise the market for discouraging racial and ethnic prejudice. Though you might restrict your social contacts, in theory at least, you can trade with whoever offers the best deal. As the economists Milton and Rose Friedman (1980) remind us, a more or less freely operating market system provides capitalist countries with the highest standards of living; in effect, they argue, the market has produced economic prosperity.

But others point to the contributions that government makes to the economy in Canada and, to a lesser extent, in the United States. Government steps in to carry out tasks that no one would do for profit. Even Adam Smith, for example, looked to government to defend the country against external enemies. Government also plays a role in constructing and maintaining public projects such as roads and utilities, as well as medical care, education, social security, public housing and other social services, safety and environmental regulation, and workers' compensation for injuries. In other words, our government plays a substantial role in the economy—one that is supported by high levels of taxation.

High taxation and the proliferation of government services and regulation go hand in hand with our widely embraced philosophies of collectivism and egalitarianism. According to Gairdner (1990:3), these policies allow the central government to "control and engineer the condition of society" in an attempt to ensure equality of outcome for all. The effect of this social engineering is to break down traditional values such as "the primacy of honesty, freedom and hard work; respect for society, authority and private property; and all related matters built upon these values." Gairdner and other supporters of free markets believe that minimal state regulation best serves the public interest.

But not everyone views the market as a positive force. For one thing, critics point out, the market has little incentive to produce anything that is not profitable. That is why few private companies set out to meet the needs of poor people since, by definition, they have little money to spend. Some analysts are critical of a freewheeling capitalist market economy, which by its nature erodes or threatens essential public services (Barlow & Campbell, 1991; Hurtig, 1991; Shields & McBride, 1994). For them, American ownership of the Canadian economy, corporate power and control, and NAFTA (which pushes us into the embrace of American capitalism) threaten Canadian values, our national identity, and the quality of life of all of our citizens. In fact, since Canada is essentially an economic union, diminishing federal involvement in the economy and in the provision of social services may even threaten national unity. Such critics look to government to curb what they see as the market system's self-destructive tendencies. Government takes a strong regulatory role, intervening in the market to control inflation (by setting interest rates), to protect the well-being of workers (by imposing workplace safety standards), and to benefit consumers (by mandating standards for product quality). Even so, advocates of a stronger role for government point out that the power of corporations in Canadian society is so great that the government still cannot effectively challenge the capitalist elite.

Because the market magnifies social inequality, the government must step in on the side of social justice. Since capitalist economies concentrate income and wealth in the hands of a few, it is necessary for government to tax the rich at a higher rate to ensure that wealth is spread over more of the population.

For a number of reasons, then, the market operating alone does not serve the public interest. While Canadians are largely supportive of the market, they also see benefits to the public through government involvement in the economy. In fact, government assists not only individual citizens but also business itself by providing investment capital, constructing infrastructure, and shielding companies from foreign competition. Yet in Canada and around the world, people continue to debate the optimal balance of market forces and government decision making.

What Do You Think?

1. How do visions of the market and government intervention in the economy fuel the debate during elections in Canada?

2. Why do defenders of the free market assert that "the government that governs best is the government that governs least"?

3. Does your family feel that income tax rates in Canada are too high or too low? Why?

information about up-coming consultation activities, and an email address for public input (www.international. gc.ca). At this point, there is no guarantee that the TPP will become a reality. It is in the nature of trade agreements that every country has to make concessions, which in turn means some loss of autonomy. Prime Minister Justin Trudeau and the major contenders in the American election of November, 2016—namely Donald Trump and Hilary Clinton—have serious reservations. If the Americans back out of the TPP, it will almost certainly collapse. If on the other hand the Americans ratify the agreement, withdrawal on our part would be extremely damaging to the Canadian economy. Since 80 percent of our exports go to the United States, any TPP-related barriers to its markets would be devastating.

What will be the long-term effects of all these changes? One thing is absolutely clear. Our economic future is not determined by our actions alone; instead, it will be played out in a global arena where Canada is only one player among many. This is illustrated by the fact that our weak Canadian dollar and general financial crisis—following the collapse in oil prices—are due to the actions of oil-producing countries far removed from our shores.

Seeing Sociology in Everyday Life

CHAPTER 16 The Economy and Work

What are the challenges of today's economy?

This chapter explains that the economy is the social institution that organizes the production, distribution, and consumption of goods and services. Because our economies are so tightly integrated, Canadians have suffered—albeit to a lesser extent—from the severe and extended recession in the United States. It's no secret that Americans are living in tough economic times that have spillover effects in Canada. Our unemployment rates are higher than they were in 2005 and will remain there for a few more years. Earning a living wage is harder than it used to be—especially in the Atlantic provinces. As C. Wright Mills might have said, the problems we face as individuals are issues that are deeply rooted in the economy. Look at the three photos and ask yourself: What changes in the North American economy create challenges for today's labour force?

Hint Industrial production has been moving from Canada (and the United States) to countries where wages are lower. In China, for example, industrial workers earn roughly 10 percent of the wages paid in North America. Since 2000, China's industrial production has increased, on average, by at least 15 percent a year. Economic activity is also expanding in India, a country that has seen striking growth in service jobs, such as those shown in the photo below of a call-centre in the city of Bangalore. Even highly skilled people such as university professors are facing challenges in today's economy. Computer technology is being used to allow professors to teach larger classes and also to allow a single faculty member to teach students in multiple classrooms—or even at home. In short, even when a corporation or organization becomes more productive, it does not always end up employing more people.

Feng Yu/Alamy Stock Photo

WALK AROUND A BIG-BOX STORE AND EXAMINE PRODUCTS TO SEE WHERE THEY ARE MADE It will not take long to see a pattern: What is it? As the share of manufactured goods made abroad rises, what happens to manufacturing jobs here in Canada?

Joerg Boethling/Alamy Stock Photo

HAVE YOU EVER CALLED AN 800 SUPPORT LINE AND WONDERED WHERE THE PERSON ON THE OTHER END OF THE LINE WAS LOCATED? IT IS NOT ONLY MANUFACTURING JOBS THAT HAVE MOVED OVERSEAS Lower wages have led corporations to relocate many service jobs—including computer programming, scientific research, and engineering—to places such as India, China, and Singapore, where service employment is skyrocketing. In short, is anyone safe from the trend we call "outsourcing"?

Dwight Cendrowski/Alamy Stock Photo

ADVANCING TECHNOLOGY MAKES OUR ECONOMY MORE PRODUCTIVE, RIGHT? GENERALLY, YES But adopting new technology can make organizations more productive with fewer employees. Have you ever taken a "distance learning" class in which the professor was not in the classroom with you? How can computer technology enable colleges to teach more students using fewer faculty?

Seeing Sociology in *Your* Everyday Life

1. Do some research to learn about the economy of your province, including the type of work people do (their occupations), the unemployment rate, the minimum wage, and the distribution of income. A good place to start is Statistics Canada (www.statcan.gc.ca). Check the most recent census and the Labour Force Survey.

2. Visit a store such as The Bay, Walmart, or Canadian Tire and do a little "fieldwork" in an area of the store that interests you. Pick 10 products and see where each is made. Do the results support the existence of a global economy?

3. Check out the occupations in your extended family and among your acquaintances. How do these occupations fit with your knowledge of the Canadian labour force?

Making the Grade

CHAPTER 16 The Economy and Work

The Economy: Historical Overview

16.1 Summarize historical changes to the economy.

The **economy** is the major social institution through which a society produces, distributes, and consumes goods and services.

In technologically simple societies, economic activity is simply part of family life.

The **agricultural revolution** (5000 years ago) made the economy a distinct social institution based on

- agricultural technology
- specialized work
- permanent settlements
- trade

The **industrial revolution** (beginning around 1750) expanded the economy based on

- new sources of energy
- centralization of work in factories
- specialization and mass production
- wage labour

The **post-industrial economy,** propelled by the **Information Revolution,** which began around 1950, is based on

- a shift from industrial work to service work
- computer technology

Three Sectors of the Economy

The **primary sector**

- draws raw materials from the natural environment
- is of greatest importance (25 percent of the economy) in low-income nations

Examples: agriculture, fishing, mining

The **secondary sector**

- transforms raw materials into manufactured goods
- is a significant share (17 percent) of the economy in low-, middle-, and high-income nations

Examples: automobile and clothing manufacturing

The **tertiary sector**

- produces services rather than goods
- is the largest sector (59 to 72 percent) in low-, middle-, and high-income countries

Examples: secretarial work, sales, teaching, medicine, website design

economy the social institution that organizes a society's production, distribution, and consumption of goods and services

post-industrial economy a productive system based on service work and high technology

primary sector the part of the economy that draws raw materials from the natural environment

secondary sector the part of the economy that transforms raw materials into manufactured goods

tertiary sector the part of the economy that involves services rather than goods

global economy economic activity that crosses national borders

Economic Systems: Paths to Justice

16.2 Assess the operation of capitalist and socialist economies.

Capitalism is based on private ownership of property and the pursuit of profit in a competitive marketplace. Capitalism results in

- greater productivity
- higher overall standard of living
- greater income inequality
- freedom to act according to self-interest

Example: Canada and the United States have mostly capitalist economies.

Socialism is grounded in collective ownership of productive property through government control of the economy. Socialism results in

- less productivity
- lower overall standard of living
- less income inequality
- freedom from basic want

Examples: The People's Republic of China and Venezuela have mostly socialist economies.

Under **welfare capitalism,**

- government may own some large industries such as transportation and the mass media
- most industry is privately owned but highly regulated by government
- high taxation of the rich helps pay for extensive government services for all

Examples: Sweden and Italy have welfare capitalist economies.

Under **state capitalism,** government works in partnership with large companies by

- supplying financial assistance
- controlling foreign imports

Examples: Japan and Singapore have state capitalist economies.

> **capitalism** an economic system in which natural resources and the means of producing goods and services are privately owned
> **socialism** an economic system in which natural resources and the means of producing goods and services are collectively owned
> **communism** a hypothetical economic and political system in which all members of a society are socially equal
> **welfare capitalism** an economic and political system that combines a mostly market-based economy with extensive social welfare programs
> **state capitalism** an economic and political system in which companies are privately owned but co-operate closely with the government

Work in Canada's Postindustrial Economy

16.3 Analyze patterns of employment and unemployment in Canada.

- Agriculture, mining, fishing, and forestry represent only 2 percent of jobs.
- Blue-collar, industrial work has declined to 17 percent of jobs.
- White-collar, service work has increased to 79 percent of jobs.

The Dual Labour Market

- Jobs in the primary labour market involve interesting work that provides high income, benefits, and job security.
- Jobs in the secondary labour market have lower pay, less job security, and fewer benefits and provide less personal satisfaction.

Self-Employment

- 12 percent of Canadian workers are self-employed.
- Many professionals (including lawyers and physicians) fall into this category, but most self-employed people have blue-collar jobs.

Unemployment

- Unemployment has many causes, including the operation of the economy itself.
- In early 2011, 7.3 percent of Canada's labour force was unemployed.
- At highest risk for unemployment are Black and Aboriginal people.

Information Technology

Information technology is changing the workplace and how people work. Computers are

- deskilling labour
- making work more abstract
- limiting interaction among workers
- increasing employers' control over workers
- allowing companies to relocate work

> **primary labour market** jobs that provide extensive benefits to workers
> **secondary labour market** jobs that provide minimal benefits to workers
> **labour unions** worker organizations that seek to improve wages and working conditions through various strategies, including negotiations and strikes
> **profession** a prestigious, white-collar occupation that requires extensive formal education
> **Self-employment** earning a living without working for a large organization
> **underground economy** economic activity involving income not reported to the government as required by law

Corporations

16.4 Discuss the importance of corporations to the Canadian economy.

Corporations form the core of the Canadian economy. Incorporation

- makes an organization a legal entity
- shields owners' wealth from lawsuits brought against the company
- can result in a lower tax rate on the company's profits

Economic Concentration and Competition

The largest corporations, which are conglomerates, account for most corporate assets and profits (e.g., Loblaw, Onyx).

- Corporations are linked through interlocking directorates.
- Recognizing that corporate linkages and the domination of certain markets by large corporations reduce competition, federal laws forbid monopoly and price fixing.

Corporations and the Global Economy

Many large corporations operate as multinationals, producing and distributing products in nations around the world.

- Modernization theorists claim that multinationals raise living standards in poor countries by offering them more jobs and advanced technology.
- Dependency theorists claim that multinationals make global inequality worse by pushing poor countries to produce goods for export and making them more dependent on rich nations.

> **corporation** an organization with a legal existence including rights and liabilities separate from that of its members
> **conglomerate** a giant corporation composed of many smaller corporations

Chapter 17
Politics and Government

Sean Kilpatrick/The Canadian Press/AP Images

⌄ Learning Objectives

17.1 Distinguish traditional, rational-legal, and charismatic authority.

17.2 Compare monarchy and democracy as well as authoritarian and totalitarian political systems.

17.3 Analyze economic and social issues using the political spectrum.

17.4 Apply the pluralist, power-elite, and Marxist models to the Canadian political system.

17.5 Describe causes of both revolution and terrorism.

17.6 Identify factors encouraging war or peace.

The Power of Society
to shape voting behaviour

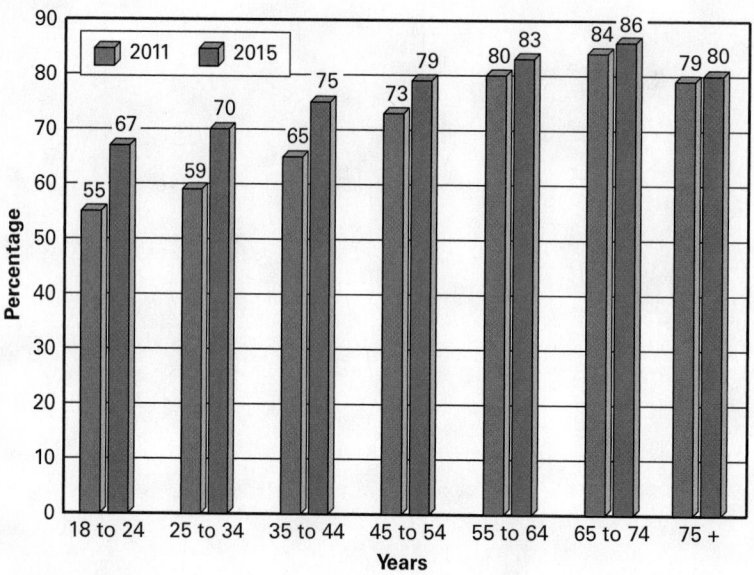

SOURCE: Statistics Canada, *The Daily*, 2016-02-22.

Does age affect the likelihood of turning out to vote? The short answer is yes. The relationship between age and voter turnout shows up clearly here—in the elections of 2011 and 2015. In both cases, people aged 18 to 24 were least likely to vote. Voter turnout increased steadily with age to its highest level among those aged 65 to 74, before dropping off among those who were older. But something unprecedented happened to voter turnout in 2015—the three youngest cohorts increased their turnout by 12, 11, and 10 percentage points respectively, while the oldest voters increased their turnout by only one point. Barack Obama inspired young voters in 2008, and Justin Trudeau did it in 2015. Americans talked about the election of 2008 as the first one that relied on the social media. Trudeau, in turn, successfully used the social media and countless "selfies" with supporters to communicate solidarity with people—particularly younger people.

Chapter Overview

Politics is the social institution that distributes power, sets goals, and makes decisions. This chapter explores politics and explains the operation of government. In addition, the chapter analyzes the character and causes of war and terrorism.

The sun has barely come up and already several thousand people have gathered at a major intersection in Manama, the capital city of Bahrain. Some have come from their homes, some have come from nearby college campuses, some have been sleeping there all night. Many people hold cellphones, checking the latest news on what is planned for the day. And over the whole scene drifts the sound of music—rap music—written by a young Tunisian known as "El Général." "Mister President," the song goes, "your people are dying.... I see injustice everywhere."

We will remember 2011 as the year when rage mixed with rap to inspire revolution throughout much of the Middle East. And added to this mix is one more key element—young people. The majority of the people in the streets of Bahrain, as elsewhere across the Middle East, are under 30. Equipped with the handheld computer technology that has defined their generation, these young people are full of ambition and hope and tired of unemployment, hunger, and having little or no voice in their political systems.

It started in Tunisia at the end of 2010 when a popular uprising forced that nation's dictator from power. The movement spread to Algeria, Jordan, Yemen, Egypt (forcing out that country's longtime leader), Libya (resulting in the death of a dictator there), as well as Syria (where yet another dictator has so far held on to power by using the military against his own people). We cannot predict the full outcome of this movement, but the goal of young people across the Middle East is clear—they are out to change the world (Al Arabiya, 2013; Ghosh, 2011; Yom and Gause, 2012; Zakaria, 2011). ∎

How power is exercised within a society—who has it and how it is used—is the focus of this chapter. What we call **politics**—or more formally, the "polity"—is *the social institution that distributes power, sets a society's goals, and makes decisions.* We will examine the bases of power and types of authority underlying the exercise of power, examine the Canadian political system and, from various perspectives, assess the extent to which our society can claim to be democratic. Then we will turn our attention to the world as a whole, including a focus on revolution, as well as the international use of power in the form of war and terrorism.

Power and Authority

17.1 Distinguish traditional, rational-legal, and charismatic authority.

Sociologist Max Weber (1978; orig. 1921) claimed that every society is based on **power**, which he defined as *the ability to achieve desired ends despite resistance from others.* The use of power is the business of **government**, *a formal*

organization that directs the political life of a society. Governments demand compliance on the part of a population; yet Weber noted that most governments do not openly threaten their people. Most of the time, people respect, or at least accept, their society's political system.

Weber pointed out that no government is likely to keep its power for very long if compliance comes *only* from the threat of brute force, because there could never be enough police to watch everyone—and who would watch the police? Every government, therefore, tries to legitimate itself in the eyes of its citizens. This brings us to Weber's concept of **authority**, *power that people perceive as legitimate rather than coercive.* How do governments transform raw power into more stable authority? Weber pointed to three ways: traditional authority, rational-legal authority, and charismatic authority.

politics the social institution that distributes power, sets a society's goals, and makes decisions

government a formal organization that directs the political life of a society

power the ability to achieve desired ends despite resistance from others

authority power that people perceive as legitimate rather than coercive

for debate; to respond otherwise would ignore the parent's traditional authority over the child and put the two on an equal footing.

Traditional Authority

Pre-industrial societies, said Weber, rely on **traditional authority**, *power legitimized by respect for long-established cultural patterns.* Woven into a population's collective memory, traditional authority means that people accept a system, usually one of hereditary leadership, simply because it has always been that way. In centuries past, Chinese emperors were legitimized by tradition, as were aristocratic rulers in medieval Europe. The power of tradition can be so strong that people come to view traditional rulers as almost godlike.

Traditional authority declines as societies industrialize. Hannah Arendt (1963) points out that traditional authority remains strong only as long as everyone shares the same beliefs and way of life. Modern scientific thinking, the specialization demanded by industrial production, and the social change and cultural diversity brought on by immigration all combine to weaken tradition. Therefore, no Canadian prime minister would claim to rule "by the grace of God," as many rulers in the ancient world did. Canada still has a monarch, Queen Elizabeth II, as its head of state, although today's more democratic culture has shifted real power to elected officials. On the recommendation of our prime minister, the queen appoints the governor-general, whose job description includes many ceremonial functions such as opening Parliament, allowing elections (by dropping the writ), and inducting people to the Order of Canada. Despite this minimal role, many Canadians are uncomfortable with any attachment to the monarchy. The recent decline in prestige suffered by the British monarchy contributed to Canada's move from deference to defiance—the Canadian revolution in attitudes described by Peter C. Newman (1995).

Traditional authority also supports *patriarchy,* the domination of women by men. This traditional form of power is still widespread, although it is increasingly challenged. Less controversial is the traditional authority that parents have over their children. As children, most of us can remember challenging a parent's demand by asking "Why?" only to hear the response "Because I said so!" Thus the parent makes clear that the demand is not open

Rational-Legal Authority

Weber defined **rational-legal authority** (sometimes called bureaucratic authority) as *power legitimized by legally enacted rules and regulations*—or power legitimized through the operation of lawful government. Weber viewed bureaucracy as the type of organization that dominates in rational-thinking, modern societies. The rational world view that promotes bureaucracy also erodes traditional customs and practices. Instead of looking to the past, members of today's high-income societies seek justice through formally enacted laws.

Rationally enacted rules also guide the use of power in everyday life. The authority of deans and classroom teachers, for example, rests on the offices they hold in bureaucratic colleges and universities. The police, too, depend on rational-legal authority. In contrast to traditional authority, rational-legal authority comes not from family background but from a position in government organization. A traditional monarch rules for life, but modern presidents or prime ministers accept and give up power according to law, which shows that their authority lies in the office, not in the person.

Charismatic Authority

Weber pointed out that power can turn into authority through charisma. **Charismatic authority** is *power legitimized by extraordinary personal abilities that inspire devotion and obedience.* Unlike traditional and rational-legal authority, charismatic authority depends less on a person's ancestry or office and more on individual personality. Charismatic leaders have surfaced throughout history, using their personal skills to turn an audience into followers. Often they make their own rules and challenge the status quo. Examples of charismatic leaders can be as different as Jesus of Nazareth and Adolf Hitler. The fact that they and others—such as India's liberator Mahatma Gandhi and American civil rights leader Martin Luther King, Jr.—succeeded in transforming the society around them explains why charismatic people are almost always highly controversial.

The prospects of politicians in Canada rise or fall according to their degree of personal charisma. Among

Types of Authority

traditional authority power legitimized by respect for long-established cultural patterns

rational-legal authority power legitimized by legally enacted rules and regulations (also known as *bureaucratic authority*)

charismatic authority power legitimized by extraordinary personal abilities that inspire devotion and obedience

THE DEATH OF PIERRE ELLIOTT TRUDEAU IN 2000, THOUGH NOT UNEXPECTED, RESULTED IN AN UNPRECEDENTED OUTPOURING OF EMOTION AND TRIBUTES FROM CANADIANS ACROSS THE COUNTRY No one—not even his sons—could have foreseen the public reaction to the death of our charismatic, infuriating, flamboyant, enigmatic former prime minister. Whatever our individual feelings about this exceptional man, it is clear that he has become part of our collective definition of what it means to be Canadian—on both national and global scales.

our more charismatic prime ministers, John Diefenbaker (1957–1963) and Pierre Elliott Trudeau (1968–1979, 1980–1984) were able to inspire Canadians with oratory and their visions of Canada. The fervour that accompanied Trudeau into his first term of office, dubbed Trudeaumania, is a phenomenon that has not been matched since. Tommy Douglas, René Lévesque, and Lucien Bouchard were also charismatic leaders.

Because charismatic authority flows from a single individual, the leader's death creates a crisis for the movement the leader has created. For the movement to survive, Max Weber explained, what must happen is the **routinization of charisma**, *the transformation of charismatic authority into some combination of traditional and bureaucratic authority*. After the death of Jesus, followers institutionalized his teachings, creating a church built on tradition and bureaucracy. Routinized in this way, the Roman Catholic Church has lasted for more than 2000 years.

Politics in Global Perspective

17.2 Compare monarchy and democracy as well as authoritarian and totalitarian political systems.

Political systems have changed over the course of history. Technologically simple hunter/gatherer societies, once found all over the planet, operated like large families without formal governments. Leadership generally fell to a man with unusual strength, hunting skill, or personal charisma. But with few resources, such leaders might control their own people but could never rule a large area (Nolan & Lenski, 2010).

Agrarian societies are larger with specialized jobs and material surpluses. In these societies, a small elite gains control of most of the wealth and power, so that politics is not just a matter of powerful individuals but a more complex social institution in its own right. This is the point in history when power passed from generation to generation within a single family and leaders start to claim a divine right to rule, gaining some measure of Weber's traditional authority. Leaders may also benefit from rational-legal authority to the extent that their rule is supported by law.

As societies grow even bigger, politics takes the form of a national government, or *political state*. But the effectiveness of a political state depends on the available technology. Centuries ago, armies moved slowly on foot, and communication over even short distances was uncertain. For this reason, the early political empires—such as Mesopotamia in what is now Iraq about 5000 years ago—took the form of many small *city-states*.

More complex technology brings about the larger-scale system of *nation-states*. Currently, the world has 195 independent nation-states, each with a somewhat distinctive political system. Generally, however, they fall into four categories: monarchy, democracy, authoritarianism, and totalitarianism.

Monarchy

Monarchy (with Latin and Greek roots meaning "one ruler") is *a political system in which a single family rules from generation to generation*. Monarchy is commonly found in the ancient agrarian societies; the Bible, for example, tells of great kings such as David and Solomon. In the world today, 26 nations have royal families;[1] some trace their ancestry back for centuries. In Weber's terms, then, monarchy is legitimized by tradition.

---

[1]In Europe: Sweden, Norway, Denmark, Great Britain, the Netherlands, Liechtenstein, Luxembourg, Belgium, Spain, and Monaco; in the Middle East: Jordan, Saudi Arabia, Oman, Qatar, Bahrain, and Kuwait; in Africa: Lesotho, Swaziland, and Morocco; in Asia: Brunei, Tonga, Thailand, Malaysia, Cambodia, Bhutan, and Japan (U.S. Department of State, 2015).

During the Middle Ages, *absolute monarchs* in much of the world claimed a monopoly of power based on divine right. Today, claims of divine right are rare, although monarchs in a number of nations—including Saudi Arabia and Oman—still exercise almost absolute control over their people, although not necessarily with divine support. Worth noting is that the leaders who managed to survive the recent uprisings in the Middle East were all monarchs rather than nontraditional leaders (Yom & Gause, 2012).

With industrialization, however, the general trend is for monarchs to gradually pass from the scene in favour of elected officials. All the European nations with royal families today are *constitutional monarchies*, meaning that their monarchs are little more than symbolic heads of state; actual governing is the responsibility of elected officials, led by a prime minister and guided by a constitution. In these nations, nobility formally reigns, but elected officials actually rule.

Fahad Shadeed/Reuters Pictures

MONARCHY IS TYPICALLY FOUND IN SOCIETIES THAT HAVE YET TO INDUSTRIALIZE The recent political unrest throughout the Middle East indicates growing resistance to this form of political system in today's world. Even so, King Abdullah and members of his royal family strengthen their control of Saudi Arabia through their support of Arabic heritage and culture.

Democracy

The historical trend in the modern world has been toward **democracy**, *a political system that gives power to the people as a whole.* More accurately, because it would be impossible for *all* citizens to act as leaders, we have devised a system of *representative democracy* that puts authority in the hands of leaders chosen by the people in elections.

Most high-income countries of the world, including those that still have royal families, claim to be democratic. Industrialization and democratic government go together because both require a literate populace. Also, with industrialization, the legitimization of power in a tradition-based monarchy gives way to rational-legal authority. Thus democracy and rational-legal authority go together, just like monarchy and traditional authority.

But even high-income countries such as Canada are not truly democratic for two reasons. First, there is the problem of bureaucracy. All democratic political systems rely on the work of large numbers of bureaucratic officials who carry out the task of public administration. In Canada, 1.2 million people work as federal, provincial/territorial, and municipal employees. These bureaucrats are not elected and, therefore, are not directly accountable to Canadians.

Second, Canada is not truly democratic because of economic inequality. In a highly stratified society, the rich will have the most political clout and will be more likely to vote. Moreover, given the even greater resources and political influence of large organizations, especially multinational corporations, how can we think that our "democratic" system responds to—or even hears—the voices of its citizens? Governments have moved to reduce the ability of large corporations to affect election outcomes; for example, corporations in Canada are now limited to donations of no more than $1000 to political parties or leadership candidates—whereas individuals can contribute more than $5000.

Still, democratic nations do provide many rights and freedoms. Global Map 17–1 shows one assessment of the extent of political freedom around the world. According to Freedom House, an organization that tracks political trends, 88 of the world's nations (with 40 percent of the global population) were "free," respecting many civil liberties, in 2015. This represents a decline in freedom for the fourth straight year, but a gain in freedom from 30 years ago when just 53 nations were considered free (Freedom House, 2015).

DEMOCRACY AND FREEDOM: CAPITALIST AND SOCIALIST APPROACHES Despite internal problems, rich capitalist nations such as ours claim to be democracies. Of course, socialist countries such as Cuba and the

monarchy a political system in which a single family rules from generation to generation

democracy a political system that gives power to the people as a whole

Window on the World

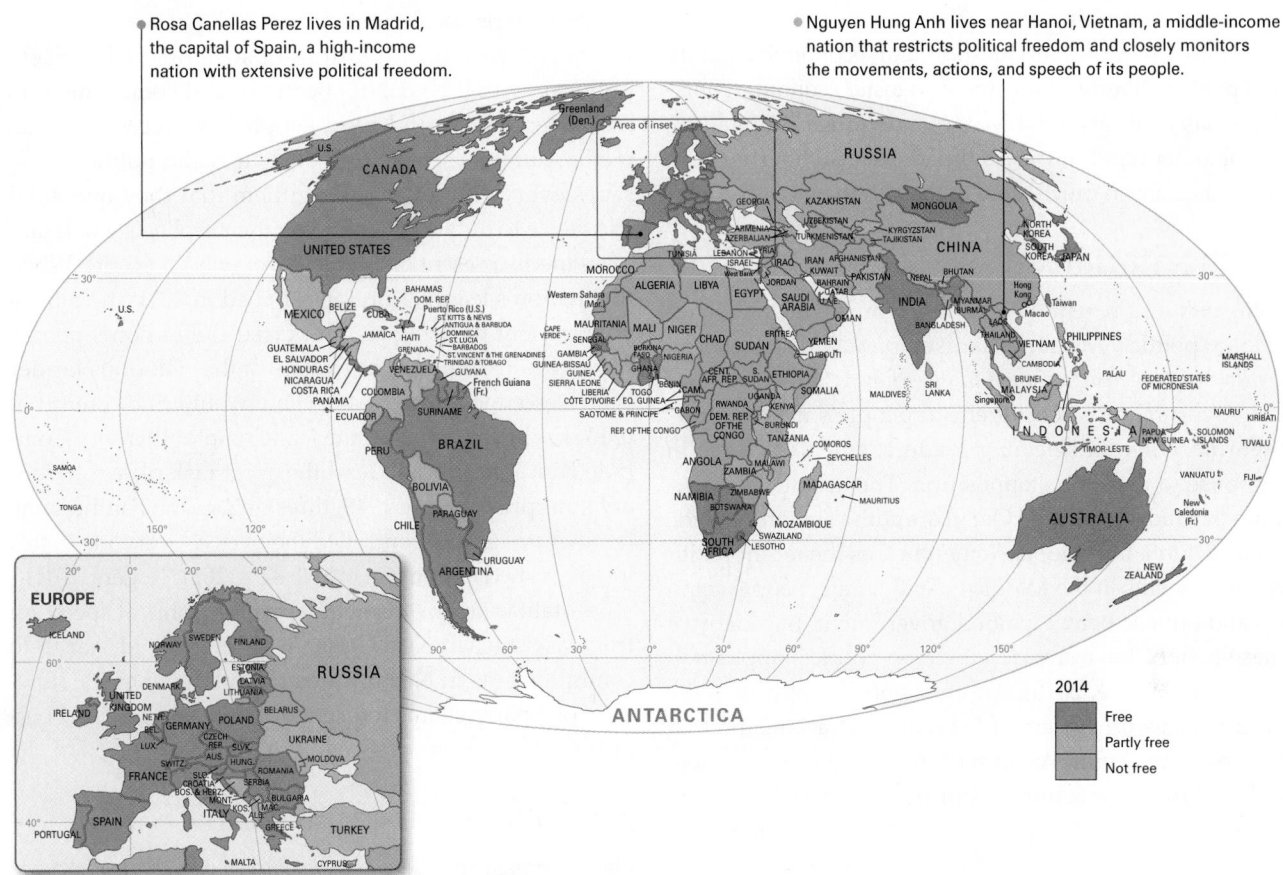

Rosa Canellas Perez lives in Madrid, the capital of Spain, a high-income nation with extensive political freedom.

Nguyen Hung Anh lives near Hanoi, Vietnam, a middle-income nation that restricts political freedom and closely monitors the movements, actions, and speech of its people.

2014
Free
Partly free
Not free

Global Map 17–1 Political Freedom in Global Perspective

In 2014, a total of 88 of the world's 194 nations, containing 40 percent of all people, were politically "free"; that is, they offered their citizens extensive political rights and civil liberties. Another 55 countries, which included 24 percent of the world's people, were "partly free," with more limited rights and liberties. The remaining 51 nations, home to 36 percent of humanity, fall into the category of "not free." In these countries, government sharply restricts individual initiative. Between 1980 and 2014, democracy made significant gains, largely in Latin America.

SOURCE: Based on Freedom House (2015).

People's Republic of China make the same claim. This curious fact suggests that we need to look more closely at *political economy*, the interplay of politics and economics.

The political life of Canada, the United States, and the nations of Europe is largely shaped by the economic principles of capitalism. The pursuit of profit within a market system requires that "freedom" be defined in terms of people's right to act in their own self-interest; therefore, the capitalist approach to political freedom translates into personal liberty, the freedom to act in whatever ways maximize personal profit or other advantage. From this point of view, "democracy" means that individuals have the right to select their leaders from among those running for office.

However, capitalist societies are marked by a striking inequality of income and wealth. If everyone acts according to self-interest, the inevitable result is that some people have much more power to get their way than others. In practice, a market system creates unequal wealth and transforms

wealth into power. Critics of capitalism claim that a wealthy elite dominates the economic and political life of the society.

By contrast, socialist systems claim that they are democratic because their economies meet everyone's basic needs for housing, schooling, work, and medical care. Though a relatively poor country, Cuba provides basic medical care to its entire population regardless of ability to pay.[2]

Critics of socialism point out that the extensive government regulation of social life in these countries is oppressive. The socialist governments of China and Cuba, for example, do not allow their people to move freely within

---

[2]Canada has universal health care because our democracy is a capitalist system tinged with socialism, but our health care system is for essential medical services; such non-essentials as cosmetic surgery, optometry, prescription drugs, some immunization and diagnostic techniques, and dental care are typically paid by private insurance (for those with employee or private health plans) or out of pocket (by the less fortunate).

or across their borders, and they tolerate no organized political opposition, freedom of speech, or freedom of the press.

These contrasting approaches to democracy and freedom raise an important question: Can economic equality and political liberty go together? To foster economic equality, socialism limits the choices of individuals. Capitalism, on the other hand, provides broad political liberties that, in practice, mean much more to the rich than to the poor.

Authoritarianism

Some nations prevent their people from having any voice at all in politics. **Authoritarianism** is *a political system that denies the people participation in government.* An authoritarian government is indifferent to people's needs, offers them no voice in selecting leaders, and uses force in response to dissent or opposition. The absolute monarchies in Saudi Arabia and Oman are authoritarian, as is the military junta in Ethiopia. Sometimes, as the recent political movements in the Middle East illustrate, people stand up and oppose heavy-handed government. But many of these nations have cracked down on political opposition (Freedom House, 2015). Another political option is the largely peaceful system of "soft authoritarianism" that thrives in the small Asian nation of Singapore—where political freedom is limited but people are secure, prosperous, and generally supportive of their government.

Totalitarianism

The most intensely controlled political form is **totalitarianism**, *a highly centralized political system that extensively regulates people's lives.* Totalitarianism emerged in the twentieth century as technological advances gave governments the ability to control their populations rigidly. The Vietnamese government closely monitors the activities of not just visitors but all of its citizens. Similarly, the government of North Korea, perhaps the most totalitarian in the world, keeps its people in poverty and uses not only police to control people but also surveillance equipment and powerful computers to collect and store information about them.

Although some totalitarian governments claim to represent the will of the people, most seek to bend people to the will of the government. As the term itself implies, such governments rely on the *total* concentration of power and allow no organized opposition whatsoever. By denying citizens the right to assemble and controlling access to information, these governments create an atmosphere of isolation and fear. In the final decades of the Soviet Union, for example, ordinary citizens had no access to telephone directories, copying

equipment, fax machines, or even accurate city maps. Only in recent years has the Cuban government allowed its citizens to own personal computers and cell phones.

Socialization in totalitarian societies is intensely political, with the goal of obedience and commitment to the system. In North Korea, people have access to social media, but they see pictures of leaders and political messages everywhere, reminding them that they owe total allegiance to the state. Government-controlled schools and mass media present only official versions of events. When that nation's leader, Kim Jong-il, died in 2011, the official government news agency reported the nation's people were in "utter despair" at the loss of the "Glorious Leader Who Descended from Heaven" but would find comfort in the "absolute surety that the leadership of [his son] Comrade Kim Jong-un will lead the great task of revolutionary enterprise." Since 1948, three generations of the same family have tightly controlled the lives of everyone in this impoverished nation (Chance & Kim, 2011; Rogers, 2011).

Totalitarian governments span the political spectrum from fascist (as in Nazi Germany during World War II) to communist (as in North Korea today). In all cases, however, one party claims total control of the society and permits no opposition.

A Global Political System?

Over the past five decades, we have seen the emergence of a global economy in which large corporations operate with little regard to national boundaries. Considering the relationship between the economy and politics—the political economy—one might ask if globalization is changing politics in the same way. On one level, the answer is no. While most of the world's economic activity is international, the planet remains divided into nation-states, just as it has been for centuries. The United Nations, founded in 1945, was a small step toward global government, but to date its political role in the world has been limited.

On another level, politics has become a global process. For some analysts, multinational corporations have created a new political order because of their enormous power to shape events throughout the world. In other words, politics is dissolving into business as corporations grow larger than governments.

Also, the Information Revolution has moved national politics onto the world stage. Email, text messaging, and Twitter mean that few countries can conduct their political affairs in complete privacy. The "WikiLeaks" controversy shows that just about anyone can transmit information—even that guarded by governments—so that it can become available to anyone and everyone. The power of electronic communication to transmit and receive information is the reason for greater efforts to control its use on the part of oppressive political regimes (Freedom House, 2015; Gellman, 2011).

authoritarianism a political system that denies the people participation in government

totalitarianism a highly centralized political system that extensively regulates people's lives

In short, social media based on computer technology add a global dimension to even local politics. Most of the young people who participated in the political opposition that swept the Middle East in 2011 and 2012 were motivated by an awareness of the greater political voice available to most people elsewhere in the world. Using cell phone networks, they rapidly spread information and quickly organized political events. It is no wonder, then, that as the Middle East drama unfolded, China clamped down on internet use, creating what some analysts called the "Great Firewall of China" (Xia, 2011; Zakaria, 2011).

As part of the global political process, several thousand *nongovernmental organizations* (NGOs) seek to advance global issues, such as human rights (e.g., Amnesty International) or an ecologically sustainable world (e.g., Greenpeace). NGOs will continue to play a key part in expanding the global political culture.

In sum, just as individual nations are losing control of their own economies, governments cannot fully manage the political events occurring within their borders.

Politics in Canada

17.3 Analyze economic and social issues using the political spectrum.

Canada's national existence comes from the other side of the political upheaval that gave birth to the United States. Seymour Martin Lipset points out: "The United States is the country of the revolution, Canada of the counterrevolution"; the Americans sought "a form of rule derived from the people and stressing individualism," while Canadians desired "free institutions within a strong monarchical state" (1991:1). "Life, liberty, and the pursuit of happiness" are the goals of our neighbours to the south; Canada chose "peace, order, and good government."

Part of the impetus for Confederation was economic, but the leaders in various parts of what was to become Canada were watching nervously, fearing economic and political absorption—if not military conquest—by the increasingly populous and aggressive United States. The colonies that formed Canada came together somewhat reluctantly: Newfoundlanders initially rejected Confederation in an 1869 election, and the people of Nova Scotia would have done the same had they been asked to vote on the issue. Nowhere did political union occur without vigorous debate and passionate opposition. Table 17–1 reveals that Canada was formed in bits and pieces from 1867 to 1949, when Newfoundlanders voted "yes" to Confederation in a referendum.

Because the provinces joined Canada at different times and through various kinds of agreements, they have never had uniform relationships with the federal government. The north, without provincial status, is composed of territories controlled by the federal government. Furthermore,

Table 17–1 Dates of Entry into Confederation

Province or Territory	Date
New Brunswick	July 1, 1867
Nova Scotia	July 1, 1867
Ontario	July 1, 1867
Quebec	July 1, 1867
Manitoba	July 15, 1870
Northwest Territories[a]	July 15, 1870
British Columbia	July 20, 1871
Prince Edward Island	July 1, 1873
Yukon Territory	June 13, 1898
Alberta	September 1, 1905
Saskatchewan	September 1, 1905
Newfoundland[b]	March 31, 1949
Nunavut[c]	April 1, 1999

[a]Rupert's Land and the North-Western Territories (including central-to-northern Ontario and Quebec, the area west to British Columbia, and north to the Arctic) was purchased from the Hudson's Bay Company in 1870. A small portion became Manitoba; the remainder, known as the North-West Territories, was governed from Ottawa. Not until the early twentieth century were northern Ontario, northern Quebec, Alberta, Saskatchewan, and the Yukon Territory transferred from the Northwest Territories.
[b]Newfoundland was officially renamed Newfoundland and Labrador in 2001.
[c]Nunavut is a federal territory carved out of lands in the eastern Northwest Territories.

SOURCES: Adapted from *Canadian Global Almanac 2003* (2002), Hall (1999), and Waite (1988).

Quebec was seen as unique from the beginning because of its French-speaking Catholic majority. Canada is a rather loose confederation in that important powers were left in provincial hands. Questions of federal/provincial jurisdiction—the centralization or decentralization of power—have been with us since 1867 and may never be fully resolved. Canada's provincial structure, its geographic size and diversity, and its immigration and settlement history add important regional dimensions to our collective identity and to Canadian politics. The presence of Quebec, the only entity with a French-speaking majority in North America, adds to our Canadian experience in terms of identity, federal/provincial relations, and unity. Our existence as a "fragile federation" (Marsden & Harvey, 1979), ever mindful of the factors that divide and unite us, is expressed in our periodic constitutional navel gazing.

Canadians are represented in Parliament by the Senate, an appointed body with 105 seats apportioned on a regional basis to the Maritimes, Ontario, Quebec, and the western provinces,[3] and the House of Commons, with 338 seats (up from 308 in the election of 2011). On the basis of population, Quebec and Ontario together elect 57 percent (191) of the 338 members of Parliament (MPs). Thus, they have a decisive impact on which party wins the most seats, and who becomes prime minister. Also, the predominance of MPs

---

[3]There are 24 seats in the Senate for each of the regions named, plus six for Newfoundland and Labrador and one each for the Yukon, Northwest Territories, and Nunavut.

from Ontario and Quebec reduces the likelihood that Parliament will pass legislation contrary to the interests of central Canada. The unhappiness of the peripheral provinces with the political clout of central Canada at both House of Commons and Senate levels was behind the quest, by the Reform Party in the early 1990s, for a Triple-E Senate (i.e., equal, effective, and elected). Equal Senate representation for all provinces would have countered Quebec/Ontario dominance in the House. The redistribution of seats, based on population growth prior to the census of 2012, provided the western provinces (Alberta in particular) with 20 of the 30 new seats. Thus, although the west did not get its Triple-E Senate, it has more political clout today because of its larger share of the seats in the House of Commons.

Culture, Economics, and Politics

Unlike Americans, who embrace individualism wholeheartedly, Canadians endorse it with ambivalence. Our individualism is tempered by a sense of communal responsibility, recognition of legitimate group interests, and the realization that we are, in the words of former Prime Minister Joe Clark, a "community of communities." When the Trudeau government gave us the *Charter*

in 1982, analysts pointed out that we had moved closer to embracing the individualism of the United States:

> The *Canadian Charter of Rights and Freedoms* is not the American *Bill of Rights*. It preserves the principle of parliamentary supremacy and places less emphasis on individual, as distinct from group, rights than does the American document. But the *Charter* brings Canada much closer to the American stress on protection of the individual and judicial supremacy—with its accompanying encouragement to litigiousness (the tendency to sue)—than is true of other parliamentary countries. (Lipset, 1991:3)

In accordance with our emphasis on collectivity, Canadians endorse a broadly interventionist government. Although in recent years Canadians have been increasingly worried about the costs of government activity, they nonetheless expect government to deal with national defence, law and order, international relations, radio and television broadcasting, stabilization of the economy, regional development, pensions, employment insurance, welfare, transportation, education (right up through university), medical care, culture and heritage, and environmental and safety standards. The federal government also has a special responsibility toward Aboriginal peoples, which, as outlined in the Thinking about Diversity box,

Thinking About Diversity: Race, Class, and Gender

Aboriginal Self-Government

Canada's Aboriginal peoples are not treated like other Canadians for historical reasons. The first European explorers and settlers encountered at least 55 *founding nations* (Dickason, 1997), distinct linguistic and cultural societies that were self-governing in their traditional territories with formal alliances among tribes. The Six Nations Confederacy (Haudenosaunee) had an elaborate constitution and *federal* structure. Fifty hereditary peace chiefs met yearly to deal with common problems and to make new laws: "The laws and decisions of the Confederacy were passed on by word of mouth and recorded in wampum, arguably the world's oldest constitution, predating the American Constitution by 200 years" (Nader et al., 1992). Some elements of this constitution were included in the *federal* structures of both the United States and Canada.

The First Nations taught the explorers and early settlers to survive on this harsh continent, introducing them to corn, squash, beans, potatoes, and tobacco. The fur trade—coordinated by the Hudson's Bay Company—depended on Aboriginal expertise, labour, and the canoe, the design of which has never been improved (Nader et al., 1992). If the Six Nations Confederacy had not sided with the British against the French in the 1750s, Canada might now be French. Furthermore, Métis historian Olive Dickason argued,

with respect to the American attack on Canada in 1812, that "Amerindian support was vital to the preservation of Britain's remaining North American colonies" (1992:217).

As settlers flowed into Canada, former fur trade partners and military allies found themselves in conflict over land. To acquire lands occupied by Aboriginal peoples and to avoid the kind of resistance to settlement that occurred in the United States, numerous treaties were negotiated—from the pre-Confederation period in the Maritimes through to 1921 in the Northwest Territories. The descendants of those who signed treaties are called Treaty Indians (or status Indians and more recently First Nations); they are subject to the *Indian Act* and remain the responsibility of Aboriginal Affairs and Northern Development Canada (formerly Indian and Northern Affairs Canada). In addition, First Nations (members of over 600 communities) are represented by their chiefs in the Assembly of First Nations or the AFN.

The terms of the treaties varied over time and across the country (Frideres & Gadacz, 2008), but most commonly they involved the surrender of lands in exchange for reserves and other guarantees (e.g., fishing and hunting rights). Interpretation of the treaties has been subject to considerable debate—but more important, in light of the current quest for self-government, is the question of whether the existence of treaties implies recognition of sovereignty. Aboriginal people believe that they were sovereign prior to the treaties and that the treaties did not extinguish that sovereignty.

Section 25 of the *Canadian Charter of Rights and Freedoms* (Canada, 1982) recognizes and affirms the existing Aboriginal and treaty rights of Native peoples, including Indian, Inuit, and Métis. In 1987, when the Meech Lake Accord was negotiated in an effort to have Quebec sign on to the constitution, the Aboriginal request for recognition of the right to self-government was ignored altogether. In response, a Cree member of the Manitoba Legislative Assembly, Elijah Harper, took steps to scuttle "Meech" just before its ratification deadline in 1990.

Representatives of four Native organizations participated in the next round of constitutional negotiation, with the result that the Charlottetown Accord of August 1992 recognized the *inherent* right to self-government: "The Aboriginal peoples of Canada, being the first peoples to govern this land, have the right to promote their languages, cultures and traditions and to ensure the integrity of their societies, and their governments constitute one of three orders of government in Canada."[4] The defeat of this accord in the referendum of October 26, 1992, was a bitter disappointment to some Aboriginal negotiators.

In the meantime, many Aboriginal communities are managing their own affairs. The Royal Commission on Aboriginal Peoples (Canada, 1996) declared that the right of Aboriginal peoples to govern themselves predates Confederation, has a basis in Canadian law, and is already protected in our constitution. Some formal self-government agreements have been negotiated between various Aboriginal peoples, the federal government, and their respective provinces or territories.

In a dramatic development, the Northwest Territories decided in a 1992 referendum to carve a new territory out of its eastern region. Nunavut, with one-fifth of Canada's land mass and a population that is 80 percent Inuit, became a distinct entity with its own territorial government in 1999. The territorial assembly is a public government and not self-government as the Assembly of First Nations would define it.[5] The development of Nunavut is enhanced by the existence of the Aboriginal Peoples Television Network, successful co-operatives, experienced Inuit business people, and sophisticated leadership. But the Inuit still face formidable challenges as they assume the tasks of territorial government.

During the Quebec separatist debate, the Grand Council of the Crees, in a report titled *Sovereign Injustice* (1995), concluded that Quebec has no right to secede from Canada or to forcibly include the Crees and their territories in a sovereign Quebec. When Quebec held its sovereignty referendum in October 1995, the Crees conducted their own, in which they almost unanimously chose *not* to be part of an independent Quebec. That referendum, and the Grand Council report (1995)—based on extensive research into international and Canadian law and precedent—signalled that others cannot continue to make decisions for the Crees.

In 2003, Minister of Indian Affairs Robert Nault found himself at loggerheads with the Assembly of First Nations over his attempt to modernize the *Indian Act*. The purpose of the proposed *First Nations Governance Act* was to provide communities with modern tools of governance, allowing them to assume substantial new powers while being accountable to their members. Despite consultation with First Nations communities regarding the proposed changes, the Assembly and its leader Matthew Coon Come argued that, once again, foreign laws and administrative practices were being forced on First Nations. The government withdrew the proposed Act. If the principle of the inherent right to self-government were taken seriously, the First Nations themselves would design and implement any new governance legislation.

In 2005, Alberta's Lubicon Cree Band sent representatives to the United Nations Commission on Human Rights in Geneva to ask for help in resolving a "long-standing land-rights dispute" (*Globe and Mail,* 2005). In 1990, the commission had criticized Canada's handling of the dispute as the Band fought for a reserve that Ottawa had promised to create in 1939. You may wonder why one of Canada's First Nations would be turning to the United Nations. The reason is that the United Nations has declared that all peoples have the right to self-determination.

In 2008, Parliament amended the *Canadian Human Rights Act* "to give over 700 000 aboriginal people, mostly residents of First Nations communities, the same protections as everyone else in Canada" (Langtry, 2012). This has allowed them to file "over 300 complaints against the federal government and their own governments" to end discrimination and improve quality of life on reserves. This change in the *Human Rights Act* allows vulnerable First Nations people to "challenge systemic and often unconscious prejudices" and provides equal opportunity for everyone.

What Do You Think?

1. Do you think that *all* Aboriginal peoples should have the right to self-determination as the United Nations declares?

2. Were you aware of the role of Aboriginal peoples in the exploration and settlement of Canada, as well as in keeping Canada British and independent of the United States?

3. How should Ottawa respond to Aboriginal land claims in populated areas such as southern Ontario and Quebec? What would you think if you owned some of the disputed land?

---

[4]Use of the word *inherent* is important because it implies that the right to self-government is neither granted by the Canadian government nor subject to repeal. Instead, the right is based on Aboriginal status and granted by the Creator. In 1984, the Canadian Parliament recognized that the right to Aboriginal self-government is inherent.

[5]The territorial government of Nunavut is a *public* government serving all of its residents, Inuit and non-Inuit alike. *Ethnic* government applies to the Inuit alone, on the lands set aside in a separate land claim agreement.

has been undergoing changes of a political nature. In fact, to the extent that we can articulate a "Canadian" identity, it is based on some of the government services that make us a tolerant and caring society. Widespread anxiety about free trade with the United States (1989)—and later with the United States and Mexico (1994)—arose partly from the fear of job loss, but also from the fear that resulting pressures to harmonize with our powerful neighbour would threaten our cultural and social welfare programs—in particular, our medicare system. We had no way of knowing that, by 2016, President Obama would have instituted Obamacare and that the two main contenders for the presidency—Donald Trump and Hilary Clinton—would be threatening to scrap NAFTA (the North American Free Trade Agreement of 1994) and to refuse to ratify the TPP (the Trans-Pacific Partnership).

Government is more involved in the daily lives of its citizens in Canada than in the United States, but this does not mean that Canadians are in complete agreement regarding the appropriateness of that involvement. Some people feel that governments should take a more activist role in areas such as child care, job creation, minority rights, employment or pay equity, and environmental protection. Others feel that government already does far too much, at too great expense, and that it should withdraw many of its programs and encourage privatization of services where feasible. These differences in perspective, which are in part a function of socio-economic status and regional subculture, are reflected in the policies and platforms of Canada's political parties. Figure 17–1 deals with the "size" of government in selected countries; people in France and Denmark get a broader range of social services from their government than Canadians, Americans, or Australians. You may be surprised to learn that Canada's government is only slightly larger than that of the United States—in that government expenditures account for 40 and 41 percent of GDP respectively.

Political Parties

Since about the time of Confederation, Canadians have joined to form **political parties**, *organizations operating within the political system that seek control of the government.* Although we take political parties for granted today as part of a democracy, the party system had tentative beginnings here—and was hotly debated in the United States, where George Washington and Benjamin Franklin, among others, feared that parties would tear their fledgling nation apart.

political parties organizations operating within the political system that seek control of the government.

Global Snapshot

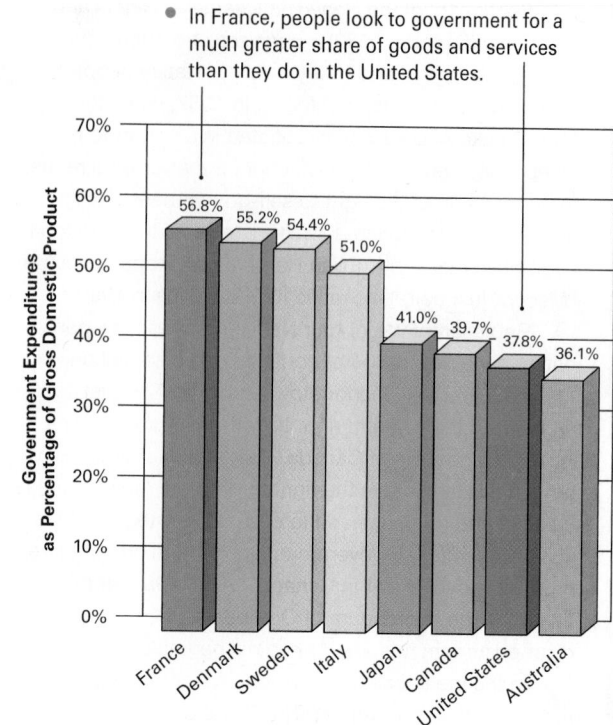

- In France, people look to government for a much greater share of goods and services than they do in the United States.

Figure 17–1 The Size of Government, 2015

Government activity accounts for a smaller share of economic output in Canada and the United States than in many other high-income countries.

SOURCE: Based on OECD (2015).

The two political parties that Canadians have known since the 1860s trace their roots to the period after 1840, when the United Provinces of Upper and Lower Canada came into being. In fact, a Liberal-Conservative coalition of factions under Sir George-Étienne Cartier and

SOME CANADIAN VOTERS VOTE FOR SPECIFIC CANDIDATES, REGARDLESS OF PARTY AFFILIATION, BUT MANY REMAIN LOYAL TO THE SAME POLITICAL PARTY FROM ELECTION TO ELECTION Party support is often shown through lawn signs, which may be subject to sabotage, as was this one in the election of 2000 (reflecting a scandal allegedly involving then prime minister Jean Chrétien).

Sir John A. Macdonald provided sufficient political stability to allow for the negotiation of Confederation. The first House of Commons had, among others, Tory (Conservative) and Grit (Liberal) factions, which, by 1867, were beginning to align themselves with specific sets of policies and supporters. The Tories were "firmly protectionist, expansionist, and pro-business," while the Grits were "anti-railroad, anti-protectionist, and pro-agrarian" (Van Loon & Whittington, 1981:326–327). After World War I, a number of minor parties appeared on the scene, the most long-lived of which was the anti-capitalism Co-operative Commonwealth Federation, which became the New Democratic Party after 1961.

In recent decades, many different parties (24 in 2015) have contested federal elections, with some of them surviving for only one election. While each of these parties had candidates running in electoral districts across the country, only the Conservative, Liberal, New Democratic, and Social Credit parties elected MPs over extended periods of time.

Two new parties turned Canadian politics upside down in the federal election of 1993, and nothing has been the same since. In that year, the Bloc Québécois and the Reform Party entered Canada's political arena and gave regionalism—in Quebec and western Canada—a new face. By 2000, after failing in its attempt to merge with the Progressive Conservatives, Reform changed its name to the Canadian Reform Conservative Alliance (Canadian Alliance, for short). Faced with the prospect of electoral annihilation by a Liberal Party led by Paul Martin, the two conservative parties made a last-ditch effort to merge in the fall of 2003. The result was the Conservative Party of Canada, with a new leader (Stephen Harper) ready to contest the federal election of 2004. The Conservatives lost the 2004 election but won in 2006 and 2008, forming a minority government each time. In 2011, Stephen Harper's Conservative Party of Canada won in a majority of the ridings (or electoral districts) and formed its first majority government.

FUNCTIONS OF POLITICAL PARTIES Political parties in Canada and elsewhere have the following societal functions:

1. *Promoting political pluralism.* Political parties create centres of power independent of the government. This is why totalitarian governments routinely quash all political parties save their own.
2. *Increasing political involvement.* Ideally, parties draw people into the political process by articulating various points of view on controversial issues. By encouraging public debate, political campaigns help make government more responsive to the people.
3. *Selection of political candidates and leaders.* Political parties nominate candidates to run for office. In Canada, at nomination meetings for each constituency, local party members choose the candidates who will run for office in the next election—unless the federal party chooses to impose its choice on specific ridings. When national or provincial parties select new leaders, riding associations elect the delegates who go to the leadership conventions—except among parties (e.g., the new Conservative Party) that forgo conventions and have party members vote individually for their leaders.

4. *Forging political coalitions.* While parties can divide a society, they often forge broad coalitions among people interested in specific issues. Party platforms usually incorporate a wide range of proposals to appeal to many people, making victory at the polls more likely. Many nations have dozens of narrowly based political parties. Canada has had two dominant federal parties—often with a weaker third party—fairly consistently since Confederation. As noted, the 1993 election introduced two new challengers (Reform and the Bloc) to vie for power with Conservatives, Liberals, and the NDP. In the election of 2008, the Green Party made its first serious inroads, gaining 6.8 percent of the votes across Canada, and in 2011 elected its first MP (party leader Elizabeth May).
5. *Maintaining political stability.* By maintaining relatively consistent positions on a number of issues, the major parties promote political stability. For this reason, of course, those who seek radical change in Canada may criticize political parties in general.

PARTIES AND THE POLITICAL SPECTRUM Political ideology is commonly viewed in terms of the political spectrum, a continuum ranging from communism on the left to extreme conservatism on the right. The *political left* in Canada, as represented by the New Democrats (NDP), can be described as anti-capitalist (or anti–big business), egalitarian, collectivist, and interventionist. It supports a broad safety net of social welfare programs, including universal child care, education, medicare, and alternative energy. Government or public ownership and regulation of major industries, unionization, inheritance taxes, and progressive taxation (that is, rates that increase with income) are also among its policies. The left opposes free trade with the United States and Mexico, because of its presumed negative effects on employment and social programs. Opposed to globalization, it favours the Kyoto Accord and supports an activist environmental agenda. In the election of 2008, the Green Party won the support of environmentalists at the expense of the NDP.

As one might expect, those on the *political right* espouse a different set of values and goals. They are in favour of private enterprise, big business, and free markets. Competitiveness, globalization, restructuring, deficit reduction, and privatization of Crown corporations are laudable goals in the eyes of the right, as are private property rights, tax exemptions for capital gains, and free trade. Those on the right generally feel that, while government expenditures on social programs are necessary, they should be restricted by society's ability to pay for them. These values are consistent with *fiscal* conservatism (or financial conservatism). The Canadian Alliance endorsed an additional set of values referred to as *social* conservatism; many of these values (including anti-abortion and anti-gay policies) are consistent with those of fundamentalist Christians. Policies referred to as *family values* are the cornerstone of social conservatism, which also embraces some American-style individual rights, such as unfettered gun ownership. For the most part, the new Conservative Party has had to steer clear of social conservatism in order to broaden its electoral support. Once it became competitive in Quebec, as evidenced in the elections of 2006 and 2008, it had to tread even more carefully.

Many Canadians conclude that there are no ideological differences among our major political parties—at least not between the Liberals and the old Progressive Conservatives. William Christian (1983) disagrees, noting that some very clear and consistent ideological strains have characterized our parties over time. Our parties and their ideological orientations are the result of our unique political history and European roots, so that they are very different from the Democratic and Republican parties of the United States. Furthermore, the ideological *mix* in our parties makes it difficult to place them accurately on a left–right continuum. For example, there were "Red" and "Pink" (meaning socialist) Tories in the Progressive Conservative Party. Whereas the stance of the Canadian Alliance was unambiguously on the right, the new Conservative Party includes some of those Red and Pink Tories. You may recall that in the election of 2015 NDP leader Thomas Mulcair moved his party away from the left towards the middle of the spectrum. This allowed Justin Trudeau to move the Liberals so far to the left that he was able to win back many of the NDP voters who created the Orange Wave with Jack Layton in the election of 2011. In other words, the ideological boundaries between our political parties are fuzzy. As a result, placing Canadian parties on a left–right continuum, as in Figure 17–2 below, is done with some hesitation—since, to some extent most parties are "mixed bags" and there is frequent movement in party positions in response to the issues of the day.

Voter Apathy

In both Canada and the United States, citizens are less likely to vote today than they were a century ago. In some U.S. presidential elections, only half of all registered voters go to the polls; in other elections, it might be 60 percent. In Canada, 70 to 90 percent of eligible voters turned out in all but five elections from 1867 to 1993. More recent federal elections had much lower voter turnout: 67 percent in 1997, 61 percent in 2000 and 2004, 65 percent in 2006, and a disappointing all-time low of 59 percent in 2008. The turnout in 2011 was only 61 percent—despite the excitement of the NDP surge (Jack Layton's Orange Wave). You may recall that the Power of Society figure at the beginning of this chapter reveals increases of 10 to 12 percentage points in voter turnout among younger people (18 to 44 years of age). Their support for Justin Trudeau and the Liberals propelled him into position of prime minister with an astonishing voter turnout of 77 percent.

Who is and is not likely to vote? Women are slightly more likely than men to cast a ballot; people older than 65 are much more likely to vote than young adults (even in 2015); and some ethnic and racial minorities are less likely to exercise their franchise than others. Generally speaking, people with a bigger stake in society—homeowners; parents with young children; people with more schooling, good jobs, and higher income—are more likely to vote. Of course, we should expect some non-voting because, at any given time, thousands of people are sick or away from home or have recently moved to a new neighbourhood. In addition, an inability to read and write discourages voting among adults with limited literacy, and those with physical disabilities that limit mobility may have difficulty getting to the polls.

Elections Canada has gone to great lengths to reach out to young voters and to facilitate voting on the part of those who are away from home or unable to get to the polls. Now, once an election has been called, you can vote ahead of time in the electoral office in your riding—or you can arrange to vote in another riding or by a mail-in ballot from abroad. If you are ill or unable to drive or walk, election workers will bring a ballot to your own home at your convenience.

Of course, there are many people, including young adults, who can make it to the polls but choose not to because of *indifference* or *alienation*. Some people fail to

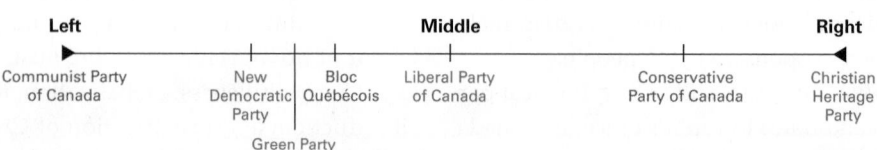

Figure 17–2 Selected Canadian Political Parties on a Left–Right Continuum

see the relevance of voting ("What's in it for me?") or to see it as one's civic duty. Others have lost faith in politicians—because of scandal or failed election promises—and the political process itself. The recent dip in turnout is also related to the competitiveness of the electoral process. If elections in your riding are won by large margins, as they often are in Canada, it's hard to see the effect of your single vote. We have also gone through a period in Canada when the Liberals were assured of victory because of vote-splitting on the right between the Reform (later, Alliance) and the Progressive Conservatives. If there is no party that can defeat the Liberals, then neither liberals nor conservatives feel a pressing need to turn out to vote (Pammett & LeDuc, 2004).

By 2006, the new Conservative Party under Stephen Harper looked as if it had a chance to form a minority government, and voter turnout increased from 61 to 65 percent. A more competitive election resulted in higher voter turnout. Of course, in 2015, the outcome of the election was unknown until the final weeks. Given that uncertainty and the perceived momentum of the Liberals, voter turnout rose to 77 percent as younger voters came out in record numbers. One other factor comes into play, and that is region. In the federal elections of 2011 and 2015, Newfoundland and Labrador had the lowest voter turnout (58 and 67 percent) while tiny Prince Edward Island—where voters know their candidates personally—had the highest turnout (81 and 86 percent in 2011 and 2015). In 2011, Manitoba and Alberta experienced also experienced relatively low voter turnout (at 66 percent) but, because they made the largest gains (10 and 11 points), their turnout in 2015 was average for the country.

PARTY SUPPORT   Although some Canadians support one political party throughout their lives, and may even come from families that have supported the same party for generations, most of us are considerably more fickle. As a result of changes in party platforms, leaders, local candidates, dominant issues, the economy, and personal social or geographic mobility, there are people who have voted for three or more parties at various points in their lives. It is also common for Canadians to vote for different parties at the federal and provincial levels, even when the elections are only weeks or months apart. Many observers of the Quebec political scene argue that the Québécois hedge their bets by voting for a separatist party (Parti Québécois) at the provincial level and the Liberals or Conservatives federally, or the Bloc Québécois federally and the Liberals provincially. As strange as it might seem to an outside observer, this kind of split voting can be the result of cool calculation rather than confusion on the part of the voter.

Recently, there have been dramatic changes in political alignment in this country, as Figure 17–3 reveals. In 1993, we turned away from a long-term three-party

ABOUT 59 TO 65 PERCENT OF ELIGIBLE VOTERS ACTUALLY VOTED IN RECENT FEDERAL ELECTIONS Observers wondered if increasing cynicism about politics and politicians would reduce turnout even further. Then along came the election of 2015, when Justin Trudeau and the Liberals inspired younger voters to turn out in unprecedented numbers and increase turnout to 77 percent.

system to embrace a mix including strong regional parties; in 1997, we confirmed the regional pattern of support (Frizzell & Pammett, 1997). As Figure 17–3 shows, the 1993 election saw the near-collapse of the Progressive

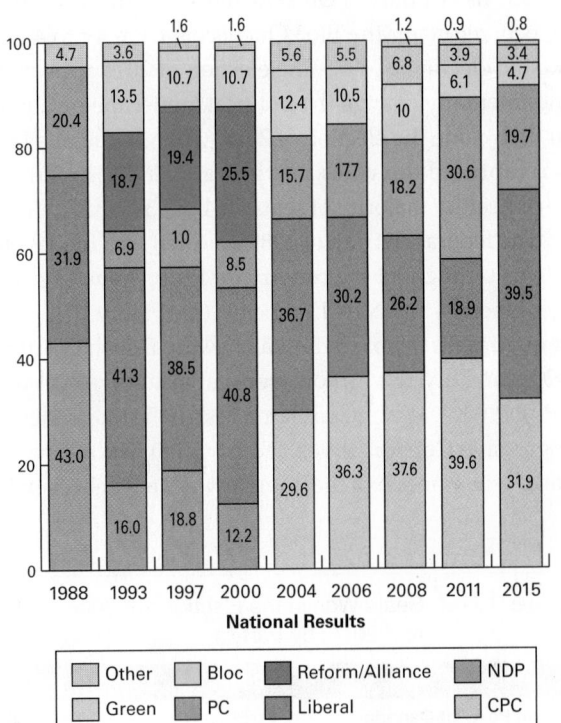

Figure 17–3 Support for Canada's Federal Political Parties, 1988, 1993, 1997, 2000, 2004, 2006, 2008, 2011, and 2015 (Percentage of the Popular Vote)

SOURCE: Compiled and adapted by L.M. Gerber from the Report of the Chief Electoral Officer, 1988, 1993, 1997, 2000, 2004, 2006, and 2008 and Elections Canada, 2011 and 2015.

Conservative and New Democratic parties, coupled with the sudden appearance of the Bloc Québécois and the Reform Party. The 1997 and 2000 results, with minor changes, suggested that Reform/Alliance and the Bloc had staying power. By 2004, the Alliance and the Progressive Conservatives had merged to form the new Conservative Party of Canada (CPC), which garnered 30 percent of the popular vote and began its breakthrough into Ontario and points east. In 2006, Stephen Harper's CPC won 36.3 percent of the vote Canada-wide, beating the seemingly invincible Liberals by 6 percentage points and 21 seats. One might describe the party system at that time as "three plus one," since three parties again dominated the country, except in Quebec where the Bloc maintained its base. The results for the election of 2008 were very similar to those of 2006, except that Green Party support increased, apparently at the expense of the Liberals.

For the first time, in 2011, Stephen Harper's CPC won enough seats (166 of Canada's 308 seats) to form a majority government (Table 17–2). Moving from two consecutive minority governments (with the most seats of any party—but not a majority), the Conservatives could propose and pass legislation without fearing defeat by the opposition parties (which would have triggered a new election). The 2011 election saw the NDP—under the leadership of the immensely popular Jack Layton—increase its support in Ontario and surge dramatically in Quebec, reducing the Bloc Québécois from 49 to 4 seats. Like the election of 1993, the election of 2011 appeared to fundamentally change the political landscape of Canada. But then came the election of 2015, when Trudeau's Liberals recaptured the votes that had gone NDP in 2011 and won a healthy majority of seats (184 of 338, or 57 percent).

The federal election of **1988** revealed varying levels of support throughout the country for Progressive Conservatives, Liberals, and New Democrats (see Figure 17–4, upper left quadrant). People in Saskatchewan, British Columbia, and especially the Yukon were most likely to vote for the NDP, while the Liberals fared best in the Maritimes. The Progressive Conservatives, led by Brian Mulroney, were able to win as much of the popular vote in Quebec—which

normally voted Liberal—as in traditionally Conservative Alberta, resulting in a majority government with 169 seats. This was to be the last two-plus-one election (Conservative/Liberal/NDP) before the Reform Party and the Bloc Québécois turned the political world inside out.

The **1993** election results present a very different picture (see Figure 17–4, upper right quadrant). Half of the vote in Quebec went to the new Bloc Québécois at the expense of the Progressive Conservatives and the NDP—which was almost obliterated. Preston Manning's Reform Party, with roots in Alberta, succeeded there with 52 percent of the vote while making substantial inroads into British Columbia, Saskatchewan, Manitoba, and even Ontario. The concentration of Bloc seats in Quebec and Reform seats in British Columbia and Alberta accentuated the regional aspects of this pivotal election. Patterns of party support in the elections of 1997 and 2000 were very similar to those of 1993, despite the fact that (by 2000) Preston Manning's Reform Party had reshaped itself into Stockwell Day's Canadian Alliance.

The appearance of two *regional parties*, the Bloc Québécois in Quebec and the Reform Party in the West (in the election of 1993), had changed Canada's political landscape to a pattern that would persist until the federal election of 2004.

Just before the election of 2004, the Progressive Conservatives and the Canadian Alliance had finally merged under the leadership of Stephen Harper, becoming the Conservative Party of Canada (CPC). The new party was unable to attract the level of support of the combined Progressive Conservative and Canadian Alliance parties in the previous election; nonetheless, its 30 percent of the popular vote was enough to give the new CPC 24 seats and that elusive breakthrough in Ontario.

By 2006, Paul Martin's Liberal government was limping badly, suffering the effects of indecision and the sponsorship scandal in Quebec (known as Adscam). In its second election, the new Conservative Party gained strength across the country (except in Manitoba) and made huge gains in Quebec (from 8.8 to 24.6 percent of the vote). The result was a *minority* Conservative government (124 of the 308 seats), with 40 seats in Ontario (up from 24) and an astounding 10 in Quebec (up from 0).

The surprise in 2008 was not that Canadians had elected another minority government; for as long as the Bloc Québécois retained its hold on Quebec, it would be difficult for any party to win a majority government. Nevertheless, the Conservative's popular vote inched up to 37.6 percent nationally. The party won 143 seats (a gain of 19), with 51 in Ontario and 10 once again in Quebec, where pundits thought the CPC would lose ground.

The election of 2011 (Figure 17–4, lower left quadrant) turned the party support patterns of the elections of 2004, 2006, and 2008 upside down once more. This time,

Table 17–2 Seats Won in the Elections of 2008, 2011, and 2015, by Party

	2008	2011	2015
Liberal Party of Canada	58	34	184
Conservative Party of Canada	143	166	99
New Democratic Party	37	103	44
Party Québécois	49	4	10
Green Party of Canada	0	1	1
Total	308	308	338

SOURCE: Elections Canada.

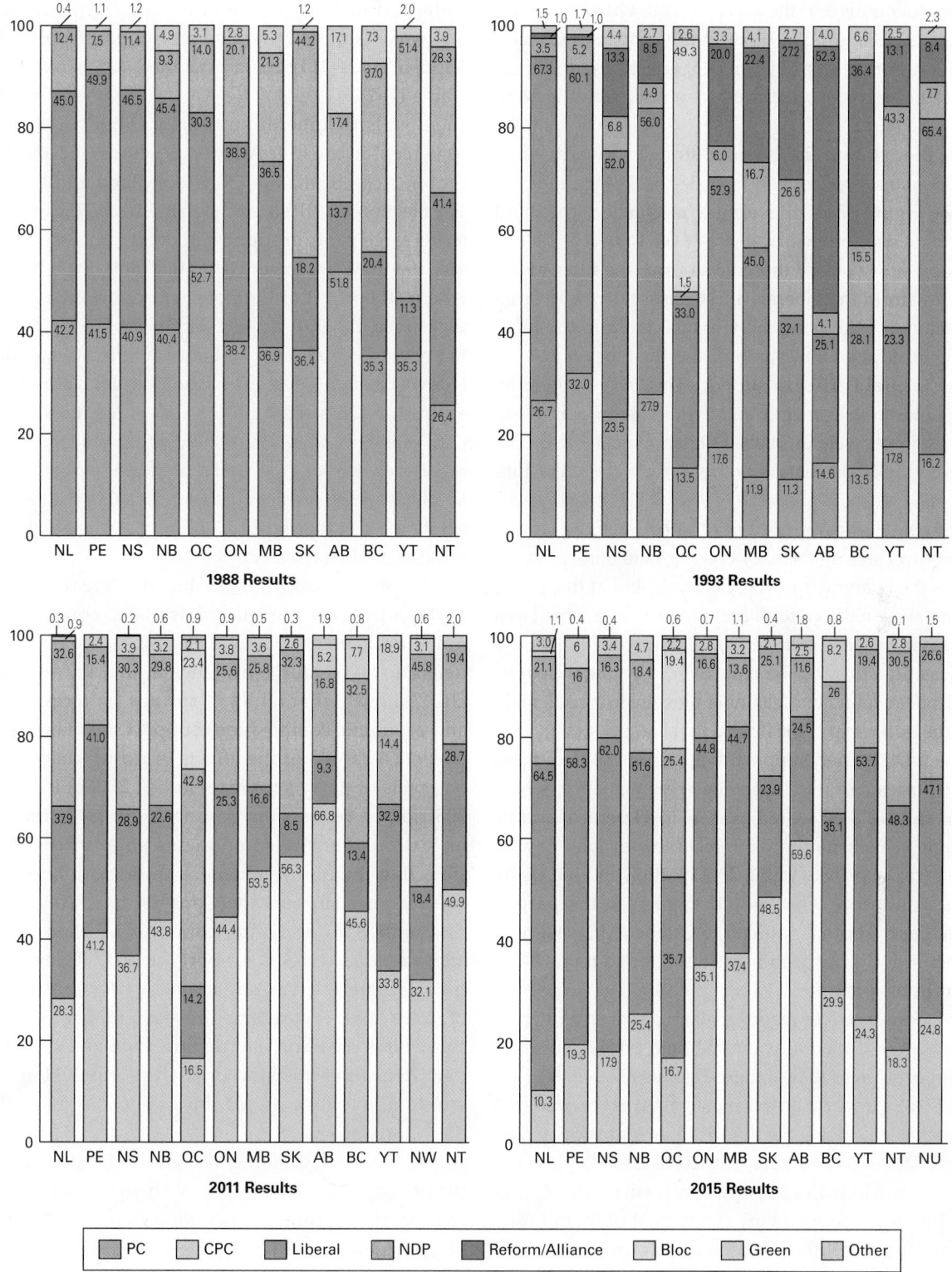

Figure 17–4 Support for Canada's Political Parties by Province and Territory 1988, 1993, 2011, and 2015 (Percentage of the Popular Vote)

SOURCE: Compiled and adapted by L.M. Gerber from the Report of the Chief Electoral Officer, 1988 and 1993 and Elections Canada, 2011 and 2015.

the Bloc Québécois and the Liberals were virtually wiped off the electoral map. The Conservative Party of Canada gained support (except in Quebec) and formed its first majority government, but the big winner was the New Democratic Party.

The Bloc story of 2011 is quite straightforward; while its level of support dropped from 38 to 23 percent of the vote (see Figure 17–4), the number of Quebec seats held by the Bloc dropped from 49 to 4 (see Table 17–2). The NDP took every one of those seats from the Bloc, along with a few from the Liberals and Conservatives. In large part because of the popularity of Jack Layton, the NDP swept Quebec and almost annihilated the Bloc.

The Liberal Party lost support—in 2011—or held its own in almost every province and territory (see Figure 17–4). Its biggest losses were in Quebec, Ontario, and New Brunswick (roughly 10 percentage points in each case). The Liberals lost 7 Quebec seats to the NDP and 27 Ontario seats, mainly to the Conservatives. Prior to 1993, the Liberals had been in power so long that they had begun to think of themselves as the "natural governing party"—but at this point, after they were reduced to 34 seats, their very survival as a party was in question (see Table 17–2). Since many Liberals felt it was time to hand the reins over to younger people, Justin Trudeau found himself under pressure to consider taking on the leadership of the Liberal Party.

The NDP gained support in a number of provinces and territories, but most spectacularly in Quebec, where support for the NDP soared from 12 to 43 percent and its *one* single seat turned into 59. NDP leader Jack Layton passed away shortly after the 2011 election and left many people wondering what would happen to the party's Quebec base. Thomas Mulcair, a Quebec MP, assumed leadership of the party and was expected to retain NDP support in the province.

The Conservatives made smaller but consistent gains across most of Canada. At the national level, Conservative support increased by a mere 2 points (37.6 to 39.6; see Figure 17–3). However, that 2-point gain translated into 23 additional seats, giving Stephen Harper his majority government. Of the 308 electoral districts in Canada, the Conservatives won in 166, or 54 percent, of them in 2011. Critics of our political system, many if not most of them Liberals, complained that the Conservatives formed a majority government with *only 39.6 of the popular vote*. They had no way of knowing that, in 2015, Justin Trudeau would form a majority government with a *mere 39.5 percent of the vote*—down 0.1 points from the CPC vote—giving him 57 percent of the seats.

During much of the long, drawn-out election campaign of 2015, it seemed to be a battle between Stephen Harper (CPC) and Thomas Mulcair (NDP). However, as election day drew near, support for Mulcair's NDP

collapsed in favour of Trudeau's Liberals. When the day was over, the Liberals had gained 21 points in the popular vote—11 of them from the NDP, 8 from the CPC (Table 17–2).

Levels of Liberal support swelled to more than 50 percent in the four Atlantic provinces (62 and 65 percent in Nova Scotia and Newfoundland and Labrador). The election of 2015 would be kind to the Liberals, registering large gains in support in every province and territory (Figure 17–4, lower right quadrant). Even in Alberta, where 60 percent of the popular vote went to the Conservatives, Liberal support surged from 9 to 25 percent. In the previous election, Liberal support was reduced to a devastating 19 percent of the popular vote; this time around, NDP support fell to 20 percent whereas the CPC managed to retain 32 percent. In Quebec, the Conservatives held on to 17 percent of the popular vote and retained *ten seats*. This is quite remarkable when one considers the fact that, prior to 2006, the Conservatives had no seats at all in Quebec.

We may think that we know a great deal about party support in various parts of the country but the dramatic changes from one election to the next are sufficient to shake our confidence in that knowledge. We also "know" what kinds of ridings (in terms of social and economic composition) support the major political parties. Analysis of the effects of riding characteristics on levels of party support (Gerber, 2006b) in Canada's 308 ridings reveals that ridings with large immigrant or visible minority components support the Liberals (rejecting the Bloc in Quebec); those with higher average incomes support the Conservatives (rejecting the Bloc and NDP); and, after controlling for income, more *highly educated* ridings support the NDP. This ecological (i.e., riding-level) analysis is consistent with the findings of individual-level research revealing that ethnicity and social class are important determinants of voting behaviour. Repeating this kind of analysis, for 2011 and 2015, would allow us to assess the stability or instability of these correlations.

In the United States, there is a sharp urban–rural divide in voting patterns, with urban areas voting Democrat and rural areas voting Republican. Looking at an electoral map of past elections might lead you to the same conclusion about Canada, as almost all of the blue (CPC) ridings are outside our three largest urban areas. However, while "the ethnically diverse metropolitan areas of Toronto, Montreal, and Vancouver failed to elect any Conservatives, voting behaviour in smaller cities across the country suggests that, in the absence of diversity, there is no rural—urban divide" (Gerber, 2006b). This means that, in the federal election of 2006, the Conservatives gained ground in all types of ridings.

They failed to win seats, despite increased support, in the multicultural ridings of our three major cities because the Liberal lead was so great.[6] In smaller cities, including Quebec City, the Conservatives were much more successful.

By 2008, the *urban* electoral map looked different. The Conservatives won no seats in Montreal (where the Liberals and Bloc Québécois hold 12 and 21 seats, respectively), but 8 of 42 Toronto ridings and 10 of 19 Vancouver ridings elected Conservatives. Many smaller cities sent only Conservatives to Ottawa. Clearly, the urban–rural divide is not as deep as it once was. In the election of 2008, the Conservatives gained support in the ridings surrounding Toronto—which they already held—and won for the first time in many central Toronto ridings. In 2015, massive Liberal wins in and around Toronto and Vancouver re-established the urban/rural divide that had appeared to be breaking down.

Political Socialization

Pierre Trudeau, Brian Mulroney, and Stephen Harper are among the prime ministers of Canada who raised young children at 24 Sussex Drive and Harrington Lake (the official residences of the prime minister). While all three of them would shield their children from many aspects of political life, their children undoubtedly learned the basic tenets of liberalism and conservatism from their parents. These families are unusual in their intense involvement in politics; as a result of more intimate exposure, one would expect their children to be very aware of politics and to have clear party affiliations. Although Justin Trudeau and Ben Mulroney have long been celebrities, it was Justin Trudeau who took the plunge into politics as a Liberal and won the Montreal riding of Papineau—one which had long been held by the Bloc Québécois. Now the grandchildren of Pierre Trudeau are being raised as children of the younger Prime Minister Trudeau.

Political attitudes, like other elements of culture, are acquired through the socialization process. Of the major agents of socialization shaping our political views—the family, the schools, and the mass media—the family is in a position to exert the earliest influence. The family is a powerful agent of socialization; not surprisingly, then, children typically come to share many opinions held by their parents. Because neighbourhoods and schools tend to be relatively homogeneous in socio-economic terms,

a child's initial peer groups are likely to reinforce ideas about the world learned at home. In Canada, many children express a partisan preference by grade 4, and by grade 8 a majority do so (Van Loon & Whittington, 1981:122). Children are more likely to learn about politics if their families are actively involved, if there is a great deal of political talk in the household, and if their families are of higher socio-economic status. Also, male children absorb political information and identify political symbols at an earlier age than their female counterparts.

Schools teach the culture's dominant political values, one of them being respect for authority. Canadian schoolchildren learn to recognize political symbols, such as the flag, the prime minister, and the queen, and, like children elsewhere, start off with positive feelings about these political icons. Interestingly, in the early 1980s, children in grades 4 and 5 overwhelmingly chose the queen as their favourite political figure (over the prime minister or governor general), and not until grade 8 did a majority (53 percent) realize that the prime minister is more powerful than the queen (Van Loon & Whittington, 1981:121). The picture today is very different because politicians, the media, and schools have downplayed the role of the monarchy or Queen Elizabeth II as our head of state. In fact, very few schools offer anything like the formal civics classes found in American schools; our political socialization appears to be both more subtle and more informal.

The mass media, too, convey values and opinions pertaining to politics. Conservatives sometimes charge the Canadian media with having a left-wing agenda, while critics on the left complain that what is packaged as "news" really amounts to support for the status quo. Specific newspapers are frequently identified as having liberal or conservative sympathies, and some of the francophone media in Quebec have been labelled separatist. Although it is not clear that they convert their readers or viewers at a basic philosophical level, there is little doubt that the media are active players in the day-to-day conduct of politics and that their involvement has changed the way in which politics is done. Good sound bites and catchy phrases are gold to a politician, especially when uttered in time for the evening news. Advertising consumes a major part of election campaign budgets, and image takes precedence over substance. (See the Sociology and the Media box for a closer look at the effects of media coverage on politics and election outcomes.)

The image projected on nightly television can help make or break a political career, as our former short-term prime ministers Joe Clark, John Turner, and Kim Campbell learned. During election campaigns, Canadian

---

[6]The Scarborough area of Toronto is recognized as the most ethnically diverse part of the world. The Scarborough ridings are as much as 66.8 percent immigrant and 84.6 percent visible minority. With Liberal support (in 2004) as high as 75.6 percent, you can see why even a gain of 15 percent in Conservative support (in 2006) would not result in a CPC win (Gerber, 2006b).

Sociology and the Media

Who Decides? The Impacts of Modern Communications

Parliamentary democracy in Canada involves political parties, party discipline, equal representation, local constituencies (where the candidate with the most votes wins), a prime minister, the Cabinet (chosen by the prime minister), and the Senate (appointed by prime ministers, present and past). In the wings, the Prime Minister's Office controls physical access as well as the flow of information to the prime minister. The net effect of these interacting components, with imperfections at each level, is a system in which our prime minister—given a majority government—has more power in decision making and implementation than the U.S. president.

Today, there is almost constant communication between politicians and the voter. Television, satellite transmission, the cell phone, the internet, email, the social media, and almost continuous opinion polling ensure that the general public can almost instantly be informed about what is going on and that politicians can continuously take the pulse of the public. Facebook, Twitter, and blogs influence both politicians and public opinion. During the 2015 election campaign, social media, the cell phone, and hundreds of selfies allowed Justin Trudeau to become one with the people—especially young people—in ways that Stephen Harper and Thomas Mulcair could not match.

Politicians are very sensitive to public opinion and wary of offending potential voters. They are still subject to all of the traditional influences and constraints, but their responses to these must be tempered by their new instant and intimate relationship with the public. We know about floods, ice storm disasters, helicopter purchases and cancellations, the Syrian refugee crisis, or suicides in First Nations communities *as events unfold*. We watch our political leaders respond to these events and we judge them—instantly and continually.

More active citizen participation—through discussions, public meetings, radio and television talk shows, letters to the editor, email, referenda, social media, blogs, and public opinion polls—serves to keep politicians on their toes. Some people applaud this spirit of active participation. After all, in a democratic system government *should* be aware of and responsive to public opinion, even as it changes during election campaigns or between elections. Clearly, these "activists" (broadly defined) counter the influence of big business, lobbyists, and senior bureaucrats. On the other hand, governments are elected by millions of voters on the basis of campaign promises. In that light, should less-representative individuals influence our politicians on an ongoing basis? Should events of the day and shifting public moods divert government action? Some argue that this kind of give and take between politicians

and the general public enhances the democratic process, while others argue that the effects, which are increasingly real and immediate, are actually ones of distortion. The most dramatic illustration of the power of the media to shape public opinion and bring down a government was that of the Quebec sponsorship scandal. In 2004, Canada's Auditor-General Sheila Fraser reported that advertising and sponsorship contracts—which were instituted by the Chrétien government in the wake of the 1995 referendum in Quebec to increase the federal presence in that province—constituted gross mismanagement. Fraser concluded that "as much as $100 million of the $250 million program budget had been siphoned off to private firms and individuals through various illegitimate schemes, including overbilling, artificial invoices, fictitious contracts, and blatant payments" (Mancuso et al., 2006). When he took over from Chrétien as Liberal leader and prime minister, Paul Martin commissioned Mr. Justice Gomery to investigate the sponsorship program in order to determine how much money had disappeared, how it was mishandled, and who was responsible.

For more than six months, Canadians were able to watch events unfold on television—first in English and then in French, after the inquiry was moved to Quebec. Politicians, bureaucrats, business executives, and administrative assistants were grilled daily—on our television screens—about their knowledge of or involvement in the mismanagement of taxpayers' money. Canadians found out that some ad agencies were given large sums of money for promotional work that was never done and that money intended for the promotion of Canada within Quebec made its way into Quebec Liberal coffers—and was used for campaign purposes. So serious are these infractions that several men were convicted of crimes. If Canadians were angry, Quebecers were furious. The implication of the sponsorship program itself was that their loyalty could be bought by paper flags and advertisements in public venues.

What about the political fallout? As Canada geared up for the 2006 election, Paul Martin's Liberal government tried desperately to hold off an election until after the publication of the second Gomery report. The first was damning, but the second would talk about how to prevent such debacles in the future. Unfortunately for the Liberal government, Adscam and government corruption were on the top of many minds, especially in Quebec. It's impossible to measure the impact of the sponsorship scandal and the televised inquiry, but Stephen Harper's Conservatives increased their share of the popular vote from 29.6 to 36.3 percent—and their seat count from 99 to 124—between 2004 and 2006. This was enough to give them a minority government and to break the Liberal lock on power that was created when the "right" splintered in 1993. In fact, the 2006 election results in Quebec surprised everyone: Conservative support rose from 8.8 to 24.6 percent, while the Party's seats increased from 0 to 10. For a time, the Conservatives competed with the Liberals as Quebec's alternative to the Bloc Québécois—*and it all started with television coverage of Adscam.*

What Do You Think?

1. Is your awareness of politics affected by the fact that politicians are on the internet? Do bloggers and the social media contribute to your political awareness and attitudes?

2. Did the media coverage of the Mike Duffy trial during the 2015 election campaign contribute to the defeat of Stephen Harper's Conservatives?

3. There are many organizations, groups, and categories of people trying to influence our politicians. Who, in your opinion, should have the most clout?

Clement Allard/The Canadian Press

Adrian Wyld/The Canadian Press

Dennis Van Tine/LFI/Photoshot/Newscom

WHEN PIERRE TRUDEAU DAZZLED US WITH HIS DIVING, SKIING, DANCING, AND WHITE-WATER CANOEING, WE BECAME CONSCIOUS OF THE PHYSICAL FITNESS OF OUR PRIME MINISTERS For the election of 1993, Jean Chrétien needed to prove that he was not yesterday's man, too old for the job, or in poor health; these concerns fell by the wayside when Canadians saw images of Chrétien water-skiing—on *one* ski. As Prime Minister Chrétien (left) fought off leadership rivals and prepared for the 2000 election, he again displayed his physical prowess, this time on the ski slopes. His opponent, Stockwell Day (centre), injected athletic competition by jet skiing, running, rollerblading, doing karate kicks, and generally showing off his muscular build. Neither Paul Martin nor Stephen Harper used the fitness card in his prime-ministerial bid, but Justin Trudeau (right) challenged Conservative Senator Patrick Brazeau to a boxing match and won. He also captivated the world by matching his father's famous yoga peacock pose.

politicians (e.g., PierreTrudeau, Jean Chrétien, Stockwell Day, and now Justin Trudeau) have engaged in displays of athleticism for the media; in contrast, some U.S. presidential candidates have displayed their religiosity. Bill Clinton tried to deflect attention from his first-term sexual troubles by being photographed emerging from church—family Bible under his arm, wife and daughter by his side. In the 2000 presidential election, George Bush and Al Gore openly claimed to be born-again Christians. Joe Lieberman (a Conservative Jew) told Americans that, when Gore called to offer him the candidacy for vice president, the two men prayed together on the phone. Canada does have politicians who are Christian fundamentalists: Preston Manning and Stockwell Day (former leaders of Reform and the Canadian Alliance) are prominent examples. Both Manning and Day believe that religion and politics should mix but had to tone down their religiosity because—as

Prime Minister Stephen Harper also learned—at the national level in Canada, overt religious expression does not play well in the media.

Opinion polls are particularly worrisome to some observers of the political scene. The timing of polls, sample size, and the wording of questions have dramatic effects on outcomes. For example, including the name of the Green Party in a question on party preference inflates the number choosing that response to almost double its actual vote yield (Marzolini, 2004). And, when the electorate is volatile and voters are waiting to make their decisions at the last minute, polls from different firms can vary wildly. Do polls reflect or shape public opinion?

Other agents of political socialization are the many organizations to which people belong. Some of these are professional, ethnic, or voluntary associations, unions, or special-interest organizations such as women's or environmental groups. From time to time, churches attempt to mobilize their members behind a particular cause, such as fighting abortion or arranging for the sponsorship of refugees. Seniors clubs, formed initially to encourage social interaction among elders, once found themselves marching on Ottawa to protest the de-indexing of pensions. Political parties themselves would normally recruit people already inclined to be political activists; once they are party members, people may increase their participation levels, political knowledge and sophistication, and partisanship. Some of these organizations are founded for political purposes; others with a wide range of non-political goals become political only as a result of circumstances.

The Participation of Women in Canadian Politics

The movement seeking the right to vote for women began in Canada in the 1880s, but, since it had to function simultaneously at the provincial and federal levels, it was subject to all "the regional conflicts and divisions that characterized other Canadian social movements" (Bashevkin, 1993:4). Despite divisions that were especially damaging to this movement, women in Canada finally acquired the right to vote at the federal level in 1918. Manitoba was the first province to extend the vote to women (in 1916), while Quebec was the last (in 1940). The extension of the vote to women set the scene for a series of political firsts. Agnes Macphail quickly ran for and won federal political office (in 1921), but she had to deal with numerous obstacles, including people who said, "We can't have a woman." It was not until 1957 that

Canada had its first female federal Cabinet minister, Ellen Fairclough; it was 1984 before women were given portfolios other than those deemed most "suited" to women, such as health, education, or the status of women. Prime Minister Brian Mulroney broke this pattern at the federal level by appointing Pat Carney to international trade, Barbara McDougall to junior finance, and Kim Campbell to the justice portfolio (Bashevkin, 1993:88). In 1989, Audrey McLaughlin became the first federal party leader (of the NDP), and Kim Campbell's leadership win in 1993 automatically made her Canada's first female prime minister. Although, in ideological and practical terms, the New Democratic Party has been most persistent in the promotion of women, these firsts involve all three of Canada's major parties.

Despite these highly visible firsts, women are still underrepresented in politics. Women tend to be the support staff of a political party rather than its candidates. The higher you look in a party's hierarchy, the less women are represented. Most female candidates run for minor parties or in ridings where wins are unlikely. As well, the proportion of females running for office and winning is greatest at the municipal level, somewhat lower at the provincial level, and lower still at the federal level.

However, there has been a steady increase in the proportion of women elected at the federal level in recent years, from 5 percent winning in the 1980 election, to 10 percent in 1984, 13 percent in 1988, 18 percent in 1993, and 21 percent in 1997 and 2000. These figures are high compared with the United States, Britain, and France, which have legislatures that are about 6 percent female, but low when compared with Finland, Sweden, Norway,

National Archives of Canada/PA30212

National Archives of Canada

NELLIE MCCLUNG (*LEFT*), MANITOBA-BORN TEACHER, AUTHOR, AND ACTIVIST, WAS WELCOMED IN MANY SETTINGS AS AN EFFECTIVE AND HUMOROUS SPEAKER She fought for women's suffrage, prohibition, factory safety, and many other reforms. She was one of the chief activists in the *Persons Case*, which involved a court battle to have women legally recognized as persons. Because of her efforts and those of her colleagues, women were given the right to vote (in 1918), to sit in the House of Commons (in 1919), and to be appointed to the Senate (in 1929) (Hallett, 1988).

AGNES MACPHAIL (*RIGHT*) WAS THE FIRST WOMAN ELECTED TO THE HOUSE OF COMMONS IN 1921, THE FIRST FEDERAL ELECTION IN WHICH WOMEN COULD VOTE Like her friend Nellie McClung, Macphail was a teacher. She was involved in the agricultural co-operative movement of Ontario, various feminist causes, and prison investigation and reform. She founded the Elizabeth Fry Society of Canada and was the first woman appointed to Canada's delegation to the United Nations. Macphail was largely responsible for Ontario's first pay equity legislation in 1951 (Black, 1988).

and Denmark, where 32 to 38 percent of their legislatures are female (Bashevkin, 1993). The 2006 federal election sent 64 women to Ottawa (21 percent of the 308 MPs); female representation was 11 percent in the Conservative caucus, 20 percent for the Liberals, 33 percent for the Bloc, and 41 percent for the New Democrats (Report of the Chief Electoral Officer, 2006). In 2011, women made up 25 percent of the legislature—mainly because 39 percent of elected NDP MPs were female. Once again, in 2015, women made up 25 percent of the legislature; furthermore, Trudeau appointed a cabinet that is 50 percent female.

Among the barriers to women's participation are socialization, lack of financing or contacts, and the electoral system itself. To the extent that gender stereotypes contribute to resistance on the part of voters and reluctance on the part of potential female candidates, the appearance (even though temporary) of Kim Campbell in the prime minister's office and of Sheila Copps as deputy prime minister may have expanded horizons. All of our parties are aware of the need to include women among Cabinet ministers. An additional, rarely noted, barrier is the geographic size of Canada. Members of Parliament have to spend much of the year in Ottawa, away from their families. While the House is sitting, MPs commute weekly, sometimes crossing two or three time zones to get to work. Considering our cultural expectations about child care and other family responsibilities, it is not surprising that few women commit to careers in federal politics. Small countries (i.e., Finland, Norway, Sweden, and Denmark) do not require such extended commutes for parliamentarians; neither do Canada's provinces or municipalities.

Theories of Power in Society

17.4 Apply the pluralist, power-elite, and Marxist models to the Canadian political system.

Sociologists have long debated how power is spread throughout society. Power is a very difficult topic to study because decision making is complex and often takes place behind closed doors. Despite this difficulty, researchers have developed three competing models of power.

The Pluralist Model: The People Rule

The **pluralist model**, closely linked to structural-functional theory, is *an analysis of politics that sees power*

as spread among many competing interest groups. Pluralists claim that politics is an arena of negotiation. With limited resources, no organization can expect to realize all of its goals. Organizations therefore operate as veto groups, realizing some success but mostly keeping opponents from achieving all of their ends. The political process relies heavily on creating alliances and compromises among numerous interest groups so that policies gain wide support. In short, pluralists see power as spread widely throughout society, with all people having at least some voice in the political system (Dahl, 1961, 1982; Rothman & Black, 1998).

In *The Vertical Mosaic: An Analysis of Social Class and Power in Canada* (1965)—a Canadian classic—John Porter addressed the question of who makes major decisions, or exercises power, in Canada. On the basis of extensive research, he concluded that there are competing elites at the top of five major organizational clusters: economic, political, bureaucratic, labour, and ideological (that is, church, education, and media). Of the five, the economic or corporate elite and the bureaucratic elite are the most powerful. While there is competition among these elites because of the opposing interests of their respective institutions, Porter pointed out that these powerful and wealthy elites are also highly integrated. To keep the system working, they are willing to accommodate one another. As a result, Canada has what one might call *co-operative pluralism.*

The Power Elite Model: A Few People Rule

The **power elite model**, based on social-conflict theory, is *an analysis of politics that views power as concentrated among the rich.* The term power elite was coined by C. Wright Mills (1956), who argued that the upper class holds the bulk of society's wealth, prestige, and power.

Mills claimed that the power elite heads the three major sectors of society: the economy, the government, and the military. The power elite includes the "super rich" (executives and major shareholders), the government, and the military.

Further, Mills explained, these elites move from one sector to another, consolidating power as they go. Political leaders often enter public life from powerful positions in the corporate world. For example, Brian Mulroney was a labour lawyer and then vice-president of Iron Ore Company of Canada before becoming prime minister. After leaving political office, he returned to Montreal to practise corporate law and sit on the boards of many influential corporations. Paul Martin was the owner and CEO of Canadian Steamship Lines (Deneault,

2006) as he was about to become our prime minister; to avoid future conflict of interest, he passed the company on to his sons.

In the 1970s, Wallace Clement (1975) argued that Canada is ruled by an increasingly powerful economic or corporate elite. This group has upper-class origins and vested interests in maintaining the capitalist system. Dense networks binding the economic, political, and bureaucratic elites blend them into one group dominated by the corporate elite. Thus, Clement rejects the pluralist model, noting that the state and private capital are complementary and mutually dependent. In effect, the state and the capitalists act as one. Power elite theorists challenge the claim that Canada is a political democracy. They maintain that the concentration of wealth and power is simply too great for the average person's voice to be heard. They reject the pluralist idea that various centres of power serve as checks and balances on one another. Instead, the power elite model maintains that those at the top encounter no real opposition.

The Marxist Model: The System Is Biased

A third approach to understanding politics is the **Marxist political-economy model**, *an analysis that explains politics in terms of the operation of a society's economic system*. The power elite model focuses on the enormous wealth and power of certain individuals; the Marxist model goes further and sees bias rooted in a country's institutions, especially its economy. Karl Marx claimed that a society's economic system (capitalist or socialist) shapes its political system. Therefore, the power elites do not simply appear out of nowhere; they are creations of capitalism itself. The problem does not lie in the people who exercise great power or the people who don't vote; the problem is rooted in the system itself, what Marxists call the "political economy of capitalism." In other words, as long as a country has a capitalist economy—as does Canada—the majority of people will be shut out of politics, just as they are exploited in the workplace.

EVALUATE

The Applying Theory table summarizes the three models of power and the political system. Which of the three models is most accurate? Over the years, research has shown support for each one. In the end, how you think our political system ought to work is as much a matter of political values as of scientific fact.

Classic research by Nelson Polsby (1959) supports the pluralist model. Polsby studied the political scene in New Haven, Connecticut, and concluded that key decisions on various issues—including education, urban renewal, and the electoral nominating process—were made by different groups. Polsby concluded that, in New Haven, no one group—not even the upper class—ruled all of the others.

Robert Lynd and Helen Lynd (1937) studied Muncie, Indiana (which they called "Middletown" to suggest that it was a typical city), and documented the fortune amassed by a single family. Their findings support the power elite position. The Lynds showed how one family dominated the city's life; in effect, the power elite boiled down to a single family.

From the Marxist perspective, the point is not to look at which individuals make decisions. Rather, as Alexander Liazos (1982:13) explains, "The basic tenets of capitalist society shape everyone's life: the inequalities of social classes and the importance of profits over people." As long as the basic institutions of society are organized to meet the needs of the few rather than the many, a democratic society is impossible.

Clearly, our political system gives almost everyone the right to participate in politics. But the power elite and Marxist models point out that our political system is far less democratic than most people think. Most citizens may have the right to vote, but the major political parties and their candidates typically support only positions that are acceptable to the most powerful segments of society and consistent with the operation of our capitalist economy.

CHECK YOUR LEARNING What is the main argument of the pluralist model of power? What about the power-elite model? The Marxist political-economy model?

APPLYING THEORY

Politics

	Pluralist Model	Power Elite Model	Marxist Political-Economy Model
Which theoretical approach is applied?	Structural-functional approach	Social-conflict approach	Social-conflict approach
How is power spread throughout society?	Power is spread widely so that all groups have some voice.	Power is concentrated in the hands of top business, political, and military leaders.	Power is directed by the operation of the capitalist economy.
Is Canada a democracy?	Yes. Power is spread widely enough to make the country a democracy.	No. Power is too concentrated for the country to be a democracy.	No. The capitalist economy sets political decision making, so the country is not a democracy.

Power beyond the Rules

17.5 Describe causes of both revolution and terrorism.

In politics, there is always disagreement over a society's goals and the means to achieve them. A political system tries to resolve these controversies within a system of rules. But political activity sometimes breaks the rules or tries to do away with the entire system.

Revolution

Political revolution is *the overthrow of one political system in order to establish another.* Reform involves change within a system, through modification of the law or, in the extreme case, a *coup d'état* (in French, literally, "stroke of the state"), in which one leader topples another. Revolution involves change in the type of system itself.

No political system is immune to revolution, nor does revolution produce any one kind of government. America's Revolutionary War (1775–1781) replaced colonial rule by the British monarchy with a representative democracy. French revolutionaries in 1789 also overthrew a monarch, only to set the stage for the return of monarchy in the person of Napoleon. In 1917, the Russian Revolution replaced monarchy with a socialist government built on the ideas of Karl Marx. In 1991, a second Russian revolution dismantled the socialist Soviet Union, and the nation was reborn as the Russian Federation, which has been moving toward a market system although it has yet to provide a greater political voice for its people.

Closer to home, one sees revolutionary potential in Quebec's quest for greater autonomy. In the referendum held on October 30, 1995, 49.4 percent of the people of Quebec voted "yes" to Quebec becoming sovereign. Had a few more people voted "yes," they would have set in motion a process that would have dismantled Canada as presently constituted and forced the creation of two or more new and very different political entities.

Despite their striking variety, revolutions share a number of traits (de Tocqueville, 1955; orig. 1856; Skocpol, 1979; Tilly, 1986):

1. **Rising expectations.** Common sense suggests that revolution is more likely when people are severely deprived, but history shows that most revolutions occur when people's lives are improving. Rising expectations, rather than bitterness and despair, make revolutions more likely. Driving the recent uprisings across the Middle East are people who may be living better than their families did a generation ago but not as well as people living in other parts of the world. Cellphones and the internet add to awareness of events and conditions in Europe and North America.

2. **Unresponsive government.** Revolutions become more likely when a government is unwilling to reform itself, especially when demands for reform by large segments of society are ignored. In Egypt, for example, the government led by Hosni Mubarak had done little to benefit the people or deal with its own corruption over many decades.

3. **Radical leadership by intellectuals.** English philosopher Thomas Hobbes (1588–1679) claimed that intellectuals provide the justification for revolution, and universities are often the centre of political change. Students played a critical role in China's prodemocracy movement in the 1990s, the uprisings in Eastern Europe, and the recent uprisings across the Middle East.

2011 BROUGHT SWEEPING CHANGE TO MANY COUNTRIES IN NORTHERN AFRICA AND THE MIDDLE EAST In Libya, a popular protest movement seeking the overthrow of longtime ruler Moammar Gadhafi turned into a civil war. Support for change also comes from high-income nations where large ethnic populations now reside. In London (*at right*), for example, hundreds of people with roots in Libya demonstrated in support of political change.

4. **Establishing a new legitimacy.** Overthrowing a political system is not easy, but ensuring a revolution's long-term success is harder still. Some revolutionary movements are held together mostly by hatred of the past regime and fall apart once new leaders are installed. For this reason, it is difficult to predict the long-term outcome of recent political changes in the Middle East. Revolutionaries must also guard against counter-revolutionary drives led by overthrown leaders. This explains the speed and ruthlessness with which victorious revolutionaries typically dispose of former leaders.

Scientific analysis cannot declare that a revolution is good or bad. The full consequences of such an upheaval depend on personal values and typically become evident only after many years. Two decades after the revolution, the future of the former Soviet Union remains uncertain.

Terrorism

The terrorist attacks on the United States on September 11, 2001, involving four commercial airliners, killed nearly 3000 innocent people (representing 68 nations), injured many thousands more, completely destroyed the twin towers of the World Trade Center in New York City, and seriously damaged the Pentagon in Washington, D.C. Not since the attack on Pearl Harbor at the outbreak of World War II had the United States suffered such a blow. Indeed, this event was the most serious terrorist act ever recorded.

Terrorism refers to *acts of violence or the threat of violence used as a political strategy by an individual or a group.* Like revolution, terrorism is a political act beyond the rules of established political systems. According to Paul Johnson (1981), terrorism has four distinguishing characteristics.

First, terrorists try to paint violence as a legitimate political tactic, even though such acts are condemned by virtually every nation. Terrorists also bypass, or are excluded from, established channels of political negotiation. Therefore, terrorism is a weaker organization's strategy against a stronger enemy. Terrorism can also be carried out by a single individual in support of some larger cause or movement.

In recent decades, terrorism has become commonplace in international politics. In 2013, there were about 9700 acts of terrorism worldwide, which claimed 17 891 lives and injured more than 32 000 people. More than half of the dead were civilians, and hundreds of victims were children. More than half of the attacks in 2013 took place in just three nations: Afghanistan, Pakistan, and Iraq (U.S. Department of State, 2014).

In Canada, the Front de libération du Québec (FLQ), which may have comprised fewer than 30 people, used terrorism to promote its goal of an independent, socialist Quebec. From 1963 to 1971, it was involved in 200 or more bombings of increasing seriousness. In 1970, its members kidnapped James Cross, the British trade commissioner, and Pierre Laporte, a Quebec Cabinet minister, whom they subsequently murdered. As was its intent, the FLQ caught the attention of the country.

Second, terrorism is used not only by groups but also by governments against their own people. *State terrorism* is the use of violence, generally without support of law, by government officials as a way to control the population. State terrorism is lawful in some authoritarian and totalitarian states, which survive by creating widespread fear and intimidation. Saddam Hussein, for example, relied on secret police and state terror to protect his power in Iraq. More recently, Syrian president Bashar al-Assad has attempted to remain in power by using the country's military against a popular uprising that has turning into a bloody civil war.

Third, democratic societies reject terrorism in principle, but they are especially vulnerable to terrorists because they give extensive civil liberties to their people and have less extensive police networks. This susceptibility helps explain the tendency of democratic governments to suspend civil liberties if they fear attack, as was done in 1970 when, in response to the murder of Pierre Laporte by the FLQ, Prime Minister Pierre Trudeau invoked the *War Measures Act* and arrested more than 450 people, many of whom were suspected of being FLQ members and sympathizers.

Since the 2001 terrorist attacks in the United States, there have been new civil rights concerns. Individuals, some of them Canadian, have been held in the United States without being charged. In 2002, Syrian-born Canadian Maher Arar was deported, based on information provided by the RCMP, by U.S. authorities to Syria, where he was imprisoned and tortured for more than a year before being returned to Canada. In 2006, a public inquiry exonerated Arar and held the RCMP responsible for giving inaccurate information to the U.S. authorities. Other Arab or Muslim Canadians, or those belonging to other visible minorities, have been subject to what looks like racial profiling as they are singled out for prolonged searches and questioning en route to the United States. Canadian author Rohinton Mistry is one of many to report such harassment.

Fourth, and finally, terrorism is always a matter of definition. Governments claim the right to maintain order, even by force, and may label opposition groups that use violence as "terrorists." Political differences may explain why one person's "terrorist" is another's "freedom fighter" (Jenkins, 2003). This is illustrated well by Che Guevara, by the Irish Republican Army, and by the Palestinian/Israeli conflict.

AP Images

IN 2011, MILITARY FORCES OF THE UNITED STATES FINALLY TRACKED DOWN AND KILLED OSAMA BIN LADEN, THE MAN BEHIND THE SEPTEMBER 11, 2001 TERROR ATTACKS THAT KILLED NEARLY 3000 INNOCENT PEOPLE Some Americans cheered the event; many felt a sense of relief. But few think that we are much closer to finding an end to global terrorism.

While hostage taking and outright killing provoke anger, taking action against terrorists is difficult. Because most terrorist groups are shadowy organizations with no formal connection to any established state, identifying the parties responsible is not easy. In addition, any military response risks confrontation with other governments. Yet, as terrorism expert Brian Jenkins warns, the failure to respond "encourages other terrorist groups, who begin to realize that this can be a pretty cheap way to wage war" (quoted in Whitaker, 1985:29).

War and Peace

17.6 Identify factors encouraging war or peace.

Perhaps the most critical political issue is **war**, *organized, armed conflict among the people of two or more nations,*

directed by their governments. War is as old as humanity, but understanding it is crucial today because humanity now has weapons that can destroy the entire planet. For almost all of the twentieth century, nations somewhere on Earth were in violent conflict. Most wars are localized, while others, like the two world wars, are widespread. Canada's involvement in several of these wars cost Canadian lives: 60 661 Canadians were killed in World War I, 42 042 in World War II, and 312 in the Korean War. In the Vietnam War, some Canadian individuals signed up to fight as part of the American forces, but Canada's official role involved serving on truce commissions and supplying medical or technical assistance. Since Vietnam, Canada has generally been involved in the world's trouble spots, such as Rwanda and Bosnia, as a peacekeeper. Once we moved into a more open combat role in Afghanistan—one that resulted in the loss of 158 members of the Canadian Forces—we had to recognize the fact that most of our peacekeeping has been accomplished with weapons.

The Causes of War

Wars occur so often that we might think there is something natural about armed confrontation. However, there is no evidence that human beings must wage war under any particular circumstances. On the contrary, governments around the world usually have to force their people to go to war. Like all forms of social behaviour, warfare is a product of *society* that is more common in some places than others. If society holds the key to war or peace, under what circumstances do humans go to battle? Quincy Wright (1987) cites five factors that promote war:

1. **Perceived threats.** Societies mobilize in response to a perceived threat to their people, territory, or culture. Leaders in the United States and the United Kingdom justified the military campaign to disarm Iraq, for example, by stressing the threat that Saddam Hussein posed to their countries.

2. **Social problems.** When internal problems generate widespread frustration at home, a society's leaders may divert public attention by attacking an external "enemy" as a form of scapegoating. While American leaders claimed that the war in Iraq was a matter of national security, there is little doubt that the onset of the war diverted attention from the struggling national economy and boosted the popularity of President Bush.

3. **Political objectives.** Poor nations, such as Vietnam, have used wars to end foreign domination. On the other hand, powerful countries, such as the United States, may benefit from a periodic show of force to increase global political standing. (Recall the

---

terrorism acts of violence or the threat of violence used as a political strategy by an individual or a group

war organized, armed conflict among the people of two or more nations, directed by their governments

deployments of troops in Somalia, Haiti, Bosnia, Afghanistan, and Iraq.)

4. **Moral objectives.** Nations rarely claim that they are going to war to gain wealth and power. Instead, their leaders infuse military campaigns with moral urgency. By calling the 2003 invasion of Iraq "Operation Iraqi Freedom," U.S. leaders tried to portray the mission as a morally justified war of liberation from an evil tyrant. Note that Canadians are deployed to active war zones as "peacemakers" whose task is to protect civilians.

5. **The absence of alternatives.** A fifth factor promoting war is the absence of alternatives. While the goal of the United Nations is to maintain international peace by finding alternatives to war, the organization has had limited success in preventing conflict between nations.

Is Terrorism a New Kind of War?

In recent years, we have heard government officials speak of terrorism as a new kind of war. War has historically followed certain patterns: It is played out according to some basic rules (Geneva Conventions); the warring parties are known to each other; and the objectives of the warring parties—which generally involve control of territory—are clearly stated.

Terrorism breaks from these patterns. The identity of terrorist individuals and organizations may not be known; those involved may deny their responsibility; and their goals may be unclear. The 2001 terrorist attacks on the United States were not attempts to defeat the nation militarily or to secure territory. They were carried out by people representing not a country but a cause. In short, they were expressions of anger and hatred, an effort to destabilize the country and create widespread fear.

Conventional warfare is symmetrical, with two nations sending their armies into battle. In contrast, terrorism is an unconventional form of warfare, an asymmetrical conflict in which a few attackers use terror—and their own willingness to die—to level the playing field against a much more powerful enemy. Although the terrorists may be ruthless, the nation under attack must exercise restraint in its response to terrorism because little may be known about the identity and location of those responsible.

The Costs and Causes of Militarism

The cost of armed conflict extends far beyond battlefield casualties. Together, the world's nations spend almost US$1.8 trillion annually for military purposes (Stockholm International Peace Research Agency, 2015) Spending this much diverts resources from the desperate struggle for survival by hundreds of millions of poor people.

After Social Security, defence is the U.S. government's second-largest expenditure, accounting for 20 percent of all federal spending. Canada's initial 20-year defence budget (2012) of $490 billion was reduced in the interests of austerity and in response to criticism by the public and the opposition. Military spending has trended down along with the size of armed forces. One reason is that more military operations are directed against terrorist targets and involve not armies but small teams of highly trained soldiers (Thompson, 2013).

For decades, American military spending went up as a result of the arms race between the United States and the Soviet Union, which dropped out of the race after its collapse in 1991. But some analysts (i.e., those who support power elite theory) link high military spending to the domination of U.S. society by a **military-industrial complex,** *the close association of the federal government, the military, and defence industries.* The roots of militarism, then, lie not only in external threats to American security but also in its institutional structures (Barnes, 2002; Marullo, 1987).

A final reason for continuing militarism is regional conflict. During the 1990s, for example, localized wars broke out in Bosnia, Chechnya, and Zambia, and tensions today run high between Israel and Palestine and between India and Pakistan. Even limited wars have the potential to grow and draw in other countries, including

ONE REASON TO PURSUE PEACE IS THE RISING TOLL OF DEATH AND MUTILATION CAUSED BY MILLIONS OF LAND MINES PLACED IN THE GROUND DURING WARTIME AND LEFT THERE AFTERWARD Civilians, many of them children, maimed by land mines receive treatment in this Kabul, Afghanistan, clinic.

Joe McNally/The LIFE Picture Collection/Getty Images

the United States. India and Pakistan—both nuclear powers—moved to the brink of war in 2002 and then pulled back. In 2003, the announcement by North Korea that it, too, had nuclear weapons raised tensions in Asia. Iran continues to develop nuclear technology, raising fears that this nation may soon have an atomic bomb.

Nuclear Weapons

Despite the easing of superpower tensions, the world still contains approximately 4000 operational nuclear warheads, representing a destructive power of several tonnes of TNT for every person on the planet. If even a small fraction of this stockpile were used in war, life as we know it would end. Albert Einstein, whose genius contributed to the development of nuclear weapons, reflected, "The unleashed power of the atom has changed everything *save our modes of thinking,* and we thus drift toward unparalleled catastrophe." In short, nuclear weapons make unrestrained war unthinkable in a world not yet capable of peace.

The United States, the Russian Federation, Great Britain, France, the People's Republic of China, Israel, India, Pakistan, and probably North Korea all have nuclear weapons. The danger of catastrophic war increases with **nuclear proliferation**, *the acquisition of nuclear weapons technology by more and more nations.* A few nations stopped the development of nuclear weapons; Argentina and Brazil halted work in 1990, and South Africa dismantled its arsenal in 1991. But the years ahead could see many more nations joining the "nuclear club." As more nations gain nuclear weapons, even the smallest regional conflict can easily threaten the entire planet.

Mass Media and War

The Iraq War was the first war in which television crews were "embedded" with U.S. and U.K. troops, reporting as the campaign unfolded. The mass media provided ongoing and detailed reports of events; cable television made available live coverage of the war 24 hours a day, seven days a week.

Media outlets critical of the war—especially the Arab news channel Al-Jazeera—tended to report the slow pace of the conflict, the casualties to coalition forces, and the deaths and injuries suffered by Iraqi civilians—information that would increase pressure to end the war. Media outlets supportive of the war, including most news organizations in the United States, tended to report the rapid pace of the war and the casualties to Saddam Hussein's forces and to downplay harm to Iraqi civilians as minimal and unintended. In sum, the power of the mass media to provide selective information to a worldwide audience means that television and other media are almost as important to the outcome of a conflict as is the military doing the actual fighting.

Pursuing Peace

How can the world reduce the dangers of war? Here are the most recent approaches to peace:

1. **Deterrence.** The logic of the arms race linked security to a "balance of terror" between the superpowers. The principle of *mutual assured destruction* means that the side launching a first-strike nuclear attack against the other will face greater retaliation. This deterrence policy kept the peace during more than 50 years of the Cold War between the United States and the Soviet Union. But this strategy fuelled an enormously expensive arms race and had little effect on nuclear proliferation, which represents a growing threat to peace. Deterrence also does little to stop terrorism or to prevent war started by a powerful nation (such as the United States) against a weaker foe (such as the Taliban's regime in Afghanistan or Saddam Hussein's Iraq).

2. **High-technology defence.** If technology created the weapons, perhaps it can also protect us from them. Such is the claim of the *strategic defence initiative* (SDI). Using this strategy, satellites and ground installations would destroy enemy missiles soon after they were launched. Critics claim that the system, which they refer to as "Star Wars," would be, at best, a leaky umbrella. Others worry that building such a system will spark another massive arms race. In recent years, the Obama administration has turned away from further development of SDI in favour of more focused defence against short-range missiles that might be launched from Iran.

3. **Diplomacy and disarmament.** Some analysts believe that the best path to peace is diplomacy rather than technology (Dedrick & Yinger, 1990). Teams of diplomats working together can increase security by reducing, rather than building, weapons stockpiles. But disarmament has limitations. No nation wants to be weakened by letting down its defences. Successful diplomacy depends on everyone involved making efforts to resolve a common problem (Fisher & Ury, 1988). Although the United States and the Soviet Union continue to negotiate arms reduction agreements, the world now faces increasing threats from other nations, such as North Korea and Iran.

4. **Resolving underlying conflict.** In the end, reducing the dangers of war may depend on resolving underlying conflicts by promoting a more just world. Poverty, hunger, and illiteracy are all root causes of war. Perhaps the world needs to reconsider the wisdom of spending thousands of times as much money on militarism as we do on efforts to find peaceful solutions (Kaplan & Schaffer, 2001; Sivard, 1988).

Politics: Looking Ahead

Change in political systems is ongoing. Several problems and trends are likely to be important as the twenty-first century unfolds.

One troublesome problem in Canada and the United States is the inconsistency between our democratic ideals and our low turnout at the polls. Perhaps, as conservative pluralist theorists say, many people do not bother to vote because they are content with their lives. On the other hand, liberal power elite theorists may be right in their view that people withdraw from a system that concentrates wealth and power in the hands of so few people. Or perhaps, as radical Marxist critics claim, people find that our political system gives little real choice, limiting options and policies to those that support our capitalist economy. In any case, the current high level of apathy undermines our claims to be democratic.

A second issue is the global rethinking of political models. The Cold War between the United States and the Soviet Union encouraged people to think of politics in terms of the two opposing models, capitalism and socialism. Today, however, people are more likely to consider a broader range of political systems that link government to the economy in various ways. "Welfare capitalism" as found in Sweden or "state capitalism" as found in Japan and South Korea are just two possibilities. In all cases, promoting the broadest democratic participation is an important goal. The Thinking Globally box helps us understand the current political transformation in the Middle East by looking at the recent political history of the world's Islamic countries.

Third, we still face the danger of war in many parts of the world. Even as the United States and the Russian Federation dismantle some warheads, vast stockpiles of nuclear weapons remain, and nuclear technology continues to spread around the world. In addition, new superpowers are likely to arise (the People's Republic of China and India are likely candidates), regional conflicts are likely to continue, and there is no end in sight to global terrorism. We can only hope for—*and vote for*—leaders who will find nonviolent solutions to the age-old problems that provoke war, putting us on the road to world peace.

Thinking Globally

Uprisings Across the Middle East: An End to the Islamic "Democracy Gap"?

The wave of popular political protest that swept across the Middle East in 2011 is the largest global political movement in the two decades since change swept through the former Soviet Union and the nations of Eastern Europe. What's going on? Why are so many nations in this part of the world erupting with political opposition?

Is there a "democracy gap" in the Middle East? Is there a lack of democracy in Islamic nations? Making any assessment of global democracy is more difficult than it may appear. For one thing, in a world marked by striking cultural diversity, can we assume that democracy and the related ideas about political freedoms are the same everywhere? The answer cannot be a simple "yes," because with their various political histories, concepts such as "democracy" and "freedom" mean different things in different cultural settings.

What have researchers found? Freedom House is an organization that monitors political freedom by tracking people's right to vote, to express ideas, and to move about without undue interference from government in nations around the world. Freedom House classifies nations in one of three categories: "not free," "partly free," and "free."

Freedom House reports that many of the nations that are classified as "not free" have populations that are largely Islamic. Around the world, 46 of 194 nations had an Islamic-majority population in 2015. Just 9 (20 percent) of these 46 countries had democratic governments, and Freedom House rated only two (4 percent)—Senegal and Tunisia—as "free." Of the remainder, 18 (39 percent) were rated "partly free" and 26 (57 percent) were "not free." Of the 148 nations without an Islamic majority, 114 (77 percent) had democratic governments, and 86 (58.1 percent) were rated as "free." When you put these facts together, countries without Islamic majorities were four times more likely

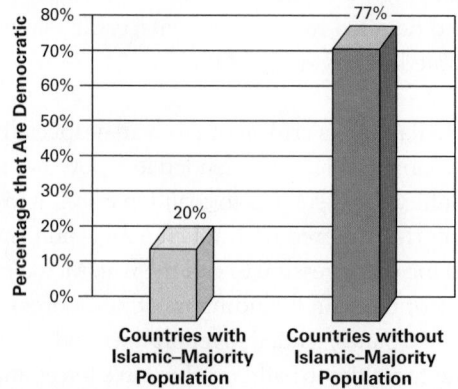

Democracy and Islam

TODAY, DEMOCRATIC GOVERNMENT IS MUCH LESS COMMON IN COUNTRIES WITH ISLAMIC-MAJORITY POPULATIONS Fifty years ago, the same was true of countries with Catholic-majority populations.

than those with Islamic majorities to have democratic governments. Based on this finding, Freedom House concluded that countries with an Islamic majority display a "democracy gap."

This relative lack of democracy was found in all world regions that contain Islamic-majority nations, including Africa, central Europe, and Asia. But the pattern was especially strong among the 16 Islamic-majority states in the Middle East and North Africa that are ethnically Arabic—as of early 2015, only Tunisia is an electoral democracy.

What explains this "democracy gap"? Freedom House points to four factors. First, countries with Islamic-majority populations are typically less developed economically, with limited schooling and widespread poverty. Second, cultural traditions rigidly control the lives of women, limiting their economic, educational, and political opportunities. Third, although most other countries restrict the power of religious elites in government, and some (including the United States) even recognize a "separation of church and state," Islamic-majority nations support a political role for Islamic leaders. In two recent cases—Iran and Afghanistan under the Taliban—Islamic leaders have actually taken formal control of the government. Fourth, the enormous wealth that comes from Middle Eastern oil plays a part in preventing democratic government. In Iraq, Saudi Arabia, Kuwait, Qatar, and other nations, this natural resource has provided astounding riches to a small number of families, money that they can use to shore up their political control.

For all these reasons, Freedom House concludes that the road to democracy for Islamic-majority nations is likely to be long. But it is worthwhile remembering that, looking back to 1950, very few Catholic-majority countries (mostly in Europe and Latin America) had democratic governments. Today, however, most of these nations are democratic.

What is the future for democracy in Islamic-majority nations? Keep in mind that 29 percent of the world's Muslims live in Turkey, Bangladesh, India, Indonesia, Germany, France, and the United States, where they already live under democratic governments. But perhaps the best indicator that change is under way is the widespread demand for a political voice now rising from people throughout the Middle East. The pace of political change is increasing.

What Do You Think?

1. How do you think the political conflict in the Middle East will turn out? Will the cause of democracy be advanced?

2. Will the "democracy gap" described here disappear? Why or why not?

3. What role should North American or European countries play in this process? Is outside intervention a force that advances democracy? Why or why not?

SOURCES: Karatnycky (2002), Freedom House (2015), and Pew Research Center (2015).

Seeing Sociology in Everyday Life

CHAPTER 17 Politics and Government

How important are you to the political process?

How important are you to the political process? Historically, as this chapter explains, young people have been less likely than older people to take part in politics. The phenomenal turnout of young voters in the federal election of 2015 was the result of Justin Trudeau's ability to connect with people in a relaxed, charming, "we're in-this-together" kind of way. He is the most open and approachable prime minister imaginable. The increased turnout of young voters in our election of 2015 suggests that, as the new leader of the Liberals, Justin Trudeau was able to appeal to young Canadians who want *their* voices heard.

> **Hint** Before the 2008 election, Elections Canada established a number of programs to engage young voters. Since voter turnout in 2008 was the lowest ever (59.1 percent of registered voters; 61.1 percent in 2011), there is little reason to believe that the Elections Canada initiatives were effective. Way back in 1968 Pierre Elliott Trudeau took university campuses by storm on a wave of Trudeaumania; almost 50 years later the son stepped into his father's shoes and rode a second wave of Trudeaumania to become the prime ministers of Canada. Justin Trudeau had done what Elections Canada failed to do—inspire a 10 percentage-point increase in voter turnout among 18- to 44-year-olds.

Paul Chiasson/The Canadian Press

YOUNG PEOPLE BY THE THOUSANDS FOUND THEIR CHAMPION IN JUSTIN TRUDEAU—A TOTALLY "WITH IT" CHARMER WHO LOVES CROWDS, TAKES SELFIES WITH ANYONE WHO MANAGES TO GET CLOSE TO HIM, AND SHARES HIS LIFE THROUGH SOCIAL MEDIA Cell phones, social networking, and the internet helped to motivate young voters in support of Barack Obama in 2008. Smartphones (think selfies) and the social media weren't just background noise in 2015. Marshall McLuhan said, "The medium is the message." In Trudeau's case smartphones and the social media said it all: This prime-minister-to-be is just like you.

YOU DON'T NEED TO BE A CAMPAIGN WORKER TO MAKE A DIFFERENCE What is the easiest—and in the end, the most important—way to be a part of the political process?

IN 2014, HARRY POTTER FILM STAR EMMA WATSON, WHO SERVES AS UNITED NATIONS WOMEN GOODWILL AMBASSADOR, SPOKE AT A UN EVENT IN SUPPORT OF GENDER EQUALITY AROUND THE WORLD Can you name other celebrities who have tried to influence the political process?

Seeing Sociology in *Your* Everyday Life

1. Go to www.elections.ca, click on Past Elections, and then choose the 42nd General Election. Here, you can check out the results of the 2015 election for Canada, the provinces and territories as well as individual ridings. See if you can find the results for your home riding and compare your riding (or electoral district) with your province. Do the proportions voting for each party differ? If so, can you explain why your riding voted the way it did?

2. With several classmates or friends, make a list of charismatic political leaders (past or present). Why is each person on the list? Do you think that charisma today is anything more than "being good on television"? What is charisma in the context of modern society? Is Justin Trudeau charismatic?

3. Talk to your friends and classmates about their attitudes toward politics. Are they interested in it, and do they plan to vote in the next election (federal or provincial)? If not, ask if they plan to take more of an interest as they grow older, become established in their occupations, and settle down in their own homes.

Making the Grade

CHAPTER 17 Politics and Government

Politics: Power and Authority

17.1 Distinguish traditional, rational-legal, and charismatic authority.

Politics is the major social institution by which a society distributes power and organizes decision making. Max Weber claimed that raw power is transformed into legitimate authority in three ways:

- Pre-industrial societies rely on tradition to transform power into authority. **Traditional authority** is closely linked to kinship.
- As societies industrialize, tradition gives way to rationality. **Rational-legal authority** underlies the operation of bureaucratic offices as well as the law.
- At any time, however, some individuals transform power into authority through charisma. **Charismatic authority** is based on extraordinary personal qualities (as found in Jesus of Nazareth, Adolf Hitler, and Mahatma Gandhi).

politics the social institution that distributes power, sets a society's goals, and makes decisions
power the ability to achieve desired ends despite resistance from others
government a formal organization that directs the political life of a society
authority power that people perceive as legitimate rather than coercive
traditional authority power legitimized by respect for long-established cultural patterns
rational-legal authority power legitimized by legally enacted rules and regulations; also known as bureaucratic authority
charismatic authority power legitimized by extraordinary personal abilities that inspire devotion and obedience
routinization of charisma the transformation of charismatic authority into some combination of traditional and bureaucratic authority

Politics in Global Perspective

17.2 Compare monarchy and democracy as well as authoritarian and totalitarian political systems.

Monarchy is common in agrarian societies.

- Leadership is based on kinship.

- During the Middle Ages, absolute monarchs claimed to rule by divine right.

Democracy is common in modern societies.

- Leadership is linked to elective office.
- Bureaucracy and economic inequality limit true democracy in high-income countries today.

Authoritarianism is any political system that denies the people participation in government.

- Absolute monarchies and military juntas are examples of authoritarian regimes.

Totalitarianism concentrates all political power in one centralized leadership.

- Totalitarian governments allow no organized opposition, and they rule by fear.
  - The world is divided into 194 politically independent nation-states, 88 of which were politically "free" in 2014. Another 55 countries were "partly free," and the remaining 51 countries were "not free." Compared to two decades ago, slightly more of the world's nations are "free."
- Multinational corporations have created a new political order because their enormous wealth gives them power to shape world events.
- In an age of computers and other new information technology, governments can no longer control the flow of information across their borders.

monarchy a political system in which a single family rules from generation to generation
democracy a political system that gives power to the people as a whole
authoritarianism a political system that denies the people participation in government
totalitarianism a highly centralized political system that extensively regulates people's lives

Politics in Canada

17.3 Analyze economic and social issues using the political spectrum.

Representation in Parliament

Quebec and Ontario elect 57 percent (191 of the 338 members of Parliament), which gives them a lot of clout and worries the other provinces and territories. The recent creation of new ridings in areas of population growth has increased the clout of western provinces, albeit only slightly.

The Political Spectrum

- The political left in Canada is represented by the New Democratic Party (along with the Green Party and the Bloc Québécois), the middle by the Liberals, and the right by the Conservatives.
- Left and right orientations involve attitudes on both economic and social issues.
- The election of 1993 was important because two new regional parties (the Bloc Québécois and Reform Party) upset the balance among our three traditional parties.
- Although the Bloc has survived, the merging of the Canadian Alliance and the Progressive Conservative party into the Conservative Party of Canada restored the traditional three-party system outside Quebec (election of 2006).

Voter Apathy

- Voter apathy in Canada seems to have increased in recent elections. Historically, 70 to 90 percent of eligible voters have turned up to vote, but the average voter turnout in the five elections prior to 2015 was about 60 percent.
- Only 61 percent of eligible voters went to the polls in the 2011 federal election—a turnout rate lower than that of the 2008 U.S. election won by Barack Obama.
- For the election of 2015, won by Justin Trudeau's Liberals, voter turnout soared to 77 percent because of increased voting among people 18 to 44 years of age.

political parties organizations operating within the political system that seek control of the government

Theories of Power in Society

17.4 Apply the pluralist, power-elite, and Marxist models to the Canadian political system.

The pluralist model

- claims that political power is spread widely in Canada
- is linked to structural-functional theory

The power-elite model

- claims that power is concentrated in a small, wealthy segment of the population
- is based on the ideas of C. Wright Mills
- is linked to social-conflict theory

The Marxist political-economy model

- claims that our political agenda is determined by a capitalist economy, so true democracy is impossible
- is based on the ideas of Karl Marx
- is linked to social-conflict theory

pluralist model an analysis of politics that sees power as spread among many competing interest groups
power-elite model an analysis of politics that views power as concentrated among the rich
Marxist political-economy model an analysis that explains politics in terms of the operation of a society's economic system

Power beyond the Rules

17.5 Describe causes of both revolution and terrorism.

Revolution radically transforms a political system.

Revolutions

- occur during periods of rising expectations and when governments are unwilling to reform themselves
- are usually led by intellectuals
- must establish a new legitimacy in the eyes of the people

Terrorism employs violence in the pursuit of political goals and is used by a group against a much more powerful enemy.

- State terrorism is the use of violence by government officials as a way to control the population.
- Who or what is defined as terrorist depends on one's political perspective.
- Terrorism is an unconventional form of warfare.

political revolution the overthrow of one political system in order to establish another
terrorism acts of violence or the threat of violence used as a political strategy by an individual or a group

War and Peace

17.6 Identify factors encouraging war or peace.

Like all forms of social behaviour, war is a product of society. Societies go to war when

- they perceive a threat to their way of life
- governments want to divert public attention from social problems at home
- they want to achieve a specific political or moral objective
- they can find no alternatives for resolving conflicts

Military spending rose dramatically in the second half of the twentieth century because of the arms race between the United States and the former Soviet Union.

Some analysts point to the domination of U.S. society by a **military-industrial complex**.

The development and spread of nuclear weapons have increased the threat of global catastrophe.

The most recent approaches to peace include

- deterrence
- high-technology defence
- diplomacy and disarmament
- resolving underlying conflict

In the end, pursuing peace means ending poverty, hunger, and illiteracy and promoting social justice for all people.

war organized, armed conflict among the people of two or more nations, directed by their governments

military-industrial complex the close association of the federal government, the military, and defence industries

nuclear proliferation the acquisition of nuclear weapons technology by more and more nations

Chapter 18
Family

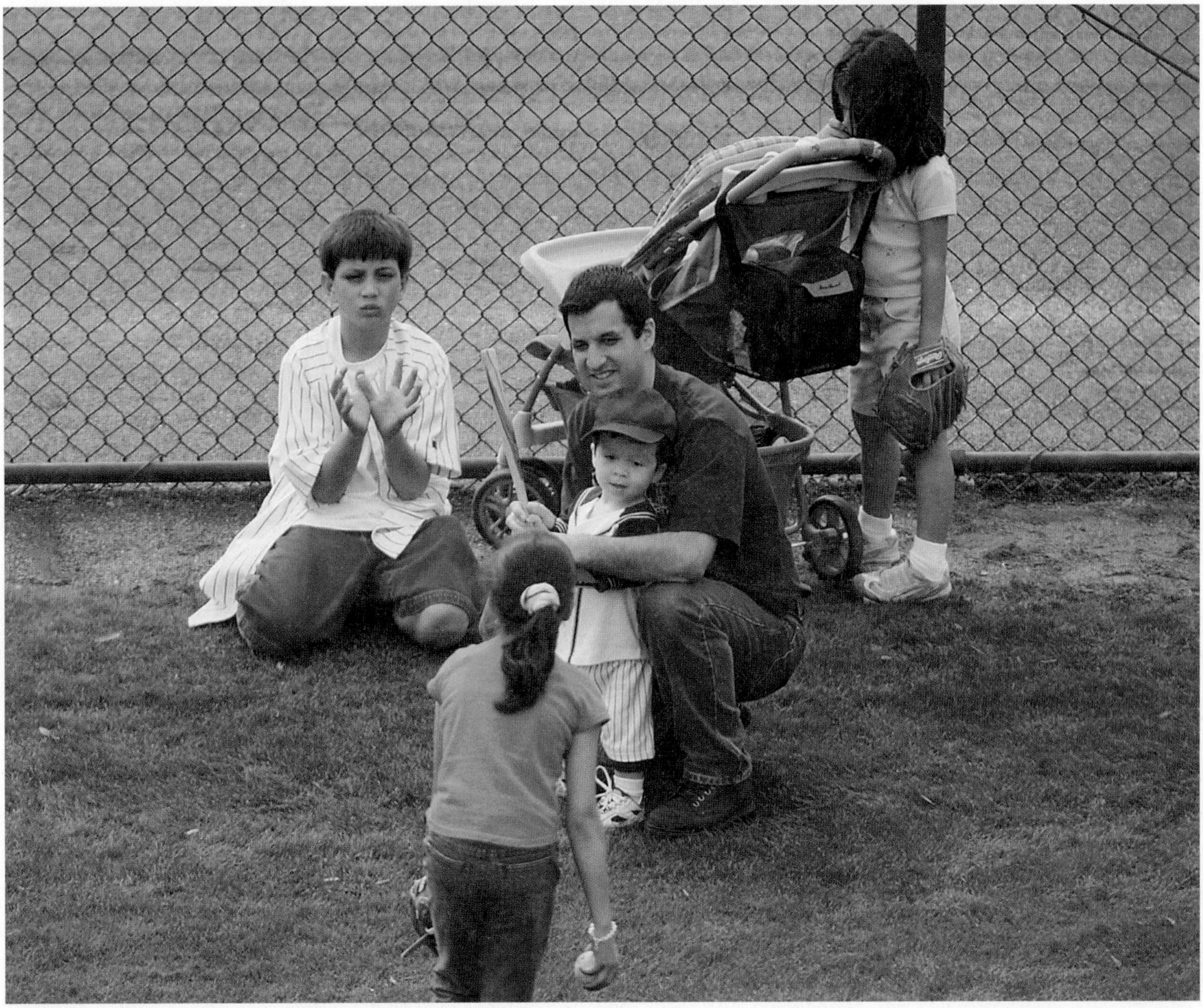

Chuck Franklin/Alamy Stock Photo

Learning Objectives

18.1 Describe families and how they differ around the world.

18.2 Apply sociology's major theories to family life.

18.3 Analyze changes in the family over the life course.

18.4 Explain how class, race, and gender shape family life.

18.5 Analyze the effects of divorce, remarriage, and violence on family life.

18.6 Describe the diversity of family life in Canada.

The Power of Society
to affect the odds of a couple having children

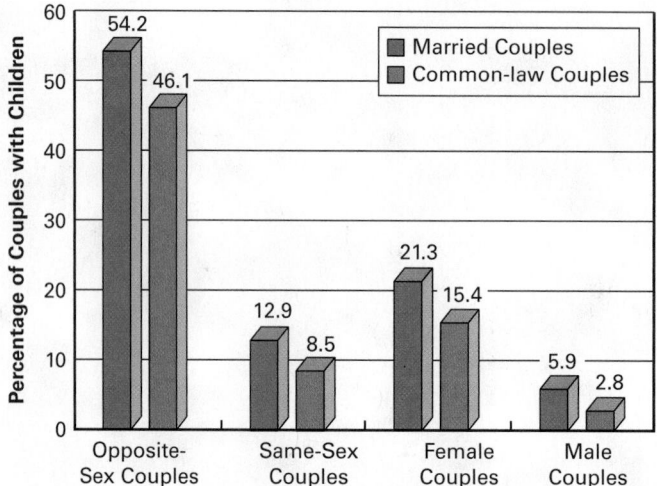

SOURCES: Compilation and calculations by L.M. Gerber based on Statistics Canada, Census 2011, Catalogue no. 98-312-XCB2011046.

Why are some couples more likely to have children than others? Surely couples make the decision to have children (or not) on the basis of their personal preferences and experiences. That may be the case, but social forces of various kinds come into play as well. One would expect to find that opposite-sex couples are more likely to have children than their same-sex counterparts—and indeed that is the case. The "facts of life" account for a large part of the difference. On the other hand, greater acceptance of same-sex relationships and the relatively recent legalization of same-sex marriage allow people to live more openly as same-sex couples. As a result, gays and lesbians may be more likely to keep children conceived in previous heterosexual unions—and even adoption is now a possibility in Canada. These two factors help to explain why female couples are more likely than male couples to have children. One other factor—a purely social construct—has a consistent impact on the presence or absence of children; opposite-sex or same-sex couples are more likely to have children if they are married rather than in common-law unions.

Chapter Overview

This chapter explores the family, a major social institution. Families are important for many reasons, and they are found in every society. The chapter begins by introducing a number of important concepts that sociologists use to describe and analyze families.

When you see a woman pushing a stroller, does it cross your mind that you might be watching a lesbian mother? By some estimates, 10 percent of women are lesbians—and 20 to 30 percent of those lesbians are mothers. In the early 1990s, gaining recognition and acceptance as mothers (i.e., as legitimate, good mothers) was not easy—especially for lesbian mothers who left heterosexual relationships and tried to gain custody of their children.

Many of these women chose not to contest custody in court because they feared defeat by a homophobic legal system. Instead, they hoped for liberal access rights. They had learned that there was an informal distinction between "good" and "bad" lesbian mothers. The "good" ones were those "who live quiet, discreet lives, who promise that they will raise their children to be heterosexual, [and] who appear to the outside world to be heterosexual single parents"—in other words, those who are completely secretive about being a lesbian. The "bad" ones were the women who viewed "their lesbianism as part of a larger challenge to society" (Arnup, 1995:331)—that is, those who had "come out."

Knowing the criteria that the courts considered in determining "the best interests of the child," lesbian mothers faced difficult choices. Most tried to appear as "straight" as possible in court to increase the chances of gaining custody, rather than be open about being lesbians.

When they gained custody of their children, lesbian mothers had to decide whether to be open about their unusual family situations—in the community, at school, at church. Now that Canada has legalized same-sex marriage, changed its formal definition of marriage, and opened the door to adoption by gay or lesbian couples, we can expect profound—though not instant—impacts on our society's acceptance of families with lesbian or gay parents. ∎

In Canada, the state of the family is a hot topic. Indeed, a rising chorus of voices charges that the family is endangered in Canada. The marriage rate within Canada is decreasing, while the divorce rate has increased. The proportion of Canadians age 15 and older who have ever been divorced doubled between 1975 and 1995—from 7 to 14 percent (Bibby, 1995:6). Marital breakdown, coupled with the increase in the number of children born to unmarried women, means that half of Canadian children born today will live with a single parent for some time before reaching age 18. Not surprisingly, the proportion of Canadian children living in poverty remains a persistent problem. This chapter looks at the rapidly changing family as well as the diversity among families here in Canada and around the world.

a social bond based on common ancestry, marriage, or adoption. All societies contain families, but exactly who people call their kin has varied through history and varies today from one culture to another. From the viewpoint of individuals, families change as children grow up and leave the families into which they were born to form families of their own.

Here, as in many other countries, families have traditionally formed around **marriage**, *a legal relationship, usually involving economic co-operation, sexual activity, and child-bearing.* The traditional belief is that people should marry before having children; this expectation is embedded in the word *matrimony*, which in Latin means "the condition of motherhood." Today, in Canada, children

Family: Basic Concepts and Global Variations

18.1 Describe families and how they differ around the world.

The **family** is *a social institution found in all societies that unites people in co-operative groups to care for one another, including any children.* Family ties are also called **kinship**,

family a social institution found in all societies that unites people in cooperative groups to care for one another, including any children

extended family a family composed of parents and children as well as other kin; also known as a *consanguine family*

nuclear family a family composed of one or two parents and their children; also known as a *conjugal family*

marriage a legal relationship, usually involving economic co-operation, sexual activity, and child-bearing

endogamy marriage between people of the same social category

exogamy marriage between people of different social categories

monogamy marriage that unites two partners

polygamy marriage that unites a person with two or more spouses

polygyny marriage that unites one man and two or more women

polyandry marriage that unites one woman and two or more men

are born to single women as well as to common-law and married couples—and many are being raised by same-sex couples. In addition, more couples are remaining childless. In effect, child-bearing is not necessarily the central focus of marriage.

Just as we have changed our definition of marriage, we are changing our understanding of "family." The 2001 census defined families as married or common-law couples with or without children, or a lone parent of any marital status with at least one child living at home. Most significantly, in 2001, a couple living common-law might be of opposite or same sex. For the 2006 census, a married couple might be of opposite or same sex. We have come a long way from the days when only a married couple with children was considered a "family."

How closely related do people have to be in order to be part of a family? In pre-industrial societies, people commonly recognize the **extended family**, *a family consisting of parents and children as well as other kin*. This large group is sometimes called the *consanguine family* because it includes everyone with "shared blood." With industrialization, however, increasing social mobility and geographic migration give rise to the **nuclear family**, *a family composed of one or two parents and their children*. The nuclear family is also called the *conjugal family*, meaning "based on marriage." While many people in our society think of kinship in terms of extended families, most people carry out daily routines within a nuclear family.

Marriage Patterns

Cultural norms, and often laws, identify people as suitable or unsuitable marriage partners. Some marital norms promote **endogamy**, *marriage between people of the same social category*. Endogamy limits potential partners to people of the same age, race, religion, or social class. By contrast, **exogamy** is *marriage between people of different social categories*. In rural areas of India, for example, people are expected to marry someone of the same caste (endogamy) but from a different village (exogamy). The reason for endogamy is that people of similar position pass along their standing to their offspring, maintaining the traditional social hierarchy. Exogamy, on the other

hand, links communities, encouraging alliances and the spread of culture.

In high-income nations, laws permit only **monogamy** (from the Greek, meaning "one union"), *marriage that unites two partners*. Global Map 18–1 shows that monogamy is the rule throughout North and South America as well as Europe. Many countries in Africa and southern Asia permit **polygamy** (from the Greek, meaning "many unions"), *marriage that unites a person with two or more spouses*. Polygamy has two forms. By far the more common form is **polygyny** (from the Greek, meaning "many women"), *marriage that unites one man and two or more women*. For example, Islamic nations in the Middle East and Africa permit men up to four wives. Even so, most Islamic families are monogamous because few men can afford to support several wives and even more children. **Polyandry** (from the Greek, meaning "many men" or "many husbands") is *marriage that unites one woman and two or more men*. This extremely rare pattern exists in Tibet, a mountainous land where agriculture is difficult. There, polyandry discourages the division of land into parcels too small to support a family and divides the work of farming among many men.

Most of the world's societies have at some time permitted more than one marital pattern. Even so, most marriages have been monogamous (Murdock, 1965; orig. 1949). This historical preference for monogamy reflects two facts of life: Supporting several spouses is very expensive, and the number of men and women in most societies is roughly equal.

Residential Patterns

Just as societies regulate mate selection, they also designate where a couple lives. In pre-industrial societies, most newlyweds live with one set of parents, who offer them protection, support, and assistance. Most common is the norm of **patrilocality** (Greek for "place of the father"), *a residential pattern in which a married couple lives with or near the husband's family*. But some societies, such as the Six Nations (Haudenosaunee), favour **matrilocality** (meaning "place of the mother"), *a residential pattern in which a married couple lives with or near the wife's family*. Societies that engage in frequent local warfare

Window on the World

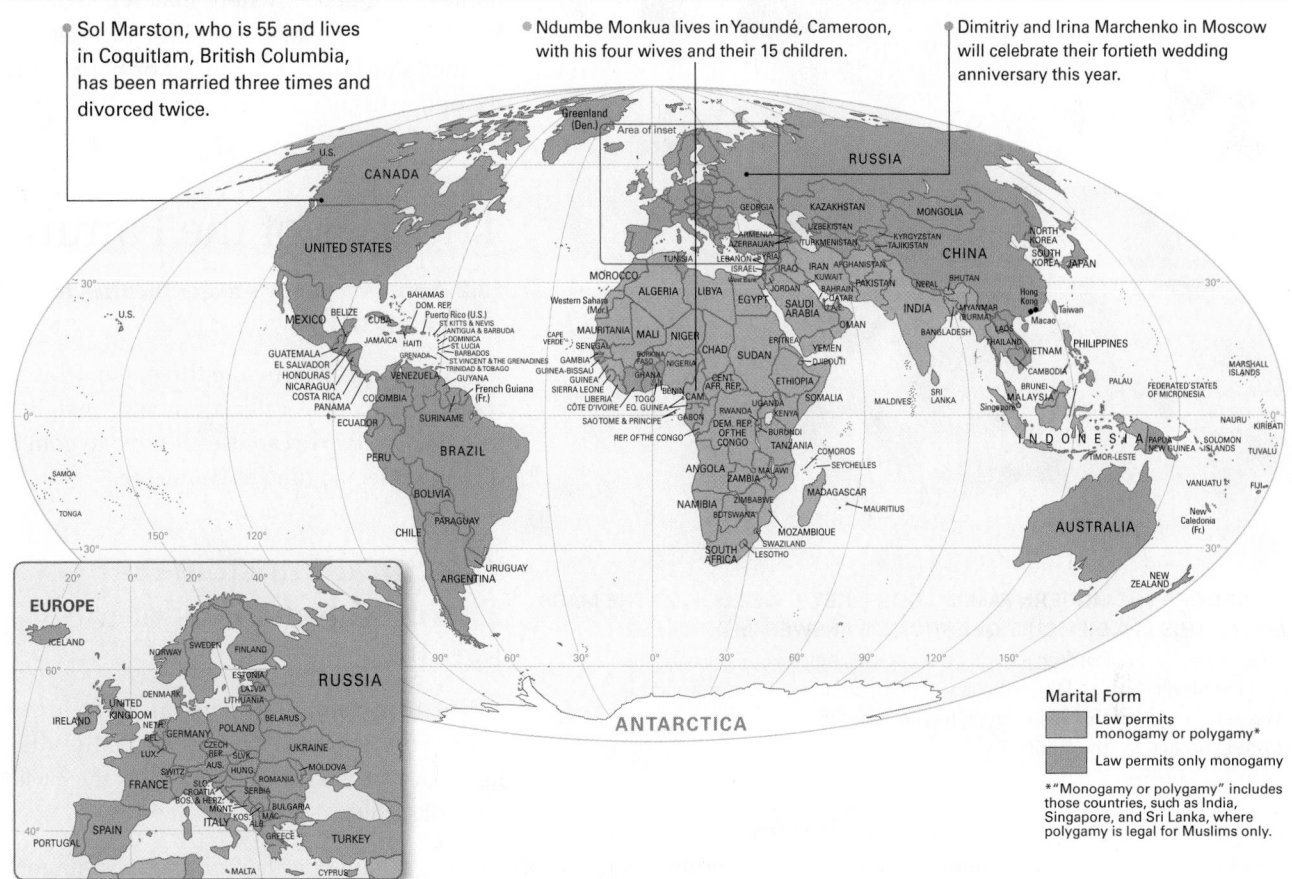

Sol Marston, who is 55 and lives in Coquitlam, British Columbia, has been married three times and divorced twice.

Ndumbe Monkua lives in Yaoundé, Cameroon, with his four wives and their 15 children.

Dimitriy and Irina Marchenko in Moscow will celebrate their fortieth wedding anniversary this year.

Marital Form

Law permits monogamy or polygamy*

Law permits only monogamy

*"Monogamy or polygamy" includes those countries, such as India, Singapore, and Sri Lanka, where polygamy is legal for Muslims only.

Global Map 18–1 Marital Form in Global Perspective

Monogamy is the only legal form of marriage throughout the western hemisphere and in much of the rest of the world. In most African nations and in southern Asia, however, polygamy is permitted by law. In many cases, this practice reflects the influence of Islam, a religion that allows a man to have up to four wives. Even so, most marriages in these countries are monogamous, primarily for financial reasons.

SOURCES: Based on Peters Atlas of the World. New York: Harper & Row, 1990 with updates by John J. Macionis.

tend toward patrilocality, so that sons are close to home to offer protection.

At the beginning of the fourteenth century, the Iroquois—in what is now southern Ontario—were involved in intensive agriculture. Because tribes were matrilocal and matrilineal, women owned all property and determined kinship. When they married, men moved in with their wives' families and their children belonged to their mother's clan (Ambert, 2012).

Industrial societies show yet another pattern. Finances permitting, they favour **neolocality** (from the Greek, meaning "new place"), *a residential pattern in which a married couple lives apart from both sets of parents.*

Patterns of Descent

Descent refers to *the system by which members of a society trace kinship over generations.* Most pre-industrial societies trace kinship through either the father's side or the mother's side of the family. **Patrilineal descent**, the more common pattern, is *a system tracing kinship through men.* In this pattern, children are related to others only through their fathers, so that fathers pass property on to their sons. Patrilineal descent characterizes most pastoral and agrarian societies, in which men produce the most valued resources.

patrilocality a residential pattern in which a married couple lives with or near the husband's family

matrilocality a residential pattern in which a married couple lives with or near the wife's family

neolocality a residential pattern in which a married couple lives apart from both sets of parents

WHAT DOES THE MODERN FAMILY LOOK LIKE? IF WE LOOK TO THE MASS MEDIA, THIS IS A DIFFICULT QUESTION TO ANSWER In the television series *Modern Family*, Jay Pritchett's family includes his much younger wife; his stepson, Manny; his daughter, Claire (who is married with three children); and his son, Mitchell (who, with his gay partner, has an adopted Vietnamese daughter). How would you define "the family"?

Less common is **matrilineal descent**, *a system tracing kinship through women.* Matrilineal descent, in which mothers pass property to their daughters, is found more frequently in horticultural societies, where women are the main food producers.

Industrial societies with greater gender equality recognize **bilateral descent** ("two-sided descent"), *a system tracing kinship through both men and women.* In this pattern, children recognize people on both the father's side and the mother's side as relatives.

The Controversy and Debate box deals with international adoption, an issue that raises a number of concerns.

Patterns of Authority

Worldwide, polygyny, patrilocality, and patrilineal descent are dominant and reflect the global pattern of patriarchy. But in industrial societies, more egalitarian family patterns evolve, especially as the share of women in the labour force increases. Even in North America, however, men are still typically heads of households, and most children are given their fathers' surnames. In Quebec, where married women keep their birth names, children may get the mother's or father's surname, or both, with the option of choosing one later on.

Theories of the Family

18.2 Apply sociology's major theories to family life.

As in earlier chapters, the three major theoretical approaches offer a range of insights into the family. We can use all three to gain a deeper understanding of family life.

Structural-Functoinal Theories: Functions of the Family

According to the structural-functional approach, the family performs many vital tasks. In fact, the family operates as the backbone of society.

1. **Socialization.** The family is the first and most important setting for child rearing. Ideally, parents help children become well-integrated, contributing members of society. Of course, family socialization continues throughout life. Adults change within marriage and, as any parent knows, mothers and fathers learn as much from their children as their children learn from them.

2. **Regulation of sexual activity.** Every culture regulates sexual activity in the interest of maintaining kinship organization and property rights. The **incest taboo** is *a norm forbidding sexual relations or marriage between certain relatives.* While the incest taboo exists in every society, exactly which relatives cannot marry varies from one culture to another. The matrilineal Dinee (or Navajo), for example, forbid marrying any relative of one's mother. Our bilateral society applies the incest taboo to both sides of the family but limits it to close relatives, including parents, grandparents, siblings, aunts, and uncles. But even brother/sister, but not parent/child, marriages existed among the ancient Egyptian, Incan, and Hawaiian nobility (Murdock, 1965; orig. 1949).

Reproduction between close relatives of any species can result in mental and physical damage to offspring. Yet only human beings observe an incest taboo, a fact suggesting that the key reason for

descent the system by which members of a society trace kinship over generations

patrilineal descent a system tracing kinship through men

matrilineal descent a system tracing kinship through women

bilateral descent a system tracing kinship through both men and women

Controversy and Debate

International Adoption

The rate of international adoption by Canadians increased rapidly from 10 per year in 1970 to roughly 2000 per year from 42 different countries in the 2000s. Citizenship and Immigration Canada, which offers assistance in adopting from abroad on its website, suggests that you should start the sponsorship process even before you find a child.

In the past, childless Canadian couples adopted the children of unwed mothers. Abortion was illegal and infrequent, and women who bore and raised children outside marriage were stigmatized. Now, abortion is legal and relatively available, and women who give birth outside marriage are increasingly likely to keep their babies. In the past, many Aboriginal children were adopted by non-Aboriginal couples; now, social workers place available children with relatives, foster homes, or adoptive parents within the Aboriginal community. As a result of these changes, between 1980 and 1990, adoptions of children born in Canada declined by almost 50 percent.

So childless couples have turned to international adoption. What does the future hold for these families? Often, the adopted child's cultural heritage differs from that of the adoptive family. For example, China's one-child policy, established in the 1980s, has led many Chinese couples to give up daughters for adoption, so that they can try again for a son to carry on the family name. Currently, about half of Canadian foreign adoptions are from China, where, because of the money involved, orphanages prefer foreign over Chinese couples—despite policies that favour domestic adoption.

Research in Canada by Westhues and Cohen (1994) indicates that most of these adoptions are successful, in terms of self-esteem, degree of integration into the adoptive family, peer relations, and the children's comfort with their own ethnic backgrounds. The unfolding stories of these adoptions and the children's adjustment to Canadian society will continue to hold great interest for Canadian researchers in the years to come.

There is another alternative to foreign adoption. Throughout Canada are 60 000 to 80 000 children under age 18 who are in government care. Instead of being adopted, these children are bounced among foster homes until they are "aged out of the system" at 19. When governments spend on media campaigns to increase awareness of these children, adoption rates spike, but government officials are reluctant to treat children as commodities.

What Do You Think?

1. Are international adoptions a good solution to Canada's lack of "adoptable" children?

2. Do you know people who have adopted children from abroad? How have these adoptions worked out?

3. What do you think of Madonna's adoption of then one-year-old David Banda from Malawi?

SOURCES: Fulton (1995), Mason (2006), Westhues and Cohen (1994), and York (2006).

OFTEN, WE EXPERIENCE MODERN SOCIETY AS COLD AND IMPERSONAL In this context, the family can be a "haven in a heartless world." Not every family lives up to this promise, of course, but people in families do live happier and longer than those who live alone.

Westend61/Newscom

controlling incest is social. Why? First, the incest taboo limits sexual competition in families by restricting sex to spouses. Second, because kinship defines people's rights and obligations toward one another, reproduction among close relatives would hopelessly confuse kinship ties and threaten social order. Third, forcing people to marry outside their immediate families creates ties within the larger society.

3. **Social placement.** Families are not needed for people to reproduce, but they help maintain social organization. Parents pass their own social identities—in terms of race, ethnicity, religion, and social class—to their children at birth.

4. **Material and emotional security.** Many people view the family as a "haven in a heartless world," offering

physical protection, emotional support, and financial assistance. Perhaps this is why people living in families tend to be happier, healthier, and wealthier than people living alone (Goldstein & Kenney, 2001).

EVALUATE

Structural-functional theory explains why society, at least as we know it, is built on families. But this approach glosses over the diversity of family life and ignores the role of other social institutions (such as government) in meeting the same human needs. Finally, structural-functionalism overlooks negative aspects of family life, including patriarchy and family violence.

CHECK YOUR LEARNING What four important functions does the family provide for the operation of society?

Social-Conflict and Feminist Theories : Inequality and the Family

Like the structural-functional approach, the social-conflict approach, including feminist theory, considers the family as central to our way of life. But rather than focusing on ways that kinship benefits society, this approach points out how the family perpetuates social inequality.

1. **Property and inheritance.** Friedrich Engels (1902; orig. 1884) traced the origin of the family to men's need, especially in the upper classes, to identify heirs so that they could hand down property to their sons. Families thus concentrate wealth and reproduce the class structure in each new generation.
2. **Patriarchy.** Feminists link the family to patriarchy. To know their heirs, men must control the sexuality of women. Families therefore transform women into the sexual and economic property of men. A century ago in Canada, the earnings of wives belonged to their husbands and, today, women still bear most of the responsibility for child rearing and housework.
3. **Race and ethnicity.** Racial and ethnic categories persist over generations because most people marry others like themselves. Endogamous marriage supports racial and ethnic hierarchies.

EVALUATE

Social-conflict and feminist theories show another side of family life: its role in social stratification. Engels criticized the family as supporting capitalism. But non-capitalist societies also have families and family problems. The family may be linked to social inequality, as Engels argued, but the family carries out societal functions not easily accomplished by other means.

CHECK YOUR LEARNING Point to three ways in which families support social inequality.

Micro-Level Theories: Constructing Family Life

Both structural-functional and social-conflict analyses view the family as a structural system. By contrast, micro-level analysis explores how individuals shape and experience family life.

SYMBOLIC-INTERACTION THEORY Ideally, family living offers an opportunity for intimacy, a word with Latin roots meaning "sharing fear." As family members share many activities over time, they build emotional bonds. Of course, the fact that parents act as authority figures often limits their closeness to younger children. Only as children approach adulthood do kinship ties open up to include sharing confidences with greater intimacy (Macionis, 1978).

SOCIAL-EXCHANGE THEORY Social-exchange analysis, another micro-level approach, describes courtship

WENN Ltd/Alamy Stock Photo

ACCORDING TO SOCIAL EXCHANGE THEORY, PEOPLE FORM RELATIONSHIPS BASED ON WHAT EACH OFFERS TO THE OTHER Generally partners see the exchange as fair or "about even." What do you think is the exchange involved in this marriage between actor Doug Hutchinson (who was 51 at the time of their marriage) and aspiring actress Courtney Stodden (who was 16)?

and marriage as forms of negotiation (Blau, 1964). Dating allows each person to assess the advantages and disadvantages of a potential spouse. In essence, exchange analysts suggest, people "shop around" for partners to make the best "deal" they can.

In patriarchal societies, gender roles dictate the elements of exchange. Men bring wealth and power to the marriage marketplace, and women bring beauty, health, and the ability to bear children (and dowries, in some societies). The importance of beauty explains women's traditional concern with their appearance. But as women have joined the labour force, they are less dependent on men to support them, and so the terms of exchange are converging for men and women.

EVALUATE

Micro-level analysis counters structural-functional and social-conflict visions of the family as an institutional system. Both the interaction and the exchange theories focus on the individual experience of family life. However, micro-level analysis misses the bigger picture: The experience of family life is similar for people in the same social and economic categories.

CHECK YOUR LEARNING How does a micro-level approach to understanding family differ from a macro-level approach? Summarize the main points of the symbolic-interaction and social-exchange theories.

The Applying Theory table summarizes what we can learn by applying each of the theoretical approaches to family life.

Stages of Family Life

18.3 Analyze changes in the family over the life course.

The family is a dynamic institution. Not only does the family itself change over time, but the way any of us *experience* family changes as well as we move through the life course. New families begin with courtship and evolve as the new partners settle into the realities of married life. Next, for most couples at least, come the years spent developing careers and raising children, leading to the later years of marriage, after the children have left home to form families of their own. We will look briefly at each of these four stages.

Courtship

November 2, Kandy, Sri Lanka. Winding through the rain forest of this beautiful island, our van driver, Harry, recounts how he met his wife. Actually, he explains, it was more of an arrangement: The two families were both Buddhist and of the same caste. "We got along well, right from the start," recalls Harry. "We had the same background. I suppose she or I could have said No. But love marriages happen in the city, not in the village where I grew up." [John J. Macionis]

In rural Sri Lanka, as in rural areas of low-income and middle-income countries throughout the world, most people consider courtship too important to be left to the young (Stone, 1977). *Arranged marriages* are alliances between extended families of similar social standing and usually involve an exchange not just of children but also of wealth and favours. Romantic love has little to do with marriage, and parents may make such arrangements when their children are very young. A century ago in Sri Lanka and India, for example, half of all girls married before reaching age 15 (Mace & Mace, 1960; Mayo, 1927). Child marriage still takes place in India and Pakistan, especially in rural areas. (See the photograph of the breastfeeding baby on her wedding day.)

Because traditional societies are more culturally homogeneous, almost all young men and women have been well socialized to be good spouses. Therefore, parents can arrange marriages with little thought about whether the two individuals involved are *personally* compatible because they know that the partners will be *culturally* compatible.

Industrialization erodes the importance of extended families and weakens tradition. Young people in industrial societies choose their own mates and delay marriage

APPLYING THEORY

Family

	Structural-Functional Theory	Social-Conflict and Feminist Theories	Symbolic-Interaction and Social-Exchange Theories
What is the level of analysis?	Macro-level	Macro-level	Micro-level
What is the importance of family for society?	The family performs vital tasks, including socializing the young and providing emotional and financial support for members.	The family perpetuates social inequality by handing down wealth from one generation to the next.	Symbolic-interaction theory explains that the reality of family life is constructed by members in their interaction.
	The family helps regulate sexual activity.	The family supports patriarchy as well as racial and ethnic inequality.	Social-exchange theory shows that courtship typically brings together people who offer the same level of advantages.

Thinking Globally

The Weakest Families on Earth? A Report from Sweden

Canadians might envy the Swedes for avoiding many of our worst social problems, including violent crime, drug abuse, and poverty. This Scandinavian nation seems to fulfill the promise of the modern welfare state with a large, professional government bureaucracy that meets virtually every human need.

But one drawback of such a large welfare state, according to David Popenoe (1991), is that Sweden has the weakest families on Earth. Because people look to the government, not spouses, for economic assistance, Swedes are less likely to marry than members of many other high-income societies. For the same reason, large proportions of Swedish adults live alone or in common-law relationships. More than half of all Swedish children are born to unmarried mothers and the average household size in Sweden (at 2.1 persons) is almost the smallest in the world. Thus, family appears to play a less central role in Swedish life than it does elsewhere.

Popenoe claims that, back in the 1960s, a growing culture of individualism and self-fulfillment, along with the declining influence of religion, began eroding Swedish families. The movement of women into the labour force also played a part. Today, Sweden has a small proportion of women who are homemakers and an exceptionally high percentage in the labour force.

John Terence Turner/The Image Bank/Getty Images

But most important, according to Popenoe, is the expansion of the welfare state. The Swedish government offers its citizens a lifetime of services. Swedes can count on the government to deliver and school their children, provide comprehensive health care, support them when they are out of work, and pay for their funerals.

Many Swedes supported this welfare state, thinking it would strengthen families. But as Popenoe sees it, government is really *replacing* families. Take the case of child-care: The Swedish government operates child-care centres that are staffed by professionals and available regardless of family income. However, the government gives nothing to parents who wish to care for their children in their own home. In effect, government benefits encourage people to let the state do what family members used to do for themselves.

But if Sweden's system has solved so many social problems, why should anyone care about the family getting weaker? For two reasons, says Popenoe. First, it is very expensive for government to provide so many "family" services; this is the main reason that Sweden has one of the highest rates of taxation in the world. Second, at any price, Popenoe says that government employees in large child-care centres cannot provide children with the same love and emotional security given by two parents living as a family. When it comes to taking care of people—especially young children—he argues that small, intimate groups do a job better than large, impersonal organizations.

What Do You Think?

1. Do you agree with Popenoe's concern that we should not allow government to replace families? Explain your answer.

2. In Canada, we have a much smaller welfare state than Sweden has. Should our government do more for its people? Why or why not?

3. With regard to children, list two specific things that you think government can do better than parents and two things that parents can do better than government. Explain your answer.

---

until they have gained the financial security needed to live apart from their parents and the experience needed to select a suitable partner.

Arranged marriages are becoming more common in Canada, particularly among Chinese and Southeast Asian families. Roughly 60 000 Canadians marry overseas annually and file international spousal sponsorship applications. In all too many cases, these marriages—contracted for up to $25 000—are terminated once the foreign partner achieves permanent residency in Canada (Jiménez, 2006).

ROMANTIC LOVE Our culture celebrates *romantic love*—affection and sexual passion for another person—as the basis for marriage. We find it hard to imagine marriage without love, and popular culture—from fairy tales like *Cinderella* to today's television sitcoms and dramas—portrays love as the key to a successful marriage. Our

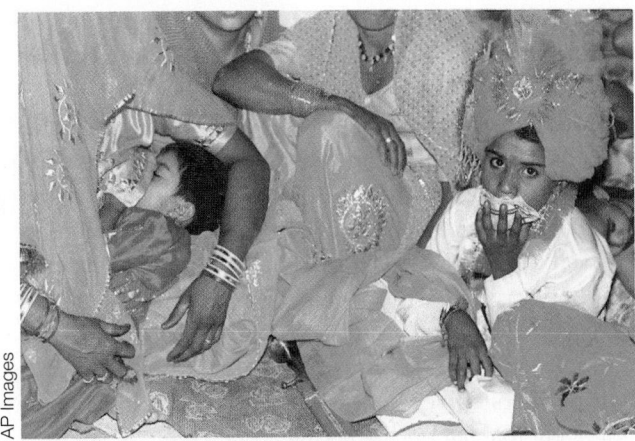

THE 18-MONTH-OLD GIRL ON THE LEFT IS BREASTFEEDING DURING HER WEDDING CEREMONY IN A SMALL VILLAGE IN THE STATE OF RAJASTHAN, INDIA; HER NEW HUSBAND IS SEVEN YEARS OLD Although outlawed, such arranged marriages involving children are still known to take place in traditional, remote areas of India.

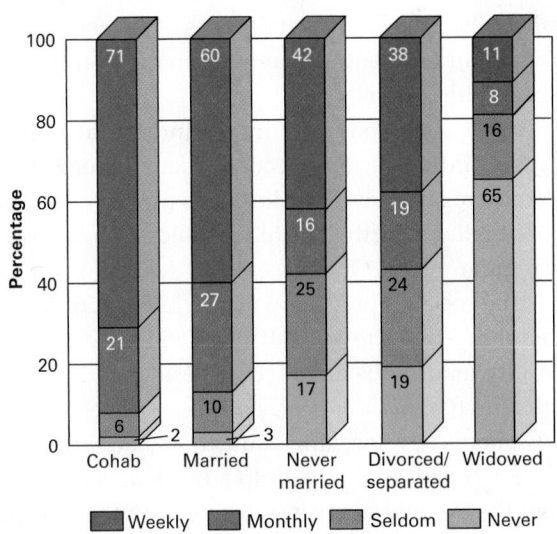

Figure 18–1 Sexual Activity by Marital Status
SOURCE: Bibby (1995:66).

society's emphasis on romance motivates young people to "leave the nest" to form new families of their own, and physical passion helps new couples through the difficult adjustments of living together. On the other hand, because feelings change over time, romantic love is a less stable foundation for marriage than social and economic considerations—which is one reason that the divorce rate is much higher in Canada than in countries with arranged marriages. But even in our country, sociologists point out, society aims Cupid's arrow more than we like to think. Most people fall in love with others of the same race, religion, social class, and similar age. Our society "arranges" marriages by encouraging **homogamy** (literally, "like marrying like"), *marriage between people with the same social characteristics.*

Settling in: Ideal and Real Marriage

Our culture gives the young an idealized, "happily ever after" picture of marriage. Such optimism can lead to disappointment, especially for women, who are taught to view marriage as the key to happiness. Also, romantic love involves a good deal of fantasy: We fall in love with others not always as they are but as we want them to be.

Sexuality, too, can be a source of disappointment. In the romantic haze of falling in love, people may see marriage as an endless sexual honeymoon, only to face the sobering realization that, over time, sex becomes less than an all-consuming passion. Although the frequency of marital sex does decline with time, about two in three married people report that they are satisfied with the sexual dimension of their relationships. In general, couples with the best sexual relationships experience the most satisfaction in their marriages. Sex may not be the key to marital bliss but, more often than not, good sex and good

relationships go together (Blumstein & Schwartz, 1983; Laumann et al., 1994). About 60 percent of married couples say that they are having sex weekly (Bibby, 1995); see Figure 18–1, which deals with sexual activity by marital status.

Infidelity—*sexual activity outside one's marriage*—is another area in which the reality of marriage does not coincide with our cultural ideal. Many Canadians support traditional marriage vows "to forsake all others." In a survey conducted in 1995, for example, 85 percent of adults said that extramarital sex is "always or almost always wrong," while only 3 percent believed that it was never wrong (Bibby, 1995). Through his research, which involved matching surveys every five years from 1975 to 1995, Bibby learned that Canadians have become *less tolerant* of extramarital sex over time—while becoming *more accepting* of non-marital (including premarital) sex and homosexual relations.

While 85 percent of Canadian adults say that extramarital sex is either "always wrong" or "almost always wrong," behaviour doesn't always conform to the ideal. Try to make sense of the discrepancy in the following Canadian figures relating to partners (not necessarily spouses): 33 and 35 percent of men and women, respectively, report that they have been cheated on by a partner; on the other hand, only 10 and 5 percent of men and women, respectively, say that they would cheat on their partners if there was no chance of getting caught (Bricker & Wright, 2005:214–215).

Child Rearing

Despite the substantial demands that children make on the time and energy of parents, almost all Canadians include at least one child in their conception of the ideal family. Today's smaller families represent a marked change from two centuries ago, when the average number of children was eight.

Big families "pay off" in pre-industrial societies because children perform needed labour. Indeed, people generally regard having children as a wife's duty and, without reliable birth-control technology, child-bearing is a regular event. Of course, high death rates in pre-industrial societies prevented many children from reaching adulthood; as late as 1900, infant and early childhood mortality made substantial contributions to those high death rates (*Canada Year Book*, 1994).

Economically speaking, industrialization transforms children from a vital asset into a burdensome liability. Today, the expense of raising a child is substantial, especially if it involves post-secondary education. This—along with the increased labour force involvement of women—helps to explain the steady drop in family size during the twentieth century to less than two children per family in Canada today. The trend toward smaller families also holds for all other industrial societies. (Canada's total fertility rate in 2012 was 1.6 children per woman, which means that we fall below the replacement level of 2.1 children per woman.) On the other hand, the picture differs sharply in low-income countries in Latin America, Asia, and especially Africa, where many women have few alternatives to bearing and raising children. In such societies, four to six children is the norm.

Parenting is expensive, and a lifetime commitment. As society affords its members greater choice in family life, more people opt to delay childbirth or to remain childless. Women also put off having children until they are older, so that they are currently giving birth three or four years later, on average, than they did in 1970. The majority of Canadian parents would like to put more time and energy into child rearing but, unless they are willing to accept a lower standard of living, economic realities demand that most parents pursue careers outside the home. Thus, the child-rearing patterns we have described reflect ways of coming to terms with economic change.

In 2006, 73.3 percent of women aged 25 to 34 (married or living common-law) were employed, while 61.3 percent of those with children at home were employed. In other words, the presence of children reduces the proportion of women working outside the home—by 12 percentage points. On the other hand, more than 60 percent of young mothers with children under age 18 worked for income outside the home. Another way of looking at this is in terms of dual-earner families. In 2014, 69 percent of couples with children had two working parents—up from 36 percent, or almost doubling from 1976 (Statistics Canada, 2015). In the same interval, the number of couples with a stay-at-home parent dropped from 1.5 million to 500 000—from over half to less than one-fifth of

couples. Most significantly, between 1976 and 2014, the proportion of men among stay-at-home parents increased from less than 2 to 11 percent.

Many men in our society are eager parents, as indicated by the increasing numbers of men who are stay-at-home fathers. In addition, more fathers are taking parental leave (Fitzpatrick, 2006). There are variations in parental leave policies across Canada, but EI benefits are split between maternity leave (17 weeks) and parental leave (35 weeks). New mothers can take leaves of at least 17 weeks and then share the remaining 35 weeks with their partners however suits them. At this point, 10 percent of eligible fathers are taking advantage of leave benefits—except in Quebec where 80 percent take advantage of five weeks of paid leave provided specifically to fathers (Huffington Post, 2016).

Ultimately, as more women join men in the labour force, parents have less time for parenting. Children of working parents spend most of the day at school or in daycare, and many school-aged youngsters are *latchkey kids* who fend for themselves after school. (The Controversy and Debate box explores related issues.) Traditionalists in the debates on "family values" caution that mothers often work at the expense of children, who receive less parenting. Progressives counter that such criticism ignores the role of fathers in parenting and unfairly faults women for seeking equal opportunity in the world of work.

Considering the changes in parenting and child-care practices over the past 20 years, it is reassuring to learn that nine in ten Canadian teens give their moms a grade of A or B, with 50 percent giving them an A. Two in three dads get a grade of A or B, with 29 percent getting an A (Bricker & Wright, 2005:172). Taking into account the normal tensions between parents and teenagers, this is indeed a good parental report card.

The Family in Later Life

Increasing life expectancy in Canada means that, barring divorce, couples are likely to remain married for a long time. By about age 50, *most* have completed the task of raising children, so the remaining years of marriage bring a return to living with only one's spouse. The departure of children requires adjustments to the "empty nest," although the marital relationship—bringing mutual understanding and companionship—often becomes closer and more satisfying in midlife.

Personal contact with children usually continues, since most older adults live a short distance from at least one of their children. Moreover, many Canadian grandparents help their daughters and sons with child care and a host of other responsibilities. On the other hand, recent developments have created new intergenerational

Controversy and Debate

The Child-Care Debate

Canadians were initially promised an affordable universal daycare system in the federal election campaign of 1993—the first election won by the Liberals under the leadership of Jean Chrétien—but it failed to appear on the political landscape until the elections of 2004 and 2006. During this period, the political right had been reunited under Stephen Harper's Conservative Party of Canada and Paul Martin's Liberal government was reeling under the impact of the sponsorship scandal in Quebec. These two factors contributed to the election of a Liberal minority government in 2004 and a Conservative minority government in 2006. Two vastly different models of child care were front and centre by the election of 2006.

In their platform for the election of 2004, the Liberals promised to spend $5 billion on child care, but "only $91 million would be spent in 2004 and $93 million in 2005" (Clarkson, 2004:44). Lawyer and former hockey player Ken Dryden, Minister of Social Development, was entrusted with the task of developing and promoting the government's child-care initiative, which would emphasize early childhood learning. He took his proposal into the 2006 election—which the Liberals lost.

Enter the Conservative Party of Canada with its child-care benefit of $100 per month ($1200 per year) for each child under six years of age. This meant that $2.5 billion *every year* would be going into the pockets of all parents of young children—to be taxed in the hands of the lower-income parent—for use for regulated daycare, nannies, sitters down the street, or relatives assuming child-care functions. Most importantly, the government would argue, for lower-income families with two or three children under age six the money might make it possible for one of the parents to stay at home instead of working part-time or full-time at some low-paid job. The Conservative plan also provided financial and tax incentives to encourage communities and organizations to create daycare spaces (e.g., workplace daycare in large corporations or office buildings). This plan provided for the creation of new daycare spaces, while giving all parents more choice in their child-care arrangements.

Quebec has a child-care plan in place that seems, at least in part, to be the model for the Liberal plan. An extensive daycare system, in which parents pay $7 per day for care, has made it more feasible for mothers of young children to enter or return to the labour force (Peritz, 2006). Table 18–1 shows that employment among women in Quebec aged 25 to 34—prime years for raising young children—increased dramatically from 1981 to 1991 and then surpassed that of women elsewhere in Canada by 2001. By 2006, women in Quebec were even more likely to be employed (76.5 percent compared to a Canadian average of 73.3).

Table 18–1 Employment among Women (25 to 34 Years of Age) with Spouse or Partner Present for Canada, Quebec, Ontario, and Alberta: 1981, 1991, 2001, and 2006*

| | Percentage Employed | | | |
	1981	1991	2001	2006
Canada	55.8	68.5	72.6	73.3
Quebec	50.5	66.5	74.1	76.5
Ontario	61.5	71.0	72.8	72.5
Alberta	57.5	69.9	71.6	70.9

*The data refer to women who are married or in common-law relationships with spouse or partner present.

SOURCE: Compilations and calculations by L.M. Gerber from Statistics Canada, Catalogue nos. 97F0012XCB2001001 and 97-559-XCB2006016.

A study of daycare in two small communities on the Ottawa River (Albanese, 2006) looked at the ripple effects of $7 per day child care (whether in home care or a larger facility). Albanese argued that allowing mothers to go to work, and in some cases get off welfare, and placing children in daycare (of either type) decreased financial pressures at home and helped children acquire social and language skills they were not learning at home.

A closer look at Table 18–1 reveals that the employment of young adult women (with a spouse or partner at home) increased between 1961 and 2006 for Canada as well as for Quebec, Ontario, and Alberta. While women's employment increased by 17.5 points for Canada as a whole, it increased more dramatically in Quebec—by 26 percentage points. In Quebec, the employment of women (25 to 34 years of age) went from five points below average in 1981 to three points above in 2006. It would be tempting to attribute the increase to the $7-per-day child care in the province, but it was not introduced until 1997, and most of the increase in women's employment took place between 1981 and 1991. One might hypothesize that the early increase was related to cultural change involved in Quebec's continuing transition from a traditional to modern society.

Although Alberta trailed behind Ontario in 1981, it was still above average in the employment of young adult women. Oddly enough, in 2006, Alberta had the worst record for the employment of women with husbands or partners at home. Quebec started off behind and ended up on top; Alberta started off well but ended up on the bottom (see Table 18–1). Is this divergence in any way related to child-care decisions?

Table 18–2 deals with employment levels for the same category of women (in 2006), taking into account the presence and ages of children. Despite the differences in employment levels between Canada and the three provinces, 86 to 89 percent of women *without* children at home are employed! These are very high levels of labour force

(continued)

Table 18–2 Employment among Women (25 to 34 Years of Age) with Spouse or Partner Present, by Presence of Children, for Canada, Quebec, Ontario, and Alberta, 2006*

	Percentage Employed			
	Canada	Quebec	Ontario	Alberta
Total	73.3	76.5	72.5	70.9
Without children at home	86.3	86.8	85.7	88.5
With children at home	66.3	71.1	65.2	61.3
Children under six years only	65.8	72.0	64.5	59.0
With at least one child under two years	61.5	68.7	59.8	54.0

*The data refer to women who are married or in common-law unions with spouse or partner present.

SOURCE: Compilations and calculations by L.M. Gerber from Statistics Canada, Census 2006, Catalogue no. 97-559-XCB2006016.

participation. For women *with* children at home, employment levels drop 15 percentage points in Quebec, 20 points in Canada and Ontario, and about 28 points in Alberta.

Since introducing "children under six years only" fails to reduce employment levels any further, we might conclude that "children at home" means "children under six at home." Introducing "at least one child under two years" to the mix does result in further declines in employment levels—three points for Canada and Quebec, five points for Ontario and Alberta. Having children at home, especially children under two years of age, gives rise to significant declines in women's employment. Most intriguing is the fact that women in Quebec are much less likely to withdraw from the labour force, in the presence of children, than are the women in Alberta.

The availability of $7 per day child care is clearly a factor allowing Quebec women to work while raising young children. For the women of Quebec, inexpensive, publicly funded daycare did exactly what advocates hoped it would do. It allowed them to make choices. Do the women of Alberta withdraw from the labour force because they lack such a daycare system? If that is all that is going on, why is there a 17.5 percentage point difference between Alberta and Canada in terms of employment levels among women with children under two?

In Alberta, which at that time had a booming economy and a shortage of workers of all types, employment of women of prime child-rearing age went from above average in 1981 to below average in 2006. Noting the same trend specifically among mothers with partners and preschool children, Brethour (2006) attempts to account for the exodus of women—even career women—from their jobs. He points out that daycare is inadequate but

attributes the disappearance of job-holding women to Alberta's prosperity. In other words, salaries are so high in Alberta that more families do well on the earnings of a single breadwinner. It is prosperity that allows mothers of pre-school children in Alberta to make choices. It's just that their choices differ from the ones made in Quebec.

So what is the best approach to child care? Quebec's best-known pediatrician, *le bon Dr. Chicoine,* argues—on the basis of attachment theory—that parents and babies need time to bond before children are sent to daycare (Wente, 2006). Children older than two or two-and-a-half benefit from the socialization that daycare offers, but Chicoine recommends daycare in moderation rather than the 60 hours per week, 52 weeks a year that is common in Quebec. He is particularly concerned about mothers in blue-collar families who have no choice but to return to work as quickly as possible, arguing that they really need a way to stay home. Those, of course, are the mothers who would benefit from the Conservatives' child benefit of $100 per month.

An article in the *Globe and Mail* titled "Mr. Harper's Child-Proof Political Strategy" (Adams, 2006) notes that, from a political perspective, the Conservatives' child-care benefit is brilliant. It is very popular among several categories of people: 64 percent of parents with children under age six favour the $1200 benefit—especially those in Quebec, where there is already a daycare program and the federal cheques cover much of the $7 per day cost. Nonetheless, Adams argues that, without institutional child-care supports, many women who would like to work cannot, and children who get a head start (early childhood education) have an advantage when they start school. A sense of fairness, he says, will eventually lead us to "a national, public child-care infrastructure."

Albanese is more critical of the universal child care benefit, noting that all hope for a universal, publicly funded child-care system was lost when the Harper government introduced the child-care benefit. She goes on to say that "children and child care are treated as private matters and individual lifestyle 'choices.' Children are not valued and mothers continue to disproportionately bear the weight of social reproduction" (Albanese, 2012:97). But social reproduction—which involves child rearing—is vitally important to our society. Brethour (2006) points out that, as the boomers retire, Canada as a whole will face labour shortages of crisis proportions. When that happens, universal daycare may be essential to prevent the economy from collapsing.

What Do You Think?

1. Which is fairer to women and families—$1200 per year for each child under age six or a subsidized daycare program?
2. Which approach would appeal most to feminists? Why?
3. Which approach would you want for your own children? Why?

challenges for Canadian families. The transition to adulthood has been extended, so that, increasingly, "midlife parenthood comprises prolonged periods of co-residence with grown young adults" (Mitchell, 2000:80). Mitchell found that, according to the 1995 General Social Survey, 27 percent of adults aged 19 to 35 had left home and returned for periods of four months or more. The termination of a job or a relationship, financial considerations, and the need to complete schooling are among the reasons for returning. Some of those who returned for financial reasons could afford to live on their own—but not at their parents' standard of living. The "crowded nest" is common to many families for the reasons outlined above, but another factor is a three-year delay in marriage for both women and men since the mid-1970s—on average, from 24 to 27 years of age for women and from 26 to 29 for men (Boyd & Norris, 2000).

Significantly, older adults can find themselves returning to child rearing: "[M]ore than 55 000 grandparents in Canada are raising their grandchildren—on their own" (Vallis, 2005). *Skip-generation households,* where grandparents are actually raising their grandchildren, are usually found in communities with high rates of poverty and unemployment—for example, inner cities and First Nations reserves (Campbell & Carroll, 2007). Since many grandparents take over child rearing to avoid foster care, they are raising at-risk children just when they might expect rest and relaxation. Social workers consider grandparents to be the first line of defence when parents, often single mothers, are incapable of raising their children (perhaps because of substance abuse or mental illness). These relationships are not always easy. Imagine raising a teenager when you are in your sixties or seventies.

The other side of the coin is that more adults in midlife must care for aging parents. The "empty nest" may be filled by a parent coming to live in the home (Che-Alford & Hamm, 2000); regardless, parents living to age 80 and beyond require practical, emotional, and financial care that can be more taxing than raising young children (Cranwick, 2000). The oldest of the baby boomers—now in their seventies—are often called the "sandwich generation" because they will spend as many years caring for their aging parents as they did for their own offspring. Some people find themselves caring for children and elderly parents at the same time. More commonly, the sandwich generation deals with raising children first and caring for aged parents later on (Ambert, 2012:305).

The final, and surely most difficult, transition in married life comes with the death of a spouse. Wives typically outlive their husbands because of women's longer life expectancy and the fact that wives are usually younger than husbands to begin with. Wives can therefore expect to spend a significant period of their lives as widows. Bereavement and loneliness accompanying the death of a spouse are extremely difficult, and the experience may be worse for men, who usually have fewer friends and may be unskilled at cooking and housework.

Recently, increased numbers of married or common-law couples—some of them same-sex couples—have not had children. They face the same problems of aging and bereavement that single or unmarried adults do, without the supportive networks that children and grandchildren might have provided.

Canadian Families: Class, Race, and Gender

18.4 Explain how class, race, and gender shape family life.

Dimensions of inequality—social class, ethnicity and race, and gender—are powerful forces that shape marriage and family life. This discussion addresses each factor in turn, but bear in mind that they overlap in our lives.

Social Class

Social class determines both a family's financial security and its range of opportunities. Interviewing working-class women, Lillian Rubin (1976) found that wives thought a good husband was one who held a steady job, did not drink too much, and was not violent. Rubin's middle-class respondents, in contrast, never mentioned such things; these women simply *assumed* that a husband would provide a safe and secure home. Their ideal husband was someone they could talk to easily, sharing feelings and experiences.

There is even a link between social class and the willingness of men to help with housework. Canada's General Social Survey reveals that only in dual-earner families where the woman earns more than $100 000 do men and women do the same amount of housework: 1.6 hours per day (Fitzpatrick, 2006).

Clearly, women's and men's aspirations for marriage are linked to social class. Much the same holds for children; boys and girls lucky enough to be born into more affluent families enjoy better mental and physical health, develop more self-confidence, and go on to greater achievement than children born to poor parents (Corak, 2000; De Broucker & Lavallée, 2000; Duncan et al., 1998).

Ethnicity and Race

Ethnicity and race are powerful social forces that can affect family life. Keep in mind, however, that the families of any racial or ethnic category do not necessarily fit particular stereotypes.

ABORIGINAL FAMILIES IN CANADA There are more than 700 Aboriginal communities in Canada—over 600 First Nations (Status Indian) reserves and dozens of non-Status Indian, Inuit, and Métis villages and settlements. Over the past few decades, increasing numbers of First Nations people have moved off the reserves—currently about half of the population. While Calgary, Edmonton, Saskatoon, and Winnipeg have substantial Aboriginal populations, residence in the major cities of Montreal, Vancouver, and Toronto is also increasing (Gerber, 1995; 2014). Given this diversity, it is impossible to discuss the family patterns of Aboriginal peoples as a homogeneous group.

Aboriginal people are among the most economically deprived members of our society and suffer discrimination and prejudice, resulting in high rates of unemployment, inadequate housing, and family instability. One researcher notes that "under these circumstances, identification with traditional cultures suffers, and their central familistic values of kin solidarity, respect for elders, and the welfare of children have been weakened" (Nett, 1993:101). Moreover, because of their political and economic subordination by Europeans and the well-known abuses of the residential school system, the family norms of many Aboriginal people have been destroyed.

Throughout the early 1900s, most Aboriginal people lived on reserves or with extended families in isolated regions. Child care was the responsibility of the extended family, and highly respected elders taught the young their languages and traditions. Christian missionaries, who had made concerted efforts to assimilate and Christianize Aboriginal peoples, took children away from their families to church-run residential schools to teach them another language, religion, and culture, and to despise their own heritage. With adults and children separated and pursuing different paths, traditional family values began to erode: Elders lost their authority; extended families lost their responsibilities for nurturing and caretaking; and young people raised outside normal family settings failed to learn parenting skills to apply later on when raising their own children. In addition, resettlement programs broke up whole communities and diminished family ties even further.

In June 2008, our federal government made a *formal* apology for "the tragedy of residential schools" (Fleras, 2001:294, 2010:176) that have done so much damage to Aboriginal family and community life. By 2003, individuals who had suffered sexual and psychological abuse in the residential school system had been offered financial compensation. However, this attempt "induced a nightmare of Orwellian proportions" in part because residential-school survivors were dying faster than their claims were being processed (with 50 of 12 000 claims being settled by 2005). Also, while huge sums have been set aside for compensation, the government was spending $4 on administration for every $1 going to the victims of abuse.

The intervention of the state and the churches in Aboriginal family life has other manifestations deriving from the lack of recognition of the role played by the extended family in providing for children when parents die or are incapacitated (Wotherspoon & Satzewich, 1993:88). From the 1950s until the mid-1970s, under the auspices of social workers employed by various Children's Aid Societies, children were taken away from parents who were no longer functioning as adequate caretakers because of poverty, unemployment, prejudice, alcohol abuse, and a variety of other social conditions. Many of these children were placed in non-Aboriginal foster homes—over 27 000 Aboriginal children are in foster homes today—where they lost contact with their remaining traditions and culture, as did the children who were adopted by non-Aboriginal families (Ambert, 2012: 49). Having observed the severe adjustment problems of many of these children, authorities now focus on keeping children with their extended families whenever possible—most often in the care of their grandparents.

Aboriginal family patterns differ from those in the larger society because they are more likely to be based on cohabitation (24 and 17 percent respectively in 2011). Furthermore, the proportion of Aboriginal families headed by lone-parents—almost always female and often teenagers—is double that of the general population (32 and 16 percent).

By 2011, Canada had roughly 650 000 status or registered Indians—the real First Nations who are subject to the *Indian Act* and represented by the Assembly of First Nations—of whom about 48 percent lived on some 630+ reserves. The remaining 1.5 million individuals with Indian, Métis, and Inuit ancestry live in rural areas, small settlements, and—for a substantial majority—urban areas including Canada's large metropolitan centres. Many Aboriginal individuals who migrate to urban areas do so as isolated individuals in search of employment opportunities, housing, schooling, trades certification, or better access to welfare. Others go to join members of their extended families, often living with them during transition (Gerber, 1976). There are also Aboriginal people—a small number—whose urban family lives are similar to those of the White middle class: "They live in single-family units as married adults with children; they have full-time employment; and they live in acceptable housing"; they have attained "a level of education, health, and well-being possessed by the vast majority of non-Aboriginal citizens of Canada" (Frideres & Gadacz, 2001:156). Many urban Aboriginals, while keeping ties with family in their communities of origin, now call their cities "home" and combine deep respect for their cultural traditions with successful urban adaptation. In fact, they exhibit cultural vitality and contribute to cultural revitalization in the urban context (Environics, 2010).

RACIAL AND ETHNIC MINORITY FAMILIES Canada's diversity—the result of its immigration history—is reflected in family forms as well. Policies favouring family class immigration (i.e., family reunification through the sponsorship of close family members) ensured a continuing stream of newcomers with strong subcultural identities and values (Li, 1996). As a result, we include a wide variety of family patterns in Canadian society.

Conversely, there are family values and practices that are common to many of these minorities. Traditional values often include religion; authoritarian or permissive parenting styles; cultural guidelines for marriage and courtship, including arranged marriage; scripted gender relations and non-mainstream notions of gender equality; prohibitions on dating or drinking; and emphasis on family rather than the individual (Fleras, 2001:181–182). In addition, immigrant families—for example, Italians and Chinese—are more likely to keep their elderly parents and grandparents at home (Gerber, 1983). More recent evidence suggests that the three-generation model no longer characterizes Chinese-Canadian families; although there is still a strong family support network, "couples tend to live near their extended family members rather than with them" (Ambert, 2012:57).

Intergenerational conflict is common in immigrant families as young people, who attend public schools, challenge the cultural values of their parents. They want the freedom to hang out with their peers and participate in party and dating scenes. Teenagers tend to feel that the constraints of their families and ethnic communities are unduly strict. You may believe that the dominant White Anglo-Saxon Protestant community is "prejudiced" and opposed to intermarriage, but some of Canada's ethnic and racial minorities push endogamy on their children. Even Finnish immigrants have been known to resist the marriage of their children to people of non-Finn heritage. In that light, recent trends in intermarriage and related attitudes are worth a look.

Mixed Marriage

Most spouses have similar social backgrounds with regard to class, race, and ethnicity, but over the course of the past century, ethnicity has mattered less and less. Thus, a man of German/French ancestry might marry a woman of Irish/English background.

On the other hand, race remains an important consideration. In 2011, visible minorities and people of Aboriginal descent represented almost 25 percent of Canada's population. The potential for mixed marriage would be unlimited if people ignored race altogether in choosing marriage partners. The fact that this is not the case reveals the continuing importance of race in social relations. Nonetheless, the number of racially mixed marriages will continue to increase as visible minorities become established over multiple generations. From 1991 to 2011, the proportion of couples in mixed unions involving visible minorities increased from 2.6 to 4.6 percent.

Table 18–3 shows that Canadians have become more accepting of intergroup marriage over time. Although the vast majority (80 to 92 percent) of Canadian adults approve of intermarriage across various racial and religious lines (Bibby, 1995:54)—or at least claim to do so—it will be some time before the extent of racial intermarriage mirrors the reported level of acceptance.

Table 18–3 Approval of Intergroup Marriage, 1975 through 1995

	1975	1980	1985	1990	1995
Whites and Aboriginal partners	75%	80%	83%	84%	84%
Whites and Asians (Oriental)	66	75	78	82	83
Whites and East Indians/Pakistanis	58	66	72	77	80
Whites and Blacks	57	64	72	79	81
Protestants and Roman Catholics	86	88	89	90	92
Protestants and Jews	80	84	84	86	90
Roman Catholics and Jews	78	81	82	85	89

SOURCE: Bibby (1995:54).

Gender

Jessie Bernard (1982; orig. 1973) said that every marriage is actually two different relationships: a woman's marriage and a man's marriage. The reason is that few marriages are composed of two equal partners. Patriarchy has weakened, but most people still expect men to be older and taller than their wives and to have more important, better-paying jobs. The persistence of the notion of man as breadwinner and wife as homemaker was illustrated in a study of steelworkers and their wives in Hamilton, Ontario. In 1979–80, when the Women Back into Stelco Committee launched a successful discrimination complaint with the Ontario Human Rights Commission, the introduction of female co-workers into the masculine world of dangerous manual labour and big machinery was resisted by the steelworkers. Detailed interviews revealed that steelmaking was seen as men's work and was linked to the notion that men must be breadwinners. This attitude was tied to men's "deeper sense of responsibility to provide for their families" (Livingstone & Luxton, 1995:187).

Such patriarchal values are associated with the persistent notion that marriage is more beneficial to women than to men (Bernard, 1982; orig. 1973). The positive stereotype of the carefree bachelor contrasts sharply with the negative image of the lonely spinster. This image is rooted in a traditional view that women are fulfilled only by being wives and mothers. However, according to Bernard, married women have poorer mental health, less happiness, and more passive attitudes toward life than single women. Married men, on the other hand, generally live longer, are better off mentally, and report being happier than single men. These differences suggest why, after divorce, men are more eager than women to remarry. Bernard concluded that there is no better assurance of long life, health, and happiness for a man than a woman well socialized to devote her life to taking care of him and providing the security of a well-ordered home. Considering the fact that divorce is so common, it might surprise you to know that less than 9 percent of our population aged 15 and over is divorced at any point in time. One reason is that people—men in particular—tie the knot again, perhaps more than once. Others may fill the gap by cohabiting or living common-law.

While families may have changed since the 1980s, recent survey responses rank "sharing of household chores" as among the most important factors contributing to a successful marriage (Pew Research Center, 2007). Research on same-sex couples found that their relationships are characterized by greater equality and role-sharing, perhaps because there is likely to be greater income equality. Since gays and lesbians are not bound by traditional masculine and feminine roles, same-sex couples end up sharing household chores more equitably (Nelson, 2010:327).

Transitions and Problems in Family Life

18.5 Analyze the effects of divorce, remarriage, and violence on family life.

Newspaper columnist Ann Landers once remarked that 1 marriage in 20 is wonderful, 5 in 20 are good, 10 in 20 are tolerable, and the remaining 4 are "pure hell." Families can be a source of joy but, for some, the reality falls far short of the ideal.

Divorce

Our society strongly supports marriage and, while 9 out of 10 people marry at some point in their lives, many of today's marriages eventually unravel. Figure 18–2

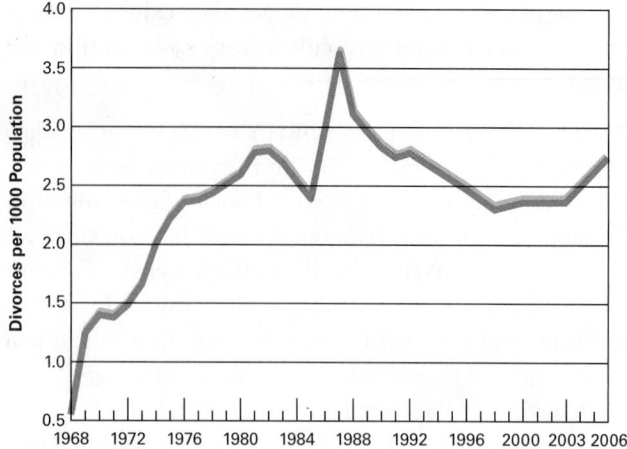

Figure 18–2 The Divorce Rate* in Canada, 1968–2006

*Divorce rates are calculated per 1000 population 15 years of age and older.

SOURCES: Compiled by L.M. Gerber from Statistics Canada, 1991, Catalogue nos. 82-003S17 and 84-213, and Statistics Canada, CANSIM tables 053-0002 and 101-651.

shows a ninefold increase in the Canadian divorce rate from 1968 to 1988, followed by gradual decline thereafter. Before 1968, divorces were granted only if one partner had committed adultery; at that time, the divorce rate was 0.4 per 1000 people. Note that, despite the peak, the divorce rate in the late 1970s is not too different from that in the 2000s. After spiking in the 1980s the rates declined from 3.6 to 2.2 per 1000 people by 2003 before going up to 2.7 in 2006.

Divorce rates in Canada and the United States rose and dropped off again in a similar pattern, though the United States still has the highest divorce rate in the world (50 percent higher than Canada's). Many researchers have tried to explain the relatively high divorce rates in the 1980s (Etzioni, 1993; Furstenberg & Cherlin, 1991; Greenspan, 2001; Popenoe, 1999):

1. **Individualism is on the rise.** Today's family members spend less time together. We have become more individualistic and more concerned about personal happiness and earning income than about the well-being of family and children.

2. **Romantic love fades.** Because our culture bases marriage on romantic love, relationships may fail as sexual passion fades. Many people end a marriage in favour of a new relationship that promises renewed excitement and romance.

3. **Women are less dependent on men.** Women's increasing participation in the labour force has reduced wives' financial dependence on husbands. Therefore, women find it easier to leave unhappy marriages.

4. **Many of today's marriages are stressful.** With both partners working outside the home in most cases,

jobs leave less time and energy for family life. This makes raising children harder than ever. Children do stabilize some marriages, but divorce is most common during the early years of marriage, when many couples have young children.

5. **Divorce is socially acceptable.** Divorce no longer carries the powerful stigma it did several generations ago. Family and friends are now less likely to discourage couples in conflict from divorcing.

6. **Legally, a divorce is easier to get.** Canada's *Divorce Act* of 1968 provided a uniform federal divorce law to replace provincial laws. The Act allowed for divorce in circumstances beyond adultery—if one of the spouses had committed a matrimonial offence (such as adultery, or emotional or physical cruelty), if one spouse had deserted, or if the spouses had lived apart for at least three years. In 1985, the Act was rewritten, making "marriage breakdown" the only reason for divorce. Marriage breakdown includes separation of at least one year, adultery, and physical and mental cruelty.

WHO DIVORCES? At greatest risk of divorce are young spouses—especially those who marry after a brief courtship—who lack money and emotional maturity. The chance of divorce also rises if the couple marries after an unexpected pregnancy, or if one or both partners use alcohol or drugs. People whose parents divorced also have a higher divorce rate themselves. Researchers suggest that a role-modelling effect is at work, as children whose parents are divorced are more likely to consider divorce themselves (Amato, 2001), and people who are not religious are more likely to divorce than those who have strong religious beliefs.

Divorce is also more common when both partners have successful careers, perhaps because of the strains of a two-career marriage, or perhaps because financially secure people (women in particular) do not feel that they have to stay in unhappy homes. Those who divorce once are more likely to divorce again, probably because high-risk factors follow them from one marriage to another (Glenn & Shelton, 1985). Interviewing people who were divorced, Ambert found that those "who had divorced only once expressed feelings of hurt, guilt, and even regret," whereas those who had divorced several times in short order gave "the impression that their marriages were part of the throw-away culture" (2012:350).

It is important to understand that rates include first-time and serial divorces. Multiple divorces mean that the same individuals contribute to annual divorce rates time and time again. For that reason, Ambert (2012:346–47) recommends calculating the risk of divorce prior to the thirtieth anniversary of marriage; using this measure, a recently married couple's risk of divorce is 38 percent. The probability of divorce is lower for first marriages and higher for people who have divorced before. The likelihood of divorce (prior to the thirtieth anniversary) depends, to some extent, on place of residence. Newfoundland and Labrador has the lowest rate (21.6 percent), less than half the rate of Quebec (48.4 percent).

For Canada as a whole, 8.5 percent of the population aged 15 and older reported being divorced at the time of NHS 2011. This means that on that day, they were divorced *and not remarried*. Some of those people have divorced only once, while others have divorced several times. Note that Quebec and Yukon have the highest levels (11 percent), while Nunavut and Newfoundland and Labrador have the lowest levels (2.7 and 5.7 percent). We know that many people who are divorced turn around and remarry, but now that we track common-law unions, we can find out how many of the officially divorced are actually living common-law. In Canada, 8.5 percent are divorced and, of those, 2.4 percent are cohabiting. They may be "divorced" but they are not living alone.

Mark J. Barrett/Creative Eye/MIRA.com

DIVORCE MAY BE A SOLUTION FOR A COUPLE IN AN UNHAPPY MARRIAGE, BUT IT CAN BE A PROBLEM FOR CHILDREN WHO EXPERIENCE THE WITHDRAWAL OF A PARENT FROM THEIR SOCIAL WORLD In what ways can divorce be harmful to children? Is there a positive side to divorce? How might separating parents better prepare their children for the transition of parental divorce?

Seeing Ourselves

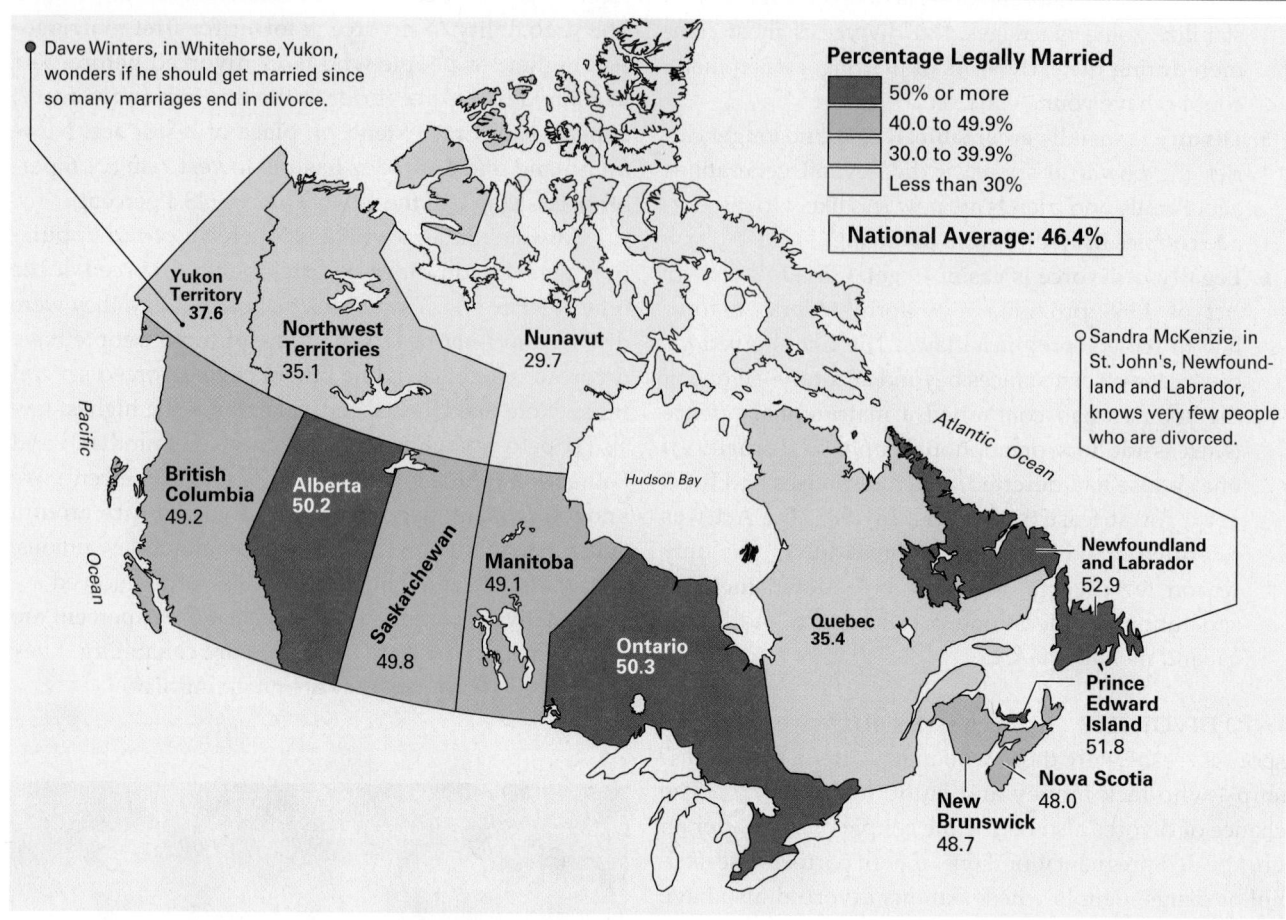

Canada Map 18–1 Percentage of Population* that is Married by Province and Territory, 2011

* Percentages are based on populations aged 15 years and over.

SOURCE: Compilation and calculations by L.M. Gerber based on Statistics Canada, Census 2011, Catalogue no. 98-312-XCB2011039.

Divorce is pronounced where religious values are weaker and where people are more likely to move often, thereby distancing themselves from the support of family and friends. People in Yukon fit both of those descriptions, forming the largest proportion claiming "no religion" and substantial migration into and out of the territory in response to changes in the resource industries. While very few Quebecers claim no religion, the province did experience rapid secularization during the Quiet Revolution, so that their attachment to the Catholic Church is relatively weak. The Quiet Revolution also involved rural–urban migration, social mobility, and the entry of women into the workforce—all of which weaken ties to old communities and networks.

DIVORCE AND CHILDREN Because mothers often gain custody of children but fathers typically earn more income, the well-being of children after a divorce often depends on fathers making voluntary or court-ordered child support payments. Yet, in any given year, half of the children legally entitled to support receive only partial payments or no payments at all. Too many "deadbeat dads" fail to support their youngsters, sometimes moving to another province to escape the system. In response, the courts can now require employers to withhold money from the earnings of fathers who fail to pay.

The effects of divorce on children go beyond financial support. Divorce can tear young people from familiar surroundings, entangle them in bitter feuding, and distance them from a parent they love. Most serious of all, many children blame themselves for the parental breakup. Divorce changes the course of their lives, often resulting in emotional and behavioural problems, and raising the risk of dropping out of school or getting into trouble with the law. Many experts counter that divorce is better for children than families torn by tension and violence. In any case, parents should remember that, if they consider divorce, more than their own well-being is at stake (Amato & Sobolewski, 2001; Popenoe, 1993b; Wallerstein & Blakeslee, 1989).

For the past two decades, Canada's divorce courts have, when possible, favoured joint custody, which deals not with access but with decision making about children. Now the results of the experiment with joint custody can be seen. When parents are able to put children first and avoid confrontation, joint custody can work very well. But too often every decision made about their children results in fights and recriminations between high-conflict parents—with "seriously traumatized children" caught in the middle. Furthermore, some fathers with joint custody agreements mistakenly assume that they should have their children half of the time. There are good reasons for revisiting the joint custody question, but it may not happen because powerful forces are aligned on both sides of the debate (Makin, 2006).

Remarriage and Blended Families

More than half of all people who divorce remarry, most within four years. Thus, a substantial portion of marriages are remarriages, at least for one partner. Men, who benefit more from wedlock, are more likely than women to remarry. Remarriage often creates *blended families*, composed of children and some combination of biological parents and step-parents. With brothers, sisters, half-siblings, a step-parent—not to mention a biological parent who might live elsewhere and be married to someone else with other children—young people in blended families face the challenge of defining many new relationships and deciding who is part of their nuclear families. When the custody of children is an issue, ex-spouses can be an unwelcome presence for people in a new marriage. Although blended families require that members adjust to their new circumstances, they offer both young and old the chance to relax rigid family roles (Furstenberg & Cherlin, 2001; McLanahan, 2002). As previously noted, in light of the increased acceptance of cohabitation, some divorced individuals are choosing common-law unions over remarriage. These of course may face the same problems of blended families as remarriage.

Family Violence

The ideal family is a source of pleasure and support. However, the disturbing reality of many homes is **family violence**, *emotional, physical, or sexual abuse of one family member by another.* Sociologist Richard J. Gelles calls the family "the most violent group in society with the exception of the police and the military" (quoted in Roesch, 1984:75).

VIOLENCE AGAINST WOMEN The common stereotype of a violent partner is a lower-class man who now and then drinks too much, loses control, and beats up his wife. In reality, although financial problems and unemployment do make the problem worse, violence against women in the home is perpetrated by men of all social classes, races, and ethnicities. Family brutality frequently goes unreported to police, but researchers estimate that 20 percent of couples (one in five) endure at least some violence each year. Many of these couples experience incidents of violence, including kicking, biting, and punching, and, more seriously, almost 30 percent of women who are murdered—compared to 6 percent of men—are killed by spouses, ex-spouses, or unmarried partners (Lupri, 1988). Overall, women are more likely to be injured by a family member than they are to be mugged or sexually assaulted by a stranger.

Violence involving current or former partners or spouses is referred to as *intimate violence,* a term that has only recently become part of our vocabulary, along with "battered wife" or "wife abuse" and "battered husbands" or "husband abuse." There are many other terms in use, but intimate violence serves well as a gender-neutral concept. What's important is that intimate violence has come out of the closet; as C. Wright Mills once wrote "private trouble" has been turned into a "public issue" (Nelson, 2010). Nelson notes that one other element of intimate violence remains largely hidden: violence in lesbian relationships. It is difficult for feminists to deal with this issue, because use of violence is considered to be a "male" phenomenon. In fact, the rate of violence is higher among same-sex couples than among heterosexuals. Gays, lesbians, and bisexuals are two to four times more likely to report being victims of spousal violence than are heterosexuals (Ambert, 2012).

In 1990, Canada's solicitor-general attempted to address the problem of crime and abuse against women by producing *Woman Alone,* a book of prevention advice. But this document ignored the situations that most frequently expose women to danger: domestic and private settings where they are threatened by men they know. One reason for this misjudgment is that victimization studies ask about "crime," and "many victims do not perceive their partners' violent actions as crimes in the legal sense" (DeKeseredy et al., 1995:479).

Physically abused women have traditionally had few options. They may want to leave home, but many—especially those with children and without much money—have nowhere to go. Most wives are also committed to their marriages and believe—however unrealistically—that they can help an abusive husband change. Some, unable to understand a husband's violence, blame themselves. Others, raised in violent families, consider assault to be part of family life. Most abused women see no way out of the family violence that makes fear the centre of their lives.

Sociology in Focus

Spousal Violence in Canada

A report on family violence in Canada reveals that an "estimated 7 percent of women and 6 percent of men in a current or previous spousal relationship encountered spousal violence during the five years up to and including 2004" (Statistics Canada, 2005c). Spousal violence rates were highest among young couples (aged 15 to 24), in relationships of three years or less, and among people who were separated and in common-law relationships.

The data indicate that "the nature and consequences of spousal violence were more severe for women than for men" and that women were more than twice as likely to be injured as men. Women were much more likely to fear for their lives and suffer more than 10 violent episodes. Heavy drinking and the presence of emotional abuse were associated with higher rates of spousal abuse as well. Furthermore, separation had an effect: "One-third (34 percent) of women who experienced violence during their relationship said that the violence increased in severity or frequency after separation." Nearly one-quarter (23 percent) of female victims reported that the most serious form of violence experienced was being beaten, choked, or threatened by having a gun or knife used against them. This was the case for 15 percent of male victims. The report on family violence notes the following:

> About 44 percent of female victims of spousal violence indicated that they suffered injury because of the violence, more than twice the proportion of 19 percent among male victims. In addition, 13 percent of female victims sought medical attention, compared with only 2 percent of male victims. Over one-third of women victims said that the violence was reported to

the police—compared to 17 percent of men victims. In addition, 38 percent of women who reported to the police also sought a restraining order—more than twice the proportion of men.

An update on spousal violence (Statistics Canada, 2008b) reveals that the 38 000 incidents of spousal violence reported to the police in 2006 represented 15 percent of all reported violent incidents. Across our provinces and territories, 8 in 10 victims of reported spousal violence were women; but, among those who *did* report incidents, men were more likely to be victims of "major assault" than women (23 percent compared to 13 percent). Quite possibly, men are more reluctant to report spousal violence than women.

Clearly, spousal violence is a major concern in Canada. We are more aware of violence perpetrated by men against women, because the consequences are generally more severe, but men also experience spousal abuse.

Postscript Since 1960, there have been about 2000 solved homicide/suicides where the perpetrator takes his or her own life after the homicide: "About three-quarters of victims of homicide/suicides were killed by a family member. . . . Over half (57 percent) of family homicide/suicides involved spouses, and, of these incidents, virtually all (97 percent) involved female victims killed by a male spouse" (Statistics Canada 2008b).

What Do You Think?

1. Were you aware that men are also the victims of spousal abuse?
2. What are the effects of spousal violence on children?
3. What can the legal system or the police do to reduce family violence?

In the past, the law regarded domestic violence as a private family matter. Now, even without separation or divorce, a woman can obtain court protection from an abusive spouse. "Stalker" legislation, introduced in 1993, protects women and children who are being threatened and followed. Some medical personnel are also more aware today of the telltale signs of spousal violence and are more likely to report such cases to police than they were in the past. Communities throughout North America have established shelters that provide counselling as well as temporary housing for women and children driven from their homes by violence. Some people who abuse their partners are also joining self-help groups in an effort to understand and control their own behaviour. In various ways, then, our society is beginning to help families with this serious problem.

It is important to understand that, when men and women are asked how often they engage in a range of

violent acts against their partners (excluding sexual assault), men are almost as likely to be victims of domestic violence as women (Lupri, 2002). While Canada, quite rightly, has mobilized to assist women and children, there is no attempt to help the male victims who also suffer severe loss of self-esteem. (For more on the topic of spousal violence, see the Sociology in Focus box.)

VIOLENCE AGAINST CHILDREN Family violence also victimizes children. One assumption is that children are abused by their parents (or step-parents), but once they start school siblings and peers are more frequently the perpetrators. Among children younger than five, 60 percent of abuse comes from parents; between ages of six and 16, peers account for 50 percent, and siblings another 25 to 30 percent. Teachers and physicians are required to report child abuse if they become aware of it, and Children's Aid Societies have the right to remove children from their homes if they find evidence of abuse (Ambert, 2012). Estimating the extent of child abuse is difficult, but Ambert cites studies showing that 31 percent of males and 21 percent of females report some family violence when they were growing up.

Child abuse entails more than physical injury; abusive adults misuse power and trust to undermine a child's emotional well-being. Child abuse is most common among the youngest and most vulnerable children (Besharov & Laumann, 1996; Straus & Gelles, 1986; Van Biema, 1994). Many abused children suffer in silence, believing that they are to blame for their own victimization. Abuse, compounded by years of guilt, can leave lasting emotional scars that prevent people abused as children from forming healthy relationships as adults.

There is clear evidence that child abuse is more common in low-income families and in neighbourhoods characterized by poverty and violence. Ambert (2012) points out that, because of the involvement of numerous social agencies, child abuse is more easily detected among the poor. Nonetheless, poverty and child abuse are clearly related. This is consistent with the following observations from the 1980s and 1990s.

In 1996, children were reported missing in Canada at a rate of one every nine minutes—more than 56 000 in that year. An alarming 78 percent of these youngsters were runaways; 57 percent of the runaways were girls; and the runaways were getting younger. Many youngsters leave home because of abuse (psychological, sexual, or physical) and neglect. In the recession of the early 1990s, more children left home because their parents said they could not afford to keep them, thereby repeating a pattern that appeared during the recession of the early 1980s. These numbers are described as an alarming sign of the increasing disintegration of the family (Mitchell, 1998).

Most child abusers are men, but they conform to no simple stereotype. Abusers, however, tend to share one trait: having been abused themselves as children. Research shows that violent behaviour in close relationships is learned. In families, then, violence begets violence (Gwartney-Gibbs et al., 1987; Widom, 1996).

Elder Abuse

Another form of family violence that society was slow to recognize is elder abuse. Parents are living longer and the costs, in terms of time and money, of caregiving into old age can be the cause of considerable stress for the "sandwich generation," which may be simultaneously caring for parents and children. Of course, the frail elderly are vulnerable to abuse (physical, psychological, and financial) because of failing mental and physical abilities. Elder abuse remains underreported because of both shame and dependence.

Alternative Family Forms

18.6 Describe the diversity of family life in Canada.

Prior to 1990, *all* families consisted of *married* (heterosexual) couples with children, because that was the census definition of "family." The next step was to include common-law couples with children as families. In Census 2001, family was defined as a married or common-law couple *with or without children*—and included a lone parent with at least one child living at home. At the same time, same-sex common-law couples were included in the definition of family and, most significantly, in 2006 a married couple could be of the same or opposite sex.

As revealed in Table 18–4, Census 2011 counted 9.4 million families comprising married and common-law couples, representing 67 and 17 percent of the total. Only 0.2 and 0.5 percent of all families were same-sex married or common-law couples. (On the other hand, 0.3 percent of marriages and 2.7 percent of common-law unions involved same-sex couples.) The proportion of families headed by lone parents increased very slightly to 16.3 in 2011—with 12.8 and 3.5 percent of all families headed by lone women or men.

These definitions of family (and the statistics) represent tremendous social change over the past 20 years that turned our traditional notions of family upside down. Personal decisions made by millions of individuals changed the structure of the social institution we call the family. So central is the family to our society that Canadian society as a whole has been transformed.

Table 18–4 Alternative Family Forms, 2011

Total families	9 389 700	100.0
Couple families	7 861 860	83.7
Married	**6 293 950**	**67.0**
Opposite-sex	6 272 935	66.8
Same-sex	21 015	0.2
Female	9475	0.1
Male	11 540	0.1
Common-law	**1 567 910**	**16.7**
Opposite-sex	1 524 350	16.2
Same-sex	43 560	0.5
Female	19 900	0.2
Male	23 660	0.3
Lone-parent families	1 527 840	16.3
Female parent	1 200 295	12.8
Male parent	327 545	3.5

SOURCE: Compilation and calculations by L.M. Gerber based on Statistics Canada, Census 2011, Catalogue nos. 98-312-X2011001 and 98-312-XCB2011046.

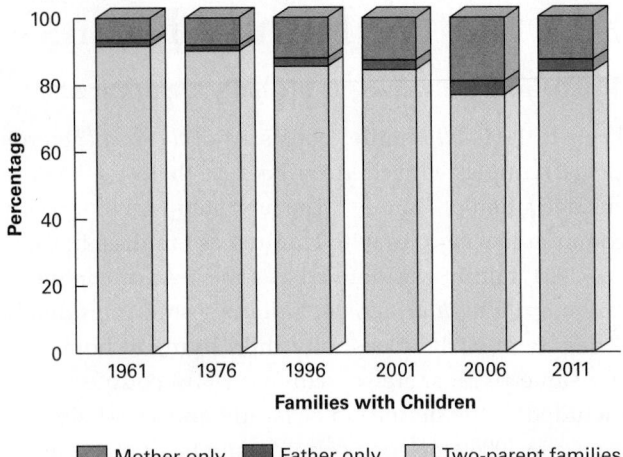

Figure 18–3 Lone-Parent Families (Female- and Male-Headed) as Proportions of the Total in Canada, 1961, 1976, 1996, 2001, 2006, and 2011.

SOURCE: Compilations and calculations by L.M. Gerber from Statistics Canada, Catalogue nos. 91-522, 97F0005XCB2001006, 97-563-XCB2006017, 98-312-X2011001.

Lone-Parent Families

As Figure 18–3 indicates, in 1961, 8 percent of Canadian families with children were headed by lone parents and 92 percent were two-parent families. By 2011—50 years later—the proportion of lone-parent families had increased to 16.3 percent of the total (with 12.8 and 3.5 percent of all families headed by women and men respectively). The proportion of lone-parent families has grown so that roughly 12 percent of children in Canada now live in these families. One-parent families, which are about four times more likely to be headed by women than men, may result from divorce or desertion, the inability to find a suitable partner, unplanned pregnancy, death, or an unmarried woman's decision to have a child.

Single parenthood increases a woman's risk of poverty because it limits her ability to work and to further her education. The converse is also true: Poverty raises the odds that a young woman will become a single mother (Trent, 1994).

Considerable research shows that growing up in a one-parent family usually disadvantages children. Some studies indicate that, because a father and a mother each make distinctive contributions to a child's social development, it is unrealistic to expect one parent alone to do as good a job. But the most serious problem among families with one parent—especially if that parent is a woman—is poverty. An astounding 70 percent of female lone-parent families with children under age 18 fall below the low-income cut-off. The comparable figure for male lone-parent families is 24 percent. On average, a child growing up in a single-parent family starts out poorer, gets less

schooling, and ends up with a lower income as an adult. Such children are also more likely to become single parents themselves (Blankenhorn, 1995; Duncan et al., 1998; Kantrowitz & Wingert, 2001; McLanahan, 2002; Popenoe, 1993b; Wu, 1996).

Cohabitation

Cohabitation is *the sharing of a household by an unmarried couple.* No longer considered to be *shacking up* or *living in sin*, the practice has become more common in Canada. Table 18–5 confirms remarkable increases across Canada in the percentage of couples living common-law between 1981 and 2011. Among provinces, the change is most dramatic in Quebec, where 8 percent of couples cohabited in 1981 and an astounding 38 percent cohabited in 2011. Data for the earlier years are not available for the territories but for 2011, their levels of cohabitation are comparable to those of Quebec. At the other end of the spectrum one finds Prince Edward Island and Ontario with only 13 percent of couples in common-law unions. There is no easy explanation for the astoundingly high rates of cohabitation in Quebec and the Territories, but one thing is certain: The cultural context within which couples of those regions choose between marriage and common-law relationships differs dramatically from that of the rest of Canada. (See the Sociology in Focus box for further discussion of this topic.)

Gay and Lesbian Couples

In 1989, Denmark became the first country to permit registered partnerships with the benefits of marriage

Table 18–5 Couples Living Common-Law by Province and Territory 1981, 2001, and 2011 (Percentage of all Couples)

	1981	2001	2011
Newfoundland & Labrador	2	10	15
Prince Edward Island	3	9	13
Nova Scotia	5	11	17
New Brunswick	4	13	19
Quebec	8	**21**	**38**
Ontario	5	8	13
Manitoba	5	9	14
Saskatchewan	4	9	15
Alberta	8	12	16
British Columbia	8	11	15
Yukon	na	na	**32**
Northwest Territories	na	na	**36**
Nunavut	na	na	**46**

SOURCE: Compilation and calculations by L.M. Gerber based on Statistics Canada, NHS 2011, Catalogue no. 98-312-XCB2011039.

Sociology in Focus

Cohabitation among Canadians

Zheng Wu (2000) has used a number of data sources—the Canadian census of various years and the General Social Surveys of 1990 and 1995—to study cohabitation. He assumes that the increase in cohabitation over the past few decades indicates a change in the norms that regulate the behaviour of families and their members.

Normative change tends to occur slowly, over long periods of time, in response to massive social and structural change. These changes challenge established lifestyles and values, forcing the development of normative solutions. Marriage and fertility trends—and ultimately cohabitation, as an alternative to marriage—are affected by economic factors, to be sure, but they also vary by language, religion, and region. Although Quebec was once Canada's most conservative province, it now stands out as the most liberal on social and welfare issues. Despite its Catholic roots, fertility and marriage rates are low—and cohabitation levels are high. Other factors affecting levels of cohabitation are referred to as age, cohort, and period effects (the effects of being born into a particular age cohort at a specific point in time).

In 1981, 8 percent of all couples were cohabiting or living common-law. By 2011, the figure had increased to 20 percent—representing 1.6 million common-law couples. These couples are to be found disproportionately in Quebec and in Aboriginal communities. In 1981, cohabitation peaked among those 20 to 24 years of age (8.2 percent); the next highest level was 7.6 percent among those aged 25 to 29. By 1996, the peak had moved up one age category to those aged 25 to 29 (with 16.9 percent cohabiting); for those aged 30 to 34, the figure was 14.1 percent. The most recent figures, from Census 2011, have cohabitation peaking—once again—among those 25 to 29 years of age at 22.4 percent. Clearly, cohabitation was pioneered by youth! But, think of it this way—the 25- to 29-year-olds of 1996 were 40 to 44 years of age in 2011; as that cohort aged, the percentage living common-law dropped from 16.9 to 14.5 or by a mere 2.4 percentage points. If an option established in youth is carried forward, we might find that about 19 percent of 40- to 44-year-olds will cohabit in 2026.

Within Canada, actual rates of cohabitation are increasing, as is approval of this alternative family form. Also, people are increasingly likely to have children within such unions. Nonetheless, cohabitation is inherently unstable. About 30 percent of these unions last for no more than three years, and only 1 in 20 lasts for 15 years. On the bright side, the reason for dissolving half of all cohabitations is the marriage of the two partners.

What Do You Think?

1. How likely are you, or your friends, to cohabit or live common-law?
2. How would your family or neighbours react if you were to live common-law?
3. Should common-law couples marry when they have children?

IN RECENT YEARS, THE PROPORTION OF YOUNG PEOPLE WHO COHABIT—THAT IS, LIVE TOGETHER WITHOUT BEING MARRIED—HAS RISEN SHARPLY This trend led to a dramatic change in the census definition of family.

for same-sex couples. This change extended social legitimacy to gay and lesbian couples and equalized advantages in inheritance, taxation, and joint property ownership. Since then, Norway (1993), Sweden (1994), Iceland (1996), Finland (2001), and the United Kingdom (2004) have followed suit. However, by 2006, only five countries had extended marriage—in name as well as practice—to same-sex couples: the Netherlands (2001), Belgium (2003), Canada (2005), Spain (2005), and South Africa (2006). Since then a number of other countries have legalized same-sex marriage nationwide—Norway (2009), Sweden (2009), Argentina (2010), Iceland (2010), Portugal (2010), Denmark (2012), Brazil (2013), Great Britain (2013), France (2013),

New Zealand (2013), Uruguay (2013), Luxembourg (2014), Finland (2015), and Ireland (2015).

In the United States, sweeping changes have taken place in just a few years. In 2004, Massachusetts became the first state to legalize same-sex marriage. Since then 13 other states have changed their laws to allow same-sex marriage, while a few more have legalized same-sex unions. In 1996, Congress passed the Defense of Marriage Act, defining marriage as joining one man and one woman. Shortly thereafter, 35 states amended their constitutions to make same-sex marriage illegal. However, in 2015, the Supreme Court required all states to extend the right to marry to both same-sex and opposite-sex couples.

As recently as 1999, the definition of marriage as the "union of one man and one woman" was endorsed overwhelmingly in the House of Commons. This definition was affirmed in Bill C-23 (June 2000), which extended to same-sex couples in committed relationships both the *benefits* and *obligations* of other unions. By 2003, after marriage laws were struck down by the courts of Ontario, British Columbia, and Quebec, the federal government submitted legislation on same-sex marriage to the Supreme Courts of Canada for review. The *Civil Marriage Act*—passed by Paul Martin's Liberal government in 2005—made same-sex marriage legal throughout the country.

Long before same-sex marriage became legal throughout Canada, questions of parental rights were raised. In 1995, gay and lesbian couples in Ontario won the right to adopt the biological children of their partners under the "step-parent adoption clause" of the *Child and Family Services Act*. Soon thereafter, in 1998, British Columbia gave separating same-sex parents equal privileges and obligations with respect to their children. As is the case with others, same-sex couples can adopt children through public agencies such as Children's Aid Societies.

Many gay and lesbian couples with children are raising the offspring of previous heterosexual unions; others have adopted children; still others have made use of reproductive technologies to have children. Gay or lesbian parenting challenges many traditional ideas, but also shows that many same-sex couples value family life as highly as heterosexuals do. By 2011, there were close to 65 000 same-sex couples—married or living common-law—in Canada. While 10 percent of same-sex couples had children, the presence of children was most likely if the couples were married females (21.3 percent).

Singlehood

In the past, at least 9 out of 10 Canadians married, so "singlehood" was seen as a transitory stage in life. Since Canada treats common-law relationships as marriages, one could think of true singlehood as being neither married nor in common-law relationships. Nonetheless, since common-law relationships are thought to be short-lived (see the Sociology in Focus box for more details) and many young women still dream of marriage and a wedding, it is worth looking at changes in the proportion of our population that never marries.

Most striking is the rising number of single young women. Throughout North America in 1960, one in four women *aged 20 to 24* was single; by 1990, the proportion was nearing two-thirds. By 2003, the figure in the United States had soared to 74 percent; while in Canada, the 2001 census revealed an astounding 89 percent. Underlying this is a recent change in the average age of marriage for men and women (up three years in each case), so that delayed marriage is a major factor. Women are going to college, university, and graduate school in greater numbers, participating in the labour force, and establishing careers. Many are marrying later—or living common-law—and having children later, while others choose to forgo marriage and children altogether. That said, in each cohort, men are more likely than women to be single. Men, it seems, have their own reasons for delaying marriage or not marrying at all.

Since most first marriages take place when people are in their late twenties or early thirties, Table 18–6 sets the pattern for the future. Note that, in the two cohorts above 55 years of age, 85 percent of men and women had married. However, women in the two oldest cohorts were less likely to be single than men and, for both older men and women, singlehood increased from 2001 to 2012. In fact, the same patterns apply to the whole of Table 18-7. First, men and women, in each census year, are less likely to be "single (never married)" with each increase in age. Second, women in each census year and age cohort are less likely to be single than men. And third, given the fact that women experience lower levels of singlehood than men, both sexes—at each age level—are more likely to be single in 2011 than in 2001.

Table 18–6 Singlehood over Generations (Percentage Never Married) by Selected Age Cohorts and Sex: 2001, 2006, and 2011

Age	Men			Women		
	2001	2006	2011	2001	2006	2011
65 to 69	6.6	6.7	7.2	5.7	5.8	6.5
55 to 59	8.3	10.8	14.3	7.0	8.8	11.2
45 to 49	16.2	21.6	25.7	12.5	16.5	19.6
35 to 39	32.7	35.3	37.1	24.0	27.2	29.8
25 to 29	71.5	76.3	78.8	57.6	63.7	67.4

SOURCE: Compilation and calculations by L.M. Gerber based on Statistics Canada, NHS 2011, Catalogue no. 98-312-XCB2011039.

Table 18–7 Singlehood over Generations (Never Married, and "in" or "not in" Common-Law Unions) by Selected Age Cohorts and Sex, 2011 (Percentages)

	Men			Women		
Age	Never Married	Not in Common-Law Unions	In Common-Law Unions	Never Married	Not in Common-Law Unions	In Common-Law Unions
65 to 69	7.2	5.7	1.5	6.5	5.5	0.9
55 to 59	14.3	10.3	4.1	11.2	8.2	3.1
45 to 49	25.7	16.6	9.1	19.6	12.0	7.6
35 to 39	37.1	22.0	15.1	29.8	17.3	12.5
25 to 29	78.8	58.1	20.7	67.4	44.3	23.1

SOURCE: Compilation and calculations by L.M. Gerber based on Statistics Canada, NHS 2011, Catalogue no. 98-312-XCB2011039.

Does this mean that—younger or older—more men and women are living alone and lonely? Not exactly. Table 18–7 makes it clear that significant proportions of the "never married" are involved in common-law unions. Roughly speaking, a third or more of the "never married"—especially below 50 years of age—have entered common-law unions instead. Table 18–6 indicates clearly that singlehood has been increasing over recent decades, and we know that the proportion of common-law relationships is increasing as well. But we do *not* know how many single (never married) individuals were in common-law relationships at some point in the past. Taken together, Tables 18–6 and 18–7 suggest that people—especially men—are more likely to be living alone with each passing census day. However, since there is no equivalent to "divorced" or "widowed" for those with past common-law relationships—no matter how long-lasting or significant—we cannot ascertain the full meaning of "singlehood."

New Reproductive Technologies and Families

Recent medical advances involving new reproductive technology are also changing families. In 1978, England's Louise Brown became the world's first "test-tube" baby. Since then, tens of thousands of children have been conceived this way. In decades ahead, 5 percent or more of the children in high-income nations may result from new reproductive technologies. Test-tube babies are the product of in vitro fertilization, in which doctors unite a woman's egg and a man's sperm "in glass" (usually not a test tube but a shallow dish) rather than in a woman's body. Doctors then either implant the resulting embryo in the womb of the woman who is to bear the child or freeze it for use at a later time.

At present, new reproductive technologies help some couples who cannot conceive by conventional means. These techniques may eventually help reduce the incidence of birth defects. Genetic screening of sperm and eggs allows medical specialists to increase the odds of having a healthy baby. But new reproductive technology also raises difficult and troubling questions. When one woman carries an embryo formed from the egg of another, who is the mother? When a couple divorces, which spouse is entitled to decide what is to be done with frozen embryos? Should parents use genetic screening to select the physical traits or even the sex of their child? Such questions remind us that technology changes faster than our ability to anticipate all the consequences of its use (Cohen, 1998; Nock et al., 1999).

And what about the relationship between sperm donors and their biological children? People who know that their fathers are anonymous donors to a sperm bank (which keeps records) are demanding information about them. If people who were adopted as children can get access to information about their biological parents, why not information about sperm-donor fathers?

There is another angle to the sperm-donor story—or rather the *known* sperm donor story—that arose in Quebec. A young woman asked her ex-boyfriend to help her get pregnant with a child she intended to raise on her own. When she died of cancer three years later, leaving the child to be raised by the grandparents, the biological father sued for custody and succeeded. That court decision sets the scene for other known sperm donors, who are commonly used by lesbian couples and single-mothers-by-choice, to demand greater access to or custody of their children. The implications of this ruling for Canadian families are huge and far-reaching (Blackwell, 2012).

Families: Looking Ahead

Family life in Canada will continue to change, and with change comes controversy. Here, as in the United States, advocates of "traditional family values" line up against those who support greater personal choice—to wed or not to wed, same-sex or opposite-sex, divorce, abortion, single parenthood. No doubt, the traditional family is threatened.

First, the divorce rate is likely to remain high. Today's marriages are about as durable as they were a century ago, when many were cut short by death. The difference is that now more couples *choose* to end marriages that fail to live up to their expectations. Thus, although the divorce rate has declined since 1990, it is unlikely to return to the low rates that marked the early decades of the twentieth century.

Second, family life in the twenty-first century will be more diverse than ever. Cohabiting couples, one-parent families, gay and lesbian families, and blended families are all on the rise. Most families are still based on marriage, and most married couples still have children. But the diversity of family forms implies a trend toward more personal choice.

Third, men will play a limited role in child rearing. In recent years, a small countertrend—the stay-at-home dad—is evident, with some older and highly educated fathers staying at home with young children, many using computer technology to continue their work. But the stay-at-home dad represents a small fraction of fathers with young children. More men are taking parental leave, but, in the end, high divorce rates and the increase in single motherhood are weakening children's ties to fathers and increasing the risk of child poverty.

Fourth, families will continue to feel the effects of economic change. In many homes, both partners work, reducing marriage and family to the interaction of weary men and women who try to fit a little "quality time" with their children into an already full schedule. The long-term effects of the two-career couple on families as we have known them are likely to be mixed. Dual-career families—and single motherhood—lead to stress and require alternatives in child care.

Fifth and finally, the importance of new reproductive technology will increase. Ethical concerns about whether what can be done *should* be done may slow these developments, but new forms of reproduction will continue to alter the traditional experience of parenthood.

Despite the changes and controversies that have shaken the family, most people still report being happy as partners, as parents, and, it seems, as children. Bibby's study of the millennial generation (2009) reveals that two-thirds of teenagers say that family is "very important" to them. They enjoy being with their parents, siblings, and grandparents. Stereotypes aside, more than 90 percent say that they have been strongly influenced by the way they were raised. They disapprove of extramarital sex and divorce, want a home like they grew up in, want to have children, and expect their marriages to last. All things considered, marriage and family life are likely to remain foundations of our society for generations to come.

Seeing Sociology in Everyday Life

CHAPTER 18 Family

How do the mass media portray the family?

Many are familiar with the traditional families portrayed in popular television shows of the 1950s such as *The Adventures of Ozzie and Harriet* and *Leave It to Beaver*. Both of these shows had a working father, homemaker mother, and two (wonderful) sons. But, as these images suggest, today's television shows present a far wider range of family types.

Hint The general pattern found in the mass media today is certainly different from that common in the 1950s, the so-called "golden age of families." Today's television shows portray careers that leave little time for families, provide fewer examples of stable marriages, and show the many ways in which people create family-like groups. Some people might say that Hollywood has an anti-family bias. Perhaps, but scriptwriters find that nonconventional family forms make for more interesting stories. To what extent do you agree with the view that most people today are capable of finding satisfying relationships, whether or not these relationships correspond to a traditional family form?

Ursula Coyote/Everett Collection

WHILE TELEVISION SHOWS 50 YEARS AGO PRESENTED THE FAMILY AS A CULTURAL IDEAL, TODAY'S SHOWS ARE FAR MORE LIKELY TO PRESENT THE REALITY OF FAMILY LIFE This means not only a variety of family types but, as shown in the popular television show *Breaking Bad*, the struggles and conflicts within families as well.

Everett Collection

IN THE SITCOM *NEW GIRL*, JESS DAY IS A TWENTY-SOMETHING TEACHER WHO NEEDS A PLACE TO LIVE AFTER ENDING A RELATIONSHIP Responding to an ad seeking a roommate, she moves in with three young men. In what ways does this group resemble a family?

Cliff Lipson/Everett Collection

THE RECENT TELEVISION SHOW *SHAMELESS* FOLLOWS THE DYSFUNCTIONAL FAMILY LIFE OF FRANK GALLAGHER, A SINGLE FATHER SUFFERING FROM ALCOHOLISM, AND HIS SIX CHILDREN, WHO TRY THEIR BEST TO COPE WITHOUT MUCH PARENTING.

Seeing Sociology in *Your* Everyday Life

1. After reading through the photo essay, list your own favorite television shows and, in each case, evaluate the importance of family life in the show. Is family life included in the show? If so, what family forms are presented? Are families a source of happiness for people or not?

2. This chapter explains that family life in today's society is more and more about making choices. What

   are the underlying reasons that family life is more varied today than it was, say, a century ago?

3. Go to www.sociologyinfocus.com to access the Sociology in Focus blog, where you can read the latest posts by a team of young sociologists who apply the sociological perspective to topics of popular culture.

Making the Grade

CHAPTER 18 Family

Families: Basic Concepts and Global Variations

18.1 Describe families and how they differ around the world.

All societies are built on *kinship*. The family varies across cultures and over time:

- In industrialized societies, *marriage* is monogamous.
- Pre-industrial societies recognize the *extended family*; industrialization gives rise to the *nuclear family*.
- Many pre-industrial societies permit *polygamy*, of which there are two types: *polygyny* and *polyandry*.
- In global perspective, *patrilocality* is most common, but industrial societies favour *neolocality*, and a few societies have *matrilocal residence*.
- Industrial societies use *bilateral descent*; pre-industrial societies are either *patrilineal* or *matrilineal*.
- *Monogamy* is the most common global pattern. In most of Africa and much of South Asia, the law also permitted polygamy.

family a social institution found in all societies that unites people in co-operative groups to care for one another, including any children

kinship a social bond based on common ancestry, marriage, or adoption

marriage a legal relationship, usually involving economic co-operation, sexual activity, and child-bearing

extended family a family consisting of parents and children as well as other kin; also known as a *consanguine family*

nuclear family a family composed of one or two parents and their children; also known as a *conjugal family*

endogamy marriage between people of the same social category

exogamy marriage between people of different social categories

monogamy marriage that unites two partners

polygamy marriage that unites a person with two or more spouses

polygyny marriage that unites one man and two or more women

polyandry marriage that unites one woman and two or more men

patrilocality a residential pattern in which a married couple lives with or near the husband's family

matrilocality a residential pattern in which a married couple lives with or near the wife's family

neolocality a residential pattern in which a married couple lives apart from both sets of parents

descent the system by which members of a society trace kinship over generations

patrilineal descent a system tracing kinship through men

matrilineal descent a system tracing kinship through women

bilateral descent a system tracing kinship through both men and women

Theories of the Family

18.2 Apply sociology's major theories to family life.

Structural-functional theory identifies major family functions that help society operate smoothly:

- socialization of children to help them become well-integrated members of society
- regulation of sexual activity in order to maintain kinship organization and property rights
- giving children a social identity within society in terms of race, ethnicity, religion, and social class
- providing material and emotional support to family members

Social-conflict theory and feminist theory point to ways in which families perpetuate social inequality.

- Families ensure the continuation of the class structure by passing on wealth to their children.
- Families perpetuate gender roles by establishing men as the heads of the household and by assigning the responsibility for child rearing and housework to women.
- The tendency of people to marry others like themselves supports racial and ethnic hierarchies.

Symbolic-interaction theory explores how family members build emotional bonds in the course of everyday family life.

Social-exchange theory sees courtship and marriage as a process of negotiation in which each person weighs the advantages and disadvantages of a potential partner.

incest taboo a norm forbidding sexual relations or marriage between certain relatives

Stages of Family Life

18.3 Analyze changes in the family over the life course.

- Arranged marriages are common in pre-industrial societies. Courtship based on romantic love is central to mate selection in modern societies.
- Large families are necessary in pre-industrial societies because children are a source of needed labour.
- Family size has decreased over time as industrialization increases the costs of raising children.
- As more women choose to go to school or join the labour force, fewer children are born.

- The "family values" debate revolves around who cares for children when both parents work outside the home.
- The departure of children, known as the "empty nest," requires adjustments to family life.
- Many middle-aged couples care for aging parents, and many older couples are active grandparents.
- The final transition in marriage begins with the death of a spouse.

homogamy marriage between people with the same social characteristics
infidelity sexual activity outside one's marriage

Canadian Families: Class, Gender, and Race

18.4 Explain how class, race, and gender shape family life.

- Social class determines a family's financial security and opportunities available to family members.
- Children born into rich families typically have better mental and physical health and go on to achieve more in life than children born into poor families.
- Ethnicity and race can affect a person's experience of family life, although no single generalization fits all families within a particular category.
- Traditional family life in First Nations (on-reserve) communities has been severely damaged by colonialism, the *Indian Act*, federal government control, European religions, and residential schooling.
- Migration of Aboriginal people to cities contributes to tremendous diversity in patterns of family life.
- The traditional pattern of extended families common to several immigrant categories is changing as they adapt to Canadian society.
- Aboriginal and visible minority communities face severe economic disadvantages, so that their families and children are more likely to be poor.
- Gender affects family dynamics because husbands dominate in most marriages.
- Research suggests that marriage provides more benefits for men than for women.
- After divorce, men are more likely than women to remarry.

Transitions and Problems in Family Life

18.5 Analyze the effects of divorce, remarriage, and violence on family life.

- The divorce rate is four times what it was a century ago; 4 in 10 of today's marriages will end in divorce. Researchers point to six causes: Individualism is on the rise; romantic love fades; women are less dependent on men; many of today's marriages are stressful; divorce is socially acceptable; legally, a divorce is easier to get.
- More than half of all people who divorce eventually remarry; remarriage creates blended families that include children from previous marriages.
- Family violence, which victimizes mostly women and children, is far more common than official records indicate; most adults who abuse family members were themselves abused as children.

family violence emotional, physical, or sexual abuse of one family member by another

Alternative Family Forms

18.6 Describe the diversity of family life in Canada.

- The proportion of lone-parent families reached 16 percent by 2011; single parenthood increases a woman's risk of poverty, which puts children at a disadvantage.
- The proportion of couples living common-law in Canada increased from 8 to 38 percent between 1981 and 2011.
- Since 2003, gay and lesbian couples in Canada have had the right to marry. With or without formal marriage, same-sex couples have been forming lasting relationships—often involving child rearing. Married same-sex couples are more likely than common-law couples to be raising children.
- The proportion of single women among those aged 35 to 39 reached 30 percent by 2011.
- This increase is result of women's greater participation in the workforce and lessened dependence on men for material support.
- Women and men may be unmarried because they are cohabiting or living common-law.

cohabitation the sharing of a household by an unmarried couple

Chapter 19
Religion

Charles Mistral/Alamy Stock Photo

Learning Objectives

19.1 Apply sociology's major theories to religion.

19.2 Discuss the links between religion and social change.

19.3 Distinguish among church, sect, and cult.

19.4 Contrast religious patterns around the world.

19.5 Analyze patterns of religiosity in Canada.

The Power of Society
to shape our values and choices

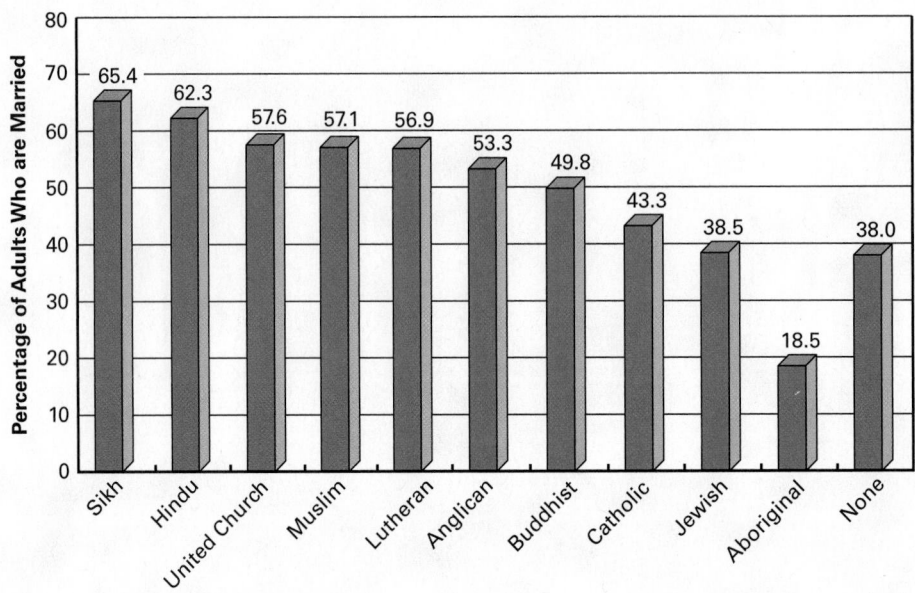

SOURCE: Compilation and calculations by LM Gerber based on Statistics Canada, NHS 2011, Catalogue no. 99-010-X2011037.

Can ones religious affiliation—or lack thereof—predict attitudes regarding marriage and family life? Does religious affiliation affect the decision to choose marriage over common-law union? This figure shows that religious affiliation has a powerful effect on the decision to marry. On the other hand, large majorities of Sikhs and Hindus—among whom 65 and 62 percent of adults are married—are immigrants whose broader cultures support marriage and prohibit non-marital relations. That said, it is worth noting that United Church and Lutheran affiliates are the only ones who, along with Sikhs, Hindus, and Muslims, have marriage rates of over 55 percent. Considering the stance of Catholic doctrine, it may surprise you to learn that only 43 percent of Catholic adults are married. In fact, Quebec, which accounts for almost half of Canada's Catholics, has the highest level of common-law union. Something in Quebec culture effectively counters the tenets of Catholicism. People of Jewish or no religious affiliation are the least likely to be married (38 percent), with the exception of those embracing Aboriginal spirituality.

Chapter Overview

This chapter explores the meaning and importance of religion, a major social institution. Although religion varies around the world, it is always based on the concept of the sacred.

"Make Jesus your CEO." These are words that you might hear at the Carruthers Creek Community Church in Ajax, Ontario. "[T]he $3.8 million, [4273 square metre] building looks more like a large, modern high school/community centre complex than one of [Toronto's] growing number of U.S.-style evangelical megachurches" (Lachaine, 2006). The church draws 900 grandparents, parents, children, *and teens* each Sunday to its distinctly unchurchy services. Congregants arrive to the sounds of soul funk wafting through the lobby and stop for a coffee under the Carruthers Creek Coffee Company logo. Children run around the huge gym before their Sunday school classes, while teens cluster in the fellowship room, which is complete with a dance floor. Everything is done to make congregants and newcomers—of any age—feel welcome.

National Post/Brent Foster

The service is a mix of the conventional and popular: "[T]he real show begins upon entry into the chapel. The lights are dim in the concert-quality theatre" with stained glass projected on the side walls and a removable wooden cross at centre stage. Musical gear—electric and acoustic guitars, a mammoth drum kit, keyboards, and an electric bass—stands ready to accompany two singers, one a teenaged girl with an alternative look, the other a middle-aged man in a sweater and gold necklace. "[T]heir harmonies send shivers down the spine [and] could easily be played on rock radio: angsty, obscure lyrics combined with modern melody" (Lachaine, 2006). Thirty-year-old Pastor Thompson, wearing an untucked shirt and jeans, delivers "his shoot-from-the-hip plainspeak in an urgent whisper, as though he's sharing the word of God with you and only you in the back room of a crowded bar. The audience is hushed and rapt for his entire 40-minute sermon" (Lachaine, 2006).

How, you might ask, does *this* church thrive when others are struggling to survive? ∎

This chapter begins by explaining religion from a sociological point of view. We then explore the changing face of religious belief throughout history and around the world, and examine the vital and sometimes controversial place of religion in today's society.

Religion: Concepts and Theories

19.1 Apply sociology's major theories to religion.

French sociologist Émile Durkheim stated that religion involves "things that surpass the limits of our knowledge" (1965:62; orig. 1915). We define most objects, events, or experiences as **profane** (from the Latin, meaning "outside the temple"), *an ordinary element of everyday life.* But we also consider some things **sacred**, *set apart as extraordinary, inspiring awe and reverence.* Setting the sacred apart from the profane is the essence of all religious belief. **Religion**, then, is *a social institution involving beliefs and practices based on recognizing the sacred.*

There is great diversity in matters of faith, and nothing is sacred to every person on Earth. Although people regard most books as profane, Jews believe that the Torah (the first five books of the Hebrew Bible, or Old Testament) is sacred, in the same way that Christians revere

profane an ordinary element of everyday life

sacred set apart as extraordinary, inspiring awe and reverence

Corbis/Getty Images

RELIGION IS FOUNDED ON THE CONCEPT OF THE SACRED—ASPECTS OF OUR EXISTENCE THAT ARE SET APART AS EXTRAORDINARY AND DEMAND OUR SUBMISSION Bowing, kneeling, or prostrating oneself are all ways of symbolically surrendering to a higher power. These Filipino Christians seek atonement for their sins in an annual Lenten ritual.

Some people with strong faith may be disturbed by the thought of sociologists turning a scientific eye on what they hold sacred. However, a sociological study of religion is no threat to anyone's faith. Sociologists study religion just as they study the family—to understand religious experiences around the world and how religion is tied to other social institutions. They make no judgments about whether a specific religion is right or wrong; rather, scientific sociology takes a more worldly approach, asking why religions take a particular form in one society or another and how religious activity affects society as a whole.

Sociologists apply the major theoretical approaches to the study of religion just as they do to any other topic. Each approach provides distinctive insights into the way that religion shapes social life.

the Old and New Testaments of the Bible and Muslims exalt the Qur'an (Koran).

But no matter how a community of believers draws its religious lines, Durkheim (1965; orig. 1915) explained, people understand profane things in terms of their everyday usefulness. We log on to the internet with our computer or turn a key to start our car. What is sacred we reverently set apart from everyday life, giving it a holy aura. Marking the boundary between the sacred and the profane, for example, Muslims remove their shoes before entering a mosque, to avoid defiling a sacred place with soles that have touched the profane ground outside.

The sacred is embodied in **ritual**, or *formal, ceremonial behaviour*. Holy Communion is the central ritual of Christianity; to the Christian faithful, the wafer and wine consumed during Communion are never treated in a profane way as food but as the sacred symbols of the body and blood of Jesus Christ.

Religion and Sociology

Because religion deals with ideas that transcend everyday experience, neither common sense nor sociology can prove or disprove religious doctrine. Religion is a matter of **faith**, *belief based on conviction rather than scientific evidence*. The New Testament of the Bible defines "faith" as "the conviction of things not seen" (Hebrews 11:1) and urges Christians to "walk by faith, not by sight" (2 Corinthians 5:7).

Structural-Functional Theory: Functions of Religion

According to Durkheim (1965; orig. 1915), society has a life and power of its own beyond the life of any individual. In other words, society itself is godlike, shaping the lives of its members and living on beyond them. While practising religion, people celebrate the awesome power of their society.

No wonder people around the world transform certain everyday objects into sacred symbols of their collective life. Members of technologically simple societies do this with a **totem**, *an object in the natural world collectively defined as sacred*. The totem—perhaps an animal or an elaborate work of art—becomes the centrepiece of ritual, symbolizing the power of society over the individual. In our society, the flag is treated with respect; it is not used in a profane way (say, as clothing) or allowed to touch the ground.

Durkheim identified three major functions of religion that contribute to the operation of society:

- **Establishing social cohesion.** Religion unites people through shared symbolism, values, and norms. Religious thought and ritual establish rules of fair play, organizing our social life.

religion a social institution involving beliefs and practices based on recognizing the sacred

faith belief based on conviction rather than on scientific evidence

- **Promoting social control.** Every society uses religious ideas to promote conformity. By defining their god as a "judge," many religions encourage people to obey cultural norms. Religion can also be used to back up the power of political systems. In the Middle Ages, royalty claimed to rule by "divine right," so that obedience was seen as doing God's will. Few political leaders in the Western world make this claim, but many publicly ask for God's blessing, implying that their efforts are right and just. Many American politicians are open about their religious beliefs, while their counterparts among Canada's parliamentarians quietly attend prayer breakfasts without drawing attention to their religious beliefs or practices.

- **Providing meaning and purpose.** Religious belief offers the comforting sense that our brief lives serve some greater purpose. Strengthened by such beliefs, people are less likely to despair in the face of change or even tragedy. For this reason, we mark major life course transitions—including birth, marriage, and death—with religious observances.

EVALUATE

In Durkheim's structural-functional analysis, religion represents the collective life of society. The major weakness of this approach is that it downplays religion's dysfunctions, especially the fact that strongly held beliefs can generate social conflict. Terrorists have claimed that God supports their actions, and nations often march to war under the banner of their god. A study of conflict in the world would probably show that religious beliefs have provoked more violence than differences of social class.

CHECK YOUR LEARNING   What are Durkheim's three functions of religion for society?

Symbolic-Interaction Theory: Constructing the Sacred

From a symbolic-interaction point of view, religion—like all of society—is socially constructed (although perhaps with divine inspiration). Through various rituals—from daily prayers to such annual religious observances as Easter, Passover, or Ramadan—people sharpen the distinction between the sacred and the profane. Peter Berger (1967:35–36) claims that placing our small, brief lives within some "cosmic frame of reference" gives us the appearance of "ultimate security and permanence."

Marriage is a good example. If two people view marriage as merely a contract, they can walk away whenever they want to. Their bond makes far stronger claims on them when it is defined as "holy" matrimony, which is surely one reason that the divorce rate is lower among people with strong religious beliefs. More generally,

whenever human beings face uncertainty or life-threatening situations—such as illness, natural disaster, terrorist attack, or war—we turn to our sacred symbols.

EVALUATE

Symbolic-interaction theory asserts that people use religion to give everyday life sacred meaning. Berger adds that the ability of the sacred to give special meaning to society depends on ignoring the fact that it is socially constructed. After all, how much strength could we gain from beliefs if we saw them merely as strategies for coping with tragedy? Also, this micro-level analysis ignores religion's link to social inequality, to which we now turn.

CHECK YOUR LEARNING   How would Peter Berger explain the fact that deeply religious people have a low divorce rate?

Social-Conflict Theory: Inequality and Religion

The social-conflict approach highlights religion's support of social inequality. Karl Marx claimed that religion serves ruling elites by legitimizing the status quo and diverting people's attention from social inequities.

Today, the British monarch is the formal head of the Church of England, illustrating the close ties between religious and political elites. In practical terms, linking church and state means that opposing the government is opposing the church and, by implication, God. Religion also encourages people to accept the difficulties of life while looking hopefully to a "better world to come." In a well-known statement, Marx dismissed religion as preventing revolutionary change. Religion, in his words, is "the sigh of the oppressed creature, the sentiment of a heartless world, and the soul of soulless conditions. It is the opium of the people" (1964b:27; orig. 1848).

Feminist Theory: Gender and Religion

Feminist theory explains that religion and social inequality are also linked through gender because virtually all of the world's major religions are patriarchal. For example, the Qur'an (Koran), the scared book of Islam, gives men social dominance over women by defining gender roles: "Men are in charge of women. . . . Hence good women are obedient . . . As for those whose rebelliousness you fear, admonish them, banish them from your bed, and scourge them" (Qur'an 4:34, quoted in Kaufman, 1976:163).

Christianity, the major religion of the Western world, also supports patriarchy. Many Christians revere Mary, the mother of Jesus, but the New Testament also includes the following passages:

A man . . . is the image and glory of God; but woman is the glory of man. For man was not made from woman,

APPLYING THEORY

Religion

	Structural-Functional Theory	Symbolic-Interaction Theory	Social-Conflict and Feminist Theories
What is the level of analysis?	Macro-level	Micro-level	Macro-level
What is the importance of religion for society?	Religion performs vital tasks, including uniting people and controlling behaviour. Religion gives life meaning and purpose.	Religion strengthens marriage by giving it (and family life) sacred meaning. People often turn to sacred symbols for comfort when facing danger and uncertainty.	Religion supports social inequality by claiming that the social order is just. Organized religion supports the domination of women by men. Religion turns attention from problems in this world to a "better world to come."

but woman from man. Neither was man created for woman, but woman for man. (1 Corinthians 11:7–9)

As in all the churches of the saints, the women should keep silence in the churches. For they are not permitted to speak, but should be subordinate, as even the law says. If there is anything they desire to know, let them ask their husbands at home. For it is shameful for a woman to speak in church. (1 Corinthians 14:33–35)

Wives, be subject to your husbands, as to the Lord. For the husband is the head of the wife as Christ is the head of the church. . . . As the church is subject to Christ, so let wives also be subject in everything to their husbands. (Ephesians 5:22–24)

Judaism has also traditionally supported patriarchy. Male Orthodox Jews say the following words in daily prayer:

Blessed art thou, O Lord our God, King of the Universe, that I was not born a gentile.
Blessed art thou, O Lord our God, King of the Universe, that I was not born a slave.
Blessed art thou, O Lord our God, King of the Universe, that I was not born a woman.

Today, Islam and the Roman Catholic Church ban women from the priesthood, as do almost half of Protestant denominations. But a growing number of Protestant religious organizations do ordain women. Judaism upholds the traditional prohibition against women serving as rabbis, but the Reform, Conservative, and Reconstructionist branches of Judaism look to both men and women as spiritual leaders.

EVALUATE

Social-conflict and feminist theories emphasize the power of religion to support social inequality. Yet religion also promotes change toward equality. For example, nineteenth-century religious groups in the United States played an important part in the movement to abolish slavery. Religious organizations and their leaders are often in the forefront, fighting for equal rights for minorities and women. Today, a number of Protestant denominations ordain women, while

Reform and Conservative (not Orthodox) Judaism look to both men and women as spiritual leaders.

CHECK YOUR LEARNING How does religion help maintain class inequality and gender stratification?

The Applying Theory table summarizes the three theoretical approaches to understanding religion.

Religion and Social Change

19.2 Discuss the links between religion and social change.

Religion can be the conservative force portrayed by Karl Marx. But, at some points in history, as Max Weber (1958; orig. 1904–1905) explained, religion has promoted dramatic social change.

Max Weber: Protestantism and Capitalism

Max Weber argued that particular religious ideas set into motion a wave of change that brought about the Industrial Revolution in Western Europe. The rise of industrial capitalism was encouraged by Calvinism, a movement within the Protestant Reformation.

John Calvin (1509–1564) was a leader in the Protestant Reformation who preached the doctrine of predestination. According to Calvin, an all-powerful and all-knowing God had selected some people for salvation but condemned most to eternal damnation. Each individual's fate, sealed before birth and known only to God, was either eternal glory or endless hellfire.

Driven by anxiety over their fate, Calvinists understandably looked for signs of God's favour in this world and came to see prosperity as a sign of divine blessing. Religious conviction and a rigid devotion to duty led

Calvinists to work all the time, and many amassed great wealth. But money was not for selfish spending or for sharing with the poor, whose plight they saw as a mark of God's rejection. As agents of God's work on Earth, Calvinists believed that they best fulfilled their "calling" by reinvesting profits and achieving ever-greater success in the process.

All the while, Calvinists practiced self-denial by living thrifty lives. In addition, they eagerly adopted technological advances that promised to increase workplace effectiveness. Together, these traits laid the groundwork for the rise of industrial capitalism. In time, the religious fervour that motivated early Calvinists weakened, leaving a profane "Protestant work ethic." To Max Weber, industrial capitalism itself arose as a "disenchanted" religion, further showing the power of religion to alter the shape of society (Berger, 2009).

Liberation Theology

Historically, Christianity has reached out to oppressed people, urging all to a stronger faith in a better life to come. In recent decades, however, some church leaders and theologians have taken a decidedly political approach and endorsed **liberation theology**, *the combining of Christian principles with political activism, often Marxist in character.* This social movement started in the 1960s in Latin America's Roman Catholic Church. Today, Christian activists continue to help people in poor nations liberate themselves from abysmal poverty. Their message is simple: Social oppression runs counter to Christian morality, so, as a matter of faith and justice, Christians must promote greater social equality.

Pope Francis has expressed support for the world's poor and also criticized the global economic system for not doing enough to assist people in need. Perhaps the current pope will steer a course that differs from that of Pope Benedict XVI and Pope John Paul II, who condemned liberation theology for distorting traditional church doctrine with left-wing politics. Nevertheless, the liberation theology movement has gained strength in the poorest countries of Latin America, where many people's

Christian faith drives them to improve conditions for the poor and oppressed (Neuhouser, 1989; Williams, 2002).

Types of Religious Organizations

19.3 Distinguish among church, sect, and cult.

Sociologists categorize the hundreds of different religious organizations along a continuum, with *churches* at one end and *sects* at the other, as shown in Figure 19–1. We can describe any actual religious organization in relation to these two ideal types by locating it on a church-sect continuum.

Church

Drawing on the ideas of his teacher Max Weber, Ernst Troeltsch (1931) defined a **church** as *a type of religious organization that is well integrated into the larger society.* Church-like organizations usually persist for centuries and include generations of the same families. Churches have well-established rules and regulations, and expect leaders to be formally trained and ordained.

Although concerned with the sacred, a church accepts the ways of the profane world. Church members think of God in intellectual terms (say, as a force for good) and favour abstract moral standards ("Do unto others as you would have them do unto you.") over specific rules for day-to-day living. By teaching morality in safely abstract terms, church leaders avoid social controversy. For example, many congregations celebrate the unity of all peoples but say little about their own lack of racial diversity; by downplaying this type of conflict, a church makes peace with the status quo (Troeltsch, 1931).

A church may operate with or apart from the state. As its name implies, a **state church** is *a church formally allied with the state.* State churches have existed throughout human history. For centuries, Roman Catholicism was the official religion of the Roman Empire, and Confucianism

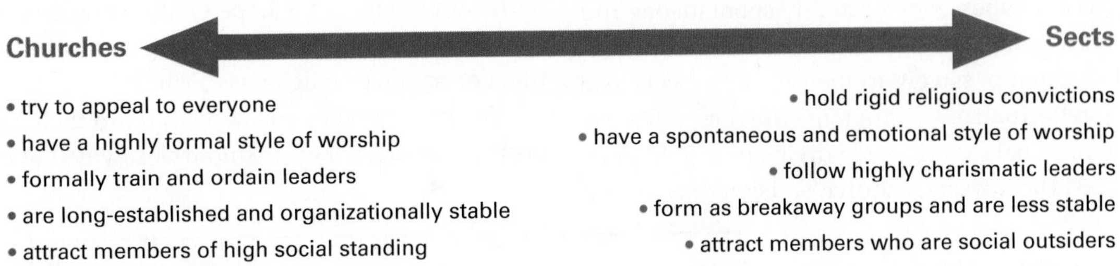

Churches	Sects
• try to appeal to everyone	• hold rigid religious convictions
• have a highly formal style of worship	• have a spontaneous and emotional style of worship
• formally train and ordain leaders	• follow highly charismatic leaders
• are long-established and organizationally stable	• form as breakaway groups and are less stable
• attract members of high social standing	• attract members who are social outsiders

Figure 19–1 Church—Sect Continuum

Churches and sects are two opposing ideal types of religious organization. Any real-life religious organization will fall somewhere on the continuum between these two concepts.

was the official religion of China until early in the twentieth century. Today, the Anglican Church is the official church of England; Islam is the official religion of Morocco, Pakistan, and Iran; and Judaism is the official religion of Israel. State churches count everyone in the society as a member, which sharply limits tolerance of religious differences.

By contrast, a **denomination** is *a church, independent of the state, that recognizes religious pluralism.* Denominations exist in nations that formally separate church and state. Canada has dozens of Christian denominations (including Catholic, United Church, Anglican, Baptist, Lutheran, and Presbyterian) as well as Muslim, Jewish, Buddhist, Hindu, and Sikh denominations. Each of these denominations adheres to its own doctrine while recognizing the right of others to do the same.

IN GLOBAL PERSPECTIVE, THE RANGE OF RELIGIOUS ACTIVITY IS TRULY ASTONISHING Members of this Southeast Asian cult show their devotion to God by suspending themselves in the air using ropes and sharp hooks that pierce their skin.

Sect

The second general religious form is the **sect**, *a type of religious organization that stands apart from the larger society.* Sect members have rigid religious convictions and deny the beliefs of others. A church tries to appeal to everyone—the term *catholic*, for instance, also means "universal"—but a sect instead forms an exclusive group. To members of a sect, religion is not just one aspect of life but a firm plan for how to live. In extreme cases, members of a sect withdraw completely from society to practise their religion without interference. The Hutterites and Old Order Mennonites are examples of Canadian sects that have remained isolated from the mainstream. Since our culture views religious tolerance as a virtue, members of sects are sometimes accused of being narrow-minded in their insistence that they alone have the true faith (Williams, 2002).

In organizational terms, sects are less formal than churches. Sect members may be highly spontaneous and emotional in worship, compared to members of churches, who tend to listen passively to their leaders. Sects also reject the intellectualized religion of churches, stressing instead the personal experience of divine power. Rodney Stark (1985:314) contrasts a church's vision of a distant god ("Our Father, who art in Heaven") with a sect's more immediate god ("Lord, bless this poor sinner kneeling before you now").

Churches and sects also have different patterns of leadership. The more churchlike an organization, the more likely that its leaders are formally trained and ordained. Sectlike organizations, which celebrate the personal presence of God, expect their leaders to exhibit divine inspiration in the form of **charisma** (from the Greek, meaning "divine favour"), *extraordinary personal qualities that can infuse people with emotion and turn them into followers.*

Sects generally form as breakaway groups from established religious organizations (Stark & Bainbridge, 1979). Their psychic intensity and informal structure make them less stable than churches, and many sects blossom only to disappear soon afterwards. The sects that do endure typically become more like churches, with declining emphasis on charismatic leadership as they become more bureaucratic.

To sustain their membership, many sects actively recruit, or *proselytize*, new members; for example, members of Jehovah's Witnesses go door to door to share their faith with others in the hope of attracting new members. Sects value highly the experience of *conversion*, a personal transformation or religious rebirth.

Finally, churches and sects differ in their social composition. Because they are more closely tied to the world,

church a type of religious organization that is well integrated into the larger society

sect a type of religious organization that stands apart from the larger society

cult a type of religious organization that is largely outside a society's cultural traditions

well-established churches tend to include people of higher social standing. Sects attract more disadvantaged people. A sect's openness to new members and its promise of salvation and personal fulfillment appeal to people who feel that they are social outsiders.

Cult

A **cult** is *a type of religious organization that is largely outside a society's cultural traditions.* Most sects spin off from conventional religious organizations. A cult, however, typically forms around a highly charismatic leader who offers a compelling message about a new and very different way of life. As many as 5000 cults exist in North America (Lottick, 2005).

Because some cult principles or practices are unconventional, the popular view is that they are deviant or even evil. The suicides in 1997 in California of 39 members of Heaven's Gate cult—people who claimed that dying was a doorway to a higher existence, perhaps in the company of aliens from outer space—confirmed the negative image that the public holds of most cults. The suicides of 53 members (in Switzerland and Quebec) of the Order of the Solar Temple in 1994, and of five more members in 1997—in the belief that death on Earth would allow transit to another planet where their lives would continue—also contributed to that negative image.

Nevertheless, there is nothing basically wrong with this kind of religious organization. Many long-standing religions—including Christianity, Islam, and Judaism—began as cults. Of course, few cults exist for very long. One reason is that they are even more at odds with the larger society than sects. Many cults demand that members not only accept their doctrine but also adopt a radically new lifestyle. This is why people sometimes accuse cults of brainwashing their members, although research suggests that most people who join cults experience no psychological harm (Kilbourne, 1983; Williams, 2002).

Religion in History and around the World

19.4 Contrast religious patterns around the world.

Like other social institutions, religion shows marked variation according to time and place. Let us look at several ways in which religion has changed over the course of history.

Religion in Pre-Industrial Societies

Early hunters and gatherers practised **animism** (from the Latin, meaning "the breath of life"), *the belief that elements of the natural world are conscious life forms that affect humanity.* Animistic people view forests, oceans, mountains, and even the wind as spiritual forces. Many Aboriginal societies in North America are animistic, which explains their reverence for the natural environment.

Belief in a single divine power responsible for creating the world began with pastoral and horticultural societies, which first appeared 10 000 to 12 000 years ago. The conception of God as a "shepherd" arose because Christianity, Judaism, and Islam had their beginnings among pastoral peoples. Religion gains importance in agrarian societies, which develop a specialized priesthood in charge of religious organizations. The central role of religion is seen in the huge cathedrals that dominated the towns of medieval Europe.

Religion in Industrial Societies

The Industrial Revolution introduced a growing emphasis on science. More and more, people looked to doctors and scientists for the knowledge and comfort they previously got from priests. But as Durkheim (1965, orig. 1915) predicted almost a century ago, religion persists in industrial societies because science is powerless to address issues of ultimate meaning in human life. In other words,

ANIMISM IS WIDESPREAD IN TRADITIONAL SOCIETIES, WHOSE MEMBERS LIVE RESPECTFULLY WITHIN THE NATURAL WORLD ON WHICH THEY DEPEND FOR THEIR SURVIVAL Animists see a divine presence not just in themselves but in everything around them. Their example has inspired "New Age" spirituality, described toward the end of this chapter.

Window on the World

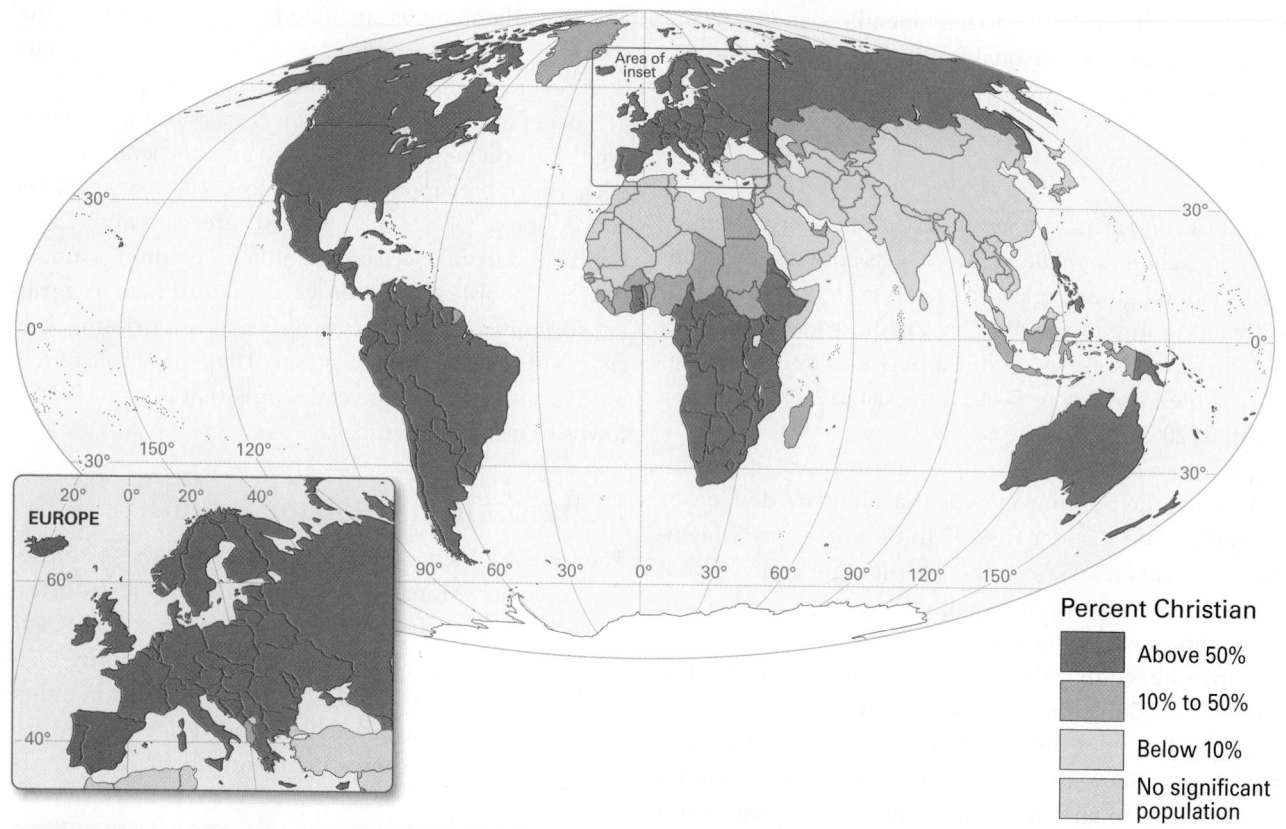

Global Map 19–1 Christianity in Global Perspective

Christianity is the dominant religion of Western Europe and became the dominant religion of the Americas and much of southern Africa and Oceania. Can you explain this pattern?

SOURCE: Based on Association of Religion Data Archives (ARDA). 2012. [Online] Available at http://www.thearda.com/.

learning how the world works is a matter for scientists, but why we and the rest of the universe exist at all is a question of faith.

World Religions

The diversity of religions in the world is almost as wide-ranging as the diversity of cultures. Many of the thousands of different religions are found in just one place and have few followers. But there are a number of *world religions,* which are widely known and have millions of adherents. We briefly describe six world religions, which together claim 5 billion believers—just about three-fourths of humanity.

Christianity

Christianity is the most widespread world religion, with 2.3 billion followers, almost one-third of the world's people. Most Christians live in Europe or the Americas; more than 75 percent of the people in the United States and Canada

identify with Christianity. As shown in Global Map 19–1, people who think of themselves as Christian represent a large share of the population in many world regions, with the notable exceptions of northern Africa and Asia. European colonization spread Christianity throughout much of the world over the past 500 years. Its dominance in the West is shown by the fact that our calendar numbers years from the birth of Jesus Christ.

As noted earlier, Christianity began as a cult, drawing elements from Judaism, a much older religion. Like many cults, Christianity was built on the personal charisma of a leader, Jesus of Nazareth, who preached a message of personal salvation. Jesus did not directly challenge the political power of his day, the Roman Empire—telling his followers to "render therefore to Caesar things that are Caesar's" (Matthew 22:21)—but his message was revolutionary all the same, promising that faith and love would triumph over sin and death.

Christianity is one example of **monotheism**, *belief in a single divine power.* As a new religion, it differed from the Roman Empire's traditional **polytheism**, *belief in*

ALTHOUGH IT BEGAN AS A CULT, CHRISTIANITY'S 2.3 BILLION FOLLOWERS MAKE IT THE MOST WIDESPREAD OF THE WORLD'S RELIGIONS TODAY.

many gods. Yet Christianity views the Supreme Being as a sacred Trinity: God the Creator; Jesus Christ, Son of God and Redeemer; and the Holy Spirit, a Christian's personal experience of God's presence.

The claim that Jesus was divine rests on accounts of his final days on Earth. Brought to trial as a threat to established political leaders, Jesus was tried in Jerusalem and sentenced to death by crucifixion, a common means of execution at the time. This explains why the cross of the crucifixion became a sacred Christian symbol. According to Christian belief, three days after his execution, Jesus arose from the dead, showing that he was the Son of God.

Jesus's followers, especially his 12 closest associates, known as the apostles, spread Christianity throughout the Mediterranean region. At first, the Roman Empire persecuted Christians. But, by the fourth century, the empire had adopted Christianity as a state church—the official religion of what became known as the Holy Roman Empire.

Christianity took various forms, including the Roman Catholic Church and the Eastern Orthodox Church, based in Constantinople (now Istanbul, Turkey). Toward the end of the Middle Ages, the Protestant Reformation in Europe gave rise to hundreds of new denominations. The United Church and Anglican Church are Canada's two largest Protestant denominations at 6 and 5 percent of our population, while the Catholics predominate at 39 percent.

Islam

Islam has about 1.6 billion followers, which is almost one-fourth of humanity. Followers of Islam are called Muslims. In 2011, Muslims (at 1.1 million) made up 3.2 percent of Canada's population. While we tend to associate Islam with Arabs in the Middle East, where the majority is Muslim, in fact most of the world's Muslims live elsewhere. Global Map 19–2 shows that most people in northern Africa and Indonesia are Muslims; in addition, large concentrations of Muslims are found in western Asia in Pakistan, India, Bangladesh, and the southern republics of the former Soviet Union. Because Muslims have a birthrate that is twice that of non-Muslims, projections are that there will be as many Muslims as Christians by about 2050, and that Islam will become the world's dominant religion soon thereafter.

Islam is the word of God as revealed to Muhammad, who was born in the city of Mecca (in what is now Saudi Arabia) about the year 570. To Muslims, Muhammad is a prophet, not a divine being as Jesus is to Christians. The text of the Qur'an, which is sacred to Muslims, is the word of Allah (Arabic for "God") as transmitted through Muhammad, Allah's messenger. In Arabic, the word *islam* means both "submission" and "peace," and the Qur'an urges submission to Allah as the path to inner peace. Muslims express this personal devotion in a ritual of prayers five times each day.

After the death of Muhammad, Islam spread rapidly. While divisions arose among Muslims, all accept the Five Pillars of Islam: recognizing Allah as the one, true God and Muhammad as God's messenger; ritual prayer; giving alms to the poor; fasting during the month of Ramadan; and making a pilgrimage at least once in one's lifetime to the Sacred House of Allah in Mecca (El-Attar, 1991; Weeks, 1988). Like Christianity, Islam holds people accountable to God for their deeds on Earth. Those who live obediently will be rewarded in heaven, and evildoers will suffer unending punishment.

Muslims are also required to defend their faith, which has led to calls for holy wars against unbelievers, in roughly the same way that medieval Christians fought in the Crusades. Recent decades have witnessed a rise in militancy and anti-Western feeling in much of the Muslim world, where many people see the United States as both militarily threatening and representing a way of life that they view as materialistic and immoral. Westerners—who typically know little about Islam and may stereotype all Muslims in terms of the terrorist actions of a few—respond with confusion and sometimes hostility (Eck, 2001; Ryan, 2001).

Window on the World

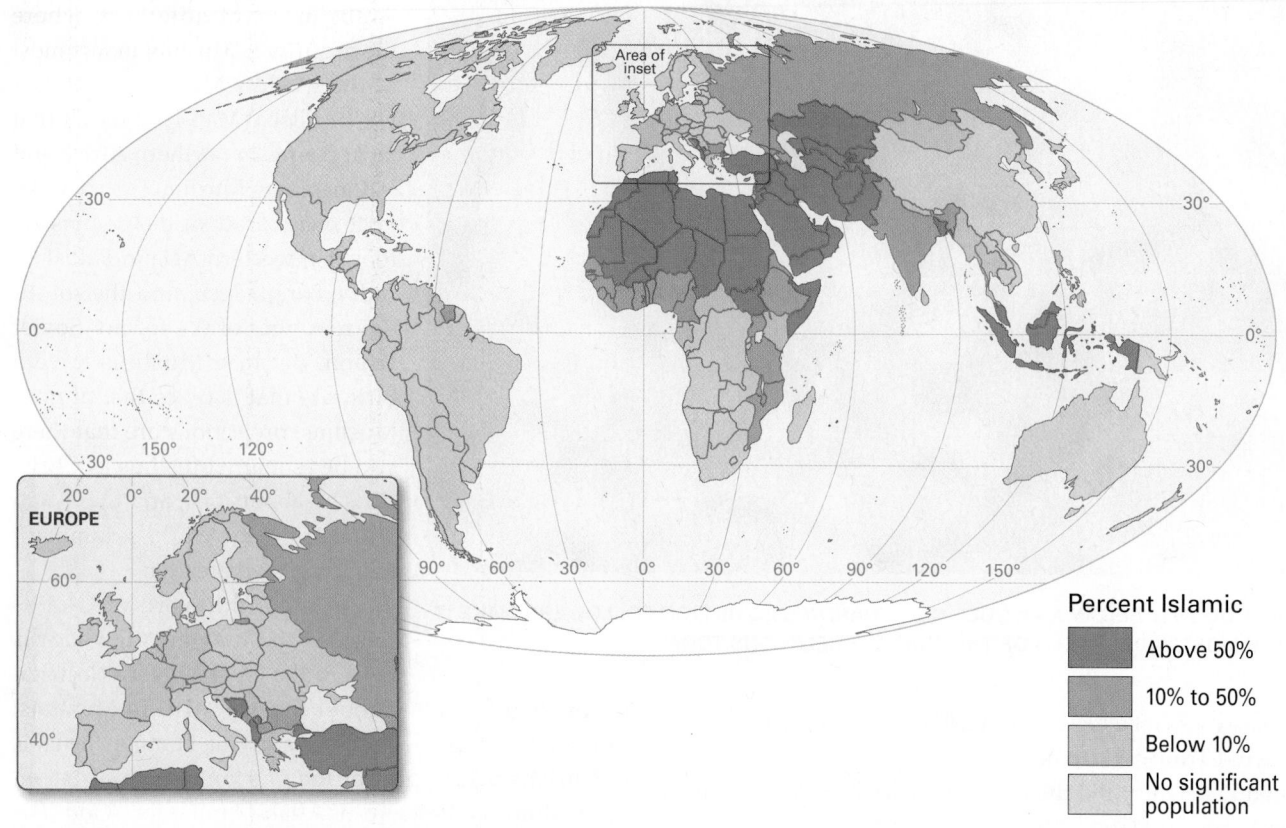

Global Map 19–2 Islam in Global Perspective

Islam is the dominant religion of the Middle East, but most of the world's Muslims live in North Africa and Southeast Asia.

SOURCE: Data from Pew Research Center. "The Future of the Global Muslim Population." 2011. [Online] Available at http://features.pewforum.org/muslim-population.

Many outsiders view Muslim women as among the world's most socially oppressed people. There are differences among Muslim nations in terms of rights given to women: Tunisia allows women far more opportunities than, say, Saudi Arabia, which does not allow women to drive a car or to vote. It is true that many Muslim women lack the personal freedoms enjoyed by Muslim men, yet many—perhaps even most—accept the mandates of their religion and find security in a system that guides the behaviour of both women and men (Peterson, 1996). Defenders of Islam also point out that patriarchy was well established in the Middle East long before the birth of Muhammad and that Islam actually improved the social position of women by requiring husbands to deal justly with their wives. For example, Islam permits a man to have up to four wives, but it requires men to have only one wife if having more would cause him to treat any woman unjustly (Qur'an, "The Women," v. 3).

Judaism

In terms of numbers, Judaism's 14 million followers worldwide make it something less than a world religion.

The followers of Judaism are referred to as Jews, who make up a majority of the population of only one country, Israel. But Judaism is of special importance to us because the largest concentration of Jews anywhere (over 5 million people) is found in North America.

Jews look to the past as a source of guidance in the present and for the future. Judaism has deep historical roots that extend 4000 years before the birth of Christ to the ancient societies of Mesopotamia (located in what is now Iraq). At that time, Jews were animistic; however, this belief changed after Jacob—grandson of Abraham, the earliest great ancestor—led his people to Egypt.

Jews survived centuries of slavery in Egypt until, in the thirteenth century BCE, Moses, the adopted son of an Egyptian princess, was called by God to lead the Jews from bondage. This exodus (this word's Latin and Greek roots mean "a marching out") from Egypt is remembered by Jews today in the annual ritual of Passover. Once liberated, the Jews became monotheistic, recognizing a single, all-powerful god.

A distinctive concept of Judaism is the covenant, a special relationship with God by which the Jews became God's "chosen people." The covenant implies a duty to

MANY RELIGIONS PROMOTE LITERACY BECAUSE THEY DEMAND THAT FOLLOWERS STUDY SACRED TEXTS As part of their upbringing, most Islamic parents teach their children lessons from the Qur'an; later, the children will do the same for a new generation of believers.

observe God's law, especially the Ten Commandments as revealed to Moses on Mount Sinai. Jews regard the Old Testament of the Bible as both a record of their history and a statement of the obligations of Jewish life. Of special importance are the Bible's first five books (Genesis, Exodus, Leviticus, Numbers, and Deuteronomy), called the Torah (a word meaning "teaching" and "law"). In contrast to Christianity's central concern with personal salvation, Judaism emphasizes moral behaviour in this world.

Judaism has four main denominations: Orthodox, Reform, Conservative, and Reconstructionist. Orthodox Jews (roughly half a million in North America) strictly observe traditional beliefs and practices, wear traditional dress, segregate men and women at religious services, and eat only kosher foods. Such traditional practices set off Orthodox Jews from the larger society, making them the most sectlike denomination. Canada's largest Orthodox community is firmly established in Montreal.

In the mid-1800s, many Jews wanted to feel a greater part of the larger society, which led to the formation of the more churchlike Reform Judaism (approaching 2 million people in North America). A third segment, Conservative Judaism (with about 1.5 million adherents in North America), has established a middle ground between the other two denominations. Finally, Reconstructionist Judaism,

with several hundred thousand followers, is the most recent and most liberal denomination, with a humanistic focus on the importance of secular Jewish culture.

Whatever the denomination, Jews share a cultural history of oppression as a result of prejudice and discrimination. A collective memory of centuries of slavery in Egypt, conquest by Rome, and persecution in Europe has shaped the Jewish identity. Jews in Italy were the first to live in an urban ghetto (this word comes, perhaps, from the Italian *borghetto,* meaning "settlement outside of the city walls"), and this residential segregation soon spread to other parts of Europe.

Jewish immigration to North America began in the mid-1600s. The early immigrants who prospered were assimilated into largely Christian communities. But as larger numbers arrived at the end of the nineteenth century, prejudice and discrimination against Jews—commonly termed *anti-Semitism*—increased. In Canada, Jews were not allowed to work in certain institutions, while other organizations maintained quotas. For instance, there were quotas on the number of Jewish students who would be admitted to Canadian universities (Abella, 1989). During World War II, German Jewish refugees were refused admittance to Canada (Abella & Troper, 1982) when anti-Semitism reached a vicious peak and the Nazi regime in Germany systematically annihilated 6 million Jews.

Today, the social standing of Jews is well above average. The University of Toronto, in its *National Report '97,* announced the endowment of two chairs in Jewish studies, an innovative and comprehensive program that reflects the belief that "the study of Jewish culture and history is critical to the understanding of Western civilization" and highly relevant to a "young, multicultural country like Canada."

Still, many Jews are concerned about the future of their religion because in the United States and Canada, only half of the children growing up in Jewish households are learning Jewish culture and ritual and perhaps half a million adults prefer to describe themselves as having "no religion." In addition, more than half of young people of Jewish background marry non-Jews. Others are more optimistic, pointing out that many secular Jews who claim no belief in God continue to attend synagogue, suggesting that a rising number of "mixed marriages" may attract new people to Judaism (Dershowitz, 1997; Goldscheider, 2004; Keister, 2003).

Hinduism

Hinduism is the oldest of all world religions, originating in the Indus River valley about 4500 years ago. Today, there are about 800 million Hindus, which is 12 percent of the world's people. Global Map 19–3 shows that Hinduism remains an Eastern religion, mostly practised in India

Window on the World

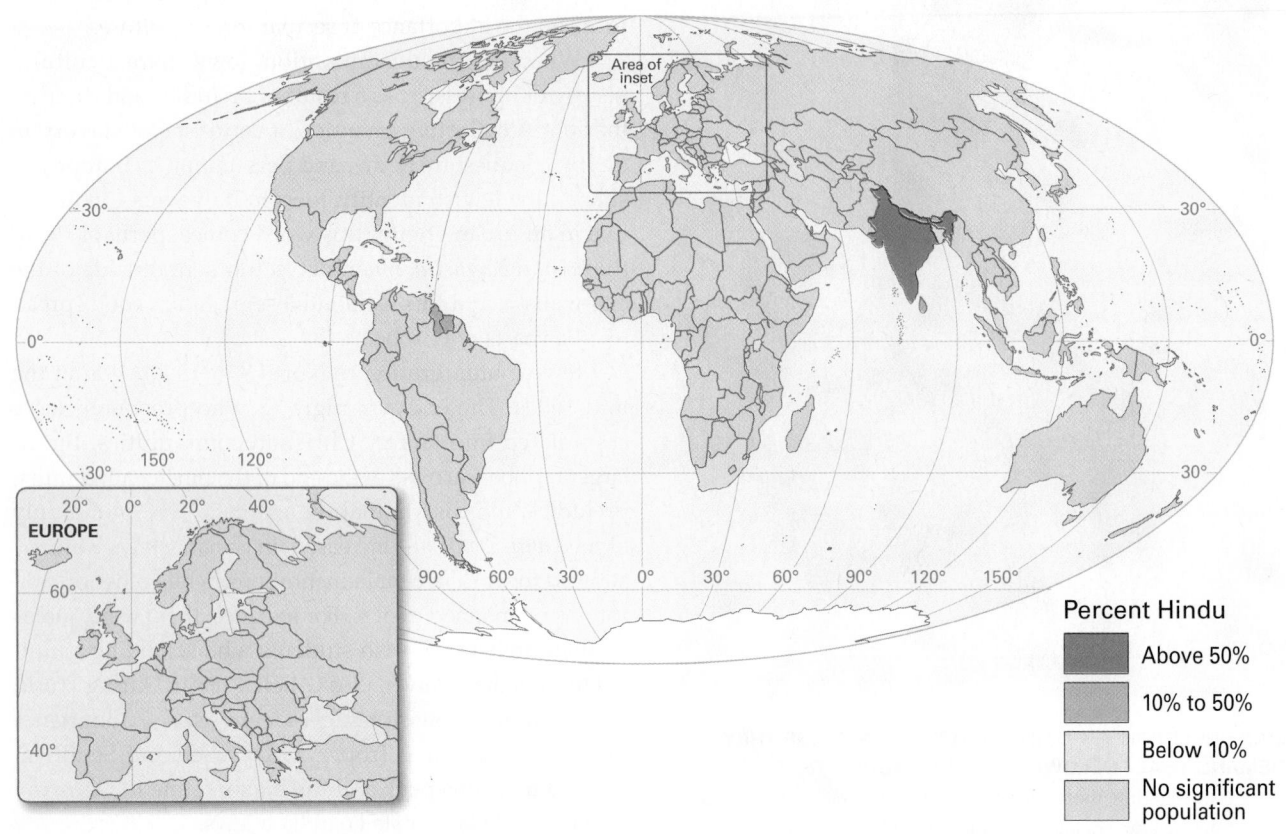

Global Map 19–3 Hinduism in Global Perspective

Hinduism is closely linked to the culture of India.

SOURCE: Association of Religion Data Archives (2012). [Online] Available at http://www.thearda.com/.

and Pakistan, but with a significant presence in southern Africa and Indonesia. Note, though, that these countries also have sizable Muslim populations.

Over the centuries, Hinduism and the culture of India have blended so that now one is not easily described apart from the other. This connection also explains why Hinduism—unlike Christianity, Islam, and Judaism—has not diffused widely to other nations. But with 1.5 million followers in North America—half a million in Canada—Hinduism is an important contributor to our cultural diversity.

Hinduism differs from most other religions in that it is not linked to the life of any single person. In addition, Hinduism envisions God as a universal moral force rather than a specific entity. For this reason, Hinduism (like other Eastern religions, as we shall show shortly) is sometimes described as an "ethical religion." Hindu beliefs and practices vary widely, but all Hindus believe that they have moral responsibilities, called *dharma*. Dharma, for example, calls people to observe the traditional caste system of India. Another Hindu principle, *karma*, involves a belief in the spiritual progress of the human soul. To a Hindu, each action has spiritual consequences and proper living results in moral development. Karma works through *reincarnation*, a cycle of death and rebirth by which a person is reborn into a spiritual state corresponding to the moral quality of a previous life. Unlike Christianity and Islam, Hinduism recognizes no ultimate judgment at the hands of a supreme god. But in the ongoing cycle of rebirth, it may be said that people get what they deserve. For those who reach *moksha,* the state of spiritual perfection, the soul will no longer be reborn.

The case of Hinduism shows that not all religions can be neatly labelled as monotheistic or polytheistic. Hinduism is monotheistic in so far as it views the universe as a single moral system, yet Hindus see this moral force at work in every element of nature. Hindus connect to this moral force through their private meditation and rituals, which vary from village to village across the vast nation of India. Many also participate in public events, such as the *Kumbh Mela,* which every 12 years brings some 20 million pilgrims to bathe in the purifying waters of the sacred Ganges River. (The ashes of Mahatma Gandhi, an Indian Hindu who gained worldwide renown for his pacifism, were spread over the Ganges.)

Window on the World

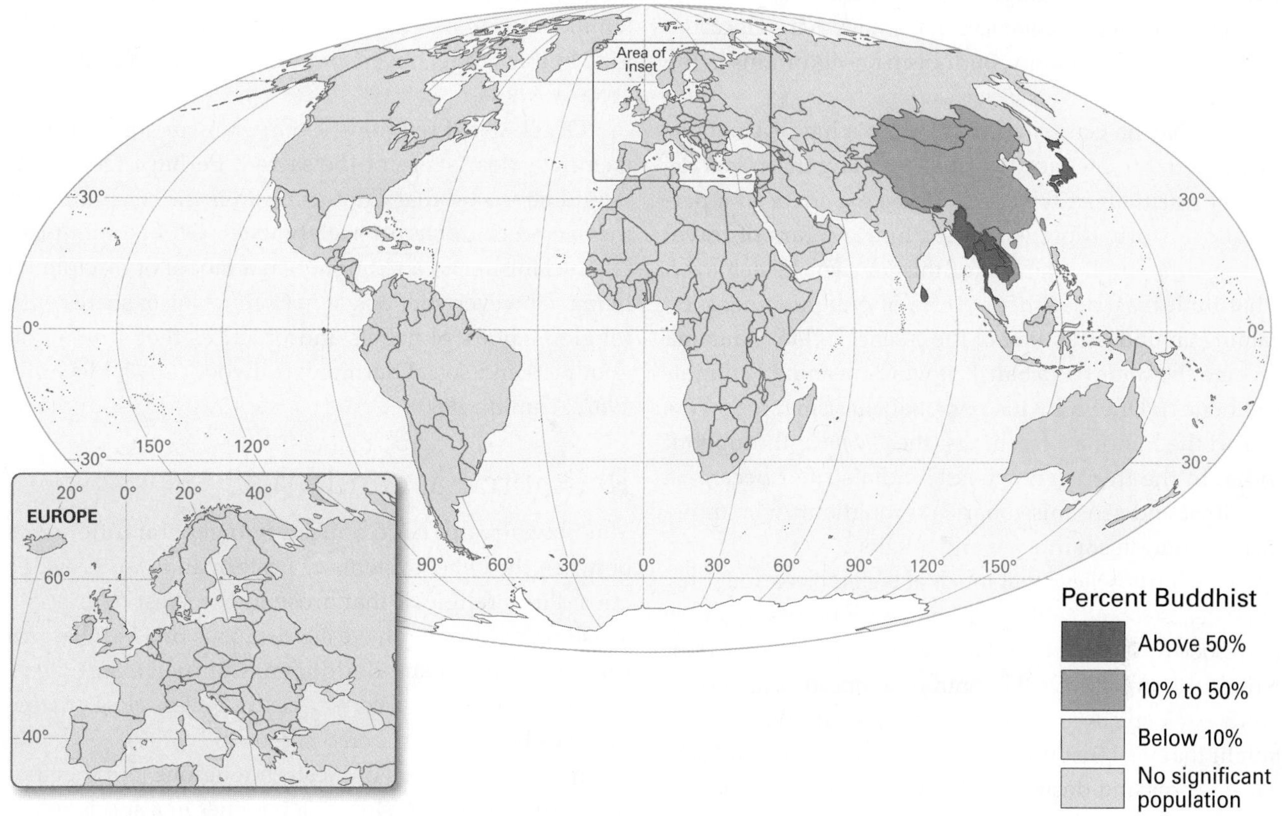

Global Map 19–4 Buddhism in Global Perspective

Buddhists represent a large part of the populations of most Asian nations.

SOURCE: Association of Religion Data Archives (2012). [Online] Available at http://www.thearda.com/.

Hinduism is not well understood in North America, although elements of Hindu thought have entered the "New Age" movement. Almost 2 million people in North America have East Indian ancestry, and the number of immigrants from India is rising; in Canada, the Indian community is composed almost equally of Hindus and Sikhs. The Hindu and Sikh religions are similar in many respects—the belief in karma and rebirth, and their roots in India—but diverse in others. Importantly, their adherents form distinct communities in Canada.

Geof Daniels/Eye Ubiquitous/Alamy Stock Photo

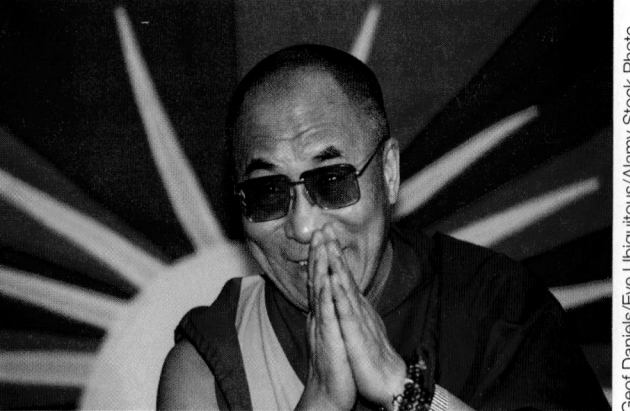

THE DALAI LAMA IS THE RELIGIOUS AND POLITICAL LEADER OF THE TIBETAN PEOPLE AND IS THE BEST-KNOWN BUDDHIST TEACHER IN THE WORLD He received the Nobel Peace Prize in 1989 for his efforts to liberate his people from Chinese control through non-violent means.

Buddhism

Twenty-five hundred years ago, the rich culture of India gave rise to Buddhism. Today, some 350 million people (5 percent of humanity) are Buddhists, and almost all live in Asia. As shown in Global Map 19–4, Buddhists are a majority of the population in Sri Lanka, Bhutan, Myanmar (Burma), Thailand, Cambodia, and Japan. Buddhism is also widespread in Vietnam, South Korea, Taiwan, and the People's Republic of China. In 2001, Canada's Buddhist population was slightly larger than the Hindu and Sikh populations—at about 300 000 people. By 2011, the Buddhist population had reached 367 000, the Sikh population 455 000, and the Hindu population 498 000 (or 1.1, 1.4, and 1.5 percent of the Canadian population).

Buddhism has much in common with Hinduism: It recognizes no god of judgment, sees each daily action as having spiritual consequences, and believes in reincarnation. But, like Christianity, Buddhism has its origins in the life of one person.

Siddhartha Gautama was born to a high-caste family in Nepal in 563 BCE. Even as a young man, he was deeply spiritual. At the age of 29, he experienced a personal transformation, which led him to years of travel and meditation. By the end of this journey, he achieved what Buddhists describe as *bodhi,* or enlightenment. By gaining an understanding of the essence of life, Gautama became the Buddha (a Sanskrit word meaning "enlightened one"). Drawn by his personal charisma, followers spread the Buddha's teachings (the *dhamma*) throughout India. In the third century BCE, India's ruler became a Buddhist and sent missionaries throughout Asia, transforming Buddhism into a world religion.

Buddhists believe that much of life involves suffering. This idea is rooted in the Buddha's own travels in a very poor society. But, the Buddha claimed, the solution to suffering is not wealth. On the contrary, a concern with money holds back spiritual development. Instead, the Buddha taught that we must use meditation to move beyond selfish concerns and desires. Only by quieting the mind can people connect with the power of the larger universe—the goal described as *nirvana,* a state of enlightenment and peace (Eck, 2001; Thomas, 1975; Van Biema, 1997).

Confucianism

From about 200 BCE until the beginning of the twentieth century, Confucianism was a state church, the official religion of China. After the 1949 revolution, the communist government of the emergent People's Republic of China repressed all religious expression. But even today, hundreds of millions of Chinese are influenced by Confucianism. China is still home to Confucian thought, although Chinese immigration has spread this religion to other nations in Southeast Asia. Perhaps 100 000 followers of Confucius live in North America.

Confucius, whose Chinese name was K'ung Fu-tzu (i.e., Master K'ung), lived between 551 and 479 BCE. Like the Buddha, Confucius was deeply moved by people's suffering. The Buddha's response was sectlike—a spiritual withdrawal from the world. Confucius took a more churchlike approach, instructing his followers to engage the world according to a code of moral conduct. In the same way that Hinduism became part of the Indian way of life, Confucianism became linked to the traditional culture of China.

A central idea of Confucianism is *jen,* meaning "humaneness." In practice, this means always placing moral principle above self-interest, looking to tradition for guidance in how to live. In the family, Confucius taught, each must be loyal and considerate. For their part, families must remember their duties to the larger community. In this model, layers of moral obligation unite society as a whole.

Of all world religions, Confucianism stands out as lacking a clear sense of the sacred. Perhaps Durkheim would have said that Confucianism is the celebration of the sacred character of society itself. Others might call Confucianism less a religion than a model of disciplined living. However you look at it, Confucianism shares with religion a body of beliefs and practices that seek moral goodness and social harmony (Ellwood, 2000; McGuire, 1987; Schmidt, 1980).

Religion: East and West

You may already have noticed two general differences between the belief systems of Eastern and Western societies. First, religions that arose in the West (Christian, Muslim, and Jewish) have a clear focus on God. Eastern religions (Hinduism, Buddhism, Confucianism), however, tend to be ethical codes; they make less clear-cut distinctions between the sacred and the profane.

Second, followers of Western religions join together in congregations, worshipping together in a special place at a regular time. Followers of Eastern religions, by contrast, express their religion in their daily lives. Temples do exist, but they are used by individuals as part of their daily routines rather than by groups according to a rigid schedule. In a country like Japan, temples are as likely to be filled with tourists along with worshippers.

Despite these two differences, however, all religions share a common element: a call to move beyond selfish everyday concerns in pursuit of a higher moral purpose. Religions may take different paths to this goal, but they all encourage a spiritual sense that there is more to life than what we see around us.

Religious Trends in Canada

19.5 Analyze patterns of religiosity in Canada.

Given that Canada is often depicted as a *secular,* or nonreligious, society—especially in comparison to the United States—it may surprise some of you to learn that 84 percent of Canadians tell pollsters that they believe in God. Furthermore, 67 percent say that "my religious faith is very important to my day-to-day life," and 69 percent believe in the resurrection of Jesus Christ (Bricker & Wright, 2005). While pointing to significant decline in religious service attendance (Bibby, 1995, 2004a), scholars

Table 19–1 Religious Affiliation and Immigrant Status for Selected Religions in Canada, 2001 and 2011

Religion	Population	Percentage of Population	Percentage Immigrant*		Percentage Recent Immigrant**	
			2001	2011	2001	2011
Canada (all religions)	32 852 320	100.0	18.4	20.6	6.2	6.6
Catholic	12 810 705	39.0	13.8	15.1	3.3	3.8
United Church	2 007 610	6.1	5.4	4.5	0.6	0.5
Anglican	1 631 845	5.0	13.7	12.9	1.5	1.4
Muslim	1 053 945	3.2	**71.7**	**68.3**	**47.6**	**36.8**
Baptist	635 840	1.9	15.5	18.0	4.9	5.6
Hindu	497 965	1.5	**71.9**	**70.4**	**39.9**	**30.9**
Pentecostal	478 705	1.5	17.7	24.7	5.7	8.6
Lutheran	478 185	1.5	21.2	17.7	1.5	1.5
Presbyterian	472 380	1.4	17.7	20.0	2.8	3.6
Sikh	454 965	1.4	**63.2**	**62.6**	**30.7**	**23.5**
Buddhist	366 830	1.1	**72.5**	**68.9**	**28.1**	**17.0**
Jewish	329 495	1.0	30.7	30.1	6.8	6.5
No religion	7 850 610	23.9	19.3	17.3	8.1	5.7

*Percentage Immigrant refers to the proportion of each population that was born outside Canada.

**Percentage Recent Immigrant refers to the proportion of each population that immigrated to Canada in the decade prior to each census.

SOURCE: Compilation and calculations by LM Gerber based on Statistics Canada, NHS 2011, Catalogue no. 99-010-X2011037.

continue to debate the extent and depth of our religiosity. While some claim that religion remains central to our way of life, others conclude that the decline of the traditional family and the growing importance of science are weakening religious faith.

Religious Affiliation

The Canadian census of 2001 revealed that 83 percent of us—compared to 85 percent of Americans—identified with a religion. As noted above, the same proportion of Canadians claimed belief in God (Bibby, 2004a). At that time, Canada was 73 percent Christian (Catholic and Protestant) with 16.6 percent declaring no religious affiliation. Ten short years later, the National Household Survey (Statistics Canada, 2011) revealed some significant changes (see Table 19–1). The proportion claiming no religious affiliation increased by 7 points to 24 percent, leaving 76 (not 83) percent to identify with one or another religion. Does this mean that fewer Canadians believe in God? Not necessarily, because "Nones" as Bibby (2004a) labels those with no religious affiliation, may still be spiritual, believe in God, and even attend religious services from time to time.

Since the proportion claiming no religion has increased by 7 percentage points and the four Eastern religions—Muslim, Hindu, Sikh and Buddhist—have increased their representation from 4.9 to 7.2 percent, it goes without saying that the mainstream Catholic and Protestant churches have lost ground. (The Sociology in Focus box deals with the question of the decline or renaissance of religion in Canada.)

Canada Map 19–1 provides clear evidence of one fact: There is nothing random about the distribution of people claiming no religious affiliation. With the exception of Nunavut, the proportion with "no religion" increases from east to west and north. Newfoundland and Labrador and Quebec have the smallest proportions at 6.2 and 12.1 percent—Nunavut at 12.9 percent. Ontario, Manitoba, and Saskatchewan have proportionately more "Nones" than Nunavut or any of the eastern provinces. The Northwest Territories and Alberta have 30 and 32 percent claiming no religion, but they come nowhere near points west. *British Columbia and the Yukon claim the distinction of having 44 and 50 percent reporting no religious affiliation.* Just think of it; the proportion claiming no religious affiliation increases from 6 percent on the east coast (in Newfoundland and Labrador) to an astonishing 50 percent on the extreme northwest (in the Yukon)!

A closer look at Table 19–1 allows for some interesting predictions of future patterns of growth or decline. The four columns on the right of the table indicate the impact of immigration on each religion or denomination.

The United Church, it appears, appeals to very few people who are born outside Canada. A mere 5 percent of its adherents are immigrants and less than 1 percent arrived in the ten years prior to each census date. Because the United Church wears a "made-in-Canada" label, it cannot rely on related congregations to supply new members through immigration. However, originating in Canada does not preclude growth through immigration. The Pentecostal Assemblies of Canada—over a thousand churches spread across the country—grew from 370 000

Sociology in Focus

Religion in Canada: Decline or Renaissance?

Reginald Bibby (1995) points out that, for the overall population of Canada, weekly attendance at religious services dropped off dramatically (from 60 to 25 percent) between 1945 and 1995. The decline was particularly dramatic for Roman Catholics in Quebec and mainline Protestant churches (United, Anglican, Presbyterian, and Lutheran) in the rest of the country. In 1995, weekly attendance was least common in Quebec and British Columbia (19 percent and 21 percent, respectively) and highest in the Atlantic region (38 percent). By 2000, weekly attendance had dropped to 22 percent (Bibby, 2004a), or 20 percent according to Ipsos-Reid polling (Bricker & Wright, 2005)—compared to 30 percent among Americans (NORC, 2003).

Michael Adams (2003, 2005), president of the polling firm Environics, carried out extensive research comparing values and social trends in Canada and the United States—revealing, through very sophisticated analysis, increasing divergence of values. Adams notes religious revival and fervour in the United States, a decline in religiosity (i.e., secularization) in Canada, and even different purposes and meanings of Canadian and American religiosity. In *Fire and Ice* (2003:186), Adams argues that, in Canada, religion is perceived as a means of "confronting the mysterious aspects of our lives" and honouring "the great imponderables of existence." In the United States, religion is the "source of strong moralist narratives and strict rules for personal conduct, [the] end of dialogue, not its beginning." In his opinion, religion, as the Americans know it, is clearly dead in Canada.

In two books, *Restless Churches* and *Restless Gods*, Reginald Bibby argues that the secularization thesis has been overstated and that there is real potential for significant religious renaissance or renewal in Canada (Bibby, 2004a, 2004b). On the basis of longitudinal research on religion in Canada, Bibby notes that, despite declining attendance, 84 percent of Canadians identify with a religion. In addition, 84 percent believe that God exists; 73 percent have spiritual needs; 68 percent believe in life after death; 47 percent have experienced God's presence; and 47 percent pray at least weekly. In a neat analysis of "Religious Nones" (the 16 percent of Canadians who declare no religion), Bibby reveals that membership in the "None" category is often temporary; furthermore, significant proportions believe in God, sometimes pray or attend church, and would consider more involvement in religious groups under certain conditions.

From Bibby's perspective, the mainline Christian churches (the Christian monopoly) can be optimistic. Very few people switch religious identities, but if they do,

they switch from one of the small religions (e.g., Jewish or Muslim) to Christianity (i.e., assimilation). People are also unlikely to switch between Christian categories. The "growth" of fundamentalist or evangelical churches is no widespread revival, as they have been singularly unsuccessful in gaining converts. Their growth stems from their ability to retain children and geographically mobile members. Fundamentalists made up 8 percent of the Canadian population from 1871 to 2001, meaning that their church growth kept pace with population growth. Since evangelical churches have the highest attendance levels, and their members are more public about their faith than other Canadians (on television and in person), they are highly visible and thus *appear* to be taking over. If the Catholic and mainline Protestant churches can figure out how to gather their own "dropouts" back into the fold *and* hold on to their children, they can generate a renaissance.

To project future attendance, Frank Jones (2000) used data from the National Longitudinal Survey of Children and Youth (1994–1995) to look at religious observance among Canadian children under age 12. He found that 23 percent of Canada's children attend religious services weekly—a level that is consistent with that in the total population—and 36 percent attend at least once a month. Jones points out that regular attendance among children varies by age, sex, region, and religious affiliation. Children in Atlantic Canada had the highest weekly or monthly attendance rate (52 percent), while those in Quebec had the lowest (19 percent). If the mainline Christian churches can hold on to these children (and, later, *their* children), a modest revival will be under way.

Three polls pegged adult weekly attendance rates at 30 percent, 26 percent, and 27 percent, bringing us very close to the American 30 percent noted above. Bibby (2004a:23) concludes, "Think of it: one in four Canadian adults in services on any given weekend . . . some five million people—plus lots of kids. There is no other group activity in Canada that begins to compare with such a level of involvement." In his latest book, Bibby (2011) revised his analysis to say that Canadians are at opposite poles on the religion continuum—from the very religious at one end to those claiming no religion at the other. He sees the potential for revitalization at one end with steadfast secularization at the other.

What Do You Think?

1. Were you under the impression that the fundamentalists or evangelicals were taking over?

2. Are you surprised to learn that American weekly attendance rates are only slightly higher than ours?

3. Do you see any signs of religious revival among the people you know?

Seeing Ourselves

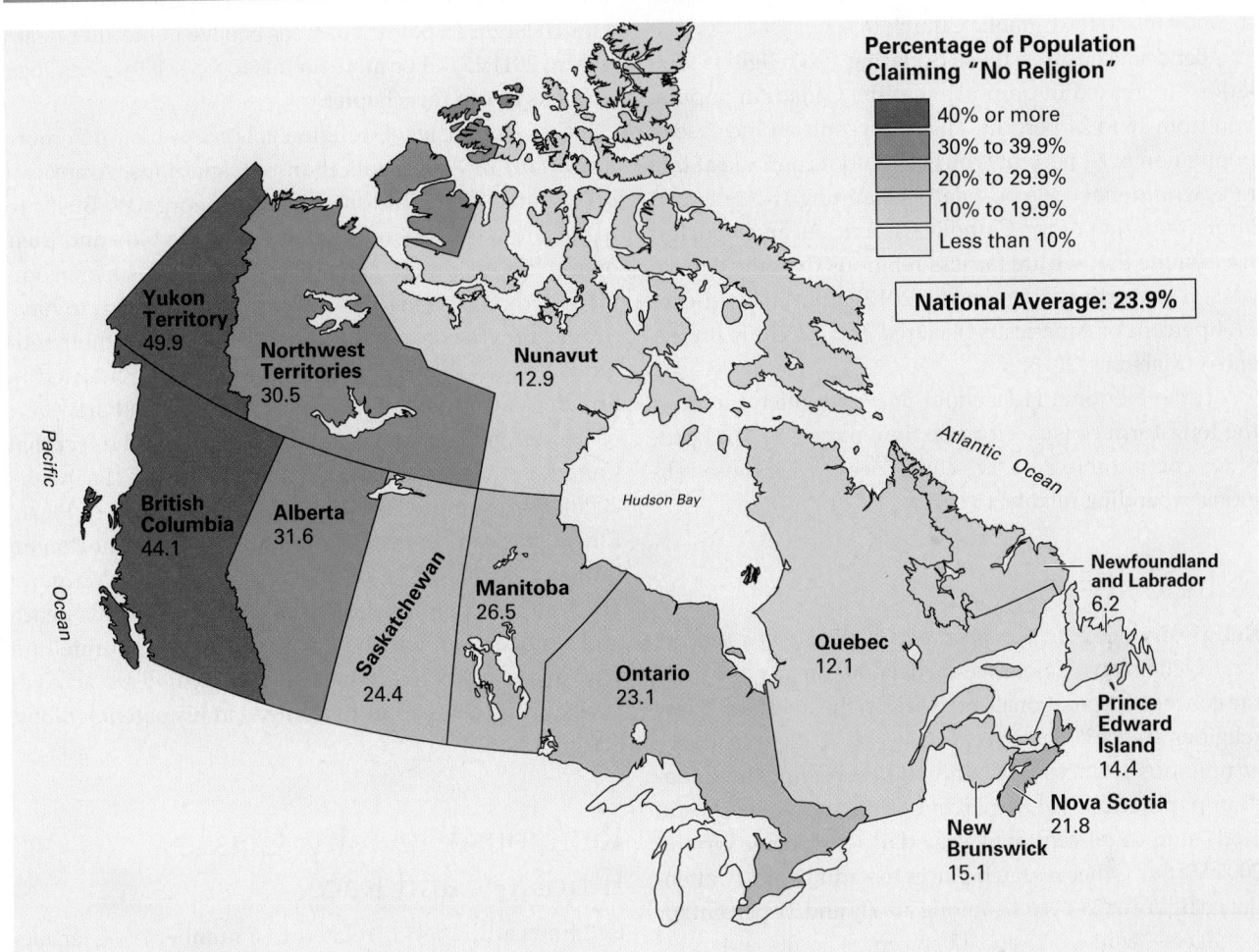

Percentage of Population Claiming "No Religion"

- 40% or more
- 30% to 39.9%
- 20% to 29.9%
- 10% to 19.9%
- Less than 10%

National Average: 23.9%

Yukon Territory 49.9

Northwest Territories 30.5

Nunavut 12.9

British Columbia 44.1

Alberta 31.6

Saskatchewan 24.4

Manitoba 26.5

Ontario 23.1

Quebec 12.1

Newfoundland and Labrador 6.2

Prince Edward Island 14.4

Nova Scotia 21.8

New Brunswick 15.1

Hudson Bay

Pacific Ocean

Atlantic Ocean

Canada Map 19–1 Canadians Claiming "No Religion" by Province and Territory, 2011

SOURCE: Compilation and calculations by LM Gerber based on Statistics Canada, NHS 2011, Catalogue no. 99-010-X2011037.

to 480 000 between census years. Pentecostals differ from other Protestants in their emphasis on direct personal relationships and communication with God. This appears to attract new recruits, including immigrants, to the point where Pentecostals have the largest proportion immigrant of any Christian denomination: 25 percent immigrant and 6 percent *recent* immigrant. As such, they will experience substantial growth in the future.

Catholics, Anglicans, Baptists, Lutherans, and Presbyterians are all extensions of European churches—the result being that immigrants can maintain ties with their churches of origin after crossing the Atlantic. These Christian churches experience moderate increases through immigration: 13 to 20 percent (Presbyterian) of their adherents are immigrants; 1.5 to 5 percent (Baptist) are recent immigrants.

The population claiming Jewish affiliation actually declined (by 500) between 2001 and 2011—despite the fact that 30 percent of the population is immigrant

and a healthy 7 percent is *recent* immigrant. Whatever the reasons for this decline—low fertility, emigration to the United States, or intermarriage—Jews are not alone. Among the Christian denominations only the Pentecostals increased their population—by 110 000.

Table 19–1 tells a very different story about the Eastern religions. All four increased their representation within the Canadian population between 2001 and 2011 through immigration—including recent immigration. Their immigrant components dwarf those of any of the other religions, ranging from 63 to 70 percent. Even more significant is the fact that their adherents include large proportions of recent immigrants—28 percent of Buddhists to a phenomenal 48 percent of Muslims. The Buddhist population grew by 22 percent, Sikhs by 63 percent, Hindus by 68 percent, and Muslims by *82 percent!* With no doubt whatsoever, one can predict continued growth for all four religions; if the rates of growth and decline persist, when questions of religious affiliation are included in the census of 2021, we may well find that Muslim affiliation surpasses that of the United Church, leaving Muslims second only to the Catholic Church in size.

Between censuses, those declaring "no religious affiliation" increased in proportion to the Canadian population from 16 to 24 percent. That represents an increase in population of 64 percent which, should it continue at that rate, would make the population claiming "no religion" larger than that of the Catholic Church. As an aside, lest we assume that we are far less religious than the Americans, it is worth noting that (in 2012) a not insignificant 21.4 percent of Americans declared "no religious preference" (Macionis, 2016).

If the National Household Survey (which replaced the long-form census—for one time only—in 2011) provides comparable data, we can expect to see these religions expanding relative to others.

Religiosity

Religiosity refers to *the importance of religion in a person's life.* Exactly how religious we are depends on precisely how the concept is operationalized. Clearly, the question "How religious are we?" has no easy answer: Weekly attendance at religious services is down to 20 percent of the Canadian population, yet 84 percent of us say we believe in God—and 45 percent of us pray daily (Bricker & Wright, 2005:80, 84). Other research places the adult weekly attendance figure at 25 percent among adults and 21 percent for teenagers—whereas 23 and 47 percent of adults and teens, respectively, never attend (Bibby, 2001:51).

If asked, most of you would assume that Americans are much more religious than Canadians. Certainly that's what the media would lead us to expect. In the 1940s, weekly church attendance in Canada "was over 60% while U.S. attendance was closer to 40%. Today U.S. attendance is still around 40%, while ours is half that" (Bricker & Wright, 2005:80). Actually, NORC (2003) puts the American figure at 30 percent. If you were to measure religiosity by church attendance, 20 percent weekly attendance would suggest that religion in Canada is almost dead, and 30 percent in the United States places American religion just behind Canada's on that downward spiral. But 81 percent of Canadians told Ipsos-Reid pollsters that "you don't need to go to church to be a good Christian" (Bricker & Wright, 2005:80). In other words, Canadians measure religiosity by more than attendance at church services.

The fact that 83 percent of us (and 85 percent of Americans) identify with a religion may mean little, but the fact that 45 percent of us (and 56 percent of Americans) pray daily is *highly* significant. People who pray daily take their religion very seriously—even if they do not attend services—so, depending on the measure you use, you could argue for religious decline or renaissance

in Canada. On another note, even though few people attend religious services weekly, 65 percent of adults and a much larger 75 percent of teens believe in life after death (Bibby, 2011:171). For more on this topic, see the Sociology in Focus box in this chapter.

On another level, religion *appears* to be much more important to Americans than to Canadians. American politicians—Bill Clinton, Al Gore, George W. Bush, to name a few—made frequent references to God and their own religious practices, and prayer breakfasts are common. Although Canadian politicians are known to have prayer breakfasts, they generally downplay their religious beliefs—as Stephen Harper did when he tried to broaden the appeal of the new Conservative Party. Part of the difference in appearances stems from the fact that Canadians are more private about their faith (Lachaine, 2006). For example, it was only after the death of Pierre Elliott Trudeau that we learned he was a devout Roman Catholic (Krauss, 2003); according to his wife, Margaret Trudeau, he spent his last days talking about his death and resurrection, which he believed would reunite him with his son Michel, who had been killed by an avalanche while cross-country skiing, and his parents (Bibby, 2004b:127).

Religious Diversity: Class, Ethnicity, and Race

Religious affiliation is related to a number of other factors, including social class, ethnicity, and race.

SOCIAL CLASS Historically, Canada has been stratified along religious lines. By and large, Protestants with high social standing are people of northern European background. Members of the Anglican Church, and later the other establishment Protestant churches, have long been among Canada's most affluent, powerful people. Anglophone political and economic dominance, and traditional Catholic doctrine, kept Catholics in Quebec subordinate and poor.

Much has changed over the years, but some of these old patterns are still apparent. Table 19–2, which provides data on educational attainment and labour force participation, is based on populations aged 25–54 for the simple reason that, by age 25, most people have completed their schooling and entered their prime working years. For each religion, the table provides data on the percentage with no certification (meaning that they have not completed high school or its equivalent), with trades or apprenticeship certificates, and with university certification at the bachelor's level or above.

The level of non-certification (lacking high school graduation) is lowest among Jews at 3 percent. The Presbyterian, Lutheran, and United Churches are also

Table 19–2 Educational Attainment and Labour Force Participation among 25- to 54-Year-Olds for Selected Religions in Canada, 2011

Religion	Population ages 25 to 54	Eductional Certification (%) None	Trades	Bachelor's or higher	Labour Force Participation (%) Participation Rate	Employment Rate	Unemployment Rate
Canada (all religions)	14 044 940	11.2	11.8	27.6	85.8	80.5	6.2
Catholic	5 409 430	11.7	**15.2**	24.4	87.4	**82.7**	5.5
United Church	689 905	8.6	10.6	26.1	**88.8**	84.7	4.6
Anglican	593 080	11.8	10.7	24.2	85.7	80.0	6.7
Muslim	481 500	10.0	5.7	**44.7**	72.6	63.7	**12.3**
Baptist	246 480	10.4	10.9	25.0	84.3	78.8	6.5
Hindu	239 615	9.8	4.3	**44.3**	82.9	75.8	**8.5**
Pentecostal	199 565	**13.3**	**12.5**	18.6	82.8	76.1	**8.1**
Lutheran	175 755	8.5	**12.2**	24.6	**89.4**	**85.8**	4.1
Presbyterian	168 955	7.7	8.5	29.2	**87.1**	**82.3**	5.5
Sikh	200 000	**13.7**	4.4	30.6	85.0	78.8	7.2
Buddhist	181 890	**21.2**	6.4	29.7	80.5	74.0	**8.2**
Jewish	116 740	3.0	3.9	**59.8**	87.8	83.2	5.3
No religion	3 702 840	11.2	10.4	28.6	85.8	80.3	6.4

SOURCE: Compilation and calculations by LM Gerber based on Statistics Canada, NHS 2011, Catalogue no. 99-010-X2011037.

unlikely to lack certification (about 8 percent); Hindus follow at 10 percent. Buddhists (at 21 percent) are the most likely to lack even high-school certification; the only others who are above average on this measure are Sikhs and Pentecostals at 14 and 13 percent.

Trades certification levels give rise to some interesting observations. Catholic (15 percent), Pentecostal (12 percent), and Lutheran (12 percent) religions have the highest levels of trade certification whereas, of all the Christian denominations, Presbyterians have the lowest (8 percent). The first three religions are more appealing to blue-collar workers than is the Presbyterian denomination with it British roots. The Jewish, Sikh, and Hindu populations have the lowest levels of trades certification of all (4 percent), followed by Muslims and Buddhists at 6 percent. The pattern is very clear: Jews have the lowest level of trades certification (3.9 percent); the four Eastern religions come next with 4.3 to 6.4 percent; Presbyterians have the lowest level of trades certification among Christian denominations (8.5 percent); while the rest range from 11 to 15 percent (among Catholics).

The Jewish population is the most highly educated of all; *60 percent* of 25- to 54-year-olds have university certification at the bachelor's level or above. The Jewish rate is more than double the Canadian average. Muslims and Hindus come next with 45 and 44 percent holding bachelor's or postgraduate certification—they are followed by Sikhs and Buddhists at 31 and 30 percent. The remarkable thing is that *all* of the Christian denominations trail behind the Jewish and Eastern religions in terms of

educational credentials. Among the Christian churches, the attainment of higher level university credentials decreases from 29 percent of Presbyterians to 19 percent of Pentecostals.

Do higher levels of educational attainment lead to greater labour force participation and employment? Not necessarily. It is important, at this point, to understand that the *employment rate* refers to the percentage of each population that was employed (full or part time) in the year prior to the census. The *unemployment rates*, often discussed in the media, are based on labour force participants—not on the total population. We exclude stay-at-home mothers, retirees, and full-time students (who are not working) from our calculation of the unemployment rate; it refers only to those who are either employed or actively seeking work.

Whereas one might expect educational attainment to be related to employment outcomes, in fact only those identifying with the Jewish religion have high levels of university education coupled with high labour force participation and employment rates—along with low unemployment rates. Almost half of Muslims and Hindus have their bachelor's degrees or postgraduate qualifications, but their employment rates are low. Despite high levels of educational attainment, Muslims have the lowest participation and employment rates of all religions (73 and 64 percent)—as well as the highest unemployment rate (12 percent or double the Canadian average). There are many possible reasons for this stark disparity: 40 percent of Muslims arrived in Canada in the ten years prior to the census, so that many may find their credentials are not recognized by employers; they may encounter prejudice and discrimination unrelated to credentials; and there may be cultural restrictions on the labour force participation of women. Being relative newcomers, it may be a decade or two before Muslim employment profiles reflect their high levels of education.

The overall pattern suggests that the *highest* participation and employment rates—as well as the *lowest* unemployment rates—are found among those adhering to the Catholic, United Church, Lutheran, Presbyterian, and Jewish religions. Anglicans and Baptists are on the second rung, just above Sikhs, Pentecostals, Hindus, and Buddhists. Muslims, at this point in time, lag behind the others—in large part because of recent immigration.

On the basis of Table 19–2, we can conclude that the major Protestant denominations, which are long-established in Canada, have high social standing that stretches back over many generations. The ranking of religious categories by education and employment reveals, until we have evidence to the contrary, that stratification along religious lines is commonplace. The old established religions—United Church, Anglican, Presbyterian, and Lutheran—have high social standing without relying on higher level educational credentials. They have been at the top of Canada's vertical mosaic for many years. Jews—and now Catholics—have broken through many of the barriers to high social status and, in all likelihood, Hindus and Muslims will follow suit.

ETHNICITY Throughout the world, religion is tied to ethnicity, mostly because a single religion stands out in specific countries or geographic regions. Islam predominates in the Arab societies of the Middle East; Hinduism is fused with the culture of India; and Confucianism runs deep in Chinese society. Christianity and Judaism do not follow this pattern; while these religions are mostly Western, Christians and Jews are found all over the world.

Religion and national identity come together in Canada, as well. We have, for example, Anglo-Saxon Protestants, Irish Catholics, Russian Jews, and Greek Orthodox adherents. This linking of nation and creed results from the influx of immigrants from nations with a single major religion, or from societies where large numbers of a particular religious group emigrated, perhaps to escape persecution. Still, nearly every ethnic category displays some religious diversity. People of English ancestry, for instance, may be Protestants, Roman Catholics, Jews, or followers of other religions.

Religion in a Changing Society

All social institutions evolve over time. Just as the economy, politics, and the family have changed over the course of the past century, so has our religious life.

Secularization

Secularization refers to *the historical decline in the importance of the supernatural and the sacred.* Secularization (from Latin, meaning "the present age") is commonly associated with modern, technologically advanced societies in which science is the major way of understanding.

Secularization was at the core of the Quiet Revolution in Quebec during the 1960s. The Catholic Church—which had administered welfare, health care, and education in addition to dealing with the spiritual needs of Quebec society—lost influence on the religious front, while giving up its social service involvement to the provincial government. Today, Canadians are more likely to experience the transitions of birth, illness, and death in the presence of physicians (with scientific knowledge) than of religious leaders (whose knowledge is based on faith). This shift alone suggests that religion's relevance to our everyday lives has declined. Harvey Cox explains:

> The world looks less and less to religious rules and rituals for its morality or its meanings. For some, religion provides a hobby, for others a mark of national or ethnic identification, for still others an aesthetic delight. For relatively few does it provide an inclusive and commanding system of personal and cosmic values and explanations. (1971:3; orig. 1965)

If Cox is right, should we expect religion to disappear some day? Most sociologists say no. As noted above, the vast majority of people in Canada and the United States still say that they believe in God, and about half of us claim to pray each day. In addition, 70 percent or more of Canadians and Americans claim a religious identification or affiliation. Canadian society is not on the road to complete secularization. While church attendance has declined, other measures of our beliefs suggest that religion is alive and well—or even undergoing a renaissance (Bibby, 2004a, 2004b).

An important measure of secularization is the proportion of the Canadian population reporting "no religion." Between 1986 and 1990, the proportion claiming "no religion" increased from 10 to 12 percent (Baril & Mori, 1991)—before climbing to 16 percent in 2001 and 29 percent in 2011. Science and higher education have been blamed for secularization, but people claiming "no religion" are spot on average in terms of percent immigrant, measures of educational attainment, and employment (see Table 19–2).

Whether religious change is good or bad is open to debate. Conservatives tend to see any weakening of religion as a mark of moral decline. Progressives view secularization as liberation from the all-encompassing belief systems of the past, giving people more choice in their beliefs. Secularization has also helped bring the practices of some religious organizations—such as ordaining only men—into line with widespread social attitudes that support greater gender equality.

According to the secularization thesis, religion should weaken in high-income nations as people enjoy higher living standards and greater security. A global perspective shows that this thesis holds for the countries of Western Europe, where most measures of religiosity have declined and are now low. But in the United States—the richest country of all—religion remains strong and may even be getting stronger. Canada, which falls between Europe and the United States on so many measures, may be closer to the Americans on the religious front than many of us realize.

"New Age" Seekers: Spirituality without Formal Religion

December 29, Machu Picchu, Peru. *We are ending the first day exploring this magnificent city built by the Inca people high in the Andes Mountains. Lucas, a local shaman, or religious leader, is leading a group of twelve travelers in a ceremony of thanks. He kneels on the dirt floor of the small stone building and places offerings—corn and beans, sugar, plants of all colours, and even bits of gold and silver—in front of him as gifts to Mother Earth as he prays for harmony, joy, and the will to do good for one another. His words and the magic of the setting make the ceremony very moving.* [John J. Macionis]

In recent decades, an increasing number of people are seeking spiritual development outside of established religious organizations, leading some analysts to conclude that we are becoming a *post-denomination society*. In simple terms, more people seem to be spiritual seekers, believing in a vital spiritual dimension to human existence that they pursue more or less separately from membership in any formal denomination.

What exactly is the difference between this focus on spirituality and a traditional concern with religion? One analysis (Cimino & Lattin, 1999:62) comments that spirituality is

> the search for . . . a religion of the heart, not the head. It's a religious expression that downplays doctrine and dogma, and revels in direct experience of the divine— whether it's called the "holy spirit" or "divine consciousness" or "true self." It's practical and personal, more about stress reduction than salvation, more therapeutic than theological. It's about feeling good rather than being good. It's as much about the body as the soul.

Millions of North Americans take part in a spirituality movement referred to as "New Age"; its adherents are called "seekers." Anthropologist and spiritual teacher Hank Wesselman (2001:39–42) identifies five core values that define this approach:

- **Seekers believe in a higher power.** There exists a higher power, a vital force that is within all things and all people. Humans, then, are partly divine.

- **Seekers believe that we're all connected.** Everything and everyone is interconnected as part of a universal divine pattern.

- **Seekers believe in a spirit world.** The physical world is not all there is; a more important spiritual reality (or "spirit world") also exists.

- **Seekers want to experience the spirit world.** Spiritual development means gaining the ability to experience the spirit world. Many seekers come to understand that helpers and teachers who dwell in the spirit world can and do touch their lives.

- **Seekers pursue transcendence.** Various techniques (such as yoga, meditation, and prayer) give people an increasing ability to rise above the immediate physical world (i.e., through the experience of "transcendence"), which is seen as the larger purpose of life.

From a traditional point of view, this New Age concern with spirituality may seem more like psychology than religion. It avoids judgments about right and wrong in favour of encouraging all of us to grow as we move through life. It has become an important new form of religious expression in the modern world—one that blends

Phil Date/Shutterstock

NEW AGE SEEKERS ARE PEOPLE IN PURSUIT OF SPIRITUAL GROWTH, OFTEN USING THE AGE-OLD TECHNIQUE OF MEDITATION The goal of this activity is to quiet the mind so that, by moving away from everyday concerns, one can hear an inner, divine voice. Countless people attest to the spiritual value of meditation; it has also been linked to improved mental and physical health. Mindfulness has taken on a life of its own in Canada, where it is recommended by health professionals, practised in some workplaces, and included in school programs.

traditional belief with modern tolerance and rationality—that is gaining popularity, especially among highly educated people (Besecke, 2003, 2005; Tucker, 2002; Wuthnow, 2003).

Religious Revival: "Good Old-Time Religion"

At the same time as New Age spirituality is becoming more popular, a great deal of change has been going on in the world of organized religion. In the United States, membership in liberal mainstream denominations (such as Episcopalian and Presbyterian) has declined steadily since 1960. During the same period, affiliation with more conservative religious organizations (including the Mormons, the Seventh-Day Adventists, and especially Christian sects) has risen steadily. In Canada, between 1981 and 1991, Presbyterian membership decreased by 22 percent, United Church by 18 percent, Anglican and Lutheran by 10 percent, and Baptist by 5 percent. In the meantime, most of the smaller, often evangelical, denominations grew significantly. Secularization itself may be self-limiting so that, as churchlike organizations become more worldly, people abandon them in favour of sectlike religious communities that offer a more intense religious experience (Stark & Bainbridge, 1981). More recently, Bibby (2004a, 2004b) notes the potential for religious renaissance among not only fundamentalist but also mainstream churches.

Religious Fundamentalism

Fundamentalism is *a conservative religious doctrine that opposes intellectualism and worldly accommodation in favour of restoring traditional, otherworldly religion.* In the United States, fundamentalism has made the greatest gains among Protestants; Southern Baptists, for example, are the largest religious community in that country. But fundamentalism has also grown among Jews (i.e., Orthodox) and Catholics (i.e., Opus Dei).

Canada has fundamentalists or evangelicals among Baptists and Lutherans; Pentecostals are evangelical, as are most of the megachurches (like the one discussed in the opener to this chapter) that have popped up all over the country. The Peoples' Church in Toronto, with a congregation of about 3000, is an example of an *old* evangelical megachurch; it already had a congregation of 2000 or more in the 1960s. An interesting thing about evangelical churches is that they made up 8 percent of our population in 1871, 8 percent in 1951, and 8 percent in 2001 (Bibby, 2004a:39). As was discussed in the Sociology in Focus box, their secret is being able to hold on to their children. Their numbers have grown in proportion to the increase in Canada's population.

In response to what they see as the growing influence of science and the weakening of the conventional family, religious fundamentalists defend what they call "traditional values." As they see it, liberal churches are simply too open to compromise and change. Religious fundamentalism is distinctive in five ways (Hunter, 1983, 1985, 1987):

- **Fundamentalists take the words of sacred texts literally.** Fundamentalists insist on a literal reading of sacred texts such as the Bible to counter what they see as excessive intellectualism among more liberal religious organizations. For example, fundamentalist Christians believe that God created the world in seven days precisely as described in the biblical book of Genesis.

- **Fundamentalists reject religious pluralism.** Fundamentalists believe that tolerance and relativism water down personal faith; therefore, they maintain that their religious beliefs are true and other beliefs are not.

- **Fundamentalists pursue the personal experience of God's presence.** In contrast to the worldliness and intellectualism of other religious organizations, fundamentalism seeks a return to "good old-time religion" and spiritual revival. To fundamentalist Christians, being "born again" and having a personal relationship with Jesus Christ should be evident in a person's everyday life.

- **Fundamentalists oppose "secular humanism."** Fundamentalists think that accommodation to the changing world weakens religious faith. They reject "secular humanism," our society's tendency to look to scientific experts rather than God for guidance about how to live. There is nothing new in this tension between science and religion; it has existed for several centuries, as the Controversy and Debate box explains.

- **Many fundamentalists endorse conservative political goals.** Although fundamentalism tends to back away from worldly concerns, some fundamentalist leaders have entered politics to oppose what they call the "liberal agenda," including feminism and gay rights. Fundamentalists oppose abortion and gay marriages, support the traditional two-parent family, seek a return to prayer in schools, and criticize the mass media for colouring stories with a liberal bias. In Canada, these were elements of fundamentalism or social conservatism in the "hidden agenda" that the Canadian Alliance (under Stephen Harper) was accused of carrying into the federal elections of 2004 and 2006.

Opponents regard fundamentalism as rigid and self-righteous. But many people find in fundamentalism, with its greater religious certainty and emphasis on the

Controversy and Debate

Does Science Threaten Religion?

About 400 years ago, Italian physicist and astronomer Galileo (1564–1642) helped start the Scientific Revolution with some startling discoveries. Dropping objects from the Leaning Tower of Pisa, he derived laws of gravity; making his own telescope, he observed the stars and found that Earth orbited the sun. Galileo was challenged by the Roman Catholic Church, which had preached for centuries that Earth stood motionless at the centre of the universe. Galileo made matters worse by responding that religious leaders had no business talking about matters of science. Soon he found his work banned and himself under house arrest. The treatment of Galileo shows that, from the start, science has had an uneasy relationship with religion.

Galileo certainly would have been an eager observer of the famous "Scopes monkey trial," when science and religion clashed over the issue of creation. In 1925, the state of Tennessee put a small-town science teacher named John Thomas Scopes on trial for teaching Darwinian evolution in the local high school. Charles Darwin's master work, *On the Origin of Species,* states that humanity evolved from lower forms of life over billions of years. But this theory counters the biblical account of creation found in Genesis, which states that "God created the heavens and the earth," introducing life on the third day and, on the fifth and sixth days, animal life—including human beings fashioned in God's own image. Tennessee state law forbade teaching "any theory that denies the story of the Divine Creation of man as taught in the Bible" and, in particular, the idea that "man descended from a lower order of animals." Scopes was found guilty and fined $100. His conviction was reversed on appeal, but the Tennessee law stayed on the books until 1967. A year later in *Epperson* v. *Arkansas,* the U.S. Supreme Court struck down all such laws as unconstitutional government support of religion.

Today—almost four centuries after Galileo was silenced—people still debate the apparently conflicting claims of science and religion. For example, a third of American adults believe that the Bible is the literal word of God and reject any scientific findings that run counter to it (NORC, 2003:157). But a middle ground is emerging: Half of Americans now accept the Bible as a book of truths inspired by God without being correct in a literal, scientific sense. That is, they recognize that science and religion are

Gary Braasch/Bettmann/Corbis

different ways of understanding different questions. While Canadians do not debate this issue as openly, some of the growth of "home schooling" can be attributed to concerns about the public school curriculum.

While Galileo and Darwin devoted their lives to investigating *how* the natural world works, religion deals with *why* we and the natural world exist in the first place. In 1992, a Vatican commission concluded that the church's silencing of Galileo was wrong. Most scientific and religious leaders now agree that science and religion represent important but different truths. Many also believe that today's rush to scientific discovery leaves our world in greater need of the moral guidance provided by religion.

But what do students think about religion, science, and the meaning of life? A survey of students at one small east coast university and one large urban campus in Ontario found that most students consider themselves to be religious (58 percent) and scientific (64 percent) (Campbell, 2005). Most also find themselves disagreeing with family or friends over religious and scientific issues (61 percent and 57 percent, respectively), while 84 percent think—often or sometimes—about the meaning of life. Significantly, 88 percent indicate that it is possible to be both religious and scientific. So questions of religion, science, and the meaning of life matter to students—and they can integrate all three in their lives.

What Do You Think?

1. Can a religious individual be an objective scientist?
2. Does the sociological study of religion challenge one's faith? Why or why not?
3. Many people think that scientific discovery is changing our lives too fast. Do you agree? Why or why not?

SOURCES: Based on Applebome (1996), Campbell (2005), Gould (1981), and Huchingson (1994).

---

emotional experience of God's presence, an appealing alternative to the more intellectual, tolerant, and worldly "mainstream" denominations (Marquand & Wood, 1997).

Which religions are fundamentalist? In recent years, the world has become familiar with an extreme form of fundamentalist Islam that is intolerant of other beliefs and even supports violence against Western cultures and people. In North America, the term is most correctly applied to conservative Christian organizations in the evangelical tradition, including Pentecostals, Southern Baptists, Seventh-Day Adventists, and Assemblies of God.

Sociology and the Media

Check the Media: Religion Is Hot!

Six hundred years ago in medieval Europe, face-to-face contact was required for transmitting religious ideas: Clerics gathered in universities or monasteries to study, later transmitting their knowledge to the masses attending religious services. Bibles and other sacred texts, hand copied by monks, were rare, until Johannes Gutenberg, a German inventor, built a movable-type press and published the first printed book—a Bible—in 1456. Within 50 years, millions of books were in print across Europe, most of them about religious matters. Printing of the Bible, the Qur'an, and other religious texts put the word of God into the hands of virtually anyone—not just the clergy, religious leaders, and scholars. Without printed Bibles, the Protestant Reformation would not have occurred.

In the twentieth century, radio (beginning in the 1920s) and television (after 1950) extended the reach of religious leaders, who founded "media congregations" no longer confined to buildings. There was a time when *100 Huntley Street* was a radio program aired only in Toronto; now it is the flagship show for the Crossroads Television System, founded by evangelist David Mainse, which broadcasts religious and family programming from its headquarters in Burlington, Ontario. This is only one of the many radio and television stations that air religious programming throughout Canada. Many listeners and viewers attend services regularly, but others may have no religious affiliation, or mobility problems make it impossible for them to attend services in person. In short, electronic communication has created what Marshall McLuhan might have called a "church without walls," allowing "live" programming to enter our homes though instant communication.

Today, we have access to a wide range of books (e.g., *Restless Gods* as well as *Restless Churches* by Canadian sociologist Reginald Bibby) and magazines dealing with religion. Newspapers keep tabs on religious developments— like the spread of evangelical megachurches, the decline of religion in a secular Canada, or the decline of organized religion with the persistence of faith or spirituality. In fact, a pervasive newspaper debate revolves around whether religion is in decline or renaissance. One of the most

watched movies of 2004 was Mel Gibson's *Passion of the Christ,* which portrays the final days of Jesus's life and his crucifixion. As well, Dan Brown's books *The Da Vinci Code* and *Angels & Demons* have sold millions of copies worldwide in multiple languages—despite the fact that the Catholic Church, Opus Dei, and other religious leaders oppose them. Kathy Reichs's *Cross Bones* picks up on a similar theme. However disturbing these books might be to the Christian establishment, they deal with basic religious issues.

It takes only a few minutes online to discover that religion is alive and well on the internet. You can find electronic Bibles, a proverb a day, and prophecies, as well as announcements of events, products, publications, and conventions. Chat groups, university or college courses, monthly magazines, and prayer groups provide opportunities for active religious participation. Today, hundreds of thousands of websites offer messages from established churches, obscure cults, and New Age organizations.

With more information out there than ever before, some analysts anticipate a new post-denominational age in which religious ideas are no longer bound by particular organizations. Electronic information technology may also usher in an age of "cyber-churches." Television has already shown that it can transmit the personal charisma and spiritual message of religious leaders to ever-larger audiences. Perhaps the internet will create "virtual" congregations, larger than any before.

What Do You Think?

1. More and more religious organizations are using the internet to spread their messages. Do you think this will strengthen or weaken religion?

2. Are you attuned to media coverage of religious issues? Is it because you are religious or spiritual? Are you just curious?

3. Have you read *The Da Vinci Code*? If so, did it change the way you think about religion?

SOURCES: Based on Adams (2005), Bibby (2004a, 2004b), Casey (2006), Lachaine (2006), and Ramo (1996).

The Electronic Church

In contrast to small village congregations of years past, some religious organizations—especially fundamentalist ones—have become electronic churches featuring "prime-time preachers" (Hadden & Swain, 1981). Electronic religion in the United States has propelled Oral Roberts, Pat Robertson, and others to greater prominence than all but a few clergy in the past. Canadian "televangelists"

David Mainse and Terry Winter, true to the "Canadian personality," were relatively low-key and have exhibited fewer public "sins" (Bibby, 1987:34–36). In Canada, about 5 percent of the national television audience regularly tunes in to religious television. Moreover, the majority of people who watch religious programs on television are also regular churchgoers, with almost 80 percent church attendance either weekly (68 percent) or monthly (11 percent). Recently, an increasing number of religious organizations are using computer technology to spread their message, a trend that Pope John Paul II termed the "new evangelism."

Religion: Looking Ahead

The popularity of media ministries, the rapid growth of religious fundamentalism, and the continuing adherence of millions more people to mainstream churches show that religion will remain a major institution of modern society. Moreover, high levels of immigration from many religious regions (e.g., Asia, India, Africa, the Caribbean, and the Middle East) will intensify and diversify the religious character of Canadian society in decades to come.

In addition, the pace of social change is accelerating. As the world becomes more complex, rapid change seems to outstrip our capacity to make sense of it all. But, rather than undermining religion, this process fires the religious imagination of people who seek a sense of religious community and ultimate meaning in life. Tensions between the spiritual realm of religion and the secular world of science and technology will surely continue.

Science is simply unable to provide answers to the most basic human questions about the purpose of our lives. Moreover, new technology that can begin and sustain life confronts us with vexing moral dilemmas as never before. Against this backdrop of uncertainty, it is little wonder that many people rely on their faith for guidance and hope.

Seeing Sociology in Everyday Life

CHAPTER 19   Religion

How religious is our society?

We may agree that the United States is quite religious for a postmodern, secular society. While we admit that Canada falls between the United States and Europe with respect to religious behaviour, we may not know that Canadians are closer to Americans than to Europeans on most measures of religiosity. Many Canadians, who do not have strong ties to the religions of their parents or grandparents, still feel the need to invoke religion, or at least its rituals, for funerals, weddings, and births—or in celebrating a wide range of "holy days" or holidays.

> **Hint** How many of us celebrate Christmas, Easter, Passover, Hanukkah, the Feast of Ramadan or Eid ul-Fitr (feasts before and after a month of fasting) for its social or traditional rather than religious significance? Each of these meals confirms the importance of family and links us to a broader society. These special occasions, which might involve gatherings of family, neighbours, and friends, usually include ritual activities as well as the sharing of specific foods and beverages.

Exactostock-1527/SuperStock

AT THANKSGIVING, FAMILIES GATHER TO SHARE A SPECIAL DINNER AND GIVE THANKS FOR THEIR GOOD FORTUNE Although Thanksgiving originated with the Pilgrims as they thanked God for bringing them safely to the New World, the concept of giving thanks can be embraced by almost anyone. Many of the people who celebrate Thanksgiving in October give little thought to its Christian origins.

IN AUGUST 2002, FRIENDS AND FAMILY GATHERED FOR A COMMITMENT CEREMONY CELEBRATING THE LOVE OF THIS SAME-SEX COUPLE Although the first ceremony was a "wedding" in all but name, it was only on the first anniversary of this ceremony that the two women were able to marry legally (when the Court of Appeal made same-sex marriage legal in Ontario).

MARRIAGE ACROSS RELIGIOUS, CULTURAL, AND RACIAL LINES IS INCREASINGLY COMMON IN POSTMODERN SOCIETIES.

Seeing Sociology in *Your* Everyday Life

1. In the United States some colleges are very religious, and many universities have religious roots. This is less obvious in Canada, but several of our universities were started by Catholics, and McMaster University (in Hamilton, Ontario) owes its existence to the educational commitments of Baptists as far back as the 1830s. McMaster has a Divinity College and houses the Canadian Baptist Archives. Investigate the place of religion on your campus. Is your school affiliated with a religious organization? Was it ever? Is there a chaplain or other religious official? Do you or your campus friends or acquaintances attend religious services?

2. Develop five questions that might be used on a questionnaire or in an interview to measure how religious people are. Present them to several people. Do your results on religiosity depend on the nature of the questions you asked?

3. Is religion getting weaker? To evaluate the claim that our society is undergoing secularization, go to the library or local newspaper office and obtain an issue of your local newspaper published 50 or 100 years ago. Compare the amount of attention given to religious activities and issues then and now. What patterns do you see?

Making the Grade

CHAPTER 19 Religion

Religion: Concepts and Theories

19.1 Apply sociology's major theories to religion.

- Religion is a major social institution based on setting the *sacred* apart from the *profane*.
- Religion is grounded in *faith* rather than scientific evidence, and people express their religious beliefs through various rituals.

profane an ordinary element of everyday life
sacred set apart as extraordinary, inspiring awe and reverence
religion a social institution involving beliefs and practices based on recognizing the sacred
ritual formal, ceremonial behaviour
faith belief based on conviction rather than on scientific evidence

Theories of Religion

Structural-functional theory describes how people celebrate the power of society through religion. Émile Durkheim identified three major functions of religion:

- Religion unites people, promoting social cohesion.
- Religion encourages people to obey cultural norms, promoting conformity.
- Religion gives meaning and purpose to life.

Symbolic-interaction theory explains that people use religion to give everyday life sacred meaning.

- People create rituals that separate the sacred from the profane.
- Peter Berger claimed that people are especially likely to seek religious meaning when faced with life's uncertainties and disruptions.

Social-conflict theory highlights religion's support of social inequality.

- Karl Marx claimed that religion justifies the status quo and diverts people's attention from social injustice.
- In this way, religion discourages change toward a more just and equal society.

Feminist theory highlights the fact that major religions have traditionally been patriarchal, supporting the domination of women by men. A number of major religious organizations bar women from serving as religious leaders.

totem an object in the natural world collectively defined as sacred

Religion and Social Change

19.2 Discuss the links between religion and social change.

- Max Weber argued, in opposition to Marx, that religion can encourage social change. He showed how Calvinism became "disenchanted," leading to a profane "Protestant work ethic" that contributed to the rise of industrial capitalism.
- Liberation theology, a fusion of Christian principles and political activism, tries to encourage social change.

liberation theology the combining of Christian principles with political activism, often Marxist in character

Types of Religious Organizations

19.3 Distinguish among church, sect, and cult.

Churches are religious organizations well integrated into their society. They formally train and ordain leaders and have a highly formal style of worship. Churches fall into two categories: *state churches* (examples: the Anglican Church in England and Islam in Morocco) and *denominations* (examples: Christian denominations such as Baptists and Lutherans, as well as various categories of Judaism, Islam, and other traditions).

Sects are the result of religious division. They are marked by charismatic leadership and members' suspicion of the larger society.

Cults are religious organizations based on new and unconventional beliefs and practices.

church a type of religious organization that is well integrated into the larger society
state church a church formally allied with the state
denomination a church, independent of the state, that recognizes religious pluralism
sect a type of religious organization that stands apart from the larger society
charisma extraordinary personal qualities that can infuse people with emotion and turn them into followers
cult a type of religious organization that is largely outside a society's cultural traditions

Religion in History and around the World

19.4 Contrast religious patterns around the world.

- Hunting and gathering societies practiced animism, viewing elements of the natural world as spiritual forces.
- Belief in a single divine power began in pastoral and horticultural societies.
- Organized religion gained importance in agrarian societies.
- In industrial societies, scientific knowledge explains *how* the world works, but people look to religion to answer questions about *why* the world exists.

World Religions

- **Christianity** is the most widespread religion, with 2.3 billion followers—almost one-fourth of the world's people.
- Christianity began as a cult built on the personal charisma of Jesus of Nazareth; Christians believe Jesus is the Son of God and follow his teachings.
- **Islam** has about 1.6 billion followers, who are known as Muslims—almost one-fifth of the world's people.
- Muslims follow the word of God as revealed to the prophet Muhammad and written in the Qur'an, the sacred text of Islam.
- **Judaism's** 14 million followers are mainly in Israel and the United States.
- Jewish belief rests on the covenant between God and his chosen people, embodied in the Ten Commandments and the Old Testament of the Bible.
- **Hinduism** is the oldest world religion and today has about 800 million adherents.
- Hindus see God as a universal moral force rather than a specific being and believe in the principles of *dharma* (moral responsibilities) and *karma* (the spiritual progress of the human soul).
- **Buddhists** number about 350 million people.
- Buddhist teachings are similar to Hindu beliefs, but Buddhism is based on the life of one person, Siddhartha Gautama, who taught the use of meditation as a way to move beyond selfish desires to achieve *nirvana*, a state of enlightenment and peace.
- **Confucianism** was the state church of China until the 1949 Communist revolution repressed religious expression. It is still strongly linked to Chinese culture.
- Confucianism teaches *jen*, or "humaneness," meaning that people must place moral principles above self-interest. Layers of moral obligations unite society as a whole.

animism the belief that elements of the natural world are conscious life forms that affect humanity
monotheism belief in a single divine power
polytheism belief in many gods

Religious Trends in Canada

19.5 Analyze patterns of religiosity in Canada.

Canada is one of the most religiously diverse nations. How researchers operationalize "religiosity" affects how "religious" our people seem to be:

- 83 percent of adults identify with a religion; 24 percent claim no religion
- 84 percent of us believe in God
- 45 percent of us pray daily
- 25 percent of Canadians attend religious services weekly

Religious affiliation is tied to social class, race, and ethnicity:

- The major Protestant denominations (United, Anglican, and Presbyterian) and Jews enjoy high social standing; lower social standing is typical of Catholics, Baptists, and Pentecostals, among others. Muslims and Hindus, with large proportions having university degrees or higher, are in a state of transition.
- Religion is often linked to ethnic background because people come to Canada from countries that have a major religion like Catholicism or Islam.
- **Secularization** involves a decline in the importance of the supernatural and sacred.
- In Canada, membership in mainstream churches has declined, whereas membership in cults and fundamentalist churches has increased.
- Spiritual seekers are part of the "New Age" movement, which pursues spiritual development outside conventional religious organizations.
- **Fundamentalism** opposes religious accommodation to the world, interprets religious texts literally, and rejects religious diversity.

religiosity the importance of religion in a person's life
secularization the historical decline in the importance of the supernatural and the sacred
fundamentalism a conservative religious doctrine that opposes intellectualism and worldly accommodation in favour of restoring traditional, otherworldly religion

Chapter 20
Education

∨ Learning Objectives

20.1 Compare schooling in high-, middle-, and low-income societies.

20.2 Apply structural-functional theory to schooling.

20.3 Apply symbolic-interaction theory to schooling.

20.4 Apply social conflict theory to schooling.

20.5 Discuss violence, dropping out, and other problems facing today's schools.

20.6 Discuss home schooling and the impact of gender on educational outcomes.

The Power of Society
to open the door to higher education

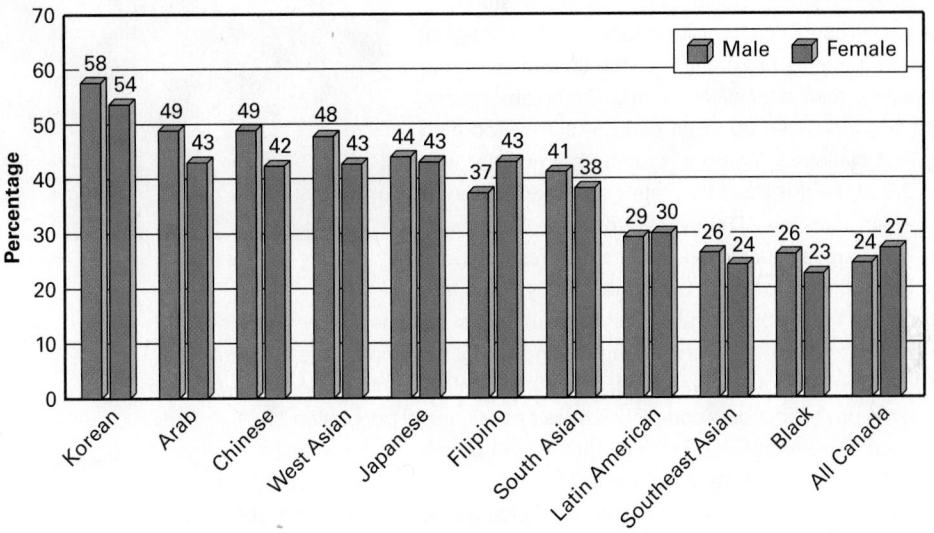

SOURCES: Compilation and calculations by LM Gerber based on Statistics Canada, NHS 2011, Catalogue no. 99-010-X2011036.

Historically, immigrants have acquired higher levels of education than the Canadian-born—so it should be no surprise to learn that this is true of our visible minorities, the majority of whom are immigrants (and even recent immigrants). In fact, men in each of the visible minorities are more likely to have certification at the bachelor's level and above than the average Canadian male. Korean, Arab, Chinese, and West Asian men are at least twice as likely to have such credentials as are Canadian men as a whole. With the exception of Southeast Asians and Blacks, visible minority women are also more likely to have university-level credentials than the average Canadian woman. In some categories women lag behind men; in others they are almost equal; and among Filipinos and "Canadians" women pull ahead of men. Not only does immigration policy favour the well-educated, but people who have the energy and ambition to immigrate tend to encourage their children to pursue higher education as well.

Chapter Overview

This chapter explains the operation of education, a major social institution. The chapter begins with a global survey of schooling and then focuses on education in Canada.

"If you're an Indian in your twenties living on a reserve, you need to leave right now." When *Globe and Mail* columnist John Ibbitson (2006) opened a column with those words, he raised many hackles—notably of readers, Aboriginal and non-Aboriginal, who oppose the forces of assimilation.

Ibbitson reached this conclusion after reading a study by Michael Mendelson of educational achievement among Aboriginal Canadians between the ages of 20 and 24—the time most young adults are completing their education. Among Canadians at that time, 16 percent of those aged 20 to 24 had not completed high school. Among First Nations living on a reserve, that number was *58 percent*—or 3.6 times the Canadian rate—and there were no signs of improvement from the 1996 census to the 2001 census. The efforts made to improve educational outcomes on reserves had not worked; so, according to Ibbitson, our education systems had "utterly failed to rescue the latest generation" of on-reserve First Nations.

There is a brighter side to this story. Young urban Aboriginal people have twice the high school completion rates of those on reserves, and Aboriginal students "who do finish high school have the same post-secondary completion rates as the general population." Furthermore, urban Aboriginal people have average incomes that are 80 percent of the average income of Torontonians, 77 percent of the average income of Montrealers, and 75 percent of the average income of Ottawa residents. However controversial Ibbitson's advice, one can see why he advised Aboriginal young people on reserves to "[p]ack your bags, say goodbye to your family and friends and get out of there. . . . Move to Toronto or Ottawa or Montreal. Find a job, any job, then get yourself back in school." ∎

Most young people in Canada dream of higher education as the passport to good jobs. But, especially for people growing up in low-income, low-education families, the odds of getting to college or university are small. Who goes on to post-secondary education in Canada? What is the impact of higher education on the type of job you get or the money you make later? This chapter answers these questions by focusing on **education**, *the social institution through which society provides its members with important knowledge, including basic facts, job skills, and cultural norms and values.* In high-income countries such as Canada, education is largely a matter of **schooling**, *formal instruction under the direction of specially trained teachers.*

education the social institution through which society provides its members with important knowledge, including basic facts, job skills, and cultural norms and values

schooling formal instruction under the direction of specially trained teachers

Education: A Global Survey

20.1 Compare schooling in high-, middle-, and low-income countries.

Currently, Canadian young people spend most of their first 18 years in school; however, in our distant past the privilege of schooling was limited to a small elite. In the 1830s in Upper Canada, only half of the children attended school—for an average of 12 months in total (Johnson, 1968:27). In low-income countries today—as was the case in Upper Canada—the vast majority of people receive little or no schooling.

Schooling and Economic Development

The extent of schooling in any society is tied to its level of economic development. In low- and middle-income countries, which are home to most of the world's people, families and communities teach young people important knowledge and skills. Formal schooling, and especially learning that is not directly connected to survival, is available mainly to wealthy people who do not need to work. After all, the Greek root of the word *school* means "leisure." In ancient Greece, famous teachers such as Socrates, Plato, and Aristotle taught aristocratic, upper-class men. The same was true in ancient China, where the famous philosopher K'ung Fu-tzu (Confucius) shared his wisdom with a privileged few.

Today, the limited schooling that takes place in lower-income countries reflects the national culture. In Iran, for example, schooling is closely tied to Islam. Similarly, schooling in Bangladesh (Asia), Zimbabwe (Africa), and Nicaragua (Latin America) has been shaped by the distinctive cultural traditions of these nations.

All lower-income countries have one trait in common when it comes to schooling: There is not very much of it. In the world's poorest nations (including several in Central Africa), more than one-fourth of all children never get to school at all (World Bank, 2015). Worldwide, more than one-fourth of all children never reach secondary school. As a result, about one-sixth of the world's people cannot read or write. Global Map 20–1 shows the extent of illiteracy around the world, and the following national comparisons illustrate the link between the extent of schooling and economic development.

Schooling in India

India has recently become a middle-income country, but people there still earn only about 10 percent of U.S. average income, and most poor families depend on the earnings of children. Even though India has outlawed child labour, many children continue to work in factories weaving rugs or making handicrafts—up to 60 hours per week, which greatly limits their chances for schooling.

Today, 97 percent of children in India complete primary school, typically in crowded schoolrooms where one teacher may face as many as 40 children. Ninety-two percent of students in India go on to secondary school, but just 25 percent enter college. Currently about a quarter of India's population is unable to read and write (UNESCO, 2015: World Bank, 2015).

Patriarchy also shapes Indian education. Indian parents are joyful at the birth of a boy, because he and his future wife will both contribute income to the family. In contrast, there are economic costs to raising a girl: Parents must provide a dowry (a gift of wealth to the groom's family), and, after her marriage, a daughter's work benefits her husband's family. Therefore, many Indians

Antony Njuguna/Reuters/Landov

IN MANY LOW-INCOME NATIONS, CHILDREN ARE AS LIKELY TO WORK AS THEY ARE TO ATTEND SCHOOL, AND GIRLS RECEIVE LESS SCHOOLING THAN BOYS But the doors to education are now opening to more girls and women. These young women are studying nursing at Somalia University in downtown Mogadishu.

see less reason to invest in the schooling of girls. What do the girls do while the boys are in school? Most of the children working in Indian factories are girls—a family's way of benefiting from their daughters while they can (UNESCO, 2015).

Schooling in Japan

Schooling has not always been part of the Japanese way of life. Before industrialization brought mandatory education in 1872, only a privileged few attended school. Today, Japan's educational system is widely praised for producing some of the world's highest achievers.

The early grades concentrate on transmitting Japanese traditions, especially a sense of obligation to family. Starting in their early teens, students take a series of difficult and highly competitive examinations. Scores on these written tests decide the future of Japanese students.

More men and women graduate from high school in Japan (99 percent) than in Canada or the United States. But Japan's competitive examinations allow just half of high school graduates to go on to post-secondary studies. Understandably, Japanese students (and their parents) take entrance examinations very seriously. About half attend "cram schools" to prepare for the exams that require very late nights completing homework.

Japanese schooling produces impressive results. In a number of fields, notably mathematics and science, Japanese students (who rank fourth in the world in science and reading and sixth in mathematics) outperform students in almost every other high-income nation, including Canada and the United States (World Bank, 2015).

Window on the World

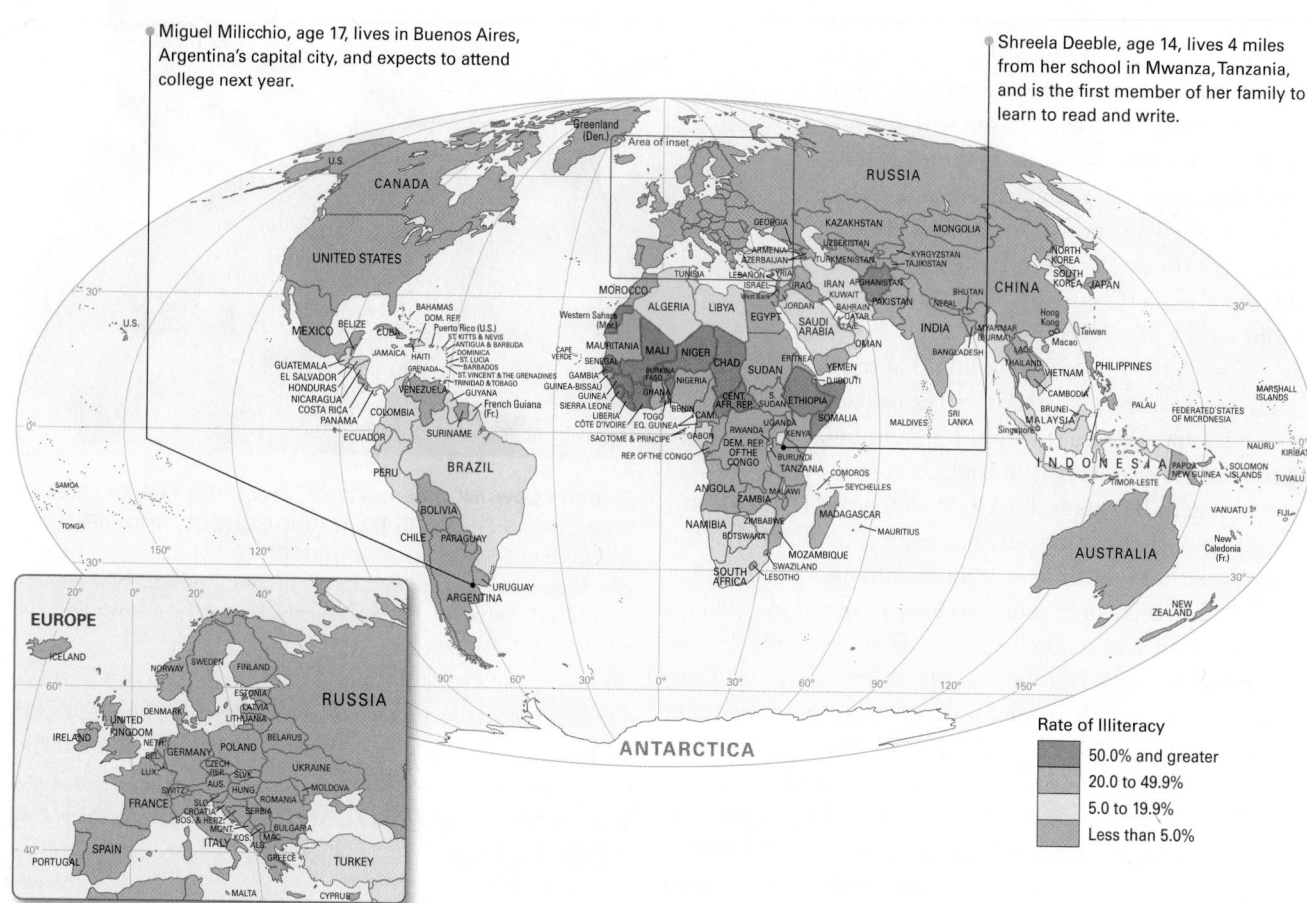

Miguel Milicchio, age 17, lives in Buenos Aires, Argentina's capital city, and expects to attend college next year.

Shreela Deeble, age 14, lives 4 miles from her school in Mwanza, Tanzania, and is the first member of her family to learn to read and write.

Rate of Illiteracy

- 50.0% and greater
- 20.0 to 49.9%
- 5.0 to 19.9%
- Less than 5.0%

Global Map 20–1 Illiteracy in Global Perspective

Reading and writing skills are widespread in high-income countries, where illiteracy rates generally are below 5 percent. In much of Latin America, however, illiteracy is more common, one consequence of limited economic development. In 14 nations—almost all of them in Africa—illiteracy is the rule rather than the exception; there people rely on the oral tradition of face-to-face communication rather than the written word.

SOURCE: Based on UNESCO (2015).

Schooling in Great Britain

During the Middle Ages, schooling was a privilege of the British nobility, who studied classical subjects, having little concern for the practical skills needed to earn a living. But as the Industrial Revolution created a need for an educated labour force and as working-class people demanded access to schools, an increasing proportion of the population entered the classroom. British law now requires every child to attend school until age 16.

Traditional class differences still affect British schooling. Most wealthy families send their children to what the British call *public schools* and we would call private boarding schools. These elite schools enrol about 7 percent of British students and teach not only academic subjects but also the special patterns of speech, mannerisms, and social

graces of the British upper class. Because these academies are very expensive, most British students attend state-supported day schools (Department for Children, Schools, and Families, 2015).

The British have tried to reduce the importance of social background in schooling by expanding the university system and by linking admission to competitive entrance examinations. For those students who score the highest, the government pays most of the costs. But many well-to-do children who do not score very well still manage to get into Oxford or Cambridge, the most prestigious British universities. Many "Oxbridge" graduates go on to positions at the top of the British power elite; for example, most of the highest-ranking members of the British government—including Prime Minister Theresa May—have "Oxbridge" degrees.

These brief sketches of schooling in India, Japan, and Great Britain show the crucial importance of economic development. In poor countries, many children—especially girls—work rather than attend school. Rich nations enact mandatory education laws to prepare an industrial workforce as well as to satisfy demands for greater equality. But a nation's history and culture still matter, as we see in the intense competition of Japanese schools, the traditional social stratification that shapes schools in Great Britain, and the practical emphasis found in Canadian schools.

Schooling in Canada

Initial developments in education in what would later become Canada took place in the early French settlements, where the three Rs—in this case, reading, writing, and religion—were taught in church-controlled schools (Johnson, 1968). By 1636, the Jesuits had established a *"collége"* that eventually became *Laval University,* which claims to be *North America's oldest institution of higher education.* By 1668, a trade or vocational school had been established in St. Joachim. In the Maritimes, an Anglican academy established in 1785 became the University of New Brunswick in 1859. The earliest primary schools in Upper Canada, which were established in the 1780s, began receiving government funding in 1792. Elite boarding schools, started in 1807, were the first step in establishing a secondary school system.

Canadian schooling in the early 1800s was heavily influenced by Britain and the Anglican Church. In addition to a Christian focus, schooling in the early years emphasized a "correct" set of values—meaning those that supported the existing stratification system—with "the grammar school curriculum for children of the upper classes emphasizing the classics and the common schools for children of the working class emphasizing learning by rote and appropriate behaviour." Of course, appropriate behaviour involved dressing neatly, carrying out routine tasks under supervision, and showing up on time. It was Egerton Ryerson (after whom Ryerson University is named) who introduced "tax-supported free schooling and secular schools within a centralized education department" (Barakett & Cleghorn, 2008:9).

Under the *British North America Act* of 1867 (now the *Constitution Act* of 1982), education was made a provincial responsibility; as a result, we now have a ministry or department of education in every province. Each provincial system incorporated separate Catholic and Protestant schools that were already in place and, in some cases, separate English and French schools (Barakett & Cleghorn, 2008).

By the time of Confederation in 1867, governments in Canada had already embraced universal education and

teacher training and put texts and curricula under the control of a department of education. Shortly thereafter, in 1883, Toronto became the second North American city to establish kindergarten within the school system. By about 1920, Canada had compulsory education to the end of elementary school or the age of 16 in most provinces. In this period, secondary schools were being established and expanded across Canada. The principle of mass education had been firmly entrenched, partly in response to the requirements of the Industrial Revolution for a literate and skilled workforce.

In Canada, the school reformers of the late 1800s were concerned that the "classical curriculum did not reflect the realities of the new economic order. Thus, education came to be viewed as an essential precondition for national economic growth" (Gilbert, 1989:105). Wide participation and universality were important goals. Canada also has a policy of universal, publicly supported primary and secondary schooling, with a separate Catholic system. We now have close to 300 publicly funded post-secondary institutions, 98 of which are classified as universities. Tuition fees at our universities cover up to 30 percent of the costs—except for specific professional programs—while government subsidies and fundraising account for the rest.

The percentage of the population aged 15 and older with university degrees rose from 6 percent in 1976 to 21 percent in 2011. In other words, over this 35-year period, the proportion of people aged 15 and older with university degrees more than tripled. Among adults aged 25 to 64, the proportion with university degrees rose from 19 percent in 1996 to 26 percent in 2011. NHS 2011 revealed that 64 percent of Canadians (aged 25 to 64) have some kind of post-secondary certification.

Besides trying to make schooling more widely accessible, Canadian society has long favoured *practical* learning—that is, education that has a direct bearing on people's lives, and especially on their occupations. Educational philosopher John Dewey (1859–1952) advanced the idea that children would readily learn information and skills they found useful. Rejecting the traditional emphasis on teaching a fixed body of knowledge to each generation of students, Dewey (1968; orig. 1938) endorsed progressive education that reflected people's changing concerns and needs. With the Quiet Revolution in Quebec in the 1960s, the classical education favoured by the religious elite was replaced by a system encouraging the study of business, engineering, and science.

Despite the overall trend toward applied or practical fields, in the early 1990s Canada lagged behind a number of other countries in awarding engineering degrees. In fact, in Canada, the proportion of degrees granted in engineering—to both men and women—was less than half that of Belgium, Portugal, Finland, Japan, Sweden,

Germany, and Denmark (Oderkirk, 1993:10). Since then, the situation has improved. From 1994 to 1998, a very short period of time, the proportion of degrees granted in engineering and applied sciences increased from 7.1 to 7.5 percent, while those granted in mathematics and the physical sciences increased from 5.4 to 5.8 percent. Although the measure is different, the 2001 census revealed that 10.2 percent of 25- to 29-year-olds with university degrees received them in engineering and applied sciences, while another 8.4 percent studied math, computer science, and the physical sciences (Statistics Canada, 2009c). Nineteen percent of university certification in 2007 was in the fields of physical/life sciences, mathematics and computer science, engineering, and related areas (Statistics Canada, 2009d). The shift toward these fields is gradual but consistent, as is the involvement of women in engineering and applied sciences—currently at 25 percent.

Another reform, which took hold in Canada as part of the French immersion movement, was initially an experiment undertaken in Montreal. A few French immersion programs (essentially pilot projects) were studied very carefully (for 16 years) by McGill University and declared both safe and successful—before Quebec's ministry of education adopted the concept for general use. The fear was that the anglophone students, schooled in French from kindergarten through grade 3, would experience negative effects in their English-language skills. Since then French immersion programs have spread to every province in Canada, involve some 400 000 students at any given time, and boast approximately 2 million people with immersion in their backgrounds (Barakett & Cleghorn, 2008:63). It is clear today, after 30 years of experience, that "immersion students outperform non-immersion students in reading," but that may be because of their higher socio-economic backgrounds (Statistics Canada, 2012d).

A report based on the Pan-Canadian Assessment Program, which tests 13-year-olds in the 10 provinces and Yukon in reading, mathematics, and science, concluded that Quebec came in significantly above the Canadian average in all three subject areas. Quebec came first in reading and mathematics, and second to Alberta in science. Ontario, which fared much worse in previous studies, has pulled up its socks to score above the Canadian average in reading and mathematics, and average in science. British Columbia is consistently below average in the three subject areas, while the Atlantic and Prairie provinces trail behind. It seems that where you live in Canada affects the quality of education you receive in the primary grades (Canada, 2007).

Despite efforts to promote literacy, Canada still has concerns in this area. It is important to note that official literacy and functional literacy are not the same.

Although Canada claims to have minimal illiteracy by international standards, educators and others have long voiced concerns about the extent to which Canadians have the literacy and numeracy skills required to cope with daily living and work—to say nothing of academic pursuits. **Functional illiteracy** is *a lack of the reading and writing skills needed for everyday living*—reading road signs or product labels and calculating tips, for example. The Thinking Critically box takes a close look at functional illiteracy in Canada.

The Functions of Schooling

20.2 Apply structural-functional theory to schooling.

Structural-functional theory looks at the ways in which formal education supports the operation and stability of society. We look briefly at five ways that this happens.

Frank Siteman/PhotoEdit, Inc.

EDUCATORS HAVE LONG DEBATED THE PROPER MANNER IN WHICH TO EDUCATE CHILDREN WITH DISABILITIES On the one hand, such children may benefit from distinctive facilities and specially trained teachers. On the other hand, they are less likely to be stigmatized as "different" if included in regular classroom settings. What do you consider to be the ramifications of the "special education" versus "inclusive education" debate for the classroom experience of all children, not only those who have disabilities?

Thinking Critically

Functional Illiteracy: Must We Rethink Education?

Imagine being unable to read the labels on cans of food, the instructions for assembling a child's toy, the dosage on a medicine bottle, or even the information on your own paycheque. These are some of the debilitating experiences of functional illiteracy, reading and writing skills inadequate for carrying out everyday responsibilities.

According to the National Literacy Secretariat, only 63 percent of Canadians have sufficient literacy and numeracy skills to deal adequately with everyday tasks; an additional 22 percent have some problems and about 15 percent have difficulty recognizing familiar words or doing simple addition and subtraction (Montigny, 1994:322). Another literacy survey revealed that by 1994 the percentages in the two lower categories had increased to 25 and 22 percent, respectively. (Keep in mind that these figures refer to literacy in English and French. Many of Canada's immigrants, especially older ones, are literate in other languages but illiterate in our two official languages.)

Functional illiteracy is a complex social problem, caused partly by an educational system that passes children from one grade to the next whether or not they learn. Community indifference and parents who offer little encouragement to learn language skills also contribute to the problem.

Functional illiteracy costs the North American economy more than $100 billion a year through decreased productivity (by workers who perform their jobs improperly) and increased accidents (by people unable to understand written instructions). It also reflects the costs of supporting those unable to read and write well enough to find work, and those who possibly end up on public assistance or in prison.

Correcting this national problem requires one approach for young people and another approach for adults. To stop functional illiteracy before it happens, the public must demand that children not graduate until they have learned basic language skills. For adults, the answer begins with diagnosis—a difficult task since many feel shame at their plight and avoid disclosure. Once such people are identified, however, effective adult education programs are required.

It should be noted that, in some cases, illiteracy is not an inability to read at all, but an inability to read in English or French (within Canada). In all countries participating in the International Adult Literacy Survey, immigrants are disproportionately represented in the lower literacy levels in the languages of the host countries. Canada has an active program teaching English as a second language to the constantly replenished body of immigrant school children and adults. Ontario has a number of programs—and qualified instructors—in place to enhance the reading, writing, and math skills of young people across the province (National

Literacy Secretariat, 2012). The importance of these skills, for the country as a whole, is reflected in this statement from the National Literacy Secretariat (2012): "Did you know that people with strong literacy skills read more books, go to the library more often, watch less television, find, get and keep jobs, and tend to be better paid than those with weak skills?" Although some people do succeed despite weak skills, the odds are not in their favour.

In November 2005, we learned that NHL coach Jacques Demers had never learned to read or write. Despite his handicap, Demers led the Montreal Canadians "to an unlikely Stanley Cup title in 1993. He also coached the Quebec Nordiques, the St. Louis Blues, the Detroit Red Wings, and the Tampa Bay Lightning" (CBC Sports, 2005). In all of these positions, he managed to hide his disability from everyone but his wife. Demers explained that he did not learn to read or write in school. He grew up in an abusive home where his father routinely beat him and his mother, and he was so anxious all the time that he could not sleep or focus in school. When asked why he revealed his illiteracy later in life, he explained that he felt free, or liberated. He also wanted parents to understand the damage that physical abuse inflicts on children. Illiteracy is one of the potential disabilities caused by violence in the home.

JACQUES DEMERS, A FORMER COACH IN THE NATIONAL HOCKEY LEAGUE, ADMITS IN A BIOGRAPHY, *En toutes lettres* **(MEANING "ALL SPELLED OUT" IN ENGLISH), THAT HE IS ILLITERATE.**

What Do You Think?

1. Do you know anyone who is illiterate? How does it affect his or her life?

2. What does it take to succeed despite illiteracy? How could Demers have hidden this disability for so long?

3. Do you see the lack of functional illiteracy as a significant social problem?

Socialization

Technologically simple societies look to families to teach skills and values and thus transmit a way of life from one generation to the next. As societies gain more complex technology, they turn to trained teachers to develop and pass on the more specialized knowledge that adults need in the workforce.

In primary school, children learn basic language and mathematical skills. Secondary school builds on this foundation and, for many, college or university allows further specialization. In addition, schools transmit cultural values and norms. Sometimes the operation of the classroom itself serves to teach important cultural lessons. Whereas in the United States spelling bees and classroom drills are intended to foster competitive individualism, in Canada there is more emphasis on activities that encourage co-operation, sharing, and team effort. Competitiveness is actually discouraged in many Canadian classrooms because of potential damaging effects on the self-esteem of those who cannot compete successfully.

Cultural Innovation

The faculty at colleges and universities create culture as well as pass it on to students. Research in the sciences, the social sciences, the humanities, and the fine arts leads to discovery and changes in our way of life. For example, medical research at major universities has helped increase life expectancy, just as research by sociologists and psychologists helps us learn how to better enjoy our lives so we can take advantage of our longevity. Marshall McLuhan foresaw the radical cultural transformation and innovation that would accompany the use of electronic media—specifically, television and the computer—in education. Suddenly, he predicted, there would be classrooms without walls; teaching, educational content, and links with the wider world would change irrevocably. His insight is now our reality.

Social Integration

Schooling moulds a diverse population into one society sharing norms and values. Canada has had a long experience with the challenges of multiculturalism and linguistic dualism, and has tried—not always successfully—to foster Canadian nationalism while accommodating a wide variety of interest groups. As a result, our educational policies have been sensitive to the problems of maintaining equality of access and unity in the face of diversity. We have been reluctant to push a national identity because of Quebec's sensitivities and our embrace of the mosaic model.

Normally, schools try to meet the challenge of social integration by establishing a common language to encourage broad communication and to forge a national identity. Of course, some ethnic minorities resist state-sponsored schooling precisely for this reason. In Canada, Hutterites, a culturally distinctive people, teach their children within their colonies; they use the Alberta provincial curriculum and speak in English for part of the day, but continue to speak their German dialect within their communities. Québécois perceive a threat to their distinct culture, resent the need to learn English for economic survival, and insist on full provincial control of education; Quebec has declared itself a unilingual province and only under special circumstances can a child be educated in English there. Aboriginal peoples in Canada have been struggling as well to establish greater control of their own schools. In each of these cases, the peoples in question resist formal schooling in the language of the majority because of very real threats to linguistic and cultural survival.

While there is understandable resistance to majority-controlled schooling by certain segments of the population, the striking cultural diversity of our country increases the importance of formal education as a path to social integration. Formal education plays a major role in integrating disparate groups, including our immigrant communities. Although our school systems seek to provide all of them with the linguistic and other skills needed for employment and daily life, Canada has not insisted that they give up their various identities completely.

GRADUATION IS AN IMPORTANT EVENT IN THE LIVES OF AN INCREASING NUMBER OF CANADIANS Young people who have reached this stage can expect to find better jobs and earn higher incomes than the peers they left behind.

Social Placement

Schools identify talent and match instruction to ability. Thus, schooling contributes to meritocracy by rewarding talent and hard work—regardless of social background—and providing a path to upward social mobility.

Latent Functions of Schooling

Schooling also serves several less widely recognized functions. It provides child care for the growing number of one-parent and two-career families. The Ontario government, for example, recently instituted full-day junior and senior kindergarten, thereby lightening the financial burden for families with young children. In addition, schooling occupies thousands of young people in their teens and twenties who would otherwise be competing for limited opportunities in the job market. High schools, colleges, and universities also bring together people of marriageable age. Finally, schools establish networks that serve as valuable career resources throughout life.

EVALUATE

Structural-functional theory stresses the ways in which formal education supports the operation of a modern society. However, this approach overlooks how the classroom behaviour of teachers and students can vary from one setting to another, a focus of the symbolic-interaction theory discussed next. In addition, structural-functional analysis fails to address the problems of our educational system and the ways in which it helps to reproduce the class structure in each generation, which is the focus of social-conflict theory, found in the final theoretical section of this chapter.

CHECK YOUR LEARNING Identify the five functions of schooling for the operation of society.

Schooling and Social Interaction

20.3 Apply symbolic-interaction theory to schooling.

The basic idea of symbolic-interaction theory is that people create the reality they experience in their day-to-day interactions. We use this approach to explain how stereotypes can shape what goes on in the classroom.

The Self-Fulfilling Prophecy

The Thomas theorem states that situations people define as real become real in their consequences. Put another way, people who expect others to act in certain ways often encourage that very behaviour. Doing so gives rise to *self-fulfilling prophecy*.

Jane Elliott, an elementary schoolteacher in the White community of Riceville, Iowa, carried out a simple experiment that showed how a self-fulfilling prophecy can take place in the classroom. In 1968, Elliot was teaching a grade 4 class when Dr. Martin Luther King, Jr. was assassinated. Her students were puzzled and asked why a national hero had been brutally shot. Elliott responded by asking her White students what they thought about Black people, and she was stunned to find out that they held many powerful and negative stereotypes. To illustrate the harmful effects of such stereotypes, Elliott performed a classroom experiment. Noting that almost all of the children had blue or brown eyes, she told the children that those with brown eyes were smarter and worked harder than those with blue eyes. To facilitate identification, a piece of brown- or blue-coloured cloth was pinned to each student's collar.

Elliott recalls the effect of this "lesson" on student behaviour: "It was just horrifying how quickly they became what I told them they were." Within half an hour, a blue-eyed girl named Carol had changed from a "brilliant, carefree, excited little girl to a frightened, timid, uncertain, almost-person." Not surprisingly, in the hours that followed, the brown-eyed students came to

HOW GOOD ARE YOU AS A STUDENT? THE ANSWER IS THAT YOU ARE AS GOOD AS YOU AND YOUR TEACHERS THINK YOU ARE The television show *Glee* demonstrates how the help of an inspiring teacher encourages students toward greater self-confidence and higher achievement—thus illustrating the process of "self-fulfilling prophecy."

Michael Yarish/FOX/courtesy Everett Collection

life, speaking up more and performing better than they had done before. The prophecy was fulfilled: Because the brown-eyed children thought they were superior, they became superior in their classroom performance—as well as "arrogant, ugly and domineering" toward the blue-eyed children. For their part, the blue-eyed children began to underperform, becoming the inferior people they believed themselves to be.

At the end of the day, Elliott explained the students' experience. She applied the lesson to race, pointing out that, if White children thought they were superior to Black children, they would expect to do better in school, just as many Black children who live in the shadow of the same stereotypes would underperform in school. The children also realized that a society that teaches these stereotypes and hatred encourages the kind of violence that ended Dr. King's life (Kral, 2000).

EVALUATE

Symbolic-interaction theory explains how we all build reality in our everyday interactions with others. When school officials define some students as "gifted," for example, we can expect teachers to treat them differently and the students themselves to behave differently as a result of having been labelled in this way. If students and teachers come to believe that one race is academically superior to another, the ensuing behaviour will be a self-fulfilling prophecy.

One limitation of this approach is that people do not make up beliefs about superiority and inferiority; rather, these beliefs are built into a society's system of social inequality, which brings us to the social-conflict approach.

CHECK YOUR LEARNING How can the labels that schools place on some students affect the students' actual performance and the reactions of others?

Schooling and Social Inequality

20.4 Apply social-conflict theory to schooling.

Social-conflict theory explains how schooling both causes and perpetuates social inequality. In this way, it can explain how stereotypes of "good" and "bad" students described in the symbolic-interaction discussion arise in the first place. In addition, social-conflict theory challenges the structural-functional idea that schooling develops everybody's talents and abilities by noting that schooling contributes to social stratification.

There is a clear link between class or power and education. Children of the elite acquire the tastes, style, language, and even the aspirations that transform cultural capital into academic capital. Where tracking is practiced, children from the lower class, who have different linguistic skills, are likely to be sorted into programs with a less demanding curriculum (Barakett & Cleghorn, 2008:37).

Traditionally, schooling was deemed more important for males than for females. The gender gap in education has decreased in recent decades—at least in terms of numbers—but women still predominate in the arts and social sciences, while men pursue mathematics and engineering. Throughout Canada, efforts have been made to provide gender-neutral texts and library materials and to remove materials that perpetuate negative stereotypes or are offensive to ethnic, racial, and religious minorities. Schools are also developing multicultural and anti-racist curricula to increase tolerance and understanding among youngsters of different backgrounds. The intent is to eradicate stereotypes, to raise the aspiration levels of those who felt excluded, and to create an environment that allows disadvantaged children to succeed (Fleras, 2012:349–53). More recently schools have gone beyond the quest for gender neutrality to recognition of diversity based on sexual orientation.

Social class background is also an important determinant of familiarity with computers, which is increasingly vital to education and employment. In the late 1980s and 1990s, home computer ownership rose, from below 30 percent to well over 60 percent, in the homes of those who are university-educated, who have high incomes, and who are professionals (Forcese, 1997:124; Goyder, 1997:70). Children from these families had an advantage as they progressed through the educational system. On the other hand, it appears that computers are available in a vast majority of households today. Statistics Canada (2010) reports internet use by age group: Among young people aged 16 to 24, 83.9 percent use the internet at least once a day; 80.7 percent of 25- to 44-year-olds do so, as do 67.5 percent of 45- to 64-year-olds. Surprisingly, 67.5 percent of people aged 65 and over do the same. Reinterpreted, the last two figures indicate that 67.5 percent of Canadians over 45 years of age use the internet at least once a day. The advantages that accrue to children who have computers at home are no longer limited to children of the well-to-do.

It is also the case that affluence itself affects the extent to which Canadians take advantage of educational opportunities. Along with gender, social class is a strong predictor of aspirations to attend university (Porter et al., 1982). In fact, a Canadian is much more likely to attend university or college if his or her parents are white-collar workers or professionals with post-secondary education (Barakett & Cleghorn, 2008; Corak, 2000; de Broucker & Lavallée, 2000; Guppy & Arai, 1993).

Regional variation in affluence and economic structure gives rise to marked differences in educational attainment. Forcese (1997:110) attributes such variation to differences

Seeing Ourselves

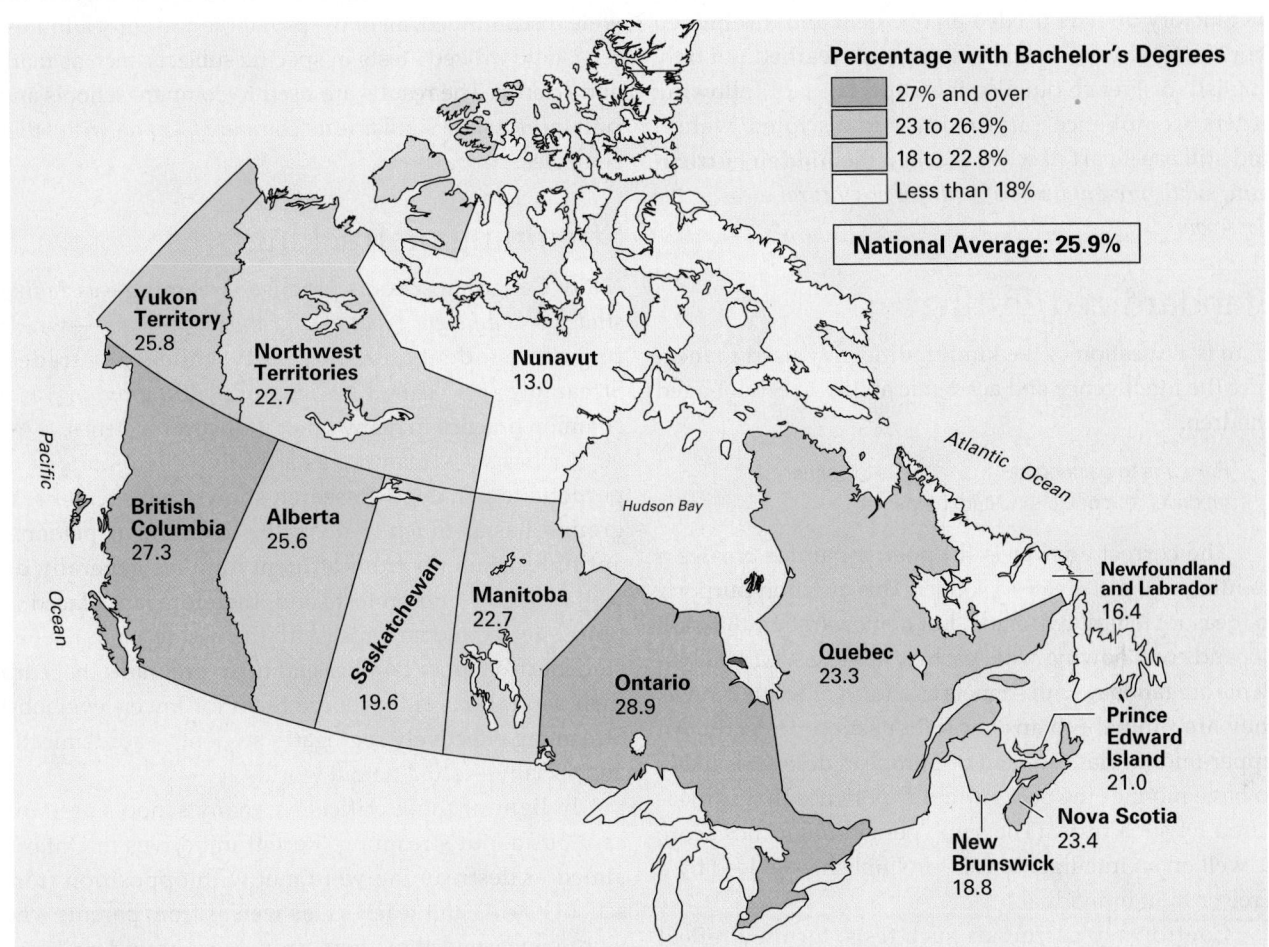

Percentage with Bachelor's Degrees

- 27% and over
- 23 to 26.9%
- 18 to 22.8%
- Less than 18%

National Average: 25.9%

Yukon Territory 25.8

Northwest Territories 22.7

Nunavut 13.0

Pacific Ocean

Atlantic Ocean

Hudson Bay

British Columbia 27.3

Alberta 25.6

Saskatchewan 19.6

Manitoba 22.7

Ontario 28.9

Quebec 23.3

Newfoundland and Labrador 16.4

Prince Edward Island 21.0

Nova Scotia 23.4

New Brunswick 18.8

Canada Map 20–1 Population Aged 25 to 64 with Bachelor's Degree or Higher by Province and Territory, 2011

SOURCE: Compilation and calculations by LM Gerber based on Statistics Canada, NHS 2011, Catalogue no. 99-010-X2011036.

in quality of education and "existing privilege," pointing out that the lowest levels of continued school attendance occur in Canada's least industrialized and urbanized provinces. The "dropout" phenomenon is "concentrated in the least prosperous areas of Canada, reinforcing the existing pattern of unskilled labour and lower-status occupations." In 1986, the Atlantic provinces had the lowest proportions with university degrees—while the highest proportions were in Ontario and Alberta. Now, Ontario and British Columbia are on the top ranks.

Canada Map 20–1 indicates the proportions of provincial and territorial populations, aged 25 to 64, with at least a bachelor's degree in 2011. As in 2006, Ontario and British Columbia were at the top, with 29 and 27 percent having bachelor's degrees (or higher); Yukon and Alberta came next at 26 percent. Quebec, Nova Scotia, Northwest Territories, and Manitoba reclaimed the middle ranks of 2006—this time with 23 percent holding bachelor's degrees. Prince Edward Island, Saskatchewan, and New Brunswick fared better than Newfoundland and

Labrador and Nunavut, with 16 and 13 percent holding bachelor's degrees. The range of educational certification at the bachelor's degree level and above—from 13 to 30 percent—is clearly associated with levels of prosperity, urbanization, and industrialization. However, the situation is different in the Yukon, which attracts much of its university-educated population from elsewhere to take jobs in government, natural resources, defence, and research.

One other factor interacts with region in determining aspirations and attainment—and that is the distance between home and the nearest college or university. Geographic isolation means that for youth in remote areas—including First Nations on reserves—higher education is not even on their radar.

Social Control

Schooling is a way of controlling people and reinforcing acceptance of the status quo. Bowles and Gintis

(1976) point out that the rise of public education in the late nineteenth century came at exactly the same time that factory owners needed an obedient and disciplined workforce. Once in school, immigrants learned not only English[1] or French but also the importance of following orders. Compliance, punctuality, and discipline were—and still are—part of what is called the **hidden curriculum**, *subtle presentations of political or cultural ideas in the classroom.*

Standardized Testing

Here is a question of the kind traditionally used to measure the intelligence and academic ability of school-aged children.

> *Painter* is to *painting* as _____ is to *sonnet*.
> (a) driver (b) poet (c) priest (d) carpenter

The correct answer is (b) poet; a painter creates a painting as a *poet* creates a sonnet. This question purports to measure logical reasoning, but demonstrating this skill depends on knowing what each term means. Unless students are familiar with sonnets as a form of written verse, they are unlikely to answer the question correctly. An upper-middle-class student of European descent is likely to have more of the background experience that is measured by such tests. (The same person might not score as well on an intelligence test—in English—devised by a Cree or Inuit individual.)

Controversy surrounds such tests, for they reflect our society's dominant culture, thereby placing the members of minorities at a disadvantage. Children raised in poverty are also disadvantaged when faced with "tests of intelligence and cognitive skills weighted in favour of middle- and upper-class children" (Porter et al., 1982:9). The motivations and attitudes transmitted by affluent parents also help children on these tests.

The organizations that create standardized tests claim that biases of these kinds have been eliminated because they carefully study response patterns and drop any question that favours one category of students over another. Critics, however, maintain that some bias based on class, race, or ethnicity is inherent in any formal testing, because questions inevitably reflect our society's dominant culture and thereby put minorities at a disadvantage (Crouse & Trusheim, 1988; Putka, 1990).

It is unlikely, in a multicultural society such as ours, that any province would use the old IQ test. From the 1950s to roughly 1970, Ontario administered provincial exams in every subject at the end of grade 13. IQ tests were used during that period as well. Although these were discontinued, all of the provinces currently administer "standardized" tests in specific subjects such as math and science. The results are used to compare schools and provinces, while similar tests compare Canada with other countries.

Streaming or Tracking

Many Canadian schools practise **streaming**—*assigning students to different types of educational programs*—which prepares students for university, college, or trades. Streaming (also called *tracking* or *ability grouping*) is a common practice in many other industrial societies.

Critics see streaming as a thinly veiled strategy to perpetuate privilege. Research shows that social background has as much to do with streaming as personal aptitude. Students from affluent families generally do well in school and on tests and, therefore, are placed in university-bound streams (with the best teachers), while students from poor families end up in programs that curb their aspirations and prepare them for lower-level jobs. Streaming effectively segregates students—academically and socially—into different worlds.

In light of these criticisms, many schools are now cautious about streaming. Recent initiatives in Ontario aimed at destreaming were met with opposition from school boards and teachers, as well as from parents who were concerned that their university-bound children would receive lower-quality education in destreamed classrooms. Streaming remains controversial, so many schools try to limit its impact by making it possible for students to move from one stream to another. Caution is required because rigid streaming has a powerful impact on student learning and self-concept. Young people in higher streams tend to see themselves as bright and able, whereas those in lower streams end up with less ambition and lower self-esteem (Bowles & Gintis, 1976; Kilgore, 1991; Kozol, 1992; Oakes, 1985).

Access to Higher Education

In industrial societies, since lawyers, physicians, dentists, or professors cannot pass credentials directly to their children, higher education is the path to occupational achievement.

Enrolment in post-secondary education has risen dramatically since World War II and in recent decades. Between 1988 and 1994, while Canada's population grew by 8.8 percent, full-time post-secondary enrolment grew by 18.1 percent (Statistics Canada, 1996). That trend has continued: "Enrolment at Canadian universities recorded its strongest increase in 28 years during the academic year

---

[1]Until Quebec passed Bill 101 in 1977, making French the sole official language in Quebec as well as the language of business, francophones had to be fluently bilingual to succeed economically. Even in Quebec, English was the language of business.

netbritish/Shutterstock

Terrie L. Zeller/Shutterstock

SOCIOLOGICAL RESEARCH HAS DOCUMENTED THE FACT THAT YOUNG CHILDREN LIVING IN LOW-INCOME COMMUNITIES TYPICALLY LEARN IN CLASSROOMS SUCH AS THE ONE SHOWN ON THE LEFT, WHERE SCHOOLS WITH LOW BUDGETS CANNOT PROVIDE ALL OF THE LATEST TECHNOLOGY FOR EACH STUDENT Children from high-income communities, who may attend private schools or better-funded schools, typically enjoy classroom experiences such as the one shown on the right, with individual access to high-technology options.

2003–04, due to a rise in the number of students aged 18 to 24, Ontario's double cohort, and a record gain in students from other countries" (Statistics Canada, 2005e). University enrolment was 990 400 in 2003–04, up 6.1 percent from the previous year and 20.4 percent from 1997–98, with enrolment hitting record highs for six consecutive years. Ten years later, in 2013/2014, university enrolment had increased to 1.3 million, college enrolment to 750 000—in both cases 75 percent of the enrolment was full time.

One area of post-secondary education that scholars tend to ignore is that of apprenticeship in the trades. According to Statistics Canada (2016), between 1991 and 2009 the number of registered apprenticeships more than doubled from 192 945 to 409 038 in 22 major trade groups. The largest of these were electricians (18.9%), carpenters (14.4%), automotive service technicians (14.1%) and plumbers, pipefitters, and steamfitters (14.4%). Apprentices are paid subsidized wages while they learn and can receive up to $4000 from Services Canada to defer the costs of travel, tools, and other expenses. By some estimates, the number of apprenticeships is increasing five times faster than college enrolments.

Statistics Canada provides statistics on full-time university enrolment by decade. Between 1997–98 and 2007–08, full-time enrolment increased from 573 099 to 796 440—or 39 percent. University enrolment grew at twice the rate of college enrolment—but *at only 40 percent of apprenticeship rate.* Fortunately for the Canadian economy, young people are turning to apprenticeships in record numbers.

Putting apprenticeships aside, it is clear that more students are gaining access to college and to university. On the other hand, young Canadians from different backgrounds do not have equal access to post-secondary education.

There are many reasons why most people in Canada do not attend and graduate from university or college. Some high school graduates enter the labour force right away; others cannot afford further education because of the costs of tuition and deferred income. Vast distances between homes and the nearest university or college are also major deterrents. In addition, many high school students become convinced that they cannot succeed at the post-secondary level.

In one respect, Canada has moved closer to the goal of equal access to higher education. As noted earlier, women are now more likely than men to attend university. Low or moderate family income, however, remains a formidable barrier to enrolment; young people with lower family incomes or fathers in blue-collar occupations are much less likely to go to university (Corak, 2000; Wotherspoon, 1991). Most universities provide financial assistance to students in the form of bursaries and scholarships, and governments make loans available to those with limited means. Nevertheless, many people cannot afford the remaining costs. The problem has been accentuated in recent years as cutbacks in government funding have forced tuition increases. Figure 20–1 deals with educational attainment among selected ethnic categories, measuring the proportions of adults 25 to 64 years of age and over with only high school certification

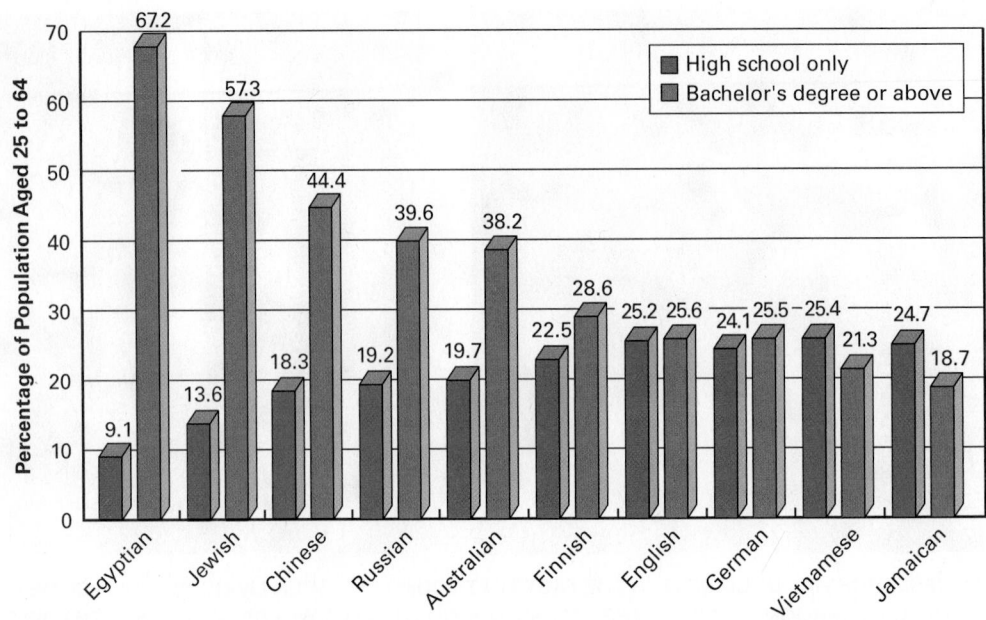

Figure 20–1 Educational Attainment for Selected Ethnic Categories Aged 25 to 64, 2011

SOURCE: Compilation and calculations by LM Gerber based on Statistics Canada, NHS 2011, Catalogue no. 99-010-X2011036.

and with at least a bachelor's degree. According to the NHS 2011, the proportions with high school diplomas only range from 9 percent among Canadians with Egyptian ancestry to 25 percent with Jamaican ancestry. The inverse is true for proportions with a bachelor's degree or above; percentages with at least bachelor's degrees *decrease* from a high of 67 percent among Egyptians to a low of 19 percent among Jamaicans.

You will notice that race is not a major—nor the only—factor determining the attainment of higher education since there are visible minorities at both ends of scale. Nor does recent immigration account for the vast differences in educational attainment. Most people claiming at least some Finnish and German ancestry have been in Canada for several generations—just like the people who report English ancestry. In fact, these three categories are clumped together with about 24 percent reporting only high school credentials and similar proportions (about 26 percent) claiming to have at least bachelor's degrees. People of Finnish, English, and German ancestry are distinguished by neither race nor recent immigration—instead their educational attainment levels are distinctly "average."

It is worth noting that with each passing census the proportion of Aboriginal people with university degrees has risen steadily—from 2 percent in 1991 to 4.4 and 8.2 percent in 2001 and 2006, respectively. Because of the prevailing stereotypes, it might surprise you to learn that, among Aboriginals in 2006, 14 555 had acquired master's degrees and 2720 had *earned doctorates*

(or Ph.D.s). In other words, *ten years ago* there were already 17 275 Aboriginal individuals in Canada who had master's degrees or Ph.D.s—and Census 2016 will reveal many more. Of all the Aboriginal groups, First Nations (registered or status Indians) lagged farthest behind in terms of educational qualifications, especially if they lived on reserve. This is due, in part, to the small size and geographic isolation of reserve communities. Another explanatory factor is the history of residential schools, which are discussed in detail in the Thinking about Diversity box (p. 577).

Education and the World of Work

Higher education, whether from university or college, expands career opportunities and increases earnings. The NHS 2011 published data on *employment* by level of educational attainment, but not on *earnings* by level of educational attainment; the same was true of Census 2006. The latest available data on earnings by education come from Census 2001. Much has changed since then—including the value of the dollar—but some observations still ring true today. Nationally, earned income among those with university-level credentials was at least twice that of people with no certification at all—while in Nunavut the average earned income of the university-educated was almost four times that of people who had not graduated from high school. The creation of Nunavut provided unprecedented opportunities to educated Inuit—especially to Inuit women.

Thinking About Diversity: Race, Class, and Gender

School Attendance among Youth across Canada: Where You Live Makes a Difference

What are the factors that encourage extended school attendance among young Canadians? Although most of the factors are discussed elsewhere in these pages, a brief review is in order. The likelihood that you will continue your schooling to high school graduation and beyond is determined, in large part, by characteristics of your family *and* the community or area in which you live.

If your family is poor, you are less likely than others to go on to post-secondary education—for a number of reasons. Your family may be unable to help you cover the expenses associated with higher education (e.g., tuition, travel, and accommodation). Since your parents are unlikely to have college or university education themselves, you lack an educated role model and may have had relatively limited exposure to computers, newspapers, and books. Under these circumstances, your parents' and your own aspirations for your future may be relatively modest.

On the other hand, if your family is upper-middle-class, it will be taken for granted that you will go to university for a bachelor's degree and perhaps postgraduate studies. One (or both) of your parents may be in a prestigious professional career—and both are likely to have at least a bachelor's degree. Not only do you have educated role models, but you will have had exposure to books, newspapers, computers, and the internet from early childhood. Your parents will cover the costs of advanced education without requiring you to work while attending school. Camp, team sports, dance or music lessons, and exotic vacations will have helped you develop a wide range of skills and broaden your horizons.

Admittedly, these are generalizations; there are many people from poor families (e.g., the children of immigrants) who reach the highest levels in terms of education, occupation, and income—just as there are others who grow up in affluence and, despite their advantages, fail to match their parents in terms of achievement and lifestyle. Nonetheless, there is a great deal of truth in the assertion, by social-conflict scholars, that family—along with other social institutions such as education—perpetuates social class from one generation to the next.

The community in which you live—rich or poor, rural or urban—will determine the quality of your school, the characteristics of your neighbours and your friends, the presence (or absence) of neighbourhood gangs, recreational options, and the nature of your exposure to and involvement in the wider world. If the local community determines your aspirations and opportunities, the region in which you live (e.g., Nunavut or urban British Columbia) will have its own effects. At the most basic level, distance from your home to the nearest community college or university is a powerful predictor of educational attainment. And, needless to say, a province with a resource-based economy inspires a very different approach to schooling than one with a vibrant industrial/post-industrial economy.

Canada Map 20–1 reveals tremendous variation in educational attainment. Ontario and British Columbia—where 29 and 27 percent of adults aged 25 to 64 have at least a bachelor's degree—lead the way in educational attainment. At the other extreme are Newfoundland and Labrador and Nunavut, where 16 and 13 percent of adults have at least a bachelor's degree. You may be surprised to learn that, at provincial or territorial levels, high educational attainment is not necessarily correlated with high income. According to the NHS of 2011, in terms of average employment income, Northwest Territories, Nunavut, and Alberta take the lead—with average earned income of $77 000, $76 000, and $70 000 respectively. At $55 000, Newfoundland and Labrador outpaces the other Atlantic provinces, Quebec, and Manitoba on earned income. If, on the other hand, one looks at total income—which includes employment insurance, welfare, or pensions along with earned income—Northwest Territories and Alberta take the lead ($55 000 and $51 000) while New Brunswick and Prince Edward Island trail on the bottom rung ($34 000). Full-time school attendance (see Table 20–1) varies across the provinces and territories in unpredictable ways. Since our population of interest is youth aged 15 to 24 years, we can expect changes in full-time school attendance (from 1991 to 2001) to give us some insight into the present. There are three provinces that were average in terms of attendance in 1991 and above average in 2001—namely Newfoundland and Labrador, Nova Scotia, and Quebec—with approximately 60 percent of youth attending school full time. In each case the proportion attending increased by 3 to 6 percentage points. Ontario's school attendance record was above average at both points in time. School attendance rates were lower everywhere west of Ontario; however, British Columbia, Northwest Territories, and most notably Nunavut increased their full-time attendance rates by 4, 5, and 13 points, respectively, in the 1991 to 2001 interval.

When the data from Census 2016 are available for analysis, the young adults who were 15 to 24 years old in 2001 will be 30 to 39 years old. We will find out if higher levels of school attendance translate into more advanced educational attainment levels (at trades, college, and university levels), greater employment, and higher earned income.

There is no relationship between level of educational attainment among populations aged 15 and over and current full-time school attendance among 15- to 24-year-olds. In effect, the data in this table turn our prior understanding upside down. What can explain these contradictory findings?

(continued)

Table 20–1 Full-Time School Attendance among Youth Aged 15 to 24 for Canada, Provinces, and Territories

Location	Year	Attending School %	Change
Canada	2001	57.1	Up 2 pts
	1991	55.4	
Newfoundland and Labrador	2001	*60.6*	**Up 5 pts**
	1991	*55.9*	
Prince Edward Island	2001	53.6	Down 2 pts
	1991	55.5	
Nova Scotia	2001	*59.1*	**Up 3 pts**
	1991	*55.9*	
New Brunswick	2001	54.5	No change
	1991	54.7	
Quebec	2001	*60.7*	**Up 6 pts**
	1991	*55.9*	
Ontario	2001	**59.7**	Up 1 pt
	1991	**58.5**	
Manitoba	2001	48.7	Down 2 pts
	1991	51.4	
Saskatchewan	2001	52.3	Down 2 pts
	1991	54.4	
Alberta	2001	48.6	Down 2 pts
	1991	51.0	
British Columbia	2001	**53.8**	**Up 4 pts**
	1991	**50.3**	
Yukon Territory	2001	51.8	Up 2 pts
	1991	49.7	
Northwest Territories	2001	**47.9**	**Up 5 pts**
	1991	**43.1**	
Nunavut	2001	**44.6**	**Up 13 pts**
	1991	**31.7**	

Note that the 2006 census did not distinguish between full-time and part-time school attendance, so only the data for 1991 and 2001 can be used for comparison. NHS 2011 has no comparable data.

SOURCE: Compilation and calculations by LM Gerber based on Statistics Canada, Census 2001, Catalogue no. 97-564-XCB2001007.

Nunavut stands out on three fronts in 2001: It had the lowest level of educational attainment, the lowest level of school attendance, as well as the largest increase in school attendance (relative to 1991). The Inuit account for about 85 percent of the population of Nunavut—the territory that came into being in 1999 when it separated from the Northwest Territories. During the negotiations that took place over the preceding decade, the Inuit people were drawn into the political and economic spheres of Canada—and were promised all kinds of opportunities in the new territory. Education took on relevance that was lacking in the past and spurred the dramatic increase in school attendance. By 2016, Nunavut and Northwest Territories had the highest average earned income in Canada.

What about Newfoundland and Labrador? It had the second lowest level of educational attainment coupled with the highest level of school attendance, which increased by a substantial five points. Newfoundland and Labrador has had a depressed economy for decades; the collapse of the cod fishery made it worse. One of the results of a depressed economy is the outmigration of young people. A steady flow of young people to Ontario and Alberta, in particular, led to population decline and aging in Newfoundland and Labrador. Clearly, the young people who migrated to the Alberta oil sands and Fort McMurray were not doing so to continue their schooling. As a result of selective migration, the young people who stayed home were those who continued their schooling.

Quebec's stellar records in educational attainment and school attendance are part of a massive change in Quebec society. Prior to 1960, Quebec was dominated by the Catholic Church and a relatively small anglophone elite. The Quiet Revolution involved rural-urban migration, secularization, and an enthusiastic embrace of higher education among francophones.

Alberta is one of the high-income provinces, with average educational attainment at the level of bachelor's and above. What explains its below-average levels of school attendance? In part, the oil industry requires few very highly educated individuals but employs thousands of workers who may have only high school, trades, or college certification. Alberta has been at the receiving end of a flow of young migrants who are not continuing their schooling from the Atlantic provinces and other parts of Canada. This inflow of migrants—many of them below 25 years of age—in search of employment reduces Alberta's school attendance level.

Indeed, where you live makes a difference. You are far more likely to continue your education in some provinces than in others. Educational aspirations are shaped by family, neighbourhood, and province or region—as well as the availability of and requirements of employment. Thus, powerful social and economic forces affect individual decisions—which in turn contribute to identifiable patterns across the country.

What Do You Think?

1. Do you recognize the impact of social forces on your own decision to pursue post-secondary education? What about your former classmates who dropped out of high school or decided not to go on to college or university?

2. Would you be willing to move across Canada because jobs in your field are available in another province?

3. If your parents were the main influence on your decision to attend college or university, how did your family's characteristics or circumstances come into the picture?

Thinking About Diversity: Race, Class, and Gender

Aboriginal Education: From Residential School to College and University

Beginning in the early twentieth century, Indians (now called First Nations) attended church-run residential schools whose intent was to "civilize" and assimilate the children by stamping out their own languages and cultures and replacing them with English or French, rudimentary reading and arithmetic, and agricultural and domestic skills.

Only recently have we become aware of the damaging consequences of the residential school experience. Removed from their communities and families, the children were ill prepared for life in the mainstream or for a return to their own communities. Inadequate and, in effect, damaging educational practices were accompanied in many of these schools by verbal, physical, and sexual abuse. By the time the residential schools were phased out in the early 1960s, several generations of First Nations youngsters had paid a very heavy price.

Vicki English-Currie describes her experience in a residential school, to which she was taken at the tender age of seven. There, the missionaries assumed total responsibility for and control over her life. She experienced the transition from home to residential school as one of total shock, enormous setback, and "the beginning of a lifetime of cultural tragedy." In this setting, her formal education was overshadowed by increasing "stress, anger, fear, and hostility" as well as loss of "self-esteem, self-determination, self-worth, pride, and confidence" (English-Currie, 1993:114–116).

When our government closed the residential schools in the early 1960s, Aboriginal youngsters were unprepared to cope with integrated provincial and territorial schools. Finding themselves two or three grades behind their peers, they dropped out.

The youngsters who were educated in residential schools suffered the long-term consequences of being separated from their families and communities, and of being wrenched from familiar cultural surroundings and thrust into an alien world in which they felt unwelcome. These same youngsters, raised outside normal families, were the ones who soon faced parenthood, for which they were ill prepared.

While 60 percent of on-reserve children now attend elementary schools operated by their own nations, the transition to high school—usually to an integrated provincial or territorial school—is still painful. As a result, the majority of Aboriginal youth do not graduate. The Royal Commission on Aboriginal Peoples points out that these youngsters "leave the school system without the requisite skills for employment [and] without the language and cultural knowledge of their people" (quoted in Schissel & Wotherspoon, 2003:59).

In their survey, Schissel and Wotherspoon found that high school students, when asked about barriers to learning, mention poverty, housing problems, violence, and racism. Although Aboriginal students express an overwhelming desire to attend university, their aspirations do not translate into reality. The authors conclude that all schools—particularly isolated rural and northern schools—need to help students understand the nature of post-secondary education, the availability of funding, and the challenges of rural/urban transition.

The importance of education to the employment prospects of Aboriginal people is clear. Tait (2000) notes that, in 1996, the unemployment rate was 40 percent for young Aboriginal adults who had not completed high school; for those with a university degree, it was 9 percent. On the basis of 2006 census data, Richards (2008) found that employment levels of Aboriginal and non-Aboriginal people are almost identical at each level of educational attainment. That's the good news. Richards also concluded that the gap between Aboriginal and non-Aboriginal attainment levels is increasing over time. Despite gains in educational attainment, Aboriginal people are not keeping up with changes in the mainstream society.

Table 20–2 compares the educational attainment levels of on-reserve and urban First Nations, all Aboriginals, and non-Aboriginals (25 to 44 years of age) in 2001 and 2006. It may help to start with a comparison of all Aboriginals and non-Aboriginals in 2006. The proportions with high school diplomas (as their highest level of attainment) are essentially equal (at 23 percent) and the levels with college-level certification are roughly comparable (at 20 and 23 percent). However, the gaps between Aboriginals and non-Aboriginals on the remaining measures of educational attainment are huge. Young adult Aboriginals are three times more likely to lack any certification whatsoever—and the tables are turned completely at the higher attainment levels. Non-Aboriginals are *three times* more likely to have bachelor's degrees or qualifications beyond the bachelor's level.

Although half of First Nations—25 to 44 years of age—*living on reserve* had not graduated from high school (in 2006), the proportions with high school diplomas more than doubled, and college, bachelor's, and postgraduate certification levels improved, however slightly, between 2001 and 2006. In comparison, *urban* First Nations fare better on all attainment measures and improved on each one between the two census years. *But* ... non-Aboriginals have twice the likelihood of acquiring bachelor's degrees (18 and 8 percent) and postgraduate or professional qualifications (2.6 and 1.0 percent).

The legacy of the residential school system is apparent in the educational record of the on-reserve population in particular. Of particular concern is the fact that the proportion of "dropouts" or those who had not graduated

(continued)

Table 20–2 Educational Attainment of On-Reserve and Urban First Nations, all Aboriginals and non-Aboriginals, 25 to 44 Years of Age, 2001 and 2006*

Certification	First Nations On-Reserve		First Nations Urban		All Aboriginals	Non-Aboriginals
	2001	2006	2001	2006	2006	2006
None	46.1	49.2	30.0	27.1	31.9	11.0
High school	7.6	17.7	10.7	25.8	23.5	22.6
College or CEGEP	11.9	13.9	18.0	20.8	19.8	22.6
Bachelor's	2.4	2.6	6.4	7.7	6.0	18.4
Postgraduate	0.3	0.5	0.7	1.0	0.8	2.6

*Comparable data from the National Household Survey, 2011, are unavailable.

SOURCE: Compilation and calculations by LM Gerber based on Statistics Canada, Census 2001 and 2006, Catalogue nos. 97F0011X2001050 and 97-560-X2006036.

from high school *increased* on reserve from 46 to 49 percent between 2001 and 2006. On the brighter side, the proportion of all Aboriginal people without at least high school certification dropped from 45 to 32 percent in one decade (1996 to 2006). The fact that half of on-reserve First Nations still fall far behind other Aboriginals in graduating from high school provides the best evidence that the legacy of residential schooling, the *Indian* Act, and federal administration continues to subject on-reserve populations to double jeopardy (Gerber, 1990).

One way to capture the differences among the categories is to total the last three numbers in each 2006 column. A full 44 percent of the non-Aboriginal young adult population graduated at the college level or above; urban First Nations came second at 30 percent, the overall Aboriginal population came 27 percent, while the on-reserve population trailed at 17 percent. Clearly, the on-reserve population suffers most from the history of residential schooling.

An editorial in the *National Post* on May 1, 2006, reported that the Canadian government agreed to compensate the victims of "Canada's shameful residential school program." More than 80 000 individuals "who were taken from their homes and forced to attend the church-run schools meant to assimilate them into the White culture" are eligible for compensation up to $10 000, plus $3000 for each year of attendance. On June 11, 2008, the Canadian government formally apologized to Aboriginal peoples (including Inuit and Métis people) for the residential school experience. As prime minister, Stephen Harper apologized, recognizing the devastating impacts of separating children

from their families and of the Indian residential schools system itself.

But this was not the end of the residential-school story. The Truth and Reconciliation Commission (TRC) was established on June 8, 2008—a few days before the formal government apology—and completed its work in December 2015. As part of their task, the commissioners spent more than six years travelling across Canada, listening to the testimony of some 6000 people who had been taken (often forcibly) from their families only to be subjected to physical, psychological and sexual abuse—and even death—while under the care and tutelage of the residential school system. The report of the TRC, which was damning on many fronts, issued 94 "Calls to Action" required for the process of reconciliation. High on its list was recognition of the United Nations Declaration on the Rights of Indigenous Peoples. In May 2016, the Liberal government of Justin Trudeau announced to the United Nations that the declaration would be fully adopted and implemented within the laws of Canada (*CBC News*, 2016).

What Do You Think?

1. What would your life be like if your parents had attended an Indian residential school?

2. Do you now have a better understanding of the barriers that Aboriginal people must overcome to make it to your college or university campus?

3. Should we do more to encourage on-reserve people to continue their schooling?

Table 20–3 shows that, in general, employment rates among 25- to 64-year-olds increase with educational attainment. This is especially true for women, among whom only 46 percent without high school certification were employed. With minor variation, men and women were more likely to have been employed in 2011 with each increase in education. Eighty-four percent of men and 78 percent of women with post-secondary credentials were employed, as were 86 and 80 percent of

men and women with bachelor's degrees. Men were *most* likely to be employed (at 89 percent) if their postgraduate training was in the medical fields of medicine, dentistry, veterinary medicine, or optometry—82 percent of women with medical qualifications were employed as well. Keep in mind that the vast majority of practitioners in these medical fields are self-employed.

We know that employment—and indeed full-time employment—increases with the attainment of a

Table 20–3 Employment of 25- to 64-Year-Olds by Level of Educational Attainment and Sex, 2011

Level of certification	Percentage employed	
	Men	Women
None	64.5	45.9
High School	78.1	65.3
Postsecondary:	83.8	77.5
Apprenticeship or trades	80.8	72.4
College or CEGEP	84.4	77.7
Bachelor's or above:	85.6	79.5
Bachelor's	85.9	79.5
Medical*	**89.1**	**82.3**
Master's	84.6	79.3
Earned doctorate (Ph.D.)	**87.2**	**83.2**

*Refers to degrees in medicine, dentistry, veterinary medicine or optometry.

SOURCE: Compilation and calculations by LM Gerber based on Statistics Canada, NHS 2011 Catalogue no. 99-012-X2011037.

bachelor's degree and even more with postgraduate certification. Furthermore, the reward for advanced education is highest in the Northwest Territories and Nunavut. Many people find schooling to be its own reward, but schooling is also a sound investment in financial terms, increasing income by hundreds of thousands of dollars over a person's working life.

While you are actively acquiring the skills that will serve you throughout your working life it makes sense to consider the skills that employers need and want. A large study called Making the Match (Evers et al., 1993), involving 20 companies and 5 universities, was designed to assess the skill development experiences of Canadian university students and graduates, as well as the fit between these skills and the needs of corporations. The skills most in demand and shortest in supply were not technical skills, such as using a computer, but a skill composite: the ability to integrate and use information, adapt to change, take reasonable risks, and conceptualize the future. Leadership and conflict management skills are

also scarce. The educational system must develop technical skills in its students *as well as* the analytical and communication skills required by employers. Interestingly, there is a link between these skills and the educational "aims and objectives" espoused by many of Canada's universities.

Privilege and Personal Merit

If, as social-conflict analysis suggests, attending university is a rite of passage for affluent men and women, then *schooling transforms social privilege into personal merit.* But given the North American cultural emphasis on individual achievement, we tend to see credentials as "badges of ability," as Sennett and Cobb (1973) put it, rather than as symbols of family affluence. When we congratulate the typical new graduate, we often overlook the social resources that made this achievement possible. In the same way, we are quick to condemn the high school dropout as personally deficient, with little thought for the social circumstances that surround that person's life. See the Sociology in Focus box for further exploration of educational attainment.

EVALUATE

Social-conflict analysis links formal education to social inequality to show how schooling transforms privilege into personal worthiness and social disadvantage into personal deficiency. However, the social-conflict approach overlooks the extent to which acquiring a degree reflects plenty of hard work or the extent to which schooling provides upward social mobility for talented women and men from all backgrounds. Further, despite the claims of many conflict theorists that schooling supports the status quo, "politically correct" educational curricula are challenging patterns of social inequality on many fronts.

CHECK YOUR LEARNING Explain several ways in which education is linked to social inequality.

The Applying Theory table provides an overview of education from the perspectives of the symbolic-interaction, structural-functional, and social-conflict approaches.

APPLYING THEORY

Education

	Structural-Functional Approach	Symbolic-Interaction Approach	Social-Conflict Approach
What is the level of analysis?	Macro level	Micro level	Macro level
What is the importance of education for society?	Schooling performs many vital tasks for the operation of society, including socializing the young and encouraging discovery and invention to improve our lives. Schooling helps unite a diverse society by teaching shared norms and values.	Teachers' expectations can affect self-image and academic performance.	Schooling maintains social inequality through unequal schooling for rich and poor. Within individual schools, streaming places privileged children into advanced or university-oriented programs.

Sociology in Focus

Explaining Educational Attainment

Over several decades, Canada has witnessed a marked increase in the number of children raised in lone-parent or blended/step-parent families. Frederick and Boyd (2000) used data from the 1994 General Social Survey to look at the impact of family structure on high school completion. They found that adults (aged 22 to 44) who had lived with both biological parents at age 15 were more likely to have completed high school (80 percent) than those from lone-parent families (71 percent) and blended or step-parent families (70 percent).

Looking at the interaction of parental education and family structure, Frederick and Boyd found that 94 percent of those who grew up with two biological parents who had completed high school were more likely to do so themselves. If neither parent had completed high school, and a child lived with both biological parents, graduation rate was 71 percent. For those who lived with only one parent, it was 59 percent. Clearly, parental education and family structure both have significant effects.

Using Canadian data from the 1994 International Adult Literacy Survey, de Broucker and Lavallée (2000) assessed the role of "inherited intellectual capital" in the acquisition of post-secondary education. Most adults aged 26 to 35 have at least as much education as their parents. Not surprisingly, young adults whose parents had post-secondary education were more likely to earn post-secondary diplomas or degrees.

Father's occupation also has an effect, in that fathers with high-status occupations have children with higher educational attainment. The literacy survey suggests that one way of passing on intellectual capital is to provide books and read to children. Parents with university degrees, regardless of income, are much more likely to read to their children, contributing to an environment that is conducive to learning.

Supportive parents can help their children achieve amazing things. Five Canadian women, Dina, Ada, Rita, Linda, and Cindy Maxwell, received their undergraduate degrees from Harvard, "where faculty and staff still talk about the Maxwell sisters from New Brunswick"

Image Source/Getty Images

because of the goodwill they generated there. Daughters of a physician from Ghana and a Canadian nurse, they attended Harvard—on scholarships, loans, and parental contributions—before going on to study medicine (Cindy and Linda) and the law (Rita, Ada, and Dina). These impressive young women explained that "their father's stern but positive guidance, combined with their mother's warm and protective support, made them the women they are today" (Reinhart & Armstrong, 2006).

For years, the top-achieving students in the Toronto public school system have been Asian—especially Chinese and increasingly South Asian: "[F]or all the hardships faced by new immigrants, their kids are the brightest of the bright" (Wente, 2006). Immigrant and first-generation children, disproportionately, are the valedictorians and—at the other extreme—the dropouts. Canadian-born youngsters are in the middle of the pack. In the United States as well as Canada, educational achievement by students of Asian ancestry is described as "stunning." Cultural capital, which is formed at home, makes ethnicity more important than any other factor—socio-economic background, curriculum, or family structure—as a determinant of educational attainment.

What Do You Think?

1. Can something as simple as reading to children affect academic aspirations and achievements? Why?

2. Living with both biological parents who are educated affects the educational attainment of children. Why?

3. Why do Canadian students of Asian backgrounds do so well in school?

Problems in the Schools

20.5 Discuss violence, dropping out, and other problems facing today's schools.

Canadians have long debated the quality of education, but, over the past decades, this debate has intensified. Perhaps because we expect our schools to do so much—teach, equalize opportunity, instill discipline, and fire

the imagination—people are divided on whether public schools are doing their job.

School Discipline and Violence

When many of today's older teachers think back to their own student days, school "problems" consisted of talking out of turn, chewing gum, breaking the dress code, or cutting class. Today, schools are grappling with serious issues such as drug and alcohol abuse, teenage pregnancy, and outright violence.

The American government estimates that several hundred thousand students and at least 1000 teachers are physically assaulted on school grounds every year. This violence at school is blamed on poverty-stricken urban environments that breed drug use as well as violence on the street and at home. All too often, violence in American communities and schools involves the use of guns.

Canada's school discipline problems are not of the same type or magnitude, but there have been many instances of assault on students and teachers; students have been found at school with knives—most often in specific schools prone to violence—but rarely with guns. At the post-secondary level, the 1989 killing of 14 female engineering students at Montreal's l'école Polytechnique shocked Canadians. In September 2006, a woman was killed in a shooting rampage at Montreal's Dawson College, which left the shooter dead and 19 other people injured. Such incidents drive home the realization that, even within our schools, we are not immune to deadly violence.

More commonly, however, the discipline problems in our schools involve students who display disdain for learning, are rude to their teachers or challenge their authority, skip classes, disrupt the classroom, or otherwise interfere with the formal education of themselves and others. Faculties of education can teach educational theory and the finer points of pedagogy but cannot prepare would-be teachers for their first field placements, where the most pressing question is how to maintain control in the classroom. Teachers, who are trained to teach but find that their energies are diverted into policing students, experience frustration and disillusionment on the job. In recent years, disruptive behaviour has become more common in college and university classes across Canada; for example, the presence of laptop computers in wired classrooms creates unique discipline problems as students check out the social media—openly and sometimes loudly—with their seatmates.

Dropping Out

If many students are disruptive in class, others are not there at all. The problem of dropping out—quitting school before completing a high school diploma—leaves young people, many of whom are disadvantaged to begin with, ill equipped for the world of work and at high risk for poverty. In a report titled *Leaving School,* which compares school leavers and high school graduates, Gilbert and colleagues (1993) note that leavers are more likely to be from single-parent families, to have parents with lower educational attainment, to be married or have children, to

have lower grades, to have failed a grade in elementary school, to have worked more than 20 hours per week during school, or to use drugs and alcohol.

Young people who drop out of school in a credentials-based society are more likely to end up unemployed or in minimum-wage jobs. Faced with this reality, as many as a quarter of school leavers return to the classroom at a later time.

Statistics Canada (2005b) notes that our high school dropout rates have been declining since the early 1990s, especially in the Atlantic provinces. The decline was greater for young women than young men, and was greater in urban centres than in small towns and rural areas. "The high school dropout rate is defined as the proportion of young people aged 20 to 24 who are not attending school, and who have not graduated from high school"; by this measure, the dropout rate for 1990–91 was 16.7 percent, declining to 9.8 percent by 2004–05. Since employers are less likely to hire high school dropouts, their unemployment rate (at 19.4 percent) is double that of others in this age group. Census 2006 and NHS 2011 reveal that, among young adults aged 25 to 34 years, 13 and 11 percent of men had not graduated from high school; this was true of 9 and 8 percent of women. In other words, while dropping out decreased for both men and women—between 2006 and 2011—men continue to be more likely to drop out than women.

While progress at the national level is encouraging, Newfoundland and Labrador and Prince Edward Island are the stars. Their rates dropped from the highest in the country (20 percent) in the early 1990s to 8 or 10 percent by 2004–05, placing them among the regions with the lowest dropout rates. Quebec and the prairie provinces have had rates above 10 percent in recent years, but these represent a decline from 16 percent and 17 percent, respectively, in the early 1990s.

Academic Standards

Canada and the United States share a growing concern with the quality of schooling. In 1983, in the United States, the National Commission on Excellence in Education prepared *A Nation at Risk,* a comprehensive report on the quality of American schools. The report noted that "nearly 40 percent of 17-year-olds cannot draw inferences from written material; only one-fifth can write a persuasive essay; and only one-third can solve mathematical problems requiring several steps" (1983:9). Furthermore, scores on the Scholastic Aptitude Test have declined steadily since the early 1960s. Few observers of the North American scene doubt that schooling has suffered a setback. *A Nation at Risk* also noted with alarm the extent of functional illiteracy. Roughly one in eight children in the United States completes secondary school without learning to read

CURRENTLY OUR SOCIETY IS DEBATING MANY STRATEGIES FOR IMPROVING EDUCATION Some parents have kept their children out of formal education altogether, believing that their youngsters can learn more at home, using information available not only in books, but also in cyberspace.

or write very well. The Thinking Critically box near the beginning of this chapter makes it clear that functional illiteracy is a major problem in Canada as well. The practice of passing youngsters to the next grade, despite reading and writing deficits, contributes to this problem.

Canadians express concerns about the quality of our educational experience, in part because of observations about the skills (or lack thereof) of graduates but also because of the lack of fit between these skills and the demands of the labour market, as indicated by unemployment levels. Concerns were heightened in 1992, when Canadian students appeared to do poorly in international mathematics tests involving a number of countries (including Japan). Barlow and Robertson (1994) assert that the results were misleading because they compared the performance of elite groups of students in some countries with a more broadly based Canadian cohort. However, media, special reports, and the business community were quick to criticize the public school systems, thereby capitalizing on public disaffection and manipulating public opinion against schools (Barlow & Robertson, 1994). The provincial and territorial governments, being responsible for education, were quick to join in the criticism of schools and the search for solutions. Using the test scores in the international study of performance in mathematics, some argued for a radical restructuring of education in Canada. Among the suggested solutions to our problems were many that are consistent with the political right and corporate interests:

- national testing and standards to measure the quality of the "product"—that is, students
- downsizing for greater efficiency so there are fewer school boards and teachers

- vouchers to allow students and families to shop for their schools
- privatization to create schools run by the private sector
- partnerships between corporations and schools or universities
- corporate sponsorship of various programs, often involving overt advertising within schools
- harmonization with educational practices in the United States

Since then, as discussed earlier in this chapter, Canada has incorporated national testing to assess the reading, mathematics, and science skills of 13-year-olds by province. These tests reveal substantial cross-country variation in skill levels, with Quebec and Ontario (and in the case of science, Alberta) ranking first and second.

Vouchers, which generally provide public funding to subsidize children who are attending private schools, are available in many U.S. states. The issue continues to be hotly debated there and was considered very seriously by Ontario in the early 2000s before being rejected. Instead, the Conservative government provided a 50 percent tax credit for tuition paid to Ontario's independent or private schools. This was subsequently cancelled by the Liberal government that followed.

Partnerships of various kinds between corporations and universities, in the areas of research or technology development and transfer, have been forged over the past decade. These partnerships are controversial because research results could be manipulated to serve corporate interests. Some of the same concerns are voiced when universities turn to the private sector for contributions to their fundraising campaigns.

Current Issues in Canadian Education

20.6 Discuss home schooling and the impact of gender on educational outcomes.

Our society's schools continuously confront new challenges. This section explores several recent and important educational issues, including school choice, home schooling, schooling people with disabilities, adult education, and the teacher shortage.

Home Schooling

Home schooling is gaining popularity in North America, where about 2 to 4 percent of school-aged children are educated at home. Home schooling is more popular in the United States than in Canada, where it involves

Andersen Ross/Blend Images/Getty Images

about 0.5 percent of children. It is legal in Canada and is used by many families stationed abroad (e.g., in the military). Each province has its own home schooling laws and provides resources to the families involved. One example is an online curriculum from kindergarten to grades 12 or 13. Provincial home-schooling associations are also available to support parents in their endeavours.

Why do parents undertake the enormous challenge of schooling their own children? Some 20 years ago, most of the parents who pioneered home schooling did so to give their children a strong religious upbringing. While religion is still a consideration, many parents today simply do not believe that public schools are doing a good job and think they can do better. To benefit their children, they are willing to forgo careers, alter work schedules, and relearn algebra and other necessary subjects. Many belong to groups in which parents pool their efforts, specializing in what each person knows best.

Advocates of home schooling point out that, given the poor performance of many public schools, no one should be surprised that a growing number of parents are willing to teach their own children. In addition, this system works; on average, students who learn at home outperform those who learn in schools (Cloud & Morse, 2001). The Sociology and the Media box, with its emphasis on cyber-school, or online learning, has real implications for home schooling.

Gender in Higher Education

Over the past two decades, across North America, colleges and universities are certifying many more women than men—increasingly in non-traditional fields such as mathematics, physics, engineering, and science. In other traditionally male programs (e.g., medicine and veterinary medicine), women make up the majority of recent graduates. Overall, North American colleges and universities are dominated by women.

The National Household Survey (NHS 2011) provides us with macro-level evidence of the gender gap in higher education. Observing the highest levels of educational attainment—among 25- to 64-year-olds—reveals that overall young women are more highly educated than young men (see Table 20–4). Men are more likely to have no certification at all, whereas women have a slight edge in post-secondary credentials. Not surprisingly, men predominate in apprenticeships or trades (16 vs 8 percent of women), while women predominate at the college level (24 vs 19 percent) and at the bachelor's level (18 to 15 percent).

However, if you want to know about recent trends, you look at 25- to 34-year-olds—who are old enough to

have finished school and young enough to reflect the "latest." The data on the younger cohort (Table 20–4) suggest that men are more likely than women to drop out before completing high school or to graduate and go no farther. Young women take the lead in acquiring post-secondary credentials (74 and 65 percent), most notably at the level of "bachelor's or above" (37 vs 27 percent). Proportionately, young women have more bachelor's, medical, and master's degrees! Women appear to be closing the Ph.D. gap as well.

So where are the men? Part of the explanation for the lack of men on Canadian (or North American) campuses may well be the old anti-intellectual male culture that discourages post-secondary education. There are numerous "male" jobs with reasonable pay that entice young men (e.g., in construction or jobs in the oil fields of Alberta). Another theory is that young men are drawn away from post-secondary education by the lure of jobs in computer science, web design, and related technologies. This pattern might be called the "Bill Gates syndrome" or the "Mark Zuckerberg syndrome" after the men who became rich and famous after dropping out of college.

Whatever the reasons for the gap in educational attainment, it raises questions about the future of gender relations. What, for example, will happen to the old notion that women should marry men who are taller, older, and better educated? What will happen if more women—it's happening already in North America and the European Union—become the breadwinners in their

Table 20–4 Highest Level of Educational Attainment by Age Cohort and Sex, 2011

	25- to 64-year-olds %		25- to 34-year-olds %	
	Men	Women	Men	Women
Population	8 984 390	7 171 140	2 108 255	2 185 695
Level of certification				
None	13.8	11.6	**11.0**	7.6
High School	22.8	23.6	**24.3**	18.7
Postsecondary:	63.4	**64.8**	64.7	**73.7**
Apprenticeship or trades	**16.0**	8.3	**14.2**	7.3
College or CEGEP	18.6	**23.8**	19.9	**24.3**
Bachelor's or above:	24.5	**27.2**	26.5	**37.1**
Bachelor's	15.1	**17.8**	18.2	**25.4**
Medical*	0.7	0.6	0.6	**0.9**
Master's	5.1	5.1	4.7	**6.3**
Earned doctorate (Ph.D.)	**1.1**	0.7	0.7	0.6

*Refers to degrees in medicine, dentistry, veterinary medicine or optometry.

SOURCE: Compilation and calculations by LM Gerber based on Statistics Canada, NHS 2011 Catalogue no. 99-012-X2011037.

Sociology and the Media

Welcome to Cyber-School

The wired planet has no boundaries and no monopolies of knowledge. The affairs of the world are now dependent upon the highest information of which man is capable…. The boundaries between the world of affairs and the community of learning have ceased to exist. The workaday world now demands encyclopedic wisdom…. Under these conditions, the old form of specialized jobs has lost meaning. It was meaningful at very low speeds, but it has now been assumed into patterns of electric speeds. This change of pace from production-line to online computer programming has been ignored, just as the shift from hardware to software accelerates, making the old categories meaningless (McLuhan and Nevitt, quoted in Benedetti & DeHart, 1996:172).

Education is responding to the arrival of computer-literate children and the demands of a drastically altered, knowledge-based economy by integrating computers and the internet throughout the education system—from kindergarten to Ph.D. The goal at primary and secondary levels is to have computers in every classroom, while universities and colleges are placing more emphasis on computer-based, interactive, self-directed learning in the context of global electronic information flow. Much of the computer-based work is specific to a single course or lab and is completed in the school, but students are also logging on to school or campus websites from home.

On campuses in Canada, it is assumed that students have computers and that they can be reached by email—although cell phones and tablets now serve to keep students in the loop. Email addresses come with their registration packages. Some private schools and colleges or university programs require laptops in class. For example, the University of Ontario Institute of Technology requires students to lease laptops as they register because so many of their programs require them. Technologically sophisticated distance-learning options and even virtual universities have been developed—while some high schools are going "paperless."

Edmonton public schools offer online learning through LearnNet (2016)—with programming based on the Alberta curriculum—to a geographically unbounded community. It is used by families who prefer home schooling or who live in remote areas—the result being that many of the students are First Nations, Métis, and Inuit. At the same time, its use by Canadian families stationed abroad is expanding (Expatriate Group, 2009). Other options for virtual education serving expatriates (and home schooling) include St. Albert Catholic High School, St. Paul's Academy, and University of Athabaska (a virtual university delivering online and distance education across Canada and worldwide).

At the university level we see computer conferencing, online courses, multimedia distance education, and more complex virtual universities (such as the University of Athabaska). Undergraduate and graduate students are relying increasingly on the internet as a means of communication and a source of information. For example, Statistics Canada data and publications increasingly are available only on the internet or on CD-ROM; its publication *The Daily,* among many other products, no longer appears on paper at all. Federal and provincial election results are available online at Elections Canada, for example, as they are through the CBC, other news channels, and major newspapers.

Academic journals in the sciences and social sciences are also available online; as of 2016, the *Canadian Review of Sociology* (CRS) is available *only* online (unless someone wants to purchase a special print copy). Most recently, purely electronic journals—several in the field of sociology—have appeared. Unlike the CRS, which is converting to that format, others are not attached to the associations of specific disciplines. In fact, they are often multidisciplinary. In most cases today, the researcher conducts computer analyses, writes a paper using a word processor, submits the paper electronically, has it sent to reviewers via the internet, and then sees it published in electronic form. Throughout this process, pen may never be set to paper. Access to information, as well as the production and dissemination of knowledge, has changed profoundly and irrevocably.

What Do You Think?

1. What are the advantages and disadvantages of the virtual university? Would you be able to function effectively in such a context?

2. Home schooling can be very traditional or technologically advanced and internet-based. What do you see as the advantages and disadvantages of home schooling?

3. Are you at the point in your studies where you do most of your reading and studying online?

families? Indeed, what will happen to Canadian society if more highly educated women choose not to marry—and not to have children? Gender relations have already changed dramatically in a trend that will undoubtedly intensify in the future.

Education: Looking Ahead

As a society, Canada is undergoing a series of changes with implications for our educational systems. First, we are dealing with increasing diversity as a result of steady immigration, cultural pluralism (partly in response to our policy of multiculturalism), ethnic nationalism (most visibly among Québécois and Aboriginal peoples), as well as continuing regional and class divisions. The fact that education falls under provincial jurisdiction complicates matters even more. In this context, the educational system is required to promote equality of access, participation, and outcome, as well as to play an integrative role, in part by fostering a Canadian identity that overrides our differences.

Second, Canada is experiencing technological change involving the expanded use of computers and the internet, which in turn has an impact on organizational patterns (e.g., the possibility of working at home while electronically hooked up to the office). The promise of this new technology goes beyond helping students learn basic skills; computers actually may improve the overall quality of learning. Interacting with computers prompts students to be more active and allows them to progress at their own pace. For students with disabilities who cannot write using a pencil, computers make self-expression possible. Using computers in schools, in some cases as early as kindergarten, also appears to increase learning speed and retention of information.

The potential for information technology to transform colleges and universities—and perhaps even high schools—is unlimited. We already have online courses and textbooks as well as virtual universities. Students around the world are taking courses and earning degrees from major western universities without leaving the comfort of their homes. Courses taught by experts in their fields (on video) are available for individual use or inclusion in existing programs at any colleges or universities that choose to adopt them. At the extreme, all of this technology may make the university lecture hall—if not the professor—obsolete.

In the meantime, the numerous benefits of computers should not blind us to their limitations. Computers will never bring to the educational process the personal insight or imagination of a motivated teacher. While the jury may be out on whether computers have improved teaching, there is no doubt that they have proliferated in the classroom. Computers have become central to the experience of students in many classes, from kindergarten through university. In some Canadian universities, all students are required to have computers and, in some programs, they are required to bring laptops to class. Because of the expense involved, this type of requirement creates a new source of inequality in access to knowledge—unless students earn credits for most if not all college or university program requirements without the expense of leaving home.

Third, we face a shrinking world of shifting political alliances, economic restructuring, multinational corporations, and global competition—wherein we strive to maintain our quality of life. Insofar as education is responsible for the development of skills relevant to the labour market, our schools must foster in students both technical skills and an ability to be innovative, flexible, and analytical. Many more students now need to "think global" even in terms of their own career options.

Education is intricately involved with change as a catalyst, an adaptive mechanism, and a force for maintaining tradition and continuity. It is simultaneously an explosive irritant and one of the ingredients in the glue that binds us together.

Seeing Sociology in Everyday Life

CHAPTER 20 Education

How much inequality is there in Canadian schooling?

Schools, of course, differ in many ways. For example, there are several tiers of schooling in Canada that reflect the social class standing of the students who enrol. The images below provide a closer look at this educational hierarchy.

At the top of the schooling hierarchy are private schools—the best of which will have large endowments, small classes, and highly dedicated teachers. Their campuses have the most up-to-date facilities and classroom technologies. If you had the means, would you want to send your child or children to a private school? Would it make a difference if you had attended a private school?

Hint Private boarding schools (many of which enrol day students as well) provide outstanding education that prepares students to succeed in university or college. Despite scholarships and bursaries provided by the school, high tuition fees put private schools beyond the reach of the average Canadian family. In contrast, many religious private schools and charter schools have substantially lower tuition fees.

In Canada, each province shapes its own curriculum, regulates class size, and sets basic standards—thereby setting the stage for regional inequalities in education. In addition, since much of the funding for public schools comes from property taxes, schools in affluent communities (with expensive real estate) are better equipped than those in municipalities with lower average incomes and less expensive homes. This is another factor contributing to educational inequity across the country.

Schooling on Canada's First Nations reserves is funded and regulated by Aboriginal Affairs and Northern Development Canada and distributed to communities through their band councils. In many, if not most, cases, the communities themselves have assumed responsibility for curriculum design and school administration. This arrangement creates another tier of schools that differs substantially from those in the public school system.

WHEN BARACK AND MICHELLE OBAMA MOVED TO THE WHITE HOUSE, THEY FACED THE CHOICE OF WHERE TO ENROL THEIR TWO YOUNG DAUGHTERS They chose a private school. Although there are prestigious private schools in Ottawa, Stephen and Laureen Harper chose to send their two children to public school. Justin Trudeau, who attended Rockcliffe Park Public School when his father was the prime minister, says that his children will go to public school as well.

Tom Hanson/The Canadian Press

Brian Summers/First Light

FOR MANY REASONS, FIRST NATIONS SCHOOLS ON RESERVES FAIL TO PREPARE ROUGHLY HALF OF THEIR STUDENTS FOR HIGH SCHOOL GRADUATION AND POST-SECONDARY STUDIES A major study conducted by a special panel—reporting to the Minister of Aboriginal Affairs and the National Chief of the Assembly of First Nations (Shawn Atleo)—made numerous recommendations for on-reserve schooling. The report pointed out that because of geographic isolation and a number of other challenges and barriers to learning, First Nations education will be more expensive than it is elsewhere.

SCHOOLS IN MANY LOW-INCOME COMMUNITIES ARE FORCED TO GET BY WITH LIMITED RESOURCES Here, students from Toronto's Parkdale Collegiate express their dissatisfaction with cuts made to their school's budget.

Ron Bull/Toronto Star/Getty Images

Seeing Sociology in *Your* Everyday Life

1. Ask your friends on campus about their high school experience. Did any of them attend private school? Do those who came through the public school system feel that their classrooms were as well equipped as those in other schools?

2. Most people feel that teaching our children is important work, yet the salaries of secondary and primary school teachers are only slightly better than the average. Do you think teachers are paid what they are worth?

3. Universities and colleges are required by law to be accessible to people with physical and learning disabilities. Do you know what is being done on your campus to meet the needs of such students?

Making the Grade

CHAPTER 20 Education

Education: A Global Survey

20.1 Compare schooling in high-, middle-, and low-income societies.

Education is the social institution for transmitting knowledge and skills, as well as teaching cultural norms and values.

- In pre-industrial societies, education occurs informally within the family.
- Industrial societies develop formal systems of schooling to educate their children.
- Differences in schooling in societies around the world today reflect both cultural values and each country's level of economic development.

> **education** the social institution through which society provides its members with important knowledge, including basic facts, job skills, and cultural norms and values
> **schooling** formal instruction under the direction of specially trained teachers
> **functional illiteracy** a lack of the reading and writing skills needed for everyday living

Schooling in India

- Despite the fact that India is now a middle-income country, patriarchy continues to shape education in India. Many more boys attend school than girls, who are often expected to work in factories at young ages.
- Today, 97 percent of children in India complete primary school, and 92 percent go on to secondary school.

Schooling in Japan

- The earliest years of schooling in Japan concentrate on transmitting Japanese cultural traditions.
- More men and women graduate from high school in Japan (99 percent) than in Canada (90 percent), but only half of high school graduates gain post-secondary education, which is determined by highly competitive examinations.

Schooling in Great Britain

- During the Middle Ages, schooling was a privilege of the British nobility. The Industrial Revolution created a need for a literate workforce.
- Traditional class differences still affect British schooling; elite schools, which enrol 7 percent of British students, provide a path for admission to the most prestigious universities.

Schooling in Canada

- Canada embraced the ideal of universal education at the time of Confederation. By 1920, Canada had compulsory education to the end of elementary school or to age 16.
- Schooling in Canada is intended to promote equal opportunity, but the opportunity to go to college or university is closely tied to family income.
- The Canadian educational system has long stressed the value of practical learning, but we lag behind other countries in awarding degrees in engineering, applied sciences, mathematics, and the physical sciences.

The Functions of Schooling

20.2 Apply structural-functional theory to schooling.

Structural-functional theory focuses on the ways in which schooling contributes to the orderly operation of society. Key functions of schooling include:

- *Socialization*—teaching the skills that young people need to succeed in life, as well as cultural values and norms
- *Cultural innovation*—providing the opportunity for academic research that leads to important discoveries
- *Social integration*—moulding a diverse population into one society by teaching cultural norms and values
- *Social placement*—reinforcing meritocracy and providing a path for upward social mobility
- *Latent functions*—providing child care and the opportunity for building social networks

Schooling and Social Interaction

20.3 Apply symbolic-interaction theory to schooling.

Symbolic-interaction theory looks at how we build reality in our day-to-day interactions.

- The "self-fulfilling prophecy" describes how self-image can have important consequences for how students perform in school. If students think they are academically superior, they are likely to perform better; students who think they are inferior are likely to perform less well.

Schooling and Social Inequality

20.4 Apply social-conflict theory to schooling.

Social-conflict theory links schooling to inequality involving class, race, and gender.

- Formal education serves as a means of generating conformity to produce obedient adult workers.
- Standardized tests have been criticized as culturally biased tools that may lead to labelling less privileged students as personally deficient.
- **Streaming** has been challenged by critics as a program that gives a better education to privileged youngsters.
- Most young people in Canada attend publicly funded schools (including Catholic schools). A small proportion of students attend elite private schools or independent religious and charter schools.
- Canadians do not have equal access to education due to the effects of social class, race, ethnicity, and geographic isolation.
- Because education is under provincial jurisdiction, provinces differ in the outcome of their educational systems; 13-year-olds in some provinces do better in tests of reading, mathematics, and science than those in other provinces.

The education of **Aboriginal people** poses real challenges for Canadian society because:

- Their levels of educational attainment lag far behind those of other Canadians.
- On average, the gap between Aboriginal and non-Aboriginal people in terms of educational attainment is increasing, despite real improvement over time.
- Almost half of on-reserve Aboriginal people do not graduate from high school.
- The legacy of the residential school system is largely responsible for the gap in educational attainment between First Nations and non-Aboriginal Canadians.

hidden curriculum, subtle presentations of political or cultural ideas in the classroom
streaming assigning students to different types of educational programs

Problems in the Schools

20.5 Discuss violence, dropping out, and other problems facing today's schools.

School discipline is difficult to maintain in the best of schools and close to impossible in others; when it breaks down schools experience disruptive classroom behaviour of all sorts, physical assault, and infrequently even murder.

- Critics charge that schools today fall short in their attempts to teach personal discipline. This is evident even in college and university classrooms.

The high school **dropout rate** leaves many young people unprepared for the world of work and at high risk of poverty.

- Dropout rates in Canada have declined over time to the point where roughly 10 percent of the Canadian population fails to graduate from high school.
- High school graduation is most common among those who lived with two biological parents at age 15 and both parents completed high school.

Declining academic standards are reflected in

- today's lower average scores on achievement tests, including international tests
- the functional illiteracy of a significant proportion of our population

Current Issues in Canadian Education

20.6 Discuss home schooling and the impact of gender on academic outcomes.

Home Schooling

- The original pioneers of home schooling turned away from public education because they wanted to give their children a strongly religious upbringing.
- Home schooling advocates today point to the poor performance of public schools, believing that parents can do a better job.
- Home schooling is legal in Canada and is supported by the provinces through the provision of online materials that meet their curriculum requirements.

Gender in Higher Education

- Historically, women were barred from pursuing higher education both formally and through cultural expectations regarding gender roles.
- Over time, women caught up with men in terms of acquiring post-secondary qualifications.
- Currently, women have overtaken men to the point where they have substantially better records than men at the post-secondary level—in college, bachelor's, medical, and master's certification.
- In contrast, men tend to drop out prior to high school graduation, at the time of graduation, or part way through college or university programs.

Chapter 21
Health and Medicine

Rostislav Sedlacek/Fotolia

⌄ Learning Objectives

21.1 Explain how patterns of health are shaped by society.

21.2 Contrast patterns of health in low- and high-income countries.

21.3 Analyze how race, class, gender, and age are linked to health.

21.4 Compare the medical systems in nations around the world.

21.5 Apply sociology's major theories to health and medicine.

The Power of Society
to shape patterns of health

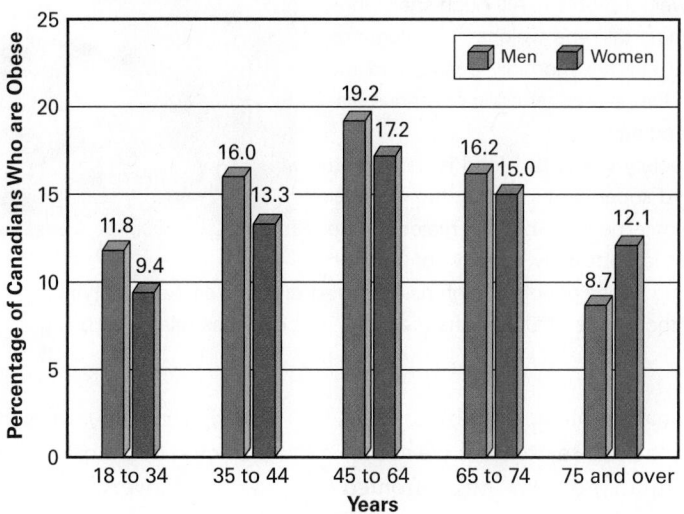

Note: Obesity is defined as a BMI of 30.0 or higher. The data here refer to the year 2000.

SOURCE: Compilation and calculations by LM Gerber based on Statistics Canada, CANSIM, Table 105-007.

The incidence of obesity—meaning a BMI or body mass index of 30.0 or higher—in Canada is barely half that of the United States. But it is concerning because, due to lifestyle changes, obesity rates are increasing over time. The pattern you see in this figure shows that the incidence of obesity varies with both age and sex. People aged 18 to 34 *or* 75 and over have the lowest rates while those in between—especially those aged 45 to 64 years—have the highest. The rates of both men and women rise and then fall as they age; *however*, there is one big difference. Women start off with substantially lower rates of obesity than men, come close to catching up by the age of 70, and surpass male levels at ages 75 and over. How can this be? Young men are supposed to be more active than women *and* they produce less estrogen—the hormone that stimulates fat storage—so why are they more likely to be obese? The higher mortality rates associated with obesity undoubtedly contribute to lower levels in old age, but men's rates drop faster. Are the effects of too much food and too little exercise more lethal for men than women?

Chapter Overview

This chapter explores health care, including medicine, a social institution of major importance. The chapter begins by explaining why health is a social issue and why sociologists have much to say about human health.

Stephanie says she cannot remember a time in her life when she was not on a diet. The 16-year-old, who lives in Winnipeg, shakes her head. "It's, like, I can't do anything about it. I know I don't look good. My mom says I shouldn't eat so much; the nurse at school says the same thing. Why can't I ever lose any weight?"

Stephanie does have a weight problem. Although she stands just 160 centimetres (63 inches) tall, she weighs 109 kilograms (240 pounds). Doctors would call her morbidly obese, and the longer she remains so heavy, the greater her odds of serious disease and even death at a young age.

She is not alone. In a society where fast food is consumed daily and people use the word *supersize* as a verb, too many of us are getting fat. Not just some people—but the majority—are overweight. Being overweight is not simply a matter of looks. It is a critical health issue, putting obese people at high risk for heart disease, stroke, and type 2 diabetes. Each year, tens of thousands of Canadians die early from diseases related to being overweight. ■

Martin Parr/Magnum Photos

Obesity is not just a personal problem; it is also a social problem. The choices we make do matter, but we are up against some powerful cultural forces. We are confronted with unhealthy fast food at every turn, and our national consumption of hamburgers, potato chips, sugar-rich soft drinks, pizza, and candy bars rises every year. The tendency to eat fast food, even in family settings, is accentuated by our lifestyles: Single-parent and dual-career families—combined with hectic schedules of sports and music and dance lessons—have precious little time for home-cooked meals at the dining-room table.

What Is Health?

21.1 Explain how patterns of health are shaped by society.

The World Health Organization defines **health** as *a state of complete physical, mental, and social well-being* (1946:3). This definition underscores the major theme of this chapter: that health is not just a matter of personal choice; nor is it only a biological issue. Patterns of well-being and illness are rooted in the organization of society.

Health and Society

Society shapes people's health in four major ways:

1. **Cultural patterns define health.** Standards of health vary from place to place. A century ago, yaws, a contagious skin disease, was so common in sub-Saharan Africa that people there considered it normal (Dubos, 1980; orig. 1965). In North America, a rich diet is so common that most adults and about one-sixth of children are overweight. "Health," therefore, is sometimes a matter of having the same disease as your neighbours (Centers for Disease Control and Prevention, 2015; Pinhey et al., 1997).

   What people see as healthful also reflects what they think is morally good. Men may think that a competitive or aggressive approach to life is "healthy" or natural because it fits with our norms of masculinity, but the resulting stress contributes to heart disease and many other illnesses. "Dangerous masculinity" may result in accidents and assault, specifically in sports such as hockey (Atkinson, 2007). People who object to homosexuality on moral grounds call this sexual orientation "sick," even though it is natural from a biological point of view. In these ways, ideas about health can act as a form of social control, encouraging conformity to cultural norms.

2. **Cultural standards of health change over time.** In the early twentieth century, some doctors warned women not to go to university because higher education strained the female brain. Others claimed that masturbation was a threat to health. We know now that both of these ideas are false. On the other hand, 50 years ago, few doctors recognized cigarette smoking or too much sun exposure as serious health risks. We are only now beginning to recognize the extent to which the high salt (or sodium) content of prepared foods is a major contributor to high blood pressure. Even basic hygiene changes over time. Today, most

of us bathe every day; 50 years ago, that would have been true of less than a third of us (Gillespie, 2000).

3. **A society's technology affects people's health.** In poor countries, infectious diseases are widespread because of malnutrition and poor sanitation. As industrialization raises living standards, health improves. But industrial technology also creates new threats to health—by overtaxing the world's resources, creating pollution, and contributing to global warming.

4. **Social inequality affects people's health.** All societies distribute resources unequally. In Canada, despite **universal medical coverage**, *a system in which the costs of essential medical services are covered by the state*, the rich have far better physical and mental health than the poor. They also live longer.

Health: A Global Survey

21.2 Contrast patterns of health in low- and high-income countries.

The impact of social factors on human well-being is apparent in the improved health associated with economic development and advanced technology. Differences in societal development are also reflected in the striking differences in health around the world.

Health in Low-Income Countries

In much of the world, severe poverty cuts decades off the long life expectancy typical of rich countries. People in most parts of Africa have life expectancies of less than 60 years, and in the poorest countries nearly one in ten newborns dies within a year and almost one in four dies before reaching the age of 30 (United Nations, 2013; World Bank, 2015).

The World Health Organization reports that 1 billion people around the world—about one person in six—suffer from serious illness due to poverty. Most poverty-linked disease occurs in low-income countries, where poverty accounts for 70 percent of all illness. In rich countries, by contrast, poverty is the cause of just 7 percent of all illness (Bloom et al., 2011; Murray et al., 2012).

How does poverty threaten health? In simple terms, poor sanitation and malnutrition kill people of all ages. A lack of safe drinking water is also common, and bad water carries a number of infectious diseases, including influenza, pneumonia, and tuberculosis, which are widespread killers in poor societies today. To make matters worse, medical personnel are few and far between; as a result, the world's poorest people—many of whom live in Central Africa—never see a physician.

In a classic vicious circle, poverty breeds disease, which in turn undermines the ability to work. When medical technology controls infectious disease, the populations of poor nations soar. Without resources to provide for the current population, poor societies can ill afford population increases. Therefore, programs that lower death rates in poor countries will succeed only if they are coupled with programs that reduce birth rates.

Health in High-Income Countries

By 1800, as the Industrial Revolution took hold, factory jobs in the cities attracted people from all over the countryside in England and Europe. Cities quickly became overcrowded, a condition that made the already poor sanitation worse. Factories fouled the air with smoke, which few recognized as a health threat until well into the twentieth century. Workplace accidents were common.

Gradually, industrialization improved health in Western Europe and North America by providing better nutrition and safer housing for most people. After 1850, medical advances began to control infectious diseases. In 1854, for example, Dr. John Snow mapped the street addresses of London's cholera victims and found that they all drank contaminated water from the same well. Not long afterwards, scientists linked cholera to a specific bacterium and developed a vaccine against the deadly disease. Armed with scientific knowledge, early environmentalists campaigned against age-old practices such as discharging raw sewage into the same rivers used for drinking water.

By the early twentieth century, death rates from infectious diseases (such as influenza and pneumonia) had fallen sharply. Chronic illnesses (such as heart disease, cancer, and stroke) now cause most deaths in North America and Europe, usually in old age.

Health in Canada

21.3 Analyze how race, class, gender, and age are linked to health.

As a rich nation, Canada's health is good by world standards, but recall that health is defined as complete physical, mental, and social well-being. By *that* standard, no country measures up. In 2003, Canada was completely unprepared to handle severe acute respiratory syndrome (SARS), the first in a series of public health threats to strike with some regularity through to 2009. The Sociology in Focus box takes a closer look at these health crises. Though we are now less vulnerable to infectious diseases, we do have our share of cancer, heart disease, and mental illnesses.

Social epidemiology is *the study of health and disease as distributed throughout a society's population*. Just as early social epidemiologists, such as Dr. John Snow, traced the

Sociology in Focus

SARS, West Nile, One Mad Cow, and Bird and Swine Flu

In March 2003, two cases of atypical pneumonia in Toronto were identified as severe acute respiratory syndrome, or SARS. Suddenly, Canada was part of a global network that eventually would include 31 countries with SARS cases. We were faced with a two-pronged threat: importation of new cases from abroad and spread from the medical facilities that were caring for active SARS cases.

Tourism in Toronto, and in Canada as a whole, was dealt a crippling blow when the World Health Organization issued a travel advisory discouraging non-essential visits to Toronto. Conferences were cancelled and individuals changed their travel plans. Toronto residents avoided public places—Chinese restaurants and businesses in particular, as several SARS patients were of Chinese ancestry. Hundreds of other residents were "voluntarily" quarantined in their homes. Until it became clear that new cases arose almost exclusively in hospitals, and not from casual contact on the subway, there was a great deal of anxiety in Toronto. In the end, 438 cases of SARS (with 38 deaths) were identified.

Next, Canada dealt with one case of "mad cow" disease on an Alberta farm. The cow appeared ill when slaughtered, but a delay of several months in testing its brain tissues complicated the task of tracking down its bovine contacts, feed sources, and offspring. Thousands of cattle linked in any way to the one identified case were slaughtered and tested for bovine spongiform encephalopathy (BSE). New regulations prohibited the use of certain tissues (e.g., brain) in animal and human foods, or of diseased carcasses in animal feed.

Whereas loyal Canadians, including politicians, continued to eat beef, our cattle industry was devastated by American steps to close the border to Canadian beef and cattle (our leading agricultural product, 80 percent of which is exported to the United States). In the fall of 2003, farmers had to decide what to do with thousands of unsold cattle. Unable to feed them through the coming winter, farmers killed and burned excess healthy livestock. Fortunately, none of the infected cattle identified in Canada or the United States entered the human food chain, where they would have threatened people with the ultimately fatal Creutzfeldt-Jakob disease.

The West Nile scare in the summer of 2003 had a happier outcome. First reported among Ontario crows and blue jays in 2001, West Nile virus was confirmed in humans only in the summer and fall of 2002, with 3 confirmed cases, 14 suspected cases, and 1 death in Ontario. Canadians braced themselves for many more cases, but the number of Ontario cases in 2003 was limited to two, and elsewhere the numbers were similarly small. Of course, there were many sub-clinical cases of West Nile infection, since the vast majority of infected people are symptom-free.

In 2005, we faced the threat of bird (or avian) flu, a pandemic said to be "long overdue," with the potential to kill millions worldwide. Starting in Asia, the flu gradually appeared in pockets in Europe and even North America. A virus called H5N1 was infecting chickens—and people handling those chickens were falling ill and dying. Because those with mild symptoms were never diagnosed, it seemed that half of all people who caught the flu (from birds) were dying. The World Health Organization declared that *human-to-human* transmission of something like H5N1 is inevitable, and here in North America we started producing and stockpiling antiviral medications (e.g., Tamiflu and Relenza).

The latest potential pandemic, which hit Canada in 2009, was swine flu or H1N1. Canada was hardest hit of all countries, with a rate of 20 cases per 100 000 population. Ranked second was Australia, at 13 cases per 100 000. Saskatchewan and Manitoba, with rates of 61 and 45 per 100 000, respectively, have large Aboriginal populations that are vulnerable because of chronic disease linked to poverty.

While 60 Canadians had died from swine flu by August 2009, 8000 Canadians die each year from infections contracted in our hospitals (the "superbug," *C. difficile,* being the main culprit). From this perspective, the swine flu pandemic and the bird flu scare of 2012 were false alarms; since flu threats are sporadic, we should turn our attention to the prevention of hospital-based infections instead.

While bird flu and swine flu threatened us, Canadians were debating who should get the limited supply of antiviral medications. Front-line responders such as doctors and firefighters are obvious choices, but how do you value babies, young adults, the elderly, or Aboriginal people? Who should receive antivirals *first* in the event of pandemic influenza?

What Do You Think?

1. What are the most serious threats to the health of Canadians?

2. Should government decide who gets antivirals, or should individuals be able to obtain them by prescription?

3. Do the media blow these health crises out of proportion? Explain your answer.

SOURCES: Canada (2006b, 2006c), Fumento (2006), Kirkey (2006), Picard (2009), and Wente (2009).

spread of infectious diseases, researchers today examine the connection between health and our physical and social environments. Patterns of health can be viewed in terms of age, gender, social class, and race.

Age and Gender

Death is now rare among young people in North America. Still, young people do fall victim to accidents and, more recently, to acquired immune deficiency syndrome (AIDS). Nonetheless, socio-cultural environments still affect the present and future health of youngsters: Canada's children, who are subject to poor diet, lack of exercise, and second-hand smoke, are tomorrow's cancer and heart patients.

Measures of self-reported health over two decades (Bibby, 1995) reveal that, by 1995, Canadian women were increasingly likely to report "excellent" or "good" health, as shown in Table 21–1. Though reported well-being drops off with age, for both genders, women fared better in 1995 than in 1975. In 1975, reported well-being among women declined after age 35; in 1995, the decline showed up only after age 55. The explanation for the gender gap in well-being after age 55 is that women live longer than men—five years longer, on average—and therefore spend more time in the stage of life when health is on the decline.

The "issue of gender differences in health and illness has gained increasing popularity as a research topic among sociologists" (Segall & Chappell, 2000:30). Gender is linked to life expectancy, major causes of death, the overall experience of health and illness, visits to physicians, and reporting of multiple health problems. Furthermore, socio-economic position, labour force participation, and earned income affect the health and well-being of men and women differently. The effects of employment, marriage, and motherhood—and the resulting role strain—on the health of women are of particular concern.

Social Class and Race

While the health of the richest children in Canada is the best in the world, our poorest children—Aboriginal

Table 21–1 Self-Reported Health: Canadian Women and Men by Age, 1975 to 1995

| | Percentage Reporting "Excellent" or "Good" Health | | | |
| | 1975 | | 1995 | |
	Women	Men	Women	Men
All adults	73	84	80	85
18 to 34	84	94	84	94
35 to 54	76	87	84	85
55 and older	58	66	63	68

SOURCE: Adapted by LM Gerber from Bibby (1995:86).

Table 21–2 Mortality and Life Expectancy, First Nations and All Canadians, 1960 and 1991*

| | 1960 | | 1991 | |
	First Nations	All Canadians	First Nations	All Canadians
Crude death rate[a]	10.9	8.0	9.2	6.0
Infant mortality rate[b]	79.0	27.3	13.0	8.0
Male life expectancy[c]	59.7	68.5	68.0	74.0
Female life expectancy	63.5	74.3	71.3	80.0

[a]Deaths per 1000 population.

[b]Deaths of children in first year of life per 1000 live births.

[c]Age to which a person can expect to live, calculated at time of birth.

SOURCE: Adapted by LM Gerber from Frideres and Gadacz (2008:73).

children, in particular—are as vulnerable to disease as those in the low-income countries of the world. Infant mortality rates (a sensitive indicator of modernization) for First Nations (registered or status Indians) dropped dramatically between 1960 and 1991 (see Table 21–2). Looking at birth and death rates combined, Frideres and Gadacz (2008:74) conclude the following: Between 1900 and the present, the Aboriginal population went through phases of high birth *and* death rates, high birth rates and *falling* death rates, and relatively low birth *and* death rates.

If we were to differentiate rates for on-reserve and off-reserve residents, we would find that on-reserve mortality rates are much higher. Surveys indicate that "residents of rural and remote communities have poorer health than people who live in urban centres" and that "the farther a community is from a large urban centre, the poorer the health of the residents" (McPherson, 2004:413). On this basis, one could say that reserve-based First Nations, most of whom live outside urban centres, suffer triple jeopardy (Gerber, 1990); they become ill and die at younger ages because they are poor, First Nations, and rural.

"Canada is, per capita, the country in the world hit hardest by H1N1, the pandemic strain of influenza formerly known as swine flu" (Picard, 2009). While the rate for Canada was 20 per 100 000 population, Saskatchewan and Manitoba were the "hot spots," with rates of 61 and 45 per 100 000, respectively. According to Picard, the reason for this is that the two provinces are disproportionately Aboriginal—and Aboriginal people suffer poverty and poor housing or sanitation along with a number of poverty-related chronic diseases such as diabetes, asthma, and obesity. Those with underlying chronic conditions are most vulnerable to swine flu.

Researchers tell us that adults in high-income families overwhelmingly report that their health is excellent or very good, but fewer than half of adults in low-income families say the same. Health and social status are strongly related in terms of the incidence of disease or longevity. Affluent people, who have more social capital, are healthier because "they have more knowledge power (from education), more purchasing power (from income) and more employment power (from prestige and access to networks)" (McPherson, 2004:412). Having higher income boosts health by improving nutrition and access to better health care, and by allowing safer and less stressful surroundings (Krueger et al., 2003; Lethbridge-Cejku & Vickerie, 2005).

General health and life expectancy tend to be higher for immigrants than for those born in Canada. The "healthy immigrant effect" is most apparent "among recent immigrants because healthier people are more likely to emigrate, and because health requirements in the *Immigration Act* screen out people with serious medical conditions" (McPherson, 2004:412). The longer immigrants live in Canada, the more their health status approaches the norm. Over time, the poverty that characterizes many ethnic groups or visible minorities takes its toll on health: "Immigrants make less use of health services, especially mental and preventive health services, than the Canadian-born population" (p. 413).

Mental Health

Prior to 1960, people who suffered from mental illness in Canada were kept in large psychiatric hospitals or "asylums." During the 1960s, patients were gradually shifted from these institutions to the community, and pharmaceutical treatment became the norm. At the same time, Canada passed laws protecting people from involuntary detention and treatment (Davis, 2006).

Given limited resources within the health care system, it is important to determine who are "mentally disordered" and who are most in need of care because of the seriousness or severity of their conditions. In defining "serious" in practice, there emerged general agreement that "two, schizophrenia and bipolar disorder (manic-depressive illness), clearly constitute serious conditions" (Davis, 2006:4). People with these two disorders will sometimes appear "visibly different and bizarre." People with other mental conditions qualify if the disorder is *persistent*, causes *functional impairment*, manifests psychotic symptoms and/or bizarre behaviour, is involuntary, and is *treatable* (p. 8). Meeting some of these criteria may qualify other conditions (such as severe depression). Lastly, if individuals come to the attention of the police or some other agency, they, too, may qualify. Thus there are "inequities in service provision, with the 'squeaky wheels' being accommodated and the quietly unwell being overlooked" (p. 9).

Missing from the severe mental illnesses just discussed are the conditions common to young people or the elderly. While people of any age can suffer from anxiety disorders, depression, seasonal affective disorder, or borderline personality disorders, a number of conditions are common to younger people. These include autism, attention deficit hyperactivity disorder (ADHD), and eating disorders (discussed later in this chapter). Among the elderly, the most widespread and debilitating conditions are the dementias (including Alzheimer's disease). The family physician often refers these cases to a pediatrician or geriatrician. The specialist then may initiate treatment or refer cases to a wide range of services, including social work and non-medical support services based in hospitals. These may be covered by medicare, as would referrals to psychiatrists. However, the services of psychologists, music therapists, or specially trained people who provide extended hours of one-on-one therapy to youngsters with autism would not be covered in most, if not all, provinces.

As the provinces prepare their budgets, they first decide how much money to allocate to education, highways and infrastructure, and health care. Then they decide how much to allocate to cancer treatment, heart surgery, and mental health and how much to give each hospital or community. When there are finite resources, no jurisdiction can do everything; again, the squeaky wheel gets the money (or the budgetary allocation).

There are other barriers to mental health care. A very important one is *stigma*, which recipients of psychiatric care (and their families) see as "the single most important factor undermining their quality of life." They also "suffer demoralization and low self-esteem due to the internalization of the stigma" (Davis, 2006:13). Many people fail to seek help because they feel they will be stigmatized.

Poverty, which can contribute to mental illness or be the result of mental illness, is another factor that gets in the way of seeking help. Men are less likely than women to approach mental health practitioners. Recent immigrants may face cultural and language barriers that make it difficult for them to take advantage of mental health services. And, lastly, Aboriginal people have suicide rates (especially among young people) that are among the highest in the world. The most isolated of all—the Inuit—have the highest rates. This is the tip of the iceberg that suggests there is a wide range of mental health issues within Aboriginal communities.

Cigarette Smoking

Cigarette smoking tops the list of preventable hazards to health. It was only after World War I that smoking became popular in Canada, remaining fashionable despite growing evidence of its dangers. Recently, among adults—but not among young people—smoking has fallen out of favour and is considered a mild form of social deviance.

Seeing Ourselves

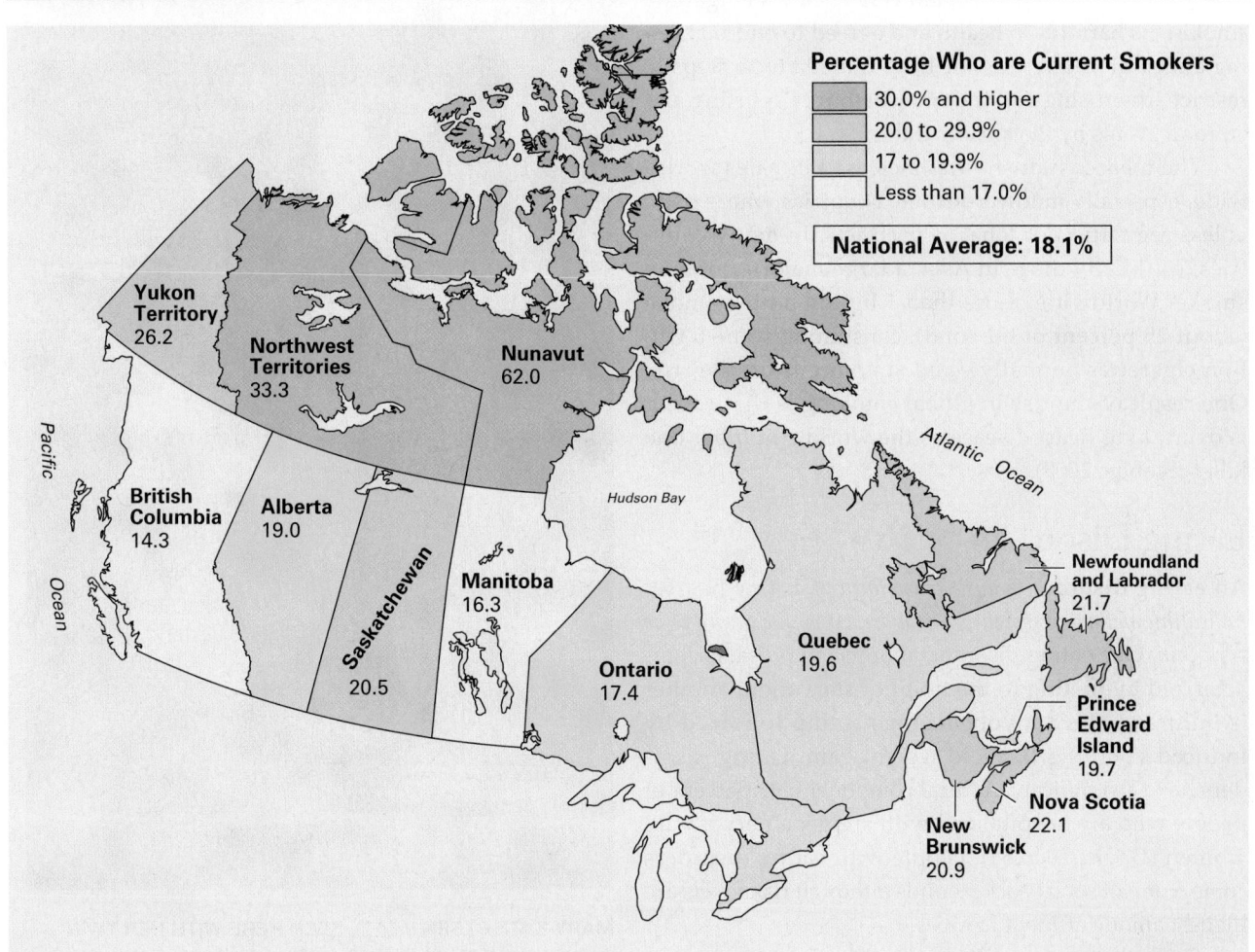

Canada Map 21–1 Percentage of Population 12 Years and Over Who are Current Smokers (2014)

SOURCE: Data compiled by LM Gerber from Statistics Canada, CANSIM, Table 105-0501.

As concern about the health effects of smoking grew, consumption of cigarettes fell from its peak in 1960, when almost 45 percent of Canadians smoked. By 2001, only 21.5 percent of Canadians were smokers; by 2014, the level had dropped to 18.1 percent. Canada Map 21–1 shows levels ranging from 14.3 percent in British Columbia to 62 percent in Nunavut. Among the provinces, Nova Scotia leads with 22.1 percent smoking, and in Quebec smoking dropped from 29.1 to 19.6 percent.

These figures suggest that, despite the addictive quality of nicotine and the difficulty of quitting, a substantial number of smokers have quit, while younger cohorts have chosen not to start. While about 24.6 percent of Canadians aged 20 to 34 smoke, this is the case among only 7.7 percent of teenagers (girls and boys) aged 12 to 19. Regardless of age, women are less likely to smoke than men, with the gender gap being largest among those aged 20 to 44 (10.0 points). For Canada as a whole, 21.4 percent of men and 14.8 percent of women are smokers.

Over the longer term, smoking by women has increased substantially, so that cigarettes have taken a larger toll on women's health. Lung cancer now competes with breast cancer as a leading cause of death among Canadian women. Worse yet, smoking is estimated to be responsible for one-quarter of deaths of men and women between 35 and 84 years of age. Smokers endure frequent minor illnesses, such as influenza, and pregnant women who smoke increase the likelihood of spontaneous abortion (miscarriage), prenatal death, and babies with a low birth weight. Even non-smokers exposed to second-hand cigarette smoke have a higher risk of smoking-related diseases.

Social factors contribute to smoking because many people smoke as a way to control stress. Smoking is more common among men, working-class people, divorced people, the unemployed, and those serving in the armed forces.

While the tobacco industry maintained that the health effects of smoking remained "an open question," laws mandating smoke-free environments spread rapidly. By 1997, the industry had conceded that cigarette smoking is harmful to health and agreed to end marketing aimed at youngsters. In 1998, Canada took steps to restrict advertising and the sponsorship of sporting and cultural events by the tobacco industry.

The tobacco industry has increased its sales worldwide, especially in lower-income countries where there is less regulation of tobacco products. In many countries, especially those in Asia, a large majority of men smoke. Worldwide, more than 1 billion adults smoke (about 25 percent of the total), consuming some 6 trillion cigarettes annually—and smoking is on the rise. One result of the rise in global smoking is that cancer is overtaking heart disease as the world's number one killer (Stobbe, 2008).

Eating Disorders

An **eating disorder** is *an intense form of dieting or other unhealthy method of weight control driven by the desire to be very thin.* One eating disorder, anorexia nervosa, is characterized by dieting to the point of starvation; another is bulimia, which involves binge eating followed by induced vomiting to avoid weight gain. Eating disorders have a significant cultural component: 93 percent of people who are hospitalized with anorexia nervosa are women (Davis, 2006:54). People with eating disorders come from all social backgrounds although risk levels are highest among affluent families.

Our culture equates slenderness with being successful and attractive. Conversely, we tend to stereotype overweight women and, to a lesser extent, men as lazy, sloppy, and even stupid (Becker, 1999). Research shows that most young women believe that "guys like thin girls" and that they are not sufficiently thin to be attractive to men. In fact, most college-aged women want to be even thinner than the men want them to be. Men, in contrast, express more satisfaction with their body shape (Fallon & Rozin, 1985). Because few achieve our culture's unrealistic standards of beauty, many women develop low self-images and diet to the point of risking their health and even their lives.

People with eating disorders contend with more than their illness. Research indicates that they are also viewed by others not as people with a mental disorder but as weak individuals who are seeking attention. In fact, the stigma attached to eating disorders was found to be more severe than the stigma attached to depression (Roehrig and McLean, 2010).

Obesity

Eating disorders such as anorexia nervosa and bulimia are not the biggest eating-related problem in North America. At the other end of the scale, we have the increasing

MARY-KATE OLSEN (*LEFT*), SEEN HERE WITH HER TWIN SISTER, ASHLEY OLSEN, IS AMONG THE MANY YOUNG WOMEN CELEBRITIES WHO HAVE STRUGGLED WITH AN EATING DISORDER To what extent do you think the mass media are responsible for encouraging young women to be so thin that some even put their lives at risk? Explain your view.

Vince Bucci/Getty Images

problem of obesity. The Canadian Community Health Survey, which directly measures the heights and weights of respondents, found that obesity rates for adults and children rose substantially over the previous 25 years. Between 1978 and 2004, obesity rates among children aged 2 to 17 rose from 3 to 8 percent, while over the same time period adult rates rose from 14 to 23 percent, the latter representing 5.5 million adult Canadians (Statistics Canada, 2005a).

Obesity is an intractable problem: Once people are overweight, they are more likely to gain further weight than to take it off. The National Population Health Survey revealed that, over an eight-year period, one-quarter of the Canadians who had been overweight at the beginning were obese by 2003, while only 10 percent dropped to normal weight. Women, younger men, and the poor were most likely to become obese. Not surprisingly, if parents are obese, children are at greater risk of obesity as well (Statistics Canada, 2005d). Unfortunately, being overweight limits physical activity and raises the risk of debilitating diseases such as heart disease, stroke, and type 2 diabetes.

What are the social causes of obesity? One factor is the jobs that keep us sitting at desks or in front of computer screens, rather than engaging in the type of physical labour that was common a century ago. Even when we are not on the job, much of the work around the house is done by machines. Children spend more of their time sitting as well—watching television or playing video games.

Then, of course, there is diet. The typical North American is eating more salty and fatty food than ever before (Wells & Buzby, 2008). And meals are getting bigger. The U.S. Department of Agriculture reported that, in 2000, the typical American adult consumed 140 more pounds (64 kilograms) of food per year than a decade earlier. Comparing old and new editions of cookbooks, recipes that used to say they would feed six now say they will feed four. The odds of being overweight go up among people with lower incomes partly because stores in low-income communities offer a greater selection of low-cost, high-fat foods and fewer healthful fruits and vegetables (Hellmich, 2002).

Sexually Transmitted Diseases

Sexual activity, though both pleasurable and vital to the continuation of our species, can transmit more than 50 kinds of *sexually transmitted diseases* (STDs). Because our culture associates sex with sin, some people regard these diseases not only as illnesses but also as marks of immorality.

STDs grabbed our attention during the "sexual revolution" of the 1960s, when infection rates rose as people began sexual activity earlier with a greater number of partners. The rise in STDs is an exception to the general decline of infectious diseases during the twentieth century. By the late 1980s, the rising dangers of sexually transmitted diseases—especially AIDS—generated a sexual counter-revolution as people moved away from casual sex (Kain, 1987; Laumann et al., 1994). The following sections briefly describe several common STDs.

GONORRHEA, SYPHILIS, AND CHLAMYDIA Gonorrhea and syphilis, among the oldest known diseases, are caused by microscopic organisms that are almost always transmitted by sexual contact. Untreated, gonorrhea causes sterility; syphilis damages major organs and can result in blindness, mental disorders, and death.

Recent increases in rates of infection of both gonorrhea and syphilis are attributed to failure to use safer-sex methods. Health Canada reports that rates of gonorrhea infection rose more than 40 percent from 1997 to 2003 and another 40 percent by 2011. The gonorrhea rate was highest in the Northwest Territories. Unfortunately,

drug-resistant strains of the disease are also on the upswing. Cases of syphilis were rare in Canada in the 1990s but, in the five years prior to 2003, the rate quadrupled, only to double again by 2011. Localized outbreaks have been reported in Vancouver, Calgary, Toronto, Ottawa, and Montreal, many within the sex trade and the gay community.

Chlamydia is the most widely reported STD in Canada especially among males and females 20 to 24 years of age. Chlamydia rates among females are twice as high as among males—and highest in the Northwest Territories, Yukon, Manitoba, and Saskatchewan.

According to the Public Health Agency of Canada (2016a) there were 1757 cases of syphilis, 11 397 of gonorrhea, and 100 044 of chlamydia reported in 2011. These represent rates of 5.1, 33.1, and 290.4 per 100 000 population respectively.

STEPHEN LEWIS, FORMER CANADIAN AMBASSADOR TO THE UNITED NATIONS AND FORMER DEPUTY EXECUTIVE DIRECTOR OF UNICEF, IS A PROFESSOR OF DISTINCTION AT RYERSON UNIVERSITY AND CHAIR OF THE BOARD OF THE STEPHEN LEWIS FOUNDATION, WHICH SUPPORTS COMMUNITY-BASED ORGANIZATIONS WORKING ON THE FRONT LINES OF THE HIV AND AIDS EPIDEMIC IN AFRICA The Foundation supports women, children orphaned by AIDS, and the indomitable grandmothers who have stepped in to care for them. He is also the co-founder and co-director of AIDS-Free World, an international advocacy organization that exposes injustice, abuse, and inequality—the social ills that underpin and continue to sustain HIV.

The Stephen Lewis Foundation

GENITAL HERPES Genital herpes is a virus that infects at least 45 million adolescents and adults in the United States (one in five). Canadian data are not available because physicians are not required to report cases. Although far less dangerous than gonorrhea and syphilis, herpes is incurable. People with genital herpes may not have any symptoms, or they may experience periodic, painful blisters on the genitals accompanied by fever and headache. Although not fatal to adults, genital herpes in pregnant women can be transmitted during a vaginal delivery, and it can be deadly to a newborn; for this reason, women with active infections are typically delivered by Caesarean section (CDC, 2009; Sobel, 2001).

ACQUIRED IMMUNE DEFICIENCY SYNDROME (AIDS) The most serious of all sexually transmitted diseases is *acquired immune deficiency syndrome* (AIDS). Identified in 1981, it is incurable and almost always fatal. It is caused by the human immunodeficiency virus (HIV), which weakens the immune system by attacking white blood cells and makes people vulnerable to a wide range of diseases that eventually cause death.

The first AIDS case in Canada was reported by the Laboratory Centre for Disease Control in February 1982. By December 1993, there had been 6187 reported deaths from AIDS in Canada, and another 2896 people documented as living with AIDS. Canada started tracking HIV infections in 1985; Table 21–3 shows that, by 1995, 35 766 HIV cases had been reported to the Public Health Agency of Canada—averaging 3426 cases in the first 11 years. From 1996 to 2004, the annual average had dropped to 2380, only to be followed by a plateau or very slight increase over the next seven years. The three years from 2012 through 2014 recorded fewer new HIV cases than any previous year—with an average of 2067 per year. But there is little here to celebrate—for in every year since 1995 more than 2000 new cases of HIV were reported. From 1985 to 2014, a total of 80 469 faced a future of HIV and AIDS.

The figures on reported AIDS cases are much lower than those for HIV (Table 21–4); between 1979 and 2004, an average of 737 men and 71 women were reported to have developed AIDS. The 811 average includes some people for whom sex was not recorded. You will notice a steady decline in newly reported AIDS cases from 2005 to 2011 and 2014. The last three years of that period averaged 152 men and 43 women who were newly diagnosed with AIDS. In 2014 there were 80 469 individuals living with HIV— 20 701 of whom had gone on to develop full-blown AIDS. Although modern medical treatments are able to delay or even prevent the onset of AIDS among those infected with HIV, the spread of HIV is complicated by the fact that an estimated 20 percent of the people infected with HIV are unaware of their status.

Table 21–3 HIV Cases Reported to PHAC, 1985 to 2014 (1985–1995, 1996–2004, 2005–2011, and 2012–2014)

Years	Number	Average
1985–1995	**35 766**	**3426**
1996	2729	
1997	2460	
1998	2290	
1999	2184	
2000	2092	
2001	2216	
2002	2460	
2003	2468	
2004	2520	
1996–2004	**21 419**	**2380**
2005	2476	
2006	2537	
2007	2439	
2008	2620	
2009	2391	
2010	2330	
2011	2290	
2005–2011	**17 083**	**2440**
2012	2081	
2013	2076	
2014	2044	
2012–2014	**6201**	**2067**
1985–2014	**80 469**	**2682**

SOURCE: Compilation and calculations by LM Gerber based on Public Health Agency of Canada, 2016.

Deaths from AIDS (Table 21–5) have declined rapidly over the years. The period between 1987 and 2004 saw a deceptively low average number of deaths from AIDS— at 864 per year. The deception arises from the fact that, in the middle of that period, the six years of the early nineties (the peak years of 1991 to 1996) had well over one thousand deaths per year from AIDS. 1995 saw the most deaths from AIDS at 1764, whereas 2011 had only 303. Significantly, the reported number of new HIV cases has been declining slowly since 1996 but still remains above 2000 per year. In that light, the steady decline in reported AIDS cases *and* deaths suggests that increasingly effective treatments rather than safer sex practices are responsible for the decline.

Women accounted for 8 percent of all AIDS cases reported in Canada from 1982 to 1984 or an average of 10 percent between 1979 and 2004 (Table 21–4). Between 2005 and 2011 women accounted for an average of 25 percent of reported AIDS cases—a proportion that increased again for the 2012–2014 period to a full 28 percent. Most of that increase took place in the last decade of that

Table 21–4 Reported AIDS Cases by Sex: 1979 to 2004; 2005 to 2011; and 2012 to 2014

Years	Men	Average	Women	Average	Total Sex	Average
1979–2004	18 418	737	1784	71	20 286	811
2005	325		90		429	
2006	307		79		395	
2007	299		61		369	
2008	277		84		365	
2009	224		57		294	
2010	214		49		273	
2011	182		40		234	
2005–2011	1828	261	460	66	2359	337
2012	172		36		222	
2013	154		52		225	
2014	129		41		187	
2012–2014	455	152	129	43	634	211
1979–2014	20 701	591	2373	68	23 279	665

SOURCE: Compilation and calculations by LM Gerber based on Public Health Agency of Canada, 2016.

Table 21–5 Deaths from AIDS, 1987 to 2011, including peak years, 1991 to 1996

Years	Number	Average	Peak Years	Number	Average
1987–2004	15 556	864			
			1991	1170	
2005	468		1992	1358	
2006	428		1993	1562	
2007	422		1994	1628	
2008	407		**1995**	**1764**	
2009	355		1996	1306	
2010	336		**1991–1996**	**8788**	**1465**
2011	303				
2005–2011	2719	388			
1987–2011	18 275	731			

SOURCE: Compilation and calculations by LM Gerber based on Public Health Agency of Canada, 2016.

period. A disturbing result of this trend is its effect on children. As of December 31, 2014 there were 650 children under the age of 15 diagnosed with HIV—and 4279 infants exposed to HIV at birth (of whom 578 were confirmed as infected). The increase in HIV infections among women has consequences for the women themselves as well as for their newborn infants (Public Health Agency of Canada, 2016b).

The exposure routes for HIV cases reported in Canada differ over time. Specifically, the proportion of HIV cases attributed to male homosexual contact declined over time—as did the proportion attributed to a combination of male homosexual contact and intravenous use. Together, these two exposure routes involving male homosexual contact accounted for close to half of the reported HIV cases in Canada; in 2014, these two exposure routes accounted for 49 percent of reported cases. Intravenous drug use was the second-largest exposure route, involving 20 percent of all reported cases; the comparable figure for 2014 is 12 percent (Gandhi, 2006; Public Health Agency of Canada, 2016a).

The next three categories involve heterosexual contact: with someone from an HIV-endemic country, with a person at risk, and by "other" routes. Among the heterosexual categories, contact with persons at risk increased most significantly over time (from 5.9 to 12.8 percent before falling back to 9 percent by 2014). Infection through "other" types of heterosexual contact also increased, from 7.9 to 11.6 percent before dropping back to 10 percent 2014. Combining the three categories reveals that HIV infection through heterosexual contact accounts for 28 percent of cases. With close to 30 percent of reported cases being attributable to heterosexual contact, it is very clear that one does not have to be homosexual or an intravenous drug user to be at risk of HIV infection.

Another disturbing trend is the spread of AIDS within the Aboriginal community. While the overall increase in AIDS cases has levelled off, the incidence within the Aboriginal population has been increasing steadily. The proportion of Aboriginal people among AIDS cases increased from 1.5 percent before 1986 to 16.4 percent in 2005. Injection drug use is responsible for 64 percent of AIDS cases among Aboriginal women and 28 percent among Aboriginal men (Canada, 2006b; Gandhi, 2006). By 2014, 3552 Aboriginal people were

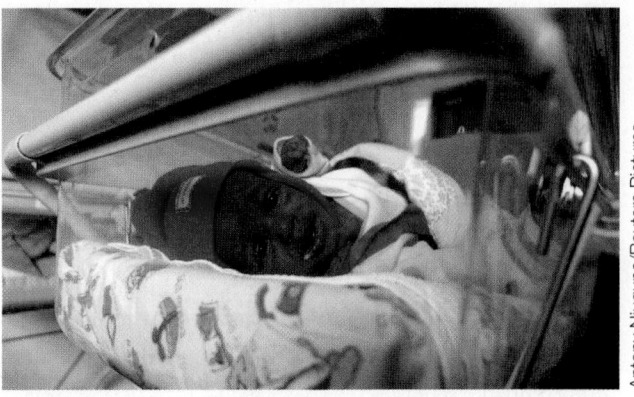

IN THE AFRICAN NATION OF KENYA, THERE ARE ABOUT 500 DEATHS FROM AIDS EVERY DAY In parts of sub-Saharan Africa, the epidemic is so great that half of all children will become infected with HIV. This young Nairobi child, who already has AIDS, is fighting for his life.

Antony Njuguna/Reuters Pictures

Table 21–6 Reported Cases of HIV by Race or Ethnicity (1998 to 2014)

	1998 to 2014		1998–2008	2009–2014
	n	%	%	%
First Nations	2643	16.5	18.5	14.3
Other Aboriginal	909	5.6	6.4	4.8
South Asian	492	3.1	2.4	3.7
Asian	739	4.6	3.5	5.8
Black	2245	14.0	10.0	18.1
Latin American	559	3.5	2.2	4.8
White	8289	51.6	56.3	46.8
Other	174	1.1	0.6	1.6
Subtotal*	16 050	100	100	100
Race not reported	23 464			
Total # of HIV cases	39 514			

*Note that the breakdown is based on only 40 percent of all reported AIDS cases. Race or ethnicity was not reported for the other 60 percent.

SOURCE: Compilation and calculations by LM Gerber based on Public Health Agency of Canada, 2016.

living with HIV—22 percent of the cases for whom race was reported. Blacks accounted for 14 percent of the HIV cases, Asians for 5 percent (see Table 21–6).

Globally, HIV infects some 37 million people—3 million of them under the age of 15—and the number continues to rise. The global AIDS death toll now exceeds 37 million (UNAIDS, 2015). Global Map 21–1 shows that Africa (especially south of the Sahara) has the highest HIV infection rate and accounts for about 70 percent of new HIV infections. A recent United Nations study found that in the nations of southern Africa, 15-year-olds face a 50-50 chance of becoming infected with HIV. The risk is especially high for girls, not only because HIV is transmitted more easily from men to women but also because many African cultures encourage women to be submissive to men. According to some analysts, the AIDS crisis now threatens the political and economic security of Africa, which in turn affects the entire world (Ashford, 2002; UNAIDS, 2015).

Upon infection, people with HIV display no symptoms at all, so most are unaware of their condition. Symptoms of AIDS may not appear for a year or longer but, during this time, an infected person may infect others. Within five years, one-third of infected people develop full-blown AIDS; half develop AIDS within 10 years, and almost all become sick within 20 years. In low-income countries, the progression of this illness is much more rapid than elsewhere.

HIV is infectious but not contagious. That is, HIV is transmitted from person to person through blood, semen, or breast milk but not through casual contact such as shaking hands, hugging, sharing towels or dishes, swimming together, or even by coughing and sneezing. The

risk of transmitting the virus through saliva (as in kissing) is extremely low. The chance of transmitting HIV through sexual activity is greatly reduced by the use of latex condoms. However, abstinence or an exclusive relationship with an uninfected person is the only sure way to avoid infection.

Specific behaviours increase the risk of HIV infection. The first is anal sex, which can cause rectal bleeding, allowing easy transmission of HIV from one person to another. *Sharing needles* to inject drugs is a second high-risk behaviour, which in turn makes sex with an intravenous drug user very risky. Intravenous drug use is more common among poor people in North America (including Aboriginal and Black people). *Using any drug,* including alcohol, also increases the risk of HIV infection to the extent that it impairs judgment. In other words, even people who understand what places them at risk of infection may act less responsibly if they are under the influence of alcohol, marijuana, or some other drug.

The American and Canadian governments responded slowly to the AIDS crisis, largely because the earliest people to be infected—gay men and intravenous drug users—were widely viewed as deviant. But funds allocated for AIDS research have increased rapidly to US$24 billion annually in the United States. In 2004, the Canadian government announced that "federal HIV/aids funding would increase to $84 million from $42.2 million annually over five years." Critics argue that Canada should be spending $100 million or $200 million on prevention alone (Gandhi, 2006). Researchers have identified some drugs, including protease inhibitors that suppress the symptoms of the disease. Nevertheless, educational programs remain the most effective weapon against AIDS, since prevention is the only way to stop a disease that so far has no cure.

Ethical Issues Surrounding Death

Now that technological advances have given us the power to draw the line between life and death, we must decide when and how to do so. In other words, medical technology has added an ethical dimension to the management of health, illness, and death.

WHEN DOES DEATH OCCUR? In the past, we knew that life ceases when breathing and heartbeat stop—but the ability to replace a heart and artificially sustain respiration makes that definition of death obsolete. Medical and legal experts now define death as an *irreversible state* involving no response to stimulation, no movement or breathing, no reflexes, and no indication of brain activity (Jones, 1998; Wall, 1980).

DO PEOPLE HAVE A RIGHT TO DIE? Today, medical personnel, family members, and patients themselves

Window on the World

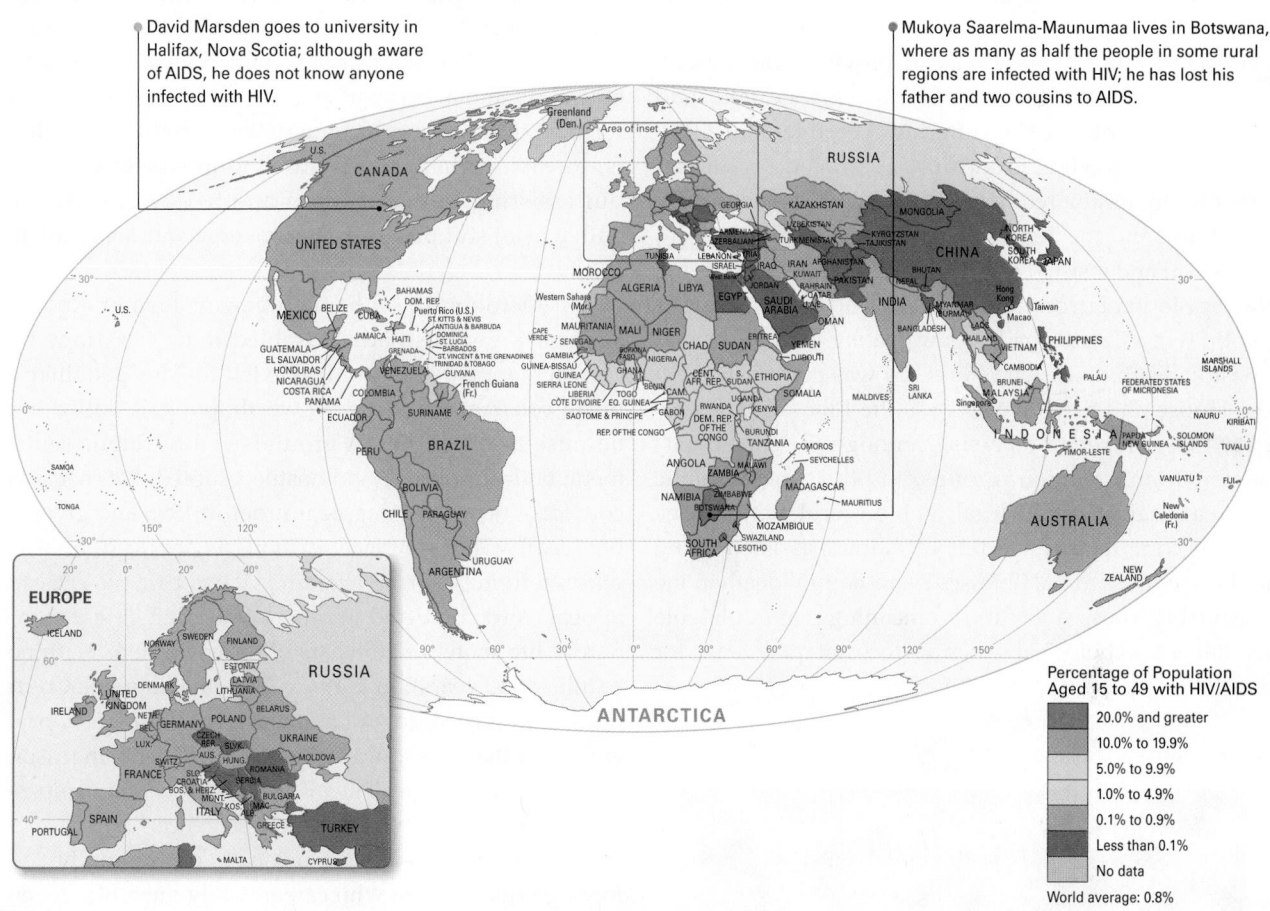

David Marsden goes to university in Halifax, Nova Scotia; although aware of AIDS, he does not know anyone infected with HIV.

Mukoya Saarelma-Maunumaa lives in Botswana, where as many as half the people in some rural regions are infected with HIV; he has lost his father and two cousins to AIDS.

Percentage of Population Aged 15 to 49 with HIV/AIDS

- 20.0% and greater
- 10.0% to 19.9%
- 5.0% to 9.9%
- 1.0% to 4.9%
- 0.1% to 0.9%
- Less than 0.1%
- No data

World average: 0.8%

Global Map 21–1 HIV/AIDS Infection of Adults in Global Perspective

Seventy-one percent of all people infected with HIV live in sub-Saharan Africa. In Swaziland, one-fourth of people between the ages of 15 and 49 are infected with HIV/AIDS. This very high infection rate reflects the prevalence of other sexually transmitted diseases and infrequent use of condoms, two factors that promote transmission of HIV. South and Southeast Asia account for about 14 percent of global HIV infections; by contrast, North America and South America taken together account for 8 percent of global HIV infections. From another angle, in Thailand, 1.1 percent of people aged 15 to 49 are now infected compared to 0.6 percent of comparable people in the United States. The incidence of infection in Muslim nations is extremely low by world standards.

SOURCES: Based on Population Reference Bureau (2012) and UNAIDS (2015).

face the agonizing burden of deciding when a terminally ill person should die. In 1992, the Parliament of Canada abolished attempted suicide as a crime but retained the prohibition against assisting suicide. Individuals periodically challenge this law, as did Sue Rodriguez, a British Columbia woman with Lou Gehrig's disease. Rodriguez eventually would have been unable to swallow, to speak, to walk, or to turn over without assistance. Eventually, she would need a respirator to breathe and would be less able to end her own life. She wanted permission for a doctor, at a given time in the future, to set up an intravenous tube filled with a lethal dose of medication. Her case spawned both widespread support and fervent opposition from churches, right-to-life activists, and provincial and federal governments (Wood, 1993). In 1993, the Supreme Court

of Canada ruled that the state's interest in protecting the sanctity of life took precedence over the individual's right to a dignified death. In the end, Rodriguez was helped to die by an anonymous physician and a friend, maverick MP Svend Robinson.

Normally, the first responsibility of physicians and hospitals is to protect a patient's life. Even so, a mentally competent person in the process of dying may refuse medical treatment or even nutrition. Moreover, laws require hospitals, nursing homes, and other medical facilities to honour the desires of a patient made earlier in the form of a living will. Thus, under certain circumstances, we already make decisions regarding when and how death will occur. In May 2016, the new Liberal government was anxious to pass Bill C-14—its assisted-dying bill—before the June 6th deadline imposed by the Supreme Court. The Court "laid out four criteria for determining who qualifies for an assisted death. The person must be a competent adult, provide clear consent, have a 'grievous or irremediable medical condition,' and be enduring 'intolerable' suffering" (Berthiaume, 2016). Having left it too late, Trudeau's government was under pressure to get the required law—Bill C-14—passed by the House and the Senate before the deadline. The Senate balked and insisted on amendments, thereby delaying the legislation beyond the deadline and leaving a short period when Canada had no law dealing with physician-assisted death. In the end, Bill C-14 was passed through the House and Senate exactly as the Liberals had proposed it. Controversy persists among physicians, parliamentarians, religious groups, and the general public about a range of ethical, legal, and technical matters. One specific complaint is that Bill C-14 limits assisted dying to those with terminal illnesses—and natural death in the reasonably foreseeable future—meaning that intolerable mental or psychological suffering does not qualify one for assistance.

NANCY MORRISON, A HALIFAX PHYSICIAN, WAS CHARGED WITH MURDERING A TERMINALLY ILL CANCER PATIENT IN NOVEMBER 1996 The judge threw out the charges, but the case reignited heated debate on the morality of mercy killing.

WHAT ABOUT MERCY KILLING? Mercy killing is the common term for **euthanasia,** *assisting in the death of a person suffering from an incurable disease.* Euthanasia (from the Greek, meaning "a good death") poses an ethical dilemma, being at once an act of kindness and a form of killing. Support for a patient's right to die (that is, passive euthanasia) is growing in North America. But assisting in the death of another person (active euthanasia) still provokes controversy and may violate the law.

In October 1993, Saskatchewan farmer Robert Latimer killed his badly disabled daughter Tracy by carbon monoxide poisoning. He felt that his daughter's life of constant pain was not worth living; he killed her because he loved her. A groundswell of public sentiment, both supportive and hostile, erupted. Latimer was convicted of second-degree murder in 1995 and given a one-year prison sentence. Although convicted, he was released from prison and confined to his farm. In 1998, an appeal court convicted Latimer of murder, with a mandatory life sentence (25 years of imprisonment, with no parole for 10 years). In January 2001, the Supreme Court of Canada turned down Latimer's appeal for a new trial and ruled that he should serve at least 10 years in prison (Beltrame, 2001). The Court would not consider compassionate grounds for a more lenient sentence.

The debate on euthanasia usually centres on the following issues. Those who categorically view life—even with suffering and disability—as preferable to death reject both passive and active euthanasia. People who recognize circumstances under which death is preferable to life endorse passive or perhaps active euthanasia, but they face the practical problem of determining just when life should be ended.

In 2012, the report of Quebec's Dying with Dignity Commission was released. The report recommends improvements in palliative care—including care at home—as well as a "final option for those who seek it" (Gurney, 2012). In light of the vociferous debate surrounding the issue, it is surprising to learn that 63 percent of Canadians—and 78 percent of Quebecers—support euthanasia; a minority of Quebec's doctors also supports the practice. Quebec has had an assisted-dying law since Dec. 10, 2015.

The Medical Establishment

21.4 Compare the medical systems in nations around the world.

Medicine is *the social institution that focuses on fighting disease and improving health.* Through most of human history, health care was the responsibility of individuals and their families. Medicine emerges as a social institution only as societies become more productive and people take on specialized work.

Members of agrarian societies today still turn to various traditional health practitioners, including herbalists and acupuncturists, who play a central part in improving health. In industrial societies, medical care falls mainly to specially trained and licensed professionals, from anesthesiologists to x-ray technicians.

The Rise of Scientific Medicine

In colonial times, doctors, herbalists, druggists, midwives, and ministers all engaged in various forms of healing arts. But not all did so effectively: Unsanitary instruments, lack of anesthesia, and simple ignorance made surgery a terrible ordeal, and physicians probably killed as many patients as they saved.

Medicine became a science when physicians learned more about human anatomy, physiology, and biochemistry. Early in the nineteenth century, medical societies appeared in Canada as doctors established themselves as self-regulating professionals (Blishen, 1991). Formal colleges of medicine offered training in the field. The increase in the number of medical schools paralleled the growth in the number of hospitals (Stevens, 1971). Medical societies required practitioners to obtain licences and enforced conformity to medical standards.

The establishment in 1865 of the General Council of Medical Education and Registration in Upper Canada signified acceptance of the scientific model of medicine. Before long, scientists had traced the cause of life-threatening illnesses to bacteria and viruses and developed the first vaccines (Blishen, 1991).

The Canadian Medical Association, established in 1867, controlled the certification process and defined the practice of medicine. Thus, doctors determined what the various "paramedical" occupations could and could not do. Before long, the practice of medicine was limited mainly to those with medical degrees, and the prestige and income of physicians rose dramatically.

Other practitioners, such as naturopaths, herbal healers, and midwives, held to their traditional roles, but at a high cost: All have been relegated to fringe areas of the medical profession. With far less social prestige and income than physicians, such professionals now have a small, if devoted, following in Canada (Blishen, 1991; Nancarrow Clarke, 1996). Treatment by chiropractors is partially covered by provincial health insurance, and midwives have been legally recognized as birth attendants in Ontario (Rajhathy & Roulard, 1994:40). Further, more than one-third of North Americans use some form of "complementary" medicine (Eisenberg et al., 1993). The rise of scientific medicine, taught in expensive, urban medical schools,

also changed the social profile of doctors. Historically, there has been overrepresentation of medical students from higher-level social backgrounds (Blishen, 1991). Traditionally, medicine was a male-dominated profession, as women were considered unfit to practise medicine (Huet-Cox, 1984; Nancarrow Clarke, 1996; Starr, 1982). While in 1992 more than 80 percent of physicians were men and some 97 percent of nurses were women, younger cohorts are changing these male/female ratios dramatically.

Holistic Medicine

In recent years, the scientific model of medicine has been tempered by the more traditional model of **holistic medicine**, *an approach to health care that emphasizes the prevention of illness and takes into account a person's entire physical and social environment.* Holistic practitioners agree on the need for drugs, surgery, artificial organs, and high technology, but they emphasize treatment of the whole person, rather than symptoms, and focus on health, rather than disease. Holistic practitioners treat patients as people in the context of lifestyle and environmental factors. Holistic medicine favours an *active* approach to *health,* rather than a *reactive* approach to *illness*—shifting responsibility for health-promoting behaviour to us as patients. In addition, holistic practitioners generally provide their personal treatment in homes, rather than in hospitals or offices. There are three foundations of holistic medicine (Gordon, 1980; Patterson, 1998):

1. Treat patients as people. Holistic practitioners concern themselves not only with symptoms but also with how environment and lifestyle affect their patients. Holistic practitioners extend the bounds of conventional medicine, taking an active role in fighting poverty, environmental pollution, and other dangers to public health.
2. Encourage responsibility, not dependency. In the scientific model, patients are dependent on physicians. Holistic medicine tries to shift some responsibility for health from physicians to people themselves by encouraging health-promoting behaviour. Holistic medicine thus favours an *active* approach to *health* rather than a *reactive* approach to *illness.*
3. Provide personal treatment. Scientific medicine locates medical care in impersonal offices and hospitals, both

medicine the social institution that focuses on fighting disease and improving health

holistic medicine an approach to health care that emphasizes the prevention of illness and takes into account a person's entire physical and social environment

disease-centred settings. By contrast, holistic practitioners favour, as much as possible, a personal and relaxed environment such as the home.

In sum, holistic care does not oppose scientific medicine but shifts the emphasis from treating disease toward achieving the greatest well-being for everyone. Because there are as many as 50 medical specialties—that deal with specific diseases or parts of the body—it is clear that there is a need for practitioners who are concerned with the whole patient.

Paying for Medical Care: A Global Survey

With medicine relying on high technology, the costs of providing medical care have skyrocketed. Countries throughout the world use various strategies to meet these costs.

MEDICINE IN SOCIALIST NATIONS   In nations with mostly socialist economies, government provides medical care directly to the people. These countries hold that all citizens have the right to basic medical care, paid for by the government using public funds. The state owns and operates medical facilities and pays salaries to doctors and other health care workers, who are government employees.

People's Republic of China   This industrializing but still mostly agrarian nation faces the immense task of providing for the health of more than 1.3 billion people. China has experimented with private medicine, but the government controls most medical care.

China's "barefoot" doctors, roughly comparable to our paramedics, bring some modern methods of health care to millions of farm workers in rural villages. Otherwise, traditional healing arts, including acupuncture and the use of medicinal herbs, are still widely practised in China. The Chinese approach to health is based on a holistic concern for the interplay of mind and body (Kaptchuk, 1985).

Russian Federation   The Russian Federation transformed a state-dominated economy into more of a market system, so health care is also in transition. Nonetheless, the state remains in charge of health care and claims that everyone has a right to basic medical care.

Russians do not choose their physicians but report to local government-operated health facilities. Physicians have much lower incomes than medical doctors in North America, earning about the same salary as skilled industrial workers. Interestingly, more than 72 percent of Russian doctors are women, compared to 39 percent in Canada.

In recent years, the Russian Federation has suffered setbacks in health care and a falling standard of living. A rising demand for medical care has strained a bureaucratic system that, at best, provides highly standardized and impersonal care. The optimistic view is that government efforts will improve the quality of medical services, but that country's medical establishment so far has resisted change (Mason, 2003; Vasilyeva, 2014; Zuckerman, 2006).

MEDICINE IN CAPITALIST NATIONS   Countries with capitalist economies tend to have people pay for health care out of their own pockets. However, because its cost puts health care beyond the reach of most people, government programs underwrite much of the expense.

Sweden   In 1891, Sweden began a mandatory, comprehensive system of government health care. Citizens pay for this program with their taxes, which are among the highest in the world. Typically, physicians are government employees, and most hospitals are government-managed. Because this medical system resembles that found in socialist societies, Sweden's system is called **socialized medicine**, *a medical care system in which the government owns and operates most medical facilities and employs most physicians.*

Great Britain   In 1948, Great Britain also established socialized medicine by creating a dual system of medical service. All British citizens are entitled to medical care provided by the National Health Service, but those who can afford to may go to doctors and hospitals that operate privately.

As shown in Figure 21–1, Canada pays about 70 percent of medical costs—less than in the United Kingdom, Sweden, Japan, and France but more than in Australia, South Africa, and the United States.

United States   The United States stands alone among industrialized nations in having no universal, government-sponsored program of health care. Instead, it has a **direct fee system**, *a medical care system in which patients pay directly for the services of physicians and hospitals.* Europeans look to government to fund 70 to 90 percent of their medical costs (paid for through taxation), but the U.S. government pays just 47 percent of medical costs (World Bank, 2015).

socialized medicine a medical care system in which the government owns and operates most medical facilities and employs most physicians

direct-fee system a medical care system in which patients pay directly for the services of physicians and hospitals

Global Snapshot

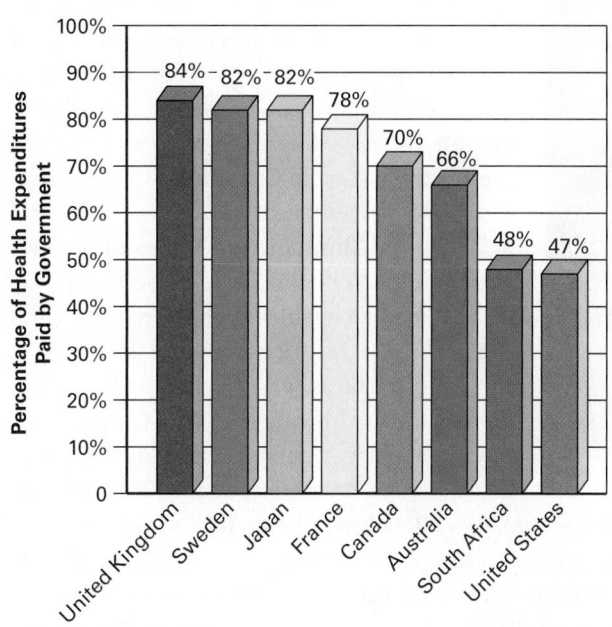

Figure 21–1 Extent of Socialized Medicine in Selected Countries

The governments of most high-income countries, including Canada, pay a greater share of medical costs than the U.S. government does.

SOURCE: Based on World Bank (2015).

In the United States, rich people can purchase the best medical care in the world; yet the poor are worse off than their counterparts in Canada and Europe. This difference explains the relatively high death rates among both infants and adults in the United States (Population Reference Bureau, 2015).

While Maine, Vermont, and Massachusetts provide health care to everyone, the United States has no national health care program. Why is this the case? Because its culture stresses self-reliance, government intervention is limited. Political support for a national medical program has not been strong, even among labour unions, which have concentrated on winning health care benefits from employers. Further, the American Medical Association and the health insurance industry have strongly and consistently opposed national medical care.

The Obama administration took office in 2009 with the promise of making health care available to all Americans. In 2010, the U.S. Congress passed a new law (the *Affordable Health Care Act* of 2010) that made significant changes to the way that country pays for health care—extending medical insurance to more people in several stages:

1. From the start, all families paid an insurance tax. Lower-income families, however, receive subsidies to help pay the cost of the insurance; high-income families pay higher taxes on their income to help fund the program.

2. Insurance companies are no longer permitted by law to drop customers because they get sick or to refuse coverage to children because of pre-existing conditions.

3. Insurance companies cannot set caps on the amount of money they will pay to any individual for medical expenses over a lifetime.

4. Parents can use their health care plans to include children up to the age of 26.

5. By 2014, insurance companies could no longer refuse coverage to anyone of any age due to preexisting health conditions.

6. By 2014, all families were required to purchase insurance coverage. Government regulates both the benefits available and the costs.

7. People who do not buy health insurance face penalties that increase over time.

In 2012, the U.S. Supreme Court declared that the penalties for refusal to buy health insurance are constitutional; in effect, it declared the penalty to be a "tax" and that the federal government has the right to tax Americans. The *Affordable Health Care Act* provides health care coverage to 32 million Americans who previously had none.

In 2016, Americans were still debating the merits of Obamacare. If you find that surprising, you should understand that, here in Canada, the "achievement of universal health care took a long, acrimonious and protracted road" (Romanow, 2012).

Medicine in Canada July 31, Montreal, Canada. I am visiting the home of an oral surgeon who appears (judging by the large home) to be doing pretty well. Yet he complains that the Canadian government, in an effort to hold down medical costs, caps doctors' annual salaries at several hundred thousand dollars (exact caps vary from province to province). Therefore, he explains, many specialists have left Canada for the United States, where they can earn much more; other doctors and dentists simply limit their practices. [John J. Macionis]

Canadians have universal medical coverage administered through provincial and territorial governments. Our provincial governments pay doctors and hospitals—which operate privately or independently—for the services they provide, according to a schedule of fees set annually by governments in consultation with professional medical associations. Thus, Canada has government-funded and -regulated medical care but—because the vast majority of physicians are in "private practice"—our medicare system is not socialized medicine. In reality,

THE AMERICAN CULTURE OF INDIVIDUALISM SUPPORTS THE NOTION THAT PEOPLE SHOULD BE RESPONSIBLE FOR THEIR OWN HEALTH AND MEDICAL CARE The 2010 health care reform in the United States is a step toward government ensuring that everyone has at least basic health care. Not surprisingly, the 2010 reforms were controversial. Why would some people be up in arms?

it is socialized medical *insurance*. (See the Sociology and the Media box further details.)

Canada's system of universal medicare has a long history, with seeds before Confederation. By 1884, Canada's *Public Health Act* required the establishment of health boards and sanitary regulations at the local level. In 1919, Prime Minister Mackenzie King introduced the idea of universal health care as part of the Liberal party platform, but it was not until 1972 that all provinces were part of a federal program providing comprehensive medical insurance—11 years after such a program was first introduced in Saskatchewan by New Democratic Premier Tommy Douglas.[1] Canada's law was shaped by the recommendations of a Royal Commission on Health Services, which reported in 1964 under Mr. Justice Emmett Hall of the Supreme Court of Canada. The law was based on four basic premises (Nancarrow Clarke, 1996:256):

- *Universality.* All residents of Canada would be eligible on equal terms, regardless of such differences as previous health records, age, income, membership, or other considerations.
- *Portability.* The benefits would be portable from province to province or territory.
- *Comprehensive coverage.* The benefits would include all necessary medical services and certain surgical services performed by a dental surgeon in hospital.

- *Administration.* The plan would be run on a non-profit basis.

Canada's system has the advantage of providing care for everyone at a total cost that is significantly lower than that needed to operate the non-universal medical system in the United States. In Canada, health expenditures, as a percentage of GDP, peaked in 1993 at 9.9 percent, dropping to 8.9 percent by 1997, mainly because of a growing economy. By 2005, Canada's health expenditures had risen to $142 billion, or 10.2 percent of GDP. In 2007, the United States was paying US$7500 per person for health care; in 2005, Canada was paying $4411 per person. Expenditures were greatest in the territories, where 136 physicians service a small, scattered population (and airlifts are common). By 2015 among the provinces, per capita health care expenditures ranged from $5655 in Quebec to $7063 in Newfoundland and Labrador—representing 10.9 percent of GDP. Spending on hospitals (29.5 percent), drugs (15.7 percent), and physician services (15.5 percent) account for more than 60 percent of total health spending in Canada (Canadian Institute for Health Information, 2015).

Keep in mind that our universal health insurance (e.g., OHIP in Ontario) does not cover all medical expenses. Depending on the province, exclusions might include cosmetic surgery, eye exams and glasses, prescription drugs, physiotherapy, chiropractics, and dentistry. Employees of large organizations (corporations or government) and unionized workers have private insurance to cover most of the exclusions as well as semi-private rooms in hospitals.

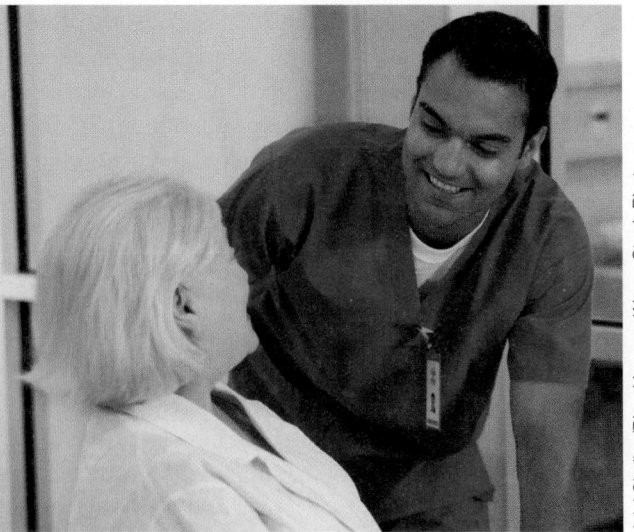

ONE STRATEGY FOR DEALING WITH A SHORTAGE OF NURSES IS TO RECRUIT MORE MEN INTO THE PROFESSION Anyone visiting a Canadian hospital today will notice a number of men on its nursing staff. Currently, about 4 percent of registered nurses are men.

---

[1]Actor Kiefer Sutherland is the son of actor Shirley Douglas, and the grandson of Tommy Douglas. In 2004, Tommy Douglas was voted "The Greatest Canadian" (in a CBC contest) for his role in bringing universal health care to Canada.

Sociology and the Media

Two-Tiered Health Care: Threat, Fact, or Fiction?

In the fall of 2000, Canadians found themselves involved in a federal election campaign, one that took a number of unexpected turns and resulted in a third majority Liberal government. Central to the Liberal campaign—and to much of the media coverage—was the attempt to instill fear of Stockwell Day and the Canadian Alliance in eastern Canada. According to the Liberals, Day and his Alliance candidates were "social conservatives" who, through a "hidden agenda," would force their religious beliefs about abortion, capital punishment, and homosexuality on the whole country. Even more damaging was the allegation that they would introduce "two-tiered medicine," resulting in separate systems of medical care for the rich and the poor. They would accomplish this by allowing *private* clinics to deliver health care.

In the weeks that followed, the Liberals, the New Democrats, and the media failed to acknowledge a reality that Stockwell Day was unable to articulate clearly. The reality is that the funding of Canada's universal medicare is public, yet its *delivery* is almost entirely private. It was not in the interests of the Liberals, the New Democrats,

MR. JUSTICE EMMETT M. HALL (1898–1995) HAD A DISTINGUISHED LEGAL CAREER LEADING TO HIS APPOINTMENT TO THE SUPREME COURT OF CANADA, FROM WHICH HE RETIRED IN 1973 AT THE AGE OF 75 Beyond his legal role, Hall helped develop public medical care in Saskatchewan—under Premier Tommy Douglas—before going on to design a system of universal health care for all of Canada, which was implemented in 1967. As the designer of our national medicare program, Hall created a social institution that is dear to our hearts and central to our Canadian identity.

The Supreme Court of Canada Collection

or the media to clarify this issue, even when, two years later, Liberal senator Michael Kirby was making exactly the same point—that public funding and private delivery are the norm in Canada. The media did pick up on Kirby's Senate Committee recommendation that "all Canadians have timely access to medically necessary health services regardless of their ability to pay." In the federal election of 2006, "wait-time guarantees" were front and centre, but neither the media nor the politicians pointed out that guaranteed services are delivered by the private sector.

It is worth noting that "wait-time guarantees" are necessary because Canadians may wait a year or even two for specific surgeries. One reason for these long wait times is that provinces have *budgets* wherein they allocate the money to pay for health care versus education, then different kinds of surgeries (e.g., hip surgeries), and ultimately the number of hip surgeries that each hospital can perform in a given year. This, in effect, is rationing. Canada and the provinces simply cannot afford to provide unlimited diagnostic or surgical procedures to everyone who needs them. When President Barack Obama promised universal, single-payer health care, many Americans worried about the necessary rationing implied (Krauthammer, 2009). Now that the promised reforms are in place—at least partially—concerns about rationing persist.

In an academic report titled "Getting What We Pay For: Myths and Realities about Financing Canada's Health Care System," Raisa Deber (2000) points out the distinction between financing and delivery. She also claims that our failure to distinguish between financing and delivery makes it difficult to diagnose the problems in our system, a point echoed by Senator Kirby's committee. We call our medicare system *public* because the government ensures its universality by paying most of the bills. Yet Canadians have failed to recognize that almost all of the delivery is *private*. Most of our hospitals are private, non-profit organizations run by independent boards. Nursing homes and home care providers are also private organizations. Physicians in Canada are not government employees but private practitioners or people in business. They bill governments for services rendered but have to pay rent, staff salaries, and equipment costs from their revenues.

As long as there is a single payer—the government—and individuals cannot pay to jump a queue for essential medical services, we do not have a two-tier system with superior services for the wealthy. Some Canadians have to be sent to the United States for cancer treatment in private clinics when services here are not available, but that does not signify unequal access—because Canadian governments pay their expenses.

In Canada, part of the debate about universality revolves around insured and uninsured services. Public funding does not cover all components of medical care; dentistry, cosmetic surgery, eye care (i.e., glasses, laser

(Continued)

surgery), and drugs are among the services left to private insurance or payment by the individual. In fact, in Canada, public expenditure on health care is only 70 percent of the total cost, compared to 88 percent in Belgium and 83 percent in the United Kingdom (Deber, 2000). The *Canada Health Act* protects only publicly "insured" services from queue jumping on the part of those willing to pay out of pocket or through private insurance. Uninsured services are funded and delivered entirely within the private sphere.

On August 23, 2006, both the *National Post* and *The Globe and Mail* covered the election of Dr. Brian Day as president of the Canadian Medical Association. This is significant because Day is the co-founder of a private, state-of-the-art surgical centre in Vancouver that operates outside Canada's publicly funded system. In other words, it is both *privately* funded and *privately* delivered; patients pay for its services personally or through their private insurance. The fear was that Day would use his one-year presidency to push for further privatization of health care—that is, increased private delivery not funded by government insurance (Greenaway, 2006b; Picard, 2006).

This brings a new dimension to the public/private debate about health care. Day says that he supports medicare and that his private clinic simply aids in the timely delivery of quality care. In 2005, the Quebec Supreme Court ruled that it is unconstitutional to stop someone from paying privately for care if the wait for public service is too long. Since governments limit the number of procedures they will or can afford to cover, we may not be able to give "wait-time guarantees" without considering the option of private funding. At this point, more Canadians are realizing the limits of our publicly funded health care and demanding privately financed services (Blackwell, 2009). The outcome of this tug-of-war will become clear in the near future.

There is an issue that might help you decide where you stand. Currently, it is possible to have your DNA sequenced to find out if there are specific hereditary diseases to which you or your children are susceptible. The original cost for sequencing the first human genome was US$500 million; with new technology, the price tag dropped to US$100 000 and then US$10 000. Today, you can submit a saliva sample and, for $250, receive a fairly extensive report on your DNA. In the past, only the wealthy could indulge their curiosity; today DNA sequencing is available to almost anyone. Would you support the right of Canadians to buy this service privately from a lab in Saskatoon?

What Do You Think?

1. What do you think of the argument that private delivery, if publicly funded, does *not* constitute a two-tier system of health care?

2. Do you think taxpayers should pick up the tab for a broader range of health care services (e.g., drugs, cosmetic surgery, vision care)?

3. Should couples have their DNA sequenced before marriage or giving birth to children?

Canada still lacks universal public insurance for prescription drugs, or "pharmacare." To avoid the loss of individuals' savings and income due to serious diseases, we have contemplated coverage for catastrophic drug costs, such as those involved for drugs needed to treat some cancers and AIDS.

The Shortage of Nurses

Another important issue in medical care is the shortage of nurses across North America and, in fact, around the world. Canada and the United States combined have over 2 million registered nurses, but many of the available jobs are unfilled. The main cause of the shortage is that fewer people are entering the nursing profession. During the past decade, enrolments in nursing programs have dropped, even as the need for nurses—driven by population aging—increases. Why this decline? Today's young women have a wide range of occupational choices, so that fewer are drawn to the traditionally female occupation of nursing. Also, many nurses are unhappy with working conditions, citing 12-hour shifts, heavy patient loads, too much required overtime, a stressful working environment, and a lack of recognition and respect from supervisors, physicians, and hospital managers. Most nurses say they would not recommend the field to others, and many are leaving nursing for other jobs.

Drastic cutbacks in funding by the Liberal government in the 1990s led hospitals to cut staff, which in turn caused many more nurses to look to the United States for employment opportunities—and much higher salaries. American hospitals actively recruit Canadian nurses with generous signing bonuses. As a result, Canada loses 15 nurses to the United States for every American nurse who comes north.

To deal with the shortage, nursing programs have almost doubled their output, from 4833 graduates in 1999 to 9447 in 2007. Dunsdon predicted we could be short 78 000 nurses by 2011 and 113 000 by 2016 (2009). Attributing the shortage of nurses to the needs of an aging population and the retirement of baby boomers (including nurses), the Canadian Nurses Association is more restrained in its estimates, saying that "Canada will have a shortfall of almost 60 000 full-time registered nurses within 12 years" (Hyslop, 2012). At this point, we are meeting the demand for more nurses by having them work more overtime; this is not ideal because of the potential consequences of fatigue but also because many

Table 21–7 The Representation of Canadian Women in Medicine by Age: 2003, 2009, 2012, and 2015.

Age*	Percentage Female			
	2003	2009	2012	2015
Under 35	50.9	55.8	61.0	60.7
35–44	40.5	44.4	46.8	50.0
45–54	31.0	37.8	39.8	41.9
55–64	17.2	24.8	29.5	33.4
65+	9.8	12.4	14.2	17.3
Unknown	27.9	28.9	31.5	38.8
Total	30.4	34.0	36.4	39.2

*Excludes physicians over 80 years of age.
SOURCE: Calculations by LM Gerber based on the Canadian Medical Association Masterfile. 2003, 2009, 2012, and 2015 (www.cma.ca).

nurses work part-time in order to deal with the extreme pressures of their jobs (Winston, 2011).

Canadian Women in Medicine

Gone are the days when physicians were almost always male. Today, roughly 40 percent of physicians are women. In 2012 *and* 2015, women represented 61 percent of physicians under 35 years of age—compared to 51 percent in 2003 (see Table 21–7). If you look carefully across each row in the table, you will see that the proportion of female physicians *in each age cohort* increases steadily—to the point where proportion of females among physicians 65 years of age or older grew from 9.8 to 17.3 percent between 2003 and 2015. Women also represent more than half of the specialists in the youngest cohort, meaning that the proportion of female specialists among physicians of all ages will increase substantially from its current level of about 30 percent. The presence of so many women in specialties means that women are willing to undertake four to six extra years of residency (beyond medical school), often postponing child bearing until their thirties or forgoing it altogether.

Over the past 40 years, first-year enrolment in Canadian medical schools has involved an increasing proportion of women. In 1968–69, women made up only 17.6 percent of first-year medical students; by 2008–09, that proportion had increased to 57.6 percent. In 20 years, the majority of Canada's physicians will be women.

Many young women doctors—especially residents in emergency departments and on hospital wards—have to correct the impression that they are nurses. The stereotypical image of doctor as male is still with us, but young people growing up today are increasingly exposed to women physicians in real life and in the mass media. As a result, 20 or 30 years from now, the stereotypical physician may well be female.

Theories of Health and Medicine

21.5 Apply sociology's major theories to health and medicine.

Each of sociology's major theoretical approaches—structural-functional theory, symbolic-interaction theory, and social conflict and feminist theories—helps us organize and interpret facts and issues concerning human health.

Structural-Functional Theory: Roles

Talcott Parsons (1964; orig. 1951) viewed medicine as society's strategy to keep its members healthy. According to this model, illness is dysfunctional because it undermines people's abilities to perform their roles.

THE SICK ROLE Society responds to sickness not only by providing medical care but also by incorporating a **sick role**, *patterns of behaviour defined as appropriate for people who are ill*. According to Parsons, the sick role releases people from normal obligations such as going to work or attending classes. To prevent abuse of this privilege, however, people cannot simply claim to be ill; they must "look the part" and, in serious cases, get the help of a medical expert. After assuming the sick role, the patient must want to get better and must do whatever is needed to regain good health, including co-operating with health professionals. This social position, defined by illness, involves a set of expectations regarding the behaviour of the sick person in relation to family and health professionals. In other words, the sick person has both rights and obligations (Segall & Chappell, 2000:23–25).

THE PHYSICIAN'S ROLE Physicians evaluate people's claims of sickness and help restore the sick to normal routines. To do this, physicians use their specialized knowledge and expect patients to co-operate with them, providing necessary information and following "doctor's orders" to complete the treatment.

EVALUATE

Parsons's analysis links illness and medicine to the broader organization of society. Others have extended the concept of the sick role to some non-illness situations such as pregnancy (Myers & Grasmick, 1989).

One limitation of the concept of the sick role is that it applies to acute conditions (e.g., flu or a broken leg) better than it does to chronic illnesses, which may not be reversible (e.g., heart disease or mental illness). In addition, a sick person's ability to assume the sick role (i.e., to take time off work to regain health) depends on the patient's resources; many working poor, for example, cannot afford to assume a sick role. On the other hand, illness is not entirely dysfunctional; it can have some positive consequences. Sometimes, a person who experiences a grave illness finds the opportunity to re-evaluate his or her life and gains a better sense of what is truly important (Ehrenreich, 2001; Myers, 2000).

Finally, critics point out that Parsons's analysis gives doctors, rather than patients, the primary responsibility for health. A more prevention-oriented approach gives each of us as individuals the responsibility to pursue health.

CHECK YOUR LEARNING Define the sick role. How does turning illness into a role in this way help society operate?

Symbolic-Interaction Theory: The Meaning of Health

According to symbolic-interaction theory, society is less a grand system than a complex and changing reality. In this model, health and medical care are socially constructed by people in everyday interaction.

THE SOCIAL CONSTRUCTION OF ILLNESS If both health and illness are socially constructed, people in a poor society may view hunger and malnutrition as normal. Similarly, many members of our own society give little thought to the harmful effects of a rich diet.

Our response to illness also is based on social definitions that may or may not square with medical facts. People with AIDS may be forced to deal with fear and prejudice that has no medical basis. Likewise, students may pay no attention to signs of real illness on the eve of a vacation but head for the campus clinic, hours before a midterm examination, with a case of the sniffles. In short, health is less an objective fact than a negotiated outcome.

How people define a medical situation may actually affect how they feel. Medical experts marvel at *psychosomatic* disorders (a fusion of Greek words for "mind" and "body"), when state of mind guides physical sensations (Hamrick et al., 1986). Our goal is to "understand the individual's definition of the situation and the social construction of reality to discover the meaning of health and illness" to that person (Segall & Chappell, 2000:28).

THE SOCIAL CONSTRUCTION OF TREATMENT Erving Goffman's *dramaturgical* approach to explain how physicians tailor their physical surroundings (their offices) and their behaviour (the presentation of self) so that others see them as competent and in charge.

Sociologist Joan Emerson (1970) further illustrates this process of reality construction in her analysis of a gynecological examination carried out by a male doctor. This situation is vulnerable to misinterpretation, since a man's touching of a woman's genitals is conventionally viewed as a sexual act and, possibly, an assault.

To ensure that people define the situation as impersonal and professional, the medical staff wear uniforms and furnish the examination room with nothing but medical equipment. The doctor's manner and overall performance are designed to make the patient feel that, to the doctor, examining the genital area is no different from treating any other part of the body. A female nurse is usually present during the examination, not only to assist the physician but also to avoid any impression that a man and a woman are "alone together."

Managing situational definitions in this way is only rarely taught in medical schools. The oversight is unfortunate because, as Emerson's analysis shows, understanding how people construct reality in the examination room is as important as mastering the medical skills required for treatment.

THE SOCIAL CONSTRUCTION OF PERSONAL IDENTITY A final insight provided by symbolic-interaction theory is an understanding of how surgery affects ones social identity. The reason that medical procedures can have a major effect on how we think of ourselves is that our culture places great symbolic importance on some organs and other parts of our bodies. People who lose a limb (say, in military combat) typically experience serious doubts about being "as much of a person" as before. The effects of surgery can be important even when there is no obvious change in physical appearance. For example, Jean Elson (2004) points out that one out of three women in the United States eventually has her uterus surgically removed in a procedure known as a *hysterectomy*. In interviews with women who had undergone the procedure, Elson found that the typical woman faced serious self-doubt about gender identity, asking, in effect, "Am I still a woman?" Only 10 percent of hysterectomies are for cancer; most are for pain, bleeding, or cysts—serious conditions but not so dangerous as to rule out other types of treatment. Perhaps, Elson points out, doctors might be more willing to consider alternative treatment if they were aware of how symbolically important the loss of the uterus is to many women.

Many women who undergo breast surgery have much the same reaction, doubting their own feminine identity and worrying that men will no longer find them attractive. For men to understand the significance of such medical procedures, it is only necessary to imagine how a male might react to the surgical loss of any or all of his genitals.

EVALUATE

Symbolic-interaction theory suggests that what people view as healthful or harmful depends on numerous factors that are not, strictly speaking, medical. This approach also shows that, in any medical procedure, both patient and medical staff engage in a subtle process of reality construction. It has helped us understand the symbolic importance of limb and other bodily organs: The loss of any part of the body—through accident or elective surgery—can have important consequences for personal identity.

By directing attention to the meanings that people attach to health and illness, symbolic-interaction theory draws criticism for implying that there are no objective standards of well-being. Certain physical conditions—arthritis, paralysis, blindness—define interpersonal relations, regardless of how we view those conditions. People who lack sufficient nutrition and safe water, for example, suffer from their unhealthy environment, whether they define their situations as normal or not.

CHECK YOUR LEARNING   Explain what it means to say that health, the treatment of illness, and personal identity are all socially constructed.

Social-Conflict and Feminist Theories: Inequality and Health

Social-conflict analysis points out the connection between health and social inequality and, taking a cue from Karl Marx, ties medicine to the operation of capitalism. Researchers have focused on three main issues: access to medical care, the effects of the profit motive, and the politics of medicine.

ACCESS TO CARE   Health is important to everyone. Yet, by requiring individuals to pay for medical care, capitalist societies allow the richest people to have the best health. The access problem is more serious in the United States than in other high-income countries because it does not have a universal medical care system.

Conflict theorists argue that capitalist health care provides excellent care for the rich but not for the rest of the population. Most of the 42 million Americans who lacked medical coverage before Obamacare had moderate to low incomes. Under capitalist health care, when illness strikes, the experience is starkly different for rich and poor.

Even Canadians, who have universal medical insurance (i.e., public financing), experience inequality of access to health care. When well-educated, affluent people visit physicians, they will have researched their symptoms or conditions on the internet. They may challenge their doctors and request referrals to specific kinds of specialists, and they can pay for their prescriptions personally or through private insurance. Poor people approach physicians very differently, are less likely to be referred to specialists, and often cannot pay for prescribed drugs. Access to care is one thing; access to good medical care is another.

THE PROFIT MOTIVE   Some conflict analysts go further, arguing that the real problem is not access to medical care but the character of capitalist medicine itself. The profit motive turns physicians, hospitals, nursing homes, home care, and the pharmaceutical industry into multi-billion-dollar corporations. The quest for higher profits encourages physicians to recommend unnecessary tests and surgery, and to rely too much on drugs, rather than focusing on improving people's lifestyles. In Canada, where medical insurance is socialized, the profit motive is attenuated but not eliminated. Physicians, pharmaceuticals, dentistry, nursing homes, and home care services are almost entirely in the private sector. Since physicians are in private practice, their earnings are determined by the extent of their billings relative to their expenses (which would include the costs of office space, equipment, receptionists or nurses, professional fees, insurance, and continuing education).

MEDICINE AS POLITICS   Although science claims to be politically neutral, scientific medicine frequently takes sides on important social issues. The American medical establishment, for example, has always strongly opposed government health care programs. The history of medicine itself shows how racial and sexual discrimination have been supported by "scientific" opinions about, say, the inferiority of women (Leavitt, 1984). Consider the diagnosis of "hysteria," a term that has its origins in the Greek word *hyster,* meaning "uterus." In choosing this word to describe a wild, emotional state, the medical profession suggested that being a woman is somehow the same as being irrational. Even today, according to conflict theory, scientific medicine explains illness exclusively in terms of bacteria and viruses, ignoring the contributing factor of poverty. In effect, scientific medicine hides the bias in our medical system by transforming this social issue into simple biology.

Over the past decade or two, physicians and politicians have engaged in an unusual medicalization issue—the medicinal use of marijuana—where *politicians* are seeking to influence appropriate medical intervention. Along with moves to decriminalize marijuana, Canada's federal government is allowing physicians to prescribe and dispense the drug to patients for control of pain, nausea, and other symptoms, especially among terminally ill patients. Doctors, in turn, are reluctant because marijuana has not gone through the normal rigorous clinical trials that establish efficacy and safety. In the end, some physicians will co-operate, while others will not—just as some refuse to prescribe birth control because of their personal beliefs.

EVALUATE

Social-conflict theory provides another view of the interactions of health, medicine, and society. According to this approach, social inequality is the reason why some people have better health than others.

Social-conflict theory also underlines the power of organized, scientific medicine. The medical profession defines and legitimizes illness, while controlling the diagnostic process and access to treatment (Segall & Chappell, 2000:26). Thus medical dominance is firmly established and maintained.

The most common objection to the social-conflict approach is that it minimizes the gains in health brought about by scientific medicine and higher living standards that have raised population health indicators in North America and Europe. Moreover, it is the profit motive that drives the tremendously expensive process of research, development, and clinical trials required to bring to market life-saving or life-enhancing drugs, such as those used to relieve HIV/AIDS. Governments, as a general rule, do not underwrite such expensive and risky endeavours.

CHECK YOUR LEARNING Explain how health and medical care are related to social classes, to capitalism, and to gender stratification.

In sum, sociology's three major theoretical approaches explain why health and medicine are social issues. The Applying Theory table sums up what they teach us.

Renowned French scientist Louis Pasteur (1822–1895), who spent much of his life studying how bacteria cause disease, said that health depends less on bacteria than on the social environment in which the bacteria are found (quoted in Gordon, 1980:7). Explaining and publicizing Pasteur's insight is sociology's contribution to human health.

Health and Medicine: Looking Ahead

In the early 1900s, deaths from infectious diseases such as diphtheria and measles were common. Because scientists had yet to develop penicillin and other antibiotics, even a small wound might become infected, and a simple infection from a minor wound was sometimes life-threatening. A century later, most of us—at least, most young people—take good health and long life for granted. Although the obesity epidemic is cause for concern, it seems reasonable to expect improvements in health to continue during the twenty-first century. Another encouraging trend is that more people are taking responsibility for their own health. Every one of us can live better and longer if we avoid tobacco, eat healthful meals, drink alcohol in moderation, and exercise regularly.

Yet certain health problems will continue to plague Canadian society in the decades to come. With no cure in sight, it seems likely that the AIDS epidemic will persist for some time. At this point, the only way to steer clear of contracting HIV is to make a decision to avoid all of the risky behaviours noted in this chapter. Furthermore, the changing social profile of people with AIDS, which increasingly afflicts the poor, reminds us that Canada falls short in addressing the health of marginalized members of our society.

We know that health problems are far greater in low-income countries than they are in Canada. The good news is that life expectancy for the world as a whole has been rising—from 48 years in 1950 to 71 years today—and the biggest gains have been made in low-income countries (Population Reference Bureau, 2014). But in much of Latin America, Asia, and especially Africa, hundreds of millions of adults and children lack not only medical attention but also adequate food and safe water. Improving health in the world's poorest societies remains a critical challenge in the years to come.

From a policy perspective, the World Health Organization and governments worldwide must prepare for the possibility of pandemic influenza (of bird, swine, or some other origin), which many analysts argue is not just a possibility but inevitable. Practical problems, such as producing massive quantities of antiviral medications, and ethical questions, such as who will get these antivirals, loom large in our future.

Another issue that raises ethical concerns is the international organ trade (see the Controversy and Debate box); too often, when patients in the wealthiest nations seek kidney "donors," the desperately poor in developing countries are enticed to sell their organs. As the demand for organs grows, the pressures on the world's poor to provide them can only increase.

Most of the challenges to health and medical care that we face in the future are the result of knowing too little—but it is also possible to know too much. Advances in genetic knowledge make it possible to check the DNA of individuals to identify abnormalities that predispose them to some forms of cancer (e.g., breast cancer), sickle-cell anemia, muscular dystrophy, Huntington's disease, and cystic fibrosis. It will also be possible to manipulate the expression of DNA segments to prevent the development of some of these diseases.

The same genetic knowledge that allows identification and perhaps removal of abnormal genes in the initial stages of human reproduction also enables us to choose the characteristics of our children. Mapping the medical destinies of individuals produces information of interest not only to scientists and physicians but also to life insurance companies and potential marriage partners.

Do we really want to look into the genetic crystal ball? That question, deceptively simple on one level, introduces numerous ethical issues (e.g., "genetic privacy" and "designer children"). Where until now we have been concerned, primarily, with what we can do, the future will raise questions of what we ought to do with unprecedented knowledge.

Controversy and Debate

Waiting for a Kidney Transplant: Canadian Patients and the International Organ Trade

What would you do under the following conditions? Your kidneys have failed; you are spending three or four hours, four days a week, in dialysis; the wait-time for a transplant in Canada is four years or more; you know that you can go abroad for an immediate transplant; *and* you can afford it.

That, in a nutshell, is the question answered by dialysis patients who were interviewed by Amanda Peters (2011) for her master's thesis at the University of Guelph. She interviewed six patients, three doctors, and three nurses in a dialysis unit to begin the process of understanding how people on the ground felt about these issues. Because she wanted to find out what people involved in dialysis thought and felt about kidney disease, treatment options, and transplants at home or abroad, she needed to be a participant observer. So she volunteered to help out in the dialysis unit—but first she submitted her proposal to the university ethics committee, got permission from hospital administration, and arranged for all of the people she would interview to give informed consent (by signing a form).

When Canadians donate organs (or blood), they do it as volunteers—meaning that they are not paid. In fact, the sale and purchase of organs or blood is illegal in Canada. A human can live with a single kidney, so, when someone is a match with a loved one (or, once in a while, a complete stranger), he or she might consent to being a live donor. The other source of kidneys is people who have died—provided that, before death, they indicated their willingness to donate their organs. This is why organs are hard to come by in Canada—and why the wait time for kidney transplants is four years or more.

But kidneys *are* readily available overseas—in developing countries where people are poor and desperate enough to sell a kidney for cash. If Canadians can afford it, they have the option of going abroad for a kidney transplant. The problem, from a social-conflict perspective, is that the people who give up their kidneys are desperately poor. By purchasing their kidneys, we are taking advantage of their desperation. This is exploitation, pure and simple.

Through her volunteering and her interviews, Peters found out that none of her respondents had made plans to go abroad for transplants, but half of them *would consider it* under the right circumstances. They would do so if they felt confident about their personal safety; the extent to which they could trust the transplant teams, their cleanliness, and their quality of care; and affordability of the procedure.

Significantly, *none* of the respondents expressed any concern for the kidney seller. No thought was given to the fact that the "buyer" would be exploiting vulnerable people—people who had no way of escaping desperate poverty other than by selling their kidneys. Given the right conditions (safety, trust, quality of care, and affordability), they would be willing to proceed without any thought for the safety or welfare of the people at the other end of their transactions.

What Do You Think?

1. What would you do if you found yourself in the position of the dialysis patient described in the first paragraph?

2. Should Canada be taking steps to make more kidneys available here at home—perhaps by increasing public awareness and encouraging more people to donate (or arrange to donate) organs when they die?

3. Do we, as Canadians, have any responsibility for the welfare of organ donors in the Philippines or India?

APPLYING THEORY

Health

	Structural-Functional Theory	Symbolic-Interaction Theory	Social-Conflict and Feminist Theories
What is the level of analysis?	Macro-level	Micro-level	Macro-level
How is health related to society?	Illness is dysfunctional for society because it prevents people from carrying out their daily roles.	Societies define "health" and "illness" differently according to their living standards.	Health is linked to social inequality with rich people having more access to care than poor people.
	The sick role releases people who are ill from responsibilities while they try to get well.	How people define their own health affects how they actually feel (psychosomatic conditions).	Capitalist medical care places the drive for profits over the needs of people.
			Scientific medicine downplays the social causes of illness, including poverty, racism, and sexism.

Seeing Sociology in Everyday Life

CHAPTER 21 Health and Medicine

How does society affect patterns of health?

Certain occupations put people at higher-than-average risk of accident or death. One example is coal mining, which has long been one of the deadliest jobs. Although the death toll from mining accidents has gone down over time, even miners who manage to avoid mine collapses or explosions typically suffer harm from years of breathing coal dust. Look at the photos below: How do they link health to a way of life?

Hint Among the most dangerous jobs in Canada are farming (dangers come from power equipment and pesticides), mining, timber cutting, truck driving, and constructing tall buildings (high-steel construction is a specialty of the Mohawk). Until their involvement ended in 2014, our troops in Afghanistan faced danger—and possibly death—on a daily basis The Association of Workers' Compensation Boards of Canada reported 919 workplace fatalities in 2014, or more than 2.5 per working day. In general, blue-collar workers are at greater risk. Furthermore, men predominate in the most dangerous jobs.

Dan Rafla/Aurora Photos, Inc.

CREWS ON FISHING BOATS SUCH AS THIS ONE SPEND MONTHS AT A TIME BATTLING HIGH SEAS, OFTEN IN FRIGID TEMPERATURES It is a rare and fortunate fishing season that brings no death or serious injury. What other jobs threaten the health and lives of workers?

Andrew Vaughan/The Canadian Press

THE WESTRAY MINE IN PICTOU COUNTY, NOVA SCOTIA, EXPLODED EARLY ON THE MORNING OF MAY 9, 1992, KILLING 26 MEN A pickaxe created sparks that ignited methane gas in the mine. Although miners had complained about safety hazards, owners and mine officials had called the new mine one of the safest in Canada.

WANG SONG/XINHUA/AP Images

ARE HIGH DEATH TOLLS IN COAL MINING A THING OF THE PAST? IN 2007, CHINA REPORTED 3786 DEATHS IN COAL MINES IN THAT COUNTRY Here, rescuers remove a body from a mine after a gas explosion killed more than 80 miners.

Seeing Sociology in *Your* Everyday Life

1. Check out the emergency service at a hospital near you. Are there people lining the hallways on stretchers? How does the staff decide which patients to see first?

2. Get a course catalogue from a medical school (or visit a school's website) and see how much, if any, of the curriculum deals with the social dimensions of medical care.

3. What have you learned from this chapter that you can use to improve your own health?

Making the Grade

CHAPTER 21 Health and Medicine

What Is Health?

21.1 Explain how patterns of health are shaped by society.

Health is a social issue because personal well-being depends on a society's level of technology and its distribution of resources.

- A society's culture shapes definitions of health, which change over time.
- A society's technology affects people's health.
- Social inequality affects people's health.

> **health** a state of complete physical, mental, and social well-being
> **universal medical coverage**, a system in which the costs of essential medical services are covered by the state,

Health: A Global Survey

21.2 Contrast patterns of health in low- and high-income countries.

Health in Low-Income Countries

- Poor nations suffer from inadequate sanitation, hunger, and other problems linked to poverty.
- Life expectancy in low-income nations is about 20 years less than in Canada; in the poorest nations, 10 percent of children die within a year of birth, and 25 percent die before the age of 30.

Health in High-Income Countries

- In the nineteenth century, industrialization improved health dramatically in Western Europe and North America.
- A century ago, infectious diseases were leading killers; today, most people in Canada die in old age of illnesses such as heart disease, cancer, or stroke.

Health in Canada

21.3 Analyze how race, class, gender, and age are linked to health.

Who Is Healthy? Age, Gender, Class, and Race

- Over 80 percent of Canadian children born today will live to at least age 65.
- Throughout the life course, women have better health than men. Our culture's definition of masculinity promotes aggressive and individualistic behaviour that contributes to men's higher rate of coronary disease as well as accidents and violence.

- People of high social position enjoy better health than the poor, a result of better nutrition, wider access to health care, and safer and less stressful living conditions.
- Poverty among Aboriginal people helps explain why they are more likely to die in infancy and to suffer the effects of violence, drug abuse, and poor health.

Cigarette Smoking

- Cigarette smoking is the greatest preventable cause of illness and premature death.
- The proportion of Canadian adults who smoke dropped from 45 to 18 percent between 1960 and 2014.
- Initially, the tobacco industry denied that smoking is a threat to health, but conceded in 1997 that it is harmful and agreed not to target advertising to youngsters. The tobacco industry now focuses on Asia and low-income countries around the world.

Eating Disorders and Obesity

- Eating disorders—anorexia nervosa and bulimia—are tied to cultural expectations of thinness; among adults, women are three times more likely than men to suffer from anorexia nervosa and five times more likely to suffer from bulimia.
- About 23 percent of Canadian adults are obese—with BMIs of 30 or more—thereby raising the risk of heart disease, stroke, and type-2 diabetes.
- Social causes of obesity include an inactive lifestyle and a diet heavy in salt and fatty foods.

Sexually Transmitted Diseases

- STDs became a matter of national concern during the Sexual Revolution beginning in the 1960s; by the late 1980s, the dangers of STDs, especially AIDS, caused a sexual counter-revolution as people turned away from casual sex.
- Specific behaviours that put people at risk of AIDS include anal sex, sharing needles, and use of any drug.

Ethical Issues Surrounding Death

- Questions about the use of medical technology have added an ethical dimension to health and illness.
- Supporters of a "right to die" argue that individuals should be able to decide for themselves when to use or refuse medical treatment to prolong their lives.

> **social epidemiology** the study of health and disease as distributed throughout a society's population
> **eating disorder** a disorder that involves an intense form of dieting or other unhealthy method of weight control driven by the desire to be very thin

euthanasia assisting in the death of a person suffering from an incurable disease; also known as *mercy killing*

The Medical Establishment

21.4 Compare the medical systems in nations around the world.

The Rise of Scientific Medicine

- Health care was historically a family concern but with industrialization became the responsibility of trained specialists.
- The model of scientific medicine is the foundation of the Canadian medical establishment.

Holistic Medicine

- Holistic medicine, focusing on prevention of illness, takes a broader and more traditional approach than scientific medicine.
- Holistic practitioners focus on health rather than disease; they emphasize treating patients as people, encourage people to take responsibility for their own health, and provide treatment in personal, relaxed surroundings.

Paying for Medical Care: A Global Survey

- Socialist societies define medical care as a right; governments offer basic care equally to everyone.
- Capitalist societies view medical care as a commodity to be purchased, although most capitalist governments help pay for medical care through socialized medicine or national health insurance.

Paying for Medical Care: Canada

- Canadians have universal medical insurance that covers essential medical care, as defined by each of the provinces. People who work for government and large organizations generally have private insurance to fill in the gaps on vision care, dentistry, and prescriptions.
- Canada's health care system differs from socialized medicine in that physicians and nurses are not government employees. Physicians are in private practice, and most nurses work for hospitals that are independent non-profit organizations.

The Nursing Shortage

- The aging of Canadian society is a major factor raising the demand for nursing.
- The wider range of occupational choices for women today has resulted in fewer young women choosing this traditionally female job. Canada is creating more spaces in nursing schools, but we lose 15 nurses to the United States for every one that comes here.

Canadian Women in Medicine

- The proportion of female medical students and physicians has increased steadily, to the point where 61 percent of physicians under 35 years of age are women. In 2016, 40 percent of all physicians are women.

medicine the social institution that focuses on fighting disease and improving health
holistic medicine an approach to health care that emphasizes the prevention of illness and takes into account a person's entire physical and social environment
socialized medicine a medical care system in which the government owns and operates most medical facilities and employs most physicians
direct fee system a medical care system in which patients pay directly for the services of physicians and hospitals

Theories of Health and Medicine

21.5 Apply sociology's major theories to health and medicine.

Structural-functional theory argues that illness is dysfunctional because it reduces people's abilities to perform their roles. According to Talcott Parsons, society responds to illness by defining roles:

- The sick role excuses the ill person from routine social responsibilities.
- The physician's role is to use specialized knowledge to take charge of the patient's recovery.

Symbolic-interaction theory shows how health and medical care are socially constructed by people in everyday interaction:

- Our response to illness is not always based on medical facts.
- How people define a medical situation may affect how they feel.

Social-conflict and feminist theories focus on the unequal distribution of health and medical care. They criticize the medical establishment for

- its overreliance on drugs and surgery
- the dominance of the profit motive
- overemphasis on the biological rather than the social causes of illness

sick role patterns of behaviour defined as appropriate for people who are ill

Chapter 22
Population, Urbanization, and Environment

Jeremy sutton-hibbert/Alamy stock photo

Learning Objectives

22.1 Explain the concepts of fertility, mortality, and migration, and their effects on population.

22.2 Analyze population trends using Malthusian theory and demographic transition theory.

22.3 Summarize patterns of urbanization in Canada and around the world.

22.4 Identify the contributions of Tönnies, Durkheim, Park, Wirth, and Marx to our understanding of urban life.

22.5 Describe the third urban revolution now under way in poor societies.

22.6 Analyze current environmental problems such as pollution and global warming or climate change.

The Power of Society
to shape our view of global warming

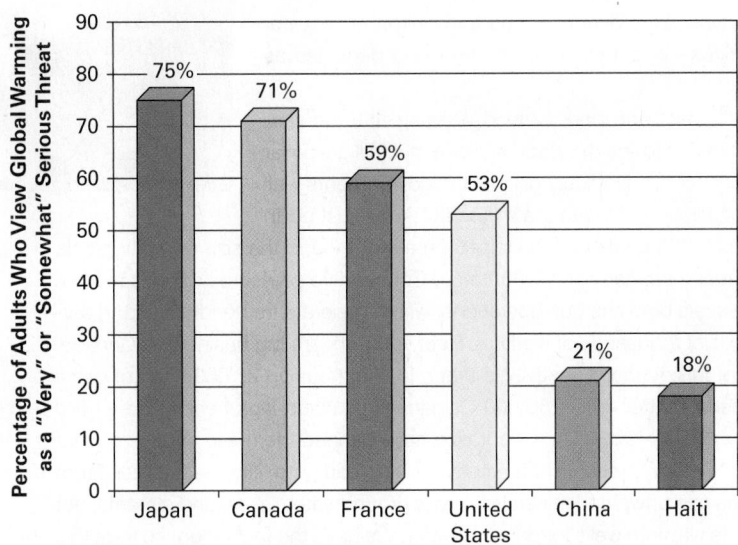

SOURCE: Data from Gallup (2011).

Are attitudes about global warming simply our personal opinions? One way to answer this question is to look around the world. Compared with Canadians, Americans are more evenly divided on the issue of global warming, with a slight majority seeing global warming as a "somewhat serious" or "very serious" threat. Canadian attitudes about global warming are more closely aligned with other high-income countries. The level of concern about global warming is far lower in low-income countries, where people are more concerned with basic needs such as food and shelter. Clearly, society has the power to shape our view on environmental issues just as it shapes so many other aspects of our lives.

Chapter Overview

This chapter explores three dimensions of social change: population dynamics, urbanization, and increasing threats to the natural environment. Not only are all three important, but they are closely linked as well.

"When Water Kills" is the title of a *Maclean's* cover story (Nikiforuk, 2000) written in the aftermath of deaths and illnesses that followed the contamination of drinking water in Walkerton, Ontario. *Escherichia coli* 0157:H7, a virulent strain of the bacterium *E. coli* that resides in the gut of animals, was responsible for the Walkerton deaths, just as it was for the deaths of a dozen children in southern Alberta between 1989 and 1991. These outbreaks, the article explains, were directly linked to monitoring of water quality and farming practices—in particular, cattle and hog densities as mapped by Health Canada.

The global demand for beef and pork to feed growing and increasingly affluent populations has led to the development of a multibillion-dollar industry in Canada: factory farms, feedlots, or, as our governments call them, "intensive livestock operations." In Alberta's "Feedlot Alley" just north of Lethbridge, as many as 25 000 cattle may be raised on a plot of land the size of a city block. Hog factory farms might house as many as 80 000 pigs. Competitive pressures force Canadian producers into these large-scale beef and hog operations, which generate tremendous export revenues and employ hundreds of thousands of workers. Beef and pork are big business in Canada.

The problem with all of this economic activity is that a feedlot housing 25 000 head of cattle produces more dung, or fecal matter, than 250 000 Calgarians. Canada lags behind the United States in regulating factory farms—Kansas and Nebraska have banned them altogether—so that almost all of our beef and hog effluent remains untreated and is spread onto fields as fertilizer. From there, runoff carries bacteria and unwanted minerals into our groundwater, lakes, and streams; not surprisingly, *E. coli* makes its way into wells for drinking water. We have the technology to treat this sewage, test water quality, and treat our water. What we do *not* have in any of our provinces is the political will to enforce the regulations that would ensure safe drinking water for all Canadians. ■

It is hard to imagine what a global population of 7 billion means. But consider this—just 50 years ago, the planet's population was less than half as large. So while we can't be sure exactly what future decades will bring, we can be certain that huge changes are under way.

Demography: The Study of Population

22.1 Explain the concepts of fertility, mortality, and migration, and their effects on population.

Some 12 000 years ago, when humans first began to cultivate plants, the world's human population numbered about 5 million—roughly equal to British Columbia's today. Very slow growth pushed the global total in 1 BCE to perhaps 300 million.

Starting around 1750, world population began to spike upward. We now add more than 86 million people to the planet each year. Today, the world's population is about 7.2 billon people (Population Reference Bureau, 2014).

The causes and consequences of this drama are the basis of **demography**, *the study of human population*. Demography (from Greek, meaning "description of people") is a cousin of sociology that analyzes the size and composition of a population and studies how and why people move from place to place. Demographers not only collect statistics but also raise important questions about the effects of population growth and suggest how it might be controlled. The following sections present basic demographic concepts.

Fertility

The study of human population begins with the number of people born. **Fertility** is *the incidence of child-bearing in a country's population*. During her child-bearing years, from the onset of menstruation (typically in her early teens) to menopause (usually in her forties), a woman is capable of bearing more than 20 children; but *fecundity*, or maximum possible child-bearing, is sharply reduced by health, cultural norms, finances, and personal choice.

Demographers often measure fertility using the **crude birth rate**, *the number of live births in a given year for every thousand people in a population*. A crude birth rate is

Global Snapshot

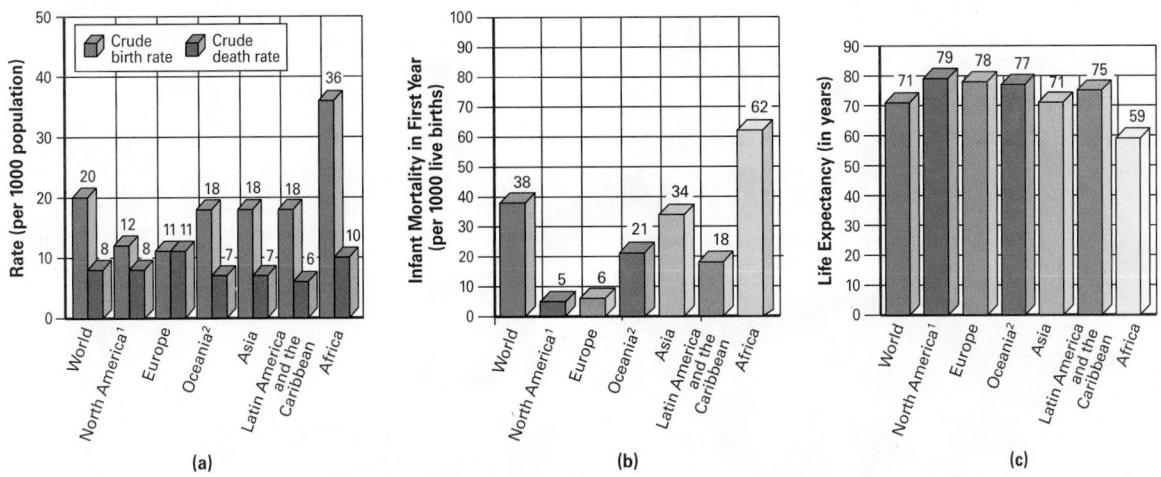

¹United States and Canada. ²Australia, New Zealand, and South Pacific Islands.

Figure 22–1 (a) Crude Birth Rates and Crude Death Rates, (b) Infant Mortality Rates, and (c) Life Expectancy around the World, 2014

By world standards, North America has a low birth rate, an average death rate, a very low infant mortality rate, and high life expectancy.

SOURCE: Data from Population Reference Bureau (2014).

calculated by dividing the number of live births in a given year by a society's total population, and multiplying the result by 1000. For example, in Canada in 2011 there were 377 636 live births in a population of 33.5 million, yielding a crude birth rate of 11.0.

Figure 22–1(a) shows that, in global perspective, the crude birth rate of North Americans is low—roughly one-third of the rate in Africa. Canada Map 22–1 reveals that fertility even within Canada varies dramatically, from lows of 8.7 and 9.3 per 1000 population in Newfoundland and Labrador and Nova Scotia to 24.9 in Nunavut. The lows in Atlantic Canada are the result of steady out-migration of young people of child-bearing age (which contributes to population aging); the high in Nunavut is due to the high fertility of the relatively young Inuit population. It is worth noting that, from 1981 to 2011, Canada's crude fertility rate declined from 14.9 to 11.0—while that of Newfoundland and Labrador started off higher than Canada's and dropped to the lowest (15.9 to 8.7). Ontario had the lowest crude birth rate in 1981 (13.9) but ended up at 0.5 below average in 2011 (at 10.5 per 1000 population).

Mortality

Population size is also affected by **mortality**, *the incidence of death in a society's population.* To measure mortality, demographers use a **crude death rate**, *the number of deaths in a given year for*

every thousand people in a population. The crude death rate is calculated as the number of deaths in a year divided by the total population, multiplied by 1000. In 2013, Canada's crude death rate was 7.2 per 1000 population—compared to 8.4 in the United States, 9.6 in Sweden, 9.5 in Japan, and 10.6 in Germany. There is an inverse relationship between crude death rates and crude birthrates; where birthrates are high, death rates are low because a young population has relatively few elders who are most likely to die (World Health Organization, 2016).

A third widely used demographic measure is the **infant mortality rate**, *the number of deaths among infants in the first year of life for each thousand live births in a given*

FERTILITY IN CANADA HAS FALLEN DURING THE PAST CENTURY AND IS NOW QUITE LOW But some categories of our population have much higher fertility rates. The Hutterites of Alberta and the Amish in the United States provide examples; it is common for such couples to have five, six, or more children.

David Turnley/Corbis Historical/Corbis

Seeing Ourselves

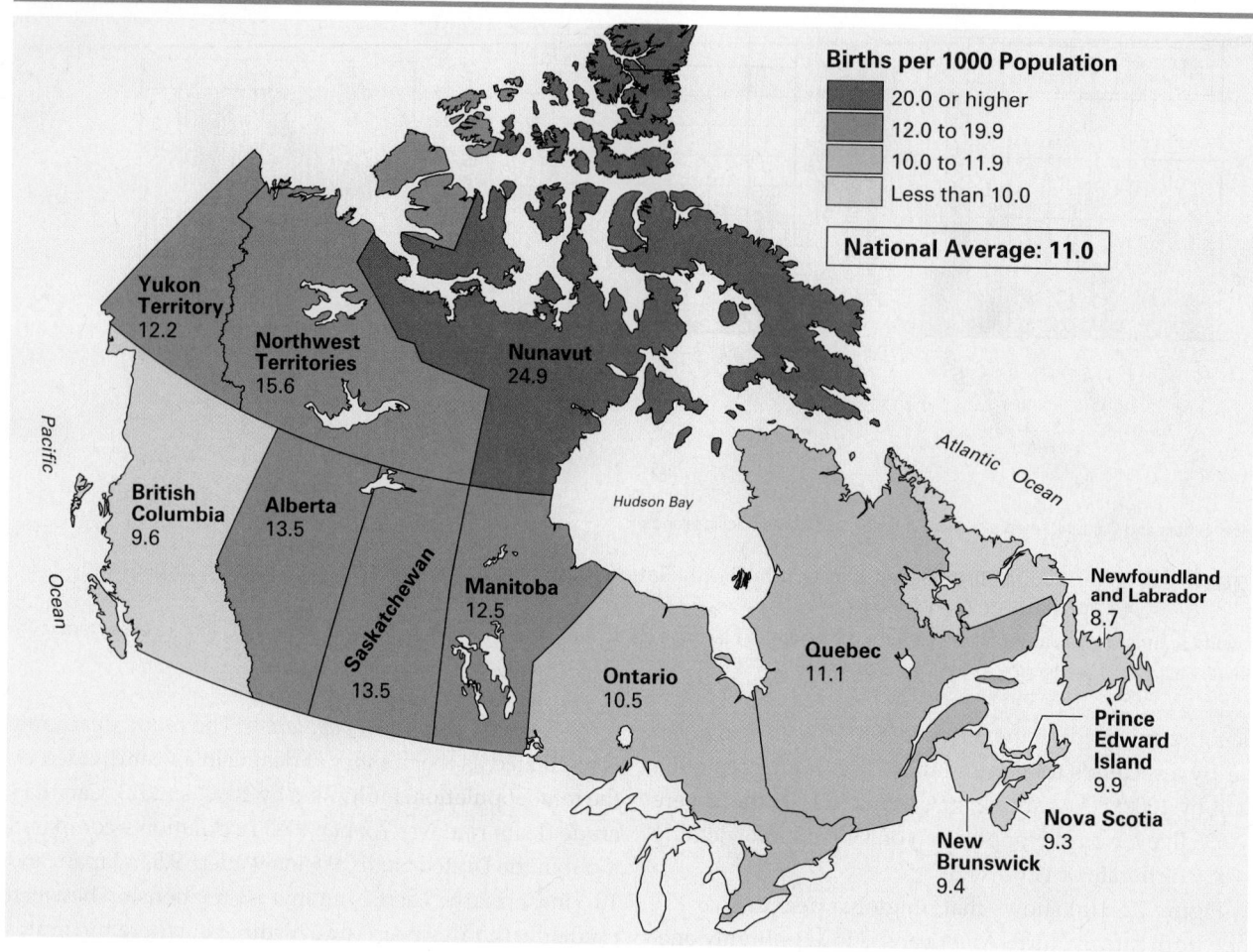

Canada Map 22–1 Crude Birth Rates (births per 1000 population) by Province and Territory, 2011

SOURCE: Compilation by LM Gerber from Statistics Canada, Canadian Vital Statistics, Catalogue no. 91-209-X.

year. This rate is calculated by dividing the number of deaths of children under one year of age by the number of live births during the same year and multiplying the result by 1000. In 2012, Canada's infant mortality rate was 4.8 per 1000 live births. This was lower than the U.S. rate (6.5), but on par with those of most European countries. Like other demographic variables, the infant mortality rate conceals considerable variation among segments of the Canadian population. For example, infant mortality rates are higher among the poor, in isolated communities, and among Aboriginal peoples. Nonetheless, infant mortality offers a good general measure of overall quality of life and, therefore, is used as one indicator of socioeconomic development. Within Canada, infant mortality rates range from a low of 2.2 in Yukon to a high of 21.4 in Nunavut. Figure 22–1(b) shows that infant mortality in North America is low by world standards.

Societies with low infant mortality rates have high **life expectancy**, *the average lifespan of a society's population.* Canadian males born in 2012 can expect to live 80 years,

while females can expect to live 84 years—two or three years longer than their counterparts in the United States. Life expectancy in rich, industrialized countries is about 20 years longer than it is in poorer societies (see Figure 22–1(c)). When countries are ranked by estimated life expectancies—for people born in 2016 (www.geoba.se)—Canada ranks 13th out of 228 countries at 81.9 years. Monaco has the highest life expectancy at a phenomenal 89.5 years, while Chad and South Africa have the lowest at 50 years. The United States ranks 53rd, with a life expectancy of 79 years.

Migration

Population size is also affected by **migration**, *the movement of people into and out of a specified territory.* Movement into an area, or *immigration,* is measured as an *in-migration* rate, calculated as the number of people entering an area for every 1000 people in the population. Movement out of an area, or *emigration,* is measured in terms of an

demography the study of human population

fertility the incidence of child-bearing in a country's population

crude birth rate the number of live births in a given year for every 1000 people in a population

mortality the incidence of death in a country's population

crude death rate the number of deaths in a given year for every 1000 people in a population

infant mortality rate the number of deaths among infants in the first year of life for each 1000 live births in a given year

migration the movement of people into and out of a specified territory

out-migration rate, the number leaving for every 1000 people. Both types of migration usually occur at once; the difference is the net migration rate.

All nations experience internal migration—that is, movement within their borders from one region to another. Within Canada, for example, Ontario, British Columbia, and Alberta—and more recently Manitoba and Saskatchewan—fairly consistently gain population at the expense of other provinces or territories. Migration is sometimes voluntary, as when people leave a small town and move to a larger city. In such cases, push/pull factors are typically at work: A lack of jobs pushes people to move, and more opportunity pulls them elsewhere—as in the move from the Atlantic provinces to Alberta prior to the collapse in oil prices. Migration can also be involuntary, such as the forcible transport of 10 million Africans to the western hemisphere as slaves, or the relocation of Aboriginal people from their ancestral lands onto reserves.

Population Growth

Fertility, mortality, and migration all affect the size of a society's population. In general, rich nations (such as Canada) grow as much from immigration as from natural increase; poor nations (such as Pakistan) grow almost entirely from natural increase.

Demographers derive the *natural growth rate* of a population by subtracting the crude death rate from the crude birth rate. For example, the natural growth rate of the Canadian population in 2009–10 was 3.8 per 1000 (the crude birth rate of 11.3 minus the crude death rate of 7.5), or 0.38 percent annually (less than half of 1 percent.) Taking net migration into account, Canada's growth rate is roughly 0.5 percent per year.

Global Map 22–1 shows that population growth in Canada and other high-income nations is well below the world average of 1.2 percent. Earth's low-growth continents are Europe (currently showing no growth) and North America (0.4 percent). Close to the global average are Oceania (1.1 percent), Asia (1.1 percent), and Latin America (1.2 percent). The highest-growth region in the world is Africa (2.5 percent).

A handy rule of thumb for estimating a nation or region's growth is to divide the number 70 by the population growth rate; this yields the *doubling time* in years. Thus an annual growth rate of 2 percent (found in the Latin American nation of Honduras) doubles a population in 35 years, and a 3 percent growth rate (found in the African nation of the Democratic Republic of Congo) drops the doubling time to just 23 years. The rapid population growth of the poorest countries is deeply troubling because these countries can barely support the populations they have now.

Population Composition

Demographers also study the makeup of a society's population at a given point in time. One variable is the **sex ratio**, *the number of males for every 100 females in a nation's population*. In 2011, the sex ratio in Canada was 96.2, or 96 males for every 100 females. Sex ratios are usually below 100 because, on average, women outlive men. In India, however, the sex ratio is 106, because many parents value sons more than daughters and may either abort a female fetus or, after birth, give more care to a male infant, raising the odds that he will live.

A more complex measure is the **age-sex pyramid**, *a graphic representation of the age and sex of a population*. Figure 22–2 presents the age-sex pyramids for Canada in 1971, 1981, 2001, and 2011. The left side indicates the distribution of males of different ages, while the right side shows the corresponding distribution of females. The rather rough pyramidal shape of these figures results from higher mortality as people age. Also note that after about age 30, women increasingly outnumber men in Canada. The bulge that moves up the pyramid from 1971 to 2011 represents the *baby boom* (born between 1947 and 1966). The contraction below age 15 on the 1981 pyramid shows that the baby boom was followed by a *baby bust* as the birth rate dipped from 28.2 in 1955 to a low of 12.7 in 1996. The bulges in the four pyramids in Figure 22–2 reveal the upward movement—or aging—of the baby boom generation over a 40-year period.

Window on the World

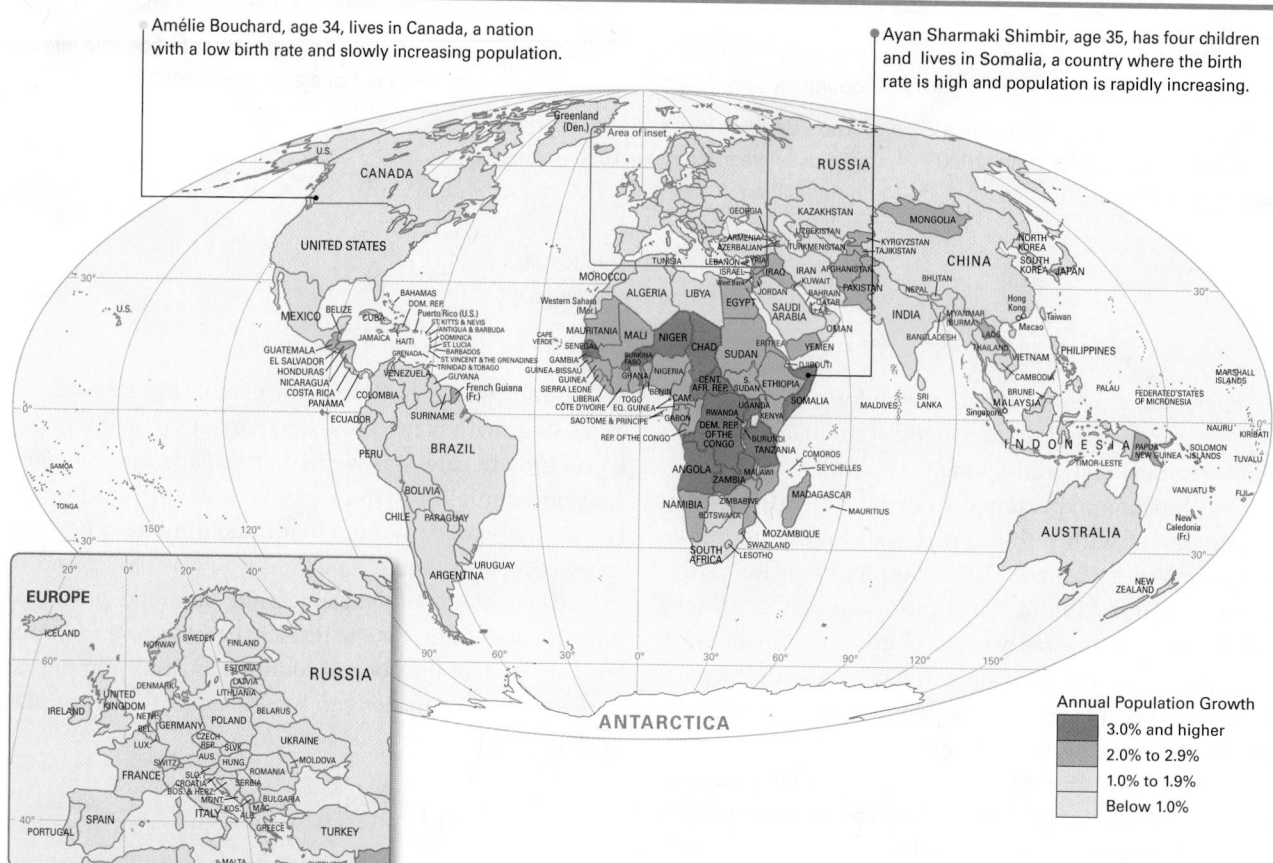

Amélie Bouchard, age 34, lives in Canada, a nation with a low birth rate and slowly increasing population.

Ayan Sharmaki Shimbir, age 35, has four children and lives in Somalia, a country where the birth rate is high and population is rapidly increasing.

Annual Population Growth
- 3.0% and higher
- 2.0% to 2.9%
- 1.0% to 1.9%
- Below 1.0%

Global Map 22–1 Population Growth in Global Perspective

The richest countries of the world—including the United States, Canada, and the nations of Europe—have growth rates below 1 percent. The nations of Latin America and Asia typically have growth rates around 1.2 percent, a rate that doubles a population in 58 years. Africa has an overall growth rate of 2.5 percent (despite only small increases in countries with a high rate of AIDS), which cuts the doubling time to 28 years. In global perspective, we see that a society's standard of living is closely related to its rate of population growth: Population is rising fastest in the world regions that can least afford to support more people.

SOURCE: Based on Population Reference Bureau (2014).

History and Theory of Population Growth

22.2 Analyze population trends using Malthusian theory and demographic transition theory.

In the past, people wanted large families because human labour was the key to productivity. In addition, until rubber condoms were invented in the mid-1800s, the prevention of pregnancy was uncertain at best. But high death rates from infectious diseases put a constant brake on population growth.

A major demographic shift began about 1750 as the world's population turned upward, reaching the 1 billion mark by 1800. This milestone—which took all of human history to reach—was repeated just more than

a century later in 1930, by when a second billion people had been added to the planet. In other words, not only was population increasing, but the *rate* of growth was accelerating. The global population reached 3 billion by 1962 (just 32 years later) and 4 billion by 1974 (only 12 years after that). The rate of world population increase has slowed recently, but our planet passed the 5 billion mark in 1987, the 6 billion mark in 1999, and the 7 billion mark early in 2012. In no previous century did the world's population even double; in the twentieth century, it *quadrupled*.

Currently, the world is gaining 87 million people each year; 98 percent of this increase is in poor countries. Experts predict that Earth's population will reach 8 billion by 2025 and will climb more slowly to about 9.5 billion by 2050 (United Nations, 2013). Given the world's

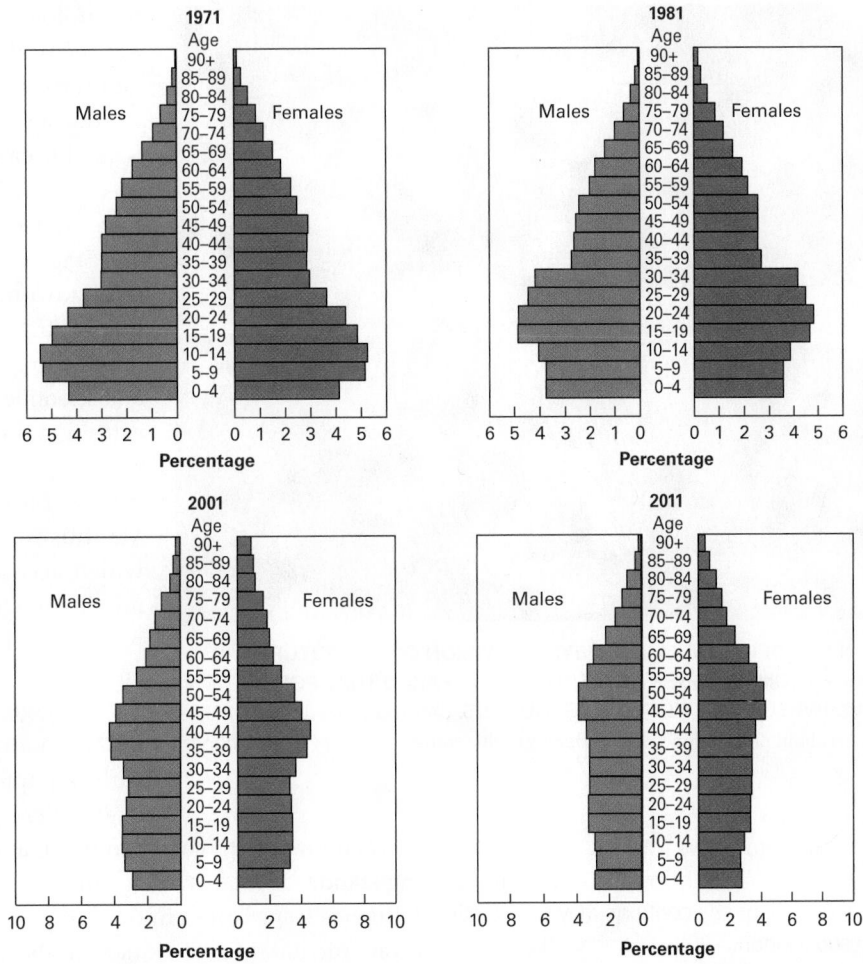

Figure 22–2 Age-Sex Population Pyramids for Canada, 1971–2011*

*Note that, in 1971, the baby boom shows up among people aged 5 to 29; by 2011, the baby boom is among people aged 45 to 64.

SOURCE: Adapted by LM Gerber from Census 1971 and 1981. Calculations for Census 2001 and 2011 are based on Catalogue nos. 95F0486XCB2001001 and 95-311-XCB2011-018.

troubles feeding the present population, such an increase is a matter of urgent concern.

Malthusian Theory

The sudden population growth 250 years ago sparked the development of demography. Thomas Robert Malthus (1766–1834), an English economist and clergyman, warned that population increase would soon lead to social chaos. Malthus (1926; orig. 1798) calculated that population would increase in what mathematicians call a *geometric progression* (e.g., 2, 4, 8, 16, 32, and so on). At such a rate, Malthus concluded, world population would soon soar out of control.

Food production would also increase, Malthus explained, but only in *arithmetic progression* (e.g., 2, 3, 4, 5, 6, and so on) because, even with new agricultural technology, farmland is limited. Thus, Malthus presented a distressing vision of the future: People reproducing beyond what the planet could feed, leading ultimately to

widespread starvation and war over what resources were available.

Malthus recognized that artificial birth control or abstinence might change his prediction. But he considered the former morally wrong and the other quite impractical. Because, in Malthus's mind, famine and war stalked humanity, he was justly known as "the dismal parson."

EVALUATE

Fortunately, Malthus's prediction was flawed. By 1850, the European birth rate began to drop, partly because children were becoming an economic liability rather than an asset and partly because people began using artificial birth control. Also, Malthus underestimated human ingenuity: Modern irrigation techniques, fertilizers, and pesticides increased farm production far more than he could have imagined (Yemma, 2011).

Some people criticized Malthus for ignoring the role of social inequality in world abundance and famine. Karl Marx (1967; orig. 1867), for example, objected to viewing suffering as a "law of nature" rather than the curse of capitalism. More

THIS STREET SCENE IN OLD DELHI, INDIA, CONVEYS THE VISION OF THE FUTURE FOUND IN THE WORK OF THOMAS ROBERT MALTHUS, WHO FEARED THAT POPULATION INCREASE WOULD OVERWHELM THE WORLD'S RESOURCES Can you explain why Malthus had such a serious concern about population? How is demographic transition theory a more hopeful analysis?

recently, "critical demographers" have claimed that saying poverty is caused by high birth rates in low-income countries amounts to blaming the victims; on the contrary, they see global inequality as the real issue (Horton, 1999; Kuumba, 1999).

Still, Malthus offers an important lesson. Habitable land, clean water, and fresh air are limited resources, and greater economic productivity has taken a heavy toll on the natural environment. In addition, medical advances have lowered death rates, pushing up world population. Common sense tells us that no level of population growth can go on forever. People everywhere must become aware of the dangers of population increase.

CHECK YOUR LEARNING What did Malthus predict about human population growth and about food production? What was his overall conclusion?

Demographic Transition Theory

A more complex analysis of population change is **demographic transition theory**, *the thesis that population patterns reflect a society's level of technological development*. Figure 22–3 shows the demographic consequences at four levels of technological development.

Pre-industrial agrarian societies (Stage 1) have high birth rates because of the economic value of children and the absence of birth control. Death rates are also high because of low living standards and limited medical

technology. Outbreaks of disease neutralize births, so population rises and falls with only a modest overall increase. This was the case for thousands of years in Europe before the Industrial Revolution.

Stage 2, the onset of industrialization, brings a demographic transition as death rates fall due to greater food supplies and scientific medicine. But birth rates remain high, resulting in rapid population growth. It was during Europe's Stage 2 that Malthus formulated his ideas, which accounts for his pessimistic view of the future. The world's poorest countries today are in this high-growth stage.

In Stage 3, a mature industrial economy, birth rate drops, curbing population growth once again. Fertility falls because most children survive to adulthood and because high living standards make raising children expensive. In short, affluence transforms children from economic assets into economic liabilities. Smaller families, made possible by effective birth control, are also favoured by women working outside the home. As birth rates follow death rates downward, population growth slows further.

Stage 4 corresponds to a post-industrial economy in which the demographic transition is complete. The birth rate keeps falling, partly because dual-income couples gradually become the norm and partly because the cost of raising children continues to increase. This trend, linked to steady death rates, means that population grows only very slowly or even decreases. This is the case today in Japan, Europe, and North America.

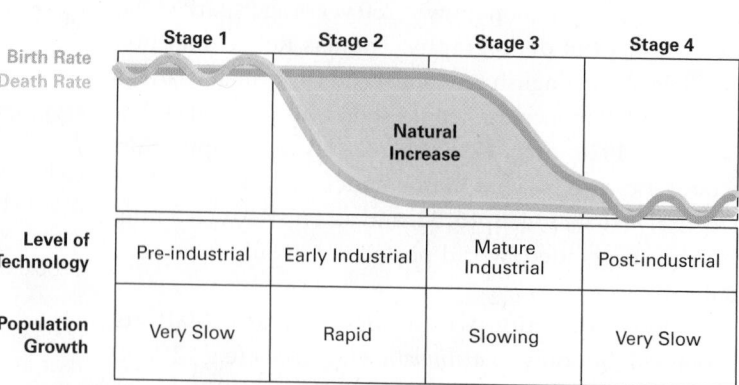

Figure 22–3 Demographic Transition Theory

Demographic transition theory links population change to a society's level of technological development.

Demographic transition theory suggests that the key to population control lies in technology. Instead of the runaway population increase feared by Malthus, this theory sees technology slowing growth and spreading material resources.

Demographic transition theory is linked to modernization theory. Modernization theorists are optimistic that poor countries will solve their population problems as they industrialize. But critics, notably dependency theorists, strongly disagree. Unless there is a redistribution of global resources, they maintain, our planet will become increasingly divided into industrialized "haves," enjoying low population growth, and non-industrialized "have-nots," struggling in vain to feed more and more people.

CHECK YOUR LEARNING Explain the four stages of demographic transition theory.

Global Population Today: A Brief Survey

What can we say about population in today's world? Drawing on the discussion so far, we can identify important patterns and reach several conclusions.

THE LOW-GROWTH NORTH When the Industrial Revolution began in the northern hemisphere, the population increase in Western Europe and North America was a high 3 percent annually. But, in the centuries since, the growth rate has steadily declined, and in 1970 it fell below 1 percent. As our post-industrial society settles into Stage 4, Canada's total fertility rate (1.7 children per woman) is less than the replacement level of 2.1 children per woman, a point demographers term **zero population growth**, *the level of reproduction that maintains population in a steady state*. In 2014, 84 nations, almost all of them high-income countries, were at or below the point of zero population growth.

Among the factors that serve to hold down population growth in post-industrial societies are the high proportion of men and women in the labour force, the rising costs of raising children, trends toward later marriage and singlehood, and the widespread use of contraceptives and abortion.

In high-income nations, then, population increase is not the pressing problem that it is in poor countries. On the contrary, many governments in high-income countries, including Italy and Japan, are concerned about a future problem of *underpopulation* because declining population is difficult to reverse and because the swelling ranks of elderly people require a younger workforce to sustain them (El Nasser & Overberg, 2011; Population Reference Bureau, 2014).

THE HIGH-GROWTH SOUTH Population is a critical problem in poor nations of the southern hemisphere. No nation of the world lacks industrial technology entirely; demographic transition theory's Stage 1 applies today to remote rural areas of low-income nations. But much of Latin America, Africa, and Asia is at Stage 2, with a mix of agrarian and industrial economies. Advanced medical technology, supplied by high-income countries, has sharply reduced death rates, but birth rates remain high. This is why poor countries now account for more than 80 percent of Earth's people and 98 percent of annual global population increase.

In some of the world's poorest countries, such as the Democratic Republic of the Congo in Africa, women still have, on average, more than six children during their lifetimes. In most poor countries, birth rates have fallen from about six children per woman (typical in 1950) to about three, but this level of fertility is still high enough to make global poverty much worse. This is why leaders in the battle against global poverty point to the importance of reducing fertility rates in low-income nations.

Notice, too, that a key element in controlling world population growth is improving the status of women. Why? Because of this simple truth: Give women more life choices and they will have fewer children. History has shown that women, who are free to decide when and where to marry, who bear children as a matter of choice, and who have access to education and to good jobs, will limit their own fertility (Axinn & Barber, 2001; Population Reference Bureau, 2014; Roudi-Fahimi & Kent, 2007).

THE DEMOGRAPHIC DIVIDE High- and low-income nations display very different population dynamics, a gap that is sometimes called the *demographic divide*. In Italy, a high-income nation with very low growth, women average just 1.4 children in their lifetimes. Such a low birth rate means that the number of annual births is less than the number of deaths. This means that, at the moment, Italy is actually *losing* population. Looking ahead to 2050, and even assuming some gains from immigration, Italy's population is projected to be about the same as it is today. But the share of elderly people in Italy—now 22 percent—will only increase as time goes on.

How different the patterns are in a low-income nation such as the Democratic Republic of the Congo. There, women still average six to seven children, so even with a high mortality rate, this nation's population will more than double by 2050. The share of elderly people is extremely low—about 3 percent—and half that country's people are below the age of 16. With such a high growth rate, it is no surprise that the problem of poverty is bad and getting worse: About three-fourths of the people are undernourished (Population Reference Bureau, 2014).

Urbanization: The Growth of Cities

22.3 Summarize patterns of urbanization in Canada and around the world.

October 8, Hong Kong. The cable train grinds to the top of Victoria Peak, where we behold one of the world's most spectacular vistas: the city of Hong Kong at night! A million bright, colourful lights ring the harbour as ships, ferries, and traditional Chinese junks churn by. Few places match Hong Kong for sheer energy. This small city is as economically productive as the state of Wisconsin or the nation of Finland. We could sit here for hours entranced by the spectacle of Hong Kong. [John J. Macionis]

Throughout most of human history, the sights and sounds of great cities such as Hong Kong, Paris, New York, and Toronto were simply unimaginable. Our distant ancestors lived in small, nomadic groups, moving as they depleted vegetation or hunted migratory game. The settlements that marked the emergence of civilization in the Middle East some 12 000 years ago held only a small fraction of the earth's population. Today, the largest three or four cities of the world hold as many people as the entire planet did then.

Urbanization is *the concentration of population into cities.* Urbanization redistributes and concentrates population within a society and transforms many patterns of social life. We will trace these changes in terms of three urban revolutions: The emergence of cities 12 000 years ago, the development of industrial cities after 1750, and the explosive growth of cities in low-income countries today.

The Evolution of Cities

Cities are a relatively new development in human history. Only about 12 000 years ago did our ancestors begin founding permanent settlements, which paved the way for the *first urban revolution.*

THE FIRST CITIES In early hunting and gathering societies people were forced to move from time to time; however, once our ancestors discovered how to domesticate animals and cultivate crops, they were able to stay in one place. Producing food in these ways created a material surplus, which freed some people from food production and allowed them to build shelters, make tools, weave cloth, and take part in religious rituals. The emergence of cities led to both job specialization and higher living standards.

The first city that we know of was Jericho, which lies to the north of the Dead Sea in what is now the West Bank. When first settled some 10 000 years ago, it was home to only 600 people. But, as the centuries passed, cities grew to tens of thousands of people and became the centres of vast empires. By 3000 BCE, Egyptian cities flourished, as did cities in China about 2000 BCE and in Central and South America about 1500 BCE. In North America, however, only a few indigenous peoples formed settlements; widespread urbanization did not occur until the arrival of European settlers in the seventeenth century.

PRE-INDUSTRIAL EUROPEAN CITIES European cities date back some 5000 years to the Greeks and later the Romans, both of whom created great empires and founded cities across Europe, including Vienna, Paris, and London. With the fall of the Roman Empire, the so-called Dark Ages began as people withdrew within defensive walled settlements and warlords battled for territory. Only in the eleventh century did Europe become more peaceful; trade flourished once again, allowing cities to grow.

Medieval cities were quite different from those familiar to us today. Beneath towering cathedrals, the narrow and winding streets of such cities as London, Brussels, and Florence teemed with merchants, artisans, priests, peddlers, jugglers, nobles, and servants. Guilds such as bakers, carpenters, and metalworkers often clustered together in distinct sections or quarters. Ethnicity also defined communities as residents tried to keep out people who differed from themselves; the term *ghetto* (from the Italian *borghetto*, meaning "outside the city walls") was first used to describe the neighbourhood in Venice in which Jews were segregated.

INDUSTRIAL EUROPEAN CITIES As the Middle Ages came to a close, steadily increasing commerce enriched a new urban middle class, or *bourgeoisie* (French, meaning "townspeople"). With more and more money, the bourgeoisie soon rivalled the hereditary aristocracy.

By about 1750, the Industrial Revolution triggered a *second urban revolution,* first in Europe and then in North America. Factories that unleashed tremendous productive power allowed cities to grow bigger than ever. London, the largest European city, reached 550 000 people by 1700 and exploded to 6.5 million by 1900 (Chandler & Fox, 1974; Weber, 1963; orig. 1899).

Cities not only grew but changed shape as well. Older winding streets gave way to broad, straight boulevards to handle the increasing flow of commercial traffic. Steam and electric trolleys soon criss-crossed expanding cities. Because land was now a commodity to be bought and sold, developers divided cities into regular-sized lots (Mumford, 1961). The centre of the city was no longer the cathedral but a bustling central business district filled with banks, retail stores, and tall office buildings.

With a new focus on business, cities became more crowded and impersonal. Crime rates rose. Especially at the outset, a few industrialists lived in grand style, but most men, women, and children barely survived by working in factories.

Organized efforts by workers to improve their lives eventually brought changes to the workplace, better housing, and the right to vote. Public services such as water, sewerage, and electricity further improved urban living. Today, some urbanites still live in poverty, but a rising standard of living has partly fulfilled the city's historical promise of a better life.

The Growth of North American Cities

Indigenous peoples who occupied North America before Europeans arrived were mostly migratory peoples who seldom created permanent settlements—the Iroquois village in what became Montreal being one exception. Villages and towns like those in Europe sprang up as a product of colonization.

In 1565, the Spanish built a settlement at St. Augustine, Florida; Samuel de Champlain founded Port Royal for the French in what is now Nova Scotia in 1605; the English founded Jamestown, Virginia, in 1607; and Champlain established a trading post at what is now Quebec City in 1608. New Amsterdam, later called New York, was established by the Dutch in 1624; Montreal was founded by de Maisonneuve in 1642; Halifax was founded in 1749 by the British to counter the French influence in North America; and York (now Toronto) was founded in 1793.

By 2000, the United States had 200 cities with a population of more than 100 000, while Canada had 40 cities of that size. Each country now has more than three-quarters of its total population living in urban areas. How North America became so urban is explained in the brief history that follows.

SETTLEMENT IN NORTH AMERICA TO 1850   New York and Boston started out as tiny villages in a vast wilderness. Dutch New Amsterdam at the top of Manhattan Island (1624) and English Boston (1630) developed along the lines of medieval towns of Europe, with narrow, winding streets that still curve through lower Manhattan and downtown Boston. New Amsterdam was walled on its north side, the site of New York's Wall Street. Boston, the largest colonial settlement, had a population of only 7000 in 1700. Economic growth soon transformed these quiet villages into thriving towns with wide streets, usually built on a grid pattern.

When York (now Toronto) was founded in 1793 by John Graves Simcoe, commander of the Queen's Rangers and later the first lieutenant-governor of Upper Canada, Montreal was already a bustling city of more than 5500. In Upper Canada, there were only about 15 settler families between Burlington Bay and the Bay of Quinte—a distance of 200 kilometres (Benn, 1993). Simcoe's intent was to move the capital from its vulnerable location at Newark (now Niagara-on-the-Lake) to one from which an American invasion could more easily be repelled. He also wanted to establish a civilian community and a naval base at York. The map in Figure 22–4 shows York Harbour, the location of the Garrison (now called Fort York), and the settlement. The gridlike settlement is near the area where Toronto's St. Lawrence Market stands today (Benn, 1993). The north/south lines above Queen Street mark the parcels of land that Simcoe granted to some of his regimental comrades and others in an effort to entice them to settle in York as a

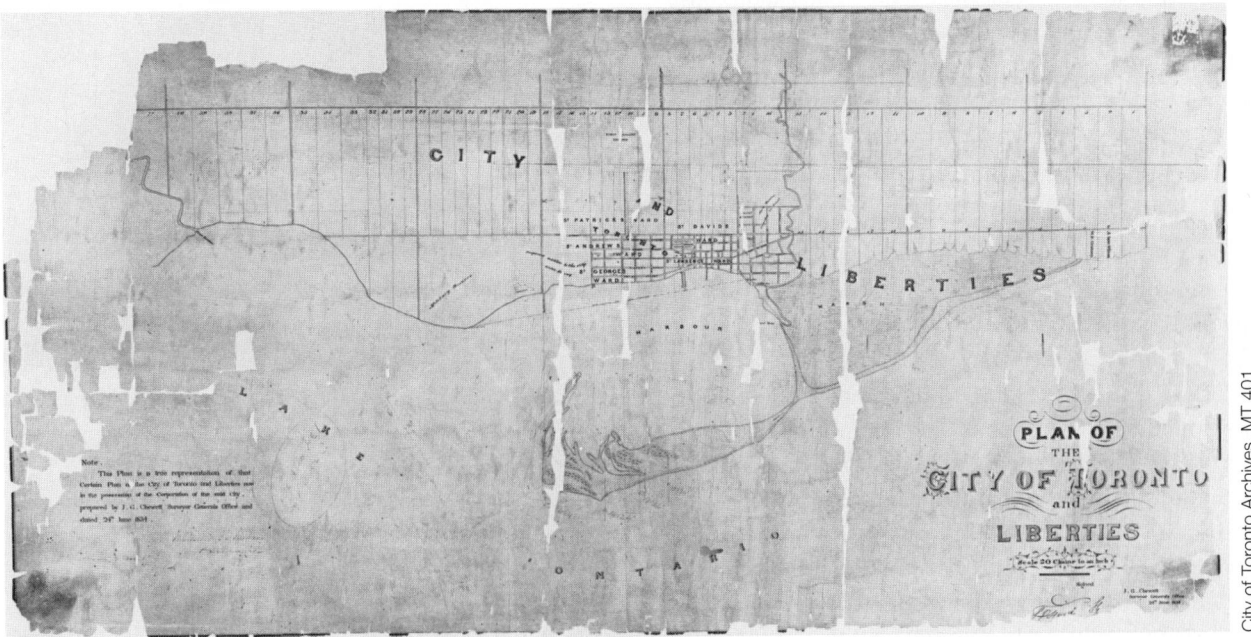

City of Toronto Archives, MT 401

Figure 22–4 Map of York (Toronto), 1834

York was designed on a grid pattern as a temporary capital for Upper Canada. It was located on a protected bay, where it could be shielded from potential attack by Americans. If you compare the map of York with a map of Toronto today, you will see that the north/south lines are major streets, such as Yonge, Bathurst, and Dufferin.

local aristocracy. The lines separating their land allotments are major north/south arteries in Toronto.

As the first settlements grew, North America remained overwhelmingly rural. In 1790, the first U.S. census counted a national population of 4 million, a scant 5 percent of whom lived in cities. By Confederation in Canada in 1867, the U.S. population of about 40 million was 20 percent urban; Canada's population of about 3 million was almost as urban at 18 percent. The vast majority of people in both countries lived on farms and in small villages. Today, both Canada and the United States are more than 80 percent urban.

URBAN EXPANSION Early in the nineteenth century, towns sprang up across North America—somewhat later in Canada than in the United States. Waterways, new roads, and railway lines encouraged this growth. British Columbia agreed to join Confederation in 1871 on the condition that a transcontinental railway was completed. The last spike was not driven until 1885, but the Canadian Pacific Railway gave a powerful boost to settlement and economic development, especially in towns and cities located along the railway. Calgary, for example, was incorporated as a town in 1884 and, by 1893, with a population of about 4000, it became a city. Harbours, too, were significant; Halifax and Vancouver grew and prospered around their harbours. The St. Lawrence River and Great Lakes system spurred the growth of Quebec City, Montreal, and Toronto as well as many smaller cities.

By 1920 and 1931, respectively, U.S. and Canadian censuses revealed that more than 50 percent of their populations were living in cities. To some, increased urbanization constituted progress toward better living, but others mourned the gradual passing of traditional agrarian life. Over time, rural/urban tensions grew more pronounced, with adversaries trading negative stereotypes that pitted "ignorant country cousins" against "shady city slickers" (Callow, 1969).

THE METROPOLITAN ERA Dizzying growth and concentration of population by the 1940s marked the coming of the **metropolis**, *a large city that dominates the surrounding area both socially and economically*. The current Canadian definition of a Census Metropolitan Area is a population of at least 100 000 spread out among one or more municipalities with economic and commuting ties. These metropolises have become the manufacturing, commercial, and residential centres of North America.

By the 1880s, industrial technology was producing steel girders and mechanical elevators so that builders were raising structures 10 storeys above the ground. This, of course, was only the beginning. In 1975, Toronto's CN Tower was completed; at 553.3 metres, it was the world's tallest free-standing structure. City centres contain these kinds of monuments as well as clusters of soaring buildings of glass, concrete, and steel, while public transit

and roadways allow for lower-density city sprawl that stretches for kilometres.

In 2011, Canada had 33 Census Metropolitan Areas (CMAs) ranging in population size from Toronto at 5.6 million to Peterborough, Ontario, at 119 000. Table 22–1 includes population data for the largest 20 CMAs in 1956 and 2011, a span of half a century. You will notice that some of the cities doubled in size over the 50-year period, while others—such as Calgary, Edmonton, and Oshawa—expanded four- or fivefold. The oil and automobile industries are major contributors to this growth.

Suburbs and Central Cities

Just as central cities flourished a century ago, we have recently witnessed the expansion of **suburbs**, *urban areas beyond the political boundaries of a city*. The first suburbanites were well-to-do but, by the late 1940s, less wealthy people also came to view a single-family house on its own piece of leafy suburban ground as the ideal lifestyle. The mobility provided by increasingly affordable automobiles made this dream come true for more and more

Table 22–1 Population of Census Metropolitan Areas* in Canada, 1956 and 2011—Top 20 Ranked by 2011 Population

	Population (000s)	
	1956	**2011**
Toronto, ON	1502.2	5583.1
Vancouver, BC	665.0	2313.3
Montreal, QC	1745.0	1824.2
Ottawa, ON/Gatineau, QC	345.4	1236.3
Calgary, AB	201.0	1214.8
Edmonton, AB	254.8	1159.9
Quebec City, QC	311.6	765.7
Winnipeg, MB	412.2	730.0
Hamilton, ON	164.2	721.1
London, ON	154.4	474.8
Kitchener-Cambridge-Waterloo, ON	451.2	477.2
St. Catharines/Niagara, ON	85.0	392.2
Halifax, NS	164.2	390.3
Oshawa, ON	62.8	356.2
Victoria, BC	133.8	344.6
Windsor, ON	185.8	319.2
Saskatoon, SK	72.8	260.6
Regina, SK	89.7	210.6
Sherbrooke, QC	61.8	201.9
St. John's, NL	79.1	197.0

*A Census Metropolitan Area is defined by Statistics Canada as a large urban area (with at least 100 000 population) together with neighbouring urban and rural areas that has a high degree of social and economic integration.

SOURCE: Compilation and calculations by LM Gerber based on Statistics Canada, NHS 2011, Catalogue numbers 99-011-X2011028, -029, -038, and -045.

people. After World War II, men and women eagerly returned to family life, igniting the baby boom. Since central cities offered little space for new housing construction, suburbs blossomed almost overnight.

Today, more than half of Canada's urbanites live in municipalities outside central cities, or in newer central cities, such as those on the Prairies, which are largely suburban in style. As a result of the overall flight to the suburbs by young families and the fact that more people are living alone in their downtown homes, vigorous construction in the central cities has not stopped the decline in some central city populations (Michelson, 1988:86). As population decentralized, businesses also began to migrate to the suburbs. Older people today can recall trips downtown to shop, but, by the 1970s, the suburban mall had replaced Main Street as the centre of retail trade. Manufacturing interests, too, moved to the suburbs, where there was relief from high taxes, escalating property costs, and traffic congestion. The result was financial difficulty for the older central cities owing to reduced tax revenue.

In 1953, in response to this disparity between the core of the city and outlying areas, Ontario created Metropolitan Toronto by combining the central city of Toronto with 12 of its suburbs. The province had to impose the solution initially, as none of the municipalities was enamoured of the prospect. But, as a result of the success of Metropolitan Toronto, other urban regions in Canada have followed suit.[1] The benefits of this model of urban development are clear when we compare Canada's situation to that of the United States. Since American cities rarely adopt a metropolitan-type government, they tend to suffer much more from decaying inner cities: "Canadian metropolitan areas suffer fewer of the glaring contrasts in welfare, infrastructure, and supportive services differentiating American central cities and suburbs" (Michelson, 1988:97).

A CENTURY AGO, AS THIS SCENE FROM THE FILM *GANGS OF NEW YORK* SUGGESTS, PEOPLE LIVING IN CITIES USED THE STREETS FOR MOST OF THEIR DAILY ACTIVITIES Today, in contrast, the idea of "living on the streets" is associated with the poor and homeless. Why do you think street life is less valued today than it was in the past?

When several adjacent metropolitan regions become so large that they bump up against each other and form a continuous urban area, they create what is called a **megalopolis**, *a vast urban region containing a number of cities and their surrounding suburbs.* Gottmann (1961) first coined the term *megalopolis* in reference to the area between and including Boston and Washington. An equivalent area in Canada, known as the Golden Horseshoe, stretches from Oshawa in the east, through Toronto, and west to St. Catharines; the Windsor–Quebec City corridor forms another, looser version. The political and economic dominance of these regions is quite apparent from the fact that the Golden Horseshoe alone contains about one-third of Canada's population, while the larger Windsor–Quebec City corridor contains about half.

Urbanism as a Way of Life

22.4 Identify the contributions of Tönnies, Durkheim, Simmel, Park, Wirth, and Marx to our understanding of urban life.

Early sociologists in Europe and the United States focused their attention on the rise of cities and the differences between rural and urban life. We briefly present their accounts of urbanism as a way of life.

Ferdinand Tönnies: *Gemeinschaft and Gesellschaft*

In the late nineteenth century, German sociologist Ferdinand Tönnies (1855–1937) studied how life in the new industrial metropolis differed from life in rural villages.

---

[1]Note that the creation of the new city of Toronto in 1997 through the amalgamation of six cities—into the Greater Toronto Area—is distinct from the creation of a metropolitan area.

metropolis a large city that dominates the surrounding area both socially and economically	**suburbs** urban areas beyond the political boundaries of a city	**megalopolis** a vast urban region containing a number of cities and their surrounding suburbs

AF archive/Alamy Stock Photo

From this contrast, he developed two concepts that have become a lasting part of sociology's terminology. Tönnies (1963; orig. 1887) used the German word **Gemeinschaft** (meaning roughly "community") to refer to *a type of social organization in which people are closely tied by kinship and tradition*. The *Gemeinschaft* of the rural village joins people in what amounts to a single primary group.

By and large, argued Tönnies, *Gemeinschaft* is absent in the modern city. On the contrary, urbanization creates **Gesellschaft** (a German word meaning roughly "association"), *a type of social organization in which people come together only on the basis of individual self-interest*. In the *Gesellschaft* way of life, individuals are motivated by their own needs rather than by a desire to help improve the well-being of everyone. City dwellers display little sense of community or common identity, and they look to others mainly when they need something. Tönnies saw in urbanization a weakening of close, long-lasting social relations in favour of the brief and impersonal ties—or secondary relationships—typical of business.

Émile Durkheim: Mechanical and Organic Solidarity

French sociologist Émile Durkheim (see the chapter on Society) agreed with much of Tönnies's thinking about cities. However, Durkheim countered that urbanites do not lack social bonds; they simply organize social life differently than rural people.

Durkheim described traditional, rural life as *mechanical solidarity*, social bonds based on common sentiments and shared moral values. With its emphasis on tradition, Durkheim's concept of mechanical solidarity bears a striking similarity to Tönnies's *Gemeinschaft*. Urbanization erodes

mechanical solidarity, Durkheim explained, but it also generates a new type of bonding, which he called organic solidarity, social bonds based on specialization and interdependence. This concept, which parallels Tönnies's *Gesellschaft*, reveals an important difference between the two thinkers. Both thought that the growth of industrial cities weakened tradition, but Durkheim optimistically pointed to a new kind of solidarity. Where societies had been built on *likeness* (mechanical solidarity), Durkheim now saw social life based on *difference* (organic solidarity). For Durkheim, urban society offered more individual choice, moral tolerance, and personal privacy than people find in rural villages. In sum, for Durkheim, something is lost in the process of urbanization, but much is gained.

Georg Simmel: The Blasé Urbanite

German sociologist Georg Simmel (1858–1918) offered a microanalysis of cities, studying how urban life shapes individual experience. According to Simmel (1964; orig. 1905), individuals perceive the city as a crush of people, objects, and events. To prevent being overwhelmed by all of this stimulation, urbanites develop a *blasé attitude*, tuning out much of what goes on around them. Such detachment does not mean that city dwellers lack compassion for others; they simply keep their distance as a survival strategy so they can focus their time and energy on those who really matter to them.

The Chicago School: Robert Park and Louis Wirth

In the 1920s and 1930s, sociologists in the United States (there were no sociology departments in Canada yet) joined the study of rapidly growing cities. Robert Park, a

PEASANT DANCE (LEFT), BY PIETER BREUGHEL THE ELDER, CONVEYS THE ESSENTIAL UNITY OF RURAL LIFE FORGED BY GENERATIONS OF KINSHIP AND NEIGHBOURHOOD By contrast, Lily Furedi's *Subway* (right) communicates the impersonality common to urban areas. Taken together, these paintings capture Tönnies's distinction between *Gemeinschaft* and *Gesellschaft*.

Pieter Breughel the Elder (c. 1525/30–1569), *Peasant Dance*, c. 1565, Kunsthistorisches Museum, Vienna/Superstock. Lily Furedi, American. *Subway*. Oil on canvas, 99 * 123 cm. National Collection of Fine Arts, Washington, DC/Smithsonian Institute.

leader of the first American sociology program at the University of Chicago, sought to add a street-level perspective by getting out and studying real cities: "I suspect that I have actually covered more ground, tramping about in cities in different parts of the world, than any other living man" (1950:viii). Walking the streets, Park found the city to be an organized mosaic of distinctive ethnic communities, commercial centres, and industrial districts. Over time, he observed these "natural areas" develop and change in relation to one another. To Park, the city was a living organism—a human kaleidoscope.

Another major figure in the Chicago School of urban sociology was Louis Wirth (1897–1952). Wirth (1938) is best known for blending the ideas of Tönnies, Durkheim, Simmel, and Park into a comprehensive theory of urban life. Wirth began by defining the city as a setting with a large, dense, and socially diverse population, traits that result in an impersonal, superficial, and transitory way of life. Living among millions of others, urbanites come into contact with many more people than residents of rural areas. So, when city people notice others at all, they usually know them not in terms of *who they are* but *what they do*—as, for instance, the bus driver, florist, or grocery store clerk. Specialized urban relationships are pleasant for all concerned, but we should remember that self-interest rather than friendship is usually the main reason for the interaction.

Limited social involvement coupled with great social diversity make city dwellers more tolerant than rural villagers. Rural communities often jealously enforce their narrow traditions, but the heterogeneous population of a city rarely shares any single code of moral conduct (Wilson, 1985, 1995).

EVALUATE

In both Europe and the United States, early sociologists presented a mixed view of urban living. Rapid urbanization troubled Tönnies, and Wirth saw personal ties and traditional morality lost in the anonymous rush of the city. Durkheim and Park emphasized urbanism's positive face, pointing to more personal freedom and greater personal choice.

One problem with all of these views is that they paint urbanism in broad strokes that overlook the effects of class, race, and gender. There are many kinds of urbanites—rich and poor; Black, White, and Aboriginal; anglophone and francophone; women and men—all of whom lead distinctive lives. As the Thinking about Diversity box explains, the proportions of Aboriginals, immigrants, and visible minorities in Canada's largest metropolitan areas increased rapidly over the past two decades.

CHECK YOUR LEARNING   Of these urban sociologists—Tönnies, Durkheim, Park, and Wirth—which were more positive about urban life? Which were more negative? In each case, explain why.

Ron Watts/First Light

MANY SMALL TOWNS HAVE GAINED POPULATION THROUGH MIGRATION FROM CITIES This "rural rebound" has been most pronounced in towns that offer spectacular natural beauty and recreational attractions, such as mountains, lakes, and ski areas. There are times when the people who actually live in the scenic town of Banff, Alberta, cannot find a parking space.

Thinking About Diversity: Race, Class, and Gender

NHS 2011: Minorities a Major Presence in Canada's Largest Metropolitan Areas

According to the results of the 2011 National Household Survey, Aboriginals, immigrants, and visible minorities constitute a major presence in Canada's largest cities. So marked is this concentration of minorities that Scarborough (now part of Toronto) has been recognized by the World Health Organization as the world's most ethno-racially diverse community (McKenzie, 2006).

New immigrants typically settle first in Toronto, Vancouver, and Montreal, where they join the "old" immigrants (i.e., those who have not moved on to other parts of Canada), thereby adding to the proportion of foreign-born people in each of the cities. Keep in mind that immigrants have come to Canada for seven decades or more—initially from Europe, then from Asia and other parts of the world. Furthermore, visible minorities are not necessarily immigrants, as 31 percent—almost one-third—are born in Canada.

Immigrants overwhelmingly arrive in Canada through Toronto, Montreal, and Vancouver—which are 46, 23, and 40 percent immigrant, respectively. Since they find their own ethnic communities established in these cities, they are likely to stay there, at least for a while. Gradually, immigrants move on to other parts of Canada, including other metropolitan areas listed in Table 22–2 (except Quebec City, which is only 4.4 percent immigrant). Calgary and Hamilton are 26 and 24 percent immigrant. Canada's visible minorities have congregated in Toronto and Vancouver, specifically—so that the two cities are 37 percent visible minority, respectively. Since they are among the more recent immigrants, they have not had as much time to spread throughout the country. Nonetheless, they are well represented in Calgary and Edmonton, which are 22 and 17 percent visible minority.

Aboriginal peoples, because of their special status within Canada, are not considered to be visible minorities. They, too, are unevenly represented in Canada's largest metropolitan areas. While 5.6 percent of Canada's population claims Aboriginal ancestry, this is true of 12 and 7 percent, respectively, of the populations of Winnipeg and Edmonton. The only metropolitan area that experienced a significant increase between Census 2006 and NHS 2011 is Ottawa-Gatineau, where Aboriginal representation increased from 4.6 to 5.1 percent. Although Montreal is only 2.6 percent Aboriginal, it stands out as the metropolitan area with the largest *number* of people claiming Aboriginal ancestry—96 700. Winnipeg has the second largest Aboriginal population—82 700—making up 11.6 percent of its population.

As suggested above, the concentration of immigrants and visible minorities is even more pronounced than Table 22–2 suggests. The five electoral districts of Scarborough are 51 to 69 percent immigrant and 43 to 85 percent visible minority. Not surprisingly, since multicultural districts are known to vote Liberal, the Scarborough ridings exhibited the highest levels of support for the Liberal Party in the federal elections of 2004 and 2006 (Gerber, 2006a, 2006b).

What Do You Think?

1. Why do Aboriginal people, immigrants, and visible minorities gravitate to some metropolitan areas and not others?

2. How do ethnic and racial diversity contribute to city life?

3. What are some specific challenges faced by cities with large populations of new immigrants?

Table 22–2 Ethnic and Racial Diversity in Canada's Ten Largest Metropolitan Areas, 2011

Metropolitan Area	Population 2011	Percent Aboriginal	Percent Immigrant	Percent Visible Minority
Toronto, ON	5 521 230	1.2	**46.0**	**37.3**
Montreal, QC	3 752 475	2.6	22.6	15.5
Vancouver, BC	2 280 700	2.8	**40.0**	**37.1**
Ottawa-Gatineau	1 215 735	**5.1**	19.4	14.6
Calgary, AB	1 199 125	3.9	26.2	**21.6**
Edmonton, AB	1 139 580	**6.6**	20.4	17.3
Quebec City, QC	746 685	2.8	4.4	2.3
Winnipeg, MB	714 639	**11.6**	20.6	15.2
Hamilton, ON	708 175	2.7	23.5	11.0
London, ON	467 260	2.8	18.8	9.9
Canada	32 852 325	5.6	20.6	15.0

SOURCE: Compilation and calculations by LM Gerber based on Statistics Canada, NHS 2011, Catalogue numbers 99-011-X2011028, -029, -038, and -045.

Urban Ecology

Sociologists—especially members of the Chicago School—developed **urban ecology**, *the study of the link between the physical and social dimensions of cities.* For example, why are cities located where they are? The first cities emerged in fertile regions where the ecology favoured raising crops. Pre-industrial people, concerned with defence, built their cities on mountains (i.e., ancient Athens was perched on an outcropping of rock) or surrounded by water (i.e., Paris and Mexico City were founded on islands). With the coming of the Industrial Revolution, economic considerations situated all major U.S. cities near rivers and natural harbours that facilitated trade.

Urban ecologists also study the physical design of cities. In 1925, Ernest W. Burgess, a student and colleague of Robert Park's, described land use in Chicago in terms of *concentric zones.* City centres, Burgess observed, are business districts bordered by a ring of factories, followed by residential rings with housing that becomes more expensive the farther it is from the noise and pollution of the city's centre.

Homer Hoyt (1939) refined Burgess's observations, noting that distinctive districts sometimes form *wedge-shaped sectors.* For example, one fashionable area may develop next to another, or an industrial district may extend outward from a city's centre along a train or trolley line.

Chauncy Harris and Edward Ullman (1945) added yet another insight: As cities decentralize, they lose their single-centre form in favour of a *multi-centred model.* As cities grow, residential areas, industrial parks, and shopping districts typically push away from one another. Few people wish to live close to industrial areas, for example, so the city becomes a mosaic of distinct districts.

Social area analysis investigates what people in particular neighbourhoods have in common. Three factors seem to explain most of the variation: family patterns, social class, and race and ethnicity (Johnston, 1976; Shevky & Bell, 1955). Families with children look for areas with single-family homes or large apartments and good schools. The rich seek high-prestige neighbourhoods, often in the central city near cultural attractions. People with a common race or ethnic heritage may cluster in distinctive communities.

Brian Berry and Philip Rees (1969) tie together many of these insights. They explain that distinct family types tend to settle in the concentric zones described by Burgess. Specifically, households with few children tend to cluster toward the city's centre, and those with more children live farther away. Social class differences are primarily responsible for the sector-shaped districts described by Hoyt—for instance, the rich occupy one side of the tracks and the poor occupy the other side. And racial and ethnic neighbourhoods are found at various points throughout the city, consistent with Harris and Ullman's multi-centred model.

Urban Political Economy

As urban problems—rioting, crime, poverty, and unemployment—proliferated, most visibly in the United States, some analysts turned away from the ecological approach to a social-conflict understanding of city life. *Urban*

JANE JACOBS, A WRITER AND ACTIVIST, WAS BORN IN THE UNITED STATES, WHERE SHE WROTE HER INFLUENTIAL BOOK *THE DEATH AND LIFE OF GREAT AMERICAN CITIES* (1961) In 1969, with her architect husband and two sons, she moved to Toronto; there, she continued writing and played an active role in urban planning. Jacobs argued that cities should be built for people, not cars. A Toronto icon since her involvement in the movement to stop the Spadina Expressway, Jacobs died in 2006, at the age of 89.

Dick Loek/Toronto Star/The Canadian Press

Paul Sancya/AP Images

THE INDUSTRIAL REVOLUTION CREATED GREAT CITIES ACROSS THE UNITED STATES In recent decades, however, the movement of industry abroad has brought decline to Detroit and other older cities in the "Rustbelt." From this abandoned warehouse, we see the headquarters of General Motors, which, in 2009, declared bankruptcy. Do we have examples of this kind of urban decline in Canada?

political economy is influenced by the thinking of Karl Marx, although the scene of social conflict shifts from the workplace to the city (Lindstrom, 1995).

The ecological approach of the Chicago School saw the city as a "natural" organism, with particular districts and neighbourhoods developing according to an internal logic. Political economists disagree, claiming that city life is defined mostly by people with power: corporate leaders and the political elite. In Canada, American multinational corporations, foreign investors, and the global capitalist system are seen as important players as well. These powerholders make the economic and political decisions that determine the location, size, shape, and character of major cities. For example, deindustrialization of the Maritime provinces, and shifts in political and economic clout up the St. Lawrence River to Montreal and then to Toronto, caused an inordinate concentration of capital, industry, population, and political power in southern Quebec and Ontario. This relatively small area—and Metropolitan Toronto, in particular—emerged as the core to the peripheral areas, or hinterland, of the country. The industrialized core dominates weaker areas, rural and urban, that are dependent on natural resources. This relationship accounts for regional inequalities, regionalism, and even threats to national unity (Brym, 1986; Goyder, 1990; Hiller, 2006; Matthews, 1983).

EVALUATE

The urban political economy paradigm has gained much attention in recent years. For one thing, compared to the older urban ecology approach, the political economy view seems better able to address the harsh realities of urban life. On the other hand, analysis based on the political economy perspective has been largely limited to capitalist societies in the modern era—and to the United States in particular. Capitalism and industrialization are assumed to cause the problems of urban life, while the environment and physical structure of cities are ignored.

Jane Jacobs (1961, 1970, 1984), a highly esteemed expert on urban development and urban life, argued that urban social problems are the result of economic stagnation, but sustaining economic development is not a simple function of the availability of capital and political will. Cities are vital to developing economies, but conditions including environment, population growth, economic differentiation, and a crucial mix of industries are required to sustain economic health. Jacobs, who was keenly interested in neighbourhoods—all kinds of them (Kelly, 2006)—asserted that cities should be built for people.

CHECK YOUR LEARNING In your own words, explain what the urban ecology theories and the urban political economy theory teach us about cities. What insight was added by Jane Jacobs?

Wilfried Krecichwost/Zefa/Corbis

THE MOST IMPORTANT INSIGHT SOCIOLOGY OFFERS ABOUT OUR PHYSICAL WORLD IS THAT ENVIRONMENTAL PROBLEMS DO NOT SIMPLY "HAPPEN" Rather, the state of the natural environment reflects the ways in which social life is organized. The greater the technological power of a society, the greater that society's ability to threaten the natural environment.

Urbanization in Poor Nations

22.5 Describe the third urban revolution now under way in poor societies.

November 16, Cairo, Egypt. People call the vast Muslim cemetery in Old Cairo the "City of the Dead." In truth, it is very much alive: Tens of thousands of squatters have moved into the mausoleums, making this place an eerie mix of life and death. Children run across the stone floors, clotheslines stretch between the monuments, and an occasional television antenna protrudes from a tomb roof. With Cairo's population increasing at the rate of 1000 people a day, families live where they can. [John J. Macionis]

As noted above, twice in its history, the world has experienced a revolutionary expansion of cities. The first revolution began about 10 000 years ago with the first urban settlements and continued until permanent settlements were in place on several continents. About 1750, the second expansion began; it lasted for two centuries as the Industrial Revolution spurred rapid urban growth in Europe and North America.

A *third urban revolution* is now under way. Today, approximately 80 percent of people in industrial societies are already city dwellers. But extreme urban growth is occurring in low-income nations. In 1950, about 25 percent of the people in poor countries lived in cities. In 2008, the world became mostly urban for the first time in history, with more than half of humanity living in cities; in 2014 the urban share reached 54 percent (United Nations, 2014).

As the global population continues to expand, the share of humanity living in urban places is also increasing. As noted earlier, global population is projected to reach 9.5 billion by 2050. Almost all of this increase will take place in cities, increasing the urban share of the world's population to about 66 percent (United Nations, 2014).

Not only are more of the world's people urban, but more cities are passing the 10 million mark. In 1975, only three cities in the world, Tokyo, New York, and Mexico City, had populations exceeding 10 million, and all three cities were in high-income nations. In 2014, 28 cities had passed this mark, and only seven of them were in high-income nations. By 2030, 13 more "megacities" will be added to the list and *none* of them will be in high-income nations (eight will be in Asia, two in Latin American, and three in Africa) (Brockerhoff, 2000; United Nations, 2014).

This third urban revolution is taking place, according to demographic transition theory, because many poor nations have entered the high-growth Stage 2 of the demographic transition. Falling death rates have fuelled population increases in Latin America, Asia, and especially Africa. For urban areas, the rate of increase is twice as high because in addition to natural increase, millions of people leave the countryside each year in search of jobs, health care, education, and conveniences such as running water and electricity.

Cities do offer more opportunities than rural areas, but they provide no quick fix for the massive problems of escalating population and grinding poverty. Many cities in less economically developed nations—including Mexico City, Egypt's Cairo, India's Kolkata (formerly Calcutta), and Manila in the Philippines—are simply unable to meet the basic needs of much of their populations. All these cities are surrounded by wretched shantytowns—settlements of makeshift homes built from discarded materials. In some countries, city dumps are home to thousands of poor people, who pick through piles of waste hoping to find enough food to make it through another day.

Environment and Society

22.6 Analyze current environmental problems such as pollution and global warming or climate change.

The human species has prospered, rapidly expanding over the entire planet. An increasing share of the global population now lives in cities, complex settlements that offer the promise of a better life than that found in rural villages.

But these advances have come at a high price. Never before in history have human beings placed such demands on the planet. This disturbing development brings us to the final section of this chapter: The interplay between the natural environment and society. Like demography, **ecology** is another cousin of sociology, formally defined as *the study of the interaction of living organisms and the natural environment.* Ecology rests on the research of natural scientists as well as social scientists. In this text, we focus on the aspects of ecology that involve familiar sociological concepts and issues.

The **natural environment** is *Earth's surface and atmosphere, including living organisms, air, water, soil, and other resources necessary to sustain life.* Like every other species, humans depend on the natural environment to survive. Yet with our capacity for culture, humans stand apart from other species; we alone take deliberate action to remake the world according to our own interests and desires, for better and for worse.

Why is the environment of interest to sociologists? Environmental problems, from pollution to acid rain to global warming, do not arise from the natural world operating on its own. Such problems are the result of specific actions of human beings, which means that they are *social* problems.

The Global Dimension

The study of the natural environment requires a global perspective. The reason is simple: Regardless of political divisions among nations, the planet is a single **ecosystem**, *a system composed of the interaction of all living organisms and their natural environments.*

The Greek meaning of *eco* is "house," reminding us that this planet is our home and that all living things and their natural environment are interrelated. A change in any part of the natural environment ripples throughout the entire global ecosystem.

Consider, from an ecological point of view, our love of hamburgers. North Americans (and, increasingly, people around the world) have created a huge demand for beef, which has greatly expanded the ranching industry in Brazil, Costa Rica, and other Latin American nations. To produce the lean meat sought by fast-food corporations, cattle in Latin America feed on grass, which requires a great deal of land. Latin American ranchers acquire grazing land by clearing thousands of hectares of forest each year. These tropical forests are vital to maintaining Earth's atmosphere. Deforestation ends up threatening everyone, including the people enjoying their hamburgers. In Canada, our cattle are raised in feedlots; see the chapter opener for a discussion of the environmental impacts of this practice.

Technology and the Environmental Deficit

Sociologists point to a simple formula: $I = PAT$, where environmental impact (I) reflects a society's population (P), its level of affluence (A), and its level of technology (T). Members of societies with simple technology—hunters and gatherers, for example—hardly affect the environment because they are few in number, poor, and use only simple technologies. On the contrary, nature defines their lives as they follow the migration of game, watch the rhythm of the seasons, and suffer from natural catastrophes such as fires, floods, droughts, and storms.

Societies at intermediate stages of technological development have greater effects on the environment. Such societies are both larger and richer. But the environmental impact of horticulture (small-scale farming), pastoralism (the herding of animals), and even agriculture (using animal-drawn plows) is limited because people still rely on muscle power for producing food and other goods.

The Industrial Revolution greatly increased the impacts of human activity on the natural environment. Muscle power gave way to engines that burn fossil fuels: Coal at first and then oil. Such machinery affects the environment in two ways: We consume more natural resources, and we release more pollutants into the atmosphere. Even more significantly, armed with industrial technology, we are able to bend nature to our will, tunnelling through mountains, damming rivers, irrigating deserts, and drilling for oil in the Arctic wilderness or on the ocean floor. This explains why people in rich nations, who represent just 24 percent of humanity, account for half of the world's energy use (World Bank, 2015).

The environmental impact of industrial technology goes beyond energy consumption. High income societies produce 100 times more goods than people in agrarian societies. Higher living standards in turn increase the problem of solid waste (since people ultimately throw away most of what they produce) as well as pollution (since industrial production generates smoke and other toxic substances).

People have long recognized the material benefits of industrial technology, but only a century after the Industrial Revolution did they begin to see the long-term effects on the natural environment. Today, we realize that the technological power to make our lives better can also put the lives of future generations at risk. Evidence is mounting that we are running up an **environmental deficit**, *profound long-term harm to the natural environment caused by humanity's focus on short-term material affluence* (Bormann, 1990). This concept of environmental deficit is important for three reasons. First, it reminds us that environmental concerns are *sociological*, reflecting societies' priorities about how people should live. Second, it suggests that much environmental damage to air, land, and water is *unintended*. By focusing on the short-term benefits of, say, cutting down forests, strip mining, or using throwaway packaging, we fail to see their long-term environmental effects. Third, in some respects, the environmental deficit is *reversible*. Inasmuch as they have created environmental problems, societies can undo many of them.

Culture: Growth and Limits

Whether we recognize environmental dangers and decide to do something about them is a cultural matter. Thus, along with technology, culture has powerful environmental consequences.

THE LOGIC OF GROWTH When you turn on the television news, you might hear a story like this: "The government reported good economic news today, with the economy growing by 3.2 percent during the first quarter of the year." If you stop to think about it, our culture almost always defines growth as good. An economy that isn't growing is "stagnant" (which is bad); one that is getting smaller is in a "depression" (which is *very* bad). More cars, more and bigger homes, more income, more spending—the idea of *more* is at the heart of our cultural definition of living well (McKibben, 2007).

One of the reasons we define growth in positive terms is that we value *material comfort,* believing that money and the things it buys improve our lives. We also believe in the idea of *progress,* thinking that the future will be better than the present. In addition, we look to *science* to make our lives easier and more rewarding. In simple terms, "having things is good," "life gets better," and "people are clever." Taken together, such cultural values form the *logic of growth.*

An optimistic view of the world, the logic of growth holds that more powerful technology has improved our lives, and new discoveries will continue to do so in the future. This logic has been the driving force behind settling the wilderness, building towns and roads, and pursuing material wealth.

However, "progress" can lead to unexpected problems, including strain on the environment. The logic of growth responds by arguing that people (especially scientists and other technology experts) will find a way out of any problem that growth places in our path. For example, before the world runs short of oil, we will come up with hydrogen, solar, or nuclear engines or some other as-yet-unknown technology to meet the world's energy needs.

Environmentalists counter that the logic of growth is flawed because it assumes that natural resources such as oil, clean air, fresh water, and topsoil will always be plentiful. We can and will exhaust these *finite* resources if we continue to pursue growth at any cost. Echoing Malthus, environmentalists warn that if we call on Earth to support increasing numbers of people, we will surely deplete finite resources, destroying the environment—and ourselves—in the process.

THE LIMITS TO GROWTH If we cannot invent our way out of the problems created by the logic of growth, perhaps we need another way to think about the world. Environmentalists counter by pointing out that growth must have limits. Stated simply, the *limits-to-growth thesis* is that humanity must put in place policies to control the growth of population, production, and use of resources in order to avoid environmental collapse.

In *The Limits to Growth,* a controversial book that was influential in launching the environmental movement, Donella Meadows and her colleagues (1972) used a computer model to calculate the planet's available resources, rates of population growth, amount of land available for cultivation, levels of industrial and food production, and amount of pollutants released into the atmosphere. The authors concede that any long-range predictions are speculative, and some critics think they are plain wrong (Simon, 1981). But right or wrong, the conclusions of the study call for serious consideration. First, the authors claim that we are quickly consuming Earth's finite resources. Supplies of oil, natural gas, and other energy sources are declining and will continue to drop, a little

faster or slower depending on the conservation policies of rich nations and the speed with which other nations such as India and China continue to industrialize. Within the next 100 years, resources will run out, crippling industrial output and causing a decline in food production.

This limits-to-growth theory shares Malthus's pessimism about the future. People who accept it doubt that current patterns of life are sustainable for even another century. Perhaps we all can learn to live with less. This may not be as hard as you might think: Research shows, for example, that an increase in material consumption in recent decades has not brought an increase in levels of personal happiness (D. G. Myers, 2000). In the end, environmentalists warn, we must either make fundamental changes in how we live, placing less strain on the natural environment, or widespread hunger and conflict will force change on us.

Solid Waste: The Disposable Society

Throughout North America, people generate a massive amount of solid waste—about 0.7 billion kilograms (1.5 billion pounds) *each and every day.* Figure 22–5 shows the composition of a typical community's trash. The data are American, but there is no reason to think that the composition of Canadian trash is any different.

As a rich nation of people who value convenience, Canada has become a *disposable society.* We consume vast numbers of products, most of which have throwaway packaging. For example, fast food is served with cardboard, plastic, and foam containers that we throw away within minutes. Countless other products, from film or toothbrushes to fishhooks, are elaborately packaged to make them more attractive to the customer and to discourage tampering and theft.

Figure 22–5 Composition of Community Trash

We throw away a wide range of material, with paper the single largest part of our trash.

SOURCE: U.S. Environmental Protection Agency (2014).

Manufacturers market soft drinks, beer, and fruit juices in aluminum cans, glass jars, and plastic containers, which not only consume finite resources but also generate mountains of solid waste. Then there are countless items intentionally designed to be disposable: pens, razors, flashlights, batteries, and even cameras. Other products, from light bulbs to automobiles, are designed to have a limited useful life and then become unwanted junk. Even the words we use to describe what we throw away—*waste, litter, trash, refuse, garbage, rubbish*—show how little we value what we cannot immediately use (Connett, 1991).

Living in rich societies, the average person in North America consumes hundreds of times more energy, plastics, lumber, water, and other resources than someone living in a low-income country such as Bangladesh or Tanzania and nearly twice as much as people in some other high-income countries such as Sweden and Japan. This high level of consumption means not only that we in North America use a disproportionate share of the planet's natural resources but also that we generate most of the world's refuse.

We like to say that we throw things "away," but most of our solid waste never goes away. Rather, it ends up in landfills, which are, quite literally, "filling" up. Material in landfills can pollute underground water supplies. In most places, laws now regulate what can be discarded in a landfill site. Nonetheless, dump sites around the world—Canada being no exception—contain hazardous materials that are polluting water both above and below the ground. In addition, what goes into landfills all too often stays there, sometimes for centuries. Tens of millions of tires, diapers, and other items buried in landfills each year do not decompose but remain as an unwelcome legacy for future generations.

Environmentalists argue that we should address the problem of solid waste by doing what many of our grandparents did: Use less and turn "waste" into a resource. Part of the solution is recycling, reusing resources we would otherwise discard. Recycling is well established in Canada, Japan, and many other nations; it is also increasingly common in the United States. Most Canadian cities have recycling programs for glass, cans, and paper. A few, like Toronto and Guelph, Ontario, collect dry and wet waste (including diapers) and convert the wet, organic waste into compost. In the past, Toronto sent its waste to Michigan—in 400 trucks a

day along Highway 401. The conversion of wet waste, including diapers, into compost allowed Toronto to drastically reduce the number of trucks going to Michigan (which is increasingly reluctant to absorb Toronto's residential waste). The nearby Regional Municipality of Halton was planning to come to Toronto's rescue with an incineration plant that would produce energy from waste, but that project was "delayed"—permanently, in fact—by howls of protest from local residents.

Water and Air

Oceans, lakes, and streams are the lifeblood of the global ecosystem. Humans depend on water for drinking, bathing, cooking, recreation, and a host of other activities.

Through the *hydrologic cycle,* Earth naturally recycles water and refreshes the land. The process begins as heat from the sun causes Earth's water, 97 percent of which is in the oceans, to evaporate and form clouds. Because water evaporates at lower temperatures than most pollutants, the water vapour that rises from the seas is relatively pure, leaving various contaminants behind. Water then falls to Earth as rain, which drains into streams and rivers and, finally, returns to the sea. Two major concerns about water for humans, then, are supply and pollution.

WATER SUPPLY Less than 0.1 percent of Earth's water is suitable for drinking. It is not surprising, then, that for thousands of years, water rights have figured prominently in laws around the world. Today, some regions of the world, especially the tropics, enjoy plentiful fresh water, using a small share of the available supply. However, high

WATER, VITAL TO LIFE, IS IN SHORT SUPPLY The state of Gujarat, in western India, has experienced a decade-long drought. In the village of Natwarghad, people crowd together, lowering pots into the local well, taking what little water is left.

Dave Amit/Reuters/Landov

demand, coupled with modest reserves, makes water supply a matter of concern in central North America and much of Asia, where people look to rivers rather than rainfall for their water. In China, deep aquifers are dropping rapidly. In the Middle East, water supply is reaching a critical level. Iran rations water in its capital city. In Egypt, the Nile River provides just one-sixth as much water per person as it did in 1900. Across northern Africa and the Middle East, as many as 1 billion people may lack the water needed for irrigation and drinking by 2030. From another angle, by that time the world will be able to provide 40 percent less water than required (United Nations Environmental Program, 2008; Walsh, 2009).

Rising population and the development of more complex technology have greatly increased the world's appetite for water. The global consumption of water—now estimated at 3800 cubic kilometres per year—has tripled since 1950 and is rising steadily. As a result, even in parts of the world that receive plenty of rainfall, people are using groundwater faster than it can be replenished naturally. In the Tamil Nadu region of southern India, for example, so much groundwater is being used that the water table has fallen 30 metres over the past several decades. Mexico City has pumped so much water from its underground aquifer that the city sank nine metres during the past century and continues to drop about five

centimetres per year. Farther north in the United States, the Ogallala aquifer, which lies below seven states from South Dakota to Texas, is now being pumped so rapidly that some experts fear it could run dry in just a few decades.

In Canada, where fresh water supplies—though diminishing—are adequate for the time being, we worry that we will become the fresh water supplier for other countries. If we were to export water to the United States for commercial purposes, the North American Free Trade Agreement would require us to keep the tap open, even as our own supplies are threatened. In light of such developments, we must face the reality that water is a valuable, finite resource. Greater conservation of water by individuals—the average North American consumes about 38 million litres in a lifetime—is part of the answer. However, households around the world account for just 10 percent of water use. It is even more crucial that we curb water consumption by industry, which uses 20 percent of the global total, and by farming, which consumes 70 percent of the total for irrigation.

WATER POLLUTION In large cities from Mexico City to Cairo to Shanghai, many people have no choice but to drink contaminated water. Infectious diseases such as typhoid, cholera, and dysentery—all caused by waterborne micro-organisms—spread rapidly through these populations. Besides ensuring ample *supplies* of water, then, we must protect the *quality* of water.

Water quality in North America is generally good by global standards. However, even here the problem of water pollution is steadily growing. According to the Sierra Club (2009), an environmental organization, rivers and streams absorb some 230 million kilograms of toxic waste each year. This pollution results not just from intentional dumping but also from runoff containing agricultural fertilizers, factory farm or feedlot pollutants, lawn chemicals, and contaminants from landfill sites. In 2006, the Kaschechewan First Nation, near the western shore of James Bay, experienced a water crisis that forced the evacuation of residents. *E. coli* had contaminated their drinking water. Canadians soon learned that

CONTRARY TO EXPECTATIONS, THE SIERRA CLUB REPORTS THAT CONSERVATIVE PRIME MINISTERS AND REPUBLICAN PRESIDENTS HAVE HAD THE BEST ENVIRONMENTAL RECORDS: "WHEN BRIAN MULRONEY WAS RECENTLY DECLARED THE 'GREENEST PRIME MINISTER' IN CANADIAN HISTORY, THERE WAS DISBELIEF THAT A RIGHT-WINGER COULD BE SO HONOURED" (HAMILTON, 2006) The Sierra Club chose Mulroney for the award because he worked effectively with President Ronald Reagan in fighting acid rain. Tory prime ministers and environment ministers have had the greenest records—along with Republican American president Richard Nixon. The administration of George W. Bush "outperformed the Canadian Liberal government in fighting pollution." For more on Canadian and American records in environmental protection, see the Sociology and the Media box.

Sociology and the Media

Environmentally Friendly Canada, Eh!

Many Canadians believe that we have come a long way on the environmental front. After all, we have recycling programs and convert organic waste to compost. Canada turns tires—banned from landfill sites for decades—into an asphalt additive or into bouncy flooring material for children's playgrounds (including "Honey, I Shrunk the Kids" at Disney World). We have environmental reviews, regulations governing the disposal of pollutants into waterways or the air, international agreements on emissions reduction, a wonderful system of national and provincial parks, and an environmentally sensitive public.

Canada's environmentalists draw public attention to the clear-cutting of forests in British Columbia or to overfishing in Atlantic coastal waters. First Nations, such as Walpole Island (in Ontario), strive for sustainable development (Jacobs, 1992; Nin.Da.Waab.Jig, 1992), and organizations such as the Wendaban Stewardship Authority blend Aboriginal and non-Aboriginal environmental knowledge to co-manage timber, land, and resource development in the Temagami area (Shute & Knight, 1995). Surely we have the right to be smug about our environmental record.

Looks can be deceiving, though! Behind the scenes, federal and provincial governments cut their environmental budgets in the late 1990s. In Ontario, environmental laws were weakened, enforcement budgets were cut, and regulatory powers were taken away (Fine, 1997). So lax was the enforcement of regulations that Ontario ranked fifth among North America's polluters, behind Ohio, Texas, Indiana, and Pennsylvania. By 1997, Ontario Hydro's nuclear energy program was in serious difficulty and the utility began to deactivate some of its plants amid daunting safety and pollution concerns (Mittelstaedt, 1997). In 1998, Toronto debated the merits of its household recycling program, as it is extremely costly and ineffective in ensuring the reuse of materials. (Some blue box deposits ended up as landfill.) In 2009, we debated the reactivation (or permanent closure) of the Chalk River nuclear reactor. This is a global issue since Chalk River produces most of the world's supply of radio isotopes for cancer treatment.

Decisions regarding environmental issues are inherently political—and controversial. Having failed to live up to its earlier promises regarding emission targets, Canada was expected to set new ones at the 1997 summit in Kyoto. The Vancouver-based David Suzuki Foundation took out full-page newspaper ads aimed at stopping global warming. In Alberta, fear-mongering reached a fever pitch because the proposed emission targets would reduce the demand for oil and natural gas—a catastrophe for the provincial economy and, by extension, the Canadian economy. Premier Ralph Klein, the resource industries, and the Alberta public were up in arms—and Prime Minister Chrétien felt pressured to accommodate them (Bercuson & Cooper, 1997).

When the Kyoto agreement was revisited in November 2000, Canada's commitment to reduce global carbon emissions remained in question. In that round, Canada proposed achieving our reduction goals by "protecting" forests (here and abroad) and buying "credits" from countries that had succeeded in reducing emissions. Notably, the federal government had no plans to reduce our emissions. Nonetheless, Canada ratified the Kyoto Accord in 2002, only to have Stephen Harper's Conservative government pull back in 2006—promising reductions through technological innovation and a clean air act put before the House of Commons in October 2006.

By this time, we learned that Canada has the *worst* record in meeting its Kyoto targets—below that of the United States, Japan, and New Zealand. Instead of declining, Canada's greenhouse gas emissions had *increased by 32 percent* over 1990 levels; American emissions had increased, too, but only by 22 percent. Two very big reasons for our inability to meet our Kyoto targets are the Alberta oil sands (a large part of our economy) and our reliance on cars and trucks to move people and products around this vast country.

Canadians have other environmental concerns. The annual shipment of hazardous or toxic waste from the United States into Canada quintupled between 1993 and 1999 (to 663 000 tonnes), while the reverse flow remained stable. Ontario and Quebec are the main recipients of this hazardous waste. Most U.S. states have increased regulations and restrictions, Mexico has banned toxic imports altogether, while Canada's regulations remained lax (Hogue, 2000).

In 2009, as the Arctic ice caps melted away, tensions regarding the ownership of the Far North were heightened—with claims made by Canada, the United States, Russia, Denmark (Greenland), and Norway. Each country covets the region's oil and gas reserves but, for Canada, the most pressing issue is control of the Northwest Passage, which is now navigable for more of the year. As traffic through the northern route increases, so does the danger of oil spills and other contamination.

In 2011, bowing to political pressure from environmentalists and others, U.S. president Barack Obama postponed the decision on a project called the Keystone Pipeline to 2013—that is, until after the November 2012 presidential election. The postponement of the decision on the pipeline, which would take oil from northern Alberta to a number of American destinations, was a devastating blow to the Canadian economy. In response, the Harper government declared its support for a pipeline—the Northern Gateway—over the Rockies to the B.C. coast (from Bruderheim, Alberta, to Kitimat). NDP leader

Thomas Mulcair was front and centre in the attack on this proposal.

The Haisla Nation, whose lands are in the Kitimat area, is taking active control of its resources by entering into formal relationships with oil and natural gas companies—to secure agreements on direct equity, revenue sharing, or royalty sharing. At the same time, the Tsleil-Waututh Nation on the North Shore of Burrard Inlet (in Vancouver) is fighting the *expansion* of an existing pipeline from Edmonton to Burnaby, which would allow the Kinder Morgan pipeline to move 750 000 barrels of oil each day to Asia and California. The band is working for "all British Columbians" in fighting the pipeline expansion (Galloway & Vanderklippe, 2012).

For many years, Canadian governments have been engaged in a high-wire act. Environmentalists at home and abroad demand greater protection for our natural environment—specifically reductions in carbon emissions. Industries, workers, and other agencies in the resource sector oppose added restrictions. *In recent months, the tide has turned*. Provincial governments—including British Columbia's—have introduced their own environmental protection programs. Ontario, under the Liberals, subsidized solar and wind installations in its attempt to reduce carbon emissions. In May of 2015, Rachel Notley was sworn in as the first NDP premier of Alberta, putting her in a position to shake up the oil industry and introduce a moderate cap and trade system to control carbon emissions. In the last few weeks before the Oct.19, 2015 federal election, it was apparent that Justin Trudeau—not Thomas Mulcair—was the greatest threat to Stephen Harper and his Conservative government. Mulcair was sideswiped by the Leap Manifesto; Premier Wynne proposed the elimination of natural gas for heating Ontario homes; and Prime Minister Trudeau endorsed the UN Declaration on the Rights of Indigenous Peoples, apparently supporting their right to a veto over any energy sector projects. Predicting the future of Canada's energy production and export is now very difficult indeed.

What Do You Think?

1. Are you willing to pay more for fuel, reduce the use of your car, turn the thermostat down in the winter and up in the summer, and take public transit whenever possible to help reduce carbon emissions?

2. Are you an environmentalist in action, in theory, or not at all?

3. Is the threat of global warming real or overblown? Explain your reasoning.

Kashechewan had suffered a boiled-water advisory for two years and that there are many First Nations communities with unsafe drinking water.

A special problem is *acid precipitation* (rain or snow made acidic by air pollution), which destroys plant and animal life. Acid precipitation begins with power plants burning fossil fuels (oil and coal) to generate electricity; this burning releases sulphuric and nitrous oxides into the air. As the wind sweeps these gases into the atmosphere, they react with the air to form sulphuric and nitric acids, which turns atmospheric moisture acidic. This is a case where one type of pollution causes another: Air pollution from industrial and hospital smokestacks contaminates water in lakes and streams that collect acid precipitation. Acid precipitation is truly a global phenomenon because the regions that suffer the harmful effects may be distant from the original pollution. For instance, British power plants have produced acid rain that has devastated forests and fish in Norway and Sweden, up to 1600 kilometres to the northeast. In Canada, the Inco smokestacks in Sudbury, Ontario, once destroyed vegetation over a vast area, including the fish habitat in the lakes of Killarney Provincial Park. Now, pollution controls in the smokestacks have allowed for the gradual revival of vegetation in the Sudbury area, in what is now known to be one of Canada's environmental success stories.

AIR POLLUTION Because we are surrounded by air, we are more aware of air pollution than contaminated water. One of the unexpected consequences of industrial technology, especially the

MEMBERS OF SMALL, SIMPLE SOCIETIES, SUCH AS THE TAN'T BATU IN THE PHILIPPINES, LIVE IN HARMONY WITH NATURE; THEY DO NOT HAVE THE TECHNOLOGICAL MEANS TO GREATLY AFFECT THEIR FOREST HOMELAND AND MAY HOLD EXTENSIVE KNOWLEDGE OF ITS LIVING COMPONENTS Although we in complex societies like to think of ourselves as superior to such people, the truth is that there is much we can—and must—learn from them.

Remi Benali/Corbis

factory and the motor vehicle, has been a decline in air quality. In London, England in the mid-twentieth century, factory smokestacks, automobiles, and coal fires used to heat homes all added to what was probably the worst urban air quality the world has ever known. What some English people jokingly called "pea-soup" fogs were in reality a deadly mix of pollutants. In the worst case, over five extremely cold days in December 1952 (when coal use soared), an especially thick haze that hung over London killed 4000 people.

Air quality improved in the final decades of the twentieth century. Rich nations passed laws that banned high-pollution heating, including the coal fires that choked London. Scientists devised ways to make factories as well as automobiles and trucks operate more cleanly. In fact, today's vehicles produce only a fraction of the pollution that spewed from models of the 1950s and 1960s. And cleaner air has improved human health; improvement in air quality over recent decades has added almost half a year to the average life span (Chang, 2009).

If people in rich countries can breathe a bit more easily than they once did, the problem of air pollution in poor societies is becoming more serious. One reason is that people in low-income countries still rely on wood, coal, peat, and other "dirty" fuels for cooking fires and to heat their homes. And nations eager to encourage short-term industrial development may pay little attention to the longer-term dangers of air pollution. As a result, many cities in Latin America, Eastern Europe, and Asia are plagued today by air pollution similar to London's pea-soup fogs of the 1950s.

Rainforests

Rainforests are *regions of dense forestation, most of which circle the globe close to the equator.* The largest tropical rainforests are in South America (notably Brazil), west-central Africa, and Southeast Asia. In all, the world's rainforests cover about 5 percent of Earth's total land surface.

Like other global resources, rainforests are falling victim to the needs and appetites of the surging world population. As noted earlier, to meet the demand for beef, ranchers in Latin America burn forested areas to increase their supply of grazing land. We are also losing rainforests to the hardwood trade. People in rich nations pay high prices for mahogany and other woods because, as the environmentalist Norman Myers (1984:88) puts it, they have "a penchant for parquet floors, fine furniture, fancy paneling, weekend yachts, and high-grade coffins." Under such economic pressure, the world's rainforests are now just half of their original size and continue to shrink by about 1 percent (165 000 square kilometres) annually.

Unless we stop this loss, the rainforests will vanish before the end of this century and with them will go protection for Earth's biodiversity and climate (The Nature Conservancy, 2015; United Nations, 2011).

Canada has the world's largest remaining coastal lowland temperate rainforest, at Clayoquot Sound on Vancouver Island. A grassroots environmental group founded in 1979, Friends of Clayoquot Sound, has lobbied governments to change forest policy and deal with First Nations rights there. Nuu-Chah-Nulth live, hunt, and fish in the Clayoquot area; they have dedicated Meares Island as a Tribal Park, hosted festivals and blockades, and worked with the Friends to change global attitudes to ancient temperate rainforests. The largest civil disobedience action in Canadian history—the Clayoquot Sound protest from July to October 1993—resulted in the arrest of 800 people, the loss of $10 million in European and American contracts by the forest products company MacMillan Bloedel, and the establishment of a government task force on a Clayoquot Sound sustainable development strategy. As a result, social justice for First Nations became an integral part of the wilderness and eco-forestry movements (Langer, 1996). Furthermore, the forest industry agreed to adjust its cutting practices in the temperate rainforest.

Global Climate Change

Why are rainforests so important? One reason is that they cleanse the atmosphere of carbon dioxide (CO_2); plants require and inspire carbon dioxide and expire oxygen—humans and other animals inspire oxygen and expire carbon dioxide. Since the beginning of the Industrial Revolution, the amount of CO_2 produced by humans—by breathing or from emissions by factories and automobiles—has risen sharply. Much of this CO_2 is absorbed by the oceans, but plants—notably trees—also take in CO_2 and expel oxygen. This is why rainforests are vital to maintaining the chemical balance of the atmosphere.

The problem is that production of carbon dioxide is rising, while the amount of plant life on Earth is shrinking. To make matters worse, rainforests are being destroyed mostly by burning, which releases even more CO_2 into the atmosphere. Experts estimate that the atmospheric concentration of CO_2 is now 40 percent higher than it was 150 years ago (Adam, 2008; National Oceanic & Atmospheric Administration, 2015).

The theory is that, high above the Earth, carbon dioxide acts like the glass roof of a greenhouse, letting heat from the sun pass through to the surface while preventing much of it from radiating away from the planet. The result of this greenhouse effect, say ecologists, is **global warming**, *a rise in Earth's average temperature due to an increasing concentration of carbon dioxide in the atmosphere.*

Over the past century, the global temperature has risen about 0.8° Celsius, and predictions are that it will continue to rise. Already, the polar ice caps are melting, and over the past century, the average level of the oceans has risen about six inches. Scientists predict that increasing average temperatures could melt so much ice that the sea level would rise enough to cover low-lying land all around the world. Some predict that such a change would create perhaps 100 million "climate change refugees." On the other hand, this same process of rising temperatures will affect other regions of the world very differently; some of the most productive agricultural regions in the world may become more arid while other regions become more productive (Gillis, 2011; McMahon, 2011; Reed, 2013).

Some scientists point out that we cannot be sure of the extent of global warming or its consequences. Even the International Panel on Climate Change revised its temperature predictions to a rise of 0.1 rather than 0.2° C per decade after a period of no increase at all. Others point to the fact that global temperature changes have taken place throughout history without the contributions of rainforests or industrialization. A few are actually optimistic, suggesting that higher concentrations of carbon dioxide in the atmosphere might speed up plant growth (since plants thrive on this gas), and this increase would correct the imbalance and push Earth's temperature downward once again. Nonetheless, much research effort focuses on the causes of and impacts of global warming or climate change on our future (Gore, 2006; Hart, 2015; International Panel on Climate Change, 2007; Kerr, 2005; Plimer, 2009; Ridley, 2012; Singer, 2007).

Declining Biodiversity

Our planet is home to as many as 30 million species of animals, plants, and micro-organisms. As rainforests are cleared and humans extend their control over nature, several dozen unique species of plants and animals cease to exist each day, reducing the planet's *biodiversity*.

Given the vast number of living species, why should we be concerned by the loss of a few? Environmentalists give four reasons. First, our planet's biodiversity provides a varied source of human food. Using agricultural high technology, scientists can "splice" familiar crops with more exotic plant life, making food more bountiful as well as more resistant to insects and disease. Certain species are even considered vital to the production of human food. Bees, for example, perform the work of pollination, a necessary stage in the growth of plants. The fact that the bee population has declined by one-third in North America and two-thirds in the Middle East is cause for serious concern. Thus sustaining biodiversity helps feed our planet's rapidly increasing population.

Second, Earth's biodiversity is a vital genetic resource used by medical and pharmaceutical researchers to produce hundreds of new compounds each year that cure disease and improve our lives. For example, children now have a good chance of surviving leukemia, a disease that was a killer two generations ago, because of a compound derived from a tropical flower called the rosy periwinkle. The oral birth control pill, used by millions of women in this country, is another product of plant research, involving the Mexican forest yam. Because biodiversity itself allows our ecosystem to control many types of diseases, it is likely that if biodiversity declines, the transmission of disease will increase.

Third, with the loss of any species of life—whether it is the magnificent California condor, the famed Chinese panda, the spotted owl, or even a single species of ant—the beauty and complexity of our natural environment are diminished. And there are clear warning signs of such loss: Three-quarters of the world's 10 000 species of birds are declining in number.

Finally, the extinction of any species is irreversible and final. An important ethical question, then, is whether we who live today have the right to destroy the world's environment and biodiversity for future generations (Capella, 2011; Keesing et al., 2010; Wilson, 1991).

Environmental Racism

Conflict theory has given rise to the concept of **environmental racism**, *the pattern by which environmental hazards are greatest for poor people, especially minorities.* Historically, factories that spewed pollution stood near neighbourhoods of the poor and visible minorities. Why? In part, the poor themselves were drawn to factories in search of work, and their low incomes often meant that they could afford housing only in undesirable neighbourhoods. Sometimes the only housing they could afford stood in the very shadow of the plants and mills where they worked.

Nobody wants a factory or dump nearby, but the poor have little power to resist. Through the years, the most serious environmental hazards have been located not near the neighbourhoods of the affluent but near those of the vulnerable and powerless. In Canada, Aboriginal communities are frequently affected. Uranium mines have contaminated ground and surface water in many areas where Aboriginal families live and hunt. Clear-cutting of forests and flooding for power generation have contaminated water and destroyed natural habitat in the James Bay region of Quebec, where Cree, in a 1975 land agreement, had been guaranteed long-term hunting and fishing rights. Lubicon Crees in north-central Alberta have been fighting since 1930 for recognition of their rights, settlement of their land claim, and the power to stop Alberta from selling timber and natural gas rights on their land. The proposal in 2000 to transport Toronto's garbage to the Adams Mine would have resulted in contamination of groundwater in Kirkland Lake and First Nations lands. And, as noted earlier, in October 2005, Kashechewan, a First Nations community of 1700 in northern Ontario, was evacuated because of widespread illness caused by contaminated drinking water. Subsequently, we learned that about half of the reserve communities in Canada have inadequate water treatment plants.

Looking Ahead: Toward a Sustainable Society and World

The demographic analysis presented in this chapter points to some disturbing trends. We see, first, that Earth's population has reached record levels because birth rates remain high in poor nations, whereas death rates have fallen just about everywhere. Reducing fertility will remain a pressing issue into the foreseeable future. Even with some recent decline in the rate of population increase, the nightmare that Thomas Robert Malthus described is still a real possibility, as the Controversy and Debate box explains.

Further, population growth remains greatest in the poorest countries of the world, which cannot meet the needs of their present populations, much less future ones. Supporting almost 87 million additional people on our planet each year, 85 million of them in economically less developed countries, will require a global commitment to provide not just food but housing, schools, and employment as well. The well-being of the entire world may ultimately depend on resolving the economic and social problems of poor, overly populated countries and bridging the widening gulf between "have" and "have-not" nations.

Urbanization is continuing, especially in poor countries. For thousands of years, people have sought out cities in the hope of finding a better life. But the sheer numbers of people who live in today's megacities—including Mexico City, São Paulo (Brazil), Lagos (Nigeria), Mumbai (India), and Manila (Philippines)—have created urban problems on a massive scale.

Around the world, humanity is facing a serious environmental challenge. Part of this problem is population increase, which is greatest in poor countries. But another part is the high level of consumption in rich nations such as our own. By increasing the planet's environmental deficit, our present way of life is borrowing against the well-being of our children and their children. Globally, members of rich societies, who currently consume so much of Earth's resources, are mortgaging the future security of the poor countries of the world.

The answer, in principle, is to create an **ecologically sustainable culture**, *a way of life that meets the needs of the present generation without threatening the environmental legacy of future generations.* Sustainable living depends on three strategies.

First, the world needs *to bring population growth under control.* The current population of 7.2 billion is already straining the natural environment. Clearly, the higher the world's population climbs, the more difficult environmental problems will become. Even if the recent slowing of population growth continues, the world will have close to 10 billion people by 2050. Few analysts think that the planet can support this many people; most argue that we must hold the line at about 7 billion, and some argue that we must decrease population in the coming decades (Smail, 2007).

A second strategy is *to conserve finite resources.* This means meeting our needs with a responsible eye toward the future by using resources efficiently, seeking

IF HUMAN INGENUITY CREATED THE THREATS TO OUR ENVIRONMENT THAT WE NOW FACE, CAN HUMANS ALSO SOLVE THESE PROBLEMS? IN RECENT YEARS, A NUMBER OF DESIGNS FOR SMALL, ENVIRONMENTALLY FRIENDLY CARS SHOW THE PROMISE OF NEW TECHNOLOGY But do such innovations go far enough? Will we have to make more basic changes to our way of life to ensure human survival in the centuries to come?

alternative sources of energy, and, in some cases, learning to live with less.

A third strategy is *to reduce waste*. Whenever possible, simply using less is the best solution, with recycling programs as part of the answer. Learning to live with less will not come easily, but keep in mind that, as consumption increased, people did not become any happier (Myers, 2000). Recycling programs, too, are part of the answer, as recycling can make everyone part of the solution to our environmental problems.

In the end, making these strategies work depends on real change in the way we think about ourselves and our world. Our *egocentric* outlook makes self-interest the standard for how to live, but a sustainable environment demands an *ecocentric* outlook that helps us see how the present is tied to the future and why we must all work together. Most nations in the southern half of the world are *underdeveloped*, unable to meet the basic needs of their people. At the same time, most countries in the northern half of the world are *overdeveloped*, using more resources than the planet can sustain over time. The changes needed to create a sustainable ecosystem will not come easily, and they will be costly. But the price of not responding to the growing environmental deficit will certainly be greater (Brown et al., 1993; Gore, 2006; Kellert & Bormann, 1991; Population Action International, 2000).

Finally, consider that the great dinosaurs dominated this planet for some 160 million years and then perished forever. Humanity is far younger, having existed for a mere 250 000 years. Compared to the rather dim-witted dinosaurs, our species has the gift of great intelligence. But how will we use this ability? What are the chances that our species will continue to flourish 160 million years—or even thousands of years—from now? The answer depends on the choices that will be made by one of the 30 million species currently living on Earth: human beings.

Controversy and Debate

Apocalypse: Will People Overwhelm the Planet?

Are you worried about the world's increasing population? Think about this: By the time you finish reading this box, more than 1000 people will have been added to our planet. By this time tomorrow, global population will have risen by 237 000. Currently, as Table 22–3 shows, there are more than four births for every two deaths on the planet, pushing the world's population upward by 87 million annually. Put another way, global population growth amounts to adding another Germany to the world each year.

It is no wonder that many demographers and environmentalists are deeply concerned about the future. Earth has an unprecedented population of 7.2 billion; the 3.2 billion people we have added since 1974 alone exceed the planet's total in 1963. Might Thomas Robert Malthus, who predicted that overpopulation would push the world into war and suffering, be right after all? Lester Brown and other *neo-Malthusians* predict a coming apocalypse if we do not change our ways. Brown admits that Malthus failed to imagine how much technology (especially the use of fertilizers and the ability to genetically modify plants) could boost the planet's agricultural output. But he maintains that Earth's rising population is rapidly outstripping its finite resources.

Families in many poor countries can find little firewood, members of rich countries are depleting the oil reserves, and everyone is draining our supply of clean water and poisoning the planet with waste. Some analysts argue that we have already passed Earth's "carrying capacity" for population and we need to hold the line or even reduce global population to ensure our long-term survival.

But other analysts, the *anti-Malthusians,* sharply disagree. Julian Simon (1995) points out that, two centuries after Malthus predicted catastrophe, Earth supports almost six times as many people who, on average, live longer, healthier lives than ever before. With more advanced technology, people have devised ways to increase productivity and limit population increase. As Simon sees it, this is cause for celebration. Human ingenuity has consistently proved the doomsayers wrong, and Simon is betting it will continue to do so.

Table 22–3 Global Population Increase, 2014

	Births	Deaths	Net Increase
Per year	143 341 000	56 759 000	86 582 000
Per month	11 945 083	4 729 917	7 215 167
Per day	392 715	155 504	237 211
Per hour	16 363	6479	9884
Per minute	273	108	165
Per second	4.5	1.8	2.7

What Do You Think?

1. Where do you place your bet? Do you think Earth can support 8 or 10 billion people? Explain your reasoning.

2. What, if anything, do you think should be done about global population increase?

3. Were Malthus alive today, would he feel relieved or would he say "I told you so!"? Explain.

SOURCES: Brown (1995), Population Reference Bureau (2014), Simon (1995), Scanlon (2001), Smail (2007), and U.S. Census Bureau (2014).

Seeing Sociology in Everyday Life

CHAPTER 22   Population, Urbanization, and Environment

Why is the environment a social issue?

As this chapter explains, the state of the natural environment depends on how society is organized, especially the importance a culture attaches to consumption and economic growth.

Hint If expansion is "good times," then contraction is a "recession" or perhaps even a "depression." Such a world view means that it is normal—or even desirable—to live in a way that increases stress on the natural environment. Sustainability, an idea that is especially important as world population increases, depends on learning to live with what we have or maybe even learning to live with less. Although many people seem to disagree, it really doesn't require a 3000-kilogram SUV to move around urban areas. Actually, it might not require a car at all. This new way of thinking requires that we do not define social standing and personal success in terms of what we own and what we consume. Can you imagine a society like that? What would it be like?

WE LEARN TO SEE ECONOMIC EXPANSION AS NATURAL AND GOOD When the economy stays the same for a number of months, we say we are experiencing "stagnation." When the economy gets smaller and the stock market falters, we say that we are in a recession. How do we know when recession has turned into a depression?

Jeff Greenberg/AGE Fotostock

WHAT WOULD IT TAKE TO CONVINCE MEMBERS OF OUR SOCIETY THAT SMALLER (RATHER THAN BIGGER) MIGHT BE BETTER? WHY DO WE SEEM TO PREFER NOT JUST BIGGER CARS BUT ALSO BIGGER HOMES AND MORE AND MORE MATERIAL POSSESSIONS?

Seeing Sociology in *Your* Everyday Life

1. Here is an illustration of the problem of runaway growth (Milbrath, 1989:10): "A pond has a single water lily growing on it. The lily doubles in size each day. In 30 days, it covers the entire pond. On which day does it cover half the pond?" When you have figured out the answer, discuss the implications of this example for population increase.

2. Each of us generates in our minds a "mental map" of cities in which we have lived. Draw a mental map of a city familiar to you with as much detail of specific places, districts, roads, and transportation facilities as you can. After you complete the map, look at what you considered to be important and try to recognize what you left out. One good way to do this is to compare your map to a street map or, better yet, compare it to a map drawn by someone else. When you make comparisons, try to account for the differences.

3. As an interesting exercise, carry a plastic bag around for a single day and collect in it everything you want to throw away. Most people are surprised to find that the average North American discards close to 2.25 kilograms of paper, metal, plastic, and other materials daily. Over a lifetime, that's about 50 tonnes.

Making the Grade

CHAPTER 22 Population, Urbanization, and Environment

Demography: The Study of Population

22.1 Explain the concepts of fertility, mortality, and migration, and their effects on population.

Demography analyzes the size and composition of a population and how and why people move from place to place.

- **Fertility** is the incidence of child-bearing in a country's population. Demographers describe fertility using the **crude birth rate**.
- **Mortality** is the incidence of death in a country's population. Demographers measure mortality using both the **crude death rate** and the **infant mortality rate**.

  - The **net migration rate** is the difference between the in-migration rate and the out-migration rate.
  - In general, rich nations grow almost as much from immigration as from natural increase; poorer nations grow almost entirely from natural increase.
  - Demographers use **age-sex pyramids** to show the composition of a population graphically and to project population trends.

> **demography** the study of human population
> **fertility** the incidence of child-bearing in a country's population
> **crude birth rate** the number of live births in a given year for every 1000 people in a population
> **mortality** the incidence of death in a country's population
> **crude death rate** the number of deaths in a given year for every 1000 people in a population
> **infant mortality rate** the number of deaths among infants under one year of age for each 1000 live births in a given year
> **life expectancy** the average life span of a country's population
> **migration** the movement of people into and out of a specified territory
> **sex ratio** the number of males for every 100 females in a nation's population
> **age-sex pyramid** a graphic representation of the age and sex of a population

History and Theory of Population Growth

22.2 Analyze population trends using Malthusian theory and demographic transition theory.

- Historically, world population grew slowly because high birth rates were offset by high death rates.

- About 1750, a demographic transition began as the world population rose sharply, mostly due to falling death rates.
- In the late 1700s, Thomas Robert Malthus warned that population growth would outpace food production, resulting in social calamity.
- **Demographic transition theory** contends that technological advances gradually slow population increase.
- Currently, the world is gaining 87 million people each year, with 98 percent of this increase taking place in poor countries. World population is expected to reach about 9.6 billion by 2050.

> **demographic transition theory** the thesis that population patterns reflect a society's level of technological development
> **zero population growth** the rate of reproduction that maintains population in a steady state

Urbanization: The Growth of Cities

22.3 Summarize patterns of urbanization in Canada and around the world.

The **first urban revolution** began with the appearance of cities about 10 000 years ago.

- By about 2000 years ago, cities had emerged in most regions of the world except North America and Antarctica.
- Pre-industrial cities have low-rise buildings; narrow, winding streets; and personal social ties.

A **second urban revolution** began about 1750 as the Industrial Revolution propelled rapid urban growth in Europe.

- The physical form of cities changed as planners created wide, regular streets to facilitate commerce.
- The emphasis on business, as well as the increasing size of cities, made urban life more impersonal.

A **third urban revolution** is now occurring in poor countries. Today, most of the world's largest cities are found in less developed nations.

In Canada, urbanization has been going on for almost 300 years.

- Urbanization came to Canada with British and French settlers.

- By 1800, hundreds of cities had been founded across the United States; in Canada, though York (now Toronto) had been founded, there were only 15 families living between Burlington Bay and the Bay of Quinte (a distance of 200 kilometres).
- Today, more than 80 percent of Canada's population is urban.
- Today, many of our cities and their suburbs are strung together in metropolitan areas.
- The Golden Horseshoe (Oshawa through Toronto to St. Catharines) contains about one-third of Canada's population, while the Windsor–Quebec City corridor contains about half.

> **urbanization** the concentration of population into cities
> **metropolis** a large city that dominates the surrounding area both socially and economically
> **suburbs** urban areas beyond the political boundaries of a city
> **megalopolis** a vast urban region containing a number of cities and their surrounding suburbs

Urbanism as a Way of Life

22.4 Identify the contributions of Tönnies, Durkheim, Park, Wirth, and Marx to our understanding of urban life.

Rapid urbanization during the nineteenth century led early sociologists to study the differences between rural and urban life. **Ferdinand Tönnies** built his analysis on the concepts of *Gemeinschaft* and *Gesellschaft*.

- *Gemeinschaft*, typical of the rural village, joins people in what amounts to a single primary group.
- *Gesellschaft*, typical of the modern city, describes individuals motivated by their own needs rather than by a desire to help improve the well-being of the community.

Émile Durkheim agreed with much of Tönnies's thinking but claimed that urbanites do not lack social bonds; the basis of social solidarity simply differs in the two settings. He described

- **mechanical solidarity**—social bonds based on common sentiments and shared moral values. This type of social solidarity is typical of traditional, rural life.
- **organic solidarity**—social bonds based on specialization and interdependence. This type of social solidarity is typical of modern, urban life.

Georg Simmel claimed that the overstimulation of city life produced a blasé attitude in urbanites.

Robert Park, at the University of Chicago, claimed that cities permit greater social freedom.

Louis Wirth saw large, dense, heterogeneous populations creating an impersonal and self-interested, though tolerant, way of life.

Karl Marx's analysis of conflict in the city is echoed in the urban political economy model.

> **Gemeinschaft** a type of social organization in which people are closely tied by kinship and tradition
> **Gesellschaft** a type of social organization in which people come together only on the basis of individual self-interest
> **urban ecology** the study of the link between the physical and social dimensions of cities

Urbanization in Poor Nations

22.5 Describe the third urban revolution now under way in poor societies.

- The third urban revolution is taking place now in low-income nations.
- Almost all global population increase is taking place in cities. Of the 28 cities with population greater than 10 million, 19 are in low- or middle-income nations.

Environment and Society

22.6 Analyze current environmental problems such as pollution and global warming or climate change.

The state of the **environment** is a social issue because it reflects how human beings organize social life.

- Societies increase the **environmental deficit** by focusing on short-term benefits and ignoring the long-term consequences brought on by their way of life.
- The more complex a society's technology, the greater its capacity to alter the natural environment.
- The *logic-of-growth thesis* supports economic development, claiming that people can solve environmental problems as they arise.
- The *limits-to-growth thesis* states that societies must curb development to prevent eventual environmental collapse.
  - 54 percent of the solid waste we throw away ends up in landfills, which are filling up and can pollute groundwater.
  - The supply of clean water is already low in some parts of the world. Industrial technology has caused a decline in air quality.

- Rainforests help remove carbon dioxide from the atmosphere and are home to a large share of this planet's living species. Under pressure from development, the world's rainforests are now half their original size and are shrinking by about 1 percent annually.
- Conflict theory has drawn attention to environmental racism by which the poor and minorities suffer most from environmental hazards.

Toward a Sustainable Society and World

- Our planet's population continues to grow due to high fertility in low-income countries coupled with declining mortality almost everywhere.

- As population increases, humanity faces environmental challenges

ecology the study of the interaction of living organisms and the natural environment

natural environment Earth's surface and atmosphere, including living organisms, air, water, soil, and other resources necessary to sustain life

ecosystem a system composed of the interaction of all living organisms and their natural environment

environmental deficit profound long-term harm to the natural environment caused by humanity's focus on short-term material affluence

rainforests regions of dense forestation, most of which circle the globe close to the equator

global warming a rise in Earth's average temperature due to an increasing concentration of carbon dioxide in the atmosphere

environmental racism the pattern by which environmental hazards are greatest for poor people, especially minorities

ecologically sustainable culture a way of life that meets the needs of the present generation without threatening the environmental legacy of future generations

Chapter 23
Collective Behaviour and Social Movements

Lightroom Photos/Photoshot/Newscom

Learning Objectives

23.1 Distinguish various types of collective behaviour.

23.2 Identify five types of crowds and three explanations of crowd behaviour.

23.3 Describe rumours, disasters, and other types of mass behaviour.

23.4 Analyze the causes and consequences of social movements.

The Power of Society

to encourage or discourage participation in social movements

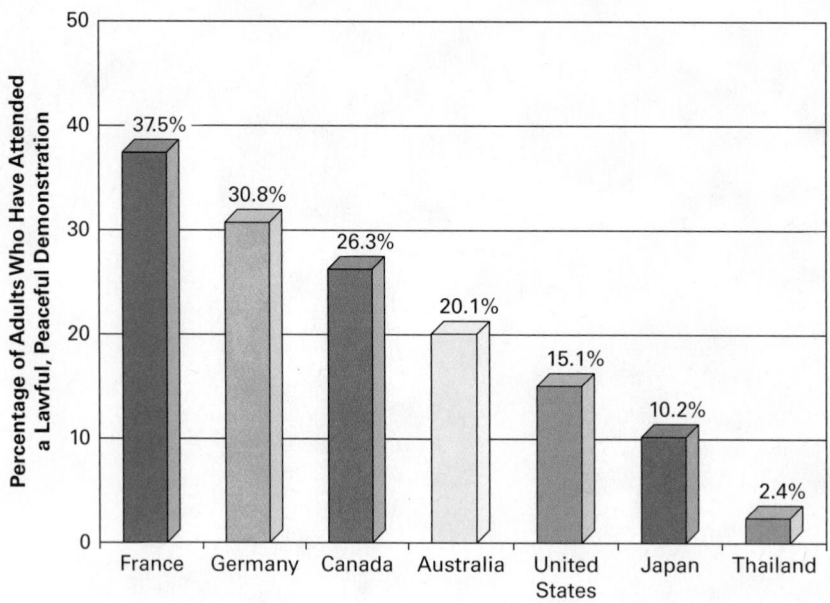

SOURCE: Based on Inglehart, Ronald, et al. "World values survey," 2013, http://www.worldvaluessurvey.org/ index_surveys.

Is active involvement in a social movement simply a matter of personal choice? When asked if they had ever attended a lawful, peaceful demonstration in support of some social movement, about 26 percent of Canadian adults said "yes." In some nations that share is much lower; 10 percent in Japan and only 2 percent in Thailand. Even Australians and Americans—at 20 and 15 percent—are less likely than Canadians to have engaged in demonstrations. Whether people "take to the streets" to show their support for a cause depends on more than personal decisions; it also reflects the culture of the larger society.

Chapter Overview

This chapter explores the wide-ranging patterns of behaviour that sociologists describe as "collective behaviour," including crowd behaviour, rumour and gossip, panics, disasters, and social movements.

The summer of 1990 was pivotal for Canada's First Nations because after Elijah Harper and Oka, the relationship between Aboriginal peoples and other Canadians would never be the same. The Meech Lake Accord was to be ratified by each of the provinces by June 23, to allow amendments to the constitution that would satisfy Quebec—and, thereafter, block constitutional changes sought by Aboriginal leaders. Newfoundland was poised to vote, and Manitoba was going through the procedural steps for ratification. The snag came in the form of Elijah Harper, a Cree Member of the Legislative Assembly, who, through dramatic delay tactics, prevented ratification by the Manitoba legislature—thereby "killing" the accord.

In the meantime, the town of Oka, Quebec, was ensuring its international visibility by proposing to expand a golf course onto lands that the people of Kanesatake considered to be a sacred burial ground. A barricade erected across a rural road in response to this threat gave rise to a five-month armed confrontation between the residents of Kanesatake, aided by Mohawk Warriors, on one side and the Quebec police and, later, the Canadian Forces on the other.

The significance of these events lay not in the fact that Aboriginal peoples and their leaders were taking decisive action to defend their interests—but in the fact that their struggle had captured the attention of the media, the general public, and Aboriginal individuals throughout the country. Suddenly, there was an outpouring of support for Elijah Harper and the people of Kanesatake in the form of letters, donations of food and money, marches, a run to bring a peace feather from British Columbia to Oka, a peace camp at Oka, and the barricade of the Mercier Bridge into Montreal by the people of Kahnawake. Daily, if not hourly, coverage of the Manitoba legislature and the tense, armed confrontation at Oka hypnotized Canadians and mobilized Aboriginal peoples in support of a cause. A growing sense of solidarity emerged as Aboriginal individuals everywhere watched events unfold. Many people who had paid little attention to their Aboriginal roots were suddenly intensely interested, proud, and somehow empowered by this new sense of movement and common cause. Raised consciousness and forged bonds had profound effects on relations among Aboriginal peoples, other Canadians, and governments. A social movement was born.

For most of the past century, sociologists focused on established social patterns such as the family and social stratification. They paid little attention to collective behaviour, considering most of it unusual or deviant. But numerous social movements that burst on the scene during the tumultuous 1960s changed all of that. As this chapter explains, a **social movement** is *organized activity that encourages or discourages social change.* Social movements are the most important type of **collective behaviour**, *activity involving a large number of people, often spontaneous, and usually in violation of established norms.* Other forms of collective behaviour—also controversial and sometimes provoking change—are mobs, riots, and crowds; rumour and gossip; public opinion; fashions and fads; and panic and mass hysteria.

Studying Collective Behaviour

23.1 Distinguish various types of collective behaviour.

Collective behaviour is difficult for sociologists to study for three reasons:

1. **Collective behaviour is diverse.** Collective behaviour involves a wide range of human action. At first glance, it is difficult to see what disasters have in common with fads, rumours, and mob behaviour.
2. **Collective behaviour is variable.** Some rumours—such as the claim in 2004 that electing Stephen Harper's Conservatives would allow him to implement a "hidden

agenda"—have consequences. Other rumours die out without impact. Why does one rumour catch on but others do not?

3. **Much collective behaviour is transitory.** Sociologists have long studied social institutions such as the family because they are continuing parts of society. Disasters, rumours, and fads, however, come and go quickly.

Some researchers point out that these problems apply not just to collective behaviour but to most forms of human behaviour (Aguirre & Quarantelli, 1983). In addition, collective behaviour is not always so surprising; anyone can predict that crowds will form at sporting events and music festivals, and sociologists can study these gatherings firsthand or record them on videotape to study later. Researchers can even anticipate some natural disasters, such as tornadoes or hurricanes, and be ready to study how people respond to such events (Miller, 1985).

As a result of their efforts, sociologists now know a great deal about collective behaviour. The most basic lesson is that all collective behaviour involves the action of some **collectivity**, *a large number of people whose minimal interaction occurs in the absence of well-defined and conventional norms.* Collectivities are of two types. A *localized collectivity* refers to people physically close to one another, as in the case of crowds and riots. A *dispersed collectivity,* or *mass behaviour,* involves people who influence one another despite being spread over a large area. Examples of this type of collective behaviour include rumours, public opinion, and fashion.

Be sure to keep in mind how collectivities differ from the familiar concept of *social groups.* Here are three key differences:

1. **People in collectivities have little or no social interaction.** People in groups interact frequently and directly. People in mobs or other localized collectivities interact very little. Most people taking part in dispersed collectivities, such as a fad, do not interact at all.

2. **Collectivities have no clear social boundaries.** Group members share a sense of identity, but people engaged in collective behaviour usually do not. People in a local crowd may have the same object of their attention, such as someone on a ledge threatening to jump, but they feel little sense of unity. Individuals involved in dispersed collectivities, such as the people who spread the rumour about the Harper government making abortion illegal, have minimal awareness of

shared membership. To give another example, people may share concerns over many issues, but usually it is difficult to say exactly who falls within the ranks of, say, the environmental or the feminist movement.

3. **Collectivities generate weak and unconventional norms.** Conventional cultural norms usually regulate the behaviour of people in groups. Some collectivities, such as people travelling together on an airplane, do observe conventional norms, but their interaction is usually limited to polite small talk with respect for the privacy of others sitting nearby. Other collectivities—such as excited fans after a game who take to the streets drinking and overturning cars—behave according to no clear guidelines (Turner & Killian, 1987; Weller & Quarantelli, 1973).

Localized Collectivities: Crowds

23.2 Identify five types of crowds and three explanations of crowd behaviour.

One major form of collective behaviour is the **crowd**, *a temporary gathering of people who share a common focus of attention and who influence one another.* Most of our

IT'S SEPTEMBER 2005: MORE THAN 5000 STUDENTS AND ALUMNI HAVE DESCENDED ON KINGSTON, ONTARIO, FOR HOMECOMING AT QUEEN'S UNIVERSITY The Aberdeen Street parties had been getting wilder over the past few years; this one turned into a riot, resulting in several overturned cars, other property damage, and more than 100 charges for liquor and other offences. The following year, Queen's incorporated this photo into a poster pointing out that several thousand onlookers were also idiots.

The Kingston Whig-Standard

---

collective behaviour activity involving a large number of people, often spontaneous, and usually in violation of established norms

collectivity a large number of people whose minimal interaction occurs in the absence of well-defined and conventional norms

ancestors never saw a large crowd. In medieval Europe, for example, about the only time large numbers of people gathered in one place was when armies faced off on the battlefield (Laslettt, 1984). Today, however, crowds of 25 000 to 500 000 are common at rock concerts and sporting events. In 2002, Toronto's World Youth Day attracted about 250 000 young Catholics to see Pope John Paul II. Various AIDS benefit concerts (e.g., Live 8), which are usually attended and/or organized by Bono of U2, have been known to draw much larger crowds. And estimates placed the size of the crowd at President Barack Obama's first inauguration at about 1.5 million (Tucker, 2009).

All crowds include a lot of people, but they differ in their social dynamics. Herbert Blumer (1969) identified four categories of crowds:

- A *casual crowd* is a loose collection of people who interact little, if at all. People lying on a beach or people who rush to the scene of an automobile accident have only a passing awareness of one another.

- A *conventional crowd* results from deliberate planning, as illustrated by a country auction, a college lecture, or a celebrity's funeral. In each case, the behaviour of people involved follows a clear set of norms.

- An *expressive crowd* forms around an event with emotional appeal, such as a religious revival, a NASCAR race, New Year's Eve at Times Square, Stanley Cup parades, or homecoming weekends at universities like Queen's. In July 2003, close to 400 000 people gathered at Toronto's Downsview Park for a Rolling Stones concert—which, at that time, was the largest ever concert in North America. Whatever the occasion, excitement is the main reason people join expressive crowds, which makes this spontaneous experience exhilarating for those involved.

- An *acting crowd* is a collectivity motivated by an intense, single-minded purpose, such as an audience rushing the doors of a concert hall or fleeing from a mall after hearing gunshots. Acting crowds are set in motion by powerful emotions, which can sometimes trigger mob violence.

Any crowd can change from one type to another. In 2001, for example, a conventional crowd of more than 10 000 fans filed into a soccer stadium in Johannesburg, South Africa, to watch a match between two rival teams. After a goal was scored, the crowd erupted, and people began to push toward the field. Within seconds, an acting crowd had formed, and a stampede began, one that ended up crushing 47 people to death (Nessman, 2001).

Deliberate action by a crowd is not simply the product of rising emotions. Participants in protest crowds—a fifth category we can add to Blumer's list—may stage marches, boycotts, sit-ins, and strikes for political purposes (McPhail & Wohlstein, 1983). The antiwar demonstrations that took place on many campuses and in many large cities during the Iraq War are examples of protest crowds. Sometimes protest crowds have the low-level energy characteristic of a conventional crowd; at other times, people become emotional enough to form an acting crowd.

Mobs and Riots

When an acting crowd turns violent, the result may be the birth of a **mob**, *a highly emotional crowd that pursues a violent or destructive goal*. Despite, or perhaps because of, their intense emotions, mobs tend to dissipate quickly. How long a mob continues to exist depends on its precise goals and whether its leadership tries to inflame or calm the crowd.

Lynching is one of the most notorious examples of mob behaviour. The term is derived from Charles Lynch, of colonial Virginia, who tried to enforce law and order in his community before there were formal police and courts; the word *lynch* soon came to mean violence and murder committed outside the law. In the United States, lynching has always been coloured by race. After the Civil War, lynch mobs terrorized newly freed slaves. Any Black person who challenged White superiority risked being hanged or burned alive by hateful Whites.

Lynch mobs—typically composed of poor Whites who felt threatened by competition from freed slaves—reached their peak between 1880 and 1930; police recorded some 5000 lynchings in that period, though many more undoubtedly occurred. Like public executions, lynchings were popular events, attracting hundreds of spectators. Some victims were killed quickly, but others were tortured before being put to death. Most of these killings took place in the American Deep South, where the farming economy depended on a cheap and obedient labour force. On the western frontier, lynch mobs targeted people of Mexican and Asian descent. In about 25 percent of reported lynchings, White mobs killed other White men. Lynching women was rare; only about 100 such cases are known, almost all involving Black women (Grant, 1975; Lacayo, 2000; White, 1969; orig. 1929).

A highly energized crowd, acting with no particular purpose, becomes a **riot**, *a social eruption that is highly emotional, violent, and undirected*. Unlike the action of a mob, a riot usually has no clear goal, except perhaps to express dissatisfaction. The cause of most riots is some

crowd a temporary gathering of people who share a common focus of attention and who influence one another

mob a highly emotional crowd that pursues a violent or destructive goal

riot a social eruption that is highly emotional, violent, and undirected

long-standing anger or grievance; more often than not, violent action is ignited by some minor incident that causes people to start destroying property and harming other persons (Smelser, 1962).

In October 2003, a crowd turned to rioting when a Montreal club announced the cancellation of a concert; the punk rock band that was to appear that night had been turned back at the border. In the few minutes before police arrived, angry young people smashed store windows, set fire to a number of cars, and overturned others. Whereas a mob action usually ends when a specific violent goal has been achieved or decisively prevented, a riot tends to disperse only as participants run out of steam or as community leaders or police gradually bring them under control.

Riots often serve as collective expressions of social injustice. Industrial workers, for example, have rioted to vent rage at their working conditions, and race riots have occurred with striking regularity. In Vancouver in 1907, in response to steady migration from China of what seemed to be unfairly competitive cheap labour and a sudden influx of more than 8000 Japanese, a riot broke out, during which

WHAT EXPLAINS THE BEHAVIOUR OF CROWDS? PEOPLE ONCE THOUGHT A CROWD TAKES ON A "MIND OF ITS OWN"; NOW, IT IS MORE CORRECT TO SAY THAT PEOPLE ARE BROUGHT TOGETHER BY SOME SHARED INTEREST In the case of this protest crowd in Quebec City, the participants are demanding that the province not cut funding to education or raise tuition fees. Exactly what happens next, however, depends on many factors that unfold as the protest proceeds.

local people lashed out violently against Japanese residents and looted their businesses. In Los Angeles in 1992, the acquittal of police officers involved in the beating of a Black motorist, Rodney King, set off an explosive riot. Violence and fires killed more than 50 people, injured thousands, and destroyed property worth hundreds of millions of dollars. These riots were followed almost immediately by race riots on the streets of Toronto.

Riots are not always fired by hate. They can also stem from positive feelings, such as the celebration of the 1993 Stanley Cup victory in Montreal, which turned into a night of looting and violence. Days later, in anticipation of further violence, the Montreal Canadiens were protected during their victory parade by hundreds of police officers and the riot squad. Similar occurrences have happened elsewhere in Canada after sporting events. As illustrated an earlier photo, in the fall of 1995 another "party" turned into a riot at the Queen's University homecoming (Doolittle, 2005).

Crowds, Mobs, and Social Change

What does a riot accomplish? One answer is "power." Ordinary people can gain power by acting collectively. The power of the crowd to challenge the status quo and sometimes to force social change is the reason crowds are controversial. Throughout history, defenders of the status quo have feared "the mob" as a threat while those seeking change have supported collective action.

Theories of Crowd Behaviour

What accounts for the behaviour of crowds? Social scientists have developed several explanations.

CONTAGION THEORY An early explanation of collective behaviour was offered by French sociologist Gustave Le Bon (1841–1931). According to Le Bon's *contagion theory* (1960; orig. 1895), crowds have a hypnotic effect on their members. Shielded by the anonymity found in large numbers, people forget about personal responsibility and give in to the contagious emotions of the crowd. A crowd thereby assumes a life of its own, stirring up emotions and driving people toward irrational, even violent, action.

> **EVALUATE**
>
> Le Bon's idea that crowds provide anonymity and can generate strong emotions is surely true. Yet, as Clark McPhail (1991) points out, a considerable body of research shows that "the madding crowd" does not take on a life of its own; its actions result from the policies and decisions made by specific individuals. In 2010, for example, 47 people were crushed to death at a German music festival when a crowd of people moving through a tunnel to gain access to the concert grounds suddenly panicked. The police described the situation as "very chaotic." Later investigation, however, revealed that the panic did not occur because the crowd suddenly and mysteriously

"went crazy" but because the police suddenly closed one end of the tunnel while people were pouring in. This action sparked a panic among those who were being crushed inside and had nowhere to go (Grieshaber & Augstein, 2010).

While collective behaviour can involve strong emotions, such feelings may not be irrational, as contagion theory suggests. Emotions, as well as action, can reflect real fear—as in the festivalgoers' panic—or result from a sense of injustice.

CHECK YOUR LEARNING Explain the contagion theory of crowd behaviour. What are the criticisms of this theory?

CONVERGENCE THEORY *Convergence theory* holds that crowd behaviour comes not from the crowd itself but from the particular people who join in. From this point of view, a crowd is a convergence of like-minded individuals. Contagion theory states that crowds cause people to act in a certain way; convergence theory states the opposite, claiming that people who wish to act in a certain way come together to form crowds. For example, the crowds that formed at demonstrations protesting globalization, as in Quebec City in 2001, did not cause participants to oppose capitalism. On the contrary, protestors came together to oppose the Free Trade Agreement of the Americas because of their political attitudes.

EVALUATE

By linking crowds to broader social forces, convergence theory rejects Le Bon's claim that crowd behaviour is irrational in favour of the view that people in crowds express existing beliefs and

values. But in fairness to Le Bon, people sometimes do things in a crowd that they would not have the courage to do alone, because crowds can spread responsibility among many people. In addition, crowds can intensify an emotion simply by creating a critical mass of like-minded people.

CHECK YOUR LEARNING Explain the convergence theory of crowd behaviour. What are two criticisms of this theory?

EMERGENT NORM THEORY Ralph Turner and Lewis Killian (1993) developed the *emergent norm theory* of crowd dynamics. These researchers admit that social behaviour is never entirely predictable but, if similar interests draw people into a crowd, distinctive patterns of behaviour may emerge.

According to Turner and Killian, crowds begin as collectivities containing people with mixed interests and motives. Especially in the case of expressive, acting, and protest crowds, norms may be vague and changing. Consider how many Iraqi citizens began looting government buildings after American troops toppled Saddam Hussein. While some citizens stole anything they could carry, others tried to stop the lawlessness. In short, people in crowds make their own rules as they go along.

EVALUATE

Emergent norm theory represents a middle ground approach to crowd dynamics. Turner and Killian (1993) explain that crowd behaviour is neither as irrational as contagion theory suggests nor as deliberate as convergence theory implies. Certainly, crowd behaviour reflects the desires of participants, but it is also guided by norms that emerge as the situation unfolds.

According to Turner and Killan, crowds begin as collectivities containing people with mixed interests and motives. Especially in the case of expressive, acting, and protest crowds, norms may be vague and changing. In the minutes and hours after the earthquake and tsunami devastated Japan, many people fled in terror. But, quickly, the Japanese came to each other's aid and soon undertook a collective effort to rebuild their lives. In short, the behaviour of people in crowds may change over time as people draw on their traditions or—as emergent norm theory predicts—make new rules as they go along.

CHECK YOUR LEARNING Explain the emergent norm theory of crowd behaviour. What are the criticisms of this theory?

John Moore/AP Photo/The Canadian Press

THE 2001 MEETING OF THE SUMMIT OF THE AMERICAS, IN QUEBEC CITY, WAS THE OCCASION FOR PROTESTS BY THOSE OPPOSED TO EXPANSION OF THE GLOBAL MARKETPLACE Specifically, the protestors wanted to derail negotiation of the Free Trade Agreement of the Americas (FTAA). Try to apply contagion, convergent, or emergent norm theory to an event such as this one. Which approach seems to make the most sense to you? Why?

Dispersed Collectivities: Mass Behaviour

23.3 Describe rumour, disasters, and other types of mass behaviour.

It is not just people clustered together in crowds who take part in collective behaviour. **Mass behaviour** refers to *collective behaviour among people spread over a wide geographic area.*

Rumour and Gossip

A common type of mass behaviour is **rumour**, *unconfirmed information that people spread informally, often by word of mouth.* People pass along rumours through face-to-face communication, of course, but today's modern technology—including cell phones, the mass media, email, and the internet—spreads rumours faster and farther than ever before. Rumour has three main characteristics:

1. **Rumour thrives in a climate of uncertainty.** Rumours arise when people lack clear and certain information about an important issue. When Trudeau said that the election of 2015 would be the last one based on our long-standing first-past-the-post system, rumours arose claiming that the Liberal-dominated committee would support ranked ballots—which in turn would ensure the election of Liberal majority governments.
2. **Rumour is unstable.** People change rumours as they pass them along, usually giving them "spin" that serves their own interests. The Conservatives and NDP circulated two very different critiques of Trudeau's electoral reform plan.
3. **Rumour is difficult to stop.** The number of people aware of a rumour increases very quickly because each person spreads information to many others. Rumours go away eventually but, in general, the only way to control them is for a believable source to issue a clear and convincing statement of the facts. Trudeau could allay the fears that give rise to rumours by stating clearly that any alternative to our first-past-the-post electoral system will be subject to a national referendum.

Rumour can trigger the formation of crowds or other collective behaviour. For this reason, officials establish a rumour-control centre during a crisis in order to manage information. Yet some rumours persist for generations, perhaps because people enjoy them. The rumour that the Beatles' Paul McCartney had mysteriously died in 1966 is a classic example—as is the persistent rumour that Elvis Presley lives on. **Gossip** is *rumour about people's personal affairs.* Charles Horton Cooley (1962; orig. 1909) explained that rumour involves some issue many people care about, but gossip interests only a small circle of people who know a particular person. This is why rumours spread widely but gossip tends to be localized.

Communities use gossip as a means of social control, using praise and blame to encourage people to conform to local norms. Also, people gossip about others to raise their own standing as social "insiders" (Baumgartner, 1998; Nicholson, 2001). Yet no community wants gossip to get so out of control that no one knows what to believe; people who gossip too much are criticized as "busybodies."

Public Opinion and Propaganda

Another form of highly dispersed collective behaviour is **public opinion**, *widespread attitudes about controversial issues.* Exactly who is, or is not, included in any "public" depends on the issue involved. Over the years in Canada, "publics" have formed over issues such as water fluoridation, greenhouse gases, the killing of seal pups, gun control, Quebec separatism, immigration, health care, same-sex marriage and, more recently, assisted death and the bathrooms to be used by transgendered individuals. As this list indicates, public issues are important matters about which people disagree. Over time, public interest rises and falls; for example, interest in women's rights in Canada was strong during the decades of the movement to secure the vote for women but declined after this right was won—federally in 1918, and provincially when Quebec became the last province to extend the vote to women in 1940. Since the 1960s, a second wave of feminism has created a public with strong opinions on gender issues.

Of course, not everyone's opinion carries the same weight. Some categories of people are more likely to be asked for their opinions, and what they say will have more clout because they are better educated, wealthier, or better connected. By forming organizations—for example, the Canadian Medical Association (CMA), the Canadian Union of Public Employees (CUPE), or Greenpeace—various categories of people increase their influence.

Political leaders and special-interest groups seek to influence public tastes and attitudes by using **propaganda**, *information presented with the intention of shaping public opinion.* Although we tend to think of propaganda in negative terms, it is not necessarily false. A thin line separates information from propaganda: The difference depends mostly on the presenter's intention. We offer *information* to enlighten others; we use *propaganda* to sway people toward our own points of view. Political speeches, commercial advertising, and even some university or college lectures may disseminate propaganda with the goal of making people think or act in some specific way. Input from Canada's business community during the 1987 debate over free trade with the United States was denounced by opponents as propaganda, as were all pronouncements of the three major federal political parties during the 1992 referendum on the Charlottetown Accord.

One way to legitimize propaganda is to show that it is consistent with public opinion, as measured by pollsters. In August 2006, headlines in *The Globe and Mail* implied that Canadians were outraged by Prime Minister Stephen Harper's decision to stand by Israel in its response to attacks by Hezbollah. According to a Globe/CTV poll, most Canadians believed that Harper supported Israel to please then U.S. President George W. Bush. Suspecting that the findings might be the result of question design, Western Standard/COMPAS conducted its own poll with very different results (COMPAS, 2006). With only "out of principle" and "domestic considerations" as alternative options, the majority of Globe/CTV respondents (53 percent of Canadians and 72 percent of Quebecers) said that Harper chose to support Israel in order to be "in line with U.S. President George W. Bush and his administration." Given a number of more specific options, such as "Israel's right of self-defence" or protection of "Canada's economic interests," Western Standard/COMPAS respondents were much less likely to cite the Bush factor (12 percent of Canadians and 11 percent of Quebecers). It should be no surprise to learn that Globe/CTV is pro-Liberal in its leanings, while Western Standard/COMPAS is pro-Conservative: The design of their respective questions had clear impacts on the results. Take a look at the actual wording of the question when you read that an overwhelming majority of people have expressed some opinion—especially when the issue is controversial.

Fashions and Fads

Fashions and fads also involve people spread over a large area. A **fashion** is *a social pattern favoured by a large number of people.* Tastes in clothing, music, and automobiles, as well as ideas about politics change often—going in and out of fashion.

In pre-industrial societies, clothing and personal appearance changed very little, reflecting traditional style. Women and men, the rich and the poor, lawyers and carpenters wore distinctive clothes and hairstyles that reflected their occupations and social standing (Crane, 2000; Lofland, 1973).

In industrial societies, however, established style gives way to changing fashion. For one thing, modern people care less about tradition and are often eager to try out new lifestyles. Higher rates of social mobility also cause people to use appearance to make statements about themselves. German sociologist Georg Simmel (1971; orig. 1904) explained that rich people are trendsetters

because they attract a lot of attention. As Thorstein Veblen (1953; orig. 1899) put it, fashion involves *conspicuous consumption* as people buy expensive products—from bottled water to Hummers—not because they need such things but simply to show off their wealth.

Ordinary people who want to look wealthy are eager to buy less expensive copies of items made fashionable by the rich. In this way, a fashion moves downward through the class structure. Eventually, a fashion loses its prestige when too many average people share a "look," so the rich move on to something new. Fashions, in short, are born at the top of the social hierarchy, rise to mass popularity in department stores, and soon are forgotten by almost everyone.

Since the 1960s, however, there has been a reversal of this pattern: Many fashions favoured by rich people are drawn from people of lower social position. This pattern began with blue jeans, which have long been worn by people doing manual labour. During the civil rights and antiwar movements of the 1960s, jeans became popular

Barbara Nitke/Lifetime/Everett Collection

FASHION REFERS TO SOCIAL PATTERNS THAT ARE POPULAR WITHIN A SOCIETY'S POPULATION In modern societies, the mass media play an important part in guiding people's tastes. For example, the popular television show *Project Runway* sets standards for attractive clothing. Fads are patterns that change more quickly. *Project Runway* is one example of the recent fad that has brought so many "reality shows" to television.

among American college students who wanted to identify with working people. Today, emblems of hip-hop culture allow wealthy entertainers and celebrities to mimic the styles that began among the inner-city poor. Even rich and famous people may identify with their ordinary roots: In one of her songs, Jennifer Lopez sings, "Don't be fooled by the rocks that I've got, I'm still, I'm still Jenny from the block."

A **fad** is *an unconventional social pattern that people embrace briefly but enthusiastically.* Fads, sometimes called crazes, are common in high-income societies, where many people have the money to spend on amusing, if often frivolous, things. During the 1950s, two young Californians produced a brightly coloured plastic hoop, a version of a toy popular in Australia, that you can swing around your waist by gyrating the hips. The "hula hoop" became a national craze. In less than a year, hula hoops all but vanished, reappearing sporadically. Pokémon cards are another example of the rise and fall of a fad (Aguirre et al., 1988).

How do fads differ from fashions? Fads capture the public imagination but quickly burn out. Because fashions reflect basic cultural values, such as individuality and sexual attractiveness, they tend to stay around for a while. Therefore, a fashion—but rarely a fad—becomes a more lasting part of popular culture. Streaking, for instance, was a fad that came out of nowhere and soon vanished; blue jeans, on the other hand, originated in the rough mining camps of the gold rush in the 1870s and are still popular today.

Panic and Mass Hysteria

Panic is *a form of collective behaviour in which people in one place react to a threat or other stimulus with irrational, frantic, and often self-destructive behaviour.* The classic illustration of panic is people streaming toward the exits of a crowded theatre after someone yells, "Fire!" As they flee, they may trample one another or block the exits so that few actually escape.

Closely related to panic is **mass hysteria** (or **moral panic**), *a form of dispersed collective behaviour in which people react to a real or imagined event with irrational and even frantic fear.* Whether the cause of the hysteria is real or not, a large number of people take it very seriously.

In recent years, Canadians have experienced panics, in local areas as well as nationwide (mass hysteria or moral panics), over a series of infectious diseases—namely, HIV/AIDS, SARS, West Nile, mad cow, avian or bird flu, swine flu, and most recently the Zika virus. One factor that makes moral panics common in our society is the influence of the mass media. Diseases, disasters, and deadly crime all get intense coverage by the media in hopes of gaining larger audiences. "The mass media *thrive* on scares; contributing to moral panics is the media's stock in trade" (Goode, 2000:549). Consider the role of the mass media in spreading panic regarding the "inevitable" bird flu pandemic; there was intensive coverage for several months and then nothing, despite the fact that a pandemic remains equally "inevitable."

A classic example of mass hysteria occurred during the evening before Halloween in 1938. A CBS radio dance music broadcast was suddenly interrupted with a "special report" of explosions on the surface of the planet Mars and, soon after, the crash landing of a mysterious cylinder near a farmhouse in New Jersey. This was a dramatization by Orson Welles of H.G. Wells's novel *War of the Worlds* (Cantril et al., 1947; Koch, 1970). The program then switched to an "on-the-scene reporter" who presented a chilling account of giant monsters equipped with death-ray weapons emerging from a spaceship. An "eminent astronomer" informed the audience that Martians had begun a full-scale invasion of Earth. At the time, North Americans relied on radio for factual news. There was an announcement to clarify that the broadcast was fiction, but about 1 million of the 10 million listeners in the United States and Canada missed this announcement and believed that the play was real. By the time the show was over, thousands were hysterical, gathering in the streets to spread news of the "invasion," while others flooded telephone switchboards with warnings to friends and relatives. Many simply jumped into their cars and fled. (Author Linda Gerber's mother listened to the Orson Wells broadcast in Winnipeg.)

---

mass behaviour collective behaviour among people spread over a wide geographic area

rumour unconfined information that people spread informally, often by word of mouth	**public opinion** widespread attitudes about controversial issues	**fashion** a social pattern favoured by a large number of people	**panic** a form of collective behaviour in which people in one place react to a threat or other stimulus with irrational, frantic, and often self-destructive behaviour	**mass hysteria** or **moral panic** a form of dispersed collective behaviour in which people react to a real or imagined event with irrational and even frantic fear
gossip rumour about people's personal affairs	**propaganda** information presented with the intention of shaping public opinion	**fad** an unconventional social pattern that people embrace briefly but enthusiastically		

Disasters

A **disaster** is *an event, generally unexpected, that causes extensive harm to people and damage to property.* Disasters are of three types.[1] The first is the *natural disaster,* such as a flood, hurricane, earthquake, forest fire, or tsunami. A second type is the *technological disaster,* which is widely regarded as an *accident* but is more accurately a failure to control technology. The massive oil spill from the *Exxon Valdez* tanker running aground off the coast of Alaska in 1989 and the nuclear explosion at the Chernobyl power plant in Ukraine in 1986 were both technological disasters. A third type of disaster is the *intentional disaster,* in which organized groups deliberately harm others. War, terrorist attacks, and genocide—as in Yugoslavia, Rwanda, and the Darfur region of Sudan—are examples of intentional disasters.

Kai Erikson (1976, 1994, 2005) has investigated dozens of disasters of all types. From the study of floods, nuclear contamination, oil spills, and genocide, Erikson reached three major conclusions about the social consequences of disasters.

First, disasters are *social* events. We all know that disasters harm people and destroy property, but most people don't realize that disasters also do damage to human community. The Saguenay flood of 1996 killed seven, levelled an entire neighbourhood, and forced the evacuation of 16 000 people. When a dam bursts or overflows, as in this case, however rapid and effective the assistance from outside, people are paralyzed by the loss of family members, friends, and an entire way of life. A decade later, parts of the community have never been rebuilt. We may know when disasters start, Erikson points out, but we cannot know when they will finally end. Often, when disasters strike, it is the poor who suffer the most. This lesson was made clear when Hurricane Katrina struck New Orleans in 2005; one year later, the middle-class and affluent neighbourhoods were returning to normal, while the poor Black neighbourhoods looked very much as Katrina left them.

Second, Erikson found that the social damage is more serious when an event involves some toxic substance, as is common with technological disasters. After the catastrophic explosion and radiation leak in 1986 at the Chernobyl nuclear plant, people in Ukraine were exposed to a dangerous substance that they feared and over which they had no control. The Thinking Globally box explores a similar example, which is still affecting people on Utrik Island, and their descendants, more than 50 years after it occurred.

Third, the social damage is most serious when the disaster is caused by the actions of other people. This can happen through negligence or carelessness (in the case of technological disasters) or through wilful action (in the case of intentional disasters). Our belief that "other people will do us no harm" is a basic foundation of social life, Erikson claims. But when others act carelessly (as in the case of the *Exxon Valdez* oil spill) or intentionally (as in genocide) in ways that harm us, those who survive typically lose their trust in others to a degree that may never go away.

---

[1]The first two types are based on Erikson (2005). The third type is added by author John Macionis.

SOCIOLOGISTS CLASSIFY DISASTERS INTO THREE TYPES The 2011 tsunami that brought massive flooding to Japan is an example of a natural disaster. The 1989 grounding of the tanker *Exxon Valdez,* which spilled 42 million litres of crude oil off the coast of Alaska, was a technological disaster. The slaughter of hundreds of thousands of people and the displacement of millions more from their homes in the Darfur region of Sudan since 2003 is an example of an intentional disaster.

Thinking Globally

A Never-Ending Disaster

It was just after dawn on March 1, 1954, and the air was already warm on Utrik Island, a small bit of coral and volcanic rock in the South Pacific that is one of the Marshall Islands. The island was home to 159 people who lived by fishing, much as their ancestors had done for centuries. The Utrik people knew only a little about the outside world: A missionary from the United States taught the local children, and two dozen military personnel lived at a small American weather station with an airstrip that received one plane each week.

At 6:45 A.M., the western sky suddenly lit up brighter than anyone had ever seen and, seconds later, a rumble like a massive earthquake rolled across the island. Some of the islanders thought the world was coming to an end. Their world—at least as they had known it—had changed forever.

About 250 kilometres (160 miles) to the west, on Bikini Island, the United States military had just detonated an atomic bomb, a huge device with a thousand times the power of the bomb used in 1945 to destroy the Japanese city of Hiroshima. The enormous blast vaporized Bikini Island and sent a massive cloud of dust and radiation into the atmosphere. The military expected winds to take the

cloud north into an open area of the ocean, but the cloud blew east instead. By noon, the radiation cloud engulfed a Japanese fishing boat ironically called *Lucky Dragon*, exposing the 23 people on board to a dose of radiation that would eventually sicken or kill them all. By late afternoon, the deadly cloud reached Utrik Island.

The cloud was made up of coral and rock dust, all that was left of Bikini Island. The dust fell softly on Utrik Island, and children who remembered pictures of snow shown to them by their missionary teacher ran outside to play in the white powder that was piling up everywhere. No one realized that it was contaminated with deadly radiation.

Three and a half days later, the U.S. military landed planes on Utrik Island and informed the people there that they would have to leave immediately, bringing nothing with them. For three months, the islanders were held on another military base, and then they were taken home. Many of the people who were on the island on that fateful morning died young, typically from cancer or some other disease associated with radiation exposure. But, even today, those who survived consider themselves and their island poisoned by the radiation, and they believe that the poison will never go away.

The radiation may or may not still be in the islanders' bodies, but it has worked its way deep into their culture. More than 50 years after the atomic bomb exploded, people on Utrik Island still talk about the morning that "everything changed." The damage from this disaster turns out to be much more than medical: It is a social transformation that has left the people with a deep belief that they are all sick, that life will never be the same, and that people could have prevented the disaster but did not.

Corbis

What Do You Think?

1. In what sense is a disaster like this one never really over?

2. In what ways did the atomic bomb test change the culture of the Utrik people?

3. What elements of global stratification do you see in what happened to the people of Utrik Island?

SOURCE: Based on K.T. Erikson (2005a).

Social Movements

23.4 Analyze the causes and consequences of social movements.

A **social movement** is *an organized activity that encourages or discourages social change.* Social movements are among the most important types of collective behaviour because they often have lasting effects on our society.

Social movements are common in the modern world, but this was not always the case. Pre-industrial societies are tightly bound by tradition, making social movements extremely rare. Conversely, the many subcultures and countercultures found in industrial and post-industrial societies encourage social movements. In North America and Europe, significant public issues are likely to give rise to social movements favouring change and to countermovements resisting it. In recent decades in Canada, for example, the gay rights movement has won the right to same-sex *marriage* and not just formal domestic *partnerships,* as is the case in many other jurisdictions that support same-sex marriage. In response, a countermovement has formed to try to turn back the clock on gay marriage.

Historically, there have been three major dynamic sources of social change in Canada: class relations, regional identity, and the bilingual and multicultural nature of our society (Marsden & Harvey, 1979:4). Many of our social movements arose from one of four sources: Quebec, where the francophone majority seeks to reshape its relationship with the rest of Canada or to achieve independence; regional interests responding to economic and political inequities; Aboriginal peoples struggling to gain recognition of the inherent right to self-government; and ethnic or racial minorities attempting to participate as equals within the larger society without completely losing their identities.

With the patriation of our constitution in 1982 and the incorporation of the *Canadian Charter of Rights and Freedoms* (Canada, 1982), we entered a new era. Numerous issues have been brought to the forefront, claiming *Charter* protection and inspiring social movements along with various degrees of social change. Earlier movements, of women or gays and lesbians—and, most recently, transgendered individuals—gained momentum and reached many goals in this period. Others, mobilized around the human rights of refugees—specifically the 25 000 Syrian refugees arriving in Canada early in 2016—and permanent residents (previously called landed immigrants), are in full force. A smaller movement endorsing euthanasia or the right to assisted death gained momentum periodically in response to the plight of specific individuals—until the Supreme Court of Canada imposed a deadline of June 6, 2016 for the enactment of legislation dealing with the criteria and framework for medically assisted death. But by far the one of greatest consequence is the environmental movement, which is focused upon the reduction—or better yet elimination—of the carbon emissions said to be responsible for global warming or climate change

Types of Social Movements

Sociologists classify social movements according to several variables (Aberle, 1966; Blumer, 1969; Cameron, 1966). One variable determines *who is changed?* Some movements target selected people, and others try to change everyone. A second variable deals with *how much change?* Some movements seek only limited change in our lives, and others pursue radical transformation of society. Combining these variables results in four types of social movements, shown in Figure 23–1:

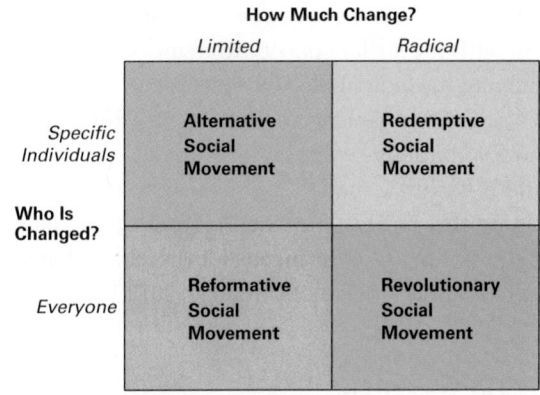

Figure 23–1 Four Types of Social Movements

There are four types of social movements based on who is changed and the extent of change.

SOURCE: Based on Aberle (1966).

- *Alternative social movements* are the least threatening to the status quo because they seek limited change in only some narrow segment of the population. Planned Parenthood, for example, encourages individuals of child-bearing age to take the consequences of sexual activity more seriously by practising birth control.

- *Redemptive social movements* also have a selective focus, but they seek radical change in those they engage. Alcoholics Anonymous, for example, is an organization that helps alcoholics to achieve a sober life.

- *Reformative social movements,* which generally work within the existing political system, seek only limited social change but encompass the entire society. They can be progressive (promoting a new social pattern) or reactionary (countermovements trying to preserve the status quo or to return to past social patterns). In the ongoing debate about abortion in Canada, both the anti-abortion and pro-choice organizations are reformative social movements. Right-wing movements such as the Western Guard, the National Citizens Coalition, and the Ku Klux Klan are examples of reactionary countermovements.

- *Revolutionary social movements* are the most extreme. They seek basic transformation of a society. Sometimes pursuing specific goals, sometimes spinning utopian dreams, these social movements reject existing social institutions as flawed, while promoting radically new alternatives. The nationalist (i.e., separatist) movement in Quebec is revolutionary because it seeks, at the very least, a radical restructuring of federal institutions to give Quebec more political and economic autonomy; failing that, Quebec nationalists would argue, the need to protect their distinct society requires the establishment of an independent state and the complete overthrow of existing institutions. As with the social conservative movement, the creation of the federal Bloc Québécois and the provincial Parti Québécois lend legitimacy to a revolutionary and potentially separatist movement by incorporating it within Canada's political structure. In effect, doing this limited the likelihood of ethnic violence by providing "a clear means for disgruntled actors to address their grievances" (Lange, 2012:123).

Claims Making

In 1981, the Centers for Disease Control and Prevention began to track a strange disease that was killing people, most of them homosexual men. It was a deadly disease, but there was little public attention and few stories in the mass media. Only about five years later did the public become aware of the rising number of deaths and begin to think of the disease as a serious social threat. The disease came to be known as acquired immune deficiency syndrome (AIDS).

The change in public thinking about AIDS was the result of **claims making**, *the process of trying to convince the public and public officials of the importance of joining a social movement to address a particular issue.* In other words, for a social movement to form, some issue has to be defined as a problem that demands public attention. Usually, claims making begins with a small number of people. In the case of AIDS, the gay community in large cities—notably San Francisco, New York, and Toronto—mobilized to convince people of the dangers posed by this deadly disease. Over time, if the mass media give an issue attention and public officials speak out on behalf of the problem, the social movement gains strength. Considerable public attention has now been given to AIDS, and there is ongoing research aimed at finding a cure for this deadly disease.

The process of claims making goes on all the time. For example, the Aboriginal rights movement tries to increase public awareness of issues relating to land claims, social justice, and quality of life. A more recent example is the student protest that began during the winter semester of 2012. Although the protest expanded—to condemn almost anything done by the Quebec Liberal government of Jean Charest—it started off as claims making in an area of specific interest to university students. Premier Charest had announced a gradual increase in tuition (over several years); initially, the students wanted to prevent the proposed tuition increases, but before long they were claiming a right to free tuition. In mid-July, the Quebec student leaders launched the Quebec–Ontario Student Solidarity Tour—by visiting 10 Ontario cities "to teach their anglo counterparts how to organize a 'Student strike, people's struggle!'" (Kheiriddin, 2012). To the extent that they succeeded in engaging Ontario university students, they were legitimizing their claim to free tuition.

Explaining Social Movements

Because social movements are intentional and long-lasting, sociologists find this type of collective behaviour easier to explain than brief episodes of mob behaviour or mass hysteria. Several theories to explain social movements have gained importance.

DEPRIVATION THEORY *Deprivation theory* holds that social movements seeking change arise among people who feel deprived. People who feel that they lack enough income, safe working conditions, basic political rights, or plain human dignity may organize a social movement to bring about a more just state of affairs (Morrison, 1978; Rose, 1982).

The rise of the Ku Klux Klan and the passage of Jim Crow laws by White people intent on enforcing segregation in the southern United States after the Civil War illustrate deprivation theory. With the end of slavery, White landowners lost a source of free labour and poorer White people lost the claim that they were socially superior to African Americans. This change produced a sense of deprivation, prompting White people to try to keep all "coloured" people "in their place" (Dollard et al., 1939). The deprivation experienced by African Americans was far greater, of course, but, as a minority in a racist society, they had little opportunity to organize. During the twentieth century, however, they organized successfully in pursuit of racial equality.

Of course, deprivation is a relative concept. Regardless of anyone's absolute amount of money and power, people feel either good or bad about their situation only by comparing themselves to some other category of people. **Relative deprivation**, then, is *a perceived disadvantage arising from some specific comparison* (Merton, 1968; Stouffer et al., 1949).

Alexis de Tocqueville's study of the French Revolution (1955; orig. 1856) offers a classic illustration of relative deprivation. Why did rebellion occur in progressive France, where feudalism was breaking down, rather than in more traditional Germany, where peasants were much worse off? De Tocqueville's answer was that, as bad as their conditions were, German peasants had known nothing but feudal servitude and, therefore, had no basis for feeling deprived. French peasants, in contrast, had seen improvements in their lives that made them eager for more change. Consequently, the French—but not the Germans—felt relative deprivation. As de Tocqueville saw it, increasing freedom and prosperity did not satisfy people as much as it sparked their desire for an even better life.

Closer to home, de Tocqueville's insight helps explain patterns of rioting during the 1960s. Protest riots involving African Americans took place not in the southern United States, where many Black people lived in miserable poverty, but in Detroit, where the auto industry was booming, Black unemployment was low, and Black home ownership was the highest in the country (Thernstrom & Thernstrom, 1998).

EVALUATE

Deprivation theory challenges our commonsense assumption that the worst-off people are the most likely to organize for change. People do not organize simply because they suffer in an absolute sense; rather, social movements arise out of a sense of *relative* deprivation. Both de Tocqueville and Marx—as different as they were in many ways—agreed on the importance of relative deprivation in the formation of social movements.

But most people experience some discontent all of the time, so deprivation theory leaves us wondering why social movements arise among some categories of people and not others. A second problem is that deprivation theory suffers from circular reasoning: We assume that deprivation causes social movements, but often the only evidence of deprivation is the social movement itself (Jenkins & Perrow, 1977). A third limitation is that this approach focuses on the cause of a social movement and tells us little about what happens after movements take form (McAdam et al., 1996).

CHECK YOUR LEARNING   State the basic idea of the deprivation theory of social movements. What are several criticisms of this theory?

MASS SOCIETY THEORY   William Kornhauser's *mass society theory* (1959) argues that socially isolated people seek out social movements as a way to gain a sense of belonging and importance. From this point of view, social movements are most likely to arise in impersonal, *mass*

societies. This theory points out the *personal* as well as the *political* consequences of social movements that offer a sense of community to people otherwise adrift in society (Melucci, 1989).

It follows, says Kornhauser, that categories of people with weak social ties are those most eager to join a social movement. People who are well integrated socially, in contrast, are unlikely to seek membership in a social movement.

Kornhauser concludes that activists tend to be psychologically vulnerable people who eagerly join groups and can be manipulated by group leaders. For this reason, Kornhauser claims, social movements are rarely very democratic.

EVALUATE

To Kornhauser's credit, his theory focuses on both the kind of society that produces social movements and the kinds of people who join them. But one criticism is that there is no clear standard for measuring the extent to which we live in a "mass society," so his thesis is difficult to test.

A second criticism is that explaining social movements in terms of people hungry to belong ignores the social justice issues that movements address. Put another way, mass society theory suggests that flawed people—rather than a flawed society—are responsible for social movements.

What does research show about mass society theory? The record is mixed. Research by Piven and Cloward (1977) supports Kornhauser's approach—finding that a breakdown of routine social patterns encourages poor people to form social movements. Also, a study of the New Mexico State Penitentiary found that, when prison programs that promoted social ties among inmates were suspended, inmates were more likely to protest their conditions (Useem, 1979).

But other studies cast doubt on this approach. Some researchers conclude that the Nazi movement in Germany did not draw heavily from socially isolated people (Lipset, 1963; Oberschall, 1973). Similarly, many of the people who took part in urban riots during the 1960s had strong ties to their communities (Sears & McConahay, 1973). Evidence also suggests that most young people who join religious movements have fairly normal family ties (Wright & Piper, 1986). Finally, researchers who have examined the biographies of 1960s political activists find evidence of deep and continuing commitment to political goals rather than isolation from society (McAdam, 1988, 1989; Whalen & Flacks, 1989).

Tom Hanson/The Canadian Press

MASS SOCIETY THEORY SUGGESTS THAT PEOPLE JOIN SOCIAL MOVEMENTS IN ORDER TO GAIN A SENSE OF MEANING AND PURPOSE IN THEIR LIVES
How well do you think this theory explains the behaviour of people in this pro-life (anti-abortion) demonstration? Why?

CHECK YOUR LEARNING   State the basic idea of the mass society theory of social movements. What are the criticisms of this theory?

STRUCTURAL STRAIN THEORY One of the most influential theories about social movements was developed by Neil Smelser (1962). His *structural strain theory* identifies six factors that encourage the development of social movements. Smelser's theory also suggests which factors encourage unorganized mobs or riots and which encourage highly organized social movements. The prodemocracy movement that transformed Eastern Europe in the late 1980s illustrates the factors in Smelser's theory:

1. **Structural conduciveness.** Social movements begin to emerge when people come to think that their society has some serious problems. In Eastern Europe, these problems included low living standards and political repression by national governments.

2. **Structural strain.** People begin to experience relative deprivation when society fails to meet their expectations. Eastern Europeans joined the prodemocracy movement because they compared their living standards to the higher ones in Western Europe; they also knew that their standard of living was lower than socialist propaganda had for years led them to expect.

3. **Growth and spread of an explanation.** Forming a well-organized social movement requires a clear statement of not just the problem but also its causes and solutions. If people are confused about why they are suffering, they will probably express their dissatisfaction in an unorganized way through rioting. In the case of Eastern Europe, intellectuals played a key role in the prodemocracy movement by pointing out economic and political flaws in the socialist system and proposing strategies to increase democracy.

4. **Precipitating factors.** Discontent may exist for a long time before some specific event sparks collective action. Such an event occurred in 1985 when Mikhail Gorbachev came to power in the Soviet Union and began his program of *perestroika* (restructuring). As Moscow relaxed its rigid control over Eastern Europe, people there saw a historic opportunity to reorganize political and economic life and claim greater freedom.

5. **Mobilization for action.** Once people share a concern about some public issue, they are ready to take action—to distribute leaflets, stage protest rallies, and build alliances with sympathetic organizations. The initial success of the Solidarity movement in Poland—helped by the Reagan administration in the United States and by Pope John Paul II in the Vatican—mobilized people throughout Eastern Europe to press for change. The rate of change grew faster and faster. What had taken a decade in Poland required only months in Hungary and only weeks in other Eastern European nations.

6. **Lack of social control.** The success of any social movement depends, in large part, on the response of

political officials, police, and the military. Sometimes the state moves swiftly to crush a social movement, as happened in the case of prodemocracy forces in the People's Republic of China. But Gorbachev adopted a policy of non-intervention in Eastern Europe, opening the door for change. Ironically, the movements that began in Eastern Europe soon spread to the Soviet Union itself, ending the historic domination of the Communist Party in 1991 and producing a new and much looser political confederation.

EVALUATE

Smelser's analysis explains how various factors help or hurt the development of social movements. Structural strain theory also explains why people may respond to their problems either by forming organized social movements or through spontaneous mob action. Yet Smelser's theory contains some of the same circularity of argument found in Kornhauser's analysis. A social movement is caused by strain, says Smelser, but the only evidence of underlying strain is often the social movement itself. Structural strain theory is incomplete, overlooking the important role that resources such as the mass media or international alliances play in the success or failure of a social movement (Jenkins & Perrow, 1977; McCarthy & Zald, 1977; Olzak & West, 1991). Canada's Aboriginal peoples have been particularly adept at gaining media coverage and winning support for their cause in the United States, Europe, and the United Nations, and among the Canadian public.

CHECK YOUR LEARNING According to structural strain theory, what six factors encourage the formation of social movements? What are two criticisms of this theory?

RESOURCE MOBILIZATION THEORY *Resource mobilization theory* points out that no social movement is likely to succeed—or even get off the ground—without substantial resources, including money, human labour, office and communications equipment, access to the mass media, and a positive public image. In short, any social movement rises or falls on how well it attracts resources, mobilizes people, and forges alliances.

Outsiders can be just as important as insiders in affecting the outcome of a social movement. Because socially disadvantaged people, by definition, lack the money, contacts, leadership skills, and organizational know-how that a successful movement requires, sympathetic outsiders fill the resource gap. In North America, well-to-do White people, including university and college students, joined the Black civil rights movement in the 1960s, and many affluent men have joined women as leaders of the women's movement.

Resources that connect people are also vital. The 1989 prodemocracy movement in China was fuelled by students, whose location on campuses clustered together in

SOCIAL MOVEMENTS CAN BE INSPIRED AND ENERGIZED
BY POWERFUL VISUAL IMAGES In June 1972, a photo of
children running from a napalm strike on their village in South
Vietnam made headline news. The image of the girl in the middle
of the picture, who had ripped the flaming clothes from her body,
mobilized Americans and people around the world in a social
movement opposing the war in Vietnam.

Beijing allowed them to build networks and recruit new
members (Zhao, 1998). More recently, the internet, including Facebook and Twitter, was an important resource that
helped organizations to mobilize hundreds of thousands
of people who took part in the political movements in

PEACE ACTIVIST KIM PHÚC PHAN THI, WHO NOW LIVES IN
THE TORONTO AREA WITH HER HUSBAND AND TWO SONS,
WAS THE GIRL IN THE FAMOUS PHOTOGRAPH Kim Phúc
endured 14 months in hospital and 17 surgeries before returning
to her village. She was educated in Vietnam and in Cuba after
the evacuation of Saigon, and asked for political asylum for
herself and her new husband when their plane landed in Gander,
Newfoundland, to refuel. She founded the Kim Foundation
International to help children who are victims of war, was named
a UNESCO Goodwill Ambassador, and in 2004 was honoured with
a Doctorate of Law from York University in Toronto.

many nations in the Middle East (Earl & Kimport, 2011;
Preston, 2011). Advanced communications technology
was also crucial to the development of social movements
in other countries—witness the activists in Egypt who
communicated and launched a social movement through
Facebook.

The availability of organizing ideas online has helped
many social movements to grow over time. Take Back the
Night, for example, is an annual occasion for rallies in
Canada and the United States at which people speak out
in opposition to violence against women, children, and
families. Using online resources, even a small number of
people can plan and carry out an effective political event
(Packer, 2003; Passy & Giugni, 2001).

EVALUATE

Resource mobilization theory recognizes that resources as well
as discontent are necessary to the success of a social movement. Research confirms the importance of forging alliances to
gain resources and notes that movements with few resources
may, in desperation, turn to violence to call attention to their
cause (Grant & Wallace, 1991; Jenkins et al., 2003).

Critics of this theory counter that "outside" people and
resources are not always needed to ensure a movement's success. They argue that even relatively powerless segments of
a population can promote change if they are able to organize
effectively and have strongly committed members (Donnelly &
Majka, 1998). Aldon Morris (1981) adds that the success of the
civil rights movement of the 1950s and 1960s was the result of
Black people drawing mostly on their own skills and resources.
A second problem with this theory is that it overstates the extent
to which powerful people are willing to challenge the status quo.
Some rich White people did provide valuable resources to the
Black civil rights movement, but, probably more often, elites
were indifferent or opposed to significant change (McAdam,
1982, 1983; Pichardo, 1995).

CHECK YOUR LEARNING What is the basic idea of resource
mobilization theory? What are the criticisms of this theory?

CULTURE THEORY In recent years, sociologists have
developed *culture theory*, the recognition that social movements depend not only on material resources and the
structure of political power but also on cultural symbols.
That is, people in any particular situation are likely to
mobilize to form a social movement only to the extent
that they develop "shared understandings of the world
that legitimate and motivate collective action" (McAdam
et al., 1996:6; see also Williams, 2002).

In part, mobilization depends on a sense of injustice,
as suggested by deprivation theory; in addition, people
must come to believe that they are not able to respond to
their situation effectively by acting alone.

Social movements gain strength as they develop
symbols and a sense of community that both build strong

EFFORTS TO CONTROL THE PROCESS OF GLOBAL WARMING ARE A CURRENT EXAMPLE OF A NEW SOCIAL MOVEMENT This movement gained ground because of the involvement of former U.S. Vice-President Al Gore, who has focused public attention on the harmful effects of change to Earth's climate.

feelings and direct energy into organized action. Media images of the burning World Trade Center towers after the terrorist attacks on September 11, 2001, helped mobilize people to support the "war against terrorism." Photos of gay couples celebrating their weddings have helped fuel both the gay rights movement and the countermovement trying to prevent the extension of same-sex marriage rights. Likewise, images of First Nations barricades at Oka, Caledonia, and other places fuel their rights movement and agitate those who feel that Canada's Aboriginal peoples are a pampered lot who deserve no special treatment. Colourful rubber bracelets are now used by at least a dozen social movements to encourage people to show support for various causes.

EVALUATE

A strength of culture theory is the reminder that social movements depend not just on material resources but also on cultural symbols. At the same time, powerful symbols—such as the flag and ideas about patriotism and respecting our leaders—help support the status quo. How and when symbols turn people from supporting the system toward protest against it are questions in need of further research.

CHECK YOUR LEARNING State the basic idea of the culture theory of social movements. What is the main criticism of this theory?

POLITICAL ECONOMY THEORY Marxist *political economy theory* also has something to say about social movements. From this point of view, social movements arise within capitalist societies because capitalism fails to meet the needs of the majority of people. Despite great economic productivity, Canadian society has had

to deal with separatism in Quebec, an ailing—and hotly debated—health care system, and unrelenting poverty, especially in Aboriginal communities.

Social movements arise in response to such conditions. Workers organize to demand higher wages or better working conditions, and young people from around the world gather to protest (and attempt to shut down) economic summits like the one proposing a Free Trade Agreement of the Americas held in Quebec City in 2001. Environmentalists and First Nations joined forces to stop the development and expansion of pipelines through northern and southern British Columbia or to established refineries in Ontario and points east. The 94 recommendations of the Truth and Reconciliation Commission and the newly-embraced UN Declaration on the Rights of Indigenous Peoples provide greater legitimacy to such Indigenous/environmental social movements.

EVALUATE

A strength of political economy theory is its macro-level approach. Other theories explain the rise of social movements in terms of traits of individuals (such as weak social ties or a sense of relative deprivation) or traits of movements (such as their available resources); this approach focuses on the institutional structures of society itself (i.e., the economic and political systems). This approach does explain social movements concerned with economic issues, but it is less helpful in understanding the recent rise of social movements concerned with such non-economic issues as obesity, animal rights, abortion, or physician-assisted death.

CHECK YOUR LEARNING State the basic idea of the political economy theory of social movements. What is the main criticism of this theory?

NEW SOCIAL MOVEMENTS THEORY A final theoretical approach addresses what are often called "new" social movements. *New social movements theory* suggests that recent social movements in the post-industrial societies of North America and Western Europe have a new focus (Jenkins & Wallace, 1996; McAdam et al., 1996; Pakulski, 1993).

First, older social movements, such as those led by labour organizations, are concerned mostly with economic issues. New social movements, however, tend to focus on improving our social and physical surroundings. The environmental movement, for example, is trying to stop global warming or climate change and address other environmental dangers.

Second, most of today's social movements are international, focusing on global ecology, the social standing of women and gay people, animal rights, and opposition to war. In other words, as the process of globalization links the world's nations, social movements are becoming global. This is illustrated by the gathering of protesters (from North America, South America, and Europe) in Quebec City in April 2001. They converged on the third Summit of the Americas to prevent the creation of the Free Trade Agreement of the Americas. Although there were subsequent meetings of the 36 countries involved, the FTAA never materialized—in part due to the Quebec City protests.

Third, most social movements of the past drew strong support from working-class people, but new social movements that focus on non-economic issues usually draw support from the middle and upper-middle classes. Many affluent people tend to be conservative on economic issues (because they have wealth to protect), but liberal on social issues (partly because of extensive education). In rich nations, the number of highly educated professionals—the people who are most likely to support new social movements—is increasing, a fact that suggests these movements are with us to stay (Jenkins & Wallace, 1996; Rose, 1997).

EVALUATE

One strength of new social movements theory is recognizing that social movements have become international along with the global economy. This theory also highlights the power of the mass media and new information technology to unite people around the world in pursuit of political goals.

However, critics claim that this approach exaggerates the differences between past and present social movements. The women's movement today, for example, focuses on many of the same issues—workplace conditions and pay—that have concerned women and labour organizations for decades. Similarly, opponents of the Free Trade Agreement of the Americas were concerned about economic issues, albeit at the global level.

CHECK YOUR LEARNING   How do "new" social movements differ from the "old" ones?

Each of the seven theories presented here offers some explanation for the emergence of social movements. The Summing Up table outlines them all.

Gender and Social Movements

Gender figures prominently in the operation of social movements. In keeping with traditional ideas about gender, more men than women tend to take part in public life—including running for political office and spearheading social movements.

While investigating Freedom Summer, a 1964 voter registration project in Mississippi, Doug McAdam (1992) found that movement members considered the job of registering African-American voters in a hostile White community dangerous and therefore defined it as "men's work." Many of the women in the movement, despite more years of activist experience, ended up working in clerical or teaching assignments behind the scenes. Only the most exceptionally talented and committed women, McAdam found, were able to overcome the movement's gender barriers.

In short, women have played leading roles in many social movements (including abolitionist and feminist movements), but male dominance has been the norm even in social movements that oppose other elements of the status quo. At the same time, the political movement that brought change to Egypt included women as well as men in the leadership, suggesting a trend toward greater gender equality (Herda-Rapp, 1998; MacFarquhar, 2011).

SUMMING UP

Theories of Social Movements

Deprivation Theory	People experiencing relative deprivation begin social movements. The social movement is a means of seeking change that brings participants greater benefits. Social movements are especially likely when rising expectations are frustrated.
Mass Society Theory	People who lack established social ties are mobilized into social movements. Periods of social breakdown are likely to spawn social movements. The social movement gives members a sense of belonging and social participation.
Culture Theory	People are drawn to a social movement by cultural symbols that define some cause as just. The movement itself usually becomes a symbol of power and justice.
Resource Mobilization Theory	People may join for all of the reasons noted above and also because of social ties to existing members. But the success or failure of a social movement depends largely on the resources available to it. Also important is the extent of opposition within the larger society.
Structural Strain Theory	People come together because of their shared concern about the inability of society to operate as they believe it should. The growth of a social movement reflects many factors, including a belief in its legitimacy and some precipitating event that provokes action.
Political Economy Theory	People unite to address the societal ills caused by capitalism, including unemployment, poverty, and inequality of opportunity. Social movements are necessary because a capitalist economy inevitably fails to meet people's basic needs.
New Social Movements Theory	People who join social movements are motivated by quality of life, not necessarily economic concerns. Mobilization is national or international in scope. New social movements arise in response to the expansion of the mass media and new information technology.

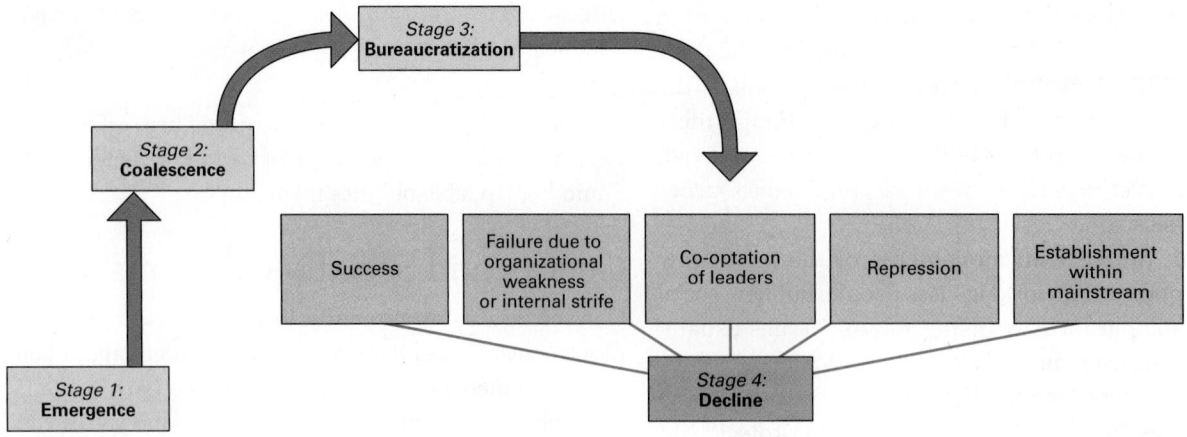

Figure 23–2 Stages in the Life of Social Movements

Social movements typically go through four stages before declining.

SOURCE: Based on Blumer, Herbert G. "Collective Behaviour." In Alfred McClung Lee, ed, Principles of Sociology. 3rd ed. New York: Barnes & Noble Books, 1969:65-121.; Mauss, Armand L. Social Problems of Social Movements. Philadelphia: Lippincott, 1975.; Tilly, Charles. From Mobilization to Revolution. Reading, Mass.: Addison – Wesley, 1978.

Stages in Social Movements

Despite the many differences that set one social movement apart from another, all unfold in roughly the same way, as shown in Figure 23–2. Researchers have identified four different stages in the life of the typical social movement (Blumer, 1969; Mauss, 1975; Tilly, 1978).

STAGE 1: EMERGENCE Social movements are driven by the perception that all is not well. Some, such as the civil rights and women's movements, are born of widespread dissatisfaction. Others emerge only as a small vanguard increases public awareness of some issue, as gay activists did with respect to the threat posed by HIV/AIDS.

STAGE 2: COALESCENCE After emerging, a social movement must define itself clearly and develop a strategy for "going public." Leaders must determine policies, select tactics, build morale, and recruit new members. At this stage, the movement may engage in collective action, such as rallies or demonstrations, to attract media attention and public notice. The movement may also form alliances with other organizations to gain necessary resources.

STAGE 3: BUREAUCRATIZATION To become an established political force, a social movement must assume bureaucratic traits. As it becomes routinized, a social movement depends less on the charisma and talents of a few leaders, instead relying more on a capable staff. When social movements do not become established in this way, they risk dissolving once the leader steps down. For example, many activist organizations on university campuses during the late 1960s were energized by a single charismatic leader and, consequently, did not last long. On the other hand, the National Action Committee on the Status of Women, despite changing leadership, is well established and offers a steady voice on behalf of

feminists in Canada. Canada's environmental movement has reached the bureaucratization stage in that we have an environmental ministry and a wide range of environmental organizations.

But becoming more bureaucratic can also hurt a social movement. Surveying the fate of various social movements, Piven and Cloward (1977) found that leaders sometimes become so engrossed in building an organization that they neglect the need to keep people "fired up" for change. In such cases, the radical edge of protest is lost.

STAGE 4: DECLINE Eventually, most social movements lose their influence. Frederick Miller (1983) suggests four reasons why this may occur:

First, if members have met their goals, decline may simply signal success. For example, the women's suffrage movement disbanded after it won the right for women to vote (in Canada and the United States). But, as was the case with the modern women's movement, winning one victory can lead to the embrace of new goals (such as employment, pay equity, or equal representation in Parliament).

Second, a social movement may fold because of organizational failures, such as poor leadership, loss of interest among members, insufficient funds, or repression by authorities. Some people lose interest when the excitement of early efforts is replaced by formal routines. Fragmentation by internal conflicts over goals and tactics is another common problem. Political parties with radical goals like those of the Parti Québécois—formed in 1968 with Quebec sovereignty as its central aim—can lose some of their more committed and activist members when they have to modify their platforms, however temporarily, to govern or to ensure re-election.

Third, a social movement can fall apart if the established power structure, through offers of money, prestige, and other rewards, diverts leaders from their goals—in other words, by co-optation or "selling out." Organizational leaders may use their positions to enrich themselves or may simply shift attention to mainstream careers once initial movement goals are met. For example, the former poverty activist and head of the Daily Bread food bank in Toronto, Gerard Kennedy, entered politics—becoming a Liberal Cabinet minister in Ontario and a political "insider," before spending much of 2006 as a candidate for the leadership of the federal Liberal Party. By contrast, some people leave lucrative or high-prestige occupations to become activists: Cat Stevens, a rock star in the 1970s, became a Muslim, changed his name to Yusuf Islam, and now promotes his religion. Stephen Lewis left Ontario politics, where he was the opposition leader, to be an activist dedicated to turning the tide of HIV/AIDS in Africa.

Fourth and finally, a social movement can collapse because of repression. Officials may crush a social movement by frightening away participants, discouraging new recruits, and even imprisoning leaders. In general, the more revolutionary the social movement, the more officials try to repress it. In Canada in the 1960s, the FLQ—a revolutionary movement aiming for an independent socialist Quebec—used bombs, kidnapping, and murder to promote its cause. In response, Prime Minister Pierre Trudeau invoked the *War Measures Act* in peacetime to suspend civil liberties and facilitate the arrest of FLQ members and sympathizers. By 1971, the FLQ had folded.

Another reason for decline, beyond those noted by Miller, is that a social movement may "go mainstream." Some movements become an accepted part of the system—typically after realizing some of their goals—to the point where they no longer challenge the status quo. The Canadian and American labour movements are now well-established parts of mainstream society; the leaders control large organizations and vast sums of money so they now have more in common with the business tycoons they once opposed than with rank-and-file workers. Until 1990, the government of South Africa, for example, banned the African National Congress (ANC), which was then a political organization seeking to overthrow the state-supported system of apartheid. Even suspected members of the ANC were subject to arrest. In 1990, the government lifted the decades-old ban and released ANC leader Nelson Mandela from prison; in 1994, Mandela became president of South Africa, by then a country moving away from apartheid.

Social Movements and Social Change

Social movements exist to encourage or to resist social change. The political life of our society is based largely on the claims and counterclaims of social movements that identify problems and suggest the right solutions.

Gender equality, still only partially realized, has been advanced by the actions of numerous women's groups in Canada and elsewhere. The gay rights movement achieved important goals in the past two decades—notably same-sex marriage—and will undoubtedly press on to advance new goals. Environmentalists, as well, have experienced major successes and have changed public awareness dramatically. The fact that the media, educators—from preschool to university—and politicians have joined the fight against global warming or climate change is clear evidence of the environmental movement's success.

Sometimes we overlook the success of past social movements and take for granted the changes that other people struggled so hard to win. Beginning a century ago, workers' movements fought to end child labour in factories, limit working hours, make the workplace safer, and establish the right to bargain collectively with employers. In addition, women now enjoy greater legal rights and economic opportunities because of the battles won by earlier generations of women.

Social Movements: Looking Ahead

Especially since the turbulent decade of the 1960s—a decade marked by widespread social protests—Canadian society has been pushed and pulled by many social movements and countermovements. Sometimes tension explodes into violence, as with the Oka standoff described at the beginning of this chapter. In other cases, the struggles are more restrained, as with mobilization for and against gay and lesbian—or LGBTQ—rights or Quebec independence (see the Controversy and Debate box). Of course, definitions of the problem and proposed solutions may differ, but social movements and the problems they address are always *political* (Macionis, 2013).

For three reasons, the scope of social movements is likely to increase. First, protest should increase as women, visible minorities, Aboriginal peoples, gays, lesbians, and other historically disadvantaged categories of people strengthen their political voices. Thus, the twenty-first century should be marked by more social movements than ever before. Second, at a global level, anyone with a television, personal computer, or cell phone can stay abreast of political events, often as they happen. Finally, new technology and the emerging global economy mean that social movements are now uniting people throughout the entire world—or throughout Marshall McLuhan's "global village." Since many problems are global in scope, we can expect the emergence of international social movements attempting to solve them.

Controversy and Debate

Are You Willing to Take a Stand?

Are you satisfied with our society as it is? Indeed, despite the fact that 92 percent of Canadians claim to be "very happy" or "pretty happy," there are many things that people would change about our way of life. Pessimism about our society is widespread. About 70 percent of Canadians believe that, in financial terms, the lot of the average person is getting worse. Only a quarter of us have "a great deal" or "quite a bit" of confidence, respectively, in our federal and provincial leaders. We feel that the rich, corporations, and politicians have too much power, and that politicians are paid too much. We fear crime. And 85 percent of us believe that the "courts do not deal harshly enough with criminals." Although these observations were made by Reginald Bibby in 1995 (Bibby, 1995), the sentiments are with us today.

When asked if people who commit crimes with handguns should face minimum 10-year sentences, 58 percent of Canadians agree. Up to 60 percent of Canadians do not trust politicians; 46 percent worry that they would not be able to meet expenses if they were to become critically ill; and 40 percent feel stressed because life is beyond control and the world is changing too quickly (Bricker & Wright, 2005).

But are we willing to take a stand to bring about social change? How many of us are willing to serve on a picket line or barricade, march in protest or in a gay pride parade, vote against our preferred party in the House of Commons, or tie ourselves to a tree to stop clear-cutting? Certainly, there are good reasons to avoid political controversy. Any time we challenge the system—whether on campus, at work, or in the larger political arena—we risk making enemies, losing a job, or perhaps even sustaining physical injury. By definition, challenging the status quo means stepping on powerful toes. For Canadians, who, traditionally, have deferred to authority more readily than Americans, such challenges in themselves may have appeared to question basic values. However, time marches on as indicated by our opening figure; when asked if they had ever participated in a "lawful, peaceful demonstration," 26.3 percent of Canadians but only 15.1 percent of Americans said that they had done so (Inglehart et al., 2013).

While it may be the case that only a small percentage of Canadians are willing to take a stand publicly on specific issues, there have been some highly visible and well-publicized instances of Canadians joining in collective action to address social problems. For example, in October 1995, three days before the referendum on sovereignty in Quebec, an estimated 150 000 Canadians from across Canada gathered at a massive "no" rally in Montreal to express their solidarity with the people of Quebec. Despite the fact that airlines and buses offered cut rates, participation required significant sacrifices. Families disrupted their routines, and people took time off from work or school. Some analysts felt that the outpouring of support from the rest of Canada

Ryan Remiorz/The Canadian Press

A RALLY HELD IN MONTREAL IN OCTOBER 1995 ENCOURAGED QUEBECERS TO VOTE "NO" IN THE SOVEREIGNTY REFERENDUM.

touched Quebecers and may have helped to bring about the "photo finish" in favour of the "no" side. Others pointed out that many Quebecers were outraged by outside interference in their affairs. In any case, Quebec's chief electoral officer declared that the politicians and corporations who organized the rally acted in contravention of Quebec's referendum laws and, therefore, behaved illegally.

Some may argue, in light of cultural values emphasizing the responsibility of individuals for their own well-being, that collective action is no remedy for social ills. Sociology, of course, poses a counterpoint to this cultural individualism. As C. Wright Mills (1959) pointed out decades ago, many of the problems we encounter as individuals are caused by the structure of society. Mills maintained that solutions to many of life's challenges depend on collective effort—that is, on people willing to join together to take a stand for their beliefs.

What Do You Think?

1. Does the reluctance of Canadians to address problems through collective action mean that they are basically satisfied with their lives and their society?

2. Have you ever participated in a political demonstration? What were its goals? What did it accomplish?

3. Identify ways in which life today has been affected by people who took a stand in the past. Think about race and ethnic relations, the environment, the status of women, and conditions of employment.

Seeing Sociology in Everyday Life

CHAPTER 23 Collective Behaviour and Social Movements

What is the scope of today's social movements?

Social movements are about trying to create (or resist) change. Some movements have a local focus, others are national in scope, and still others tackle international or global issues.

> **Hint** Every social movement makes a claim about how the world should be. In just about every case, some people disagree, perhaps giving rise to a countermovement. Whatever the goal of the movement (lesbian and gay rights, financial aid or concessions to the world's poorest countries, fighting HIV/AIDS in Africa or elsewhere), there will always be people who oppose its efforts. It is worth remembering that, to the extent that we are part of the "global village" (as Marshall McLuhan would say), local problems in any part of the world have implications for the rest of us.

IN 2005, THE LESBIAN AND GAY RIGHTS MOVEMENT ACHIEVED A VERY IMPORTANT GOAL—THE GOVERNMENT OF CANADA REDEFINED MARRIAGE FROM THE UNION OF A MAN AND A WOMAN TO THE UNION OF TWO PERSONS, THEREBY LEGALIZING SAME-SEX MARRIAGE The movement has gone on to fight for the rights of transgendered individuals.

BONO CAME TO TORONTO IN 2003 TO ATTEND A LIBERAL PARTY CONVENTION He had joined the Drop the Debt campaign—which aims to get rich countries to forgive the debt owed to them by the world's poorest countries—and was there to make sure that Canada's prime minister, Paul Martin, was on board.

AVRIL LAVIGNE AND SARAH MCLACHLAN PERFORMED IN THE UNITED AGAINST AIDS CONCERT IN MONTREAL (SEPTEMBER 2007)—AN EVENT HOSTED BY BEN MULRONEY These celebrities were part of a larger social movement aimed at treating and eliminating HIV/AIDS.

Seeing Sociology in *Your* Everyday Life

1. With 10 friends, try this experiment. One person writes down a detailed "rumour" about someone important and then whispers it to the second person, who whispers it to the third, and so on. The last person to hear the rumour writes it down again. Compare the two written versions of the rumour. Are you surprised by the results of your experiment? Why?

2. With other members of the class, identify recent fads or fad products. What makes people want them? Why do people lose interest in them so quickly?

3. What social movements are represented by organizations on your campus? Talk to some of their leaders about the goals and strategies of their groups.

Making the Grade

CHAPTER 23 Collective Behaviour and Social Movements

Studying Collective Behaviour

23.1 Distinguish various types of collective behaviour.

Collective behaviour differs from group behaviour:

- Collectivities contain people who have little or no social interaction.
- Collectivities have no clear social boundaries.
- Collectivities generate weak and unconventional norms.

social movement organized activity that encourages or discourages social change.
collective behaviour activity involving a large number of people, often spontaneous, and usually in violation of established norms
collectivity a large number of people whose minimal interaction occurs in the absence of well-defined and conventional norms

Localized Collectivities: Crowds

23.2 Identify five types of crowds and three explanations of crowd behaviour.

Crowds, an important type of collective behaviour, take various forms:

- casual crowds
- conventional crowds
- expressive crowds
- acting crowds
- protest crowds

Mobs and Riots

Crowds that become emotionally intense can create violent mobs and riots.

- Mobs pursue a specific goal; rioting involves unfocused destruction.
- Crowd behaviour can threaten the status quo, which is why crowds have figured heavily in social change throughout history.

Theories of Crowd Behaviour

Social scientists have developed several explanations of crowd behaviour:

- **Contagion theory** views crowds as anonymous, suggestible, and swayed by rising emotions.
- **Convergence theory** states that crowd behaviour reflects the desires people bring to them.
- **Emergent-norm theory** suggests that crowds develop their own behaviour as events unfold.

crowd a temporary gathering of people who share a common focus of attention and who influence one another
mob a highly emotional crowd that pursues a violent or destructive goal
riot a social eruption that is highly emotional, violent, and undirected

Dispersed Collectivities: Mass Behaviour

23.3 Describe rumour, disasters, and other types of mass behaviour.

Rumour and Gossip

Rumour—unconfirmed information that people spread informally—thrives in a climate of uncertainty and is difficult to stop.

- Rumour, which involves public issues, can trigger the formation of crowds or other collective behaviour.
- Gossip is rumour about people's personal affairs.

Public Opinion and Propaganda

Public opinion consists of people's positions on important, controversial issues.

- Public attitudes change over time, and at any time on any given issue, a small share of people will hold no opinion at all.
- Special-interest groups and political leaders try to shape public attitudes by using **propaganda.**

Fashions and Fads

People living in industrial societies use fashion as a source of social prestige.

- Fads are more unconventional than fashions; although people may follow a fad with enthusiasm, it usually goes away in a short time.
- Fashions reflect basic cultural values, which make them more enduring.

Panic and Mass Hysteria

A panic (in a local area) and mass hysteria (across an entire society) are types of collective behaviour in which people respond to a significant event, real or imagined, with irrational, frantic, and often self-destructive behaviour.

Disasters

Disasters are generally unexpected events that cause great harm to many people. Disasters are of three types:

- *natural disasters* (Example: the 2015 earthquake in Nepal)

- *technological disasters* (Example: the Lac-Mégantic runaway train and crude oil explosion, 2013)
- *intentional disasters* (Example: Syrian conflict and plight of the refugees, 2015)

---

mass behaviour collective behaviour among people spread over a wide geographic area

rumour unconfirmed information that people spread informally, often by word of mouth

gossip rumour about people's personal affairs

public opinion widespread attitudes about controversial issues

propaganda information presented with the intention of shaping public opinion

fashion a social pattern favoured by a large number of people

fad an unconventional social pattern that people embrace briefly but enthusiastically

panic a form of collective behaviour in which people in one place react to a threat or other stimulus with irrational, frantic, and often self-destructive behaviour

mass hysteria (moral panic) a form of dispersed collective behaviour in which people react to a real or imagined event with irrational and even frantic fear

disaster an event, generally unexpected, that causes extensive harm to people and damage to property

---

Social Movements

23.4 Analyze the causes and consequences of social movements.

Social movements are an important type of collective behaviour.

- Social movements try to promote or discourage change, and they often have a lasting effect on society.

Types of Social Movements

Sociologists classify social movements according to the range of people they try to involve and the extent of change they try to accomplish:

- *Alterative social movements* seek limited change in specific individuals. (Example: Planned Parenthood)
- *Redemptive social movements* seek radical change in specific individuals. (Example: Alcoholics Anonymous)
- *Reformative social movements* seek limited change in the whole society. (Example: the environmental movement in its fight against climate change)

- *Revolutionary social movements* seek radical change in the whole society. (Example: Quebec separatism)

Explaining of Social Movements

- *Deprivation theory:* Social movements arise among people who feel deprived of something, such as income, safe working conditions, or political rights.
- *Mass-society theory:* Social movements attract socially isolated people who join a movement in order to gain a sense of identity and purpose.
- *Culture theory:* Social movements depend not only on money and resources but also on cultural symbols that motivate people.
- *Resource-mobilization theory:* Success of a social movement is linked to available resources, including money, labour, and the mass media.
- *Structural-strain theory:* A social movement develops as the result of six factors. Clearly stated grievances encourage the formation of social movements; undirected anger, by contrast, promotes rioting.
- *Political-economy theory:* Social movements arise within capitalist societies that fail to meet the needs of a majority of people.
- *New social movements theory:* Social movements in post-industrial societies are typically international in scope and focus on quality-of-life issues.

Stages in Social Movements

A typical social movement proceeds through consecutive stages:

- *emergence* (defining the public issue)
- *coalescence* (entering the public arena)
- *bureaucratization* (becoming formally organized)
- *decline* (due to failure or, sometimes, success)

---

social movement an organized activity that encourages or discourages social change

claims making the process of trying to convince the public and public officials of the importance of joining a social movement to address a particular issue

relative deprivation a perceived disadvantage arising from some specific comparison

Chapter 24
Social Change: Traditional, Modern, and Postmodern Societies

Bloomberg/Getty Images

Learning Objectives

24.1 State four defining characteristics of social change.

24.2 Explain how culture, conflict, ideas, and population patterns direct social change.

24.3 Apply the ideas of Tönnies, Durkheim, Weber, and Marx to our understanding of modernity.

24.4 Contrast analysis of modernity as mass society and as class society.

24.5 Discuss postmodernism as one type of social criticism.

24.6 Evaluate possible directions of future social change.

The Power of Society
to shape our view of science

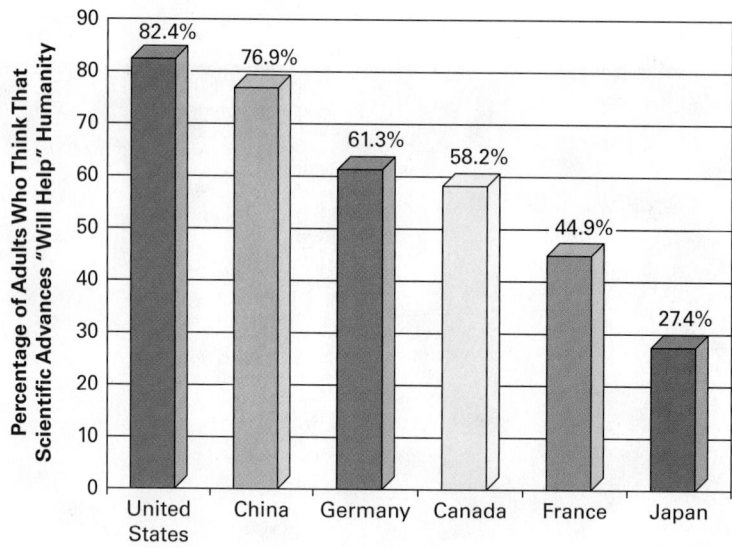

Survey Question: "In the long run, do you think the scientific advances we are making will help or harm humanity?"

SOURCE: Data from World Values Survey.

Doesn't everyone agree that science is useful to humanity? Americans overwhelmingly—at 82 percent—have faith in science; in fact, they are more likely than any other country to claim that scientific advances benefit humanity. Most European countries as well as Canada are more divided over whether science is helpful or harmful. Among high-income countries, the Japanese (the only people to experience the horrors of the atomic bomb in war) are least positive about the impacts of science. Clearly, attitudes about scientific advances and other dimensions of change are not simply personal; they also reflect the type of society in which one lives.

Chapter Overview

This chapter explores social change, explaining how modern societies differ from earlier traditional societies. It begins by describing the process of social change and identifying many of its causes.

Firelight flickers in the gathering darkness as Kanhonk sits, as he does at the end of the day, ready to begin an evening of animated talk and storytelling. Kanhonk is chief of the Kaiapo, about 7000 people indigenous to the Xingu River area of Brazil's Amazon rainforest. This is the hour when the Kaiapo celebrate their heritage; because the Kaiapo are a traditional people with no written language, the elders rely on evenings by the fire to teach their culture and instruct the grandchildren. In the past, evenings like this were filled with tales of brave Kaiapo warriors fighting off their neighbours or Portuguese traders in pursuit of slaves and gold.

As the minutes pass, only a few older villagers assemble for the evening ritual. "It is the Big Ghost," one man grumbles, to explain the poor turnout. The Big Ghost has indeed descended on them, its bluish glow spilling from windows of homes throughout the village. The Kaiapo children—and many adults as well—are watching television. Installing a satellite dish in the village several years ago has had greater consequences than anyone imagined. In the end, what their enemies failed to do with weapons, the Kaiapo may well do to themselves with prime-time programming.

Kaiapo are among 230 000 Indigenous people who inhabit Brazil. They stand out because of their striking body paint and ornate ceremonial dress. Recently, they have become rich from gold mining and the harvesting of mahogany trees. Now they must decide if their new-found fortune is a blessing or a curse. To some, affluence means the opportunity to learn about the outside world through travel and television. Others, like Chief Kanhonk, are not so sure.

Sitting by the fire, he thinks aloud: "I have been saying that people must buy useful things like knives and fishing hooks. Television does not fill the stomach. It only shows our children and grandchildren White people's things." The oldest priest, Bebtopup, nods in agreement: "The night is the time the old people teach the young people. Television has stolen the night" (Simons, 2007). ◼

The story about television in Kaiapo society raises profound questions about the causes and consequences of change. Kaiapo villagers may be edging toward modernity, but does a higher standard of living necessarily improve their lives? The drama that is changing Kaiapo life is being played out around the globe as more and more traditional cultures are being transformed by the materialism and affluence of rich societies.

Within Canada, people are grappling with similar issues—and the influence of television in particular. In Nunavut, Inuit were concerned about the damaging effects of television programming that originates in the south. With financial assistance from the federal government, they created the Inuit Broadcasting Corporation, which produces news, documentaries, children's programs (including cartoons and puppet shows), and talk shows that deal with issues of relevance to Inuit—in their own language, Inuktitut. Unlike the Kaiapo, through their own broadcasting, the Inuit have been able to mitigate some of the intrusive and damaging impacts of television on their culture. More recently, all Canadians have had access to the Aboriginal Peoples Television Network by cable or satellite. In January 2001, the network increased its international content from 10 to 30 percent to include more programming about Indigenous peoples around the world.

This chapter examines social change as a process with both positive and negative consequences. Of particular interest to us are *modernity*, changes brought about by the Industrial Revolution, and *postmodernity*, recent transformations sparked by the Information Revolution and the post-industrial economy. Whatever the consequences, one thing is clear—the rate of change has never been faster than it is now.

What Is Social Change?

24.1 State four defining characteristics of social change.

In earlier chapters, we examined relatively fixed or *static* social patterns, including status and role, social stratification, and social institutions. We also looked at the *dynamic* forces that have shaped our way of life, ranging from innovations in technology to the growth of bureaucracy and the expansion of cities. These are all dimensions of **social change**, *the transformation of culture and social institutions over time.* The process of social change has four major characteristics:

1. **Social change happens all the time.** "Nothing is constant except death and taxes" goes the old saying. Yet even our experience with death has changed dramatically as life expectancy doubled over the course of a century. In 1900, people paid little or no tax on their earnings; over the course of the twentieth century, taxes increased dramatically, along with the size and scope of government. In short, just about everything is subject to the twists and turns of change.

   Still, some societies change faster than others—hunter/gatherer societies change quite slowly, whereas members of today's high-income societies experience significant change within a single lifetime.

   It is also true that, in a given society, some cultural elements change faster than others. William Ogburn's (1964) theory of *cultural lag* states that material culture usually changes faster than nonmaterial culture; that is, things change faster than ideas and attitudes. For example, the genetic technology that allows scientists to alter and perhaps even to create life has developed more rapidly than our ethical standards for deciding when and how to use it.

2. **Social change is sometimes intentional but often unplanned.** Industrial societies actively promote many kinds of change. For example, scientists seek more efficient forms of energy, and advertisers try to convince us that life is incomplete without this or that new gadget. Yet rarely can anyone envision all of the consequences of the changes that are set in motion. In 1900, when people relied on horses for transportation, many people looked ahead to motorized vehicles that would carry them in a single day distances that took them weeks or months. But no one could see how much the mobility provided by automobiles would alter people's lives, scattering family members, threatening the environment, and reshaping cities and suburbs. Nor could automotive pioneers have predicted that close to 40 000 people would die each year as a result of car accidents in North America.

3. **Social change is controversial.** The history of the automobile shows that social change brings both good and bad consequences. Capitalists welcomed the Industrial Revolution because new technology increased productivity and swelled profits. However, workers feared that machines would make their skills obsolete and resisted the push toward "progress."

   Today, as in the past, changing patterns of social interaction between racial and ethnic minorities and the majority, between women and men, and between gays or lesbians and heterosexuals are welcomed by some people and opposed by others.

4. **Some changes matter more than others.** Some changes (such as clothing fads) have only passing significance; others (such as the invention of computers) may change the entire world. Will the Information Revolution turn out to be as important as the Industrial Revolution? Like the automobile and television, the computer has both positive and negative effects, providing new kinds of jobs while eliminating old ones, isolating people in offices while linking people in global electronic networks, offering vast amounts of information while threatening personal privacy.

Causes of Social Change

24.2 Explain how culture, conflict, ideas, and population patterns direct social change.

Social change has many causes. In a world linked by sophisticated communication and transportation technology, change in one place often sets off change elsewhere.

Culture and Change

There are three important sources of cultural change. First, *invention* produces new objects, ideas, and social patterns. Rocket propulsion research, which began in the 1940s, has produced spacecraft that reach toward the stars. Today we take such technology for granted; during this century, a significant number of people—not just astronauts—may well have the opportunity to travel in space.

Second, *discovery* occurs when people take note of existing elements of the world. Medical advances, for example, offer a growing understanding of the human body. Beyond their direct effects on human health, medical discoveries have stretched life expectancy, setting in motion the "greying" of society. Third, *diffusion* creates change as products, people, and information spread from one society to another. Ralph Linton (1937) recognized that many familiar elements of our culture came from other lands. Cloth used to make our clothing, for

THESE YOUNG MEN ARE PERFORMING IN A HIP-HOP DANCE MARATHON IN HONG KONG Hip-hop music, dress style, and dancing have become popular in Asia, a clear case of cultural diffusion. Social change occurs as cultural patterns move from place to place, but people in different societies don't always have the same understanding of what these patterns mean. How might Chinese youth understand hip-hop differently from the young African Americans who originated it?

example, was developed in Asia; the mechanical clocks we see all around us were invented in medieval Europe; and the coins we carry in our pockets were devised in what is now Turkey.

In general, material things diffuse more easily than cultural ideas. That is, new breakthroughs, such as the science of cloning, occur faster than our understanding of when—and even whether—they are morally desirable.

Conflict and Change

Inequality and conflict in a society also produce change. Karl Marx saw class conflict as the engine that drives societies from one historical era to another. In industrial-capitalist societies, he maintained, the struggle between capitalists and workers pushes society toward a socialist system of production. More than a century later, this model has proved simplistic. Yet Marx correctly foresaw that social conflict arising from inequality—involving not just class but also race and gender—would force changes in every society, including our own, to improve the lives of working people.

Ideas and Change

Max Weber also contributed to our understanding of social change. Although Weber agreed that conflict could bring about change, he traced the roots of most social change to ideas. For example, people with charisma—such as Martin Luther King, Jr.—can carry a message that changes the world.

Weber also highlighted the importance of ideas by showing how the religious beliefs of early Protestants set the stage for the spread of industrial capitalism. The fact that industrial capitalism developed primarily in areas of Western Europe where the Protestant work ethic was strong revealed to Weber (1958; orig. 1904–05) the power of ideas to bring about change.

Ideas also direct social movements. Change occurs when people join together in the pursuit of a common goal, such as cleaning up the environment or improving the lives of oppressed people.

Demographic Change

Population growth places escalating demands on the natural environment while altering cultural patterns. While Canada enjoys a bounty of physical space, urbanization and industrialization have changed our way of life and will continue to do so. More than three-quarters of Canadians live in cities, which cover only a small percentage of the land surface.

Profound change is also taking place as our population, collectively speaking, grows older. In 2011, more than 15 percent of Canadians were over age 65—more than double that proportion of the population in 1901. Statistics Canada estimates that, by 2031, seniors will account for almost *one-quarter* of the Canadian population. Medical research and health care services will increasingly focus on elderly people, and life will change in countless additional ways as homes and household products are redesigned to meet the needs of older consumers.

Migration within and among societies is another demographic factor that promotes change. Since the early 1800s, millions of people have come to Canada—initially to fish or participate in the fur trade or to establish farming homesteads, and more recently, to seek a better life in the growing urban areas. Immigrants to Canada's urban centres were joined by a steady flow of migrants from rural Canada, where high fertility and changes in the structure of agriculture resulted in surplus population. As a result of immigration and rural/urban migration, Canada's urban population grew from 18 percent of the total population in 1871 to 80 percent by 2011. In 140 years, Canada was transformed from a nation of settlers to an urban-industrial society with one of the world's largest economies.

Nave Nave Moe (Sacred Spring), 1894 (oil on canvas), Gauguin, Paul (1848–1903)/State Hermitage Museum, St. Petersburg, Russia/ Bridgeman Images

IN RESPONSE TO THE ACCELERATING PACE OF CHANGE IN THE NINE-TEENTH CENTURY, PAUL GAUGUIN LEFT HIS NATIVE FRANCE FOR THE SOUTH SEAS, WHERE HE WAS CAPTIVATED BY A SIMPLER AND SEEM-INGLY TIMELESS WAY OF LIFE He romanticized this environment in his painting *Nave Nave Moe (Sacred Spring)*.

Visions of Modernity

24.3 Apply the ideas of Tönnies, Durkheim, Weber, and Marx to our understanding of modernity.

A central concept in the study of social change is **modernity**, *changes brought about by the Industrial Revolution*. In everyday usage, *modernity* (its Latin root means "lately") refers to the present in relation to the past. Sociologists include in this catch-all concept all of the social patterns set in motion by the Industrial Revolution, which began in Western Europe in the 1750s. **Modernization**, then, is *the process of social change begun by industrialization.*

Four Dimensions of Modernization

Peter Berger (1977), in his influential study of social change, identified four major characteristics of modernization:

1. **The decline of small, traditional communities.** Modernity involves "the progressive weakening, if not destruction, of the … relatively cohesive communities in which human beings have found solidarity and meaning throughout most of history" (1977:72). For thousands of years, in the camps of hunters and gatherers and in the rural villages of Europe and North America, people lived in small communities where social life revolved around family and neighbourhood. Such traditional worlds gave each person

a well-defined place that, although limiting range of choice, offered a strong sense of identity, belonging, and purpose.

Canada has a land mass of close to 10 million square kilometres—second in size only to Russia—with a population density of just 2.8 persons per square kilometre. Since about 80 percent of our population lives within 160 kilometres of the U.S. border, there is a great deal of space through which to scatter other communities. Small, isolated communities—many with fewer than a hundred members, and many of them Aboriginal—still exist in Canada, but they are now home to only a small percentage of the overall Canadian population. Even so, cars, telephones, television, and the internet give most remote rural families the pulse of the larger society and connect them to the entire world.

2. **The expansion of personal choice.** Members of traditional, pre-industrial societies view their lives as shaped by forces beyond human control: gods, spirits, or simply fate. As the power of tradition weakens, people come to see their lives as an unending series of options, a process Berger calls *individualization*. Canadians, for example, may choose a lifestyle—or even adopt one after another, showing an openness to change. Indeed, a common belief in our modern culture is that people *should* take control of their lives.

Widespread support for greater personal choice has political consequences. A cultural orientation embracing individualism means that modern, high-income societies are likely to be democratic (Inglehart & Welzel, 2010).

3. **Increasing social diversity.** In pre-industrial societies, strong family ties and powerful religious beliefs enforce conformity and discourage diversity and change. Modernization promotes a more rational, scientific world view as tradition loses its hold and people gain more and more freedom of choice. The growth of cities, the expansion of impersonal bureaucracy, and the social mix of people from various backgrounds combine to foster diversity of belief and behaviour.

4. **Orientation toward the future and a growing awareness of time.** Pre-modern people focus on the past, but people in modern societies think more about the future. Modern people are not only forward-looking but also optimistic that new inventions and discoveries will improve their lives.

Traditional people organize their lives around sunlight and seasons. With the introduction of clocks in the late Middle Ages, Europeans began to think not in terms of sunlight and seasons but in terms of days, hours, and minutes. Preoccupied with personal gain, modern people demand precise measurement of time and are likely to agree that "time is money." Berger (inspired by Weber) points out that one good indicator of a society's degree of modernization is the extent to which people wear wristwatches.

Recall that modernization touched off the development of sociology itself. The discipline originated in the wake of the Industrial Revolution in Western Europe, where social change was proceeding most rapidly. Early European and American sociologists tried to analyze the rise of modern society and its consequences, good and bad, for human beings.

Finally, in comparing industrial societies with those that came before, it is easy to assume that *everything* in our world is new. Of course, this is not the case. The Sociology in Focus box on page 688 illustrates that fact with a historical look at a favourite form of modern clothing—jeans.

Ferdinand Tönnies: The Loss of Community

German sociologist Ferdinand Tönnies (1855–1937) produced a lasting account of modernization in his theory of *Gemeinschaft* and *Gesellschaft* Like Peter Berger, whose work he influenced, Tönnies (1963; orig. 1887) viewed modernization as the progressive loss of *Gemeinschaft,* or human community. As Tönnies saw it, the Industrial Revolution weakened the social fabric of family and tradition by introducing a businesslike emphasis on facts, efficiency, and money. European and North American societies gradually became rootless and impersonal as people came to associate mostly on the basis of self-interest—the state Tönnies termed *Gesellschaft.*

Early in the twentieth century, much of Canada approximated Tönnies's concept of *Gemeinschaft.* For generations, families lived in small villages and towns, bound together in a hardworking, slow-moving way of life. Telephones (invented in 1876) were rare; not until 1915 could one place a coast-to-coast call. Living without television—introduced commercially in the 1920s but not widespread until after 1950—families entertained themselves, often gathering with friends in the evening to share stories, sorrows, or song. Without rapid transportation—Henry Ford's assembly line began in 1908, but cars became commonplace only after World War II—your community was your entire world.

Inevitable tensions and conflicts divided these communities of the past. But, according to Tönnies, because of the traditional spirit of *Gemeinschaft,* people were "essentially united in spite of all separating factors" (1963:65; orig. 1887).

Modernity turns societies inside out so that, as Tönnies put it, people are "essentially separated in spite of uniting factors" (1963:65; orig. 1887). This is the world of *Gesellschaft,* where, especially in large cities, most people live among strangers and ignore the people they pass on the street. Trust is hard to come by in a mobile and anonymous society where people tend to put their personal needs ahead of group loyalty and, increasingly, adults believe "you can't be too careful" in dealing with others. No wonder researchers conclude that, even as we become more affluent, the social health of modern societies has declined (Myers, 2000).

The high level of geographic mobility in modern societies contributes to a sense of rootlessness. Over a single year, one in nine Canadians (12.4 percent) changes his or her place of residence. According to the National Household Survey of 2011 (see Table 24–1), 39 percent of Canadians had moved over the previous five-year period, 21 percent within the same municipality and 7 percent from outside the province, territory, or country. As you might expect, the people most likely to have moved are 25 to 34 years of age (70 percent); the least likely to have moved are aged 65 and older (18 percent). Among those young adults, 14 percent moved to their

GEORGE TOOKER'S 1950 PAINTING *THE SUBWAY* DEPICTS A COMMON PROBLEM OF MODERN LIFE: WEAKENING SOCIAL TIES AND ERODING TRADITIONS CREATE A GENERIC HUMANITY IN WHICH EVERYONE IS ALIKE YET EACH PERSON IS AN ANXIOUS STRANGER IN THE MIDST OF OTHERS.

Sociology in Focus

Tradition and Modernity: The History of Jeans

Sociologists like to contrast "tradition" and "modernity." Tönnies, Durkheim, Weber, and even Marx developed theories (discussed in various sections of this chapter) that contrasted social patterns that existed "then" with those that exist "now." Such theories are enlightening. But thinking in terms of "tradition versus modernity" encourages us to think that the past and the present have little in common.

All the thinkers discussed in this chapter saw past and present as strikingly different. But it is also true that countless elements of today's society—ranging from religion to warfare—have been part of human society for a very long time. It is also the case that many cultural elements that we think of as "modern" turn out to have been around much longer than many of us realize.

One element of today's culture, popular among today's college students, that we think of as distinctly modern is jeans. This piece of clothing, which is common enough to be considered almost a "uniform" among young people, moved to the centre of popular culture when it swept across the college campus in the late 1960s.

But many people would be surprised to learn that jeans have been worn for centuries. To understand more, consider the original meanings of the words used to define this type of clothing. The term *dungarees,* a common name for jeans before the 1960s, is derived from the Hindi word *dungri,* a district of the Indian city Mumbai (formerly Bombay) where the coarse cloth is thought to have originated. From there, the fabric spread westward into Europe. The term *jeans* can be traced back to the name of the Italian city of Genoa, where the cotton fabric was widely worn in the 1650s. Another word for the fabric, *denim,* refers to the French city of Nîmes, reflecting the fact that, somewhat later, people described the cloth as being "de Nîmes."

In art from the 1500s, we see poor people wearing "jeans." By the 1800s, jeans had become the uniform for the western cowboy. By the 1960s, jeans became the clothing of choice on the campus. More recently, corporate executives (especially in tech companies) have made jeans acceptable in the workplace.

Art historians have identified paintings from the sixteenth century that show people—typically the poor—wearing jeans. In the 1700s, British sailors used this fabric not only for making sails but also for constructing hammocks to sleep in and for fashioning shipboard clothing.

More than a century later, in 1853, U.S. clothing manufacturer Levi Strauss sold dungarees to miners who were digging for gold in the California gold rush. The familiar blue-and-white woven fabric is very strong and durable. Jeans became the clothing of choice among people who had limited budgets and who did demanding physical labour.

After gaining popularity among gold miners, jeans became popular among cowboys all across the western United States. By the beginning of the twentieth century, jeans were worn by almost all working people. By the 1930s, most prisoners across the country also wore denim.

This pattern made jeans a symbol of lower social standing. This fact is surely the reason that many middle-class people looked down on such clothing. As a result, especially in higher-income communities, public school officials banned the wearing of dungarees.

By the 1960s, however, a youth-based counterculture was emerging in the United States. This new cultural orientation rejected the older pattern of "looking upward" and copying the styles of the rich and famous and, instead, began "looking downward" and adopted the look of working people and even the down and out. By the end of the 1960s, rock stars, Hollywood celebrities, and college students favoured jeans as a way to make a statement that they identified with working people—part of the era's more left-leaning political attitudes.

Of course, there was money to be made in this new trend. By the 1980s, the fashion industry was cashing in on the popularity of jeans by promoting "designer jeans" among more well-off people who probably had never entered a factory in their lives. A teenage Brooke Shields helped launch Calvin Klein jeans (1980), which became all the rage among people who were able to spend three and four times as much on jeans as ordinary people.

Galerie Canesso

H. Mark Weidman Photography/Alamy Stock Photo

Mantel/Sipa/Newscom

IN ART FROM THE 1500S, WE SEE POOR PEOPLE WEARING "JEANS" By the 1800s, jeans had become the uniform for the western cowboy. By the 1960s, jeans became the clothing of choice on the campus. More recently, corporate executives (especially in tech companies) have made jeans acceptable in the workplace.

By the beginning of this century, jeans had become an accepted form of dress not only in schools but also in the corporate world. Many of the CEOs of U.S. corporations—especially in the high-tech fields—now routinely wear jeans to work and even to public events.

As you can see, jeans turn out to have a very long history. The fact that jeans existed both "then" and "now," all the while taking on new and different meanings, reveals the limitation of characterizing cultural elements as either "traditional" or "modern" in a world in which societies invent and reinvent their way of life all the time.

What Do You Think?

1. Is your attitude toward jeans different from that of your parents? If so, how and why?

2. Do you think the changing trend in the popularity of jeans suggests broader changes in our society before and after the 1960s? Explain.

3. How popular is wearing jeans on your campus? What about among your professors? Can you explain these patterns?

SOURCE: Based, in part, on Brazilian (2011).

new residences from *outside* the province or the country—compared to only 2 percent of the oldest cohort. These findings are consistent with earlier analysis based on the General Social Survey (Statistics Canada, 1985). Among Canadians, the most frequently stated reasons for moving were to purchase or build a home, to live in a larger home, to live in a better neighbourhood, to live near work, and to establish an independent household. Each of these top-ranked reasons is consistent with movement among young adults, who are leaving the homes of their parents, getting married, having children, and moving to larger homes to accommodate their children.

EVALUATE

Tönnies's theory of *Gemeinschaft* and *Gesellschaft* is the most widely cited model of modernization. The theory's strength lies in combining various dimensions of change: growing population, the rise of cities, and increasing impersonality in social interaction. But modern life, though often impersonal, still has some degree of *Gemeinschaft*. Even in a world of strangers, modern friendships can be strong and lasting. Some analysts also think that Tönnies favoured—perhaps even romanticized—traditional societies while overlooking bonds of family, neighbourhood, and friendship that continue to flourish in modern societies.

CHECK YOUR LEARNING As types of social organization, how do *Gemeinschaft* and *Gesellschaft* differ?

Table 24–1 Residential Mobility in the Five-year Period Prior to NHS 2011 by Age

Age	Movers* %	Non-migrants** %	Interprovincial and Extenal Migrants*** %
15–24 years of age	43.0	22.3	8.1
25–34 years of age	70.2	36.4	13.5
35–44 years of age	48.2	26.2	9.2
65 years and over	17.7	9.9	1.9
Total population	38.6	20.9	6.6

*Changed residence in the five years prior to NHS 2011.

** Moved within the same municipality.

*** Moved from another province/territory or from outside Canada.

SOURCE: Compilation and calculations by L.M. Gerber based on NHS 2011, Catalogue number 99-010-X2011036.

Émile Durkheim: The Division of Labour

French sociologist Émile Durkheim shared Tönnies's interest in the profound social changes that resulted from the Industrial Revolution. For Durkheim (1964b; orig. 1893), modernization is defined by an increasing **division of labour**, or *specialized economic activity*. Every member of a traditional society performs more or less the same daily round of activities; modern societies function by having people perform highly specific roles.

Durkheim explained that pre-industrial societies are held together by *mechanical solidarity,* or shared moral sentiments; in other words, members of pre-industrial societies view everyone as basically alike, doing the same kind of work and belonging together. Durkheim's concept of mechanical solidarity is virtually the same as Tönnies's *Gemeinschaft*. With modernization, the division of labour becomes more and more pronounced. To Durkheim, this change means less mechanical solidarity but more of another kind of tie: *organic solidarity,* or mutual dependency between people engaged in specialized work. Put simply, modern societies are held together not by likeness but by difference: All of us must depend on others to meet most of our needs. Organic solidarity corresponds to Tönnies's concept of *Gesellschaft*.

Despite obvious similarities in their thinking, Durkheim and Tönnies viewed modernity somewhat differently. To Tönnies, modern *Gesellschaft* amounts to the loss of social solidarity, because modern people lose the "natural" and "organic" bonds of the rural village, leaving only the "artificial" and "mechanical" ties of the big industrial city. Durkheim had a different view of modernity, even reversing Tönnies's language to bring home the point. Durkheim labelled modern society "organic," arguing that modern society is no less natural than any other, and he described traditional societies as "mechanical" because they are so regimented. Durkheim viewed modernization not as the loss of community but as a change from community based on bonds of likeness (kinship and neighbourhood) to community based on economic interdependence (the division of labour). Durkheim's view of modernity is thus both more complex and more positive than Tönnies's view.

EVALUATE Durkheim's work, which resembles that of Tönnies's, is a highly influential analysis of modernity. Of the two, Durkheim was more optimistic; still, he feared that modern societies might become so diverse that they would collapse into **anomie**, *a condition in which norms and values are so weak and inconsistent that society provides little moral guidance to individuals.* Living with weak moral norms, modern people can become egocentric, placing their own needs above those of others and finding little purpose in life.

Evidence supports Durkheim's contention that anomie plagues modern societies. Suicide rates, which Durkheim considered a prime index of anomie, have risen over the past century in both Canada and the United States; in Canada, the rates have doubled. Suicide rates are especially high in Aboriginal communities, which are still experiencing rapid social change.

Even though modernization is associated with numerous indicators of stress or distress, shared norms and values are still strong enough to give the majority of people a sense of meaning and purpose. Whatever the hazards of anomie, most people seem to value the personal freedom modern society gives us.

Check Your Learning Define mechanical and organic solidarity. In his view of the modern world, what makes Durkheim more optimistic than Tönnies?

Max Weber: Rationalization

For Max Weber, modernity meant replacing a traditional world view with a rational way of thinking. In pre-industrial societies, Weber explained, tradition acts as a constant brake on change. To traditional people, "truth" is roughly the same as "what has always been" (Weber, 1978:36; orig. 1921). To modern people, however, "truth" is the result of rational calculation. Because they value efficiency and have little reverence for the past, modern people adopt whatever social patterns allow them to achieve their goals.

Echoing Tönnies and Durkheim, who held that industrialization weakens tradition, Weber declared modern society to be "disenchanted." The unquestioned truths of an earlier time had been challenged by rational thinking. In short, modern society turns away from the gods. Throughout his life, Weber studied various modern "types"—the capitalist, the scientist, the bureaucrat— all of whom share the detached world view that Weber believed was coming to dominate humanity.

MAX WEBER MAINTAINED THAT THE DISTINCTIVE CHARACTER OF MODERN SOCIETY WAS ITS RATIONAL WORLD VIEW
Virtually all of Weber's work on modernity centred on types of people he considered typical of their age: the scientist, the capitalist, and the bureaucrat. Each is rational to the core: The scientist is committed to the orderly discovery of truth, the capitalist to the orderly pursuit of profit, and the bureaucrat to orderly conformity to a system of rules.

EVALUATE

Compared with Tönnies and especially Durkheim, Weber was critical of modern society. He knew that science could produce technological and organizational wonders but worried that science was turning us away from more basic questions about the meaning and purpose of human existence. Weber feared that rationalization, especially in bureaucracies, would erode the human spirit with endless rules and regulations.

Some of Weber's critics think that the alienation he attributed to bureaucracy actually stemmed from social inequality. That criticism leads us to the ideas of Karl Marx.

CHECK YOUR LEARNING How did Weber understand modernity? What does it mean to say that modern society (think of scientists, capitalists, and bureaucrats) is "disenchanted"?

Karl Marx: Capitalism

For Karl Marx, modern society was synonymous with capitalism; he saw the Industrial Revolution as primarily a capitalist revolution. Marx traced the emergence of the bourgeoisie in medieval Europe to the expansion of commerce. The bourgeoisie gradually displaced the feudal aristocracy as the Industrial Revolution gave it a powerful new productive system.

Marx agreed that modernity weakened small communities (as described by Tönnies), sharpened the division of labour (as noted by Durkheim), and fostered a rational world view (as Weber claimed). But he saw all of these simply as conditions necessary for capitalism to flourish. According to Marx, capitalism draws population from farms and small towns into an ever-expanding market system centred in cities, specialization is needed for efficient factories, and rationality is exemplified by the capitalists' endless pursuit of profit.

Earlier chapters have painted Marx as a spirited critic of capitalist society, but his vision of modernity also includes a good bit of optimism. Unlike Weber, who viewed modern society as an "iron cage" of bureaucracy, Marx believed that social conflict in capitalist societies would sow seeds of revolutionary change, leading to an egalitarian socialism. Such a society, as he saw it, would harness the wonders of industrial technology to enrich people's lives and also rid the world of social classes, the source of social conflict and so much suffering. Although Marx's evaluation of modern capitalist society was negative, he imagined a future of human freedom, creativity, and community.

EVALUATE

Marx's theory of modernization is a complex theory of capitalism. But he underestimated the dominance of bureaucracy in modern societies. In socialist societies in particular, the stifling effects of bureaucracy turned out to be as bad as, or even worse than, the dehumanizing aspects of capitalism. The upheavals in Eastern Europe and the former Soviet Union in the late 1980s and early 1990s reveal the depth of popular opposition to oppressive state bureaucracies.

CHECK YOUR LEARNING How did Marx understand modern society? Of the four theorists just discussed—Tönnies, Durkheim, Weber, and Marx—who was the most optimistic about modern society? Who was the most pessimistic? Explain your answer.

Theories of Modernity

24.4 Contrast analysis of modernity as mass society and a class society,

The rise of modernity is a complex process involving many dimensions of change, as described in the Summing Up table that appears on the following page. How can we make sense of so many changes going on all at once? Sociologists have developed two broad explanations of modern society, one guided by the structural-functional approach and one based on social-conflict theory.

Structural-Functional Theory: Modernity as Mass Society

One broad approach—drawing on the ideas of Ferdinand Tönnies, Émile Durkheim, and Max Weber—depicts modernization as the emergence of *mass society* (Berger et al., 1974; Kornhauser, 1959; Nisbet, 1966; Pearson, 1993). A **mass society** is *a society in which prosperity and bureaucracy have weakened traditional social ties.* A mass society is highly productive; on average, people have more income than ever. At the same time, it is marked by weak kinship and impersonal neighbourhoods, which contributes to social isolation. Although many people have material plenty, they are spiritually weak and often experience moral uncertainty about how to live.

THE MASS SCALE OF MODERN LIFE Mass-society theory argues, first, that the scale of modern life has greatly increased. Before the Industrial Revolution, Europe and North America formed a mosaic of countless rural villages and small towns. In these small communities, which inspired Tönnies's concept of *Gemeinschaft,* people lived out their lives surrounded by kin and guided by a shared heritage. Gossip was an informal yet highly effective way to ensure conformity to community standards. These small communities, with strong moral values and low tolerance of social diversity, exemplified the state of mechanical solidarity described by Durkheim.

For example, before 1690, English law demanded that everyone participate regularly in the Christian ritual of Holy Communion (Laslett, 1984); later, among the

Thinking Globally

Indonesian Democracy and Development: Welcome but Unexpected!

When Hans Bakker defended his Ph.D. thesis at the University of Toronto (in 1979) he did not feel very optimistic about the future of Indonesia, the country he had studied. He tried to understand Indonesia's underdevelopment and the powerful role of the military in administrative affairs. Its pre-colonial and colonial histories pointed to a lack of sufficient modern cultural capital and infrastructural development. Many scholars argued that colonialism and imperialism had significantly reduced the probability of Indonesian society escaping wide-scale poverty. Clifford Geertz even argued that agriculture had taken a few steps backwards during the nineteenth century—a phenomenon he called "involution." In the 1970s and 1980s it was not at all clear that the nation-state of Indonesia would undergo profound political and economic changes. The debates concerning "modernization" suggested that the global "South" would never really develop. The assumptions of modernization theorists like Walter Rostow—recall his theory of stages of growth and economic "takeoff"—were widely criticized. Nevertheless, there appeared to be opportunities for relatively small-scale improvements. Bakker worked for the Canadian government, especially CIDA (the Canadian International Development Agency), on integrated rural development projects in various parts of Indonesia, especially the island of Sulawesi—where rural areas needed significant improvement. Urban planning was required, as was the development of health care, education, and other basic services.

Somewhat surprisingly, Indonesia today is a highly developed and democratic country. There have been many political changes since the fall of President Suharto, but, despite numerous challenges, Indonesia remains a secular country. That means that there is separation of "church" (temple) and "state" in Indonesia, as there is in India. The constitution recognizes five "world religions" as equally valid: Hinduism, Buddhism, Protestant Christianity, Roman Catholicism, and Islam. Although there are many Muslims in Indonesia it is not an "Islamic state" of the kind represented by Iran or Saudi Arabia. While there is still poverty in Indonesia and while no one would claim that all of its major political and economic issues have been overcome, it is remarkable how far Indonesia has come since the early 1980s.

What Do You Think?

1. Does Canada have a role to play in the development of countries such as Indonesia?

2. How might the separation of "church" and "state" contribute to the economic development of a country?

3. How might tradition stand in the way of modernization in such countries?

SOURCES: Bakker (1979, 1992, 2009) and Geertz (1963).

SUMMING UP

Traditional and Modern Societies: The Big Picture

Elements of Society	Traditional Societies	Modern Societies
Cultural Patterns		
Values	Homogeneous; sacred character; few subcultures and countercultures	Heterogeneous; secular character; many subcultures and countercultures
Norms	Great moral significance; little tolerance of diversity	Variable moral significance; high tolerance of diversity
Time orientation	Present linked to past	Present linked to future
Technology	Pre-industrial; human and animal energy	Industrial; advanced energy sources
Social Structure		
Status and role	Few statuses, most ascribed; few specialized roles	Many statuses, some ascribed and some achieved; many specialized roles
Relationships	Typically primary; little anonymity or privacy	Typically secondary; much anonymity and privacy
Communications	Face to face	Face-to-face communication supplemented by mass media
Social control	Informal gossip	Formal police and legal system
Social stratification	Rigid patterns of social inequality; little mobility	Fluid patterns of social inequality; high mobility
Gender patterns	Pronounced patriarchy; women's lives centred on the home	Declining patriarchy; increasing number of women in the paid labour force
Settlement patterns	Small scale; population typically small and widely dispersed in rural villages and small towns	Large scale; population typically large and concentrated in cities

Social Institutions		
Economy	Based on agriculture; much manufacturing in the home; little white-collar work	Based on industrial mass production; factories become centres of production; increasing white-collar work
State	Small-scale government; little state intervention in society	Large-scale government; much state intervention in society
Family	Extended family as the primary means of socialization and economic production	Nuclear family retains some socialization functions but is more a unit of consumption than of production
Religion	Religion guides world view; little religious pluralism	Religion weakens with the rise of science; extensive religious pluralism
Education	Formal schooling limited to elites	Basic schooling becomes universal, with growing proportion receiving advanced education
Health	High birth and death rates; short life expectancy because of low standard of living and simple medical technology	Low birth and death rates; longer life expectancy because of higher standard of living and sophisticated medical technology
Social Change	Slow; change evident over many generations	Rapid; change evident within a single generation

New England colonies, only Rhode Island tolerated religious dissent. In general, because social differences were repressed in favour of conformity to established norms, subcultures and countercultures were few, and change proceeded slowly.

Increasing population, the growth of cities, and specialized economic activity driven by the Industrial Revolution gradually altered this pattern. People came to know one another by their jobs (e.g., as "the doctor" or "the bank clerk") rather than by kinship or home town. People looked on most others as strangers. The face-to-face communication of the village was eventually replaced by the impersonal mass media: newspapers, radio, television, and computer networks. Large organizations steadily assumed more and more responsibility for seeing to the daily tasks that had once been carried out by family, friends, and neighbours; schools took on education; police, lawyers, and courts supervised a formal justice system. Even charity became the work of faceless bureaucrats working for various social welfare agencies.

Geographic mobility and exposure to diverse ways of life all weaken traditional values. People become more tolerant of social diversity, defending individual rights and freedom of choice. Treating people differently because of race, sex, or religion is defined as unacceptable. As a result, minorities at the margins of society gradually gain greater power and broader participation in public life. The election of Barack Obama as president of the United States was a clear indication of the modernity of American society.

The mass media give rise to a dominant culture that may wash over traditional differences that set off one region from another or one country from another. This is part of a process called harmonization that critical sociologists claim will lead to the Americanization of Canadian culture. The separate French-language media in Quebec allow it to resist inclusion in the generic mass society characterizing the rest of North America.

THE EVER-EXPANDING STATE   In the small-scale pre-industrial societies of Europe, government amounted to little more than the local noble. A royal family formally reigned over an entire nation, but, without efficient transportation or communication, even absolute monarchs had far less power than today's political leaders.

Technological innovation allowed government to expand, and the centralized state grew in size and importance. At the time of confederation in 1867, federal and provincial governments had limited functions. Since then, government in Canada has entered more and more areas of social life—establishing publicly owned enterprises in the areas of transportation, communication, and natural resources; regulating wages and working conditions; establishing standards for products of all kinds; educating the population; delivering medical care; protecting the environment; and providing financial assistance to ill, disabled, aged, and unemployed Canadians. To pay for such programs, taxes have soared, so that today's average worker labours for six months each year just to pay for the broad array of services that the government provides.

In a mass society, power resides in large bureaucracies, leaving people in local communities little control over their lives. For example, government officials mandate that local schools must have a standardized educational program, local products must be government-certified, and every citizen must maintain extensive tax records. While such regulations may protect people and advance social equality, they also force us to deal more and more with nameless officials in distant and often unresponsive bureaucracies, and they undermine the autonomy of families and local communities.

EVALUATE

The growing scale of modern life certainly has positive aspects, but at the price of losing some of our cultural heritage. Modern societies increase individual rights, tolerate greater social differences, and raise standards of living (Inglehart & Baker,

2000). But they are prone to what Weber feared most—excessive bureaucracy—as well as Tönnies's self-centredness and Durkheim's anomie. Modern society's size, complexity, and tolerance of diversity all but doom traditional values and family patterns, leaving individuals isolated, powerless, and materialistic. Voter apathy is a serious problem in the United States and more recently in Canada despite the differences in our political systems—in part because individuals in vast, impersonal societies think that no one person can make much of a difference.

Critics sometimes say that mass-society theory romanticizes the past. They remind us that many people in small towns were actually eager to set out for a higher standard of living in cities. Moreover, mass-society theory ignores problems of social inequality. Critics say this theory attracts conservatives who defend conventional morality and overlook the historical inequality of women and other minorities.

CHECK YOUR LEARNING In your own words, state the mass-society theory of modernization as well as two criticisms of this theory.

....

Social-Conflict Theory: Modernity as Class Society

The second interpretation of modernity derives largely from the ideas of Karl Marx. From a social-conflict perspective, modernity takes the form of a **class society**, *a capitalist society with pronounced social stratification*. That is, although agreeing that modern societies have expanded to a mass scale, this approach views the heart of modernization as an expanding capitalist economy, marked by inequality (Buechler, 2000; Habermas, 1970; Harrington, 1984).

CAPITALISM Class-society theory follows Marx in claiming that the increasing scale of social life in modern society results from the growth and greed unleashed by capitalism. Because a capitalist economy pursues ever-greater profits, both production and consumption steadily increase.

According to Marx, capitalism rests on "naked self-interest" (Marx & Engels, 1972:337; orig. 1848). This self-centredness weakens the social ties that once united small communities. Capitalism also treats people as commodities: a source of labour and a market for capitalist products.

Capitalism supports science, not just as the key to greater productivity but as an ideology that

class society a capitalist society with pronounced social stratification

mass society a society in which prosperity and bureaucracy have weakened traditional social ties

justifies the status quo. That is, modern societies encourage people to view human well-being as a technical puzzle to be solved by engineers and other experts rather than through the pursuit of social justice. For example, a capitalist culture seeks to improve health through scientific medicine rather than by eliminating poverty, which is a core cause of poor health.

Business also raises the banner of scientific logic, trying to increase profits through greater efficiency. Today's capitalist corporations have reached enormous size and control unimaginable wealth as a result of "going global" as multinationals. From the class society point of view, the expanding scale of life is less a function of *Gesellschaft* than the inevitable and destructive consequence of capitalism.

PERSISTENT INEQUALITY Modernity has gradually eroded the rigid categories that set nobles apart from commoners in pre-industrial societies. But class-society theory maintains that elites persist—albeit now as capitalist millionaires rather than as the nobles of an earlier era. The distribution of income is skewed in our country—to the point that, from 1961 to 2011, the proportion of all income received by the top quintile (20 percent) of

SOCIAL-CONFLICT THEORY SEES MODERNITY NOT AS A MASS SOCIETY BUT AS A CLASS SOCIETY IN WHICH SOME CATEGORIES OF PEOPLE ARE SECOND-CLASS CITIZENS This family lives without electricity or running water, a situation shared by many Aboriginal families. In both Canada and the United States, Aboriginal peoples are among the last to experience the benefits of modernity.

Alison Wright/Corbis Documentary/Getty Images

SUMMING UP

SUMMING UP

Two Interpretations of Modernity

	Mass Society	Class Society
Process of modernization	Industrialization; growth of bureaucracy	Rise of capitalism
Effects of modernization	Increasing scale of life; rise of the state and other formal organizations	Expansion of the capitalist economy; persistence of social inequality

families increased from 38 to 44 percent. Over the same five decades, the percentage of all income earned by families in the lowest quintile decreased from 6.6 to 4.8 percent. In other words, the top quintile earned at least twice its share, while the lowest quintile earned roughly a quarter of its share. This pattern was remarkably stable over the 50-year period and is only marginally better than the American record.

What of the state? Mass society theorists contend that the state works to increase equality and to combat social problems. Marx was skeptical that the state could accomplish more than minor reforms because, as he saw it, the real power lies in the hands of capitalists who control the economy. Other class society theorists add that, to the extent that working people and minorities enjoy greater political rights and a higher standard of living today, these changes are the fruits of political struggle, not expressions of government goodwill. Therefore, they conclude, despite our pretensions of democracy, power still rests primarily in the hands of those with wealth and influence.

EVALUATE

Class-society theory dismisses Durkheim's argument that people in modern societies suffer from anomie, claiming instead that they suffer from alienation and powerlessness. Not surprisingly, then, the class society interpretation of modernity enjoys widespread support among liberals and radicals who favour greater equality and call for extensive regulation (or abolition) of the capitalist marketplace.

A basic criticism of class-society theory is that it overlooks the increasing prosperity of modern societies and the fact that discrimination based on race, ethnicity, and gender is now illegal and is widely viewed as a social problem. In addition, most people in North America—especially in the United States—are not committed to an egalitarian society, preferring instead a system of unequal rewards that reflects personal differences in talent and effort.

Based on the failure of socialism to generate a high standard of living, few observers think that a centralized economy would cure the ills of modernity. Many of the problems in predominantly capitalist societies—from unemployment, hunger, and industrial pollution to unresponsive government—are also found in socialist nations.

CHECK YOUR LEARNING In your own words, state the class-society theory of modernity. What are the criticisms of this theory?

The Summing Up table above contrasts these two interpretations of modernity. Mass-society theory focuses on the increasing scale of social life and the growth of government; class-society theory stresses the expansion of capitalism and the persistence of inequality.

Modernity and the Individual

Both mass society and class society theories look at the broad societal changes that have taken place since the Industrial Revolution. But from these macro-level approaches we can also draw micro-level insights into how modernity shapes individual lives.

MASS SOCIETY: PROBLEMS OF IDENTITY   Modernity liberated individuals from the small, tightly knit communities of the past. Most people in modern societies, therefore, have privacy and freedom to express their individuality. Mass-society theory suggests, however, that extensive social diversity, isolation, and rapid social change make it difficult for many people to establish coherent personal identities (Berger et al., 1974; Riesman, 1970, orig. 1950; Wheelis, 1958). Proximity to the United States, regional tensions, and bilingualism make it even more difficult for Canadians to establish clear self-definition (Hiller, 2006; Taras et al., 1993). Canadians also have had considerable difficulty articulating a collective identity, to the point where national identity "is the quintessential Canadian issue" (Lipset, 1991:42). Marshall McLuhan, when asked if there is such a thing as a Canadian identity said, "No, there is no Canadian identity. Canadians are the only people in the world who have learned to live without a national identity" (cited in Colombo, 2001:1).

If personality or personal identity is largely the product of social experience, what are the impacts of traditional or modern mass society? The small, homogeneous, and slowly changing societies of the past provided firm, if narrow, foundations for building personal identities. The traditional Hutterite communities that flourish in Alberta teach young men and women "correct" ways to think and behave—and most learn to embrace this life as "natural" and right. Everything is shared—property, work, meals—in these tiny communal societies that have perpetuated the Hutterite way of life, largely unchanged for more than 400 years. Under these circumstances, which contrast sharply with those of modern mass society, it is relatively easy to establish a secure sense of personal identity.

Mass societies, with their characteristic diversity and rapid change, provide only shifting sands on which to build a personal identity. Left to make their own life decisions, many people—especially those who are wealthier—confront a bewildering range of options. Freedom of choice has little value without standards to help us make good choices and, in a tolerant mass society, people may find little reason to choose one path over another. Not surprisingly, many people shuttle from one identity to another, changing their lifestyle, relationships, and even religion in search of an elusive "true" self; without a moral compass, people lack the security and certainty once provided by tradition.

For David Riesman (1970; orig. 1950), modernization brings changes in **social character**, *personality patterns common to members of a particular society*. Pre-industrial societies promote what Riesman terms **tradition-directedness**, *rigid conformity to time-honoured ways of living*. Members of traditional societies model their lives on what has gone before so what is "good" is equivalent to "what has always been."

Tradition-directedness corresponds to Tönnies's *Gemeinschaft* and Durkheim's mechanical solidarity. Culturally conservative, tradition-directed people think and act alike. Unlike the conformity found in modern societies, this uniformity is not an attempt to mimic one another. Instead, people are alike because everyone draws on the same solid cultural foundation. Hutterite women and men exemplify tradition-directedness; in Hutterite culture, tradition ties everyone to ancestors and descendants in an unbroken chain of communal living "as ordained by God."

social character personality patterns common to members of a particular society

tradition-directedness rigid conformity to time-honoured ways of living

other-directedness a receptiveness to the latest trends and fashions, often expressed by imitating others

Members of diverse and rapidly changing societies think of a tradition-directed personality as deviant because it seems so rigid. Modern people, by and large, prize personal flexibility and sensitivity to others. Riesman calls this type of social character **other-directedness**, *a receptiveness to the latest trends and fashions, often expressed in the practice of imitating others*. Because their socialization occurs within societies that are continuously in flux, other-directed people develop fluid identities marked by superficiality, inconsistency, and change. They try on different "selves" almost like new clothing, seek out role models, and engage in varied "performances" as they move from setting to setting (Goffman, 1959). In a traditional society, such "shiftiness" marks a person as untrustworthy, but in a changing, modern society, the ability to fit in virtually anywhere—like a chameleon changing its colours to match its environment—is very useful.

In societies that value the up to date rather than the traditional, people look to others for approval, using members of their own generation rather than elders as role models. Peer pressure can be irresistible to people without enduring standards to guide them. Modern society urges individuals to be true to themselves, but when social surroundings change so rapidly, how do people develop the selves to which they should be

MASS-SOCIETY THEORY RELATES FEELINGS OF ANXIETY AND LACK OF MEANING IN THE MODERN WORLD TO RAPID SOCIAL CHANGE THAT WASHES AWAY TRADITION This notion of modern emptiness is captured in the photo on the left. *Class-society theory*, in contrast, ties such feelings to social inequality, by which some categories of people are made into second-class citizens (or not made citizens at all), as expressed in the photo on the right.

Sociology in Focus

The True North LGBT: We're "Post-Gay"

In July 2012, the *National Post* ran a two-page spread—under the above title—on what it called the "landscape of gay Canada." A Forum Research poll, commissioned by the *National Post,* provided the most comprehensive snapshot to date of the LGBT community and Canadian attitudes toward them and same-sex marriage.

Here are some of their findings:

- Whereas 5 percent of Canadians *self-identified* as lesbian, gay, bisexual, or transgender, this is true of 10 percent between 18 and 34 years of age.

- While 21 percent of the respondents over 65 said that a *family member* is gay, lesbian, bisexual, or transgender, this is true of 33 percent of people 18 to 44 years of age.

- When asked if they *know someone* who is gay, lesbian, bisexual, or transgender, 81 and 63 percent of the younger and elder cohorts, respectively, said yes.

- Women were slightly more likely to answer yes to the second and third issues above, and were equally likely to answer the one on self-identification.

- Quebecers are most likely, and Albertans are least likely, to have personal knowledge of or to have family members who are gay, lesbian, bisexual, or transgender.

- Although Green Party supporters are most likely to be self-identifiers (10 percent), this is true of 1 percent of Liberal supporters and 3 percent of Conservatives. (Also, Liberals and Conservatives are matched but lag behind the others on all three measures combined.)

On questions regarding same-sex marriage, the responses were as follows:

- Respondents aged 18 to 34 *and 65 or over* are the most likely to be in same-sex marriages (at 2.9 and 2.4 percent, respectively, compared to less than 1 percent of the other cohorts).

- Women are more likely than men to be in same-sex marriages (2.2 and 1.0 percent, respectively), to have a family member or to know someone in such a marriage, and to approve of same-sex marriage.

- Despite that fact that Alberta has the most respondents in same-sex marriages (3.4 percent) or with same-sex marriages among family members, it has the lowest approval rate of same-sex marriage itself.

- Except for the Bloc, Conservatives have the highest proportion of supporters in same-sex marriages (1.5 percent)—but they are least likely to approve of such unions.

The findings of this survey are highly significant. Despite variation by age, sex, province, and political orientation, Canadians overwhelmingly support same sex-marriage (at roughly 65 percent). Albertans, who have the largest proportion of people involved in same-sex marriage, are the least likely to support it. Albertans and Conservatives are the only categories in which less than half of the respondents support same-sex marriage (i.e., 46 percent in each case). In other categories, support runs as high as 80 or 85 percent. When taking into account the fact that, before the law was changed, support hovered around 35 percent, the current situation is nothing less than astounding. In less than a decade, support for same-sex marriage has increased from 35 to 65 percent. It is this level of support and the speed at which change occurred that led to the conclusion that we are now "post gay." Being gay, lesbian, bisexual, or transgender is only one of the relevant characteristics shaping interaction across increasingly porous social boundaries.

What Do You Think?

1. Where do you fit into the picture revealed by these survey results?

2. Are you surprised by the findings or are they consistent with your understanding of changing attitudes?

3. Are we now "post gay"?

SOURCE: Adapted from Carlson (2012).

---

true? This problem is at the root of the identity crisis so widespread in industrial societies today. "Who am I?" is a question that many of us struggle to answer. In truth, this problem is not so much psychological as sociological, reflecting the inherent instability of modern mass society.

CLASS SOCIETY: PROBLEMS OF POWERLESSNESS

Class-society theory paints a different picture of modernity's effects on individuals. This approach maintains that persistent social inequality undermines modern society's promise of individual freedom. For some people, modernity serves up great privilege but, for many, everyday life means coping with economic uncertainty and a growing sense of powerlessness (Ehrenreich, 2001; Newman, 1993).

For racial and ethnic minorities—particularly Aboriginal peoples—the problem of relative disadvantage looms even larger. Similarly, although women participate more broadly in modern societies, they continue to run up against traditional barriers of sexism. This approach rejects the claim by mass-society theory that people suffer from too much freedom. According to class-society theory, our society still denies a majority of people full participation in social life.

The expanding scope of world capitalism has placed more of Earth's population under the influence of multinational corporations. As a result, about 59 percent of the world's income is concentrated in high-income nations, where only 24 percent of its people live. Is it any wonder, class society theorists ask, that people in poor nations seek greater power to shape their own lives?

The problem of widespread powerlessness led Herbert Marcuse (1964) to challenge Max Weber's statement that modern society is rational. Marcuse condemned modern society as irrational for failing to meet the needs of so many people. Modern capitalist societies produce unparalleled wealth, but poverty remains the daily plight of more than 1 billion people. Marcuse adds that technological advances further reduce people's control over their own lives. Sophisticated technology gives a great deal of power to a small core of specialists—not the majority of people—who now dominate the discussion of issues such as computing, energy production, and medical care. Countering the common view that technology solves the world's problems, Marcuse argues that science causes them. In sum, class-society theory asserts that people suffer because modern, scientific societies concentrate both wealth and power in the hands of a privileged few.

Modernity and Progress

In modern societies, most people expect—and applaud—social change. We link modernity to the idea of *progress* (from Latin, meaning "moving forward"), a state of continual improvement. We see stability as stagnation.

PEOPLE TODAY ARE BETTER OFF ECONOMICALLY THAN PAST GENERATIONS Nonetheless, there has been no long-term increase in measures of personal happiness. How can you explain this contradiction?

This chapter began by describing Kaiapo villagers in Brazil, for whom social change has broadened opportunities but weakened traditional heritage; with its advantages and disadvantages, change cannot be equated simply with progress. Whether we see a given change as progress depends on our values. Although it is not the case in all societies, in North America modernity has made our lives longer and more comfortable. At the same time, today's fast pace is very stressful—often at the expense of downtime or family time.

Not surprisingly, measures of happiness have declined while material prosperity has increased. Scholars who study happiness have found that happiness—measured by the response "very happy" in surveys—increases somewhat with higher family income, but only to the $75 000 mark (beyond which there is no further increase). Intriguingly, experiments have shown that people—even small children—are happier if they spend on or share their bounty with others. Even when income is controlled, people who are married (with children), religious, and politically conservative are four times more likely to be "very happy" than their secular, liberal, single, and childless counterparts. In other words, it is not how much money you have but what you do with it that determines your level of happiness (Brooks, 2012; Dunn & Norton, 2012; Inglehart et al., 2009; Myers, 2000).

Social change is both complex and controversial. Modern society's recognition of basic human rights is valued by most people. The assertion that individuals have rights simply by virtue of their humanity is a distinctly modern idea that can be found in the *Canadian Charter of Rights and Freedoms*, the American Declaration of Independence, and the United Nations's Declaration of Human Rights; but we now have something of a "culture of rights" that overlooks the duties and obligations we have to one another. In principle, we might agree that people have the right to shape their own lives, but as people exercise that right, they inevitably challenge the social patterns cherished by others. For example, people may choose not to marry, to live with someone without marrying, to bear children out of wedlock, or to enter into a same-sex partnership or marriage. To those who support individual choice, such changes symbolize progress; to those who value traditional family patterns, however, these developments signal societal decay.

New technology has always provoked controversy. A century ago, the introduction of automobiles and telephones allowed more rapid transportation and efficient communication. But the same technology weakened traditional attachments to home towns and even to families. Today, it appears that computer technology is doing the same thing—providing access to people around the world while shielding us from the communities outside our doors. The internet simultaneously provides unprecedented access to information and threatens our privacy.

Whether good or bad for society—progress or not—social change comes faster all the time. For more on the transformation of Canadian society by the Information Revolution, see the Sociology and the Media box.

Modernity: Global Variation

October 1, Kobe, Japan. Riding the computer-controlled monorail high above the streets of Kobe or the 320-kilometre-per-hour bullet train to Tokyo, we see Japan as the society of the future; its people are in love with high technology. Yet the Japanese remain strikingly traditional in other respects: Few corporate executives and almost no senior politicians are women; young people still show seniors great respect; and public orderliness contrasts with the chaos of many U.S. cities. [John J. Macionis]

Japan is a nation at once traditional and modern. This contradiction reminds us that, although it is useful to contrast traditional and modern societies, the old and the new often coexist in unexpected ways. In the People's Republic of China, ancient Confucian principles are mixed with contemporary socialist thinking. In Saudi Arabia and Qatar, the embrace of modern technology is mixed with respect for the ancient principles of Islam. Likewise, in Mexico and much of Latin America, people observe centuries-old Christian rituals even as they struggle to move ahead economically. In short, combinations of traditional and modern are far from unusual; rather, they are found throughout the world.

Postmodernity

24.5 Discuss postmodernism as one type of social criticism.

If modernity was the product of the Industrial Revolution, is the Information Revolution creating a postmodern era? A number of scholars think so, and they use the term **postmodernity** to refer to *social patterns characteristic of post-industrial societies.* Precisely what postmodernism is remains a matter of debate. The term has been used for decades in literary, philosophical, and even architectural circles. It moved into sociology on a wave of social criticism that has been building since the spread of left-leaning politics in the 1960s. While there are many variants of postmodern thinking, all share the following five themes (Hall & Neitz, 1993; Inglehart, 1997; Rudel & Gerson, 1999):

1. **In important respects, modernity has failed.** The promise of modernity was a life free from want. As postmodernist critics see it, however, the twentieth century was unsuccessful in solving social problems such as poverty. Poverty is widespread and, even in the richest countries, many people still lack financial security. In Canada, our Aboriginal peoples stand out as glaring evidence of exclusion in the face of prosperity. Living conditions on many isolated reserves are intolerable—with families surviving in tents or dilapidated shacks and coping with contaminated drinking water. The fastest-growing segment of our population is being left behind by slow progress on the education front; in 2011, 29 percent of Aboriginals aged 25 to 64 years had not graduated from high school. The comparable figure for First Nations is 35 percent; for non-Aboriginals it is 12 percent. In other words, First Nations are three times more likely to have no certification than their non-Aboriginal counterparts. The original inhabitants of our rich country are least likely to have experienced the promise of modernity or to be educated for the jobs of tomorrow (Fay, 2012; Peacock, 2012).

2. **The bright light of "progress" is fading.** Modern people look to the future, expecting that their lives will improve in significant ways. However, members (and even leaders) of postmodern societies are less confident now about what the future holds. The optimism that carried society into the modern era more than a century ago has given way to stark pessimism; over the past decade or two, Canadians and Americans have come to share that pessimism, believing that life is getting worse (Bibby, 1995:8; Bricker & Wright, 2005; Smith et al., 2013:402).

3. **Science no longer holds the answers.** The defining trait of the modern era was a scientific outlook and a confident belief that technology would make life better. But postmodern critics argue that science has not solved many old problems (such as poor health) and has even created new problems (such as pollution, global warming, and the threat of a flu pandemic).

   Postmodernist thinkers discredit science, claiming that it implies a singular truth. On the contrary, they maintain, there are many ways to view "reality" or to socially construct the world.

4. **Cultural debates are intensifying.** Now that more people have all of the material things they really need, ideas are taking on more importance. In this sense, postmodernity is also a postmaterialist era, in which more careers involve working with symbols and in which issues such as social justice, the natural environment, and animal rights command more and more public attention.

5. **Social institutions are changing.** Just as industrialization brought a sweeping transformation to social institutions, the rise of a post-industrial society is remaking society all over again. For example, the

Sociology and the Media

The Canadian Revolution through the Information Revolution: The Point of No Return

Journalist and author Jeffrey Simpson opens his book *Faultlines* (1993) with the following passage:

> Canada's traditional political culture in the 1980s cracked like river ice in spring. No single current produced the crack-up; it arose from the confluence of powerful new economic, demographic and political factors and the resurgence of older currents. By the early 1990s, a country that had always been at heart a political arrangement—for it had never been a cultural union or a natural economic entity—found its governmental institutions discredited and indebted, its national parties widely reviled, its political leaders mocked, its Constitution the source of division rather than pride, its economy battered by pressures from abroad, its habitual optimism dimmed.

The relative stability of the past, based on elite accommodation, brokerage politics, and deference to authority, had been shattered. Peter C. Newman traced the radical transformation of Canada's political, social, cultural, and economic landscape in *The Canadian Revolution, 1985–1995: From Deference to Defiance* (1995). Political scientist Neil Nevitte used the World Values Survey to reveal changes in Canadian values during the volatile 1980s in his book *The Decline of Deference* (1996). These authors agree that Canada and Canadians have changed profoundly.

Through the 1980s and early 1990s, Canadians lost faith in many of the country's major institutions: organized religion, marriage, the Canada Pension Plan, the monarchy, political parties, the Red Cross, the military and peacekeepers, the Grey Cup, Canada Post, the railways, Ontario Hydro, banks, and corporations. Canadians are less inclined to believe in the inevitability of progress, in the ability of governments to solve our problems, or in corporations as the basis for investment or long-term careers.

Refusing to defer to traditional leadership and authority, Canadians turned inward for solutions to their problems, seeking information and making decisions—often in defiance of the elite. For example, a majority said "no" to the Charlottetown Accord—and "no" to the Conservatives in the 1993 federal election, reducing them from 169 seats to 2. Influential pollster Allan Gregg (1998) notes that, through the 1980s and 1990s, Canadians went from being the most deferential people in the Western world to seeking new rights and taking decision making away from leaders.

Marshall McLuhan predicted the radical transformation of Canadian society in the 1960s and early 1970s (Benedetti & DeHart, 1996) as the result of the development of the electronic media. Television was invading homes and classrooms during that period, and computers—room-sized monstrosities at the time—were changing information processing. We moved into a world of instantaneous all-at-onceness: "Time, in a sense, has ceased as space has vanished…. [W]e now live in a global village of our own making, a simultaneous happening … created by instant electronic information movement" (quoted in Benedetti & DeHart, 1996:40). McLuhan foresaw the walls coming down between families, nations, and economies as people became intensely involved in the affairs of everyone else, everywhere. He predicted that electronic data would become indispensable to all decision making in business, politics, and education; education would be completely transformed; students from around the world would develop a sense of unity; people would forge personal identities in the context of the new simultaneous world; violence would escalate in the quest for identity and people (even children) would kill to feel real; privacy would be a thing of the past; and one could be both superhuman and nobody simultaneously.

As early as 1971, McLuhan said that the "wired planet has no boundaries and no monopolies of knowledge," that specialized jobs had lost meaning, and that we might return to a "cottage economy" again because one could run the world's largest factory from a kitchen computer. *Individuals* now have instant access to information, data, or knowledge, at the same time that these are available to the traditional elites: decision makers and leaders in business, government, education, or religion. Deference to these traditional authorities is difficult to maintain under these conditions. Knowledge is power, and knowledge—through the electronic media—is available to the masses.

Peter C. Newman (1995) also saw the electronic media as a central force for social change:

> The invisible hand of technology had provided citizens with the ammunition for their Revolution. The advent of saturation television coverage of real-time news events, such as the raw footage of the Aboriginal standoff at Oka, Quebec, left politicians with no place to hide. The new rules were to be openly negotiated. But by the decade's end, television, which had been the dominant technological force at the beginning of the decade, was being supplanted by the computer. A full-scale rout of authority was guaranteed by the advent of the power of the internet. Unregulated access to unlimited, cheap information meant the computer channel that was signing up thousands of Canadian recruits daily had changed their world—and ours—by dramatically empowering its users.

Information technology is so central to the transformation we have experienced that a new basis for social class appears to be evolving. In the post-industrial world, control of "the means of production"—using Marxist terms—means access to information, primarily through the use of computers. Affluent families are more likely to have computers, and children who grow up using computers have a head start as they further develop their computer skills at school. Growth in employment is taking place almost entirely in the knowledge-based sector. The result is a new privileged class made up of superbly educated, computer literate men and women (Newman, 1995; also Forcese, 1997; Goyder, 1997).

A *Globe and Mail* editorial (Globe and Mail, 2006) illustrates the Information Revolution in its discussion of Wikipedia: "the wildly popular online encyclopedia that has turned conventional wisdom about reference sources on its head." Where experts or authorities once wrote encyclopedia entries, *anyone* can contribute or modify items in Wikipedia. By making all of us potential authors or editors, the revolutionary Wikipedia "puts a question mark over the whole idea that information must move from credentialed producer to passive consumer."

What Do You Think?

1. Is the above an accurate description of the transformation of the past two decades?
2. Do you consult Wikipedia? Do you check information you find there in other sources? Is it a reliable reference, in your opinion?
3. Is the Information Revolution good or bad for society?

postmodern family no longer conforms to any single pattern—as individuals are choosing among many new family forms.

EVALUATE

Analysts who claim that high-income societies are entering a postmodern era criticize modernity for failing to meet human needs. In defence of modernity, there have been marked increases in longevity and living standards over the course of the past century. Even if we accept postmodernist views that science is bankrupt and progress is a sham, what are the alternatives? There are those who would argue that Canada and the United States have taken two different paths into modernity, while others argue that the differences have been overplayed, (See the Controversy and Debate box.)

CHECK YOUR LEARNING In your own words, state the characteristics of postmodern society.

Modernization and Our Global Future

24.6 Evaluate possible directions of future change.

Imagine the entire world reduced to a village of 1000 people. About 90 residents of this "global village" live in high-income countries and earn half of all income. Another 113 people are so poor that their lives are at risk.

The tragic plight of the world's poor suggests that the planet is in desperate need of change. There are two competing views of why more than 1 billion people around the world are so poor. *Modernization theory* claims that, in the past, the entire world was poor and that technological change, especially the Industrial Revolution, enhanced human productivity and raised living standards in many nations. From this point of view, the solution to global poverty is to promote technological development and market economies around the world.

For reasons suggested earlier, however, global modernization may be difficult. Recall that David Riesman portrayed pre-industrial people as *tradition-directed* and likely to resist change; therefore, modernization theorists argue that the world's rich societies must help poor countries grow economically. Industrial nations can speed development by exporting technology to poor regions, welcoming students from these countries, and providing foreign aid to stimulate economic growth.

A review of modernization theory points to some success with policies in Latin America and to greater success in the small Asian countries of Taiwan, South Korea, Singapore, and Hong Kong (since 1997, part of the People's Republic of China). But jump-starting development in the poorest countries of the world poses greater challenges. And, even where dramatic change has occurred, modernization involves a trade-off. Traditional people, such as Brazil's Kaiapo, may gain wealth through economic development, but they lose their cultural identity and values as they are drawn into a global "McCulture" based on Western materialism, pop music, trendy clothes, and fast food. One Brazilian anthropologist expressed hope for the future of the Kaiapo: "At least they quickly understood the consequences of watching television.... Now [they] can make a choice" (Simons, 2007:253).

But not everyone thinks that modernization is really an option. According to a second approach to global stratification, *dependency theory*, today's poor societies have little ability to modernize, even if they want to. From this point of view, the major barrier to economic development is not traditionalism but global domination by rich capitalist societies.

Controversy and Debate

We're Different, Eh?

There are many Canadians who believe that, in important ways, we differ from Americans. Michael Adams, in *Fire and Ice* (2003), argues that Americans are retrenching—they defer to authority, believe that the father is the master of the house, and embrace fundamentalist religion—while Canadians are moving in a different direction. Others argue that Canadians are becoming more like Americans; globalization, the dominance of the American media, and free-trade agreements have led to homogeneity or value convergence.

Is the United States a nation in decline? Clearly, by some measures, it is thriving. Between 1960 and 1995, for example, the nation's economic output tripled and median family income, controlled for inflation, climbed by more than one-third. During the same time span, the official poverty rate dropped by half. By 2004, infant mortality had declined further, life expectancy had increased, and poverty among elderly people had been greatly reduced. High school dropout rates declined and college completion rates improved. And Americans continue to volunteer and give to charity much more generously than do Canadians.

Nonetheless, other indicators paint a more disturbing picture of American life. Between 1960 and 1995, violent crime shot up fourfold; the number of children born to single mothers as well as the number of children supported by welfare rose more than fivefold; the divorce rate doubled; and teen suicide tripled. Television viewing increased dramatically, and academic achievement, as measured by test scores, declined. By 2004, child abuse had increased fourfold, average weekly wages had declined in real dollars, and the income gap between rich and poor had widened. Voter turnout declined steadily. Between 1970 and 2004, the proportion of Americans without health care coverage increased from 10 to 16 percent.

The economic crisis of 2008–09 ushered in a serious recession in the United States, involving job losses in many sectors (e.g., financial institutions and the automobile industry) as well as the loss of homes through bank foreclosures. As a result, some of the gains made in earlier years had been eroded (albeit temporarily). Although Canada weathered the recent economic downturn relatively well—at least in terms of our banks, other financial institutions, and mortgages (which are structured very differently from those in the United States)—our natural resource exports were hit hard and we did lose jobs. But, even before the recent crisis, Canadians had concerns regarding our society that mirrored those of the Americans. In the mid-1990s, we lost confidence in our economy, at least with respect to job creation and job security. Taking inflation into account, our average family income declined after 1989, and recovered fully only by 1998. Despite our improving economy, about 15 percent of Canadian families, especially Aboriginal families, continued to fall below the poverty line. Violent crime and homicide rates increased initially and then declined through the late 1990s and early 2000s, yet Canadians are increasingly fearful about their safety. We are cynical about politicians and worried about the quality of our schools and the survival of the family as we know it. Our political will to ensure universal and timely access to medical care is in question. Voter turnout is declining here, too, particularly among young people. Like Americans, we live in an age of entitlement rather than one of duty, an age of individual rights rather than responsibility for one's community. To many observers, it seems as though we are simply a few steps behind the United States with respect to the growth of social problems.

Despite these changes, Canadians seem to have retained certain moral and social values. While we are less likely to attend religious services, 84 percent of us believe in God and 45 percent pray daily. Honesty and reliability are "very important" to about 90 percent of Canadians, and family life is important to 86 percent. Cultural, racial, and religious intermarriage is approved by 80 to 90 percent of Canadians, suggesting that we have become quite tolerant. And, of course, Canada legalized same-sex marriage. Furthermore, our level of social compassion has remained quite high, as evidenced by our beliefs that people who are poor deserve adequate income and medical care (84 percent and 96 percent, respectively). If ours has become a more cynical and dangerous society, it is clear that we have not rejected our basic social values. Keep in mind, though, that professing beliefs and values is not the same as putting them into action.

Anti-American sentiment has been out in the open, but much of it was directed at the U.S. government, President George W. Bush, and the war in Iraq and not against Americans themselves. About a million of us favour Canada becoming part of the United States, while many more support political and economic union. Among employed Canadians, 19 percent (24 percent in British Columbia and Quebec) would prefer to work and live in the United States, and 70 percent support our participation in the North American Free Trade Agreement. Only 15 percent of Canadians say they are "anti-American" at heart, while 70 percent agree that "I value and respect the United States and its citizens" (Bricker & Wright, 2005). Furthermore, we have no qualms about immersing ourselves in American culture—its books, magazines, movies, and television programs—thereby failing to support Canadian culture through our choices.

We may define ourselves as "*not* American" and disagree with many things that Americans do, but—despite differences in attitudes and values—deep down, the average Canadian has not been *anti*-American. Canadians were undoubtedly more comfortable with their

American neighbours during the eight years when Barack Obama was the president. But, by the time of writing, the U.S. election of 2016 had—to the astonishment of almost everyone and the dismay of many—propelled Donald Trump into the role of president-elect. Pundits, pollsters, and the media had failed to detect the depth of the anger or the level of distrust and animosity towards the established elite that was bubbling to the surface. Similar undercurrents—to which Canada is not immune—can be detected throughout the European Union. It is too early to predict the fate of NAFTA, but Prime Minster Trudeau was quick to suggest an early meeting of American and Canadian trade negotiators in an effort to ward off the worst potential consequences of a Trump-inspired rift in

or collapse of our long-standing trade agreement. Love it or hate it, anything that happens in the United States matters to Canadians.

What Do You Think?

1. Are Canadians superior to Americans? How?

2. Would you consider working and living in the United States? Do you have relatives, friends, or acquaintances doing so?

3. How do we get the impression that Canadians are anti-American?

SOURCES: Adams (2003), Bennett (1993), Bibby (1995), Bricker and Wright (2005), and Sauvé (1994).

Dependency theory asserts that rich nations achieved their modernization at the expense of poor ones, plundering poor nations' natural resources and exploiting their human labour. Even today, the world's poorest countries remain locked in a disadvantageous economic relationship with rich nations, dependent on wealthy countries to buy their raw materials and in return provide them with whatever manufactured products they can afford. According to this view, continuing ties with rich societies only perpetuate current patterns of global inequality.

Whichever approach you find more convincing, keep in mind that change in North America or Western Europe is no longer separate from change in the rest of the world. At the beginning of the twentieth century, most people in today's high-income countries lived in relatively small settlements with limited awareness of the larger world. Now, a century later, the entire world has become one huge village because the lives of all people are increasingly linked.

The twentieth century witnessed unprecedented human achievement. Yet solutions to many problems of human existence—including finding meaning in life, resolving conflicts between nations, and eliminating poverty—have eluded us. To this list of pressing matters new concerns have been added, such as controlling population growth and establishing an environmentally sustainable society. In the next hundred years, we must be prepared to tackle these problems with imagination, compassion, and determination. Our growing understanding of human society gives us reason to be hopeful that we can get the job done.

Seeing Sociology in Everyday Life

CHAPTER 24   Social Change: Traditional, Modern, and Postmodern Societies

Is tradition the opposite of modernity?

Conceptually, this may be true. But as this chapter explains, traditional and modern social patterns merge in all sorts of interesting ways in our everyday lives.

Look at the photographs below, and identify elements of tradition and modernity. Do they seem to go together, or are they in conflict? Why?

> **Hint** Although sociologists analyze tradition and modernity as conceptual opposites, every society combines these elements in various ways. People may debate the virtues of traditional and modern life, but the two patterns are found almost everywhere. Technological change always has social consequences—for example, the use of cell phones changes people's social networks and economic opportunities; similarly, the spread of McDonald's changes not only what people eat but also where and with whom they share meals.

paul prescott/Alamy Stock Photo

THESE YOUNG GIRLS LIVE IN THE CITY OF ISTANBUL IN TURKEY, A COUNTRY THAT HAS LONG DEBATED THE MERITS OF TRADITIONAL AND MODERN LIFE What sets off traditional and modern ways of dressing? Do you think such differences are likely to affect patterns of friendship? Would the same be true in Canada?

WHEN THE FIRST MCDONALD'S RESTAURANT OPENED IN THE CITY OF KIEV IN UKRAINE, MANY PEOPLE STOPPED BY TO TASTE A HAMBURGER AND SEE WHAT "FAST FOOD" WAS ALL ABOUT As large corporations expand their operations around the world, do they tip the balance away from tradition in favour of modernity? How?

IN RIYADH, SAUDI ARABIA, THIS YOUNG COUPLE IS SHOPPING FOR THE LATEST IN CELL PHONES Does such modern technology threaten a society's traditions?

Seeing Sociology in *Your* Everyday Life

1. Ask an elderly relative or friend to name the most important social changes that occurred during his or her lifetime. Do you think your world will change as much during your lifetime?

2. Ask your friends and classmates to make five predictions about Canadian society in 2050, when you will be senior citizens. Compare notes. On what issues is there agreement?

3. What do you see as the advantages of living in a modern society? What are the drawbacks?

Making the Grade

CHAPTER 24   Social Change: Traditional, Modern, and Postmodern Societies

What Is Social Change?

24.1 State four defining characteristics of social change.

Social change is the transformation of culture and social institutions over time. Every society changes all the time, sometimes faster, sometimes more slowly. Social change often generates controversy.

> social change the transformation of culture and social institutions over time

Causes of Social Change

24.2 Explain how culture, conflict, ideas, and population patterns direct social change.

Culture

- *Invention* produces new objects, ideas, and social patterns.
- *Discovery* occurs when people take notice of existing elements of the world.
- *Diffusion* creates change as products, people, and information spread from one society to another.

Social Conflict

- Karl Marx claimed that class conflict between capitalists and workers pushes society toward a socialist system of production.
- Social conflict arising from class, race, and gender inequality has resulted in social changes that have improved the lives of working people.

Ideas

Max Weber traced the roots of most social changes to ideas:

- The fact that industrial capitalism developed first in areas of Western Europe where the Protestant work ethic was strong demonstrates the power of ideas to bring about change.

Demographics

Population patterns play a part in social change:

- The aging of Canadian society has resulted in changes to family life and the development of consumer products to meet the needs of the elderly.
- Migration within and between societies promotes change.

Visions of Modernity

24.3 Apply the ideas of Tönnies, Durkheim, Weber, and Marx to our understanding of modernity.

Modernity refers to the social consequences of industrialization, which include

- the decline of traditional communities
- the expansion of personal choice
- increasing social diversity
- focus on the future

Ferdinand Tönnies described modernization as the transition from *Gemeinschaft* to *Gesellschaft*, a process characterized by the loss of traditional community and the rise of individualism.

Émile Durkheim saw modernization as a society's expanding division of labour. *Mechanical solidarity*, based on shared activities and beliefs, is gradually replaced by *organic solidarity*, in which specialization makes people interdependent.

Max Weber saw modernity as the decline of a traditional world view and the rise of rationality. Weber feared the dehumanizing effects of modern rational organization. Karl Marx saw modernity as the triumph of capitalism over feudalism. Capitalism creates social conflict, which Marx claimed would bring about revolutionary change leading to an egalitarian socialist society.

> modernity changes brought about by the Industrial Revolution
> modernization the process of social change begun by industrialization
> division of labour specialized economic activity
> anomie Durkheim's term for a condition in which norms and values are so weak and inconsistent that society provides little moral guidance to individuals

Theories of Modernity

24.4 Contrast analysis of modernity as mass society and as class society.

Structural-Functional Theory: Modernity as Mass Society

- According to mass-society theory, modernity increases the scale of life, enlarging the role of government and other formal organizations in carrying out tasks previously performed by families in local communities.

- Cultural diversity and rapid social change make it difficult for people in modern societies to develop stable identities and to find meaning in their lives.

Social-Conflict Theory: Modernity as Class Society

- According to class-society theory, modernity involves the rise of capitalism into a global economic system resulting in persistent social inequality.
- By concentrating wealth in the hands of a few, modern capitalist societies generate widespread feelings of alienation and powerlessness.

Modernity and the Individual

Both mass-society theory and class-society theory are macro-level approaches; from them, however, we can also draw micro-level insights into how modernity shapes individual lives.

Mass Society: Problems of Identity

- Mass-society theory suggests that the great social diversity, widespread isolation, and rapid social change of modern societies make it difficult for individuals to establish a stable social identity.

David Riesman described the changes in social character that modernity causes:

- Pre-industrial societies exhibit **tradition-directedness**: Everyone in society draws on the same solid cultural foundation, and people model their lives on those of their ancestors.
- Modern societies exhibit **other-directedness**: Because their socialization occurs in societies that are continuously in flux, other-directed people develop fluid identities marked by superficiality, inconsistency, and change.

Class Society: Problems of Powerlessness

- Class-society theory claims that the problem facing most people today is economic uncertainty and powerlessness.
- Herbert Marcuse claimed that modern society is irrational because it fails to meet the needs of so many people.
- Marcuse also believed that technological advances further reduce people's control over their own lives.
- People suffer because modern societies have concentrated both wealth and power in the hands of a privileged few.

Modernity and Progress

Social change is too complex and controversial simply to be equated with progress:

- A rising standard of living has made lives longer and materially more comfortable; at the same time, many people are stressed and have little time to relax with their families; there have been no increases in measures of personal happiness over recent decades.
- Science and technology have brought many conveniences to our everyday lives, yet many people are concerned that life is changing too fast; the introduction of automobiles and advanced communications technology has weakened traditional attachments to hometowns and even to families.

> **mass society** a society in which prosperity and bureaucracy have weakened traditional social ties
>
> **class society** a capitalist society with pronounced social stratification
>
> **social character** personality patterns common to members of a particular society
>
> **tradition-directedness** rigid conformity to time-honoured ways of living
>
> **other-directedness** a receptiveness to the latest trends and fashions, often expressed in the practice of imitating others

Postmodernity

24.5 Discuss postmodernism as one type of social criticism.

Postmodernity refers to the cultural traits of post-industrial societies. Postmodern criticism of society centres on the failure of modernity, and specifically science, to fulfill its promise of prosperity and well-being.

> **postmodernity** social patterns characteristic of post-industrial societies

Modernization and Our Global Future

24.6 Evaluate possible directions of future social change.

Modernization theory links global poverty to the power of tradition. Rich nations can help poor countries develop their economies.

Dependency theory explains global poverty as the product of the world economic system. The operation of multinational corporations makes poor nations economically dependent on rich nations.

Glossary

abortion   the deliberate termination of a pregnancy

absolute poverty   a deprivation of resources that is life-threatening

achieved status   a social position that someone assumes voluntarily and that reflects personal ability and effort

activity theory   the idea that a high level of activity increases personal satisfaction in old age

age-sex pyramid   a graphic representation of the age and sex of a population

age stratification   the unequal distribution of wealth, power, and privilege among people at different stages of the life course

ageism   prejudice and discrimination against older people

agriculture   large-scale cultivation using ploughs harnessed to animals or more powerful energy sources

alienation   the experience of isolation and misery resulting from powerlessness

animism   the belief that elements of the natural world are conscious life forms that affect humanity

anomie   a condition in which norms and values are so weak and inconsistent that society provides little moral guidance to individuals

anticipatory socialization   learning that helps a person achieve a desired position

ascribed status   a social position that someone receives at birth or assumes involuntarily later in life

asexuality   a lack of sexual attraction to people of either sex

assimilation   the process by which minorities gradually adopt patterns of the dominant culture, thereby becoming more similar to the dominant group

authoritarianism   a political system that denies the people participation in government

authority   power that people perceive as legitimate rather than coercive

beliefs   specific statements that people hold to be true

bilateral descent   a system tracing kinship through both men and women

bisexuality   sexual attraction to people of both sexes

blue-collar occupations   lower-prestige jobs that involve mostly manual labour

bureaucracy   an organizational model rationally designed to perform tasks efficiently

bureaucratic inertia   the tendency of bureaucratic organizations to perpetuate themselves

bureaucratic ritualism   a focus on rules and regulations to the point of undermining an organization's goals

capitalism   an economic system in which natural resources and the means of producing goods and services are privately owned

capitalists   people who own and operate factories and other businesses in pursuit of profits

caregiving   informal and unpaid care provided to a dependent person by family members, other relatives, or friends

caste system   social stratification based on ascription, or birth

cause and effect   a relationship in which change in one variable causes change in another

charisma   extraordinary personal qualities that can infuse people with emotion and turn them into followers

charismatic authority   power legitimized by extraordinary personal abilities that inspire devotion and obedience

church   a type of religious organization that is well integrated into the larger society

claims making   the process of trying to convince the public and public officials of the importance of joining a social movement to address a particular issue

class conflict   conflict between entire classes over the distribution of a society's wealth and power

class consciousness   workers' recognition of themselves as a class unified in opposition to capitalists and ultimately to capitalism itself

class society   a capitalist society with pronounced social stratification

class system   social stratification based on both birth and individual achievement

cohabitation   the sharing of a household by an unmarried couple

cohort   a category of people with something in common, usually their age

collective behaviour   activity involving a large number of people, often spontaneous, and usually in violation of established norms

collectivity   a large number of people whose minimal interaction occurs in the absence of well-defined and conventional norms

colonialism   the process by which some nations enrich themselves through political and economic control of other nations

communism   a hypothetical economic and political system in which all members of a society are socially equal

community-based corrections   correctional programs operating within society at large rather than behind prison walls

concept   a mental construct that represents some part of the world in a simplified form

concrete operational stage   the level of human development at which individuals first see causal connections in their surroundings

conglomerates   giant corporations composed of many smaller corporations

conspicuous consumption   buying and using products because of the "statements" they make about social position

control   holding constant all variables except one in order to see clearly the effect of that variable

corporate crime   the illegal actions of a corporation or people acting on its behalf

corporation   an organization with a legal existence including rights and liabilities apart from those of its members

correlation   a relationship in which two (or more) variables change together

counterculture   cultural patterns that strongly oppose those widely accepted within a society

crime the violation of a society's formally enacted criminal law

criminal justice system organizations—police, courts, and prison officials—that respond to alleged violations of the law

criminal recidivism subsequent offences by people previously convicted of crimes

critical sociology the study of society that focuses on the need for social change

crowd a temporary gathering of people who share a common focus of attention and who influence one another

crude birth rate the number of live births in a given year for every thousand people in a population

crude death rate the number of deaths in a given year for every thousand people in a population

cult a religious organization that is largely outside a society's cultural traditions

cultural integration the close relationship among various elements of a cultural system

cultural lag cultural elements changing at different rates, causing various degrees of disruption in cultural systems

cultural relativism the practice of judging a culture by its own standards

cultural transmission the process by which one generation passes culture to the next

cultural universals traits that are part of every known culture

culture the ways of thinking, the ways of acting, and the material objects that together shape a people's way of life

culture shock personal disorientation when experiencing an unfamiliar way of life

Davis-Moore thesis social stratification has beneficial consequences for the operation of a society

deductive logical thought reasoning that transforms general theory into specific hypotheses suitable for testing

democracy a political system that gives power to the people as a whole

demographic transition theory the thesis that population patterns reflect a society's level of technological development

demography the study of human population

denomination a church, independent of the state, that recognizes religious pluralism

dependency theory a model of economic and social development that explains global inequality in terms of the historical exploitation of poor nations by rich ones

dependent variable the variable that changes

descent the system by which members of a society trace kinship over generations

deterrence the attempt to discourage criminality through punishment

deviance the recognized violation of cultural norms

direct fee system a medical system in which patients pay directly for the services of physicians and hospitals

disaster an event, generally unexpected, that causes extensive harm to people and damage to property

discrimination unequal treatment of various categories of people

disengagement theory the idea that society functions in an orderly way by disengaging people from positions of responsibility as they reach old age

division of labour specialized economic activity

dramaturgical analysis the study of social interaction in terms of theatrical performance

Durkheim, Émile society is defined by type of solidarity

dyad a social group with two members

eating disorder an intense form of dieting or other unhealthy method of weight control driven by the desire to be very thin

ecologically sustainable culture a way of life that meets the needs of the present generation without threatening the environmental legacy of future generations

ecology the study of the interaction of living organisms and the natural environment

economy the social institution that organizes a society's production, distribution, and consumption of goods and services

ecosystem a system composed of the interaction of all living organisms and their natural environments

education the social institution through which society provides its members with important knowledge, including basic facts, job skills, and cultural norms and values

ego a person's conscious efforts to balance innate pleasure-seeking drives with the demands of society

empirical evidence information we can verify with our senses

endogamy marriage between people of the same social category

environmental deficit profound long-term harm to the natural environment caused by humanity's focus on short-term material affluence

environmental racism the pattern by which environmental hazards are greatest for poor people, especially minorities

ethnicity a shared cultural heritage

ethnocentrism the practice of judging another culture by the standards of one's own

ethnomethodology the study of the way people make sense of their everyday surroundings

Eurocentrism the dominance of European cultural patterns

euthanasia assisting in the death of a person suffering from an incurable disease

exogamy marriage between people of different social categories

experiment a research method for investigating cause and effect under highly controlled conditions

expressive leadership group leadership that focuses on the group's wellbeing

extended family a family consisting of parents and children as well as other kin

fad an unconventional social pattern that people embrace briefly but enthusiastically

faith belief based on conviction rather than scientific evidence

false consciousness explanations of social problems as the shortcomings of individuals rather than as the flaws of society

family a social institution found in all societies that unites people in co-operative groups to care for one another, including any children

family violence emotional, physical, or sexual abuse of one family member by another

fashion a social pattern favoured by a large number of people

feminism the advocacy of social equality for women and men, in opposition to patriarchy and sexism

feminization of poverty the trend by which women represent an increasing proportion of the poor

fertility the incidence of child-bearing in a country's population

folkways norms for routine or casual interaction

formal operational stage the level of human development at which individuals think abstractly and critically

formal organizations large secondary groups organized to achieve their goals efficiently

functional illiteracy a lack of the reading and writing skills needed for everyday living

fundamentalism a conservative religious doctrine that opposes intellectualism and worldly accommodation in favour of restoring traditional, otherworldly religion

Gemeinschaft a type of social organization in which people are closely tied by kinship and tradition

gender the personal traits and social positions that members of a society attach to being female or male

gender identity traits that females and males, guided by their culture, incorporate into their personalities

gender roles (sex roles) attitudes and activities that a society links to each sex

gender stratification the unequal distribution of wealth, power, and privilege between men and women

gender-conflict approach a point of view that focuses on inequality and conflict between women and men

generalized other widespread cultural norms and values we use as a reference in evaluating ourselves

genocide the systematic killing of one category of people by another

gerontocracy a form of social organization in which older people have the most wealth, power, and prestige

gerontology the study of aging and elderly people

Gesellschaft a type of social organization in which people come together only on the basis of individual self-interest

global economy expanding economic activity that crosses national borders

global perspective the study of the larger world and our society's place in it

global stratification patterns of social inequality in the world as a whole

global warming a rise in Earth's average temperature due to an increasing concentration of carbon dioxide in the atmosphere

gossip rumour about people's personal affairs

government a formal organization that directs the political life of a society

groupthink the tendency of group members to conform, resulting in a narrow view of some issue

hate crime a criminal act against a person or a person's property by an offender motivated by racial or other bias

Hawthorne effect a change in a subject's behaviour caused simply by the awareness of being studied

health a state of complete physical, mental, and social well-being

heterosexism a view that labels anyone who is not heterosexual as "queer"

heterosexuality sexual attraction to someone of the other sex

hidden curriculum subtle presentations of political or cultural ideas in the classroom

high culture cultural patterns that distinguish a society's elite

high-income countries nations with the highest overall standards of living

holistic medicine an approach to health care that emphasizes the prevention of illness and takes into account a person's entire physical and social environment

homogamy marriage between people with the same social characteristics

homophobia the dread of close personal interaction with people thought to be gay, lesbian, or bisexual

homosexuality sexual attraction to someone of the same sex

horticulture the use of hand tools to raise crops

hunting and gathering the use of simple tools to hunt animals and gather vegetation

hypothesis a statement of a possible relationship between two (or more) variables

id the human's basic drives

ideal culture social patterns mandated by cultural values and norms

ideal type an abstract statement of the essential characteristics of any social phenomenon

ideology cultural beliefs that justify particular social arrangements, including patterns of inequality

incest taboo a norm forbidding sexual relations or marriage between certain relatives

income occupational wages or salaries, earnings from investments, and government transfer payments (e.g., welfare)

independent variable the variable that causes the change

inductive logical thought reasoning that transforms specific observations into general theory

industrialism the production of goods using advanced sources of energy to drive large machinery

infant mortality rate the number of deaths among infants in the first year of life for each thousand live births in a given year

infidelity sexual activity outside one's marriage

in-group a social group toward which a member feels respect and loyalty

institutional completeness the complexity of community organizations that meet the needs of members

institutional prejudice and discrimination bias built into the operation of society's institutions, including schools, hospitals, the police, and the workplace

instrumental leadership group leadership that focuses on the completion of tasks

intergenerational social mobility upward or downward social mobility of children in relation to their parents

interpretive sociology the study of society that focuses on the meanings people attach to their social world

intersection theory the interplay of race, class, and gender, often resulting in multiple dimensions of disadvantage

intersexual people people whose bodies, including genitals, have both female and male characteristics

interview a series of questions a researcher asks respondents in person

intragenerational social mobility a change in social position occurring during a person's lifetime

kinship a social bond based on common ancestry, marriage, or adoption

labelling theory   the idea that deviance and conformity result not so much from what people do as from how others respond to those actions

labour unions   worker organizations that seek to improve wages and working conditions through various strategies, including negotiations and strikes

language   a system of symbols that allows people to communicate with one another

latent functions   the unrecognized and unintended consequences of any social pattern

Lenski, Gerhard and Jean   society is defined by level of technology

liberation theology   the combining of Christian principles with political activism, often Marxist in character

life expectancy   the average lifespan of a society's population

looking-glass self   a self-image based on how we think others see us

low-income countries   nations with a low standard of living in which most people are poor

macro-level orientation   a broad focus on social structures that shape society as a whole

manifest functions   the recognized and intended consequences of any social pattern

marriage   a legal relationship, usually involving economic co-operation, sexual activity, and child-bearing

Marx, Karl   society is defined by type of social conflict

Marxist political-economy model   an analysis that explains politics in terms of the operation of a society's economic system

mass behaviour   collective behaviour among people spread over a wide geographic area

mass hysteria (moral panic)   a form of dispersed collective behaviour in which people react to a real or imagined event with irrational and even frantic fear

mass media   the means for delivering impersonal communications directed to a vast audience

mass society   a society in which prosperity and bureaucracy have weakened traditional social ties

master status   a status that has exceptional importance for social identity, often shaping a person's entire life

material culture   the physical things created by members of a society

matriarchy   a form of social organization in which females dominate males

matrilineal descent   a system tracing kinship through women

matrilocality   a residential pattern in which a married couple lives with or near the wife's family

measurement   a procedure for determining the value of a variable in a specific case

mechanical solidarity   strong social bonds, based on common sentiments and shared moral values, among members of pre-industrial societies

medicalization of deviance   the transformation of moral and legal deviance into a medical condition

medicine   the social institution that focuses on fighting disease and improving health

megalopolis   a vast urban region containing a number of cities and their surrounding suburbs

meritocracy   social stratification based on personal merit

metropolis   a large city that dominates the surrounding area both socially and economically

micro-level orientation   a close-up focus on social interaction in specific situations

middle-income countries   nations with a standard of living about average for the world as a whole

migration   the movement of people into and out of a specified territory

military-industrial complex   the close association of the federal government, the military, and defence industries

minority   any category of people distinguished by physical or cultural difference that a society sets apart and subordinates

miscegenation   biological reproduction by partners of different racial categories

mob   a highly emotional crowd that pursues a violent or destructive goal

modernity   changes brought about by the Industrial Revolution

modernization   the process of social change begun by industrialization

modernization theory   a model of economic and social development that explains global inequality in terms of technological and cultural differences between nations

monarchy   a political system in which a single family rules from generation to generation

monogamy   marriage that unites two partners

monotheism   belief in a single divine power

moral panic   see *mass hysteria*

mores   norms that are widely observed and have great moral significance

mortality   the incidence of death in a society's population

multiculturalism   social policy designed to encourage ethnic or cultural heterogeneity

multinational corporation   a very large business that operates in many countries

natural environment   Earth's surface and atmosphere, including living organisms, air, water, soil, and other resources necessary to sustain life

neocolonialism   a new form of global power relationships that involves not direct political control but economic exploitation by multinational corporations

neolocality   a residential pattern in which a married couple lives apart from both sets of parents

network   a web of weak social ties

nonmaterial culture   the ideas created by members of a society

non-verbal communication   communication using body movements, gestures, and facial expressions rather than speech

norms   rules and expectations by which a society guides the behaviour of its members

nuclear family   a family composed of one or two parents and their children

nuclear proliferation   the acquisition of nuclear weapons technology by more and more nations

objectivity   personal neutrality in conducting research

oligarchy   the rule of the many by the few

operationalize a variable   specifying exactly what is to be measured before assigning a value to a variable

organic solidarity social bonds based on specialization and interdependence that are strong among members of industrial societies

organizational environment factors outside an organization that affect its operation

organized crime a business that supplies illegal goods or services

other-directedness receptiveness to the latest trends and fashions, often expressed in the practice of imitating others

out-group a social group toward which a person feels a sense of competition or opposition

panic a form of collective behaviour in which people in one place react to a threat or other stimulus with irrational, frantic, and often self-destructive behaviour

participant observation a research method in which investigators systematically observe people while joining them in their routine activities

pastoralism the domestication of animals

patriarchy a form of social organization in which males dominate females

patrilineal descent a system tracing kinship through men

patrilocality a residential pattern in which a married couple lives with or near the husband's family

peer group a social group whose members have interests, social position, and age in common

personal space the surrounding area over which a person makes some claim to privacy

personality a person's fairly consistent patterns of acting, thinking, and feeling

plea bargain a legal negotiation in which the prosecution reduces a defendant's charge in exchange for a guilty plea

pluralism a state in which racial and ethnic minorities are distinct but have social parity

pluralist model an analysis of politics that sees power as spread among many competing interest groups

political parties organizations operating within the political system that seek control of the government

political revolution the overthrow of one political system in order to establish another

politics the social institution that distributes power, sets a society's goals, and makes decisions

polyandry marriage that unites one woman and two or more men

polygamy marriage that unites a person with two or more spouses

polygyny marriage that unites one man and two or more women

polytheism belief in many gods

popular culture cultural patterns that are widespread throughout society

population the people who are the focus of research

pornography sexually explicit material that causes sexual arousal

positivism a way of understanding based on science

positivist sociology the study of society based on systematic observation of social behaviour

post-industrial economy a productive system based on service work and high technology

post-industrialism technology that supports an information-based economy

postmodernism an approach that is critical of modernism, with a mistrust of grand theories and ideologies, that can have either a micro or macro orientation

postmodernity social patterns characteristic of post-industrial societies

power the ability to achieve desired ends despite resistance from others

power elite model an analysis of politics that views power as concentrated among the rich

pre-operational stage the level of human development at which individuals first use language and other symbols

prejudice a rigid and unfair generalization about an entire category of people

presentation of self a person's efforts to create specific impressions in the minds of others

primary group a small social group whose members share personal and lasting relationships

primary labour market jobs that provide extensive benefits to workers

primary sector the part of the economy that draws raw materials from the natural environment

primary sex characteristics the genitals, organs used for reproduction

profane an ordinary element of everyday life

profession a prestigious white-collar occupation that requires extensive formal education

proletarians people who sell their labour for wages

propaganda information presented with the intention of shaping public opinion

property crimes crimes that involve theft of property belonging to others

prostitution the selling of sexual services

public opinion widespread attitudes about controversial issues

queer theory a growing body of research findings that challenges the heterosexual bias in Western society

questionnaire a series of written questions that a researcher presents to subjects

race a socially constructed category of people who share biologically transmitted traits that members of a society consider important

race-conflict approach a point of view that focuses on inequality and conflict between people of different racial and ethnic categories

racism the belief that one racial category is innately superior or inferior to another

rainforests regions of dense forestation, most of which circle the globe close to the equator

rational-legal authority power legitimized by legally enacted rules and regulations

rationality a way of thinking that emphasizes deliberate, matter-of-fact calculation of the most efficient way to accomplish a particular task

rationalization of society the historical change from tradition to rationality as the main mode of human thought

real culture actual social patterns that only approximate cultural expectations

reference group a social group that serves as a point of reference in making evaluations and decisions

rehabilitation a program for reforming the offender to preclude subsequent offences

relative deprivation a perceived disadvantage arising from some specific comparison

relative poverty the deprivation of some people in relation to those who have more

reliability consistency in measurement

religion a social institution involving beliefs and practices based on recognizing the sacred

religiosity the importance of religion in a person's life

replication repetition of research by other investigators

research method a systematic plan for doing research

resocialization efforts to effect radical change in an inmate's personality by carefully controlling the environment

retribution an act of moral vengeance by which society makes the offender suffer as much as the suffering caused by the crime

riot a social eruption that is highly emotional, violent, and undirected

ritual formal, ceremonial behaviour

role behaviour expected of someone who holds a particular status

role conflict conflict among the roles connected to two or more statuses

role set a number of roles attached to a single status

role strain tension among the roles connected to a single status

routinization of charisma the transformation of charismatic authority into some combination of traditional and bureaucratic authority

rumour unconfirmed information that people spread informally, often by word of mouth

sacred set apart as extraordinary, inspiring awe and reverence

sample a part of a population that represents the whole

Sapir-Whorf hypothesis people perceive the world through the cultural lens of language

scapegoat a person or category of people, typically with little power, whom people unfairly blame for their own troubles

schooling formal instruction under the direction of specially trained teachers

science a logical system that bases knowledge on direct, systematic observation

scientific management the application of scientific principles to the operation of a business or other large organization

scientific sociology the study of society based on systematic observation of social behaviour

secondary analysis a research method in which a researcher uses data collected by others

secondary group a large and impersonal social group whose members pursue a specific goal or activity

secondary labour market jobs that provide minimal benefits to workers

secondary sector the part of the economy that transforms raw materials into manufactured goods

secondary sex characteristics bodily development, apart from the genitals, that distinguishes biologically mature females and males

sect a type of religious organization that stands apart from the larger society

secularization the historical decline in the importance of the supernatural and the sacred

segregation the physical and social separation of categories of people

self the part of an individual's personality composed of self-awareness and self-image

self-employment earning a living without working for a large organization

sensorimotor stage the level of human development at which individuals experience the world only through their senses

sex the biological distinction between females and males

sex ratio the number of males for every 100 females in a nation's population

sex roles see *gender roles*

sexism the belief that one sex is innately superior to the other

sexual harassment comments, gestures, or physical contact of a sexual nature that is deliberate, repeated, and unwelcome

sexual orientation a person's romantic and emotional attraction to another person

sick role patterns of behaviour defined as appropriate for people who are ill

significant others such as parents, who have special importance for socialization

social change the transformation of culture and social institutions over time

social character personality patterns common to members of a particular society

social conflict the struggle between segments of society over valued resources

social-conflict approach a framework for building theory that sees society as an arena of inequality that generates conflict and change

social construction of reality the process by which people creatively shape reality through social interaction

social control attempts by others to regulate people's thoughts and behaviour

social dysfunction any social pattern that may disrupt the operation of society

social epidemiology the study of health and disease as distributed throughout a society's population

social functions the consequences of any social pattern for the operation of society as a whole

social group two or more people who identify with and interact with one another

social institutions the major spheres of social life, or societal subsystems, organized to meet human needs

social interaction the process by which people act and react in relation to others

social mobility a change in position within the social hierarchy

social movement organized activity that encourages or discourages social change

social protection rendering an offender incapable of further offences either temporarily through incarceration or permanently by execution

social stratification a system by which a society ranks categories of people in a hierarchy

social structure any relatively stable pattern of social behaviour

socialism an economic system in which natural resources and the means of producing goods and services are collectively owned

socialization the lifelong social experience by which people develop their human potential and learn culture

socialized medicine a medical care system in which the government owns and operates most medical facilities and employs most physicians

society people who interact in a defined territory and share a culture

societal protection rendering an offender incapable of further offences either temporarily through incarceration or permanently by execution

socio-cultural evolution changes that occur as a society gains new technology

socio-economic status a composite ranking based on various dimensions of social inequality

sociobiology a theoretical approach that explores the ways in which human biology affects how we create culture

sociological perspective seeing the general in the particular

sociology the systematic study of human society

spurious correlation an apparent but false relationship between two (or more) variables that is caused by some other variable

state capitalism an economic and political system in which companies are privately owned but co-operate closely with the government

state church a church formally allied with the state

status a social position that a person holds

status consistency the degree of consistency in a person's social standing across various dimensions of social inequality

status set all of the statuses that a person holds at a given time

stereotype a simplified description applied to every person in some category

stigma a powerfully negative label that greatly changes a person's self-concept and social identity

streaming assigning students to different types of educational programs

structural social mobility a shift in the social position of large numbers of people owing more to changes in society itself than to individual efforts

structural-functional approach a framework for building theory that sees society as a complex system whose parts work together to promote solidarity and stability

subculture cultural patterns that set apart some segment of a society's population

suburbs urban areas beyond the political boundaries of a city

superego the cultural values and norms internalized by an individual

survey a research method in which subjects respond to a series of statements or questions in a questionnaire or an interview

symbolic-interaction approach a framework for building theory that sees society as the product of the everyday interactions of individuals

symbols anything that carries a particular meaning recognized by people who share culture

technology knowledge that people use to make a way of life in their surroundings

terrorism acts of violence or the threat of violence used as a political strategy by an individual or a group

tertiary sector the part of the economy that involves services rather than goods

theoretical approach a basic image of society that guides thinking and research

theory a statement of how and why specific facts are related

Thomas theorem situations we define as real become real in their consequences

total institution a setting in which people are isolated from the rest of society and manipulated by an administrative staff

totalitarianism a highly centralized political system that extensively regulates people's lives

totem an object in the natural world collectively defined as sacred

tradition values and beliefs passed from generation to generation

traditional authority power legitimized by respect for long-established cultural patterns

tradition-directedness rigid conformity to time-honoured ways of living

transgendered people see *transsexuals*

transsexuals people who feel they are one sex even though biologically they are the other

triad a social group with three members

underground economy economic activity involving income or the exchange of goods and services that is not reported to the government as required by law

universal medical coverage a system in which the costs of essential medical services are covered by the state

urban ecology the study of the link between the physical and social dimensions of cities

urbanization the concentration of population into cities

validity actually measuring exactly what you intend to measure

values culturally defined standards that people use to decide what is desirable, good, and beautiful, and that serve as broad guidelines for social living

variable a concept whose value changes from case to case

victimless crimes violations of law in which there are no obvious victims

violent crimes crimes against people that involve violence or the threat of violence

war organized, armed conflict among the people of two or more nations, directed by their governments

wealth the total amount of money and other assets, minus outstanding debts

Weber, Max society is defined by ideas/mode of thinking

welfare capitalism an economic and political system that combines a mostly market-based economy with extensive social welfare programs

white-collar crime crime committed by persons of high social position in the course of their occupations

white-collar occupations higher-prestige jobs that involve mostly mental activity

zero population growth the level of reproduction that maintains population in a steady state

References

Chapter 1

Benedetti, Paul, and Nancy Dehart, Eds. *On McLuhan: Forward Through the Rearview Mirror.* Scarborough, ON: Prentice Hall, 1996.

Berger, Peter L. *Invitation to Sociology.* New York: Anchor Books, 1963.

Breton, Raymond. "Institutional Completeness of Ethnic Communities and the Personal Relations of Immigrants." *American Journal of Sociology.* Vol. 70 (1964):193–205.

Breton, Raymond, and Jeffrey G. Reitz. *Ethnic Relations in Canada: Institutional Dynamics.* Montreal: McGill-Queen's University Press, 2007.

Canada. *Canadian Charter of Rights and Freedoms,* enacted as Part I of the *Constitution Act, 1982,* being Schedule B to the *Canada Act, 1982* (U.K.), 1982, c.11.

Centers for Disease Control and Prevention. "Deaths: Final Data for 2010 (tables only)." 2012. Available at http://www.cdc.gov/nchs/data/dvs/deaths_2010_release.pdf.

Clark, Campbell. "Rampage by U.S. soldier shatters trust that Canadian forces built." *The Globe and Mail* (March 12, 2012):A1.

Clement, Wallace. *The Canadian Corporate Elite: Economic Power in Canada.* Toronto: McClelland & Stewart, 1975.

———. "Comparative Class Analysis: Locating Canada in a North American and Nordic Context." *Canadian Review of Sociology and Anthropology.* Vol. 27, No. 4 (1990).

Comte, Auguste. *Auguste Comte and Positivism: The Essential Writings.* Gertrud Lenzer, ed. New York: Harper Torchbooks, 1975.

Corbeil, Jean-Pierre. "Sport Participation in Canada." In Statistics Canada, *Canadian Social Trends. Volume 3.* Toronto: Thompson Educational Publishing, 2000.

De Tocqueville, Alexis. *The Old Regime and the French Revolution.* Stuart Gilbert, trans. Garden City, NY: Anchor/Doubleday Books, 1955; orig. 1856.

Du Bois, W.E.B. *The Philadelphia Negro: A Social Study.* New York: Schocken Books, 1967; orig. 1899.

Durkheim, Émile. *Suicide.* New York: Free Press, 1966; orig. 1897.

Eichler, Margrit. "Women Pioneers in Canadian Sociology: The Effects of a Politics of Gender and a Politics of Knowledge." *Canadian Journal of Sociology.* Vol. 26, No. 3 (2001):375–403.

Foucault, Michel. *Power/Knowledge.* ed. Colin Gordon. New York: Pantheon Books, 1980.

Goffman, Erving. *The Presentation of Self in Everyday Life.* Garden City: NY: Anchor Books, 1959.

———. *Asylums: Essays on the Social Situation of Mental Patients and Other Inmates.* New York: Doubleday Anchor, 1961.

———. *Stigma: Notes on the Management of Spoiled Identity.* Englewood Cliffs, N.J.: Prentice-Hall, 1963.

Goyder, John. *Technology and Society: A Canadian Perspective.* Peterborough, ON: Broadview Press, 1997.

Innis, Harold A. *The Fur Trade in Canada.* Toronto: University of Toronto Press, 1930.

Lengermann, Patricia M., and Jill Niebrugge-Brantley. *The Women Founders: Sociology and Theory, 1830 to 1930.* Toronto: McGraw Hill, 1998.

Maki, Allan. "Nothing Stops Woolstencroft." *The Globe and Mail* (November 8, 2011): S5.

McDonald, Lynn. *The Women Founders of the Social Sciences.* Ottawa: Carleton University Press, 1994.

Mills, C. Wright. *The Sociological Imagination.* New York: Oxford University Press, 1959.

Porter, John. *The Vertical Mosaic: An Analysis of Social Class and Power in Canada.* Toronto: University of Toronto Press, 1965.

Skelton, Chad. "Decide Military's Role, Ottawa Told." *The Globe and Mail* (August 12, 1997):A4.

Smith, Dorothy. *Institutional Ethnography: A Sociology for People.* Toronto: AltaMira Press, 2005.

United Nations. *Human Development Report 2014.* [Online] Available July 29, 2016, at https://issuu.com/unpublications/docs/hdr2014/62.

Winslow, Donna. *The Canadian Airborne Regiment in Somalia. A Socio-cultural Inquiry.* Ottawa: Commission of Inquiry into the Deployment of Canadian Forces to Somalia, 1997.

Chapter 2

Albas, Daniel, and Cheryl Albas. "Studying Students Studying: Perspectives, Identities and Activities." In Mary Lorenz Dietz, Robert Prus, and William The Shaffir, eds. *Doing Everyday Life: Ethnography as Human Lived Experience.* Mississauga, ON: Copp Clark Longman, 1994.

American Sociological Association. "Code of Ethics." Washington, DC: American Sociological Association, 1997.

Anderson, Doris. *The Unfinished Revolution.* Toronto: Doubleday Books, 1991.

Bakker, J.I. (Hans). "Wilhelm Dilthey: Classical Sociological Theorist." *Quarterly Journal of Ideology: A Critique of Conventional Wisdom.* Vol. 22, No. 1–2 (1999).

Baltzell, E. Digby. *Puritan Boston and Quaker Philadelphia.* New York: Free Press, 1979.

Benjamin, Lois. *The Black Elite: Facing the Color Line in the Twilight of the Twentieth Century.* Chicago, IL: Nelson-Hall, 1991.

Berger, Peter L., and Hansfried Kellner. *Sociology Reinterpreted: An Essay on Method and Vocation.* Garden City, NY: Anchor Books, 1981.

Bibby, Reginald W. *The Bibby Report: Social Trends Canadian Style.* Toronto: Stoddart, 1995.

———. *Canada's Teens: Today, Yesterday and Tomorrow.* Toronto: Stoddart, 2001.

Cafb. Canadian Association of Food Banks. Annual Report. 2004. [Online] Available at http://www.cafb-acba.ca/documents/04annual_report.pdf.

Canada. Royal Commission on Aboriginal Peoples. *Ethical Guidelines for Research.* 8 pp. Ottawa: Supply and Services Canada, 1993.

———. Final report of the Royal Commission on Aboriginal Peoples. 6 Vols. Ottawa: Ministry of Indian Affairs and Northern Development, 1996.

———. Social Sciences and Humanities Research Council of Canada. Tri-Council Policy Statement: Ethical Conduct for Research Involving Humans. 2003 (includes updates to 2005). [Online] Available at http://www.pre.ethics.gc.ca/english/policystatement/policystatement.cfm.

Eichler, Margrit. *Nonsexist Research Methods: A Practical Guide.* Winchester, MA: Unwin Hyman, 1988.

Feagin, Joe R., and Vera Hernán. *Liberation Sociology.* Boulder, CO: Westview Press, 2001.

Fischer, Claude W. *The Urban Experience.* 2nd ed. New York: Harcourt Brace Jovanovich, 1984.

Gerber, Linda M. *Minority Survival: Community Characteristics and Out-Migration from Indian Communities Across Canada.* Toronto: University of Toronto Press, 1976.

———. "Multiple Jeopardy: A Socio-economic Comparison of Men and Women among the Indian, Métis and Inuit Peoples of Canada." *Canadian Ethnic Studies.* Vol. xxii, No. 3 (1990):69–84.

Giovannini, Maureen. "Female Anthropologist and Male Informant: Gender Conflict in a Sicilian Town." In John J. Macionis and Nijole V. Benokraitis, eds. *Seeing Ourselves: Classic, Contemporary, and Cross-Cultural Readings in Sociology.* 2nd ed. Englewood Cliffs, NJ: Prentice Hall, 1992. pp. 27–32.

Haney, Craig, Curtis Banks, and Philip Zimbardo. "Interpersonal Dynamics in a Simulated Prison." *International Journal of Criminology and Penology.* Vol. 1 (1973):69–97.

Hess, Beth B. "Breaking and Entering the Establishment: Committing Social Change and Confronting the Backlash." *Social Problems.* Vol. 46, No. 1 (February 1999):1–12.

Klein, Daniel B., and Charlotta Stern. "How Politically Diverse Are the Social Sciences and Humanities? Survey Evidence from Six Fields." National Association of Scholars. 2004. [Online] Available January 13, 2005, at http://www.nas.org/aa/klein_launch.htm.

Lavin, Danielle, and Douglas W. Maynard. "Standardization vs. Rapport: Respondent Laughter and Interviewer Reaction during Telephone Surveys." *American Sociological Review.* Vol. 66, No. 3 (June 2001):453–79.

Lorenz, Frederick O., and Brent T. Bruton. "Experiments in Surveys: Linking Mass Class Questionnaires to Introductory Research Methods." *Teaching Sociology.* Vol. 24, No. 3 (July 1996):264–71.

Luxton, Meg. *More Than a Labour of Love.* Toronto: Women's Press, 1980.

Mackie, Marlene. *Exploring Gender Relation.* Toronto: Butterworths, 1983.

Matthews, Ralph. *"There's No Better Place Than Here": Social Change in Three Newfoundland Communities.* Toronto: Peter Martin Associates, 1976.

McDonald, Lynn. *The Women Founders of the Social Sciences.* Ottawa: Carleton University Press, 1994.

Nelson, E.D., and Barry W. Robinson. *Gender in Canada.* Scarborough, ON: Prentice Hall, 1999.

Neuman, W. Laurence. *Social Research Methods: Qualitative and Quantitative Approaches.* 3rd ed. Boston: Allyn & Bacon, 1997; 4th ed. 2000.

Perrucci, Robert. "Inventing Social Justice: SSSP and the Twenty-First Century." *Social Problems.* Vol. 48, No. 2 (May 2001):159–67.

Prus, Robert. "Approaching the Study of Human Group Life: Symbolic Interaction and Ethnographic Inquiry." In Mary Lorenz Dietz, Robert Prus, and William Shaffir, eds. *Doing Everyday Life: Ethnography as Human Lived Experience.* Mississauga, ON: Copp Clark Longman, 1994.

Rademacher, Eric W. "The Effect of Question Wording on College Students." *The Pittsburgh Undergraduate Review.* Vol. 8, No. 1 (Spring 1992):45–81.

Roethlisberger, F.J., and William J. Dickson. *Management and the Worker.* Cambridge, MA: Harvard University Press, 1939.

Smith, Dorothy E. "Women, the Family and Corporate Capitalism." In M. Stephenson, ed. *Women in Canada.* Don Mills, ON: General Publishing, 1977. pp. 32–48.

———. "Women's Inequality and the Family." Department of Sociology, Ontario Institute for Studies in Education, Mimeograph, 1979.

———. "Women, Class and the Family." In R. Miliband and J. Saville, eds. *The Socialist Register*. London, UK: Merlin Press, 1983.

Sniderman, Paul M., David A. Northrup, Joseph F. Fletcher, Peter H. Russell, and Philip E. Tetlock. "Psychological and Cultural Foundations of Prejudice: The Case of Anti-Semitism in Quebec." *Canadian Review of Sociology and Anthropology*. Vol. 30, No. 2 (May 1993):242–70.

Thomas, W.I., and F. Znaniecki. *The Polish Peasant in Europe and America*. New York: Octagon Books, 1971; orig. 1919.

Wendell, Susan. "Toward a Feminist Theory of Disability." In E.D. Nelson and B.W. Robinson, eds. *Gender in the 1990s: Images, Realities, and Issues*. Toronto: Nelson Canada, 1995. pp. 455–56.

Whyte, William Foote. *Street Corner Society*. 3rd ed. Chicago, IL: University of Chicago Press, 1981; orig. 1943.

Zimbardo, Philip G. "Pathology of Imprisonment." *Society*. Vol. 9 (April 1972):4–8.

Chapter 3

Abley, Mark. "Losing Our Languages." *National Post* (February 14, 2006): A18.

Barash, David. *The Whispering Within*. New York: Penguin Books, 1981.

Barovick, Harriet. "Tongues That Go Out of Style." *Time* (June 10, 2002):22.

Bellah, Robert N., Richard Madsen, William M. Sullivan, Ann Swidler, and Steven M. Tipton. *Habits of the Heart: Individualism and Commitment in American Life*. New York: Harper & Row, 1985.

Berteau, Celeste. "Disconnected Intimacy: AOL Instant Messenger Use among Kenyon College Students." Senior thesis. Kenyon College, 2005.

Bricker, Darrell, and John Wright. *What Canadians Think . . . about Almost Everything*. Toronto: Doubleday Canada, 2005.

Central Intelligence Agency. "CIA World Factbook." 2009. Available at https://www.cia.gov/library/publications/the-world-factbook/index.html

Chagnon, Napoleon A. *Ynomamö: The Fierce People*. 4th ed. Austin, TX: Holt, Rinehart and Winston, 1992.

Darwin, Charles. *On the Origin of Species*. London, UK: Penguin, 1968; orig. 1859.

Fontaine, Phil, Reuven Bulka, and Sylvain Abitbol. "Two Solitudes Break Their Isolation Together." *The Globe and Mail* (July 31, 2008):A15.

Fretz, Winfield. *The Waterloo Mennonites: A Community in Paradox*. Waterloo, ON: Wilfrid Laurier Press, 1989.

Hall, John R., and Mary Jo Neitz. *Culture: Sociological Perspectives*. Englewood Cliffs, NJ: Prentice Hall, 1993.

Harris, Marvin. *Cultural Anthropology*. 2nd ed. New York: Harper & Row, 1987.

Hayden, Thomas. "Losing Our Voices." *U.S. News & World Report* (May 26, 2003):42.

Helin, David W. "When Slogans Go Wrong." *American Demographics*. Vol. 14, No. 2 (February 1992):14.

IBM. "Web Site by Country/Region and Language." 2012. Available at http://www.ibm.com/planetwide/select/selector.html.

Kay, Paul, and Willett Kempton. "What Is the Sapir–Whorf Hypothesis?" *American Anthropologist*. Vol. 86, No. 1 (March 1984):65–79.

Keller, Helen. *The Story of My Life*. New York: Doubleday, Page, 1903.

Lederman, Marsha. "A New Native Art." *The Globe and Mail* (February 29, 2012):R1.

Lenhart, Amanda. "Adults, Cell Phones, and Texting." Pew Research Center Publications. [Online] Available September 2, 2010, at http://pewresearch.org/pubs/1716/adults-cell-phones-text-messages.

Lewis, M. Paul, ed. *Ethnologue: Languages of the World*. 16th ed. Dallas, Tex: SIL International, 2009.

Linton, Ralph. "One Hundred Percent American." *The American Mercury*. Vol. 40, No. 160 (April 1937):427–29.

Lipset, Seymour Martin. *Canada and the United States*. Charles F. Donan and John H. Sigler, eds. Englewood Cliffs, NJ: Prentice Hall, 1985.

Lynd, Robert S. *Knowledge For What? The Place of Social Science in American Culture*. Princeton, NJ: Princeton University Press, 1967.

Maclean's/CTV Poll, 1994. January 2, 1995. Cited in Rathus, Spencer A., Jeffrey S. Nevid, Lois Fischner-Rathus, and Edward S. Herold. *Human Sexuality in a World of Diversity*. Canadian Edition. Toronto: Pearson Canada, 2004. p. 424.

Maclennan, Hugh. *Two Solitudes*. Toronto: McClelland & Stewart, 2008; orig. 1945.

Marx, Karl, and Friedrich Engels. *The Marx-Engels Reader*. 2nd ed. Robert C. Tucker, ed. New York: Norton, 1978; orig. 1859.

Murdock, George Peter. "The Common Denominator of Cultures." In Ralph Linton, ed. *The Science of Man in World Crisis*. New York: Columbia University Press, 1945. pp. 123–42.

National Post. "Our G-G: Gracious and Gutsy." (May 29, 2009):A14.

Ogburn, William F. *On Culture and Social Change*. Chicago, IL: University of Chicago Press, 1964.

Parsons, Talcott. *Societies: Evolutionary and Comparative Perspectives*. Englewood Cliffs, NJ: Prentice Hall, 1966.

Pevere, Geoff, and Greig Dymond. *Mondo Canuck: A Canadian Pop Culture Odyssey*. Scarborough, ON: Prentice Hall Canada, 1996.

Philp, Margaret. "Aboriginal Languages Nearing Extinction: Expert." *The Globe and Mail* (May 13, 2000):A7.

Pinker, Steven. *The Language Instinct*. New York: Morrow, 1994.

Rubin, Joel. "E-mail Too Formal? Try a Text Message." Columbia News Service. March 7, 2003. [Online] Available April 25, 2005, at http://www.jrn.columbia.edu/studentwork/cns/2003-03-07/85.asp.

Sapir, Edward. "The Status of Linguistics as a Science." *Language*. Vol. 5 (1929):207–14.

———. *Selected Writings of Edward Sapir in Language, Culture, and Personality*. David G. Mandelbaum, ed. Berkeley: University of California Press, 1949.

Sauvé, Roger. *Borderlines: What Canadians and Americans Should—but Don't—Know About Each Other*. Whitby, ON: McGraw-Hill Ryerson, 1994.

Sowell, Thomas. *Migrations and Cultures: A World View*. New York: Basic Books, 1996.

Statistics Canada. "Electronic Commerce and Technology," *The Daily*, April 2, 2003. [Online] Available at http://www.statcan.ca/Daily/English/030402/td030402.htm.

———. Imports and exports (International trade statistics). 2012. http://www.statcan.gc.ca/trade-commerce/data-donnee-eng.htm.

Sumner, William Graham. *Folkways*. New York: Dover, 1959; orig. 1906.

UNESCO. Data reported in "Tower of Babel Is Tumbling Down—Slowly." *U.S. News & World Report* (July 2, 2001):9.

Whorf, Benjamin Lee. "The Relation of Habitual Thought and Behavior to Language." In *Language, Thought, and Reality*. Cambridge, MA: Technology Press of MIT; New York: Wiley, 1956:134–59; orig. 1941.

Williams, Robin M., Jr. *American Society: A Sociological Interpretation*. 3rd ed. New York: Knopf, 1970.

World Values Survey. "Latest Publications: Predict 2005—FIGURE." 2004. [Online] Available April 25, 2005, at http://www.worldvaluessurvey.com/library/index.html.

Chapter 4

Bell, Daniel. *The Coming of Post-Industrial Society: A Venture in Social Forecasting*. New York: Basic Books, 1973.

Berger, Peter. "Faith and Development." *Society*. Vol. 46, No. 1 (January/February 2009):69–75.

Boulding, Elise. *The Underside of History*. Boulder, CO: Westview Press, 1976.

Clarkson, Adrienne. "Installation Speech." In David Taras and Beverly Rasporich, eds. *A Passion for Identity: Canadian Studies for the 21st Century*. 4th ed. Scarborough, ON: Nelson, 2001.

Durkheim, Émile. *The Division of Labor in Society*. New York: Free Press, 1964a; orig. 1895.

———. *The Rules of Sociological Method*. New York: Free Press, 1964b; orig. 1893.

———. *Suicide*. New York: Free Press, 1966; orig. 1897.

———. *Sociology and Philosophy*. New York: Free Press, 1974; orig. 1924.

Fisher, Elizabeth. *Woman's Creation: Sexual Evolution and the Shaping of Society*. Garden City, NY: Anchor/Doubleday, 1979.

Gerber, Linda M. "Referendum Results: Defining New Boundaries for an Independent Quebec." *Canadian Ethnic Studies*. Vol. xxiv, No. 2 (1992):22–34.

Gerth, H.H., and C. Wright Mills, Eds. *From Max Weber: Essays in Sociology*. New York: Oxford University Press, 1946.

Grand Council of the Crees. *Sovereign Injustice: Forcible Inclusion of the James Bay Crees and Cree Territory into a Sovereign Quebec*. Nemaska, QC: The Grand Council, 1995.

Hamilton, Anita. "Speeders, Say Cheese." *Time* (September 17, 2001):32.

Hiller, Harry H. *Canadian Society: A Macro Analysis*. 5th edition. Toronto: Pearson Education Canada, 2006.

Leacock, Eleanor. "Women's Status in Egalitarian Societies: Implications for Social Evolution." *Current Anthropology*. Vol. 19, No. 2 (June 1978):247–75.

Lenski, Gerhard, Patrick Nolan, and Jean Lenski. *Human Societies: An Introduction to Macrosociology*. 7th ed. New York: McGraw-Hill, 1995.

Lichter, S. Robert, Stanley Rothman, and Linda S. Lichter. *The Media Elite: America's New Powerbrokers*. New York: Hastings House, 1990.

Marx, Karl. Excerpt from "A Contribution to the Critique of Political Economy." In Karl Marx and Friedrich Engels, *Marx and Engels: Basic Writings on Politics and Philosophy*. Lewis S. Feurer, ed. Garden City, NY: Anchor Books, 1959. pp. 42–46.

———. *Karl Marx: Early Writings*. T.B. Bottomore, ed. New York: McGraw-Hill, 1964a; orig. 1844.

Marx, Karl, and Friedrich Engels. "Manifesto of the Communist Party." In Robert C. Tucker, ed. *The Marx-Engels Reader*. New York: Norton, 1972; orig. 1848. pp. 331–62.

Nolan, Patrick, and Gerhard Lenski. *Human Societies: An Introduction to Macrosociology*. 9th ed. Boulder, CO: Paradigm, 2004.

Reid, Scott. *Canada Remapped: How the Partition of Quebec Will Reshape the Nation*. Vancouver: Pulp Press, 1992.

Statistics Canada. 2011. National Household Survey, Catalogue no. 99-010-X2011036.

Weber, Max. *The Protestant Ethic and the Spirit of Capitalism*. New York: Charles Scribner's Sons, 1958; orig. 1904–05.

———. *Economy and Society*. G. Roth and C. Wittich, eds. Berkeley, CA: University of California Press, 1978; orig. 1921.

Chapter 5

American Psychological Association. *Violence and Youth: Psychology's Response*. Washington, DC: American Psychological Association, 1993.

Ariès, Philippe. *Centuries of Childhood: A Social History of Family Life*. New York: Vintage, 1962.

Baldus, Bernd, and Verna Tribe. "The Development of Perceptions and Evaluations of Social Inequality Among Public School Children." *Canadian Review of Sociology and Anthropology*. Vol. 15, No. 1 (1978):50–60.

Begley, Sharon. "Gray Matters." *Newsweek* (March 7, 1995):48–54.

Best, Raphaela. *We've All Got Scars: What Boys and Girls Learn in Elementary School*. Bloomington: Indiana University Press, 1983.

Canada. House of Commons. Standing Committee on Communications and Culture. *Television Violence: Fraying our Social Fabric*. Issue No. 6. Ottawa: Supply and Services Canada, 1993.

Chodorow, Nancy. *Femininities, Masculinities, Sexualities: Freud and Beyond*. Lexington, KY: University of Kentucky Press, 1994.

Cooley, Charles Horton. *Human Nature and the Social Order*. New York: Schocken Books, 1964; orig. 1902.

Curtiss, Susan. *Genie: A Psycholinguistic Study of a Modern-Day "Wild Child."* New York: Academic Press, 1977.

Davis, Kingsley. "Extreme Social Isolation of a Child." *American Journal of Sociology*. Vol. 45, No. 4 (January 1940):554–65.

———. "Final Note on a Case of Extreme Isolation." *American Journal of Sociology*. Vol. 52, No. 5 (March 1947):432–37.

Davies, Mark, and Denise B. Kandel. "Parental and Peer Influences on Adolescents' Educational Plans: Some Further Evidence." *American Journal of Sociology*. Vol. 87, No. 2 (September 1981):363–87.

Donovan, Virginia K., and Ronnie Littenberg. "Psychology of Women: Feminist Therapy." In Barbara Haber, ed. *The Women's Annual 1981: The Year in Review*. Boston, MA: G.K. Hall, 1982. pp. 211–35.

Dunlop, Garfield. *Hansard*, Ontario. December 1, 2003:236.

Edwards, Peter. "Boot Campers Get Cool Welcome." *Toronto Star* (August 1, 1977): A1.

Ellison, Christopher G., John P. Bartkowski, and Michelle L. Segal. "Do Conservative Protestant Parents Spank More Often? Further Evidence from the National Survey of Families and Households." *Social Science Quarterly*. Vol. 77, No. 3 (September 1996):663–73.

Erikson, Erik H. *Childhood and Society*. New York: Norton, 1963; orig. 1950.

Fellman, Bruce. "Taking the Measure of Children's T.V." *Yale Alumni Magazine* (April 1995):46–51.

Finkelstein, Neal W., and Ron Haskins. "Kindergarten Children Prefer Same-Color Peers." *Child Development*. Vol. 54, No. 2 (April 1983):502–08.

Frideres, James S. "Ethnogenesis: Immigrants to Ethnics and the Development of a Rainbow Class Structure." *Canadian Issues* (Spring 2005):58–60.

Gibbs, Nancy. "What Kids (Really) Need." *Time* (April 30, 2001):48–49.

Gilligan, Carol. *In a Different Voice: Psychological Theory and Women's Development*. Cambridge, MA: Harvard University Press, 1982.

———. *Making Connections: The Relational Worlds of Adolescent Girls at Emma Willard School*. Cambridge, MA: Harvard University Press, 1990.

Goffman, Erving. *Asylums: Essays on the Social Situation of Mental Patients and Other Inmates*. Garden City, NY: Anchor Books, 1961.

Goldberg, Bernard. *Bias: A CBS Insider Exposes How the Media Distort the News*. Washington, DC: Regnery, 2002.

Goldsmith, H.H. "Genetic Influences on Personality from Infancy." *Child Development*. Vol. 54, No. 2 (April 1983):331–35.

Gorman, Christine. "Stressed-Out Kids." *Time* (December 25, 2000):168.

Hareven, Tamara K. "The Life Course and Aging in Historical Perspective." In Tamara K. Hareven and Kathleen J. Adams, eds. *Aging and Life Course Transitions: An Interdisciplinary Perspective*. New York: Guilford Press, 1982:1–26.

Harlow, Harry F., and Margaret Kuenne Harlow. "Social Deprivation in Monkeys." *Scientific American*. Vol. 207 (November 1962):137–46.

Human Rights Watch. "Children's Rights: Child Labor." 2004. [Online] Available August 29, 2005, at http://www.hrw.org/children/labor.htm.

Hymowitz, Kay S. "Kids Today Are Growing Up Way Too Fast." *Wall Street Journal* (October 28, 1998):A22.

Jordan, Ellen, and Angela Cowan. "Warrior Narratives in the Kindergarten Classroom: Renegotiating the Social Contract?" *Gender and Society*. Vol. 9, No. 6 (December 1995):727–43.

Kohlberg, Lawrence. *The Psychology of Moral Development: The Nature and Validity of Moral Stages*. New York: Harper & Row, 1981.

Kohlberg, Lawrence, and Carol Gilligan. "The Adolescent as Philosopher: The Discovery of Self in a Postconventional World." *Daedalus*. Vol. 100 (Fall 1971):1051–86.

Kohn, Melvin L. *Class and Conformity: A Study in Values*. 2nd ed. Homewood, IL: Dorsey Press, 1977.

Kubler-Ross, Elisabeth. *On Death and Dying*. New York: Macmillan, 1969.

Lareau, Annette. "Invisible Inequality: Social Class and Childrearing in Black Families and White Familes." *American Sociological Review*. Vol. 67, No. 5 (October 2002):747–76.

Larossa, Ralph, and Donald C. Reitzes. "Two? Two and One-Half? Thirty Months? Chronometrical Childhood in Early Twentieth-Century America." *Sociological Forum*. Vol. 166, No. 3 (September 2001):385–407.

Lever, Janet. "Sex Differences in the Complexity of Children's Play and Games." *American Sociological Review*. Vol. 43, No. 4 (August 1978):471–83.

Mead, George Herbert. *Mind, Self, and Society*. Charles W. Morris, ed. Chicago, IL: University of Chicago Press, 1962; orig. 1934.

Meltzer, Bernard N. "Mead's Social Psychology." In Jerome G. Manis and Bernard N. Meltzer, eds. *Symbolic Interaction: A Reader in Social Psychology*. 3rd ed. Needham Heights, MA: Allyn & Bacon, 1978.

NORC. *General Social Surveys, 1972–2006: Cumulative Codebook*. Chicago: National Opinion Research Center, 2007.

Obasogie, Osagie K. *Blinded by Sight: Seeing Race Through the Eyes of the Blind*. Stanford, Calif.: Stanford University Press, 2013.

Press, Andrea L. Review of *Enlightened Racism: "The Cosby Show," Audiences, and the Myth of the American Dream*, by Sut Jhally and Justin Lewis. *American Journal of Sociology*. Vol. 99, No. 1 (July 1993):219–21.

PricewaterhouseCoopers. "Filmed Entertainment Industry in Canada the Fastest Growing in World," September 13, 2003. [Online] Available at http://www.pwcglobal.com/extweb/ncpressrelease.nsf/docid/B8AC0264872F898085256D9B00634DB6.

Richards, Karen. *The Aboriginal Peoples Television Network: An Institutional Model of Empowerment*. MA thesis. Department of Sociology. Guelph: University of Guelph, 2006.

Rothman, Stanley, Stephen Powers, and David Rothman. "Feminism in Films." *Society*. Vol. 30, No. 3 (March–April 1993):66–72.

Rymer, Russ. *Genie*. New York: HarperPerennial, 1994.

Sheehan, Tom. "Senior Esteem as a Factor in Socioeconomic Complexity." *The Gerontologist*. Vol. 16, No. 5 (October 1976):433–40.

Statistics Canada. "2001 Census: Age and Sex," *The Daily*, July 16, 2002. [Online] Available at http://www.statcan.ca/Daily/English/020716/td020716.htm.

———. "Average Hours per Week of Television Watching, Fall 2001," Canadian Statistics, December 2, 2002a. [Online] Available at http://www.statcan.ca/english/Pgdb/arts23.htm.

———. "Television Viewing," *The Daily*, December 2, 2002b. [Online] Available at http://www.statcan.ca/Daily/English/021202/d021202a.htm.

———. Census 2011. Catalogue no. 96-311-XWE-2011002. http://www12.statcan.gc.ca/census-recensement/2011/dp-pd/hlt-fst/as-sa/index-eng.cfm?Lang=E.

Tierney, John. "Adultescent." *New York Times* (December 26, 2004).

Weitzman, Lenore J. *The Divorce Revolution: The Unexpected Social and Economic Consequences for Women and Children in America*. New York: Free Press, 1985.

———. "The Economic Consequences of Divorce Are Still Unequal: Comment on Peterson." *American Sociological Review*. Vol. 61, No. 3 (June 1996):537–38.

Williams, T. *The Impact of Television: A Natural Experiment in Three Communities*. New York: Academic Press, 1986.

Wilson, Barbara. "National Television Violence Study." Reported in Julia Duin, "Study Finds Cartoon Heroes Initiate Too Much Violence." *Washington Times* (April 17, 1998):A4.

Chapter 6

Atwood, Margaret. "True Trash." In *Wilderness Tips*. Toronto: McClelland & Stewart, 1991. pp. 1–30.

Bakalar, Nicholas. "Reactions: Go On, Laugh Your Heart Out." *New York Times* (March 8, 2005). [Online] Available March 11, 2005, at http://www.nytimes.com/2005/03/08/health/08reac.html.

Baker, Patricia S., William C. Yoels, Jeffrey M. Clair, and Richard M. Allman. "Laughter in the Triadic Geriatric Encounters: A Transcript-Based Analysis." In Rebecca J. Erikson and Beverly Cuthbertson-Johnson, eds. *Social Perspectives on Emotion*. Vol. 4. Greenwich, CT: JAI Press, 1997:179–207.

Benokraitis, Nijole, and Joe Feagin. *Modern Sexism: Blatant, Subtle, and Overt Discrimination*. 2nd ed. Englewood Cliffs, NJ: Prentice Hall, 1995.

Berger, Peter L. *Redeeming Laughter: The Comic Dimension of Human Experience*. Berlin: Walter de Gruyter, 1997.

Colombo, John Robert. *The Penguin Book of Canadian Jokes*. Toronto: Penguin, 2001.

Davies, Christie. *Ethnic Humor Around the World: A Comparative Analysis*. Bloomington: Indiana University Press, 1990.

Ebaugh, Helen Rose Fuchs. *Becoming an Ex: The Process of Role Exit*. Chicago: University of Chicago Press, 1988.

Ekman, Paul. "Biological and Cultural Contributions to Body and Facial Movements in the Expression of Emotions." In A. Rorty, ed. *Explaining Emotions*. Berkeley: University of California Press, 1980a. pp. 73–101.

———. *Face of Man: Universal Expression in a New Guinea Village*. New York: Garland Press, 1980b.

Flaherty, Michael G. "A Formal Approach to the Study of Amusement in Social Interaction." *Studies in Symbolic Interaction*. Vol. 5. New York: JAI Press, 1984. pp. 71–82.

———. "Two Conceptions of the Social Situation: Some Implications of Humor." *The Sociological Quarterly*. Vol. 31, No. 1 (Spring 1990).

Garfinkel, Harold. *Studies in Ethnomethodology*. Cambridge: Polity Press, 1967.

Globe and Mail, The. "Your Morning Smile." (August 2, 1997):A1.

Goffman, Erving. *The Presentation of Self in Everyday Life*. Garden City, NY: Anchor Books, 1959.

———. *Interactional Ritual: Essays on Face to Face Behavior*. Garden City, NY: Anchor Books, 1967.

Goyder, John. *Technology and Society: A Canadian Perspective*. Peterborough, ON: Broadview Press, 1997.

Haig, Robin Andrew. *The Anatomy of Humor: Biopsychosocial and Therapeutic Perspectives*. Springfield, IL: Charles C. Thomas, 1988.

Henley, Nancy, Mykol Hamilton, and Barrie Thorne. "Womanspeak and Manspeak: Sex Differences in Communication, Verbal and Nonverbal." In John J. Macionis and Nijole V. Benokraitis, eds. *Seeing Ourselves: Classic, Contemporary, and Cross-Cultural Readings in Sociology*. 2nd ed. Englewood Cliffs, NJ: Prentice Hall, 1992:10–15.

Hochschild, Arlie Russell. "Emotion Work, Feeling Rules, and Social Structure." *American Journal of Sociology*. Vol. 85, No. 3 (November 1979):551–75.

———. *The Managed Heart*. Berkeley, CA: University of California Press, 1983.

Johnson, Cathryn. "Gender, Legitimate Authority, and Leader-Subordinate Conversations." *American Sociological Review*. Vol. 59, No. 1 (February 1994):122–35.

Linton, Ralph. "One Hundred Percent American." *The American Mercury*. Vol. 40, No. 160 (April 1937):427–29.

Macionis, John J. "A Sociological Analysis of Humor." Presentation to the Texas Junior College Teachers Association, Houston, 1987.

McLuhan, Marshall. *The Gutenberg Galaxy*. New York: New American Library, 1969.

Merton, Robert K. *Social Theory and Social Structure*. New York: Free Press, 1968.

Monk, Katherine. "Instant Communication Can Mean Instant Confrontation." *National Post* (May 8, 2009):PM3.

Ontario. *Words That Count Women Out/In*. Toronto: Ontario Women's Directorate, 1992.

Powell, Chris, and George E.C. Paton, eds. *Humour in Society: Resistance and Control*. New York: St. Martin's Press, 1988.

Primeggia, Salvatore, and Joseph A. Varacalli. "Southern Italian Comedy: Old to New World." In Joseph V. Scelsa, Salvatore J. LaGumina, and Lydio Tomasi, eds. *Italian Americans in Transition*. New York: The American Italian Historical Association, 1990. pp. 241–52.

Sansom, William. *A Contest of Ladies*. London, UK: Hogarth, 1956.

Shively, Joellen. "Cowboys and Indians: Perceptions of Western Films Among American Indians and Anglos." *American Sociological Review*. Vol. 57, No. 6 (December 1992):725–34.

Simmel, Georg. *The Sociology of Georg Simmel*. Kurt Wolff, ed. New York: Free Press, 1950:118–69; orig. 1902.

Smith-Lovin, Lynn, and Charles Brody. "Interruptions in Group Discussions: The Effects of Gender and Group Composition." *American Journal of Sociology*. Vol. 54, No. 3 (June 1989):424–35.

Thomas, W.I. "The Relation of Research to the Social Process." In Morris Janowitz, ed. *W.I. Thomas on Social Organization and Social Personality*. Chicago, IL: University of Chicago Press, 1966; orig. 1931. pp. 289–305.

Thorne, Barrie, Cheris Kramarae, and Nancy Henley, Eds. *Language, Gender and Society*. Rowley, MA: Newbury House, 1983.

Turner, Jonathan. *On the Origins of Human Emotions: A Sociological Inquiry into the Evolution of Human Emotions*. Stanford, CA: Stanford University Press, 2000.

Vowell, Sarah. "Canuck Yuks." *Salon*, January 27, 1999. [Online] Available http://www.salon.com/ent/music/vowe/1999/01/27vowe.html.

Yoels, William C., and Jeffrey Michael Clair. "Laughter in the Clinic: Humor in Social Organization." *Symbolic Interaction*. Vol. 18, No. 1 (1995):39–58.

Chapter 7

Asch, Solomon. *Social Psychology*. Englewood Cliffs, NJ: Prentice Hall, 1952.

Baron, James N., Michael T. Hannan, and M. Diane Burton. "Building the Iron Cage: Determinants of Managerial Intensity in the Early Years of Organizations." *American Sociological Review*. Vol. 64, No. 4 (August 1999):527–47.

Bassett, Isabel. *The Bassett Report: Career Success and Canadian Women*. Toronto: Collins, 1985.

Bedard, Paul. "Washington Whispers." *U.S. News & World Report* (March 25, 2002):2.

Blau, Peter M. *Inequality and Heterogeneity: A Primitive Theory of Social Structure*. New York: Free Press, 1977.

Blau, Peter M., Terry C. Blum, and Joseph E. Schwartz. "Heterogeneity and Intermarriage." *American Sociological Review*. Vol. 47, No. 1 (February 1982):45–62.

Bobo, Lawrence, and Vincent L. Hutchings. "Perceptions of Racial Group Competition: Extending Blumer's Theory of Group Position to a Multiracial Social Context." *American Sociological Review*. Vol. 61, No. 6 (December 1996):951–72.

Breton, Raymond. "Institutional Completeness of Ethnic Communities and the Personal Relations of Immigrants." *American Journal of Sociology*. Vol. 70 (1964):193–205.

Brooks, David. *Bobos in Paradise: The New Upper Class and How They Got There*. New York: Simon & Schuster, 2000.

CBC, "Muscovites mad for McDonald's," CBC Digital Archives, Jan. 31, 1990, http//archives.cbc.ca, accessed on March 23, 2012.

Curtis, James E., Douglas E. Baer, and Edward G. Grabb. "Nations of Joiners: Explaining Voluntary Association Membership in Democratic Societies." *American Sociological Review*. Vol. 66, No. 6 (December 2001):783–805.

Etzioni, Amitai. *A Comparative Analysis of Complex Organization: On Power, Involvement, and Their Correlates*. Rev. and enlarged ed. New York: Free Press, 1975.

Fernandez, Roberto M., and Nancy Weinberg. "Sifting and Sorting: Personal Contacts and Hiring in a Retail Bank." *American Sociological Review*. Vol. 62, No. 6 (December 1997):883–02.

Fife, Sandy. "The Total Quality Muddle." *The Globe and Mail: Report on Business* (November 1992):64–74.

Florida, Richard, and Martin Kenney. "Transplanted Organizations: The Transfer of Japanese Industrial Organization to the U.S." *American Sociological Review*. Vol. 56, No. 3 (June 1991):381–98.

Green, Gary Paul, Leann M. Tigges, and Daniel Diaz. "Racial and Ethnic Differences in Job-Search Strategies in Atlanta, Boston, and Los Angeles." *Social Science Quarterly*. Vol. 80, No. 2 (June 1999):263–0.

Gwynne, S.C., and John F. Dickerson. "Lost in the E-Mail." *Time*. Vol. 149, No. 15 (April 21, 1997):88–90.

Hagan, Jacqueline Maria. "Social Networks, Gender, and Immigrant Incorporation: Resources and Restraints." *American Sociological Review*. Vol. 63, No. 1 (February 1998):55–67.

Halberstam, David. *The Reckoning*. New York: Avon Books, 1986.

Hamilton, Anita. "Speeders, Say Cheese." *Time* (September 17, 2001):32.

Helgesen, Sally. *The Female Advantage: Women's Ways of Leadership*. New York: Doubleday, 1990.

Hightower, Jim. *Eat Your Heart Out: Food Profiteering in America*. New York: Crown, 1975.

Hoerr, John. "The Payoff from Teamwork." *Business Week*. No. 3114 (July 10, 1989):56–62.

Hurtado, Sylvia, Alexander W. Austin, William S. Korn, and Kathryn M. Mahoney. *The American Freshman: National Norms for Fall 2004*. Los Angeles: UCLA Higher Education Research Institute, 2004.

Ide, Thomas R., and Arthur J. Cordell. "Automating Work." *Society*. Vol. 31, No. 6 (September–October 1994):65–71.

Janis, Irving. *Victims of Groupthink*. Boston: Houghton Mifflin, 1972.

———. *Crucial Decisions: Leadership in Policymaking and Crisis Management*. New York: Free Press, 1989.

Kanter, Rosabeth Moss. *Men and Women of the Corporation*. New York: Basic Books, 1977.

Kanter, Rosabeth Moss, and Barry A. Stein. "The Gender Pioneers: Women in an Industrial Sales Force." In R.M. Kanter and B.A. Stein, eds. *Life in Organizations*. New York: Basic Books, 1979. pp. 134–60.

Lewis, Lionel S. "Madoff's Victims and Their Day in Court." *Society*. Vol. 45, No. 5 (September/October 2010):439–0.

Lin, Nan, Karen Cook, and Ronald S. Burt, eds. *Social Capital: Theory and Research*. Hawthorne, N.Y.: Aldine de Gruyter, 2001.

Maddox, Setma. "Organizational Culture and Leadership Style: Factors Affecting Self-Managed Work Team Performance." Paper presented at the annual meeting of the Southwest Social Science Association, Dallas, Texas, February 1994.

Mahoney, Jill. "Web skeptics take note: The sky hasn't fallen." *The Globe and Mail* (January 26, 2006a):A8.

Markoff, John. "Remember Big Brother? Now He's a Company Man." *New York Times* (March 31, 1991):7.

Merton, Robert K. *Social Theory and Social Structure*. New York: Free Press, 1968.

Michels, Robert. *Political Parties*. Glencoe, IL: Free Press, 1949; orig. 1911.

Milgram, Stanley. "Behavioral Study of Obedience." *Journal of Abnormal and Social Psychology*. Vol. 67, No. 4 (1963):371–78.

———. "Group Pressure and Action Against a Person." *Journal of Abnormal and Social Psychology*. Vol. 69, No. 2 (August 1964):137–43.

———. "Some Conditions of Obedience and Disobedience to Authority." *Human Relations*. Vol. 18 (February 1965):57–76.

———. "The Small World Problem." *Psychology Today* (May 1967):60–67.

Miller, Arthur G. *The Obedience Experiments: A Case of Controversy in Social Science*. New York: Praeger, 1986.

Mollenhorst, Gerald. "Networks in Contexts: How Meeting Opportunities Affect Personal Relationships." Ph.D. Dissertation. University of Utrecht, 2009.

O'Harrow, Robert, Jr. "ID Theft Scam Hits D.C. Area Residents." [Online] Available February 21, 2005, at http://news.yahoo.com.

Ouchi, William. *Theory Z: How American Business Can Meet the Japanese Challenge*. Reading, MA: Addison-Wesley, 1981.

Petersen, Trond, Ishak Saporta, and Marc-David L. Seidel. "Offering a Job: Meritocracy and Social Networks." *American Journal of Sociology*. Vol. 106, No. 3 (November 2000):763–816.

Philadelphia, Desa. "Tastier, Plusher—and Fast." *Time* (September 30, 2002):57.

Pinchot, Gifford, and Elizabeth Pinchot. *The End of Bureaucracy and the Rise of the Intelligent Organization*. San Francisco, CA: Berrett-Koehler, 1993.

Podolny, Joel M., and James N. Baron. "Resources and Relationships: Social Networks and Mobility in the Workplace." *American Sociological Review*. Vol. 62 No. 5 (October 1997):673–3.

Reskin, Barbara F., and Debra Branch McBrier. "Why Not Ascription? Organizations' Employment of Male and Female Managers." *American ociological Review*. Vol. 65, No. 2 (April 2000):210–33.

Ridgeway, Cecilia L. *The Dynamics of Small Groups*. New York: St. Martin's Press, 1983.

Ritzer, George. *The McDonaldization of Society: An Investigation into the Changing Character of Contemporary Social Life*. Thousand Oaks, CA: Pine Forge Press, 1993.

———. *The McDonaldization Thesis: Explorations and Extensions*. Thousand Oaks, CA: Sage, 1998.

———. "The Globalization of McDonaldization." *Spark* (February 2000):8–9.

Schofer, Evan, and Marion Fourcade-Gourinchas. "The Structural Contexts of Civil Engagement: Voluntary Association Membership in Comparative Perspective." *American Sociological Review*. Vol. 66, No. 6 (December 2001):806–28.

Scott, D.B. "Lean Machine." *Report on Business Magazine, The Globe and Mail* (November 1992):90–99.

Semma, Monika. *A Cultural and Historical Analysis of Tattooing.* Honours Thesis, University of Guelph, 2012.

Schlosser, Eric. *Fast-Food Nation: The Dark Side of the All-American Meal.* New York: Perennial, 2002.

Shipley, Joseph T. *Dictionary of Word Origins.* Totowa, NJ: Roman & Allanheld, 1985.

Simmel, Georg. *The Sociology of Georg Simmel.* Kurt Wolff, ed. New York: Free Press, 1950:118–69; orig. 1902.

South, Scott J., and Steven F. Messner. "Structural Determinants of Intergroup Association: Interracial Marriage and Crime." *American Journal of Sociology.* Vol. 91, No. 6 (May 1986):1409–30.

Stouffer, Samuel A., Arthur A. Lumsdaine, Marion Harper Lumsdaine, Robin M. Williams, Jr., M. Brewster Smith, Irving L. Janis, Shirley A. Star, and Leonard S. Cottrell, Jr. *The American Soldier.* Volume 1 *Adjustment During Army Life.* Princeton, NJ: Princeton University Press, 1949.

Sullivan, Barbara. "McDonald's Sees India as Golden Opportunity." *Chicago Tribune* (April 5, 1995):B1.

Tajfel, Henri. "Social Psychology of Intergroup Relations." *Annual Review of Psychology.* Palo Alto, CA: Annual Reviews, 1982. pp. 1–39.

Tannen, Deborah. *Talking from 9 to 5: How Women's and Men's Conversational Styles Affect Who Gets Heard, Who Gets Credit, and What Gets Done at Work.* New York: Wm. Morrow, 1994.

Taylor, Frederick Winslow. *The Principles of Scientific Management.* New York: Harper Bros., 1911.

Tolson, Jay. "The Trouble with Elites." *The Wilson Quarterly.* Vol. XIX, No. 1 (Winter 1995):6–8.

Torres, Lisa, and Matt L. Huffman. "Social Networks and Job Search Outcomes among Male and Female Professional, Technical, and Managerial Workers." *Sociological Focus.* Vol. 35, No. 1 (February 2002):25–42.

Watts, Duncan J. "Networks, Dynamics, and the Small-World Phenomenon." *American Journal of Sociology.* Vol. 105, No. 2 (September 1999):493–527.

Weber, Max. *Economy and Society.* G. Roth and C. Wittich, eds. Berkeley, CA: University of California Press, 1978; orig. 1921.

Wellman, Barry, and Milena Gulia. "Net-Surfers Don't Ride Alone: Virtual Communities as Communities." In Barry Wellman, ed. *Networks in the Global Village: Life in Contemporary Communities.* Boulder, CO: Westview Press, 1999. pp. 331–66.

White, Ralph, and Ronald Lippitt. "Leader Behavior and Member Reaction in Three 'Social Climates.' "In Dorwin Cartwright and Alvin Zander, eds. *Group Dynamics.* Evanston, IL: Row, Peterson, 1953. pp. 586–611.

Wildavsky, Ben. "Small World, Isn't It?" *U.S. News & World Report* (April 1, 2002):68.

Yeatts, Dale E. "Creating the High Performance Self-Managed Work Team: A Review of Theoretical Perspectives." Paper presented at the annual meeting of the Southwest Social Science Association, Dallas, February 1994.

Chapter 8

Alan Guttmacher Institute. "U.S. Teenage Pregnancy Statistics: National and State Trends and Trends by Race and Ethnicity." Rev. September 2006. [Online] Available on May 8, 2007, at http://www.guttmacher.org/pubs/2006/09/12/USTPstats.pdf.

Angier, Natalie. "Sexual identity predominates: Case of boy raised as girl underscores importance of prenatal events, MDs say." *The Globe and Mail* (March 14, 1997):A1.

Armstrong, Jane. "RCMP Scour Second Site." *The Globe and Mail* (July 21, 2003):A1.

Belle, Marilyn, and Kevin Mcquillan. "Births Outside Marriage: A Growing Alternative." In Statistics Canada, *Canadian Social Trends. Volume 3.* Toronto: Thompson Educational Publishing, 2000.

Benedict, Ruth. "Continuities and Discontinuities in Cultural Conditioning." *Psychiatry.* Vol. 1 (May 1938):161–67.

Bibby, Reginald W. *The Bibby Report: Social Trends Canadian Style.* Toronto: Stoddart, 1995.

———. *Canada's Teens: Today, Yesterday and Tomorrow.* Toronto: Stoddart, 2001.

———. *The Boomer Factor: What Canada's Most Famous Generation is Leaving Behind.* Project Canada Books: Lethbridge, AB. 2006.

———. *The Emerging Millennials: How Canada's Newest Generation Is Responding to Change and Choice.* Lethbridge, Alberta: Project Canada Books, 2009.

Bielski, Zozia. "Why teen pregnancy is on the rise again in Canada (and spiking in these provinces). *The Globe and Mail* (Jan. 29, 2013). http://www.theglobeandmail.com/life/health-and-fitness/health/why-teen-pregnancy-is-on-the-rise-again-in-canada-and-spiking-in-these-provinces/article7927983/.

Blackwood, Evelyn, and Saskia Wieringa, Eds. *Female Desires: Same-Sex Relations and Transgender Practices across Cultures.* New York: Columbia University Press, 1999.

Bricker, Darrell, and John Wright. *What Canadians Think . . . about Almost Everything.* Toronto: Doubleday Canada, 2005.

CBC News. "Catholic University in Ottawa opposes free condoms." [Online] Available March 15, 2012, at http://www.cbc.ca/news/canada/ottawa/story/2012/03/14/ottawa-condoms-catholic-university.html.

Chauncey, George. *Gay New York: Gender, Urban Culture, and the Making of the Gay Male World, 1890–1940.* New York: Basic Books, 1994.

Colton, Helen. *The Gift of Touch: How Physical Contact Improves Communication, Pleasure, and Health.* New York: Seaview/Putnam, 1983.

Cousens, Cynthia, and Sylvia Durand. "Cynthia Cousens & Sylvia Durand Contact Page." [Online] Available March 2012 at http://www.reocities.com/westhollywood/5605.

Crossette, Barbara. "Female Genital Mutilation by Immigrants Is Becoming Cause for Concern in the U.S." *New York Times International* (December 10, 1995):11.

Davidson, Julia O'Connell. *Prostitution, Power, and Freedom.* Ann Arbor, MI: University of Michigan Press, 1998.

Davis, Kingsley. "Sexual Behavior." In Robert K. Merton and Robert Nisbet, eds. *Contemporary Social Problems.* 3rd ed. New York: Harcourt Brace Jovanovich, 1971:313–60.

Dekeseredy, Walter S., and Ronald Hinch. *Woman Abuse: Sociological Perspectives.* Toronto: Thompson Educational Publishing, 1991.

Diamond, Milton. "Sexual Identity, Monozygotic Twins Reared in Discordant Sex Roles and a BBC Follow-Up." *Archives of Sexual Behavior.* Vol. 11, No. 2 (April 1982):181–86.

Dryburgh, Heather. "Teenage Pregnancy" *Health Reports.* Vol. 12, No. 1 (October 1, 2003). Statistics Canada Catalogue 82-003. [Online] Available at http://www.statcan.ca/english/kits/preg/preg3.htm.

Dworkin, Andrea. *Intercourse.* New York: Free Press, 1987.

Estes, Richard J. "The Commercial Sexual Exploitation of Children in the U.S., Canada, and Mexico." Reported in "Study Explores Sexual Exploitation." [Online] Available September 10, 2001, at http://news.yahoo.com.

Ford, Clellan S., and Frank A. Beach. *Patterns of Sexual Behavior.* New York: Harper & Row, 1951.

Foucault, Michel. *The History of Sexuality: An Introduction.* Vol. 1. Robert Hurley, trans. New York: Vintage, 1990; orig. 1978.

Gagné, Patricia, Richard Tewksbury, and Deanna McGaughey. "Coming Out and Crossing Over: Identity Formation and Proclamation in a Transgender Community." *Gender and Society.* Vol. 11, No. 4 (August 1997):478–508.

Gates, Gary. "How Many People Are Lesbian, Gay, Bisexual, and Transgender?" The Williams Institute. April 2011. Available at http://williamsinstitute.law.ucla.edu/wp-ontent/uploads/Gates-How-Many-People-LGBT-Apr-2011.pdf.

Geertz, Clifford. "Common Sense as a Cultural System." *The Antioch Review.* Vol. 33, No. 1 (Spring 1975):5–26.

Giddens, Anthony. *The Transformation of Intimacy.* Cambridge: Polity Press, 1992.

Gordon, Sol, and Craig W. Snyder. *Personal Issues in Human Sexuality: A Guidebook for Better Sexual Health.* 2nd ed. Boston: Allyn & Bacon, 1989.

Greenberg, David F. *The Construction of Homosexuality.* Chicago, IL: University of Chicago Press, 1988.

Hamer, Dean, and Peter Copeland. *The Science of Desire: The Search for the Gay Gene and the Biology of Behavior.* New York: Simon & Schuster, 1994.

Hass, Ann P., Philip L. Rodgers, and Jody L. Herman. "Suicide Attempts Among Transgender and Gender Non-Conforming Adults." The Williams Institute. January 2014. Available at http://williamsinstitute.law.ucla.edu/research/suicide-attempts-among-transgender-and-gender-non-conforming-adults.

Hennenberger, Melinda. "Old People F—-ing: Does an Elderly Couple Have a Right to a Sex Life?" *National Post.* (June 14, 2008):A26.

Huffman, Karen. *Psychology in Action.* New York: Wiley, 2000.

Humphreys, Adrian. "First Gay Marriage Legal, for Now." *National Post* (January 15, 2001):A1.

Johnson, Holly. *Dangerous Domains: Violence Against Women in Canada.* Toronto: Nelson Canada, 1996.

Johnston, W.R. Historical abortion statistics, Canada. 2014. "http://www.johnstonsarchive.net/policy/abortion/ab-canada.htm" www.johnstonsarchive.net/policy/abortion/ab-canada.htm.

Jonas, George. "Baby, you haven't come such a long way after all." *National Post* (April 21, 2012):A12.

Kinsey, Alfred, et al. *Sexual Behavior in the Human Male.* Philadelphia, PA: Saunders, 1948.

———. *Sexual Behavior in the Human Female.* Philadelphia, PA: Saunders, 1953.

Kinsman, Gary. *The Regulation of Desire: Homo and Hetero Sexualities.* Montreal: Black Rose Books, 1996.

Kluckhohn, Clyde. "As an Anthropologist Views It." In Albert Deuth, ed. *Sex Habits of American Men.* New York: Prentice Hall, 1948.

Laumann, Edward O., John H. Gagnon, Robert T. Michael, and Stuart Michaels. *The Social Organization of Sexuality: Sexual Practices in the United States.* Chicago, IL: University of Chicago Press, 1994.

Levay, Simon. *The Sexual Brain.* Cambridge, MA: MIT Press, 1993.

Lunman, Kim. "National Response Needed, Cauchon Maintains." *The Globe and Mail* (June 11, 2003):A4.

Mahoney, Jill. "Canadians happier in the bedroom than Americans." *The Globe and Mail* (April 20, 2006b):A3.

Makin, Kirk. "Gay Marriage Is Legalized." *The Globe and Mail* (June 11, 2003):A1.

Mathews, T.J., and Brady E. Hamilton. "Trend Analysis of the Sex Ratio at Birth in the United States." *National Vital Statistics Reports.* Vol. 53, No. 20 (June 14, 2005). Hyattsville, MD: National Center for Health Statistics.

Miracle, Tina S., Andrew W. Miracle, and Roy F. Baumeister. *Human Sexuality: Meeting Your Basic Needs.* Upper Saddle River, NJ: Prentice Hall, 2003.

Murdock, George Peter. *Social Structure.* New York: Free Press, 1965; orig. 1949.

Murray, Stephen O., and Will Roscoe, Eds. *Boy-Wives and Female-Husbands: Studies of African Homosexualities.* New York: St. Martin's Press, 1998.

National Conference of State Legislatures. "Same Sex Marriage, Civil Unions and Domestic Partnerships." 2015. Available at http://www.ncsl.org/issues-research/human-services/same-sexmarriage.aspx.

Nelson, Adie. *Gender in Canada*. 4th ed. Toronto: Pearson Canada, 2010.

Nelson, E.D., and Augie Fleras. *Social Problems in Canada: Issues and Challenges*. 2nd ed. Scarborough, ON: Prentice Hall, 1998.

Nelson, E.D., and Barry W. Robinson. *Gender in Canada*. Scarborough, ON: Prentice Hall, 1999.

NORC. *General Social Surveys, 1972–1998: Cumulative Codebook*. Chicago, IL: National Opinion Research Center, 1999.

———. *General Social Surveys, 1972–2002: Cumulative Codebook*. Chicago, IL: National Opinion Research Center, 2003.

———. *General Social Surveys, 1972–2012: Cumulative Codebook*. Chicago: National Opinion Research Center, 2013.

Olyslager, Femke, and Lynn Conway. "On the Calculation of the Prevalence of Transsexualism." 2007. Available at http://ai.eecs.umich.edu/people/conway/TS/Prevalence/Reports/Prevalence%20of%20Transsexualism.pdf.

Peritz, Ingrid. "Sex-Change Soldier Hails Canada's Liberal Attitudes." *The Globe and Mail* (February 22, 2000):A1.

Press, Jordan. "Gender protection legislation unveiled: Bill outlaws discrimination based on identity." *National Post* (May 18, 2016): A4.

Rotermann, Michelle. "Trends in teen sexual behaviour and condom use." Statistics Canada Catalogue no. 82-003-X, September 2008. [Online] Available http://www.statcan.gc.ca/pub/82-003-x/2008003/article/10664-eng.pdf.

Singer, Peter, and Agata Sagan. "He or she: Does it really matter?" *The Globe and Mail* (April 17, 2012):A11.

Society of Obstetricians and Gynaecologists of Canada. 2006. [Online] Available at http://www.sexualityandu.ca.

Statistics Canada. Census 2011a, Catalogue no. 98-312-XCB2011045.

———. Census 2011b. Catalogue no. 98-312-XCB2011046.

———. *Crime Statistics in Canada, 2005*. Catalogue no. 85-002-XIE, Vol. 26, no. 4. Accessed online in May 2009a.

Storms, Michael D. "Theories of Sexual Orientation." *Journal of Personality and Social Psychology*. Vol. 38, No. 5 (May 1980):783–2.

Tewksbury, Richard, and Patricia Gagné. "Transgenderists: Products of Non-normative Intersections of Sex, Gender, and Sexuality." *Journal of Men's Studies*. Vol. 5, No. 2 (November 1996):105–29.

Ventura, Stephanie J., Joyce C. Abma, William D. Mosher, and Stanley K. Henshaw. "Estimated Pregnancy Rates by Outcome for the United States, 1990–2005: An update." *National Vital Statistics Reports*, Vol. 58, No. 4 Hyattsville, MD: National Center for Health Statistics. 2009. [Online] Available http://www.cdc.gov/nchs/data/nvsr/nvsr58/nvsr58_04.pdf.

Verma, Sonia, "Same-sex couples should get married." *The Globe and Mail* (May 10, 2012):A1.

Weinberg, George. *Society and the Healthy Homosexual*. Garden City, NY: Anchor Books, 1973.

Weeks, Carley. "Is it time to have that talk a little earlier?" *The Globe and Mail*, October 24, 2012:L1.

Wolff, Lee, and Dorota Geissel. "Street Prostitution in Canada." In Statistics Canada, *Canadian Social Trends. Volume 3*. Toronto: Thompson Educational Publishing, 2000.

Chapter 9

Akers, Ronald L., Marvin D. Krohn, Lonn Lanza-Kaduce, and Marcia Radosevich. "Social Learning and Deviant Behavior." *American Sociological Review*. Vol. 44, No. 4 (August 1979):636–55.

Amnesty International. "Abolitionist and Retentionist Countries." [Online] Available on June 4, 2005, at http://web.amnesty.org/pages/deathpenalty-countries-eng.

Anderson, Elijah. "The Code of the Streets." *Atlantic Monthly*. Vol. 273 (May 1994):81–94.

———. "The Ideologically Driven Critique." *American Journal of Sociology*. Vol. 197, No. 6 (May 2002):1533–50.

Atkinson, Michael. "It's Still Part of the Game: Masculinity, Crime and Victimization in Ice Hockey." In L. Fuller, ed. *Sport, Rhetoric, Gender and Violence: Historical Perspectives and Media Representations*. New York: Palgrave MacMillan, 2007.

BBC. "Sudan 'Trousers Woman' Released." *BBC Mobile News*. [Online] Available September 8, 2009, at http://news.bbc.co.uk/2/hi/8244339.stm.

Becker, Howard S. *Outside: Studies in the Sociology of Deviance*. New York: Free Press, 1966.

Blau, Judith R., and Peter M. Blau. "The Cost of Inequality: Metropolitan Structure and Violent Crime." *American Sociological Review*. Vol. 47, No. 1 (February 1982):114–29.

Blumberg, Abraham S. *Criminal Justice*. Chicago, IL: Quadrangle Books, 1970.

Boritch, Helen. *Fallen Women: Female Crime and Criminal Justice in Canada*. Toronto: ITP Nelson, 1997.

Buffone, Sonya. *Heroic Crime Fighters: A Phenomenological Analysis of Police Officers' Idealistic Role Construct*. Master of Arts Thesis. Guelph: University of Guelph. 2011.

Canada. Royal Commission on Aboriginal Peoples. *Choosing Life: Special Report on Suicide among Aboriginal People*. Ottawa: Minister of Supply and Services Canada, 1995.

———. Correctional Service Canada. 2006a. [Online] Available at http://www.csc-scc.gc.ca.

Carrigan, D. Owen. *Crime and Punishment in Canada: A History*. Toronto: McClelland & Stewart, 1991.

Carroll, James R. "Congress Is Told of Coal-Dust Fraud UMW; Senator from Minnesota Rebukes Industry." *Louisville Courier Journal* (May 27, 1999):1A.

Chase, Steven, and Paul Waldie. "Cool welcome awaits Lord Black." *The Globe and Mail* (May 2, 2012):A1.

Cloward, Richard A., and Lloyd E. Ohlin. *Delinquency and Opportunity: A Theory of Delinquent Gangs*. New York: Free Press, 1966.

Cluff, Julie, Alison Hunter, and Ronald Hinch. "Feminist Perspectives on Serial Murder: A Critical Analysis." Homicide Studies. Vol. 1, No. 3 (1998):291–308.

Cohen, Albert K. *Delinquent Boys: The Culture of the Gang*. New York: Free Press, 1971; orig. 1955.

Currie, Elliott. *Confronting Crime: An American Challenge*. New York: Pantheon Books, 1985.

Davis, Stephen Spencer, and Alisa Mamak. "Throughout Our Communities." *The Globe and Mail* (June 9, 2012):A17.

Derber, Charles. *The Wilding of America: Money, Mayhem, and the New American Dream*. 3rd ed. New York: Worth, 2004.

Depew, Robert. "Policing Native Communities: Some Principles and Issues in Organizational Theory." *Canadian Journal of Criminology*. Vol. 34 (1992).

Durkheim, Émile. *The Division of Labor in Society*. New York: Free Press, 1964a; orig. 1895.

———. *The Rules of Sociological Method*. New York: Free Press, 1964b; orig. 1893.

Eboh, Camillus. "Nigerian Woman Loses Appeal against Stoning Death." [Online] Available August 19, 2002, at http://news.yahoo.com.

Elias, Robert. *The Politics of Victimization: Victims, Victimology and Human Rights*. New York: Oxford University Press, 1986.

Erikson, Kai T. Lecture delivered at Kenyon College, Gambier, Ohio, February 7, 2005a.

Fiorillo, Isabella. *Crisis in the Criminal Justice System: Over-Representation and Over-Classification of Aboriginal Women in Canadian Prisons*. Master of Arts (major research paper). Guelph: University of Guelph. 2012.

Fleras, Augie. *Unequal Relations: An Introduction to Race, Ethnic, and Aboriginal Dynamics in Canada*. 6th ed. Toronto: Pearson Canada, 2010.

Francis, Diane. *Bre-X: The Inside Story*. Toronto: Key Porter Books, 1997.

Frideres, James S., and René Gadacz.
Aboriginal Peoples in Canada. 8th ed. Toronto: Pearson Prentice Hall, 2008.

Garfinkel, Harold. "Conditions of Successful Degradation Ceremonies." *American Journal of Sociology*. Vol. 61, No. 2 (March 1956):420–24.

Glueck, Sheldon, and Eleanor Glueck. *Unraveling Juvenile Delinquency*. New York: Commonwealth Fund, 1950.

Goffman, Erving. *Stigma: Notes on the Management of Spoiled Identity*. Englewood Cliffs, NJ: Prentice Hall, 1963.

Gottfredson, Michael R., and Travis Hirschi. "National Crime Control Policies." *Society*. Vol. 32, No. 2 (January–February 1995):30–36.

Hagan, John, and Patricia Parker. "White-Collar Crime and Punishment: The Class Structure and Legal Sanctioning of Securities Violations." *American Sociological Review*. Vol. 50, No. 3 (June 1985):302–16.

Herpertz, Sabine C., and Henning Sass. "Emotional Deficiency and Psychopathy." *Behavioral Sciences and the Law*. Vol. 18, No. 5 (September/October 2000):567–80.

Hirschi, Travis. *Causes of Delinquency*. Berkeley, CA: University of California Press, 1969.

Hope, Trina L., Harold G. Grasmick, and Laura J. Pointon. "The Family in Gottfredson and Hrischi's General Theory of Crime: Structure, Parenting, and Self-Control." *Sociological Focus*. Vol. 36, No. 4 (November 2003): 291–311.

Houpt, Simon, and Steve Ladurantaye, "Playoff mayhem stirs concern, but the fans are glued." *The Globe and Mail* (April 19, 2012):A12–13.

Howlett, Karen, et al. "Enron Deception Aided by CIBC: U.S. Report." *The Globe and Mail* (July 29, 2003):A1.

Inciardi, James A. *Elements of Criminal Justice*. 2nd ed. New York: Oxford University Press, 2000.

Jacobs, David. "Inequality and Police Strength." *American Sociological Review*. Vol. 44, No. 6 (December 1979):913–25.

Jones, Judy. "More Miners Will Be Offered Free X-Rays; Federal Agency Wants to Monitor Black-Lung Cases." *Louisville Courier Journal* (May 13, 1999):1A.

Kallen, Evelyn. *Ethnicity and Human Rights in Canada*. Don Mills, ON: Oxford University Press, 2003.

Kalish, Carol B. "International Crime Rates." Bureau of Justice Statistics Special Report, May. Washington, DC: U.S. Government Printing Office, 1988.

King, Kathleen Piker, and Dennis E. Clayson. "The Differential Perceptions of Male and Female Deviants." *Sociological Focus*. Vol. 21, No. 2 (April 1988):153–64.

Kingston, Anne. Let's be clear, this isn't "great theatre." *Maclean's*. (February 15 and 22, 2016):11–12.

Kittrie, Nicholas N. *The Right to Be Different: Deviance and Enforced Therapy*. Baltimore, MD: Johns Hopkins University Press, 1971.

Kline, Jesse. "Don Cherry is right—fighting is part of what makes hockey great." *National Post* (October 13, 2011):A3.

Langbein, Laura I., and Roseana Bess. "Sports in School: Source of Amity or Antipathy?" *Social Science Quarterly*. Vol. 83, No. 2 (June 2002):436–54.

Laprairie, Carol P. "Community Types, Crime and Police Services on Canadian Indian Reserves." *Journal of Research in Crime and Delinquency.* Vol. 25, No. 4 (1988):375–91.

———. "Aboriginal Over-Representation in the Criminal Justice System: A Tale of Two Cities." *Canadian Journal of Criminology.* Vol. 44 (2002):181–208.

Laprairie, Carol, and J. Roberts. "Circle Sentencing, Restorative Justice and the Role of the Community." *Canadian Journal of Criminology.* Vol. 34 (1997):40–52.

Lavelle, Marianne. "Payback Time." *U.S. News & World Report* (March 11, 2002):36–40.

Lemert, Edwin M. *Social Pathology.* New York: McGraw-Hill, 1951.

———. *Human Deviance, Social Problems, and Social Control.* 2nd ed. Englewood Cliffs, NJ: Prentice Hall, 1972.

Lemonick, Michael D. "The Search for a Murder Gene." *Time* (January 20, 2003):100.

Leonard, Eileen B. *Women, Crime, and Society: A Critique of Theoretical Criminology.* New York: Longman, 1982.

Li, Peter S. *Destination Canada: Immigration Debates and Issues.* Toronto: Oxford University Press Canada, 2003.

Liazos, Alexander. "The Poverty of the Sociology of Deviance: Nuts, Sluts and Perverts." *Social Problems.* Vol. 20, No. 1 (Summer 1972):103–20.

Liska, Allen E., and Barbara D. Warner. "Functions of Crime: A Paradoxical Process." *American Journal of Sociology.* Vol. 96, No. 6 (May 1991):1441–63.

Little, Craig, and Andrea Rankin. "Why Do They Start It? Explaining Reported Early-Teen Sexual Activity." *Sociological Forum.* Vol. 16, No. 4 (December 2001):703–29.

Lupri, Eugene. "Intimate Violence: Male Abuse." Unpublished manuscript. University of Calgary, 2002.

MacDonald, Nancy. "Justice is not blind," *Maclean's* (February 29, 2016):16–23.

Martin, John M., and Anne T. Romano. *Multinational Crime: Terrorism, Espionage, Drug and Arms Trafficking.* Newbury Park, CA: Sage, 1992.

Merton, Robert K. "Social Structure and Anomie." *American Sociological Review.* Vol. 3, No. 6 (October 1938):672–82.

———. *Social Theory and Social Structure.* New York: Free Press, 1968.

Messing, Philip. "City Crime Plummets." *New York Post* (September 5, 2003). [Online] Available at http://www.nypost.com/news/regionalnews/5020 .htm.

Miller, William J., and Rick A. Matthews. "Youth Employment, Differential Association, and Juvenile Delinquency." *Sociological Focus.* Vol. 34, No. 3 (August 2001):251–68.

Moffitt, Terrie E., et al. "A Gradient of Childhood Self-Control Predicts Health, Wealth, and Public Safety." *Proceedings of the National Academy of Sciences of the United States of America.* Available January 30, 2011, at http://www.pnas .org/content/early/2011/01/20/1010076108.

Ontario. *The Report of the Commission on Systemic Racism in the Ontario Criminal Justice System.* Toronto: Queen's Printer for Ontario, 1996.

Parnaby, Patrick, and Myra Leyden. "Dirty Harry and the Station Queens: A Mertonian Analysis of Police Deviance." In Lorne Tepperman and Angela Kalyta, eds. *Reading Sociology: Canadian Perspectives.* 2nd ed. Don Mills, Ontario: Oxford University Press. 2011:77–81.

Paperny, Anna Mehler. "Gangs smaller—but packing more heat." *The Globe and Mail* (June 9, 2012):A17.

Pinker, Steven. "Are Your Genes to Blame?" *Time* (January 20, 2003):98–100.

Quinney, Richard. *Class, State and Crime: On the Theory and Practice of Criminal Justice.* New York: David McKay, 1977.

Reckless, Walter C., and Simon Dinitz. "Pioneering with Self-Concept as a Vulnerability Factor in Delinquency." *Journal of Criminal Law, Criminology, and Police Science.* Vol. 58, No. 4 (December 1967):515–23.

Reid, Sue Titus. *Crime and Criminology.* 6th ed. Fort Worth, TX: Holt, Rinehart & Winston, 1991.

Reiman, Jeffrey H. *The Rich Get Richer and the Poor Get Prison: Ideology, Class, and Criminal Justice.* 3rd ed. New York: John Wiley & Sons, 1990.

Scheff, Thomas J. *Being Mentally Ill: A Sociological Theory.* 2nd ed. New York: Aldine, 1984.

Schellenberg, Kathryn. "Policing the Police: Technological Surveillance and the Predilection for Leniency." *Criminal Justice and Behavior* (1995).

Scott, Hannah. *The Female Serial Killer: A Well-Kept Secret of the "Gentler Sex."* Master's thesis. University of Guelph, 1992.

Sheldon, William H., Emil M. Hartl, and Eugene McDermott. *Varieties of Delinquent Youth.* New York: Harper, 1949.

Sheley, James F., Joshua Zhang, Charles J. Brody, and James D. Wright. "Gang Organization, Gang Criminal Activity, and Individual Gang Members' Criminal Behavior." *Social Science Quarterly.* Vol. 76, No. 1 (March 1995):53–68.

Sherman, Lawrence W., and Douglas A. Smith. "Crime, Punishment, and Stake in Conformity: Legal and Informal Control of Domestic Violence." *American Sociological Review.* Vol. 57, No. 5 (October 1992):680–90.

Simon, Rita J., and N. Sharma. "Women and Crime: Does the American Experience Generalize?" In F. Adler and R.J. Simon, eds. *Criminology of Deviant Women.* Boston: Houghton Mifflin, 1979.

Smith, Douglas A. "Police Response to Interpersonal Violence: Defining the Parameters of Legal Control." *Social Forces.* Vol. 65, No. 3 (March 1987):767–82.

Smith, Douglas A., and Patrick R. Gartin. "Specifying Specific Deterrence: The Influence of Arrest on Future Criminal Activity." *American Sociological Review.* Vol. 54, No. 1 (February 1989):94–105.

Smith, Douglas A., and Christy A. Visher. "Street-Level Justice: Situational Determinants of Police Arrest Decisions." *Social Problems.* Vol. 29, No. 2 (December 1981):167–77.

Spitzer, Steven. "Toward a Marxian Theory of Deviance." In Delos H. Kelly, ed. *Criminal Behavior: Readings in Criminology.* New York: St. Martin's Press, 1980:175–91.

Stack, Steven, Ira Wasserman, and Roger Kern. "Adult Social Bonds and the Use of Internet Pornography." *Social Science Quarterly.* Vol. 85, No. 1 (March 2004):75–88.

Statistics Canada. *Juristat Service Bulletin.* Catalogue No. 85-002. Ottawa: Statistics Canada, 1994a.

———. "Homicides, 2002." *The Daily,* October 1, 2003a. [Online] Available at http://www.statcan.ca/Daily/English/031001/d031001a.htm.

———. "Police-reported hate crime in Canada, 2010." *Juristat.* 2012a. No. 85-002-X. [Online] Available http://www.statcan.gc.ca/pub/ 85-002-x/2012001/article/11635-eng.htm#a3.

———. *Juristat.* Catalogue No. 85-002-x. Ottawa: Statistics Canada, 2015.

Sutherland, Edwin H. "White Collar Criminality." *American Sociological Review.* Vol. 5, No. 1 (February 1940):1–12.

Sutherland, Edwin H., and Donald R. Cressey. *Criminology.* 10th ed. Philadelphia, PA: J.B. Lippincott, 1978.

Szasz, Thomas S. *The Manufacturer of Madness: A Comparative Study of the Inquisition and the Mental Health Movement.* New York: Dell, 1961.

———. *The Myth of Mental Illness: Foundations of a Theory of Personal Conduct.* New York: Harper & Row, 1970; orig. 1961.

———. "Cleansing the Modern Heart." *Society.* Vol. 40, No. 4 (May/June 2003):52–9.

——— "Protecting Patients against Psychiatric Intervention." *Society.* Vol. 41, No. 3 (March/April 2004):7–0.

Thornberry, Terrance, and Margaret Farnsworth. "Social Correlates of Criminal Involvement: Further Evidence on the Relationship Between Social Status and Criminal Behavior." *American Sociological Review.* Vol. 47, No. 4 (August 1982):505–18.

Tittle, Charles R., Wayne J. Villemez, and Douglas A. Smith. "The Myth of Social Class and Criminality: An Empirical Assessment of the Empirical Evidence." *American Sociological Review.* Vol. 43, No. 5 (October 1978):643–56.

Valdez, A. "In the Hood: Street Gangs Discover White-Collar Crime." *Police.* Vol. 21, No. 5 (May 1997):49–50, 56.

Vold, George B., and Thomas J. Bernard. *Theoretical Criminology.* 3rd ed. New York: Oxford University Press, 1986.

Waldie, Paul, and Karen Howlett. "Reports Reveal Tight Grip of Ebbers on WorldCom." *The Globe and Mail* (June 11, 2003):B1, B7.

Warr, Mark, and Christopher G. Ellison. "Rethinking Social Reactions to Crime: Personal and Altruistic Fear in Family Households." *American Journal of Sociology.* Vol. 106, No. 3 (November 2000):551–78.

Wente, Margaret. "Welcome back, Conrad!" *The Globe and Mail* (May 3, 2012):A19.

Wolfgang, Marvin E., Terrence P. Thornberry, and Robert M. Figlio. *From Boy to Man, From Delinquency to Crime.* Chicago, IL: University of Chicago Press, 1987.

Wright, Richard A. *In Defense of Prisons.* Westport, CT: Greenwood Press, 1994.

Chapter 10

Baltzell, E. Digby. *The Protestant Establishment: Aristocracy and Caste in America.* New York: Vintage Books, 1964.

Beeghley, Leonard. *The Structure of Social Stratification in the United States.* Needham Heights, MA: Allyn & Bacon, 1989.

Bian, Yanjie. "Chinese Social Stratification and Social Mobility." *Annual Review of Sociology.* Vol. 28 (2002):91–116.

Brinton, Mary C. "The Social-Institutional Bases of Gender Stratification: Japan as an Illustrative Case." *American Journal of Sociology.* Vol. 94, No. 2 (September 1988):300–34.

Brym, Robert J. "The Canadian Capitalist Class, 1965–1985." In Robert J. Brym, ed. *The Structures of the Canadian Capitalist Class.* Toronto: Garamond, 1985:1–20.

Clark, Margaret S., Ed. *Prosocial Behavior.* Newbury Park, CA: Sage, 1991.

Clement, Wallace. "Comparative Class Analysis: Locating Canada in a North American and Nordic Context." *Canadian Review of Sociology and Anthropology.* Vol. 27, No. 4 (1990).

Dahrendorf, Ralf. *Class and Class Conflict in Industrial Society.* Stanford, CA: Stanford University Press, 1959.

Davis, Kingsley, and Wilbert Moore. "Some Principles of Stratification." *American Sociological Review.* Vol. 10, No. 2 (April 1945):242–49.

Francis, Diane. *Controlling Interest: Who Owns Canada?* Toronto: Macmillan, 1986.

French, Howard W. "Teaching Japan's Salarymen to Be Their Own Men." *New York Times* (November 27, 2002):A4.

Geiger, John. "A matter of class." *The Globe and Mail* (April 13, 2012):A8,9.

Gerber, Theodore P., and Michael Hout. "More Shock than Therapy: Market Transition, Employment, and Income in Russia, 1991–1995." *American Journal of Sociology.* Vol. 104, No. 1 (July 1998):1–50.

Humphreys, Adrian. "He Is no Longer an Unknown Child." *National Post* (November 7, 2002):A3.

Johnson, Ian. "China's Aristocratic Class Wields Its Influence to Shape Politics." *New York Times* (November 13, 2012).

Keister, Lisa A., and Stephanie Moller. "Wealth Inequality in the United States." *Annual Review of Sociology.* Vol. 26 (2000):63–81.

Kuznets, Simon. "Economic Growth and Income Inequality." *The American Economic Review.* Vol. xlv, No. 1 (March 1955):1–28.

———. *Modern Economic Growth: Rate, Structure, and Spread.* New Haven, CT: Yale University Press, 1966.

Lenski, Gerhard E. *Power and Privilege: A Theory of Social Stratification.* New York: McGraw-Hill, 1966.

Liu, Melinda, and Duncan Hewitt. "The Rise of the Sea Turtles." *Newsweek* (August 18, 2008):29–31.

Lord, Walter. *A Night to Remember.* Rev. ed. New York: Holt, Rinehart & Winston, 1976.

Marx, Karl, and Friedrich Engels. "Manifesto of the Communist Party." In Robert C. Tucker, ed. *The Marx-Engels Reader.* New York: Norton, 1972; orig. 1848. pp. 331–62.

Mason, David S. "Fairness Matters: Equity and the Transition to Democracy." *World Policy Journal.* Vol. 20, No. 4 (Winter 2003-04). 2004. [Online] Available February 21, 2008, at http://www.worldpolicy.org/journal/articles/wpj03-4/mason.html.

Matthews, Ralph. *The Creation of Regional Dependency.* Toronto: University of Toronto Press, 1983.

McKee, Victoria. "Blue Blood and the Color of Money." *New York Times* (June 9, 1996):49–50.

Newman, Peter C. *Titans: How the New Canadian Establishment Seized Power.* Toronto: Penguin, 1998.

Norbeck, Edward. "Class Structure." In *Kodansha Encyclopedia of Japan.* Tokyo: Kodansha, 1983. pp. 322–25.

OECD (Organisation for Economic Co-operation and Development). "Stat. Extracts." 2012, 2015. Available at http://stats.oecd.org/index.aspx.

Parry, Wynne. "Titanic's Unknown Child Given a New, Final Identity" in Live Science. April 25, 2011. http://www.livescience.com/13859-titanic-unknown-child-identification-sidney-goodwin.html.

Richburg, Keith B. "China's Communist Rulers Find Newly Rich a Headache." *The Richmond Times-Dispatch* (September 14, 2011):A2.

Scott, Graham F. "Canada's Top 100 highest-paid CEOs." *Canadian Business.* 2016. Available March 2016 at http://www.canadianbusiness.com/lists-and-rankings/richest-people/canadas-top-100-highest-paid-ceos-2016/.

Smith, Dorothy E. *The Everyday World as Problematic: A Feminist Sociology.* Toronto: University of Toronto Press, 1987.

Statistics Canada. 2006 Census of Population, Catalogue no. 97-564-XCB2006005.

Tumin, Melvin M. "Some Principles of Stratification: A Critical Analysis." *American Sociological Review.* Vol. 18, No. 4 (August 1953):387–94.

———. *Social Stratification: The Forms and Functions of Inequality.* 2nd ed. Englewood Cliffs, NJ: Prentice Hall, 1985.

United Nations. "International Human Development Indicators." 2014. Available at http://hdrstats.undp.org/en/indicators/default.html.

Vallis, Mary. "Opulence at Home." *National Post* (May 6, 2006):A3.

Wendle, John. "Russia's Millionaires Keep Their Heads Up." *Time* (January 12, 2009):4.

Williamson, Jeffrey G., and Peter H. Lindert. *American Inequality: A Macroeconomic History.* New York: Academic Press, 1980.

Williamson, Samuel H. "Six Ways to Compute the Relative Value of a U.S. Dollar Amount, 1790 to Present." *Measuring Worth.* 2015. Available at http://www.measuringworth.com/index.html.

World Bank. "World DataBank: World Development Indicators." 2012, 2014, 2015. Available at http://data.worldbank.org/data-catalog/world-developmentindicators.

Wotherspoon, Terry, and Vic Satzewich. *First Nations: Race, Class, and Gender Relations.* Scarborough, ON: Nelson, 1993.

Zuckerman, Mortimer B. "The Russian Conundrum." *U.S. News & World Report* (March 13, 2006):64.

Chapter 11

Adams, Patricia F., Whitney K. Kirzinger, and Michael E. Martinez. "Summary Health Statistics for the U.S. Population: National Health Interview Survey, 2011." National Center for Health Statistics. *Vital Health Statistics.* Vol. 10, No. 255. 2012. Available at http://www.cdc.gov/nchs/data/series/sr_10/sr10_255.pdf.

Banfield, Edward C. *The Unheavenly City Revisited.* Boston: Little, Brown, 1974.

Bassuk, Ellen J. "The Homelessness Problem." *Scientific American.* Vol. 251, No. 1 (July 1984):40–45.

Blishen, Bernard R. "The Construction and Use of an Occupational Class Scale." *Canadian Journal of Economics and Political Science.* Vol. xxiv (1958):519–25.

Blishen, Bernard R., W. Carroll, and C. Moore. "The 1981 Socio-Economic Index for Occupations in Canada." *Canadian Review of Sociology and Anthropology.* Vol. 24 (1987):465–88.

Bohannan, Cecil. "The Economic Correlates of Homelessness in Sixty Cities." *Social Science Quarterly.* Vol. 72, No. 4 (December 1991):817–25.

Bott, Elizabeth. *Family and Social Network.* New York: Free Press, 1971; orig. 1957.

Clement, Wallace. *The Canadian Corporate Elite: Economic Power in Canada.* Toronto: McClelland & Stewart, 1975.

Counts, G.S. "The Social Status of Occupations: A Problem in Vocational Guidance." *School Review.* Vol. 33 (January 1925):16–27.

Cowan, James. "Toronto asks its $90,000 question." *National Post* (April 20, 2006):1.

Creese, Gillian, Neil Guppy, and Martin Meissner. *Ups and Downs on the Ladder of Success.* Ottawa: Statistics Canada, 1991.

Duffy, Ann, and Nancy Mandell. "The Growth in Poverty and Social Inequality: Losing Faith in Social Justice." In Dan Glenday and Ann Duffy, *Canadian Society: Meeting the Challenges of the Twenty-First Century.* Toronto: Oxford University Press Canada, 2001.

Food Banks Canada, 2016. www.foodbankscanad.ca. Accessed on March 26, 2016.

Francis, Diane. *Controlling Interest: Who Owns Canada?* Toronto: Macmillan, 1986.

Gerber, Linda M. "The Development of Canadian Indian Communities: A Two-Dimensional Typology Reflecting Strategies of Adaptation to the Outside World." *Canadian Review of Sociology and Anthropology.* Vol. 16, No. 4 (1979):123–50.

———. "Multiple Jeopardy: A Socio-economic Comparison of Men and Women among the Indian, Métis and Inuit Peoples of Canada." *Canadian Ethnic Studies.* Vol. xxii, No. 3 (1990):69–84.

———. "Education, Employment, and Income Polarization among Aboriginal Men and Women in Canada: Stagnation and Progress." *Canadian Ethnic Studies.* Vol. 46, No. 1 (2014):87–110.

Gilbert, Dennis, and Joseph A. Kahl. *The American Class Structure: A New Synthesis.* 3rd ed. Homewood, IL: The Dorsey Press, 1987.

Goyder, John. *Technology and Society: A Canadian Perspective.* Peterborough, ON: Broadview Press, 1997.

———. "The Dynamics of Occupational Prestige: 1975–2000." *The Canadian Review of Sociology and Anthropology.* Vol. 42, No. 1 (2005):1, 23.

Goyder, John C., and James E. Curtis. "Occupational Mobility in Canada over Four Generations." In James E. Curtis and William G. Scott, eds. *Social Stratification: Canada.* 2nd ed. Scarborough, ON: Prentice Hall, 1979.

Goyder, John, Neil Guppy, and Mary Thompson. "The Allocation of Male and Female Occupational Prestige in an Ontario Urban Area: A Quarter-Century Replication." *The Canadian Review of Sociology and Anthropology.* Vol. 40, No. 4 (2003):417.

Hodge, Robert W., Donald J. Treiman, and Peter H. Rossi. "A Comparative Study of Occupational Prestige." In Reinhard Bendix and Seymour Martin Lipset, eds. *Class, Status, and Power: Social Stratification in Comparative Perspective.* 2nd ed. New York: Free Press, 1966. pp. 309–21.

Kaufman, Leslie. "Surge in Homeless Families Sets Off Debate on Cause." *New York Times* (July 29, 2004). [Online] Available March 24, 2005, at http://www.researchnavigator.com.

Kuitenbrouwer, Peter. "The uncounted ones." *National Post* (April 20, 2006):A15.

Kohn, Melvin L. *Class and Conformity: A Study in Values.* 2nd ed. Homewood, IL: Dorsey Press, 1977.

Lareau, Annette. "Invisible Inequality: Social Class and Childrearing in Black Families and White Familes." *American Sociological Review.* Vol. 67, No. 5 (October 2002):747–76.

Lewis, Oscar. *The Children of Sanchez.* New York: Random House, 1961.

Lin, Nan, and Wen Xie. "Occupational Prestige in Urban China." *American Journal of Sociology.* Vol. 93, No. 4 (January 1988):793–832.

Macionis, John J. *Sociology,* 15th ed. United States of America: Pearson Education, 2014.

Mahoney, Jill. "Single mother has more money, less cash." *The Globe and Mail* (March 31, 2006c):A8.

Mcfarland, Janet. "Executive compensation rankings for Canada's 100 biggest companies." *The Globe and Mail* (May 29,2011). [Online] Available at http://www.theglobeandmail.com/report-on-business/careers/management/executive-compensation/executive-compensation-rankings-for-canadas-100-biggest-companies/article2038022.

Mcleod, Jay. *Ain't No Makin' It: Aspirations and Attainment in a Low-Income Neighborhood.* Boulder, CO: Westview Press, 1995.

Michelson, William. "Urbanization and Urbanism." In James Curtis and Lorne Tepperman, eds. *Understanding Canadian Society.* Toronto: McGraw-Hill Ryerson, 1988:73–104.

Pelley, Lauren. "Canada's richest make Forbes' 2015 billionaires list." (2015). thestar.com. Accessed on March 23, 2016.

Richler, Jacob. "Last night, I walked in another's mismatched shoes." *National Post* (April 20, 2006):A15.

Ryan, William. *Blaming the Victim.* Rev. ed. New York: Vintage Books, 1976.

Scoffield, Heather. "Growth spurs decline in poverty." *The Globe and Mail* (March 31, 2006):A1.

Singh, Gopal K. "Child Mortality in the United States, 1935–2007: Large Racial and Socioeconomic Disparities Have Persisted Over Time." Rockville, Md.: U.S. Department of Health and Human Services. 2010. Available at http://www.hrsa.gov/healthit/images/mchb_child_mortality_pub.pdf.

Statistics Canada. Canadian Statistics. "Characteristics of household Internet users." 2006. [Online] Available at http://www40.statcan.ca/l01/cst01/comm10a.htm.

———. "Persons in low income before tax (In percent, 2007 to 2011)." CANSIM Table 202-0803. Available at http://www.statcan.gc.ca/tables-tableaux/sum-som/l01/cst01/famil41a-eng.htm.

———. "Canadian Internet use survey, Internet use, by age group, Internet activity, sex, level of education and household income occasional (percent)."

CANSIM Table 358-0153. 2011. Available at http://www5.statcan.gc.ca/cansim/a26?lang=eng&id=3580153.

Tepperman, Lorne. "Status Inconsistency in the Toronto Elite of the 1920s." In James Curtis and William G. Scott. *Social Stratification: Canada*. 2nd ed. Scarborough, ON: Prentice Hall, 1979.

Walker, Karen. "'Always There for Me': Friendship Patterns and Expectations among Middle- and Working-Class Men and Women." *Sociological Forum*. Vol. 10, No. 2 (June 1995):273–96.

Weitzman, Lenore J. "The Economic Consequences of Divorce Are Still Unequal: Comment on Peterson." *American Sociological Review*. Vol. 61, No. 3 (June 1996):537–8.

White, Patrick. "Rescue in the Frigid River: Split-Second Decision Gives Homeless Hero Second Chance." *The Globe and Mail*. May 6, 2009:A1.

Whitman, David. "Shattering Myths about the Homeless." *U.S. News & World Report* (March 20, 1989):26, 28.

Wotherspoon, Terry, and Vic Satzewich. *First Nations: Race, Class, and Gender Relations*. Scarborough, ON: Nelson, 1993.

York, Geoffrey. "UN Body Chastises Canada on Poverty." *The Globe and Mail* (June 25, 1993):A1-2.

Zagorsky, Jay. "Divorce Drops a Person's Wealth by 77 Percent." Press release (January 18, 2006). Available January 19, 2006, at http://www.eurekalert.org/pub_releases/2006-01/osu-dda011806.php.

Chapter 12

Anti-Slavery International. "Slavery in Mauritania" 2015. Available at http://www.antislavery.org/english/what_we_do/antislavery_international_today/award/2009_award_winner/slavery_in_mauritania.aspx.

Aponiuk, Natalia. "Some Comments on This Special Issue." *Canadian Ethnic Studies. Ethnicity, Civil Society, and Public Policy: Engaging Cultures in a Globalizing World*. Vol. 39, No. 3 (2007).

Bangladesh Garment Manufacturers & Exporters Association. 2012. Available at http://www.bgmea.com.bd/home/pages/aboutus.

Bauer, P.T. *Equality, the Third World, and Economic Delusion*. Cambridge, MA: Harvard University Press, 1981.

Bearak, Barry. "Lives Held Cheap in Bangladesh Sweatshops." *New York Times* (April 15, 2001):A1, A12.

Berger, Peter L. *The Capitalist Revolution: Fifty Propositions About Prosperity, Equality, and Liberty*. New York: Basic Books, 1986.

Bonanno, Alessandro, Douglas H. Constance, and Heather Lorenz. "Powers and Limits of Transnational Corporations: The Case of ADM." *Rural Sociology*. Vol. 65, No. 3 (September 2000):440–60.

Bricker, Jesse, Lisa J. Dettling, Alice Henriques, Joanne W. Hsu, Kevin B. Moore, John Sabelhaus, Jeffrey Thompson, and Richard A. Windle. "Changes in U.S. Family Finances from 2010 to 2013: Evidence from the Survey of Consumer Finances." *Federal Reserve Bulletin* (September 2014):1–40. 2014. Available at http://www.federalreserve.gov/econresdata/scf/files/BulletinCharts.pdf.

Burkett, Elinor. "God Created Me to Be a Slave." *New York Times Magazine* (October 12, 1997):56–60.

Bussolo, Maurizio, Rafael E. Dehoyos, Denis Medvedev, and Dominique Van De Mensbrugghe. *Global Growth and Distribution: Are China and India Reshaping the World?* Policy Research Working Paper No. 4392. New York: World Bank, 2007.

Canada. Canadian International Development Agency. *Sharing Our Future: Canadian International Development Assistance*. Ottawa: Ministry of Supply-and Services Canada, 1987.

———. "Economic Impact of International Education in Canada." Global Affairs Canada, March 30, 2016. [Online] Available at international.gc.ca.

Chen, Shaohua, and Martin Ravallion. "An Update to the World Bank's Estimates of Consumption Poverty in the Developing World." *World Bank*. 2012. Available at http://siteresources.worldbank.org/INTPOVCALNET/Resources/Global_Poverty_Update_2012_02-29-12.pdf.

Chen, Shahua, and Martin Ravallion. "The Developing World Is Poorer than We Thought, but No Less Successful in the Fight against Poverty." 2008. [Online] Available at http://go.worldbank.org/C9GR27WRJ0.

Classen, Lauren, Sally Humphries, John Fitzsimons, and Susan Kaaria. "Opening Participatory Spaces for the Most Marginal: Learning from Collective Action in the Honduran Hillsides." *World Development*. Vol. 36, No. 11 (2008):2402–2420.

Consortium for Street Children. "Street Children Statistics." 2009. [Online] Available at http://www.streetchildren.org.uk/_uploads/resources/Street_Children_Stats_FINAL.pdf.

Davies, James, Rodrigo Lluberas, and Anthony Shorrocks. "Credit Suisse Global World Databook, 2014." 2014. Available at https://publications.credit-suisse.com/tasks/render/file/?fileID=5521F296-D460-2B88-081889DB12817E02.

Davies, James B., Susanna Sandstrom, Anthony Shorrocks, and Edward N. Wolff. *The World Distribution of Household Wealth*. Helsinki: United Nations University/World Institute for Development Economics Research, March 2008.

Finnis, Elizabeth. "Why Grow Cash Crops? Subsistence Farming and Crop Commercialization in the Kolli Hills, South India." *American Anthropologist* Vol. 108, No. 2 (2006):363–369.

———. "'Now It Is an Easy Life': Women's Accounts of Cassava, Millets, and Labour in South India." *Culture and Agriculture*. Vol. 31, No. 2 (2009):88–94.

Firebaugh, Glenn. "Growth Effects of Foreign and Domestic Investment. "*American Journal of Sociology*. Vol. 98, No. 1 (July 1992):105–30.

———. "Does Foreign Capital Harm Poor Nations? New Estimates Based on Dixon and Boswell's Measures of Capital Penetration." *American Journal of Sociology*. Vol. 102, No. 2 (September 1996):563–75.

———. "Empirics of World Income Inequality." *American Journal of Sociology*. Vol. 104, No. 6 (May 1999):1597–1630.

Firebaugh, Glenn, and Frank D. Beck. "Does Economic Growth Benefit the Masses? Growth, Dependence, and Welfare in the Third World." *American Sociological Review*. Vol. 59, No. 5 (October 1994):631–53.

Firebaugh, Glenn, and Dumitru Sandu. "Who Supports Marketization and Democratization in Post-Communist Romania?" *Sociological Forum*. Vol. 13, No. 3 (September 1998):521–41.

Fisher, Max. "The Country Where Slavery Is Still Normal." *The Atlantic* (June 28, 2011). Available at http://www.theatlantic.com/international/archive/2011/06/the-country-where-slavery-is-still-normal/241148.

Forbes. "The World's Billionaires." 2015. Available at http://www.forbes.com/wealth/billionaires.

Frank, André Gunder. *On Capitalist Underdevelopment*. Bombay: Oxford University Press, 1975.

Frayssinet, Fabiana. "Agribusiness Driving Land Concentration." Inter Press Service News Agency. [Online] Available October 5, 2009, at http://ipsnews.net/news.asp?idnews=48734.

Galano, Ana Maria. "Land Hungry in Brazil." August 1998. [Online] Available December 4, 2008, at http://www.unesco.org/courier/1998_08/uk/somm/intro.htm.

Galloway, Gloria. "MPs debate doing more in Darfur." *The Globe and Mail* (May 2, 2006):A11.

Goesling, Brian. "Changing Income Inequalities within and between Nations: New Evidence." *American Sociological Review*. Vol. 66, No. 5 (October 2001):745–61.

Gregg, Allan R. "What tsunamis tell us about our changed world." *The Globe and Mail* (January 7, 2005):A15.

Hossain, Naomi. "Exports, Equity, and Empowerment: The Effects of Readymade Garments Manufacturing Employment on Gender Equality in Bangladesh."

Humphries, Sally. "The Intensification of Traditional Agriculture among Yucatec Maya Farmers: Facing up to the Dilemma of Livelihood Sustainability." *Human Ecology*. Vol. 21, No. 1 (1993):87–102.

IGBE (Instituto Brasileiro de Geografi a e Estat[[iacute]]stica). Census of Agriculture, 2006. [Online] Available at http://www.ibge.gov.br/english/presidencia/noticias/noticia_visualiza.php?id_noticia=1464&id_pagina=1.

International Labour Organization. "Forced Labour." 2012. Available at http://www.ilo.org/global/topics/forced-labour/lang-en/index.htm.

———. "Global Child Labour Trends 2008 to 2012." 2013. Available at http://www.ilo.org/ipecinfo/product/viewProduct.do?productId=23015.

Kentor, Jeffrey. "The Long-Term Effects of Globalization on Income Inequality, Population Growth, and Economic Development." *Social Problems*. Vol. 48, No. 4 (November 2001):435–55.

Landesa Center for Women's Land Rights. 2011. Available at http://www.landesa.org/women-and-land.

Lappé, Frances Moore, and Joseph Collins. *World Hunger: Twelve Myths*. New York: Grove Press/Food First Books, 1986.

Lappé, Frances Moore, Joseph Collins, and Peter Rosset. *World Hunger: Twelve Myths*. 2nd ed. New York: Grove Press, 1998.

Leopold, Evelyn. "Sudan's Young Endure 'Unspeakable' Abuse: Report." [Online] Available April 19, 2007, at http://www.news.yahoo.com.

Levinson, F. James, and Lucy Bassett. "Malnutrition Is Still a Major Contributor to Child Deaths." Population Reference Bureau. 2007. [Online] Available December 4, 2008, at http://www.prb.org/pdf07/Nutrition2007.pdf.

Lindauer, David L., and Akila Weerapana. "Relief for Poor Nations." *Society*. Vol. 39, No. 3 (March/April 2002):54–58.

Milanovic, Branko. "Global Inequality Recalculated: The Effect of New 2005 PPP Estimates on Global Inequality." World Bank. 2009. Available at http://siteresources.worldbank.org/INTDECINEQ/Resources/Global_Inequality_Recalculated.pdf.

———. "Global Income Inequality: New Results and Implications for 21 st Century Policy." World Bank. 2011. Available at http://siteresources.worldbank.org/EXTABCDE/Resources/7455676-1292528456380/7626791-1303141641402/7878676-1306699356046/Parallel-Sesssion-6-Branko-Milanovic.pdf.

Moore, Wilbert E. "Modernization as Rationalization: Processes and Restraints." In Manning Nash, ed. *Essays on Economic Development and Cultural Change in Honor of Bert F. Hoselitz*. Chicago, IL: University of Chicago Press, 1977. pp. 29–42.

———. *World Modernization: The Limits of Convergence*. New York: Elsevier, 1979.

Orhant, Melanie. "Human Trafficking Exposed." *Population Today*. Vol. 30, No. 1 (January 2002):1, 4.

Parsons, Talcott. *Societies: Evolutionary and Comparative Perspectives*. Englewood Cliff s, NJ: Prentice Hall, 1966.

Partridge, John. "Balanced Foreign Aid Policy Urged." *The Globe and Mail* (October 8, 2003). [Online] Available at http://www.globeinvestor.com/servlet/ArticleNews/story/LAC/20031008/RCONFERENCE.

Perry, Alex. "Africa Rising." *Time*. Vol. 180, No. 23 (December 3, 2012):48–2.

Pomfret, Richard. *The Economic Development of Canada*. Toronto: Methuen, 1981.

Population Reference Bureau. *2010 World Population Data Sheet.* 2010. [Online] Available at http://www.prb.org/Publications/Datasheets/2010/2010wpds.aspx.

———. "Datafinder." 2012. Available at http://www.prb.org/DataFinder.aspx.

———. "World Population Data Sheet." 2012. Available at http://www.prb.org/pdf12/2012-population-data-sheet_eng.pdf.

———. "World Population Data Sheet 2014." 2014. Available at http://www.prb.org/Publications/Datasheets/2014/2014-world-population-data-sheet.aspx.

Rostow, Walt W. *The Stages of Economic Growth: A Non-Communist Manifesto.* Cambridge: Cambridge University Press, 1960.

———. *The World Economy: History and Prospect.* Austin: University of Texas Press, 1978.

Sala-i-Martin, Xavier. "The World Distribution of Income." Working Paper No. 8933. Cambridge, Mass.: National Bureau of Economic Research, 2002.

Smyth, Julie. "Earning less, feeling more." *Maclean's.* (March 14, 2016):26.

Statistics Canada. 2011. CANSIM Table 380-0027.

Tomlinson, Brian. "Development in the 1990s: Critical Reflections on Canada's Economic Relations with the Third World." In Jamie Swift and Brian Tomlinson, eds. *Conflicts of Interest: Canada and the Third World.* Toronto: between the lines, 1991.

United Nations. Department of Economic and Social Affairs. "World Population Prospects: The 2012 Revision." 2013. Available at http://esa.un.org/unpd/wpp/unpp/panel_indicators.htm.

United Nations. Food and Agriculture Organization. "The State of Food Insecurity in the World." Rome: Food and Agriculture Organization of the United Nations. 2010. [Online] Available at http://www.fao.org/publications/sofi/en.

———. Food and Agriculture Organization, Statistics Division. "Prevalence of Undernourishment in Total Population." Food Security Statistics. 2014. Available at http://www.fao.org/economic/ess/ess-fs/fs-data/en.

United Nations Development Programme. *Human Development Report 2007–08.* 2008. [Online] Available at http://hdr.undp.org/en/reports/global/hdr2007-8.

———. "International Human Development Indicators." 2012. Available at http://hdrstats.undp.org/en/indicators/default.html.

———. "International Human Development Indicators." 2014. Available at http://hdrstats.undp.org/en/indicators/default.html.

U.S. Census Bureau, Foreign Trade Division. "Foreign Trade Statistics." 2012. Available at http://www.census.gov/foreign-trade/index.html.

Vogel, Ezra F. *The Four Little Dragons: The Spread of Industrialization in East Asia.* Cambridge, MA: Harvard University Press, 1991.

Wallerstein, Immanuel. *The Modern World-System: Capitalist Agriculture and the Origins of the European World-Economy in the Sixteenth Century.* New York: Academic Press, 1974.

———. *The Capitalist World-Economy.* New York: Cambridge University Press, 1979.

———. "Crises: The World Economy, the Movements, and the Ideologies." In Albert Bergesen, ed. *Crises in the World-System.* Beverly Hills, CA: Sage, 1983:21–36.

———. *The Politics of the World Economy: The States, the Movements, and the Civilizations.* Cambridge: Cambridge University Press, 1984.

Weber, Max. *The Protestant Ethic and the Spirit of Capitalism.* New York: Charles Scribner's Sons, 1958; orig. 1904–05.

Wente, Margaret. "A+ for cultural capital." *The Globe and Mail* (June 27, 2006):A15.

World Bank. *2008 World Development Indicators.* Washington, DC: World Bank, 2008.

———. "World DataBank: Health, Nutrition, and Population Statistics." 2012. Available at http://data.worldbank.org/data-catalog/health-nutrition-andpopulation-statistics.

———. "World DataBank: World Development Indicators." 2012. Available at http://data.worldbank.org/data-catalog/world-development-indicators.

———. "The State of the Poor: Where Are the Poor and Where Are They Poorest?" April 17, 2014. Available at http://www.worldbank.org/content/dam/Worldbank/document/State_of_the_poor_paper_April17.pdf.

———. "World DataBank: Health, Nutrition, and Population Statistics." 2014, 2015. Available at http://data.worldbank.org/data-catalog/health-nutritionand-population-statistics.

———. "World DataBank: World Development Indicators." 2014, 2015. Available at http://data.worldbank.org/data-catalog/world-developmentindicators.

———. "Povcal Net." 2015. Available at http://databank.worldbank.org/data/views/variableSelection/selectvariables.aspx?source=poverty-and-inequalitydatabase.

Worsley, Peter. "Models of the World System." In Mike Featherstone, ed. *Global Culture: Nationalism, Globalization, and Modernity.* Newbury Park, CA: Sage, 1990. pp. 83–95.

Chapter 13

Anderssen, Erin. "We have a record number of female MPs, but hold the applause." *The Globe and Mail:* (October 21, 2014). http://www.theglobeandmail.com/life/we-have-a-record-number-of-female-mps-but-hold-the-applause/article26887164/. Accessed April 5, 2016.

Armstrong, Elisabeth. *The Retreat from Organization: U.S. Feminism Reconceptualized.* Albany, NY: State University of New York Press, 2002.

Atkinson, Michael. "It's Still Part of the Game: Masculinity, Crime and Victimization in Ice Hockey." In L. Fuller, ed. *Sport, Rhetoric, Gender and Violence: Historical Perspectives and Media Representations.* New York: Palgrave MacMillan, 2007.

Bascaramurty, Dakshana. "This is how we do it: Hazel's pointers for T.O." *The Globe and Mail,* November 17, 2012:M3.

———. Dakshana, "Former Mississauga mayor Hazel McCallion lands a new job." *The Globe and Mail:* February 23, 2015. http://www.theglobeandmail.com/news/toronto/former-mississauga-mayor-hazel-mccallion-lands-new-job/article23163563/. Accessed April 5, 2016.

Baydar, Nazli, and Jeanne Brooks-Gunn. "Effect of Maternal Employment and Child-Care Arrangements on Preschoolers' Cognitive and Behavioral Outcomes: Evidence from Children from the National Longitudinal Survey of Youth." *Developmental Psychology.* Vol. 27 (1991):932–35.

Bem, Sandra Lipsitz. *The Lenses of Gender: Transforming the Debate on Sexual Inequality.* New Haven, CT: Yale University Press, 1993.

Bernard, Jessie. *The Female World.* New York: Free Press, 1981.

Bibby, Reginald W. *The Bibby Report: Social Trends Canadian Style.* Toronto: Stoddart, 1995.

Bishop, Mary F. "Birth Control." In *The Canadian Encyclopedia.* 2nd ed. Vol. 1. Edmonton: Hurtig Publishers, 1988:231–32.

Bonner, Jane. Research presented in "The Two Brains." Public Broadcasting System telecast, 1984.

Canada. Royal Commission on the Status of Women in Canada. *Report of the Royal Commission on the Status of Women in Canada.* Ottawa: Information Canada, 1970.

———. *Canadian Charter of Rights and Freedoms,* enacted as Part I of the Constitution Act, 1982, being Schedule B to the *Canada Act, 1982* (U.K.), 1982, c.11.

CBS News Polls. "Poll: Women's Movement Worthwhile." [Online] Available October 23, 2005, at http://www.cbsnews.com/stories/2005/10/22/opinion/polls/main965224.shtml.

Coltrane, Scott, and Melinda Messineo. "Mass Mediated Inequality: Images of Race and Gender in 1990s' Television Advertising." *Sex Roles.* Vol. 42, No. 5/6 (2000):363–9.

Cortese, Anthony J. *Provocateur: Images of Women and Minorities in Advertising.* Lanham, MD: Rowman & Littlefield, 1999.

Davis, Donald M. Cited in "T.V. Is a Blonde, Blonde World." *American Demographics,* special issue: Women Change Places. Ithaca, NY, 1993.

Doyle, James A. *The Male Experience.* Dubuque, IA: Wm. C. Brown, 1983.

Dubé, Francine. "Magna's Political Matchmaker." *National Post* (October 18, 2003):A1.

Dworkin, Andrea. *Intercourse.* New York: Free Press, 1987.

Ehrenreich, Barbara. *The Hearts of Men: American Dreams and the Flight from Commitment.* Garden City, NY: Anchor Books, 1983.

———. "The Real Truth About the Female Body." *Time.* Vol. 153, No. 9 (March 15, 1999):56–65.

Engels, Friedrich. *The Origin of the Family.* Chicago, IL: Charles H. Kerr & Company, 1902; orig. 1884.

Evans, Mark. "A beacon in the urban jungle." *National Post* (March 8, 2003):PW6.

Farrell, Warren. *Why Men Earn More: The Startling Truth Behind the Pay Gap— and What Women Can Do About It.* New York: American Management Association, 2005.

Ferree, Myra Marx, and Beth B. Hess. *Controversy and Coalition: The New Feminist Movement across Four Decades of Change.* 3rd ed. New York: Routledge, 1995.

Fitzpatrick, Meagan. "Record number of women elected." CBCnews/Politics. [Online] Available May 3, 2011, at http://www.cbc.ca/news/politics/canadavotes2011/story/2011/05/03/cv-election-women.html#.

Fleras, Augie. *Unequal Relations: An Introduction to Race, Ethnic, and Aboriginal Dynamics in Canada.* 7th ed. Toronto: Pearson Canada, 2012.

Forster, Merna. *100 Canadian Heroines: Famous and Forgotten Faces.* Toronto: The Dundurn Group, 2004.

Francis, Diane. "Canadian women raise the bar." *National Post* (March 8, 2003):PW1.

Freedman, Estelle B. *No Turning Back: The History of Feminism and the Future of Women.* New York: Ballantine Books, 2002.

French, Marilyn. *Beyond Power: On Women, Men, and Morals.* New York: Summit Books, 1985.

Fuller, Rex, and Richard Schoenberger. "The Gender Salary Gap: Do Academic Achievement, Intern Experience, and College Major Make a Difference?" *Social Science Quarterly.* Vol. 72, No. 4 (December 1991):715–26.

Gelles, Richard J., and Claire Pedrick Cornell. *Intimate Violence in Families.* 2nd ed. Newbury Park, CA: Sage, 1990.

Gerber, Linda M. "Multiple Jeopardy: A Socio-economic Comparison of Men and Women among the Indian, Métis and Inuit Peoples of Canada." *Canadian Ethnic Studies.* Vol. xxii, No. 3 (1990):69–84.

———. "Education, Employment, and Income Polarization among Aboriginal Men and Women in Canada: Stagnation and Progress." *Canadian Ethnic Studies.* Vol. 46, No. 1 (2014):87–110.

Gewertz, Deborah. "A Historical Reconsideration of Female Dominance among the Chambri of Papua New Guinea." *American Ethnologist.* Vol. 8, No. 1 (1981):94–106.

Gibbs, Nancy. "What Kids (Really) Need." *Time* (April 30, 2001):4–49.

Goffman, Erving. *Gender Advertisements.* New York: Harper Colophon, 1979.

Goldberg, Steven. *The Inevitability of Patriarchy.* New York: William Morrow, 1974.

Gooding, Gretchen E., and Rose M. Kreider. "Women's Marital Naming Choices in a Nationally Representative Sample." *Journal of Family Issues.* Vol. 31, No. 5 (2010): 681–01.

Gulli, Cathy. "The richer sex: One-third of women now earn more than their husbands, and not everyone is happy." *MacLean's.* [Online] Available March 8, 2012, at http://www2.macleans.ca/2012/03/06/the-richer-sex.

Hampson, Sarah. "The ultimate hockey mom." *The Globe and Mail* (May 8, 2012):L1.

Haney, Lynne. "After the Fall: East European Women since the Collapse of State Socialism." *Contexts.* Vol. 1, No. 3 (Fall 2002):27–36.

Hasselback, Drew. "The queens of diamonds." *National Post.* (March 8, 2003): PW3.

Henley, Nancy, Mykol Hamilton, and Barrie Thorne. "Womanspeak and Manspeak: Sex Differences in Communication, Verbal and Nonverbal." In John J. Macionis and Nijole V. Benokraitis, eds. *Seeing Ourselves: Classic, Contemporary, and Cross-Cultural Readings in Sociology.* 2nd ed. Englewood Cliffs, NJ: Prentice Hall, 1992:10–15.

Herman, Dianne. "The Rape Culture." In John J. Macionis and Nijole V. Benokraitis, eds. *Seeing Ourselves: Classic, Contemporary, and Cross-Cultural Readings in Sociology.* 5th ed. Upper Saddle River, NJ: Prentice Hall, 2001.

Jeffrey, Pamela. "The path to power." *Financial Post Magazine* (December, 2011):42–75.

Lengermann, Patricia Madoo, and Ruth A. Wallace. *Gender in America: Social Control and Social Change.* Englewood Cliffs, NJ: Prentice Hall, 1985.

Lever, Janet. "Sex Differences in the Complexity of Children's Play and Games." *American Sociological Review.* Vol. 43, No. 4 (August 1978):471–83.

Lewin, Tamar. "Girls' Gains Have Not Cost Boys, Report Says." *New York Times* (May 20, 2008). [Online] Available December 7, 2008, at http://www.nytimes.com/2008/05/20/education/20girls.html?partner=permalink&exprod=permalink.

Lupri, Eugene. "Intimate Violence: Male Abuse." Unpublished manuscript. University of Calgary, 2002.

Mackie, Marlene. *Exploring Gender Relations: A Canadian Perspective.* Toronto: Butterworths, 1983.

Marathonguide.com. "Marathon Records." 2015. Available at http://www.marathonguide.com/history/records/index.cfm.

Marshall, Susan E. "Ladies Against Women: Mobilization Dilemmas of Antifeminist Movements." *Social Problems.* Vol. 32, No. 4 (April 1985):348–62.

Martin, Carol Lynn, and Richard A. Fabes. Research cited in Marianne Szegedy-Maszak, "The Power of Gender." *U.S. News & World Report* (June 4, 2001):52.

Mckenzie, Judith. *Pauline Jewett: A Passion for Canada.* Montreal and Kingston: McGill-Queen's University Press, 1999.

Mead, Margaret. *Sex and Temperament in Three Primitive Societies.* New York: William Morrow, 1963; orig. 1935.

Merrit, Susan E. *Her Story: Women from Canada's Past.* St. Catharines, ON: Vanwell Publishing, 1993.

Messineo, Melinda. "Does Advertising on Black Entertainment Television Portray More Positive Gender Representations Compared to Broadcast Networks?" *Sex Roles.* Vol. 59, No. 9/10 (2008):752–4.

Milan, A., L. Keown, and C. Urquijo. 2010. "Families, Living Arrangements, and Unpaid Work." Statistics Canada, Publication 89-503-X.

Morrow, Adrian, and Caroline Alphonso. "Women make the grade, but not the money." *The Globe and Mail* (Sept. 8, 2010):A1.

Mundy, Liza. *The Richer Sex: How the New Majority of Female Breadwinners Is Transforming Sex, Love, and Family.* Toronto: Simon and Schuster. 2012.

Murdock, George Peter. "Comparative Data on the Division of Labor by Sex." *Social Forces.* Vol. 15, No. 4 (May 1937):551–53.

Nelson, Adie. *Gender in Canada.* 4th ed. Toronto: Pearson Canada, 2010.

Nelson, E.D., and Barry W. Robinson. *Gender in Canada.* Scarborough, ON: Prentice Hall, 1999.

NORC. *General Social Surveys, 1972–2002: Cumulative Codebook.* Chicago, IL: National Opinion Research Center, 2003.

Nolan, Patrick, and Gerhard Lenski. *Human Societies: An Introduction to Macrosociology.* 10th ed. Boulder, CO: Paradigm, 2007.

O'Toole, Megan. "Don't call time just yet." *National Post*, November 17, 2012:A15.

Ovadia, Seth. "Race, Class, and Gender Differences in High School Seniors' Values: Applying Intersection Theory in Empirical Analysis." *Social Science Quarterly.* Vol. 82, No. 2 (June 2001):341–56.

Pappas, Stephanie. "Americans Like Baby Boys Best." *Live Science* (June 24, 2011). Available at http://news.yahoo.com/s/livescience/20110624/sc_livescience/americanslikebabyboysbest.

Parsons, Talcott. "Age and Sex in the Social Structure of the United States." *American Sociological Review.* Vol. 7, No. 4 (August 1942):604–16.

———. *Essays in Sociological Theory.* New York: Free Press, 1954.

———. *The Social System.* New York: Free Press, 1964; orig. 1951.

Perkins, Tara. "Nobody's Saviour." *The Globe and Mail Report on Business* (May 2009):40.

Popenoe, David. "Parental Androgyny." *Society.* Vol. 30, No. 6 (September/October 1993):5–11.

———. "American Family Decline, 1960–1990: A Review and Appraisal." *Journal of Marriage and the Family.* Vol. 55, No. 3 (August 1993b):527–55.

Population Reference Bureau. "Female Genital Mutilation/Cutting: Data and Trends: Update 2010." 2010. Available at http://www.prb.org/pdf10/fgm-wallchart2010.pdf.

———. "Datafinder." 2014. Available at http://www.prb.org/DataFinder.aspx.

Pratt, Laura. "Madame Chief Justice: Passing judgment." *National Post* (March 8, 2003):PW1.

Raphael, Ray. *The Men from the Boys: Rites of Passage in Male America.* Lincoln, NE, and London, UK: University of Nebraska Press, 1988.

Ridgeway, Cecilia L., and Lynn Smith-Lovin. "The Gender System and Interaction." *Annual Review of Sociology.* Vol. 25 (August 1999):191–216.

Roesch, Roberta. "Violent Families." *Parents.* Vol. 59, No. 9 (September 1984):74–76, 150–52.

Rosendahl, Mona. *Inside the Revolution: Everyday Life in Socialist Cuba.* Ithaca, NY: Cornell University Press, 1997.

Rossi, Alice S. "Gender and Parenthood." In Alice S. Rossi, ed. *Gender and the Life Course.* New York: Aldine, 1985:161–91.

Shellenbarger, Sue. "The Name Change Dilemma." *Wall Street Journal* (May 13, 2011). Available at http://finance.yahoo.com/family-home/article/112736/name-change-dilemma-women-marriage-wsj?mod=family-love_money.

Shupe, Anson, William A. Stacey, and Lonnie R. Hazlewood. *Violent Men, Violent Couples: The Dynamics of Domestic Violence.* Lexington, MA: Lexington Books, 1987.

Smith, Graeme. "What is wrong with the girls of Melfort?" *The Globe and Mail* (June 12, 2004): F3.

Smith, Tom W., Peter Marsden, Michael Hout, and Jibum Kim. "General Social Surveys, 1972–012." National Opinion Research Center; The Roper Center for Public Opinion Research, University of Connecticut; Computer-assisted Survey Methods Program, University of California. June 2013. Available at http://www.norc.org/GSS+Website.

Smolowe, Jill. "When Violence Hits Home." *Time.* Vol. 144, No. 1 (July 4, 1994):18–25.

St. Jean, Yanick, and Joe R. Feagin. *Double Burden: Black Women and Everyday Racism.* Armonk, NY: Sharpe, 1998.

Stacey, Judith. *Patriarchy and Socialist Revolution in China.* Berkeley, CA: University of California Press, 1983.

Stasiulis, Daiva. "Feminist Intersectional Theorizing." In Peter Li (ed.) *Race and Ethnic Relations in Canada.* 2nd ed. Toronto: Oxford University Press, 1999:347–397.

Statista. "Revenue of the Cosmetic Industry in the United States from 2002 to 2016." 2015. Available at http://www.statista.com/statistics/243742/revenueof-the-cosmetic-industry-in-the-us.

Statistics Canada. *Violence Against Women Survey.* Ottawa: Minister of Industry, Science and Technology, 1994b.

———. *Women in Canada: A Statistical Report.* 3rd ed. Catalogue No. 89-503E. Ottawa: Statistics Canada, 1995.

———. "Canadian Community Health Survey: Obesity among children and adults." *The Daily.* July 6, 2005a. [Online] Available at http://www.statcan.ca/Daily/English/050706/d050706a.htm.

Straus, Murray A., and Richard J. Gelles. "Societal Change and Change in Family Violence from 1975 to 1985 as Revealed by Two National Surveys." *Journal of Marriage and the Family.* Vol. 48, No. 4 (August 1986):465–79.

Tannen, Deborah. *You Just Don't Understand: Women and Men in Conversation.* New York: Morrow, 1990.

———. *Talking from 9 to 5: How Women's and Men's Conversational Styles Affect Who Gets Heard, Who Gets Credit, and What Gets Done at Work.* New York: Wm. Morrow, 1994.

Tasker, John Paul. "Top ranks of Canadian Forces get shake-up with new army, navy commanders." CBC News. (January 19, 2016). http://www.cbc.ca/news/politics/vance-new-army-navy-commanders-1.3410474.

Tavris, Carol, and Carol Wade. *Psychology in Perspective.* 3rd ed. Upper Saddle River, NJ: Prentice Hall, 2001.

Udry, J. Richard. "Biological Limitations of Gender Construction." *American Sociological Review.* Vol. 65, No. 3 (June 2000):443–57.

United Nations Development Programme. *Human Development Report 2010.* 2010. [Online] Available at http://hdr.undp.org/en/statistics/data.

United Nations Development Programme. "Human Development Report 2014." Statistical Tables. Available at http://hdr.undp.org/en/statistics/data.

U.S. Census Bureau. "Current Population Survey." 2014. Available at http://www.census.gov/cps.

Vogel, Lise. *Marxism and the Oppression of Women: Toward a Unitary Theory.* New Brunswick, NJ: Rutgers University Press, 1983.

World Health Organization, Department of Reproductive Health and Research. "Female Genital Mutilation and Other Harmful Practices: Prevalence of FGM." 2015. Available at http://www.who.int/reproductivehealth/topics/fgm/prevalence/en.

Wotherspoon, Terry, and Vic Satzewich. *First Nations: Race, Class, and Gender Relations.* Scarborough, ON: Nelson, 1993.

Chapter 14

Adorno, Theodor W., Else Frankel-Brunswick, Daniel J. Levinson, and R. Nevitt Sanford. *The Authoritarian Personality.* New York: Harper & Brothers, 1950.

Allen, Terry, The General and the Genocide: General Romeo Dallaire, 2002. [Online] Available at http://www.thirdworldtraveler.com/Heroes/Gen_Romeo_Dallaire.Html.

American Sociological Association. *The Importance of Collecting Data and Doing Social Scientific Research on Race.* Washington, DC: American Sociological Association, 2003.

Anderson, Alan B., and James S. Frideres. *Ethnicity in Canada: Theoretical Perspectives.* Toronto: Butterworths, 1981.

Barrett, Stanley R. *Is God a Racist? The Right Wing in Canada.* Toronto: University of Toronto Press, 1987.

Beaujot, Roderic, and Kevin Mcquillan. *Growth and Dualism: The Demographic Development of Canadian Society.* Toronto: Gage, 1982.

Bibby, Reginald W. *The Bibby Report: Social Trends Canadian Style.* Toronto: Stoddart, 1995.

Bissoondath, Neil. *Selling Illusions: The Cult of Multiculturalism in Canada.* Toronto: Penguin Books, 1994.

Bogardus, Emory S. "Comparing Racial Distance in Ethiopia, South Africa, and the United States." *Sociology and Social Research.* Vol. 52, No. 2 (January 1968):149–56.

Breton, Raymond. "Institutional Completeness of Ethnic Communities and the Personal Relations of Immigrants." *American Journal of Sociology.* Vol. 70 (1964):193–205.

———. *Why Meech Failed: Lessons for Canadian Constitutionmaking.* Toronto: C.D. Howe Institute, 1992.

Butterworth, Douglas, and John K. Chance. *Latin American Urbanization.* Cambridge: Cambridge University Press, 1981.

Canada. *Canadian Charter of Rights and Freedoms,* enacted as Part I of the *Constitution Act, 1982,* being Schedule B to the *Canada Act, 1982* (U.K.), 1982, c.11.

Carmichael, Stokely, and Charles V. Hamilton. *Black Power: The Politics of Liberation in America.* New York: Vintage Books, 1967.

CBC. Residential School Package. [Online]. Available on November 23, 2005.

Coleman, William D. *The Independence Movement in Quebec, 1945–1980.* Toronto: University of Toronto Press, 1984.

Cottrell, John, and The Editors Of Time-Life. *The Great Cities: Mexico City.* Amsterdam: 1979.

Dickason, Olive Patricia. *Canada's First Nations: A History of Founding Peoples from Earliest Times.* 2nd ed. Toronto: Oxford University Press, 1997.

Dollard, John, Neal E. Miller, Leonard W. Dood, O.H. Mower, and Robert R. Sears. *Frustration and Aggression.* New Haven, CT: Yale University Press, 1939.

Driedger, L., and G. Church. "Residential Segregation and Institutional Completeness: A Comparison of Ethnic Minorities." *Canadian Review of Sociology and Anthropology.* Vol. 11, No. 1 (1974):30–52.

Fleras, Augie. *Unequal Relations: An Introduction to Race, Ethnic, and Aboriginal Dynamics in Canada.* 6th ed. Toronto: Pearson Canada, 2010.

Frideres, James S. *First Nations in the Twenty-First Century.* Don Mills. ON: Oxford Univeristy Press, 2011.

Frideres, James S., and René Gadacz. *Aboriginal Peoples in Canada.* 8th ed. Toronto: Pearson Prentice Hall, 2008.

———. *Aboriginal Peoples in Canada.* 9th ed. Toronto, ON: Pearson Canada, 2012.

Fulford, Robert. "Multiculturalism's eloquent enemy." *National Post* (August 15, 2005):A16.

Gerber, Linda M. "The Development of Canadian Indian Communities: A Two-Dimensional Typology Reflecting Strategies of Adaptation to the Outside World." *Canadian Review of Sociology and Anthropology.* Vol. 16, No. 4 (1979):123–50.

———. "Ethnicity Still Matters: Socio-Demographic Profiles of the Ethnic Elderly in Ontario." *Canadian Ethnic Studies.* Vol. xv, No. 3 (1983):60–80.

———. "Community Characteristics and Out-Migration from Canadian Indian Communities: Path Analyses." *Canadian Review of Sociology and Anthropology.* Vol. 21 (1984):145–65.

———. "Multiple Jeopardy: A Socio-economic Comparison of Men and Women among the Indian, Métis and Inuit Peoples of Canada." *Canadian Ethnic Studies.* Vol. xxii, No. 3 (1990):69–84.

———. "Referendum Results: Defining New Boundaries for an Independent Quebec." *Canadian Ethnic Studies.* Vol. xxiv, No. 2 (1992):22–34.

———. "Indian, Métis, and Inuit Women and Men: Multiple Jeopardy in a Canadian Context." In E.D. Nelson and B.W. Robinson, eds. *Gender in the 1990s: Images, Realities, and Issues.* Scarborough, ON: Nelson Canada, 1995. pp. 466–77.

———. "The Visible Minority, Immigrant, and Bilingual Composition of Ridings and Party Support in the Canadian Federal Election of 2004." *Canadian Ethnic Studies* Vol. 38, No. 1 (2006a): 65-82.

———. "Urban Diversity: Riding Composition and Party Support in the Canadian Federal Election of 2004." *The Canadian Journal of Urban Research.* Vol. 15, No. 2 (2006b):105–18.

———. "Educational, Employment, and Income Polarization among Aboriginal Men and Women in Canada," unpublished manuscript, 2012.

Geschwender, James A. *Racial Stratification in America.* Dubuque, IA: Wm. C. Brown, 1978.

Gotham, Kevin Fox. "Race, Mortgage Lending, and Loan Rejections in a U.S. City." *Sociological Focus.* Vol. 31, No. 4 (October 1998):391–405.

Harris, David R., and Jeremiah Joseph Sim. "Who Is Multiracial? Assessing the Complexity of Lived Race." Vol. 67, No. 4 (August 2002):614–27.

Hill, Mark E. "Race of the Interviewer and Perception of Skin Color: Evidence from the Multi-City Study of Urban Inequality." *American Sociological Review.* Vol. 67, No. 1 (February 2002):99–108.

Hiller, Harry H. *Canadian Society: A Macro Analysis.* 2nd ed. Scarborough, ON: Prentice Hall, 1991.

Inciardi, James A., Hilary L. Surratt, and Paulo R. Telles. *Sex, Drugs, and HIV/AIDS in Brazil.* Boulder, CO: Westview Press, 2000.

Isajiw, Wsevelod W. "Definitions of Ethnicity." In Rita M. Bienvenue and Jay E. Goldstein, eds. *Ethnicity and Ethnic Relations in Canada.* 2nd ed. Toronto: Butterworths, 1985. pp. 5–18.

Jorde, Lynn B., and Stephen P. Wooding. "Genetic variation, classification and 'race.'" *Nature Genetics.* Vol. 36 (2004):S28-S33.

Kaufman, Robert L. "Assessing Alternative Perspectives on Race and Sex Employment Segregation." *American Sociological Review.* Vol. 67, No. 4 (August 2002):547–572.

Knowles, Valerie. *Strangers at Our Gates: Canadian Immigration and Immigration Policy, 1540–1990.* Toronto: Dundurn, 1997.

Latouche, Daniel. "Québec." In *The Canadian Encyclopedia.* 2nd ed., Vol. 3. Edmonton: Hurtig Publishers, 1988. pp. 1793–802.

Lautard, Hugh, and Neil Guppy. "Revisiting the Vertical Mosaic: Occupational Stratification among Canadian Ethnic Groups." In Peter S. Li. *Race and Ethnic Relations in Canada.* 2nd ed. Don Mills, ON: Oxford University Press, 1999. pp. 219–252.

Li, Peter S. *Ethnic Inequality in a Class Society.* Toronto: Wall and Thompson, 1988.

———. "Race and Ethnicity." In Peter S. Li. *Race and Ethnic Relations in Canada.* 2nd ed. Don Mills, ON: Oxford University Press, 1999. pp. 3–20.

———. *Destination Canada: Immigration Debates and Issues.* Toronto: Oxford University Press, 2003.

Lipset, Seymour Martin. *Continental Divide: The Values and Institutions of the United States and Canada.* New York: Routledge, 1991.

Mackie, Marlene. "Ethnic Stereotypes and Prejudice: Alberta Indians, Hutterites and Ukrainians." *Canadian Ethnic Studies.* Vol. x (1974):118–29.

Matthiessen, Peter. *Indian Country.* New York: Viking Press, 1984.

McAll, Christopher. *Class, Ethnicity and Social Inequality.* Montreal and Kingston: McGill-Queen's University Press, 1990.

Merrit, Susan E. *Her Story: Women from Canada's Past.* St. Catharines, ON: Vanwell Publishing, 1993.

Mooney, Erin. "Presence, *ergo* Protection? UNPROFOR, UNHCR, and the ICRC in Croatia and Bosnia and Herzegovina." *International Journal of Refugee Law.* Vol. 7, No. 3 (1995).

Nader, Ralph, Nadia Milleron, and Duff Conacher. *Canada Firsts.* Toronto: McClelland & Stewart, 1992.

Olzak, Susan. "Labor Unrest, Immigration, and Ethnic Conflict in Urban America, 1880–1914." *American Journal of Sociology.* Vol. 94, No. 6 (May 1989):1303–33.

Porter, John. *The Vertical Mosaic: An Analysis of Social Class and Power in Canada.* Toronto: University of Toronto Press, 1965.

Ramcharan, Subhas. *Racism: Nonwhites in Canada.* Toronto: Butterworths, 1982.

Reitz, Jeffrey G. *The Survival of Ethnic Groups.* Toronto: McGraw-Hill Ryerson, 1980.

Reitz, Jeffrey G., and Raymond Breton. *The Illusion of Difference: Realities of Ethnicity in Canada and the United States.* Toronto: C.D. Howe Institute, 1994.

Richards, Karen. *The Aboriginal Peoples Television Network: An Institutional Model of Empowerment.* MA thesis. Department of Sociology. Guelph: University of Guelph, 2006.

Sale, Kirkpatrick. *The Conquest of Paradise: Christopher Columbus and the Columbian Legacy.* New York: Alfred A. Knopf, 1990.

Statistics Canada. National Household Survey 2011. Catalogue no. 91-010-X2011028.

———. National Household Survey 2011. Catalogue no. 99-010-X2011029.

Steele, Shelby. *The Content of Our Character: A New Vision of Race in America.* New York: St. Martin's Press, 1990.

Thomas, W.I. "The Relation of Research to the Social Process." In Morris Janowitz, ed. *W.I. Thomas on Social Organization and Social Personality.* Chicago, IL: University of Chicago Press, 1966; orig. 1931. pp. 289–305.

Truth and Reconciliation Commission of Canada. 2015. *Honouring the Truth, Reconciling for the Future.* (Executive Summary). http://www.trc.ca/reports.php. (Accessed April 2016).

Ujimoto, K. Victor. "Postwar Japanese Immigrants in British Columbia: Japanese Culture and Job Transferability." In Jean Leonard Elliott, ed. *Two Nations, Many Cultures: Ethnic Groups in Canada.* Scarborough, ON: Prentice Hall, 1979.

Ujimoto, K. Victor. "Studies of Ethnic Identity, Ethnic Relations, and Citizenship." In Peter S. Li. *Race and Ethnic Relations in Canada.* 2nd ed. Don Mills, ON: Oxford University Press, 1999. pp. 253–90.

Walker, James W. St. G. *A History of Blacks in Canada.* Ottawa: Ministry of Supply and Services Canada, 1980.

Wotherspoon, Terry, and Vic Satzewich. *First Nations: Race, Class, and Gender Relations.* Scarborough, ON: Nelson, 1993.

Chapter 15

Ariês, Philippe. *Western Attitudes toward Death: From the Middle Ages to the Present.* Baltimore: Johns Hopkins University Press, 1974.

Atchley, Robert C. *Aging: Continuity and Change.* Belmont, CA: Wadsworth, 1983.

Baltes, Paul B., and K. Warner Schaie. "The Myth of the Twilight Years." *Psychology Today.* Vol. 7, No. 10 (March 1974):35–39.

Bess, Irwin. "Widows Living Alone." In Statistics Canada, *Canadian Social Trends. Volume 3.* Toronto: Thompson Educational Publishing, 2000. pp. 165–69.

Butler, Robert N. *Why Survive? Being Old in America.* New York: Harper & Row, 1975.

Brend, Yvette. "Why History Lives in Old Crow." *The Globe and Mail* (November 11, 1997):A2.

Callahan, Daniel. *Setting Limits: Medical Goals in an Aging Society.* New York: Simon & Schuster, 1987.

Canada. *Demographic Aging: The Economic Consequences.* Ottawa: Ministry of Supply and Services, 1991.

Carriére, Yves. "Population and Hospital Days: Will There be a Problem?" In Ellen M. Gee and Gloria, M. Gutman, eds. *The Overselling of Population Aging: Apocalyptic Demography, Intergenerational Challenges, and Social Policy.* Don Mills, ON: Oxford University Press, 2000, pp 26–44.

CBC News. "Quebec's new assisted-dying law leaves doctors struggling to adapt." (Feb. 17, 2016). http://www.cbc.ca/news/canada/montreal/quebec-medical-assisted-dying-euthanasia-quebc-1.3452366. (Accessed in April, 2016).

Che-Alford, Janet, and Brian Hamm. "Under One Roof: Three Generations Living Together." *Canadian Social Trends. Volume 3.* Toronto: Thompson Educational Publishing, 2000. pp. 161–64.

Cohen, Elias. "The Complex Nature of Ageism: What Is It? Who Does It? Who Perceives It?" *Gerontologist.* Vol. 41, No. 5 (October 2001):576–78.

Cortez, Michelle Fay. "Memory Loss Grows Less Common among Older Americans, Study Says." Bloomberg.com. February 20, 2008. [Online] Available January 8, 2009, at http://www.bloomberg.com/apps/news?pid=2060 1103&sid=a667F2gzkXoE&refer=us.

Crompton, Susan, and Anna Kemeny. "In Sickness and in Health: The Well-Being of Married Seniors." *Canadian Social Trends.* Toronto: Thompson Educational Publishing, 2000:45–50.

Cumming, Elaine, and William E. Henry. *Growing Old: The Process of Disengagement.* New York: Basic Books, 1961.

Cutcliffe, John R. "Hope, Counseling, and Complicated Bereavement Reactions." *Journal of Advanced Nursing.* Vol. 28, No. 4 (October 1998):754–62.

Danforth, Marion M., and J. Conrad Glass Jr. "Listen to My Words, Give Meaning to My Sorrow: A Study in Cognitive Constructs in Middle-Aged Bereaved Widows." *Death Studies.* Vol. 25, No. 6 (September 2001):413–30.

Erikson, Erik H. *Childhood and Society.* New York: Norton, 1963; orig. 1950.
———. *Identity and the Life Cycle.* New York: Norton, 1980.

Foliart, Donne E., and Margaret Clausen. "Bereavement Practices among California Hospices: Results of a Statewide Survey." *Death Studies.* Vol. 25, No. 5 (July 2001):461–68.

Foot, David K. *Boom, Bust and Echo 2000: Profiting from the Demographic Shift in the New Millennium.* Toronto: Macfarlane Walter & Ross, 1998.

Friedan, Betty. *The Fountain of Age.* New York: Simon and Schuster, 1993.

Gardyn, Rebecca. "Retirement Redefined." *American Demographics.* Vol. 22, No. 11 (November 2000):52–57.

Gerber, Linda M. "Ethnicity Still Matters: Socio-Demographic Profiles of the Ethnic Elderly in Ontario." *Canadian Ethnic Studies.* Vol. xv, No. 3 (1983):60–80.

Gillon, Raanan. "Euthanasia in the Netherlands: Down the Slippery Slope?" *Journal of Medical Ethics.* Vol. 25, No. 1 (February 1999):3–4.

Gross, Jane. "Under One Roof, Aging Together Yet Alone." *The New York Times* (January 30, 2005).

Hawthorn, Tom. "107 years young, she still loves to dance." *The Globe and Mail* (May 10, 2006):A3.

Hennenberger, Melinda. "Old People F—ing: Does an Elderly Couple Have a Right to a Sex Life?" *National Post.* (June 14, 2008):A26.

Jones, D. Gareth. "Brain Death." *Journal of Medical Ethics.* Vol. 24, No. 4 (August 1998):237–43.

Keith, Julie, and Laura Landry. "Well-being of Older Canadians." In Craig McKie and Keith Thompson, eds. *Canadian Social Trends.* Toronto: Thompson Educational Publishing, 1994.

Kübler-Ross, Elisabeth. *On Death and Dying.* New York: Macmillan, 1969.

Lah, Kyung. "Report: More Elderly Japanese Turn to Petty Crime." CNN.com/Asia. December 24, 2008. [Online] Available April 20, 2009, at http://www.cnn.com/2008/WORLD/asiapcf/12/24/elderly.shoplifters.

Lee, Felicia R. "Long Buried, Death Goes Public Again." *New York Times* (2002). [Online] Available November 2, 2002, at http://www.research-navigator.com.

Lipovenko, Dorothy. "Golden Handshakes Launch New Careers." *The Globe and Mail* (January 29, 1996):A1, A6.

Longino, Charles F., Jr. "Myths of an Aging America." *American Demographics.* Vol. 16, No. 8 (August 1994):36–42.

Lund, Dale A. "Conclusions about Bereavement in Later Life and Implications for Interventions and Future Research." In Dale A. Lund, ed. *Older Bereaved Spouses: Research With Practical Applications.* London, UK: Taylor-Francis-Hemisphere, 1989. pp. 217–31.

Lund, Dale A., Michael S. Caserta, and Margaret F. Dimond. "Gender Differences Through Two Years of Bereavement Among the Elderly." *The Gerontologist.* Vol. 26, No. 3 (1986):314–20.

MacDonald, Jo-Anne. "Home for the Grey and Gay." *National Post* (August 15, 2005).

McDaniel, Susan. "Emotional Support and Family Contacts of Older Canadians." In Craig McKie and Keith Thompson, eds. *Canadian Social Trends. Volume 2.* Toronto: Thompson Educational Publishing, 1994. pp. 129–32.

Mcpherson, Barry D. *Aging as a Social Process: An Introduction to Individual and Population Aging.* 2nd ed. Toronto: Butterworths, 1990.
———. *Aging as a Social Process: Canadian Perspectives.* 4th ed. Don Mills, ON: Oxford University Press, 2004.

Metz, Michael E., and Michael H. Miner. "Psychosexual and Psychosocial Aspects of Male Aging and Sexual Health." *Canadian Journal of Human Sexuality.* Vol. 7, No. 3 (Summer 1998):245–60.

Moen, Phyllis, Donna Dempster-Mcclain, and Robin M. Williams. "Successful Aging: A Life-Course Perspective on Women's Multiple Roles and Health." *American Journal of Sociology.* Vol. 97, No. 6 (May 1992):1612–38.

Nelson, E.D., and Barry W. Robinson. *Gender in Canada.* Scarborough, ON: Prentice Hall, 1999.

Nett, Emily M. *Canadian Families: Past and Present.* 2nd ed. Toronto: Butterworths, 1993.

Neugarten, Bernice L. "Grow Old with Me. The Best Is Yet to Be." *Psychology Today.* Vol. 5 (December 1971):45–48, 79, 81.
———. "Personality and Aging." In James E. Birren and K. Warner Schaie, eds. *Handbook of the Psychology of Aging.* New York: Van Nostrand Reinhold, 1977. pp. 626–49.

Newman, Peter C. *Titans: How the New Canadian Establishment Seized Power.* Toronto: Penguin, 1998.

Norton, Phillip. "Jackrabbit Johannsen: The Pioneer of Skiing in Canada." *Canadian Geographic* (April/May 1997):18–23.

Ogawa, Naohiro, and Robert D. Retherford. "Shifting Costs of Caring for the Elderly Back to Families in Japan: Will It Work?" *Population and Development Review.* Vol. 23, No. 1 (March 1997):59–95.

Ogden, Russel D. "Nonphysician-Assisted Suicide: The Technological Imperative of the Deathing Counterculture." *Death Studies.* Vol. 25, No. 5 (July 2001):387–402.

Palmore, Erdman. "Predictors of Successful Aging." *The Gerontologist.* Vol. 19, No. 5 (October 1979):427–31.

Parini, Jay. "The Meaning of Emeritus." *Dartmouth Alumni Magazine* (July/August 2001):40–43.

Patients Rights Council, 2016. "Euthanasia & Assisted Suicide in Canada." (2016). http://www.patientsrightscouncil.org/site/canada/. (Accessed in April 2016.)

Rubenstein, Eli A. "The Not So Golden Years." *Newsweek* (October 7, 1991):13.

Savishinsky, Joel S. *Breaking the Watch: The Meanings of Retirement in America.* Ithaca, N.Y.: Cornell University Press, 2000.

Segall, Alexander, and Neena L. Chappell. *Health and Health Care in Canada.* Toronto: Prentice Hall, 2000.

Shapiro, Joseph P. "Back to Work, on Mission." *U.S. News & World Report* (June 4, 2001).

Sheehan, Tom. "Senior Esteem as a Factor in Socioeconomic Complexity." *The Gerontologist.* Vol. 16, No. 5 (October 1976):433–40.

Schultz, R., and J. Heckhausen. "A Lifespan Model of Successful Aging." *American Psychologist.* Vol. 7, No. 7 (July 1996):702–714.

Smart, Tim. "Not Acting Their Age." *U.S. News & World Report* (June 4, 2001): 54–60.

Spitzer, Steven. "Toward a Marxian Theory of Deviance." In Delos H. Kelly, ed. *Criminal Behavior: Readings in Criminology.* New York: St. Martin's Press, 1980:175–91.

Statistics Canada. *Lone-Parent Families in Canada.* Catalogue No. 89-522E. Ottawa: Statistics Canada, 1992.
———. CANSIM, table 102-0512 and Catalogue no. 84-537-XIE, 2012b. [Online] Available June 13, 2012, at http://www.statcan.gc.ca/tables-tableaux/sum-som/l01/cst01/health26-eng.htm.

Streib, Gordon F. "Are the Aged a Minority Group?" In Bernice L. Neugarten, ed. *Middle Age and Aging: A Reader in Social Psychology.* Chicago, IL: University of Chicago Press, 1968. pp. 35–46.

Tindale, Joseph A. "Older Workers in an Aging Workforce." Ottawa: Statistics Canada, 1991.

Todd, Douglas. "Giving Old Age Meaning." *National Post* (July 28, 2003):A11.

Treas, Judith. "Older Americans in the 1990s and Beyond." *Population Bulletin.* Vol. 50, No. 2 (May 1995). Washington, DC: Population Reference Bureau.

Wall, Thomas F. *Medical Ethics: Basic Moral Issues.* Washington, DC: University Press of America, 1980.

Walsh, Mary Williams. "No Time to Put Your Feet Up as Retirement Comes in Stages." *New York Times* (April 15, 2001):1, 18.

Wolfe, David B. "Targeting the Mature Mind." *American Demographics.* Vol. 16, No. 3 (March 1994):32–36.

Yudelman, Montague, and Laura J. M. Kealy. "The Graying of Farmers." *Population Today.* Vol. 28, No. 4 (May/June, 2000):6.

Znaimer, Moses. "Age of Enlightenment." *Zoomer.* July/August 2012:10–11.

Chapter 16

Adams, Tracey L. "Profession: A Useful Concept for Sociological Analysis?" *Canadian Review of Sociology* 47,1 (2010):49–70.

Albrecht, William P., Jr. *Economics.* 3rd ed. Englewood Cliffs, NJ: Prentice Hall, 1983.

Bakker, J.I. (Hans), and Anthony Winson. "Rural Sociology." In Peter S. Li and B. Singh Bolaria, eds. *Contemporary Sociology: Critical Perspectives.* Toronto: Copp Clark Pitman, 1993. pp. 500–17.

Barlow, Maude, and Bruce Campbell. *Take Back the Nation*. Toronto: Key Porter Books, 1991.

Berger, Peter L. *The Capitalist Revolution: Fifty Propositions About Prosperity, Equality, and Liberty*. New York: Basic Books, 1986.

Breton, Raymond. "Regionalism in Canada." In David Cameron, ed. *Regionalism and Supranationalism*. Montreal: Institute for Research on Public Policy, 1981.

Brodie, Janine. "The Political Economy of Regionalism." In Wallace Clement and Glen Williams, eds. *The New Canadian Political Economy*. Montreal: McGill-Queen's University Press, 1989. pp. 138–59.

Bronson, Harold. "Economic Concentration and Corporate Power." In Peter S. Li and B. Singh Bolaria, eds. *Contemporary Sociology: Critical Perspectives*. Toronto: Copp Clark Pitman, 1993:203–22.

Brym, Robert J., Ed. *Regionalism in Canada*. Toronto: Irwin, 1986.

Canada. *The Economic and Fiscal Update*. Ottawa: Department of Finance, October 1997.

Clement, Wallace. *The Canadian Corporate Elite: Economic Power in Canada*. Toronto: McClelland & Stewart, 1975.

Computer Industry Almanac. "Worldwide Internet Users Top 1.5 Billion in 2008." (press release), May 10, 2009. [Online] Available at www.c-i-a.com/pr_info.htm.

Côté, James E., and Anton L. Allahar. "Youth: The Disinherited Generation." In Dan Glenday and Ann Duffy, eds. *Canadian Society: Meeting the Challenges of the Twenty-First Century*. Toronto: Oxford University Press, 2001.

Dahrendorf, Ralf. *Class and Class Conflict in Industrial Society*. Stanford, CA: Stanford University Press, 1959.

Dalglish, Brenda. "Cheaters." *Maclean's* (August 9, 1993):18–21.

Dixon, William J., and Terry Boswell. "Dependency, Disarticulation, and Denominator Effects: Another Look at Foreign Capital Penetration." *American Journal of Sociology*. Vol. 102, No. 2 (September 1996):543–62.

Evans, M.D.R. "Immigrant Entrepreneurship: Effects of Ethnic Market Size and Isolated Labor Pool." *American Sociological Review*. Vol. 54, No. 6 (December 1989):950–62.

Firebaugh, Glenn, and Frank D. Beck. "Does Economic Growth Benefit the Masses? Growth, Dependence, and Welfare in the Third World." *American Sociological Review*. Vol. 59, No. 5 (October 1994):631–53.

Firebaugh, Glenn, and Dumitru Sandu. "Who Supports Marketization and Democratization in Post-Communist Romania?" *Sociological Forum*. Vol. 13, No. 3 (September 1998):521–41.

Forbes. "The Global 2000." 2014. Available at http://www.forbes.com/global2000/list.

Francis, Diane. *Controlling Interest: Who Owns Canada?* Toronto: Macmillan, 1986.

Fraser Institute. *Canadians Celebrate Tax Freedom Day on June 10, 2015*. [Online] https://www.fraserinstitute.org/studies/canadians-celebrate-tax-freedom-day-on-june-7-2016.

Frideres, James S., and René R. Gadacz. *Aboriginal Peoples in Canada*, 9th Edition. Toronto, ON: Pearson Canada. 2012.

Friedman, Milton, and Rose Friedman. *Free to Choose: A Personal Statement*. New York: Harcourt Brace Jovanovich, 1980.

Gairdner, William D. *The Trouble With Canada*. Toronto: Stoddart Publishing, 1990.

Gardner, Arthur. "Their Own Boss: The Self-Employed in Canada." In Statistics Canada, *Canadian Social Trends. Volume 3*. Toronto: Thompson Educational Publishing, 2000.

Gerber, Linda M. "Multiple Jeopardy: A Socio-economic Comparison of Men and Women among the Indian, Métis and Inuit Peoples of Canada." *Canadian Ethnic Studies*. Vol. xxii, No. 3 (1990):69–84.

———. Unpublished analysis based on Statistics Canada Microdata for enumeration areas in Burlington, Ontario, 1991.

Gerlach, Michael L. *The Social Organization of Japanese Business*. Berkeley and Los Angeles, CA: University of California Press, 1992.

Glenday, Dan. "Off the Ropes: New Challenges and Strengths Facing Trade Unions in Canada." In Dan Glenday and Ann Duffy, eds. *Canadian Society: Meeting the Challenges of the Twenty-First Century*. Toronto: Oxford University Press, 2001.

Globe and Mail, The. "The Top 1000," Report on Business. (July/Aug. 2006b).

Goode, William J. "Encroachment, Charlatanism, and the Emerging Profession: Psychology, Sociology and Medicine." *American Sociological Review*. Vol. 25, No. 6 (December 1960):902–14.

Greenaway, Norma. "Canada losing more than it's gaining." *National Post* (July 4, 2006a):A4.

Greenhouse, Steven. "Many Entry-Level Workers Find Pinch of Rough Market." *New York Times*, September 4, 2006.

Hareven, Tamara K., and Randolph Langenbach. *Amoskeag: Life and Work in an American City*. New York: Pantheon Books, 1978.

Herman, Edward S. *Corporate Control, Corporate Power: A Twentieth Century Fund Study*. New York: Cambridge University Press, 1981.

Hill, Mark E. "Race of the Interviewer and Perception of Skin Color: Evidence from the Multi-City Study of Urban Inequality." *American Sociological Review*. Vol. 67, No. 1 (February 2002):99–108.

Howden, Daniel. "Latin America's New Socialist Revolution." *New Zealand Herald* (December 20, 2005). [Online] Available February 13, 2006, at http://www.nzherald.co.nz.

Hurtig, Mel. *The Betrayal of Canada*. Toronto: Stoddart Publishing, 1991.

IBM. "Focus on E-business." *The Globe and Mail* (January 28, 1998): Section C

Ignatius, Adi. "The Beauty of Everyday Economics." *U.S. News & World Report* (January 28, 2008):14.

International Labour Organization. "Key Indicators of the Labour Market." 2012, 2014. #http://www.ilo.org/empelm/what/WCMS_114240/lang--en/index.htm#.

Janigan, Mary. "How can we be innovative enough to keep our best brains?" *The Globe and Mail*, January 2, 2006: A5.

Kalleberg, Arne L., Barbara F. Reskin, and Ken Hudson. "Bad Jobs in America: Standard and Nonstandard Employment Relations and Job Quality in the United States." *American Sociological Review*. Vol. 65, No 2 (April 2000): 256–78.

Kasarda, John D. "Entry-Level Jobs, Mobility and Urban Minority Employment." *Urban Affairs Quarterly*. Vol. 19, No. 1 (September 1983):21–40.

Kelly, Karen, Linda Howatson-Leo, and Warren Clark. "I Feel Overqualified for My Job," *Canadian Social Trends*. Toronto: Thompson Educational Publishing, 2000:182–87.

Kentor, Jeffrey. "The Long-Term Effects of Foreign Investment Dependence on Economic Growth, 1940–1990." *American Journal of Sociology*. Vol. 103, No. 4 (January 1998):1024–46.

Livingstone, David W. "Public Education at the Crossroads: Confronting Underemployment in a Knowledge Society." In Dan Glenday and Ann Duffy, eds. *Canadian Society: Meeting the Challenges of the Twenty-First Century*. Toronto: Oxford University Press, 2001.

Macgregor, Roy. "Why in the world did you move here from California?" *The Globe and Mail*. (December 28, 2004):A2.

Marlios, Peter. "Interlocking Directorates and the Control of Corporations: The Theory of Bank Control." *Social Science Quarterly*. Vol. 56, No. 3 (December 1975):425–39.

Matas, Robert. "UBC scores academic coup by luring Nobel physicist." *The Globe and Mail* (March 20, 2006):A1.

Matthews, Ralph. *The Creation of Regional Dependency*. Toronto: University of Toronto Press, 1983.

Mills, C. Wright. *White Collar: The American Middle Classes*. New York: Oxford University Press, 1951.

Montaigne, Fen. "Russia Rising." *National Geographic*. Vol. 200, No. 5 (September 2001):2–31.

Moore, Gwen. "The Structure of a National Elite Network." *American Sociological Review*. Vol.44, No. 5 (October 1979):673–92.

Nelson, Adie. *Gender in Canada*. 4th ed. Toronto: Pearson Canada, 2010.

Nelson, Joel I. "Work and Benefits: The Multiple Problems of Service Sector Employment." *Social Problems*. Vol. 42, No. 2 (May 1994):240–55.

Newman, Peter C. *Titans: How the New Canadian Establishment Seized Power*. Toronto: Penguin, 1998.

Ontario College of Trades. "Bring the voices of the skilled trades together." Included as a flyer in the *National Post*, June 16, 2010.

Perkins, Tara. "Nobody's Saviour." *The Globe and Mail, Report on Business* (May 2009):40.

Peters, Susan. "At General Electric, a Culture of Risk." *The New York Times* (Sunday, March 18, 2012): BU 5.

Preibisch, Kerry. "Interrogating Racialized Global Labour Supply: An Exploration of the Racial/National Replacement of Foreign Workers in Canada." *The Canadian Review of Sociology and Anthropology*. Vol. 44, No. 1 (February 2007):5–36.

———. "Migrant Workers and Changing Work-place Regimes in Contemporary Agricultural Production in Canada." *International Journal of Sociology of Agriculture & Food*. Vol. 19. No. 1 (2011):62–82.

Ritzer, George, and David Walczak. *Working: Conflict and Change*. 4th ed. Englewood Cliffs, NJ: Prentice Hall, 1990.

Robinson, Allan. "Inco Sends in the Robo-Miners." *The Globe and Mail* (January 3, 1998):B1.

Rule, James, and Peter Brantley. "Computerized Surveillance in the Workplace: Forms and Delusions." *Sociological Forum*. Vol. 7, No. 3 (September 1992):405–23.

Scott, John, and Catherine Griff. *Directors of Industry: The British Corporate Network, 1904–1976*. New York: Blackwell, 1985.

Shields, John, and Stephen McBride. "Dismantling a Nation: The Canadian Political Economy and Continental Free Trade." In Les Samuelson, ed. *Power and Resistance: Critical Thinking About Canadian Social Issues*. Halifax, NS: Fernwood Publishing, 1994. pp. 227–60.

Simon, Carl P., and Ann D. Witte. *Beating the System: The Underground Economy*. Boston: Auburn House, 1982.

Simpson, Jeffrey. *Star-Spangled Canadians: Canadians Living the American Dream*. Toronto: Harper Collins, 2000.

Smith, Adam. *An Inquiry into the Nature and Causes of the Wealth of Nations*. New York: The Modern Library, 1937; orig. 1776.

Statistics Canada. *Perspectives on Labour and Income*. Catalogue No. 71-202. Ottawa: Statistics Canada, 1990.

———. "Electronic Commerce and Technology," *The Daily*, April 2, 2003b. [Online] Available at http://www.statcan.ca/Daily/English/030402/td030402.htm.

———. "Electronic Commerce and Technology." *The Daily*. April 24, 2008a.

———. 2009b. http://www.cbc.ca/money/story/2005/04/22/unionization-050422.html.

———, 2012c. *Indicators of Well-being in Canada: Work—Unionization Rates*. Human Resources and Skills Development Canada (www.hrsdc.gc.ca).

Tim Hortons. 2016. "World's Third Largest Quick Service Restaurant Company Launched with Two Iconic and Independent Brands: Tim Hortons and Burger King." http://www.timhortons.com/ca/en/corporate/news-release.php?id=825.

Toronto Star. "Saks Fifth Avenue to open two GTA stores." (Nov. 17, 2015). http://www.thestar.com/business/2015/11/17/saks-fifth-avenue-to-open-two-gta-stores.html.

Ubelacker, Sheryl. "Finally, more doctors returning to Canada than leaving." *The Globe and Mail.* (August 25, 2005):A13.

United Nations Development Programme. *Human Development Report 1990.* New York: Oxford University Press, 1990.

Useem, Michael. "The Social Organization of the Corporate Business Elite and Participation of Corporate Directors in the Governance of American Institutions." *American Sociological Review.* Vol. 44, No. 4 (August 1979):553–72.

Vallas, Stephen P., and John P. Beck. "The Transformation of Work Revisited: The Limits of Flexibility in American Manufacturing." *Social Problems.* Vol. 43, No. 3 (August 1996):339–61.

Vieira, Paul. "Tax Lures Hortons Home." *National Post* (June 30, 2009):FP1.

Visser, Jelle. "Union Membership Statistics in 24 Countries." *Monthly Labor Review* (January 2006):38–49. [Online] Available June 2, 2006, at http://www.bls.gov/opub/mlr/2006/01/art3full.pdf.

Wall Street Journal/Heritage Foundation. "Index of Economic Freedom." 2015. Available at http://www.heritage.org/index/Default.aspx.

Wallerstein, Immanuel. *The Capitalist World-Economy.* New York: Cambridge University Press, 1979.

Walton, John, and Charles Ragin. "Global and National Sources of Political Protest: Third World Responses to the Debt Crisis." *American Sociological Review.* Vol. 55, No. 6 (December 1990):876–90.

Wells, Jennifer. "Jobs." *Maclean's* (March 11, 1996):12–16.

Whitman, Janet. "Canadian Coffee Giant Set to Open in Big Apple." *National Post* (June 30, 2009):FP1.

Wikipedia. *Tax Freedom Day around the World.* [Online] Available Aigust 22, 2016, at http://en.wikipedia.org/wiki/Tax_Freedom_Day.

Wiles, P.J.D. *Economic Institutions Compared.* New York: Halsted Press, 1977.

Winson, Anthony. *The Intimate Commodity: Food and the Development of the Agro-Industrial Complex in Canada.* Toronto: Garamond Press, 1993.

World Bank. "World DataBank: Health, Nutrition, and Population Statistics." 2012. Available at http://data.worldbank.org/data-catalog/health-nutrition-andpopulation-statistics.

———. "World DataBank: World Development Indicators." 2012. Available at http://data.worldbank.org/data-catalog/world-development-indicators.

———. "Countries." 2015. Available at http://www.worldbank.org/en/country.

———. "World DataBank: World Development Indicators." 2012, 2015. Available at http://data.worldbank.org/data-catalog/world-developmentindicators.

Wotherspoon, Terry, and Vic Satzewich. *First Nations: Race, Class, and Gender Relations.* Scarborough, ON: Nelson, 1993.

Chapter 17

Al Arabiya. "Syria Video Shows Assad Militia Stabbing and Stoning Victims." Al Arabiya News. January 2, 2013. Available at http://english.alarabiya.net/articles/2013/01/02/258348.html.

Arendt, Hannah. *Between Past and Future: Six Exercises in Political Thought.* Cleveland, OH: Meridian Books, 1963.

Barnes, Julian E. "War Profiteering." *U.S. News & World Report* (May 13, 2002):20–24.

Bashevkin, Sylvia B. *Toeing the Lines: Women and Party Politics in Canada.* 2nd ed. Toronto: Oxford University Press, 1993.

Black, Naomi. "Agnes MacPhail." In *The Canadian Encyclopedia.* 2nd ed. Vol. 2. Edmonton: Hurtig Publishers, 1988. p. 1281.

Canada. *Canadian Charter of Rights and Freedoms,* enacted as Part I of the *Constitution Act, 1982,* being Schedule B to the *Canada Act, 1982* (U.K.), 1982, c.11.

———. Final report of the Royal Commission on Aboriginal Peoples. 6 Vols. Ottawa: Ministry of Indian Affairs and Northern Development, 1996.

Chance, David, and Jack Kim. "North Korea Mourns Dead Leader, Son Is 'Great Successor'." Reuters. December 19, 2011. Available at http://news.yahoo.com/north-koreastate-tv-says-kim-jong-il-031257363.html.

Christian, William. "Ideology and Politics in Canada." In John H. Redekop, ed. *Approaches to Canadian Politics.* 2nd ed. Scarborough, ON: Prentice Hall, 1983.

Clement, Wallace. *The Canadian Corporate Elite: Economic Power in Canada.* Toronto: McClelland & Stewart, 1975.

Dahl, Robert A. *Who Governs?* New Haven, CT: Yale University Press, 1961.

———. *Dilemmas of Pluralist Democracy: Autonomy vs. Control.* New Haven, CT: Yale University Press, 1982.

Dedrick, Dennis K., and Richard E. Yinger. "MAD, SDI, and the Nuclear Arms Race." Manuscript in development. Georgetown College, 1990.

Deneault, Alain. *Paul Martin and His Companies.* Vancouver: Talonbooks, 2006.

de Tocqueville, Alexis. *The Old Regime and the French Revolution.* Stuart Gilbert, trans. Garden City, NY: Anchor/Doubleday Books, 1955; orig. 1856.

Dickason, Olive Patricia. *Canada's First Nations: A History of Founding Peoples from the Earliest Times.* Toronto: McClelland & Stewart, 1992.

———. *Canada's First Nations: A History of Founding Peoples from Earliest Times.* 2nd ed. Toronto: Oxford University Press, 1997.

Fisher, Roger, and William Ury. "Getting to yes." In William M. Evan and Stephen Hilgartner, eds. *The Arms Race and Nuclear War.* Englewood Cliffs, NJ: Prentice Hall, 1988. pp. 261–68.

Freedom House. "Freedom in the World Comparative and Historical Data." 2015. Available at http://www.freedomhouse.org/report-types/freedom-world.

Frideres, James S., and René Gadacz. *Aboriginal Peoples in Canada.* 8th ed. Toronto: Pearson Prentice Hall, 2008.

Frizzell, Alan, and Jon H. Pammett, eds. *The Canadian General Election of 1997.* Toronto: Dundurn Press, 1997.

Gellman, Barton. "Julian Assange." *Time.* Vol. 176, No. 26 (December 27, 2010–January 3, 2011):90–94.

Gerber, Linda M. "Urban Diversity: Riding Composition and Party Support in the Canadian Federal Election of 2004." *The Canadian Journal of Urban Research.* Vol. 15, No. 2 (2006b):105–18.

Ghosh, Bobby. "Rage, Rap, and Revolution." *Time.* Vol. 177, No. 8 (February 28, 2011):32–37.

Globe and Mail, The. "Canadian aboriginals ask UN for help in land battle." (October 17, 2005):A8.

Grand Council of the Crees. *Sovereign Injustice: Forcible Inclusion of the James Bay Crees and Cree Territory into a Sovereign Quebec.* Nemaska, QC: The Grand Council, 1995.

Hallett, M.E. "Nellie McClung." In *The Canadian Encyclopedia.* 2nd ed. Vol. 2. Edmonton: Hurtig Publishers, 1988. p. 1257.

Jenkins, J. Craig. *Images of Terror: What We Can and Can't Know about Terrorism.* Hawthorne, NY: Aldine de Gruyter, 2003.

Johnson, Paul. "The Seven Deadly Sins of Terrorism." In Benjamin Netanyahu, ed. *International Terrorism.* New Brunswick, NJ: Transaction Books, 1981. pp. 12–22.

Kaplan, David E., and Michael Schaffer. "Losing the Psywar." *U.S. News & World Report* (October 8, 2001):46.

Karatnycky, Adrian. "The 2001–2002 Freedom House Survey of Freedom: The Democracy Gap." In *Freedom in the World: The Annual Survey of Political Rights and Civil Liberties, 2001–2002.* New York: Freedom House, 2002:7–8.

Langtry, David. "More relevant than ever: The acting chief commissioner of the Canadian Human Rights Commission speaks out." *The Globe and Mail.* June 19, 2012:A12.

Liazos, Alexander. *People First: An Introduction to Social Problems.* Needham Heights, MA: Allyn & Bacon, 1982.

Lipset, Seymour Martin. *Continental Divide: The Values and Institutions of the United States and Canada.* New York: Routledge, 1991.

Lynd, Robert S., and Helen Merrell Lynd. *Middletown in Transition.* New York: Harcourt, Brace & World, 1937.

Mancuso, Maureen, Michael M. Atkinson, André Blais, Ian Greene, and Neil Nevitte. *A Question of Ethics: Canadians Speak Out.* Don Mills, ON: Oxford University Press, 2006.

Marsden, Lorna R., and Edward B. Harvey. *Fragile Federation: Social Change in Canada.* Toronto: McGraw-Hill Ryerson, 1979.

Marullo, Sam. "The Functions and Dysfunctions of Preparations for Fighting Nuclear War." *Sociological Focus.* Vol. 20, No. 2 (April 1987):135–53.

Marzolini, Michael. "Public Opinion Polling and the 2004 Election." In Jon H. Pammett and Christopher Dornan (eds.) *The Canadian General Election of 2004.* Toronto: The Dundurn Group, 2004. pp. 290–313.

Mills, C. Wright. *The Power Elite.* New York: Oxford University Press, 1956.

Nader, Ralph, Nadia Milleron, and Duff Conacher. *Canada Firsts.* Toronto: McClelland & Stewart, 1992.

Newman, Peter C. *The Canadian Revolution, 1985–1995: From Deference to Defiance.* Toronto: Penguin Books, 1995.

Nolan, Patrick, and Gerhard E. Lenski. *Human Societies: An Introduction to Macrosociology.* 11th ed. Boulder, Colo.: Paradigm, 2010.

Pammett, Jon H., and Lawrence LeDuc. "Behind the Turnout Decline." In Jon H. Pammett and Christopher Dornan (eds.) *The Canadian General Election of 2004.* Toronto: The Dundurn Group, 2004. pp. 338–60.

Pew Research Center. "Political Survey, March 2015." 2015. Available at http://www.peoplepress.org/2015/03/30/more-approve-than-disapprove-of-iran-talks-butmost-think-iranians-are-not-serious.

Polsby, Nelson W. "Three Problems in the Analysis of Community Power." *American Sociological Review.* Vol. 24, No. 6 (December 1959):796–803.

Porter, John. *The Vertical Mosaic: An Analysis of Social Class and Power in Canada.* Toronto: University of Toronto Press, 1965.

Report of the Chief Electoral Officer of Canada on the 39th General Election of January 23, 2006. http://www.elections.ca/content.aspx?section=res&dir=rep/off/sta_2006&document=index&lang=e.

Rogers, Martin. "In Memory of Kim Jong-Il: Dear Leader, G.O.A.T." *The Daily Take* (December 21, 2011). Available at http://www.thepostgame.com/blog/daily-take/201112/memory-kim-jong-il-dear-leader-and-goat.

Rothman, Stanley, and Amy E. Black. "Who Rules Now? American Elites in the 1990s." *Society.* Vol. 35, No. 6 (September/October 1998):17–20.

Sivard, Ruth Leger. *World Military and Social Expenditures, 1987–88.* 12th ed. Washington, DC: World Priorities, 1988.

Skocpol, Theda. *States and Social Revolutions: A Comparative Analysis of France, Russia, and China.* Cambridge, UK: Cambridge University Press, 1979.

Stockholm International Peace Research Institute (SIPRI). "SIPRI Yearbook, 2014." 2015. Available at http://www.sipri.org/yearbook.

Thompson, Mark. "Reshaping the Army." *Time.* Vol. 182, No. 19. (November 4, 2013):34–40.

Tilly, Charles. "Does Modernization Breed Revolution?" In Jack A. Goldstone, ed. *Revolutions: Theoretical, Comparative, and Historical Studies.* New York: Harcourt Brace Jovanovich, 1986:47–57.

U.S. Department of State. "Country Reports on Terrorism." 2014. Available at http://www.state.gov/j/ct/rls/crt/2010/index.htm.

U.S. Department of State, Bureau of Intelligence and Research. "Independent States in the World." 2015. Available at http://www.state.gov/s/inr/rls/4250.htm.

Van Loon, Richard J., and Michael S. Whittington. *The Canadian Political System: Environment, Structure and Process*. 3rd ed. Toronto: McGraw-Hill Ryerson, 1981.

Weber, Max. *Economy and Society*. G. Roth and C. Wittich, eds. Berkeley, CA: University of California Press, 1978; orig. 1921.

Whitaker, Mark. "Ten Ways to Fight Terrorism." *Newsweek* (July 1, 1985):26–29.

Wright, Quincy. "Causes of War in the Atomic Age." In William M. Evan and Stephen Hilgartner, eds. *The Arms Race and Nuclear War*. Englewood Cliffs, NJ: Prentice Hall, 1987:7–10.

Xia, Renee. "In China, Activists Watch and Cheer." *Wall Street Journal*. [Online] Available March 12, 2011, at http://online.wsj.com/article/SB1000 14240527870482300457 6192_642010298086.html.

Yom, Sean L., and F. Gregory Gause III. "Resilient Royals: How Arab Monarchies Hang On." *Journal of Democracy*. Vol. 23, No. 4 (October 2012):74–8.

Zakaria, Fareed. "Why It's Different This Time." *Time*. Vol. 177, No. 8 (February 28, 2011):30–31.

Chapter 18

Adams, Michael. "Mr. Harper's child-proof political strategy." *The Globe and Mail* (May 2. 2006):A15.

Albanese, Patrizia. "Small Town, Big Benefits: The Ripple Effect of $7/Day Child Care." *The Canadian Review of Sociology and Anthropology*. Vol. 45, No. 2 (2006):125–40.

———. "The More Things Change…the More We Need Child Care: On the Fortieth Anniversary of the *Report on the Royal Commission on the Status of Women*." In Lorne Tepperman and Angela Kalyta, eds. *Reading Sociology: Canadian Perspectives*. 2nd ed. Don Mills, Ontario: Oxford University Press, 2012. pp. 95–98.

Amato, Paul R. "What Children Learn from Divorce." *Population Today*. Vol. 29, No. 1 (January 2001):1, 4.

Amato, Paul R., and Juliana M. Sobolewski. "The Effects of Divorce and Marital Discord on Adult Children's Psychological Well-Being." *American Sociological Review*. Vol. 66, No. 6 (December 2001):900–21.

Ambert, Anne-Marie. *Changing Families: Relationships in Context*. 2nd ed. Toronto: Pearson Canada, 2009.

Arnup, Katherine. "'We Are Family': Lesbian Mothers in Canada." In E.D. Nelson and B.W. Robinson, eds. *Gender in the 1990s: Images, Realities and Issues*. Scarborough, ON: Nelson Canada, 1995. pp. 330–45.

Bernard, Jessie. *The Future of Marriage*. New Haven, CT: Yale University Press, 1982; orig. 1973.

Besharov, Douglas J., and Lisa A. Laumann. "Child Abuse Reporting." *Society*. Vol. 34, No. 4 (May/June 1996):40–46.

Bibby, Reginald W. *The Bibby Report: Social Trends Canadian Style*. Toronto: Stoddart, 1995.

———. *The Emerging Millennials: How Canada's Newest Generation is Responding to Change and Choice*. Lethbridge, Alberta: Project Canada Books, 2009.

Blackwell, Tom. "When can a sperm donor be called a father?" *National Post*, April 11, 2012: A1.

Blankenhorn, David. *Fatherless America: Confronting Our Most Urgent Social Problem*. New York: HarperCollins, 1995.

Blau, Peter M. *Exchange and Power in Social Life*. New York: Wiley, 1964.

Blumstein, Philip, and Pepper Schwartz. *American Couples*. New York: William Morrow, 1983.

Boyd, Monica, and Norris, Doug. "Crowded Nest? Young Adults at Home." *Canadian Social Trends*. Vol. 3. Toronto: Thompson, 2000. pp. 161–64.

Brethour, Patrick. "The Boardroom or Romper Room?" *The Globe and Mail* (May 1, 2006):A1.

Bricker, Darrell, and John Wright. *What Canadians Think... about Almost Everything*. Toronto: Doubleday Canada, 2005.

Campbell, Lori D., and Michael Carroll. "Aging in Canadian Families Today." In David Cheal, ed. *Canadian Families Today: New Perspectives*. Don Mills, Ontario: Oxford University Press, 2007: pp. 117–33.

Canada Year Book. Ottawa: Statistics Canada, 1994.

Che-Alford, Janet, and Brian Hamm. "Under One Roof: Three Generations Living Together." *Canadian Social Trends. Volume 3*. Toronto: Thompson Educational Publishing, 2000. pp. 161–64.

Clarkson, Stephen. "Disaster and Recovery: Paul Martin as Political Lazarus." In Jon H. Pammett and Christopher Dornan, eds. *The Canadian General Election of 2004*. Toronto: The Dundurn Group, 2004. pp. 28–65.

Cohen, Adam. "Test-Tube Tug-of-War." *Time* (April 6, 1998):65.

Corak, Miles. "Getting Ahead: Does Your Parents' Income Count?" In *Canadian Social Trends. Volume 3*. Toronto: Thompson Educational Publishing, 2000.

Cranwick, Kelly. "Canada's Caregivers." *Canadian Social Trends*. Vol. 3. Toronto: Thompson, 2000. pp. 121–25.

De Broucker, Patrice, and Laval Lavallee. "Getting Ahead: Does Your Parents' Education Count?" In Statistics Canada, *Canadian Social Trends. Volume 3*. Toronto: Thompson Educational Publishing, 2000.

Dekeseredy, Walter S., Ronald Hinch, Hyman Burshtyn, and Charles Gordon. "Taking Woman Abuse Seriously: A Critical Response to the Solicitor General of Canada's Crime Prevention Advice." In E.D. Nelson and B.W. Robinson, eds. *Gender in the 1990s: Images, Realities, and Issues*. Scarborough, ON: Nelson Canada, 1995. pp. 478–89.

Duncan, Greg J., W. Jean Yeung, Jeanne Brooks-Gunn, and Judith R. Smith. "How Much Does Childhood Poverty Affect the Life Chances of Children?" *American Sociological Review*. Vol. 63, No. 3 (June 1998):406–23.

Engels, Friedrich. *The Origin of the Family*. Chicago, IL: Charles H. Kerr & Company, 1902; orig. 1884.

Environics Institute. 2010. *Urban Aboriginal Peoples Study*. Toronto, ON: Environics Institute. [Online] Available at http://uaps.ca/wp-content/uploads/2010/03/UAPS-Main-Report.pdf.

Etzioni, Amitai. "How to Make Marriage Matter." *Time*. Vol. 142, No. 10 (September 6, 1993):76.

Fitzpatrick, Meagan. "Housework begins to sink in with men." *National Post* (July 20, 2006):A12.

Fleras, Augie. *Social Problems in Canada: Conditions, Constructions, and Challenges*. Toronto: Pearson Education Canada, 2001.

———. *Unequal Relations: An Introduction to Race, Ethnic, and Aboriginal Dynamics in Canada*. 6th ed. Toronto: Pearson Canada, 2010.

Frideres, James S., and René Gadacz. *Aboriginal Peoples in Canada: Contemporary Conflicts*. Toronto: Prentice Hall, 2001.

Furstenberg, Frank F., Jr., and Andrew Cherlin. *Divided Families: What Happens to Children When Parents Part*. Cambridge, MA: Harvard University Press, 1991.

———. "Children's Adjustment to Divorce." In Bonnie J. Fox, ed. *Family Patterns, Gender Relations*. 2nd ed. New York: Oxford University Press, 2001.

Gerber, Linda M. *Minority Survival: Community Characteristics and Out-Migration from Indian Communities Across Canada*. Toronto: University of Toronto Press, 1976.

———. "Ethnicity Still Matters: Socio-Demographic Profiles of the Ethnic Elderly in Ontario." *Canadian Ethnic Studies*. Vol. xv, No. 3 (1983):60–80.

———. "Indian, Métis, and Inuit Women and Men: Multiple Jeopardy in a Canadian Context." In E.D. Nelson and B.W. Robinson, eds. *Gender in the 1990s: Images, Realities, and Issues*. Scarborough, ON: Nelson Canada, 1995. pp. 466–77.

———. "Education, Employment, and Income Polarization among Aboriginal Men and Women in Canada: Stagnation and Progress." *Canadian Ethnic Studies*. Vol. 46, No. 1 (2014):87–110.

Glenn, Norval D., and Beth Ann Shelton. "Regional Differences in Divorce in the United States." *Journal of Marriage and the Family*. Vol. 47, No. 3 (August 1985):641–52.

Goldstein, Joshua R., and Catherine T. Kenney. "Marriage Delayed or Marriage Forgone? New Cohort Forecasts of First Marriage for U.S. Women." *American Sociological Review*. Vol. 66, No. 4 (August 2001):506–19.

Greenspan, Stanley I. *The Four-Thirds Solution: Solving the Child-Care Crisis in America*. Cambridge, MA: Perseus, 2001.

Gwartney-Gibbs, Patricia A., Jean Stockard, and Susanne Bohmer. "Learning Courtship Agression: The Influence of Parents, Peers, and Personal Experiences." *Family Relations*. Vol. 36, No. 3 (July 1987):276–82.

Huffington Post. "Paternity Leave: Why So Few Canadian Dad's Take Time Off." (2016). http://www.huffingtonpost.ca/2015/05/25/paternity-leave_n_7421960.html.

Jiménez, Marina. "Arranged marriages becoming more common, officials say." *The Globe and Mail* (May 11, 2006):A12.

Kantrowitz, Barbara, and Pat Wingert. "Unmarried with Children." *Newsweek* (May 28, 2001):46–52.

Laumann, Edward O., John H. Gagnon, Robert T. Michael, and Stuart Michaels. *The Social Organization of Sexuality: Sexual Practices in the United States*. Chicago, IL: University of Chicago Press, 1994.

Li, Peter S. *The Making of Post-War Canada*. Toronto: Oxford University Press, 1996.

Livingstone, D.W., and Meg Luxton. "Gender Consciousness at Work: Modification of the Male Breadwinner Norm Among Steelworkers and Their Spouses." In E.D. Nelson and B.W. Robinson, eds. *Gender in the 1990s: Images, Realities, and Issues*. Scarborough, ON: Nelson Canada, 1995. pp. 172–200.

Lupri, Eugene. "Male Violence in the Home." In Craig McKie and K. Thompson, eds. *Social Trends in Canada*. Toronto: Thompson Educational Publishers, 1988. pp. 170–72.

———. "Intimate Violence: Male Abuse." Unpublished manuscript. University of Calgary, 2002.

Mace, David, and Vera Mace. *Marriage East and West*. Garden City, NY: Doubleday (Dolphin), 1960.

Macionis, John J. "Intimacy: Structure and Process in Interpersonal Relationships." *Alternative Lifestyles*. Vol. 1, No. 1 (February 1978):113–30.

Makin, Kirk. "Split decisions." *The Globe and Mail* (July 29, 2006):F1.

Mayo, Katherine. *Mother India*. New York: Harcourt, Brace, 1927.

Mclanahan, Sara. "Life without Father: What Happens to the Children?" *Contexts*. Vol. 1, No. 1 (Spring 2002):35–44.

Mitchell, Alanna. "More Children Running Away Younger, Statscan Says." *The Globe and Mail* (February 13, 1998):A3.

Mitchell, Barbara A. "The Refilled 'Nest.'" In Ellen M. Gee and Gloria M. Gutman, eds. *The Overselling of Population Aging: Apocalyptic Demography, Intergenerational Challenges, and Social Policy*. Don Mills, ON: Oxford University Press, 2000.

Murdock, Geroge Peter. *Social Structure*. New York: Free Press, 1965; orig. 1949.

Nelson, Adie. *Gender in Canada*. 4th ed. Toronto: Pearson Canada, 2010.

Nett, Emily M. *Canadian Families: Past and Present*. 2nd ed. Toronto: Butterworths, 1993.

Nock, Steven L., James D. Wright, and Laura Sanchez. "America's Divorce Problem." *Society*. Vol. 36, No. 4 (May/June 1999):43–52.

Peritz, Ingrid. "Public daycare helps fuel Quebec work force." *The Globe and Mail* (May 1, 2006):A4.

Pew Research Center. "As Marriage and Parenthood Drift Apart, Public Is Concerned about Social Impact." July 1, 2007. [Online] Available January 31, 2009, at http://pewsocialtrends.org/pubs/542/modern-marriage.

Popenoe, David. "Family Decline in the Swedish Welfare State." *Public Interest*. No. 102 (Winter 1991):65–77.

———. "American Family Decline, 1960–1990: A Review and Appraisal." *Journal of Marriage and the Family*. Vol. 55, No. 3 (August 1993b):527–55.

———. "Can the Nuclear Family Be Revived?" *Society*. Vol. 36, No. 5 (July/August 1999):28–30.

Roesch, Roberta. "Violent Families." *Parents*. Vol. 59, No. 9 (September 1984):74–76, 150–52.

Rubin, Lillian Breslow. *Worlds of Pain: Life in the Working-Class Family*. New York: Basic Books, 1976.

Statistics Canada. "Family violence in Canada: A statistical profile." *The Daily*. July 14, 2005c. [Online] Available at http://www.statcan.ca/Daily/English/050714/td050714.htm.

———. "Family Violence: Spousal Violence in Canada." *The Daily*. October 9, 2008b. Available at www.statcan.gc.ca/daily-quotidien/081009/dq081009b-eng.htm.

———. "Study: Employment patterns of families with children, 1976 to 2014." *The Daily*, June 24, 2015. http://www.statcan.gc.ca/daily-quotidien/150624/dq150624a-eng.htm.

Stone, Lawrence. *The Family, Sex and Marriage in England, 1500–1800*. New York: Harper & Row, 1977.

Straus, Murray A., and Richard J. Gelles. "Societal Change and Change in Family Violence from 1975 to 1985 as Revealed by Two National Surveys." *Journal of Marriage and the Family*. Vol. 48, No. 4 (August 1986):465–79.

Trent, Katherine. "Family Context and Adolescents' Expectations About Marriage, Fertility, and Nonmarital Childbearing." *Social Science Quarterly*. Vol. 75, No. 2 (June 1994):319–39.

Vallis, Mary. "When grandkids don't leave." *National Post* (October 8, 2005):A1.

Van Biema, David. "Parents Who Kill." *Time*. Vol. 144, No. 20 (November 14, 1994):50–51.

Wallerstein, Judith S., and Sandra Blakeslee. *Second Chances: Men, Women, and Children a Decade After Divorce*. New York: Ticknor & Fields, 1989.

Wente, Margaret. "A+ for cultural capital." *The Globe and Mail* (June 27, 2006):A15.

Westhues, Anne, and Joyce S. Cohen. "International Adoption in Canada: Predictions of Well-Being." In *Child Welfare in Canada: Research and Policy Implications*, ed. Joe Hudson and Burt Galaway. Toronto: Thompson Educational Publishing, 1994.

Widom, Cathy Spatz. "Childhood Sexual Abuse and Its Criminal Consequences." *Society*. Vol. 33, No. 4 (May/June 1996):47–53.

Wotherspoon, Terry, and Vic Satzewich. *First Nations: Race, Class, and Gender Relations*. Scarborough, ON: Nelson, 1993.

Wu, Lawrence L. "Effects of Family Instability, Income, and Income Instability on the Risk of a Premarital Birth." *American Sociological Review*. Vol. 61, No. 3 (June 1996):386–406.

Wu, Zheng. *Cohabitation: An Alternative Form of Family Living*. Don Mills, ON: Oxford University Press, 2000.

Chapter 19

Abella, Irving. *A Coat of Many Colours: Two Centuries of Jewish Life in Canada*. Toronto: Lester and Orpen Dennys, 1989.

Abella, Irving, and Harold Troper. *None Is Too Many: Canada and the Jews in Europe, 1933–1948*. Toronto: Lester and Orpen Dennys, 1982.

Adams, Michael. *Fire and Ice: The United States, Canada and the Myth of Converging Values*. Toronto: Penguin Canada, 2003.

———. "My Canada doesn't include religiosity." *The Globe and Mail* (January 10, 2005):A13.

Applebome, Peter. "70 Years after Scopes Trial, Creation Debate Lives." *New York Times* (March 10, 1996):1, 10.

Baril, Alain, and George A. Mori. "Leaving the Fold: Declining Church Attendance." *Canadian Social Trends*. No. 22, 1991:21–24.

Berger, Peter L. *The Sacred Canopy: Elements of a Sociological Theory of Religion*. Garden City, NY: Doubleday, 1967.

———. "Faith and Development." *Society*. Vol. 46, No. 1 (January/February 2009):69–5.

Besecke, Kelly. "Speaking of Meaning in Modernity: Reflexive Spirituality as a Cultural Resource." *Sociology of Religion*. Vol. 62, No. 3 (2003):365–81.

———. "Seeing Invisible Religion: Religion as a Societal Conversation about Transcendent Meaning." *Sociology Theory*. Vol. 23, No. 2 (June 2005):179–96.

Bibby, Reginald W. *Fragmented Gods: The Poverty and Potential of Religion in Canada*. Toronto: Irwin, 1987.

———. *The Bibby Report: Social Trends Canadian Style*. Toronto: Stoddart, 1995.

———. *Canada's Teens: Today, Yesterday and Tomorrow*. Toronto: Stoddart, 2001.

———. *Restless Churches: How Canada's Churches Can Contribute to the Emerging Religious Renaissance*. Toronto: Novalis. 2004a.

———. *Restless Gods: The Renaissance of Religion in Canada*. Toronto: Novalis, 2004b.

———. *Beyond the Gods and Back: Religion's Demise and Rise and Why it Matters*. Lethbridge, AB, 2011.

Bricker, Darrell, and John Wright. *What Canadians Think... about Almost Everything*. Toronto: Doubleday Canada, 2005.

Campbell. Robert A. "Students' Views on the Relationship between Religion and Science: Analyses of Results from a Comparative Survey." *The Canadian Review of Sociology and Anthropology*. Vol. 42, No. 3 (August 2005):249–66.

Cimino, Richard, and Don Lattin. "Choosing My Religion." *American Demographics*. Vol. 21, No. 4 (April 1999):60–65.

Cox, Harvey. *The Secular City*. Rev. New York: Macmillan, 1971; orig. 1965.

Dershowitz, Alan. *The Vanishing American Jew*. Boston: Little, Brown, 1997.

Durkheim, Émile. *The Elementary Forms of Religious Life*. New York: Free Press, 1965; orig. 1915.

Eck, Diana L. *A New Religious America: How a "Christian Country" Has Become the World's Most Religiously Diverse Nation*. San Francisco, CA: Harper San Francisco, 2001.

El-Attar, Mohamed. Personal communication with John J. Macionis. 1991.

Ellwood, Robert S. "East Asian Religions in Today's America." In Jacob Neusner, ed. *World Religions in America: An Introduction*. Louisville, KY: Westminster John Knox Press, 2000:154–71.

Goldscheider, Calvin. *Studying the Jewish Future*. Seattle: University of Washington Press, 2004.

Gould, Stephen J. "Evolution as Fact and Theory." *Discover* (May 1981):35–7.

Huchingson, James E. "Science and Religion." *Miami Herald* (December 25, 1994):1M, 6M.

Hadden, Jeffrey K., and Charles E. Swain. *Prime Time Preachers: The Rising Power of Televangelism*. Reading, MA: Addison-Wesley, 1981.

Hunter, James Davison. *American Evangelicalism: Conservative Religion and the Quandary of Modernity*. New Brunswick, NJ: Rutgers University Press, 1983.

———. "Conservative Protestantism." In Philip E. Hammond, ed. *The Sacred in a Secular Age*. Berkeley, CA: University of California Press, 1985. pp. 50–66.

———. *Evangelicalism: The Coming Generation*. Chicago, IL: University of Chicago Press, 1987.

Jones, Frank. "Are Children Going to Religious Services?" In Statistics Canada, *Canadian Social Trends. Volume 3*. Toronto: Thompson Educational Publishing, 2000.

Kaufman, Walter. *Religions in Four Dimensions: Existential, Aesthetic, Historical, and Comparative*. New York: Reader's Digest Press, 1976.

Keister, Lisa A. "Religion and Wealth: The Role of Religious Affiliation and Participation in Early Adult Asset Accumulation." *Social Forces*. Vol. 82, No. 1 (September 2003):175–207.

Kilbourne, Brock K. "The Conway and Siegelman Claims Against Religious Cults: An Assessment of Their Data." *Journal for the Scientific Study of Religion*. Vol. 22, No. 4 (December 1983):380–85.

Krauss, Clifford. "In God We Trust... Canadians Aren't So Sure." *New York Times* (March 26, 2003). [Online] Available at http://www.nytimes.com/2003/03/26/international/americas/26LETT.html?ex=1049718839&ei=1&en=7b6d16eaa7fa6364.

Lachaine, Pierre. "Make Jesus your CEO." *National Post* (March 25, 2006):TO12.

Lottick, Edward A. "Prevalence of Cults: A Review of Empirical Research in the U.S.A." International Cultic Studies Association, Universidad Autonoma de Madrid. 2005. Available at http://www.pressbox.co.uk/detailed/Health/Prevalence_of_Cults_in_the_USA_32794.html.

Macionis, John J. (2014) Sociology. 15th ed. United States of America: Pearson Education, Inc.

Marquand, Robert, and Daniel B. Wood. "Rise in Cults as Millennium Approaches." *Christian Science Monitor* (March 28, 1997):1, 18.

Marx, Karl. *Karl Marx: Selected Writings in Sociology and Social Philosophy*. T.B. Bottomore, trans. New York: McGraw-Hill, 1964b; orig. 1848.

McGuire, Meredith B. *Religion: The Social Context*. 2nd ed. Belmont, CA: Wadsworth, 1987.

Neuhouser, Kevin. "The Radicalization of the Brazilian Catholic Church in Comparative Perspective." *American Sociological Review*. Vol. 54, No. 2 (April 1989):233–44.

NORC. *General Social Surveys, 1972–2002: Cumulative Codebook*. Chicago, IL: National Opinion Research Center, 2003.

Peterson, Scott. "Women Live on Own Terms behind the Veil." *Christian Science Monitor* (July 31, 1996):1, 10.

Ryan, Patrick J. "The Roots of Muslim Anger." *America* (November 26, 2001):8–16.

Schmidt, Roger. *Exploring Religion*. Belmont, CA: Wadsworth, 1980.

Stark, Rodney. *Sociology*. Belmont, CA: Wadsworth, 1985.

Stark, Rodney, and William Sims Bainbridge. "Of Churches, Sects, and Cults: Preliminary Concepts for a Theory of Religious Movements." *Journal for the Scientific Study of Religion*. Vol. 18, No. 2 (June 1979):117–31.

———. "Secularization and Cult Formation in the Jazz Age." *Journal for the Scientific Study of Religion*. Vol. 20, No. 4 (December 1981):360–73.

Statistics Canada, National Household Survey 2011, Catalogue no. 99-010-X2011037.

Thomas, Edward J. *The Life of Buddha as Legend and History*. London, UK: Routledge & Kegan Paul, 1975.

Troeltsch, Ernst. *The Social Teaching of the Christian Churches*. New York: Macmillan, 1931.

Tucker, James. "New Age Religion and the Cult of the Self." *Society*. Vol. 39, No. 2 (February 2002):46–51.

Van Biema. "Buddhism in America." *Time*. Vol. 150, No. 15 (October 13, 1997):71–81.

Weber, Max. *The Protestant Ethic and the Spirit of Capitalism*. New York: Charles Scribner's Sons, 1958; orig. 1904–05.

Weeks, John R. "The Demography of Islamic Nations." *Population Bulletin*. Vol. 43, No. 4 (December 1988). Washington, DC: Population Reference Bureau.

Wesselman, Hank. *Visionseeker: Shared Wisdom from the Place of Refuge*. Carlsbad, CA: Hay House, 2001.

Williams, Peter W. *America's Religions: From Their Origins to the Twenty-First Century*. Urbana: University of Illinois Press, 2002.

Wuthnow, Robert. *All in Sync: How Music and Art Are Revitalizing American Religion*. Berkeley, CA: University of California Press, 2003.

Chapter 20

Barakett, Joyce, and Allie Cleghorn. *Sociology of Education: An Introductory View from Canada.* Toronto: Pearson Prentice Hall, 2008.

Barlow, Maude, and Heather-Jane Robertson. *Class Warfare: The Assault on Canada's Schools.* Toronto: Key Porter, 1994.

Benedetti, Paul, and Nancy Dehart, Eds. *On McLuhan: Forward Through the Rearview Mirror.* Scarborough, ON: Prentice Hall, 1996.

Bowles, Samuel, and Herbert Gintis. *Schooling in Capitalist America: Educational Reform and the Contradictions of Economic Life.* New York: Basic Books, 1976.

Canada. *PCAP 2007: Report on the Assessment on 13-Year-Olds in Reading, Mathematics, and Science.* Toronto: Council of Ministers of Education, 2007.

CBC News. "Canada removing objector status to UN Declaration on the Rights of Indigenous Peoples." May 8, 2016. http://www.cbc.ca/news/aboriginal/canada-position-un-declaration-indigenous-peoples-1.3572777.

CBC Sports. "Former NHL coach Jacques Demers admits he's illiterate." 2005. [Online] Available at http://www.cbc.ca/sports/story/2005/11/03/demers051103.html.

Cloud, John, and Jodie Morse. "Home Sweet School." *Time* (August 27, 2001):46–54.

Corak, Miles. "Getting Ahead: Does Your Parents' Income Count?" In *Canadian Social Trends. Volume 3.* Toronto: Thompson Educational Publishing, 2000.

Crouse, James, and Dale Trusheim. *The Case Against the SAT.* Chicago, IL: University of Chicago Press, 1988.

de Broucker, Patrice, and Laval Lavallée. "Getting Ahead: Does Your Parents' Education Count?" In Statistics Canada, *Canadian Social Trends. Volume 3.* Toronto: Thompson Educational Publishing, 2000.

Department for Children, Schools, and Families (UK). "DCSF: Pupil Characteristics and Class Sizes in Maintained Schools in England." 2015. Available at http://www.education.gov.uk/rsgateway/DB/SFR/s000925/index.shtml.

Dewey, John. *Experience and Education.* New York: Collier Books, 1968; orig. 1938.

English-Currie, Vicki. "An Education of Oppression." In Jeanne Perreault and Sylvia Vance, eds. *Writing the Circle.* Edmonton: NeWest Press, 1993.

Evers, Frederick T., James C. Rush, Jasna A. Krmpotic, and Joanne Duncan-Robinson. *Making the Match: Phase II* (Final Technical Report). Universities of Guelph and Western Ontario, 1993.

Expatriate Group. "Lifestyle." 2009. www.expat.ca/education.htm.

Fleras, Augie, *Unequal Relations: An Introduction to Race, Ethnic, and Aboriginal Dynamics in Canada.* Don Mills, Ontario: Pearson, 2012.

Forcese, Dennis. *The Canadian Class Structure.* 4th ed. Toronto: McGraw-Hill Ryerson, 1997.

Frederick, Judith A., and Monica Boyd. "The Impact of Family Structure on High School Completion." In Statistics Canada, *Canadian Social Trends. Volume 3.* Toronto: Thompson Educational Publishing, 2000.

Gerber, Linda M. "Multiple Jeopardy: A Socio-economic Comparison of Men and Women among the Indian, Métis and Inuit Peoples of Canada." *Canadian Ethnic Studies.* Vol. xxii, No. 3 (1990):69–84.

Gilbert, S.N. "The Forgotten Purpose and Future Promise of University Education." *Canadian Journal of Community Mental Health.* Vol. 8, No. 2 (1989):103–22.

Gilbert, Sid, Lynn Barr, Warren Clark, Matthew Blue, and Deborah Sunter. *Leaving School: Results from a National Survey Comparing School Leavers and High School Graduates 18 to 20 Years of Age.* Catalogue No. LM-294-07-93E. Ottawa: Queen's Printer, 1993.

Goyder, John. *Technology and Society: A Canadian Perspective.* Peterborough, ON: Broadview Press, 1997.

Guppy, Neil, and A. Bruce Arai. "Who Benefits from Higher Education? Differences by Sex, Social Class, and Ethnic Background." In James E. Curtis, Edward Grabb, and Neil Guppy, eds. *Social Inequality in Canada: Patterns, Problems, Policies.* 2nd ed. Scarborough, ON: Prentice Hall, 1993. pp. 214–32.

Ibbitson, John. "A bleak choice for young Indians." *The Globe and Mail* (August 3, 2006):A4.

Johnson, F. Henry. *A Brief History of Canadian Education.* Toronto: McGraw-Hill, 1968.

Kilgore, Sally B. "The Organizational Context of Tracking in Schools." *American Sociological Review.* Vol. 56, No. 2 (April 1991):189–203.

Kozol, Jonathan. *Savage Inequalities: Children in America's Schools.* New York: Harper Perennial, 1992.

Kral, Brigitta. "The Eyes of Jane Elliott." *Horizon Magazine.* 2000. [Online] Available June 8, 2005, at http://www.horizonmag.com/4/jane-elliott.asp.

LearnNet (Online Learning) 2016. https://epsb.ca/programs/homeeducation/learnnetonlinelearning/.

Literacy and Numeracy Secretariat, Government of Ontario, [Onlline] Available July 1, 2012, at http://www.edu.gov.on.ca/eng/literacynumeracy/moreinfo.html.

Montigny, Gilles. "Reading Skills." In Craig McKie and Keith Thompson, eds. *Canadian Social Trends: A Canadian Studies Reader. Volume 2.* Toronto: Thompson Educational Publishing, 1994. pp. 111–19.

National Commission on Excellence in Education. *A Nation at Risk.* Washington, DC: U.S. Government Printing Office, 1983.

National Literacy Secretariat, Government of Canada. [Online] Available July 1, 2012, at http://www.collectionscanada.gc.ca/read-up-on-it/015020-6022-e.html.

Oakes, Jeannie. *Keeping Track: How High Schools Structure Inequality.* New Haven, CT: Yale University Press, 1985.

Oderkirk, Jillian. "Education Achievement: An International Comparison." *Canadian Social Trends* (Autumn 1993):8–12.

Porter, John, Marion Porter, and Bernard R. Blishen. *Stations and Callings.* Toronto: Methuen, 1982.

Putka, Gary. "SAT to Become a Better Gauge." *Wall Street Journal* (November 1, 1990):B1.

Reinhart, Anthony, and Jane Armstrong. "One by one, sisters earn Harvard honours." *The Globe and Mail* (June 26, 2006):A1.

Richards, John. *Closing the Aboriginal/Non-Aboriginal Education Gaps.* Toronto: CD Howe Institute, 2008. [Online] http://www.cdhowe.org/pdf/Backgrounder_116.pdf.

Schissel, B., and T. Wotherspoon. *The Legacy of School for Aboriginal People: Education, Opression, and Emancipation.* Toronto: Oxford University Press, 2003.

Sennett, Richard, and Jonathan Cobb. *The Hidden Injuries of Class.* New York: Vintage Books, 1973.

Statistics Canada. "Social Indicators." *Canadian Social Trends* (Spring 1996).

———. "Education Matters: Trends in dropout rates among the provinces." *The Daily.* December 16, 2005b. [Online] Available at http://www.statcan.ca/Daily/English/051011/d051011b.htm.

———. "University enrolment." *The Daily.* October 11, 2005e. [Online] Available at http://www.statcan.ca/Daily/English/051011/d051011b.htm.

———. Census 2001. Catalogue Nos. 95F0419XCB1001004 and 97F0017XCB2001003, 2009c.

———. "University Degrees, Diplomas and Certificates Granted, by Program Level and Instructional Program." Census 2006. http://www40.statcan.gc.ca/l01/cst01/educ52a-eng.htm.2009d.

———. "Canadian Internet use survey, Internet use by age group and frequency of use." CANSIM Table 358-0155. 2010. [Online] Available July 1, 2012, at http://www5.statcan.gc.ca/cansim/a05?lang=eng&id=3580155&pattern=3580155&searchTypeByValue=1&p2=35.

———. "French immersion 30 years later." *Education Matters.* catalogue no. 81-004-XIE. 2012d. [Online] Available July 1, 2012, at http://www.statcan.gc.ca/pub/81-004-x/200406/6923-eng.htm.

———. 2016. Trends in Registered Apprenticeship Training in Canada, 1991 to 2009. http://www.statcan.gc.ca/pub/81-004-x/2011003/article/11538-eng.htm#a

Tait, Heather. "Educational Achievement of Young Aboriginal Adults." In Statistics Canada, *Canadian Social Trends. Volume 3.* Toronto: Thompson Educational Publishing, 2000.

UNESCO Institute of Statistics. "Data Centre." 2015. Available at http://stats.uis.unesco.org/unesco/tableviewer/document.aspx.

Wente, Margaret. "A+ for cultural capital." *The Globe and Mail* (June 27, 2006):A15.

World Bank. "World DataBank: Education Statistics." 2015. Available at http://data.worldbank.org/data-catalog/ed-stats.

Wotherspoon, Terry. "Transforming Canada's Education System: The Impact on Educational Inequalities, Opportunities and Benefits." In B. Singh Bolaria, ed. *Social Issues and Contradictions in Canadian Society.* Toronto: Harcourt Brace Jovanovich, 1991. pp. 448–63.

Chapter 21

Ashford, Lori S. "Young Women in Sub-Saharan Africa Face a High Risk of HIV Infection." Population Today. Vol. 30, No. 2 (February/March 2002):3, 6.

Atkinson, Michael. "It's Still Part of the Game: Masculinity, Crime and Victimization in Ice Hockey." In L. Fuller, ed. *Sport, Rhetoric, Gender and Violence: Historical Perspectives and Media Representations.* New York: Palgrave MacMillan, 2007.

Becker, Anne E. "The Association of Television Exposure with Disordered Eating Among Ethnic Fijian Adolescent Girls." Paper presented at the annual meeting of the American Psychiatric Association, Washington, DC, May 19, 1999.

Beltrame, Julian. "Latimer's Last Chances for Earlier Release Appear Slim." *Maclean's* (January 29, 2001).

Berthiaume, Lee. "'Clarity' urged as assisted-dying bill remains in limbo." *National Post,* May 21, 2016:A10.

Bibby, Reginald W. *The Bibby Report: Social Trends Canadian Style.* Toronto: Stoddart, 1995.

Blackwell, Tom. "Prognosis for Profit." *National Post* (June 27, 2009):A1.

Blishen, Bernard R. *Doctors in Canada.* Toronto: University of Toronto Press, 1991.

Bloom, D. E., et al. *The Global Economic Burden of Non-Communicable Diseases.* Geneva: World Economic Forum, September 2011.

Canada. Health Canada. 2006b. [Online] Available at http://www.hc-sc.gc.ca.

Canadian Institute for Health Information. 2015. *National Health Expenditure Trends, 1975 to 2015.* https://www.cihi.ca/en/spending-and-health-workforce/spending/national-health-expenditure-trends1.

Centers for Disease Control and Prevention (CDC). "Behavioral Risk Factor Surveillance System." 2015. Available at http://www.cdc.gov/brfss/index.htm.

Davis, Simon. *Community Mental Health in Canada.* Vancouver: UBC Press, 2006.

Deber, Raisa. "Getting What We Pay For: Myths and Realities about Financing Canada's Health Care System." *Dialogue on Health Reform.* University of Toronto. 2000. [Online] Available at http://www.utoronto.ca/hlthadmn/dhr.

Dubos, René. *Man Adapting.* New Haven, CT: Yale University Press, 1980; orig. 1965.

Dunsdon, Nicole. "Nursing Shortages Make Colleges Get Creative in Training RNs." *The Globe and Mail* (April 8, 2009).

Ehrenreich, Barbara. *Nickel and Dimed: On (Not) Getting By in America.* New York: Henry Holt, 2001.

Eisenberg, David M., Ronald C. Kessler, Cindy Foster, Frances E. Norlock, David R. Calkins, and Thomas L. Delbanco. "Unconventional Medicine in the United States: Prevalence, Costs and Patterns of Use." *New England Journal of Medicine.* Vol. 328, No. 4 (1993):246–52.

Elson, Jean. *Am I Still a Woman? Hysterectomy and Gender Identity.* Philedelphia: Temple University Press, 2004.

Emerson, Joan P. "Behavior in Private Places: Sustaining Definitions of Reality in Gynecological Examinations." In H.P. Dreitzel, ed. *Recent Sociology.* Vol. 2. New York: Collier, 1970. pp. 74–97.

Fallon, A.E., and P. Rozin. "Sex Differences in Perception of Desirable Body Shape." *Journal of Abnormal Psychology.* Vol. 94, No. 1 (1985):100–5.

Frideres, James S., and René Gadacz. *Aboriginal Peoples in Canada.* 8th ed. Toronto: Pearson Prentice Hall, 2008.

Gandhi, Unnati. "The War on AIDS hits home." *The Globe and Mail.* (August 8, 2006):A4.

Gerber, Linda M. "Multiple Jeopardy: A Socio-economic Comparison of Men and Women among the Indian, Métis and Inuit Peoples of Canada." *Canadian Ethnic Studies.* Vol. xxii, No. 3 (1990):69–84.

Gillespie, Mark. "Trends Show Bathing and Exercise Up, TV Watching Down." January 2000. [Online] Available April 9, 2006, at http://www.gallup.com.

Gordon, James S. "The Paradigm of Holistic Medicine." In Arthur C. Hastings *et al.*, eds. *Health for the Whole Person: The Complete Guide to Holistic Medicine.* Boulder, CO: Westview Press, 1980. pp. 3–27.

Greenaway, Norma. "Physicians signal frustration, elect private-care chief." *National Post* (August 23, 2006b):A6.

Gurney, Matt. "Euthanasia a right long denied." *National Post.* [Online] Available May 22, 2012, at http://fullcomment.nationalpost.com/2012/03/22/matt-gurney-euthanasia-a-right-long-denied.

Hamrick, Michael H., David J. Anspaugh, and Gene Ezell. *Health.* Columbus, OH: Merrill, 1986.

Hellmich, Nanci. "Environment, Economics Partly to Blame." *USA Today* (October 9, 2002):9D.

Huet-Cox, Rocio. "Medical Education: New Wine in Old Wine Skins." In Victor W. Sidel and Ruth Sidel, eds. *Reforming Medicine: Lessons of the Last Quarter Century.* New York: Pantheon Books, 1984:129–49.

Hyslop, Lucy. "Recruiters bracing for nursing shortage." *Postmedia News.* [Online] Available November 8, 2010, at http://www.canada.com/business/Recruiters+bracing+nursing+shortage/3800234/story.html.

Jones, D. Gareth. "Brain Death." *Journal of Medical Ethics.* Vol. 24, No. 4 (August 1998):237–43.

Kain, Edward L. "A Note on the Integration of AIDS into the Sociology of Human Sexuality." *Teaching Sociology.* Vol. 15, No. 4 (July 1987):320–23.

Kaptchuk, Ted. "The Holistic Logic of Chinese Medicine." In Shepard Bliss et al., eds. *The New Holistic Health Handbook.* Lexington, MA: The Steven Greene Press/Penguin Books, 1985:41.

Krauthammer, Charles. "Health Rationing, Obama-style." *National Post* (April 22, 2009):A12.

Krueger, Patrick M., Richard G. Rogers, Robert A. Hummer, Felicia B. Leclere, and Stephanie A. Bond Huie. "Socioeconomic Status and Age: The Effect of Income Sources and Portfolios on U.S. Adult Maturity." *Sociological Forum.* Vol. 18, No. 3 (September 2003):465–82.

Laumann, Edward O., John H. Gagnon, Robert T. Michael, and Stuart Michaels. *The Social Organization of Sexuality: Sexual Practices in the United States.* Chicago, IL: University of Chicago Press, 1994.

Leavitt, Judith Walzer. "Women and Health in America: An Overview." In Judith Walzer Leavitt, ed. *Women and Health in America.* Madison: University of Wisconsin Press, 1984. pp. 3–7.

Lethbridge-Cejku, Margaret, and Jackline Vickerie. *Summary Health Statistics for U.S. Adults: National Health Interview Survey, 2003.* Vital and Health Statistics, Series 10, No. 225. Hyattsville, MD: National Center for Health Statistics, 2005.

Mason, David S. "Fairness Matters: Equity and the Transition to Democracy." *World Policy Journal.* Vol. 20, No. 4 (Winter 2003). Available February 21, 2008, at http://www.worldpolicy.org/journal/articles/wpj03-4/mason.html.

Mcpherson, Barry D. *Aging as a Social Process: Canadian Perspectives.* 4th ed. Don Mills, ON: Oxford University Press, 2004.

Murray, Christopher, et al. "Disability-Adjusted Life Years (DALYs) for 291 Diseases and Injuries in 21 Regions, 1990–2010: A Systematic Analysis for the Global Burden of Disease Study 2010." *The Lancet.* Vol. 380, No. 9859 (December 15, 2012):2197–23. Available at http://www.thelancet.com/journals/lancet/article/PIIS0140-6736(12)61689-4/fulltext.

Myers, David G. *The American Paradox: Spiritual Hunger in an Age of Plenty.* New Haven, CT: Yale University Press, 2000.

Myers, Sheila, and Harold G. Grasmick. "The Social Rights and Responsibilities of Pregnant Women: An Application of Parsons' Sick Role Model." Paper presented to Southwestern Sociological Association, Little Rock, AR, March 1989.

Nancarrow Clarke, Juanne. *Health, Illness & Medicine in Canada.* 2d ed. Toronto: McClelland & Stewart, 1996.

Parsons, Talcott. "Age and Sex in the Social Structure of the United States." *American Sociological Review.* Vol. 7, No. 4 (August 1942):604–16.

Patterson, Elissa F. "The Philosophy and Physics of Holistic Health Care: Spiritual Healing as a Workable Interpretation." *Journal of Advanced Nursing.* Vol. 27, No. 2 (February 1998):287–93.

Peters, Amanda. *Making the Choice, Organ Transfer or Trade: An Analysis of Values and the Political Economy of Care.* Master's thesis, 2011. University of Guelph. [Online] Available at http://atrium.lib.uoguelph.ca.

Picard, André. "Future CMA head says he supports medicare." *The Globe and Mail* (August 23, 2006):A5.

———. "Time to Draw Up a Better Plan of Attack against H1N1." *The Globe and Mail* (July 2, 2009):L1.

Pinhey, Thomas K., Donald H. Rubinstein, and Richard S. Colfax. "Overweight and Happiness: The Reflected Self-Appraisal Hypothesis Reconsidered." *Social Science Quarterly.* Vol. 78, No. 3 (September 1997): 747–5.

Population Reference Bureau. "Datafinder." 2012, 2014, 2015. Available at http://www.prb.org/DataFinder.aspx.

Public Health Agency of Canada. 2016a. "Executive Summary—Report on Sexually Transmitted Infections in Canada: 2011." http://www.phac-aspc.gc.ca/sti-its-surv-epi/rep-rap-2011/index-eng.php.

———. 2016b. *HIV and AIDS in Canada: Surveillance Report to Dec 31, 2014.* http://healthycanadians.gc.ca/publications/diseases-conditions-maladies-affections/hiv-aids-surveillance-2014-vih-sida/index-eng.php?page=10#t21.

Rajhathy, Judith, and David Roulard. "Victory for Health Freedom." *Health Naturally* (June/July 1994).

Roehrig, James P., and Carmen P. McLean. "A Comparison of Stigma Toward Eating Disorders Versus Depression." *International Journal of Eating Disorders.* Vol. 43, No. 7 (November 2010):671–4.

Romanow, Roy. "Medicare is part of us." The Globe and Mail (July 2, 2012): A9.

Segall, Alexander, and Neena L. Chappell. *Health and Health Care in Canada.* Toronto: Prentice Hall, 2000.

Sobel, Rachel K. "Herpes Tests Give Answers You Might Need to Know." *U.S. News & World Report* (June 18, 2001):53.

Starr, Paul. *The Social Transformation of American Medicine.* New York: Basic Books, 1982.

Statistics Canada. "Canadian Community Health Survey: Obesity among children and adults." *The Daily.* July 6, 2005a. [Online] Available at http://www.statcan.ca/Daily/English/050706/d050706a.htm.

———. "National Population Health Survey—Obesity: A growing issue." *The Daily.* April 7, 2005d. [Online] Available at http://www.statcan.ca/Daily/English/050407/d050407a.htm.

Stevens, Rosemary. *American Medicine and the Public Interest.* New Haven, CT: Yale University Press, 1971.

Stobbe, Mike. "Cancer to Be World's Top Killer by 2010, WHO Says." *Yahoo News* (December 9, 2008). [Online] Available December 10, 2008, at http://news.yahoo.com/s/ap/20081209/ap_on_he_me/med_global_cancer.

UNAIDS. "AIDSinfo." 2015. Available at http://www.unaids.org/en/dataanalysis/datatools/aidsinfo.

United Nations, Department of Economic and Social Affairs, Population Division. "World Population Prospects: The 2012 Revision." 2013. Available at http://esa.un.org/unpd/wpp/unpp/panel_indicators.htm.

Vasilyeva, Nataliya. "Russian Doctor Rebellion Causes Headache for Putin." Associated Press (November 28, 2014). Available at http://bigstory.ap.org/article/c747606267694e11b9ea77e8b5e53062/russian-doctor-rebellion-causesheadache-putin.

Wall, Thomas F. *Medical Ethics: Basic Moral Issues.* Washington, DC: University Press of America, 1980.

Wells, Hodan Farah, and Jean C. Buzby. *Dietary Assessment of Major Trends in U.S. Food Consumption, 1970–2005.* Economic Information Bulletin No. (EIB 33). Washington, DC: U.S. Department of Agriculture, March 2008.

Winston, Iris. "Nursing shortages a national concern." *Postmedia News.* [Online] Available February 18, 2011, from http://www.canada.com/health/Nursing+shortages+national+concern/4288871/story.html.

Wood, Daniell. "Death Wish: Would You Choose an Assisted Suicide?" *Chatelaine* (July 25–29, 1993):94.

World Bank. "World DataBank: Health, Nutrition, and Population Statistics." 2015. Available at http://data.worldbank.org/data-catalog/health-nutritionand-population-statistics.

World Health Organization. *Constitution of the World Health Organization.* New York: World Health Organization Interim Commission, 1946.

Zuckerman, Mortimer B. "The Russian Conundrum." *U.S. News & World Report* (March 13, 2006):64.

Chapter 22

Adam, David. "World CO_2 Levels at Record High, Scientists Warn." *Guardian* (May 12, 2008). [Online] Available July 16, 2008, at http://www.guardian.co.uk/environment/2008/may/12/climatechange.carbonemissions.

Axinn, William G., and Jennifer S. Barber. "Mass Education and Fertility Transition." *American Sociological Review.* Vol. 66, No. 4 (August 2001): 481–505.

Benn, Carl. *Historic Fort York, 1793–1993.* Toronto: Natural Heritage, 1993.

Bercuson, David, and Barry Cooper. "A New Tax on Energy Is Unacceptable." *The Globe and Mail* (November 8, 1997):D2.

Berry, Brian L., and Philip H. Rees. "The Factorial Ecology of Calcutta." *American Journal of Sociology.* Vol. 74, No. 5 (March 1969):445–91.

Bormann, F. Herbert. "The Global Environmental Deficit." *BioScience.* Vol. 40 (1990):74.

Brockerhoff, Martin P. "An Urbanizing World." *Population Bulletin.* Vol. 55, No. 3 (September 2000):1–44.

Brown, Lester R. "Reassessing the Earth's Population." *Society.* Vol. 32, No. 4 (May/June 1995):7–0.

Brown, Lester R., et al., Eds. *State of the World 1993: A Worldwatch Institute Report on Progress Toward a Sustainable Society.* New York: Norton, 1993.

Brym, Robert J., Ed. *Regionalism in Canada.* Toronto: Irwin, 1986.

Callow, A.B., Jr., Ed. *American Urban History.* New York: Oxford University Press, 1969.

Capella, Peter. "UN Alarmed at Huge Decline in Bee Numbers." Yahoo.com [Online] Available March 10, 2011, at http://news.yahoo.com/s/afp/20110310/sc_afp/unenvironment_speciesanimalfarmbee_20110310124832.

Chandler, Tertius, and Gerald Fox. *3000 Years of Urban History*. New York: Academic Press, 1974.

Chang, Alicia. "Study: Cleaner Air Adds 5 Months to U.S. Life Span." *Yahoo News* (January 21, 2009). [Online] Available April 10, 2009, at http://www.newsvine.com/_news/2009/01/21/2339450-study-cleaner-air-adds-5-months-to-us-life-span.

Connett, Paul H. "The Disposable Society." In F. Herbert Bormann and Stephen R. Kellert, eds. *Ecology, Economics, and Ethics: The Broken Circle*. New Haven, CT: Yale University Press, 1991. pp. 99–122.

El Nasser, Haya, and Paul Overberg. "U.S. Growth Slows, Still Envied." *USA Today* (January 7–9, 2011):1A.

Fine, Gary Alan. "Nature and the Taming of the Wild: The Problem of 'Overpick' in the Culture of Mushroomers." *Social Problems*. Vol. 44, No. 1 (February 1997):68–88.

Galloway, Gloria, and Nathan Vanderklippe. "Resources rewrite first nations priorities." *The Globe and Mail* (July 14, 2012): A3.

Gerber, Linda M. "The Visible Minority, Immigrant, and Bilingual Composition of Ridings and Party Support in the Canadian federal Election of 2004." *Canadian Ethnic Studies*. 38:1 (2006a):65-82.

———. "Urban Diversity: Riding Composition and Party Support in the Canadian Federal Election of 2004." *Canadian Journal of Urban Research*. Vol. 15, No. 2 (2006b):105–18.

Gillis, Justin. "Sea-Level Science." *Conservation*. Vol. 12, No. 1 (Spring 2011):44–45.

Gore, Al. *An Inconvenient Truth: The Crisis of Global Warming*. Emmaus, PA: Rodale Books, 2006.

Gottmann, Jean. *Megalopolis*. New York: Twentieth Century Fund, 1961.

Goyder, John. *Essentials of Canadian Sociology*. Toronto: McClelland & Stewart, 1990.

Hamilton, Graeme. "Tory blue has shades of green." *National Post* (April 20, 2006).

Harris, Chauncey D., and Edward L. Ullman. "The Nature of Cities." *The Annals*. Vol. 242 (November 1945):7–17.

Hart, Michael. *Hubris: The Troubling Science, Economics, and Politics of Climate Change*. Ottawa, ON; Compleat Desktops Publishing, 2015.

Hiller, Harry H. *Canadian Society: A Macro Analysis*. 5th ed. Toronto ON: Pearson Prentice Hall, 2006.

Horton, Hayward Derrick. "Critical Demography: The Paradigm of the Future?" *Sociological Forum*. Vol. 14, No. 3 (September 1999):363–67.

Hogue, Cheryl. "U.S. Exports of Hazardous Waste to Canada Continue to Rise." *Chemical and Engineering News* (November 13, 2000):26.

Hoyt, Homer. *The Structure and Growth of Residential Neighborhoods in American Cities*. Washington, DC: Federal Housing Administration, 1939.

International Panel On Climate Change. *Climate Change, 2007*. New York: United Nations, 2007.

Jacobs, Dean. "Walpole Island: Sustainable Development." In Diane Engelstad and John Bird, eds. *Nation to Nation: Aboriginal Sovereignty and the Future of Canada*. Concord, ON: House of Anansi Press, 1992. pp. 179–85.

Jacobs, Jane. *The Death and Life of Great American Cities*. New York: Random House, 1961.

———. *The Economy of Cities*. New York: Vintage Books, 1970.

———. *Cities and the Wealth of Nations*. Toronto: Random House, 1984.

Johnston, R.J. "Residential Area Characteristics." In D. T. Herbert and R. J. Johnston, eds. *Social Areas in Cities. Vol. 1: Spatial Processes and Form*. New York: Wiley, 1976. pp. 193–235.

Keesing, Felicia, et al. "Impacts of Biodiversity on the Emergence and Transmission of Infectious Disease." *Nature: International Weekly Journal of Science*. Vol. 468, No. 7324. Available December 2, 2010, at http://www.nature.com/nature/journal/v468/n7324/full/nature09575.html.

Kellert, Stephen R., and F. Herbert Bormann. "Closing the Circle: Weaving Strands among Ecology, Economics, and Ethics." In F. Herbert Bormann and Stephen R. Kellert, eds., *Ecology, Economics, and Ethics: The Broken Circle*. New Haven, Conn.: Yale University Press, 1991:205–10.

Kelly, Deirdre. "The places that mattered to Jane Jacobs." *The Globe and Mail* (April 29, 2006):M3.

Kerr, Richard A. "Climate Models Heat Up." *Science Now* (January 26, 2005):1–3.

Kuumba, M. Bahati. "A Cross-Cultural Race/Class/Gender Critique of Contemporary Population Policy: The Impact of Globalization." *Sociological Forum*. Vol. 14, No. 3 (March 1999):447–63.

Langer, Valerie. "It Happened Suddenly (Over a Long Period of Time): A Clayoquot History." 1996. [Online] Available at http://www.ancient rainforest.org/history.htm.

Lindstrom, Bonnie. "Chicago's Post-Industrial Suburbs." *Sociological Focus*. Vol. 28, No. 4 (October 1995):399–412.

Malthus, Thomas Robert. *First Essay on Population 1798*. London, UK: Macmillan, 1926; orig. 1798.

Marx, Karl. *Capital*. Friedrich Engels, ed. New York: International Publishers, 1967; orig. 1867.

Matthews, Ralph. *The Creation of Regional Dependency*. Toronto: University of Toronto Press, 1983.

McKenzie, Judith I. "The Inner Suburbs of the Greater Toronto Area." In *Health, Governance, and Citizenship in Four Canadian Cities*, ed. Karen B. Murray. Vancouver: University of British Columbia Press, 2006.

McKibben, Bill. *Deep Economy: The Wealth of Communities and the Durable Future*. New York: Times Books, 2007.

McMahon, Bucky. "Vanishing Point." *Conservation*. Vol. 12, No. 1 (Spring 2011):40–48.

Meadows, Donella H., Dennis L. Meadows, Jorgan Randers, and William W. Behrens, III. *The Limits to Growth: A Report on the Club of Rome's Project on the Predicament of Mankind*. New York: Universe, 1972.

Michelson, William. "Urbanization and Urbanism." In James Curtis and Lorne Tepperman, eds. *Understanding Canadian Society*. Toronto: McGraw-Hill Ryerson, 1988:73–104.

Milbrath, Lester W. *Envisioning a Sustainable Society: Learning Our Way Out*. Albany: State University of New York Press, 1989.

Mittelstaedt, Martin. "Change Unavoidable for Ontario Hydro." *The Globe and Mail* (August 18, 1997):A1.

Mumford, Lewis. *The City in History: Its Origins, Its Transformations, and Its Prospects*. New York: Harcourt, Brace & World, 1961.

Myers, David G. *The American Paradox: Spiritual Hunger in an Age of Plenty*. New Haven, CT: Yale University Press, 2000.

Myers, Norman. "Humanity's Growth." In Sir Edmund Hillary, ed. *Ecology 2000: The Changing Face of the Earth*. New York: Beaufort Books, 1984. pp. 16–35.

National Oceanic & Atmospheric Administration, 2015.

Nature Conservancy The. "Facts About Rainforests." 2015. Available at http://www.nature.org/ourinitiatives/urgentissues/rainforests/rainforests-facts.xml.

Nikiforuk, Andrew. "When Water Kills." *Maclean's* (June 12, 2000).

Nin.Da.Waab.Jig. Walpole Island Heritage Centre. "Walpole Island in 2005: A View from the Future." In Diane Engelstad and John Bird, eds. *Nation to Nation: Aboriginal Sovereignty and the Future of Canada*. Concord, ON: House of Anansi Press, 1992. pp. 186–96.

Park, Robert E. *Race and Culture*. Glencoe, IL: Free Press, 1950.

Plimer, Ian. *Heaven and Earth; global warming, the missing science*. Toronto, ON: Taylor Trade Publishing, 2009.

Population Action International. *People in the Balance: Population and Resources at the Turn of the Millennium*. Washington, D.C.: Population Action International, 2000.

Population Reference Bureau. "Datafinder." 2014. Available at http://www.prb.org/DataFinder.aspx.

——— "World Population Data Sheet." 2014. Available at http://www.prb.org/Publications/Datasheets/2014/2014-world-population-data-sheet/population-clock.aspx.

Reed, Brian. "Could People from Kiribati Be 'Climate Change Refugees'? *The Two-Way*. National Public Radio news blog. [Online] Available February 27, 2011, at http://www.npr.org/templates/archives/archive.php?thingId=131216964.

Ridley, Matt. "Cooling Down the Fears of Climate Change." *Wall Street Journal* (December 19, 2012):A19.

Roudi-Fahimi, Farzaneh, and Mary Mederios Kent. "Challenges and Opportunities: The Population of the Middle East and North Africa." *Population Bulletin*. Vol. 65, No. 2 (June 2007). Washington, D.C.:Population Reference Bureau, 2007.

Scanlon, Stephan J. "Food Availability and Access in Less Industrialized Societies: A Test and Interpretation of Neo-Malthusian and Technoecological Theories." *Sociological Forum*. Vol. 16, No. 2 (June 2001):231–2.

Shevky, Eshref, and Wendell Bell. *Social Area Analysis*. Stanford, CA: Stanford University Press, 1955.

Shute, Jeremy J., and David B. Knight. "Obtaining an Understanding of Environmental Knowledge: Wendaban Stewardship Authority." *The Canadian Geographer*. Vol. 39, No. 2 (1995):101–11.

Sierra Club. "Clean Water." 2009. [Online] Available February 11, 2009, at http://www.sierraclub.org/cleanwater/overview.

Simmel, Georg. "The Metropolis and Mental Life." In Kurt Wolff, ed. *The Sociology of Georg Simmel*. New York: Free Press, 1964:409–24; orig. 1905.

Simon, Julian. *The Ultimate Resource*. Princeton, NJ: Princeton University Press, 1981.

———. "More People, Greater Wealth, More Resources, Healthier Environment." In Theodore D. Goldfarb, ed. *Taking Sides: Clashing Views on Controversial Environmental Issues*. 6th ed. Guilford, CT: Dushkin, 1995.

Singer, S. Fred. "Global Warming: Man-Made or Natural?" *Imprimis*. Vol. 36, No. 8 (2007):1–5.

Smail, J. Kenneth. "Let's *Reduce* Global Population!" In John J. Macionis and Nijole V. Benokraitis, eds. *Seeing Ourselves: Classic, Contemporary, and Cross-Cultural Readings in Sociology*. 7th ed. Upper Saddle River, NJ: Prentice Hall, 2007.

Tönnies, Ferdinand. *Community and Society (Gemeinschaft und Gesellschaft)*. New York: Harper & Row, 1963; orig. 1887.

United Nations, Department of Economic and Social Affairs. "The State of Forests in the Amazon Basin, Congo Basin and Southeast Asia." June 2011. Available at http://www.fao.org/forestry/fra/70893/en.

———, Department of Economic and Social Affairs. "World Population Prospects: The 2012 Revision." 2013. Available at http://esa.un.org/unpd/wpp/unpp/panel_indicators.htm.

———, Department of Economic and Social Affairs. "World Urbanization Prospects: The 2014 Revision." 2014. Available at http://esa.un.org/unpd/wup.

U.S. Census Bureau. "American Community Survey." 2014. #http://www.census.gov/acs/www/#lation/metro.

———. "Population Estimates." 2014. Available at http://www.census.gov/popest/data/index.html.

———. "State and County Quick Facts." 2010, 2014. Available at http://www.fedstats.gov/qfd/index.html.

United Nations Environmental Programme. "Vital Water Graphics: An Overview of the State of the World's Fresh and Marine Waters." 2nd ed. 2008. [Online] Available February 9, 2009, at http://www.unep.org/dewa/vitalwater/article186.html .

Weber, Adna Ferrin. *The Growth of Cities.* New York: Columbia University Press, 1963; orig. 1899.

Wilson, Edward O. "Biodiversity, Prosperity, and Value." In F. Herbert Bormann and Stephen R. Kellert, eds. *Ecology, Economics, and Ethics: The Broken Circle.* New Haven, CT: Yale University Press, 1991. pp. 3–10.

Wilson, Thomas C. "Urbanism and Tolerance: A Test of Some Hypotheses Drawn from Wirth and Stouffer." *American Sociological Review.* Vol. 50, No. 1 (February 1985):117–23.

———. "Urbanism and Unconventionality: The Case of Sexual Behavior." *Social Science Quarterly.* Vol. 76, No. 2 (June 1995):346–3.

Wirth, Louis. "Urbanism as a Way of Life." *American Journal of Sociology.* Vol. 44, No. 1 (July 1938):1–24.

World Health Organization. 2016. Global Health Observatory. http://apps.who.int/gho/data/view.main.CBDR2040.

Yemma, John. "As the World's Population Heads Toward a Peak, Malthusian Worries Reemerge." *The Christian Science Monitor.* [Online] Available February 7, 2011, at http://www.csmonitor.com/Commentary/editors-blog/2011/0207/As-world-population-heads-toward-a-peak-Malthusian-worries-reemerge.

Chapter 23

Aberle, David F. *The Peyote Religion Among the Navaho.* Chicago, IL: Aldine, 1966.

Aguirre, Benigno E., and E.L. Quarantelli. "Methodological, Ideological, and Conceptual-Theoretical Criticisms of Collective Behavior: A Critical Evaluation and Implications for Future Study." *Sociological Focus.* Vol. 16, No. 3 (August 1983):195–216.

Aguirre, Benigno E., E.L. Quarantelli, and Jorge L. Mendoza. "The Collective Behavior of Fads: Characteristics, Effects, and Career of Streaking." *American Sociological Review.* Vol. 53, No. 4 (August 1988):569–84.

Baumgartner, M.P. "Introduction: The Moral Voice of the Community." *Sociological Focus.* Vol. 31, No. 2 (May 1998):105–17.

Bibby, Reginald W. *The Bibby Report: Social Trends Canadian Style.* Toronto: Stoddart, 1995.

Blumer, Herbert G. "Collective Behavior." In Alfred McClung Lee, ed. *Principles of Sociology.* 3rd ed. New York: Barnes & Noble Books, 1969. pp. 65–121.

Bricker, Darrell, and John Wright. *What Canadians Think . . . about Almost Everything.* Toronto: Doubleday Canada, 2005.

Cameron, William Bruce. *Modern Social Movements: A Sociological Outline.* New York: Random House, 1966.

Canada. *Canadian Charter of Rights and Freedoms,* enacted as Part I of the *Constitution Act, 1982,* being Schedule B to the *Canada Act, 1982* (U.K.), 1982, c.11.

Cantril, Hadley, Hazel Gaudet, and Herta Herzog. *Invasion from Mars: A Study in the Psychology of Panic.* Princeton, NJ: Princeton University Press, 1947.

COMPAS. 2006. "Explaining the Globe's misleading anti-Harper poll." http://www.compas.ca/data/060814-ExplainingGlobesMisleadingAnti-HarperPoll-EPCB.pdf.

Cooley, Charles Horton. *Social Organization.* New York: Schocken Books, 1962; orig. 1909.

Crane, Diana. *Fashion and Its Social Agenda: Class, Gender, and Identity in Clothing.* Chicago: University of Chicago Press, 2000.

de Tocqueville, Alexis. *The Old Regime and the French Revolution.* Stuart Gilbert, trans. Garden City, NY: Anchor/Doubleday Books, 1955; orig. 1856.

Dollard, John, Neal E. Miller, Leonard W. Dood, O.H. Mower, and Robert R. Sears. *Frustration and Aggression.* New Haven, CT: Yale University Press, 1939.

Donnelly, Patrick G., and Theo J. Majka. "Residents' Efforts at Neighborhood Stabilization: Facing the Challenges of Inner-City Neighborhoods." *Sociological Forum.* Vol. 13, No. 2 (June 1998):189–213.

Doolittle, Robyn. "Queen's may not be very amused." *The Toronto Star* (September 26, 2005):A16.

Earl, Jennifer, and Earl Kimport. *Digitally Enabled Social Change: Activism in the Internet Age.* Massachusetts Institute of Technology, 2011.

Erikson, Kai T. *Everything in Its Path: Destruction of Community in the Buffalo Creek Flood.* New York: Simon & Schuster, 1976.

———. *A New Species of Trouble: Explorations in Disaster, Trauma, and Community.* New York: Norton, 1994.

———. Lecture delivered at Kenyon College, Gambier, Ohio, February 7, 2005.

Goode, Erich. "No Need to Panic? A Bumper Crop of Books on Moral Panics." *Sociological Forum.* Vol. 15, No. 3 (September 2000):543–52.

Grant, Donald L. *The Anti-Lynching Movement.* San Francisco: R and E Research Associates, 1975.

Grant, Don Sherman, II, and Michael Wallace. "Why Do Strikes Turn Violent?" *American Journal of Sociology.* Vol. 96, No. 5 (March 1991):1117–50.

Grieshaber, Kirsten, and Frank Augstein. "Death Toll Rises After Stampede at Festival." *The Huffington Post.* [Online] Available July 25, 2010, at http://www.huffingtonpost.com/2010/07/24/germany-love-parade-trage_n_658216.html.

Herda-Rapp, Ann. "The Power of Informal Leadership: Women Leaders in the Civil Rights Movement." *Sociological Focus.* Vol. 31, No. 4 (October 1998):341–55.

Inglehart, Ronald, et al. "World Values Survey: Online Data Analysis." Available February 2013, at http://www.wvsevsdb.com/wvs/WVSAnalizeQuestion.jsp.

Jenkins, J. Craig, David Jacobs, and Jon Agone. "Political Opportunities and African-American Protest, 1948–1997." *American Journal of Sociology.* Vol. 109, No. 2 (September 2003):277–303.

Jenkins, J. Craig, and Charles Perrow. "Insurgency of the Powerless: Farm Worker Movements (1946–1972)." *American Sociological Review.* Vol. 42, No. 2 (April 1977):249–68.

Jenkins, J. Craig, and Michael Wallace. "The Generalized Action Potential of Protest Movements: The New Class, Social Trends, and Political Exclusion Explanations." *Sociological Forum.* Vol. 11, No. 2 (June 1996):183–207.

Kheiriddin, Tasha. "We don't need no solidarity: Quebec's student protest movement isn't likely to catch on in Ontario." *National Post* (July 12, 2012):A14.

Koch, Howard. *The Panic Broadcast: Portrait of an Event.* Boston: Little, Brown, 1970.

Kornhauser, William. *The Politics of Mass Society.* New York: Free Press, 1959.

Lacayo, Richard. "Blood at the Root." *Time* (April 10, 2000):122–23.

Lange, Matthew. "Education, Ethnonationalism, and Non-Violence in Quebec." In Lorne Tepperman and Angela Kalyta, eds. *Reading Sociology: Canadian Perspectives.* 2nd ed. Don Mills, Ontario: Oxford University Press, 2012.

Laslett, Peter. *The World We Have Lost: England Before the Industrial Age.* 3rd ed. New York: Charles Scribner's Sons, 1984.

Le Bon, Gustave. *The Crowd: A Study of the Popular Mind.* New York: Viking Press, 1960; orig. 1895.

Lipset, Seymour Martin. *Political Man: The Social Bases of Politics.* Garden City, NY: Anchor/Doubleday, 1963.

Lofland, Lyn. *A World of Strangers.* New York: Basic Books, 1973.

Macionis, John J. *Social Problems.* 5th ed. Upper Saddle River, N.J.: Pearson Prentice Hall, 2013.

MacFarquhar, Neil. "After Revolt, Egyptians Try to Shape New Politics." *New York Times.* [Online] Available March 18, 2011, at http://www.nytimes.com/2011/03/19/world/middleeast/19egypt.html?scp=5&sq=Women%20and%20Cairo&st=cse.

Mauss, Armand L. *Social Problems of Social Movements.* Philadelphia, PA: Lippincott, 1975.

Marsden, Lorna R., and Edward B. Harvey. *Fragile Federation: Social Change in Canada.* Toronto: McGraw-Hill Ryerson, 1979.

McAdam, Doug. *Political Process and the Development of Black Insurgency, 1930–1970.* Chicago, IL: University of Chicago Press, 1982.

———. "Tactical Innovation and the Pace of Insurgency." *American Sociological Review.* Vol. 48, No. 6 (December 1983):735–54.

———. *Freedom Summer.* New York: Oxford University Press, 1988.

———. "The Biographical Consequences of Activism." *American Sociological Review.* Vol. 54, No. 5 (October 1989):744–60.

———. "Gender as a Mediator of the Activist Experience: The Case of Freedom Summer." *American Journal of Sociology.* Vol. 97, No. 5 (March 1992):1211–40.

McAdam, Doug, John D. Mccarthy, and Mayer N. Zald. Eds. *Comparative Perspectives on Social Movements: Political Opportunities, Mobilizing Structures, and Cultural Framings.* New York: Cambridge University Press, 1996.

McCarthy, John D., and Mayer N. Zald. "Resource Mobilization and Social Movements: A Partial Theory." *American Journal of Sociology.* Vol. 82, No. 6 (May 1977):1212–41.

McPhail, Clark. *The Myth of the Madding Crowd.* New York: Aldine, 1991.

McPhail, Clark, and Ronald T. Wohlstein. "Individual and Collective Behaviors Within Gatherings, Demonstrations, and Riots." *Annual Review of Sociology.* Vol. 9. Palo Alto, CA: Annual Reviews, 1983. pp. 579–600.

Melucci, Alberto. *Nomads of the Present: Social Movements and Individual Needs in Contemporary Society.* Philadelphia, PA: Temple University Press, 1989.

Merton, Robert K. *Social Theory and Social Structure.* New York: Free Press, 1968.

Miller, David L. *Introduction to Collective Behavior.* Belmont, CA: Wadsworth, 1985.

Miller, Frederick D. "The End of SDS and the Emergence of Weatherman: Demise Through Success." In Jo Freeman, ed. *Social Movements of the Sixties and Seventies.* New York: Longman, 1983. pp. 279–97.

Mills, C. Wright. *The Sociological Imagination.* New York: Oxford University Press, 1959.

Morris, Aldon. "Black Southern Sit-In Movement: An Analysis of Internal Organization." *American Sociological Review.* Vol. 46, No. 6 (December 1981):744–67.

Morrison, Denton E. "Some Notes Toward Theory on Relative Deprivation, Social Movements, and Social Change." In Louis E. Genevie, ed. *Collective Behavior and Social Movements.* Itasca, IL: Peacock, 1978. pp. 202–9.

Nessman, Ravi. "Stampede at Soccer Match Kills 47." [Online] Available April 11, 2001, at http://news.yahoo.com.

Nicholson, Nigel. "Evolved to Chat: The New Word on Gossip." *Psychology Today* (May/June 2001):41–45.

Oberschall, Anthony. *Social Conflict and Social Movements.* Englewood Cliffs, NJ: Prentice Hall, 1973.

Olzak, Susan, and Elizabeth West. "Ethnic Conflict and the Rise and Fall of Ethnic Newspapers." *American Sociological Review.* Vol. 56, No. 4 (August 1991):458–74.

Packer, George. "Smart-Mobbing the War." *New York Times Magazine* (March 9, 2003):46–49.

Pakulski, Jan. "Mass Social Movements and Social Class." *International Sociology.* Vol. 8, No. 2 (June 1993):131–58.

Passy, Florence, and Marco Giugni. "Social Networks and Individual Perceptions: Explaining Differential Participation in Social Movements." *Sociological Forum.* Vol. 16, No. 1 (March 2001):123–53.

Pichardo, Nelson A. "The Power Elite and Elite-Driven Countermovements: The Associated Farmers of California During the 1930s." *Sociological Forum.* Vol. 10, No. 1 (March 1995):21–49.

Piven, Frances Fox, and Richard A. Cloward. *Poor People's Movements: Why They Succeed, How They Fail.* New York: Pantheon Books, 1977.

Preston, Jennifer. "Movement Began with Outrage and a Facebook Page That Gave It an Outlet." *New York Times.* [Online] Available February 5, 2011, at http://www.nytimes.com/2011/02/06/world/middleeast/06face.html?_r=1.

Rose, Jerry D. *Outbreaks.* New York: Free Press, 1982.

Rose, Fred. "Toward a Class-Cultural Theory of Social Movements: Reinterpreting New Social Movements." *Sociological Forum.* Vol. 12, No. 3 (September 1997):461–94.

Sears, David O., and John B. Mcconahay. *The Politics of Violence: The New Urban Blacks and the Watts Riot.* Boston: Houghton Mifflin, 1973.

Simmel, Georg. "Fashion." In Donald N. Levine, ed. *Georg Simmel: On Individuality and Social Forms.* Chicago, IL: University of Chicago Press, 1971; orig. 1904.

Smelser, Neil J. *Theory of Collective Behavior.* New York: Free Press, 1962.

Stouffer, Samuel A., Arthur A. Lumsdaine, Marion Harper Lumsdaine, Robin M. Williams, Jr., M. Brewster Smith, Irving L. Janis, Shirley A. Star, and Leonard S. Cottrell, Jr. *The American Soldier.* Volume 1 *Adjustment During Army Life.* Princeton, NJ: Princeton University Press, 1949.

Thernstrom, Abigail, and Stephan Thernstrom. "American Apartheid? Don't Believe It." *Wall Street Journal* (March 2, 1998):A18.

Tilly, Charles. *From Mobilization to Revolution.* Reading, MA: Addison-Wesley, 1978.

Tucker, Maria. "How Big Was the Inaugural Crowd? Good Question." *News & Observer* (January 21, 2009). [Online] Available April 28, 2009, at http://www.sacbee.com/inauguration/story/1563105.html.

Turner, Ralph H., and Lewis M. Killian. *Collective Behavior.* 2nd ed. Englewood Cliffs, NJ: Prentice Hall, 1972; 3rd ed. 1987; 4th ed. 1993.

Useem, Michael. "The Social Organization of the Corporate Business Elite and Participation of Corporate Directors in the Governance of American Institutions." *American Sociological Review.* Vol. 44, No. 4 (August 1979):553–72.

Veblen, Thorstein. *The Theory of the Leisure Class.* New York: The New American Library, 1953; orig. 1899.

Weller, Jack M., and E.L. Quarantelli. "Neglected Characteristics of Collective Behavior." *American Journal of Sociology.* Vol. 79, No. 3 (November 1973):665–85.

Whalen, Jack, and Richard Flacks. *Beyond the Barricades: The Sixties Generation Grows Up.* Philadelphia, PA: Temple University Press, 1989.

White, Walter. *Rope and Faggot.* New York: Arno Press and New York Times, 1969; orig. 1929.

Williams, Peter W. *America's Religions: From Their Origins to the Twenty-First Century.* Urbana: University of Illinois Press, 2002.

Wright, Stuart A., and Elizabeth S. Piper. "Families and Cults: Familial Factors Related to Youth Leaving or Remaining in Deviant Religious Groups." *Journal of Marriage and the Family.* Vol. 48, No. 1 (February 1986):15–25.

Zhao, Dingxin. "Ecologies of Social Movements: Student Mobilization during the 1989 Prodemocracy Movement in Beijing." *American Journal of Sociology.* Vol. 103, No. 6 (May 1998):1493–1529.

Chapter 24

Adams, Michael. *Fire and Ice: The United States, Canada and the Myth of Converging Values.* Toronto: Penguin Canada, 2003.

Bakker, J. I. (Hans). 1979. Patrimonialism and Imperialism as Factors in Underdevelopment: A Comparative Historical Sociological Analysis of Java, with Emphasis on Aspects of the Cultivation System, 1830–1870. Toronto: unpublished Ph.D. dissertation.

———. 1992. "Resettlement of Bajo 'Sea Nomads': Rapid Rural Appraisal of an IRD-IAD Project in Sulawesi, Indonesia." Integrated Rural Development Review 1:129–166.

———. 2009. "The Netherlands Indies in Aceh, Bali and Buton: Degrees of Resistance and Acceptance of Indirect and Direct Rule." *Leidschrift* (Journal of the Leiden History Department) 24 no. 1:83–103.

Benedetti, Paul, and Nancy Dehart, Eds. *On McLuhan: Forward Through the Rearview Mirror.* Scarborough, ON: Prentice Hall, 1996.

Bennett, William J. "Quantifying America's Decline." *Wall Street Journal* (March 15, 1993).

Berger, Peter L. *Facing Up to Modernity: Excursions in Society, Politics, and Religion.* New York: Basic Books, 1977.

Berger, Peter, Brigitte Berger, and Hansfried Kellner. *The Homeless Mind: Modernization and Consciousness.* New York: Vintage Books, 1974.

Bibby, Reginald W. *The Bibby Report: Social Trends Canadian Style.* Toronto: Stoddart, 1995.

Brazilian, Alexa. "Forever in Blue Jeans." *Wall Street Journal* (January 8, 2011). Available at http://online.wsj.com/article/SB10001424052748704111504576060150008236490.html.

Bricker, Darrell, and John Wright. *What Canadians Think . . . about Almost Everything.* Toronto: Doubleday Canada, 2005.

Brooks, Arthur C. "Why Conservatives are Happier than Liberals." *The New York Times* (July 8, 2012):SR 4.

Buechler, Steven M. *Social Movements in Advanced Capitalism: The Political Economy and Cultural Construction of Social Activism.* New York: Oxford University Press, 2000.

Carlson, Kathryn Blaze. "The true north LGBT: We're 'post-gay.'" *The National Post* (July 7, 2012):A1.

Colombo, John Robert. *The Penguin Book of Canadian Jokes.* Toronto: Penguin, 2001.

Dunn, Elizabeth, and Michael Norton. *The New York Times* (July 8, 2012):SR 1.

Durkheim, Émile. *The Rules of Sociological Method.* New York: Free Press, 1964b; orig. 1893.

Ehrenreich, Barbara. *Nickel and Dimed: On (Not) Getting By in America.* New York: Henry Holt, 2001.

Fay, Stephen. "Educating indigenous youth for the jobs of tomorrow." *The National Post* (June 21, 2012):A14.

Forcese, Dennis. *The Canadian Class Structure.* 4th ed. Toronto: McGraw-Hill Ryerson, 1997.

Geertz, Clifford. 1963. Agricultural Involution: The Process of Ecological Change in Indonesia. Berkeley, CA: University of California Press.

Globe and Mail, The. Editorial. (May 1, 2006).

Goffman, Erving. *The Presentation of Self in Everyday Life.* Garden City, NY: Anchor Books, 1959.

Goyder, John. *Technology and Society: A Canadian Perspective.* Peterborough, ON: Broadview Press, 1997.

Gregg, Allan R. "Brave New Epoque." *Maclean's* (April 6, 1998):56–60.

Habermas, JüRgen. *Toward a Rational Society: Student Protest, Science, and Politics.* Jeremy J. Shapiro, trans. Boston, MA: Beacon Press, 1970.

Hall, John R., and Mary Jo Neitz. *Culture: Sociological Perspectives.* Englewood Cliffs, NJ: Prentice Hall, 1993.

Harrington, Michael. *The New American Poverty.* New York: Penguin Books, 1984.

Hiller, Harry H. *Canadian Society: A Macro Analysis.* 5th ed. Toronto, ON: Pearson Prentice Hall, 2006.

Inglehart, Ronald. *Modernization and Postmodernization: Cultural, Economic, and Political Change in 43 Societies.* Princeton, NJ: Princeton University Press, 1997.

Inglehart, Ronald, and Wayne E. Baker. "Modernization, Cultural Change, and the Persistence of Traditional Values." *American Sociological Review.* Vol. 65, No. 1 (February 2000):19–51.

Inglehart, Ronald and Christian Welzel. "World Values Survey." Inglehart-Welzel Cultural Map of the World. 2010. Available at http://www.worldvaluessurvey.com.

Inglehart, Ronald, Christian Welzel, and Roberto Foa. "Happiness Trends in 24 Countries, 1946–2006." 2009. [Online] Available February 15, 2009, at http://margaux.grandvinum.se/SebTest/wvs/articles/folder_published/article_base_106.

Kornhauser, William. *The Politics of Mass Society.* New York: Free Press, 1959.

Laslett, Peter. *The World We Have Lost: England Before the Industrial Age.* 3rd ed. New York: Charles Scribner's Sons, 1984.

Linton, Ralph. "One Hundred Percent American." *The American Mercury.* Vol. 40, No. 160 (April 1937):427–29.

Lipset, Seymour Martin. *Continental Divide: The Values and Institutions of the United States and Canada.* New York: Routledge, 1991.

Marcuse, Herbert. *One-Dimensional Man.* Boston: Beacon Press, 1964.

Marx, Karl, and Friedrich Engels. "Manifesto of the Communist Party." In Robert C. Tucker, ed. *The Marx-Engels Reader.* New York: Norton, 1972; orig. 1848. pp. 331–62.

Myers, David G. *The American Paradox: Spiritual Hunger in an Age of Plenty.* New Haven, CT: Yale University Press, 2000.

Nevitte, Neil. *The Decline of Deference.* Peterborough, ON: Broadview Press, 1996.

Newman, Katherine S. *Declining Fortunes: The Withering of the American Dream.* New York: Basic Books, 1993.

Newman, Peter C. *The Canadian Revolution, 1985–1995: From Deference to Defiance.* Toronto: Penguin Books, 1995.

Nisbet, Robert A. *The Sociological Tradition.* New York: Basic Books, 1966.

Ogburn, William F. *On Culture and Social Change.* Chicago, IL: University of Chicago Press, 1964.

Peacock, Kerry. "Setting a new course for Aboriginal education." *The National Post* (June 21, 2012):A14.

Pearson, David E. "Post-Mass Culture." *Society.* Vol. 30, No. 5. (July/August 1993):17–22.

Riesman, David. *The Lonely Crowd: A Study of the Changing American Character.* New Haven, Conn.: Yale University Press, 1970; orig. 1950.

Rudel, Thomas K., and Judith M. Gerson. "Postmodernism, Institutional Change, and Academic Workers: A Sociology of Knowledge." *Social Science Quarterly.* Vol. 80, No. 2 (June 1999):213–28.

Sauvé, Roger. *Borderlines: What Canadians and American Should—but Don't—Know About Each Other.* Whitby, ON: McGraw-Hill Ryerson, 1994.

Simons, Marlise. "The Price of Modernization: The Case of Brazil's Kaiapo Indians." In John J. Macionis and Nijole V. Benokraitis, eds. *Seeing Ourselves: Classic, Contemporary, and Cross-Cultural Readings in Sociology.* 7th ed. Upper Saddle River, NJ: Prentice Hall, 2007.

Smith, Tom W., Peter Marsden, Michael Hout, and Jibum Kim. "General Social Surveys, 1972–2012." National Opinion Research Center. The Roper Center for Public Opinion Research, University of Connecticut, Computer-assisted Survey Methods Program, University of California. June 2013. Available at http://www.norc.org/GSS+Website.

Statistics Canada. General Social Survey. "Social support and aging." 1985.

Taras, David, Beverly Rasporich, and Eli Mandel. *A Passion for Identity: An Introduction to Canadian Studies.* Scarborough, ON: Nelson, 1993.

Tönnies, Ferdinand. *Community and Society (Gemeinschaft und Gesellschaft).* New York: Harper & Row, 1963; orig. 1887.

Weber, Max. *The Protestant Ethic and the Spirit of Capitalism.* New York: Charles Scribner's Sons, 1958; orig. 1904–05.

———. *Economy and Society.* G. Roth and C. Wittich, eds. Berkeley, CA: University of California Press, 1978; orig. 1921.

Wheelis, Allen. *The Quest for Identity.* New York: Norton, 1958.

Author Index

Subject Index

Note: Entries for tables, figures, maps, and footnotes are followed by "t," "f," "m,"and "n" respectively.

and social mobility, 295
social-conflict approach, 579
structural-functional approach, 579
summary, 588–589
symbolic-interaction approach, 579
efficiency, 187
ego, 120, 121, 140
egocentric outlook, 649
Egoyan, Atom, 154
Eichler, Margrit, 41
Einstein, Albert, 489
Ekman, Paul, 156–157
elder abuse, 415, 519
elderly people. *See also* aging
    caregiving, 414–415
    cohorts of, 405
    emotional support for, 400
    happiness, 410*t*
    living arrangements, 411*t*
    as minority, 416
    retirement, 411–413
    and sex, 412–413
    social isolation, 410–411
electronic church, 554–555
elites, 438
Elliott, Jane, 569–570
embarrassment, 155
emergence, of social movement, 674
emigration, 624–645
emotion management, 157
emotions
    biological side of, 156–157
    cultural side of, 157
    on the job, 157
    summary, 164
empirical evidence, 34, 60
employment. *See also* work
    and education, 446, 447*t*, 549, 574–579, 579*t*
    and ethnicity, 385*t*, 449
    and gender, 447, 447*t*
    in government, 180*m*, 184
    and religion, 549–550, 549*t*
    statistics, Canadian, 439*f*
    underemployment, 446–449
    unemployment, 447–449
    of women, 509*t*, 510, 510*t*
Employment Equity Act, 376, 378, 383
empty nest, 508
enclosure movement, 13
endogamous marriage, 260
endogamy, 500, 527
energy, 429
engagement theory, 416
Engels, F., 100, 358
English-Currie, Vicki, 577
Enron, 235
environment
    air pollution, 645–646
    biodiversity, 647
    and culture, 640–641
    environmental racism, 647–648
    in everyday life, 650–651
    future of, 648–649
    global climate change, 646–647
    global dimension, 640
    rainforests, 646
    and society, 639
    solid waste, 641–642, 641*f*
    summary, 653
    and technology, 640
    water, 642–645
environmental deficit, 640, 654
environmental racism, 647–648, 654
Epperson v. Arkansas, 553
Equal Rights Amendment, 336, 360
Erikson, Erik H.
    eight stages of development, 125, 140
    the elderly, 410
eros (life instinct), 120
Escherichia coli, 622, 643
"Essays on the Art of Thinking" (Martineau), 42
ethics, sociological investigation and, 44, 61
ethnic cleansing, 382
ethnicity
    and AIDS, 602*t*
    in Canada, 373–374, 374*t*, 375, 382–394, 398
    categories of, 372–373

and class society theory, 697–698
and crime, 242–243
defined, 374, 397
and education, 385*t*, 574*f*, 580
and employment, 385*t*
in everyday life, 395–396
and family, 504, 511–513
future of, 393–394
and identity, 127–129
and income, 385*t*
mixed marriage, 513, 513*t*
overview, 374–375
and poverty, 279, 297–298
and religion, 550
and social standing, 385–386
and social stratification, 287
and socialization, 127
special status societies. *See* special status societies
summary, 397
and unemployment, 449
and voting behaviour, 478
and work, 427, 439
ethnocentrism, 80–81, 81*f*, 89
ethnographies, 50
ethnomethodology, 149–150, 164
Etzioni, Amitai, 179
Eurocentrism, 78, 89
euthanasia, 416, 419, 604, 619
evolution, 84–85
evolutionary change, 99
exclusion, 184
exes, 148
existing sources, 52–54
exogamy, 500, 527
experimental group, 45
experiments
    defined, 44, 61
    described, 44–45
    Hawthorne effect, 46
    Stanford County Prison, 46–47
    summary, 56*t*
experts, 33
explicit consent, 238
export-oriented economies, 324
expressive crowd, 659
expressive leadership, 170, 192
expressive qualities, 356
extended family, 499, 500, 527
extramarital sex, 205, 507

F

facial expressions, 156
factory work, 441
fads, 664, 680
Fairclough, Ellen, 482
faith, 33, 532, 558
false consciousness, 99, 102, 115
familiar, 4–5
family. *See also* marriage
    alternative forms of, 519–523, 519*t*, 528
    authority patterns, 502
    basic concepts, 499–502
    blended families, 517
    child rearing, 507–508
    cohabitation, 520
    courtship, 505–507
    defined, 499, 527
    descent patterns, 501–502
    and education, 580
    feminist approach, 504, 505
    formation of, 148
    future of, 523–524
    gay and lesbian couples, 520–552
    in later life, 508–511
    lone-parent families, 520, 520*f*
    in the mass media, 525–526
    micro-level theories, 504–505
    and new reproductive technologies, 523
    problems related to, 514–519, 528
    and race and ethnicity, 504, 511–513, 528
    and remarriage, 517
    residential patterns, 500–501
    and security, material and emotional, 503–504
    and sexual activity, regulation of, 502–503
    singlehood, 522–523, 522*t*, 523*t*
    size of, 508